John Edwin Fagg

Professor of History, New York University

LATIN AMERICA

A General History

THE MACMILLAN COMPANY, NEW YORK
COLLIER-MACMILLAN LTD., LONDON

FOREWORD

THIS BOOK originated when I began to write up my lectures for courses given at New York University on the history of Latin America. An exercise undertaken to clarify my presentation of the subject, it led me to deeper reading and research, and to much re-writing. As the work progressed, it appeared to be different enough from other general studies of Latin America to justify publication as a textbook. In certain portions, archival investigations of my own or a reading of other primary sources have resulted in new material, and the secondary works used as a basis for most of this book have sometimes been re-interpreted. I have also been able to visit nearly every country where the Spanish and Portuguese languages are used. Necessarily, some of my personal impressions from these travels have found their way into this account.

The extensive treatment of the colonial period and the Wars of Independence is, I believe, necessary to a proper understanding of Latin American history. In the case of the post-independence period, I have sought to compress many details of the nineteenth century and to emphasize, rather, the twentieth century, when developments of greater significance seem to be leading the peoples of Latin America toward a climax of crises and, one hopes, of brilliant achievements. My effort has been to be realistic and to keep the history of these lands constantly in a world perspective.

My gratitude to those who have inspired or assisted me in this undertaking extends to many persons. My parents, Mr. and Mrs. E. E. Fagg of San Saba, Texas, have generously shared their home with me for the past four summers while I typed the manuscript. Miss Helen Lidstone first awoke my interest in history. The late Rafael Altamira y Crevea gave me many ideas and repeatedly encouraged me to pursue the study of Spain and Latin America. My major professors at the University of Chicago, Bernadotte E. Schmitt, J. Fred Rippy, and Louis Gottschalk, trained me in historical scholarship and endowed me with a lifelong ambition to justify their confidence.

The officials and attendants of the New York University libraries, the

New York Public Library, the Hispanic Society of America, the Bancroft Library at the University of California, the University of Texas Library, the Archivo General de Indias in Sevilla, and the Public Record Office in London have been helpful beyond the normal call of their obligations. In particular, I wish to thank Dr. Nettie Lee Benson of the Latin-American Collection at the University of Texas for countless acts of assistance.

Among the authorities who have read parts or all of the manuscript, I owe much to Professors Irving A. Leonard, C. Alan Hutchinson, James Ferguson King, Alan K. Manchester, Bailey W. Diffie, H. B. Parkes, Leo Gershoy, Carleton Sprague Smith, and Jordan Young and to Mrs. Ysabel Fisk Rennie and Mr. Martin R. R. Goldman. While their suggestions were not invariably heeded, they usually were, and they were indeed valuable. The editors at The Macmillan Company with whom I have worked most closely, Roger Howley, Eugene Becker, and W. Carter Hunter, have been helpful and understanding.

Finally, my students at New York University have been a constant source of stimulation and pleasure as we have studied Latin American history together over the past fifteen years.

John Edwin Fagg

October, 1962

TABLE OF CONTENTS

SECTION I

Background

I

The Original Americans

ANY study of the history of Latin America must inevitably consider the aboriginal inhabitants and the way they lived before the Europeans came. The intrinsic interest of the subject is justification enough: since the day Columbus waded ashore in the Bahamas and greeted the brown-skinned natives he called Indians, the cultures of these early Americans have fascinated men. Beyond the fascination there is this reality: the Indians have outlasted their European conquerors, often with little change in activity and outlook, and now they are showing their strength in countries like Mexico, Guatemala, and the Andean republics. Their civilizations, however much stunted and redirected by the Spaniards, have also survived in some ways.

The question of the origin and nature of the Indians confronts us at once with tantalizing and frustrating problems. Ever since Columbus mistakenly took them for inhabitants of the Indies, the American Indians, or Amerinds, have been identified as Asians. For centuries Europeans have found seeming resemblances between Amerinds and Asians in color, bone structure, hairiness, palm lines, eye folds, and, still more dubiously, temperament. But the methods of comparison used are more tried than scientifically true. The Indians of the Americas differ from one another to such a degree that almost any generalization about their kinship to Asians breaks down under the weight of exceptions. No one can yet prove that all Amerinds stemmed from Asian stock.

Most recent scholars have argued that the western hemisphere was peopled by immigrants who came by the northern route from Asia. Is there any proof? Yes, with qualifications. Substantial if not overwhelming archaeological evidence indicates that a steady stream of Asians flowed into America by way of Siberia after the end of the last Ice Age, between ten and twenty thousand years ago. At that time the water level was lower, so that a land or ice crossing was possible for centuries. Even in later periods men might have used small boats to cross the Bering Strait and the waters about the Aleutian Islands. The pioneers apparently went up the Yukon Valley and down the eastern Rockies through present-day Canada and the United States. Occasional findings make us reasonably sure of this route. Also, we can accept the opinion universally held by specialists in the field that most of the Indians have the physical traits of Mongoloids. As for the motives of those who migrated, we can only guess whether they were following game, fleeing from dangers in Asia, or merely adventurous.

Did the human race, then, enter America from the northwest and move all the way down to the Antarctic? Were the settlers so primitive that they lost all contact with their original homeland and all recollection of this migration? This seems to be the case. Still, a few students believe it is not the whole story. Several excavations, some of them very recent, have turned up apparently human remains beside those of animals that, according to radiocarbon dating methods, have been extinct for 30,000 years. A slight possibility exists, therefore, that a few men may have survived the last Ice Age in America. Some students persuade themselves—but almost no one else—that human beings also reached the New World from Africa and Europe in the remote past. This of course does not rule out the near certainty that most of the Indians are of Asian descent. More plausible are theories that men sailed or drifted to America from the islands of Australasia, probably much later than the crossings into Alaska. But thus far all these speculations lack proof. Philologists may some day find a link between some Indian tongues and languages in other regions. Archaeologists are steadily uncovering evidence. Meanwhile, the safest course is skepticism about all hypotheses that seek to answer too much.

Since we do not know the extent of early American immigration and are not sure of the routes, except for movements across Alaska, we cannot fix the origin and age of such cultures as the Maya, Aztec, Pueblo, and Inca. Perhaps they developed gradually and independently over a long period, building upon the achievements of earlier cultures. Possibly, but only possibly, they got inspiration or assistance from each other or even from European or Asiatic visitors. We also have to be very cautious about estimating how many Indians lived in America when the Europeans came. The early Spaniards had the medieval habit of giving a specific high figure when they only meant to suggest large numbers. Hence most students reject their statements about quantities of soldiers fought, converts made, or natives overcome. In our age the standard estimate of Amerind population in the New World is based on the admirable studies of the Argentine scholar, Ángel Rosenblat, who puts the number at about 13,000,000. Yet exhaustive investigations of specific localities, such as those in central Mexico of the Americans Sherburne F. Cook, Lesley Byrd Simpson, and Woodrow Borah, indicate a much higher population. When experts disagree, no layman can draw confident conclusions. But our lack of knowledge about fundamental points in the story of the ancient Americans need not spoil the pleasure of learning as much as we can. We may go ahead, certain that a study of their ways will yield some insight into the problems of Latin America.

The Maya

WE begin with the Maya, in many ways the most admirable and surely the most brilliant of the ancient cultures. This civilization arose in a region that is lightly populated today—northern Guatemala, British Honduras, and southeastern Mexico. For at least fifteen centuries the area was the scene of civilized activity that approached contemporaneous European cultures in architecture and sculpture, surpassed them in mathematics and astronomy, and may have rivaled them in providing sustenance and public order. Though we cannot be sure, the Maya was probably the first civilization to flourish in the western hemisphere. Its influence on the ancient cultures of Mexico was large, if immeasurable, but it apparently had no effect on the growth of civilization in Peru.

Appreciation of the Maya has been relatively recent. The conquering Spaniards found a decadent, disorganized society of brown-skinned, round-headed, stocky people who cherished recollections of the better days their ancestors had known but were patently less advanced than the Aztecs or Inca. Around 1560, Bishop Diego de Landa went about the peninsula of Yucatan uncovering startling evidence of a highly developed civilization by then all but dead. Like most of the pioneering Spanish clerics, he was repelled by the signs of paganism and destroyed idols and heathen writings with such vigor that for centuries his fame has been infamy. Yet the most important Maya manuscripts we have we owe to his efforts, and in 1949 a forgotten collection in the Vatican library turned out to be priceless Maya relics the abused bishop had not destroyed at all but had salvaged and shipped to Europe.

During the long Spanish colonial period the Maya area had few inhabitants and drew little attention. Early in the nineteenth century a Spanish army officer and an eccentric English nobleman explored the jungles and discovered tantalizing evidence that rekindled interest in the dead civilization. A young American diplomat named John Lloyd Stephens conducted further explorations during the 1840's. His writings, together with the sketches of Frederick Catherwood, advertised a few of the magnificent temples and amphitheaters that rain forests had hidden for centuries. Later, a number of adventurous scientists, some of them exceedingly bizarre characters, turned up more remains. The growing taste for chewing gum in the outside world furnished still another motive for charting the wilderness; long-forgotten ruins came to light as men hunted out the sapodilla tree, source of chicle sap. By the beginning of this century large-scale, systematic excavations carried out by trained archaeologists were under way.

For years now the ruins have drawn the interest of scientist and layman alike, and, as a result, our understanding of the baffling Maya culture has deepened, though much patient work remains to be done. Unfortunately, the descendants of the Maya have known little of their great forefathers and their ways. Nor have archaeologists been able to decipher enough of the early writings to reconstruct a reliable history, assuming that is possible at all. A few students believe these writings had only numerical significance, but most credit the Maya with something more and think they can translate a few words.

The question at once arises as to how people living in the Central American jungle could become civilized in the first place. The southern part of the region was the least advanced, though it has the best climate and the most fertile soil. It was in the central area that the Maya reached his peak of greatness. Yet this area has an enormous rainfall, dense jungles that become savannahs filled with stubborn grasses when cleared, and an enervating climate. Its only manifest advantage is an abundance of the limestone that went into the great buildings. From the fourth to the tenth centuries after Christ, the Maya gloried in their Classic period, sometimes called the Old Empire, centered on this unpromising region. Between the tenth and the thirteenth centuries they flourished farther north, in the Mexican peninsula of Yucatan, during a less brilliant phase variously known as the post-Classic, Mexican, or New Empire period. This region also has defects; it is hot, dry, and not particularly fertile. Instead of rivers and lakes there are great natural wells, or *cenotes*, where the limestone has cracked and permitted an opening to the underground drainage system. Nothing about either Maya area suggests the Nile, Tigris-Euphrates, Ganges, or other famous river valleys of ancient cultural splendor. They do not even resemble the cool, rich uplands of Mexico and Peru, where later Indian societies reached a high stage. The growth of the Maya civilization in such an unpromising setting may well support Arnold Toynbee's famous theory that a people confronted with a challenge powerful enough to inspire them but not harsh enough to discourage them can respond with a disciplined, protracted effort that will civilize them. The challenge certainly existed in Central America. Difficulties of terrain stimulated a peo-

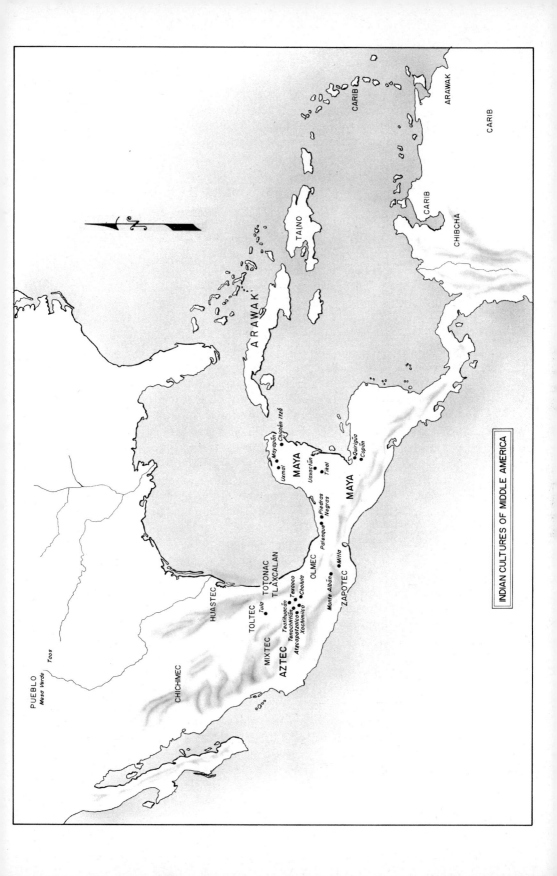

INDIAN CULTURES OF MIDDLE AMERICA

PUEBLO
Mesa Verde
Taos

CHICHIMEC

HUASTEC

TOLTEC
Tula
TOTONAC
TLAXCALAN
MIXTEC
AZTEC
Teotihuacán
Tenochtitlán
Texcoco
Atzcapotzalco
Xochimilco
Cholula
OLMEC
ZAPOTEC
Monte Albán
Mitla

MAYA
Uxmal
Mayapán
Chichén Itzá
Uaxactún
Tikal
Palenque
Piedras Negras

MAYA
Quiriguá
Copán

ARAWAK

TAINO

CARIB

ARAWAK

CARIB

CARIB

CHIBCHA

ple who wished to grow corn or maize into making an organized, intelligently-directed, and ultimately successful effort over a long period. Success in turn gave them the confidence necessary for progress in many other directions. •The Maya must also have produced that utterly unpredictable essential for civilization: a supply of geniuses.

The Classic or Old Empire Period

AFTER what must have been hundreds or thousands of years of growth a distinctive culture took shape around 300 A.D. in the present lands of Guatemala and British Honduras. During the next six centuries it became more elaborate and spread into other parts of Central America and into Mexico, where four or five different culture areas were in various stages of development. Very impressive centers—Tikal, Uaxactun, Copán, Quirigua, Calakmul, Palenque, and dozens more—along with numerous towns were constructed in what appears to have been a generally peaceful atmosphere. The absence of large fortifications and mention of warfare on monuments suggests that the settlements got along with a minimum of blood-letting. The great centers were not cities in our sense of the word; they contained stone temples, lofty pyramids, astronomical observatories, sculptured monuments, marketplaces, ballcourts, stucco-covered and brilliantly painted amphitheaters—but not residences. People dwelt outside the centers, the upper classes in handsome suburbs, the rest in villages scattered about the area. They went to the centers for purposes of worship, business, culture, and pleasure but lived near the fields where they grew the corn that provided most of their diet. Obviously, they had abundant leisure to build and adorn their great public works.

As some of these Maya centers have come into view, with moss scraped off and jungle growth torn away except for the great roots that have penetrated the foundations, their architecture above all has commanded admiration. Why? First and foremost, because these ruins are beautiful, far more so than those of ancient Mexico and Peru. The Maya cut white limestone to fit his needs, made bricks, and used mortar to erect the multi-storied buildings that are often still sturdy. Since each story is smaller than the one below, the constructions look like pyramids. Graceful stairs, columns, and ornate carvings attest to a high artistic skill. Inside were murals and large chambers roofed with corbeled vaults, though unaccountably the Maya failed to grasp the use of the keystone and so never achieved the true arch. They did not build as well as the Europeans of their time, but they were talented craftsmen who had a sense of beauty unmatched among the early Americans. They raised up great numbers of limestone shafts with carvings, or *stelae,* as monuments. These too offer mute testimony of a sophisticated culture. Some of the Maya buildings, always well-proportioned, were huge. Their amphitheaters were large enough to accommodate enormous crowds at religious or athletic events. Ballcourts and stands indicate the popularity of games played with rubber balls. The streets, broad and paved, must have been stately—wide ribbons tying together a marvelous composition of shining white buildings, blue lakes, and purple mountains.

Architecture aside, the Maya had many other outlets for their artistic bent. Wood carvings, pottery, work in jade and turquoise, and paintings of a unique blue shade all command the respect of modern students of art. Some of the stone sculptures emphasize serpents, bats, jaguars, lizards, and fantastic creatures in a manner often sinister, often playful. Others give good representations of the human face and figure, both in repose and in action. On a lower level, the Maya instinct for art showed itself in blankets, domestic articles, knives, and humbler ornaments of feathers and stones. Clearly, the cult of beauty reached down to the lowest class.

No other culture has been as obsessed with time and its mysteries as the Maya. Time was personified as benevolent or harsh according to the day or month. The past won respectful study as a guide to the future, for the cycles of climate and the movement of heavenly bodies were known to have a pattern that might reveal to each man his fate. For fatalism is the key to the Maya's preoccupation with time. What had been would be again. The weather would predictably change, the planets would orbit on schedule. It was not unusual for a primitive people to understand that the solar year had 365 days, but the Maya went beyond that to work out a calendar more accurate than any then used in Europe. The Maya year consisted of eighteen months of twenty days, with five days left over at the end—five days regarded as unlucky for any undertaking, even being born. The calendar also made adjustments for the extra day we put in our leap year.

The evidence of observatory remains and chronological calculations running back hundreds of millions of years shows that the Maya had a remarkably professional approach to the measurement of time. All this is especially noteworthy because a rainy climate made it very difficult to chart the skies, and in any case there was no glass for telescopes. We can only infer a high degree of cooperation among astronomers in different localities and an unbroken tradition from one generation to the next. Apparently the Maya did not measure minutes or hours as we do, but their concern with time led them far enough into advanced mathematics to discover the zero before the Europeans learned of it through the Arabs from the Hindus. They also worked out a vigesimal system, counting by twenties instead of tens. The Maya created numerals less clumsy than the Roman, but their method of computing time is defective from our point of view because it does not enable us to tell centuries apart—as if 1492, 1776, and 1984 were rendered only 92, 76, and 84. Hence much of our confusion about the sequence of Maya history even when we identify some years and names.

Writing was another achievement which distinguished the Maya from all other Americans. Primitive peoples often use pictures, as in Mexico, where a fairly advanced system of pictographs served as a way of writing. A further step is rebus writing, such as the drawing of an eye for "I." Much more sophisticated is ideographic writing, the use of symbols for ideas. This the Maya had, though they did not progress to the European stage of phonetic writing, in which characters stand for sounds. The Maya carved on their *stelae* dates, names, and possibly summaries of events. We can read only the calendric notations. The *stelae*, understandably, have proved rather durable, but, as noted, many or most of the manuscripts have disappeared. These were usually on paper made from fig tree bark, and it is reasonable to suppose that had more survived we might have learned to decipher the inscriptions. As matters stand, scholars may never come to understand the records that we have. The common Maya, of course, did not write. As in Europe, writing was a special skill restricted to a small educated minority.

Whether the Maya believed in one supreme god is uncertain. They appear to have credited creation to one deity, but many gods filled their pantheon. All were associated with time periods, and it was important for men to bargain with them. This was the origin of the sacrifice of human beings, animals, and birds, and the offering of one's own blood, obtained by pricking holes in the flesh at various times. The sun in particular was thought to require human blood if it were to be restored to life each morning after passing below the earth through a region of death. Human sacrifice was a standard practice but on a small scale. A certain dignity characterized this awful custom in that the victims were often willing, people who had agreed to play their part in propitiating the gods for the good of mankind. Furthermore, those who gave their all had the benefit of being drugged before they were drowned or had their hearts cut out.

The Maya believed that the world had been created and destroyed four or five times, and that it would again be destroyed. Obviously, prayer, ritual, fasting, and other means of placating the gods seemed urgent. The great centers had a primarily religious function, and the priestly class held so much power that many scholars think it long constituted the ruling group. Religion filled the life of the common man. Like most American Indians, he endowed his labor with reverent purpose, raising corn and working on buildings not entirely because he needed sustenance or because others forced him to, but because what he did was the right, the holy, thing to do. The Maya believed in five hells for punishment and thirteen pleasanter places for the afterlife. On the whole, the modern student has to be cautious about summarizing the cosmography and religious practices of the Maya, otherwise the effort may prove as confusing as an attempt to make a quick capsule statement of Europe's religious development from St. Peter to Martin Luther.

Many questions about the great period of the Maya remain unanswered. How were the people ruled? The Maya world may have consisted of a number of city-state theocracies living together in peace, more or less. If there were great kings or warriors we do not know of their deeds. An occasional historical figure appears in inscriptions or chronicles, but we find it hard to identify him or to be sure why he was honored. Did the large centers have intimate ties with each other? Apparently they did. Roads connected them, and the ruins are alike enough to indicate mutual influences. How was the land apportioned? There is no answer. We can only assume that the people worked well together and produced enough to support a large population. How was this society stratified? We have little to go on, though clearly some classes lived better than others. The questions multiply, for each new excavation unearths more mysteries than answers.

The greatest puzzle, however, is why the Old Empire or Classic period ended so abruptly. Between 800 and 925 the centers one by one suddenly stopped building, often in the midst of important work. Disaster must have overwhelmed them, but what it was, we have no idea. A surprise invasion from the outside world seems likely, for there is little evidence to suggest the violence and mutual destruction of civil war. Epidemics may have swept the population away, but this hypothesis is highly arguable. Soil exhaustion, climatic changes, droughts, and the like are often listed as possibilities. A favorite recent theory holds that the ruling priesthood lost its grip on the people because of a natural disaster and that an uprising followed. Somehow, in some way, the Maya broke away from the civilized path that had brought them so far. Mass deaths or flight created ruin, for the remnant of the population had only inadequate machetes or digging sticks to fend off a rampaging Nature. Just a year or two of neglect was enough time for the jungle or tough grass to take over the corn fields. Once this happened, if it did, the Maya could not restore what they had lost. The jungle moved in and blanketed the centers and towns until modern archaeologists arrived to tear it away. Whatever the cause of this ninth century calamity, it extinguished the brilliance of the central Maya area forever.

The New Empire, Post-Classic, or Mexican Period

As the great central Maya civilization sank into baffling decline, the borderland area in Yucatan climbed to its zenith. By the end of the tenth century this parched, sunnier area was heavily populated, perhaps with migrants from Guatemala, and a second outburst of Maya glory had begun. The buildings were, if anything, larger and more ornate than those of the Old Empire period, and the geometric designs adorning them were more advanced. Chichén Itzá, Mitla, Uxmal, and Mayapán became great centers and, after a century or two, real cities with thousands of inhabitants.

Scholars differ widely in interpreting the politics of the period. Undoubtedly, a strong Mexican influence was at work, as seen in the use of the bow and arrow, the ubiquity of the feathered serpent symbol, and the worship of the benevolent Kukulcan, who must have been the Quetzalcoatl expelled by the Toltecs of Mexico. Quetzalcoatl may actually have lived and conquered part of Yucatan about 1000. Or possibly a people known as the Itzá had absorbed the cult of Quetzalcoatl from the Mexicans before establishing themselves as the rulers of Yucatan. Whatever may have happened, we cannot say for sure whether the peninsula was united or divided into several sovereign nations. Emphasis on militarism in monuments and buildings suggests a ruling class of soldiers instead of priests. In any event, the Maya renaissance was a brilliant period.

About 1200, if not sooner, the city of Mayapán apparently established a mastery over all Yucatan which lasted until 1441. This seems to have been a period of stagnation. Even the ball courts for some reason fell into disuse. As the cultural level of the Maya slipped, that of the Mexicans rose. In all probability the Mexicans made good use of the knowledge and techniques they acquired through contacts with the Maya until the pupils surpassed their teachers. An outbreak of civil war in Yucatan in the fifteenth century hastened the dreary process of Maya downfall. The New Empire degenerated into a confused collection of warring city-states and tribes, and suffered a drastic decline in the arts, commerce, and population. Cities were abandoned, and learned groups disappeared. The surviving natives, cultivating corn as usual and fighting civil wars, almost lost touch with their heritage.

The Spaniards found the Maya in this sad state when, in 1511, a shipwrecked group reached the shores of Yucatan. Such European contacts may account for the epidemic of 1515–1516, which wiped out much of the remaining population. In 1517, 1518, and 1519, Spanish expeditions from Cuba explored the coastline. The intruders marveled

at the pyramids and colonnaded temples but were deterred from landing by the bellicosity of the natives and the greater lure of Mexico.
Later, after his famous victory over the Aztecs, Hernán Cortés himself
led a force south from Mexico through Maya territory into Honduras,
and his lieutenant, Pedro de Alvarado, conquered Guatemala, which
had long been in decay. In 1527 Francisco de Montejo undertook the
conquest of Yucatan, which proved unexpectedly difficult and required
nineteen years to complete. Montejo and his associates were as humane
as conquistadors ever could be, but the Maya fought furiously and
suffered dreadful losses in the struggle. Some of them managed to hold
out free in the Guatemalan jungles until 1697.

The Maya never re-established a link with their glorious past. Broken
in spirit, greatly reduced in numbers, and enslaved or scattered, they
labored for the Europeans in Yucatan and Guatemala or lived in isolation. As late as the 1840's, the Mexican Republic cruelly put down a
Maya revolt and deported thousands to slavery in Cuba. In very recent
times a strong stirring of the Guatemalan Maya has brought about a
resurgence of pride and a determination to win material advantages and
even political power. But this movement has little but romance to
connect it with the golden days of the Old and New Empires.

The mystery of what went wrong with the Maya is as great as that
of their original emergence. Civilizations simply rise and fall, and men
ponder why. The Maya, with their architecture, system of writing, mathematics, and astronomy, remain a fascinating enigma to any student of
the Americas. Did the achievements for which we honor them somehow
rule out more practical creations that would have saved them, such as
weapons and better tools? Whatever the final judgment, if any, the
brilliance of Maya culture shows some of the potential of the Indian before the European shackled him.

ANCIENT MEXICO

North of Maya territory, in the present republic of Mexico, were cultures that may have reached an advanced state about the time of Julius
Caesar. Their sequence we do not know, though the new method of
determining age by radiocarbon dating promises to clear up some major
points. Some authorities contend that these societies antedated and influenced the Maya. Others hold that the flow of civilization ran in the
opposite direction, particularly after 1000, when the Mexicans conquered parts of Yucatan. If the latter surmise is correct, the civilizing
of the Mexicans by the Maya paralleled the education of the militaristic
Romans by the cultured Greeks. While this theory seems the sounder at
present, it is possible that Mexican and Maya may have stemmed from

a still more ancient mother culture. Archaeologists are constantly making new finds and advancing new hypotheses, all of them highly tentative and open to revision. The student now can only balance his curiosity with skepticism until or unless the best authorities reach agreement.

The names given to some of the ancient Mexican cultures come from men of later periods who spoke different tongues. They may therefore in no way resemble the names used by the creators of those societies. Labels aside, the Aztecs are well-known, since they were dominant at the time of the Spanish invasion. Near the Gulf Coast were the Olmecs and Totonacs, who at one time in the distant past may have been very advanced. Recent excavations indicate that they were the heirs of an earlier culture we call La Venta, which perhaps flourished before the Maya. In southern Mexico near the Pacific coast are the awesome remains of the city of Mitla, center of Mixtec civilization, and towns of the Zapotecs, whose splendor has come to be appreciated only recently, since the excavation of graceful temples and rich tombs at Monte Albán. Other tribes or nations, such as the Zacatecans and the Toltecs, had traditions that intimated a great past, but their legends were confusing. What writings the Spanish found were too spare to clear up their history. Buildings had often survived, but the invader could not be sure who had erected them. Apparently, a backward group named the Chichimecs had forced their way into central Mexico and displaced more advanced peoples. In any case, the Spaniards were confused. They comprehended the present but could only guess at the past. They faced the same problem that might today confront visitors from outer space who could grasp political conditions on Earth but would become greatly bewildered if they heard of the Holy Roman Empire, Napoleon, Hitler, the League of Nations, or the Confederate States of America.

The Toltecs

PERHAPS the most mystifying of these early Mexicans were the Toltecs, a group so nebulous we are not sure whether they were a nation at all. When the Spaniards arrived, individuals said to be Toltecs enjoyed the respect of the Aztecs and received credit for great past achievements. It may well be that they created a culture or integrated previous cultures while dominating the richest part of Mexico about the time of the Old Empire of the Maya. Tula, which lies about fifty miles north of Mexico City, was one of their main centers, perhaps, if the Toltecs were a genuine nation, their political capital. More impressive was Teotihuacán, probably the most-visited of all the historic Indian cities in the Americas. This may have been the Toltec religious center, a built-up area more than six square miles in size and containing the soaring Pyramid of the Sun—probably the largest in the world—and several smaller pyramids, amphitheaters, monuments, and paved streets. The enormous ruins of Teotihuacán are likely to inspire the modern tourist with their sheer magnitude rather than their beauty, for its builders did not equal the Maya in delicate artistry. The tourist is also likely to sense the doom that awaits all great cultures eventually, a rather unsettling feeling. Another awesome Toltec center was Cholula, which may have supplanted Teotihuacán as a religious capital. Later, the Spanish saw to it that numerous—guides always say the number was 365 —Christian churches were erected in this pagan citadel.

Of Toltec government and society we know next to nothing. It may be that this was a nation that ruled the major part of Mexico for a time and conquered Yucatan from the Maya. If there were great warriors and statesmen we cannot chronicle their doings, Toltec pictographs being neither numerous nor informative enough for the purpose. We have more evidence of an influential god or ruler in the cult of Quetzalcoatl, which the Aztecs took over after a fashion. This figure may have been a dim folk hero who ruled wisely and well, a sort of father of his peoples, preacher of virtue and ethics, and teacher of mechanical skills. The tradition that he was white and bearded is cloudy but may have some substance. According to the story, Quetzalcoatl departed dramatically with a promise to return. He had either committed the sin of incest and exiled himself or was overthrown through the sorcery of a rival god, Tezcatlipoca. The timing of this event, just before 1000, coincides with the appearance of Kukulcan in Yucatan and the collapse of the Toltecs before new invaders. It is a plausible guess that the ousted ruler and his followers had enough arms to establish themselves in Maya territory and introduced the strong Mexican influences in Yucatan we have noted. As to whether Quetzalcoatl-Kukulcan was really white and bearded, and therefore a European, conjecture is tempting but fruitless. Certainly the Spanish exploited the legend for all it was worth, for the widespread belief among the Indians that the god would return proved very useful to the white, bearded conquistadors.

The Aztecs

A LITTLE more than a century after the departure of Quetzalcoatl, the Toltecs disappeared altogether as a ruling group. Apparently invaders from the north moved into central Mexico and dragged down the cultural level of the area. Whether these Chichimecs introduced the Nahuatl language, the basic tongue of this region, or learned it from the Toltecs is disputed. In time they lost some of their barbaric ways and fused with the defeated peoples. Greatness was the destiny of one of these nations from the north, the Aztecs. Our knowledge of this people is fairly substantial because the Spanish studied them before administering the fatal blow that destroyed their independence. Also, various clergymen and officials compiled comprehensive if somewhat credulous accounts of their ways after the Conquest. The seized pictographs were of some assistance in learning of their past. Finally, the Spanish government drew up codes of Aztec practices to facilitate the process of adapting the conquered people to their rule.

According to their own official history, the Aztecs were a primitive tribe of nomads living in the arid north when, in 1168, they began to wander toward the heartland of Mexico, a 7000-foot high, cool, fertile basin ringed by spectacular mountain ranges then known as Anáhuac and now usually as the Valley of Mexico. An ugly little pot-bellied idol named Huitzilopochtli gave them excellent advice about military matters. In 1248 or sooner, these Aztecs penetrated Anáhuac. This splendid territory had long been the goal of land-hungry tribes and at this time was occupied by Chichimecs and Toltecs and other competing groups who had built cities along the shores of the great salt water lake and several smaller fresh water bodies. The Aztecs forced their way in, another of a long series of intruders. For three or four generations these rude, prolific warriors served as mercenaries and allies to stronger tribes until they established themselves as a potent nation in their own right, absorbing all the while some of the civilization of their enemies. The Aztecs had many adventures, some hilarious and others gruesome as their state histories record them, while they contended with other groups in Anáhuac, where international morality was at least as low as it was in Europe. After a particularly base deed of treachery they had to flee for their lives in 1325 into the islands of the salt water lake. There a favorable sign appeared to them: an eagle with a serpent in its beak, perched on a cactus on a tiny island—the emblem now of the Mexican nation.

True to the sacred forecast, the settlement in the lake prospered. The Aztecs multiplied and grew rich in predatory wars and raids on the mainland. Their warlike zeal was made all the more formidable by the conviction that Huitzilopochtli craved the sacrifice of vast numbers of prisoners of war. The Aztec haven in the islands became a great city, Tenochtitlán, with artificial islands being constructed when needed and causeways several miles long connecting them with the mainland. Countless dirt-covered rafts, "floating gardens," provided homes and vegetables for many persons. A spectacular temple housed Huitzilopochtli and other idols on what is now the Zócalo, the principal plaza of Mexico City. Great, truncated pyramids in the Toltec style were erected, their whitewashed steps contrasting with the bright red rivulets of human blood that ran ominously down from the sacrificial altars on their tops. Enormous markets served the commercial requirements of the population. Aqueducts brought in fresh water. Paved streets, portable bridges. and canals enabled the people to circulate by foot or canoe. Splendid palaces, temples, and civic centers gleamed in the brilliant Mexican sun. Luxurious homes for the upper classes and numerous houses of more humble type sheltered a population probably larger than that of Sevilla, Spain's biggest city. This enchanted Venice, set in a shining lake with majestic mountain ranges and a smoking volcano in the distance, seemed impregnable to invasion. Its inhabitants were amphibious, able to descend on their rivals by canoe or causeway as they willed and to shut themselves up behind their defenses.

During the reign of Itzcoatl, 1428–1440, Tenochtitlán came to dominate some of the mainland in alliance with two other cities, Tlacopán and Texcoco. Under Montezuma I, 1440–1487, the Aztecs successfully waged war eastward to the Gulf and southward to the Pacific, compelling the defeated tribes and nations to pay heavy tribute for the glorification of Tenochtitlán. This imperialistic expansion continued under the three succeeding rulers until Texcoco and Tlacopán were dependent allies rather than partners and nearly all of southern and central Mexico came under Aztec rule. Only two islands of independence withstood the Aztec tide, the Tarascans to the west and, significantly, the Tlaxcalans to the east. In 1503 the chieftainship of this imperial nation went to Montezuma II, who thereby became autocrat of Tenochtitlán, masterful ally of two other great cities, and overlord of at least thirty-eight tributary provinces.

The government of the Aztecs centered in the monarch, whom the Spanish later chose to call "emperor." Elected from a large royal family by an august council of a hundred military leaders, prelates, and civil dignitaries, this emperor was to serve, as they said, as father and mother to his people, to dispense justice, and to assure the fruits of the earth for his subjects. Though he was treated with great deference and lived in splendor that a European monarch might have envied (Montezuma II had several palaces, many gardens and zoos, and at least 2,000 personal servants), the Aztec ruler was not regarded as a divinity. His authority was circumscribed in routine governmental affairs by the many duties performed by a vice-emperor and in war and other matters of high policy by the advice of a council. The large and well-endowed clergy also occupied a position of eminence in statecraft. Finally, the twenty or so tribes who composed the Aztec nation had leaders who were consulted on important matters and who themselves took the major decisions regarding the economic welfare of their own groups. These tribes were further subdivided into *calpullis,* or land-holding clans, whose leaders intimately controlled the destinies of the common people in both war and peaceful pursuits. While it may have been that no nobility of the European type had developed, a sort of hereditary aristocracy existed in the upper classes of officials, war leaders, and clergy. Yet social mobility, in the way of opportunity for a warrior to rise into a higher class, prevailed, and the Aztec society was democratic to this extent.

Since the fundamental purpose of this society was imperialistic—to expand and exploit at the expense of neighboring peoples—the government was largely absorbed in cultivating military skills and in accumulating weapons. The Aztec soldier was encouraged to be brave and tough. He flaunted his militarism in the way he painted his body and displayed colorful, feathery clothing, not really uniforms since much individual decoration was permitted. The men did not drill, but they constantly kept themselves in condition through hunting and athletics and, of course, by working. When war came they sprang to the arsenals and grouped around the clan leaders. Their major weapons were a heavy wooden club with an obsidian blade and the javelin, both of which were fearfully effective when wielded by shouting Aztecs with their superb morale and tradition of victory. Bows and arrows, spears, slings, knives, and hatchets were secondary weapons, and the Aztecs made extensive use of protective helmets and quilted cotton shields for their chests. War with another nation at times involved the usual amount of treachery and surprise, yet a certain ceremony might prevail with the formal exchange of warnings and messages, truces, and even an element of chivalry if the going were not too rough. The desirability of taking prisoners instead of exterminating the enemy perhaps accounts for some battlefield courtesy.

One battle usually determined the outcome of war. The defeated tribe would see its young men led off as prisoners to be sacrificed, its temples defiled, and its attractive women and goods seized. Then it was likely to settle down as a tribute-paying satellite of the Aztecs. It would live as it had before, but no longer could it make war on its own, and periodically Aztec tax collectors would arrive, demanding such tribute as clothes, war implements, eagles, skins, feathers, jade, turquoise, corn, cacao, honey, chile, tobacco, construction materials, furniture, incense, live birds, and, regrettably, other human beings to be offered in sacrifice. By the time the Spanish came, the power of Tenochtitlán was well respected throughout southern and central Mexico. Montezuma's demands were to be honored, cost what they may, and hatred for the arrogant Aztecs was as deep as the fear they inspired. It was not an integrated empire, such as the Inca in Peru ruled, but a matter of a master nation and cowed dependencies.

As might be expected, the economy of Aztec Mexico centered about the raising of corn. The Aztecs had the choice lands, which were parceled out among the tribes and then re-divided among the component clans. There seems to have been no sense of permanent land ownership among the Indians, and fields were awarded to families within the clans by the elders to be tended as long as they could or would do so. If the land itself belonged to the state or nation, its produce went to the family who worked it. Apparently the system functioned well enough to feed and satisfy the population, at least of the favored tribes and clans, and it offered an elemental amount of security. In fact, it was the duty of the rulers to see that a young man who married received land. In addition to the strips or fields thus divided out, common lands, or *ejidos*, reinforced the economy and provided opportunity for those who did not enjoy occupancy of distinct plots. It is this revival of the *ejido* in modern Mexico that has brought hope to many formerly landless peons. On the whole, the economy of ancient Mexico was something of a mixture of feudalism, private ownership, and primitive communism. It was far superior to slavery, and it provided the population with as much nutrition, clothing, and housing as the average European of the time had. This economy may easily have been more productive and just than any other the Mexicans were to enjoy until recent times.

If the raising of corn and other vegetables basic to the support of the population—beans, peppers, squashes, avocados, tomatoes, and many others—absorbed the peacetime energies of the bulk of the population, the growth of commerce indicated the development of a more sophisticated economy. Traders carried articles of luxury from various parts of Mexico to the cities for the benefit of the ruling groups. In time this process might have signified the creation of something resembling an Indian middle class, but the Spanish conquest cut it off. If the commercial group did not succeed in organizing a large distributive system in ancient times, the exchange of articles among the Indians went on continuously before and after the Europeans arrived. Market places varied from the humble assembly of women in villages to magnificent exchanges in the cities. Goods were usually bartered, but in some cases the cacao bean served as a unit of exchange, a sort of money. There was even a tendency for certain towns or sections of the country to specialize in various types of handicraft which could be traded for others, painted pottery for feathery clothes, delicately wrought silver and gold for the more precious jade ornaments, processed food for furniture or blankets, and so on. All this permitted a considerable variety in clothing and food for the common population as well as a high standard of living for the upper classes. The Mexicans had as wide a choice of plant food as the Europeans had, their stone and adobe huts were surely no more inadequate, and their clothing, while simple, was as colorful and comfortable as that worn by equivalent classes in the Old World. If they had less meat to eat—none but the turkey and such game as they killed—and no dairy products, they enjoyed in tobacco a comfort other peoples were later to covet to an amazing degree. Their alcoholic vice was pulque, a mild intoxicant made from the juices of the maguey plant.

The class system on which this economy rested was not greatly different from that of other parts of the world. The august ruling groups and their luxuries compared to those of European or Asian societies, the warrior, priest, and administrator being duly privileged, though perhaps having less sanctity based on long tradition. The Mexican soil tiller had no domesticated animals to ease his labor and his implements were inferior, but his way of life was apparently no more debased than elsewhere in the world. At the bottom of the social scale were the plebeians, who fashioned the pottery and blankets and other articles, and a slave class. This latter group does not compare explicitly to contemporaneous Europe, where slavery persisted and, of course, serfdom was very general. In ancient Mexico a person was not born into slavery but fell into this state through being captured in war, minor crimes, debts, social ostracism of one type or another, or even by committing himself to a wealthier person for the sake of protection and livelihood as in the earliest days of European feudalism. The labor of such a slave, but not his whole being, belonged to the owner, and a slave could achieve freedom or own other slaves while in servitude.

Aztec justice was as harsh as it was everywhere else. Husbands ruled their wives, polygamy being a privilege permitted males of the upper classes and easy divorce and re-marriage constituting for men of the lower classes a benefit almost as great. Fathers ruled sons absolutely unless the clan elders chose to impose their greater authority in family matters. Elected lower courts handled much of the justice for the common people, while superior tribunals dealt with crimes among the upper classes. Punishment was likely to be fierce, as it was everywhere until the last two centuries. For murder, theft, or witchcraft death penalties were apt to be inflicted. Slanderers would have their lips cut off, and sex offenders might be mutilated. Curiously, drunkenness outside of legitimate festivities or ceremonies brought severe punishment and disgrace except for old people, who were exempted from such penalties. Fundamentally, the object of justice was to discourage crime and any act regarded by the group as anti-social. If possible, the wrongdoer was forced to make restitution to his victim.

The pictographic writing of the Aztecs, those colorful comic strips relating historical events as later generations idealized them, represents the bulk of the literature that is still available. Oratory was very popular but by its nature has not come down to us. In addition, poems and plays and perhaps other forms of literature expressed the feelings of the people and offered entertainment. Obsession with death and tragedy in these forms may suggest something about the pessimistic, doom-soaked atmosphere of ancient Mexico. Yet the same conclusion might be drawn about the literary expression of any other society, including our own, at almost any period.

The Aztecs made music with drums, whistles, flutes, rattles and trumpets—music for moments of frivolity and romance but more for the stately ceremonies that played such a part in their life. We know little of it, other than the fact that it was widespread, for European instruments and forms quickly eclipsed the Indian. The dance was also a matter of general entertainment and reverent patriotic-religious exhibition. In the regular ceremonies about the pyramids thousands of Indians, usually segregated by sex and under the influence of alcohol, swayed and moved according to majestic patterns while gods were invoked and human beings sacrificed. Less grim were the popular athletic events involving the usual efforts to excel and great crowds of spectators. One of their games resembled modern basketball except that the rubber ball could be knocked through hoops only with knees and hips, surely a most difficult proceeding. The Aztecs were also fond of dressing up like birds and flying about high poles, with cords linking their bodies to the tops.

It was a brilliant if barbaric society the Aztecs had. The Spanish were properly astonished as they beheld cities larger than they had seen in Spain with a scale of living that, class for class, in so many respects equalled that of Europe. The pyramids, temples, amphitheaters, bridges, palaces, and even the ordinary homes bespoke a society of much technical skill. Popular appreciation of the arts and a widespread cult of beauty attested to a long-maturing culture. A political system that enforced the will of the rulers, an economy that sufficed to support a large population in comparative plenty, a society that lived according to established rules—all this seemed generally familiar. Aztec skill in construction and in reckoning time—based on the calendar also used by the Maya and the Toltecs—seemed to surpass much of the European. But wonder and respect turned to horror as the invaders grasped the true nature of the religious rituals. It was offensive enough to these Christians that a multiplicity of idols and vicious gods was worshiped, that the fate of man on this planet was deemed to depend upon the whims of hideous deities. Yet even illiterate Spanish soldiers knew that the Christian faith did not prevail in all corners of the earth, a condition they earnestly hoped to remedy. Many had seen pagans and idols before. What seemed so utterly unspeakable to them in Mexico was the massively organized system for slaughtering human beings to propitiate these false gods.

The Aztec religion was truly a horrifying affair by the standards of any time. In centers all over Mexico prisoners waited in cages until the grim Aztec officials arrived to send them on to Tenochtitlán. In that spectacular city, at least every twenty days groups were dragged or forced up the pyramid steps while yelling, drunken Aztecs danced gruesomely about the base. The usual method of sacrifice was for the priests to throw the victim on his back upon a large stone, break open his chest with a dull obsidian blade, and tear out his heart. The heart might then be eaten by the clergy, the victim's skin taken and used for dress in jest, mockery, or even in reverence, and his skull placed in a hideous collection that grew to monstrous proportions. Macabre variations to this procedure featured the ceremonies at the beginning of each of the eighteen months. Sometimes the victim would have to fight with feathers against armed warriors until they killed him by degrees. One particularly cruel celebration involved roasting the prisoners before they were finally killed. Some of the victims were children, a few were women, a still smaller number were honored persons, but by far the most were anonymous prisoners of war. They died by the thousand. In the reign of Montezuma II, 20,000 were said to have been killed in a single ceremony. These mass executions were occasions for great rejoicing by the Aztec population. Those who died deserved their fate, they believed, or at least the taking of their lives pleased the gods. It seems almost certain that these mass sacrifices at frequent intervals were typical only of the Aztecs, not of other nations who had once prevailed in Middle America. If so, the Aztec indeed represented a retrogression from other cultures who had known gentler and more noble rituals.

Some of these monthly ceremonies seem purely sadistic with mass gloating over pain and bloodshed. Others had an exalted dramatic quality. Children were sacrificed early in the solar year with the hope that their tears would assure a rainy season. On another occasion a credulous woman would be told that a noble warrior desired her and suddenly find herself being dragged up the pyramid to death as her betrayers laughed. A fine youth, chosen among the prisoners of war, would be allowed to live out a year in honor and pleasure, only to pay for it at the end by a solemn sacrifice of his own heart. In one monthly ceremony the clergy would dance about in the skins of the men they had just executed. The biggest massacres took place as the annual war season began, when great numbers, hundreds or even thousands, of captured soldiers from previous campaigns were ripped open to placate Huitzilopochtli. Yet the ritual was not all brutality. The return of the gods from their annual retreat was a time of dramatic suspense and then great exultation when their footprints were "observed" by the waiting clergy. And every fifty-two years a cycle ended in which it was problematical whether life would be renewed or the world destroyed. All the fires in the land went out, and the entire population was supposed to fast and pray until the terrible tension ended with the movement of the stars to a designated position. Then the sacred fire would be re-lit, and torch bearers would race through the land carrying the joyous tidings that another fifty-two-year lease on life had been granted the human race.

Dreadful as the sacrifices were, and it seemed they were becoming more rather than less numerous as time went on, the Aztecs' practices have been defended. They believed, as many other peoples have, that their own gods had found eternal life through pain and death, and so would humanity. They demanded the lives of men in order to permit the rest of the race to live on earth awhile longer. Hence it was an honor to give one's heart that others might continue to live. Sometimes the victims were willing to do so, and usually a certain amount of dignity and good will prevailed in these grisly ceremonies. The atmosphere has been likened to modern war, when men face death in the hope that their fellows may survive.

Aztec religion was pervaded with pessimism. All was decided by fate, but modifications might be obtained by humoring the proper god. As in other religions, superstitions, charms, signs, portents, and such were much employed. Yet the soul went to one of the five hells or thirteen heavens on the basis of predetermination, conduct in this life having little to do with one's ultimate destination except for warriors killed in battle or women dead in childbirth, who went to heaven. Not all of the clergy spent their time tearing open chests and eating human flesh. Some were important advisors in matters of state, others were holy men and healers, some taught and compiled sacred works, some lived lives of contemplation, and most of them pulled sticks or strings through their ears, tongues, and nostrils to draw blood that would appease the gods.

It is easy to see why the hardened Spanish conquistadors were revolted by the religion of the Aztecs, and why Christian clergymen exulted in releasing prisoners, overturning idols, and burning sacred literature. To their credit, as soon as possible they compelled the Aztecs to desist from their bloody practices. It is also easy to understand why the satellite tribes of the Aztecs detested their masters and were so readily persuaded to join in overthrowing them. Once the Conquest was finished, the Aztecs themselves quickly abandoned their hideous divinities and, in many cases, embraced the nobler religion of their conquerors with hysterical joy.

THE PRESENT AMERICAN SOUTHWEST

The Pueblos

MORE than a thousand miles to the north of the Aztec domain, across the mountains and deserts that separate the modern United States and Mexico far more truly than the Rio Grande, a minor Indian culture developed between the time of Christ and 1300. Its survivals today, in the Hopi, Zuñi, and other reservations of the American Southwest, are the focus of attention from archaeologists and anthropologists as well as oil and uranium seekers and tourists.

The generic name for the culture is Pueblo. A few students believe it was a parent civilization for the societies farther south, but this is distinctly a minority point of view. In any event, the Pueblos are much admired. After centuries of wandering they settled in communities on top of the buttes and mesas of the Southwest, where the women raised corn and wove baskets and the men fought and hunted. Perhaps around 800, they began to build adobe houses and kivas, or large, underground religious chambers, where, women and children were told, live gods resided. Boys found out better during the brutal puberty ceremonies but apparently kept the secret. The people lived in comparative safety on these high points, pondered the sky and the great stretches of sagebrush and cactus, and became ardent conformists, seeking above all to harmonize their ways with nature.

By about 1100 they were quite advanced in pottery and construction. Their homes were windowless rooms in enormous apartment houses, where they lived intimately with other families. Then, as we can trace best in Mesa Verde (Colorado), they forsook the open mesa tops and built intricate homes in caves that dotted the rocky cliffs, most of them also in the style of apartment houses or wasp nests. They danced in a stately fashion, worshiped, painted their skins, and seemingly stayed to themselves, a strange people almost like sleepwalkers.

Between 1276 and 1299, as we know from a study of tree rings, a terrible drought afflicted the Southwest. Leaving their homes in an orderly fashion, the cliff-dwellers and mesa people descended into the river valleys of modern New Mexico and Arizona.[1] There they constructed villages, again in the apartment house style. They lived on, probably fewer than 100,000 of them all told, when the Spanish ar-

---

1. Of course, there is always the pos-   their migration.
sibility that other reasons accounted for

rived under Coronado in 1540. They were organized only on a community basis and could put up no effective resistance to the intruder. The same was true fifty years later when the Spanish came back to make permanent settlements. And yet, in 1680, they carried out one of the very rare successful rebellions of Indian against white. The Spanish were expelled for more than ten years. They came back, of course, but the Pueblos ignored them as much as they could, as later they spurned the Mexican and the American. Even today they live apart, their ways little modified by centuries of contact with Western civilization except for a fondness for the automobile.

The Plains and Coastal Indians
of the Present United States

THE savage nomads who lived on the Great Plains played a much larger role in the history of the United States than they did in the Spanish empire. Their lives centering about the buffalo and deer, they moved as hunting necessities dictated, developing only the most elemental skills. The Spanish made contact with them during Coronado's adventure and a few other incursions, but they cared little whether these fierce people were civilized into Europeans or not, and there was no question of making them settle down to labor for the white man. Late in the eighteenth century the Plains Indians received guns and horses from Englishmen and Frenchmen, not always as gifts, and proceeded to raid frontier Spanish settlements in Texas, New Mexico, and northern Mexico. They continued to be a menace until the Americans exterminated them or herded them into reservations. Somewhat nostalgically, modern people think of them as leading lives of drama and adventure.

Along the shores of California lived natives of the lowest culture. Nature was so kindly they had no need to work systematically. So they picked berries, fished, and hunted rabbits and deer. They had no permanent villages, and some of the first Spaniards who visited them concluded they were the basest of creatures. These coastal Indians were largely let alone by the white men, at least until the late eighteenth century. Then, the Spanish became fearful that the Russians would colonize California and forestalled them by dispatching Franciscan friars into American California. The Indians were soon rounded up in a string of missions, whereupon they died off, ran away, or settled down quietly as humble plebeians. Low as their culture was, they did not wish to improve it nor live as the white man wanted them to.

ANCIENT SOUTH AMERICA

Inca Civilization in Peru

IN THE central Andean region of South America developed an Indian culture which seems in many ways the most peculiar and haunting of all those the Spaniards invaded. Much of it has persisted in spite of more than four centuries of the white man's occupation—the Quechua and Aymará languages, many humble customs of daily life, mystical attitudes, and a sullen separateness from the European that has prevented the widescale mixing of the races as that in Mexico. The new method of determining dates by Carbon 14 has pushed back our reckoning of the beginnings of this culture, or at least of its basis in farming, to perhaps 3000 B.C., making it almost as old as the most ancient civilizations anywhere in the world. Perhaps it antedated the Indian societies in Middle America. It is remotely possible that sporadic landings of men from Polynesia and Melanesia who sailed the Pacific brought some influences. All we can be sure of now is that men practiced agriculture and built extraordinary cities for many centuries before Columbus and that the Europeans found the entire region stretching from the present republic of Ecuador down into Chile and Argentina, between the Amazon jungles and the Pacific Ocean, united under a uniquely effective government. The elaborate political and economic organization that prevailed gave internal peace and material security to perhaps as many people as live in the central Andes region today. The word "Inca" is our name for it, though, confusingly enough, it also means the master nation which dominated the area, the large royal family which claimed descent from the sun, and merely the monarch himself.

That a civilization should develop in the Andes is not quite so strange as the puzzle posed by the growth of Maya culture in Central America. The climate in these mountains, which rank after the Himalayas as the highest in the world, is sunny and cool during most of the daylight hours, like a fine October day in the United States. Between the lofty ranges are fertile valleys and plateaus where a great number of small plants grow. A strip of desert along the Pacific coast and the edge of the vast Amazon basin to the east permit a considerable variety in game and plants. Guinea pigs and small dogs, deer, and above all, those disdainful members of the camel family—the llama, guanaco, alpaca, and vicuña—along with fish provide additional food. Once the earliest men learned to settle down and to cultivate crops of potatoes, corn, grain, and the usual foods common to the Americas, they were well on the road to civilization. Contact with one another broadened their

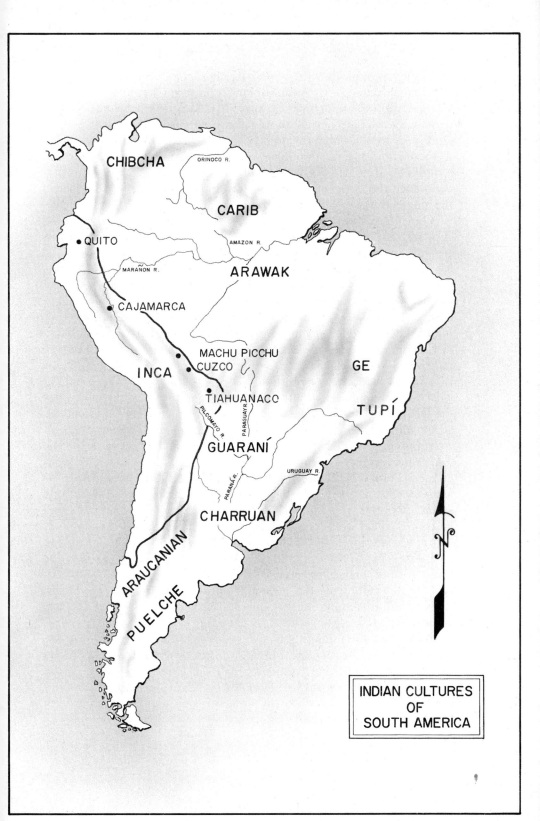

INDIAN CULTURES
OF
SOUTH AMERICA

skills and stock of knowledge. Perhaps immigrants from across the Pacific brought new plants and techniques. Or it may have been the other way around, for the dramatic voyage in 1949 of the balsa raft *Kontiki* with its Scandinavian crew proved the possibility of sailing two thousand miles west from South America. Contacts with other culture areas, if they ever existed, were long since broken before the Europeans came. The Inca rested complacently on the misconception that they dominated the entire earth and all its peoples but for a few savages in the jungles to the east and the forests to the south.

Our information about the Andean cultures is exasperatingly scant, even for the Inca society itself. No system of writing, not even the pictographs of the Aztecs nor the largely undecipherable hieroglyphics of the Maya, served to inform the curious European.[2] The Spaniards who conquered the Inca were a rather bad lot, committing the inexcusable barbarity of failing to commit to writing the facts and statistics that might have been enlightening. The few who troubled to record what they found did so tardily and incompletely except for that methodical soldier, Pedro de Cieza de León, who was not in the first wave of the conquistadors. Many years later, two mestizos of Inca and Spanish ancestry, Blas Valera and Garcilasso Inca de la Vega, compiled useful accounts of what they had heard as youths. In the 1570's, forty years or more after the first contact with the Inca, Pedro Sarmiento de Gamboa assembled all the information he could from surviving Inca elders. Important as his contribution proved, it was distorted by his palpable effort to justify the rule of the Spanish by depicting the Inca as usurping tyrants. The Jesuit fathers Montesinos, Cobo, and Acosta wrote significant accounts in the late sixteenth and the seventeenth centuries, but they were necessarily remote from the great times of Inca superiority, and Montesinos, though he copied a useful work, was singularly unreliable. All of these records and others dealing with the ancient Inca are full of contradictions and inconsistencies. In recent times, particularly during the last two decades, the science of archaeology has contributed enormously to our appreciation of the culture of the ancient Andeans. Much more knowledge should be forthcoming so that our information may someday be less vague and tentative.

Aware of these inhibiting factors, we may proceed to sketch the rise of the fantastic Inca empire which the Spanish overthrew in 1532. By 1200 B.C. an identifiable culture we call the Chavín prevailed in the northern highlands of modern Peru. Its emphasis on feline deities and fantastic monsters carved out of stone suggests a preoccupation with frightening spirits and unwholesome worship of power but also exhibits

2. A slight possibility exists that some of the pre-Inca groups had a system of writing, but the evidence is so thin it should not yet be accepted.

a commendable striving for perfection. Chavín influences are seen in much of the highlands and coasts of Peru as pottery, temples, and monuments are excavated. From a few centuries before the birth of Christ to a few centuries afterward, a period roughly corresponding with the rise and fall of Rome, large centers or cities were built along the desert coast of Peru and deep in the bleak highlands of Bolivia around Lake Titicaca. Their contacts with one another must have been largely military, for fortresses and extensive walls on the order of the Great Wall of China are conspicuous. Because of the extreme dryness of the climate, many of these remains are in good condition, once they are detected and unearthed. Nazca and Paracas on the southern and Mochica on the northern coast were great centers, and Pachacamac in the central coastal region near modern Lima perhaps flourished as early as this. Near Nazca in the desert wastes are enormous man-made lines that have only recently been discerned from airplanes. Whether they had a calendric purpose or were built to please the gods in the sky or for some other reason is a mystery. Pachacamac is huge, a partially buried city to challenge the archaeologist and to excite wonder in the tourist. The artistic remains of Mochica stress the macabre and erotic. As strange as the others are the megalithic survivals in the barren highlands near Lake Titicaca, the center or city we call Tiahuanaco.

It may have been between 400 and 1000 A.D. that Tiahuanaco came to dominate all of Peru. At least, its influences are seen in most cities. Yet Nazca continued to flourish, its textiles and weaving becoming as fine as any in the world and its geometric designs on pottery uncommonly beautiful. In the north, Mochica shared with another culture, the Chimu, a fruitful period. Real cities developed out of an elaborate economy, and the rich archaeological findings have revealed much about the life of the population, their practicality and their frank realism which often becomes brutality. Perhaps the Tiahuanaco culture unified all Peru for a time and then lost its control, leaving the various areas to develop along regional lines. Then it seems to have made a comeback, again dominating the coastal areas in the south until the rise of the Inca. In any event, there were times when all of these ancient cultures were in close contact with each other and times when they were isolated. Whether they were centered in the highlands, the coastlands, or the irrigated river valleys near the Pacific, all succumbed eventually to the Inca, who of course borrowed heavily from them. Once Inca authority was established over the whole area, a determined and, unhappily, successful effort was made to blot out the memory of these cultures. The physical remains are all we have to interpret.

It is probable that the Inca were inferior to the peoples they defeated, at least in the beginning. In time, however, they created an official myth-history flattering to themselves. According to this record as the early Spaniards understood it, the world was created by Viracocha. Afterward he invented mankind, but, displeased with its behavior, he turned all human beings into stones and flooded the world. Later he emerged from Lake Titicaca and tried another experiment, creating a smaller race of men and the sun and the moon. Jealous of the moon, the sun threw ashes in its face and dimmed its luster. Mankind, however, apparently multiplied. Viracocha eventually went through Peru and Ecuador in disguise, performing miracles, teaching, and preaching, and then walked westward into the Pacific and disappeared over the horizon.[3] After some lapse of time a remarkable family emerged from three caves close to the deep valley of Cuzco, four brothers and four sisters. One of the brothers proved so troublesome the others sealed him in a cave, and one of the sisters was so terrifying she conquered the early inhabitants of Cuzco. The eldest, Manco Capac, established himself in Cuzco as the first emperor of the Inca line, blessed by the ruling Sun, his ancestor and protector. This may have happened about 1200 A.D.

For several reigns the Inca ruled little but Cuzco, as well-defended by nature in its way as the Aztec capital in the lake. "The navel of the universe," Cuzco lay in one of the extremely steep, high valleys in the Andes, protected by mountains and watered by streams that could be manipulated to the advantage of the defenders. It is so high (about 11,000 feet) that it is cool all the time. Its inhabitants, like those of the highlands of Peru and Bolivia, have barrel chests, outsized lungs, and more blood and larger hearts than most other people. Only in this way could the fittest survive in the thin mountain air. Not only did the Cuzqueños survive, but early in the fifteenth century they began to expand under an emperor who took the name of his god, Viracocha. Almost defeated in an epic attack on Cuzco, the Inca Viracocha was saved by his son, Pachacuti, who took the offensive and began the fabulous career of Inca imperialism. Emperor himself after a time, Pachacuti rebuilt Cuzco and stabilized the calendar, which was less accurate than the Maya but which served well. He conquered his neighbors, which is enough to make any ruler "great" by his nation's standards, and expanded the realm of the Inca in all directions. Then his son, Topa Inca Yupanqui, continued the conquests into Ecuador, Bolivia, and the coast of Peru and made a distant voyage to islands in the Pacific, probably the Galápagos, and returned. Eventually becoming tenth emperor himself, Topa Inca Yupanqui built the enormous fortress-shelter of Sac-

bearded man. It may have been that the Spaniards were eager to believe this and the Mexican Quetzalcoatl is added the point that Viracocha was a white, reached the Americas and left these

3. To this similarity with the career of that the Indians were insincere when they told them so. On the other hand, a European leader might somehow have legends.

sahuaman, whose ruins near Cuzco offer a marvelous example of Inca engineering skill. He also fixed the tribute for his subjects, created a perpetual class of servants known as the *yanacona*, and collected the finest girls in the realm to serve as Chosen Women. By this time, about 1492, the Inca firmly ruled the bulk of creation as they knew it. They had conquered nearly everyone in reach and had learned from their victims. So sure were they of their power they now began a policy of conciliation to make the defeated peoples forget their past and cooperate with the new ruling group. The Quechua language was becoming the general tongue throughout the Andes.

Huayna Capac succeeded Topa Inca Yupanqui in 1493. In the Inca fashion he was the son of the preceding monarch and that dignitary's sister. Huayna Capac extended the Inca realm to its greatest size, penetrating Ecuador, the western edges of the Amazon basin, and central Chile. Apparently he was a great ruler, and with his reign the Inca empire reached its peak of strength and morale. Not long before Huayna Capac died, in 1526, he learned of white bearded men sailing down the coast of Peru and, possibly, penetrating overland from the east. He caught a pestilence (one wonders if germs from these Europeans caused it) and became mortally ill. Somehow he failed to name his heir in an unequivocal way. According to some, he made his legitimate son Huascar successor to the fringe of red tassels that served as a crown. Others declared that he split his realm, leaving the northern portion to a son by a wife other than the principal one, to Atahualpa, who had often accompanied him on hunts and military campaigns. The rest of his domains went to Huascar. Whatever Huayna Capac willed, Huascar assumed power in Cuzco after the spectacular funeral ceremonies, and Atahualpa took over in Quito. At this point partisanship clouds the issue so that villain and hero cannot be identified. Not unnaturally, Huascar and Atahualpa were soon at war. In 1532, just as the Spaniards were preparing to enter the interior of Peru from the coast, Huascar was badly defeated and captured. Insulted, taunted, and forced to witness the hanging of his wives, children, generals, and officials, the beaten emperor was being brought to Atahualpa at the city of Cajamarca when Francisco Pizarro abruptly terminated the independence of Inca Peru.

INCA GOVERNMENT

Political administration was closely integrated with all other aspects of organized life in ancient Peru. Governmental, religious, economic, and social functions were embodied in the Sapa Inca, or emperor who, in contrast to the Aztec chieftain, was a true monarchical despot, an adored figure supposed to be the son of the Sun. In fact the son of the Inca emperor and his chief sister-wife, named heir presump-

tive during his father's lifetime, he "took the fringe," the modest head-
dress that denoted his sovereignty, in a gorgeous coronation ceremony.
He had to construct a new palace, for each monarch rated a residence
of his own choice, and acquire thousands of new servants, for those who
waited on his late father had all been made drunk and killed during
the funeral, along with the bereaved widows and concubines. The Inca
ruler traveled on a litter, an elaborate contraption carried at a slow,
steady pace by a tribe whose sole occupation was this stately function,
and the populace knelt and averted its gaze from the brilliance of his
divine figure, very much as the Japanese did prior to 1945 when their
emperor passed. Even high-ranking officials spoke to him through a
screen and did so with trepidation, for the emperor could have anyone killed without excuse or warning. There was no true limit to his authority other than his sense of duty and self-restraint. He lived in
splendor, had all the wives he wanted, ruled as he saw fit, and confessed
only to the Sun, admittedly his superior. All authority channeled up to
this august personage, a matter which proved ruinous in 1532 when the
Spanish took Atahualpa prisoner.

Four subordinates immediately responsible to the Inca emperor resided in imperial Cuzco, each a prefect or a viceroy of one-quarter of the
Inca realm. Next in the hierarchy were governors of provinces—once independent nations—usually if not always members of the hereditary nobility, who wore distinctive headbands and earplugs. After them were
chieftains, or *curacas*, some of them Inca nobility and others local
monarchs who had been won over to the conquering Inca. The most
important of these ruled 10,000 adult males. Under them were *curacas*
for 5,000, 1,000, 500, and 100, and then foremen or commissars for fifty
and ten taxpayers. Each official was responsible to his immediate superior and was watched by spies and secret inspectors. The lowest officials
were often not aristocratic but men of ability and firmness who were
loyal to the system and sought to integrate into it the basic kin group,
the *ayllu*. Authority came from above, duty from below. No cross-wise
operations in this bureaucratic pyramid were permitted, so that the military concentration of power narrowing upward to the emperor was theoretically perfect. It was an amazingly precise system, and it kept a large
area of South America under the tightest political control it has ever
known.[4]

The Inca system was not in the least democratic, though men of ex-
ceptional ability may have been recruited for choice positions in the

4.   Some authorities bitterly dispute this
description of Inca government, based as
it is on confusing Spanish records. This
account generally follows John Howland
Rowe, "Inca culture at the Time of the
Spanish Conquest," in J. H. Steward
(ed.), *Handbook of South American Indians*, II, Washington, D.C.: Government Printing Office, 1947, 262–64.

army or even in the bureaucracy. Probably this process was fairly common during the period when the Inca spread their control so rapidly under Pachacuti and Topa Inca Yupanqui. But the privileges and dignity of the born aristocrats were well-protected and leveling of classes was not a purpose of the system in any way. It should be noted that the nobility performed real functions, not only in warfare and administration but in ceremonial physical labor. It was not a class of parasites but simply of high-ranking servants or slaves of the emperor.

With much wisdom the Inca sought to win to their side the chieftains of smaller nations or tribes. If possible, such collaboration would mean the peaceable incorporation of their subjects within the empire. If not, efforts were made to win over the conquered people after the war. Sons of the old tribal aristocracy were brought to Cuzco and trained, and idols and other sacred objects were concentrated in the temples of the capital both as hostages and out of respect for the defeated peoples. If a tribe proved recalcitrant to collaboration, its most troublesome members might be scattered among other regions and loyal colonists, or *mitimae*, moved in. The Inca were apparently very successful in obliterating the historical lore of their subjects and in inducing them to learn the Quechua language, far more so than recent imperial nations which have tried to unify their overblown empires.

The effectiveness of the Inca political system depended originally and ultimately on the army, obviously an exceedingly good one. Repeated victories not only heightened its self-confidence but swelled its numbers through the affiliation of conquered peoples until it enjoyed a towering supremacy in the Andean area. Its weapons were typical—slings, spears, bows and arrows, axes, star-headed clubs, and knives—but the Inca genius in logistics endowed it with a matchless supply system. As in other areas, Inca discipline probably accounted for some of its high quality. Banners and martial music stimulated military fervor, but more important were the tradition of victory and a high morale induced by a mystic belief that the gods inevitably favored the expansion of Incadom. This missionary impulse was not to be surpassed until the Spanish Christians arrived. Inca soldiers enjoyed a position of honor in society. They were well led and cared for, and their defensive helmet and quilted jackets, like those of the Aztecs, offered them some protection from the hazards of battle.

Another important factor that enabled the system to work was the Inca network of roads, which excite marvel even today.[5] In engineering skill they probably surpassed Roman roads, the best in Europe until Napoleon's time, for the Inca surmounted natural obstacles instead of circumventing them. From Cuzco great stone paths stretched out straight

5. *Ibid.*, pp. 220–39.

for hundreds of miles to the chief centers of the empire. One major road ran north-south down the desert coast and another parallel to it in the highlands, with several connecting crossovers. On the desert it was as wide as fifteen feet, with some shade and water supplies provided for. In the loneliest stretches it might consist only of markers linked by ropes so the runners would not lose their way. The narrower highland roads ran straight across cliffs, canyons, plateaus, and mountains. The steepest places had only carved footholds. Tunnels and culverts smoothed out other obstacles. At the deepest streams were intricately matted or woven suspension bridges which swayed terrifyingly in the wind. Every few miles was a storehouse and shelter. The Inca had no wheeled vehicles and the llama refused to pull loads, so these highways were used by men—soldiers marching to conquer or put down rebellion, refugees who were being resettled or colonists going to new homes, drafted laborers on their way to carry out public works, licensed merchants, and officials going about their business. No one else could use the highway, for the subjects of the Inca were supposed to stay where the state wanted them and not to travel as they pleased. Government runners were an interesting class. They carried messages and freight from one part of the empire to another in relays, shouting out their words or handing over parcels as they breathlessly approached a shelter, where another began his run. In this fashion 150 miles a day might be covered. It took three days to cover the distance from Cuzco to the Lima area by runner, not bad time for an automobile today in that rugged 420-mile stretch.

The keeping of records was incredibly difficult for a people who had no system of writing, yet the Inca at all times had a comprehensive statistical picture of their empire. They knew all about their garrisons, the work of the bureaucracy, the populations of various areas, and even the classification of men and women for purposes of labor. A device called the *quipu* facilitated prodigious feats of memory. This rope or string had a comb-like attachment of other strings with various colors and knots as mnemonic aids, so that a professional memory specialist would know what each knot and string stood for. By devoting himself to remembering this data, he could inform the officials of all the details for which he was responsible. The *quipu* was also a sort of catalogue of historical events, or at least the kind of history the ruling group wished to have remembered. A trained class of wise men performed these labors. It is nothing less than tragic that the Spanish neglected to take advantage of their knowledge and record it in a form we could understand today.

Inca justice was as harsh as might be expected for the times in any part of the world. Treason, as always, was the worst crime. A high-born traitor was imprisoned with wild beasts and loathsome serpents and insects. Murderers and thieves were likely to be executed by having heavy stones dropped on them. Exile and torture were lesser punishments. It is suggestive that public rebukes were much dreaded: this might indicate that the Inca system worked so well and morale was so high that an official humiliation for failure brought great anguish. There is also reason to believe that crime was comparatively rare, that the subjects of Incadom were generally honest and restrained. That trials were held in public and the accused had the right of defense suggest a high degree of assurance on the part of the governing classes.

THE INCA ECONOMY

In the economic field the Inca were organized more and better than any of the other Indians of the Americas. It may well be that they achieved a higher degree of production and a better living standard in Peru than any of the governments that have followed them. The high, fertile valleys and plateaus that lay between the several ranges of the Andes were well-populated with people who were skilled in agriculture and were adequately housed and clothed. Much of the coastal desert was irrigated by the torrents that spring out of the mountains and produced crops that could not be grown in the highlands. The variety of food was even greater than that of the Mexicans, for it included among other items the white potato, which has since become the most important single article of food in the world. Furthermore, by scientific irrigation, terracing, and fertilization[6] the land was kept productive. In general, the various settled areas among the mountains were divided into three zones: one for the Inca emperor and his government, another for the Sun or the clerical establishment, and a third for the inhabitants. When planting time came, the population would proceed to the ruler's zone, singing, chanting, and apparently willing, to dig with spade-like sticks and to sow. Then they moved over to the zone of the Sun and planted the crop. In these fields they worked as a community and were fed from the storehouses of the government and the church. Then they prepared the lands reserved to themselves, probably performing the labor as a group but realizing that certain strips were reserved for each family when harvest time came and rotating them from year to year in the interest of equality. The crops were tended during the growing season as the local foremen or straw bosses dictated, at least in the zones of the Inca and the Sun. Communal labor continued during the harvest, when the crops of the Inca and the Sun were placed in

---

6. The Inca well knew the value of *guano*, the dried bird droppings on the islands off the desert coast. Not until the Peruvian republic was well launched was extensive use again made of this fertilizer.

the appropriate storehouses. Then each family gathered its own crop and consumed it or placed it in the community storehouse for future needs. In this fashion the government and clergy were well-supplied, and the common people apparently received enough for their needs. It was not intended that their needs proliferate, for luxury was the privilege of the upper classes, but the rulers seemed conscious of an obligation to see that everyone should receive sustenance.

Fundamental to the Inca system was the requirement that every able-bodied subject pay taxes or tribute. Since there was no medium of exchange, not even the cacao bean used in Middle America, this obligation was discharged in the form of labor. Usually this meant work on the fields of the Inca and the Sun as described, and everything was done to make such toil seem honorable and dignified as well as agreeable. Everyone was supposed to work and to take joy and pride in doing so. Toil was not only a patriotic but a religious duty, and, with allowance for human frailty and individualism, it seems that the population generally responded with sincerity. Other forms of labor taxation were tending the herds of llamas and kindred beasts which produced wool and dried meat for the upper classes, the manufacture of weapons, pottery, clothing, ornaments, liquor, and furniture, as well as mining, since the Inca used copper and tin and cherished articles of gold and silver. For public works which lay outside the specialty of any one province, a draft called up a small percentage of men from all parts of the empire and transported them on the highways to the cities, where they constructed the mammoth temples, palaces, and fortresses and filled in the ranks of the army. This *mita*, which the Spanish were later to abuse to such a shocking degree, operated fairly gently in Inca times, only a small number of men being taken from any one area and not being held for more than a short period. Sometimes the government had no work for them to do, in which case they moved mountains or performed other useless labor. When a group or an area complained that it possessed no labor force to contribute for public purposes it might be condemned to cram cane joints with lice, just to show the emperor that it was "willing" to fulfill its obligation to him.

The Inca economy has been much admired. A large, labor-conscious population obviously produced well and consumed adequately. On the other hand, some critics have felt that the element of compulsion must have been brutal at times, since laziness is natural to much of the human race. Hence charges that ancient Incadom was a veritable penitentiary harshly kept in order by arrogant overlords. The common people indeed had to spend much time toiling for their rulers. They could not move from one community to another by their own volition. Their houses were (and usually still are) mere stinking stone huts with no comforts or beauties that might make them homes instead of shelters. Even if they accumulated some wealth they were not supposed to enjoy luxuries. Yet the only fair judgment is to compare them with equivalent classes in other parts of the world, and here the verdict must favor the Inca system. The fact that Inca economic methods continued on their own momentum long after the Spaniard came and that many Indians still cling to them also buttresses a favorable view.

CUSTOMS

Life among the common people included some pleasures. When work periods were over, relaxation and fun were permitted. Among their comforts were music, with the instruments typical of the Indians generally, and dancing, which seems to have been fairly simple. Athletics were not as common as in Mexico or the Maya area. The Incas were too serious-minded for that. Tobacco was enjoyed, usually in the form of snuff or chewing. Liquor was, and still is, concocted in a method highly offensive to squeamish moderns. Women chewed up corn kernels and spat into large jugs, where the juices fermented. Later diluted, sweetened, and colored, it was the famous *chicha*, a potent intoxicant. Yet drunkenness here, as among most of the Indians, was a religious act to be indulged in only during special occasions. The narcotic coca leaves assuaged hunger, thirst, and cold and seemingly gave energy to those who chewed them. The Inca apparently succeeded in reducing the cultivation of the coca plant to certain imperial plantations and in limiting the use of the drug among the people. All this was to change with the Conquest, and today the Peruvian and Bolivian Indians are widely addicted to this vice.

The Inca encouraged marriage, if for no other reason to produce more laborers. Every year an official paired off youths and young girls, who lined up in the plazas of the towns, those couples who had already been attracted to each other arranging to stand in the proper place to effect a junction with the chosen one when they reached the official. The inevitable disputes would be settled in due course by this bureaucrat, and the weddings took place under family auspices. Arbitrary as the system was, there must have been few single adults in Incadom.

INCA ARCHITECTURE AND OTHER WONDERS

As builders the Inca surpassed the Maya, Toltecs, and Aztecs in engineering skill though not in beauty and artistic grace. Their buildings were huge and located often in exceedingly difficult places—on the tops of mountains or the sides of steep valleys. The mysterious element of their mammoth ruins lies largely in the question as to how great stones were moved from distant quarries up and down mountain ranges, across streams, and up canyon walls. No machines or animals could have been used to transport them. Even the pulley was unknown to the Inca, though he probably made use of wooden rollers, long since rotted. Assuming, as we must, that thousands of human laborers dragged these large pieces over long stretches of rugged country, a further wonderment faces us in the way they cut them up on the scene of construction. Possibly some bronze or even iron chisels were used, but most of the cutting was done by stone. The uneven size of the stones when they were put together was the result of a deliberate plan, indicating a knowledge of stress and balance that suggests a very advanced acquaintance with mathematics and the principles of engineering. Cement was seldom used; the stones were cut so they would fit perfectly. The reason for this was the need to defeat the earthquakes which frequently shake the area. This became apparent when the first Spanish buildings collapsed during tremors while the Inca structures merely separated, gave with the convulsions of the earth, and fell back into place. Even today Inca walls withstand earthquakes that bring down all other types of buildings. They were severely utilitarian, as befitted a hard-working society, with very little beautification inside or out. The construction of these strange buildings was probably designed and supervised by an aristocratic class whose greatness was not appreciated for a long time, until they had died out and their secrets had been lost. The best examples for Inca construction can still be studied in Cuzco, and other locations in its vicinity, such as Pisac, Ollantaytambo, and the fabulous Inca hideout Machu Picchu on the mountaintops.

The Inca were expert at making terraces on steep hillsides, and very long irrigation channels, some of which seem to the untrained eye to flow the water uphill, carried melted snow to the fields.

The Inca also knew a great deal about healing. Much of their knowledge was brushed aside and forgotten by the Spaniards, for it was based on pagan beliefs that spirits caused illness, but eventually quinine and cocaine were adopted. Embalming and mummifying were superior to European methods of the time. From some of the mummies recently uncovered we know that the Inca were able somehow to cut into the skull, apparently for brain surgery or the release of evil spirits, though it seems incredible that even a drugged patient could have survived, if indeed any did,[7] in view of the medical instruments of the time.

7. Apparently they did, according to studies of bone repair which indicate the patients recovered from these operations and died later of other causes.

INCA RELIGION

Inca religion centered about the sun, as is natural in an agricultural society and in the high, clear atmosphere where the sun seemed so close. Some authorities believe that the upper classes worshiped the creator-god Viracocha as the true deity and thus had monotheism, a mark of an advanced culture. Whether they did or not, the general population was saturated with worship for many gods, some which they had before the Inca conquered them and others introduced by the victors, who were agreeable to flexible religious practices. Shrines and sacred places were everywhere, almost anything which excited wonder or awe being endowed with the quality of a *huaco*, or holy object. While many temples stood, worship was mostly in the open, at several times during the day in the fields or in military campaigns. The twelve months were duly ushered in by religious ceremonies. Yet reverence for the sun stands out as the chief feature of Inca religion. One's destiny in the after-life depended on pleasing it.

The clergy was not particularly numerous as a class but it was highly important. Clerics presided over ceremonies and served as healers, sages, and holy men. On rare and greatly important occasions they performed human sacrifice, such as the coronation of an emperor, when two hundred children were killed, or at the beginning of a military campaign, when several young people were offered in sacrifice.

The Chosen Women were an unusual feature of Inca society. Every year thousands of the most beautiful and healthy girls of eight or nine were picked from all parts of the empire and sent to schools, where for about five years they learned to sew, weave, make *chicha*, and perform religious rites. When they reached womanhood, they were sent to Cuzco, where many became Virgins of the Sun, attendants in temples and caretakers of sacred objects. Others had a less restricted fate, being sent to the emperor's collection of concubines or given out by him as presents to important officials. It was considered a high honor and not a degradation to be selected for the Chosen Women. Only the most promising girls could qualify.

SUMMARY

Students of the Inca have always divided radically in assessing the ultimate effects of their system in the central Andes. Critics regard them as a mere warlike nation which overwhelmed several more advanced cultures, dulled their brilliance, and then sought to transform the whole area into a beehive or an antbed. The conquering Spaniards were pleased to belittle the Inca's constructive achievements and to emphasize the harsh features of his rule. A romantic, or at least a favorable, view developed among the Indians themselves long after the fall of the Inca. This attitude accounts for some of the restlessness of the natives in the late eighteenth century, and in modern Peru the tendency is to glorify the ancient culture. In all, it would seem that an admiring point of view is tenable. The Inca managed a society of several million people with perhaps as much order and discipline as has ever prevailed in the central Andes. The inhabitants carried out an intelligent routine and wrested from nature the necessities they required to provide economic security for all. Their general welfare was such that they had little reason to question the righteousness of their stratified class system and the Inca who presided over it. Religion buttressed the economic-political authority, which commanded respect for its own success. The Indians who lived in the empire possessed an explanation satisfactory to them of life and its purpose. The ruling Inca had every reason for self-satisfaction. They had conquered the world as they knew it. Alone in the universe as they believed, subject to the sun and other explicable gods, they must have been comparatively happy in their lonely civilization.

Other Indian Groups in South America

IMMEDIATELY south of the Inca empire lived a numerous and virile nation known as the Araucanian. About half of these hardy people were included in Incadom, though they were far from absorbed in its culture, and the others defied the conquerors from the thick rain forests and mountainous islands of southern Chile. While the Araucanians were a primitive people, their ferocity checked the Inca at the River Maipú in central Chile and was strong enough to deter the Spaniards. They were never entirely conquered in the colonial period. In fact, not until the late nineteenth century were the Chileans able to reduce them. The epic struggle of the Araucanian for freedom has won him a place of honor in South American lore.

At the very tip of South America were very backward tribes whose life centered about the canoe, seals, penguins, sea lions, and beached whales. To the north of them in the Patagonian region of southern Argentina were other nomads—who are charitably called "cultural tarriants" by anthropologists—Tehuelches and Puelches, who hunted the ostrich-like rhea and the guanaco and who spent much of their energy seeking to protect themselves in skin tents from the cold, shrieking winds that blow eastward across the Andes. One distinction they deserve: almost alone of American Indians they avoided tobacco and all forms of alcohol. These people were not worth conquering, neither by the Inca, the Spaniard, the occasional Dutch or British intruder, nor even by the Argentines until the 1870's.

In the region about Buenos Aires and Uruguay, now one of the richest and best-developed sections on earth, were other wild and fierce nomads, chief among whom were the tall, cannibalistic Charruans. They had heard of the Inca, but the compliment was apparently not returned. These savages were ready to offer a rough reception to the Spaniards and Portuguese when they dared to land.

A native group destined to play a large part in the colonial empires of Spain and Portugal and in modern Paraguay, the Guaraní, lived in a fertile, humid country between the Río de la Plata and the highlands of Bolivia. This region, called the Chaco, was and is naturally rich, with deep topsoil and very few rocks. It is still largely undeveloped. On the eve of the Conquest a number of primitive tribes churned about, fighting one another and hunting. The Inca had not bothered to conquer them, probably because men from the highlands are miserably uncomfortable in the torrid Chaco, as the war between Paraguay and Bolivia in the 1930's demonstrated. The Guaraní were the least bellicose of these groups and perhaps the most numerous. Spanish Jesuits and Portuguese *paulistas* made them docile, a quality which a generous nature had already encouraged, and modern dictators of Paraguay have found them easy to rule.

The Aymará are still very much alive in the bleak highlands of modern Bolivia. Most of them had been conquered by the Inca in a series of wars but, then as now, the Aymará was unadaptable, dour, unsmiling, and unwilling to mix with the Quechua. Resentfulness has been the most conspicuous characteristic of these people. Perhaps they are descendants of the earliest men who built the great stone structures of Tiahuanaco and cherish a pride they refuse to explain to outsiders. In any event, they were sullen members of the Inca empire and for centuries have stood aloof from the European. Capable of fierce outbursts of violence on rare occasions, these Bolivian Indians have recently been on the resurgence.

The enormous sub-continent of modern Brazil, which was larger than the United States until the annexation of Alaska, contained hundreds of backward tribes. For most of them life was simple enough, a matter of collecting berries, nuts, and fruits supplied by an ample nature, fishing, and hunting. Naked wanderers little attracted to sedentary life, the men allowed the women to perform such work as needed to be done, the making of pottery and cultivation of manioc, their basic food. Males found it more important to fight one another, spear fish, hunt with blowguns, and honor the gods with periodic orgies. Husbands suffered piteously during childbirth, lying in hammocks groan-

ing amid sympathetic friends while their wives quietly produced the
baby and promptly went back to work. The paramount skill of these
natives was navigational. They moved great distances in fast canoes up
and down the numerous streams with which Brazil is endowed. The
most important linguistic group was the Tupí, which anthropologists
link with the Guaraní. These were the natives the Portuguese were to
encounter in greatest number. While the Tupí were not particularly
hostile to the white invaders, they proved uncooperative in adapting
themselves to his requirements, for the Tupí disliked labor as much as
the Portuguese. A more advanced group whom the Tupí had chased
into the highlands of southeastern Brazil were the Ge, or the "Tapu-
yans," as the Portuguese called them. Perhaps the Ge were more inclined than the Tupí to engage in farming and to live in palisaded
villages, but they shared with their persecutors a fondness for eating
human flesh.

The Amazon basin, which even today is not well explored, spawned
among many others two important linguistic groups, the Arawak and
the Carib. The Arawak apparently developed first and migrated to
the coast of northern South America and populated the islands of
the Caribbean. Not a nation at all, but tribes speaking the same basic
language, the Arawaks were strung out from the Chaco to the Bahama
Islands. The first natives Columbus met in 1492 were members of
this stock. Deceptively as it turned out, they seemed to be child-like
innocents who were eager to accommodate the visitors. Later, the Spanish came to despise them for their pagan practices and their nakedness,
lewdness, and occasional sex perversions. Less numerous than the Arawak but more vigorous were the tribes in central Brazil, the Guianas,
and the lesser Antilles who belonged to a linguistic group the Spanish
labeled "Carib," for cannibal. Fiercely hostile and addicted to the
torturing and consumption of fellow human beings, the Caribs had apparently routed the gentler Arawak folk from the string of islands that
connects South America with the Greater Antilles. They were beginning to penetrate Puerto Rico when the Spanish burst in upon the Indian world. While the Arawaks of the Caribbean islands quickly died out
in the shock of the Conquest, the Caribs defied the Spanish, who
tampered with them to their own disaster, for more than a century. Finally left alone by the Spaniards, the Caribs succumbed in the seventeenth century to the English, Dutch, and French when these nations
occupied the lesser Antilles and the Guianas. Some Carib tribes survive in modern Brazil, adding to the perils of exploration in the remote
parts of that country.

The tribes along the Caribbean shores of Venezuela and Colombia,
the Spanish Main of the colonial period, were also warlike and primi-

tive. They offered much resistance to the Spanish and were not truly intimidated until the phase of exploration gave way to massive settlement. With poison-tipped arrows and the advantage of concealing themselves in the jungle, they withstood the slavers and missionaries long after better organized societies had been overcome.

Back from the Colombian coast was an advanced nation, the Chibcha, who have been treated too generously by writers who rank them almost with the Inca and Aztecs. It is true that they were in the process of consolidating into two states, one ruled by a *Zipa* and the other by a *Zaque,* but their political system was still very primitive. Their agriculture was reasonably advanced in the cool highlands of central Colombia, but their buildings and works of art were not notable. Their greatest fame lay in the legend of *El Dorado* (the gilded man), apparently a priest or noble who covered himself with gold dust and dove into a lake in a dramatic ceremony, after which the people would hurl emeralds and chunks of gold in the water. Reports of these activities were enough to assure persistent searches into the northern Andes by the white man and, of course, the conquest of the Chibcha.

South of them, in modern Ecuador, were the Aucas and head-shrinking Jívaros, who still offer hostility to invaders, however altruistic. But the largest group in that region, the Quito, had been subjected to Inca imperialism by the time the Spanish arrived and were both civilized and prepared to form a submerged class in the new order.

Odious as comparisons may be, they often serve to clarify and to place things in perspective. In this spirit we may conclude that the highest Indian cultures in the Americas prior to the coming of the white man ranked substantially below their contemporaries in Europe and most of Asia. In many respects they were more backward than African societies of the time. In reaching this judgment we may point to the absence of many items that facilitate superior civilizations, perhaps even spell them. The wheel, for example, was not in use unless we count the wooden rollers of the Inca and toys. No animals in the New World were suitable for extensive use in labor, with a reservation for dogs in the case of the Plains savages and the very limited employment of llamas by the Inca. This lack was no fault of the American Indians, but it greatly retarded them. Iron seems to have been used scarcely at all, though limited quantities were available. Absent from Amerind cultures were the plow, the true arch, the compass, the printing press, and gunpowder. Only the Maya had an advanced system of writing, itself inferior to European or Asian. Thus intellectual achievements except in mathematics were greatly restricted. Religious practices were at their worst grossly barbarous and at their best full of cruelty and superstition, though comparisons on this point might produce parallels unflattering to Old World cults. No conception of personal liberty seems to have shone through the political system. Everywhere there was despotism, oppression, contempt for human life. The Amerinds abused and exploited one another with little compassion. The masses were passive and given to dissimulation long before the Europeans came, like people who never dreamed of progress.

This estimate must be balanced with other considerations. The New World had much to offer the Old, above all, the potato, which helps account for the striking increase in Europe's population. Of incalculable importance have been corn, beans, tomatoes, squash, pumpkins, chocolate, tapioca, vanilla, turkeys, rubber, tobacco, and perhaps petroleum.[8] The outside world greatly profited from cocaine and quinine, though it disregarded Indian surgical techniques and healing methods we might label psychosomatic medicine. The more we learn of Indian art the higher we raise our admiration of these peoples, who were not merely puttering with crude materials but attaining profundities in creative expression we can scarcely grasp.

Something else occurs to modern man as he reflects on the ancient cultures of America. These Amerinds seem to have enjoyed a way of life that harmonized with nature instead of seeking to master it. The restless, insatiable citizen of the industrialized world looks with admiration at the orderly life of the Indian, his spirit at peace with the unseen forces that direct the universe and man's place in it. The Indian appears moderate in checking his tendency to greed and self-indulgence, even virtuous in a fashion and austere. His society, whether it was a mere nomadic tribe or a formidable empire, integrated religion, economy, political life, and artistic expression in a way the unsettled, insecure man of Western civilization has not known for centuries.

The tragedy of the Conquest surpasses description. In vain we may speculate about the course of the Indian cultures, what they might have achieved had the Europeans left them alone for a few more centuries. It was to be otherwise. From the day in 1492 that Columbus carried away a few natives to use as interpreters until the present, the Amerind has undergone fear, pain, disorganization, and oppression at the hands of alien intruders. But the story is not all sad. These same alien intruders have done much for the Indian, themselves, and the human race in general.

8. It is not certain the Indian utilized oil.

2

The Iberian Background

So MANY of the differences between the Americans north of the Rio Grande and those south of it are popularly ascribed to the peculiar Iberian background of the Latin Americans. If political ideals are very similar, practices are not. The rhythm of anarchy and tyranny in Spanish and Portuguese lands on both sides of the Atlantic perplexes the rest of the world, which is never quite satisfied with the explanations presented for this condition. Nor is it easy for outsiders to understand why the immense resources of those countries are utilized so ineptly, why the historic poverty-in-wealth situation is so unyielding century after century and now, with the population explosion assuming such large proportions, threatens to become even worse. In a world in which class lines have blurred and poverty, at least in some nations, is disappearing, the Hispanic lands still have elite groups of elegant, cultured, and rich people, and huge masses of the destitute. The condition does not change if the actors do, whether autocratic Spain, democratic Argentina, or socialistic Mexico is examined from this angle. In attitudes toward life, manners, religion, and everyday habits, the Hispanic world has its own distinctiveness. Naturally, one looks to the Iberian heritage to supply some of the reasons.

SPAIN

Spain Against the World

THE feeling that the Spanish are different in their outlooks and ways from other peoples is not limited to the New World. It is age-old in Europe too. Nor is it altogether a matter of foreigners failing to ap-

preciate values cherished south of the Pyrenees. The Spaniards themselves have long agreed with foreign critics or enthusiasts who say they
are unlike Europeans and North Americans. This has been especially
true since the defeat of Spain at the hands of the United States in 1898,
a jolt so unexpected and so humiliating it set the responsible thinkers
of the peninsula to seek to identify the unique qualities of their nation.
Most of them assume, as others do, that Spain is a land where the max-
ims that govern other peoples do not apply, where the rules are suspended. The mental image of man and his destiny which many Spaniards hold differs in important ways from that accepted by so many of
their fellows in the Western world. They employ phrases, such as "to
live by denying oneself," whose meaning eludes many foreigners. Their
cult of the heroic stance, of action for its own sake regardless of material
consequences, their proud refusal to compete with others and to accept
rebukes for not playing the game, their long spells of indifference to issues that agitate the outside world—these attitudes fascinate many foreigners and alienate still more. Yet, through the centuries and very much
in our own time, the Spaniard flaunts his isolation and could not care
less what outsiders think. Those elements in Spain who are exceptions
to this pattern seldom dominate the country for long.

The Spanish are very much aware, perhaps too much so, of what they
call the Black Legend, a collection of myths or facts assembled over a
long period by Spain's foes and victims and perpetuated through prejudice. The list of enemies is long. The Jews and Moslems who were
expelled from the peninsula have not forgotten nor forgiven the homeland which they loved and, some declare, still long for. Lutherans and
Calvinists have added many an item of atrocity to the Black Legend.
Italy and the Netherlands were long occupied and mistreated by the
Spanish. France and England warred with Spain for generations, and
their historians have had much to say of her cruelty and perfidy. Then,
the lost colonies have, in the usual fashion, turned on the mother country and blamed it for years of oppression and, often, for most of their
own shortcomings. This harsh depiction or misrepresentation of Spain's
imperialism persisted until recently and is by no means extinct. It affected public opinion in the United States until well into this century.
The Spanish, then, maintain they have been maligned and vilified by
spiteful enemies through this Black Legend. It is because of such prejudice that so much of the outside world regards them as unusually cruel,
caste-minded, slothful, and given to procrastination or the derided
mañana habit. Spanish reactions to these criticisms have given them the
reputation for disliking foreigners, though Spain is a proverbially hospitable land to visitors. Finally, in matters of religion there is the least
possibility of reconciling critic and apologist. Spain ousted the Jew and

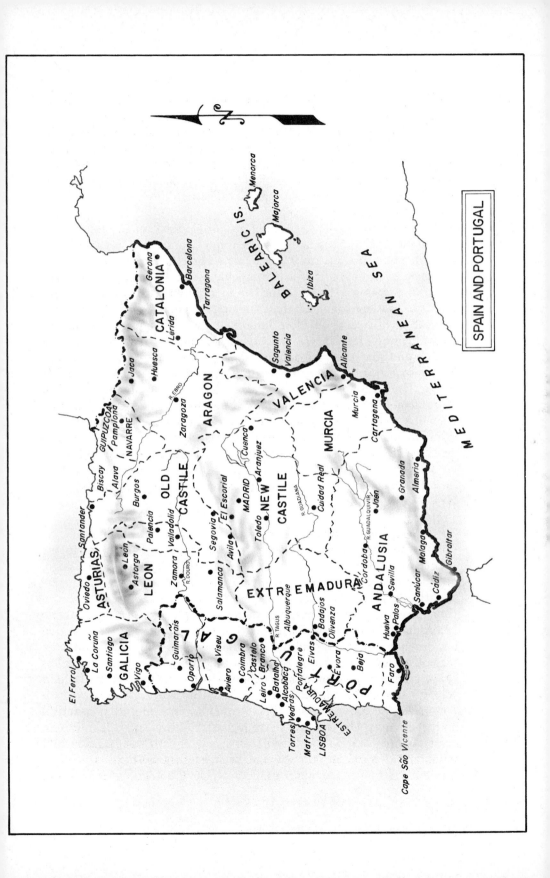

SPAIN AND PORTUGAL

Moslem, steadfastly fought the Protestant, and overwhelmed the many paganisms with which she came into contact. The Inquisition has been an evil memory for centuries, and Spaniards have resisted idealistic philosophies not specifically rooted in Roman Catholicism. Mysticism permeates all classes profoundly, to the bewilderment of more worldly outsiders. To charges of bigotry or fanaticism the Spaniard's typical reply is that he takes his religion seriously. And to a degree unknown in the rest of Christendom, he does.

The paradoxes which Spain and its people pose for the foreign student both repel and fascinate. Speculations about national character or collective traits are less fruitful than a study of the locale and history of this people, who have left such an indelible stamp on a great part of the world. Something is to be learned from the period of Roman occupation, the Moslem conquest, the Christian reconquest, and the ultimate unification of Spain. Of more importance for our purposes is the sixteenth century, for this was the time when much of America was conquered and the mold for eighteen Spanish-speaking nations was cast. Some aspects of the sixteenth century are part of the living past today. As the United States traces many of its ideals to the original period of its settlement by seventeenth-century Englishmen who left or fled from a country torn by religious and constitutional troubles, so Latin America shows many effects of Iberian institutions and attitudes of the previous century. Much as the Latin American republics flaunt their independence, they too still feel the effects of Spanish and Portuguese rulers who have long been dead. In spite of all, Spain and Portugal linger in the New World.

Geographically and in many other ways the Iberian peninsula resembles northern Africa more than Europe, lending foundation to the French taunt that Africa begins at the Pyrenees. Much of Spain is high, arid, and full of great, bleak spaces. Mountain chains almost wall in the country. Spectacular as they are, especially in Granada and in the north, they run wrong for the purposes of rainfall. The dry heartland of the peninsula, Old and New Castile, is therefore suitable more for grazing and mining than for agriculture and forestry. The glare, the winds, the play of shadow and color on the yellow-brown expanses, and the treeless towns give an impression of melancholy which perhaps induces a certain sobriety among the inhabitants. This is Tawny Spain, the Spain which dominates the other sections. These other sections are often beautiful and charming. The northwestern region, Galicia, and the northern coast, Asturias, have a wild, turbulent character with woods, mists, and mountains that run into the sea. The triangle of the northeastern corner, Catalonia, strongly resembles France, which it borders. It is rich and fertile and by far the most European of the several sections. Valencia, to the south of Catalonia on the Mediterranean coast, is something like southern Italy or Greece. Granada and Andalusia, in the south, are semi-tropical and, when irrigated, lush productive areas of great beauty. Portugal resembles these areas, but it also contains features of the rest of Spain, such as arid stretches and mountains. On the whole, it is less harsh than most of Spain. The rivers of the peninsula are seldom navigable for long distances, and the variety of the whole area makes for difficult communication and for the fostering of localism. If nature has not been entirely kind to the Iberians, it still would seem that their peninsula might be as productive as California or Israel if they enjoyed the proper direction.

Ancient Times

THIS peninsula, which in modern times is an almost abandoned bridge between Europe and Africa, has been a scene of human activity from time immemorial. The famous drawings of Altamira cave are among the oldest preserved works of prehistoric Cro-Magnon man. But to link these ancients with later peoples is as formidable a problem as tracing the sequence of Indian cultures in the Americas. We have written records of the Celts, who once occupied the western half of Europe, including Iberia. At some time in the dim past another white group invaded Spain, perhaps from Africa, a people we call the Iberians. The resulting mixture, Celt-Iberian, slowly developed a culture little if any more advanced than the ones we have considered in early America. The Celt-Iberians (or according to other students of the problem, their predecessors, whoever they were) felt the effects of contacts with the more advanced people of the Levant, such as the Phoenicians and Hebrews, who occasionally sailed to the peninsula and planted colonies. These Semitic invaders introduced writing and engaged in mining and commerce. Another ancient people, whether invaders or descendants of early man, managed to retain their identity through the ages. These are the mysterious Basques, who still live in the western Pyrenees and speak a language that baffles those who would relate it to any other tongue. They employ this difficult language today not only as a mark of their self-proclaimed superiority but as a convenience in the smuggling business. Basque influence in Latin America has not been light.

After the Greeks began to penetrate the western Mediterranean and venture past the Pillars of Hercules into the Atlantic, important cities and commercial colonies developed along the Iberian coastline. These contacts brought advanced engineering and architecture into the peninsula and in many other ways elevated the cultural level of the Celt-Iberians. Then came the Carthaginians, heirs of the Phoenicians, who in the third century before Christ wrested most of the Greek colonies from their owners and proceeded to conquer the wild inhabitants in the hinterland. This proved a difficult process, for the Celt-Iberians put up a ferocious resistance. One of the earliest Spanish traditions centers about the heroic but doomed defense of the city of Sagunto, a symbol of the warlike fury and spirit of survival that on so many occasions the Hispanic people have demonstrated. Carthage had only a few decades to attempt the colonization of the Iberian peninsula. Her defeats at the hands of Rome during the Punic Wars exposed the region to the legions of the republic, who, to be sure, filled no mere vacuum but fought determinedly for nearly two centuries to overcome the fierce Celt-Iberians. The siege of Numantia in 134 B.C. became another inspiring memory to Spain of a later time, if like Sagunto it was a lost battle.

When at last the peninsula was subdued, it became and remained for about four centuries a firm, loyal component of the Roman Empire known as Hispania. It received a plenitude of new racial stocks and was filled with roads, buildings, theaters, and aqueducts. A leading province of the Roman Empire, Hispania contributed rulers such as Trajan, Hadrian, Theodosius, and Marcus Aurelius; writers such as Seneca, Lucian, Martial, and Quintilian; as well as soldiers for the legions, officials for the bureaucracy, and fruits and minerals.

The impress of these four hundred years or more of Roman civilization explains much of Spain and Portugal and of Latin America today. The very memory of a united peninsula helped draw fragmented sovereignties of later times into a unified Spain which longed to incorporate Portugal. While the strong urban tradition in the Hispanic world has several explanations, a major one was the Roman tendency to civilize and rule through cities, as the Spanish would do in the New World. Roman law still prevails in its fundamental aspects throughout the peninsula and Latin America, the law of a strong empire in which the executive truly rules and tolerates little obstruction from parliaments or courts or local governments. And it is a law which endows the father and husband with great power over the family, which exalts the military and the police and values order more than democratic ideals. Even the languages of the peninsula (except Basque)—Castilian, Catalan, and Portuguese, and the dialects that derive from them—are corrupted Latin. Finally, Hispania became Christianized as Rome did and preserved a special quality of missionary zeal and rigidity that played such a great part in the conquest of America.

The Visigoths

THE first crack in the Roman imperial system as far as Hispania was concerned occurred in 409 A.D., when the barbarian Vandals, Alans, and Suevi poured into the peninsula from the north. Five years later came the formidable Visigoths, who had wandered from the Ukraine through the Balkans, Italy, and France and had become adherents of the Arian heresy of Christianity. Pushing the Suevi up into the rugged northwestern corner of Spain and the Vandals through Andalusia, which took its name from them, into North Africa, the Visigoths occupied with little fighting the places of profit and power from the demoralized inhabitants. They brought little into Hispania but themselves, for their cultural level was low. Until their leader, Reccared, accepted Catholicism in 587, the difference in religion was a source of disagreement and made the invaders all the more odious to the Latinized populations. Scarcely a word of the Visigothic language, very few buildings or articles of utility or artistic value have been preserved. By overpowering the Romans they pushed Hispania into a dark age of semi-barbarism and stagnation. The cities all but disappeared, economic life fell to a primitive level, and most men of learning died out or lost touch with the brilliant past. A few decades of Roman or Byzantine restoration on the eastern coasts, from 554 to 621, were not sufficient to revive Hispania, which languished for three centuries under the depressing control of the Visigoths.

The Visigothic domination did not signify retrogression in every way. Among many classes the proud Roman tradition persisted, and Latin, though corrupted, remained the basic language of the peninsula. Two of the early "fathers" of the church, Orosius and St. Isidore of Sevilla, were Spaniards who wrote during this period. For all their crudeness the Visigoths made some contributions to the development of Iberia. They brought with them the Germanic ideal of chivalry and the principle of leadership, by which warriors grouped themselves around admired figures somewhat in the fashion that Latin Americans defer for a time to an outstanding political-military *caudillo,* or leader. While they debased Roman law along with other aspects of civilization, the Visigoths codified in a *Fuero Juzgo* their own savage practices so that an eventual amalgamation modified Roman legal traditions with feudal concepts. Kingship was a major contribution of the Visigoths, much as it was to evolve in the subsequent periods of Spanish history. And so was official anti-Semitism, which was destined to bring such tragedy to the large Jewish population of the peninsula.

The Moslems

THE Visigoth phase ended abruptly when hordes of North African warriors, fired by the new religion of Mohammed the Prophet and an imperialistic urge to conquer, crossed the Strait of Gibraltar in 711. While this invasion was a phase of the sensational explosion of the Islamized Arabs and Berbers, who quickly overran territory from France to India, in Spain it was often attributed to Jews seeking relief from Visigothic oppression or to various traitors who intended to spite their enemies. The rotten Visigothic domain, broken by now into many competing local monarchies, collapsed almost at once. A few Visigothic leaders with their more devoted followers took refuge in the mountains of the north while the Moslems swept deep into France. There they were finally checked by Charles Martel in 732 at the battle of Tours and settled back to rule Spain. The only Christian victory in the peninsula was won by Pelayo at the cave of Covadonga, where a few hundred of his men, with divine aid—or so the hallowed tradition has it—defeated thousands of Mohammedans. In any event, it was to prove significant that a few Christians were able to hold out in the mountainous north, where to this day political refugees and fugitives from the law find sanctuary. The single Christian success did not prevent enormous numbers of North Africans, Arabs, and Levantines—all of whom the Spanish refer to as "Moors"—and many Jews from pouring into the peninsula. This infusion of new blood greatly altered the racial stock of Hispania, and the resulting new culture which flourished accounts more than anything else for the differences between Iberians and other Europeans.

For more than three and a half centuries the Moslems dominated most of the peninsula, and they held rich territories until January 1492. At first their area was an emirate of the Caliphate of Damascus, but in 755, the Abbassid family ousted the Ommayyad dynasty from the throne, whereupon a royal Ommayyad refugee fled to Spain and established himself as monarch. This split in the Moslem empire made Spain independent of Damascus but did not cut it off from eastern cultural and economic influences. By 929 Ommayyad Spain was powerful enough to rival the older territories in the east and the monarch created the Caliphate of Cordova, which lasted for more than a century before the "Moors" broke up into splinter monarchies.

While the entire "Moorish" period was characterized by brilliance and plenty, the century of the Caliphate represented the peak. Cordova was probably the largest and most wealthy city in Europe, far outclassing London or Paris and even Rome and Constantinople. The capital with its gorgeous court, mosques, schools, palaces, and business houses was only part of the story. Moslem Spain was heavily populated with hard-working settlers who made this region more productive than it has ever been since. Irrigation, stock breeding, and the cultivation of rice, sugar cane, cotton, silk, and fruits characterized a flourishing economy. So did the thriving towns and cities, supported by an extensive commerce and a great variety of manufacturing. Excellent schools and a large learned class introduced the superior culture of the East and, in time, brought a knowledge of Greek classics to a Christian Europe that had almost forgotten it. For generations students of western Europe went as disciples to the academies and libraries of Cordova to establish contact with a manifestly superior civilization. Life seemed good in the Caliphate for men of all faiths. The Mohammedans were clearly the ruling class, but they amiably tolerated Jews and Christians as long as there was no likelihood of rebellion and were amazingly gentle when there was.

The contributions of the Moslems to the development of Spain and Portugal were countless. We may note such items as metallurgy, stock-raising, and important crops that were to play such a role when the Iberians went to the New World. Much of the Hispanic attitude toward women, both in its romantic aspects and its harsher phases, has obvious "Moorish" origin. A list of Arabic words in the Spanish and Portuguese languages would run to many pages. Medical knowledge was advanced and gave the Spanish something of a superiority over other colonizing peoples. Architecture, with the thick walls, patios, fountains, marble and plaster plaques, tiles, brilliant colors, ingenious designs, and other features we think of as typically Hispanic, was greatly influenced or even fashioned by the invaders. The custom of the *siesta* came from the North Africans who moved to Spain. Above all, the racial composition of the whole peninsula was greatly affected by the heavy immigration from Africa and Asia. Many a patriotic, ardently Christian Spaniard of later times was descended from Mohammedans or Jews who came from Morocco, Egypt, Syria, and other lands of the Arabic world.

The Reconquest

IF THE brilliant Moslem period brought many peoples and techniques to the Iberian peninsula, the effect of them on the free Christians who finally prevailed after eight centuries was also of enormous importance. As Américo Castro has described in abundant detail,[1] these eventually victorious remnants of Latin and Visigothic Spain who escaped envelopment in the Moorish tide became what they are largely

1. *The Structure of Spanish History*, Princeton, 1954.

as a reaction to this Moslem civilization, which at once abashed them because of its superiority and yet inspired them to try to be different. During the long centuries of contact the Christians outside the Moslem domain learned a great deal from the infidel. But they spurned his industrious ways and his bent for technology. The Christian wanted to be a man of action, a warrior, and not a farmer or artisan or trader. If this attitude implied a weakness on the part of the Christian, he readily translated it into a moral superiority, of which he became more assured as it slowly brought triumphs in the way of military victories. And the victories came his way. The survival of groups like those who fought with Pelayo ultimately signified the protracted frontier war which resulted in total reconquest of the peninsula.

Some impetus to this Reconquest came with the invasion of northeastern Spain by Charlemagne in 777. While the great monarch abandoned his crusade as too difficult, some of the region we know as Catalonia long remained attached to France and came to resemble that country in many ways. A lesser result was the famous *Song of Roland,* a literary achievement associated with his campaign. Of much importance was the supposed discovery about 900 of the remains of St. James the Greater, a half-brother of Jesus, on the northwestern coast in Galicia, a discovery which was reputed to come about through a miracle of a star remaining still until believers located the grave. Christendom was thrilled by this spectacular event, and the town of Compostela became one of the great attractions for pilgrims during the Middle Ages. Even the Mohammedans respected the site when they temporarily occupied Compostela in 997. The effect on the free Christians was incalculable. They believed St. James protected and blessed their arms, that in difficult battles his white horse would appear in the skies to assure victory. Their war cry, *Santiago* (for Santo Iago or St. James), rang throughout the Reconquest of the peninsula and the Conquest of America.

Before about 1000, when the balance began surely to tip in the Christians' favor, the wars were local and seasonal, a matter of raids not only for the glory of Christ but for land and laborers, and gains were very slow. Urbanism like that of Roman times developed again, for cities with their walls and guards were safer than the countryside. Then, town charters were offered by Christian rulers to encourage growth of such concentrations, and in time the towns became jealous of their privileges and rather independent of outside authority. Furthermore, feudalism of the familiar western European type failed to take shape, for serfs were encouraged by promises of freedom to join the armies, and besides, farm or manor life was unsafe when there were so many raids and so much scorching of the earth. The Christians took on a Moorish custom that was to reach startling proportions in America: the allocation of a fifth of the spoils from a victorious campaign for the monarch. Above all, the character of these early Spanish Christians was affected. They fought with an intensified religious faith that could and did slide easily into a militant fanaticism. They cultivated glory, adventure, striving for the impossible, action regardless of risk, and extravagant virility. Physical courage and daring were admired, labor not. Only infidels and women were supposed to work with their hands.

Despite all the glorification of physical violence and manliness in the Reconquest, we may be sure that many people switched sides, intermarried with the enemy, and ran from combat. It is even likely that many Christians engaged in manual labor. The semi-legendary El Cid Campeador, who died in 1099 after a life of heroic achievements romanticized in the usual medieval way, dealt with the Moslems and shifted his allegiance. Yet the tradition of the Reconquest is still a robust influence among the Spanish, affecting them at least as much as the *Drang nach Osten* has the Germans or the more recent westward movement inspires the modern citizen of the United States.

As the momentum of Christian imperialism gathered in the eleventh century, the "Moors" fell on bad days. The disappearance of the Caliphate of Cordova in 1035 was followed by political fragmentation and then, in 1086, by an invasion from North Africa of warlike, primitive Almorávides. These rude fanatics came with the intention of containing the Christians, who had just taken Toledo and moved their line almost halfway down the peninsula. The Africans decided the Hispanic Moslems were too lax and tolerant and proceeded to stiffen them. The effect was at once to dim the brilliance of Moslem culture and to frighten the Christians into more cooperation with one another. Another invasion by the Almohades in 1146 had a similar effect. The Christians were held for a time, but by now the Crusades were stimulating all western Europe and much foreign assistance in the way of pilgrims and knights strengthened the Hispanic faithful. The creation of military orders of devout, crusading knights in the twelfth century introduced a new element into the Reconquest, privileged groups who were competent fighters. These orders of Calatrava, Santiago, and Alcántara proved generally effective, occupied powerful political positions, and disposed of much wealth.

Political power was passing into the hands of Christian monarchs as the institution of kingship developed. The first community to attain the rank of kingdom was Leon in 944, though the strength of its monarch was diminished by the custom of dividing his possessions among his children. Later in this century Navarre became a kingdom and temporarily united all the Spanish Christian states, only to fall back to the status of a small "saddlebags" state straddling the Pyrenees, where it tempted ambitious rulers in both France and Spain. In the northeast,

Aragon evolved into an aggressive kingdom and absorbed the County of Catalonia. Most important was the growth of Castile, which acquired Leon in the eleventh century, lost it for two periods, and then definitely united with it in the thirteenth century. Castile was to carry out Spain's destiny in the peninsula and America. Playing a tricky game of war and dynastic marriage with its Christian neighbors and often cooperating with Moorish potentates, it absorbed the entire northwest and then thrust itself into the bleak heartland of the peninsula (New Castile).

One accident of the Reconquest was the award of the County of Portugal to a French crusader, Henry of Burgundy, whose heir won complete independence in the twelfth century. While the rulers of Portugal often intermarried with the royal house of Castile and intrigues for union of the two crowns were frequent, the little western state accentuated its own individuality and went its own way. The American historian, Roger B. Merriman, is one of the many who have lamented the tricks of fate that separated Portugal from Castile, for they were very much alike and might have proved a more fortunate combination than the one that took place, Castile and Aragon.[2]

The expansion of Christendom associated with that most powerful of popes, Innocent III, included momentous triumphs in Spain. The great pontiff fairly compelled the Christian states to cooperate in an offensive against the Moslem which culminated in the battle of Las Navas de Tolosa in 1212. Now the "Moors" were reduced to the southern areas of the peninsula, rich and heavily populated and still formidable. But the Christian campaigns continued under Fernando of Castile, later canonized as St. Fernando, who in 1236 took Cordova itself and in 1248, Sevilla. Simultaneously, Portugal had completed the task of expelling the Moslem in the western area of the peninsula. All the Mohammedans had left was Granada, a highly developed province with strong natural defenses against the Christians.

Instead of completing the crusade by taking Granada, which managed to remain in Moslem hands until 1492, Castile underwent more than two centuries of medieval anarchy. Some of it was the consequence of the follies of Alfonso the Wise, who won the great honor of election to the throne of the Holy Roman Empire but was never able to be crowned or, for that matter, to rule his own kingdom of Castile effectively. He was deposed in 1284, but his reputation as a scientist and man of letters has compensated for his failure as a political leader. Furthermore, he issued an influential codification of laws known as *Las siete partidas* which largely restored the prominent features of Roman law after centuries of Visigothic and Moslem domination. Thus Spain, and

2. *The Rise of the Spanish Empire*, 4 vols.; New York, 1918–34 I, 73.

eventually Latin America, were to develop within the framework of the ideals of justice and order of the Roman Empire.

The Later Middle Ages

CONFUSING and depressing as the internal history of Castile was between St. Fernando and Isabel the Catholic, a period extending from 1252 to 1474, it was nonetheless a time of growth and ferment. A weak monarchy was almost the plaything of the great nobles or grandees, but it persisted and eventually came into its own. The lesser nobles, *hidalgos* and *caballeros*, were also powerful and turbulent, engaging in private wars and stealing one another's subjects, so that serfdom practically disappeared. The clergy was numerous and powerful, often a law unto itself, and the great military orders were strong and rich. Franciscans and Dominicans and other regular orders performed much humanitarian and educational work. Towns and cities were largely autonomous. At times they seemed to be developing in a democratic direction. Lands conquered from the Moslem were populated, and when Jews and Mohammedans elected to remain in the Christian zones they were comparatively well-treated, even if they were segregated. Still, the Christians failed to develop much agriculture. They preferred the military life or banditry, the clergy, or mining and ranching. The prestige of livestock raising over farming was stressed in the privileges accorded the *Mesta*, a guild or association of sheepowners who could move their animals across the peninsula irrespective of the damage they wrought on crops. In all, Castile during this long period was scarcely an integrated state. Each major group flaunted its *fueros* or privileges, developing a peculiar pride that would manifest itself in Latin America long after strong monarchs had concentrated real power in their hands. And much of the institutional and psychological preparation for the occupation of America was taking form as empty areas in south central Spain, especially Extremadura and La Mancha, were being populated by Christians. The process was scarcely completed when the New World would offer a larger field for settlement, and a disproportionate number of its colonists would come from these frontier regions in Spain.

On the east coast things were considerably different. Aragon, having absorbed Catalonia, made the ancient city of Caesar Augustus (Zaragoza) its capital and joined Castile in the great offensives of the thirteenth century that confined the Moslems to Granada. King Jaime the Conqueror won Valencia, Majorca, the chief island of the Baleares, and pushed over the Pyrenees into France during a long reign that spanned the years 1213-1276. Cut off from peninsular expansion by the strength of Castile, the Aragonese later conquered Sardinia, Minorca, Corsica, and Sicily, this last acquisition involving them in Italian affairs until the Napoleonic wars. Interest in overseas territories and an affinity for trade led the Catalans to establish themselves for a time in Greece and Asia Minor while the Byzantine Empire was prostrate. These extensive contacts made the Aragonese monarchy seem more European than the Castilian. Serfdom and other institutions of feudalism gave the kingdom an atmosphere typical of other states of the period, and the northeastern part of Spain still resembles France or Italy in ways that Castile does not. It even seemed for a time that the *cortes*, or assembly of nobles, clergy, and urban delegates, was likely to establish parliamentary rule. But Aragon was not destined to become an England. Cosmopolitan, prosperous, and liberal-minded though it was, Aragon's fate was to be a junior partner of Castile.

The Catholic Kings and the Unification of Spain

IN 1469 a highly important royal marriage took place when Fernando, the heir to the throne of Aragon, was united with Isabel, the heiress presumptive to the Castilian crown. This notable couple eventually became *los reyes católicos*, a title given them by the pope, but only after many difficulties and brushes with failure. Isabel's claim was threatened when a daughter was born to the wife of her half-brother, King Enrique the Impotent. Countless intrigues, much display of energy, and several dramatic horseback rides through Castile were necessary before Isabel organized the forces that supported her rights. In 1474 she won and became queen. This spirited but dignified woman with her round face, blue eyes, and red hair was touched with greatness. Her courage and imagination—and her luck—had much to do with Spanish and American history. Fernando was quite different. To his contemporaries he seemed crafty, calculating, tricky, mendacious, and dishonest. These traits brought him the dubious honor of being praised (or obliquely damned) in an entire chapter of Machiavelli's *The Prince*. But combined with Isabel's qualities, they helped bring unparalleled fortune to the royal couple, their heirs, and to Spain. Fernando did not come into his inheritance until 1479. For that reason, because he enjoyed powers in Castile as Isabel's husband that she did not wield in Aragon as his consort, and because the Castilian monarchy was stronger than the Aragonese, the pair emphasized the more absolutist Castile. Thus Castile's predominance waxed steadily, though for more than a century the Aragonese domains were legally separate, united only by the crown. With the reign of Fernando and Isabel it becomes easier if not altogether accurate to refer to "Spain," since these monarchs and their heirs increasingly ruled the area as one kingdom.

The growth of royal power in Spain was in line with developments in France under Louis XI, England under Henry VII, and Portugal under João II, who were contemporaries of the Catholic Kings. Still, it took much energy, persistence, and skill to accomplish, for it was something new and was by no means inevitable. The nobles found themselves overawed and out-maneuvered by the monarchs and transformed rather rapidly into allies or servants of the royal pair during these years. Many were attracted into a royal guard or into government service. Others were defeated in battle, had their castles razed, their privileges annulled, and their peasants encouraged to move away. The three great military-clerical orders, which had helped establish Isabel, were persuaded or intimidated into naming Fernando as their head, thus bringing more reins into the hands of the monarch. The proud, often defiant towns had to bend before the royal will personified by officials known as *corregidores*, who were later used in America. The *cortes* seldom met, thus discouraging any movement toward parliamentary assertiveness.

Even the formidable forces of the clergy fell under royal control. Beginning in 1482, a series of bulls conceded by popes who needed Fernando's support for Italian or personal affairs or who were unable to withstand pressure made the Church in Spain almost a national organization, subject to Rome only in matters of doctrine. The government collected tithes, supervised ecclesiastical affairs, and nominated Church officials. These powers, known as the *patronato real*, were to be employed extensively in creating the great Church establishment in America. To her credit, Isabel was concerned with more than aggrandizing her authority. With the aid of the great Cardinal Ximenes de Cisneros, she disciplined unworthy clergymen and insisted that the Church abide by her own high-minded if intolerant ideals. The effect was to reform the Spanish Church years before the Reformation started, and Protestantism was never to attract many Spaniards. Moreover, the Spanish clergy was zealous and efficient when the discovery of America brought the magnificent challenge to Christianize millions of pagans. In 1478 Isabel, and, in 1481 Fernando, obtained papal permission to establish the Inquisition in their domains under their own control. This agency assisted in the task of eliminating unworthy ecclesiastics and enforcing conformity to doctrine, but under the Grand Inquisitor Tomás de Torquemada it also began the persecution of persons whose Christianity was suspect, a long and terrible chapter of Spanish history that has fattened the Black Legend.

All of this concentration of power in royal hands was facilitated by rallying the soldiers and common people to the cause of the monarchy. This was largely accomplished by a protracted national effort against the remaining Moors in the densely populated kingdom of Granada. This cause, the last stage of the Reconquest that had inspired the Spaniards for nearly eight centuries, was by no means easy to fulfill. An enormous army, many financial sacrifices, the use of gunpowder, and the almost constant presence of Fernando and Isabel were required, and yet it was more than ten years before Boabdil, the last of the Moorish monarchs, surrendered in January 1492. The final victory brought an ecstatic national feeling to Spain and won the applause of Christendom.

So thankful was Isabel for this richly satisfying victory that she decided to illustrate her gratitude by "purifying" her kingdom, and Fernando agreed to the project, which was nothing less than requiring all Jews to become Christians within four months or to leave Spain. Barbarous as the measure was, France and England had done the same thing two centuries before, and while Spain had generally been tolerant and cosmopolitan, popular violence directed at the Jews had been growing rapidly. In any event, Isabel felt righteous about the whole matter. The number of those who became converted, sincerely or otherwise, is not known. Perhaps 150,000 sold out hurriedly and left for Portugal, where they were fleeced further and then sent away to the Ottoman Empire, Italy, the Netherlands, and elsewhere. A large number chose conversion, but this course exposed them to sinister ministrations of the Inquisition and resulted in further sufferings. So successful did the measure seem to Isabel that ten years later she commanded the half-million or more Moslems in Castile to embrace Christianity or leave. For a century or so Spaniards were inclined to think the expulsions were fine achievements, since Spain became the greatest nation in Europe. Yet we know that in the long run the loss of about a tenth of her population, the most hard-working and skilled element at that, was ruinous. And the enormity of the crime has never been lived down.

It is problematical whether the Catholic Kings might have pursued an imperialistic crusade in Africa had they not been diverted by the discoveries of Columbus. As it turned out, for more than a decade they concerned themselves with the "Indies," the rather unpromising islands and shores of a mysterious New World, which did not prove especially valuable during their lifetimes.

Greater prizes seemed to be in their reach through the dynastic alliances they made for their children. In some respects they were dogged by bad luck. Their sons died without heirs. Two daughters were "wasted" in a futile effort to bring about a union with Portugal. Another

was married to the heir to the English crown, and, when he died, to
his brother, the future Henry VIII. This daughter was the unfortunate
Catherine of Aragon, who achieved neither marital happiness nor closer
ties between England and Spain nor, as it happened, the strengthening
of Catholicism. But fortune compensated liberally in the case of another
tragic daughter, Juana the Mad, whose marriage with Philip the Handsome of the house of Habsburg greatly changed the destinies of Europe,
for better or for worse. For when Isabel died in 1504, Juana and Philip
came to Castile to take over the kingdom and the Americas, such as they
were then. But Philip soon died and Juana became insane, though
romantics have tried from time to time to make out that she was victimized for holding liberal ideas. There is little or no reason to doubt
that she was desperately mad and that she had to be confined for the
rest of her long life, to 1555. Her father, Fernando of Aragon, assumed
the direction of Castile and her overseas possessions until his death in
1516, a somewhat unedifying period in the early history of America.
Meanwhile, his crooked diplomacy and the tough Spanish armies led by
the "Great Captain," Gonsalvo de Córdova, brought him Navarre and
Naples. Aragon, or Spain, thus established a hegemony in Italy that was
to last for more than two centuries and an influence that endured much
longer, and along with them an involvement in European affairs that all
the silver of America could not finance.

The Emperor Charles V

BY THE time Fernando the Catholic died, the first son of Juana
the Mad and Philip the Handsome was nearly old enough to come into
his full rights. From his grandmother, Isabel the Catholic, he inherited
Castile and the expanding possessions in the New World. Fernando
bequeathed him Aragon, Navarre, much of Italy, and the islands of the
western Mediterranean. From his father's mother, Mary of Burgundy,
the young heir received lands now included in the Netherlands, Belgium,
and parts of eastern France and western Germany, then as now one of
the richest areas on earth. His paternal grandfather, Maximilian of Habsburg, left him Austria, assorted territories in central Europe, the likelihood of following him as Holy Roman Emperor, and the prestige of the
name of Habsburg. This young man, who became Carlos I of Spain but
is better known as the Emperor Charles V, eventually acquired titular
possession to as much real estate as almost any other person in history.
He stood as the nearest thing to a universal ruler that Europe was to
know between Charlemagne and Napoleon and came close to unifying
western Europe. With all of it, he was a profound and sensitive man,
a humanist of rich culture, a friend of learning, and altogether one of

Europe's noblest monarchs. If it proved unfortunate that Spain should become involved in European affairs just as she was taking over much of the New World, the Spanish contemporaries of Charles V were gratified by the majesty of their king and the imperial greatness that had come to their backward and isolated peninsula.

The first visit of young Carlos I to Spain in 1517–1520 was not particularly promising. At that time a clumsy, slow-moving youth, ugly with his pronounced underslung jaw, speaking Flemish, and surrounded by luxury-loving Lowlanders who ate and drank too much, the new king seemed very un-Spanish. As soon as he departed to be crowned Holy Roman Emperor and for his dramatic meeting with Martin Luther at Worms, a serious revolt broke out in Castile. Like so many Spanish rebellions it was called a *comunero* movement, chiefly because its impulse came from towns seeking to cast off royal authority, but it developed the characteristics of a social rebellion against the landed nobility, especially when it spread into Valencia. This feature probably killed the movement, since the privileged groups rallied to monarchical authority, and Spain was to experience little in the way of social or democratic unrest for another three centuries. The monarchy was to be absolute.

Charles V was out of Spain for much of his reign. He had several wars to fight against France, which was almost hemmed in by Habsburg power and had to fight for survival, allying herself with Protestants, Mohammedans, and anyone else who opposed the emperor. Much of the warfare took place in Italy, a circumstance that brought Charles into conflict with the pope on occasion and once, in 1527, resulted in the deplorable sacking of Rome by his unpaid troops. When France associated herself with that formidable infidel, Suleiman the Magnificent of the Ottoman Turks, Charles became heavily involved in naval warfare in the Mediterranean, land campaigns in the Danube basin, and attempts to seize North African strongpoints. These wars distracted the emperor from his efforts to deal with the Protestant Reformation, which grew more menacing with the Lutheran successes in central and northern Europe and the spread of Calvinism into France and the Low Countries, apart from the peculiar developments in England sponsored by his erstwhile uncle by marriage, Henry VIII, and Edward VI.

When at last Charles V accepted a stalemate with France and the Turks in order to deal with the Protestants, the matter was out of hand. In the 1540's he finally pressed the reluctant pope to undertake the reform of the Roman Catholic Church and collected a great army to deal with the German Lutherans. Victory seemed assured in 1547, and some sort of reconciliation was believed possible, one that would keep the universal church together through concessions to the Protestants. But an unexpected Protestant victory in 1552 undid Charles' labors.

Narrowly escaping capture, the emperor had to admit failure. Four years later he astonished the world and grieved his subjects by abdicating voluntarily and retiring to a monastery in southern Spain, where he died in 1558. Spaniards have always been proud that the great monarch came to regard Spain as his true home, or in his own words, his garden, fortress, treasury, and sword.

In spite of the many distractions that tore at Charles, he devoted considerable time and thought to his overseas empire. It was he who supported, as Isabel the Catholic had, the more humane policies advocated by the clergy to protect the Indians from exploitation and to make them Christians. He wisely backed the conquistadors while they were winning new kingdoms for him and cashiered them as soon as he could in favor of obedient officials who would be scrupulously loyal to the crown. Charles fashioned the fundamental machinery by which Spain would rule the Americas for many generations: the Council of Indies, the viceroys, the missions, the convoys, the mining regulations, and many other instruments. On the other hand, the wealth of the American possessions helped finance his wars in Europe and buttressed the national position of Spain and the international prestige of Habsburgs. The Counter-Reformation, which was to salvage so much from the disintegration of the Roman Catholic Church, owed its beginning to the wisdom of Charles and the financial support he drew from Mexico and Peru. So it was with the cultural greatness of Spain, its *siglo de oro*, partially inspired by the impact of the New World on European imagination and facilitated by the flow of gold and silver from abroad.

Felipe II, the Prudent King

WHEN Charles V abdicated he turned over to his brother Ferdinand the Habsburg possessions in central Europe, not only because he felt there was too much for one man to rule but because Ferdinand was in a position to bring great pressure for this partition. The remaining lands were indeed valuable, and the emperor's son had no reason to consider himself disinherited. Felipe II (1556-1598) had assisted his father for years in ruling the spreading Spanish monarchy and was husband of the queen of England, "Bloody" Mary. Now he assumed the thrones of Castile and her expanding empire in the New World and in the countless islands of the Pacific Ocean, Aragon, Navarre, Sardinia, Sicily and Naples, Milan, the Low Countries, and the Franche Comté in eastern France. In 1580 he became king of Portugal and her extensive possessions along the coasts of Brazil, the Atlantic and Indian sides of Africa, and fortified places in Persia, India, Malaya, China, and many islands of the Far East.

By far the most formidable monarch of his time, Felipe II had many enemies. He has long been regarded as the man a modern liberal loves to hate, a gloomy bigot, a despot, a cruel hypocrite. For generations men have related that he gloated over the persecution of heretics by the Inquisition; that he killed his own son, Don Carlos; that he took revenge on the only woman he loved, Ana de Mendoza, by confining her to her house and having the windows bricked in; that he laughed only once, when he heard of the massacre of Protestants in France on St. Bartholomew's Day in 1572; that he brutally exterminated the liberties Aragon had enjoyed for so long; and that he hired assassins to fell inconvenient opponents. If only the first of these accusations rises above slander Felipe II did embody most of the characteristics that made the sixteenth-century Spaniard so detested. He was sober and melancholy and often wrong-headed and self-righteous. But he was keenly aware of his great responsibilities before God and posterity. Felipe worked tirelessly, insisting on knowing everything and deciding everything about his empire, seeking above all to make it operate in accordance with his religious ideals. Greatness is seldom lovable.

Felipe II was not a great innovator but rather a conserver, hence his informal title, "the prudent." In the New World he created few important institutions, though the establishment of the Inquisition and the dispatch of the Jesuits there had large consequences. For the most part he perfected the operation of the great imperial apparatus that had been in the making since the days of Columbus. The sharp attention Felipe II gave to details and the close supervision he inflicted on administrators affected the way the viceroys, governors, *corregidores*, bishops, missionaries, treasury officials, and other members of the bureaucracy functioned long after the Prudent King was dead. His example and his methods remained an ideal after it was apparent that more flexibility was needed. The very atmosphere of his 42-year reign was too heavy to be dissipated during the remainder of the colonial period. To some students it seems that the spirit of Felipe II still broods over Latin America.

The European problems that Felipe II faced had important repercussions in the Americas. The real force behind the Catholic Counter-Reformation, which became so powerful after the Council of Trent in 1564, the austere king imparted to such faraway places as the Philippines, Mexico, and Peru a passion to hunt down heretics and to keep the faith pure. Along more positive lines, the resurgent Church pursued the conversion of Indians with great energy and improved Catholic education in the New World.

Felipe II continued the wars against the Turks. With the great naval victory of Lepanto in 1572, Christian Spain virtually concluded her eight and a half centuries of warfare against the Moslem. Perhaps with this victory, as many historians have declared, Spain lost that special quality of inspiration which had driven her to greatness. The Dutch rebelled against Felipe II in 1567 and themselves rapidly attained greatness, thriving on the enmity of the detested king. For most of the ensuing eighty years the traders, pirates, and armed expeditions of the doughty Lowlanders worked havoc on the Hispanic empires. The long duel between Elizabeth I of England and Felipe II, which culminated in the disastrous experience of the Spanish Armada in 1588, opened a nearly continuous warfare or competition that ended only when Latin America became free, or perhaps with the victory of the United States over Spain in 1898. Felipe's acquisition by force of the crown of Portugal in 1580 had long-range effects, many of them injurious to Spain, that he did not foresee.

In all of these international developments the overseas Spanish possessions played a part, sometimes as victim, sometimes as prize, even on occasion as beneficiary. Spain had to tighten her control or risk losing the colonies, and this she did to a degree that fulfilled her purpose, if eventually it proved burdensome to the Americans. Moreover, the so-called Indies provided much of the treasure that enabled Felipe II to dominate or threaten Europe for so long, and that gave Spain the reputation for power that lasted after the power itself had vanished. The silver galleons helped finance the artistic wonders of the *siglo de oro*, especially the palaces, cathedrals, and cloisters that were erected all over the peninsula. Felipe II chose Madrid for his capital and appropriately adorned it, thanks to American metallic treasures. His personal residence and eventually the tomb of Spanish kings, the bleak Escorial, was testimony of the transatlantic sources of wealth. These architectural splendors long outlasted the ships that sailed against England and the Turks, the famous Spanish infantry that fought all over Europe, and the spies and purchased officials in foreign courts who worked Felipe's will, who also were financed by the silver of Mexico and Peru.

The death of this dreaded and strangely admirable king in 1598 is a convenient point to mark the end of Spain's material grandeur. Yet a decline had set in years before, for the healthful and degenerative forces in a state, as in an organism, operate simultaneously before one or the other gains dominance. Something had gone wrong in Spain while she was at the peak of her strength. Whatever it was, it proved malignant and rendered the nation sickly for centuries, with no period of recuperation proving sufficient to restore her. The mystery of Spain's decline has long tantalized her own sons and foreign students. Plausible explanations abound, but few agree as to their position in the hierarchy of causes. Looking at the problem from an international point of view, one may insist that Spain was largely diverted from her true destiny in North Africa by Columbus, that she should never have abandoned the land crusade against the Moslem. Or that the inheritance of Charles V embroiled Spain in European affairs so that she wasted her strength on causes that brought her no lasting advantages. The loss of inspiration after the victory at Lepanto has been mentioned. Spain's efforts to hold the Dutch down, to interfere in France, the Germanies, and Italy, and to contain the English drained her while releasing the energies and firing the determination of others. Perhaps she tried to do too much and ended up by collapsing, by becoming, as Ortega y Gasset has said, the dust left by a great people who once galloped down the highway of destiny. Could it even be that Spain was a bogus power, a backward peninsula that through accidents of discovery and dynastic inheritance became inflated, but which always lacked the fundamental resources that nourish greatness? Or should we be content with philosophizing that a century or so of first-rank strength is about all that any modern European nation has been able to sustain?

  If one rejects all such explanations a number of reasons related to Spain's internal situation come to mind. The rigid character of her royal autocracy may have been beneficial while the empire was growing but unsuitable for a long period of stability, especially when the caliber of the kings declined so sharply, as it did between 1598 and 1700, The religious intolerance that expelled the Jews and Moslems (and later, the converted Moslems) and badgered the populace into conformity or timidity is a favorite explanation. The emphasis on pastoral and mining industries obstructed the development of agriculture and manufacturing as well as commerce. The influx of treasure from America led to an inflation that injured many groups and, in the long run, enriched Spain's rivals more than herself. Something was at odds in a society which stressed war and religiosity at the expense of plain, humble labor. Does the answer lie in false ideals, collective character defects, or in circumstances the wisest of statesmen could not control? Outsiders and Spaniards alike ponder these imponderables, and no single answer seems to fit.

  Having said all this, we must not dismiss Spain too easily after the passing of the Prudent King. For nearly a half-century more Spain, or her ghost, enjoyed great military prestige in Europe. The annihilation of her fleets in 1637–1639 and the catastrophic defeat of her army at Rocroi in 1643 did not altogether overthrow Spain as a respected power. She continued to occupy much of Italy and the Netherlands, and her enormous empire remained loyal and productive. Very little of it was lost to her stronger enemies, the English, Dutch, and French. And then in the eighteenth century Spain underwent a considerable revival under a new dynasty, the Bourbons. Somehow, the vast and peculiar world empire continued operating on the momentum imparted to it by Isabel the Catholic, Charles V, and Felipe II. The imperial machinery never quite collapsed during the seventeenth century. It must have been soundly conceived and not altogether repugnant to its subjects.

Spain's Golden Age

A CULTURAL flowering of large proportions began during Spain's period of overseas expansion and lingered for several generations after the decline had set in, thus offering support both for those who claim that great artistic and literary expression coincides with national greatness and for those who contend it characterizes the aftermath of such periods. It was natural enough that Spanish explorers and conquistadors should write about their achievements, inadequately as they did so for our purposes. They sometimes recorded the facts faithfully but often were partisan and too prone to describe non-existent marvels and supernatural miracles. Only by inadvertence did they set down most of the facts the modern anthropologist or social and economic historian would like to know. Also, the Spanish wrote books on navigation, geography, metallurgy, and mining that were regarded as authoritative. The collection of important papers dealing with the New World and the recording of its history from the conqueror's point of view were also done with a sense of responsibility. The sudden enrichment of Spain and the profound stimulation of the senses brought about by the great discoveries surely encouraged the establishment of universities. Perhaps thirty or more institutions in the peninsula merited the name of university by the death of Felipe II, and while some of them provided degrees and intellectual pretensions to ignorant graduates, others furthered the growth of academic traditions and standards we can admire.

Such matters, however, constitute no more than the normal or predictable effects of a period of national greatness. There was more to Spain's *siglo de oro* (golden century) than that. Genius, always unaccountable, appeared in many forms during the sixteenth and seventeenth centuries. Above all was Miguel de Cervantes Saavedra (1547–1616), that warrior and man of action whose worthy poems, novels, and essays are overshadowed by his great *Don Quijote*. The dramatist Félix Lope de Vega (1562–1635) wrote so many plays with so many different plots, full of such superlative lyric verse, that he entertained his contemporaries and has influenced dramatists of his own and other nations ever since. Pedro Calderón de la Barca (1600–1681), with his lofty absorption in religion and philosophy, was a prolific genius whose lyrical dramas are masterpieces of beauty and profoundly stirring to the spirit. Tirso de Molina (1571–1648) produced an admirable variety of dramas of possibly less depth but often of more interest in the interplay of human passions. Along with these towering figures of literature were great numbers of lesser lights whose verses, stories, and plays enjoyed much popularity in Spain and America. Whether they are chivalrous, pastoral, or picaresque, many of them strike us today as shallow and silly, but then the transient works of literature usually are. Until the appearance of *Don Quijote* in 1605–1611, most Spaniards who read (or listened to readings) were influenced above all by the Portuguese chivalric romance. *The four books of Amadis of Gaul*, with its extravagant treatment of improbable deeds in remote places, was full of meaning to a nation engaged in world-wide explorations. It was fantastic and exaggerated, but the people doted on it. Not a little of the posturing and strutting of the conquistadors may be attributed to the influence of this work.

A plentiful supply of Spanish geniuses rose to the religious issues posed by the Discovery and the Reformation. The political scientists, jurists, and historians we shall consider in later pages as they dealt with the problems of the Americas. St. Ignatius Loyola (1491–1556), and his *Spiritual Exercises* affected many a Jesuit who buttressed the Spanish monarchy in five continents and other devout souls, some of them in high positions of the government, who felt the need of such rigid self-discipline. Spanish mystics have long commanded the respect, often grudging, of the outside world. Outstanding among them was St. Teresa de Jesús (1515–1582), who reformed the Carmelites in the face of many obstacles and wrote powerfully of the blazing ecstasy one may achieve in approaching an awareness of God. St. John of the Cross (1542–1591), her follower and also a Carmelite, described the way to reach spiritual bliss and the joys of mystical experience. While comparatively few people were capable of such discipline, these mystics were loved and respected by the populace at large on both sides of the Atlantic. A strong strain of Spanish mysticism persists in much of the Hispanic world, often serving as another barrier to the sympathetic understanding of this world by outsiders with different religious traditions.

The memorable period of Spanish painting came after the peak of imperial greatness, though the way for it had been prepared by the cultured Charles V and his sponsorship of artists and by Felipe II and his tendency to collect meritorious works of art. El Greco (1541–1614), a Greek or Cretan named Domenico Theotocopuli, painted for years in Toledo his delicate, haunting portraits and scenes that seem to typify the gravity, dignity, and religiosity of the Spaniard. José de Ribera (1588–1652) was able to depict both the spiritual exaltation and the human cruelty that Spaniards displayed in their period of domination. Diego Velásquez (1599–1660) was court painter to Felipe IV and a superlative master of his craft. Serene and realistic, his portraits immortalized the mediocre Habsburgs of the mid-seventeenth century and the characters who frequented their court, something their own achievements fell short of doing. There were many other famous names, certainly those of Zurbarán and Murillo, whose works endowed Spanish painting with its great reputation and furnished inspiration and material for imitation by many artists of the Spanish empire in America, who themselves were often gifted, if not outstanding. In all, the New World partially stimulated and endowed the Golden Age and certainly shared in its glories.

THE RISE OF IMPERIAL PORTUGAL

The section of western Hispania known as Lusitania in Roman times shared the experiences of the rest of the Iberian peninsula and was not attributed any particular distinctiveness from its other inhabitants. After the peak of the Moslem period, while the Reconquest was gathering momentum, a town at the mouth of the Douro River and its surrounding area came to be called *Portucale*. Somehow the name later denoted the western part of the Iberian peninsula while the modern city is known as Oporto, Portugal's second port and metropolis. The County of Portucale was awarded to a French crusader, Henry of Burgundy, for his important services to the crown of Leon in fighting the Moslems, and about 1100 Henry was claiming virtual independence. His son, Afonso Henriques, continued the crusade by enlarging the county to include Lisbon and began to call himself king of Portugal in 1140. One legend is that he won this right in a tournament, very much as the fate of a great business might be decided by the outcome of a dice game. Certainly, a great deal of fighting and intrigue attended the process of Portugal's becoming an independent kingdom, and it was because of personal and dynastic accidents that it did so, not because of the inevitable assertion of a unique nationality. For there was little to distinguish the Portuguese from the Castilians but a dialect that has over the centuries become a language differing radically in pronounciation but little in writing. As has been noted, many writers have regretted this turn of affairs, holding that a union of Castile and Portugal would have been far more wholesome than that of Castile and Aragon.

Destiny decreed otherwise, and few who are acquainted with the Portuguese would wish to quarrel with fate in this respect. The Portuguese have nearly always been more pleasing to foreigners than the Castilians, more flexible and less stern, more lovable and less reserved.

Much as they resemble the Castilians in their poetic cult of heroism and action regardless of material consequences, the Portuguese have been far less inclined to religious intolerance. They seem to smile more, to be more human and agreeable. Yet, fundamentally, they are very much like the other Iberians. Their efforts to accentuate their distinctiveness and to develop their peculiarities have not erased the profound similarities of Spaniard and Portuguese. Being different from Spain has been Portugal's chief justification for existing. In most of the wars of modern times Portugal has been on the side opposed to her large neighbor. Yet the rhythm of her internal history—in political, economic, and cultural affairs alike—has been almost identical with that of Spain.

By 1249 the kingdom of Portugal had reached the southern shores that have ever since confined her expansion in Europe. With the Moslem no longer in easy reach, the little nation began the preliminary oceanic explorations that were to take it so far. Also, it received much outside influence through the frequent use of Lisbon by sailors from England and France. During the next century it appeared that Portugal might move back into union with Castile and Leon through dynastic ties. But a timely rebellion by the warlike nobles led to the establishment of a new dynasty, the house of Avis, in 1385. In the following year Portugal and England signed an alliance, the Treaty of Windsor, which has stood through the centuries with few lapses and is the oldest diplomatic tie in Europe. Its true meaning has been the general cooperation of the two maritime powers to their mutual profit and invaluable English assistance in enabling Portugal to remain free from Spain. Without it, even in very recent times, Portugal might have been incorporated by her stronger neighbor.

The new dynasty of Avis was full of crusading fervor, as befitted a royal house in the twilight of the age of chivalry. A dazzling exploit was planned in great secrecy, an overseas expedition to capture the city of Ceuta in Morocco, near the Strait of Gibraltar. In 1415 this enterprise was carried out with brilliant success. While Ceuta itself failed to yield the economic advantages the Portuguese expected, its capture stimulated the idea of making further conquests in Africa to shake the Moslems and to establish contacts with dark-skinned traders deep in the Sahara who were reputed to deal in exotic articles the Europeans craved. It was Prince Henrique, "Henry the Navigator" as foreigners called him, who personified these ambitions. His long and highly important career will be dealt with in the next chapter, but here it may be noted that explorations until his death in 1460 brought the Portuguese two thousand miles down the western coast in Africa, acquainted them with the techniques of deep ocean sailing, and entrenched them in fortified places along the coast where they dealt very profitably with Negro and Arabic traders. Portugal became one of the most exciting places in Europe for men of great dreams and the spirit of adventure. She was prosperous and active and clearly engaged in undertakings to inspire traders, missionaries, and heroes.

The Avis kings, who were usually both able and interesting as individuals, had more to think about than the exploits of their sailors, promising as these were. Above all, they needed to centralize royal power at the expense of the nobility, a process that was carried to a successful conclusion in Spain, France, and England during the last decades of the fifteenth century. It is necessary here to record only that Portugal, too, became an autocratic monarchy at this time, particularly after João II (1481–1495) foiled an assassination plot directed at his royal self. It was this same João, called "the Perfect," who listened with interest to the overtures of Christopher Columbus but finally turned him down. With the return of Bartolomeu Dias in 1488, he was satisfied that the Portuguese would reach the true Indies by sailing around Africa. Later he had the mixed pleasure of hearing from Columbus' own lips about the supposed discovery of the short westward route to Asia, but he let his guest proceed to Spain without molestation and contented himself with dividing the seas and newly-found lands with Castile in the Treaty of Tordesillas of 1494, which he regarded as a great triumph for Portugal.

Manoel I, "the Fortunate," ruled from 1495 until 1521. One of his first measures was taken in connection with his marriage to a daughter of Fernando and Isabel, the expulsion of the numerous and powerful Portuguese Jews. As it turned out, the number forced to leave was comparatively small, for most of the Jews were compelled to accept Christianization by brutal physical pressures. These New Christians continued to play a large role in the life of Portugal, in the African slave trade, and as will be seen, in Brazil. More fortunate were Manoel's sponsorship of the expeditions that expanded Portugal's interests and rule, the epochal voyage of Vasco da Gama to India in 1497–1499, Cabral's discovery of Brazil in 1500 and subsequent voyage to India, and the brilliant career in the East of the great viceroy, Afonso de Albuquerque, in 1507–1515. Albuquerque consolidated Portugal's base in India at Goa, which until 1962 was a Portuguese city, and developed the enormously rich commercial channels which brought the goods of the East to Lisbon. He also established a strong point at Malacca, north of the modern city of Singapore, from which the Portuguese were able to acquire a dominant position in the trade of the East Indies, China, and Japan. Under Albuquerque the Portuguese bested the Arabs in India and the Indian Ocean, though they did not entirely eliminate these detested competitors. The capture of Ormuz on the Persian Gulf in 1515 gave Portugal another foundation stone for the commercial empire she was building, and the unsuccessful assault on Aden weakened if it did not block the Arabic trade channel through the Red Sea. While many Portuguese lost their lives in creating and operating this overseas empire, the oldest and most enduring in the world, some enriched themselves. Strangely enough, the far-flung Asiatic empire did not prove particularly profitable to the government, but it brought fame and influence.

João III reigned from 1521 to 1557, a period which saw the tightening of the hold on the African coasts, the continued development of a mercantile empire in the Orient, and the true beginnings of Brazil. Rather tardily, and no doubt because of the Spanish example, Portugal began to take more seriously the opportunities for missionary work among the peoples she dealt with. The Jesuits embarked on their spectacular career in Asia and Brazil. Beset with Protestantism and Turkish advances in Europe, the papacy was glad enough to turn over to the Portuguese crown, as it had to the Spanish, the right to manage the ecclesiastical establishment. As in the Spanish empire, the arrangement was not at all harmful to the spread of Roman Catholicism in distant lands. The Inquisition came to Portugal in 1536 at the urgent request of its king but never achieved the dread reputation its counterpart won in the Spanish monarchy.

The death of João III in 1557 found Portugal suffering from the effects of overexpansion. A small country without rich natural resources and only a million and a half population, its young men had for years gone to sea and to distant lands. The abuse of the Jews and New Christians had done the country no good from the standpoint of developing a mercantile class. Indeed, many of the middlemen who received the products of Asia, Africa, and America were not Portuguese at all, and in sending these articles to better distribution centers in northern Europe they gave Portugal little chance to profit. And now, by the middle of the sixteenth century, the coveted goods from afar were being carried again through the old land channels and Italian routes over the Mediterranean. Portugal's control of the trade had never been complete and was by 1560 only an advantage, not a monopoly.

Coinciding with this period of national exhaustion and depression was the reign of a boy king, Sebastião, 1557–1578, whose unbalanced mind was made feverish by a romantic proposal to conquer Morocco. Exalted by religious fanaticism and crusading zeal, the young monarch disappeared in a disastrous battle on Moroccan soil in 1578. The fact that no one saw him die caused a troublesome situation to plague Portugal for sixty years or more,[3] as claimants appeared from time to time to assert they were the lost king.

The passing of Sebastião in his tragic crusade found the house of Avis without a suitable heir. An aged great-uncle of Sebastião took the throne for the last two years of his life as king. Already a cardinal, the old man was ineligible to marry, and efforts to obtain papal permission for him to retract his vows and take a wife dragged on until it was too late. A Duke of Braganza had some claim to the inheritance, but more legitimate heirs were available, among them Felipe II of Spain, whose mother was a Portuguese princess. As Felipe is supposed to have said, he inherited, bought, and conquered the Portuguese throne. His claim to the inheritance was as good as any. Certainly he used "Mexican bullets," or silver pesos, to bribe many influential Portuguese, and in 1580 he sent the Duke of Alba into Lisbon with an overpowering army to assure his accession as Felipe I of Portugal. Soon afterward the Prudent King swore that he would respect Portuguese laws and liberties, that the colonial empires of Spain and Portugal would be kept separate, and that the vast monarchy of Portugal would be connected with Spain only through the person of a common king. Thus began the 60-year period of union which the Portuguese characterize as "the Babylonian captivity."

Portugal's cultural development during her great age of expansion reached impressive heights, a veritable Golden Age like that of Spain. Her architecture and painting were impressive in the technical skill that expressed the burgeoning imagination of Portuguese artists of the period. In music, Portugal's greatest distinction came later, in the eighteenth century. It was in letters that the Portuguese achieved their greatest glory, drawing the inevitable comparison with ancient Greece in that both countries, beautiful but poor, produced a literature of appealing originality. While poets and historians abounded during the great years of imperialism, by far the most important figure was Luis de Camões (1524–1580), whose epic poem, The Lusiads, glorified the voyage of Vasco da Gama. Compared by his admirers with Shakespeare and Cervantes, this versatile genius and curiously poetic man of action stands at the head of Portugal's national literature. If the creative output of the little kingdom during its period of fame was astonishingly large because of talented individuals, it is notable that the populace at large often understood and appreciated their achievements.

3. The miraculous Sebastião was also supposed to have stirred a backwoods rebellion in Brazil during the 1890's.

Discovery and Conquest

3

The Discovery

The Expansion of Europe

As we come to the decisive events in which Spain reached out and established contact with the primitive civilizations of America it is imperative to state the obvious so we will be reminded of the great significance of the voyage of Columbus and all that has flowed from it. This is the stage of modern history called the Expansion of Europe. Shortly before 1500, Europe, which we may equate with Christendom, was a comparatively unpromising, insignificant civilization when we consider the state of the entire globe. This Europe was and has remained politically disunited. Its religion was split between Roman Catholicism and Greek Orthodoxy, and the former was about to be shaken fundamentally by the Protestant Reformation. The European world was undergoing a period of discouragement and seemed to be threatened with progressive impoverishment. While it surpassed the Aztec and Inca societies and those of Africa in most respects, it was less advanced than contemporaneous cultures in the Middle East, India, and the Far East by many standards. There was little to suggest that Europe was about to explode and establish a leadership that would become a real domination of the world until the mid-twentieth century, when the process would go into reverse.

During the long interval between the Iberian voyages of discovery and the recent German wars, the Christians of Europe peopled much of northern Asia, the Americas, and the islands of Oceania. Africa was subjugated and in parts colonized, and millions of its inhabitants were forced to emigrate to America. The sophisticated societies of the Middle and Far East were intimidated and compelled to defer to the European nations in commerce, technology, and diplomacy. Europe itself became more divided in government and religion but proved able nonetheless to achieve a fantastic position of leadership for four hundred years. In the process its peoples rose to unparalleled heights of wealth and culture, and the civilization we know as Western would become one of the glories of the human race.

It is no simple matter to identify the factors of history or the qualities of the European Christians themselves that explain this "four-hundred year boom," as Walter Prescott Webb has called it. There is no obvious factor on the technological side. The Asians had gunpowder, artillery, and other weapons which might have protected their independence or even enabled them to conquer Europe. They knew as much or more about sailing and employed larger ships. They enjoyed every advantage in numbers and wealth. Their disunity was scarcely more pronounced than that of Europe. Perhaps the answer is that these Asian societies were spent—though the Ottoman Turks were certainly an exception—that the fires of their might and civilization were burning low. Their self-satisfaction led them to underestimate the "Goths" or "Franks" they understood to live in a state of near-barbarism in the small western peninsula of Asia called Europe. Already these supposed primitives had exhibited strong powers of survival and had struck back at their invaders in Russia and Spain and during the Crusades. Was it that the Christians of 1500 were fired by a missionary spirit, that they could not rest until they had taken their religion to other peoples, while the ancient religions of the East were less obsessed with the impulse to proselyte? For ages the Europeans had sought to convert Far Eastern potentates by means of emissaries, and failure had not in the least diminished their ambition.

The ultimate reason for the expansion of Europe may have been a humble materialistic factor: the Europeans coveted goods the Asians had. This yearning of the rather backward Europeans for the silks, drugs, lacquers, spices, perfumes, and sugar of the East dates back at least to Roman times. It was not lost during the long dismal period that followed, and the Crusades served to intensify it. For much of the later Middle Ages and the Renaissance it seemed that overland trade might suffice to bring these articles of luxury and refinement to the few Europeans who could afford them. In some volume they came to Constantinople and the Levant, where Italian ships carried them to markets in the west. With their population and standards of living generally rising, the Europeans greatly relished these goods and demanded more. But the supply via overland caravans became irregular when China began her policy of exclusiveness soon after the overthrow of the Mongols in 1368. The depredations of Tamerlane in the Middle East also harmed the channels of trade, and the Ottoman Turks, who conquered Constantinople in 1453, often made passage by overland caravans hazardous. A water route through the Red Sea served to connect Italian distribution centers with Arabia and India, but local rulers in this area levied vexatious duties and otherwise raised obstructions. Toward the end of the fifteenth century the Europeans were more eager than ever for Asian luxuries, and they found themselves often frustrated.

Had it been the other way around, had the Asians sought European goods, then the Chinese might have sailed about Africa and seized Lisbon or Cadiz. But the Easterners scarcely reciprocated the European desire for contact. Europe had little or nothing that Asia wanted. As it was, the Europeans became more and more curious about the Far East. Missionaries, traders, and adventurers grappled relentlessly with the problem of reaching the splendid courts and fabled cities of the East. The most famous of these was the celebrated Venetian, Marco Polo, whose long visit at the court of the Great Khan in Peking and to Japan and India (1271–1295) came to be recorded after his return and was circulated until it was part of the folklore of Italy, well-known to illiterate boys like Columbus. Even if many people regarded Marco Polo as a liar, and he certainly exaggerated, they had a mental image of the fabulous East that made them all the more curious. The Italian Renaissance, with its spirit of adventure and its generally unsettling influence, further heightened this eagerness of the European to reach out for riches and romance.

The Portuguese Pioneers

IT WAS one of the most backward and insignificant kingdoms of Christendom that solved the problem of establishing regular contact with the East. This was Portugal, whose location and long duel with the Moslems had stimulated an impulse to sail southward in the hope of encircling Africa, as according to legend the Phoenicians had done many centuries earlier. The key figure in this undertaking was Prince Henrique, usually known as "Henry the Navigator." As a young man he had participated in the capture of Ceuta, in Morocco, in 1415 by the Portuguese in a stunningly successful expedition. Probably there he became interested in the mystery of Prester John, a Christian monarch long reputed to rule a formidable kingdom deep in Africa. This Prester John was never satisfactorily identified, though he must have been the monarch of Ethiopia, who then as now professed the Coptic type of Christianity. At any rate, the idea of reaching Prester John and placing the Moslems between two enemies appealed to this young prince, who had no political ambitions or amorous inclinations to distract him and was free to dedicate his life to the enterprise. As head of the Order of Christ, a successor to the Knights Templar, he represented the crusading spirit. Then too, he must have heard of the romantic caravan traffic in the Sahara and tales of rivers of gold in Africa. Near Cape St. Vincent, the extreme southwestern corner of Europe, the pious prince established a center that attracted cosmographers, navigators, marine architects, mathematicians, and adventurers from all over the Mediterranean.

In time Prince Henry had a veritable headquarters for exploration. While his missionary zeal burned bright, we cannot doubt that the pure joy of scientific discovery became one of his chief inspirations. Strangely, he stayed home himself, but almost every year an expedition he had carefully assembled sailed out into the Atlantic. Madeira and the Azores Islands were explored and later populated with Portuguese. After years of effort Henry's men passed the long, barren desert coasts and rounded Cape Bojador and then pushed on to Senegal, Gambia, the Cape Verde Islands, and, by the time Prince Henry died in 1460, around the paunch of Africa. Knowledge of currents, improved seamanship, new marine instruments, and the development of the caravel for high-seas sailing were some of the fruits of these voyages. Of almost equal importance was the conquest of superstition on the part of his sailors, who had feared they would turn black if they sailed too far southward or that they would encounter monsters, the edge of the world, or circular currents from which they could never extricate themselves.

Apart from the zest of exploration, the Portuguese monarchy developed a very tangible interest in furthering Prince Henry's policies and in keeping his findings secret. The crown granted monopolies of sectors along the African coasts and the islands to wealthy traders who established fortified posts. Here they exchanged cloth, horses, saddles, bowls, pots, mirrors, scissors, needles, combs, beads, tools, and grain for gold, salt, ivory, and spices that often had been brought hundreds of miles from the interior over ancient commercial routes. Furthermore, most of the local kings and chieftains owned slaves, usually young prisoners of war, whom they were willing to sell to the Portuguese. Prince Henry had come to disapprove of such purchases, but others were eager to obtain Africans to labor on farms in Portugal, where so many areas were underpopulated. Under the able and bellicose King João II, "the Perfect," the little Lusitanian kingdom energetically expanded her activities. The pope gave Portugal the exclusive right to convert and trade in these pagan areas, and other Christians were supposed to keep out. In particular, Castile agreed to do so in 1479 through a treaty that supported her title to the Canary Islands, which she had conquered early in the century. Explorers sailed up the rivers of western Africa in search of more slaves and goods. They hopefully coasted eastward after they passed the hump, only to find that the shore dismayingly turned southward for thousands of miles. But more trading posts were created, and Lisbon became a thriving port full of rumors and foreign mariners, as Columbus found when he went there about 1476.

Finally, in 1487–1488, Bartolomeu Dias rounded the Cape of Good Hope, while a compatriot of his, Pedro de Covilhã, reached India by land and explored the eastern coast of Africa. The Portuguese knew they had found the route to India. It was nine years before they were in a position to verify their theory, which they did through the epochal voyage of Vasco da Gama in 1497–1499. Da Gama's cargo was not particularly rich, and he mistakenly reported that the Hindus were Christians. On their part, the Indians were not impressed by the arrival of the Portuguese, whose voyage deceptively seemed to signify so little to the complacent Easterners. But official circles in Lisbon were elated, and they immediately made ready to exploit the new route. Men in Venice, Genoa, and Egypt who had previously handled the Oriental trade were overcome with gloom at the Portuguese feat. And Spain had at that time only the Canaries and some paltry islands across the Atlantic which she called "the Indies" with more hope than reason. Little Portugal had done it! She had reached the Far East and established herself profitably on the coasts of Africa.

The "Discovery" of America

IT IS generally accepted that the Spanish landing in America in 1492 was an accident in the quest for a sea route to the East. Did the Portuguese precede the Spanish? With much emotion many Portuguese and not a few Brazilians will assert they did. It stands to reason that the Portuguese might have landed in South America. They certainly had the capacity to sail that far, and they wandered over much of the Atlantic from Prince Henry's time on. When asked for proof, all the defenders of this theory can produce is that King João II urgently demanded that the papal line of demarcation of 1493 be pushed to the west. He wanted to make sure that Brazil was included in his part, they say. But if he knew about America, why is there no written evidence? Here, the Portuguese can only point to the policy of secrecy which Portugal wisely followed to keep foreigners from intruding or, if pushed, to the fact that so many records were destroyed in the great earthquake of 1755 that devastated much of Lisbon. We can only regard their assertions as logical, but utterly lacking in substantiation.

Did others reach America before Columbus? Claimants for Japan, China, and even Africa are heard from time to time, but they can supply no convincing basis for their contentions. We are reasonably sure, of course, that primitive peoples migrated to America from Asia, but they apparently kept no contact with their previous homelands. As for Europe, legends persisted for centuries about strange lands to the west, Antilia, St. Brendan's Isle, Atlantis, the Fortunate Isles, and others which might have arisen from ancient relations with America, but again we have no facts to support them. Irish monks were great sailors in the sixth to eighth centuries, and they have partisans who allege that traditions of white gods in ancient America date from such contacts. Even Christians driven from Spain by the Moslems are said to have fled to the New World. But all of this is conjecture, fruitless if pleasant. There is no doubt that the Vikings or the Norsemen reached Greenland about 981, and little doubt that Leif Ericson went to Canada about 1000. There is really no reason to deny the possibility that the Norse sailed farther down the eastern coast of North America or into Hudson Bay, but neither is there reason to be sure they did. Hoaxes which from time to time have purported to show that these hardy Scandinavians reached the Great Lakes or the coast of Georgia have given such claims an air of the ludicrous they do not deserve, for the Norse could have gone almost anywhere. But even if they sailed widely about North America and made extensive settlements, they lost touch with the New World and there was no continuity to their activities.

CHRISTOPHER COLUMBUS

About the exploits of Columbus, there is no doubt. His voyage of 1492–1493 made the impression on Europe that the first round-trip from Earth to other planets may well have. Since his second voyage, Spanish civilization and the Christian religion have flourished in the Americas. Furthermore, some of his policies, adopted under the pressure of events, helped to shape the fundamental structure of the long-lived Spanish empire. His career is so dramatic and so full of sublimity, anguish, and defeat in victory that curiosity about the man himself has been acute and has led to disagreements. He came of humble stock and later in life made cryptic, enigmatic, and probably untruthful statements about his youth, thus creating an air of mystery about his origins and, in fact, his first forty years. Some Spaniards can scarcely bear the thought that this great man was not Spanish and have sought to "prove" that he was. The brilliant essayist and historian Salvador de Madariaga has made a persuasive but not truly convincing case for Columbus as the descendant of Christianized Jews who fled Spain for Genoa. The soundest of recent studies of the discoverer's life, Samuel Eliot Morison's *Admiral of the Ocean Sea*, attempts to restore the traditional conception of Columbus, relying largely on the writings of his son, Fernando, and his friends,

Bartolomé de Las Casas, Peter Martyr, and Fernández de Oviedo. Yet many mysteries remain and controversies refuse to die.

The usually accepted story of Columbus is that he was born in 1451 in Genoa of a simple family of weavers named Colombo. As a boy he took to the sea, a natural thing for a Genoese to do, and he sailed to various points in the Mediterranean. In 1476 or thereabouts he went to Portugal, his ship being wrecked after a tangle with a Moslem raider. Columbus is supposed to have waded ashore in Portugal naked, destitute, illiterate, and friendless. Within several years he was a prosperous sea captain, able to read two or three languages, and married to a lady of the lower nobility. All of this is so improbable that questions force themselves on any student. Madariaga may be correct in guessing that Columbus established contacts with Portuguese Jews or fellow converted Jews who sponsored his rise in state. Perhaps it was pure good luck in the exciting atmosphere and fluid conditions that prevailed in Lisbon. It may be simply that Columbus' impressive personality, manifest abilities, and fortunate marriage brought him up so rapidly in the world. In any event, he sailed widely, going far down the west coast of Africa and then to a distant northern island, possibly Iceland. Apart from acquiring experience in deep seas sailing and much knowledge of currents and navigation, he learned a great deal from other mariners about the rumors and realities of new lands that were stirring the Portuguese. This tall, blue-eyed, red-haired man not only listened but read enthusiastically. His markings of passages of the Bible and antique books of geography and prophecy show how his thoughts were moving.[1]

Soon he was a dedicated man, one of those unreasonable, tiresome, and yet often decisive makers of history. Columbus was convinced that a comparatively but not impossibly long voyage west from Lisbon would bring a ship to the Far East. This idea was not altogether revolutionary, for most educated people knew the world was round. But no one had done such a thing, or at least lived to tell about it. Technically it seemed feasible but very difficult, as interplanetary travel does today. Still, there were skepticism, inertia, and superstitious fears about the dangers of such a voyage. The difficulties were really psychological and monetary, apart from the unsuspected fact that the great land barrier we call America obstructed the route. The more Columbus was challenged the more difficult he became. Always proud and sensitive, he insulted those who

---

1. As is true of every stage of Columbus' life to 1492, some controversy remains here. Cecil Jane has made out a case that Columbus was illiterate as late as 1492, learned to read a little in later years but affected to be learned in several languages, and marked these passages long after his first voyage (Introduction to *Select Documents Illustrating the Four Voyages of Columbus*, London: Printed for the Hakluyt Society, 1930–1933).

disagreed with him and provoked useless antagonism, a tendency he exhibited all his life. When, in 1484, he formally presented his proposal to João II, that monarch's advisers finally decided against Columbus on the correct grounds that the Orient was several times more distant from Portugal than he had represented and that no ship could possibly make such a voyage. Only three years later João's sailors went around the southern tip of Africa and seemed to justify his unwillingness to support Columbus.

In 1485 Columbus, now a widower, went to Spain, accompanied by his son Diego. Soon he secured a sponsor in the Duke of Medina Celi, who introduced him to Fernando and Isabel. The latter, who resembled Columbus in many ways, was impressed with his idea, but the demands of the war against Granada made it impossible to underwrite so expensive and problematical an enterprise. So Columbus remained near the royal court, pressing his beliefs and making enemies, while his brother went to sound out the monarchs of England and France. In 1490 the committee of experts who advised Queen Isabel concluded that the East was too far, there was no way to get back, and there were no inhabitable lands in between. They knew all this because St. Augustine had said so! In their defense it should be acknowledged that Columbus made extremely extravagant demands for titles, profits, and powers while offering nothing more than his personal conviction that large results could be obtained. Embittered, Columbus was on the point of departing when a friend of his, a former confessor of the queen, caused him to press his case again. Once more Isabel seemed about to approve, but early in 1492, just as the Moors were finally defeated, she veered back to the position of her advisers. This time Columbus was truly disgusted with the long years he had wasted in Spain, and with his son he set off for France. Somehow Queen Isabel changed her mind and sent a rider to fetch Columbus from the road.

Agreeing quickly after so much uncertainty, Columbus and the monarchs, for by now Fernando was acquiescent and possibly enthusiastic, laid plans for the sensational enterprise. It was not necessary for Isabel to pawn her jewels in order to finance the voyage, though she considered it. Instead, the little seaport of Palos was commanded to fit out the necessary ships, for it had somehow incurred royal wrath and owed a fine. Isabel and her husband also signed the Capitulations of Santa Fe on 17 April 1492, which authorized Columbus to sail westward, avoiding the Portuguese preserve in Africa, to use the titles of Don and Admiral of the Ocean Sea if he were successful, and to become viceroy and recipient of one-tenth of all royal revenues from any new lands he might discover. The absence of any mention of the Far East in these capitulations has caused speculation that Columbus had something else in mind, but his passport expressly stated that he would navigate the Indies, and he carried a letter from the monarchs to the Great Khan (who had been nonexistent for more than a century).

After a good deal of pressure and frenetic exertions, Columbus assembled his fleet, the *Santa María* and the smaller *Pinta* and *Niña*, a crew of ninety men and boys from the neighborhood of Palos, nearly all of whom have been identified through the industry of an American lady in recent years.[2] They proved equal to the job, if troublesome on occasion, and several of them became famous mariners. The ships were only small caravels with square, rigged sails, sitting high on the water, the *Santa María* displacing perhaps 120 tons and the others about half that many. Their military equipment was pathetically limited: some primitive iron cannon which made a great deal of noise and would hurl rounded rocks a fair distance, a few muskets, cross-bows, and other weapons typical of the time. Had the party encountered the Aztecs or Inca, they quite likely would never have gotten back to Spain. Certainly they could not have impressed the potentates of the Orient.

The little expedition sailed from Palos on August 3, 1492. Columbus went directly to the Canary Islands, which Castile had partially colonized, and tarried with the notorious Doña Beatriz, who had murdered her husband and taken his place as governor. Then began the daring part of the voyage, the 33-day sailing across the Atlantic to the Bahama Islands. Europeans had sailed as many days before, but they had seldom done it so far from land and in a great unknown ocean. Columbus rose superbly to the occasion. He was a great navigator, as we know from his journal (assuming it is authentic) and the careful checks made on his calculations when Morison in 1939 sailed over the same route. His principal problem had to do not with nature but with human beings, for the men became more restive as each day carried them farther from home and the supplies diminished. While the faith of Columbus seems not to have wavered, especially as signs of nearby land appeared, his men threatened him with a mutiny in October, and he won from them an agreement to continue for two or three more days. Near the end of this period a light was sighted, not by Columbus to his chagrin and later to his dishonor, for he claimed he had been the first to see it, but by one of the crew. On the next day, October 12, 1492, an island came into view.

In one of the most dramatic moments of human history, Columbus went ashore and planted the banner of Isabel the Catholic and a cross. The naked brown savages who greeted him seemed very agreeable folk, anxious to give him anything he wished and, after they had developed a means of communicating, to hear about his religion and his queen and

2. Miss Alice Quincy Gould, whose posthumous work has not yet been published.

to assure him that anything he said was true. Thus Columbus believed what he wished, that he was close to Asia and that these islands were the Indies and the inhabitants therefore Indians. His nomenclature for these people lasted longer than his first impression of their nature, for he was sure they were noble savages, a gentle people who were only too eager to worship Jesus and to acknowledge the queen of Castile. Carrying away some of the natives to use as interpreters, Columbus toured other islands and heard his men announced as "the people from Heaven," another first impression which was not destined to endure. He went on to the northern coasts of Cuba and Haiti, finding not Oriental spendors but friendly folk who gladly offered their feathers, cloth, and bits of gold. On Christmas Eve his largest ship, the *Santa María*, ran aground, and thirty-nine men had to be left at a spot called Navidad, since there was not sufficient space to carry them back. The commander of the *Pinta*, Martín Alonso Pinzón, defied Columbus by sailing off on his own, but he eventually rejoined him to go back home.

The homeward voyage was also full of adventure, including a storm so threatening that Columbus sealed an account of his discovery and cast it into the waters in case he failed to survive, and a stop in the Azores, where the Portuguese tried to arrest the crew. Columbus had rightly sailed far to the north from Haiti and entered the Gulf Stream, which carried him rapidly eastward. Just as the two ships approached the Iberian peninsula another storm separated them. Pinzón made it to northwestern Spain, where he sent word that Columbus was lost and that he himself had carried the expedition through to success. Columbus was not lost, however, but in Lisbon, where for some uneasy days he wondered whether João the Perfect was going to do away with the man who had first offered to serve Portugal. Either good sportsmanship or fear of Fernando and Isabel won out, and the king let Columbus sail on to Palos.

The return of the Discoverer was a unique time for the Europeans, a moment that kindled wonder, excited greed, stimulated missionary zeal, and fired the inspiration to do great things overseas that motivated Western civilization for so long. News reports went to Italy, where wise men pondered the implications of Columbus' feat, though they disagreed as to exactly what he had accomplished. As Columbus himself walked or rode the 600 miles across Spain from Palos to Barcelona with some of his crew, examples of wild life from "the Indies," and several natives, the first American tourists to Europe, many a child witnessed the dramatic pageant, later to turn up as a conquistador or missionary in the lands the Discoverer had found.

In Barcelona the Catholic Kings accorded him an effusive welcome. It was Columbus' most triumphant, if not exactly his finest, hour. His critics were confounded, his own prophecies seemingly justified. Assuring the monarchs he had found the sea route to Asia, he requested and received almost unlimited authority to establish a great base on the island where he left the crew of the *Santa María*.[3] Then contact could be effected with the Great Khan and other Oriental rulers. Trade would flow and the modern Christopher, like the saint for whom he was named, would carry Christ across to the distant shore. Columbus was exultant over his deed, reverently grateful to God, and full of plans to achieve great things in the supposed Indies.

The Line of Demarcation

AS SOON as they heard of Columbus' return the Catholic Kings approached the pope to award them exclusive rights in the newly discovered lands on the order of the privileges he had previously granted the Portuguese in Africa. On many occasions in the past popes had extended to Christian princes such rights over pagan lands, and it was generally assumed under such international law as prevailed that this was within the papal prerogative. Pope Alexander VI, an Aragonese whose family and properties were under Fernando's control, readily obliged for this reason and, perhaps, because he was satisfied that Isabel would convert the inhabitants of the new lands. Also, the pope had incurred the displeasure of the Catholic Kings for befriending the expelled Spanish Jews. His concessions, dated May 4, 1493 though some of them were actually made later, granted to the crown of Castile control over pagan lands west of a line running from pole to pole 100 leagues west of the Azores and Cape Verde Islands. Isabel had the obligation of bringing the inhabitants into the Christian faith. The Portuguese monarch, who in the meantime had mobilized a fleet in protest, was then given the same rights east of that line.

King João II was still not satisfied with the concession of Alexander VI, whom he knew to be subject to undue pressure from the Spanish rulers. He may have known about Brazil and realized that the line did not include it. Vague phraseology in these and previous awards might be interpreted to block Portuguese expansion south of the Cape Verdes around African waters, and the Spanish might seek to colonize the Far East by sailing west, which they undoubtedly hoped to do. João II was not a ruler to be trifled with, and the Catholic Kings prudently negotiated with him the Treaty of Tordesillas of 1494, which moved the line 370 leagues west of the Cape Verdes. Thus Portugal was left free to sail around Africa to India and, as it turned out, to colonize Brazil. Compli-

3. This island, which now contains Haiti and the Dominican Republic, was called *la isla española*, or Hispaniola in English.

cations regarding the line of Tordesillas on the other side of the world were not settled until 1529, when Spain finally sold her claims to the Molucca Islands. Even so, the Philippines were destined to be Spanish even though they were on Portugal's side of the line.

Sketching the Outline of the New World

FOR the moment, Columbus had the initiative, which he exploited by fitting out the largest of his expeditions. Seventeen vessels and 1500 men left with him on September 25, 1493 in the expectation of creating a large base in the "Indies" from which lucrative contacts might be established with the fabled monarchs of the Orient, all of this undertaken with the unrestrained support of the Catholic Kings and public opinion. The colonizing aspects of this second Columbian voyage we may leave until later. Otherwise, the Discoverer expertly made his way back to Haiti, touching islands of the lesser Antilles, where the wild inhabitants exploded the noble savage myth, and the lovely island of Puerto Rico. Later Columbus discovered Jamaica and probed about Cuba, which he hoped and tried to prove was a peninsula stretching out from the Asian mainland. He returned to Spain in June 1496, greatly disheartened over the refusal of Japan and China to appear in Caribbean waters and the unhappy experiences he had undergone as a colonizer.

Before the great Discoverer was ready to sail again, foreigners were investigating for themselves the secrets of the new lands, which some suspected might not be the Indies at all. The Portuguese may have penetrated the area about Newfoundland or Labrador, though as usual we have no documentary proof of it. King Henry VII of England, possibly inspired by one of these Portuguese mariners or acting on his own, ignored the papal grant and sent an Italian whom the English called John Cabot into the North Atlantic to Newfoundland in 1497 and 1498. On the second voyage Cabot and his son, Sebastian, may have sailed far down the eastern coast of the present United States. The king was not impressed with their findings and reputedly paid them off with an absurdly small sum and lost interest in exploration. Fishermen from Normandy and Brittany in France may have sailed to Newfoundland about this time or soon after, but it was Brazil which was to tempt the French more in the next generation.

Columbus undertook his third voyage in May 1498, with a modest expedition of four ships and a crew made up of many convicts. He touched South America, being perhaps the first European to do so, and he thought he discovered the site of the Garden of Eden. It was typical of him that he made so much of this hypothesis but neglected to follow up an opportunity to exploit the great source of pearls which lay just off the coast. Others were to gain these riches which might have restored Columbus' deflated reputation. Meanwhile, the Portuguese had reached India through Vasco da Gama's expedition in 1497–1499, making a mockery of the pretensions of Columbus, who was having a wretched time of it in his base. And in 1500 the Portuguese made good their claim to Brazil when Pedro Alvares Cabral landed there. In 1500–1502 Gaspar and Michael de Corte Real lost their lives in the Arctic wastes north of Newfoundland, which further substantiated the Portuguese belief that there was little point in sailing westward to reach the Indies.

Fernando and Isabel were so disenchanted with Columbus' efforts by 1499 that they violated their capitulations of 1492 by permitting others to go out on their own and see if they could find something worthwhile. Alonso de Ojeda, Amerigo Vespucci, Pero Alonso Niño, Cristóbal and Luis Guerra, Vicente Yáñez Pinzón, Diego de Lepe, Alonso Velez de Mendoza, Rodrigo de Bastidas, and Juan de la Cosa were the most illustrious of these mariners who coasted along the northern shores of South America between 1499 and 1502. If they sometimes fixed pompous names to the physical features of this area, such as calling the Orinoco or the Amazon the Ganges, and had amusing and horrifying experiences with the fierce natives, they found little of value but pearls. Surely Columbus was wrong about the proximity of these lands to Asia, just as he had greatly misread the character of the inhabitants and the potentialities of wealth.

Yet the Discoverer was not finished. In 1502–1504 a last, exhausting effort took him to Central America. Bad luck continued to dog him, for he missed the Maya centers and failed to hear of the great ocean across the isthmus of Panama, where he languished for months. A long-drawn-out agony while stranded in Jamaica, a painful snub from the dying Isabel, poor health, mockery from his numerous critics, and official deprecation from Fernando embittered his last years. In 1506, this noble, poetic, and prickly man died, prosperous but stripped of his powers. It was for posterity to appreciate him.

A lull in exploration followed. Spain finally developed a satisfactory base on the island of Hispaniola. The occupation of Puerto Rico, Jamaica, and Cuba was accomplished between 1508 and 1511. In 1512 Juan Ponce de León explored the coasts to the north as far as the Carolinas. In 1513 Vasco Núñez de Balboa "discovered" the South Sea (or the Pacific Ocean, as it was later named), a body of water long known to the civilized Asians and, if only Europeans are to be considered, seen by the Polos about 1290 and by the Portuguese in 1511 from the other side of the world. The outlines of South America were discerned

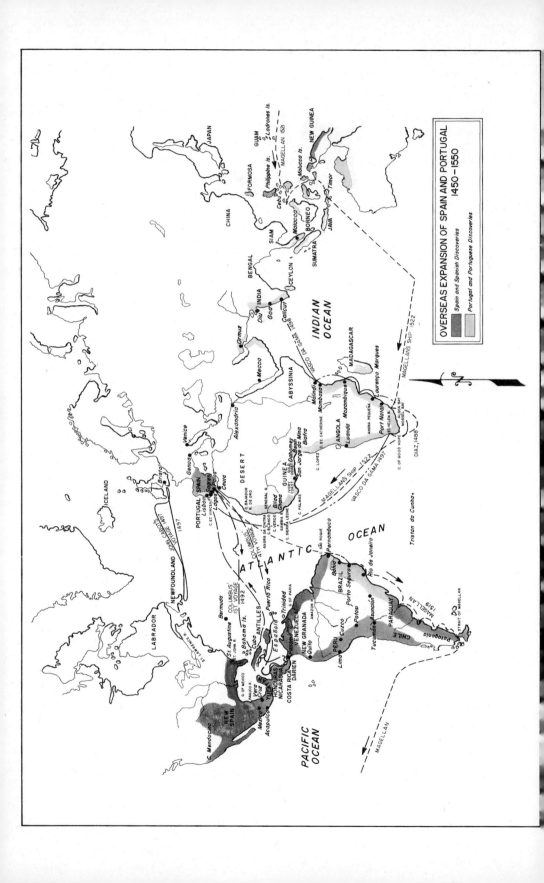

OVERSEAS EXPANSION OF SPAIN AND PORTUGAL
1450-1550

Spain and Spanish Discoveries

Portugal and Portuguese Discoveries

by Juan Díaz de Solís in 1515–1516, who got as far as present-day Argentina and was killed. Ferdinand Magellan was there and beyond in 1519–1520. The Gulf Coast was explored by Hernández de Córdoba in 1517, by Juan de Grijalva in 1518, by Hernán Cortés in 1519, and by Álvarez de Pineda in 1519. The Spaniards Lucás Vásquez de Ayllón, Pedro de Quexos, and Estéban Gómez probed about the eastern coastline of the present United States between 1520 and 1526, finding nothing to suggest the area was worth the trouble of conquering. It was obvious that these new lands were extensive and far from Asia. Many later explorers were due to break their hearts or lose their fortunes and lives in penetrating the mysteries of this New World. Thirty years after Columbus' first voyage, its main outlines were known.

The First Circumnavigation of the Globe

FERDINAND MAGELLAN, as he is called in English, played a decisive role in fixing the true place of the New World. As a young Portuguese nobleman he went out to India in 1504, and he may have been among his countrymen who saw the Pacific Ocean from the East Indies several years before Balboa saw it. Returning to Portugal after various adventures, Magellan found himself under a cloud for alleged misdeeds or indiscretions involving the Moslems. A maladroit effort to repair things with King Manoel the Fortunate ended unhappily, with the monarch telling Magellan he had no further use for him and would not care if he offered his services to another lord. This fit of temper was indeed unfortunate for Manoel, for Magellan went to Spain and soon became involved in a highly complicated scheme to break Portugal's near-monopoly of the Indian trade by sending a Spanish expedition to Asia through a strait that must exist somewhere in America. Surely, some of the valuable commercial depots in the East were on Spain's side of the Line of Tordesillas, perhaps Malacca itself. Magellan helped sell the plan to young King Carlos I (who was soon the Emperor Charles V) and at royal expense gathered an expedition of five ships. It was difficult to collect a crew, for at this time disenchantment with the supposed Indies hung over Spain.

At long last, in September 1519, the fleet sailed from Sanlúcar de Barrameda. Magellan soon learned of a conspiracy to depose him in favor of representatives of financial interests who hoped to cheat him of the anticipated profits that would fall to the commander. When the plot came to a head in what are now Argentine waters, he rose to the occasion by throttling the mutiny, losing one of his ships in the process. Then the four remaining vessels sailed into Antarctic waters, marveling at the whales, seals, penguins, and big-footed natives on the shore of a territory in Argentina that still bears the name Patagonia in honor of these last. Finally they came upon the coveted strait, whereupon another ship was lost through desertion. For thirty-eight days the little fleet bumped and bounced through the long passage, riding the 40-foot Atlantic tides for awhile and then meeting the watery surges from the west, circling about terrifyingly in the great cold whirlpools, and finding to their horror that on one side of the strait the tides might run eastward and on the other westward. On both sides were craggy mountains and stark rocks that seemed to dare the three ships to crash into them. At night the primitive natives lit fires, which caused Magellan to name this the Land of Fire (*Tierra del Fuego*). Suddenly the fleet emerged from the turbulent cold waters and screeching gales into a calm ocean Magellan called Pacific. The strait, of course, retained his own name.

Jubilation over this momentous passage was slowly dissipated during the following ninety-nine days. Only two small islands were sighted, and they were uninhabited. As food and fresh water gave out, the crew sickened and died. They were surely the loneliest men on earth, and the most despairing, when they came upon Guam, an island Spain was to own until 1898. Naming this island and its neighbors the Ladrones (thieves) from the habits of the natives, Magellan sailed on to the Philippines. There, after an apparently successful effort to convert the inhabitants to Christianity, a rebellion occurred and Magellan was killed. The remnants of the expedition went southward to the Spice Islands, where the Portuguese made difficulties. Finally, one ship, the *Victoria*, under the command of Sebastián de Elcano, got away, crossed the Indian Ocean, came up the Atlantic, and returned to Sanlúcar almost exactly three years after the departure. Its cargo amply paid for the cost of the entire expedition. If the first circumnavigation of the world had been completed,[4] Magellan's route to the true Indies was not attractive enough to encourage emulation on a large scale.

The Naming of the New World

FOR half the colonial period or even longer the Spanish referred to their transatlantic empire as "the Indies," as Columbus had done. In a just world the Discoverer's name would have been eventually fixed to the area. But the name that stuck came from abroad, and gradually the Spaniards and the peoples of the Indies accepted it. Much controversy surrounds the career of Amerigo Vespucci, whose name came to be fastened to the New World through no conscious effort on his

4. Probably the first man to circumnavigate the globe was Magellan's Asian slave, Enrique de Malacca, whose starting point was the Far East.

part. He may have been a mere meat supplier who helped provision some of the first expeditions and then a part-time sailor, who wrote wildly fantastic accounts of his more or less imaginary adventures when he went along with Ojeda's party in 1499 and with a Portuguese group in 1501–1502. Probably he was more than that, as the recent Argentine scholar Roberto Levillier and the Colombian writer Germán Arciniegas have sought to prove.[5] This Italian who resided in Spain may actually have made a voyage in 1497 to check up on Columbus and explored the coasts from Central America to Chesapeake Bay, though most students of the problem doubt it very much. Perhaps he was a commander on one of his voyages, and perhaps not. Scholars differ as to whether he was a great navigator or a mere charlatan, though his appointment as chief pilot for Spain in 1508 is in his favor, and Columbus himself seems to have thought well of him. It was his writings about four supposed voyages to the New World that brought him fame abroad, circulated as they were among rulers and other persons interested in world affairs. These writings are colorful, somewhat exaggerated, and vague. One of them fell into the hands of Martin Waldseemüller, who was illustrator of a book on cosmography being gotten up by a group of monks in Lorraine. When the book appeared in 1507, a map of the New World had Amerigo's name fixed to part of South America. The name caught on outside of Spain, and by 1538 it was applied to the northern continent too. "America" was an agreeable word, and much as one may deplore the injustice to Columbus or the undeserved honor accorded Amerigo Vespucci, few regret the name of the two great continents.

5. Levillier, *América la bien llamada,*   *and the New World,* New York: 1955.
Buenos Aires: 1948; *Arciniegas, Amerigo*

4

Birth of the Spanish Empire

Columbus as a Colonizer

IN OCTOBER 1493, Columbus arrived for the second time in the Caribbean Sea. The crossing had been beautifully executed by the Admiral of the Ocean Sea, and the island of Hispaniola was where it was supposed to be. Now he had 1,500 men with him, volunteers paid by the crown, who were to create a powerful base on the island from which the rich civilizations of the East could supposedly be reached. Seeds, plants, domestic animals, working implements, bricks, and lime were in adequate supply for this purpose, and clergymen were along to begin the conversion of the natives. The high hopes of the expedition fell a little when Navidad, the site of the wreckage of the *Santa María*, was located. No beginnings of a colony, no crops, no Spaniards in fact, were there to facilitate the mission of the new expedition. Only mystery, and Indian friends "sick" or in hiding remained where nine months before thirty-nine Spaniards and hundreds of friendly allies had waved farewell to Columbus. After much investigation the Admiral learned that the Spaniards had broken his rules by bullying the natives and had all been massacred. So the gentle pagans could fight back! Had the Spaniards drawn the proper inference, they might have acted with more wisdom in the months ahead.

Columbus coasted eastward along the northern shores of Hispaniola into what is now the Dominican Republic and chose another site for his base, which he named Isabela. The men were eager to get started, but not to dig, build, and plant. They were *hidalgos*, or wanted to be, and such tiresome labor was for infidels and other inferiors. The Spanish had come to gain easy wealth and to do great things. Columbus lacked the will and the talent to compel these men to construct the houses and pens and start the planting that might supply sufficient food in the months to come. Instead, he led a gorgeous procession, the first of count-less Spanish *entradas* in the New World, into the charming interior of the island, which he thought might be the Land of Sheba. The natives continued to exhibit great friendliness, offering the white men gold, when they saw it was prized, but helping themselves to Spanish articles when they could, for they had no sense of private property. Returning to Isabela after this excursion, the Admiral tried to crack down on his men and force them to build the base, but the complaints were long and loud and the work was only half done.

Apart from the psychological reluctance of the Spanish to perform manual toil, other factors were at work. Men from temperate zones suddenly transplanted to the tropics often fall sick or lose their energy. This was abundantly demonstrated in World War II when American forces went into the islands of the South Pacific. Long after Columbus' time Spaniards reaching torrid regions in the New World after long voyages became weak and lethargic. The heat, humidity, sand flies, mosquitoes, and new diet accounted for much of this physical degenera-tion and the irritable temper which went with it. But there was some-thing else, a painful disease called *bubas*, the descriptions of which sound very much like syphilis. It has long been debated whether or not this affliction was an unwitting revenge the American Indians took on the European. Most students of the problem now believe the Americans had suffered from it so long that it had become a mild dis-ease with them. But it was new to the Europeans, who found it acutely painful and often died of it. Soon syphilis was spreading over Europe with the force of a terrible plague, and while it is not certain that the epidemic originated in America after the first contacts with the Indians, or in Spain through the Indians Columbus had brought back with him, it is a plausible hypothesis.

Columbus was not at his best in trying to administer a colony of sick, unruly Spaniards. By nature a compulsive explorer, he was impa-tient to go find the Great Khan. Leaving his pious brother Diego in charge, he sailed off in April 1494 to Jamaica and Cuba. Much as he loved the palm-fringed coasts and the flower-scented air of these lands, the Admiral was sick at heart because they refused to become China and Japan. In September he returned to Isabela, to find that Diego had been unable to control the settlers, who had lain about grumbling or ranged all over Hispaniola committing outrages of theft, extortion, rap-ine, and brutality. A food shortage was becoming serious, for the Span-iards consumed far more than the natives. Their own supplies were low, and new crops were not coming along satisfactorily. The natives were in bewilderment and misery over the behavior of their guests and the disorganization of their paradise.

One heartening feature was the return of a dozen ships, which Columbus had earlier dispatched to Spain, with enough provisions to postpone the food crisis. The Admiral's brother Bartholomew was among the new arrivals, and Columbus appointed him *adelantado,* a title used for military rulers of frontier areas. Queen Isabel was annoyed by Columbus' presumption, but she eventually confirmed Bartholomew's position. It was different with another action taken by the Admiral on his own initiative. No one realized better than he that his explorations had brought him no closer to the empires of the Far East. For all the expense and promise of his expedition, there was little to show, only some gold dust, a few ornaments, pieces of cloth, and wood that had little material value. Hoping to demonstrate that he was making good, Columbus knowingly stretched Isabel's instructions regarding kind treatment of the natives by shipping home five hundred Indians as slaves. To make matters worse, these were people who had been "tamed" and started on the path to Christianization by the clergy. Some of them were being sold in Sevilla when the queen heard about it. The royal wrath was impressive. Far from being pleased at the profits, Isabel the Catholic ordered the slaves freed and returned to Hispaniola. At about the same time a group of disgruntled colonists, including the chaplain, stole a ship and sailed to Spain, where they spread tales about Columbus' mismanagement. Soon an official, Juan de Aguado, came to Hispaniola to investigate what seemed more and more a messy situation. He eventually reported on it, but Columbus' hour had not quite come.

Columbus' shipment of slaves to Spain had another unhappy result. The various native chieftains on Hispaniola had witnessed for more than a year the progressive ruination the white men were bringing to their island, and provoked by the slave incident, they organized a full-scale revolt to oust the invader. As far as numbers were concerned, they should have overwhelmed the Europeans. Yet the pattern was to be the same as nearly all subsequent Indian rebellions in America would reveal: much secrecy, a frightening ambush with superior numbers, and victory of the white man. Nothing the Indians could do offset the advantages of the invader in noisy cannon and muskets, lances, swords, crossbows, suits of armor, horses, and dogs. This rebellion, like most of the others would be, was a fiasco. The Spaniards shattered the native forces mercilessly and hunted down the runaways until a peace of death prevailed.

Now in a thoroughly evil humor, Columbus determined to compel the Indians to perform the work the Spaniards would not. The physical toil of construction, farming, and livestock raising could be taken care of now by captured prisoners of war, who were in reality slaves. Producing the gold he knew was on the island called for a more ingenious scheme, one which fitted in with Spanish historical experience and, as Columbus saw it, common sense. These Indians were subjects of the queen, as she insisted. Then, let them pay taxes or tribute, like her other subjects! His plan was that every male Indian over fourteen should find enough gold dust to fill one of the bells the Indians liked so well, that he should do this every three months, turning it over to his chieftain, who would bring it to the Admiral. When the man paid, he was to be given a token. If he failed to produce, he was subject to the death penalty. In lieu of gold dust he might pay twenty-five pounds of cotton cloth as his tribute. This system, instituted by the Discoverer in 1495, was destined to continue in one fashion or another until the end of the Spanish colonial period, and in some countries, far into the nineteenth century.

The anguish that Columbus' scheme brought can scarcely be imagined. In a short time the natives surrendered, if they had not already seen them seized, the accumulations of centuries. Then, they had to pick gold from the streams and dig for it in caverns and river beds. These sources were soon exhausted. Finally, they had to mine for it by deep extractions under the supervision of a few mining experts sent out from Spain. This last was too much, for the Indians had never labored in this fashion and were not physically equal to persistent toil. Some ran off to the hills or woods and were hunted down. If they were not killed on the spot, they were chained up as slaves. Others managed to escape to neighboring islands. Suicide by drinking a poison fluid of the cassava plant, which also was a source for meal, became prevalent, and so did infanticide. All of this misery was bad enough, coming as it did after a crushing military defeat. But the natives were dying off at an appalling rate because of food shortages, work, grief, massacre, and above all, on account of such European diseases as smallpox, measles, and probably the common cold. Diseases new to the Indians, they proved deadly. If we can accept any approximation of contemporary estimates, the population of Hispaniola declined by one-third in the years 1494–96 and by nine-tenths in the first twenty years of the occupation. The Indian race almost disappeared from the Caribbean islands in a few decades, for Puerto Rico, Cuba, and Jamaica had a similar experience with extortionate Spaniards and the germs they introduced.

While the tribute system produced enough gold to make Columbus a rich man and to maintain Spanish interest in the colony, the Admiral himself was thoroughly disheartened by 1496. He knew he was in deep trouble with his monarchs, since so many colonists had gone home with bitter reports to make, and no doubt he was shaken by the sufferings of the island. In 1496 he ordered the relocation of Isabela to a healthier spot and better harbor on the south coast, founding a town that became Santo Domingo, the oldest European settlement in the Americas, and left the remaining Spaniards under the charge of the *adelantado*, Bartholomew Columbus. Then the Admiral sailed back to Spain with his ships overcrowded by a very disenchanted group of ex-settlers. He found a cool reception. At home they had soon gotten over the sensation that Columbus had discovered anything of immense value. The Admiral himself was in a humble frame of mind and put in some months doing penance. In view of his own mood and that of his contemporaries, it is easy to overlook the basic fact that Columbus did not do altogether badly. He really had established a base, inadequate as it was, which endured. From this base the conquest not of the East, but of America, would be achieved. And from his second voyage to the present day, Spanish civilization and Christianity have thrived in the New World.

During the two-year absence of Columbus the little colony did poorly. The natives scratched for gold and continued to die off at a fearful rate. Bartholomew was unable to dominate the two or three hundred tough Spaniards on the island, as probably anyone else would have been. When the Admiral came back in August 1498 with his crew of convicts, he found the Spanish party split by the revolt of one Francisco Roldán. Failing to defeat or win him over, Columbus made peace with Roldán by agreeing to change the tribute system so that the natives would pay and labor for individual Spaniards. The plan was based on the *encomienda*, which the Spaniards had instituted during the Reconquest in lands newly won from the infidels. In Hispaniola it simply meant that each Spaniard strong enough to make himself respected would be placed in charge of a certain number of natives. It was little better than a system of slavery or feudalism at its crudest stage, but it provided a basis to satisfy the Spaniards and to control the Indians.

The queen was offended again at the way Columbus presumed to divide her subjects up among his supposed lieutenants, and her anger mounted when she learned that outright slavery persisted in spite of her commands, that Columbus had even dared to send some more captives to Spain to be sold. The standing of Columbus was now very low, both in Spain and in Hispaniola. Former settlers had many complaints to make of these foreigners, the Columbus brothers, whose tyranny and incompetence were said to be at the root of Hispaniola's troubles. It was symptomatic of the Admiral's decline that the crown gave permission in 1499 for several expeditions to explore this baffling region, though Columbus was supposed to be viceroy of all the newly-discovered area.

By 1500 conditions were so confusing that Columbus asked for a royal official to come adjudicate the disputes among the Spaniards. He obtained more than he requested, for the Catholic Kings dispatched no mere judge, but an imposing *visitador* or inspector with full powers to assume command if necessary. This official, Francisco de Bobadilla, reached Santo Domingo in August 1500. As he entered the port, he saw gallows and signs of recent executions, and, as soon as he landed, the Spaniards pressed about him with accusations against the Admiral, who was out of town. Bobadilla at once took charge, arresting Bartholomew and Diego Columbus and ordering the Admiral to return. When Columbus remonstrated, he too was arrested and placed in irons. The three brothers went to Spain in fetters, the great Discoverer being so hurt and grieved that he declined an offer of the ship's captain to remove the chains, and later he directed that they be buried with him as a symbol of man's ingratitude.

Once Columbus arrived in Spain the Catholic Kings ordered the removal of the fetters and came as close to apologizing as royalty could permit itself. They were sincerely distressed at the high-handed way Bobadilla had acted. Yet they parried Columbus' demands that he be reinstated in his command. Though he continued to draw his one-tenth of all the royal revenue as promised in the capitulations of 1492 and became a wealthy man, the riches were poor compensation for a man of Columbus' temperament, and he suffered grievously at the flouting of his right to rule the lands he had found. When, two years later, he went back on his fourth voyage, he was ordered not to set foot on Hispaniola.

Consolidation of Hispaniola

BOBADILLA did little better than Columbus as a governor. The Spaniards were still defiant of authority and accustomed to abusing the natives, who continued to die off at a shocking rate. He managed to collect an impressive amount of gold, but it was lost along with himself, the troublemaker Roldán, and many other Spaniards when a hurricane devastated their fleet on the return voyage to Spain in 1502.

The official who supplanted Bobadilla was the true founder of Hispaniola as a successful base, Nicolás de Ovando, who arrived in 1502 with a monster fleet of thirty-two ships and 2,500 men. This expedition was the final effort of Isabel the Catholic to create a sound colony and to effect the Europeanization of the Indians, a cause so dear to the queen.

Ovando stayed for seven years, and he abundantly accomplished the first of these purposes. Fusing the original idea of a royal plantation developed along mercantilistic lines with Castilian historical experience in repopulating conquered lands, this small, red-bearded knight with an air of authority was eminently successful. During his term as governor, perhaps ten thousand Spaniards came over as settlers, many of them bringing their womenfolk. Some of them still hoped to live off the labor of Indians held in *encomienda,* but it was more and more apparent that there was little future in this direction. Pressures grew to capture natives from adjoining islands and even to import African slaves to compensate for the loss of the original population. Gold mining was still the most attractive field. In order to stimulate production the crown agreed to let the miners retain four-fifths of their findings, thus instituting the famous "royal fifth" which was to prevail so long in America and to enrich the monarchs of Spain. It was clear that of all the crops the Spaniards introduced, sugar cane flourished the best, an encouraging fact in view of the insatiable appetite of Europe for sweets. Bananas, oranges, lemons, rice, and figs grew well enough to provision the colonists and bring in profits. And peninsular livestock multiplied in this salubrious isle, hogs and chickens from the very first, and horses, cattle, and donkeys under more care. By the end of Ovando's term, Hispaniola contained a dozen or more towns and numerous thriving farms and ranches. Without the food this island produced, and above all without the horses, the subsequent conquests of Mexico and Peru might not have been possible at all.

Ovando's successor was the son of Columbus, Diego, who arrived in 1509 with an imposing court including many of his relatives. Diego was in the process of suing the crown to live up to its agreement with his father in 1492 and permit him to rule as viceroy over all the newly-discovered lands and to draw one-tenth of all the revenues. For the present he was not a true viceroy of the Indies, but only governor of Hispaniola, his appointment being due as much to his wife's prestigious family connections in Spain as to King Fernando's willingness to show a conciliatory attitude toward the Columbus family claims. Diego built a substantial palace in Santo Domingo and attempted to control all of the Indies, but his authority was steadily clipped by the crown. He was not allowed to dominate Cuba, Puerto Rico, nor the settlements on the mainland, and in 1511 his powers on Hispaniola itself were humiliatingly curbed by the establishment of a high court, the *audiencia,* the first of many such important institutions in the New World. At length Diego went back to Spain to prosecute his suit against the crown, which involved a welter of claims by other explorers who sought to minimize the achievements of Christopher Columbus, and died in 1526. In 1536 his widow finally settled this protracted case by accepting the title of Duke of Veragua for her son and a large financial grant. Had the crown given in, Columbus' heirs might have ruled all the Americas as viceroys and received enormous profits. Even now a wealthy nobleman in Spain bears the title of Duke of Veragua, a memento of the Discoverer's sufferings in Central America on his fourth voyage.

Under the long but largely nominal governorship of Diego Columbus, Hispaniola experienced a drastic diminution in importance through no fault of his. The Indians practically disappeared, and even the Spanish rushed off to Puerto Rico, Jamaica, Cuba, Florida, and the mainland of South America. A few years later, when Mexico and Peru were opened up, the more energetic Spaniards were attracted to the great opportunities there, leaving the middle-aged, the elderly, and the more timid settlers on Hispaniola. It became a relatively quiet colony, disturbed occasionally by escaped slaves, pirates, new expeditions which drained off the young men, and foreign enemies in the three centuries that remained of the colonial period. Immigrants were mostly unwilling Africans who were imported to cultivate sugar, Spanish or Canarian farmers, merchants, and officials. Santo Domingo developed into a small but fairly beautiful city with government buildings, churches, cloisters, residences, fortifications, and even a university, the first in the New World, which was set up in 1538. The colony had served its purpose as a base for the conquest of the other islands and the mainland. Little of its history until the close of the eighteenth century concerns us.

CHRISTIAN AND PAGAN

At this point we should recapitulate certain aspects of a most important problem which the Spanish contended with for centuries, for better or for worse, and which other imperialistic powers have still not settled to general satisfaction: the relationship of the European to backward native populations. As we have seen, Columbus was at first convinced that the so-called Indians were a gentle, unspoiled people who were eager to accept Christianity and to serve the monarch. Isabel and the pope at once endorsed this view, and the policy of both the Spanish crown and the Catholic Church was enunciated in 1493, to the effect that the Indians were subjects of the monarchy morally equal to those in the peninsula and that they should become Europeanized Christians as rapidly as possible. This official policy persisted despite many setbacks and disappointments. In a way we might say that it was finally fulfilled, for most of the American Indians have become Christians and civilized in the European fashion. But such a long view, while we should never lose sight of it, omits too many crimes and tragedies that account largely for Spain's bad reputation.

Most of the Spaniards who came into contact with the Indians of the Caribbean developed extremely unfavorable attitudes toward them. They saw these natives naked, worshipping idols, unmindful of private property, cannibalistic, idle, and engaging in grossly obscene mating and homosexual practices. In their revulsion the Spaniards were likely to conclude that the Indians were not even human in the sense that they themselves were. Furthermore, since they needed the natives as a labor force, it was easy to rationalize that such disgusting people had no feelings or rights; it was natural for them to serve the white man. Natives who were willing to accept such a relationship might settle down as a submerged proletariat incapable of progress, and those who resisted should be killed or chained up as chattel slaves. Naturally, the Spaniard was tempted to exaggerate the baseness of the Indian in order to justify his exploitation, but nonetheless, most of the white men in the New World sincerely believed the Indians were their inferiors and that the altruistic purpose of the Church and the crown emanated from well-meaning persons a long way off who did not understand what they were talking about. Judged by his actions, Columbus himself adopted this point of view, and so did almost every other conquistador, even when Indians far more advanced than those of the islands were encountered.

To her credit, Isabel the Catholic clung to her original attitude. We have seen how indignant she was with Columbus for enslaving the natives. When Ovando went out in 1502, she instructed him to treat the Indians lovingly, to leave them free, and to pay them if they worked. The queen retreated somewhat after Ovando informed her that the natives refused to toil, and she gave him permission to employ the *encomienda* as a temporary measure in order to bring the Indian under the tutelage of the supposedly more civilized Spaniard. On her deathbed the famous queen expressed kind thoughts and high hopes for her Indian subjects.

Unfortunately, King Fernando was less solicitous of the natives during the years that he ruled Castile and the Indies for his mad daughter Juana. He wanted the colonial venture to pay off, regardless of humane considerations; this required human labor. If the Indians would not work for pay, then they might be captured and enslaved on the grounds that they were cannibals or that they resisted conversion to Christianity. These grounds became quite flexible, for the king received a share of the slaves, and the Indians were disappearing so rapidly they became all the more valuable. Finally, the king encouraged slave-catching expeditions to seize Indians on the other islands or the mainland. In the Bahamas, where the natives seemed to be uselessly enjoying life, were thousands of potential slaves whom the Spaniards carried off, many of the Indians believing they were going to Hispaniola to meet their dead ancestors in paradise. To be sure, most of them soon expired there, and the Bahamas were depopulated.

Meanwhile, intellectuals in Europe were immensely curious about this newly-found type of the human race. They had little information to go on, only a few specimens and the reports of such correspondents as Peter Martyr and Amerigo Vespucci. Those who actually saw some Indians or talked extensively with returned Spaniards inevitably disagreed among themselves about the fundamental nature of the American aborigines. Some insisted on believing they were grotesque creatures unlike mankind. A great many educated persons followed the sacrosanct Aristotle in holding that some men were born to be servile and concluded that this category fitted the Indians. This group was reinforced from time to time as Spaniards came back from the New World with tales of native depravity and incorrigibility. Yet those students of the problem who were generally the best respected and the most influential maintained that the American Indians were human beings like other men, who had been unfortunate in not being exposed earlier to Christianity and to civilization. A fringe of thinkers idealized the Indians as noble savages, superior in every respect save religion to the warlike, mercenary, over-organized European. These and other points of view were hotly debated almost from the time Columbus returned from his first voyage, in universities, royal courts, cloisters, and streets. By the middle of the sixteenth century the controversies still excited intellectuals, but then they died down. The Church and the crown went on proclaiming the Indians were rational beings who should be assisted in becoming civilized Christians. Most of the Spanish settlers in the Americas and some of their partisans at home continued to believe the natives were little better than talking animals who could never fit into a Europeanized society except as inferiors.

Montesinos

A REALISTIC aspect of the problem came up in 1511, when a Dominican friar confronted the Spaniards in Santo Domingo and later pricked the conscience of King Fernando. Clergymen, mostly Franciscans, had been in Hispaniola since 1493, but little was heard of them. Probably they had been intimidated by the other Spaniards and had become convinced there was little use in trying to convert the Indians. But in 1510 a small group of Dominicans arrived, representing an intellectual order which was equipped to discern and contend with fundamental moral problems. One of them, Antonio de Montesinos, was so incensed at the callous disregard for Indian humanity that he preached a fiery sermon in the church at Santo Domingo around Christmas, 1511.

He shocked his congregation by telling its members they were in danger of mortal sin because of the way they had warred on the natives, worked them to death, and failed to instruct them. The bold friar was threatened with physical violence, but he repeated his accusations the following Sunday and announced he would not give absolution to any Spaniard who failed to repent of his crimes against the Indians. The uproar was too much. The colonists wanted to lynch Montesinos, and Governor Columbus was offended, as were King Fernando and the leading figures in the Dominican Order in Spain when they heard of the scandal. Montesinos was shipped back to Spain. There he or someone briefed by him managed to talk to Fernando and shocked him with a blunt description of the horrors in Hispaniola.

It was well known that Fernando the Catholic was no humanitarian; yet his sensibilities were truly affected, and he called his wise men to ponder the situation. Montesinos was soon out of the picture, but other reporters were available, and it was apparent that the Spaniards in Hispaniola had abused the Indians dreadfully. Considering the length of time required for legislation to be enacted in any age, the king's advisers moved quickly. In December 1512, just a year after Montesinos' sermons in Santo Domingo, the so-called laws of Burgos were promulgated. According to this legislation the Indians were to be removed to new villages, where they could be closely supervised by Spanish *encomenderos*. They should all be baptized, given religious instruction, and encouraged to marry. They were not to dance, get drunk, paint or bleed themselves, nor go about naked. The natives might be required to work for a maximum of nine months of the year for the Spanish, but only adult males were to be called upon for this purpose, and they were to be paid adequately and never beaten. The laws of Burgos assumed that the natives were wayward and inclined to idleness and vice, but with these safeguards they might learn to live like Europeans. The colonists in Hispaniola were displeased by the legislation, which they regarded as much too favorable to the Indian.

Another measure was taken by Fernando's court at this time to protect the natives in other areas that the Spanish might conquer. This was a curious document known as the *Requerimiento* of 1513, which was to be read to all natives before the Spanish could make war on them or establish suzerainty. It consisted of a brief history of the world as devout Christians understood it, beginning with the Creation. It went on to state that Christ had named St. Peter the first pope, and that the successor of St. Peter had awarded part of the world to the monarch of Castile and her successors. The Indians were then to be informed with appropriate gravity that they resided in a land that belonged to those royal figures,

Queen Juana the Mad and Fernando the Catholic, whereupon they were summoned to acknowledge these lawful rulers and the blessed religion they professed. If the natives did so, the Spanish would then move in on them and peacefully establish a civilized state. If not, they were to be reduced by fire and sword, their rulers and idols overthrown, their property seized, and their persons enslaved. This quaint *Requerimiento* was seriously intended, and it was read with solemnity on many occasions in Latin or Spanish to uncomprehending natives during the next few decades all over America. So strong was the Spaniard's sense of legalism that it was often read from aboard ships or at other points too distant for listening or translation or even after battles of conquest had begun. The few natives who understood its implications probably felt like doing what the Inca monarch actually did when he heard it in 1532: he interrupted and angrily rejected it. Outrageous or hilarious as the *Requerimiento* might seem, its effect on the Spanish who were about to perform the invasions may have been similar to that of the righteous proclamations to which modern soldiers are treated on the eve of important offensives.

Bartolomé de las Casas, Protector of the Indians

SOON after the laws of Burgos and the *Requerimiento* were drafted, a far more famous friar than Montesinos rose up to voice the anguish of a good Christian at the brutal disregard for the natives. This was Bartolomé de las Casas, whose long life of humanitarian endeavors makes him one of the few Spaniards of the colonial period to be revered today throughout Latin America. As a youth in the University of Salamanca, Las Casas enjoyed the services of an Indian slave brought back to him by his father from Columbus' second voyage. He himself went to Hispaniola probably in 1502, and he stayed to prosper. He began to take instruction as a Dominican friar, and he may have been the first priest to be ordained in the New World, but he was apparently not particularly devout for some time afterward. Then, in 1511, he joined in the conquest of Cuba, which proved to be one of the more cruel of these operations from the standpoint of native relations. His crucial year was 1514, when he underwent a religious experience of such profundity that he remained until his death in 1566 a man of God. He gave up his own slaves and prospects for wealth and took his religious vows seriously. The decimation of the Indians in Hispaniola, the slave-catching excursions to other islands, and the horrors of the conquest of Cuba now repelled him to an unbearable degree. The laws of Burgos struck him as too weak, and as for the *Requerimiento*, he said he did not know whether to laugh or to cry. In view of Montesinos' ineffectuality in Santo Domingo, Las Casas decided to go straight to Spain and bring pressure there.

He arrived too late to influence Fernando the Catholic, who died in 1516, but he won the ear of the regent, Cardinal Ximenes de Cisneros, the strong and upright cleric who had done so much to reform the Church in Spain. For the first time Las Casas demonstrated what he was to repeat on many occasions in the next fifty years, the ability to command the respect of the highest figures in the land and to have his way. The cardinal-regent was greatly moved by the importunities of the Dominican, and he named him Protector of the Indians, which proved to be a meaningless title but which was intended to endow him with vast powers over the natives. Next, Cisneros suspended Diego Columbus as governor of Hispaniola and appointed in his stead a committee of three friars. Since such rivalry existed between the Dominicans and the Franciscans, the Order of St. Jerome nominated a group from which Las Casas picked the three to rule. It all seemed to be a marvelous opportunity for a humanitarian experiment: Las Casas as Protector of the Indians and the Jeronymite friars as governors, backed firmly by the cardinal-regent!

Yet the experience was a sad one, in its broad outlines typical of the defeats the well-meaning were to experience in the face of realities in the New World. In the first place the Jeronymites found Las Casas personally unbearable, so despotic and oppressive was this noble altruist. They sailed on different ships and avoided him once they reached the Indies, late in 1516. In Santo Domingo the gentle governors proceeded to conduct an investigation in which they sought the opinions of Spanish settlers and ecclesiasts about the nature of the Indians. The colonists replied unanimously that the natives were inferior beings who would revert to paganism if the Spanish did not keep them under strict control. Then, the good friars attempted to round up the remaining Indians in villages, offering them livestock and tools and a chance to live under their own leaders with only clerical supervision. But the Spanish settlers would have none of it. They protested to Spain against the friars and obstructed them at every turn. Perhaps they even brought the monkish governors around to their way of thinking. By 1520 the Jeronymites asked to be, and were, relieved. Las Casas had long since gone home to discredit them, and it was apparent they had accomplished little. The situation seemed hopeless, the Indians almost extinct and the Spaniards unwilling to keep their hands off them as long as any survived.

One solution to Hispaniola's chronic labor shortage seemed obvious: the importation of Negro slaves. Already a few had arrived in the colony and had displayed great adaptability, especially in cultivating sugar. It seemed to everyone that Negroes were fully capable of performing the labor which the Spaniards would not and the Indians could not do. Even the humanitarian Protector of the Indians seriously submitted a proposal to bring in African slaves to replace the Indians, and in 1517 the king granted to a Fleming an *asiento,* or privilege to import African slaves. It was some years before Las Casas came to see how illogical it was to regard Negroes as natural slaves while Indians and Europeans should be free, and three centuries before most other people did.

PUERTO RICO

The island of Puerto Rico, which Columbus discovered, was a pleasant semi-tropical homeland for many natives called Boriquén before the Spanish occupied it. Las Casas said it was as populous as a beehive, as lovely as an orchard, and considerable competition prevailed among the leading Spaniards in Hispaniola for the privilege of conquering it. It was Juan Ponce de León who won the approval of Fernando the Catholic, and in 1508 landed with perhaps no more than fifty conquistadors. Thanks to the technological and psychological advantages the Spanish always enjoyed, he was able in a very short time to bring the natives under control. It was not long until the Indians realized that Spanish domination was not altogether a blessing. Yet they feared the Spaniards were supernatural beings, very likely immortal. An experiment of holding an *hidalgo* under water for several hours convinced them otherwise, and a fearful uprising occurred. All but twenty of the white men were killed. And yet these twenty Spaniards, still led by Ponce de León, were able to reconquer the island, their guns, suits of armor, horses, and dogs (one of these terrible hounds was said to be the equal of a hundred men in battle) overcoming the vast disparity in numbers. Once the Indians had been defeated and parceled out among the victors, they began to perish, just as they did in the other islands.

Ponce de León was not content to develop Boriquén, or Puerto Rico. Instead, he was lured by rumors of wealth and magic elsewhere. In particular, he credited stories of a Fountain of Youth in Bimini, or present-day Florida. In doing this he was no more superstitious than most men of his time. Even the sophisticated Peter Martyr wrote that he doubted there was such a thing as a fountain of youth, but that many intelligent men believed in it. But Ponce de León's energetic pursuit of this illusion has made him a pathetic symbol of gullibility. He organized two expeditions to Florida, in 1512 and in 1520, on the second of which he received a mortal wound. His experiences confirmed the bad reputation of the peninsula, which contained hostile Indians and, strange as it sounds today, a most disagreeable terrain.

Meanwhile, Puerto Rico was neglected. For one thing the Spaniards found the storms perpetrated, according to the natives, by the god *Huracán*, a threat to life and property. The enticements of Mexico and South America drew off most of the energetic Spaniards, despite urgent efforts by the crown to colonize the island. The aborigines did not benefit by these departures, for the Spanish had already broken up their way of life and introduced deadly diseases. They continued to die out, and the fierce man-eating Caribs entered in considerable numbers by island-hopping from the lesser Antilles in the southeast. Puerto Rico amounted to little in the Spanish world until about 1600, when pirates and foreign enemies made it necessary to fortify the island and to build up its capital, San Juan. Then, sugar planting and Negro slavery developed, and Puerto Rico became a modestly valuable if somewhat somnolent colony.

JAMAICA

Jamaica was also discovered by Columbus, and on his fourth voyage he was compelled to spend many months there because his ships were in an unseaworthy condition. It was on this occasion that he frightened the Indians out of a planned massacre by accurately predicting an eclipse, thus demonstrating supernatural powers to their satisfaction. He did and found little else in the island that pleased him, and other Spaniards left it alone except for minor exploratory visits. Finally, in 1509, it was conquered by Juan de Esquivel, acting for Diego Columbus, who still asserted the right of his family to do all the exploring in the New World. This particular conquest added little to the importance of the Columbus family or Spain. It was a lovely island, grassy and cool for the tropics. It was a good place to raise horses and cattle. But the natives were few and of low culture. No treasures were in evidence. And after the conquest of Mexico and Peru there were not enough Spaniards to develop it. Thus Jamaica assumed little importance in the Spanish monarchy except in providing horses for expeditions to the mainland. These noble beasts flourished in Jamaica, and it was much better to purchase them there than to try to ship them all the way from Spain. In 1655 the English occupied it in what they hoped would be the first phase of the seizure of South America. If this ambitious plan was never realized, Jamaica remained in the hands of the English and grew valuable.

CUBA

Columbus discovered Cuba on his first voyage, and he revisited it in 1494. On the second occasion the Discoverer deduced that it was really an island, but so eager was he to prove he was in the Orient he pressed his crew into swearing that it was a peninsula on the dubious theory that people would think a peninsula must be an appendage of the Asian mainland. For some years this land, which Columbus named Fernandina and others called Juana, was regarded as a mysterious place. That it was an island was definitely established in 1508 when it was circumnavigated. Rumors persisted that untold wealth was hidden there. King Fernando may have suspected that the Columbus family had concealed a cache of treasure on the island, and he pondered long before deciding which conquistador he could trust enough to conquer it. At length Diego Velásquez received this mission, at first from Diego Columbus but then from the king, whereupon he severed his connection with Diego. Velásquez was one of the wealthiest and most successful of the settlers in Hispaniola, and his prestige was high.

In 1511 Velásquez began his conquest with about 300 men, including Las Casas and two other men who presently became famous, Hernán Cortés and Pánfilo de Narváez. It proved fairly easy to subdue the island, which the Spanish began to call "Cuba" because they understood that was its Indian name. The natives were primitive like the other island Indians and offered little effective resistance. Yet the later stages of the conquest were brutal in the extreme. Since the Spanish found little treasure, they took out their chagrin on the hapless natives, whom they regarded as little more than base creatures who were better off digging for gold than sitting about idle. Swarms of Spaniards who had not satisfied themselves in Hispaniola came to seek new fortunes in Cuba. The Indians were divided out in *economiendas* to those conquistadors Velásquez favored and were put to work. Then, the usual tragedies occurred. From grief, mistreatment, food shortages, and the new diseases, the natives began to die out, just as they had on Hispaniola. It was apparent that the Indian population would soon disappear, and the Spaniards undertook slave-catching expeditions to the mainland, which in turn were to lead to further explorations and conquests.

Except for the harsh treatment of the Indians which Velásquez permitted, he proved an effective ruler. Dutifully he sent to Fernando the Catholic a fifth of the gold dust and other wealth that he found, an amount smaller than he had expected to find but still substantial enough to maintain Spanish interest in the Indies. With Santiago de Cuba, in the southeastern part of the island, as his main base, he imported cattle, horses, hogs, seeds and plants, Negro slaves, and Spanish women. Within five years seven towns stood in Cuba, really mere villages but laid out strictly according to plans sent from Spain, with streets the prescribed size, plazas, churches, government buildings, and warehouses. For some years they exhibited sparks of democratic feeling, with popularly elected representatives gathering at Santiago to petition the crown. Ranches, mines, and farms had a good potentiality.

Cuba might have developed in an orderly fashion into a stable colony but for the intriguing suggestions brought back by slave-catchers and explorers that great native kingdoms existed on the mainland. As things turned out, Velásquez began to assemble a large force to investigate the rumors about Yucatan and Mexico. After Cortés made off with this expedition in 1518, Velásquez raised a larger one to apprehend him in 1520. These undertakings and the subsequent exodus of Spaniards to the mainland almost stripped Cuba, as the Cuban enterprise had almost depopulated Hispaniola and Puerto Rico of active white men. By the time Velásquez died in 1524, humiliated and broken over the way Cortés had thwarted him in Mexico, Cuba was no thriving, stable colony but a shambles. Conquistadors had raked through it rapidly, started and abandoned the task of building, and gone on to greater things, leaving the desolated island to older and weaker white men.

This emigration of the Spanish to Mexico occurred too late to benefit the Indians, whose island paradise had been plundered beyond hope of restoration. The Spanish crown attempted to do something in behalf of the natives in 1526, when a Franciscan friar was empowered to free as many as he legally could. The colonists obstructed him for a time, and, after their opposition was overruled, the Indians revolted, fruitlessly, of course, and many afterward hanged themselves. Finally, an epidemic swept away a third of those who had survived to that point. In 1535 the crown ordered that all Indians in Cuba be liberated. By that time only a handful remained. All efforts to save the aboriginal population had been mocked by bad luck.

Cuba was a desolate place indeed when Hernando de Soto became governor in 1538, following his dramatic adventures in the conquest of Peru. De Soto transferred the seat of government from Santiago to Havana, which had a fine protected harbor adjacent to the Gulf Stream, the best current for sailing from Mexico to Spain. De Soto was a man of first-class calibre, and he might have restored Cuba to prosperity but for his penchant for exploration, which if successful was always more pleasant than the tedious processes of economic development. His expedition into what is now the southeastern part of the United States during the years 1539 to 1542 brought him death and again skimmed from Cuba hundreds of men who might have become planters, ranchers, and miners had they stayed at home.

Now there remained only a few rude settlers who occasionally shipped hides and wood to Spain. Havana was subject to occupation occasionally by Frenchmen, some of them Protestant corsairs and others in the service of their king. One of Cuba's governors, Pedro Menéndez de Avilés, ended this phase of violence with the fleet system he organized and through the brutal massacre of Huguenot settlers near St. Augustine,

Florida, in 1565. But then the English loomed as threats, and Spain began the permanent defenses of Havana, the most famous of which were the *Fuerza*, or fortress, which may be the oldest inhabited building in America, and Morro Castle, which guards the entrance to the harbor. The Spanish made extensive use of Havana as a base to repair their ships and to assemble them in convoys for the long voyage home, a journey always likely to be eventful because of the treasure the galleons carried and the outlaws or national enemies who coveted it. In 1589 the city officially became the capital of Cuba, as it had been in fact for some time. By the seventeenth century Cuba began to revive. The cultivation of sugar cane, which is still its chief activity, flourished wonderfully and with it, sadly enough, Negro slavery. Cuba became an inconspicuous but worthy colony, and, then as now, it had considerable strategic importance in the endless game of international rivalry.

PANAMA

The establishment of a Spanish settlement on Tierra Firme, the northern coast of South America, was a giant step in the expansion of Spain's empire into the Pacific, Central America, Peru, and the rest of the continent. For ten years Columbus, Ojeda, Vespucci, Solís, Guerra, and others had coasted about the southern shores of the Caribbean. The eyes of fierce cannibals stared through the jungles as these Spanish parties probed about. Showers of poisoned-tipped arrows greeted some of those who landed for fresh water or food. The caravels and brigantines that came too close to land might be so full of arrows they looked like pin cushions. The Spanish sometimes met friendly natives but proceeded to alter their attitude by booming their cannon to make them jump into the water like frogs, seizing them as slaves, and making free with their womenfolk, who to be sure were often as cordial to the visitors as the men were broad-minded. All these expeditions had yielded in the way of value were pearls, which Ojeda had exploited with great vigor, and minor articles such as monkeys, parrots, and fine woods. The manpower of the mainland was tempting to the planters of Hispaniola, whose own Indians were perishing, and always the possibility that great riches might be found attracted the more venturesome souls. In 1508 Alonso de Ojeda and Diego de Nicuesa obtained permission to organize a large expedition to settle some of the coast, Ojeda in the east and Nicuesa in the west. They were to convert the natives, establish a permanent settlement, and see what could be found beyond the shores.

This Ojeda was a romantic character, small and handsome. Once he had walked out a twenty-foot plank protruding from a window of the tower of the Giralda in Sevilla and done an about-face before the eyes of a terrified but admiring Isabel the Catholic. With Columbus on the second voyage, he had put down a mutiny, captured a tough Indian king through a ruse (enticing him to try on a pair of beautiful bronze hand-cuffs), made himself troublesome to the Admiral by pillaging the natives as he pleased, and generally displayed a buoyant independence of spirit. Nicuesa was different, a more elegant, pompous, and richer man. Their joint expedition was organized after many contretemps in His-paniola, but hundreds of Spaniards joined and sailed off in high hopes. Ojeda began his settlement with a landing on the gulf of Urabá, where modern Panama and Colombia come together on the Caribbean. His colony was soon called Darien. Nicuesa sailed to Panama, which bore the hopeful name of Golden Castile.

The horrors that afflicted these parties became a legend in the Indies. Very uncooperative Indians, land crabs, flies, jungle cats, crocodiles, mosquitoes, and a host of other enemies combined with fever and food shortage to reduce the 900 or so Spaniards to a bad-tempered few dozen within a year. Even Ojeda's spirit broke after he was wounded, and he returned to Hispaniola, the admired tough man becoming a trembling monk who soon died. His group scrapped shamelessly among themselves at Darien. Nicuesa underwent still worse. In Panama his men split into factions and perished of starvation or Indian hostility. Finally, a party from Darien went to search for Nicuesa and found him almost a skeleton. Quickly reviving, and possibly by now mad, Nicuesa insisted that he should take over Darien and the gold and pearls that the surviving con-quistadors had collected. This threat was understandably repugnant to the men of Darien, who chased Nicuesa away and put him out to sea, where he disappeared. Then they organized a "city" and elected the ablest man adelantado, completing their follies by permitting an official who was legally in charge to sail away. Eventually he arrived in Spain and informed the king of the defiant attitude of Darien, to which, oddly enough, more volunteers found their way from Hispaniola.

The man chosen to lead the remnant of the colony was Vasco Nú-ñez de Balboa, who had originally joined the expedition as a stowaway fleeing his creditors in Santo Domingo. A blond, outdoor fellow from Extremadura, the southwestern region of Spain that spawned so many of the early conquistadors, Balboa was a man of real stature. He pos-sessed the qualities, so rare in those circumstances, to dominate his un-ruly men and to make sincere friendships with Indian chieftains. Soon the colony was comfortably housed and fed, and the native neighbors were trustworthy allies. How he did all this is a mystery, one of those se-crets that distinguish great leaders from the rest of mankind.

With Darien in order, Balboa undertook to investigate the reports of a great sea to the west, mountains of pearls, and powerful kingdoms deeper in the interior. In September 1513, he set out with 190 Spaniards, nearly a thousand native guides and porters, some of those formidable hounds the Spanish found so helpful, including his own magnificent dog Leoncico,[1] and no horses at all. Penetrating the swamps and jungles where even today no road has been constructed, the party made it to the mountainous ridge that separates the great oceans. The only memorable incident was coming upon a colony of sex deviates, whom the Spaniards righteously massacred by having the dogs tear them apart. Approaching the crest of the ridge, not really a "peak" as the poets say, Balboa went ahead by himself and became the first European on record to see the Pacific Ocean from the east. With a moving ceremony the Spaniards took possession of this "South Sea" for Spain, erecting a cross and taking the usual affidavit of all the participants that the discovery had occurred on that day, September 25, 1513.

There was no question that this was a great ocean. It stretched out as far as men could see, the Indians had sailed out long distances in it, and great surfs and tides suggested the might of this body of water. Descending to the shore, Balboa found other cooperative Indians who showed him the islands where pearls in unlimited number were to be found, though the explorer was unable, because of storms, to see them for himself. With a liberal gift of gold and pearls from the Indians his expedition went back to Darien. It has been a model exploration. Only one Spaniard was lost, and on the way home, significantly, the Indians were still friendly. Usually this was not the case once the Spaniards had passed through an area. From Darien, Balboa composed a long letter to the king relating his discovery and assembled an impressive treasure for the royal fifth. But the ship was too late in reaching Spain to divert Fernando the Catholic from another plan, one which spelled ruin for Balboa and tragedy for Darien and Panama.

In Spain the tales of Ojeda's and Nicuesa's disastrous efforts were well circulated. It was clear that a firm hand was needed to dominate the Spaniards who had expelled the lawful authorities. And the supposed wealth of Darien had been exaggerated, so that far more Spaniards wanted to go than could be accommodated. After more than six months of hectic preparations, a brilliant expedition of nineteen ships and 2,000 men sailed in April 1514. Second in size only to Ovando's fleet in 1502, this expedition was under the command of an elderly, strong-willed man, Pedro Arias de Ávila, whose name was shortened to Pedrarias. With him were such luminaries of later years as Hernando de Soto, Diego de Almagro, Sebastián de Belalcázar, Hernando de Luque, and Francisco de Coronado, all of whom were to play notable roles in the conquest of America. Also with Pedrarias was the *Requerimiento*, which the crown

1. Leoncico, it is said, drew the pay of an army captain. He probably earned it.

theologians and lawyers hoped would win the Indians over peacefully. Balboa was dismayed when Pedrarias and his enormous force landed; but he made the best of the situation and tried to cooperate. It was impossible; Pedrarias was the kind of man that could deal only with abject servants. His temper did not improve when the crown, now aware of Balboa's success, made him *adelantado* of the South Sea and ruler of Panama but under Pedrarias' over-all command. In 1515 Balboa wrote a long letter to King Fernando relating the misdeeds of Pedrarias: how he had broken the morale of the Spaniards, failed to take effective measures to provide for the colony, promoted discord, cheated the crown of revenues, displayed shameless greed, and, worst of all, ruined all the Indian alliances Balboa had woven, turning the natives from "sheep" into "fierce lions." Fernando the Catholic may never have seen this letter, and in any event he was soon dead.

Making allowances for a proud man who saw his masterpiece spoiled, Balboa was apparently not too far from the truth. Darien was doing miserably, heat, epidemics, and food shortages aggravating a bad situation. Balboa was soon caged in Pedrarias' house but finally made peace through marrying, by proxy, the old governor's daughter in Spain and removing himself to Panama. There he spent about three years constructing ships, for the natives confided to him that fabulous kingdoms lay somewhere down the coast of the South Sea. Jealous because the ablest men of the colony chose to join Balboa instead of remaining in the dreary atmosphere of Darien, Pedrarias invited his son-in-law for a friendly conference at the town of Acla, treacherously seized him, and had him beheaded for treason. The personal tragedy of Balboa has long excited sympathy, but perhaps the greater pity is that this able, understanding conquistador did not carry out the conquest of Peru instead of the lesser men who finally did.

Pedrarias continued to dominate the scene until his death at an advanced age in 1531.[2] A replacement duly turned up but immediately died, and the old despot ruled on. After Balboa's death he transferred the seat of the capital from Darien to Panama, on the coast of the South Sea, and typically chose a torrid, dank location and laid out the streets so that the morning and afternoon sun filled them with an unwonted heat the year around. When Spaniards from Cortés' group invaded Guatemala and Honduras in 1522, Pedrarias sent large forces to contest the control of these areas. While many Spaniards suffered and died in this sordid competition, it was the Indian population who paid the worst penalties. The Maya and their neighbors were cruelly victimized by

---

2. Though nearly everyone reviles Pedrarias, a doctoral dissertation by Dominic Salandra, *Pedrarias Dávila and the* *Spanish Beginnings on the Isthmus* (Berkeley, 1933) offers a favorable interpretation of his career.

Spaniards fighting for their property and labor. When at last, in 1527, Pedrarias was removed as governor of Panama, he continued on as governor of Nicaragua, where his legacy was ill feeling among the Spanish and oppression of the Indians. Several years after Pedrarias' death Father Las Casas went to Nicaragua to demonstrate that missionaries could turn recalcitrant Indians into peaceable Christians. Despite the hoots and jeers of the hardened Spaniards, Las Casas seemingly succeeded, but after he departed the natives quickly went back to their pagan ways. Conditions of life degenerated again into sullen warfare and tyranny.

As for Panama, it became the springboard for the conquest of Peru in 1531 and after. Soon it was swarming with Spaniards who were heading for the land of the Inca. Nearly all Spanish traffic with Peru passed across the isthmus and the port of Panama, and the area developed the characteristics of a place of transit which it still possesses, with emphasis on pleasure, vice, shady business transactions, and gouging of travelers. The Atlantic side of the isthmus was the seat of fairs where Peruvian merchants bought goods from Europe. It was also the focus of pirates and foreign enemies who coveted the silver being brought from Peru for shipment to Spain. Since the Indians died off or escaped to jungle hideaways, Negro slavery became the prevailing form of labor. From time to time men wondered about digging a canal between the oceans, but theological and engineering objections were insurmountable until long after Spain's rule had ended. Until then, Panama remained a place of the highest strategical significance but ugly, chaotic, and sordid.

VENEZUELA

Another Spanish foothold on the mainland proved less rewarding, at least in the short run, than Darien and Panama. The northern coast of South America, which foreigners came to call the "Spanish Main," intrigued Columbus, when on his third voyage he thought he had discovered the Garden of Eden. Subsequent explorations west of the mouth of the Orinoco brought the Spanish to a group of native villages built on stilts in the water and inspired them to name the area "little Venice," or Venezuela, surely a far-fetched compliment to the Queen of the Adriatic, then at its most gorgeous. The name stuck, however, outlasting the official "New Andalusia." At first the pearl fisheries drew the Spaniards to the off-coast islands of Cubagua and Margarita. They overworked the native divers by forcing them to jump too often and remain too long, thus killing off the experts and discouraging others from trying this trade. It turned out they even overworked the oysters, who ceased to produce pearls in those waters after a few years. Then it was a matter of trying to pick up Indians for the insatiable labor requirements of Hispaniola.

Since many of the natives were cannibals, all of them could legally be enslaved. But the Indians were usually able to fight back successfully or hide in the interior, and Venezuela seemed to hold little future for the white man.

An opportunity thus loomed for the missionaries. In 1513 a group of Dominicans persuaded some Indians in Venezuela to settle down in villages. Scarcely had they been "tamed" when a party of slavers carried them off. In 1518 Las Casas proposed to settle the New World with families of farmers from Spain, who would live side by side with the Indians and teach them by example to live like Europeans while the missionaries brought them the blessings of Christianity. This plan failed despite his heroic efforts, the few families of farmers jumping ship in Santo Domingo and electing to try their hand at being conquistadors. Not easily discouraged, the indefatigable friar obtained permission in 1520 to escort a select group of pious soldiers, "Knights of the Golden Spur" he called them, into Venezuela. There they were expected to induce thousands of Indians to live in villages, learn European ways, and pacify the entire region for the crown. This plan was not altogether foolish, much as it was derided at the time. Later experiments in America were to show how well it could work under favorable circumstances, and experiences of other imperial powers in dealing with barbarians have brought no better methods. In this instance it turned out to be a fiasco. The fifty young men Las Casas assembled found the friar insufferable and quarreled with him on the way over. They wanted to be rich men, not saints. Most of them deserted as soon soon as they reached Santo Domingo and joined slave-catching parties. When Las Casas went on to Venezuela and encountered a sobered remnant of his group who had floundered rather badly in the slave business, he induced them to set up some villages. Again, slavers descended on the settlement and carried some of the Indians away. Those who escaped understandably turned on the Spanish and would have no further dealings with them except warfare. Las Casas underwent one of his rare fits of despondency and entered a monastery in Santo Domingo, to the joy of the colonists he had badgered. But he was to emerge a few years later, as full of fight and plans as ever.

The years passed and little was done with Venezuela. In 1528 Charles V turned over the area to the Welsers, a banking family of the Germanies. His immediate purpose was to pay off some of his debts,[3] but the emperor hoped that Germans might succeed where Spaniards had failed. In 1529 an expedition of nearly 500 men, half of them Spaniards, arrived with the purpose of establishing a commercial colony and converting the In-

3. Charles had borrowed fantastic sums   him as Holy Roman Emperor.
in order to bribe the electors to choose

dians. It must be admitted that this group did as badly as unmixed Spaniards had on other occasions. The Indians were brutally mistreated, not altogether because the Europeans were wicked but also because the natives were extremely inhospitable after their previous experiences. Massacre, rapine, seizures, and violent quarrels among the invaders characterized the whole sad effort. One defiant party under Nikolaus Federmann went off to the west and after three years of the usual tribulations, or worse, reached the Chibcha area of modern Colombia in 1539, just after a Spanish force had appeared in the area. Except for this feat, which brought Federmann no reward but rather a term in prison, the Welser colony was a total failure. No towns were founded, no revenues flowed to the bankers, and few if any Indians were Christianized. It was a story of quarrels and killings from start to finish. Finally, in 1548, Charles V revoked the grant. Four centuries later the Nazis pointed to this dismal experiment as a harbinger of further imperialism they hoped to carry out in Latin America, a historic German "claim" to Venezuela.

Venezuela remained a neglected area as far as Spain was concerned. In 1567 the town of Caracas was established, but it long remained a mere village. A few sugar and indigo planters found a way to make a living and colonized some of the coastline, but there was nothing to attract a significant number of settlers. The Caribs and other Indians continued very hostile. During the seventeenth century the pirates, Dutch, and English made considerable use of the coast as bases and even put some farms into operation to provide food for themselves and cash crops such as tobacco. The Dutch exploited the salt pits and found ways to smuggle goods into other parts of the Spanish empire from the Venezuelan coast. But Spain was unable and unwilling to expend much effort there until the eighteenth century, when suddenly a splendid colony developed.

By 1519 the Spanish had touched most of the coast line on the Atlantic side from Maryland to the Argentine. They had solid bases in Hispaniola and Cuba and at least a foothold in Jamaica and Puerto Rico. They had gone into Florida and Venezuela, and they had a firm grip on the important isthmus of Panama as well as Darien. The gold dust, woods, and pearls of the Indies—for they persisted in using this name, though most of them knew they were in a somewhat unwelcome New World—had proved valuable enough to encourage the crown to hold what it had and to explore further. Thousands of Spaniards had lost their lives, but enough had found fortune to inspire others to adventure. The missionary impulse, to be sure, had slackened greatly in the midst of the primitive, hostile natives of the Caribbean area. Yet in Spain the leading figures of the court were hardening in their determination to salvage what they could of the Indian population and to compel the conquistadors to do better. Then, in 1519, Hernán Cortés landed in Mexico and found opportunities for missionaries, gold-seekers, and soldiers of the king that equaled the dreams of Columbus.

5

The Conquest of Mexico

THE PROMISE OF THE MAINLAND

IN SPITE of all the disappointments the Spanish had encountered in the New World, occasional suggestions that wealthy civilizations might be found far in the interior of the mainland still received credence. These fabled lands could not be the monarchies of the Orient, most men realized, but they might equal or surpass the profitable territories already taken, the pearl fisheries and alluvial gold deposits. These hints of imposing kingdoms came altogether from the natives, and by now the Spanish had grasped the fact that the Indians often made fools of them, telling the invader anything to make him happy or to get rid of him. And yet, could there be something to these rumors?

In 1517 Governor Velásquez of Cuba sent Hernández de Córdoba on a modest expedition whose real purpose was to pick up slaves. Córdoba was blown farther to the west than he expected and found himself on an unfamiliar shore, the coast of Yucatan. In the distance he could see the architectural wonders of the Maya, obviously something far superior to the poor thatched huts of the natives heretofore encountered. The inhabitants were no naked savages but well-dressed, armed members of organized societies who exhibited their advancement by killing half the Spanish party and wounding all the others, including Córdoba, who soon perished. The remaining invaders made it back to Cuba with a few well-made ornaments of gold and eye-popping stories. Velásquez promptly dispatched another expedition, this one under the command of his nephew, Juan de Grijalva, and consisting of two hundred men. Grijalva left in May 1518 and landed on the island of Cozumel, from whence he coasted about Yucatan, Tabasco, and up the Gulf shores of Mexico. Finding overwhelming confirmation of Córdoba's report, Grijalva was too cautious to permit his men to operate for long on the mainland and made them sleep at night on board their ships, much to their dissatisfaction, for they saw a good opportunity to make a settlement in this "New Spain." At length Grijalva sent a vessel back to Cuba with some dazzling examples of native wealth. This was enough to set the colony to buzzing.

Velásquez at once undertook to organize a formidable party. From his superiors, the Jeronymite friars in Santo Domingo, he won permission to trade with the natives on the mainland, but he sent to Spain for royal authority to establish a colony. Meanwhile, the preparations proceeded apace, Velásquez probably paying for most of them, though this point came to be a matter of sharp dispute, and hundreds of adventurers flocked to Santiago to join up. Grijalva finally returned, only to find himself abused by his uncle for sticking literally to his instructions and merely trading with the Indians instead of creating a fortified settlement. It seemed clear that a bolder, less scrupulous man was needed to lead the next expedition.

HERNÁN CORTÉS

Such a man was available in the person of Hernán Cortés, a personable, daring, and imaginative officer already well-known to the governor. This Cortés came, as so many conquistadors did, from Extremadura, of an *hidalgo* family better endowed with pride than wealth. He had gone to the University of Salamanca for a couple of years, long enough to convince himself that he preferred to be a man of action. Scheduled to sail with Ovando in 1502, he was injured in some amorous scrape and forced to miss the boat. In 1504 he made it to Hispaniola, and in 1511 he went with Velásquez into Cuba. His record there was mixed. He seemed to be a good fellow, popular and full of fun, and yet obviously capable. One of the governor's secretaries, he fell into bad grace over his reluctance to marry a Spanish girl to whom he was betrothed and was accused of plotting against Velásquez. After two escapes from prison and other daredevil activities, Cortés was restored to good favor, whereupon he married the girl and settled down to the life of a planter. In 1518 he was about thirty-three years of age.

Cortés displayed tremendous energy in assembling this new expedition at Santiago de Cuba. As its designated captain-general he was, of course, in full authority, but somehow his zeal or utterances disturbed Velásquez, who decided to replace this ambitious man whose loyalty he once before had doubted. From here on the circumstances are confused by conflicting testimony. Judged by his actions, Cortés must have been in the wrong. In November 1518 he made a bombastic speech to his followers (like Napoleon, Cortés is credited with many dramatic exhortations at critical moments, which may have been written into the record afterward), looted the slaughterhouse of meat, hurriedly loaded his ships, and sailed away before Velásquez could relieve him of command. Moving about the coast of Cuba, he stopped to pick up more supplies and volunteers, rejecting all orders from the governor to return. In Havana, far out of Velásquez' reach, he completed his preparations and sailed away toward Mexico in February 1519. Cortés had his reasons for such behavior, which his men endorsed and which even the crown finally accepted after he repaid Velásquez for his investment in the fleet. Yet it seems that Cortés stole the expedition by appealing to the men and acting fast.

Cortés' force was one of the largest that had ever been assembled in the New World, and with luck and skill it proved equal to the task of penetrating the Aztec Empire. Yet it was pitifully small. Counting all of the soldiers and sailors, there may have been nearly 700 men. They had only sixteen or seventeen horses, ten cannon, thirteen guns, and other less effective weapons. The ships numbered eleven. Their Cuban base was now enemy territory, for Velásquez was determined to arrest the group and bring them to justice. The authorities in Spain were likely to take a dim view of Cortés' actions. Even within the expedition the men were divided, both by factions and in their own minds, about the prudence of what they had done, and they might be persuaded to switch back to Velásquez. And they were sailing against a hostile continental shore behind which stood the might of the warlike Aztecs who had conquered countless enemies.

They reached Cozumel and then probed along the coast of Yucatan. The ruins of the Maya temples and idols both offended the Spanish and whetted their desire to conquer the people who had constructed them. As a skirmish indicated, these people were not going to be easy to punish. A piece of good luck came Cortés' way. A Spaniard named Jerónimo de Aguilar joyfully emerged from the mainland to join his compatriots after eight years of living with the Indians. Lost on a voyage from Darien to Hispaniola, he and several others had reached Yucatan. Now, only he and another man survived, and the second preferred to remain with the natives. Before long the Spanish acquired a slave girl, who became famous as Doña Marina. An Aztec noble who had been sold to the Maya by her mother, this girl knew both Nahuatl and Maya, and with Aguilar's knowledge of Maya and Spanish it became possible for the Spaniards to speak with the natives. Marina was to prove herself useful in other ways, as mistress of Cortés, as a shrewd adviser, and as a magnetic figure who wielded a peculiar power over the Indians.

Everything the Spanish saw and heard during the spring of 1519 heightened their sense of anticipation. They picked the brains of Indians and gravely accepted gifts. Cortés wisely circulated among the men all the favorable information he received about the wealth of the Aztecs, and he pondered profoundly what he had learned of Aztec superstitions. By the last of April they reached Aztec territory. There, on the hot, mosquito-infested beaches, Cortés disembarked his forces and deliberated about the future. His own illegal position made it unthinkable to send back for massive reinforcement. So he induced his more trusted followers to organize a municipality, *La villa rica de la Vera Cruz,* "the rich town of the True Cross," which was then only an encampment with a gallows. To this entity the men voted to endow full authority until the king's commands arrived, thus freeing themselves, as they thought, from Velásquez' claims. After an appropriate show of reluctance, Cortés acceded to their inspired request to become captain-general and to lead them to the Aztecs. The magistrates of this "town" drew up a long letter to the king relating the supposed misdeeds of Velásquez. Cortés forced the men to cough up all the treasure they had thus collected, including some magnificent golden discs, and shipped it along with the explanatory letter to Spain. The ship stopped briefly in Cuba, contrary to Cortés' orders, and one sailor escaped to tell Velásquez what had happened. Then it sailed into the Gulf Stream and made for Spain, where the court was impressed with the treasure but skeptical about the proceedings. All shipments to this New Spain were interdicted, and it was three years before the king, absent from Spain and beset by the *comunero* revolt, finally consented to legalize Cortés' position. Until then the great conquistador was an outlaw leader of a gang of filibusters, not that it really mattered.

Cortés sailed up the coast a little farther and debarked near the present city of Vera Cruz, where a fortified position was erected. He was well aware that his movements were being carefully watched and noted by artists, who made sketches of the ships, horses, and fire-spitting guns. Cortés exploited the opportunity by exhibiting all his power in its full terror. Soon, rich gifts came from the Aztec ruler, Montezuma, together with a courteous request that the invaders depart. This was, of course, exactly the wrong psychology, especially as Cortés was well-informed by now of the Quetzalcoatl legend and the belief that this god would return. These messages from Montezuma continued during the course of the famous march on Tenochtitlán, their tone varying from pleadings to threats. Aware that many of his men were thinking second thoughts about penetrating the interior, Cortés had his remaining ships dismantled and scuttled. Now there was no choice but to follow his leadership. Cortés realized he would not be left stranded on the beaches, for sooner than he desired ships would surely come after him from Cuba or Spain. Still, the boldness of his action compels admiration.

In August 1519 he was ready for the great march on the Aztec capital, which he himself recorded with sober pride and pardonable exaggeration in his letters to Charles V. Another conquistador, Andrés de Tapia, wrote an account, and Francisco Cervantes de Salazar afterward compiled memorials from the survivors of the famous march. The contemporary historians Las Casas, Peter Martyr, Gonzalo Fernández de Oviedo, and Francisco López de Gómara wrote excellent but not first-hand accounts. So did some of the early Franciscan friars, Sahagún, Mendieta, and Motolinía. The story of a participant, Bernal Díaz del Castillo, has recently enjoyed wide circulation in the United States. Compiled in his old age to prove that Cortés was not alone in the great endeavor, the old warrior's flavorful "true history" nonetheless casts much flattering light on the captain-general. The story of the conquest has never been told better than by the blind American historian William H. Prescott, whose book was published in 1843. A more recent publication by Henry R. Wagner utilized evidence unknown to Prescott, but its effort to read too much into the testimony of contemporaries and to belittle Cortés is insufficient to overthrow the traditional interpretation that he was one of the great captains of all times.

The skill of this remarkable conquistador manifested itself in difficult situations throughout the conquest. To maintain his leadership over such a band of tough individualists and to bend them to his will required the highest talents. No less impressive was the way he dealt with Indian chieftains and warriors on the way. Some he flattered and cajoled. From all of them he wrung respect. He soon learned that it was unwise to smash idols and otherwise blaspheme the religion of these people, though he did what he could to halt human sacrifice. He also comprehended that Aztec rule was hated, that the Spanish could pose as liberators from these dreaded gatherers of taxes and human sacrificial victims. Thus he was able to secure useful information about the country and the services of Indian allies and porters. At the same time the Aztec emissaries were persuaded that Cortés had supernatural powers, that he was benevolent, and that come what would, he would have his way.

Of the many famous incidents of the march on Tenochtitlán, two stand out. Nestling high in the mountains and protected by a long wall, the "Swiss of Mexico," the Tlaxcalans, had for generations withstood Aztec assaults. Montezuma's comment later that the Aztecs used the Tlaxcalans for live target practice and did not desire their defeat can scarcely be credited. At first, these sturdy people resisted the Spanish. After a horrifying battle, one in which the Spaniards were nearly overwhelmed by human sea tactics, the beaten Tlaxcalans became trusty allies and stayed with Cortés even when he was expelled from Tenochtitlán in 1520, for which they enjoyed privileges all during the colonial period. The Cholulans tried different tactics. Genuinely attached to the Aztecs, they made a show of welcoming the Spaniards but, once the invaders were settled, planned a wide-scale ambush. They even dug pits to catch the horses which had hitherto proved so formidable. Marina, so the story went, learned of it and warned Cortés. Himself a master of deceit, the captain-general induced the Cholulan leaders to gather and suddenly had them slaughtered. This show of terror ridded him of a hostile nation and removed the fight from the Aztecs, who had planned the original ambush and were now left face to face with the gentlemen from Spain.

Apart from the serious business of fighting Indians and negotiating with allies and foes, the Spanish underwent many changes of mood during their epic march. The scenery of Mexico has always impressed visitors, especially when they entered from the torrid beaches of Vera Cruz, passed through the scented jungles with their brilliant birds and plants, climbed into the rich uplands with their fields of maguey and corn, and then ascended the magnificent mountains with their cedars and pines, their mists and snow. The Spanish had never seen anything like the Toltec pyramids and temples in Cholula nor the smoking volcano of Popocatepetl. Some of the Indians disgusted or frightened them. Others had the kindly ways that make Mexicans so easy to like. Clearly, these were the subjects of an organized society, the heirs of generations of settled peoples, barbarians in a way—certainly in their loathsome religion— but not notably more primitive than Europeans even if they had never seen a horse, coat of armor, or gun before. At last the invaders reached the rim of the great basin of Anáhuac and paused. With vast purple mountains in the distance, glittering lakes, woods, fields, and the largest cities they had ever seen, the view thrilled the Spaniards in a way Columbus had expected but not experienced. It was a great and terrible moment.

The reception was to be friendly. Montezuma had passed through moods of despondency, defiance, and panic since he had learned of the strangers. The defeat of the Cholulans had crushed his spirit. Now he took comfort in his religion. The visitors were to be received in fulfillment of ancient prophecy, as agents of the supernatural. As they reached the shores of Lake Texcoco, the monarch's brother offered lavish hospitality. Then, on November 8, 1519, the Spanish began their cavalcade across the five-mile earth causeway, Cortés leading on horseback. Thousands of natives watched the strange procession from their canoes, rafts, and "floating gardens." As it neared the city a splendid aggregation of Aztec officials awaited, in their center on a bejeweled litter the gorgeously arrayed Montezuma. The monarch stepped down and, after some moments of awkwardness over protocol, greeted Cortés with a poignant speech about how the Aztecs had long known that a departed god or his descendants would return. Cortés may have told Montezuma what he reported he said, that he represented a great ruler overseas. Or possibly he led Montezuma to think that he himself was Quetzalcoatl. In any event, Cortés was master of the situation. The Spaniards were led to one of Montezuma's palaces, near the site of the president's offices on the main plaza of present-day Mexico City. The magnificence of their quarters and the evidences of luxury and wealth were doubtless greater than any this particular group of Spaniards had ever known.

THE OVERTHROW OF THE AZTECS

It did not take Cortés long to perceive that he needed to take control of Montezuma's person. His own Spaniards were for the moment filled with wonderment but were likely to become restive in the presence of so many riches and repellent religious practices. Another danger was that Montezuma would change his mind about the Spaniards being gods. Just a few days after his arrival Cortés and a small party paid a dramatic visit to Montezuma's palace. He laid before the monarch a choice: immediate death or coming to live in Cortés' quarters as a guest. Realizing the implications full well, the tragic Indian ruler wept, and it is said that even Cortés shed tears of sympathy. Montezuma gave in and quieted his guards when they expressed wonderment at his removal.

Once installed as a puppet monarch, Montezuma was submissive and obedient. His Spanish captors became fond of him, for the noble pagan had many attractive qualities and his anguish was pitiable. From all over the country his officials reported to him and brought in valuable gifts, which were turned over to Cortés. Montezuma obligingly furnished his conqueror with information about the treasures of Mexico and the political operations of his domain. He even escorted Cortés on hunting parties and on a memorable sight-seeing tour of the residence of the most sacred Mexican idols, a dread temple that made Cortés' blood run cold. So things went for several months, Mexico being dominated by the Aztecs, who still obeyed Montezuma, who in turn deferred to Cortés. There was scarcely any parallel to this extraordinary situation until 1945, when General Douglas MacArthur assumed direction of Japan and the lands it occupied through Emperor Hirohito.

This peaceful control of Mexico was shaken in May 1520 when Cortés learned that Governor Velásquez of Cuba had sent a large force to arrest him. Already, signs of Aztec unrest had appeared. Chieftains from the provinces had been called in and imprisoned, the Christians had taken over and defiled some of the sacred places, and Montezuma himself had begun to show a little spirit. Now, Cortés had to take his best soldiers and leave the capital in the hands of a small force led by Pedro de Alvarado, of whom nothing favorable could be said except that he was a fierce soldier. The expedition from Cuba was indeed awesome. With 900 men, eighty horses, and twenty guns they far outmatched Cortés' group, and they had a reputable commander in the person of the confident, boom-voiced Pánfilo de Narváez. And yet Cortés' luck held, aided not a little by his guile in playing on human emotions. He captured a few of Narváez' men and told them of the achievements to date, and then let them go to advertise these feats to their companions. His own spies entered the rival camp and told of the great wealth now available, how Cortés had the whole country from Montezuma on down eating out of his hand. After this type of psychological warfare had weakened the loyalty of Narváez' men, Cortés executed a dazzling blow. Racing toward the coast he found Narváez negligently defended near Cempoalla. Just after a rainstorm, at night, Cortés descended on his rival's quarters and seized him. When Narváez' men were offered the option of being blown to bits by their leader's guns or sharing the riches of Mexico, they made the inevitable choice. All the men joined Cortés, and the ships too. Narváez, who lost an eye in the tussle, spent two years in Vera Cruz as a prisoner and in 1528 led an expedition to a disastrous end on the coasts of Texas.

When he returned to Tenochtitlán, Cortés found the Spaniards isolated and the natives sullen. He learned that Pedro de Alvarado had massacred a large group of Aztec nobles at a religious ceremony which he mistook for an uprising. Now the air was thick with resentment, and the Mexicans were refusing to supply the invaders with food. Cortés sought to mollify the people by releasing prisoners, among them Montezuma's half-brother, Cuitlahua. But instead the august council of the Aztec nation deposed Montezuma and elected Cuitlahua emperor, and violence began. This time Cortés had Montezuma appear before his people and ask them to desist, but a shower of stones greeted him, and the fallen monarch soon died from a blow. Everywhere the noise of war cries and drums filled the air. The Spanish were faced with starvation.

Finally, Cortés made the reluctant decision to evacuate such an exposed position. On the night of June 30, 1520, the Spaniards began their exodus, staggering under all the loot they could carry. The causeway itself was vulnerable, with thousands of arrows, javelins, and stones pelting it from canoes and rafts. Bolder natives climbed up and dragged Spaniards into the water. Large cuts in the causeway made the use of a portable bridge necessary, and when it proved inadequate, swimming through the infested waters or, in the case of the dashing Alvarado, a famous leap with the help of a lance. Cortés and Marina narrowly escaped death, all the horses and most of the treasure were lost, and a majority of the Spaniards were killed, the remainder all being injured. This *noche triste* was a "sorrowful night" the Spaniards long remembered.

At last across the causeway on the mainland, the Spanish might yet have been massacred had their Indian allies not proved faithful and the Aztecs unable to take the offensive. After a few days of binding up their wounds and collecting the wreckage, Cortés, well-flanked by the Tlaxcalans, led his embittered party back to the homeland of his allies. The thoughts of Narváez' erstwhile men may well be imagined. So this was Mexico! For the remainder of 1520 the Spaniards stayed in Tlaxcala, safe from the pursuing Aztecs, from the helpless, broken Velásquez in Cuba, and even from Spain, which was having its own difficulties in the *comunero* revolt.

Again Cortés demonstrated his greatness. Taking control of the situation with a firm hand, he built up his forces from the several Spanish garrisons he had placed between Vera Cruz and the interior and received welcome replenishment as Spaniards from Jamaica and Hispaniola poured in to share in the spoils, bringing their horses and guns. Cortés was still legally an outlaw, but his leadership shone. After a few months his forces were reorganized and re-equipped. Now came the most imaginative stroke of all, the construction of European-style ships or brigantines, accomplished by the Indians under Spanish supervision and then carried over the mountains to the lakes. By May 1521 he was ready to besiege the Aztec capital.

Meanwhile, a smallpox epidemic, reputedly introduced by a Negro slave, carried off countless numbers of Indians, a fateful illustration of the impact of European disease on American aborigines. Among the victims was Cuitlahua, whose successor was the last of the Aztec line, Cuauhtémoc. This heroic figure put up a magnificent fight, leading his nation to an honorable ruin. The thousands of Aztec canoes could not beat back the eighteen Spanish brigantines. Barricades on the causeways were no match for cannon. When the causeways were cut and control of the lake passed to the invader, there was no way to supply Tenochtitlán with the food it required. Occasional victories in skirmishes were encouraging, as when sixty-two Spaniards were captured and dragged up the bloody pyramids to be sacrificed in full sight of their compatriots. But no Aztec weapon could deter the Spaniards, who, thanks to their naval supremacy, seized bits of the city, destroyed the buildings to make room for their horses to maneuver, and then took other blocks. One by one the stone and abode houses were battered down and the combustible rafts and huts burned. A decisive battle on August 13, 1521 broke the back of Aztec resistance. The survivors sought to escape in mass flight via canoe but were slaughtered or captured. Among the prisoners was the monarch Cuauhtémoc. It was a dreadful finale to the history of the warlike Aztecs, their former subjects rejoicing in their overthrow, their capital in ruins, and their chieftain a prisoner. Cuauhtémoc gave a fine example of heroism in refusing to tell under torture what had happened to the treasures lost during the *noche triste*, most of which were never located. He is much honored in Mexico today, while not a marker commemorates Cortés.

6

The Founding of New Spain

Cortés as a Colonizer

Hernán Cortés had won historic fame through his conquest of the heartland of Mexico. Now, with his forces exhausted following the long siege of Tenochtitlán and without any word, favorable or otherwise, as to whether the king intended to legalize his position or arrest him, he undertook the reorganization and pacification of the fantastic territories the Spanish were already calling "New Spain."

Cortés established a second claim to greatness through the energy, imagination, and above all the vision which he brought to this constructive work, for he was an imperialist in the best sense of the word. His over-all purpose was to create a hybrid European-Indian state which would preserve the lives and achievements of the natives while adapting them to the higher civilization he represented, to conciliate the vanquished, and to heal the wounds of the conquest. Thus there must occur no repetition of the enslavements and depopulations that had characterized Spanish imperialism in the Indies up to this point. The fundamental humanitarianism of their conqueror was sensed by the natives, who revered him as a benevolent if determined ruler. Even the Spaniards, those hundreds of hard young men who poured into Mexico in the wake of the conquest, generally obeyed the restraints imposed by Cortés to a far greater degree than they were to do in any other major enterprise of this type. The conquistadors were supposed to become true settlers, bound to the community and bringing their wives from Spain if they had them or marrying Mexican girls within eighteen months. This Cortés was no mere conqueror, but a builder of states.[1]

1. This is the traditional attitude toward Cortés. For a minority point of view, see H. R. Wagner, *The Rise of Fernando Cortés* (Berkeley, 1944), especially pp. 447–465.

The specific problems which faced the captain-general would have taxed the most experienced of administrators. It required all of Cortés' famed skill in handling men to curb his own Spaniards, who stalked through the ruins of the Aztec state in search of wealth. They were indignant almost to the point of mutiny when Cortés forced them to turn over a fifth of their collections to forward to Spain and then another fifth for himself. The new arrivals coveted a share of the loot, and thus an antipathy between them and the conquistador party began and continued to disturb the peace of Mexico for many years. The danger of the Aztec uprising, desperate as it would have been, remained a threat in the minds of the Spanish for some time. The former subject tribes and nations who now jeered at the fallen Aztec were showing signs of casting off all controls and renewing the internecine warfare that had characterized the history of Mexico. Something needed to be done to restore the food supply and to reduce the effects of the epidemics that always accompanied Spanish invasion. Improvisation was often necessary, to build ships, to cast cannon, to acquire sulphur for ammunition by descending into the center of Popocatepetl. Such mundane problems occupied the new conqueror in his day-to-day labors.

Somehow he remained in control of the situation. The Spaniards responded to his discipline, grumble as they did. The former subject tribes were induced to continue their payment of tribute, though not in human beings, and the Aztecs sank into the apathy of the defeated. Cortés began the rebuilding of a new capital on the ruins of Tenochtitlán[2] and planned the conversion of the Mexicans and the creation of a stable economy based on ancient methods and Spanish technological advantages. The ordinances he issued would do credit to any statesman.

The matter of his official standing nagged him from 1518, when he sailed away from Velásquez in Santiago de Cuba, until 1523, when he received word that in October 1522 the Emperor Charles V had named him governor and captain-general of New Spain. The long delay was attributable not so much to indecision as to the absence of the emperor from the country and the *comunero* revolt. With Cortés' long letters and the sweetening provided by his shipment of treasure tipping the balance in his favor, the emperor reluctantly decided to accept accomplished facts. Yet he was not unmindful of Cortés' earlier defiance of his superiors, and his reservations later led to Cortés' demotion. For the time being, the emperor left the conqueror in power but sent an overseer and fiscal officers to look into matters. The overseer proved of no use at all;

2. This decision had much wisdom, laying the basis as it did for an amalgamation of Spanish and native culture. Lima, on the contrary, was a specially-created city and always remained aloof from the Indian society of Peru, with the effect that Peru has never achieved the racial and cultural synthesis of Mexico.

his credentials were questioned in New Spain and his determination smothered by bribes. The fiscal officers found that Cortés had not cheated the emperor of the royal fifth, but discovered other ways to make themselves troublesome.

Along with the announcement of Cortés' authority came instructions to avoid the establishment of the *encomienda* system. Charles V and his court were mindful of the tragic fate of the natives of the islands and Panama, which they did not wish to see duplicated in New Spain. The award of Indians to individual Spaniards for personal service seemed the root of the evil, and some other method might save the native population. Cortés suppressed the order, an action which the crown swallowed with deep misgivings. As he explained to Charles V, the ablest conquistadors had to be rewarded for their deeds. The treasures of Mexico were insufficient for this purpose. Many of them had been lost, and they were too easily gambled away. If the men received no Indians to serve them, they might become rebellious. Besides, the Aztec system had been harsh, with slavery being permitted and subjugated tribes being required to contribute to the master nation. The Indians were used to this sort of thing and would not work without it. Cortés reminded the emperor that he had lived in Hispaniola and Cuba and knew the *encomienda* system could be abused, but that he would seek earnestly to avoid its evils in New Spain. Many *encomiendas* were passed out to conquistadors Cortés deemed deserving. These Spaniards took their places at the top of the Indian society, receiving labor and tribute from their subjects and often intermarrying with the aristocracy, for they did not always pretend to racial superiority. Tribes who refused to acknowledge Spanish rule were beaten down and enslaved, but those who accepted Cortés in place of Montezuma paid tribute and permitted Christian missionary activities and lived very much as they had before. If anything, the new regime was more agreeable than the Aztec despotism.

To adapt the Indians of New Spain to the new master nation required much flexibility and attention to detail, both of which Cortés exhibited. He also oversaw the exploration of the country, the *entradas* to the Pacific provinces, the northern areas, Oaxaca, and Central America. The work of converting the Indians got under way, especially after the arrival of three Franciscan friars from Flanders, among whom was Pedro de Gante, reputedly the illegitimate half-brother of Charles V, in 1523. A year later twelve Franciscans walked from the coast to Mexico City to be greeted humbly by Cortés himself, who knelt and kissed their dusty robes. Soon the Franciscans were teaching Indian youths, smashing idols, tearing up the bloody temples, and, sadly enough, burning up numerous manuscripts of pagan Toltec and Aztec pictographs. Word quickly got around that the new religion was vastly superior to the old one, which manifestly was unequal to the task of saving Tenochtitlán, and the good brothers were swamped with converts.

Cortés also busied himself with the reconstruction of Mexico City, using as a foundation the stones from shattered temples and idols, which modern archaeologists would be happy to have. He was fired by the economic possibilities of the new kingdom, the silver and gold and precious stones to be acquired, the construction to be done, and the introduction of European animals and plants to elevate the standards of living. For three years, from 1521 to 1524, Cortés capably supervised the creation of the great Hispano-Indian state that became the greatest of Spain's colonies and the largest of her heirs. Then he chased off on a fruitless errand.

It was unfortunate if understandable that Cortés dreamed that other cultures lay within his grasp. The forces he dispatched in all directions turned up items of interest but nothing on the order of Tenochtitlán. The return of Magellan's ship in 1522 had greatly excited the Spaniards, who still did not appreciate how far Asia was from America. One expedition dispatched by Cortés in 1527 eventually reached the Moluccas but could not return to America. Central America seemed promising, though Pedro de Alvarado encountered stout resistance from the Indians and became entangled with the forces of Pedrarias sent up from Panama. Another lieutenant, Cristóbal de Olíd, angered Cortés greatly by penetrating Honduras and then shifting his allegiance to the detested Velásquez. When a party was sent after him and appeared to fail, Cortés himself determined to apprehend the rebel, not without the hope that he might stumble upon another great culture. The expedition took two years of his life and removed him from Mexico where he was needed.

In 1524 he set out, taking Marina and the captured Cuauhtémoc with him. Moving overland through southeastern Mexico they missed the principal Maya centers and found only hostile natives, jungles, marshes, rocks, and countless streams. At one point an Indian ambush seemed imminent and Cortés accused Cuauhtémoc of instigating it, whereupon he hanged the unfortunate Aztec hero. To this day Mexico is occasionally stirred by the discovery of graves which are alleged to contain his remains. After a hideously difficult march, Cortés arrived in Honduras only to find that Olíd had already been killed. No riches to gather up, no splendid barbarians to rob, not even rebels to punish! Sick and dispirited, the captain-general sailed back to Vera Cruz, where he was greeted as one returned from the dead. A triumphal advance to Mexico City over the road that so many future viceroys were to take brought him back to his capital.

Things had degenerated sadly while he was gone. The royal officials sent by Charles V had ruled for a time but had fallen out among themselves. Believing Cortés was lost, they had confiscated his property and discriminated against many of the original conquistadors (or so it was charged—the conquistadors being great litigants and advancing extravagant claims for alleged services for the rest of their lives). The robbing of graves, seizures of goods, and exploitation of Indian labor had taken a severe turn for the worse. The constructive projects had made little progress. Obviously, the removal of Cortés from the scene had been disastrous. Scarcely had the captain-general restored order when an official arrived from Spain to investigate his conduct. This officer presently died, and so did the man he had named to replace him. The crown had always been suspicious of Cortés, and now there were ominous grounds. It was even charged that Cortés had murdered his wife, who also had died under unusual circumstances shortly after she arrived from Cuba. And the great fortified home of the captain-general in Mexico City as well as his airs of royalty suggested that he was dreaming of independence. Sick of the rumors and worried about his standing in Spain, Cortés gladly accepted an invitation from Charles V to visit the imperial court.

The conqueror of Mexico arrived in Spain in 1528. Applause and honors showered on him, and he straightened out the points at issue. Charles V was kind, even solicitous. Grandly, he made Cortés Marquis of the Valley of Oaxaca with its rich lands and numerous Indians, and Captain-General of New Spain and the coasts of the South Sea, and gave him permission to make discoveries in this South Sea, or Pacific Ocean. But he was no longer governor of New Spain and still less, viceroy.[3] Charles V was clearly embarked on the Habsburg course of ingratitude to the conquistadors, removing them from effective power once their successes were secure. He may well have been wise. Cortés' own record and the character of the lesser conquistadors might justify this imperial hardness of heart.

If Cortés was grievously disappointed at the reward offered him by the crown, he was yet to accomplish many useful things in New Spain. Returning in 1530 with a young bride, he received a touching welcome from the Indians, who affectionately called him "Malinche," as they had Marina. He chafed when he learned he was not to enter Mexico City for fear of creating disturbances and when he found that his powers as captain-general did not support the title. For ten years he contended with the men who ruled New Spain for the emperor, though the relationship was outwardly polite. Yet he achieved a great deal in his reduced role. Still very wealthy, he built a handsome palace in Cuernavaca, a cool and beautiful town, and devoted himself to managing his properties and

3. The crown hesitated, perhaps because the litigation with Columbus' heirs was still in progress, to grant the title of viceroy until 1535, when it went to Antonio de Mendoza.

to exploration. His exemplary treatment of the Indians did much to preserve his good reputation and to justify their fondness for him. Seeds, plants, and animals were brought in from Spain to find a magnificent hospitality in the Mexican soil, and more than any other man he helped provide Mexico with mules and mulberry trees for silkworms. He built a shipyard on the Pacific and went into debt constructing vessels he hoped would find Asia. All they did, however, was deplete his resources and explore the western coasts of Mexico and the Gulf of California, which for a time bore the name, "Sea of Cortés." He even sent a small force to Peru by ship when word reached him of the dangerous native rebellion against Pizarro. In spite of these activities the marquis' position in New Spain was awkward, for he necessarily attracted critics of the new regime. In 1540 he went back to Europe, hoping to restore his position. Instead, he wore himself out in military service and at court, where he joined the other conquistadors begging for fuller recognition. He died in 1547.

Government by Committee

AS CORTÉS prepared to leave New Spain in 1527, his successor was picked: another *audiencia*, the second in the Indies. This ranking court with executive functions had operated well enough in Hispaniola since 1526. Perhaps another would clear up the quarrels among the Spaniards in conquered Mexico, or at least would assert the crown's will in a way no brilliant hero was inclined to do. The president of this body was a cultured, affable gentleman of good family named Nuño de Guzmán. No one anticipated that he would turn out to be a swinish despot whose infamy would rival that of Pedrarias in Panama. As governor of Pánuco, on the northern Gulf coast of Mexico, he had already displayed a tyrannical temper and had sent many shiploads of Indian slaves to the islands, but all this was unknown to the authorities in Spain. His four companions in the *audiencia* were men of similar stripe, or at least they were too cowed by the president to exhibit any difference. By 1529 this unholy team was united and in full control. The pattern was clear: rapid enrichment of themselves, abuse of the Indians, and discrimination against the conquistadors, whose activities had brought Mexico under Spanish rule. Within a few months the colony was demoralized. The corruption of Guzmán and his cohorts discouraged all decent elements. Indians were forced to pay more and more tribute, to work as slaves in any way the Spanish desired. Their chieftains were summoned to Mexico City for conferences, only to be tortured and killed. Fines, seizures, imprisonments, and levies infuriated the conquistadors.

The only man in New Spain strong enough to stand up against this carnival of gangsterism was the noted Franciscan, Juan de Zumárraga. A

Basque more than fifty years old, he had been picked out of obscurity by Charles V as a result of a favorable impression he had made on the emperor during a brief encounter and named bishop of Mexico. Since Rome had shortly before been sacked by Charles V's troops, the pope refused to consecrate this appointment, among others, an omission which Zumárraga's critics did not fail to exploit. Whether he was a mere friar or bishop of Mexico, Zumárraga acted as the conscience of New Spain. With no particular authority he established an Indian court, where natives swarmed with their charges against the Spanish, and he energetically furthered the work of converting the heathen and educating the native youth.

Nuño de Guzmán jeered at his efforts and pushed the Franciscans aside whenever they seriously interfered with his policies. Finally, he sponsored a libel which was circulated both in New Spain and the peninsula, in which the righteous old man was accused of countless misdeeds, among them the improbable charge that he had gotten a number of Indian girls pregnant. At bay, the Franciscans attempted to expose Guzmán in public to his face very much as Montesinos had confronted the Spaniards in Santo Domingo in 1511. The effort did not succeed. The preacher was dragged from his pulpit, and the Franciscans were chased out of the church into hiding. But Zumárraga walked all the way to the coast and entrusted to a fellow Basque a detailed letter revealing Guzmán's outrages. In time, this missive was smuggled to Spain, where it produced immediate results.

Nuño de Guzmán and his companions were all removed in 1530 and replaced by another *audiencia*, this one a stellar group of "upright judges," as Lesley Byrd Simpson styles them, under the presidency of Bishop Sebastián de Fuenleal, who had served on the *audiencia* of Santo Domingo. Rather than face an inquest, Guzmán collected about 500 of the worst rowdies in Mexico City and pushed out into the west, along with his loot. It was not long until familiar tales of villages burned, women raped, men branded and chained up as slaves, graves robbed, and native chieftains tortured and hanged, reached the capital. This memorable trail of terror penetrated the scenic mountain and lake country between the capital and the Pacific and then up the coast, as the villainous leader sought the land of the Amazons or the Lost Seven Cities and other illusions. For several years he maintained himself as extra-legal governor of Nueva Galicia, defying Fuenleal, interfering with Cortés' expeditions to California, and pillaging the Indian communities. Odious as Guzmán's name was, he extended Spanish control far into the west and northwest. In 1548, a decade after he had been brought to justice, another *audiencia* was established for this area in the important colonial city of Guadalajara.

Fuenleal and his associates were greatly taxed between 1530 and 1535 by the problem left by the first *audiencia*. Above all, it was necessary to re-establish the authority of the Spanish government among the white settlers, for it was well understood that Spaniards, not Indians, were the ones who produced wealth for the royal treasury, and if they declined to follow the policies of the home government no plantations, ranches, mines, or businesses would benefit the monarchy. Nor would the Church, now under such attack in Europe, enlarge the ranks of Christendom. This aspect of the problem yielded to the firmness and probity of the *audiencia*. Perhaps the Spaniards were too deeply imbued with loyalty to think seriously of cutting themselves adrift from home.

Another face of this problem, however, stared at the monarch and tempted his advisers to test the loyalty of the overseas Spaniards. This was the responsibility of Christian to heathen. It was well known in Spain that so far the contacts with Indians had resulted in disaster to the native and a damaged conscience for the European. On the islands the Indians had all but vanished. On the coasts of Florida and Venezuela, in Darien and Panama, little had been achieved to soothe the sense of guilt that disturbed the more sensitive Europeans. Now, Mexico and Guatemala were at the white men's mercy, and though they did not know it yet, soon the ancient cultures of South America would pose at least as great a challenge. Was the same sorry story to be continued? Were all the Indians doomed to extinction? The news from New Spain had been disheartening; Cortés had instituted the ill-famed *encomienda* system, Guzmán had piled abuse upon abuse, and epidemics were sweeping away vast numbers of potential Christians and loyal subjects. Dominicans in high places in Spain and Franciscans on the spot in New Spain persisted in dramatizing the plight of the native, and now the recipient of these pressures was not Charles V, who was out of the country, but his wife, the kindly Empress Isabel.

As soon as Fuenleal and the *audiencia* had reasserted Spanish control, the empress yielded to the humanitarians. The *encomienda*, important as it was to reward the conquistadors, must go. Slavery, whether the Aztecs had permitted it or not, whether it was suitable for cannibals and debased savages or not, must be abolished. Exploitation of the Indians must cease. Somehow the natives must be brought into Christianity and European civilization by decent methods that would preserve them as a race and reconcile them to Spanish rule. Instructions to this effect went from the imperial court in Spain to the *audiencia* in New Spain. While they were secret, intimations of their tenor reached the settlers and produced consternation. Already stirred by the news from Peru, the colonists believed they had a strong moral case to preserve their control over the Indian. Had they not conquered the area from horrid barbarians? Were they not risking everything to settle in this death-soaked land? The only way the crown could repay them was to permit them to collect tributes from the Indians and to force these childish pagans to work, to build cities and churches, and develop ranches, mines, and farms whose products would enrich the whole Spanish empire! If that soft-hearted woman and her impractical advisers took away the Indians from their "rightful" owners the settlers would desert the place and let it relapse into the pagan horrors it deserved.

Such arguments convinced the *audiencia* and carried much weight in Spain. When Charles V returned, he cancelled his wife's decrees, probably because of the mounting nature of the problem now that Peru was conquered. With such an opportunity facing him, he could scarcely disregard the almost unanimous opinions of trusted men in the field and provoke the colonists. Even at his own court were representatives of the conquistadors with earnest arguments and ample purses to bribe those whom they could not convince. Charles V had not dropped the problem, as will be seen, and still less had the Dominicans. But for the time being no drastic changes were forthcoming.

Still, all was not lost from the standpoint of the humanitarians. In New Spain the *audiencia* freed numbers of Indians whose status as slaves or subjects of *encomiendas* could not be proved. The tribute was lowered so that it would be less oppressive. Regulations forbidding the Indians to be used as pack-carriers were issued, though they were largely disregarded. With more Franciscans, Dominicans, and, after 1533, Augustinians coming into the country, it was possible to leave many Indian communities alone but for a clergyman and a supposedly protective royal official. And it was heartening to see how avidly the natives were accepting Christianity, particularly after it came to be believed that the Virgin Mary had appeared in Indian form at Guadalupe.

The First Viceroy, Antonio de Mendoza

THE royal government of New Spain took definite shape, the one which it held for nearly three centuries, with the reign of the first viceroy, the great Antonio de Mendoza. This impressive personage arrived in 1535 and remained until 1550. A member of one of the most aristocratic families of Spain, a distinguished servant of the crown for some years, Mendoza established a model for the viceroy in much the same way as George Washington set an example for presidents of the United States. While Mendoza once said in a moment of cynicism that a good ruler should do little, and do that slowly, his career in New Spain belied this philosophy. He administered firmly and with a sure touch. He was energetic, imaginative, resourceful, and above all, obedient to the king he served. If the crown had long hesitated to appoint a viceroy after its experience with Columbus, Mendoza abundantly justified the office. His powers were formidable indeed. He was, of course, the chief executive, the king in Mexico. As president of the *audiencia* he had judicial functions. As vice-patron of the Church he oversaw the rapidly growing ecclesiastical establishment. He was commander of the armed forces (not really garrisons, but Spanish settlers and trusted Indians who could be called upon) and supervisor of the royal treasury. He was, in fact, the embodiment of the monarch in New Spain, and as such he received royal honors wherever he went and lived like a king.

The fifteen-year reign of Mendoza was the period of consolidation after the conquest. Things fell into place and largely remained there. This was the crucial time, the time of setting the pattern for the future. Its importance, and with it Mendoza's success, can only be assessed when the experience of Peru is considered. Thousands of Spaniards were immigrating into New Spain, bringing the skills, attitudes, plants, and animals that shaped the country's history. It was a magnificent period of expansion for miner and missionary, for explorer and entrepreneur. Among the less important events of this reign was the establishment of a royal mint, where two billion silver dollars were to be coined under the regulations he framed, dollars which became the staple currency of Europe, America, and even Asia for almost two centuries. About the same time a press went into operation, the first in the New World, though its significance was something less than overwhelming. Other famous incidents included the polite duel with the Marquis of the Valley of Oaxaca, Hernán Cortés, who finally realized that Mendoza meant to rule New Spain and went to the home country to attempt to unseat his august rival. Also, Nuño de Guzmán came to Mexico City to see Mendoza, only to be arrested and spend two years in the common jail and to be sent home to obscurity and death.

Among the more important events was another effort to deal with the agonizing question of native relations. Mendoza found the former Aztec heartland of New Spain full of Indians awarded to aging conquistadors. These veterans were often united by marriage with the Aztec aristocracy. They lived in power and comfort among Indians who paid them tribute and performed work for them. Supposedly, the *encomenderos* protected their Indians and saw that they were converted to Christianity and acquainted with European techniques. They expected to live in this fashion all their days and to pass on to their descendants the tribes they had won. That was the way it had happened in Spain during the Reconquest, and the rough veterans of Cortés confidently expected to be revered as founders of a new aristocracy. Then, there were hostile natives who furiously resisted the white men in Yucatan, the mountains, and above all, in a huge central portion of the country contemptuously called "Gran Chichimeca," a term implying barbarism and depravity of the worst sort. If caught they were liable to branding and enslavement as common chattel slaves for the crime of opposing "peaceful" Spanish efforts at civilization and conversion. The friars were beginning to control Indian communities for those who responded to Spanish overtures. Still, the overall Indian situation was unsettled, and further efforts at stabilization were at hand.

The New Laws of 1542

IN SPAIN the humanitarians had never accepted their quasi-defeat following the return of Charles V. Las Casas, fresh from his apparent victory in effecting peaceful conversion in Nicaragua, was back at the court agitating for better treatment of the Indians. The papacy again asserted, this time in a bull of 1537, that the Indians were rational beings, a point many a settler in America stoutly disputed. After much deliberation Charles V issued in 1542 a body of statutes that came to be known as "the New Laws." According to these commands, further enslavements under any pretext must cease forthwith, and holders of Indian slaves must prove beyond doubt they owned cannibals or natives who were captured in "just" wars. No further *encomiendas* were to be granted, and at the death of the present holder the Indians of each *encomienda* must revert to the crown. So much, then, for the would-be founders of a new aristocracy! Then there were many regulations to protect the Indians from the whites under all circumstances.

Political complications also attended the issuance of the New Laws. A formidable official, Tello de Sandoval, brought them to New Spain in 1544 in his capacity of *visitador*, an ominous type of inspector reminiscent of Bobadilla's intrusion on Columbus in 1500. Appalled both by the New Laws and the *visita*, Mendoza blamed the former on idealistic Dominican reformers and the latter on Cortés. The viceroy wisely gave way to Tello de Sandoval, removing himself from the capital and letting it be known that he highly disapproved of the New Laws, while bringing pressure at the court in Spain, where it would do the most good. The *visitador* found little to criticize in Mendoza's management of New Spain, much as he tried, but he too was sobered by the threatening attitude of the settlers. They would have none of the New Laws! Not daring to suggest rebellion, they indicated they would leave the country altogether if the crown went through with this project. Even the clergy, the Dominicans whose brothers in Spain had largely inspired the legislation and such well-known friends of the Indians as the Franciscans, including Bishop Zumárraga, whole-heartedly agreed with the colonists. If the situation in Mexico was very grave, it was equally so in Guatemala and worse in Peru, where the viceroy bearing the New Laws was killed and an independence movement took definite shape. Before such unanimous opposition not even Charles V could prevail, especially since he was on the eve of an offensive against the German Lutherans and urgently required American treasure. The emperor capitulated, repealing the statute concerning the expiration of the *encomienda* and letting it be known that most of the New Laws would not be enforced. Tension then subsided, and Tello de Sandoval left New Spain with such dignity as he could muster. Mendoza resumed his duties with heightened prestige, and the Spanish element rejoiced over a victory at the expense of the reformers.

The Silver Strike

THE connection between the modification of the New Laws and the flow from the Indies to Spain of gold, silver, pearls, and precious stones was easy enough to perceive. Even during the most discouraging phases of her adventures in the New World, Spain had derived enough profit to justify continuance of the empire. After Cortés opened up Mexico, dazzling treasures went to Spain to provide attractive toys for the imperial court and fortunes for individuals but not enough to spell the difference between penury and plenty for the government. Now all this was to change. New Spain first, and then Peru, were to begin the regular dispatch of hard wealth that was to support the Spanish monarchy during generations of wars and imperialism.

It began in 1546 when a small party of soldiers, settlers, and friars scouted the stark mountains of the Gran Chichimeca, that unpromising land of stunted shrubs, cactus plants, magueys, and the wildest of Indians. A range of mountains near Zacatecas turned out to be incredibly rich in silver ore, enough so to produce one-fifth of all the silver mined throughout the world during the next 250 years. Indian dangers or no, a silver rush ensued, and the area was soon the scene of frantic activity.

Viceroy Mendoza took firm charge of the affair, at once making it clear that the government would impose order and administer the extraction of ore. His mining regulations prevailed in most respects for most of the colonial period. By the Roman law which Spain followed, the monarch owned all subsoil wealth. In order to encourage exploration and extraction he permitted the miner to retain four-fifths of his findings, reserving only the customary royal fifth. Mendoza saw to it that hard-headed royal inspectors were present in the mining area to examine, usually on Sundays, the week's output. The miners had to bring their silver to a central place for smelting, whereupon it was weighed, cast into bars, and stamped. Long caravans of mules carried the precious bars over hundreds of miles through Chichimec country to the royal mint at Mexico City, where much of it was turned into coins. Assuring the passage of the royal fifth from the mines to the ships at Vera Cruz came to be the most important function of the viceroys of New Spain, the very standard by which their success was judged. Mendoza's regulations were generally effective in minimizing cheating on the part of the miners. His successors enjoyed a further check after mercury was imported from Europe to facilitate the smelting, for by the amount of mercury a miner bought a fair estimate of his operations could be calculated.

The Zacatecas strike assured the ultimate occupation of the Gran Chichimeca, for savage Indians skilled in human torture could not deter silver prospectors. The discoveries at Guanajuato and other localities during the 1550's intensified Spanish interest in this hostile area. Not only had the silver to pass southward, but merchandise and settlers had to move into the mining areas over the long trails. Yet fifty years of bitter warfare between Spaniard and Indian was to take its toll in fear, pain, and death before the Gran Chichimeca was finally calmed. The decisive force, as it proved, was not so much the soldier or the missionary, but the creation of colonies of loyal Indians, such as the Tlaxcalans, to fill the exposed regions.

All of these exertions were worthwhile, at least from the standpoint of the mine owners and the crown. No one will ever know how many individuals profited, but hundreds of private fortunes were made, and Mexico City became filled with handsome homes. As for the crown, figures are available, though it is almost impossible to state their equivalents in modern terms. Suffice it to say that in the quarter-century following the discovery at Zacatecas in 1546, royal income from New Spain increased seven-fold over the preceding twenty-five years, and in the third quarter-century, trebled again. This fabulous outpouring made New Spain so valuable to the mother country that no chances could be taken with its loyalty, whatever the settlers did to the natives.

Exploration: Coronado, De Soto, the Pacific

VICEROY Mendoza could not escape the exhilarating mood of the times for continued exploration. If the true position of the Indies on the globe was understood after Magellan's expedition of 1519–1522, many luring possibilities remained. Rich island groups might wait in the South Sea for a lucky explorer. Further native cultures like the Aztec and Inca might be added to the empire of Charles V. And for generations men hoped the northern continent in places might prove to be as thin as Panama, or that it might contain a northwest passage to Asia.

Many a sailor was to suffer and perish in the Arctic wastes in vain efforts to locate this shortcut to the Orient, a route not negotiated until the twentieth century.

Meanwhile, men could not be kept from trying. Would-be conquistadors were plentiful in New Spain and inclined to be credulous. These adventurers were likely to think in heroic terms, to imagine themselves glorious knights serving Christ and king like the great leaders in medieval romances. The spell of the Middle Ages was still strong on these sons of Spain. Even if they were illiterate, they listened to tales from *Amadis of Gaul* and other dramatic adventure stories not greatly unlike the comic books read by soldiers in modern times. On a more practical level, it was clear that the explorers most likely to succeed were those who had survived the fevers and other hazards of the New World after an apprenticeship in the islands, Panama, Mexico, or Peru. And their leaders needed to be men with capital or credit from previous stints as conquistadors, men with the ability to attract Indians as allies, guides, and porters, and certainly with high qualities of leadership to control their own followers. After enduring many hardships and testing their courage repeatedly, these conquistadors were likely to meet an early death, or perhaps merely heartbreak, bankruptcy, and wrecked health. A few were successful, and they inspired the rest.

It was the north that beckoned men in Mendoza's time. Nuño de Guzmán, Hernán Cortés, and Pedro de Alvarado were eager to explore this mysterious region, but events played into Mendoza's hands, little good as he derived from them. Soon after he assumed the viceroyalty Mendoza learned of the arrival of Alvar Núñez Cabeza de Vaca after eight years of wanderings. Cabeza de Vaca and several others had been stranded on the Gulf Coast during the disastrous expedition of Pánfilo de Narváez in 1528. Walking through Texas and New Mexico, sometimes as a slave to the Indians and then as a venerated miracle-worker and medicine man, he had finally reached Mexico City. Little as his experiences should have encouraged him, he told Mendoza of fantastically rich cities he had heard of and went to Spain for permission to explore the Gulf area again. As it happened, Hernando de Soto was ahead of him and thus won the right to ruin himself there, and Cabeza de Vaca had to be satisfied with the authority to colonize Paraguay, which brought him little better reward.

But the tales he had told in Mexico City titillated the colony, and Mendoza vowed to take the lead in investigating the north. Ever prudent, he first sent scouts, Friar Marcos de Niza, a zealous and hardened explorer, and an African slave, Estéban, who had been with Cabeza de Vaca. Estéban went on ahead and for a time hugely enjoyed being lionized by the Indians, whereupon they suddenly killed him. Sobered by this misfortune, Friar Marcos steered clear of the natives but claimed he penetrated the north to a point where he could see in the distance cities "larger than Mexico" with golden rooftops like those Marco Polo had reported in China.

His reports were enough for the restless hopefuls in Mexico City. Mendoza now acted fast, for there was still danger that De Soto, Cortés, Alvarado, or someone else might attempt to beat him to the area. A large and well-organized expedition was assembled under the command of Francisco Vásquez de Coronado, a glamorous young man who was governor of a western province. Another party was to sail up the Gulf of California and meet Coronado in the Seven Cities of Cíbola or whatever they were. Mexico was full of excitement, so much so that the frontier region was almost depopulated of Spaniards, with the result that the Mixtón Indians revolted. Before they were put down Pedro de Alvarado had been defeated and fatally injured, and Viceroy Mendoza himself had to take the field.

Coronado left in February 1540 with about 350 Spaniards, hundreds of Indians, and perhaps 1500 horses, cattle, mules, and sheep. Well-planned as his effort was, hard luck pursued him all the way. Nothing resembling golden cities appeared in the arid spaces of New Mexico and Arizona, only evil-smelling adobe towns of the sullen Hopi and Zuñi Indians. One detachment discovered the Grand Canyon, but its scenic wonders failed to compensate for the tales of Friar Marcos, who finally had to admit he had stretched things a bit. With only a few pieces of silver and turquoise along with many beautiful but valueless rocks to show for their efforts, the expedition settled down for a dreary season among the Pueblo Indians who were aloof (and have continued to be) from the white invaders. At last Coronado heard of splendid communities far to the north, across the Staked Plains, from an Indian called "the Turk." Following this false guide across the Texas and Oklahoma Panhandles into Kansas, they found only the tent cities of the savage Wichitas. The Turk had lied. Now there was nothing to do but head for home, about 2,000 miles away. A bedraggled, dispirited expedition finally returned in 1542. Coronado's effort had proved something: the continent was very wide and there was nothing in the north to interest the Spanish. Soon Mendoza received sour instructions from Spain to stop wasting money on useless expeditions.

While Coronado was proving the apparent worthlessness of the present southwestern part of the United States, Hernando de Soto was demonstrating the low value of the southeast. In 1539 this noted conquistador, fresh from his success in Peru, brought about 600 men from Spain to Cuba, where he was the new governor, and proceeded to collect settlers, horses, and supplies for a tremendous effort in Florida. It all turned out very badly. Storms, fevers, food shortage, and fiercely hostile Indians disenchanted the conquistadors. They went from the site of modern Tampa across Georgia into South Carolina, then to or near the sites of present-day Chattanooga, Mobile, and Memphis, where a huge muddy stream stood in their way. Pitifully ragged and weak by now, they went downstream and, in 1542, De Soto died and was buried in the river that was to mean so little to Spain and so much to immigrants from other nations. The remnants of his expedition continued down the Mississippi, a few of them finally reaching home.

Surely, there was nothing to attract the Spaniards in the lands covered by Coronado and De Soto. Florida seemed a veritable graveyard of explorers and missionaries. After Spain learned that a group of French Huguenots had the impudence to establish a base near the present Jacksonville in 1564, where not only a detested religion mocked His Catholic Majesty but some danger to Spanish treasure fleets might result, Pedro Menéndez de Avilés was entrusted with the founding of an opposing settlement at St. Augustine, which he did in 1565. The French were soon killed or otherwise removed, and the Spanish attempted to build up a line of missions into Virginia. It was a difficult business and had to be abandoned, but St. Augustine remained even after a sacking at the hands of Francis Drake. Florida, flanking the Gulf Stream over which the silver-laden galleons went to Spain, had strategic value and nothing else for a long time. As for New Mexico, it was forty years after Coronado before missionaries or explorers in New Spain could be interested again. During the 1580's alluring reports reached the viceregal capital, and few were old enough to remember the earlier disappointments. Juan de Oñate finally won permission to investigate these sensational stories and departed in 1598 with about 200 settlers. This time a permanent colony was established, Santa Fe being founded in 1610, but the story was reminiscent of the 1540's: no wealth, disagreeable Indians, loneliness, and disappointment.

Greater rewards derived from Spanish sailings into the Pacific. In 1542 Viceroy Mendoza seized the crude, home-made ships of the late Pedro de Alvarado and sent them under the command of Ruy López de Villalobos toward the true Indies. Touching probably at Hawaii, they reached the archipelago they named the Philippines for the heir presumptive to the Spanish throne, though it lay on Portugal's side of the Line of Tordesillas.[4] Villalobos was unable to sail back to America. At the same time a voyage by Juan Rodríguez Cabrillo seemed to prove that California was lacking in value to the white man.

It was not until 1564 that another expedition left New Spain under

4. Matters were eventually adjusted by the Treaty of Madrid in 1750, when Spain recognized Brazil's enlargement in exchange for the Philippines.

Miguel López de Legazpi for the promising Oriental islands. This time Spanish rule was assured, and Manila was founded. The Portuguese being difficult about intruders in the Indian Ocean, it was important to find a way back to New Spain across the Pacific. An elderly sailor turned Augustinian friar, Andrés de Urdaneta, discovered the route. It was simple enough, a matter of sailing north almost to Japan and hitting the current that swiftly carried the vessel to California and on down to Acapulco.[5] It was a notable discovery, one which Spain kept secret for nearly two centuries. Now it was possible for regular sailings to link New Spain and the Philippines. Eventually, a captaincy-general of Manila was placed under the supervision of the viceroy of New Spain. The silver of Zacatecas went to the Far East and purchased enough silk to swamp the nascent industry in New Spain. Spain had at last established the Oriental trade Columbus had promised.

New Spain, 1550–1600

IN 1550 Mendoza was finally relieved of his post in New Spain and sent down to Peru, where it was hoped he could stabilize that turbulent viceroyalty too. His successor was Luis de Velasco, another capable official, who reigned until 1564. Affable, a great horseman and lover of sports, he proved one of the rare viceroys who enjoyed popularity as well as prestige. He needed popularity for carrying out one important policy, the implementation of what was left of the New Laws. It was too late to think of doing anything drastic in behalf of the Indians, for it was apparent by now that New Spain was too valuable to shake by provoking the Spanish element. Yet Velasco relentlessly pursued his duty. When titles to chattel slaves (usually the captured terrorists or their families from the Gran Chichimeca) could not be justified, he freed the Indians. Thousands of them were taken from their owners and turned over to the crown. And *encomenderos* were made to realize they must pay their Indians for labor they performed and treat them decently. Velasco accomplished his purpose without antagonizing the settlers to a dangerous degree.

At Velasco's death in 1564 a serious situation developed. Three sons of Hernán Cortés had arrived in New Spain to take over their vast properties, the legitimate heir as Marquis of the Valley of Oaxaca. Before the next viceroy arrived a hiatus in the government tempted a few surviving conquistadors or their sons to assert themselves. Some of the talk was quite seditious, aiming at nothing less than the independence of New Spain under the young marquis. Talk they did, extensively and for

5. Soon after World War II, airplane pilots discovered a similar atmospheric current that sped their eastward flights to the United States from Japan.

months. A conspiracy of sorts was drafted, a plan insane enough to succeed. The marquis hesitated too long, almost two years, and in 1566 the royal officials struck, arresting him by a subterfuge and shipping him off to Spain, where it took years to clear himself. His illegitimate half-brother, the son of Cortés and Marina, was tortured and imprisoned, but he was either innocent or able to withstand this cruelty, for they learned little from him. At length the whole affair blew over, with varying estimates of its seriousness. While the tension between the early conquistadors and their heirs with the officials sent out from Spain continued all through the colonial period, this was the last notable instance of independence sentiment in New Spain for two hundred years.

Another long viceregal reign brought order to New Spain, that of Martín Enríquez between 1568 and 1583. Arriving in Vera Cruz just after a group of English smugglers had anchored, the new viceroy chastised the intruders and inadvertently opened the protracted period of violence that saw Englishmen and Spaniards fighting each other off and on until 1808. During his reign two memorable institutions came to New Spain, the Inquisition, which at once went to work on the captured English seamen, and the Society of Jesus, which soon outdistanced all the other orders in effectiveness and royal favor. Another line of development was the settlement of the northeast through an able governor, Luis de Carvajal. Unfortunately, Carvajal's settlers proved to have a large complement of Jews among them, and, Jews of course being illegal throughout the Spanish monarchy, great tragedy eventually came to most of them, including Carvajal himself.

Also, a stronger approach was made to the nagging question of Indian raids on the route from Zacatecas to Mexico City through the Gran Chichimeca. Roads were better patrolled so the mule trains could get through, *presidios*, or small forts, were built to shelter soldiers and travelers or to imprison captured Indians, and the migration of friendly natives into this area was encouraged. Enríquez institutionalized a custom begun by Mendoza forty years before, that of encouraging Indians to visit him on certain days and complain about the Spaniards. The Indians loved to do this, for they seem from the first to have shown a bent for litigation, and while Mendoza himself had grown skeptical of the tales they told him, he realized the value of his custom as a safety valve for Indian resentment and as a means of learning the worst about the Spaniards. Now, a General Indian Court was set up. Any Indian could come before it and accuse a Spaniard. Generally, this court was sympathetic to the Indian and often gave him redress.

Toward the end of the sixteenth century another ambitious effort was made to reconcile the European conscience with the practical requirements of the Spanish settler. By then many Indians were entering mission towns operated by the friars. This was all to the good, according to the Spanish crown, for the brothers would convert them and teach them European techniques, and then turn them over to the state. "Wild" Indians, those outside the Spanish pale, were still subject to slavery if caught, and there was no intention of permitting them to defy the Cross and the crown indefinitely. Indians held in *encomiendas* were now fairly well-supervised, though abuses were still too common. The crown was now resigned to the idea that the *encomienda* would persist for a long time. The experiences with the New Laws had been too frightening.

Other human dilemmas puzzled the authorities, the mestizo for instance. Was this half-Spaniard, half-Indian a European or a native? No one knew, certainly not the mestizo himself. He was proud of not being an Indian, yet the whites rejected him. To be sure, he was often illegitimate, and this was a shameful condition in most countries until about 1800. The tendency in New Spain around 1600 was to deplore the mestizo as a mongrel, a bastard, and a criminal type, but he was not officially classified. Negro slaves were few in New Spain, for the simple reason that most of them managed to run away and join the free Indians.

Stabilization of the Indian Situation

FOR fifty years or more after the Spanish conquered Mexico, Indian labor abounded. Household servants, field and mine workers, porters, and laborers for construction projects seemed overwhelmingly abundant. It was simple enough to build thousands of homes, public buildings, churches, and monasteries. By the 1570's labor had grown short, and the building boom notably slackened. Landowners began to compete for Indian workers in a way they had never done before in New Spain. The number of *encomiendas* fell from 721 to 140 between 1574 and 1602. A shocking explanation may lie in the recent studies of Sherburne F. Cook, Lesley Byrd Simpson, and Woodrow Borah. Employing materials hitherto unknown to students, they believe the pre-Cortes population of central Mexico may have been eleven million, and that by 1597 it was only two and a half million. We cannot be sure of these statistics. Even current census figures in Latin America are notoriously unreliable, and in colonial times it was to the advantage of many crown officials and encomenderos to minimize the number of Indians they controlled so they could pocket funds the crown was supposed to receive. Yet if the decline in native population was anything on the order these studies indicate, we can understand better why New Spain throve in the first half-century of the Spanish presence and then, with great epidemics of 1576 and after, suffered depression. We can also comprehend better why this often seemed a tragic and death-obsessed land.

Toward the end of the sixteenth century the government, never losing sight of its ultimate purpose of making natives a reservoir of free labor working for wages, strenuously sought to re-group the Indian population so that it could be managed better. More and more it took over Indian groups from *encomenderos* or missions and called them "crown" Indians. They lived under their hereditary or elected chieftains, who obeyed the Spanish officials or else lost their positions, but they were ultimately subjects of the king of Spain. Hence they paid him tribute, a silver peso or its equivalent a year for each adult male. Furthermore, they must perform public works in the interest of the state and, if the general welfare demanded it, labor at times for private individuals who needed to gather their crops. What this situation amounted to was that crown officials or private owners who needed a labor force would notify the Indian chieftains in their locality. In turn, the native ruler would pick out a number of men and hire them to the white overlord. As finally legalized in ordinances of 1609, only a small proportion of a given tribe was supposed to be called up for this draft at one time. The workers were not to be taken too far from their homes, they were to be treated well and provided for, and they were to be paid in the presence of a crown official. The period of work was not supposed to last longer than two or three weeks for any given group of draftees.

While this system was taking shape for crown Indians, a far-reaching resettlement of the native population occurred. Below a line stretching from Tampico to Guadalajara countless Indians were compelled to move into villages especially built to congregate them for the convenience of the Spaniard. In a few years after the first major congregation in 1598 begun by the Viceroy Monterrey, this process was completed. The problems must have been formidable. First, the towns had to be built along Spanish, not Indian, patterns. Then the repopulation had to be effected, surely a heart-rending affair and one strongly resisted in some instances. Yet it was done, and for the remainder of the colonial period the natives of central Mexico lived mostly in villages located for the purpose of assuring an adequate supply of labor. The population decline slowed down, halted, and then changed to a gradual increase during the seventeenth century, and the crown Indians settled into the social system as a submerged proletariat living to themselves most of the year but subject to call whenever the needs of the state—liberally interpreted—demanded them.

After the crucial period of its formation, New Spain is of interest to us less as the scene of great events than as an enormous laboratory where Europeans and their culture were fused with the Amerind society. Spanish immigrants came in a steady stream. Trade with Spain, the Philippines, and Peru stimulated economic development. The introduction of such humble creatures as cows, chickens, and pigs revolutionized the standard of living. The effect of the horse, mule, sheep, and donkey was enormous if not easily traced. Such foods as the banana, sugar cane, and numerous European fruits and vegetables improved the diet of the population, though corn remained the chief staple. The silk industry flourished, and then languished after Asian imports and labor shortages made it economically shaky. Shipyards on the Pacific coast greatly increased the potential of New Spain. The manufacture of furniture, tiles, blankets, cotton goods, and European bricks permitted a better standard of dress and housing. The continuous extraction of silver affected New Spain and the world in ways so profound we must assess them later in detail. The viceroyalty was a success, an immensely valuable producer of wealth and the scene of an Hispano-Indian experiment that eventually produced a great nation.

Central America Is Added to the Spanish Empire

THE conquest of Central America is a confusing, sordid, and imperfectly known story. The area was an obscure colony of Spain for nearly three centuries, and its development in modern times has been so chaotic as to deter all but the most persistent students from following it. Central America was less a bridge than an obstacle to contacts between North and South America, and its native population—so admirable in distant Maya times—distinguished itself only by managing to survive the horrors of Spanish conquest and exploitation. Briefly, its reduction by Spain began in 1523 when Cortés sent his red-headed lieutenant, Pedro de Alvarado, overland into Guatemala. Alvarado was a fine figure of a man, outwardly frank, and unquestionably an able soldier. Yet he stands with Pedrarias and Nuño de Guzmán as one of the villains of the conquest period. His experiences in fighting the Aztecs had not imbued him with compassion or patience for the Indians. Thus, when he found resistance in Guatemala, he proceeded to torture, slay, and burn in the worst tradition of the conquistador. His fury was partly a matter of tactics, for he believed the Indians responded only to terror, but he was also chagrined that the country offered little but rich soils, fine woods, volcanoes, mountains, and lakes. In these he had little interest.

While Alvarado was crashing through Guatemala, Cortés himself, as has been seen, went to Honduras to support his own interests against those of his old enemy, Governor Velásquez of Cuba, who had won over a previous expedition sent by Cortés into the area. The errand proved unnecessary. Most of the first group were dead and the survivors were living in wretchedness in that wooded land, still one of the most backward in all America. Francisco de Montejo, whose conquest of Yucatan was going so slowly, involved himself without notable effectiveness in Honduras. Despite several other incursions of conquistadors and royal officials Honduras failed to become a sound colony, and eventually it was annexed to Guatemala. It remained a wilderness, a territory full of refugee Indians and foreign badmen.

Meanwhile, Pedrarias, the governor of Panama, had sent forces northward to contest Alvarado's and Cortés' men from New Spain. A squalid series of fraternal conflicts among the Spaniards, confused by treacheries and lawlessness, ruined many of the whites and great numbers of the natives. In 1527 Pedrarias became governor of Nicaragua, a position he held until his death in 1531. His tenure lived up to his reputation. Spaniards were tyrannized and Indians were robbed and abused on a hideous scale. In 1537 Father Las Casas appeared on the scene to demonstrate his theory that Indians might respond better to kindness than to cruelty, persuading a group of warlike Indians to settle down peacefully and accept his teachings. But when he departed after two years, the Devil, as the Spanish said, got the upper hand again. In any event, the Indians were reluctant to let the Spanish settlers rule them as long as they could help themselves. In the next decade Nicaragua was the scene of an independence effort led by the Contreras brothers, Pedro and Hernando. With their defeat in 1550, Nicaragua too became a disorderly, little-known appendage of Guatemala.

Farther south the Spaniards encountered little but hardships in fixing their claim. Nuevo Cartago, or Costa Rica, was the scene of a colonizing effort in 1540. The familiar obstacles—disease, mutinies, food shortages, and Indian hostility—made it a terrible experience. Yet the Spanish foothold proved enduring, and in time farmers and ranchers crept in to find few Indians and a very inviting, temperate land. Costa Rica thus developed into a white settlement with a number of independent landholders. Its growth was slow but sound, resembling more the English colonization of North America than the Spanish occupation of New Spain.

Another colonizing effort proved totally unrewarding. After the Columbus family surrendered its claim to all the Indies for a financial settlement and the marquisate of Veragua, agents arrived in present-day northern Panama to establish a colony. But this region was too forbidding, as Columbus himself, Nicuesa, and even recent immigrants have found. The Columbus family had to content itself with the title, but not the actuality, to rule Veragua.

Pedro de Alvarado remained the key figure in the Central American scene for twenty years, with intervals for visits to Spain, Peru, and New Spain. Somehow he was able to surmount his critics and obtain the title of governor and captain-general of Guatemala. This magnificent tyrant aspired to win himself a share of the Peruvian booty, but as will be seen, he was disappointed. He also sought to explore the South Sea and built a fleet for this purpose from the excellent timber of Nicaragua. At the time of the Coronado expedition he was in New Spain, to the nervousness of Coronado and Viceroy Mendoza. His career was cut short in 1541, when he was called upon to assist Viceroy Mendoza in putting down the Mixtón rebellion. Defeated for once by the despised Indians, Alvarado was retreating when a horse rolled on him and crushed him. His bride in Guatemala managed to have herself acknowledged as governor. An orgy of public mourning, surely insincere, followed, for Alvardo was unlamented by nearly everyone. His widow even stained her house black and saw that the little capital, Santiago de los Caballeros, was decked out with black banners. The macabre situation lasted only a few weeks. Santiago had been built on the side of an extinct volcano with a crater full of water, something like Crater Lake in Oregon. A heavy rain tore the side of the mountain, and the grieving widow, the town, and most of the Spaniards were swept to their destruction.

A new capital was built farther north, and then another, Guatemala City. Order of a sort had scarcely been imposed when the New Laws were issued. As in New Spain and Peru, the colonists threatened to desert or even to rebel. With the repeal of the most offensive clauses of the New Laws, an *audiencia* attempted to assert the power of Spain. But much confusion ensued as to the boundaries of its jurisdiction, which at times reached far into Mexico and Panama, and again was restricted to a smaller area, while the *audiencias* in Santo Domingo, Panama, and Mexico City sought to extend their sway. At last, by 1570, the *audiencia* found a permanent home in Guatemala City, and the area we know as Central America, with some discrepancies, remained the captaincy-general of Guatemala. Nominally under the supervision of the viceroy of New Spain, Guatemala was to function during the colonial period almost as a little viceroyalty itself.

7

Spanish Occupation of
South America

Francisco Pizarro

A s THE Spanish had probed about the jungles of Darien and
Panama, intimations reached them through the Indians of
a highly advanced society in the interior of the continent. Similarly, the
explorers of the tributaries of La Plata heard of a wealthy, formidable
state high in the Andes. While few Spaniards still believed they were in
the Orient and not many more credited Indian tales, which were so often
transparent lies to lure the white men to doom, these rumors of Biro or
Peru were plausible enough to excite as experienced a conquistador as
Balboa. This capable leader was preparing an expedition to sail down
the western coasts of South America when Governor Pedrarias seized and
killed him in 1519. Fortunately, the villainous Pedrarias had his hands
full with Panama and Central America and was not able to explore the
possibilities to the south. Nor were many others in his colony eager to
involve themselves with adventures in that direction, with the notable
exception of one Francisco Pizarro.

Francisco Pizarro was one of those dedicated fanatics who convince
themselves that an improbability is true and, if they are right about it, are
acknowledged as great men. He was sure that a fabulous culture comparable to or better than the Aztec awaited conquest in the central
Andes. Despite lack of interest on the part of the authorities and the
scoffing of Spaniards who had had enough of Indian rumors, Pizarro
would not be discouraged. A voyage by Pascual de Andagoya in 1522,
which brought back only more rumors and real evidence of endless
swamps, insects, vicious animals, and hostile natives, did not change Pizarro's mind.

If he had been born in 1470, as he thought, Pizarro was by now more than fifty years old, a venerable age for a conquistador. He was illegitimate—a dreadful disadvantage in those days—the son of an army officer, technically a gentleman, and a humble girl of Extremadura. As a youth he had tended pigs; he never quite lived down the ignominy of having been a swineherd. He left Spain for adventure and probably because of some kind of trouble—motivations that were only too typical of the other explorers in the New World. It is probably stretching things to say that he was illiterate, though he had no formal education and certainly read and wrote poorly. Having survived the hazards of the Caribbean for some years, this tough character had already demonstrated qualities of leadership. At one critical juncture in the occupation of Darien he had assumed command of the beleaguered force of Spaniards and acquitted himself well. If he has been frequently called an illiterate, illegitimate swineherd, this son of Extremadura combined the traits of dreamer and leader of men of action that circumstances required.

Pizarro organized a sort of triumvirate consisting of himself, Diego de Almagro, and a priest, Hernando de Luque, to undertake an expedition to Peru. Permission was granted with typical lack of grace by Pedrarias. Funds and volunteers had to be raised by exhortation, particularly on the part of Luque, who enjoyed considerable influence. Two forces sailed between 1524 and 1526 with results that could not have been more daunting. The little ships fought the strong, cold northward current for hundreds of miles as they sailed down South America's western coast. On the shore stretched an appalling jungle full of fierce natives and animals. Behind them were forested mountains often shielded by cloud. Land explorations seemed to produce little but curses and casualties. Most of the men who got back to Panama never wished to hear anything more of the area, nor of Pizarro and his partners. Yet a more formidable effort was somehow assembled in 1527–1528, when Pizarro sailed even farther down the coast and again met disaster and distress. Badly shaken, his party finally was marooned on Rooster Island, or Gallo, until a relief expedition dispatched by Almagro arrived. Even then Pizarro insisted, like Columbus during the last days of his famous voyage in 1492, that just a little more effort would bring results. Twelve men accepted his challenge to remain on Gallo after Pizarro theatrically drew a line across the sand and reminded them of the ugliness of Panama and the promise of Peru. The "thirteen of fame" were all eventually ennobled, and ancestry is proudly traced back to them.

After seven months of waiting on the island, another relief expedition came to rescue the Thirteen of Fame. Instead of going back to Panama, they seized a ship and sailed to the south, to Túmbez, where they saw forts and houses that gave unmistakable evidence of an advanced civilization. The natives did not seem particularly impressed by the white men nor by any means hospitable. Finally, after talking with a few of them and some who had been taken off an Indian raft, Pizarro felt he had enough evidence, together with some llamas, examples of goldwork, woolen cloth, and fine feathers. He also picked up a native boy, Felipillo, who was to serve as interpreter and in some ways as troublemaker.

Returning to Panama in 1528, Pizarro found the authorities and the rank and file still dubious. His partners stood with him, however, and when it was apparent they could not raise any more funds or sufficient forces, they agreed to send Pizarro to Spain. The rather seedy would-be conquistador had scarcely set foot on his native land when he was arrested for some ancient debt. Finally released, he went to the court of the Emperor Charles V, who proved far more easy to convince than the tough-minded settlers in Panama. It cost the crown little to let these explorers operate, and if they were fortunate, the rewards were enormous. Thus Pizarro was given the necessary capitulation to explore, conquer, and convert. He became an *hidalgo* and *adelantado*, and if he succeeded he would be governor and captain-general of a large area, stretching about six hundred miles south of Panama, to be called New Castile. Almagro would be second in command and would receive Túmbez. Luque would become bishop of Túmbez and protector of the Indians. It is very likely that Pizarro went beyond his compact with the other triumvirs, for they had expected to share and share alike. But Pizarro was in Spain and they were in Panama.

Also in Spain Pizarro encountered Hernán Cortés, just back from Mexico. It would be interesting to know what Cortés told Pizarro. Very likely he gave him good advice about the importance of seizing the persons of Indian potentates and of resisting officials sent out by the home government to snoop. Pizarro also collected four of his half-brothers, Hernando, Gonzalo, Martín, and Juan, all of whom became famous but had reason to regret their participation in the Peruvian venture. In January 1530, with the expedition still not completed, the Pizarros sailed precipitately from Spain, reportedly because they feared an investigation. Flights from the law, imprisonment, accusations of fraud, and charges of bad faith—these seemed to follow the Pizarro brothers in both hemispheres.

Back in Panama a bitter quarrel at once developed from the terms of the emperor's capitulation. So Francisco Pizarro was to be commander and chief beneficiary! That was not the way the other partners had understood matters. Almagro, a diminutive homely, low-born fellow who nonetheless kindled affection among his followers, was particularly upset. Things were patched up after a fashion, but the ill feeling remained.

So low was the credit and reputation of Pizarro that when he left Panama in January 1531 his expedition was still under strength, as it had been when he quit Spain a year before. He had only 180 men and twenty-seven horses.

Pizarro again sailed down the coast off western South America. Stupidly, he did not sail far enough to reach Túmbez but landed somewhere on the coast of modern Ecuador. For many weeks his men floundered in the torrid swamps and jungles. The natives were as hostile as ever, and the conquistadors were obliged to take refuge on the island of Puná near the present city of Guayaquil. There they waited until Hernando de Soto, one of the few men of stature in the Peruvian expedition, arrived with reinforcements. Then they went to Túmbez, but found it devastated by recent fighting which proved to be the terrible civil war between Huascar, the legitimate heir of the late Inca ruler, and his usurping illegitimate half-brother Atahualpa. Pizarro learned that the war was now over and that Atahualpa had won, Huascar was a prisoner, and Atahualpa was in the interior at Cajamarca consolidating his victorious army in preparation for his reign over the vast Inca realm.

Pizarro had by now been in Peru a year and a half. There was no evidence that Atahualpa feared him or in any way dreaded the appearance of the white, bearded men who had horses and large ships. The Spaniards had not fired their guns enough to cause consternation among the Inca. One may only conjecture what Atahualpa was thinking about these strange creatures who had coasted along the shore line and made weak penetrations of his realm. From his actions, it may be inferred that he was not impressed. Perhaps he imagined himself lord of the known world and regarded the Spaniards as odd beings who somehow had escaped being included in the Inca regime. With his luck holding and his cunning functioning well, Pizarro decided on the boldest possible course: to take his little force deep into Peru and capture Atahualpa himself. He began by establishing the inevitable "city," San Miguel, which furnished a base for reinforcement he expected from Panama and some psychological support for his men, who were reassured by this legal evidence of Spain's backing.

The march required several weeks. Crossing the desert, the stark brown and purple mountains, the roaring streams in deep chasms, and the occasional fertile valleys, the little force of about sixty horsemen and a hundred foot soldiers with a few cannon and muskets could have been cut off at several points, had the Inca elected to obstruct them. The cutting of rope bridges, rolling of stones, or creation of ambushes might have made short work of Pizarro's group. Yet Pizarro had sent word that he wished only to pay his respects to the triumphant Atahualpa. His men had orders not to fire their guns nor to do anything to frighten or antagonize the natives. The Inca apparently waited in curiosity, their self-confidence firm.

Finally, in November 1532, the Spaniards reached Cajamarca, which they found deserted. On the heights beyond the city were many thousands of Inca soldiers, the victorious army of Atahualpa at peak strength. The ruler himself was fasting and perhaps recuperating from the recent civil war. Taking over the city, Pizarro sent his brother Hernando, De Soto, Felipillo, and perhaps fifty horsemen up to see the great monarch. Nothing in the behavior of Atahualpa and his entourage suggested more than mild curiosity about the visitors. They remained stolid even after the Spaniards gave them a dazzling equestrian exhibition, having the horses race to the throne and then stop immediately before Atahualpa and rear upon their hind legs. The pagan monarch agreed, however, to meet with Pizarro the next day in Cajamarca.

During the night and day that followed, the Spaniards planned their reception with the thoroughness of a gang of bank robbers. Each man was concealed and well-instructed as to how he would react when the signal was given. Yet, the day, November 16, 1532, was passing without the Inca arriving. The Spaniards grew increasingly nervous and feared an ambush. Late in the day the Inca began to move down from the heights, a gorgeous cavalcade of feathered, robed, and armed warriors. Behind the advance guard, treading on flowers dropped for the monarch, came a group of noblemen bearing a huge litter, on which the august Atahualpa sat in majesty. The monarch stopped in the deserted square where the chaplain, Friar Valverde, approached with Felipillo and read out to Atahualpa the *Requerimiento*. As he heard for the first time through Felipillo's doubtful translations about Adam and Eve, Christ and the Resurrection, St. Peter and the Roman Church, and finally the grant of Pope Alexander VI which placed Peru in the possession of Queen Juana, the Inca ruler grew more and more incensed. He remonstrated angrily that he had never heard of any of those personages or events and that he himself was lord of creation, subject only to the Sun which was now sinking in the west. Snatching a prayer book from Friar Valverde and throwing it contemptuously to the ground, Atahualpa himself gave the signal for the Spanish to carry out their plot.

With shots ringing, swords clashing, and horses rushing out from hiding places the square was suddenly a scene of terror. Shouting their victory cry, *¡Santiago!*, the Spaniards dispersed the bewildered Inca, who dropped the litter, and killed or captured the bejeweled nobles. Atahualpa himself fought and might have been struck by a Spaniard had Pizarro himself not got in the way, thereby incurring a wound that made him the only Spanish casualty of the day. It was all over in a few minutes. Atahualpa and many of his guard were prisoners. The others were dead, wounded, or in flight. Perhaps a more stupefying scene has never been enacted. The god-king of a large state, the economic and political autocrat over millions of people, was abruptly made the prisoner of creatures who might well have come from outer space!

There was no one else on whom Atahualpa's authority could devolve. Even as a captive he enjoyed the obedience of his subjects. Accordingly, Pizarro saw to it that he was treated considerately, allowed to see his officials and to be attended by his servants and concubines. As in the case of Montezuma, some of the Spaniards came to admire and like the imprisoned monarch. Pizarro followed the presumed advice of Cortés to the extent of permitting Atahualpa to carry on public business, thereby learning the extent and nature of the Inca realm. Seeking to free himself, Atahualpa made a fateful offer to fill one room with gold and another with silver, for he detected that the Spaniards were fond of these commodities. Pizarro agreed, and orders went out by means of runners to all parts of the Inca monarchy to collect the ransom. As the objects poured in, some of them of immense artistic value, Pizarro had them melted and cast in bars, the easier to divide with his followers.

Meanwhile, the stricken Inca realm was suffering grief and bewilderment in a way that can only be imagined. Spaniards were roving about the country, abusing the natives and seizing what they wished. Pizarro either did not care particularly or, unlike Cortés, was unable to enforce discipline. De Soto went far to the south toward the great capital, Cuzco, with its large population and its great fortresses, temples, and palaces. On his way he stopped to interview the imprisoned Huascar. Fearing that Huascar and the Spaniards might strike a bargain, Atahualpa ordered the execution of the deposed monarch, which was promptly carried out by drowning. When he learned of this action, Pizarro affected to be greatly scandalized. The ransom was almost in. All of his men had enough (until gambling effected a redistribution) to make them rich for life. If he now released Atahualpa in accordance with his promise, the restored Sapa Inca might make trouble. Therefore, Pizarro decided to get Atahualpa out of the way by charging him with the murder of his brother and with such violations of Christian morality as polygamy. The cheated monarch was sentenced to die—since he was a pagan, to be burned. On the way to the stake Friar Valverde persuaded Atahualpa to accept baptism and to be strangled by the *garrote* instead.

When he learned of the Inca's execution, De Soto bitterly criticized Pizarro for committing an unjust, stupid blunder. Pizarro himself soon realized the need for a puppet Inca monarch and had a son of Huascar crowned. But this ruler soon died, and another had to be found, this time Manco Inca. For two years Manco Inca affected to serve willingly as a puppet, but it was apparent that the moral authority of the Inca system had broken down. That was the fault of the system: too much concentration at the top. When the Sapa Inca was imprisoned or whenever his legitimacy was questioned, the whole tightly-organized apparatus began to be unstrung. This disintegration at first affected only the nobility and the bureaucracy, but in time it affected the masses. Contributing to this tragic process was the anarchy of the Spaniards roaming about the land, committing rapine, theft, seizures, and other forms of brutality. Few of the Spaniards in the conquest of Peru rose above the level of greedy extortionists. As in the early days of the West Indies, the clergymen were cowed or indifferent and the commanders were ineffectual in preventing dreadful abuses.

Spaniards poured into Peru in great volume as soon as they heard of Atahualpa's fall. Diego de Almagro arrived with his force from Panama, determined to win as much as Pizarro had. Riffraff from Panama, Central America, Mexico, the islands, and Spain itself heard of the new discovery and made their way as best they could. Most of them had been left out of previous divisions of the spoils and were in no mood to be temperate. The conquest of Peru saw the Spaniard at his worst. The adventurers seemed utterly heartless as they seized and terrified. About 500 of these immigrants came in 1534 with Pedro de Alvarado, the old comrade of Cortés who was now governor of Guatemala. No one had invited Alvarado to Peru, but down he sailed. On the Ecuadorian coast he debarked with his forces and climbed the icy Andes into the Quito area. Breathless and exhausted, they encountered there fresh invaders who had come overland from Peru, led by Sebastián de Belalcázar. After some parleying Alvarado agreed to sell out for a handsome sum,[1] left his men in the area, and withdrew to Guatemala.

As for Pizarro, the aging commander lacked the natural authority over men to dominate the situation, though some writers detect evidences of statesmanship in his rule. He oversaw after a fashion the award of hundreds of *encomiendas* to his followers, many of whom looked after their own interests without his blessing. He sent his brother Hernando back to Spain with an account of the conquest and the emperor's royal fifth of Atahualpa's ransom. He also directed the conquest of Cuzco, which elected to defend itself after the initial reconnaissance by De Soto, and this victory brought more spoils.

Needing a headquarters within easy reach of ships, for seapower was the key Spanish advantage, he chose a site a few miles from the coast, which came to be called Lima (from a corruption of the name of its river, the Rimac). Founded on the feast of the Epiphany in January

1. The old story that he received worthless coins that had been gilded is too good to be true.

1535, this capital also bore the majestic title of City of the Kings. Since it is covered several months each year by a thick cloud bank which tells heavily on the nerves of its inhabitants, *limeños* have long joked bitterly about the trick the Indians played by encouraging Pizarro to build his capital there. Even so, Lima developed rapidly after the usual Spanish colonial pattern, with immigrants, plants, seeds, and domesticated animals from the metropolis being acclimated very successfully.

Hernando Pizarro returned from Spain with strengthened authority for his brother, who now was a marquis. Francisco Pizarro was to have 270 leagues for his captaincy of New Castile, and Almagro was to be *adelantado* of a 200-league stretch to the south which briefly bore the name of New Toledo. Almagro had already departed with a large force in the general direction of the Antarctic, an expedition we shall consider presently, and so Pizarro took it for granted that the populous area around Cuzco and the city itself were on his side of the line, all this without consulting his partner. Hernando took possession of Cuzco with a small force in accordance with his brother's orders, which, as it turned out, were correct, for Cuzco was in reality in the Pizarro grant.

Pizarro had no opportunity to consolidate his control during Almagro's absence, for Manco Inca, the puppet sovereign who for two years had seemed perfectly accommodating, one day gaily rode away on a horse and issued a call for an Inca uprising. With great alacrity the natives obeyed him, massacring isolated Spaniards by the hundreds and laying siege to Lima and Cuzco. Pizarro sent out desperate calls for reinforcement and in time received military assistance from Panama, the islands, and from those two rivals in New Spain, Viceroy Mendoza and Hernán Cortés. Lima was soon safe enough. Cuzco, however, underwent a ten-month siege, surrounded by possibly as many as 180,000 Inca warriors. Yet the formula so familiar since the time of Columbus remained as sound as ever. Uncountable native soldiers could not stand up to a few dozen Spaniards with horses, steel, and gunpowder, though it seems Manco Inca should have won in this instance. He was also injured by food shortages and the ancient Inca habit of going back to farmlands at a regular season. Deterred before Cuzco for months, his armies melted away to gather food and plant crops. Soon, Manco Inca himself departed for the mountains, where his government in exile still commanded many of the Indians of Peru. Great numbers of them followed him to the east. Others left their homes and wandered up and down the highways they had never been allowed to use in Inca times, a vast floating proletariat who were often hungry, unsettled, and on the whole, of little use to the Spaniards as a labor force. They were beaten, and they knew it.

Almagro returned in 1537 from his disheartening incursion into central Chile. Angry over the paltry rewards for the epochal hardships endured, his group decided to make short work of Pizarro's claim to Cuzco. They seized the city after a brief battle with Hernando Pizarro and his small force. It was now the turn of Francisco Pizarro in Lima to reason with his old partner and to insist on royal demarcation of their respective grants, but to no purpose. The Almagro party, "the men of Chile," had never forgiven the Pizarros for feathering their nest in Spain in 1529. Finally, the matter was settled by the Battle of the Salt Pits, waged in full view of the Indians who relished the sight of Spaniards slaughtering one another. The Pizarros won. After a trial by a kangaroo court staged by Hernando Pizarro, Almagro was convicted and strangled. Hernando went back to Spain with an elaborate justification of these doings and another increment of treasure. But the court had heard enough of the violence and questionable behavior of the Pizarros. It was Hernando's fate to be imprisoned for more than twenty years for his role in the killing of Almagro. Allowed to enjoy his wealth and even to marry while a captive (his bride being a daughter of Francisco Pizarro and granddaughter of Huayna Capac, the last great Inca monarch), this tough old character lived nineteen years following his release. He must have been a centenarian, support of the theory that the good die young.

Spain's Uncertain Hold on Peru

IT IS very likely that Charles V would have deposed Francisco Pizarro had the uncouth marquis lived long enough. As ruler of Peru he had shown himself weak and negligent, or perhaps simply old. He had not taken charge the way Cortés had in Mexico but had allowed anarchy to thrive, and along with it, crime among the Spaniards and tragedy for the Indians. Possibly innocent of Almagro's death, he was still the target for the embittered followers of his lovable old partner and rival. One day in 1541 a group of them burst in on Pizarro at his home in Lima, the site of the present presidential palace, and killed him. Rallying about Almagro's half-breed son, Diego "the Lad," they hoped to avenge themselves on the Pizarro element and to win royal approval for ruling Peru. This expectation was, of course, futile. In the next year a royal investigator arrived with full powers to assume control. A brief battle finished this phase of the story; the Almagro faction was scattered and young Diego executed. It is revealing to observe how the lawless, grasping adventurers in Peru rallied to the king's representative. Turbulent as they were, the conquistadors shrank from defying too baldly the authority of a monarch thousands of miles away.

And yet the awesome hold of the Spanish monarch on the minds of his subjects in Peru went through a dangerous test. As has been related,

Charles V authorized the New Laws for the imminent termination of the *encomienda* late in 1542. By 1544 the first viceroy to Peru reached South America. This Blasco Núñez Vela may have been the priggish tyrant he was said to be. He was also a devoted royal servant who believed in his mission. In Panama, where he arrived with nearly a thousand officials and immigrants, he announced the tenor of the New Laws as though he expected instant and total obedience, which no doubt he did. All slaves who were not manifest cannibals or recalcitrants were to be liberated at once. Those who held *encomiendas* might retain them with certain safeguards until the end of their lives, whereupon the Indians would revert to the crown and not to the survivors of the present owner. This one clause undermined the expectation of the conquerors that they were founding veritable dynasties in Peru, but an additional article stipulated that anyone who had participated in the recent strife between the Almagro and Pizarro factions would forthwith lose all his holdings. This involved nearly all of the *encomenderos* in Peru. If the New Laws themselves were threatening enough, rumors of secret regulations circulated quickly down the western coast of South America, convincing the Indians they would soon have no subservience whatever to the white man—and the Spaniards of precisely the same thing. Then who would wait on them, tend their flocks, raise their crops, and go into the mines? Had they waded through danger and death just to make the Indians happy?

The long weeks required for the viceroy's journey by sea and land from Panama to Lima gave the conquistadors time to collect their thoughts. By the time the viceroy arrived, he found them firm and defiant. The Indians, on the other hand, were restless and acted as though all controls were off. From his hideaway in the Andes, Manco Inca hopefully envisioned the freedom of his erstwhile subjects. After a few energetic discussions, the white settlers disarmed the viceroy and placed him aboard a ship. This act of outright rebellion called for a leader, who appeared in Gonzalo Pizarro, the last of the five fateful brothers to remain alive and free. Aided by Francisco de Carbajal, a very fat, eighty-year-old officer who was nonetheless quite capable, Gonzalo organized the settlers to fight for their fortunes. Things went his way for a time. Viceroy Núñez Vela talked the ship captain into liberating him off the Ecuadorian coast and collected forces to march on Lima, still vowing he would enforce the New Laws. Gonzalo Pizarro sailed up to defeat and kill the viceroy in battle.

What now? Some of Gonzalo's followers urged him to declare Peru independent of Charles V and to make himself king. The Spanish element was almost unanimous in its determination not to submit to the New Laws, and news from Mexico and Guatemala indicated there was little thought of submission there. At this point Charles V backed down with as much dignity as he could. The New Laws would remain, but the offensive articles that threatened rapid termination of the *encomienda* would be withdrawn. By 1547 another royal emissary reached Panama, no arrogant viceroy but a long-legged priest with a deceptively gentle manner, Father Pedro de la Gasca. Supported not by soldiers but with pardons and blank orders signed by the emperor which he could fill in, La Gasca confided the altered nature of the New Laws. Almost at once, the colonists in Panama and the Pacific fleet went over to him. It was unthinkable in the sixteenth century that men should long consider such sin and treason as to renounce their monarch, and certainly not for one of the Pizarro brothers! Down toward Peru sailed the priest, cruel and cunning as some have described him, noble and righteous as others see him. From New Granada, Quito, and Chile the Spaniards rallied to him when they learned of his mission. In Peru itself most of the settlers welcomed a chance to bask again in the rule of their true monarch. Gonzalo Pizarro had never declared for independence, but he had gone much too far to be forgiven. His supporters deserted him wholesale, and, in a one-sided battle, he was killed.

La Gasca proved a prudent governor, pacifying a turbulent frontier colony where violence had been the norm for fifteen years. Frightened at themselves for their boldness, the settlers readily accepted pacification. La Gasca assured them the home government was mindful of their interests, a matter all the more definite now that a great mountain of silver ore had been discovered at Potosí. Reconciliation was effected largely by redistributing the *encomiendas* so as to win over the strongest men, a process that resulted in some discontent, for the most loyal elements felt they were discriminated against in order to appease the former rebels. In any event, La Gasca calmly and surely carried out his program and departed in three years.

In 1551 Antonio de Mendoza, the great viceroy of New Spain from 1535 to 1550, arrived in Lima. He was expected to perform the prodigies of organization in Peru that he had in the northern viceroyalty, but he lived only long enough to make an extensive tour of Peru and to outline the many measures that needed to be taken. When he died in 1552, power went for four years to the *audiencia* of Lima, which had been functioning as a court for several years. This form of committee rule, often resorted to during interregnums in the colonial period, seldom produced satisfactory results. This one was protracted by the defeat of Charles V by the Lutherans and his abdication. It was also made difficult by a well-meaning effort of the *audiencia* to enforce a royal decree of 1549, an afterglow of the New Laws. By this measure personal service by the Indian was supposed to be abolished, leaving the *encomenderos* with tributes only, but not with the forced labor of their wards. Again the colonists asserted themselves. Rallying about Francisco Hernández Girón they threatened violence and talked of independence if their "rights" were not respected. The usual pattern worked itself out. The *audiencia* relaxed its pressure to enforce the decree, the settlers went over to the crown, and Girón was executed by being pulled apart by horses.

A strong viceroy arrived in 1556 and reigned for four years. This Marqués de Cañete had some success in organizing royal rule in Peru, winning over the leading Inca pretender and reconciling other members of the former aristocracy. A second *audiencia* went into operation at the city of Charcas to bring Spanish law into southern Peru and the land we know as Bolivia. Cañete sent his son to Chile as governor to strengthen the beleaguered Spaniards in that frontier. His chief accomplishment was hanging, shooting, or exiling one-tenth of the Spaniards in the vice-royalty. He estimated the total European population at 8,000; of these some 500 held *encomiendas* and a thousand others had substantial property. The impoverished remainder swelled the ranks of criminals and vagabonds. Under the aforementioned decree of 1549, the state might encourage these footloose whites to work for wages the same as Indians, but few of them cared to avail themselves of this alternative. And it was no longer permissible to get rid of them by organizing expeditions into unknown territory, for the crown at this time was reconsidering the problems of just conquests and had interdicted such adventures. Hence the harsh measures of the Viceroy Cañete.

In 1561 the Conde de Nieve took over the viceregal position and ruled for three years, whereupon his career was cut short in a mysterious nocturnal brawl. Found dead, the late viceroy was the subject of much gossip involving a romantic affair. Succeeding him was Lope García de Castro, president of the *audiencia* of Lima, who for some reason was not given the dignity of viceroy. Possibly King Felipe II was experimenting or, as usual, was simply slow. The five-year rule of this official saw some progress in constructing the apparatus of government, and again the leading Inca pretender was persuaded to leave his exile and accept property, honors, and Christian baptism in the Spanish zone. An expedition led by Pedro Sarmiento de Gamboa explored much of the Pacific, discovering the Solomon Islands. The silver mines were proving exceedingly productive. Animals from Europe were multiplying with great rapidity in Peru except for the camel, who refused to propagate. Since nearly anything will grow in Peru, Spanish grain, fruits, and vegetables were doing well, though Spaniards paid little attention to Inca experience in using guano for fertilizer or in terracing the mountainsides and in irrigation. Despite its performance in silver and its promise in agriculture and ranching, Peru was still not a satisfactory colony. Royal control was tenuous and likely to snap with any strain. The Indians were potentially powerful and often displayed resentfulness. The Spaniards were still anarchical and needed a strong hand. For nearly forty years Peru had been the scene of tragic disorders.

The Consolidation of Spanish Rule in Peru

THE turning point came with the viceregal reign of Francisco de Toledo between 1569 and 1581. Beginning the way successful administrators usually do, this impressive official saw things for himself, widely touring the vast and rugged viceroyalty. So much was wrong. The royal bureaucracy was very inadequate and scarcely functioning. Many of the officials were dishonest, and all of them needed guidance. The record of the clergy was, with some outstanding exceptions, a sorry one. They were grievously understaffed and often lacking in zeal. Scarcely a beginning had been made in Christianizing the natives, in shocking contrast to New Spain, where the Indians had been converted by the million in the first few years. As for the whites, for forty years they had been running wild, terrorizing the natives, grabbing wealth and women, and fighting among themselves. The saddest spectacle of all was the common Indian, torn from his over-organized Inca culture but not assimilated to the European, unsettled, fearful, impoverished, and his numbers reduced by half since the day Atahualpa fell.

Toledo addressed himself to these challenges with great effectiveness, deserving the informal titles he was to receive, solon of Peru and consolidator of the conquest. It was first necessary to staff the administrative machine with royal finance officers and *corregidores*, these last being assigned specific districts and dealing immediately with the population. Toldeo had some success in establishing good discipline and morale in the bureaucracy, an achievement few later viceroys could approach. The creation of a Holy Office of the Inquisition in Lima meant not only persecution for suspected heretics and witches but needed discipline for unworthy clergymen. At least some improvement in the clergy was apparent, though the task of converting the masses was not undertaken until the middle of the next century. The arrival of the Jesuits during Toledo's reign also signified the injection of a new, hard force to spur the other clerics. The University of San Marcos de Lima, which had been authorized in 1551 but had scarcely functioned, began to educate lawyers, officials, scholars, doctors, and clergymen. A formidable collection of regulations issued from Toledo's hands, decrees dealing with a variety of situations. They were so well-conceived that in later years the monarch gave most of them the force of law. All of these measures gave

a tone not only to officialdom but to the settlers as a whole. They were inspired to regard themselves as participants in a going concern, not merely
wreckers or transient exploiters.

The greatest problem with which Toledo contended was that of the
Indians. Those who had survived the shock of conquest, perhaps half the
number of 1532, were a demoralized, insecure population. Countless
thousands had joined the *yanacona*, a drifting proletariat who tramped
about the land and worked as servants or menials for the Spaniard when
they needed food. With Inca controls gone, they often drank to excess
and drugged themselves with coca. Those who continued to live in the
ancient homelands under their tribal leaders were parceled out among
the *encomenderos*, who numbered nearly a thousand in Toledo's time.
Compelled to pay tribute, they had little to offer but labor and humble
goods. It has been argued that their tribute was much lower than in Inca
times, but even if this is true, the system was harsh. No one, as events
had shown, could control the *encomendero* if he chose to be extortionate. The opening up of mines in southern Peru intensified the need for
human labor, and it was work of a man-killing type. Great numbers of
Indians had not remained to see their communities subjected to *encomenderos* but had fled to the *Montaña*, the hills and jungles east of
the Andes. There they got lost in the wilderness or attempted to revive a
semblance of the life they had known in Incadom.

This last group adhered to the neo-Inca state, as did many in the
Spanish pale when they were able to choose. As long as Inca monarchs
with warriors, officials, and a court survived in the mountain fastnesses
near Cuzco, it was very difficult for the Spanish to make their rule respected. Even within Spanish territory killings, robberies, church-burn-
ings, and other atrocities could be traced to incitement from the *Montaña*. Manco Inca had begun this chronic warfare with his unsuccessful
rebellion in 1535–1536. After retreating to his hideout, quite likely the
fabulous Machu Picchu which the white man never located until 1911,
he continued to stir up rebellions. A group of Almagro's followers took
refuge with the Inca after their leader was killed and helped spread dis-
sension among the Spaniards in Peru. In 1545 they treacherously murdered Manco Inca, probably in the hope of winning pardon from the ill-
fated viceroy, Núñez Vela. The murderers were themselves slaughtered,
and another monarch followed Manco Inca as wearer of the fringe.

For some years the Spanish negotiated with him, offering him estates
and honors if he would become a Christian and remove to Spanish territory, where he might reign as a puppet. He finally agreed, but death
soon and suspiciously cut short his career in this capacity, and the Spanish had to begin all over again with his successor. The same tale was re-
enacted, leaving by 1571 a third heir of Manco Inca living in the hideout.

This Tupac Amarú was a young man who resisted all blandishments of missionaries, Indian collaborators, and Spanish emissaries. When he seemed to be stirring up the Indians with some success, Viceroy Toledo characteristically undertook strong measures. By now the Spanish knew the general location of the hidden Inca fortresses. One day in 1571 they trapped Tupac Amarú when he was outside his defenses. Faced with the dreary prospect of fleeing into the Amazon jungle or taking his chances with the Spaniards, the young monarch chose the second course. It proved a mistake, for Toledo had him humiliated by appearing in chains in Cuzco and then, before thousands of grieving Indians, beheaded. A terrible groan, one which haunted the Spaniards for years, is said to have arisen as the natives saw their monarch killed.

Toledo hunted down all the relatives of the fallen dynasty who might make trouble and had them exterminated. It seemed that the line of the Sun was finally extinct. Yet pretenders appeared from time to time, and it may be that an Inca court continued to function in secrecy at Machu Picchu, that fantastic retreat, now a tourist attraction a half-day from Cuzco by primitive railroad. A splendid fortress and residence commanding a magnificent view, this establishment is invisible from the valley a traveler would necessarily use. It may have housed generations of refugee Inca nobility; no one knows. Somehow they disappeared, and the buildings were overcome by growth until Hiram Bingham discovered them in 1911.

On the whole, the drastic action of Toledo produced the results he wished. The neo-Inca state ceased to be important. The Indians settled down, for the most part, into the Spanish system. Inca nobles had long since been put out of the way or had gone over to the Spanish side, intermarrying often with the white immigrants. Curiously, they perpetuated the Huascar-Atahualpa feud for generations, but usually in bloodless ways. Justifiable as Toledo's measures may have been, they failed to endear him to his own master, Felipe II, who objected to regicide for obvious reasons.[2] Nearly ten years after the killing of Tupac Amarú the sullen Felipe coldly reproached Toledo for this action, and the former viceroy is supposed to have been keenly hurt, even to the point of hastening his death.

As part of his campaign against the Inca, Toledo undertook to discredit their traditions, which by then were assuming the glamour of "the good old days." It was also his purpose to undermine those troublesome intellectuals in Spain who were always insisting that the Indians had many virtues, in contrast to the settlers who exploited them. The explorer Sarmiento de Gamboa was commissioned to collect from surviving Inca

2. This would not rule out his own desire to have Elizabeth I of England assassinated. But then Felipe had reason to regard her as an illegitimate monarch.

wise men and officials a group of *informaciones* which would embody the facts of the old regime. Altered somewhat by the editor, this product satisfied the viceroy, for it stressed the dubious origin of the Inca dynasty which pretended to be divine, the terrible wars it had perpetrated, the debasement of human beings who lived under its system, and the general bleakness of the Inca rule. The book is still a good antidote for those who would glorify the Inca, but its prejudiced nature was recognized in Spain, where it was not published for a long time, and by infuriated heirs of the Inca. Among the latter was the mestizo, Inca Garcilasso de la Vega, whose literary labors in Spain did much to create a high admiration for his mother's ancestors.

The most fundamental of Toledo's reforms was the regularization of Indian labor. He found the system a hodge-podge, though each method did not vary from the basic fact that Spaniards usually made the Indians work for them. Toledo had participated in crown councils in Spain concerning this problem and was familiar with the intention to have the natives work for the "republic," as the state was often called, carrying out public construction and assisting private individuals who temporarily needed a labor force in their mines, vineyards, ranches, and farms. Yet all this must be under safeguards to protect the Indian from mistreatment. It remained to put these principles into action. After long study Toledo decided to resurrect much of the Inca system. The natives had been accustomed to paying tribute to the Inca. Now this tribute was regularized so that, at least in theory, it was kept in modest proportion. Indians of an *encomienda* paid coins, goods, or labor to their master, and those who belonged to the crown outright paid directly to royal officials. *Corregidores* made the collections, and *encomenderos* were ordered to stay away from their Indian subjects.

In addition to tribute, the Inca had required each able-bodied Indian male to take his turn (*mita*) in carrying out public works or in military service. The Indians had long been accustomed to this draft, and by the 1570's it still persisted in some localities and was probably remembered by many who no longer were summoned. Toledo sought to reinstate the practice everywhere and to apply it to all kinds of labor for the good of the viceroyalty. Certainly, the Indians of Peru were willing to work, for they were not children of nature like the natives of Brazil and the West Indies. The climate was good, they were hardy, and they regarded labor as a virtue, shiftless as many of them had become since the Spanish had disrupted their familiar system. Toledo's method was to work through tribal chieftains or nobles, most of whom were Christianized and pleased to associate themselves with the white men as rulers over other Indians. Spanish owners who needed workers applied to *corregidores*, who in turn notified the tribal leaders. The Indians were thereupon drafted and marched off to toil for a few months (longer than in Mexico) under supposedly benevolent supervision and for wages. After this stint the Indian was to be let alone for a few years.

The *mita* was not to function that neatly, as we shall see when we return to Peru in a later chapter, but it served to standardize the labor situation and to get the work of the country done. Toledo has been widely admired for dealing with the problem so effectively, for seeing the crux of the issue and blending the old and the new. Yet he had many critics of his own time, when Indians remonstrated against the brutality of instituting his system, which they regarded as a perversion of the Inca method, and even in the Council of Indies. And modern historians have often condemned him. Yet in the context of the time and place, he served the interests of Spain well. In dealing so pragmatically with a chaotic situation he made perhaps the least cruel of possible choices. Toledo cannot be fairly blamed if future officials and Indian chieftains turned the *mita* into a hellish institution for exploiting the natives, while ignoring his humanitarian safeguards.

The reign of Toledo represents the watershed of the history of colonial Peru, its shift from a silver-rich but violent frontier community to a more or less settled state that became Spain's deepest root in South America. From Lima the lands now included in Chile, Argentina, Paraguay, Bolivia, Uruguay, Ecuador, Colombia, and Peru proper were long ruled. Not only the chain of royal command from Madrid, but, at least in theory, most of the commerce ran from Lima to the outlying provinces. And the silver flowed from Spanish South America to Peru, leaving sediment in the way of elegant homes, prosperous business houses, a pretentious if insular high society, institutions of culture, and a majestic officialdom in the City of the Kings. The viceroyalty seemed to be functioning at last. It was a grievous shock to the Spanish when, in 1580, Francis Drake dared to sail past Cape Horn into the Pacific and singe Felipe II's beard in coastal towns before carrying his impudence into New Spain and beyond. Despite the vulnerability of the western coast which Drake revealed, and which the Spanish took strong measures to counteract, Peru and her satellite provinces remained for almost 250 years secure in the Spanish empire.

CHILE

Diego de Almagro had hoped to discover in New Toledo, his grant to the south of Pizarro's, a treasure house like Peru. The Indians had led him to expect this outcome, for there was no better way of ridding a land of Spaniards than to circulate tales of riches in distant places. Leaving in 1535 with about 600 conquistadors and countless Indians as guides, porters, auxiliaries, and servants, as well as the usual complement of cattle, swine, llamas, and man-chasing dogs, Almagro led his expedition through a fiasco. They went southward by the high road, the loftiest peaks of the Andes, and returned by the low road, the terrible desert strip that lies between the mountains and the Pacific. Their sufferings were monumental—altitude sickness and cold in the glaciers, heat and glare on the coast. True, in Chile they found a delicious land, one that later generations have valued. Yet its loose treasure was scanty, and the Araucanian Indians resisted with such vigor it seemed hopeless to create a settlement. Almagro's men took out their rage on such natives as they conquered and headed back to Peru, where they seized Cuzco and warred disastrously with the Pizarro brothers.

Not long before he was killed, Francisco Pizarro granted another conquistador permission to explore and exploit the temperate region Almagro had covered. This was Pedro de Valdivia, a gentleman of high birth with an impressive military record from wars in Europe. In 1540 Valdivia collected 150 Spaniards, all he could attract because of the evil memory of Almagro's expedition, 3,000 Indians, and his mistress, Inéz Suárez. The 2,000-mile journey was as taxing as the pessimists had predicted. The Araucanians were still inhospitable, and the Spaniards suffered serious casualties. For a long time most of them were besieged on the hill of Santa Lucía, now a park and cherished national monument in downtown Santiago. Despite the courage of Valdivia and Inéz, the party might have disappeared but for the timely arrival of ships from Peru. This was indeed a fortunate circumstance for the skin-clad, starving Spaniards and for the future colonization of Chile. Overland contact between Chile and Peru is even now so difficult as to be prohibitive. It was the sea connection that made it possible for Spain to extend her hold into Chile permanently.

Reinforced as he was, Valdivia proved an excellent pioneer. He compelled his colonists to plant crops while fighting off Indians, in the best tradition of the United States at a much later day. The climate was ideal for growing wheat, and vineyards and orchards flourished at least as well as they did in Peru. A modest amount of gold was turned up, not enough to stimulate a rush but sufficient to justify an imperial effort. In 1547 Valdivia played a cruel practical joke on some of his colonists. Summoned to Peru to help Father La Gasca against Gonzalo Pizarro, Valdivia persuaded a dozen of the settlers to accompany him. They loaded the ship with their accumulations of gold and then attended an alcoholic party on the beach, whereupon their leader rowed off to the vessel and sailed away. Father La Gasca eventually made Valdivia repay his victims and, as a further gesture of morality, to see that Inéz Suárez was married.

By 1553 Chile was a frontier colony of some stability. Perhaps a thousand Spaniards lived there, and six forts and towns stood in the fertile valley almost enclosed by the awesome *cordillera*. The Indians were unhelpful, only those who were chained and guarded serving the Spanish. The freedom-loving Araucanians made life adventurous for the invaders with their harassment. Skillfully employing the *bola*, a rock attached to a long cord, they captured many an armored Spaniard and, what was more serious, tripped the horses. Soon they learned how to make use of horses and guns taken from their enemies. One tale of Indian revenge burned deep into the consciousness of South America. This had to do with Lautaro, an Araucanian boy who had served as a groom for Valdivia until he ran off. In 1554 Lautaro was leader of a group of natives who captured Valdivia himself. After exquisite mental torture at the hands of his former servant, the stalwart Valdivia was put to a cruel death, perhaps by having his arms and legs amputated by seashells and roasted and eaten while he watched. Whether the legend is accurate in detail or not, the Araucanian's love of independence made him the symbol of defiance for the soldier who would conquer him, the settler who would exploit him, the friar who would save his soul. A grudging admiration for these Araucanians developed in South America, where plotters for independence in the nineteenth century created secret Lautaro lodges. And the most famous literary work to come out of the Conquest, Alonso Ercilla y Zúñiga's epic poem *La Araucana*, glorified this nation to the approval of Spaniards on both sides of the Atlantic.

After Valdivia came the son of the viceroy of Peru and a string of other governors, some of whom won promotion to the viceregal post in Lima after proving themselves in Chile. In 1567–1573 an *audiencia* at Concepción graced the colony, though it was withdrawn and replaced later, in 1609, with a more enduring court at Santiago. The economy of the colony depended mainly on agriculturists and ranchers, the gold being limited and copper having little value then. Yet, though the climate was excellent and the soil fertile in places, Chile remained a marginal investment for Spain. She cost nearly as much as she produced because of the chronic Indian warfare. Despite truces, efforts at extermination by both sides, and occasional efforts to divide the land at the Bío-Bío River, Chile was a drain on the treasury, one of the extremely few localities in a vast monarchy where a regular garrison was required. Not even the Jesuits were able to pacify the Araucanians, though they were highly successful in creating large farms with Negro slaves and in operating various business enterprises.

Spain persisted in holding Chile through the viceroy of Peru and the sea connection. It was not in the nature of the Spanish empire to surrender territory but further, if the Spanish did not occupy Chile, others were ready to attempt it. The Dutch were the most troublesome of these rivals, especially during the days of the Dutch West India Company and its exploits in Brazil. Dutch traders long knew they would find a welcome in Chilean ports for contraband. A permanent base in Chile might lead to intimate contacts with the silver areas deep in the Andes, and so the Spanish stubbornly fought back. Nor were the English reluctant to intrude. Francis Drake's spectacular raids in 1580 encouraged others, particularly smugglers. And enterprising traders knew that English goods unloaded in Brazil or Buenos Aires could be carried in profitable volume across the plains of the Argentine and through passes of the Andes into Chile, where the settlers avidly purchased them in preference to the costlier, tax-laden articles that came from Spain by way of Panama and Peru. Thus Chile remained a drain and a problem to the Spanish authorities, of little value in itself but worth holding to interdict rivals. Somehow this troublesome colony finally became one of the finest heirs of Spain.

QUITO AND THE AMAZON

While the Spaniards were possessing themselves of the Peruvian highlands during 1533, Pizarro sent a body of nearly 300 men led by one of his favorites, Sebastián de Belalcázar,[3] into the northern province, the land of the Quito Indians. Belalcázar invaded this region, so recently the base of Atahualpa, with a strong sense of anticipation. To be sure, he found marvelous scenery, noble mountain ranges, and a veritable avenue of volcanoes stretching south toward Peru. The uplands were fertile and the Indians easily defeated. Yet the haul of treasure was disappointing. As we have noted, Pedro de Alvarado invited himself to share in the conquest of South America and brought his gasping forces from the torrid coastlands of present-day Ecuador into the frigid heights of Quito. Belalcázar's men were in better condition, and he was soon reinforced from Peru, so Alvarado allowed himself to be bought off. If the rival was gone, Belalcázar still felt unsatisfied with the picturesque land of the Quito. Without the approval of his superiors he pushed on northward into what is now the prosperous interior of the republic of Colombia, where he had further adventures we shall discuss presently.

Other Spanish forces followed Belalcázar's trail into Ecuador but turned up no treasure. Instead, rumors of El Dorado and forests of spices in country romantically called the Land of the Cinnamon Tree titillated the conquistadors. Since stranger things had been uncovered

3. Often written Benalcázar. Actually, neither was his name, but it does not matter. The man apparently did not know his real name. Posterity has been content to call him Belalcázar or Benalcázar.

in the New World, these men are not to be ridiculed for investigating such tales. In 1540 Gonzalo Pizarro was appointed governor of Quito by his brother. In the following year Gonzalo collected an expedition of 200 or more Spaniards, several thousand natives, and the usual multitude of swine and dogs to go exploring in the east. The icy *cordillera* diminished his forces considerably, but worse was to follow. Endless miles of thick jungle and dank forests and head-shrinking Indians drew the determination from the stoutest. They finally found the cinnamon trees, but the natives were dwindling through death and escape, and there was no way to bring the bark back; the spice trade from this region was never destined to ruin the commerce of the Far East. When about half of Gonzalo's Spaniards limped back to Peru they apparently never wished to hear anything more of this green hell.

During the expedition it was observed that all streams seemed to flow away from the Pacific. At one low point of despair, an officer named Francisco de Orellana volunteered to take a party down one of the rivers to search for food. More than fifty men went with him. On makeshift rafts they began to float downstream. On and on they drifted, the river flowing into another and then into one larger still. Everywhere there were curious birds, animals, and insects, but the jungle did not recede. When it became clear they could not return to Gonzalo Pizarro without hacking their way back through the terrible growth or, unthinkably, rowing upstream, the party heard Orellana's proposition. If they would organize a municipality, appoint him leader, and then order him to continue down the stream, all would be legal. Gonzalo and his waiting group could shift for themselves. This the men did, and a historic journey ensued. The river was, of course, the Amazon, so named because the Spanish thought they saw colonies composed entirely of fierce female warriors.

After seven months they emerged from the mouth of this "Sweet Sea" and prudently decided not to report back to Peru. Instead they sailed for Spain, where much satisfaction was expressed that the great river and its basin lay on the Spanish side of the Line of Tordesillas. Orellana was not destined to carve out a captaincy there, despite the acclaim he won and the permission he received. Just as he returned with a larger force, his boat turned over and he was drowned in the mouth of the Amazon. Other Spaniards sought to explore the river and its tributaries, but despite noble sufferings and the basest of crimes, they made little progress. It remained for the Portuguese in Brazil and not the Spanish in Peru to assert an effective claim to the mammoth river.

As for Quito, or the land we know as Ecuador, the Spanish eventually populated it to the extent of settling *encomenderos*, who divided up most of the sedentary natives and constituted an enduring ruling class. Royal officials and clergymen carried on the usual functions, winning neither great distinction nor particular notoriety. In 1563 the town of Quito became the seat of an *audiencia,* and from then on the area was known in the Spanish empire as the presidency of Quito, the head of the *audiencia* being the executive of the province under the viceroy at Lima. Quito eventually developed into a beautiful and quaint colonial city. It even became a modest cultural center, with a university, a school of painting, and a collection of savants. Its rival, Guayaquil, located on the torrid coast, came to resemble some of the teeming ports of the tropical Orient in that it was muddy, crowded, diseased, poor, and colorful. It was a shipbuilding center of considerable importance during much of the colonial period and the shipping point for the products of the hinterland. By the time of independence Guayaquil was worth competing for, as Bolívar and San Martín demonstrated.

NEW GRANADA

Discovery and Conquest: Quesada

THE various expeditions which touched the northern, Caribbean coasts of South America often had cause to regret their curiosity. Seeking slaves, loose treasure, or adventure, most of them found extreme danger and hardship. In some of the early efforts along the shores of the present republic of Colombia, probably more than half the explorers perished. Not only were the natives belligerent, but they were cannibalistic and equipped with poison-tipped arrows, which the Spanish indignantly regarded as unfair weapons. These Indians were difficult to defeat in the usual manner because of the jungles that grew thick right up to the beaches. Moreover, land crabs, alligators, jaguars, and insects tormented the intruders, and anyone who escaped the visible perils of the coastlines was likely to succumb to deadly fevers.

It is small wonder that such early settlements as Darien broke up when better locations in Panama became available. Yet Spaniards of this period were hard to deter. They knew that spectacular mountain ranges lay behind the terrible shores, that a vast river emptied into the Caribbean from sources that might lie in the land of the Inca, for they did not know how far they were from Peru. Occasional pieces of gold or emeralds found on captured Indians encouraged all sorts of speculations. If one could penetrate the jungles and cross the mountains, he might find the land of El Dorado, where a gilded man threw chunks of gold in a lake and precious metals were as common as dirt. Hardships or not, men were willing to gamble their lives away to investigate these possibilities.

By the time Peru was being overrun, two small settlements stood on the Caribbean coast of the present Colombia, Santa Marta and Cartagena. The first was only a dreary town of huts, where a hundred or so sickly Spaniards raised a few animals and crops and listened to Indian rumors. Cartagena, whose peninsula and harbor would soon make it one of Spain's prize bases, had more energetic leadership in the person of its founder, Pedro de Heredia, who penetrated the interior for some distance in 1533 and looted Indian graves of vast amounts of gold. Heredia's great haul, which some say surpassed in value the first seizures of Cortés or Pizarro, did him little good, for he soon fell afoul of jealous associates or royal justice, the two often being confounded. In any event, it was clear that gold was to be had.

In 1535 a large expedition arrived in Santa Marta from Spain under the command of Alonso Fernández de Lugo, a wealthy man who had been governor of the Canary Islands. His first incursions into the interior produced the usual fatalities and sufferings but also an encouraging amount of gold. At this point Lugo's son elected to enjoy his life and sailed away to Spain with the treasure. The betrayed elder Lugo rallied from this blow by organizing a large expedition to march into the mountains, entrusting its command to Gonzalo Jiménez de Quesada, a lawyer who had come out with him from Spain and who seemed, despite his brief experience in the New World, a natural leader. The old man's judgment was sound. Quesada addressed himself to the assignment as though he were a seasoned conquistador, and in April 1536 he began one of the most admirable campaigns in the conquest of America.

It is not necessary to labor the point that the drenching rains, heat, fevers, serpents, insects, alligators, and cats of the jungle harassed the 800 Spaniards who set out with Quesada. Indians were plentiful as enemies, not as allies and porters as they had been for Cortés. At last the bedraggled party reached the wide Magdalena, where they finally established contact with a shred of the surviving naval force that had sailed from Santa Marta to meet them. Then up the river, across swamps, swollen tributaries, and forests. Despite a fearful death rate the invaders became encouraged. Land where villages, food, salt, emeralds, and gold were available seemed to be ahead. Their course now took them away from the river and upward through cool, steep mountain country. At last they debouched on a fertile, grassy plateau. If Quesada now had only 160 of his original 800 Spaniards, he was well supplied with horses, dogs, and guns.

"Pacification," as it was called, of the highlands where the Chibcha people lived did not prove particularly difficult, though much credit must go to Quesada's abilities and occasional displays of generosity. During the last months of 1537 and in 1538, he defeated or won over most of the tribes, who, it will be recalled, were not very numerous nor tightly organized. The foremost chief, the *Zipa*, was killed in a skirmish. Quesada marred his record by torturing to death the secondary ruler, the *Zaque*, who refused to reveal the location of his treasure. Of gold there was a plenitude, though of course not enough to satisfy the conquistadors, who were nonetheless pleased to find themselves alive after the long march and well endowed with treasure, food, cotton clothes, servants, and women. At this stage chiggers were their most detested enemies. Quesada appears to have kept his men well in hand and to have enjoyed their respect. Calling the beautiful plateau the "New Kingdom of Granada" and its capital "Santa Fe de Bogotá," he had by the end of 1538 brought the stamp of Spain to an area that long adorned the monarchy.

Then a most unusual situation took shape. Quesada learned that a Spanish force was approaching from the southwest. This was the army of Belalcázar, which had left Peru and pushed through Ecuador and up the fertile valley of the Cauca, now one of the richest areas of South America. Expecting to find El Dorado, Belalcázar was now approaching the New Kingdom. But this was not all. Even more surprising was the appearance of a party of Spaniards and Germans led by Nikolaus Federmann, agent of the great banking house of Welser, who had spent three years of dreadful hardships crossing the present area of Venezuela and then climbing the Andes at one of their steepest points, anticipating the famous march of Simón Bolívar in 1818–1819. Stranger yet was the fact that all three parties had almost exactly the same number of men, 160. By 1539 they had converged, the splendidly equipped and expensively dressed warriors from Peru, the cotton-clothed conquerors of Quesada, and the representatives of the rich Welsers, clad in animal skins. A squalid melee might have occurred had Quesada not exhibited tact and firmness and indicated that he was fully in control of matters. Besides, all three leaders were in a dubious legal position: Federmann having disobeyed orders by going off to find El Dorado and leaving his superior in the lurch; Belalcázar stretching beyond a tolerable point his authority from Pizarro in Peru; and Quesada, now learning that the elder Lugo was dead, determined to have himself named governor of the New Kingdom. In a statesmanlike fashion the three men agreed to leave their forces in the cool tableland of the Chibchas and to sail to Spain to lay their respective claims before Charles V.

Exemplary as this course seems, it was not altogether fortunate for the commanders. The Habsburgs were never noted for gratitude, and reports from Peru at this time seemed to show that conquistadors should not be trusted with government. Federmann was disposed of quickly. Turned over to his German superiors, he went to prison. Belalcázar was made governor of Popayán, the western area of modern Colombia. He went back to the scene of his conquests but was soon in trouble and died before it was straightened out. As for Quesada, he neglected to share the royal fifth with the king and revealed a frivolous side of his nature by dissipating his fortune in four countries. It was the junior Lugo who came out best, and all Quesada got after years of litigation was the title of marshal and permission to live in the land he had won for Spain. This he did, surviving until 1579. He is said to have written a great deal, but few of his efforts have come to light. If he was the finest of the conquistadors, as many believe, certain mysteries about his career justify a few reservations.

Early Colonization

THE new acquisition was usually called New Granada for the entire colonial period. It was for Simón Bolívar to do justice to the Discoverer by introducing the name, "Colombia," but not until 1863 was the modern republic officially and finally christened. The colony occupied a strategic position of great significance for the Spanish empire, along with Panama linking Peru to Spain. The Chibchas in the uplands rather quietly acquiesed as the Spanish system was fastened on their culture. Gold, emeralds, salt, fine woods, and later, platinum made the area valuable. The hot coastlands of the Caribbean had much promise for sugar planting, and with it, inevitably, Negro slavery. Popayán grew slowly but soundly as a ranching and farming region. In 1549 an *audiencia* was established in Santa Fe de Bogotá, and in 1563 New Granada became a captaincy-general. Cartagena developed into a major port and center for commerce and revenue.

Yet the area remained for most of the colonial period a second-rate possession, its disadvantages being powerful enough to retard its growth. Its government for nearly 200 years was chaotic, with teams of officials flowing in at intervals, finding things in bad shape and arresting their predecessors, and then succumbing to the same treatment as they were replaced. It was too far from Lima for effective supervision to be imposed. It was too easy for crown officials to cheat on revenue collecting and to abuse the natives. Communications were fantastically complicated. Santa Fe de Bogotá could scarcely be reached except by a long, eventful voyage up the Magdalena and then a very steep climb. Except for the area around Bogotá, the Indians were likely to be rebellious, and most of New Granada remained unoccupied by the Spaniards until the eighteenth century. Even the Caribbean coast, which developed rapidly once it was settled, tempted so many foreign enemies and pirates that it too became a lawless region of uncertain prosperity.

Formless and monotonous as the early colonial history of New Granada was, lines of fundamental growth can be discerned. The relatively small capital of Santa Fe de Bogotá gradually nurtured in its cool isolation a colony of cultured souls who appreciated literature and applied themselves to science and the arts. The fertile Cauca valley was the scene of a steady if slow spread of handsome estates and even small farmers. The sugar plantations on the coast were often productive, despite the danger from foreign depredators. Timber and mineral extraction went on regularly, and in the long run New Granada contributed substantially to the riches Spain derived from the New World. Above all, the missionaries tamed and Europeanized many Indians. Natural resources, slow economic growth, a steady mixture of the races, and intelligent leadership would eventually make New Granada a sound colony and a respected nation.

PARAGUAY AND THE ARGENTINE

The early explorers who coasted far down the Atlantic side of South America had found little to lure them into making full-scale penetrations of the interior, nothing like the Maya buildings in Yucatan or the Inca establishment at Túmbez. If the shores were free of deserts, jungles, and mountains, the natives were exceedingly primitive and obviously as inhospitable as they were poor. In 1516 the famous mariner Juan de Solís had attempted to set up a Spanish base beyond Portugal's side of the dividing line, a green flat area where the coast curves sharply to the west in a temperate region. The inhabitants on these grassy plains were wildly aroused and drove off the Spanish with many casualties, Solís himself being killed and eaten. Three years later Magellan's expedition examined the entire coastline of the future Argentina without being impressed. In 1526 Sebastian Cabot (as his former English employers had corrupted his Italian name, Gabotto) sailed for Charles V in the hope of locating a strait to the Pacific less difficult than Magellan's. Cabot penetrated the muddy estuary that is formed by the drainage system of the southeastern part of the continent, finding little but belligerent natives of the utmost poverty. Yet some tales he picked up regarding a silvery kingdom somewhere beyond, surely the Inca monarchy, led him to fix the grotesque name of Río de la Plata (silver) to this ugly arm of the sea. A few members of his party probably reached the Inca domain, only to look and flee, but this was long after Cabot had returned to Spain.

Not until 1535 were the Spanish in a mood to invest in another major attempt in the Platine region. This time they hoped to find a better route to Peru, which had just been conquered, and also to contain the Portuguese, who were showing signs of solidifying their claim to Brazil. An imposing nobleman, Pedro de Mendoza, received permission to fit out a large expedition at his own expense to create a colony. With one of the largest forces ever to sail from Spain to the Indies, Mendoza should have been well-prepared to accomplish this purpose. But his expedition suffered from the prime defect that nearly all of his men came straight from Europe without the years of conditioning in the New World that the men of Cortés and Pizarro had undergone. The Mendoza effort was a sad mess. The Indians had no treasure to be seized and they were defiant and skillful fighters. Despite the fabulous fertility of the land the expedition ran short of food. After two-thirds of his men perished in three years, Mendoza sent a party up the Paraná river and started home with the other survivors. He died on the voyage to Spain. All that remained of his fiasco was that party and a stockade named Buenos Aires on the breezy banks of the estuary.

The little group who sailed up the river had a better destiny. Led by Juan de Ayolas, they encountered the smiling land of Paraguay with its rather docile Guaraní Indians. Ayolas crossed the Gran Chaco and reached Peru but soon was killed. His heir was Domingo Martínez de Irala, who settled down in the town of Asunción and presently had a competent frontier colony operating. His men seemed reasonably contented in this warm, fertile country. The Indians worked for them, and polygamy was legalized by their thoughtful leader.

But their paradise was threatened in 1542 with the arrival of a new *adelantado* armed with the authority of Charles V. This was Alvar Núñez Cabeza de Vaca, whose remarkable wanderings in North America had inspired the ill-fated Coronado expedition and gained for himself the command in Paraguay. Cabeza de Vaca's fleet was in such poor condition he disembarked on the shores of Brazil and walked or rode a thousand miles westward to Asunción. For nearly two years he sought to rule the turbulent Spaniards, most of whom resented the supercession of Irala and, above all, the new *adelantado's* efforts to treat the Indians better. In 1544 they revolted and jailed Cabeza de Vaca, confining him cruelly for almost a year in a dark hut before shipping him down the river and to Spain, where it was some years before he cleared himself. Meanwhile, Irala resumed his rule and managed competently until his death in 1556.

Irala's colony was sturdy enough to survive, thanks largely to the agreeable Indians who served the Spanish. Early in the seventeenth century, as will be seen, the crown turned over large sections of Paraguay to the Jesuits for one of the most interesting and probably the largest efforts of all time to Europeanize an entire nation of barbarians.

The settlement at Buenos Aires disappeared soon after Mendoza founded it. Years later, in 1580, an armed party from Asunción reestablished the town largely to forestall compatriots who were infiltrating from Peru, but it remained a very unpretentious village for nearly two centuries, little more than a smuggling point where English and Portuguese traders brought wares that could be transported illegally into Chile, Paraguay, and even Peru.

A more vigorous development occurred in what is now northwestern Argentina, a semitropical land of high fertility and sedentary Indians who could be put to use by the Spaniards. Here a colony, briefly called Nueva Inglaterra in commemoration of Felipe II's marriage to Mary I of England, was begun by settlers from Peru. Later, the towns of Córdoba, Tucumán, and Mendoza grew up as colonists spilled over from Peru or Chile, some of them troublesome characters who had been expelled from the older provinces. Not too far from the silver districts of the Andes, these towns gradually took on the typical Spanish colonial character with white owners and Indian workers, agriculture and ranching, and the apparatus of government and church. Not Buenos Aires but Lima served as their connection with the government and economy of the Spanish monarchy.Until very late in the colonial period there was no intimation that the region now included in Argentina would one day comprise a great nation, that Buenos Aires would become the queen of Spanish-speaking cities.

In reviewing the conquest of South America by the Spanish, one is necessarily attentive to the deeds of brave and colorful individuals. In less than a decade following Pizarro's final departure from Panama, the conquistadors had overthrown powerful native rulers and fastened the hold of Charles V on the lands we know as Peru, Bolivia, Chile, Ecuador, Colombia, Paraguay, and Argentina. It was one of the most exhilarating outbursts of energy in the history of the human race, and certainly one of the most consequential. As long as individual heroism is admired, these events will command attention.

Similarly, the tragedy of the conquered peoples remains strong in the memory of Latin Americans today. This is true even if the Europeans often elevated the conditions of life for the Indians and brought them opportunities. In perspective, one can see that the continent of South America was congeries of thousands of clashing tribes and the home of a remarkable, if weird, despotism under the Incas. The Spanish moved in on this area with stunning effect and slowly reduced the disunity and violence under which the inhabitants had lived. Then a European-oriented despotism dominated the political and economic life of the population and finally gave it the standards and ideals of Western civilization. The colonial period saw the fructification of this process, after which Latin America was thrown open to other influences whose effects are working themselves out as destiny dictates.

8

The Founding of Brazil

Portugal's Foothold

COMMANDING the second Portuguese fleet to India, Pedro Alvares Cabral sailed or drifted much farther to the west than previous pioneers and on May 8, 1500 landed in Brazil. Much as his motives have been debated, it is likely that navigational reasons account for his going so far to the west, though it may be that he deliberately did so in order to lay claim to the suspected land mass. After probing around a bit and losing some of his men to cannibalistic natives, Cabral sent a ship back to Lisbon with the information that he had discovered a large island on Portugal's side of the Line of Tordesillas, a land he named Vera Cruz (True Cross), and proceeded on to India. While Portugal was a small country already absorbed in her trading posts in Africa and the prospects of commerce with India, King Manoel I fully intended to assert his rule over the new discovery, and he courteously informed Spain to this effect. The king changed its name to Santa Cruz (Holy Cross), and of course it was soon known that the land was no island at all but a part of the southern continent. Whether Cabral's landfall was a bona fide discovery or not has long been debated. Almost certainly Columbus, Ojeda, and Vespucci had touched some of the territory now included in the Brazilian nation, and the old question of Portuguese explorations of South America before 1492 remains seemingly insoluble.

In any case Portugal proceeded to establish her control. In 1501 a fleet carrying the articulate Amerigo Vespucci, whose writings would soon result in the fixing of his name to the New World, made further investigations. The chief attractions of the area were its woods, for the variety and quality of which Brazil is still unsurpassed. In particular, a scarlet or rose-colored wood useful for making cabinets and for red dyes was plentiful. It was from this brasilwood that the entire land eventually took its name. Furthermore, the Europeans were interested in the monkeys and parrots, nuts and fruits, exotic plants and insects, and the very primitive natives who might be enslaved or converted. Even if India offered the Portuguese fantastic opportunities, this Brazil was worth the trouble of occupying, if only to prevent other kingdoms from enjoying its riches and establishing themselves on the flanks of the route to the East.

For the first thirty years following Cabral's landing, Portugal devoted just enough attention to Brazil to accomplish this purpose. She lacked the resources for a more ambitious effort. Her ablest investors and mariners were absorbed in exploiting the India commerce, and such surplus effort as remained to deal with Brazil consisted of the second- or third-rate entrepreneurs who failed to establish themselves in the East. These men were mostly interested in bringing back brasilwood and curious plants or creatures for sale in Europe. This they did under a royal monopoly which assured the crown a generous share of their profits. In addition, Brazil was a convenient place to dump *degredados*, men who had been convicted, not necessarily for crime but for being dissenters or otherwise troublesome to the authorities. Often converted Jews or New Christians fell in this category, for the Portuguese were slowly following Spain's policy of making life unbearable for the supposed converts who remained in the country following the expulsion of the Jews. In 1502 a wealthy nobleman of Jewish background, Fernão de Noronha, received permission to trade in Brazil, and his profitable activities attracted modest numbers of New Christians to the territory.

It was apparent very early that Portugal was not to be allowed to develop her American colony at her own pace. France, already fretful over missing out on the great discoveries and openly contemptuous of the papal awards to Spain and Portugal, quickly intruded at the point of least resistance, which seemed to be Brazil. Enterprising shipmasters from Normandy and Brittany were encouraged by the French crown to exploit Brazil as well as they could, and for much of the sixteenth century some likelihood stood that France rather than Portugal would ultimately colonize eastern South America. Yet the effort was not on a sufficient scale to eliminate the Portuguese, who could on occasion give a good account of themselves on land or sea. Besides, Brazil was so large and its wood so plentiful that both French and Portuguese traders could operate without serious clashes. The English also displayed some aggressive intent in the region during the reign of Henry VIII, but they satisfied it by occasional trading expeditions. Portugal's suspicions of Spain, despite the Treaty of Tordesillas, remained chronic during these early years, but Spanish energies soon found sufficient outlets in Mexico and Peru.

During this first thirty-year period the Portuguese became acquainted with the Stone Age natives of Brazil, who, it will be remembered, were among the most backward in America. Of four major groupings, Tupí-Guaraní, Ge or Tapuyan, Arawak, and Carib, these Amerinds were in fact divided into hundreds of tribes with differing languages and habits. Perhaps a million lived in the area now embraced in Brazil. They usually fought one another regularly after the fashion of the Amerind primitives, and in time the Europeans were able to establish friendly relations with some tribes by helping them to defeat their hereditary enemies. The Portuguese complained, as the English would do in North America, that the French were devilishly effective in winning the alliances of natives. Whether this was altogether true or not, both the Portuguese and the French found it possible to build up a network of tribal allies that enabled them to achieve their commercial purposes. Of course, many Europeans were captured and eaten by the Indians, and on occasion the white men would voluntarily go native.

The economic stake of the Europeans grew as the licensed traders showed up year after year along the coast to fill their vessels with brasilwood, nuts, parrots, and monkeys. Such Indians as were friendly would greet the white men and bring them the products they desired in exchange for trinkets and other useful or curious items. In time, they might be persuaded to cut trees, dress logs, and load the ships on a barter arrangement. Little outright slavery prevailed at this time, though this institution seemed normal to the Portuguese after their long contacts with Africa. And, to be sure, the natives had slavery themselves as a result of their chronic wars. Barter, however, seemed the most reliable method for getting the work done. As the Indians absorbed some of the technique of the white men, so the Europeans learned something from the natives about hunting, gathering food, cooking, and medicine. Most enduring of all contributions from the Brazilian natives was the hammock, whose advantages in a hot climate were readily comprehended.

These early Portuguese sailors, traders, and *degredados* found Brazil a sexual paradise, very much as the Spaniards had the Caribbean islands. Unless a tribe were irrevocably hostile to the invaders, its women were likely to greet the disembarking white men with overwhelming cordiality. Since a general polygamy prevailed among the Indians, the native men seldom seemed to object. From the first a half-breed stock developed rapidly, a group called *mamelucos,* or mamelukes, by the Portuguese. As time went on, the daughters of the Portuguese and Indians made acceptable wives or concubines for later settlers. Yet the amount of Indian stock in modern Brazil is probably very small compared to the mestizo countries of Spanish America, for the Negro was soon to displace the Indian to a very high degree. Brazil early came to enjoy a reputation among the Portuguese as a good place to visit or live, and the growth of the mameluke element facilitated the establishment of Portugal's control over much of the coast. The most famous instance of this process came about through the prodigious Diogo Alvarés, who took the native name of Caramurú. Shipwrecked near the later site of the capital, Bahia, in 1510, Caramurú became a ruler over a group of Indians and reputedly sired incredible numbers of offspring. For more than a generation the coastal region under his control was known to be a safe place for Portuguese to land and do business, as opposed to other areas where natural or French-incited hostility would make disembarkation dangerous.

The Experiment with Grants

PORTUGAL had probably devoted as much attention to Brazil as she could afford early in the sixteenth century. By 1530 it was apparent that a more strenuous effort was going to be necessary if French woodcutters and traders were to be contained. Uneasiness with respect to Spanish and English intentions and a heightened awareness of Brazil's strategic importance to the India route also contributed to a more vigorous policy. In that year the Portuguese king, João III, dispatched a five-ship expedition with about 400 persons commanded by Martin Afonso de Souza to drive out the French and to survey the possibilities of strengthening the colony. This force founded a definite colony, as opposed to the more or less improvised trading settlements, below the red bluffs at São Vicente, which is not far from the present-day metropolis of São Paulo, and in January 1531 reconnoitered the beautiful Guanabara Bay where Rio de Janeiro was eventually built. On his return to Portugal Souza worked out with the monarch a thoroughgoing plan to transform Brazil from a mere trading area into a strong colony. The time seemed opportune, for the India commerce was suffering from a relapse after too rapid expansion, and it was known that the Spanish were contemplating a strong effort in the region of the Río de la Plata to the south of Brazil.

The scheme was a pragmatic mixture of feudalism and early capitalism, based on common sense and on Portugal's experience in the Azores and Madeira. Her claim along the Atlantic coast would be divided into fifteen captaincies of varying size, all of them stretching from the ocean back to the Line of Tordesillas. As it turned out, these captaincies were awarded to twelve parties, called *donatários*, who were wealthy men, in some cases nobles, willing to make the investment. The *donatário* was expected to finance himself in obtaining ships, soldiers, supplies, artisans, and colonists. He was to make his grant a true settlement, self-sufficient and capable of defending itself against foreigners. He could make subgrants to followers of his own choice and had almost a free hand in governing his captaincy, collecting taxes, and administering justice. The Portuguese crown reserved the right to pass on death penalties and to inspect fiscal affairs, as well as to collect the royal fifth, tithes, and customs duties and to maintain a few monopolies. The rights of the prospective colonists were explicated in some detail so as to make settlement attractive. Since the grants to the *donatários* were hereditary and could be revoked only in the event of high crime or rank neglect, and since the captaincies could trade with Catholic foreigners, the system might, had things gone as planned, have resulted in the creation of thriving, semi-independent states.

The *donatário* system was largely a failure, at least from an administrative point of view. Between 1534 and 1549 six of the captaincies achieved some success in luring settlers to Brazil and in creating towns, food farms, ranches, lumber businesses, and even sugar plantations. But by the end of a dozen or so years, all but three of the fifteen original grants were bankrupt. The task had been underestimated. Several *donatários* had not even gotten started. Others had run out of funds, for the capitalists with the most resources had long since invested in the Far East, and only those with limited credit or funds were available for the Brazilian venture. Too, some of the 3,000 or so colonists complained to the crown of abuses at the hands of the *donatários*, and Lisbon was becoming sensitive to clerical criticism about the enslavement of Indians. (As usual, Portugal was following Spain, where a great furor over this issue had led to the New Laws of 1542.) The French were by no means expelled from Brazil; in fact, they seemed as bold as ever. The Spanish had won Peru, Chile, New Granada, and Paraguay and made a major, though disastrous, effort to colonize Buenos Aires in the years since Sousa's visit of 1530. It was apparent that Portugal needed to exert herself more strenuously if she was to retain Brazil, a matter all the more important to her now that the prosperity of the Oriental trade had begun to wane. Yet the fact remains that dozens of towns had been founded, a few thousand settlers had gone to Brazil, and sugar cultivation had opened up very promising prospects. The *donatário* system was not, when considered in perspective, a total failure but a large step in assuring Portuguese civilization of a firm foothold in America. It has often been observed that the Portuguese worked their way along the coast of Brazil like crabs, unlike the Spanish, who plunged for the rich interiors. The crabs won a good hold, it must be admitted.

The Captaincy-General

IN 1549 João III sent Tomé de Souza, one of his ablest officers, to take over the twelve captaincies that had failed or never gotten under way and to assume political authority over those which remained, notably at São Vicente in the south and Pernambuco in the eastern corner. With him went about a thousand colonists, soldiers, and *degredados*, and soon afterward the queen thoughtfully dispatched shiploads of orphan girls who were expected to become wives of the settlers. Tomé de Souza's directive was formidable. He was to make the colony pay, stop the enslavement of the natives, and keep the French out. His achievements matched his assignment in most respects. As captain-general, he set up his capital at Bahia, where the useful Caramurú welcomed him. This mud-walled village became the seat of government for most of Brazil for 200 years and developed into a large, colorful city now known as São Salvador. It was a good choice, for it had a fine harbor and was located midway between São Vicente, in the area where the population, later known as *paulistas*, were already showing the dynamism that has made them the marvel of South America, and Pernambuco, where the sugar industry was in the first stages of a great development. Souza began to take over the lapsed captaincies, though one line of the *donatários* survived far into the eighteenth century. He provided as strong government and as much direction for the long string of settlements as circumstances would allow.

In one respect Souza faltered before a problem which defeated many another administrator in colonial America: the reconciliation of the commands of the crown and the Church with the desires of the settlers in dealing with the natives. As long as the Portuguese merely appeared in Brazil at odd intervals to acquire wood and other native articles, it was usually possible to obtain Indian labor by means of barter. Now that farms and sugar plantations were being established by permanent colonists, the question of labor loomed large. The Portuguese had not the slightest intention of performing this hard work. Even in temperate zones they had long scorned manual toil, and their contacts with African slaves had fortified their belief that physical labor should be carried out only by colored peoples. To be sure, the climate of much of Brazil also made it difficult for Europeans to adjust to a strenuous life even if they had been disposed to do so. But the Indians did not care to work, either. Indian men were hunters and warriors, not farmers. Their womenfolk were accustomed to homemaking and in some cases to limited farming. Yet the Portuguese tried to create a labor force of the native males, and they failed badly, as the Spaniards had done in the West Indies. The only recourse seemed to be to enslave the Indians, but this policy antagonized the natives as a whole, and, besides, the Indians often died rather than work.

Into this perplexing situation now intruded the awakened conscience of the Portuguese crown and, more important, the determination of the Church to prevent Indian slavery. The instruments of the latter were among the passengers Souza brought with him in 1549, six members of the new Company of Jesus, headed by the redoutable Manoel de Nóbrega. The king of Portugal now enjoyed powers over the Church similar to those of the king of Spain. The Jesuits were more than willing to carry out his orders to save the Indians from slavery. Nóbrega, like so many of the early Jesuits, was remarkably successful in converting the natives to Christianity and in persuading them to abandon their nomadic ways in favor of living in towns supervised by the order. Here they would learn to dress like Europeans and to employ the techniques of a more advanced culture. Curiously, they found it easier to give up polygamy than cannibalism, which remained a problem in Brazil for a long time. Yet, the mission system sometimes facilitated the spread of epidemics and undermined such culture as the Indians had without necessarily giving them a substitute. While Nóbrega was making great headway in northern Brazil, the Jesuit José de Anchieta was performing a similar service in the southern area, making wholesale conversions and resettlements and finding time for compiling a Tupí grammar and for creative literature.

Both Nóbrega and Anchieta are heroic figures in the history of Brazil for their services to the Indians. But the colonists learned to detest them, the Jesuits, and missionaries in general. Indians shielded in church-protected villages were unavailable for labor. Tomé de Souza wrestled with the dilemma without success, though at times he modified official policy in favor of the colonists, and his successors were to waver between carrying out orders of the crown and the urgent demands of the Brazilian whites.[1] The introduction of Negro slaves, which may have begun on a small scale in the 1530's and which grew to a great volume by the 1570's, served to satisfy some of the colonial clamor for a labor force and, strangely enough, the sensibilities of the monarchs and the clergy.

In 1555 France responded to Portugal's vigorous activity in Brazil by dispatching about 600 colonists, some of them convicts, to establish a permanent settlement in the area of Rio de Janeiro. This effort has speculative interest in what might have happened had France been successful in this area. It also draws attention as an early experiment in religious toleration. At that time the Huguenots were becoming power-

1. As in the Spanish colonies, Indian enslavement was permissible if the Indians were cannibals or if they were captured in a "just war." The meaning of the latter term, especially, could be stretched according to the pressures of the time.

ful in France but were far from acquiring domination. The commander of this group, Nicholas Durand de Villegaignon, was interested in Protestantism when he left France and was backed by important Huguenots. At first he seems to have been mainly concerned, as was proper, in setting up a sound colony called "Antarctic France," a rather inappropriate name for the humid Rio de Janeiro. Once his party had landed he sent back for reinforcements and is said to have written a letter to John Calvin, the eminent Protestant leader. Several Huguenot preachers and a few more colonists arrived, thus setting the stage for an adventure in tolerance.

The Portuguese settlers reacted fiercely to this French incursion, but they were long unable to do more than prevent its expansion. Convinced that Villegaignon was truly a Protestant and was bent on winning Brazil for his heresy, the Jesuits Nóbrega and Anchieta directed great numbers of their Indian wards in attacks on the French settlement. It is altogether possible the French might have resisted indefinitely had their home government supported them energetically and if they had refrained from religious strife. But the monarch was suspicious of Villegaignon, and in Brazil the Catholics and Huguenots divided into two warring camps. Each accused Villegaignon of betrayal, probably with reason, for he played a strange game. In 1560 the able Portuguese captain-general Mem de Sá broke up the principal French settlement, but not until 1567 were all of the intruders expelled. Remnants of the colony finally wound up in Maranhão, an inaccessible province on the northern coast, where they remained until 1615.

Brazil was growing steadily during the mid-sixteenth century. True, she offered no sudden riches like India, Mexico, or Peru to fortunate conquerors. But word circulated in Portugal that a good living might be gained, or at any rate a good time, by young men who were willing to risk the ocean trip and the uncertainties of the New World. The white population growth was sufficient so that by 1580 Brazil had perhaps 35,000 Portuguese and as many mamelukes (who, speaking Portuguese and being Catholics, could count as European-oriented) as well as thousands of Negro slaves and Indians who were under immediate Portuguese control. The towns were small and squalid, for the great fortunes were still to be made. But they enjoyed regular contact with Portugal and occasional commerce with other nations, and they even felt the influence of the India trade, for such articles as parasols, porcelain, and Eastern spices arrived by way of Lisbon. Bahia was easily the largest city, with sixty-two churches and three monasteries.

The economic foundations of the colony were sound, in some respects more so than the envied Spanish settlements which were built upon minerals and more civilized native states. Wood was and remained a source of steady business activity, for the European market for dyes and high-class timber steadily grew. Cattle, hogs, sheep, and horses were multiplying. Profitable commerce could be enjoyed in such articles as tobacco, cotton, cacao, pepper, citrus fruits, and even in whales. Vineyards could flourish in Brazil as in Portugal, and with them wine and brandy. The revenues of the colony were perhaps only one-tenth those the king of Spain derived from his American possessions, but then Portugal was only one-sixth as populous as Spain and had many other resources. Above all, by the last quarter of the century, loomed the sugar industry. This article was easy to cultivate in the vast eastern corner of Brazil, around Pernambuco, Olinda and Bahia, and already enormous estates were taking shape. Separated from each other by the still-plentiful woods and jungles, the owners were able to live in almost complete isolation from neighbors and government: the king's law stopped at the gates of the plantation. As time went on, these plantation owners assumed a position of autocracy over their families, workers, and slaves, and of defiance toward the government. Royal officials or traders in the coastal towns concerned them but little, only when they exported their sugar products or purchased slaves and European or Asian articles.

The importance of this monoculture and the attitudes that went with it can scarcely be overstressed. They dominated the atmosphere of Brazil throughout the colonial and in much of the national period. They are not entirely extinct even today in northeastern Brazil. As significant as the creation of an enriched landed class, which gradually became more cultured and elegant, was the social system over which they presided. As in the Spanish empire, it was one in which a natural tension existed between the Brazilian-born white and the peninsular immigrant, one where the half-breed mameluke held himself superior to the Indian but was not accepted as white, and above all, one which the Negro influenced more and more, as slaves were imported from Africa. It was, as it has been aptly called, the society of the big house and the slave hut. Apart from the sugar plantation were the little villages on the coast, the Indian missions of the interior, and the rather feeble apparatus of the government.

The "Babylonian Captivity"

THE sensational expansion of Portugal since the days of Prince Henry the Navigator had brought the influence of the little kingdom not only to the long coastline of Brazil but into the Azores, Madeira, and Cape Verde Islands, to both the Atlantic and Indian shores of Africa, to India, and deep into the so-called Far East,[2] where the Spice Islands,

2. A term often resented by its inhabitants, who inquire, "Far from what?"

Formosa, China, and Japan were penetrated. The epic of Portuguese activity stands as one of the most amazing explosions of energy in the long history of imperialism. If the exultant pride and wealth of the Lusitanian monarchy anticipated that of Britain at a later date, other monuments stood too: the forced and unequal trade the Asians were compelled to accept at the hands of Europeans, the commercial torpor of the once-active Italian cities, and the terrible traffic of Africans to the western hemisphere. While Portugal's achievement in Brazil had its seamy side, it was far more constructive and permanent than the others.

The back of this far-flung monarchy was broken, as we have noted, in 1580, with the extinction of the royal house of Avis. Felipe II of Spain made short work of the dispute over the inheritance by invading Portugal and persuading some of the nobles to proclaim him king. For sixty years the monarchs of Spain were also rulers of Portugal and her world-wide empire, except for a few years in the Azores, where a rival claimant held out. The Spanish Habsburgs generally respected their vows to regard Portugal and her possessions as independent of Spain. This is not to say the connection was popular in Portugal, where fear of Spanish pressure was keen and the name of the period, the "Babylonian Captivity," suggests an unhappy memory. Apart from the ignominy of having to refer to Madrid for ultimate decisions in important matters, the Portuguese suffered grievously by inheriting Spain's enemies, who regarded the Portuguese empire as fair pickings. The English, for so long the allies of Portugal, carried out seizures at sea and occasional attacks on cities or trading posts, but for most of the "Babylonian Captivity" their strongest aggressions were directed at Spain. The French had harassed the Portuguese all along and continued to do so under the joint monarchy. Most serious of all were the Dutch, whose rebellion against Spain in the 1560's had brought strength and riches to the Protestant provinces. After Spain compelled Portugal to ban Dutch traders, the Lowlanders undertook the seizure of Portugal's main possessions, as will be seen.

The Spanish monarchs did not alter the government of the Portuguese empire, but they tightened it up and gave it more energetic direction. Spaniards have always regarded the Portuguese as too easygoing and neglectful, and it was natural that a new, serious look at the government of Brazil should result in improvements. The captain-general at Bahia was required to display more vigor in collecting revenues and enforcing the law. Other provinces in Brazil were not so much under his control but directly under that of Lisbon, or perhaps Madrid. Governors were systematically appointed and with them *capitães-mores*, whose functions were a great deal like those of Spanish *corregidores* in Peru. In 1604 a Council of Indies was established in Portugal to unify the rule of the overseas empire somewhat as its sister council in Madrid acted for the Spanish empire.[3] It is not surprising that the Spanish kings took the inquisitorial activities of the Holy Office more seriously than their Portuguese predecessors had and that more persecutions took place, though no Holy Office was set up in Brazil and accused persons were usually sent to Europe for trial. The Spanish also tightened up the Portuguese system of ship caravans in 1611 so that it resembled more the rigid Spanish fleet system. Spain's naval power was also available to assist the Portuguese. To be sure, it was needed more than ever before, for Portugal's enemies had multiplied. Brazilian town councils, the *cámaras*, which perhaps enjoyed more authority than their counterparts in the Spanish empire, the *cabildos*, functioned on a more orderly basis under the Habsburgs. In fine, Brazil received stronger and perhaps better government as a result of the Spanish connection, but no fundamental changes in structure occurred.

Of the far-reaching effects of the "Babylonian Captivity" two stand out as the most important: 1) Portugal acquired Spain's foes, who sheared her of most of her empire in the Far East and wrought great damage to her possessions in Africa and Brazil, so that Portugal never again enjoyed the position she occupied in 1580, and 2) the Line of Tordesillas no longer having any relevance, the Amazon basin was opened to Portuguese penetration, though it really lay on Spain's side. Curiously, the Portuguese were generally able to keep Spaniards out of their empire except when they needed help. On the other hand, the Portuguese (among them many crypto-Jews and New Christians) fairly swarmed into Spain and the Spanish empire in America, upsetting Spanish trade channels and overtaxing the Inquisition.

THE NEGRO IN BRAZIL

The subject of Negro influence in Brazil must be approached with diffidence, for so many of the basic facts are unknown and unknowable and because so many myths becloud the subject. As for the facts, we are still largely ignorant of the history of Africa and its peoples, despite the great and increasing claim it makes on our attention. It is revealing that anthropologists, with their concern for customs, culture, and folkways, have more to say on the subject than historians, with their predilection for documentary evidence. The Brazilians have not helped matters by their gesture of burning the records dealing with the slave trade and the slave system, which they did as a way of expiating the shameful past soon after the republic was set up in 1889. We have little to go on

3. This council lasted for only ten years, but it was revived after Portugal recovered her independence.

with respect to the history of African tribes and states, the mechanics of the slave trade from Africa to the Americas, and the way the institution of slavery functioned in Brazil. Furthermore, the student must contend with legends, which may contain truth but which are often misleading. Among these would be the Portuguese myths that a favor was done the Negroes by removing them from pagan African slavery to Christian Brazilian slavery, or that the native Africans were so low in culture that slavery in Brazil represented an advancement for them. Countering these attitudes is the tendency to glorify the Negro by insisting that he was often superior to the European in civilization and that it was the African who really built Brazil. In Brazil itself writers divide radically in attempting to minimize the Negro contribution as something to be ashamed of or in magnifying it out of all proportion. When knowledge is so scanty, passion and racialism can interpret the history of Brazil as they will without fear of refutation.

Africans were forcibly imported into Brazil at a steady rate from the 1530's to the 1850's. Responsible students differ widely in their estimates of the numbers, ranging from 3,000,000 to 18,000,000 for the three centuries. At the time Brazil became independent, in 1822, a number of contemporaries guessed that half her population was full-blooded Negro. Now it is claimed that the proportion is something like one-tenth, keeping in mind that in Brazil a Negro is defined as a black person with no white ancestry and not, as in much of the United States, as a person with some Negro blood. It may also be assumed that few if any of the Africans came to Brazil willingly and that they performed nearly all of the hard work in the colony. Their influence on Brazilian habits, speech, attitudes, and culture can only be estimated with hesitancy, but it must have been very great.

Long before Brazil loomed as an insatiable market for African labor the Portuguese had been involved in the slave trade. From the first expedition of Prince Henry the Navigator down the west coast of Africa (and probably before) the Portuguese were eager to enslave the pagan or Islamized black people they encountered. Much of the trade seems to have been easy to manage. The various African kingdoms or tribes fought one another most of the time, the way the American Indians and the Europeans did. Nearly every ruler had slaves in the persons of prisoners of war. In exchange for bangles and trinkets he might turn them over to Portuguese ship captains, who would bring them home and sell them. Also, parents sometimes sold their children in the hope they would go to lands where they would have enough food. It is remarkable how few people thought the traffic was immoral or un-Christian. And it was convenient to have slaves to work the fields of the richer landlords, who found the native Portuguese disinclined to labor. As the trade proved so lucrative, more contacts were established, and finally regular stations, or *feitoras*, dotted the African coasts, so that slavers could count on a supply of human beings each voyage. No doubt the time came when the whites had to exert pressure on the tribal leaders to fill their quotas, or to engage in slave-catching expeditions themselves.

Apart from the profit inherent in these activities, there was the threat of competition from Spanish, English, Dutch, or French intruders who desired to participate, As Brazil, the West Indies, and the English colonies in North America developed, the sinister business became exceedingly valuable. The privilege of participating in it was worth large sums to the dealers who purchased permission from their respective governments. Yet Portugal generally maintained her lead in the traffic until well after the Napoleonic wars. By that time Britain, alone of the great powers, had become convinced that it was immoral and began to drive the slavers out of business.

The Africans preferred by planters in Brazil were able-bodied young men, who would count as a "piece." Youths, women, cripples, or older men might have to be combined to compose a "piece." Women were supposed to be young and healthy enough to bear future slaves, but their desirability went beyond that consideration, since the white owner liked to reserve the most attractive young Negresses for his own attentions. Once purchased or seized from the African holder, the Negroes would be branded and baptized. The conjunction of these two operations appears barbarous to the modern man, but the slave dealers piously said and perhaps believed that baptism was a benefit to compensate for any suffering in this life. Next would come the most frightful experience of all, the voyage in the hold of a slave ship. The dealers naturally wanted to deliver alive as many of their passengers as they could, but they persisted in overcrowding the ships to an inhuman degree, for the profits were enormous. If an epidemic broke out, the fatalities might wipe out the profit from the voyage. A storm might cause terror to the extent of producing mass insanity. On occasion the Negroes would gain control of the ship and return to Africa or take their chances elsewhere (Sometimes a crew of only ten white men ran a ship with hundreds of slaves). Loneliness, grief, fear, anger, suicides, and seasickness surely characterized most of the tragic voyagers. Yet on the trade went, for more than 300 years. Conditions on the slave ships were little better in the nineteenth century than in the fifteenth or sixteenth.

Once in Brazil the Africans would be displayed in public marts, where bidding would result in sales and in the division of families and friends, or, one may hope, occasionally in their reunion. Whether the master was kind or harsh, whether the conditions of life were better or worse than in Africa, the abrupt uprooting of the Negroes, the branding and the humiliating voyage, the sale and adjustment to a new situation must have been a tragedy, repeated millions of times, that lies beyond description. One of the most poignant aspects about it is that such experiences usually befell the flower of Africa, the captured young warriors and the most attractive young women.

A reconsideration of the role of the Negro has led modern Brazilians to understand what the planters always knew, that most of the Africans were at least semi-civilized and that they possessed a wide variety of skills. Few of them were primitive savages on the low level of the native Indians of Brazil. The Negroes from the vast Sudan area of western Africa were the most numerous and the most important in Brazil. As a group they adapted quickly and well to life in the New World. Already affected by Moslem civilization, to the extent that a substantial number were Mohammedans, they were usually monotheists. Their governments were organized monarchies perhaps as advanced as those of the Inca or Aztecs. Most of them knew something about agriculture or handling cattle and other domesticated animals. Often they had some experience in systematic trade and in working with iron, which even the most advanced American Indians lacked. The Bantus of the Congo and East Africa were perhaps on a lower level than the Sudanese, but they were skilled in agriculture and in animal husbandry. And there were more backward types, the Kaffirs and Hottentots, the Bushmen and others. Bringing to Brazil their habits, knowledge, and skills, these Negroes were no helpless savages, but valued immigrants who often knew more than the Portuguese did.

The Portuguese (and the English, Spanish, Dutch, and French in the Americas) were certainly glad to receive these human cargoes, and they paid handsome prices to obtain them. The Negro was usually accustomed to a hot and humid climate and would labor where the Indian could not and the Portuguese would not. Generally stronger, larger, and more healthy than the racial types already in the colony, he was regarded as better-natured and more extrovertive than other laborers. When placed on a sugar plantation, he was likely to adjust to life in the manorial village and add a great deal to its gaiety. It was usually not difficult to teach him to cultivate sugar and to operate the sugar mills, which sometimes required the cooperative labor of a hundred men. In time he would learn some Portuguese and pick up a little of the terminology and ritual of the Catholic Church. Or, the Negro immigrant might be sent to one of the grain farms or ranches in the south, where he was also likely to prove useful. In time, the abler and more cooperative slaves might assume duties of a managerial nature, while others might sink into the most menial and degrading occupations. This general picture of Negro adaptability in colonial Brazil needs many qualifications and exceptions, but the eagerness of the whites to import Africans is convincing testimony that the Negroes were highly useful.

The life of slaves in Brazil struck observers who had some opportunity to make comparisons as being less harsh than in other slaveocracies. Whether this impression is altogether sound or not, several factors lend it plausibility. Brazil resembled in climate and geography much of Africa from which the Negroes came. The Portuguese generally are and have been less color-conscious than the English, Dutch, or French, and therefore more likely to regard the Negro as something more than a subhuman, despite his status as a slave. The languid atmosphere of colonial Brazil, its low pressure, slow pace, and often the slothfulness, negligence, and indifference of persons in authority—all of these may have made life easier for the slave, at least when compared to the more energetic, businesslike colonies to the north. Certainly, all was not gloom in the slave compounds. Dances of a type still in vogue, songs full of joy and love of life, romance and mating, exuberant religious practices, and such indicate that elements of happiness available to most of mankind were not denied expression in Brazil.

And yet, no one can seriously question that slavery was a hateful system in Brazil. It permeated the colony and dragged down her moral and cultural plane. Already inclined to be preoccupied with sex, the Portuguese slaveowner, living in the tropical isolation of northeastern Brazil, was likely to take advantage of any Negress to whom he was attracted. White boys would usually have their first erotic experiences with Negro girls and were likely, regardless of marriage, to continue promiscuous relations as they willed. Brazil earned and has never entirely lost the reputation of being the most licentious country in the world. Vast numbers of illegitimate children swarmed about the plantations and towns. Mulattoes for the most part, they would be free if their white fathers owned them and chose to grant manumission. With no fixed place in society, they would probably drift about the country as they became grown, neither slave nor owner, and likely to contribute to the atmosphere of a sex-obsessed society.

White women in Brazil had, at least according to tradition, a dull time of it. Daughters of white couples were likely to wind up in convents, for a certain prestige attached to families which placed the most girls in the religious orders. If they married, it was at a very early age. While they themselves were rigidly shielded, even to barred windows, from contacts with males of any race and generally under the Islamic type of seclusion suffered by Portuguese women, their husbands probably had free access to many Negro women. By the time she was thirty, the colonial wife might be fat and oily from the foods she ate, no longer needed to bear children, neglected and embittered. Such a white woman might tyrannize female Negro slaves who worked about her house. Yet even domestic autocracy could be defeated by passive resistance or by the infuriating mock stupidity the slaves were often good at displaying. It is said that many a colonial wife could be reduced to nervous collapse by the clever disobedience of her slaves.

Slavery debased Brazil in other ways. The tendency of the white men not to work was, of course, encouraged. Instincts of cruelty or sadism could be indulged, for there was no clerical or governmental authority pervasive enough to protect the slaves from mistreatment. Furthermore, many of the unwilling African immigrants were proud men, perhaps royal or noble figures in their own lands. They were often able to rebel successfully and to run away, to help release other members of their tribes and to take to the jungles, where they organized colonies called *quilombos*. Then it might be the hapless Indians who would be enslaved or the whites who were kidnaped and held for ransom. While isolated instances of slave rebellions were frequent in the history of colonial Brazil, no large-scale upheavals ever shook it. This was true even after Negroes were armed and organized to fight Indians, foreign invaders, or other Negroes. And not until the nineteenth century was there an emancipation movement of any consequence in Brazil.

The Dutch in Brazil

THE stunning success of the Dutch on the high seas during the last years of the sixteenth century made the loose confederation of the Protestant states of the Netherlands the chief naval power of the world. Fighting for independence against Felipe II was the challenge that brought forth an incredible outburst of energy. The rise of the Dutch was as sensational as the emergence of Portugal itself at an earlier date, and of Japan at a later one. With Spain badly mauled in European and Caribbean waters, the turn of Portugal soon came. Now the dynamic Lowlanders saw themselves as the true inheritors of the Hispanic empires, their ambition and greed justified to themselves by the Protestant religious cause they championed. Around 1600, fleets of Dutchmen penetrated the Indian Ocean on a very large scale and found the Portuguese defenses flabby. Capturing hundreds of galleons and carracks with little effort, the Dutch proceeded in 1602 to organize the East India Company under official sponsorship to take over the main sources of the Oriental trade. Establishing a headquarters at Batavia, in Java, they blockaded or seized the principal Portuguese ports at Goa, Malacca, Macao, Mozambique, and Ceylon. The Spanish and Portuguese fought back, sometimes with great skill, but during the first half of the seventeenth century Portugal was all but ousted from the Far East and the

Indian Ocean. Bits of Africa were also detached from her control, including the tip of the continent named the Cape of Good Hope. By the end of the "Babylonian Captivity," Portugal possessed only dots on the map, which had long since lost their value as reminders of the once-fabulous *Asia portuguesa*.

Brazil could not be expected to escape the attentions of the Dutch. For many years individual Dutchmen had traded there with little interference, and the general outlines of the colony were known in Amsterdam. Until the end of the twelve-year's truce in 1621, half or more of the goods which reached Brazil were of Dutch origin, having arrived via legal channels. The sugar industry and the profitable slave trade, as well as other commercial opportunities, were enticing. Spain and Portugal combined were demonstrating an inability to keep foreign depredators out of the Caribbean early in the seventeenth century. And so a group of merchants and capitalists authorized by Their High Mightinesses, the Seven Provinces, and by His Highness, the Prince of Orange, organized the Dutch West India Company in 1621. The Dutch hoped, of course, to strip Portugal in the New World as they had in the Far East.[4] If they could establish a strong foothold in Brazil, they might be in a position to plan the conquest of Peru with all its silver. If a clinching argument was needed, the early stages of the Thirty Years' War seemed to assure Iberian preoccupation in Europe for a long time.

In 1624 the first heavy blow was struck. Holland's brilliant admirals, Jacob Willekens and Piet Hein, in command of twenty-six ships and 3,300 men, sailed into Bahia and seized it handily. This was a staggering loss for the Iberian powers. The Dutch had hoped Spain would not be overly concerned over a misfortune to Portugal, for she had taken philosophically the loss of the great Portuguese port of Ormuz in the Persian Gulf to the English, and they believed the colonists in Bahia would welcome them as liberators. Instead, the Spanish rallied and sent to Brazil the largest force they had ever dispatched to America—fifty-two ships and 12,000 men led by Fadrique de Toledo. To the chagrin of the Dutch this expedition proved equal to the task and ejected the invaders. Then came the dreary business of punishing the Brazilians who had collaborated with the Dutch, including some who had revealed Protestant or Jewish sympathies. Piet Hein and the tough Lowlanders returned in 1627 and plundered Bahia and seized sugar boats by the hundreds. Then, in 1628, came Piet Hein's famous capture of the Spanish treasure fleet off Cuba, an event which enabled the Dutch West India Company to declare a 75 per cent dividend and cost the hapless Spanish commander his head after a lengthy trial in Spain. Thus enriched, the

4. The company was also involved in settling the Hudson River Valley and other areas in the vicinity of New York.

company sent sixty-seven ships and 7,000 men late in 1629 to the sugar area of northeastern Brazil. For two years the Brazilians, with Spanish-Portuguese assistance, contained the Dutch to a relatively limited area, but in 1631 the invaders broke out and overran approximately one-fourth of the settled area in Brazil, including parts of seven captaincies. The Iberian powers were unable now to do more than harass the Dutch, but they prudently strengthened Bahia so that it stood up under repeated attacks.

With the richest part of Brazil under control, the Dutch undertook with characteristic energy to organize a permanent colony. This time they were wise enough to refrain from antagonizing the Catholic feelings of the inhabitants, and they enunciated and generally practiced a policy of toleration except for the Jesuits. Still, many Brazilians forsook their homes, burned their crops, and withdrew to "free" territory. Perhaps 8,000 of them did so, but a larger number remained in the conquered area. Meanwhile, Dutchmen and Jews, the latter descendants of those who had been expelled from Spain and Portugal and welcomed by the company to live as traders in the colony, arrived by the hundreds. Religious friction occurred despite the official policy, and occasional Dutch efforts to make their authority respected brought charges of atrocity on the part of the Catholic Brazilians. Naturally, the Catholics wondered how long they would be tolerated if the immigration continued. Some of the conflicts between Dutch and Portuguese were neither religious, nationalistic, nor economic. The Portuguese were disgusted by the gluttony and excessive drinking of the Dutch, who on their part could not appreciate the casualness with which the abstemious Portuguese committed murder and adultery.

In 1637 the company stepped up its efforts by sending out as governor Johan Maurits, Prince-Count of Nassau and one of the renowned commanders of the Thirty Years' War. Maurits, who was captivated by Brazil from the beginning, expected to make the company's great foothold permanent through continued investment and immigration and to enlarge it. The Portuguese element would be treated decently, but it would have to accept absorption in a predominately Dutch Brazil. A key to the situation was the slave trade. Already the Dutch had seized hundreds of Portuguese ships. Now they dislodged their opponents from several of the major slave procurement bases in Africa, notably those in the Gold Coast and Angola. The Dutch imported slaves in a volume the Portuguese had never attained. Furthermore, they treated the Indians better in the hope of winning them to the new regime. Under Maurits the Dutch West India Company enjoyed several good years of high profits. The sugar business functioned effectively, and the Dutch were in a far better position to sell the much-desired sweet than the Portuguese had ever been. Energy and direction were apparent in the government and economy alike. Dirty coastal towns took on a Dutch appearance, with scrubbed sidewalks and steps, neat brick buildings, clipped trees and hedges, canals, and parks. Like other colonizing powers, the Dutch ignored the climate and attempted to make their settlements look as much like home as they could. Meanwhile, Spain and Portugal gathered a mighty expedition of eighty-seven ships and 6,000 or more men. In 1639–1640 this force disintegrated during the protracted battle of Itamaraca. Spain had no naval power of significance for another century.

Still, Brazil was not destined to become Dutch. Bahia had managed to maintain itself, valiantly fighting off the armies of Negro slaves and Indians Maurits sent against it. The sugar lords in Dutch territory remained Portuguese in sympathy and sullen under the efficient Calvinists. The company tended, like all such enterprises, to be extortionate and heedless of the feelings of its subjects and agents alike. Outside the Dutch pale, the Brazilian colonials were determined to regain the lost lands and to recapture the slave sources in Africa. A steady bush warfare drained Dutch strength. It might have been different had the Lowlanders been more numerous and willing to people the torrid area. Despite Maurits' pleas for more investors and settlers, it was apparent that the company had shot its bolt. The Seven Provinces simply had no more energy to pour into Brazil. They were already doing so well in the Far East and the Caribbean that they were not tempted to strain themselves further in the hot dampness of Brazil.

Maurits realized he was failing and that the company was losing confidence in the whole enterprise. In 1644 he asked to be, and was, recalled. By that time a curious situation had taken shape. Portugal had revolted in 1640 against Spain and proclaimed the Duke of Braganza as King João IV. Spain was not to recognize this loss until 1668, and much warfare was to take place. This circumstance made free Portugal and the Netherlands natural allies against Spain, whereupon a truce was negotiated. In Brazil both the Dutch and Portuguese elements regarded the truce as betrayal, and reconciliation was not furthered by the unsportsmanlike action of the Dutch in expanding their African holdings between the negotiation of the truce and the time it came into effect. Rather than permit the home governments to cut the ground from under them, both sides in Brazil continued the fight. It was a formless, frontier type of war, most of the fighting being done by Indians and Negroes who would remain in bondage no matter who won. The Brazilians were exhibiting a passion that can only be called patriotism; hence the term "Iliad" which their historians later gave this phase of history. Outside the Dutch territory they organized and directed the fighting. Inside it they borrowed money from the company in the belief they would never have to repay, annoyed the occupiers, and in 1645, rebelled in force.

An energetic group of Brazilians led by Salvador de Sá struck at the heart of the Dutch system by recapturing the great African slave post of Luanda in 1648. In the next year the Portuguese organized the Company of Brazil, forcing New Christians to invest in it and buying many ships which helped regain control of the slave trade. From then on it was apparent that the Brazilians had the upper hand. Soon the Dutch West India Company was knifed by the political authorities in Amsterdam, who were annoyed at its losses and its refusal to implement the truce. Shortly thereafter the Dutch met their match in Cromwell's England, who greatly reduced their naval power. Over-extended, outfought, and disowned by their sponsors, the Dutch in Brazil finally surrendered Recife, one of their chief cities, in 1654. Not until 1662 did the Dutch recognize their defeat by signing a treaty with Portugal. They received some compensation for their losses, the right to trade in the Portuguese empire on the same basis as the English and recognition of their seizures from Portugal in the East.[5]

In a narrow sense, the generation or so of the Dutch intrusion seems to be a mere episode in the expansion of Europe, intriguing as the possibilities of a Protestant and Dutch Brazil might appear. Few permanent effects on Brazil remained, save for some curious, Dutch-style buildings in the area around Pernambuco. Yet, the whole affair gave the colonists a sense of being in command of their own destiny and probably kept them from accepting much direction from the restored Portuguese monarchy. There were other consequences, one of them being that the outright Jews (as opposed to the New Christians) were evacuated. One congregation found its way to New Amsterdam, where a distinguished future awaited it. Hundreds or perhaps thousands of Dutch owners and managers removed to the West Indies with many of their slaves and most of their machinery. Soon, the West Indies bested Brazil in the sugar markets of Europe, and Brazil underwent a long period of stagnation. Countering this effect in some measure was the increased demand in Europe for sugar, whether it was Brazilian or West Indian, and with it stronger channels of commerce. In any event, Brazil was Portuguese, more firmly so than ever.

Brazil by the Mid-Seventeenth Century

THE Braganza monarchs made few changes in their reduced colonial empire. Their remaining bases in the Far East were now insignifi-

5. During the Napoleonic wars, England was to play the same part with respect to the Dutch empire as the Provinces had played during Portugal's "captivity" by Spain.

cant compared to the slave sources in Africa and the prospects of the sub-continent of Brazil. In view of the spirit exhibited by the Brazilians in ejecting the Dutch, it was not safe to attempt to crack the whip over them. One alteration was the granting of the more august title of viceroy to the captain-general at Bahia. Yet this was mostly an honorific distinction, for he was not to enjoy for more than a century anything like the authority of the Spanish viceroys in Peru and Mexico. The several provinces continued to be ruled by governors sent from Lisbon and not from Bahia. It was, in fact, faster and simpler for the provinces to communicate by sea with Portugal than by land with the supposed capital of Brazil. *Capitães-mores*, treasury officials, and a few other authorities were in evidence, but their power was usually limited by the genuine authority enjoyed by the plantation owners. As opposed to the Spanish empire, the Portuguese were more likely to award governmental posts to colonials instead of peninsulars. Another change, which was also more formal than real, was the freeing of all Indian slaves. Negro slavery was so well-intrenched by now, and Jesuit control of the Indians so complete, that the crown felt it could bow to the humanitarians by making this gesture. As will be seen, many Brazilians disagreed and made their opposition respected at times. One further matter should be noted. In 1660 Catherine of Braganza married Charles II of England, an occasion for a treaty which renewed the ancient alliance of Portugal and England and gave the British preference in commerce and the Portuguese some security against Spain.

It has been noted that the period of Spanish control, 1580–1640, permitted the Brazilians to spread far west of the Line of Tordesillas. At first this process was accidental, ejecting the French from "Equinoctal France" in 1615 and the Dutch in the 1650's. But nature had decreed that the enormous Amazon basin was more easily reached from the east than from Peru, where a few hardy explorers had learned how difficult it was to surmount the barrier of the Andes to sail down the great river. Furthermore, most of the streams back from the immediate coast of Brazil flow westward and northward into the Amazon, which is more than a stream, but rather a huge structural depression. In chasing Indians or escaped slaves, or simply in exploring for the sake of it, Brazilians were far more likely to penetrate it than Spaniards in Peru or New Granada. This process had largely been carried out by 1640. The chief step had been taken in 1637 when Pedro Texeira was sent by the governor of Maranhão up the Amazon into Peru. Soon afterward the whole river basin was claimed by the Brazilians and Portuguese, and Spain was unable to challenge the assertion. More than a century later, in 1750, Spain officially recognized the enormous inflation by the Portuguese of their original rights under the Treaty of Tordesillas.

The expansion of Brazil was partially attributable to the need to forestall foreign enemies. But the real impetus was something else, the roamings of an adventurous equestrian group in southern Brazil who came to call themselves *paulistas*, from the town of São Paulo, or *bandeirantes* from the banners each company carried. The little village and Jesuit mission of São Paulo stood back from the coast near São Vicente, the colony Sousa had planted in 1530. São Paulo was on a very high plateau which gave it a perpetually cool and energetic climate, in contrast to the torrid coastal towns, and it attracted a number of miscellaneous frontier characters, who for some reason did not choose to live in the more settled areas. Often of mixed blood, they easily took to exploration to find easy riches, which for a long time eluded them. Of more immediate profit was the business of catching Indian slaves for use by the farmers and ranchers who were filling up the choice regions to the northeast of São Paulo. This undertaking brought the *paulistas* into conflict with the Jesuits, who learned eventually to organize their Indian wards into armies to defend themselves. But many an Indian was carried away before the Jesuits made their defenses respected. Furthermore, escaped Negro slaves were valuable, and they too were hunted down. When no human prey was available the *paulistas* rode or sailed deep into the vastness of Brazil seeking other forms of adventure and profit. The spirit of enterprise and exuberant activity long characterized the *paulistas*, and to this day the aggressive business men of São Paulo pride themselves on their ancestors, or at least their predecessors in this area. At this point, it is necessary only to note that the *paulistas* were expanding the frontier of Brazil far to the west, north, and south, and were laying the foundation for the burgeoning state of São Paulo.

The core of the colony remained the sugar planters of the hot northeast. Living like autocrats on large plantations, surrounded by Negro slaves, they enjoyed a generally dependable prosperity, and their lands may have comprised the most stable area in the Americas for many generations during the colonial period. The coastal towns continued to be small and dirty, if colorful, and, with their immigrants and mixed races, somewhat democratic, since the rich lived on their plantations in the hinterland. The Jesuits had their vast missions farther back, and with the other orders (Franciscans, Capuchins, Carmelites, Benedictines, and Augustinians) had a few convents, monasteries, and occasional schools in the towns. In southern Brazil, ranches and vineyards were developing slowly, but the active *paulistas* claim the most attention in that region. In the enormous Amazon basin lived Indians who had escaped white control and growing colonies of escaped Negroes, some of whom were imperialistic in their own right. Legally, the whole unorganized assemblage of towns, plantations, missions, ranches, and farms belonged to the king of Portugal, whose authority was haphazardly exerted. Flowing into the area almost constantly were shiploads of African slaves and, on a regular basis, Portuguese ships with immigrants of white stock and goods largely of English origin. Flowing out were enormous quantities of sugar products, wood, hides, and miscellaneous items from the jungles or forests. Compared to the Spanish viceroyalties, Brazil was not a brilliant colony. It was even backward and unglamorous. It was only in the early stages of tapping its greatness.

The Institutions of Imperialism

9

Administration of the Spanish Empire

For three centuries Spain dominated the major part of the Americas. During the period of her union with Portugal from 1580 to 1640, she may have ruled the largest colonial empire of all time. Certainly it was among the most enduring, for she held important territories in the West Indies and the Pacific until 1898, and even now she has a diminutive empire in Africa. As for effectiveness in transplanting their institutions, the Spanish are rivaled only by the British and perhaps the Russians. In fine, the history of the Spanish empire is a success story. It is not a mere affair of the forcible construction of an administrative machine over backward natives, a few generations of exploitation, and then a well-deserved wrecking. One should approach the study of Spain's imperial methods with humility and respect. Any system that could cover so much territory, hold it so well, last so long, and leave so many traces must have been soundly conceived and, all things considered, well-operated.

The Indies as Property of the Monarch

SPAIN was not, and had no reason to be, prepared in 1492 for the fantastic career of overseas imperialism which Columbus began. For a few years after the Discovery, the peculiar islands of the Indies were regarded as mere personal estates of Queen Isabel, property whose title was authorized by the pope and accepted by the rival Portuguese. Beginning in 1493 the queen entrusted her business affairs for these lands to Juan Rodríguez de Fonseca, dean of the cathedral at Sevilla and later archbishop. Fonseca managed quite capably until 1520, at least from the standpoint of his monarchs' interests and the growth of the royal estates. Nor did he fail to profit personally from his position and to employ his authority ruthlessly. If such heroes as Columbus, Balboa, Magellan, and Cortés found much to complain of in his management of affairs, Fonseca successfully saw the American possessions through the difficult transition from royal plantation to true colonial empire.

The great conquests on the mainland added an enormous dimension to the concept of proprietary lands belonging to the monarch of Castile. Charles V was the ruler most involved in this fundamental change. Yet, he too continued the policy of regarding the Indies as personal possessions of himself and not of Castile or Spain. Now there were two major Indian realms, hundreds of lesser tribes, and millions of subjects under his imperial sway. Charles met the situation by transferring institutions of the peninsula to the New World and by withdrawing power from the conquistadors. By the time the great emperor abdicated, in 1556, the outlines of the imperial system were well established. Under Felipe II they were elaborated and strengthened, to remain almost unchanged until late in the eighteenth century.

While the Indies, stretching from the Kingdom of New Mexico to the Kingdom of Chile, were owned outright by the monarch, it was inevitable that his European subjects serve as his instruments for converting and ruling the inhabitants. For a very few years in the beginning, it looked as though Italian business men might carry out this function, for they were well-prepared in mercantile matters and were eager to participate. Even the Aragonese had some experience in overseas imperialism. However, Queen Isabel rather instinctively fell back upon her Castilian subjects as the choice servants for developing the islands. During his period of regency even King Fernando realized the preferability of Castilians to his own Aragonese subjects as royal agents, probably because the latter were too much aware of traditions of liberty and might be less obedient. Charles V experimented with letting his German, Flemish, and Italian subjects function in the New World, but after a time he reverted to the old policy of restricting the area to Castilians. Felipe II made no change in this respect, and by the time he died Aragon had been so curbed that it made little difference from what part of the peninsula migrants to the Indies originated. In the long run the king's holdings in America were operated almost altogether by Spaniards, particularly Castilians. Yet they performed this function not as Spaniards but as agents of the king. The monarch, not Spain, owned the sprawling overseas possessions. The distinction is not a slight one. After the virtual kidnaping of the monarch in 1808, prominent Americans could plausibly claim that their connection with a distant kingdom known as Spain had come to an end.

Guadalajara
1548

Mexico
1528

Santo Domingo

VICEROYALTY OF NEW SPAIN

Guatemala
1543

SANTO DOMINGO
1511

Panama

PANAMA
1538

Santa Fe
de Bogotá
1549

Quito

QUITO
1563

Manaos, 1674

Garupá, 1623

Pará,
1619

Santa Maria, 1614

Ceará, 1612

Natal, 1597
Parahyba, 1583
Olinda, 1535
Pernambuco, 1536
Penedo, 1620

LIMA
1542

Lima

VICEROYALTY OF PERU

Port Seguro

CHARCAS
1559

La Plata

Ouro Preto, 1698

Espírito Santo, 1535

São Paulo, 1532

São Vicente
1532

Santos, 1545

Rio de Janiero, 1555

Laguna, 1654

Santiago
1609

Buenos Aires

N

POLITICAL DIVISIONS
IN THE
SPANISH EMPIRE AND BRAZILIAN TOWNS
OF THE
16TH, 17TH AND EARLY 18TH CENTURIES
(DATES FOR AUDIENCIAS)

The Morality of Imperialism

IT is very much to the credit of Spain's monarchs, clergy, and intellectuals that the question of the justice of moving in upon pagan peoples and changing their ways greatly perturbed them. Few baldly asserted that the discovery and conquest of these lands gave them the right to rule as they pleased. From the very first, Isabel sought and obtained the pope's permission to extend her rule over Columbus' discoveries, making it clear that conversion of the heathen was one of her major purposes. The pious queen seems sincerely to have regarded the Indies in this respect as a challenge as much as an opportunity for enrichment. During his regency from 1506 to 1516 King Fernando was not altogether indifferent to the moral issues of the conquest. The agitation of the Dominicans caused him, as we have seen, to summon some of the best theologians and jurists to deliberate upon the rights of Christians in pagan lands. These discussions of 1512 and 1513 resulted in the laws of Burgos and Valladolid and the *Requerimiento*. Still, as the able professors Matías de Paz and Palacio Rubios averred, it was assumed that the pope's award in 1493 entitled the king to dispatch his servants into these new lands, where the population would be absorbed into a Christian community.

But was the papal award itself legitimate? From the outset various foreign students of theology and law, and, more to the point, envious rulers, had ridiculed the rightness of Alexander VI's demarcation in 1493. That pontiff was by no means a model pope, and his subservience to Spain was known to have an unworthy basis. Such doubts among foreigners and the large issues raised during the Reformation after 1517 about the papacy itself might not have agitated Spaniards unduly. But the shrill charges of Las Casas and the conquests of Mexico and Peru brought sensitive Spaniards more and more to face the fundamental problem: Did anything really justify the invasion of foreign lands, the overthrow of native rulers, the seizure of property, and the reduction of the inhabitants to servitude? Even Spaniards openly questioned the right of the pope to give title to foreign lands when such consequences ensued.

The question of the king's title to the Indies was, of course, closely linked with the whole matter of Spanish-Indian relations. Those who assumed the racial inferiority of the Amerinds found it easy to accept the papal award as the last word. Someone ought to look after those pagans, it seemed, and the pope had given Castile the task. A moderate position was that the pope had justified the title of Isabel and her successors to the discoveries in the belief that they would bring Christian civilization to people who had been unfortunate in not receiving it sooner. Hence all but the worst excesses of the conquest could be defended. In time, the blessings of true religion and a higher culture would compensate for the present sufferings of the natives. And yet an articulate and prestigious group of radicals, many of them Dominicans, argued that the pope had no right to endow the monarch of Castile with ownership of people who already had their own rulers, people who may have been backward but were not inferiors. The Spanish should do nothing but approach these pagans through kindly missionaries and traders. Force should never be employed, existing systems of government and property never disturbed.

Influential as Las Casas was in focusing attention on these problems, he was by no means alone. In the universities, the law courts, and the royal residence itself a number of individuals pondered the bases of imperialism, their consciences pricked as realization widened that the Indians of the islands had been wiped out, that half the population of Mexico was dying, that dreadful disorders in Peru threatened a worse fate, and that the conquistadors everywhere were making a mockery of the monarch's high-minded objectives. The influence of the humanitarians brought about ameliorative legislation during the 1520's and 1530's and the celebrated New Laws of 1542. The failure of these measures resulted in heightened pressure to renounce the Indies. Charles V listened and often half-agreed to these arguments. At times, as in 1539, he ordered the faculty at Salamanca to cease debating his rights overseas. On other occasions he favored the eminent Francisco de Vitoria, one of the founders of modern international law, who cogently pleaded for peaceful imperialism and no other. Then he rejected such pressures when the realities of the American situation intruded upon him. After the upheavals concerning the New Laws the emperor called off all further conquests in the New World.[1] In 1550–1551 a memorable debate took place at Valladolid on the moral issues of the Spanish presence in the Indies. Las Casas was there, to summarize his thinking of the past half-century. His principal opponent was the classical scholar, Juan Ginés de Sepúlveda, who made much of the revered Aristotle's doctrine that some people were basically inferior and ought to serve their betters. Most of the learned men present agreed with Las Casas but could not force the government to act accordingly. If their views had been followed, the Spanish would have been ordered out of the Indies but for missionaries and unarmed traders. Futile as the famous debate was, this was not the meanest hour in Spanish history.

Of course, the realities of politics and economics served to drown out these cries of conscience, as they always had. The silver of Mexico and

1.   They were resumed a few years later as "pacifications."

Peru was now urgently needed by the emperor after 1552, when the Lutherans suddenly reversed the military situation in Germany to their advantage and very nearly captured Charles. It defied common sense to believe that the Indians in America would long tolerate defenseless preachers and businessmen, and besides, their own systems had been torn apart beyond repair. The Spanish settlers had already shown their determination to withstand the idealistic reforms of the monarch and his high-minded advisers. It was truly unthinkable for Charles V to renounce his title. About this time the arguments over his right to rule began to die down. In the last analysis, a sensitive conscience could always be calmed by the papal award. This useful point served to silence most critics within Spain, and as for outsiders, Spaniards have seldom cared what they thought. Many years after the Valladolid debate the great jurist Juan de Solórzano Pereira summarized matters by asserting that Spanish rule should be accepted because it was beneficent, checking the greed of the conquistadors and correcting the vices of the Indians. Also, it would be worse if some other power had gone into the Indies. Finally, God is the judge, and, by implication, men should stop bothering about these issues. Indeed men had ceased to search their souls by that time over the rights of imperialism, or most of them had. Other countries were well launched in careers of empire-building, and few of their rulers or thinkers raised the points that so long agitated Charles V, Las Casas, and the university professors of Castile.

The Monarch and the Indies

LEGALLY, the various kingdoms in the Americas and the peninsula, as well as the assorted possessions of the Habsburgs in other parts of Europe and the outposts of Asia, Africa, and Oceania, were equal under the crown as a sort of commonwealth of nations. One major aspect we have considered, the employment of Castilians as royal agents and settlers in the Indies. Another was the more exalted position of the monarch in the New World than he enjoyed in older, more advanced lands. In Spain the king was restrained by traditions and precedents. He was curbed by natural law, a term used by philosophers but grasped by common men too. The king was to rule only so long as he obeyed custom, morality, and what might be called constitutional law. If he flagrantly violated his powers, the people were justified in opposing him, for tyrannicide was still openly threatened in sixteenth-century Spain. An unjust law was said not to be law at all. Many a privileged group proudly asserted its "liberty," as special right was labeled in Spain. Free speech was still widespread; powerful as he was, Felipe II was often the recipient of very blunt criticisms to his face. Divine-right monarchy had not reached in Spain the theoretical perfection it was later to achieve in the France of Louis XIV. The king might be God's vassal or agent, but he had better act like one.[2]

In the Indies the monarch suffered no such inhibitions. He owned the whole area outright, and he ruled or misruled as he would. No historical or constitutional obstacle stood in his way in the Indies. Nobles went to the Americas at his pleasure, or if they were Americans, achieved their status through his favor and not because of some ancient incident involving their ancestors. The clergy was directly under his control. All the officials were his creations, the land was his, and the population were all his subjects—Spanish, Indian, Negro, or any mixture thereof alike. This situation was not usually distasteful to the inhabitants of the Indies. The king seemed a benevolent, distant figure, especially to the lowly Indians, who until the last regarded him as their protector, ineffectual as he was. Anything that went wrong was blamed on the officials of the crown, not the king himself. If the Indians in their way loved the remote lord in Madrid, the whites well understood that their position depended largely on the unity of the Spanish element under the monarch. No revolts openly aimed at the king and exceedingly little agitation against him took place until well after 1800.

Spanish Monarchs of the Seventeenth Century

THE high character and great abilities of the sixteenth-century sovereigns of Spain have been in evidence during the discussion of the Conquest and the period of consolidation. Isabel the Catholic, Charles V, and Felipe II were as fortunate a line of rulers as any human arrangement could be expected to produce. So well had they done their work the vast Spanish commonwealth survived a century of poor monarchs. First of these was Felipe III (1598–1621), who came to the throne while young. He reacted against his somber father and developed into a frivolous, profligate man, easily influenced in the wrong ways. He did nothing to arrest the decline of Spain that had already set in, a task perhaps too formidable for the wisest of statesmen. His favorite, the Duke of Lerma, who governed the country in fact, encouraged corruption and extravagance. The whole public administration sagged into demoralization and inefficiency. Lerma's chief contribution to Spain's decay was his decision to debase the coinage, creating copper money to replace silver and gold and thus worsening the inflation the land had long suffered.

So many other things went wrong, so many serious errors in state-

2. The Spanish Jesuit, Francisco Suá-rez (d. 1617), articulated even stronger views than these regarding limitations on the king's authority. His teachings were useful to the Spanish Americans when they sought to justify the independence movement, particularly after 1808.

craft. Siding as usual with the Austrian Habsburgs, the Spanish government became involved in the first stages of what came to be the Thirty Years' War, a dreadful series of conflicts that concerned north central Europe far more than the Iberian peninsula. Felipe III made the popular but cruel and unfortunate decision to expel the *moriscos*, a quarter-million people who were of Moorish origin but supposedly Christianized. Living mostly along the Mediterranean coasts of Spain, they seemed a fifth column to tempt African war lords into raiding or invading the peninsula. Probably they constituted something of a military danger, but their expulsion removed a productive element of the population when Spain could least afford the loss. Conditions steadily became worse. Depopulation continued; miserable rural folk moved into the cities, where they often took to crime and vagrancy. Not even the monasteries could feed these hordes of unemployed. Finally, Felipe III allowed the Inquisition to increase its activities, and his administration to become excessively clericalized. All this sapped the vigor of the monarchy and encouraged the Church to over-expand in material ways and thus lose much of its purpose in an atmosphere of wealth. The Americas felt these tendencies almost as much as the peninsula.

Felipe IV (1621–1665) was an even more disastrous sovereign. Also a youth when he became king, he neglected his duties shamefully for half his reign, leaving true power in the hands of the Count-Duke of Olivares, who occasionally undertook reforms but quickly abandoned them. The entire atmosphere of the royal court was hostile to austerity and even to efficiency. It seemed easier to drift, to sell public offices on a large scale, to allow the Church to usurp governmental positions, and, always with regrets, to debase the coinage again and again. Spain's world situation became worse as the Thirty Years' War dragged on. The blood of the peninsula and the treasure of America were lavished on military campaigns in central Europe to contain the Lutherans. While these efforts were partially successful, it was different when Spanish forces attempted to beat down the Netherlands and to restrain France, now emerging with such force under the leadership of Cardinals Richelieu and Mazarin. The Spanish defeat at Rocroi in 1643 terminated a century and a half of military supremacy. And the fleets of Spain had been destroyed by the Dutch off Brazil and in the English Channel a few years previously. These naval losses and other disasters had their effects in the Indies, where the fleets were unable to supply the colonists or bring the treasure to Spain. The outbreak of revolts in Portugal, Catalonia, Sicily, and Naples during the 1640's seemed to presage the utter disintegration of the Spanish monarchy.

And yet Felipe IV got through this desperate decade. He dismissed Olivares and became earnest about his kingly duties. The king was, to be sure, a great gentleman, a sensitive soul, and a man of considerable ability, though all of these qualities were neutralized by his weakness of character. Spain fought on, stubborn as ever, against Catalonia, who finally gave in, against Sicily and Naples, who likewise capitulated, against Portugal to 1668, who retained her freedom. Felipe acknowledged Dutch independence in 1648, after more than eighty years of war, and he persisted in fighting France until 1659, eleven years after the close of the Thirty Years' War.

Admirable as his persistence may have been, he left Spain almost in ruins. Everywhere stalked poverty and despondency. It was bad enough that agriculture and ranching had declined. But so had commerce with the Indies supposedly held in monopoly, and the treasures of America had almost ceased to arrive. The population seemed to be disappearing, not only in rural areas but in cities. Those who remained were more impoverished than ever. An increasing intellectual proletariat had no place to go but into the Church, already swelled with insincere clerics, and into the bureaucracy, which was likewise large and inefficient. And, of course, many of them became vagabonds and criminals along with unemployed peasants and workers.

Worse was to follow. The death of Felipe IV, the once carefree cavalier king who became a morbid, haunted figure of tragedy, brought to the throne his four-year-old son, Carlos II (1665–1700). This unhappy creature was the product of too many intermarriages among the Habsburgs and remained for the next thirty-five years a medical curiosity. Bald, lame, nearly blind, and probably impotent, the pitiful king was also weak-minded. Occasionally he had flashes of insight and spurts of energy, but most of the time he was unaware of what was going on about him. For some years his mother reigned after a fashion, deferring at first to her confessor and then to her lover, neither of whom was capable. When she was displaced by the king's older half-brother, the illegitimate Don John José, the reign showed signs of promise. But then John José died shortly, and the king came to be dominated by his French wife and, after she died, his Austrian wife, by neither of whom could he have children. He had no heirs whatever. The government was shockingly corrupt and ineffective. Morale throughout the vast Spanish monarchy sank into despondency. Business depression was chronic, periods of inflation and spurts of deflation alike bringing misery. Poverty, bigotry, decadence in all lines of activity, and hopelessness characterized peninsular Spain. Other powers warred on her and tore off rich provinces, Louis XIV being particularly hostile. Surely the Spanish monarchy would have been partitioned but for the rivalry of the other powers and the knowledge that Carlos II had no direct heirs. For years European diplomacy was kept in a state of nervous suspense over the prospective break-up of the Spanish inheritance. The longer Carlos "the bewitched," as so many believed he was, lingered, the higher the tension grew.

Despite the steady decline of kingship since the great days of Felipe II, the enormous bureaucracy over which the monarch nominally presided continued to function in the Americas under its own momentum. Every year, on the average of a thousand or so settlers migrated to the Indies, and the hold of Spanish culture on the New World deepened regardless of the dismal political situation at home. The seventeenth century, "the forgotten century" in the history of the Spanish empire in America, was surely no period of great strides in territorial expansion and institutional development. Rather, it was a time of monotony, with racial and economic forces working themselves out along the patterns set during the period of vigorous government.

The Council of Indies

WHETHER the king was able or incapacitated, absorbed in American affairs or unconcerned with them, a prestigious institution carried out his duties as autocrat of the Indies. Sometimes it was a mere rubber stamp, doing what the king commanded. At other times, especially during the seventeenth century, it ruled almost as sovereign. This agency was the Royal and Supreme Council of Indies, created officially in 1524, though it had functioned under a less dignified title for some years previously. It grew out of the unofficial colonial empire long run by the venal Archbishop Fonseca until his disgrace about 1520 and continued his policy of centralizing all imperial matters. Ranking second only to the august Council of Castile, this body remained near the royal court, which settled down in Madrid in the 1560's, and deliberated several hours each day "without haste, without rest." Its membership was composed mainly of clergymen during the first years, but later lawyers who were supposed to be of noble birth and God-fearing came to dominate. Military and naval officers, and of course individuals who purchased their offices, filled up the Council of Indies in the seventeenth century. Often, successful administrators who had been in the New World were appointed to this agency upon their return.

Its functions were awesome in their scope. Depending on the king's will or indifference, it simply ruled the Indies. It was the legislative body for the empire, its decrees having the force of law. Nearly half a million of these regulations were issued during the first century of the Council's existence, to be reduced after forty years of fine legal scholarship into that monument of imperialism copied by other colonizing powers, the *Recopilación de las leyes de Indias* with its mere 6,000 laws. Nearly every appointment of any importance was made, or sold, by the Council of Indies. It had supreme financial and economic control over the overseas empire, supervising the *Casa de Contratación* in Sevilla, where such matters were centralized, and handling the final audits. In judicial affairs the Council of Indies was the ultimate court of appeals for lawsuits from the high courts, or *audiencias*, in America. As the king's instrument it constituted the supreme executive and military authority. All matters affecting the ecclesiastical establishment passed through the Council, which decided whether or not to transmit directives from Rome to America and which named the clerical officials who were to carry out the work of the Church. In fact, no area of activity in the Indies escaped the attention of this body. Its prestige remained high and its powers potentially or actually enormous almost to the end of the empire.

Viceroys

THOUGH Aragon had long used viceroys in Italy and elsewhere, the experience with Columbus discouraged the introduction of this office in America until 1535, when the situation in New Spain called for a forceful executive. The successful reign of Antonio de Mendoza demonstrated the efficacy of the position, and it was continued until the end of the mainland empire in 1824. During the entire colonial period[3] 170 viceroys reigned. All but four of them were peninsular Spaniards by origin, most of them belonged to the nobility or at least were of high birth, and many of them were archbishops and generals. The viceroy was the personification of the royal majesty of the king. Hence he commanded the fleet on which he sailed to America. He was received with royal honors and surrounded by pomp and pageantry designed to impress the population with the glory of the monarchy. He dwelt in a handsome palace and had a small but dressy guard. From the time he received the symbols of office from the outgoing viceroy until the lengthy inquest at the end of his term, he seemed a brilliant and very dignified official. His salary and expense account, together with the other perquisites of this office, enabled him to live in splendor, probably better for his times than most modern heads of state in ours. Cynically, it was said that he needed to make three fortunes, one to buy his position, another to maintain himself in state, and a third to buy off the inquest at the end of his term. In reality, this is unfair, for most of the viceroys were men of acceptable probity and honor.[4] Perhaps he was more likely

3. Despite the discussions regarding the Indies being kingdoms equal with Spain, they came to be, in fact, colonies, and use of the term "colonial" is both correct and unavoidable.

4. Of course, this point must be qualified by the reminder that viceroys usu-ally interpreted things to their advantage. In the same way respected officials and legislators of modern democratic republics, including our own, often accept gifts and favors and use privileged official information for private business transactions.

to violate another law of the Indies which stipulated that he must avoid avarice, asperity, and ire, that he must be affable and easy in granting audiences, and just, prompt, and careful about carrying out ceremonies.

The viceroy was the executive head of the government in his domain: enforcer of laws, military commander-in-chief, vice-patron of the Church, inspector general, and superintendent of finances. He was to guard the food supply, health, and morals of his subjects. He was to supervise Indian affairs, and detailed instructions stipulated how he was to protect the natives from exploitation by the whites. As governor and captain-general of the capital city and its surrounding province, he was all-powerful in his immediate command. As president of the *audiencia* he might interfere in lawsuits or criminal trials, though he seldom did. In all, the majesty of the viceregal position, and the numerous specific or implied powers that went with it, offered an outlet for men of energy and talent. The others could merely enjoy their splendor while it lasted and seek genteel methods to increase their personal fortunes.

It is clear that the viceroy's position was often equivocal. He served only at the pleasure of the king and had to contend with detractors at court who might covet his position. His term was likely to be short, three years according to the letter of the law but usually a little longer. The powers of the Council of Indies necessarily restricted the viceroy. He had been appointed by that body, received its detailed instructions, and gave it a thorough accounting after his term ended. Hence few viceroys dared to undertake important enterprises without the express authorization of the Council. Major decisions had to be referred to Madrid. And what must have been very frustrating to an ambitious viceroy was the fact that so many of his nominal subordinates were appointed by the Council of Indies and not by himself, especially after 1678. Such officials might be respectful to the viceroy and even obey him when the chain of command ran straight and true. But they knew the viceroy would probably not remain in office as long as they would, and besides they did not owe their appointment to him. There were ways to drag matters out so that a vigorous viceroy would find the administrative machine unresponsive to his will. Nor could he build up a powerful following within his own realm among the American-born, who might welcome a chance to chastise the lesser Spanish officials. Viceroys were not supposed to cultivate popularity among their subjects. The Spanish government was to be feared and respected, not beloved. Thus, the viceroy was to be aloof from his people, a symbol of might rather than affection. These dignified figures came and went regularly, few of them having an opportunity to emblazon their names on the historical record of the viceroyalties. This long procession seems to have left little impression on the minds of the Americans other than the haughtiness of the Spanish government.

Anonymous automatons of a malevolent character they appeared to their subjects, but that was the way the system was supposed to work, and it must be acknowledged that it served the purposes of the Spanish monarchy for a very long time.

The *Audiencia*

IN 1511 a high court with considerable administrative powers, an institution destined to become the second most important governmental institution in the Indies, was set up in Santo Domingo. Enlarged and strengthened in 1526, this *audiencia*, as it was called, supervised justice and participated in governmental affairs. A second *audiencia* was established in Mexico City in 1528, and others followed as the Spanish deepened their hold on the Americas: Panama in 1538, Lima in 1542, Guatemala in 1543, Guadalajara in 1548, Santa Fe de Bogotá in 1549, Charcas in 1559, Quito in 1563, Manila in 1583,[5] Santiago de Chile in 1609, Buenos Aires in 1778, Caracas in 1786, and Cuzco in 1787. In the viceregal capitals (Mexico City, Lima, Bogotá, and Buenos Aires) the *audiencia* was somewhat under the influence of the viceroy, its nominal president, and it also exercised restraint on him. In the last analysis, however, the viceroy could disregard the *audiencia* if he dared. Outside the viceregal capitals the *audiencias* had presidents from their own membership and, therefore, more freedom to participate in public affairs. Supposedly they supplemented the authority of the viceroy or governor, but often they sought to usurp power or, to put it more charitably, to enlarge their functions. The areas over which they had judicial jurisdiction foreshadowed the boundaries of the future Latin American republics more than the viceroyalties did.

The size of the *audiencia* varied. There were at least four *oidores*, or judges, a fiscal agent or two, attorneys, clerks, guards, and a chaplain. The judges usually sat as a body in important cases and often went on circuit to hear cases in various parts of their district. Occasionally they specialized in certain types of cases. Spanish justice was far from simple; in addition to the usual criminal and civil suits there were special courts for Church affairs, the army, the guilds, the *mesta*, or livestock association, Indians, and sometimes other entities. Appeals from all such courts might reach the *audiencia*, whose decision was final except in extraordinary criminal cases or civil suits involving very large sums; these went often to the Council of Indies in Madrid.

Like other Spanish officials, the members of the *audiencia*, were usually middle-aged or elderly men whose families and chief interests remained in Spain. After a tour of duty in America, the judge was likely to

5. Not in the Americas, of course, but vaguely under the sway of New Spain.

be transferred to another *audiencia* or to go back home. While he was in the New World he was forbidden to marry, engage in business, borrow or loan, or even attend weddings and funerals. It was not his purpose to become a popular figure but to represent the majesty of the Spanish monarchy in judicial matters. Yet, as it happened, many of the judges seem to have remained in the Indies after the close of their terms, quite likely because they had illegally established business and personal ties. If they were seldom genial figures to the populace over whom they presided, they did much to make the Spanish empire in America a civilized area. Applying for generation after generation the laws of the Indies (or in lieu of such laws, those of Castile), they fashioned the juridical structure which in the main persists—the concepts of family, property, land tenure, native relations, business affairs, and in fact the order and justice of Europe. Seldom beloved, *audiencias* were looked to for justice, and they often provided it.

Provincial Rulers

THE king might own the Indies, the Council of Indies enunciate high policy, the viceroy strut briefly about his capital, and the *audiencia* in its dignified seclusion build up a tradition of law, but perhaps the most immediately important officials were the rulers of towns and districts. These might be compared to the sergeants in an army, tough, independent, and often arbitrary, outwardly respectful to superior authority but in fact exercising the closest control over the rank and file as they willed. Under the Spanish imperial system the nomenclature for such officials varied, as did their powers and effectiveness. Some were *adelantados*, officers of high rank who wielded virtually unchallenged power in the frontier districts, dealing with Indians and protecting the white missionaries and settlers. Another official of exalted position was the captain-general, who was practically a little viceroy over areas like Guatemala, Chile, Venezuela, or Cuba. Independent of the viceroys except for matters of the utmost importance, such as defense in time of war, the captain-generals ruled as much like autocrats as their short terms permitted.

Of lesser rank were the governors, who were appointed in Spain but were nominally under the supervision of the viceroys. The governor was an important enough official, highly paid and enjoying considerable dignity. If the viceroy was not in a position to oversee him, the governor was likely to be something of a tyrant in his province. No council or local government was robust enough to resist his authority, though the *audiencia* and the ecclesiastical establishment might at times rival him. Similarly, but on a lesser scale, ruled the *alcalde mayor*, who had a smaller area under his control. As executive and military chieftain of his province, this figure was already extremely powerful, and he often legislated by issuing decrees or commands and even served as effective judicial officer. He too was under the viceroy in the chain of command, a circumstance that did little to mitigate his tyranny over his own district. Similar to the *alcalde mayor* was the *corregidor,* who ruled Spanish towns and their immediate territory and Indian towns. The *corregidor* for Spaniards was not supposed to facilitate the growth of self-government, and he was rarely likely to wish to do so. Unless the viceroy curbed him he was practically an autocrat. The *corregidor de indios* saw to it that Indian tribal rulers collected tributes and labor drafts. He also distributed goods to the natives under well-meaning laws that intended to facilitate the spread of European tools and articles among the Indians. Naturally, this process was open to much abuse, the *corregidor* often forcing the natives to purchase worthless goods he had bought up at low cost and now sold at a profit. The Indian tribal rulers cooperated with him or lost their positions.

These provincial officials were subject to the usual personal restrictions. They were mostly peninsular Spaniards, often bonded and always forbidden to participate in social and business affairs in America. More often than the higher officers of the crown, they could disregard the letter of the law with considerable safety. They were to serve three to five years in one district and then be transferred to another. After a career in America they were expected to return to Spain, but many of them remained in the New World to enjoy the property they had illegally amassed. Until 1678 most of the *corregidores* were named by the viceroy, but then the Council of Indies took over more their appointment, possibly because it could sell these positions. This tendency further weakened the control of the viceroy over his supposed subordinates and encouraged the *corregidores* to behave like despots. All in all, the functions of the provincial rules intensified the Latin American tradition of autocratic government, a tradition already established under the ancient Indian system, and the system helps explain the *caciquismo,* or bossism, of the future.

The *Cabildo*

IF THERE were no germs of popular government in the Spanish imperial system with its king, Council of Indies, viceroys, *audiencias,* and provincial rulers, an interesting municipal institution held some possibility that the creoles, or whites born in America, might develop some self-government. At the outset, however, we should note that this promise was not fulfilled. Spain had had a strong urban tradition from Roman times or the period of the Reconquest,[6] and the towns acquired a great deal of autonomy during the later Middle Ages. The Catholic Kings undertook to diminish municipal independence but had not completed the process when the settlement of the Americas began. It seemed natural to the Spaniards to establish a town as the first step in colonization. Not only was a town useful as a base and protected spot, but it provided authority for activities which had not been approved by the monarch. Thus Balboa, Cortés, Pizarro, Orellana, and other conquistadors solemnly founded paper cities with councils which legalized the actions they wished to take. As villages and towns sprouted in the West Indies and the mainland coasts, Spain issued laws to make them uniform. Physically, they were to conform to a set pattern, with a plaza, straight streets of a designated width, and rectangular blocks, and with a church, governmental house or palace, convent, arsenal, prison, and warehouse built according to specifications laid down in Spain. Then, each town was to have a council, or *cabildo*, (or *ayuntamiento*) elected by the adult white males of property who controlled the urban area and the countryside around it.

Spanish towns in America were thus created outright instead of growing up naturally as the area surrounding them developed. Once they were functioning, they became centers of Spanish culture, legal authority, church activities, and business and military power. Perhaps as many as 250 such towns had been founded by 1600, and the process continued as the Spanish pale expanded. In the early years it seemed that the *cabildos* were going to wield considerable authority, for they conferred with one another in the islands and formulated demands that crown officials sometimes found difficult to resist. Furthermore, they obtained the privilege of communicating directly with the king, by-passing *adelantados*, governors, and other officials. However, Charles V had a frightening experience with rebellious Spanish towns during the *comunero* movement of the 1520's, and he determined to extinguish the autonomy of *cabildos* on both sides of the Atlantic. Accordingly, the towns in the Indies were commanded to cease concerted action with one another. Soon, *corregidores* were placed over the *cabildos* to assure the power of the crown and the inactivity of the councils in important matters. Thus the promising political growth of the *cabildos* was cut off, apparently with little opposition from the townspeople themselves.

The members of the town council, the *regidores*, numbered twelve for large cities and six for smaller ones. They met in a sturdy and imposing building known as the *cabildo*. As long as they did not collide with

6. A protracted and somewhat futile controversy has raged among scholars as to whether Spanish urbanism dates from the Roman period or from the Reconquest.

the wishes of the *corregidor*, they were allowed to regulate such matters as police, sanitation, salt and timber supplies, market conditions, prices, hospitals, education, local justice and taxes, epidemics, dangers from Indians or foreigners, and the sale or use of public lands outside the urban area. In the event of an emergency, the leading white male citizens might be invited to join the *regidores* in an open town meeting, or *cabildo abierto*. It is evident that the *cabildo* performed important duties and potentially offered the American whites an instrument for asserting political power. Yet the authority of the royal *corregidor* and the spirit of the imperial government—and the favor usually given to rural aristocrats —served to keep them in their place. On very rare occasions did a *cabildo* disregard the will of the Spanish government. One factor in its lack of aggressiveness may have been the practice of selling lifetime and hereditary positions as *regidores*, which attracted the wealthiest and most loyal creoles and, of course, robbed the *cabildo* of any democratic character it might have possessed.

The *cabildo*, then, failed to develop into a powerful organ of creole political activity. As the empire grew, the citizens of the towns showed little restlessness over the relatively insignificant position of the *cabildos*. To be sure, the *cabildo* possessed prestige; rich men were eager to win or buy positions as *regidores*, and purely local affairs were sometimes absorbing enough for their political instincts. But there was no question of the creoles seeking to usurp real power from the royal bureaucracy. As for the privilege of corresponding directly with the king, this was usually a matter of soliciting titles, such as "most loyal and regal" and the like, or coats of arms for the city or dispatching gifts of money when a new king came to the throne, a royal heir was born, a prince knighted, or an infanta married. Rarely did a *cabildo* seek to circumvent the *corregidores* or viceroys by dealing directly with His Catholic Majesty in Madrid.

In a way it is strange that the *cabildos* were so lacking in assertiveness. It is also puzzling that they displayed so little public spirit. If the city had a few handsome buildings and if ceremonies were carried out properly, the town fathers seemed little disturbed by its defects, such as the poverty of its population and the sordidness of its slums. The *cabildo* seemed to grow weaker as the empire grew older. Some of these councils were undermanned by the eighteenth century. They occupied themselves with trifling matters. Yet, the *cabildo* remained the only organ of government open to creoles, and the tradition of open meetings was never forgotten. When the king was captured in 1808 and the top-heavy imperial system faltered, the creoles came forward to assert themselves through the *cabildo*. This nearly moribund institution quickly revived, and it made history.

PECULIARITIES OF
SPANISH ADMINISTRATION IN AMERICA

Merely to state the main functions of the chief governmental organs in the Spanish empire leaves much unsaid. So many of the attitudes behind the great administrative machine must be considered, for they had significant historical consequences and many of them still linger. First, we should ponder the enduring policy of entrusting the government of the empire only to peninsular Spaniards, men who were born in Spain and still rooted there. Quite likely this policy largely explains the longevity of the overseas empire, for American-born Spaniards were unable to wrest the centers of power from the peninsulars until after the collapse of metropolitan Spain in 1808. Yet this policy also explains why the creoles were so full of resentment by that time, why they seized the opportunity to break the connection with Europe. The basis for the policy was at first common sense, the quite defensible belief that conquistadors were too turbulent to obey the crown when it was not to their interest to do so. Thus, Charles V steadily removed the men who had conquered the Indies and replaced them with loyal servants of his own. It also became part of the lore of the mother country that men degenerated in the Indies, which were said to be tropical. Of course, most of the population centers were located in the cool, dry altitudes, and the theory did not make sense. But it persisted, to the increasing irritation of the creoles as time went on. Reversing the attitude of English America, where the earlier immigrants have felt themselves superior to later arrivals, in the Spanish empire a person fresh from Europe held an advantage not only in snobbery but in almost any kind of preferment. The creoles were always looked upon as inferiors simply because they were born on the wrong side of the Atlantic. Their competence and indeed their loyalty were impugned by the government; they were seldom deemed fit to occupy responsible posts in the administration, the Church, and often in business firms. [7] Any peninsular, however low-born or ignorant, automatically was favored over Americans who might have been educated, rich descendants of the conquistadors and Indian royalty. Naturally, the creoles grew steadily more bitter about this situation. It is striking to observe how many of the leaders during the wars of independence personally experienced the scorn of peninsulars, and how it burned their souls.

Another general policy of the Spanish monarchy was secrecy or exclusiveness. This too was instinctive common sense, at least in the be-

7. There is, of course, much substance to the Spanish argument that peninsulars were more likely to be objective in carrying out governmental duties because they were free from local interests and less subject to improper pressures.

ginning. Portugal had long found it wise to conceal the extent of her explorations and the sources of treasures from envious foreigners, and Spain learned after the first two voyages of Columbus not to advertise her discoveries. When the treasure sources became truly productive, such as the pearl fisheries in the Caribbean and the mines of New Spain and Peru, it was imperative to keep foreigners and Spanish outlaws as much in the dark as possible. The policy spread to include the location of the best ports, the currents, and the richest bases. Spain had no reason to make things easy for pirates and her national enemies. Yet, as time went on, this secrecy contributed to ignorance on the part of peninsular and American Spaniards, who might have performed important work for the monarchy had they been better informed. As late as 1800, the Spanish government strove to prevent foreigners from seeing the riches of the empire. Probably it was wise to do so.

Both in Spain and in Austria, the Habsburgs have long been accused of a policy of divide and rule, keeping national minorities and other groups so disunited and contentious that they could not organize to challenge the crown. The criticism is often unfair, for any autocracy, perhaps any democracy, needs to prevent combinations that will overpower the government. To outsiders it appeared that the Spanish crown deliberately fostered competition among various privileged groups so as the better to control them all. Hence the military and civilian authorities, the Church and the laiety, the viceroys and the *audiencias*, the provincial governors and their subordinates, and the various territorial units often quarreled with one another. Too frequently the crown permitted these disputes to continue unresolved, though it is perhaps too much to say it fomented them. Much of the disunity was natural. The Spanish empire was not the only place where coastal populations were suspicious of interior folk, or country people of townsmen, or Americans of Europeans, or members of one economic or racial group of another. Yet it is fair to point out that the royal power which all acknowledged often drew vague boundaries and created hazy lines of demarcation between the duties of different authorities. The crown could have prevented or stopped much of the wrangling in America had it chosen to do so.

Another general feature of Spanish imperial government that has often been criticized is its slowness. Here again, some case can be made for the crown on the grounds that the distances were so great that a year might pass before a condition in the Indies could be reported to Madrid and another year go by before instructions could reach the scene. Napoleonic efficiency would not have overcome such obstacles imposed by the distances and awkward means of communication. The government of the Spanish empire was never, it must be acknowledged, characterized by Napoleonic efficiency. It was notorious for its delays, red tape, pedantry, and opportunities for litigation and avoidance of decision. During the first half century of the Conquest it may have been as competent as was humanly possible. Beginning with Felipe II, however, who had to see every paper and pass on each problem, an exasperatingly sluggish tempo affected the entire government. The habit continued, furthered by the usual bureaucratic tendencies to complicate all public business. From the late sixteenth to the late eighteenth century the imperial machine could be counted on to move very deliberately. It should be observed that this situation sometimes brought a curious benefit, for it offered a built-in defense against tyranny. A great deal could be gotten away with before the government acted, and when it did, the situation might have changed so much that punishment was impossible. From the standpoint of administrative excellence, however, it is clear that the creeping paralysis of the imperial system was unfortunate.

The whole Spanish monarchy was permeated by a mania for rank, titles, honors, and official recognition, deserved or not. On the whole, the crown was slow to convince when it came to making awards to creoles, and it was very difficult for an American to obtain a title even during the most corrupt period of the monarchy. Thus, honors were all the more coveted. Spats over who should precede whom or who should have the more horses for his carriage or who should wear what decoration sometimes resulted in violence. But then, this was scarcely a peculiarity of the Spanish system, despite the unique character of some of the incidents. An aristocratic disdain for one's supposed inferiors based on birth, color, or position in the Spanish empire was also typical of European and Oriental societies of the time. It was practiced among Indians and Negroes too, who had a carefully stratified hierarchy of their own, and is not unknown in modern democracies or Soviet republics.

Spain and her daughters in America have long been afflicted with a passion known as *empleomanía,* an inordinate desire to attach oneself to the public payroll. During periods of economic depression in the United States, this tendency becomes prevalent, and it is common enough in welfare states with the eagerness of individuals to secure pensions, sinecures, and other grants. *Empleomanía* reflects perhaps not so much national character as business conditions. Certainly, schemes to obtain official positions and preferments were constantly a feature of the Spanish system. Graft and corruption were not peculiarly Spanish, of course, despite distinctive manifestations of these evils. The sale of offices was begun by Felipe II and continued until 1812, though it declined sharply under the reforming Bourbons of the eighteenth century. Enough competent men to operate the imperial system were simply not available. Thus, in selling offices (which usually meant a lifetime income and status) the crown raised a little revenue and filled positions in the bureaucracy with men who had money or credit and thus might be assumed to be capable. Evil and undignified as the practice seems, no less a student than Montesquieu defended office-selling in 1748. Other features of the Spanish imperial system included the ancient and modern institution of the lobby, which exerted pressure usually in Spain for favors. There was also the *mordida*, the "bite," a gratuity by which a subject encouraged an official to take some action he might otherwise not or a "rake-off" taken by an officer simply for doing his duty.

Paternalism was a characteristic of the Spanish empire that has affected the free Latin American nations ever since. It was taken for granted that the government should regulate anything and everything. The subject existed for the state, and property was at the disposal of the "republic," or society. Few or no limits to the authority of the government were admitted. The king owned the land and awarded it on a limited basis to those who operated the mines, farms, and industries. All the inhabitants were his subjects and could be placed under the control of one another as the monarch chose. Any independent action, such as the Conquest itself, was under the ultimate disposition of the king. The all-pervasiveness of the state was common enough during the Renaissance in Europe, as later it would be under mercantilism, absolute monarchy, and modern totalitarianism, but again, the Spanish system had its own individuality in this respect. Such paternalism restricted initiative and encouraged too much dependence on a government which was not always wise nor energetic. Inevitably, it led to overextension of royal authority and thus to ineffectiveness in many areas. It also inspired the people to devise ways to defeat the all-powerful state through passive resistance, mendacity, corruption, hypocrisy, and the famous Spanish dictum, *Obedezco pero no cumplo* (I obey but do not carry out). Also, clever individuals could operate rackets that would beat a system that attempted to do too much.

Two interesting practices of the Spanish government acted sometimes as checks on abuses by officials, the *visita* and the *residencia*. The first resembled the activity of a modern bank examiner or an inspector general in the army, being sudden, unannounced, and secret. Often the *visitador* had full authority to assume the office of his victim temporarily and to find out anything he could. His inspection might result in exoneration or punishment based on the facts, but too often it was a matter of his being bribed to report that nothing was wrong. Even the highest officials, the Council of Indies itself or the viceroys, might be subjected to this practice. The *residencia* was an old Spanish institution transferred after some hesitation to the bureaucracy in the New World.

A formal affair coming at the end of the tour of duty of any important official, the *residencia* was public. Any man could present the judge of this inquest with evidence that the official in question had ruled ill. The official would have to reply in detail to all charges against him and, usually, remain in a state of detention until the *residencia* was finished. While each situation differed, it became all too common for the judges of the *residencia* to be bribed and to announce that the subject of their inquest had cleared himself. Yet, enough fines and other punishments were inflicted to make the *residencia* at least a psychological barrier to misgovernment. An official had either to be righteous or cloak his actions so that it would appear that he had been.

In summary, Spanish rule was autocratic but often ineffective. It was most harsh in the midst of the advanced Indian cultures, where tyranny was imposed rigidly to control the natives, and most egalitarian and democratic in such frontier regions as Venezuela and the Argentine. The Spanish system was the product of the sixteenth century and was therefore wedded, as time went on, to the past and not capable of much flexibility as conditions changed. Unlike much of the English establishment on the Atlantic coast of North America, it was not the work of refugees from oppression but rather of warriors and officials. Nor was it linked to a home government that often ignored the colonists as England did but to a monarchy which needed its products and was determined to make its will felt. Much of the tradition of Isabel the Catholic, Charles V, and Felipe II remained robust, a tradition that emphasized executive, military-type authority, privilege based on birth, strong government and the by-products of hypocrisy, corruption, disrespect for law, and inexperience for the creoles in self-government.

Authorities have always differed in evaluating the Spanish system. Bourne pointed out that the overseas empire was as well-governed as Spain itself and better governed than the Latin American republics since independence. Rippy concluded that, on the whole, the empire was badly governed. Haring approvingly repeated a statement that the government was never insufferably bad, never vigorously good. Madariaga stressed the commonwealth aspect of the Spanish monarchy and the superiority of the Spanish Indies to other empires in America. Roscher showed how the Spanish system was effective, was imitated by other colonial powers, and brought wealth and historic fame to Spain. The variety of opinions could be prolonged indefinitely. With all its defects, the amazing administrative feat in setting up so quickly a vast governmental machine compels admiration. This machine functioned for 300 years well enough to insure Spain's control and to permit the steady peopling of the Americas by Iberians. The Americas were not held by force, at least in the sense of large garrisons holding down unwilling populations. Extremely few rebellions against the authority of Spain took place until 1810. Whether the longevity of the empire was the product of inherent virtue in the imperial system or the inertia of the peoples, it speaks for itself.

10

The Church in the Spanish Empire

MORE than any other institution the Church kept the Spanish empire united and cohesive. Established in so many varied sections of the New World, the settlers remained solidified in their attachment to Roman Catholicism to an even greater degree than they did with respect to the monarchy. The Church tied the inhabitants of the Indies together in many intimate, personal ways and linked them with Europe. It pervaded everything. No aspect of life was beyond its control. No one in the occupied areas was remote for long from contact with clergymen or the sound of church bells. Furthermore, the Church was the chief agency for the transmittal of Western civilization to the Amerinds. Far more than any other instrument, it changed the ways of many aborigines and imparted to them those of Europe. Also, the ecclesiastical establishment steadily attempted and sometimes succeeded in restraining the whites from the worst acts of arrogance while removing the more barbaric features of Indian culture. It was the Church in the Indies, as elsewhere during these centuries, that performed most of the functions of the modern state in education and welfare. And clergymen, more than anyone else, learned from the Indians and perpetuated some of their knowledge or lore for the benefit of the Europeans.

The period of discovery and conquest that opened in 1492 came just when the religiosity of the Spanish had attained a peak of intensity. The ten-year war against the Moors in Granada had concentrated the passions of the Castilians and Aragonese in a patriotic-religious fervor that found an immediate outlet in spreading the faith across the Atlantic. To deny or belittle the deep crusading feelings of the discoverers and conquistadors, even while they committed acts that belied their religion, would be to miss much of the significance of the Conquest. It would be as though we derided the patriotism of famous leaders in recent wars because we knew of weaknesses or failings in their citizenship. The conquistadors were not being merely theatrical when they knelt in public and addressed the Creator aloud, when they ordered mass held before an operation, or when they issued grandiose invitations to pagans to accept Christianity. They truly believed they were bringing to the Indian a hope of eternal salvation and a better life on this earth. This feeling was shared by the tough, illiterate, and grasping men of the ranks as well as by their leaders and the authorities in Spain. Whether the missionary impulse is admired or deplored, its reality during the occupation of the Americas must not be discounted.

In another respect Spain was exceedingly well-prepared for spreading her religion over the New World, a process that occurred, as devout writers like to point out, just as the Protestant Reformation was tearing away so much of the Catholic structure in the Old World. In the peninsula the religious establishment had extraordinary strength and virtue. Isabel and her successors had labored with zeal and intelligence to rid the Church of unworthy clerics. The Inquisition had been authorized in 1478 to promote this purpose along with others less commendable, and the reforming measures later carried out by Cardinal Ximenes de Cisneros brought the Spanish Church to a state of high effectiveness. The abuses which initially provoked Martin Luther, John Calvin, and other reformers scarcely existed in Spain. Nor were Spanish monarchs tempted to supplant the pope the way kings did in England, the Germanies, and Scandinavia, because in Spain the sovereign already possessed vast powers in religious matters. Under the *real patronato* the sovereign chose the prelates who filled the highest positions by nominating them to the pope for installation. The kings decided whether or not to publish in the Spanish realms bulls and decrees emanating from Rome, though matters of doctrine still remained in the pope's control. This relationship might have been ruinous for the Church, leading to a permanent break with Rome or a variety of Protestantism, had not the Spanish monarchs been so devoutly Catholic themselves. More often than not Charles V and Felipe II were more Catholic than the pope and pushed the pontiff into taking measures against the infidels and heretics. It was a remarkable partnership, this alliance of throne and altar. The crown guarded the orthodoxy of Catholicism, supported the clergy generously, and fought wars in behalf of the Church. On its part the Church preached the divine right of kings, extended the realms of the Spanish kings in pagan territories, and effected most of the labor in transforming Amerinds into Spanish-speaking Christians.

STRUCTURE OF THE CHURCH
IN THE SPANISH MONARCHY

When Columbus returned from his voyage, the religious establishment in Spain was already firmly in the hands of the monarchs. The papal award in 1493 further endowed Queen Isabel with authority to direct the conversion of the newly-found pagans in the Indies. By 1501 another papal concession granted the crown power to collect tithes in the Indies, provided the monarch would support the Church. Another pope, Julius III, shortly thereafter attempted to withdraw some of these concessions, but King Fernando, then ruling both Castile and Aragon, stoutly resisted and in 1508 obtained a far-reaching bull which confirmed previous privileges and enumerated in detail the paramount position of the crown in clerical matters in the Indies. Thereafter, the kings of Spain were practically heads of the Church in their realms and, as in other matters, stronger in the overseas empire than in Spain itself. Why had Rome thrown away so much power? One reason was that the papacy was then weak and susceptible to pressure. Another was that the popes were glad to be free of such challenges as the Amerinds posed, when such willing Catholics as the Iberian rulers were ready to take over the responsibility. Finally, it was surely true that the papacy failed to guess the magnitude of the Indies and was therefore unaware of how much it was giving away. During the centuries that followed, Rome sometimes attempted to modify its earlier concessions, maintaining that the original grants could be altered or revoked as easily as they had been made in the first place. The Spanish monarchy contended that as long as the crown upheld the Church and carried out its duties, the papacy was bound as by a contract. After the Spanish American states won their independence, much confusion in Church-state relations arose. The new republics maintained that control of the Church went with sovereignty, while Rome held that the concessions expired with the authority of the monarch.

In exercising these extraordinary powers over the Church in the Indies the Spanish monarchs through Felipe III usually took a personal interest. With much care they picked the clergymen who were to carry out their will. In matters which the monarchs did not personally supervise, the Archbishop of Sevilla wielded authority, very much as other officials in Sevilla dominated economic affairs in the Indies. Then, the monarchs desired to centralize Church affairs of the Indies in the hands of a patriarch. A post was actually created, yet it became mostly an empty honor, probably because the pope hoped to obtain the authority over the Church in America which his predecessors had so lightly given the Spanish kings. Thus real control continued to be exercised by the monarchs themselves or by that useful agency, the Council of Indies. Especially after the late sixteenth century, the Council of Indies selected the archbishops and bishops of the secular clergy for America, the generals and provincial presidents for the regular orders, and inquisitors of the Holy Office. Often these dignitaries entered upon their duties even before Rome approved the appointments, which it nearly always did in its own time. The king or the Council of Indies also decided whether or not to forward bulls and decrees from the pope to the Indies, though sometimes papal channels circumvented this obstruction.

On the American side the viceroys exercised the royal power in their capacity as vice-patrons of the Church. Appointment of priests to parishes and of abbots to convents were made by the viceroy after the appropriate prelate had submitted to him the names of three nominees for each position. The viceroy also took charge of arriving clerics and assigned them to parishes or monastic establishments as he deemed best. If he wished, he attended Church councils or synods and prevented publication of their conclusions if they were obnoxious to him. Lower clergymen could not resign or be removed unless the viceroy approved. Naturally, some viceroys were bored by ecclesiastical affairs and paid little attention to the routine functioning of the Church. Others eagerly interfered in every detail, especially when the viceroy happened to be an archbishop though, curiously enough, the crown came to believe that episcopal viceroys were likely to become overly absorbed in political affairs at the expense of ecclesiastical. No viceroy could neglect the collection of the tithe, a duty which was on the whole honestly accomplished by the state. At least, the crown seldom cheated the Church by taking more than the one-ninth of the income allowed itself. And in agreeing to the construction of the fortress-style churches and monasteries that filled the Indies, it is apparent that the viceroys acted liberally on behalf of the ecclesiastical plant.

EXPANSION OF THE CHURCH IN THE NEW WORLD

With the reports from Columbus and the papal award on hand, Queen Isabel summoned the heads of several religious orders in 1493 for advice and volunteers in dealing with the challenge of the New World. It was the first of many solemn councils assembled from time to time as the Conquest proceeded and the problems multiplied, problems of the royal title, the nature of the Amerinds, the ways to bring them into Christianity, and the limits that should be imposed on the

Spaniards in dealing with them. Certainly, the results in the first twenty years were disheartening, despite the missionaries who went back with Columbus in 1493. The work of conversion lagged, and the Indians died away. As has been seen, the dispatch of Dominicans in 1510 resulted in Montesinos' shocking revelations and remedial legislation in 1512 and 1513, as well as equipping the conquistadors with the *Requerimento*. And then, of course, came the long labors and agitations of Father Las Casas. Yet, as Christians or pagan, the aborigines of the West Indies failed to survive. On the mainland coasts prior to 1521, efforts at conversion were seldom notable.

In Mexico, or New Spain, the opportunity was met with better results. Cortés himself administered the labors of the missionaries with considerable effectiveness. In 1521 the Franciscan order received papal permission to give sacraments to Indians as though its friars were priests. The first Franciscans arrived in 1523, only three of them, but including Peter of Ghent, who soon exerted vast influence through a school for Aztec nobles he conducted for years. In 1524 twelve more barefooted Franciscans reached Mexico City. To dramatize their importance, the great Cortés himself knelt before them and soon permitted himself to be whipped in public for neglecting to go to mass. Almost incredible results followed the efforts of these and other monks who came into New Spain during the next few years. A veritable frenzy gripped the country as multitudes of Indians sought to be baptized in a religion that was obviously more potent than their own. For had the Christians not routed the Aztecs? The good brothers were swamped by converts and overtaxed to the point of exhaustion. Some even fled from pursuing would-be Christians. Apart from these nominal conversions, the regular orders quickly abolished human sacrifice and other horrid practices. Unhappily, they destroyed many idols and manuscripts that anthropologists would like to have now, though they salvaged more than they have been given credit for. The missionaries compromised with native religious practices, retaining much of their gaiety and introducing songs and emblems from Spain that attracted the Indians.

The phenomenal labors of Bishop Zumárraga we have already considered. One of the founders of New Spain, he was justly revered by Indian and Spaniard alike. Peter of Ghent's school did much to bring influential Aztec aristocrats over to Christianity, and other contemporary educational institutions flourished during the first exhilarating half-century of the viceroyalty. Vasco de Quiroga is in many ways the most interesting example of all. A member of the second *audiencia* in Mexico, the one which restored order in the early 1530's, this upright jurist later took orders as a Franciscan and set out to create a communal Christian community in western New Spain, where so much blood had been shed. His efforts were notably successful. Dozens of villages accepted his faith and lived peaceably for generations, each town specializing in a craft or crop that gave it economic stability. Besides these men of action were the friars of scholarly interests, men who not only taught and preached but learned what they could of ancient Mexico and set it down in priceless historical works. We can appreciate them all the more when we realize how few persons took the trouble to do this in Peru during the early days.

Finally, New Spain was greatly stirred by the Virgin of Guadalupe. Many skeptics have attributed the Guadalupe devotion to the practical guile of the clergy, who fostered the story in the belief the Indians would gladly believe that Mary had appeared to an Indian as an Indian herself. The fact that a cult of the Virgin of Guadalupe had long flourished in Extremadura has also been used as evidence that the miracle was bogus. Yet millions of Mexicans have long believed the traditional story and have rallied to the Virgin of Guadalupe as a national patroness, the Mother of God in Indian form. This union of Christian miracle and Mexican nationalism was a very potent force during the wars of independence, and even today, after decades of anti-Catholic persecution in Mexico, the shrine of Guadalupe with the portrait supposedly given to Juan Diego is the most sacred spot in the nation.

If Christianization proceeded very rapidly in the former Aztec realms, the story was quite different in Peru. Comparatively little effort was made to convert the masses in the overturned Inca society, a matter that brought forth much criticism of the clergy in that area. While Inca nobles were soon converted and absorbed in the new regime, the others largely went about their ways as pagans. Of course, Inca paganism was far less offensive to the Spaniards than Aztec, and perhaps by the time Peru was stabilized many white men had become skeptical of the value of preaching to natives. At any rate, Peru's lower classes did not usually flock to Christianity nor allow themselves to be forced into it until the seventeenth century, when an energetic effort suddenly brought great results. In New Granada the gentle conquistador, Quesada, began the missionary work at the outset, and the Indians readily accepted the new faith. Christianization went slower in Guatemala, and slower still in Venezuela and Chile and La Plata. In Paraguay a peculiar situation developed which we must consider separately.

By the end of the first wave of conquest in the middle of the sixteenth century, the Cross had been planted from Paraguay to northern Mexico, and millions of natives had been affected by the new faith. Most of the expansion had been carried out initially by chaplains on expeditions and by the missionaries who went to live among the Indians. Then it was time to implant the church in more conventional form, and so bishoprics were created soon after political institutions. In 1546–1567 archbishops were established in Lima, Mexico City, and Santo Domingo. By the end of the century there were five archbishops and twenty-seven bishops in the Indies, and by 1800, ten archbishops and thirty-eight bishops. It proved much easier to staff the dioceses with bishops than to fill the more lowly parishes. During most of the colonial period a shortage of parish priests prevailed, all this despite the notorious overmanning of the clergy in Spain itself. Generally, the secular clergy served the white and mestizo elements.

It was the regular clergy which carried out the work of converting the Indians. Here a new institution was shaped, in contrast to the apparatus of the secular branch which was typical of Europe. There stood no clear precedent for mass conversion of countless numbers of pagans with varying degrees of willingness to listen to Christian preaching. By 1521 it was clear from experience that the friars were most likely to be available for such labors and that they required for the purpose more authority than they had. Accordingly, the pope gave the Franciscan order (and later others) permission for selected friars to administer sacraments, as only priests did. Then it was easier for the Franciscans in New Spain to carry out evangelization and to entrench themselves in Indian communities. The mission system grew out of the needs of the time and from the experiments of Father Las Casas. Soon, the Franciscans had large groups of Indians living in villages under their supervision, isolated from the white settlers. So phenomenal was their success that the Dominicans, Augustinians Mercederians, Carmelites, and lastly and most significantly, the Jesuits, likewise established missions on the frontiers. The chain of command for these orders remained free from the secular clergy to a great extent. Each order had its own method of government, ranging from the monk or nun to the abbot or prioress, then upward to provincial presidents and generals for the order in Mexico City or Lima and in Madrid and Rome.

Altogether, the religious establishment was large enough to rival the political authority extending from the viceroy down to the *corregidores* and other officials of the administration. The Church was, of course, supposed to be under the viceroy's control, but this situation did not give lesser political officers the power to interfere with it. So willful were many of the Church leaders and so powerful was their hold on the minds of the inhabitants that the Church often enjoyed more prestige than the government. It was inevitable that competition should result, that archbishops should dispute with viceroys or captain-generals, bishops with governors, abbots with *corregidores*, missions with towns. Officially, the crown could have settled these quarrels, but the distances were so great, the issues so tangled, and the government so slow that contentious situations often never cleared up. Throughout most of the Spanish empire during the colonial period a tug-of-war was chronic between the civil and clerical authorities. The issues often took the form of ridiculous spats and unedifying pettiness, but underneath they were quite serious, involving nothing less than control of native labor and the sources of wealth. No true resolution of this condition occurred until close to the end of the colonial period, when the Church was compelled to accept the subordinate position it had legally held all along. Even so, clerical immunity to civil courts permitted the clergy a very high degree of independence.

Controversies abounded within the Church, as must be expected in any institution which wields so much power. The regular orders had gotten into the dangerous zones first and had performed the real work of conversion. Naturally, they tended to look down on the seculars who came in after the area was pacified. The secular clergy often resented the authority of the orders over the natives, in particular their power to give sacraments. Furthermore, the regulars were supposed to move farther into the frontier, to extend the "rim of Christendom," as soon as they had civilized and Christianized an Indian community. Legally, the period for accomplishing this was ten years. Yet the friars often became attached to the natives and localities. Better than anyone else they knew their labors had only begun, that ten years was far from enough. The more materialistic among them might wish to remain in missions or monasteries they had made comfortable, caring little for the risks of starting all over again in a raw district. Those who were fond of their Indian charges no doubt feared what would happen once the missions were abandoned, for the white settlers were usually eager to get their hands on a new labor supply. The secular clergy usually favored extending the tithe to the Indians, while the regulars stoutly opposed it. The compromise solution reached in many areas was for natives to pay tithes only on income from European crops. In 1574 the Spanish crown firmly reiterated the subordination of the clergy to the viceroy. In time, this signified victory for the seculars, and the regular orders lamented they had been used and demoted by the crown, just as Columbus, Cortés, and a host of other pioneers had been.

Manning the huge ecclesiastical establishment taxed the Spanish in some ways, full of clergymen as the peninsula was. The shortage of priests for both Spanish and Indian towns seldom abated for long, and there was always more work for the missionary friars than could be handled. As in other spheres, it was customary to insist that the most important posts go to peninsulars. Presumably they were more loyal, better-trained, and less likely to degenerate in the "tropics," as the Spanish officially regarded the Americas, than individuals who were

born on the "wrong" side of the Atlantic. Thus, nearly all of the archbishops and bishops were Spanish-born, perhaps only one out of seven
being creoles during the entire colonial period. The officers of the regular
orders were likewise mostly peninsulars. Many of the rank and file came
to be American-born, particularly after universities developed in the
Indies and after the Jesuits began the work of educating priests.
Mestizos were allowed to enter the regular orders and in some instances
to become priests, and in very rare cases so were full-blooded Indians.[1]
On the whole, the peninsulars held key posts, creoles composed a majority of the clergy of all types, and mestizos and Indians occupied only
the humblest positions.

The quality of the clergy in colonial America has been much debated. If it is remembered that a very large number of persons went
into the clergy in both Spain and the Indies, it is easier to comprehend
that the group as a whole reflected the entire society. Many younger
sons of good families became clergymen because they could inherit no
property or because they had failed to make the grade in the army or
government service. Great numbers of girls were dispatched to convents
by families who believed it was a mark of distinction to have daughters
who were nuns. Naturally, the clergy included many individuals whose
primary motivation was not necessarily a call to offer themselves in
sacrifice. That many of them should continue to behave like laymen
is not surprising. Furthermore, the Church in Spain followed a practice
that military establishments have adopted in recent times, sending both
their best and their worst to overseas posts. The finest went because they
were needed to carry out important tasks, the others because they were
troublesome. Arrivals from the peninsula were likely to represent the
extremes. Idealistic men of energy and ability were zealous to carry
the Cross and meet the challenge of the Indies. Others went because
they were shipped away, or because they had heard about the wealth,
women, and freedom they might enjoy in the New World.

Condemnation of the clergy in Spanish America was frequent, even
continuous, covering all areas and the whole colonial period. Viceroys
often found much to criticize, and so did other officials. Very damning reports went back to Spain from clergymen themselves, who were
well aware of the misbehavior of some of their fellows. Prelates were
likely to be accused of being ambitious to usurp the power of political
officials and to acquire an improper hold on the population. Priests
were often charged with neglecting their religious duties and involving
themselves in business affairs, owning or controlling farms and factories
and exploiting native labor. Fees charged by the priests for clerical

1. Spaniards contended that Indians
and mestizos were less likely to obey the
rule of chastity than whites, among other
failings.

services and the sales of images, relics, indulgences, and articles used in the frequent festivals so beloved by the population gave rise to tales of indecent enrichment. Friars or monks who lived among the Indians had little supervision and were open to temptations to acquire concubines and business advantages. This was particularly true in mission villages, where two or three friars lived as virtual dictators and could, if they wished, indulge themselves freely without being exposed for a long time, if ever. Many monasteries and nunneries were handsome establishments with quarters for luxurious living, abundant servants, and opportunities for immoral behavior. That many of such criticisms derived from persons interested in undermining the monks—jealous members of rival orders, the secular clergy, rapacious Spaniards who coveted the labor or wealth for themselves, or merely mischievous gossips—can be well understood. But then, some of it must have been valid.

The increase in the wealth of the Church has long been a target of condemnation. Generous awards of lands and city property were made by the early rulers, who were anxious to settle the Indies. As this attitude weakened, the Church continued to acquire productive areas through opening up the frontier and through gifts and bequests. Often the clergy was accused of frightening persons on their death beds into changing their wills in behalf of the Church, or in extorting rich gifts by playing on the superstitions or the sense of guilt of the donor. Yet it is obvious that many individuals wished to endow the Church just as people do today, making generous gifts not only to the Church as a holy institution but to further the many charitable and educational works it performed. Church wealth also accumulated through the extensive farms, orchards, vineyards, and grazing areas which had been developed by the clergy and their Indian charges. Capital was built up from such activities, and until the eighteenth century the Church was more likely to be in a position to make investments and loans than any other agency. The construction of magnificent or gaudy Church buildings, handsome episcopal palaces, splendid abbeys and convents, and many other attributes to house the ecclesiastical establishment has often been condemned by modern men, but in that period people were usually sincere in wishing to express their faith and the glory of God in this manner. The total value of the wealth of the colonial Latin American Church can scarcely be estimated in terms that have any meaning now. Possibly as much as half the productive property of the Indies was in Church hands through outright ownership or mortgages, and usually it could not be sold because of mortmain.

Two important aspects of this vast wealth should be credited. One is that the Church created so much of it, that it was veritably a pioneer in economic affairs. The very fact that at any time a million or more

Indians lived in mission villages and devoted themselves to productive pursuits was the result of long, patient, and hazardous labor on the part of the friars. Imparting to them the skills of Europe, together with the production of marketable plants and animals, greatly enriched the Indies. No other institution could, or did, obtain such results from the Indians. The second consideration is that the Church performed much of the work now undertaken by the state: education, defense of mission areas by armed natives, and what is now called "welfare"—medical care, homes for the aged, crippled, orphaned, and indigent, and many other charitable functions. Obviously, a vast amount of property and income was necessary to support these activities in lieu of the taxes and contributions with which contemporary societies are very familiar. No mortal should presume to measure the spiritual achievements of the Church in the Spanish Indies. Its activities in mundane affairs were enormously important and on the whole humanitarian.

THE INQUISITION

Few institutions have as evil a reputation in the history of Western civilization as the Spanish Inquisition. Much of its unreasonableness and cruelty appear in a different light when contemporaneous instruments of persecution in other lands are considered, and surely it is right to judge historical processes in comparative terms. Furthermore, our own times have excelled the intolerant sixteenth and seventeenth centuries in the massive sufferings inflicted upon victims of political fanaticisms, chiefly in totalitarian countries. Even so, the facts of the Inquisition in Spain are hideous enough. Beginning with the Catholic Kings, the Holy Office of the Inquisition preyed on supposedly insincere Jewish and Moslem converts to Christianity. Under Charles V, its activities were fairly moderate in Spain itself, though it turned on Protestants in the Netherlands. It was Felipe II who stepped up the terrible volume of punishment against potentially rebellious *moriscos* in the peninsula, Protestants in Italy and Belgium, heretics in the overseas empire, and evildoers wherever he could apprehend them. Under the reigns of Felipe III, Felipe IV, and Carlos II, the toll tended to increase. Not only suspected infidels or heretics, but great numbers of accused witches and assorted sinners and transgressors were brought before the dreaded tribunal. Yet these numbers were not particularly large when compared to the persecutions in France during the religious civil wars of the late sixteenth century, or those in England during the time of Mary I, Elizabeth I, and Oliver Cromwell, or in some of the German and Scandinavian states. Even the English colonies in America took shameful measures against supposed witches and hounded unpopular religious minorities. Yet, the Spanish Inquisition caught the imagination of the world and has become, along with atrocities against the Indians, the central source of the Black Legend.

In the Indies the problem of non-Christians was appallingly large. At first the authorities ignored or punished Indian blasphemers as circumstances ruled. The bishops were given inquisitorial powers, but rather early and sensibly, the Church decided that Indians should not properly be brought under such discipline for their lingering pagan ways. The few who were punished provoked outcries in Spain, where it was generally believed that Indians could not be expected to free themselves from their unfortunate heritage for a long time. The question of white heretics remained, indeed grew, as colonists arrived and as foreign interlopers began to appear in Spanish American ports. One measure to deal with the problem was to tighten up to an extreme degree the surveillance at Sevilla so that no suspicious person would reach the Indies on the fleets. As for those who illegally entered or who developed heresies while they were overseas, the Inquisition was planted in Lima in 1570 and in Mexico City in 1571. After so many English and Dutch freebooters got into the Caribbean, a third office was set up in Cartagena in 1610.

The methods of the Holy Office remain a rebuke to fair play and to plain justice. A secret denunciation might bring any white person but the viceroy, who enjoyed an immunity while he held office, before the tribunal. The inquisitors, who were clergymen of high rank and prestige and who were subject to inspection by superior authority, might decide to disregard the charges, especially if they were anonymous or if the victim were too influential to be prosecuted without a great scandal. Again, they might have him arrested and confined in a dark cell for an extensive period, isolated from family and friends and ignorant of the nature of the accusations. The day of the hearing would finally arrive. The accused appeared on his knees before the robed inquisitors while witnesses entered the building through hidden doors or tunnels, whispered their evidence from behind a screen, and then disappeared. The defendant could then admit the truth of the charges and be sentenced. If he denied his guilt, torture was administered, usually by stretching him on a rack or by filling him up with great quantities of water. Cruelly enough, the accused had to pay his torturers a fee for these services. Broken and in pain, he might now acknowledge guilt. If he persisted in upholding his innocence, the inquisitors might believe him, for they were no more foolish or hardened than other judges. Or, they might sentence him despite his protestations.

The gross unfairness of these proceedings shocks those of later times who have never experienced mistreatment at the hands of a totalitarian government. It would be a mistake, however, to assume that inquisitors were necessarily fiends or gullible fanatics who credited any testimony against a prisoner. Arrests were not likely to be made unless the evidence was convincing. Much of the long delay in bringing the accused to trial resulted from thoroughgoing efforts to assemble testimony. Defense witnesses were heard and their evidence weighed.

Unfortunate persons convicted of being Protestants, Jews, or Moslems—and therefore traitors—were usually sentenced to death unless they recanted, in which case the penalty was imprisonment. Those who were found guilty of making pacts with the devil or practicing witchcraft were likely to fare as badly. So were sex perverts and priests who seduced women during the confessional. Lesser offenders were whipped in public or sent to the galleys or prisons for stated terms. These were likely to be fake mystics, wayward clerics, and persons who made wild statements or prophecies that endangered public order. People who robbed or desecrated houses of worship also fell into this category.

Every two or three years an *auto de fe* would be held to dramatize the heinousness of such offenses. Stands were erected in the central plaza of Mexico City, Lima, or Cartagena. With great dignity the viceroy and other ranking officials proceeded to the scene. Lesser officers paraded in their robes from another direction to the plaza and took their places. Drums and bells furnished a background for the gravity of the occasion. Then the prisoners were brought through the streets, tied and wearing the detested *sanbenito*, or cover, to signify their disgrace, a garment attached afterward to family burial places to perpetuate the evil memory. The crowds were in a holiday mood, very much like the throngs who watched the cart pass to the guillotine during the French Revolution. They jeered at the prisoners and pelted them with rotten fruit or stones. To the population it appeared that the world was ridding itself of dangerous persons. They rejoiced at the victory of a godly society over evildoers. After hours of mounting tension, the ceremony reached its climax with the reading of sentences. At this point the inquisitors had completed their task. Not they but the crown administered punishment. Thus the prisoners were given over to the police to be taken to jails, galleys, public whipping posts, or execution points. Gay and relieved as the crowds seemed on these occasions, they must have been impressed with the underlying terror of the proceedings, as it was intended they should be. If they drew pleasure from the screams of traitors, heretics, and witches in the flames, they must also have realized how watchful they must be of their own conduct.

For all the horror and injustice, the Inquisition in the New World persecuted on a far smaller scale than similar agencies in western Europe and the English colonies in America during the same period.[2] As has been observed, Indians were not subject to its attentions after the first years of the colonial period. Nor were Negroes, except for flagrant cases of sorcery. During its entire history, running from 1570 to 1820 (with a suspension in 1812–1814), the American Inquisitions heard about 6,000 cases. Of these no more than one hundred resulted in burnings in person at the stake. Those who were burned in effigy presumably suffered no discomfort. Others went to prison or were flogged or fined. A few were acquitted, and a considerable number died under torture or awaiting trial. The Holy Office confiscated their property and sought to extend the stigma to the families and unborn descendants of the victims. And yet the volume of punishment was very small compared to more enlightened areas in Europe. In single days more persons were put to death for heresy in England or France or other countries than the Spanish American Inquisitions counted in two and a half centuries. It must not be overlooked that many victims of the Holy Office would be punished, though not always so severely, even today for such crimes as treason, gross immorality, and desecration of religious houses. Civilized countries are no longer concerned with witchcraft, but a third of the human race lives under systems that savagely persecute heresy in political matters.

Another duty of the Inquisition was to censor reading material and public entertainments, activities which the most enlightened democracies of the present day find it necessary to practice in some way or other. All books or other reading matter were supposed to be checked at Sevilla and scrutinized at the port of entry in the Indies to see that works subversive of religion, patriotism, and public morals were kept out. The Spanish had practiced this type of censorship even before the Inquisition went into operation in the Indies and prior to the famous Index of Prohibited Works compiled by the Council of Trent in 1563. In fact, the Spanish index continued long after the papal index began and was more thoroughgoing. The supervision of plays and musical shows was lax, judged by the crudeness of many of them, except when material of a political or religious nature pricked the inquisitors. The conclusion is warranted that over the long stretch of the colonial period, the Inquisition did not take its censorship duties very seriously. Or, possibly, the colonials were extremely clever in outwitting the authorities. In any event great numbers of books of all types reached the Indies and were read and discussed. Censorship in the Indies resembled sumptuary laws of other times in that it was always a potential threat and an

2. This being the only fair comparison. Treason and heresy were certainly punished fiercely in the non-Western world, as were many other offenses.

inhibiting factor, but that in the long run the people did what they pleased.

THE MISSION SYSTEM

The ease with which Christianity spread in much of the New World can be attributed to several mundane factors, apart from questions regarding the truth of this faith and the will of God that it be extended. One of the most important elements was the manifest impotence of the Indian deities, who had failed to protect their followers from defeat and conquest by the white men. Also, some of the legends credited by the Indians concerning creation and miracles of the past resembled those in Hebreo-Christianity, so much so that many Spaniards convinced themselves that Christian missionaries had somehow reached America in the distant past. It is barely possible that they had, but this explanation is not necessary to account for the widely prevailing beliefs of ancient floods, tempters, prophets, and supernatural beings. All the Indians apparently believed in an after-life before they heard of Christianity. Most of them had holy days, temples, rituals, fasting therefore, stretching the mentality of the Indians too much when the clerics adapted the beliefs and practices of Christianity to their traditional religions. It was only in removing idols, abolishing cannibalism, and limiting polygamy that the missionaries encountered persistent resistance.

Present on most of the *entradas* that penetrated pagan areas were friars or priests. The *Requerimiento* read and the Indians defeated, the loving work of conversion would begin. The substitution of the cross and other Christian symbols was usually easy enough. At times ludicrous situations developed when Indians overwhelmed the clergy with demands to be baptized. Once the area had settled down, the work of the priest or friar was to instruct the sons of Indian nobles, in the well-founded expectation that this work would pay large dividends in the future. An *encomendero* was likely to desire the services of a clergyman to convert the natives under his control, at least if no pressures were exerted to treat the Indians better.

Such methods were somewhat haphazard but reasonably effective in areas where the Indians were sedentary and fairly advanced. Eventually, most of them became Christians after a fashion. But for the countless primitives who lived beyond these settled regions, another system was necessary. Here the crown and Church developed a new institution, periods, and practices resembling confession and penance. It was not, the mission village as pioneered by Father Las Casas in Venezuela and Nicaragua. Natives congregated in supervised communities ruled by a few friars would adopt Christianity—a genuine ambition for most

Spaniards—and become adaptable to the economic requirements of a Europeanized society. After ten years or so, as the Law of the Indies came to specify, these Hispanicized Christians were supposed to be absorbed into the colonial system and the friars would move farther out in the wilderness to continue the process. This extraordinary system got under way on a large scale in the middle of the sixteenth century and reached a fantastic extent within a century. After a pause, it made further inroads in the pagan world during the eighteenth century. The advantages to the crown were obvious, for the more the rim of Christendom was pushed back, the more land the Spaniards could occupy and the more civilized subjects would become available to work and to create wealth. Thus the mission system was a highly effective instrument of both Spanish imperialism and Catholic expansion.

The real brunt of this scheme fell upon the first friars who made the original penetrations. They might easily be killed or driven back by hostile natives, and many of them were. Others, unarmed and manifestly peaceable, would gain a friendly audience and gradually overcome distrust of the white man. After the friar and his one or two partners, for usually they operated in very small groups, had learned some of the language and gained confidence, they might relate a simplified story of the Christian religion, probably using tales of hell fire to instill awe and heavenly rewards to kindle hope. Fireworks, candy, gadgets, and tricks might create a favorable atmosphere. At length the natives might be induced to settle down and construct a village. Usually the friars could draw on government supplies to acquire tools, seeds, plants, and domesticated animals to demonstrate the many advantages of accepting European ways. The Indians might soon tire of the proceedings and kill the missionaries. But in very many instances they consented to build the village as directed, with a plaza, church, warehouse, and homes laid out in checkerboard pattern. If things went well, the fields would produce useful crops and the animals would multiply. The friars had the opportunity to instruct their wards in Christian ways, persuading them to attend Church services, to marry (often this meant having one wife at a time in lieu of polygamy), and to accept European standards of morality. Also, the brothers knew a great deal about agriculture and animal husbandry which, together with Indian knowledge, resulted in flourishing fields, orchards, vineyards, gardens, and stocked pasturelands. Later would come instruction in lowly skills and handicrafts as well as in music and sports. Life went on at a leisured pace, without too much toil and with festivals, music, celebrations, and games. The attraction of community life itself was so great that once a village was operating, the Indians were unlikely to resume their roving existence.

The friars needed an element of force behind this work of loving instruction. This was provided by the crown, which had every ideological and material reason for supporting the experiment. Little squads of soldiers, usually about a half dozen, patrolled the mission areas to discourage attempts at flight and to keep hostile Indians and troublesome whites at a respectful distance. These soldiers themselves, riding about or encamped in a tiny base known as a *presidio*, posed problems for the friars, for they often coveted Indian women or derided the efforts of the clerics. But the system worked well enough. Usually the Indians remained in the mission and became, at least superficially, Europeanized Christians.

The mission system slowly covered enormous areas in northern and western New Spain, spreading from the rich valley of the Aztecs to the Pacific coast and north to El Paso del Norte and up the Rio Grande into Pueblo territory. Penetrating Florida, Texas, and California, the missions fixed the hold of Spain as dangers from other European powers loomed. In Central America the process was less dramatic, though many friars were martyred. In the grassy outposts of Venezuela the missions long stood as Spain's only true hold on the area. The Green Hell of the Amazon basin extending east of the Andes in Peru and New Granada was slowly reduced. The mission system came close to utter failure in Chile, where the pugnacious Araucanians refused to yield to Spanish force or preachments with a spirit that compels admiration. Nor were the primitive tribes of the Argentine receptive to the blandishments of the proselytizers until late in the colonial period. But in Brazil and Paraguay the results of the system almost tax credulity.

The Jesuit Reductions in Paraguay

NOWHERE did the phenomenal successes of the Jesuits shine more brilliantly than in Paraguay. Even Voltaire, the deadly foe of all organized religions and cruel critic of the Society of Jesus, pointed to their achievement in Paraguay as "a triumph for humanity" and treated it favorably in one of Candide's adventures. Other writers of the Enlightenment praised this undertaking, almost alone of the works of the Catholic Church, in extravagant terms. Montesquieu described the Paraguayan reductions as the healing of a wound, the righting of the wrong of the Conquest. D'Alembert believed the experiment showed how a population could be happy without recourse to force. The Scottish historian James Robertson, who was so biting in his criticisms of the work of Spain, and the Frenchman Raynal, whose historical work defamed Spanish imperialism, had praise for the accomplishments of the detested Jesuits in far-off Paraguay. The Jesuits themselves have not been reticent in writing about this celebrated achievement.

In 1605 the crown turned over to the Society of Jesus an enormous area which embraces most of the present republic of Paraguay and rich sections of Argentina and a corner of Brazil. The only Spanish settlements of any consequence in that part of South America then were Asuncion and the little port of Buenos Aires. A major purpose behind this grant was to determine whether missions on a very large scale could transform a populous area. At this time the Jesuits were in high favor with the crown and in a position to obtain this coveted assignment. Into the area they went, encountering the placid Guaraní and Tapes Indians, who seldom offered difficulties to their rulers, then and afterward. The soil was fertile, the climate warm but not tropical. In only a few years the Jesuits congregated perhaps 100,000 Indians in thirty "reductions" or communities. Sturdy stone houses stood on the gridiron pattern of the streets; warehouses, storerooms, and churches were erected. Outside the reductions were gardens, pastures, vineyards, and common fields. Perhaps the Jesuits copied the Inca system as they understood it. Or it may have been a matter of pragmatic adaptation of Christian social philosophy to Indian ways. Anyhow, the whole region was quickly pacified.

It was not long until the slave-hunters of São Paulo, the *bandeirantes*, learned of the tamed natives whose services could be so useful in other capacities. A series of raids proved rewarding, and soon large-scale incursions were stripping the reductions of their wards.[3] Perhaps 60,000 Indians were so seized and carried away. Never inclined to accept defeat, the Jesuits removed their settlements in 1627–1631 in a marvel of logistics downriver past the Iguassú Falls. Their control over this migration indicates how firmly the Indians trusted and obeyed the brothers. Finally relocated in a more distant area, the Jesuits set about to arm their wards and teach them to fight back. As usual, they were magnificently successful. Under Jesuit leadership the Guaranís fought off the *paulistas* until they ceased to be molested, and then dutifully put away their guns and went back to work. No suggestion of revolt against the Jesuits themselves is indicated. Later, these armies were effective against Spanish would-be enslavers from Asunción and against organized armies of both Spain and Portugal.

As the reductions were reorganized, the mission way of life resumed. Each morning the Indians were awakened by the ringing of a bell. After attending religious services, the men marched out to the fields, swinging along and singing as though they enjoyed it, for the Jesuits were wise enough to associate labor with celebration, as the Indians did before the

3. It should be noted that a patriotic school of Brazilian writers holds, not very convincingly, that this traditional picture of *paulista* wolves and Indian lambs is badly distorted.

Conquest. Work in the fields and pastures was not long, four to six hours a day, and then the men would return. While they had been gone, women were about their work and children were attending school, most of them to learn handicrafts and the elementary aspects of using and repairing machinery. The few very gifted children were taught Latin and Spanish and prepared for future leadership. The rest of the day was a matter of resting or recreation. Organized games and Spanish-style sports were popular, and of course there were further religious services, singing, dancing, and other simple pleasures.

The economy of the land was communal up to a point, with everyone working for everyone else. But in the distribution of fabricated articles and the reserves in the storehouses, those who had contributed the most received the most. In some cases the Indians worked bits of land they considered their own, though the Jesuits shifted them about as they deemed best. Apart from raising and making everything they needed, the reductions produced *yerba maté*, the Paraguayan tea which was becoming so popular in southern South America, which they exported along with cotton and woolen articles. Roads, some of which still remain, united the reductions and permitted such commerce as was necessary. The Society had its own system of disciplined government, but the Indians were encouraged to elect *regidores* and *alcaldes*, somewhat as schoolchildren choose their own officers.

As in other mission areas, it was imperative to keep out all whites but for the 200 or so Jesuits and an occasional trader or inspector. On the whole the whites bitterly resented this situation, as well as the spectacle of the Society occupying an enormous province with thousands of wards. All kinds of rumors were circulated to discredit the Jesuits: that they had great reserves of gold or silver; that they sent money directly to Rome, bypassing the king; that they lived lives of luxury and sin; that they overworked and abused the natives; and so on. None of these tales, as it turned out, was true. The area was rich, but only in agricultural and pastoral industries. The brothers seemed to have been virtuous to an inhuman degree, as Jesuits in the Indies generally were. The natives were far from overworked, and they had plenty and seemed contented.

Yet, as events were to prove when the Jesuits were ousted in 1768, the generations of training built up little attachment to civilization or Christianity among the Guaranís. They quickly reverted to paganism and to a semi-savage state once the brothers vanished. Their static society had been a little paradise while it lasted, but it had no dynamism of its own. The natives were treated like children, and they acted like children once the controls were gone. Much as can be said in favor of the mission system, the experience of Paraguay suggests many shortcomings.

II

Economic Affairs

IMPERIAL ECONOMIC POLICY

S PAIN's economic policies in her overseas empire are usually
described as mercantilistic, though many qualifications and
exceptions must be acknowledged. Naturally, conditions changed a great
deal between the time of Columbus and the era of Bolívar, and in any
period the effects of economic measures in the various regions were different. As in other aspects of Spanish colonial history, a natural dividing
line is the mid-eighteenth century, when a new dynasty brought about
many changes in the economic system. Centering our attention on the
earlier period, we may treat two general categories of Spain's economic
relations with the Indies.

First is the well-known attitude that Castile or Spain immediately
adopted toward the kingdoms in America, a selfish attitude, one that
took for granted the right of peninsulars to make large profits from their
activities in the New World. The risks were so great that no one but
missionaries or compulsive adventurers would be tempted to explore unless potential rewards were of a large scale. Further, it was deemed right
and proper that Spain should obtain riches from the overseas possessions
and use them for her own glorification. Thus Spaniards and no others
should have access to the treasures of America. They should enjoy a
monopoly of the products of the Indies, have a closed market for their
own exports, and see to it that Spain received more than she sent. These
attitudes had long been typical of the Italian states and the Hanseatic
League. Later, the most advanced monarchies in Europe would systema-
tize them in the policy of mercantilism. It was natural, then, for the
Spaniard to adopt these points of view and even to be unaware of their
arrogance. Also, the crown was able in economic affairs, just as it was in

political matters, to establish a more autocratic system overseas than it could enforce in Spain itself.

In exploiting the New World for treasure, there is no doubt that Spain did exceedingly well for herself, much as she wasted her income. In more narrowly commercial affairs, Spain was largely unsuccessful, at least when her opportunities are considered. Adopting from the beginning an unconsciously mercantilistic policy, and then a consciously mercantilistic attitude, the mother country proposed to ship to the colonies only such goods as it cared to spare. These should be sold at advantageous prices without competition, and raw materials and precious metals should be returned as cheaply as possible. Even during the best days of the imperial system things did not work out quite so simply. The common sense and ingenuity of the Americans served to defeat so one-sided an arrangement in many instances, and after the Spanish homeland became weak, they made a mockery of it. It should be noted that Spain did not notably attempt to force her own goods on the Indies, because she did not manufacture many articles desired by the colonials and because she feared that exports raised prices at home. Nor did Spain often try to eliminate colonial production, though she sometimes sought to restrict it. Even so, her commercial policies must be regarded as both selfish and unsuccessful in the main. The Americans purchased widely outside the system and produced what they could. The enemies of the Spanish monarchy enriched themselves on the produce of the overseas colonies, and by 1700 Spain herself was a desperately poor country.

The second broad aspect of Spanish economic policy has been less emphasized than the exploitative, and correctly so. It was less important than profit-taking; until recently most students have ignored it altogether. But we of the contemporary world generally believe that the elevation of the economies of backward lands brings not only humanitarian satisfaction but also material rewards. It is easier for us, therefore, to grasp the fact that many Spaniards likewise cherished this idea. To improve the New World by transferring European settlers, skills, technology, domestic animals, and plants and by instructing the natives was a continuing policy of the crown. Life in the Indies was indeed transformed and enriched. Nor was this change merely an incidental consequence of an otherwise hateful imperialism. From the start Queen Isabel and Columbus aspired to raise the standard of living of the Indians. Cortés was a notable builder in the economic sphere, as were other early leaders in New Spain. In Peru, too, and in other lands overrun by the Spaniards, warriors were followed by settlers who brought livestock, seeds, and tools. The crown insisted that they do this, for imperialism meant not only adding new subjects to the monarch's collection and increasing the hold of Christendom, but also providing these new subjects with the advantages of the more advanced Europe. Spaniards took satisfaction in the growth of cities in the Americas and in the flourishing mines, farms, herds, orchards, vineyards, and other aspects of a sound economy. This mixture of enlightened selfishness and altruism facilitated the growth of a Europe-oriented society from Santa Fe in New Mexico to Buenos Aires in the Argentine in a comparatively short time.

SPANISH-AMERICAN COMMERCE

The Machinery for the Control of Commerce

THE CASA DE CONTRATACIÓN

When Columbus returned to the Indies on his second voyage, his expedition was prepared under the supervision of Juan Rodríguez de Fonseca, dean of the cathedral at Sevilla. Fonseca tightened his control during the following years and became a veritable colonial minister. In 1503 a special agency, the *Casa de Contratación*, which might roughly be translated as House of Trade, was set up to co-ordinate his various duties. In Sevilla until 1717, the *Casa de Contratación* became the key to Spain's overseas empire, though at times it seemed rather a bottleneck. All persons and articles bound for the Indies and all coming from there to Spain were supposed to be channeled through this one agency. Its functions were somewhat like those of a port of embarkation in modern wartime. Fantastic as it was for the Spanish monarchy to supervise all trade with the Americas through the *Casa de Contratación*, it seems that the institution worked comparatively well for much of the colonial period.

The Casa had its difficulties. Merchants in Cadiz demanded a share in the Indies trade and had to be placated with a branch of the agency and a fixed amount of ship space. Not until 1717 did they succeed in obtaining its transfer to their city, which in truth was much more exposed than Sevilla to foreign attack. After Fonseca's disgrace about 1520 and the creation of the Council of Indies, it looked as though the Casa would be abolished. Instead, it retained its autonomy but came under the general supervision of the Council of Indies. Later, Charles V threatened its pre-eminence by opening several ports in northern Spain for the Indies trade, but he found the experiment unsatisfactory and reverted to the centralization at Sevilla. Felipe II and his Habsburg successors saw no reason to alter the situation. Thus, for more than two centuries the *Casa de Contratación* enjoyed a unique importance in Spanish-American commerce. Like all other Spanish offices it was

accused of slowness and procrastination, addiction to red tape and pedantry, and corruption.

As it finally evolved, the Casa had such duties as these: 1) Each ship
bound for the Indies had to be registered, fitted, loaded, and often armed
under its supervision. The papers of each emigrant, whether he was official, clergyman, trader, or settler, were supposed to pass its scrutiny.
2) All returning ships were to unload their passengers and cargoes where
officials of the Casa could "process" them and sort them out. As the
flood of treasure from the New World expanded, this responsibility became the most important, and the Casa fulfilled it in its own way and
in its own time, an exasperatingly deliberate pace in most instances. Not
only such treasure, but monies belonging to private individuals and shipments of goods were examined, often with great suspicion and care.
3) After 1508 the Casa operated a school for pilots, its first director being
Amerigo Vespucci, where mariners received instruction and where a
great body of nautical information, charts of currents, and maps of the
Indies were accumulated. 4) Finally, it had a court of law to deal with
crimes on the high seas and for nearly all suits regarding trade between
Spain and the Indies.

THE CONSULADOS

Complementing the *Casa de Contratación* was an organization
or guild of merchants in Sevilla which became in 1543 a *consulado*.
These business firms were not slow to grasp the fact that the settlers in
the New World were likely to be money-rich and goods-poor. Hence
the key to great profits was to send as few goods as possible and to charge
excessive prices. This characteristic bit of mercantilistic thinking, which
was poor business in the long run, could be implemented best if shortages
were created over several years in order to bring demand to a peak. Then,
at last, the cargo would reach the Indies, to be sold quickly for outrageous prices. In order to carry out such maneuvers over a period of years
it was important that the *consulado* of Sevilla enjoy intimate, even corrupt, relations with the *Casa de Contratación*.[1] It was also important
that merchants in Mexico City and Lima and other main distribution
centers cooperate. In time, *consulados* were established in the leading
cities of the Indies, often to fix prices, manipulate demand, and otherwise fleece the consumers, all in connivance with the powerful *consulado*
of Sevilla. For many years this crudely extortionate system worked, and
the *consulados* became wealthy. Their fluid capital enabled them to
serve as credit institutions and to affect economic life in America in

1. The Casa was usually housed in the
Moorish Alcázar. Close by, during much
of the colonial period, was the *consulado*
in the handsome palace designed by
Herrera known now as the General Ar-
chive of the Indies, the mecca of scholars
interested in Spain's relations with her
overseas empire.

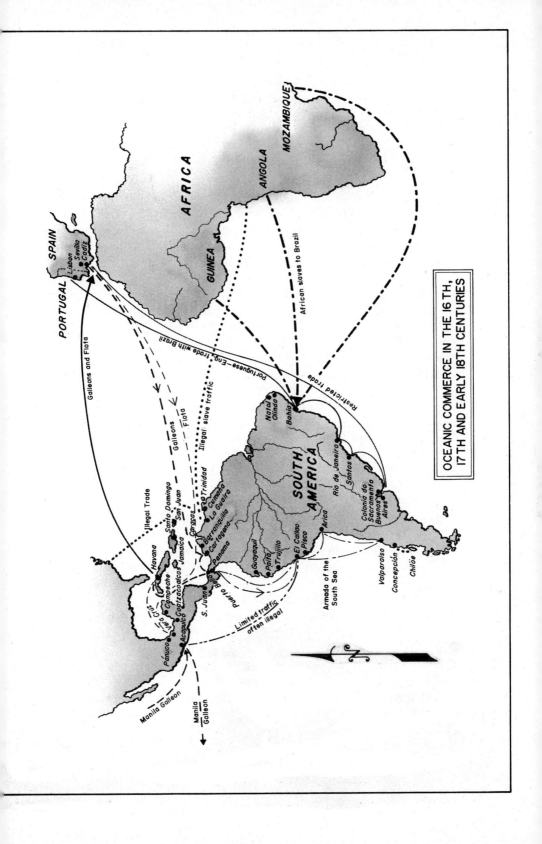

OCEANIC COMMERCE IN THE 16TH, 17TH AND EARLY 18TH CENTURIES

other ways. The colonists, however, realized that to defend themselves against such exploitation they would have to manufacture many goods themselves and trade illegally with foreign or domestic smugglers. By the latter half of the seventeenth century the monopolists were in decline.

THE FLEETS

One of the most fascinating aspects of the imperial commercial system was the employment of massive fleets or convoys. As early as 1526 the crown had directed that ships between Spain and the Indies sail in pairs or three to guard against capture, for already French privateers had molested occasional Spanish vessels, among them one loaded with Aztec treasures sent by Cortés. As news of Mexican and Peruvian riches circulated through Europe, the menace mounted. Shipowners clamored for help. As a result the vessels were enlarged and armed, and squadrons of warships patrolled the waters off southern Spain and the Caribbean. Depredations, especially by pirates, became worse, and in the 1540's the Spanish began to consolidate all ships going to America in mammoth fleets protected by fast warships with soldiers who could board enemy attackers. And then those returning to Spain required such defenses. The system was perfected in the 1560's by Menéndez de Avilés, the governor of Cuba, so that two fleets would depart each year, deliver their passengers and goods in America, load the silver, combine in the Caribbean, and return as one huge convoy to Sevilla.

This system, in its regularity and majesty so typical of Felipe II, functioned on an annual basis for about half a century. After Spain's control of the seas weakened in the early seventeenth century, a year or two might be skipped. The fleets diminished greatly in number, but the ships were much larger. Not only was Spain unable to send them across regularly by that time, but the Americans were discovering other ways to obtain merchandise. By the last half of the seventeenth century the fleet system operated on a very uncertain basis. An effort was made to restore the annual convoys in the eighteenth century, but by then individual sailings were more profitable and, late in the colonial period, all pretense of maintaining the system was abandoned. Despite its spotty effectiveness over the centuries, this cumbersome process brought to the New World thousands of Spanish colonists and officials as well as many supplies, and it returned to Spain incredible quantities of silver and other riches.

The pattern was for the American-bound ships to gather in the Guadalquiver River at Sevilla or in smaller seaports at its mouth each spring. There they would be loaded under the usually watchful officials of the *Casa de Contratación*. Probably in May or June vessels of the first fleet, the *flota*, would sail seventy miles downriver, carefully negotiating the sand bars and other hazards, and join warships once they were at sea. Always they paused at the Canary Islands, where illegal emigrants often boarded, and began the eventful voyage across the ocean. Two months after leaving Sevilla they would, if lucky, reach the lesser Antilles. Vessels with cargoes for Cuba, Puerto Rico, Hispaniola, and Honduras might detach themselves, while the main fleet moved toward New Spain. There would be much excitement at Vera Cruz as the *flota* approached, and merchants would be preparing to receive the wares in Jalapa, a cool town not far from the torrid port. The *flota* anchored in the harbor, protected by the fortress of San Juan de Ulúa on its eastern side. Then the passengers debarked and the goods were carried up to Jalapa, where a huge fair staged by the *consulados* of Sevilla and Mexico City permitted the distribution of the merchandise. Very much in evidence at this occasion were gamblers, thieves, and loose women.

Meanwhile, the second fleet, known for no particular reason as the "galleons," was being readied in Sevilla. Often sailing late in the summer, it was likely to make the westward voyage with little difficulty save for the hazards of ocean travel. Pirates and privateers were not particularly interested in such prosaic cargoes as clothing, furniture, tools, livestock, and seeds. After entering the Caribbean, a few galleons would pull away for small ports on the South American mainland, while the principal fleet proceeded to Cartagena, a beautiful, defended city in New Granada. While some unloading took place there to serve the immediate area, the ships remained mostly at anchor with their cargoes intact while a messenger was sent to the viceroy in Lima. That official was supposed to have a smaller fleet loaded and ready to sail up the Pacific from Callao. At the signal from Cartagena these ships left for Panama, also in convoy, and unloaded their cargoes and passengers. Negro slaves and mule trains carried the silver or other freight about fifteen miles across the spine of the isthmus and ferried them down the Chagres River to the Caribbean side, to Nombre de Dios or Puerto Bello. By that time the galleons had sailed over from Cartagena. The merchandise they had brought from Europe was sold to buyers from Lima at a fair which surely rivaled Jalapa in vice, merriment, and frenzied spending.

European goods and passengers from Spain had thus been delivered. It remained for them to be trans-shipped to Lima or Mexico City and make their way to smaller towns in the Indies or embark for the Philippines. From the standpoint of the Spanish crown, this operation was less important that the one which followed, the transportation of precious metals to Europe. Both the viceroy of New Spain and the *audiencia* in Panama took very seriously, as well they might, the careful loading of the treasure in the homeward-bound ships. Then the two fleets converged on Havana, whose spacious harbor afforded security and provided facilities for repair and refitting. After the hurricane season passed, the *flota* and the galleons combined, usually, in one monster fleet shaped something like a leaf fan with warships protecting the rear. The course was the Gulf Stream between the Bahamas and Florida, for it was difficult for sailing vessels to leave the Caribbean at any other opening, then to the northeast, past the Azores, and on to the mouth of the Guadalquiver. High adventure usually attended this operation. Pirates lurked in the islands, especially in the numerous cays of the Bahamas, hoping for a silver-laden ship separated from the main fleet. At times foreign warships engaged the whole convoy or picked at exposed flanks or stragglers. The capture of one silver vessel alone might enrich a crew for life. Thus the rewards justified enormous risks, and at times the whole Atlantic seemed to the Spaniards a veritable gauntlet. Even the waters off Spain were likely to be unsafe, thanks to Moslem bases in North Africa. Despite all these perils, most of the silver reached Spain. Only one entire fleet was lost, in 1628 off Cuba. Others suffered damage, but the wonder is that so many got through intact. Ponderous as the fleet system was, it functioned satisfactorily for several generations.

A miniature fleet of similar type operated in the Pacific, or the "South Seas," as the Spanish usually called it. This was the so-called Manila Galleon, ordinarily two galleons rather than one, which composed one of the most picturesque shipping lines that ever functioned. These vessels, usually large ones, left Acapulco, New Spain, for the Philippines with silver, mail, agents of the Spanish crown and Church, and a little European or Mexican merchandise. Mexican pesos were the most valued items in their cargoes. The tiny fleet stopped at Guam, a Spanish outpost, where the natives greeted the sailors from bamboo boats. Then it proceeded to Manila, where the Chinese merchants who dominated the business life of the Philippines were eager to receive the silver in exchange for the Oriental goods the Europeans had long coveted. Undoubtedly, more than two vessels could have been utilized profitably in this trade, but the Sevilla monopolists favored restriction of goods to bring the highest of prices. Also, they took a dim view of silk competion from the Far East. They succeeded in having the crown forbid Oriental trade with Peru, even by way of Acapulco, but such commerce went on surreptitiously notwithstanding. The return voyage from Manila followed the course discovered by Friar Urdaneta in 1567, a route almost to Japan and then across to California and down to Acapulco that sometimes required four months to cover. Most of the silk remained in New Spain, with some illegally reaching Peru, while passengers, mail, and a few goods were transported to Vera Cruz and then to Spain.

The *Casa de Contratación*, the *consulados*, the fleets and galleons, and the fairs and merchants were crucial components of the famous Spanish commercial machine. Finished goods went from Europe to the Indies, precious metals and raw materials came back; silver reached the Philippines and silk went to New Spain. On and on the process went. We must not forget the human cargoes. Carefully as the *Casa de Contratación* kept records, it is obvious that many persons reached the Indies who were not registered. Perhaps they were wife deserters, unattached women, runaway couples, former convicts, debtors, and people whose racial or religious purity would not satisfy the Inquisition. These and the emigrants we know about—the officials, clergymen, soldiers, merchants, servants, farmers, and technicians—may have averaged about a thousand a year, though we cannot be sure. Packed tightly on the small sailships, they endured the two-month voyage as well as they could. Often they passed the time reading aloud, singing, playing games, having religious services, and staging wrestling matches and mock bull-fights. At last they hit one of the lesser Antilles, usually Deseada or Dominica. A cheer would go up, and grateful prayers. Whether these immigrants were running away from difficulties in the Old World or seeking opportunity in the New, they were likely to be young and hardy. Most of them came from the extreme south or the extreme north of Spain, not from Aragon, Catalonia, Valencia, or New Castile. They manned the imperial administration that ruled the Indies and the ecclesiastical establishment. They built towns, started businesses, operated mines, planted crops, raised livestock, and propagated. This constant stream of immigrants, most of them anonymous and humble, had more to do with fashioning Spanish America than all the prestigious officials and the laws of the Indies.

The Indies As a Source of Revenue

CONSISTENT with the theory that all of the states belonged to the king of Spain and were equal under his rule, it followed that revenues from these kingdoms be used as His Catholic Majesty thought best in carrying out his duties to God, to Whom alone he was accountable. It did not appear unjust or paradoxical that funds taken from the hides of creoles or Indians in America should be employed to fight Turks in the Mediterranean, Frenchmen in Italy and the Netherlands, Lutherans in the Germanies, and Englishmen on the high seas. The monarchy was a family of nations with, presumably, common interests. The Indies provided so much hard money that peninsular Spain long cut a splendid figure on the world stage, one far out of line with her real strength. It was not a matter of the gold washings from Hispaniola, the pearls of

Panama, and the easy pickings from Aztec and Inca wrecked empires providing these means so much as the steady flow of treasure and revenue for more than two and a half centuries.

First in importance was the royal fifth, the celebrated *quinto*, an ancient practice by which the monarch was entitled to one-fifth of the profits on findings of treasure and the sale of slaves. It was applied to the mining industry as an inducement to prospectors, for the king owned the subsoil and could have claimed all its proceeds by the Roman law which the Spanish perpetuated. It still complicates legal matters in drilling for oil in some parts of the United States once under Spanish rule. By demanding only a fifth, the crown encouraged enterprisers to locate the veins, and at times the royal share was reduced to a tenth or rebated altogether in order to stimulate discoveries. Over the three centuries of the Spanish empire, the *quinto* was the leading source of royal revenue from the Americas.

Import and export duties, the *almojarifazgo*, were another steady source of income. At Sevilla an export tax on goods destined for America of two-and-one-half per cent and an import duty of five per cent on articles arriving from America were levied after 1543. On the American side of the ocean, duties of ten per cent on imports and two-and-one-half per cent on exports were enforced. In calculating the *almojarifazgo* on either side of the Atlantic, the basis was nearly always the price in the Indies, which was twice or more the price in Spain. During the seventeenth century changes in assessing the tax led to bulk, rather than price, serving as the criterion, and in the eighteenth century the *almojarifazgo* in American ports ceased to be collected. Imposts of this type were also levied between some of the provinces in the Americas as "dry customs," notably on the mountainous road between Lima and Buenos Aires. While it seems odd to modern students that customs barriers prevailed between Spain and her colonies and among the colonies themselves, this type of revenue-producer was very common in most nations until the French Revolution or even later.

A detested tax was the *alcabala*, a device learned from the Mohammedans, which was something like a modern sales or transactions tax. Ten per cent in Spain, it was usually less than five per cent in the Indies when, indeed, it existed at all. So stout was resistance to this tax, even powerful viceroys hesitated to impose it. The *alcabala* did not affect Indian goods nor such items as bread, books, horses, and arms. Nevertheless, it was so unpopular that it must be counted a remote cause of the independence movement.

The tribute, a poll or head tax, had ample precedent in European history and had been levied on Indians since the colonial effort of Columbus in Hispaniola. The theory supporting it was that any subject of the crown ought to pay something for the privilege of being ruled. One was charged for his membership in the state. In America the tribute went to the *encomenderos* as cash or, more likely, as goods, crops, or services. When the *encomiendas* shrank, or disappeared, the tribute continued, but now it went to the crown instead of the *encomendero*. Like most imposts, this one tended to grow, from a peso a year or its equivalent in the sixteenth century to eight pesos annually by the close of the eighteenth. Tribute was supposed to be paid by all able-bodied adult males under fifty-five, though collectors often stretched the definitions. It was ordinarily the only tax the Indians paid.

Whites and mestizos were obliged to tithe, to give the Church a fraction of their income from the fruits of the earth, usually farming and ranching. In some localities Indians were compelled to pay the tithe, but no uniformity prevailed and most of them seem to have been excused from it. The crown had the privilege of collecting the tithe for the Church and, but for the one-ninth of the proceeds that it was entitled to retain, was honest in devoting this income to ecclesiastical purposes, or generally was.

Other sources of royal income from the Indies would include the sale of offices, which came to be quite lucrative in the seventeenth century. Then, there were the *mesada* and *media anata*, kickbacks of one month's or a half year's salary from recipients of positions in the government and the Church. Also, the sale of titles and honors brought in money for the crown, but this source was not especially abused. Always there were many wealthy creoles who sought to purchase these dignities, which the crown distributed with considerable parsimony. Money came into the royal coffers from popular gifts to the king, some of them solicited with great abnegation and others practically extorted, this last being an evil precedent for the dictators of the nineteenth century. The crown also resorted to another dubious expedient, that of exchanging bullion belonging to individuals as it entered Sevilla for copper coins or paper certificates, a device regarded with little enthusiasm by the owners.

The application of the royal fifth to the sale of imported Negro slaves brought considerable revenues, especially after the slave trade to the Caribbean area grew to such large proportions. The government also had monopolies of certain articles much in demand, such as gunpowder, mercury, legal paper, coca, tobacco (late in the colonial period), playing cards, salt, and snow that was packed and hurried down from the mountains by runners to cool the drinks of the rich. Taxes on liquor were, as always, productive of revenue. It is doing the Spanish no great injustice to point out that Indians were encouraged to drink excessively in order to increase this income, though possibly they needed no incitement. Previously, it will be recalled, the Indian became intoxicated mainly during religious ceremonies. Now, chronic alcoholism became a large social problem.

While any listing of taxes seems hateful, it should be observed that the Spanish imposed no land tax at all, and no income tax unless the tithe be so regarded. Furthermore, tax rates were much lower in the rich Indies than they were in the impoverished peninsula. Their imposition without representation and their collection, often by corruptible royal revenue agents and professional tax farmers with legendary hard hearts, were typical of nearly all governments in the world at the time. While taxation did not make the inhabitants of the Americas happy, they were really less burdened than almost any of their contemporaries.

Disposition of the Income from America

ONCE the imperial system was operating with regularity from northern Mexico to Buenos Aires, approximately half the royal revenues remained in the Indies to finance it. As the government grew, as it did to meet the increasing needs of the empire and in the strange way of all governments, the share that remained overseas sometimes amounted to eighty per cent. Important as the American income was, it was never more than one-fourth the total revenues that reached the Spanish crown, though this was enough to spell the difference between an inactive and an aggressive foreign policy for several reigns. The exact amount cannot be ascertained precisely nor expressed in meaningful ways, but we have some idea of the proportions of this income from estimates responsible scholars have made. During the 1530's, prior to the spectacular silver discoveries, the crown received from New Spain alone something on the order of 100,000 pesos annually. By 1600 it was obtaining 1,500,000 pesos a year. The volume tapered off slowly during the seventeenth century, a dismal period of bad government and foreign attacks, but it rose to new heights during the eighteenth century and reached a peak just after 1800, amounting to 20,000,000 pesos a year. Peru and New Granada were also very productive, and the income of private individuals must have been several times that of the government.

What became of all this money? As has been noted, much remained in the Indies, where the extensive bureaucracy and defense needs absorbed it. The plethora of public buildings and churches and convents throughout Spanish America required huge sums. And the thousands of handsome homes in American cities and those on plantations, as well as the elegant way of life that went with them, testify to expenditures by wealthy individuals. Also, enormous quantities went to Spain by means of the stately fleets.[2] This is the saddest part of the story, a lost opportunity. The income was not used so much for creating better means of production, for factories or roads or irrigation, as for ostentation. Government buildings, palaces, expensive residences, monuments, and religious edifices went up on a lavish scale. Spanish fleets and armies were committed in wars to further Habsburg imperialism, and mercenaries and spies were purchased for this end. Suddenly, there was not money enough, despite the influx from the New World. The silver all too quickly filtered through Spain into Italy, France, the Low Countries, the Germanies, and England, where men were better prepared to make intelligent use of it. The building of ornate edifices in Spain slowed down. The royal court itself was often pitifully, or comically, short of petty cash. Peninsular Spain was hardly more than a sieve.

To be sure, the American windfall greatly shook the primitive economy of Spain, forcing prices up abruptly and steeply. For two or three generations men failed to understand why prices rose. Europe had been suffering from a shortage of precious metals on the eve of the Discovery. Now, ships were pulling into Sevilla laden with silver and gold. Of course, inflation followed for reasons that seem obvious to us. But contemporaries long blamed the weather, witches, malevolent foreigners, greedy colonials who offered high prices for goods, and almost everything but the true cause, the startling increase in bullion. The cost of merchandise went up faster than wages, with the result that the lower classes underwent great deprivation. Further, monopolistic merchants in Sevilla were unable to supply the settlers in the Indies with the goods they craved and were too lacking in economic statesmanship to create means of increased production. Instead, they purchased articles from other lands and shipped them from Sevilla, thus sending bullion out of Spain and doing nothing to build up local industries on the scale required. The long-range effect of the influx from America was to impoverish the peninsula, to retard its own development, and to channel the treasure to countries which knew, or could learn, how to manufacture the goods so much in demand in the Spanish Indies. To nearly all Spaniards who did not own property in America or trade there, the income proved a curse. It should be added that the New World treasure caused inflation and dislocations as it passed into countries beyond Spain, but most of them turned it to their advantage. With better direction than Spain enjoyed, they developed capitalism with such success that their own standards of living grew and their national power soon surpassed Spain.

2. Between 1503 and 1660, about 200 tons of fine gold and 18,600 tons of fine silver are known to have entered Spain as registered imports. The value was more than one billion U.S. dollars of the mid-twentieth century.

This was only the first act of a continuing drama that has seen the Americas contribute mightily to the well-being of Europe. Through this enrichment and reinforcement of the heartland of Western civilization the two American continents have benefited themselves, receiving immeasurable advantages in culture, technology, and immigrants. For 300 years the treasure of the Iberian empires flowed to Europe and largely financed its spectacular growth. After the empires were lost, Europeans made enormous profits through investments in the Americas. When that phase ended with World War I, loans, grants, and many other types of assistance from the United States and Canada—no longer from the Hispanic states—continued the tradition that the New World rescues and bolsters the Old.

COLONIAL ECONOMIC DEVELOPMENT

Intercolonial Trade

MERCHANDISE purchased at the fairs in Jalapa, Cartagena, and Puerto Bello found its way in due course to the principal cities of the Spanish empire and then to the less populated areas and the frontier. This process, simple in essence, was extremely slow and costly. Indian trade routes were not very helpful to the Europeans, for there had never been any of great complexity and they were unsuited for the white man and his mules, donkeys, oxen, horses, and wheeled vehicles. The Spaniards had to create roads for the wagons and coaches. They long hired or forced natives to carry goods on their backs, despite urgent orders from the crown not to do so, but in the long run mule trains and wheeled vehicles replaced the human porters. The means of distribution centered about the merchant guilds or *consulados* of the large cities, smaller traders with shops in the towns, local fairs, open markets, and numerous peddlers. Prices rose all the higher as the distance grew. The cost of transportation, the profits of middlemen, and intercolonial customs houses added to the price of merchandise. An article that cost one peso in Spain might bring two or three pesos in the fair of Puerto Bello, five or six in Lima, and eight or ten in Buenos Aires. Should a smuggler turn up along the way and offer the same product at lower cost, the American would not hesitate long before buying it.

Products of one colony would, of course, be sold in another. Ordinarily the mining areas were well endowed with loose money but very poor in goods, especially luxuries. Thus, sugar, liquor, tallow, furniture, clothing, leather goods, cacao, and high quality woods would flow into the mining districts. The route might be long and dangerous, across the dreaded Chichimeca country in New Spain or the Andes in Peru. It might run across the flat, grassy pampas of the Argentine and then steeply up the glacial mountains of Upper Peru. Yet the prices justified the effort, for the mining regions spent money freely. Wheat flourished in Chile and was shipped to Peru, where it refused to grow. The wines of Chile and western Argentina had markets ranging from Brazil to Panama. In general, a modest exchange of foodstuffs, tobacco, and finished goods took place throughout the Indies. Compared to the trading that had gone on in pre-Columbian Indian societies, this commerce would seem very heavy. If it is compared to trade within Europe, of course it seems paltry.

Mining

THE attracting power that precious metals had for Europeans does not need to be stressed as a factor in the Conquest. For the first half-century the Spaniards enriched themselves on the ornaments of the Indians, in addition to gold washings and pearl fisheries of the Caribbean. These brought substantial but not vastly important increases in wealth to the monarchy as a whole. The native treasures were soon looted and distributed. The pearl fisheries were exhausted after a few years. And the shallow gold mines in Hispaniola, Venezuela, New Granada, and Panama affected only a comparatively few Spanish enterprisers and their slaves. Then came the fantastic discoveries of large silver veins. It was probably in 1544 that an Andean Indian found that the cone-shaped mountain of Potosí in what is now Bolivia was almost solid silver. This reddish, snow-topped peak rising 17,000 feet above sea level was soon the scene of frantic digging on the part of thousands of Spaniards and Indians. The fires from their furnaces gave the mountain at night the appearance of a mammoth Christmas tree. While many persons were eager to extract the ore for high wages, it was important to assure an abundant labor force by bringing in great numbers of Indians in relays. Hence the *mita* was applied, so that natives from many Andean communities would at any time be quartered in the huge compound, often with their wives, at the base of the mountain. The workers descended like ants into the openings, tearing out the silvery rocks in chunks, climbing up wide ladders, and going back in again. The mortality rate was shockingly high, from overwork, the cold, fumes from the tallow candles, dust from the digging, and epidemics. Yet nothing could be allowed to interfere with this labor, for Potosí was long the most valuable single possession of Spain. It is said to have produced 800,000,000 pesos' worth of silver during the colonial period.

At almost the same time Potosí was discovered, a party of Spaniards ran across another larger silver vein in the mountains at Zacatecas, northwest of Mexico City about 300 miles. A little later, another was developed at Guanajuato, between Zacatecas and Mexico City, and dozens of others were located in this general vicinity. The silver rush resulted in the eventual pacification of the Chichimeca territory and the growth of flourishing mining settlements, as well as a stupendous increase in the world's supply of silver. Zacatecas alone produced one-fifth of this supply during the following two and a half centuries. While Potosí, Zacatecas, and Guanajuato were the largest and the most renowned silver mines, many smaller ones were opened in the central Andes near Lake Titicaca and the Sierra Madre Occidental ranges in western New Spain. Fortune was so kind at this point that another mammoth silver mine, at Guadalcanal, came into operation in 1550 in peninsular Spain itself. Gold mining was much less important, amounting to about one-tenth the value of silver, but it was pursued with great energy in western New Granada and in Chile.

The Spanish had little knowledge of silver mining when the strikes were made. Not since Roman times had much extraction of this ore taken place in the peninsula. The best experts were German and Italian, and even they relied heavily on methods used by the ancient Egyptians. In 1528 Charles V sent twenty-four German technicians to the Welser colony in Venezuela, and in 1536 a few others were dispatched to New Spain. But their specialty was gold, which was not then abundant, and no great progress was evident. However, fortune was again benign. During the 1550's the Spanish learned of new techniques for reducing silver ore by employing quicksilver, or mercury. This *patio* process, as it was called, was probably developed by Germans or Flemings and was introduced into New Spain by one Bartolomé de Medina. It was found to be highly effective, for American silver ore was less rich than European and required superior methods of smelting. The ore would be ground to a fine powder, sifted, and mixed with mercury. Then it was wetted in troughs and trampled until it became a thick mud, after which it was dried in piles. The resulting cakes went into a furnace where the mercury was oxidized, and the remaining silver was hung in leather bags to harden into white loaves or was cast into bars. At this point a royal official was supposed to be present to assure the subtraction of the *quinto* and to stamp on the hard silver the weight as well as a figure denoting its fineness. Afterward, the silver went by pack train to the mint to be coined or straight to the seaport for shipment to Spain.

It proved fortunate for the crown that mercury was required for the *patio* process. This commodity came only from a mine in Austria, one in the peninsula, and after 1570, from Huancavelica in Peru. The crown established a monopoly and distributed the mercury in sheepskin bags carried by mules or llamas into the mining districts. Sold by officials to mine operators, it was easy to calculate approximately how much silver was being extracted by the amount of mercury purchased by each individual, a far better index than his oath. Though we may be sure that much bullion was bootlegged, the royal monopoly on mercury kept the situation under some control.

After a wild period when the mines were first discovered, the affected regions settled into routine. Of the great number of adventurers attracted by the strikes, many had to be satisfied with something less than easy riches and become merchants, farmers, ranchers, or technicians to serve the mining industry. Therefore, mining had the effect of populating and developing areas that might otherwise have been unoccupied for a long time, as California and Alaska were before the gold rushes. The crown made strenuous efforts to impose its will on the mining areas so as to secure its share of the production. This meant the establishment and policing of the long, dangerous lines of communication. Officials also had to be plentiful and well-supported in order to pacify the mining regions and to collect the king's due. Potosí seems to have been the most difficult district to tame. For a generation after the strike it was not only the largest white settlement in the Americas but the rowdiest. Gamblers, prostitutes, entertainers, sharpsters, slavers, and coca peddlers gave it a reputation for wickedness and extravagence which it surely deserved. So bleak that plants would not grow, so cold that flies could not survive, this barren city offered fantastic rewards to men who could bring foodstuffs, merchandise, entertainment, and labor forces. The arch-type of a mining boom town, it exulted in crude prosperity for a few decades, and then, like so many of its kind, declined until it was scarcely more than a ghost community.

Nearly every aspect of colonial Latin America was touched by the mining industry. Regions that would otherwise have been neglected were occupied and cultivated. The enrichment of the Spanish crown and those who robbed its treasure ships had large consequences in the history of the great powers. Thousands of families enjoyed fortunes, most of them residing far from the sordid mining towns. They built splendid homes in Lima or Mexico City or went back to Spain. Absentee ownership and the graces of easy living became factors in the social scene, and have remained so in modern Latin America. Mining lubricated the economic life of the Indies in other ways, offering markets to sugar producers, cotton raisers, lumbermen, traders, and ranchers who provided dried meat, hides, and the millions of tallow candles consumed annually in the mines. Loose coins were so abundant that foreign traders and national enemies created opportunities to sell to the Indies or to raid them. Mining left a deep mark on the mentality of colonial society. But it is the fate of the Indians which haunts anyone who studies this period, the tens of thousands of Andean natives in particular who were called up under the *mita*, marched to the mines, and sent inside to labor for long periods in the dark coldness. So many perished there. Perhaps conditions were not quite so bad in other localities, where free labor was more likely to prevail, but mining exacted a terrible price in human suffering, however much it did for the growth of the world's economy.

Agriculture

IF THE mines of the Americas stimulated the growth of the Spanish empire and changed the course of world history, agricultural development there was, in the long run, still more significant. The importance of white potatoes, beans, corn,[3] vanilla, squash, peppers, chocolate, tomatoes, and many other staples in the diet of Europe cannot be over-stressed. Further, the success in America of sugar, coffee, bananas, rice, wheat, and livestock brought fortunes to European owners and traders, along with a higher standard of living for the common man in many parts of the world. The slow but geometrical growth of the tobacco habit may not be counted altogether a blessing, but it has added indeed to the pleasures of the European. These articles enriched Europe more than the flow of bullion. They account in important ways for its vigor and rise in population.

On the other side of the picture is the introduction of plants, seeds, tools, and domestic animals which revolutionized the way of life of the American natives. Slow as they have been to accept the iron plow and the hoe, the Indians have profited from the superior technology of Europe. If the white man often failed to appreciate the irrigation and fertilizing methods of the Indians, he more than compensated by bringing in pack animals, iron implements, and a greater variety of vegetables and fruits. It was not only the European whose diet was enriched by contact with another continent. The process worked both ways, to mutual advantage. Receiving from the invaders cattle, pigs, chickens, wheat, sugar, grapes, citrus fruits, bananas, and new vegetables—to list but a few—the Amerinds were not short-changed.

The agricultural system introduced by the Spaniards disrupted the procedures of the Indians in the more advanced areas. *Encomenderos* often became owners of great estates, though not to the degree they originally expected, for the crown insisted that an *encomienda* did not involve property rights. Other settlers won grants of land from the crown or bought them from the *cabildos*. By whatever process it occurred,

3.   Corn or maize has rarely attracted Europeans as something to be eaten, but it has been very useful in feeding their livestock.

wealthy and influential Spaniards became great landowners in regions once managed by the Indians. *Latifundia*, or the system of great estates worked by servile labor, was early fastened on the choice agricultural areas of Latin America and still prevails in most of them. Through the *mayorazgo*, or entailment of estates, the system of bequeathing large properties undivided to the eldest son also tended to perpetuate an aristocratic society. Much as modern men are tempted to speculate that small farmers would have been better builders, or that the Indian system should not have been disrupted, *latifundia* was the normal condition in most of the world until recently. Also, the large landowners were often true pioneers in creating sugar plantations on the Caribbean coasts, vineyards and grain farms in Chile, ranches in New Spain, and food farms all over. Without the incentive to become virtual lords, these entrepreneurs might never have developed the Indies as they did. Once *latifundia* was a fact in the productive areas, however, the incentive to improve methods was weakened. Owners lived on in comparative wealth, often away from their properties, and Negro slaves and servile Indians carried on the work with an understandable indifference.

Ranching

IF THE superimposition of Spanish methods in agriculture was not always a blessing, the introduction of livestock-raising brought large benefits and few disadvantages to the Americas. Beginning with the second voyage of Columbus, oxen, asses, cattle, horses, sheep, goats, pigs, and poultry (the Indians had turkey but not chicken or geese) arrived in the Indies and multiplied. They furnished the food and transportation that enabled the conquistador to carry through the occupation. Then they served all the population to some degree. Often running wild, the herds and flocks migrated to the north into the present United States, where longhorns, mustangs, broncos, and razorbacks greeted the "Anglo" settlers moving westward. They filled up northern New Spain, where great ranches and the colorful *vaqueros*, or cowboys, served the mining districts and the Indian missions. They moved into the pampas of the Argentine, finding there a veritable cow paradise. Most important of all, domestic animals added to the diet and, with their skins, to the clothing and housing of the mixed populations of the Americas.

While most of the grazing area was not held by individual owners in colonial times, their herds roaming over great spaces attended by a few "hands," a curious institution known as the *mesta* was introduced into the Indies to serve the rancher. In the peninsula the *mesta* was a guild of livestock owners who enjoyed the right to move their herds over crops to reach the best grazing area for the season. It was truly a

serious handicap to Spanish agriculture. While the same privilege prevailed in much of America for members of the *mesta*, the consequences
were not so harmful, no doubt because there was so much space for
these migrations. Further, the *mesta* regulated such matters as brands
and ethics among the livestock owners. It had its own court to enforce
compliance. In the Americas the *mesta* was less aristocratic than in
Spain, for owners of twenty cows or 300 sheep or goats could belong.

Not until the late eighteenth century was there much of a market
outside the Americas for hides, though foreign traders sometimes
carried them to Europe when they could obtain nothing better. Meat
could not, of course, be transported to Europe and remain edible. Spain
and most of the rest of Europe had no need to import wool. Within
the Indies hides were used on a very large scale, as were tallow, wool,
and mohair. The consumption of meat was no longer a luxury for the
upper classes or for fortunate hunters, as it had been before the Conquest. Meat became a staple of diet for the entire population, though
dairy products most Latin Americans have always spurned. Pigs and
chickens became almost too intimately associated with the formerly
vegetarian Indians, living in and around their dwellings. There was, of
course, little incentive for improving livestock through scientific breeding and still less inclination. Such developments awaited modern times.

Forestry

LATIN AMERICA has almost a third of the world's forested areas
today and has been a source of fine woods for Europeans since 1500.
While the greatest plenitude was in Brazil, Central America and sections of New Granada and New Spain had fine resources in dyewoods,
cedars, ebonies, hardwoods, and spice trees. Most of this timber was
utilized in the Americas, often being transported long distances into
the arid mining regions. This was true also of the shipbuilding industry,
which flourished from the earliest days in Panama and Ecuador. Dye-
woods had a good market in Europe and so did cochineal (clusters of
insects on cactus plants that produced red and orange tints). Since
Spain was not well-endowed with forests, her wealthier families imported mahogany, rosewood, rare spruce, and pines for the handsome
furniture that still graces so many homes and for the extraordinary
woodwork found in peninsular churches.

Among other forest products were sarsaparilla, cinnamon, and
quinine, this last an Indian remedy for fevers which the Spanish were
tardy to appreciate. Coca leaves, chewed regularly by the natives of the
Andes to deaden the pain of cold, work, and life in general, also came
to be welcome in Europe as cocaine. If the fruit of the tapioca tree won

approval in the outside world, the common cassava plant or manioc, so much utilized by the Indians, was not relished by the white man or the African unless he were very hungry. Not even *pulque*, the fiery drink fermented from the juice of the maguey plant, won many admirers, popular as it continues to be among the Indians of Mexico. Except for iron cutting implements and wheeled vehicles for transporting timber, the European contributed little to the forest industry. He did, however, introduce new types of trees, such as the olive, which did well in Peru and provided the inhabitants with the cooking oil they preferred. The lemon, lime, apricot, peach, orange, and grapefruit made handsome orchards and penetrated the woods and jungles, all to the advantage of a growing population.

Manufacturing

AFTER the Conquest the Indians persisted in making the articles which they had fabricated from time immemorial, the blankets, capes, pottery, and other homely goods. Additional techniques came from the hands of the Europeans, who brought knives, axes, plows, and wheels of iron and taught the Indians how to use them. In fact, nearly everything the Spanish knew was imparted to the Indians, so that cloth and leatherwork, silver-, copper-, and goldsmithing, soap- and furniture-making, and construction skills quickly spread all over the Indies and displaced many native methods. Food processing was known to both whites and Indians, and the combination of their methods meant that dried or jerked beef, sugar preserves, and dried vegetables were widely used. While the crown fostered the transmission of these techniques, commanding its white subjects to teach its colored subjects, more credit for their spread goes to the common sense and everyday requirements of the population.

Shipbuilding was one of the first and most important industries in the New World. Since it was almost prohibitively difficult to bring vessels around Cape Horn or through the Straits of Magellan, it seemed more feasible to construct them on the Pacific coast, where abundant timber resources were available. This was done in a large scale, mainly in Nicaragua and Guayaquil, from the earliest days of the Conquest. Ship repair was of the utmost importance in the open ports of the Gulf of Mexico and the Carribbean, particularly at Havana, where the fleets were readied for the dangerous voyage to Spain.

The Spanish crown seldom attempted to discourage manufacturing in the overseas empire. This was due in part to the fact that Spain had such a modest industrial establishment, one with less influence on the crown than the commercial interests, as well as to the power of the *consulados.* And it was believed that exportation of Spanish goods created scarcities at home that resulted in intolerable price increases. Generally, the Indies were free to fabricate anything they could. The combined skill of both Spaniards and Indians permitted them to satisfy most of their requirements for necessities. Most luxuries, however, had to come from Europe or the Philippines by legal or illegal channels. A few rather large factories grew up in the Indies, mainly in Mexico, along with countless small units of production in homes and Indian villages and missions. They served to give the population of the empire a standard of living not greatly inferior to that of Spain itself.

While the most discriminating customers continued to prefer clothing of European or Asiatic materials, cloth-making became a large industry in the Indies. Nearly every city had an *obraje,* or sweatshop, where Indians were locked in and forced to stay on the job by all kinds of compulsion, including stocks, chains, and whippings. It must be remembered that exceedingly harsh labor conditions prevailed in most parts of the world until the late nineteenth century and, in the case of totalitarian systems, into the present age. However evil working conditions were, the *obraje* was part of the continuing social scene in colonial Spanish America. Allied to cloth-making is the somewhat mysterious situation with reference to silk manufacture. It may have been Cortés himself who started silk-making in New Spain by importing mulberry trees. Soon a boom of great proportions was on, and silk guilds made ribbons, taffeta, thread, clothes, altar cloths, and other fine articles. Later in the sixteenth century the entire industry faltered and almost died out. Perhaps it could not stand the competition of Filipino imports. Or labor troubles and the sharp decline in Indian population may have caused its diminution. Once the industry had declined, but not before, the crown discouraged it. The monopolists at Sevilla are usually blamed for this restriction.

The craft guild was another feature of manufacturing in Spanish America. In nearly every city the guilds sought and usually achieved a monopoly of a certain type of industry, such as silverworking, goldworking, and the manufacture of church bells, artillery, candles, carriages, glass, fine clothes, and furniture. These guilds tended to be aristocratic, as they were in Europe, limiting production to certain families of whites. Indians or mestizos could serve only in humble capacities and seldom rise to the distinction of master. Typically, the guilds carried out other social functions, such as disciplining their members, assisting sick colleagues, helping the bereaved when a member died, and holding regular entertainments. While they may be criticized now for restraining production and for racial discrimination, they maintained a high standard of craftmanship that the modern world might well regard with envy.

12

Foreign Rivalry and Outlaws

THE Spanish monopoly in the Indies was fashioned not only by the theories of the times but from the necessity of defense against national enemies and plain criminals. The same necessity led Spain to tighten her system more and more, to turn the screws even harder to keep out the interlopers. Finally, the machine disintegrated, as much from the obstinate efforts of the Spanish to force it to operate in an impossible way as from the hammering on the outside by these enemies. Yet the pretense that a monopoly was in force went on for generations, until the Bourbons of the mid-eighteenth century undertook extensive repairs, indeed, remade the machine. A few decades later the whole Spanish monarchy fell apart from other causes.

The activities of the national heroes, pirates, corsairs, privateers, and buccaneers who hacked away at the Spanish monopoly have earned a major place in the literature of adventure. Historians too have tended to treat them as valiant, or at least romantic, figures who are to be admired for making life miserable on the Spanish Main. Of fun and adventure and deeds of great courage carried out with high spirit and marvelously rewarded there were plenty. Also, there was terror, cruelty, sadism, and wreckage. If bigoted, vain Spanish officials were vexed, so also did thousands of innocent passengers on ships and peaceable inhabitants of towns endure horror at the hands of predators who seem so glamorous in fiction. The larger historical results of this long period of violence can be summarized by pointing to the gaping leaks in the Spanish commercial system, the enrichment of smugglers and thieves, a tradition of lawlessness, the accumulation of capital in northern Europe, and the acquisition by England, the Netherlands, and France of rich colonies in the Caribbean, most of which they still hold. The perpetrators of atrocities in connection with these developments will presumably continue to enjoy a favored position in literature.

Perhaps it should never have been pretended that the western hemisphere could be divided by Spain and Portugal and left isolated from the course of world events. The wars and constant diplomatic dueling of the rising nations of Europe were bound to affect the Indies, as were the religious struggles of the Reformation, particularly whenever such sea powers as England and Holland fought Spain. Then, the very riches of the Indies—not only in loose treasure and commerce but in the production of sugar, tobacco, and chocolate—served to bring the New World into the arena of international politics. And the action of enterprising individuals could not be curbed by any law or policy. Almost from the first, the Americas were drawn into Europe's affairs.

EARLY THREATS TO THE
IBERIAN MONOPOLY

The papal award of 1493 and the Treaty of Tordesillas in 1494 produced indignation not unmixed with mirth in Paris and London, loyally Catholic though they were. Monarchs in both capitals dispatched expeditions to investigate the New World, Cabot sailing to the shores of Canada and French privateers to Brazil. Deducing that there was little of value across the Atlantic, France and England lost interest for a time, though their mariners hopefully sailed in waters claimed by Spain. The English dropped out of the scene until the reign of Elizabeth I (1558–1603). Frenchmen molested Spanish treasure ships occasionally and continued to cut brazilwood in Portugal's sphere. Verrazano mapped some of the eastern coast of the present United States for France, but nothing came of his efforts and he was soon killed by the Spanish. French challenges assumed a new dimension during the long series of wars between Charles V and the Valois kings of France. During the 1530's French warships sought out Spanish treasure ships, sacked ports in the Caribbean, and captured a few vessels. At this time Jacques Cartier violated the pre-emptive claims of Spain in North America by exploring the St. Lawrence River. Despite his belief that certain glassy stones were diamonds, he found little to inspire further French activity in that area for seventy years. The decade of the 1540's was likewise a period of small-scale French picking at Spain and Portugal. In the 1550's corsairs and sailors of France terrorized the West Indies, sacking open towns and seizing Spanish ships. One notorious character, Peg-leg LeClerc, carried out much of this pillaging while his Lutheran lieutenant plundered Havana. And, as has been seen, Villegaignon attempted to establish a colony in Rio de Janeiro while other Huguenots created a settlement along the present coast of Georgia.

Much as these activities annoyed the Spanish and Portuguese, they were not truly formidable. No permanent losses were suffered. In 1559 the Habsburg-Valois conflict closed with the Treaty of Cateau-Cambrésis. Since France flatly refused to recognize Spain's monopoly in the New World, the two powers made a verbal agreement of a most curious sort. A "line of amity" running along the Tropic of Cancer and the 30th meridian would serve as a sort of veil. South and west of this line, the subjects of France and Spain could kill and despoil each other as they wished without the home governments taking official notice. Eventually, the Line of Amity applied to other powers and, though never reduced to writing, it became a well-known bit of international law for more than a century. Thus, outright battles could take place beyond the Line without causing war in Europe. Hypocritical as it was, the agreement was useful at times in keeping American affairs from disrupting the peace of Europe.

If the Iberian powers had retreated from their pretensions to own all the New World, they nonetheless asserted themselves with vigor. The French were soon ejected from "Antarctic France" in Rio and exterminated in Georgia. France gave up her role as a tormentor of Spain and Portugal for half a century, her own civil wars and religious disturbances keeping her weak and divided.

It was England who now loomed as a challenger. Prior to 1562 the English had rarely molested the Spanish, and the two kingdoms were traditionally friendly. In that year an enterprising merchant named John Hawkins won the support of Queen Elizabeth and a few London speculators for an extraordinary experiment. Its purpose was to persuade Felipe II that English trade in Spanish America might be mutually profitable. Demonstrating this theory, Hawkins sailed down to Africa, seized slaves, and ferried them across the Atlantic to Hispaniola, where he paid the port dues and solemnly observed every courtesy. The colonists were puzzled by his appearance and knew it was illegal to trade with foreigners, but all the same they eagerly purchased the human cargo. Paid off with hides and cash, Hawkins now had the impudence to send some of his merchandise to Spain for sale and to write a familiar letter to Felipe II. Far from seeing the light, the Prudent King confiscated Hawkins' wares and ordered punishment of the colonials who had dealt with him.

Hawkins went back on a similar mission in 1564–1565, exchanging slaves for hides, pearls, and gold along the northern coast of South America. Again, Felipe II proved stubborn. One result of this royal reaction

was that henceforth the colonists learned to pretend they had been co-
erced into illegal trading. The wise smuggler would shoot several volleys
into space and send a bloodthirsty threat in writing to the colonists,
who, apparently helpless and cowed, would finally agree under "duress"
to buy his goods. Another trick was for the smuggler to pretend his ship
was about to sink. Out of humanitarian motives it would be admitted to
the port, where business rather than repairs would absorb attention.
Royal investigators might be convinced that the colonists were innocent
victims of wily foreigners. Or the officials might not be fooled but have to
admit the colonists had a good case. And, of course, officials liked to make
money too. Thus hypocrisy spread into another area of the relations between rulers and subjects.

In 1568–1569 Hawkins made still another effort at peaceful trade,
hoping to trick Felipe II into thinking he was plotting treason against
Elizabeth. This time he found the colonists fearful of dealing with him,
and he had the bad luck to encounter a hurricane, which drove his fleet
of six ships into the port of Vera Cruz. The next day a tense situation
arose when the annual Spanish fleet carrying the new viceroy, Martín
Enríquez, entered the same harbor. After some uncertainty, firing began,
and four of the English ships were sunk or captured. The other two,
Hawkins' and another commanded by his cousin, Francis Drake, got
away under conditions suggestive of desertion. Things were never the
same again after this incident between England and Spain. The Vera
Cruz episode convinced everyone that English trade in the Spanish empire was an impossibility. Henceforth, Englishmen would make no pretense of doing Felipe II a good turn, but instead would exult in singeing
his whiskers.

Elizabeth I versus Felipe II

BY 1570 it was evident that Spain and England were opponents.
Felipe II finally abandoned hope that Elizabeth would become his bride
and bring England back into the Roman Catholic Church. Yet another
seventeen years passed before open warfare broke out. In the meantime
almost continuous violence occurred between their subjects. Having
learned their way to the Indies and sampled their wealth, Elizabeth's
sailors zestfully raided Spanish ships and colonial towns. Many of them
were aristocratic young men who enjoyed themselves in the process and
acquired fortunes. When their outrages were reported to Elizabeth she
feigned indignation and threatened punishment, but in fact she encouraged and even helped to finance them. Few were deceived by her pose,
least of all Felipe II, who retaliated by plotting the overthrow of the

Virgin Queen and by sending Spanish ships up to give English coastal towns a taste of beard-singeing.

By far the most illustrious, or notorious, of Elizabeth's freebooters was Francis Drake, known in the Indies as *El Draque*, still a name to frighten children. Like most of his confederates Drake was no mere criminal. He was a warrior of some gallantry, who behaved like a gentleman even while he burned homes and kidnaped women. In 1570 he conceived a project typically Elizabethan in its daring: the capture of the annual accumulation of silver as it awaited shipment in Panama. To this end he planned long and carefully. A secret base was established on the jungled Caribbean coast of New Granada. The Indians there were cooperative, as were the escaped Negroes, for they were glad to do the Spanish a bad turn. With seventy-three Englishmen and many native allies Drake emerged from his lair in 1572 and stole into the rear of Nombre de Dios. The surprised inhabitants were relieved of their movable property, saw their churches looted, and stood helpless while the storehouses were sacked of silver. It was heart-breaking to the invaders that some of the silver bars were too long and heavy to be carried off. Yet the remaining booty was impressive, and the audacious frolic ended with the English eager to undertake another. In the spring of 1573 Drake again left his hideout with eighteen well-briefed Englishmen and many Indian collaborators, picked his way in secrecy across the isthmus of Panama, and became the first of his nationality to see the Pacific Ocean. The party descended on the city of Panama and helped themselves to the silver stored in the warehouses. As luck would have it, however, most of the treasure was still in ships riding anchor in the harbor and escaped seizure. Even so, the English captured a mule train and its bullion and had more than they could transport. Silver bars and coins had to be buried hurriedly and the withdrawal deftly accomplished, for the Spanish rallied quickly. After this feat Drake went back to England with many fortunes of stolen Spanish property—all this at a time when England and Spain were nominally at peace, at least on the European side of the Line of Amity.

The Londoners gave him a hero's welcome. The queen did not seem particularly angry that a friendly power had been pillaged. Further, the wealth of the Indies was given much advertisement, and worse, so was its vulnerability. Many a sailor decided to emulate Drake. It was not always easy. John Oxenham and others were caught by the Spanish after attempting to raid Panama and were executed by the Inquisition in Lima as heretics. Admiral Drake, as he now was, returned to the Indies in 1577, this time to reach into the Antarctic past Cape Horn, ravage towns in Chile and Peru, shoot up a few surprised Spanish ships, and after upsetting Viceroy Toledo, who found such impudence incredible, to move northward in search of the Land of Anian. Eventually, Drake explored the California coasts and brought his flagship, the *Golden Hind,* across the Pacific and Indian Oceans and home to England. He was the first commander to circumnavigate the globe. Knighted and more than ever a national hero, he left in 1585—while Sir Walter Raleigh was violating Spain's title to North America by trying to establish a colony on Roanoke Island—for more adventures. With thirty ships, two of them Royal Navy, Drake plundered the peninsular port of Vigo and vainly sought to trap the returning treasure fleet. Then he crossed the Atlantic to take the town of Santo Domingo from the rear, a staggering blow to Spain's prestige. Its inhabitants stood under guard outside and watched the English burn down house after house. Finally convinced there was no alternative, they paid the ransom Drake demanded. Sir Francis tried the same trick at Cartagena, where, incidentally, he was infuriated to find among the governor's papers a description of himself as a pirate. The citizens of that port, however, held out more stubbornly and escaped for a fifth of Drake's original demand. On his way back to England with about two million pesos and hundreds of pieces of Spanish artillery, Drake paused long enough to burn St. Augustine, Spain's outpost in Florida.

War between Spain and England finally became official in 1587, after Elizabeth had Mary Queen of Scots, her Catholic rival for the English throne, beheaded. The fate of Felipe II's monster armada in 1588 is well known. If the tipping of the naval balance in England's favor was not as abrupt as it is sometimes depicted, it was a fact nonetheless. The English rose to new heights of confidence while the heartsick Felipe II and his over-extended monarchy lost spirit. As privateers and mere corsairs the English romped over the Caribbean. So did the Dutch, who had long been in rebellion against Spain and who suddenly surged forward as the foremost maritime power. *El Draque* was still in the picture. In 1595 he assembled a force of 2,500 men to seize Panama and make it a permanent base from which Peru might be conquered. But the time was now past for such adventures. The Spanish had good shore defenses and alert garrisons in key spots. Drake reached Panama, but his men suffered from disease and ill fortune. Chiggers are said to have made them especially miserable as they clanked about the jungles in suits of armor. Drake died during the enterprise, and the whole affair fell through. The last major efforts of this phase of the Anglo-Spanish duel were the seizure of San Juan in Puerto Rico in 1598 by the Earl of Cumberland and the inconclusive explorations by Raleigh in the Guianas in 1595 and 1617–1618 as he sought El Dorado.[1]

1. The second Raleigh expedition does not belong in this phase. Sir Walter promised to avoid any action that might injure Spain, now friendly. Allegedly violating this vow, he was executed soon after he returned to London.

A pause followed these spectacular English incursions of the Eliza-bethan period. James I and Felipe III made peace and attempted to be friendly for a generation. Spain chose to ignore English colonization in Virginia as well as French activities in Quebec. Even the Dutch agreed to a truce in 1609. While Spain had suffered, she was capable of recovery. Her fleets bore more silver across the Atlantic than they ever had before. They could still force their way into and out of the Caribbean on their annual voyages. Often substituting fast frigates for the lumbering gal-leons, the Spanish could win respect not only from national enemies but from corsairs. Tough officials were placed in key positions to strengthen the will of the colonists. Very costly fortifications went up in Havana, Santo Domingo, San Juan, Cartagena, Vera Cruz, and Puerto Bello, this last a replacement for Nombre de Dios in Panama. An office of the In-quisition was established in Cartagena to deal with foreign heretics. The Spanish also undertook such drastic measures as depopulating forcibly the northwestern third of Hispaniola to prevent the inhabitants from receiving smugglers. This action proved short-sighted, for outlaws began to move into the abandoned farms of this area. To discourage the Dutch, who had bought tobacco from colonists on the Spanish Main, the Spaniards burned tobacco fields and forced the inhabitants to move. Also, the salt pits the Dutch had exploited were poisoned. Spain could fight back, even to the extent of mutilating her own possessions.

THE PLANTING OF PERMANENT COLONIES IN THE WEST INDIES BY SPAIN'S ENEMIES

By the 1620's the European situation had degenerated into the ter-rible sequence of conflicts known as the Thirty Years' War. Spain fur-nished most of the financial support and many of the troops to aid the Catholic and Habsburg cause as the Bohemians, Palatines, Danes, Swedes, and French were resisted. England did not participate but in-stead sought opportunities overseas. Spain's truce with the Dutch ended in 1621 with this extraordinary people now in its prime. France was re-surgent, rising under Cardinal Richelieu's leadership to the position of Europe's greatest power.

Almost at the same time businessmen in London, Paris, and Amster-dam discerned profitable possibilities in the cultivation and sale of to-bacco, a weed to whose effects increasing numbers of Europeans were making slaves of themselves. It seemed that joint stock companies with official backing could send unlimited numbers of poor whites—debt-ors, beggars, idlers, and minor criminals—to the Americas to raise this crop. The opportunity was compelling, for Spain was absorbed in mid-European wars. The English colony in Virginia was successful, and the

Dutch West India Company was preparing for massive adventures in Brazil. The smaller islands of the Caribbean which Spain had never occupied offered a strong temptation to these enterprisers who dreamed of lucrative tobacco production.

Things did not go quite as simply as the optimists hoped, nor were the profits as large. True, the adventure got under way in the 1620's with great impetus. Thousands of unfortunates were shipped from the slums and jails of Europe to the lesser Antilles. These fragrant islands often contained man-eating Carib Indians who had to be disposed of. Spain was not so supine that she could not occasionally dislodge or injure the interlopers. Also, the English, French, and Dutch disputed among themselves in a small-minded way. Nor did the human outpourings readily take to toil in the tropics and exhibit any great determination to succeed as small farmers. Even so, within the first generation of the experiment the Dutch solidified a hold on Curaçao, Saba, St. Martin's, and St. Eustatius and on the mainland coast at Surinam. After much turbulence, France was entrenched on Martinique, Tobago, and Guadaloupe. The English held St. Kitt's, Barbados, Nevis, Barbuda, Antigua, and Montserrat. For a few years English Puritans and pirates jointly occupied two small islands off the coast of Nicaragua until the Spanish removed them in 1641.

And yet the tobacco enterprise did not succeed. Virginia offered stiff competition, and the motley population of the islands were not inclined to build permanent colonies. The squabbling of the national groups and, after 1640, that of English royalists and Puritans among themselves, was damaging to productivity. Soon after 1650 it became obvious that nature had created the lesser Antilles to provide sugar, not tobacco, for Europe. The Dutch demonstrated this point effectively when they were ousted from Brazil and relocated their slaves and machinery in the West Indies. It was apparent that large plantations with African slaves could produce sugar far more profitably than small tobacco patches with degenerate whites could enrich the stockholders. The transformation was quickly effected, and the sugar boom has not yet terminated. As island after island converted from tobacco to sugar, the European settlers, always surly and ungovernable, joined gangs of pirates and took to a life of crime.

While this transition was taking place, Spain was almost helpless. The loss of her fleet in successive disasters in the English Channel and off the coast of Brazil made it impossible to dispatch the annual convoys after 1640. When the galleons sailed, they were few and likely to be bottled up in ports for long periods. That Spain did not endure worse losses in territory during these years was due to quarrels among her enemies. During the 1640's the English were split between partisans of Charles I and Oliver

Cromwell. After that decade Cromwell in the 1650's and Louis XIV and Charles II in the 1660's destroyed the naval might of the Dutch, who had really inflicted the most damage on the Iberian empires. Dutch efforts to employ Brandenburg and Denmark as fronts for their capital and energies had no permanent result other than the Danish title to the Virgin Islands. If Holland was permanently demoted as a great power, she still held a few productive islands in the West Indies and a base on the Spanish Main which engaged in an enormous illicit trade with Venezuela and New Granada until the mid-eighteenth century.

Cromwell was not so absorbed with the Dutch that he neglected Spain, the favorite Puritan enemy. Republican England was inflamed during this period by Thomas Gage, a former Dominican friar who had resided in New Spain and Guatemala for years. Gage had returned to England and loudly announced his conversion to Protestantism, possibly in order to claim an inheritance. He traveled widely, denouncing the abuses of the Spanish system and the horrors of the Romish religion, emphasizing all the while the vulnerability of the Spanish empire in America. His agitations had great effect on the Puritans, and in 1654 Cromwell grandly called upon Felipe IV to grant freedom of religion and to open the Indies to English traders. The reply being what he anticipated, the dictator dispatched a force of 9,000 men to conquer Santo Domingo, then Panama, and finally Peru, following the sequence of the Spanish Conquest. As it turned out, the Puritan expedition was ill-managed and full of delusions. It failed miserably to capture Santo Domingo, whereupon it moved over to Jamaica and seized that grassy island from a few hundred Spanish ranchers. That was as far as the Puritan conquest of the Indies was fated to go.

In the last third of the seventeenth century France became Spain's worst enemy, with important repercussions in America. Already in possession of rich sugar islands in the Carribean and a foothold in the moist Guianas, the French were then broadening their interests in the area of the St. Lawrence, Great Lakes, and Ohio. After La Salle sailed down the Mississippi in 1680, he conceived a plan of magnificent grandeur, one equal to Cromwell's dream of seizing Peru. This was nothing less than the capture of the silver mines of New Spain, which La Salle represented as being quite close to the Mississippi. While Louis XIV was less sanguine about this scheme, he, like Spanish rulers of the preceding century, was willing to let his subjects take chances for such large results. Accordingly, La Salle attempted to colonize an area on the Gulf from which he could conquer Mexico. His pitiful wanderings in Texas and his death in 1685 terminated the scheme with a salutary lesson in geography to the French. France, however, had a claim to the Mississippi basin, and her interests in the West Indies were so lucrative they tended to obscure other opportunities. When the wars of Louis XIV against Spain finally ceased in 1697, France extracted Spanish acceptance of her title to the colony of St. Domingue (Haiti), the western third of Hispaniola which Spain had depopulated. This proved a fine colony indeed for France. Negro slaves were brought in vast numbers to create the richest sugar production area in the world, until they rose up and eliminated the French a century later.

THE BUCCANEERS AT THEIR BOLDEST

While the maritime powers were contending with one another in the Caribbean during the mid-seventeenth century, a crime wave of unprecedented proportions was bringing loss and injury to thousands of persons. Pirates had long been a nuisance in the Indies, but their activities had been limited until the Thirty Years' War. Early in the seventeenth century, when the Dutch largely displaced the Portuguese from the Indian Ocean, the desperado empire of pirates, long tolerated by the easygoing Portuguese, shifted its headquarters from Madagascar to the West Indies. Easier pickings were available in the new scene of operations, and the confused fighting of the European powers together with the immigration of many sorry characters from Europe made the Caribbean an ideal locality for kidnapers and thieves. Their ranks grew rapidly after so many whites were replaced by Negro slaves in the islands.

The life of the pirates has been much romanticized. Indeed, it had its colorful aspects. Men of all nations were likely to maintain that they had canceled all obligations—to creditors, wives, and kings—once they had reached the New World. There, they drifted or were pressed into gangs of outlaws, who obeyed natural leaders. These bands sometimes had specialties, such as attacking treasure-laden vessels, raiding missions, plundering coastal towns, or kidnaping wealthy persons for ransom or Negroes and children for slaves. Often they served as mercenaries, a sort of foreign legion, for the great powers in their frequent wars. Occasionally they might do a little work, settling on Tortuga, Haiti, one of the smaller islands, or the empty coasts of the Spanish Main for a few years. Here they raised crops, hunted, sold illicit goods, and recuperated between orgies of plunder. These outlaws had a code of honor of sorts. Some were religious fanatics, others the most primitive of pagans. Their dress tended to be garish. Private property could not be respected much in a society of fugitive scoundrels who specialized in theft and gambling. Nor was life itself. They took enormous risks and killed readily. It was their method of barbecuing whole cattle or hogs on a circulating gridiron (*boucan*) that gave them the name by which they were commonly known, the "buccaneers."

To the Spanish settlers in the Indies there was little about the buccaneers that could be considered romantic or picturesque. Peaceful folk were likely to be pulled off their ships or dragged from their homes and tortured or held for ransom, and to see their cargoes robbed and their towns sacked by these fearful characters, who raped nuns, burned homes, desecrated churches, seized property, and killed or mutilated out of sadism. Scarcely a town near the coast in Hispaniola, Puerto Rico, Cuba, Venezuela, New Granada, Panama, and New Spain escaped these dreadful incursions. While the settlements of other European nations were less likely to suffer such treatment, they too were sometimes terrorized. For much of the seventeenth century the only precaution was to abandon coastal towns and move far back into the interior, and this the Spanish did.

Henry Morgan

ILLUSTRATING the activities of the buccaneers at their worst was the career of the Welshman, Henry Morgan. Soon after England took Jamaica, Morgan and his cohorts, most of them men who had been expelled from more civilized areas, moved into the island to establish a base of criminal operations at Port Royal. A natural leader of men, one who loved life and yet loved to kill, Morgan had many engaging traits. Like most nasty people he could be winning when he cared to be, attractive and capable of making others admire him. By 1668 he was in command of fifteen ships and about 2,000 outlaws. In that year he carried out a brilliantly planned operation to take Puerto Bello from behind, thus avoiding the Spanish fortifications facing the sea. In order to disarm Spanish soldiers in the towers he forced nuns to plant ladders and climb up, hoping in vain the Spaniards would not shoot them. The population was crammed into churches, where women were raped on the altars, men mutilated, and everyone suspected of concealing property tortured. It is said that the buccaneers even tortured animals for the perverted pleasure this gave them.

In 1670 Morgan went back to the isthmus, this time leading 1,800 men across to the Pacific, where the rich but ugly city of Panama lay helpless. The Spaniards fought as well as they could, attempting as a last resort to stampede cattle in the direction of the outlaws. It was no use. Morgan knew every trick and had every advantage. Soon he occupied the capital for a 28-day ordeal. After gratifying their instincts for inflicting pain and grabbing wealth, the pirates loaded their ships in the Chagres River. At this point the English increment betrayed the French element by sailing away with the booty. After a period of rest Morgan went on to England, where he faced an inquest by the Lords of

Trade. Coming clear from this "trial," which King Charles II attended as moral support for Morgan, the buccaneer chieftain was knighted and named lieutenant governor of Jamaica. Several times he served as acting governor, and in 1685 Sir Henry won damages in a libel suit against a writer who had had the impudence to describe him as a pirate.

Despite Morgan's triumphs the day of the buccaneer was closing. If Spain could do little to defend herself, France and England could, and these two powers were developing prosperous sugar industries in the islands which required freedom from molestation by criminals. By the 1680's the several European maritime nations concerned were cooperating to end the nuisance of piracy. The suppression did not take long. Most of the buccaneers were pressed into the respective navies or forced to take their activities into other areas, such as South Carolina and New England. Jamaica became an orderly colony and Sir Henry Morgan a patriarchal official. It seemed symbolical that Port Royal, the headquarters for so much piracy in years past, slid into the sea during an earthquake in 1692.

Life for the Spanish in those days seemed one misfortune after another. Having weathered the shocks of the buccaneer period and enjoying, during the 1690's, some respite from French and English aggression, Spain was compelled to face another challenger, Scotland. In 1690 the Edinburgh Company was created for the purpose of establishing a monopoly of the type that had proved so lucrative for the Dutch and English. A lesser objective was to carry into the priest-ridden Spanish Empire the truths of Calvinism. The company planned to build a large base at Darien, where the Spanish had fumbled in the sixteenth century and even Drake had failed to create a permanent settlement. The baleful attitude of the English served to heighten the determination of the Scots, and they proceeded with exemplary thoroughness. A large expedition, well-financed and abundantly equipped, reached the humid coasts of New Granada and set up a base. Then, everything began to go wrong. The clothing the Scots brought proved unsuitable for the tropics, admirable as it was for the Highlands. The same was true of the liquor. The men became sick and surly. The Indians were pleased to annoy the Spanish, but they had little interest in toiling for the Scots or in hearing about Calvinism. The opposition of the home government proved awkward, for Scotland and England had a common monarch, and London could make its disapproval, or jealousy, felt. After several dreary years the Scots had to admit failure. Spanish opposition, Indian indifference, the climate, and financial distress took a toll that Scottish nationalism could not redress. Eventually, the Scots found a satisfactory outlet for their imperialistic urges in the large share they won in managing the British Empire.

On the eve of the eighteenth century, when a new dynasty was to bring renovation to Spain and the competition for empire would take on different dimensions, the Spanish had cause for feeling proud of their position in America. Despite the long generations of warfare and violence, they had lost no territory they had occupied but for Jamaica and a few islands of the lesser Antilles. It is true that they had abandoned their pretension to rule all the New World west of the Line of Tordesillas, but this hurt them little. They had never occupied Virginia, New England, New France, Louisiana, Guiana, or New York, and they had deliberately withdrawn from Haiti. Their empire was almost intact. Their coastal cities were now well-fortified. If their fleets carried only one-fourth the tonnage they had brought a century before, they still came and went. Badly as the imperial system was creaking, it nonetheless still functioned, and the Americans were devoted to the king, even the pathetic Carlos II. The forthcoming War of the Spanish Succession would show how strong were the ties between peninsular and American Spain.

On the other hand, the areas in the Caribbean and North America that other powers had taken were destined to prove extremely rich and important. The intrusion in the Guianas would remain. Worst of all from the Spanish point of view was the fact that the commercial monopoly was almost in ruins. Only one-tenth of the imported goods bought by Spanish colonials were products of peninsular Spain. The rest were either brought to Sevilla and trans-shipped or were introduced by smugglers whose boldness knew few limits. The home country was in a state near collapse. The great powers were tensely awaiting the demise of Carlos II, when it seemed likely that a contest for the Spanish inheritance would have to take place.

SECTION IV

The Iberian Empires in Maturity

13

Regeneration in the Eighteenth Century

The War of the Spanish Succession

Toward the end of the seventeenth century the Spanish monarchy was the sick man of both Europe and America. At its head, symbolically enough, reigned a sick man, Carlos II, last of the Spanish Habsburgs. The governmental machine had become a dismal mess of corruption and indifference. Nearly all the trade with the Indies was in foreign hands, and the scanty revenues that reached Spain were mortgaged to creditors long in advance. The fleet was unequal to the task of providing annual convoys, even small ones. The army had lost its reputation in repeated defeats. Its morale was wretched and the garrisons in Madrid could scarcely put on a good parade. Appalling poverty and backwardness characterized the peninsula. Its population had greatly declined since the days of Felipe II. Not only were the masses ragged and undernourished, but even the royal court was so short of ready funds it could not always finance its seasonal migrations from palace to palace. Obscurantism and fanaticism filled the official atmosphere, and a very high percentage of the adult manhood of the country was in the clergy, often because there was no other way to secure a livelihood. This was Spain of the Black Legend, foolishly proud of its insularity, impoverished, weak, haughty, and affecting to disdain material welfare while malignantly seeking to oppress the Americas, Italy, and Belgium.

If Spain was so badly off, then why did she survive? Probably the true reason is the one that explains why several decrepit empires have drifted along for decade after decade: the competition of the would-be heirs. Since Carlos II had no close relatives, the prospects were that his inheritance would fall to an Austrian Habsburg, a Bavarian Wittelsbach, or a French Bourbon, all of whom had family claims of equal validity. For years spies haunted the court at Madrid to influence the dim-witted king. His French wife and later his Austrian wife plotted to direct the legacy toward their dynasties. Frequent crises in the health of Carlos II produced situations of morbid comedy, of conspiracies and the alerting of the great powers to stand ready for the windfall. Certainly, the stakes were high enough to justify such activities. Yet time after time Carlos recovered, and people widely believed he was bewitched and that chasing the devils from the palace accounted for his revival. Carlos thought so too. After twenty years of such tension, the two strongest monarchs got together to avert a war of succession by agreeing to treaties of partition. These rulers, Louis XIV of France and William III of England, who was also Stadholder of Holland, painstakingly prepared a division of the vast Spanish monarchy, completing the second of these treaties in 1700, under which the Austrian archduke, Charles, would become king of Spain and the Indies, and other possessions went this way and that. Late in that year Carlos II finally expired, whereupon it was revealed that a few weeks earlier he had drawn up a will leaving everything to Philip of Anjou, a grandson of Louis XIV. The motive of the dying Spanish king, who occasionally had periods of lucidity, must have been to protect the integrity of his dominions. No one had done more than Louis XIV to injure Spain during his reign; yet the Bourbon dynasty seemed to offer the best assurance against partition.

For a few weeks after the testament of Carlos II was announced, an awful pause interrupted the course of affairs in the courts of the mighty. Two great questions must be resolved. First, would the varied Spanish dominions honor the will of Carlos II? Would the inhabitants of Buenos Aires and Brussels, Manila and Milan, Bogotá and Barcelona, Naples, Guatemala, Mexico, Lima, Havana, Madrid, and all the others accept a Bourbon as king? The answer was quickly seen to be affirmative. So steeped were the Spanish in monarchical tradition they proclaimed the seventeen-year-old Philip as Felipe V with scarcely a whisper of dissent, in contrast to the wild opposition they were to display spontaneously in 1808 when a Bonaparte was thrust on their throne. The second question was more fateful. Would the great powers stand by the statesmanlike treaty of partition? It was for Louis XIV to decide. The *Grande Monarque* wrestled with his conscience and won. Regardless of his word of honor, he could not resist this fabulous windfall to his dynasty. Rushing his grandson off to Madrid he may well have exulted, as Voltaire says, "The Pyrenees no longer exist!" The cheated hopefuls elected to fight, not only because of their private disappointments but because the accretion of the Spanish monarchy to the already formidable possessions of the Bourbons destroyed the balance of power. William of England and Holland took the initiative in assembling a coalition: Portugal would oppose Spain as usual, Austria agreed to support her archduke, and Savoy and several German states joined the great alliance, which generally had the support of such world opinion as there was.

The War of the Spanish Succession rocked Europe and affected the Americas from Newfoundland to Cape Horn. Its strategic outline was determined by the great push for Vienna undertaken in 1704 by Louis XIV. Unlike Napoleon 101 years later, the Sun King failed, his forces beaten by the Duke of Marlborough at Blenheim. For several years thereafter Marlborough and Prince Eugene of Savoy wore down France on her own territory until Louis XIV asked for peace. Political changes in Great Britain, as England and Scotland were now known, and the unexpected accession of the Archduke Charles to the throne of the Holy Roman Empire made the allies amenable to peaceful overtures. After tedious negotiations a series of pacts known collectively as the Treaty of Utrecht was drawn up between 1712 and 1715. Felipe V was to remain king of Spain and the Indies, with the proviso that the French and Spanish thrones were never to be united. The Austrian Habsburgs were consoled by the acquisition of Belgium, Milan, Naples, and Sardinia. The house of Savoy obtained Sicily, which it soon exchanged for Sardinia. And Great Britain was rewarded with Gibraltar, Menorca, Newfoundland, Nova Scotia, the Hudson Bay territories, and the right to send a 500-ton ship of merchandise and 4,800 "pieces" of slaves to the Spanish empire every year for thirty years. For such results had France exhausted herself to the point of ruin. Even the tarnished Sun King sadly counted the cost.

Spain had been deeply involved in the struggle, which marks the arrest of her decline and the beginning of her recovery. In 1702 Admiral George Rooke sank the treasure fleet before it could be unloaded at Vigo, where to this day men dive for silver. No fleets sailed between Spain and the Indies until 1706, and the seizures and smuggling of the allies largely paid for their war against the Bourbons. An Anglo-Dutch force landed in Portugal and took Madrid in 1706. The Archduke Charles had already installed himself in Barcelona, where Catalan nationalism was stirring again, and he removed to Madrid to reign for a few months as "Carlos III." Ejected by the Castilians, he forced his way back to the capital in 1710, only to be expelled for the second time. Most Spaniards had enthusiastically rallied around young Felipe V. Meanwhile, Admiral Rooke took the rock of Gibraltar, to the eternal discomfiture of Spain, and the island of Menorca, which England held until 1783. Destructive as the fighting had been, the peninsula was galvanized by all the activity, the influx of foreigners, and the shock of new methods. The strong loyalties aroused for Felipe V gave the new dynasty an auspicious start.

An Infusion of Energy

THE new king and his advisers zestfully proceeded with the work of renovating the antiquated Spanish monarchy, now strengthened rather than debilitated by the loss of its possessions in Italy and northwestern Europe. So long isolated, and glad to be so, the Spaniards suddenly confronted energetic, confident men of the type who had brought France to greatness while Spain had been sinking into stagnation. Annoyed and abashed, they reacted finally by accepting leadership from these obviously more competent foreigners. The war itself and the aliens who shamed or prodded the Spanish people into utilizing their latent energies brought a new atmosphere to the peninsula, and soon to America. Perhaps this atmosphere was un-Spanish or even anti-Spanish, as many grumbled and some still do. Material progress, vigor, and efficiency came to be prized in many quarters, especially in the upper reaches of the government. Men who knew how to do things, who were not afraid to imitate foreigners, who could think creatively, and who had ideas began to replace the haughty hacks who had somnolently managed the imperial machine until it had almost, but not quite, run down by 1700.

Under Felipe V, Frenchmen manned the major posts of the government until the war was safely over. Then, the new administrative type began to appear, most of them well-born but not nobles, military men who had displayed capacity during the war. As their power grew throughout the century, that of the old aristocracy declined. The number of nobles decreased by half, in contrast to the signal rise in population. They remained rich and prestigious, but, often ignored by the Bourbons, they responded by disdaining the government and living in splendid isolation. Felipe V by-passed the ancient councils of Spain by creating five ministries to centralize administration. The intendant system long used in France was imported and by 1749, when it was completed, served to bring into the king's hands effective control over the provinces. Tax farming ended in favor of royal collectors. The army and navy continued to thrive after the war was over, and the merchant marine received lavish attention. Monopoly companies were established to develop backward areas, particularly in the overseas empire. Subsidies to industries, protective tariffs, importation of foreign technical experts, and the repopulation of deserted areas were introduced as orthodox mercantilistic measures, which had served France so well in the time of Colbert. New styles, as signified by the wig and silk stockings, captivated the upper classes. French classicism in architecture, painting, and literature quickly assumed domination in Spain and the Indies, so much so that for a long time Spanish artistic creativity almost dried up. Scholarship blossomed with the establishment of such institutions as the Spanish Academy, the Royal Library, the Academy of Medicine, and the Academy of History. The viceroyalties overseas came to benefit from these advances.

Felipe V was no dynamic progressive, nor was his influential second wife, Isabel Farnese, but they allowed the refreshing breezes to blow with good effect. Heartening as the advances in Spain were, Felipe underwent a period of melancholia in 1724 and resigned the crown to his young son, Luis I, who died a few months later, whereupon he succumbed to urgent pressures to resume the kingship and reigned until his death in 1746. In mockery of the fears of the great alliance during the War of the Spanish Succession, Felipe V proved by no means a puppet of France. On the contrary, he competed with his cousin, Louis XV, and may even have intrigued to take his throne. In the Americas the effects of this tension between the two Bourbons manifested themselves by serious and not always bloodless rivalries over West Florida and Texas. Finally, in 1733, Felipe V formed a close diplomatic tie with France that continued, with the usual ups and downs of such relationships, until after the French Revolution had begun. The occasion for this family compact was the War of the Polish Succession, which had the odd results of reinstating the Spanish Bourbons on the thrones of Naples and Sicily while dislodging the French choice for the Polish crown.

Great Britain loomed more and more as the arch-enemy of the two Latin empires overseas. The privilege to import slaves, the *asiento*, was stretched considerably beyond the 4,800 annual limit, and British agents who were supposed to supervise this traffic in Spanish-American ports exceeded their functions by furthering illicit trade. Furthermore, the 500-ton annual ship that was to supply Panama became, or so the Spaniards charged, a veritable floating warehouse anchored almost constantly while its stocks were sold and replenished from Jamaica. Spanish measures to contain the British, and very likely some high-handedness of their own invention, produced more abuses and aggressions, attaining an absurd degree in 1739 when a shipmaster named Jenkins widely exhibited in London a detached ear, which he claimed the Spanish had cut off.[1] Britain finally declared war on Spain, frankly acknowledging her intention to expand her trade in the Americas and going so far as to foster independence sentiment in the Spanish viceroyalties. This War of Jenkins' Ear soon merged in the War of the Austrian Succession (1740–1748). As far as Spain was concerned, the war was by no means inglorious. Admiral Vernon and a huge expeditionary force sacked Puerto Bello and

1.   Skeptics maintained that Jenkins had two perfectly good ears under his wig.

Venezuelan ports and undertook a massive effort to seize Cartagena, which the Spanish and New Granadans beat off. Various coastal towns on the Pacific underwent assaults, and Lord Anson captured the Manila galleon with all its Mexican silver as it approached the Philippines. Yet the Spanish gave a very satisfactory account of themselves. Their revived fleet and merchant marine and their fortifications in the Indies proved equal to British threats. As for the British ambition to detach the Americans from the Spanish monarchy, the idea was not only premature, but ridiculous. Everywhere the Americans proved their loyalty. Their desire for British merchandise still had no political implications whatever. By the Treaty of Aix-la-Chapelle in 1748, the Spanish empire remained intact, and the *asiento* was cancelled.

Felipe V had died before this war was over and had been succeeded by Fernando VI, whose short rule (1746–1759) was a generally productive and serene period. It was characterized by prosperity, good government, enlightenment, philanthropy, and after 1748, by peace. In both the peninsula and America (the term "Indies" was being superseded by this time) capable, serious-minded men operated the vast imperial machine and undertook to repair its weaknesses. The Treaty of Madrid in 1750 finally acknowledged the claim of Portugal to Brazil west of the Line of Tordesillas and attempted to adjust the border of what is now Uruguay. In 1753, a concordat with the Church again asserted the authority of the Spanish monarchs to dominate ecclesiastical activities, even in some matters of dogma, restoring conditions to what they had been under the first Habsburgs. The music-loving Fernando VI patronized Domenico Scarlatti and other artists. Meanwhile, the pungent writings of the monk Feyjóo affected a few but influential persons in the direction of accepting scientific attitudes and modernizing the educational system. In government, diplomacy, economic affairs, and cultural life Spain was making a comeback.

The Peak of the Recovery

THE long reign of Carlos III concluded the period of good rule under the Bourbons by bringing the Spanish monarchy to its highest state since the best days of Felipe II. This king was personally colorless, his expression being sheep-like, as the celebrated lover Casanova, himself goat-like, once observed. The court painter, Francisco Goya, depicted Carlos' ungainly features without mercy. Homely and uninteresting a personality as he was, this monarch was one of the ablest rulers of the Age of Enlightened Despots and possibly the finest king Spain ever had. Having served a long apprenticeship in philanthropic autocracy as king of the Two Sicilies, he came to Madrid in 1759 to succeed Fernando VI, his half-brother. While French and English influences were running strong in the peninsula, the Italian strain that entered with Carlos III further enriched the Enlightenment. Yet these foreign currents, together with an overdue attempt to curb crime in Madrid, provoked an ugly riot in 1766; Carlos III learned the lesson and thereafter proceeded with caution, taking care to replace foreign advisers with Spaniards.

The great ministers of Carlos III left a strong mark on Spain and the Americas. One of the most notable was the Count of Aranda, foe of the Jesuits and the Inquisition, friend of Voltaire and other luminaries of the Age of Reason, and a man of vision who advised the king to decentralize the American empire by sending his sons over to rule as kings under the aegis of an emperor in Madrid.[2] The Count of Floridablanca sponsored the creation of economic societies to spread modern agricultural and industrial knowledge, and with them the humanitarian ideas of the age. In general, he undermined the antique, obscurantist tradition of Spain during a long career that was to end with his horrified reaction to the French Revolution. Another great light of this period was the Count of Campomanes, as he was finally titled, who favored protection of industries, interior colonization, free trade within the Spanish empire, and measures to restrict the guilds, Church, and landed aristocracy. Gaspar Melchor Jovellanos did much to improve education and to stimulate the universities both in Spain and America. He proposed agricultural reforms and popularized the physiocratic doctrines of economic laissez-faire. José de Gálvez, Marquis of Sonora, made a memorable tour of New Spain and returned to the peninsula to carry out far-reaching reforms in the administration of the Americas. These and lesser ministers both typified and advertised the exhilarating ideas of the Enlightenment, more so than Spanish intellectuals, who were by no means lacking or silent. Carlos III did not always act as they advised. Nor did the conservative forces notably acquiesce in all these projects. The tendencies of that hopeful age were clear, however, and Spain's official circles rejoiced in them.

In foreign affairs Carlos III was less successful, though Spain's strength and prestige were restored to a level they had not known for a century and a half and would never know again. In 1761 Carlos allowed himself to be persuaded to help France in the last stages of the Seven Years' War, a world conflict that was costing Louis XV most of his colonies in India and North America. During the final year of this struggle Spain shared the French defeats at the hands of a surging Britain. Both Manila and Havana were occupied. By the Peace of Paris in 1763

2. There has been a great deal of controversy on the point. Recent studies offer persuasive testimony that Aranda did, in fact, present such a plan.

Spain recovered Manila but had to cede Florida to Britain in order to regain Havana. Hoping to salvage something from the expanding British and to compensate Carlos III for his losses, Louis XV gave Spain the western half of Louisiana, a gift of dubious advantage to Spain, who had much difficulty in asserting her rights there.

During the 1770's Carlos III had friction with Portugal over the boundaries between her Platine colonies and Brazil. Finally, by establishing a viceroyalty in Buenos Aires and undertaking an expensive military offensive, he succeeded in pushing the Portuguese for a time out of the present Uruguay. Another conflict was also equivocal in outcome, that over a group of islands near the Antarctic labeled *"las islas Malvinas"* on Argentine maps today, though called the Falkland Islands by everyone else and colored with the British red on non-Argentine maps. This circumstance dates back to a confused situation when British whalers took possession of the barren group. In 1774 the Spanish ousted the intruders but failed to fortify the islands, and in 1833, long after the king of Spain had ceased to rule the Argentine, the British came back to stay. Argentina still asserts to an indifferent world that the islands are legally hers.

The American Revolution brought a dangerous opportunity to France and Spain. They were greatly tempted to assist the rebellious colonies and thus take revenge upon Britain, who had done them so much harm. Yet if they helped and the revolution failed, a reunited British Empire might turn on Latin America, which it had coveted so long. If the Latin powers failed to help and the Americans won their independence, the new country might become aggressive on its own and urge the Spanish and French colonies to sever their European ties. After weighing the possibilities, France in 1778 and Spain in 1779 took the plunge, deciding that punishment of Britain was worth the other hazards. Their intervention was decisive. Without it the American Revolution might have dragged on for years and even been defeated. Spain's fleet was very useful in hampering British naval activity, and her conquest of Florida not only gratified her national pride but increased the prestige of Spanish arms throughout the Americas. On the other hand, a massive effort against Gibraltar failed. In the Peace of Versailles of 1783 Carlos III won suitable rewards for his efforts. Florida was returned to Spain, Menorca was recovered, and the British agreed to remove themselves from Honduras, where they had been cutting logwood for more than a century. Yet the success of the American Revolution was exceedingly unfortunate for the Spanish monarchy. Both its example and the aggressiveness of the United States helped bring ruin to the overseas empire of the kings of Spain. If the French Bourbons, whose financial chaos led to the calling of the Estates-General in 1789, suffered more dramatically from their ill-advised assistance to the Americans, the long-range effects on the Spanish Bourbons were almost as terrible.

The last years of Carlos III were signally happy ones for the Spanish monarchy, a period that would later loom as "the good old days" to many on both sides of the Atlantic. Prosperity was general; a sharp rise in American income, a spectacular increase in Catalan industry, and a general improvement in agricultural methods gave the peninsula an appearance of economic well-being. Madrid and Barcelona had grown rapidly, becoming great cities. In fact, the population had doubled, if we may credit the census of 1787, since the Bourbons had mounted the throne. A middle class was assuming a significant size and developing modest ambitions. Cultural life was flourishing, greatly affected by the Enlightenment but still orthodox and loyal. Defects in the regime did not inspire revolutionary protest but rather a confident determination to bring about improvements through the prevailing system.

Yet, Spain was still Spain, impractical, disdainful of the foreigner, and unwilling to exert herself but for the most exalted causes. The energetic monarch and his ministers still encountered much passive resistance to modernity from a population that often regarded them as un-Spanish. If the privileges of the nobility and the clergy had been nibbled away for decades, those that remained were formidable. The number in these groups equalled that of France, which had more than twice the population of Spain. The urban proletariat and the great rural masses still existed in dreadful poverty, as they did nearly everywhere else. The spectacular progress wrought by the Bourbons had not yet brought the population to the point that they could discern how much more ought to be done, and could be done. France was about to offer some impressive lessons when, late in 1788, Carlos III died.

THE COLONIAL REVIVAL

Familiar as the historical stereotype regarding the Bourbons may be —that they learned nothing and forgot nothing—it is apparent that the first three Spanish kings of this family enabled their subjects to discard many of their former ways and to adopt much that was new. Peninsular Spain itself experienced this change of mood and spirit much sooner than the American viceroyalties did, and it was in the metropolis that improvements were most striking. The Americas felt little in the way of institutional progress during the reign of Felipe V but received abler and more dedicated officials.

At first, the new monarch had to insure the loyalty of the overseas empire during the War of the Spanish Succession. This proved simple enough, since Spaniards in the Indies no less than in Spain accepted the testament of Carlos II as binding. Only whispers of intrigues in behalf of the Archduke Charles disturbed the political atmosphere. Then, Felipe V required funds to wage war against his numerous enemies. As usual, the Americans were invited, and then begged, to contribute large gifts. The success of these appeals demonstrated the loyalty of the empire. As oceanic connections were cut for the first four years of the war, it was necessary to find some way to supply the colonists with merchandise and to bring their treasure to the peninsula. While Spain's enemies were only too eager to assume these functions, and to some extent did, the allied French were able to save what remained of the markets and to fetch the treasure. Ironically, American bullion largely financed both sides in the war, the French through legal trade and ferrying the silver, the English and Dutch through illicit commerce and seizures.

When peace came Felipe V acted to restore the Spanish monopoly, which for so long had been a bitter joke to those who knew its real weaknesses. In 1717 the *Casa de Contratación* was transferred from the riverport Sevilla to the seaport Cadiz, a move that had long been indicated but which the historic business houses in Sevilla had obstructed. Cadiz almost at once began to expand and became the third largest city in Spain, its facilities making it possible to handle a much larger volume of the American trade. Felipe V also planned the re-establishment of the famous annual fleet system. This proved very difficult, for the Spanish merchant marine did not grow rapidly enough to meet the needs of the colonists, who in any case continued to trade with the British, usually illegally. Fleets went out not annually, but with some regularity, though they were smaller than those of a century before. The method was simply too cumbersome for a power no better endowed than Spain. So Felipe V liberally authorized private registries or individual sailings. This became the chief means of carrying on the commerce between Spain and the colonies. In 1740 the annual fleet to Panama was abandoned altogether, with salutary results for the volume of trade between Cadiz and the ports of South America. Just after the Seven Years' War, in 1765, the crown threw open the principal islands of the West Indies to individual sailings, Louisiana in 1768, Yucatan in 1770, and New Granada in 1776. The results were so encouraging that in 1778 a sort of free trade within the Spanish commonwealth was proclaimed. Spanish subjects in any area were now able to engage in commerce with most of the imperial ports except for Mexico and Venezuela, which remained under monopoly control until 1789. It also proved fruitful to reduce the taxes on commerce, which responded by burgeoning further in volume. This stunning growth in inter-Spanish trade toward the end of the eighteenth century meant that foreign traders, who had long dominated American commerce, were losing out rapidly. It also resulted in the dramatic expansion of mercantile classes in the large cities, whose leaders were so pleased with the new prosperity they could not keep from wondering how much better it would be if they were still more free, even independent altogether of the Spanish monarchy.

Commerce was by no means the only beneficiary of the Bourbon improvements. Colonial agriculture, mining, stockraising, and industry also experienced decades of growth. In every area—New Spain and Peru, the Argentine and New Granada, Guatemala and Venezuela—the over-all pattern was the same. Higher productivity, increase in wealth and ambition on the part of the creoles, and heightened revenues for the crown characterized nearly every section of Spanish America. While much of this growth came about as part of the momentum of a Western civilization that was generally prosperous, the intelligent encouragement by the crown cannot be minimized. Viceroys and lesser officials performed their duties better. They know they would be respected for stimulating activities other than the output of silver, although that activity was still highly regarded. The *encomienda* finally died out altogether. Land-owning increased, both by whites and Indians, as new territories were populated. Improved commercial methods made it possible to sell American articles in Europe with greater facility. As will be seen, the crown encouraged the application of new scientific methods to mining with startling success, especially in New Spain. While it must not by any means be assumed that a century of economic growth and general prosperity benefited every inhabitant of the Americas or the peninsula, the broad outline was clear. Spain and her empire were advancing rapidly toward higher standards of living.

Reform and Autocracy in America

WHILE most structural changes in the government of Spanish America awaited the reign of Carlos III, an important alteration was made in 1714 with the creation of the Ministry of Marine and Indies, which lasted until 1790. This prestigious office handled nearly all the affairs in America that came within the monarchical prerogative, assuming the position at the king's right hand previously enjoyed by the Council of Indies. To be sure, the Council of Indies continued as an august body in which membership was a conspicuous honor, but policy matters fell under the direction of the Ministry. In 1717 the crown experimented in another respect, this time less happily, by organizing a new viceroyalty, that of New Granada, which consisted of the present republics of Colombia, Panama, Ecuador, and Venezuela. It soon proved difficult to pull together the administration of such a sprawling, underpopulated area, and the bureaucracy of the viceroyalty of Peru intrigued against the new creation, which seemed a rival for importance and profits. In 1723 the effort was abandoned and the several territories reverted to control from Lima. However, in 1739, as war with Britain began and a major British offensive against New Granada was known to be impending, the viceroyalty was restored, to endure until the wars of independence. Similarly, the possibility of war with Britain and the actuality of chronic conflicts with Portugal over the southern boundary of Brazil led to the creation of the viceroyalty of La Plata in 1776, composed of the modern republics of Argentina, Bolivia, Paraguay, and Uruguay. With four viceroyalties now instead of two, the Spanish empire in America had achieved a salutary decentralization. The amazing prosperity of La Plata and New Granada in the following years justified the step.

So it was with the up-grading of the office of captain-general, a term familiar in the New World since the days of Cortés. After the War of the Spanish Succession, Felipe V punished Catalonia, Aragon, and Valencia for their attachment to the Archduke Charles by replacing viceroys with captains-general, whose positions were less honorific but more autocratic. In America the office took the form of a small-size viceroy, as Caracas in 1777, Havana in 1728, and Chile in 1778 were subjected to captains-general, as Guatemala and the Philippines long had been. Furthermore, the crown detached most of New Spain north of the mining region in 1776 and formed a commandancy-general, which was expected to grow into a viceroyalty. Within these entities now, modernized bureaucracies staffed by comparatively efficient officers developed, and a certain nationalism took shape.

A major step toward redistributing the viceregal power in the interest of better government, as the crown regarded it, or of autocracy, as many colonists felt, was the long-debated creation of intendancies in America. The intendant system had justified itself in the peninsula since the last days of Felipe V, but the crown hesitated to transfer it to the New World. After the Seven Years' War it was experimentally introduced into Cuba in 1764. Working satisfactorily there, it was extended to the Platine area in 1782, to Peru in 1784, and finally to Chile and New Spain in 1786. The measure was indeed far-reaching. Viceroyalties and captaincies-general were divided into districts, or intendancies, that foreshadowed the states of the future republics. Over each was placed an officer of high rank, the intendant, who was virtually an autocrat. He was responsible for the operation of the government, the administration of justice, the promotion of industry, agriculture, and commerce, military defense, supervision of cities, overseeing church affairs, collection of the revenues, and the general fostering of the economy and social welfare of the population. In nearly every case he was a peninsular Spaniard, for the Bourbon reformers had no intention whatever of handing power over to the Americans, even if they piously insisted the appointments were made purely on the basis of merit and that creoles were eligible. Each intendancy was divided into smaller districts ruled by sub-delegates who answered to the intendants.

It is clear that this system weakened the authority of the viceroys and captains-general, who tended to resist its introduction and to criticize its operation.[3] Such powers as they had exerted over *corregidores*, *alcaldes mayores*, and governors vanished as these officials were swept away in favor of the intendants and sub-delegates. The effect of the system on the municipal *cabildos* was uneven. Some found themselves under stricter regulation; others discovered a power vacuum and asserted themselves. The mission communities were generally brought under closer supervision by the crown. In all, however, it is impossible to make a responsible assessment of the intendant system, for it had scarcely begun to function on a regular basis when the entire Spanish monarchy started to disintegrate. In purpose and design it was typical of the Bourbons, producing clear lines of authority, promising more efficient rule, and manifestly tightening up the autocracy wielded in Madrid. It is worthy of note that by this time the Bourbons seldom spoke of their American possessions as kingdoms on the same level as metropolitan Spain. Without admitting it, they were moving more and more toward an outright colonialism in which the American territories were both legally and in reality under the rule of the peninsular kingdom.

Curbing the Church

THE French advisers who swarmed into Spain at the accession of Felipe V were prepared to disapprove of the all-pervading Church. France had long since curbed the role of the clerics. Moreover, she was the leader of European thought and fashion that were beginning to have, and would soon glory in, skepticism toward all organized religion. This "advanced" attitude did not affect the Bourbon rulers of Spain, who themselves were notably devout, so much as the more mundane determination to restore the subordinate status of the ecclesiastical establishment that the later Habsburg monarchs had permitted to get out of hand. To the newcomers it seemed that the Church in Spain had far outgrown its official position, that its size, wealth, and influence even overshadowed the government.

Much was done in the way of enforcing existing rules of discipline for the clergy and in making better appointments to the chief posts. It was necessary for the king to recover his right of nominating clergymen,

3. Some students now hold that the intendant system did not in reality diminish the power of viceroys as much as they feared it would.

for Rome had been permitted in recent years to fill two-thirds of the positions. As the century wore on, the Bourbon kings and ministers brought about gradually a reduction in the Spanish clergy, which declined by half but still, as has been noted, was as large as that of France, who had more than twice the population of Spain. In 1717 Felipe V decreed that no new convents be established in the Indies, for every report on the subject suggested that there were far too many already. A few years later, in 1734, the crown ordered that for ten years no one in New Spain should be allowed to enter a religious order. Clergymen were warned about participating in drawing up wills, lest still more property accrue to the Church through the benefactions of people with guilty consciences. The friars lost the special privileges they had enjoyed since the Conquest of administering the rites of the Church in lieu of the secular clergy. Plan after plan was presented by the enlightened ministers of Carlos III to contain or reverse the process of Church acquisition of property and to end mortmain, though comparatively little progress was made. Despite all of these measures, which in retrospect appear somewhat timid, both Spain and the Indies remained fervently Catholic.

Though the regular orders seem to have borne the brunt of Bourbon anti-clerical policies, this period was one of vast achievement in missionary activity, possibly for the very reason that the crown prodded them out of their comfortable missions and monasteries. Again and again the political authorities used the friars to expand the frontier of Christendom, which also spread the control of the kings of Spain. To forestall the troublesome Dutch in Venezuela an outburst of conversion and mission construction pushed the Spanish Capuchins deeper into the Orinoco basin. In the Argentine, at last, the missions began to make progress in taming the nomadic Indians. Texas and Florida, endangered by French encroachment, became the scenes of energetic activity by the Franciscan friars. Most significant of all was California, which was reduced to Spanish control with amazing speed in order to keep the British and the Russians out.

One "reform" of Carlos III which greatly injured the Spanish establishment in the Americas and which still creates puzzlement was the expulsion of the Jesuits. The great services of the Order of Jesus, founded by the Spaniard Loyola, for the kings of Spain have repeatedly been noted. But the Jesuits lost popularity in high places during the eighteenth century for reasons good and bad. They were accused of distorting the true faith in order to further their own ends, of being too ambitious to control royal courts in the interest of Rome, of being too successful, fond of meddling, and absorbed in material riches, and of operating a hidden super-government. The unpopularity of the Jesuits with rival orders and with powerful elements of the Catholic Church was a long-standing affair. The spreading of the Enlightenment damaged them further, for the *philosophes* rightly discerned in the Jesuits their deadliest opponents. Then, the various monarchs resented the mysterious methods of an elite religious order which so often intrigued and got its own way. Whatever the distinction between sound and false reasons, the society was at bay by mid-century. The chief complaint in America as far as the Spanish government was concerned was that the Jesuits were disobedient, that they had frustrated the attempted demarcation of Spanish and Portuguese boundaries by leading their Indian wards in armed resistance following the treaty of 1750.

It was not Spain but Portugal who took the first measure to destroy the Jesuits. In 1759 José Carvalho, later the Marquis of Pombal, who was virtual dictator of Portugal, alleged the Jesuits had attempted to assassinate the king and summarily expelled them. The shocking measure succeeded, the Jesuits obediently going into prison or departing for exile from both Portugal and Brazil. Carlos III observed the results with satisfaction. He suspected the Jesuits of instigating the riot of 1766 in Madrid that unnerved him so, and possibly for that reason decided to oust the Society from all his dominions in 1767. Carlos III declined to explain his step, even to the pope, to whom he wrote that the true reason was locked in his breast. Whatever the cause, he issued the order with great secrecy, saw it carried out brutally, and never seems to have repented. France, the Two Sicilies, and Austria likewise turned the Jesuits out, and in 1773 the pope was pressured into abolishing the order.[4]

Gratified as the Enlightened Despots were by the expulsion, and delighted as the *philosophes* were, the results were sad in the New World. Only the universities, where the Jesuits were often hostile to the new currents, may have profited. Otherwise, the expulsion removed the best teachers, missionaries, and Church officials from the Iberian empires and left many thousands of Indian wards without competent guidance. Also, the black-robed exiles bitterly resented the treatment they received at the hands of Spain and Portugal, and some of them labored for years to foment rebellious sentiments in their colonial empires.

The pressure of the Bourbons against the Church was shown in many other ways. The concordat of 1753 permitted, among other matters already described, the Spanish crown to tax Church property. And during the last quarter of the century the authorities did not halt the circulation of anti-clerical literature, most of it outwardly gentle but sometimes

4. The Jesuits were supposed to enter other orders. Many simply went underground or took refuge in Prussia and Russia. After the Napoleonic wars, the Society was restored. About 6,000 Jesuits were expelled from Spain and 1,500 from America.

very stinging. Curiously enough, the two most effective writers of works subversive of clerical authority were clergymen, Friar Feyjóo and the witty and satirical Father Isla. The Peruvian, Pablo de Olavide, did much to undermine reverence for the Church in Spain and abroad, and many nobles and high officials diminished the prestige of the Church by adopting an amused or patronizing attitude toward it. The Inquisition still functioned, but fewer and fewer cases came before it. Except for disciplinary actions against wayward clergymen, the Holy Office almost went out of business. In Spanish America only one person was executed for heresy between the advent of the Bourbons and the French Revolution. People referred slightingly to this benighted institution, and though it still had latent power, its prestige was small and its functions were derided.

It is clear that the eighteenth century was a period of growth and prosperity for Spain and, particularly after the end of the Seven Years' War in 1763, for America. The changes were most dramatic in the peninsula. If the nobility and the Church still controlled two-thirds of the productive lands in Spain, they had long been on the defensive by the end of the period. The lower classes had participated slightly in the general improvements. And a middle class had taken shape as a potent political and intellectual force, as the nineteenth century would reveal. Roads, canals, irrigation facilities, factories, efficient mines, and better business conditions had wrought great changes on the face of Spain. When Carlos III died in 1788 it seemed that the country had accomplished much of the preparatory work for entering the Industrial Age. The government was autocratic but enlightened. The navy was the third best in the world, after those of Britain and France. As the repeated wars with Britain had demonstrated, Spanish armies and fleets were still capable of defending an extensive world empire. Yet all these conditions were so soon to change. Spain was at the end of a splendid period, not at the beginning. The modernizers had not won. They had succeeded only in splitting Spain into two personalities which are still at war with one another.

In the Americas the renovators had left much to admire. The viceroyalties and captaincy-generals all seemed to be thriving, even to be developing traces of national spirit that boded ill for colonialism. If their governments were despotic they were effective. Intellectual and artistic life flourished among many Americans. Man-made beauty, opulence, and other outward manifestations of wealth and sophistication characterized many localities. The older cities were by now real centers of civilization. And raw new towns were promising: San Francisco, Los Angeles, Albuquerque, San Antonio, New Orleans, and Pensacola in the north, and Montevideo, Rancagua, and the revived Buenos Aires in the south. Spanish immigrants had arrived by the tens of thousands during the century, and the population was rising. There may have been as many as 3,000,000 Europeans in Spanish America, 95 per cent of whom were creoles. The mestizos, numbering possibly 5,000,000, already surpassed the whites by head count and were exhibiting some ambition for political fulfillment. Under Spanish rule lived probably 8,000,000 Indians, though we must always be skeptical of population figures, and almost 1,000,000 Negroes. A majority of these shared, at least superficially, the language and religion of Spain.

So much progress had been made during the eighteenth century. So much cried out to be made. Education, humanitarian measures, sanitation, practice in self-government, increase in productivity, better distribution of wealth, improved standards of living—all these and other matters drew the attention and kindled the imaginations of thoughtful men. The Bourbon reforms were a beginning in the right direction. Yet they had fatally damaged the power of the viceroys, the Church, the guilds, the monopolists, and the old hierarchy which had so long held the empire together. Not enough time was to be allowed for the renovated imperial system to develop its own strength.

14

The Viceroyalty of New Spain
at its Zenith

FOR the nearly two centuries after the establishment of the viceroyalty of New Spain, its history rather deceptively offers an impression of suspended activity. The dramatic events of Cortés' victory over the Aztecs and the creation of the Spanish imperial apparatus between the Rockies and the Central American tropics appear to be followed by generations of monotony. Life went on sluggishly in the same pattern. Royal officials arrived and departed, contending during the interval with problems that seem drearily repetitious. Clergymen went about their labors, or in some cases neglected them, in the familiar way. Spanish immigrants arrived steadily, taking over much of the land and creating new businesses, until about half the European population of the Spanish empire lived in New Spain. The Indians continued to endure imperialistic control, or fled from it, or simply mixed with the whites. At least they ceased to die out, hard as life was. While much of the monotony is real, it should be acknowledged that the comparative paucity of historical works covering this period leaves us ignorant of many important developments.

Much more happened after the Bourbons took over Spain and her overseas dominions. Yet the impact of this regeneration did not affect New Spain seriously until the middle of the reign of Carlos III. Then, a welter of reforms altered the structure of the great viceroyalty. Prosperity became dazzling, at least for many individuals and for the monarchy as a whole. A new mood was evident in both official circles and among the numerous creoles. Important as these changes were, they did not mark the beginning of a new imperialistic phase of any duration. Rather, the old order was undermined, and the new system did not have time enough to become entrenched. It scarcely got beyond the restless, creative stage when New Spain became the Mexican nation.

GENERAL FEATURES OF
THE MID-COLONIAL PERIOD

The apparatus of government changed very little. The viceroys of New Spain reigned over a vast and incredibly varied territory stretching from New Mexico to Guatemala. In military and financial matters their authority included some measure of control over the Philippines, Central America, Cuba, Puerto Rico, Santo Domingo, and sometimes over Venezuela. Impressive dignitaries though they were, the viceroys lost real powers as the bureaucracy operated year after year on its own momentum and, like the population, came to regard their titular ruler as a transient figure who could do little before he was recalled to Spain.

More long-lived, and in many ways more effective as agents of European control, were the *audiencias* in Mexico City, Guadalájara, Guatemala, Santo Domingo, and Manila. Checking a reigning viceroy at times and usually assuming full powers during a hiatus between viceroys, the *audiencias* seemed more continuous and enduring. As the highest of colonial courts they steadily wove and strengthened a fabric of Spanish law which affected life more than the actions of the viceroys. Beneath the viceroy and the *audiencias* were rulers of specific areas. If they were on the frontier, they might bear the ancient title of *adelantado*. If they ruled large provinces, they might be governors; if small ones, *alcaldes mayores* or *corregidores*. For most of the colonial period New Spain had somewhat more than a hundred of these officials at any given time. Often they were real autocrats, ignoring as much as they dared the viceroy in Mexico City and seeking to remain in favor with Madrid, where they had usually purchased their appointments. Some of these lesser figures were creoles, and they were the most corrupt and tyrannical of all.

The Growth of the Church

THE ecclesiastical establishment had grown tremendously since the days of Bishop Zumárraga and Vasco de Quiroga. Much of the power and wealth of New Spain gravitated to the Church during the period of the weak later Habsburgs. Its prestige was greater than the government's, and though the viceroy remained vice-patron, the same factors that had weakened his political authority served to reduce his effective control over the vast clerical arm. At the head of the secular clergy stood the archbishop of New Spain, a formidable figure who might serve as viceroy during an interregnum and who was likely to attract critics of a viceroy to such an extent that a system of checks and balances might seem to operate. As shall be seen presently, an archbishop was by no means certain to lose out in a dispute with a viceroy. Eight bishops presided over their dioceses beneath the archbishop. These episcopal dignitaries were likewise powerful and prestigious, frequently pulling more weight in the administrative system than the governors with whom they often clashed. The number of parish priests in New Spain always seemed insufficient, though it seldom fell below 4,000. They were likely to serve the white element, leaving the Indians to the friars, and to concentrate in Mexico City, where most of the Europeans lived. Remote towns continually complained of a shortage of priests, and observers in the capital were likely to lament the plenitude and resulting idleness of these curates.

The members of the regular orders had far more contact with the non-whites and the areas away from the capital. Proud of their historical connection with the great missionaries of the sixteenth century, they frequently resented the priests as late arrivals who were trying to deprive themselves of their earned position. It was particularly galling to have an area they had settled and developed pronounced Hispanicized enough for the secular clergy to take over. In such cases the friars were expected to leave their comfortable monasteries and beloved wards and advance farther into the frontier. To be sure, this process went on very slowly, despite official prodding. In general, the western areas of New Spain were in the hands of the Jesuits, the central was Franciscan territory, and the eastern Dominican. Augustinians, Carmelites, and others were squeezed among the larger orders. The various orders had their own provincial officials and vicars-general in Mexico City and were controlled from Europe less through crown officials than by their own chain of command emanating from resident generals in Rome and Madrid. This circumstance produced considerable tension with the political authorities, who in a showdown would have their way. Further, the orders competed not only with the secular clergy but with each other, sometimes in friendly rivalry to convert the Indians but too often in a more sordid ambition to monopolize the choice lands. Even within the orders creoles disputed the practice of staffing the key positions with peninsulars and resisted the desire of mestizos to win entrance. Judged by the complaints of royal officials, the friars were contentious and often lived luxuriously and immorally. Such matters would naturally be reported more faithfully than the patient work of most of the friars, who numbered between six and eight thousand, in teaching, healing, caring for the helpless, and in going about their devotions. Whatever the failings of the friars and nuns, it was they who expanded the rim of Christendom from Mexico City to

Santa Fe and transformed millions of pagans and barbarians into semi-civilized, partially Christianized Spanish subjects. Their deeds of heroism and self-sacrifice are too repetitive and unverifiable to be recorded here, but judged by results, they must have been literally countless.

If the secular clergy had the most support from the crown and the regulars performed most of the work, a third pillar of the Church was the most feared. This was the Holy Office of the Inquisition, which was established in Mexico City in 1571 and functioned with a sinister vigor for more than a century. Theoretically, anyone but the viceroy or an Indian might be charged with heresy or sin and arrested, tortured, given an unfair trial, and punished. Things were not quite as bad as that, however. In New Spain the total number of persons burned was not above fifty during the entire colonial period. These were foreign sailors who had been captured or subjects charged with heresy, witchcraft, or sex perversion. Hundreds probably perished under torture or while awaiting trial, and many received public whippings and sentences to prison or the galleys. A few were acquitted. The most famous case in New Spain concerned the family of Luis Carvajal, governor of Nuevo Leon toward the end of the sixteenth century. This official and more than a hundred of his relatives were accused, correctly so in some cases, of reviving a dormant Hebrew tradition and were punished with a cruelty that was long remembered. Another governor, Diego de Peñalosa of New Mexico, was exiled for blasphemy and heresy in the seventeenth century. This dignitary avenged himself by going to France and furthering the schemes of La Salle to despoil the Spanish empire. While most of the Inquisition's victims were obscure persons and were not, when all is considered, particularly numerous, the Holy Office long stood as a formidable barrier to freedom of expression. But then it was intended to serve this function.

The pervasiveness of the Church in colonial Mexico can scarcely be grasped today. In every locality the ringing of bells dominated the daily schedule. Prominent in the scene of almost any part of the well-populated sections were houses of worship, monasteries, convents, shrines, and fine clerical residences. The Church offered sanctuary for nearly any lawbreaker, and woe to the official who failed to respect it. A person excommunicated by a clergyman became a pariah, a repulsive thing to be avoided. When, as rarely happened, an interdict was laid upon a whole district, the bells stopped ringing and divine services ceased. It seemed that a dreadful curse hung over all the inhabitants. However unrespected an individual clergyman might be, the ancient and mighty Church he represented demanded obedience. The occasional *auto-de-fe* in the capital, which attracted thousands of sightseers and thrill-seekers, was an objective lesson in the awful potentiality of the Church in this world, to say nothing of its ability to gain or deny entrance into the next one. Open irreverence or impiety was almost unknown in New Spain. Conspicuous symbols of Christianity likewise dominated the Indian areas within the Spanish pale. The ordered mission towns were veritable theocracies ruled absolutely by a handful of friars. The horrors of the primitive religions that shocked Cortés and his men were now gone; yet grotesque superstitions and other remnants of paganism persisted. Christianity was practiced perhaps more imperfectly among the Indians than among the whites and mestizos. If the Spanish venerated the Virgin of Los Remedios, the Indians more warmly and with less orthodoxy looked to the Virgin of Guadalupe.

Apart from its power over the minds of all men, the Church steadily became wealthier. Properties were donated or willed to it, its own lands became richer as native labor developed them, and fluid capital was sometimes available for investments and speculations. Sourly as laymen often commented on this expanding richness of the Church, it was not unearned. More than any other force, the Church held the sprawling viceroyalty together and served the crown by coercing both natives and white men. And, of course, it performed most of the welfare and educational functions which are now the responsibility of the state.

THE ECONOMY AND INDIAN LABOR

The growth of New Spain's agriculture was gradual and unspectacular between the first years of the viceroyalty and the last decades of the colonial period, from about 1570 to 1770. The ancient Indian crops of corn, beans, and peppers continued as staples of diet for most of the population. The European immigrants had brought grain, sugar cane, bananas, gardenstuffs, and new types of fruit. Much as these new food crops added to the diet, the growth of population during this period kept pace with the increased production, and Mexico remained what it had always been and still is, a land of hunger. Not even the plow and the increased variety of foodstuffs could assure a reliable supply of necessities. Agriculture suffered from the monopolistic practices that went with colonialism, the concentration of land in the hands of a few and marketing procedures that favored high prices for small volume. Furthermore, transportation difficulties hindered an easy transfer of food from one district to another even in time of acute need. Not even the promise of European markets could stimulate production enough to count heavily. The only crops that could be exported profitably were cotton, tobacco, chocolate, and vanilla, and they in modest quantities most of the time. Other forces worked to the detriment of agriculture. Sugar might have been a highly lucrative item in the torrid coastlands but for the fact that

Negro slaves found it easy to escape to the jungles of the interior, an opportunity not so available to the Africans in the islands of the West Indies. Grape vines and mulberry trees might have flourished in New Spain, but crown support of peninsula wines and Far Eastern silk served to restrict the producers in Mexico. And so, subsistence agriculture mainly characterized the viceroyalty.

A slowly growing prosperity was apparent in the case of ranching. Cattle men followed the explorers, missionaries, and miners into the arid northern region. Odd as it seems to regard the rough *vaquero*, or cowboy, as an agent of civilization, his long-range effect was something on this order. The great northern wastes received a Spanish veneer. The livestock association known as the *mesta* was imported from Spain and regulated brands and watering rights among the owners. Cattle, sheep, goats, horses, and donkeys multiplied abundantly in New Spain. In time, the most downtrodden Indian could have or hope to have an animal of his own. The owner of the great haciendas in the ranching county might possess magnificent herds, many of which were wild and moved up into the present American West to become the prey of savage Indians. The impact of the livestock industry can scarcely be measured. Obviously, it greatly increased the supply of food, reluctant as Mexicans always have been to consume dairy products. Hides permitted better clothing and shelters, and, even to a greater extent, so did wool. Pigs and chickens offered much insurance against starvation. Important as all these creatures were to diet and transportation, only hides offered an opportunity for increasing exports to Europe. The rest raised the standard of living in New Spain and helped support the growing population.

In contrast to agriculture and ranching, mineral production had little immediate effect on most of the inhabitants and was enormously significant in the world's economy. Nine-tenths of the exports of New Spain consisted of silver. Toward the last of the colonial period, one-half of the world's bullion production came from New Spain, from the 3,000 or so mines concentrated in Guanajuato. Zacatecas, Guadalajara, San Luis Potosí, Pachuca, and Taxco. While this treasure served to lubricate the economy of the whole viceroyalty and to enrich a few thousand families, as well as to make of it by far the most solvent country on the globe, it was important more to Spain than to New Spain itself. Whatever the vexations of holding a distant colony, Spain had every reason to exert herself to the utmost to maintain the flow of silver. Apart from revenue sent to Europe the precious minerals supported an expensive bureaucracy in New Spain and made up deficits for the Philippines, the West Indies, and Venezuela. They enriched many families in both Spain and New Spain. Still, the great majority of Mexicans felt few direct benefits of this fabulous industry. Other minerals were plentiful in New Spain, oil, iron, lead, and copper, but no particular use could be made of them until modern times. Silver was the great treasure, and then gold.

Commerce and manufacturing in New Spain developed at a respectable rate. The Indians continued to make the homely articles they always had. The Spaniards created cloth factories and centers for making furniture, tiles, bricks, and articles of metal. Shipbuilding had gone on since the earliest days of the viceroyalty. The more specialized crafts were in the hands of guilds, which operated very much as they did in Europe to assure excellence of product and the welfare of the members. The factories were mostly small, often financed by the clergy and invariably employed Indians for the menial labor. Since many of the workers were malefactors of one type or another, working conditions in these *obrajes* were extremely severe. The *obrajes* were even worse than sweatshops of the industrial age. Perhaps it was just as well that New Spain was comparatively backward in manufacturing.

All imported articles were supposed to come from Spain or the Philippines by means of the regulated galleons. Those that arrived from Spain were more than two-thirds of foreign origin, having been purchased in Sevilla or Cadiz from other European countries, at least until after the middle of the eighteenth century. The wealthy merchant guild, or *consulado*, of Mexico City presided profitably over this legal trade. Smugglers could scarcely be prevented from coasting up to either shore of New Spain and selling their goods. And British traders penetrated the Spanish monopoly from Jamaica and Honduras while French merchandise sometimes leaked into New Spain from Louisiana and the West Indies. The authorities were unable to prevent Spanish subjects from carrying on a much-forbidden traffic between Peru and Acapulco.

The population of New Spain evolved along familiar lines. Peninsular Spaniards arrived in a steady if unknown volume during good times and bad. With rare exceptions they staffed the positions of power in the government and Church, and they usually enjoyed a social prestige which gave them an easier access to business opportunities. Sorry as many of them must have been, leaving Spain for sordid reasons, immigrants often had a push or ambition that made for success in the New World. The creoles were developing something akin to national feeling and resented the airs of the peninsulars. Many creoles had become wealthy mineowners, ranchers, or planters who lived in style and proudly, if often inaccurately, traced their ancestry back to the conquistadors and Aztec royalty.[1] To be sure, some of them were debauched by their wealth, but whether they were constructive or dissipated subjects of the king, they knew that even the meanest peninsular disdained them. Similarly, persons of European blood looked down upon those with any amount of

1.   Which, ironically, would make them mestizos, not creoles.

Indian ancestry unless it was very remote Aztec royalty. The mestizos had multiplied rapidly since the Conquest and would outnumber the Europeans by the end of the colonial period. A mestizo suffered from his usually illegitimate origin and was torn between two cultures, that of his father, which despised him, and that of his mother, which he spurned. Secure members of neither world, the mestizos labored in the mines, plantations, and ranches and often drifted into the towns, where they constituted the lowest classes unless there were enough Indians to form an even lower category. Free men, the mestizos would occasionally rise in the economic scale and win a certain respectability. As time went on, they craved official positions but seldom achieved more than membership among the lower orders of the Church. Not until Mexico broke with Spain did the mestizo win much recognition.

The Indian Problem

THE Indians remained the basic stock of New Spain. If half the natives had perished during the first fifty years of the Spanish presence, the remainder rallied and survived. As has been seen, the authorities concentrated the bulk of the Indian population in specially-designated areas of central Mexico, where most of them had lived previously, and froze the hereditary Indian aristocracy so that a stable political structure resulted. The Spanish-oriented native chieftains kept their peoples in order and accepted direction from the invaders. Liberty was as little known or desired as it had been in Aztec times. The great number of "crown" Indians lived in villages which no white man but a clergyman and the *corregidor* could visit for long. Adult males paid a tribute or poll tax once a year. Delinquents had to work out their tribute or have their relatives pay. The crown wished to encourage the use of clothing and implements known to the more advanced Europeans and, with the highest of motives, stipulated that its agents could force the natives to purchase articles of this type. Often, however, this process became a pell-mell distribution of useless items or junk which the Indians had to buy. The *corregidor* turned a nice profit, one that justified his purchase of office in the first place. Crown Indians were also required to work for pay in order to keep the economy of the country going. This might take the form of natives being hired out as gangs by contractors, more or less freely. More likely it would take place under the *cuatequil* system, by which all able-bodied males were to work for two weeks four times a year on state projects or be farmed out to Spanish employers for various types of labor. Legally, this method was carefully controlled as to conditions of labor, payment, and dignified treatment. The fact was that the Indians were often overworked, abused, and underpaid through the collusion of *corregidores*, employers, and Indian chieftains. Even so, the *cuatequil* system was less brutal than outright slavery. The Indians worked for certain periods and were then left alone, when they could care for their own needs or loaf. It is not stretching things too far to note a parallel between the operation of the *cuatequil* system in colonial days and the present habits of the hundreds of thousands of Mexicans who come into the United States to work a few weeks and then go back home to spend the money they earn and to do nothing in particular until they need funds again.

As the several orders pushed into the frontier gradually but surely, the number of mission Indians grew tremendously, possibly numbering nearly one and a half million at the height of the system. Ten years of mission life was supposed to qualify the neophytes to become crown Indians, but in fact the missions tended to remain decade after decade with the same wards. When the friars finally had to surrender their charges to the state the Indians were supposedly Spanish-speaking Christians with the basic skills of European artisans and peasants. Another semi-educational system, the *encomienda*, was disappearing. The crown overlooked few opportunities to dispossess the *encomenderos*, who had long enjoyed tribute and labor from their subjects. By the eighteenth century nearly all the large *encomiendas* had lapsed to the state. The Indians were absorbed in the regular labor force, and the *encomendero* usually held title to vast tracts of land. Indian slavery had also become nearly extinct, the Aztec type entirely so and the prisoners of "just" wars remaining only on the frontier, where other untamed Indians made life difficult for the white settlers. The increasing boldness of the free Indians is accounted for largely by the horse and the gun, both of which were forbidden to the Hispanicized Indians. The defiant natives acquired them often by theft and raids. Then, too, the French, who had split the Spanish empire in the 1680's by establishing themselves on the Gulf of Mexico, often armed and incited the Indians against the Spaniards.

Toward the end of the colonial period a new form of Indian servitude began to flourish, one which became the prevailing system until recently. This was debt peonage, in which a planter or rancher would provide homes and jobs for Indians but keep them perpetually in debt by advancing them money. It was not greatly superior to slavery. Whatever the type of labor the Mexican Indian lived under, he was indeed a third-class subject of the king, regardless of what the law said. He was looked upon with disdain by anyone with some amount of white blood. Indians were not regarded as *gente de razón*, or rational men. They comprised a submerged class who did the hard work of the country for little recompense or else existed as starving beggars in the cities. Poverty, drunkenness, semi-starvation, indignities, and crime characterized the lot of the race and aggravated the scorn which the whites and mestizos bore it. Yet the race survived and grew more numerous. In the long run most of the Indians learned Spanish and became Christians.

A CHRONICLE OF EVENTS

It is instructive and sometimes entertaining to read the official records of the viceroys, the "instructions" they left nominally to edify their successors but also to impress the Council of Indies with their achievements. These accounts give us the flavor of the period, an impression of the mood of official circles, the real and imagined dangers, the vexations and satisfactions. Often naive, they sometimes offer an unconsciously revealing portrait of the men and the times.

The Early Years

BY NO means typical was the stormy reign of the Marquis of Gelves between 1621 and 1624. This exemplary official undertook to tone up the government following a few years of slackness, in particular attacking clerical corruption, banditry, and tax evasion. Soon the whole community seemed aroused, and the archbishop of Mexico served as the focus for dissidents. Not only were the immediate beneficiaries of bad government critical of the viceroy, but other pillars of the system, such as the *audiencia* and the *cabildo*, joined the opposition. A quarrel over the viceroy's violation of the right of sanctuary gave the archbishop an opportunity to humble the king's most important agent. Excommunication and that dreaded measure, the interdict, were proclaimed in 1624. Gelves' enemies became bolder, and the masses were frightened. Creole dislike of peninsular flared up. Finally, a mob attacked the viceregal palace and the marquis had to flee for his life. Eventually, the Council of Indies vindicated the viceroy, and in truth he seems more wronged than otherwise. The implications of the incident were truly disturbing: that a viceroy could be chased out of the capital within an inch of his life, that an archbishop should become the leader of a mobocracy, that the government should split into factions, that creoles could rally mestizos and Indians against the crown. All these implications might suggest an impending collapse of the imperial system. Yet that was not the case at all. If anything was proved by the Mexico City riot of 1624, it was that a viceroy should be very careful when he proceeded to carry out reforms. That a mob could perpetrate dreadful damage scarcely needed to be demonstrated anywhere.

Another crisis arose during the reign of the Duke of Escalona, viceroy in 1640–42. His assumption of power coincided with a crisis in the relations of the bishop of Puebla, Juan de Palafox, and the Jesuits. Palafox was attempting a number of reforms within the ecclesiastical establishment, which was enough to create many enemies, and also had the temerity to suggest that the Indian wards of the Jesuits should pay the tithe. The new viceroy sided with the Jesuits after studying the controversy at some length. Just as he was prepared to act, news arrived that Portugal and Catalonia had revolted against the Spanish crown. The Duke of Escalona was believed to have many ties, personal and commercial, with the swarms of Portuguese who had moved into New Spain during the "Babylonian Captivity." Bishop Palafox rallied patriotic and anti-Jesuit forces in the viceroyalty and ousted Escalona. The duke's eventual vindication in Spain removed the force from many of the charges of corruption and disloyalty, but meanwhile the archbishop, as Palafox now was, served as acting viceroy for several years. Yet no real precedent was established. Viceroys of New Spain were not to be deposed again except by the crown itself until 1808.

Much more typical than those troubled reigns was that of the gross-looking Duke of Albuquerque in 1653–1660. This was a period when the Spanish monarchy seemed very shaky, following the losses of the Thirty Years' War and the revolts of the 1640's. The viceroy's duty was to defend not only New Spain but the Caribbean from what seemed a mortally dangerous assault from Cromwell's England. That only Jamaica was lost to the Puritans was a relief to the Spaniards. Albuquerque was honored by the planting of a town in New Mexico that bears his name. The Inquisition was busy during his reign, punishing Portuguese crypto-Jews and on one occasion burning thirteen sex perverts. Crime, in particular highway banditry, was a major problem which he and almost all other viceroys mentioned in their instructions. Also, he dutifully recorded the elaborate celebrations of royal marriages, births, and birthdays when appropriate. The frequent and fervent attention given to such ceremonies was supposed to demonstrate the viceroy's enthusiasm for his monarch. More than that, it gave the lonely Europeans in New Spain a sense of belonging to a great monarchy and the Indians a good show.

The Marquis of Leyva reigned from 1660 to 1664. This viceroy had many troubles: Popocatepetl erupted and terrified his subjects; an Indian uprising occurred on the torrid isthmus of Tehuantepec; the English attacked Santiago de Cuba; a scandalous duel took place when the son of a prominent subject insulted Mexico; and a violent popular protest followed an effort of the vicereine to alter the route of a religious procession so she could watch it from the palace. The poor Marquis of Leyva soon gave up and retired to a monastery in Spain. His successor, the Marquis of Mancera, ruled from 1664 to 1673. It was his gratifying task to complete the massive cathedral of Mexico City a century after it had been begun. He was also unusually competent at raising funds and collecting revenues. Much effort went into the public mourning for the death of King Felipe IV and subsequently into jubilation over the accession of Carlos II. In the former case, black-clad messengers read out the message in plazas all over New Spain while bells tolled mournfully for days. After an appropriate demonstration of grief, the populace devoted a week or more to drinking, dancing, and fireworks in honor of the new king.

The Duke of Veragua had been named to succeed Mancera. This heir of the great Columbus died within a week after his arrival and was followed by the Archbishop Enríquez de Rivera, who reigned from 1673 to 1680. Like so many of his predecessors and successors, he was troubled by the incursions of English logwood cutters in Campeche. These outlaws, as most of them were, sailed from Jamaica to saw the great hardwood trees and carry off the precious wood to Europe. Viceroys of New Spain steadily bewailed these activities and tried to obstruct them, but they were singularly ineffective. British Honduras is a standing reminder of this profitable business and Spain's failure to stop it. In the last year of the archbishop's reign one of the very rare successful revolts of Indian against white man occurred. The sullen Pueblo tribes in New Mexico had long grumbled at the slow build-up of Spanish haciendas and ranches and missions in the upper valley of the Rio Grande. An Indian named Popé wove a net of conspiracy, capitalizing on general resentment against measures the Spanish were taking to punish native magicians. On August 10, 1680, the Indians of Taos and neighboring communities fell upon the friars and settlers, killing more than 400, and burned Spanish houses and fields and profaned their churches. The remaining 2,000 or so Spaniards herded themselves together and effected an orderly retreat down the river, where they founded the town of El Paso del Norte.

The Marquis of La Laguna, popularly if cruelly known as *Brazo de Plata* because of his artificial silver arm, tried without success to reconquer New Mexico. He was also unable to act effectively when a gang of international outlaws led by a Dutch pirate occupied Vera Cruz for several evil days in 1683, an event of outstanding brutality even for the age of the buccaneers, then fortunately coming to a close. It was also during this reign that La Salle attempted to establish a colony in Texas which he believed would enable the French to capture the silver mines of Zacatecas. The famous explorer was, of course, much farther from the mining districts than he imagined, and he lost his life in the venture.

Of much more grateful memory is La Laguna's patronage of Sor

Juana Inéz de la Cruz (1651–1695), then a lovely nun in her thirties who had first appeared as a child prodigy at the viceregal court during the reign of Mancera. Once, when she was sixteen, she had given an exhibition of academic knowledge before forty of Mexico's most eminent men that people still spoke of with awe. Now in her prime, this woman, so joyful in her intellectual and religious life, wrote lyric verses of such intensity that she stands as the foremost poet of the entire colonial period, the "Tenth Muse." She was also an accomplished musician, and she apparently remembered everything she ever read in the 4,000 books she acquired—and eventually gave away as a penance. Nearly everyone was entranced with her erudition, artistic gifts, wisdom, and sparkling personality. A few years later she would become a recluse, devoting herself to mysticism but for one excursion into theological polemics when she challenged, perhaps refuted, the noted Portuguese Jesuit Antonio Vieira. An incredible adornment of colonial Mexico, Sor Juana Inéz de la Cruz reflected credit on the several viceroys who befriended her, most of all on La Laguna and his vicereine.

After a two-year reign of the Count of Monclova from 1686 to 1688, the Count of Galve arrived to serve for eight years. It was a dangerous period, for France was knocking Spain about in Europe and establishing settlements along the Gulf Coast and in Haiti. From the mouth of the Mississippi it seemed that the colonial empire of this virile power might swell indefinitely into the present Texas, Mississippi, and Alabama. Yet, a spirited reaction by New Spain served to contain the French at both the Texas and Florida flanks. And Coahuila and Chihuahua were made more secure by soldiers, missionaries, prospectors, and settlers. Fathers Eusebio Kino and Juan María Salvatierra pioneered Spanish occupation of Sonora and Lower California. Then, New Mexico was reconquered, the Pueblos apparently having wearied of independence after fifteen years and scarcely putting up a fight. From El Paso the authority of Spain went back to Santa Fe, Taos, and Albuquerque, and this time more attention was paid to their defenses. Soon the annual caravans were moving up the *camino real*, or royal highway, from Mexico City to supply the outposts of empire in New Mexico.

New Spain had another world-famous luminary in Carlos de Sigüenza y Góngora (1645–1700), whose distinguished career had now reached its peak. This savant's range of activity included astronomy, mathematics, engineering, urban planning, Aztec antiquities, and exploration. Often an adviser to the viceroy, he was made royal cosmographer by the king of Spain after being offered a position by Louis XIV. He was a minor poet—perhaps more, for much of his literary output has been lost—and a philosopher whose stature has increased with the years. Deeply Christian, he pioneered a scientific approach to the study of the physical world

and universe, one more modern than that of most of his European contemporaries. He suggests comparison with Renaissance intellectuals who
sought to master all knowledge, or with eighteenth-century men of
learning who seemed to know everything.

Despite a generally successful reign, the Count of Galve underwent
in 1692 a desperate trial that resembled a revolution. A total eclipse of
the sun, which delighted Sigüenza y Góngora, frightened many of the
population out of their wits, a reaction typical of countries far more advanced than New Spain. Then a sudden flood drowned out much of Mexico City, where the Spaniards had been trying to create a drainage system
since the days of Cortés. A shortage of grain led to the usual rumors of
hoarding by officials. Passions found an outlet when thousands of hungry and drunken Indians (if food was scarce *pulque* was plentiful) went
on a frenzied demonstration. The mobs looted the public granary and
then sacked the viceregal palace, the *audiencia* chambers, and other symbols of Spanish rule. For a time the viceroy himself was in great danger,
but the crowds finally allowed themselves to be dispersed. It was not
really a rebellion. Rather, the latent violence of the populace had given
a fearful exhibition of its potentiality. Mexico City was something like
many Arabic cities of our times, uneasy and full of discontents that
might be channeled into explosive actions. Once the demonstration was
over, the people settled down into their customary sullenness, the Spaniards in their part of the city, the mestizos in their proletarian section,
and the Indians in their segregated native quarters. In time the crown
took measures to guard against a recurrence of such riots. They must
have been effective, for no similar upheavals were to take place until
Mexico was an independent republic.

The Count of Montezuma, whose wife claimed descent from the Aztec monarch, was viceroy in 1701 when news arrived of the accession of
Felipe V and the Bourbons to the throne. In one of the very rare instances of suspected disaffection to the new dynasty, who were welcomed
all over the far-flung monarchy, whispers said that Montezuma favored
the Archduke Charles, Felipe's rival. While the rumors were never verified, the prompt removal of Montezuma suggests they were taken seriously in Madrid. Succeeding him was the Duke of Albuquerque II,
the first of the generally distinguished Bourbon appointees. He reigned
from 1702 to 1710 and introduced into Mexico City some of the glamor
of Versailles, such as wigs, new styles of dresses and uniforms, more re-
fined tastes, modern protocol, and the admiration for luxury which characterized the court of Louis XIV. Of greater significance was his businesslike determination to provide better rule and collect revenues. The
War of the Spanish Succession endangered Spain's hold in America in a
military way, but the loyalty of the colonial population was reassuring.

Forced loans, genuine gifts, and sincere attachment to the new dynasty proved invaluable. Mexican silver was highly important in the success of the Bourbons in holding the throne against a powerful array of enemies. Albuquerque also illustrated the new trends by ordering that Negro slaves be dressed and cared for as Christians and, further, warning the clergy not to persuade dying persons to alter their wills to the advantage of the Church. The chronic problem of crime on the roads he approached with good results in creating the *acordada*, a special court and law enforcement body which eventually covered most of New Spain. Accused highway robbers and bandits were likely to be tried hurriedly and executed promptly. As time went on, the *acordada* undoubtedly became too high-handed, arresting and hanging suspects without proper regard for justice, and in many localities the highway patrols became arrogant vigilantes. The authorities and perhaps the general populace accepted such injustices as necessary to reduce banditry. For a century New Spain enjoyed considerable internal peace.

The Duke of Linares, viceroy between 1710 and 1716, continued the strong rule introduced by his predecessor. During his reign the last person was burned by the Inquisition in New Spain. The institution rapidly lost vigor and prestige as the modernists gained the upper hand in government, though its latent power remained a barrier to extreme expressions of unorthodox ideas. Linares had the satisfaction of chasing the English logwood cutters out of Campeche, only to be distressed when he learned they had turned up in Belize. Nothing Spain could do served to stop these incursions. His graphic criticisms of the bloated numbers and low morals of the clergy were typical of the anti-clerical attitude of the Bourbons, who were determined to stop abuses and restore the superiority of the state over Church.

The Marquis of Valero, viceroy from 1716 to 1722, attacked the widespread vice of gambling, which, despite spasms of reform, persists in all Spanish countries. The first newspaper or gazette began publication in Mexico City. A simple and often newsless affair, it provided a few basic facts of world events to enlighten the growing educated class. Valero was also concerned with the renewed danger of French expansionism on the Gulf Coast, for France and Spain were not the close allies the great powers had feared they would be. Texas was secured by the dispatch of soldiers who constructed *presidios* and maintained small garrisons, by Franciscans who created a few mission settlements, and by silver prospectors who wandered widely. The French threat remained for some years, but Spain's hold was strong enough. Similarly, the Spanish sent more soldiers and missionaries into Florida, which, after two centuries of resistance, finally became a relatively safe province. Most of the Indian tribes yielded to the white man, and the Spanish built a base at Pensacola. The French captured this outpost but had to give it up because of a European peace settlement. Their own base at Mobile, much as it seemed to jeopardize Spanish Florida, proved the limit of their expansion in that region. The Spaniards also had reason to be nervous about British colonizing efforts in Georgia during this period.

Considerable excitement greeted the news that the next viceroy was American-born. This Marquis of Casafuerte, who reigned from 1722 to 1734, was indeed a creole, having been born while his father served a tour of duty in Lima, but there was no reason for New Spain's creoles to regard him as more American than Spanish. Casafuerte's long reign continued the Bourbon policies of strengthening Texas and Florida, improving the administration, and collecting revenues more vigorously. His successor was the Archbishop Juan Antonio de Vizarrón, who held the viceregal post from 1734 to 1740. The most notable event of these years was a terrible plague of *matlazahuatl*, perhaps typhus, which contemporaries averred carried off two-thirds of the population. This could not be true, but the grief and terror were only too genuine. Credit for stopping the epidemic went to the Virgin of Guadalupe, who was with great fervor proclaimed protectress of New Spain. More than ever she was adored by the Indians and mestizos and seemed the focus of Mexican national feeling. Perhaps because of the plague, this decade was one of religious revival during a century in which such was not the general rule. Unusual agitation among the natives occurred when an Indian prophet predicted the Spanish would be turned into stones when he was hanged. The hanging took place on schedule, and great was the disappointment when the prophecy failed.

The Duke of La Conquista arrived to become viceroy in 1740, just as the War of Jenkins' Ear and the Austrian Succession brought immense danger to the Spanish empire from the British, who planned nothing less than the creation of independent states in America. But the duke was without his proper papers. It seems that he had deserted his family and left his credentials in Puerto Rico because the British were likely to capture him. When at length he arrived in New Spain, the *audiencia* tried to prevent his taking office. The outgoing archbishop, however, inducted him, and he reigned for a few months. He died soon, either from a rebuke he received from the king for his cowardice, as people said, or, more likely, from yellow fever. The Count of Fuenclara followed La Conquista, serving from 1742 to 1746. These were years of war with the usual forced loans and more or less forced gifts. The British threat to the Spanish empire proved slight, for few colonials were prepared to think of independence with or without British sponsorship. A sensation was caused by the activities of Lord George Anson, who desperately tried to capture the Manila galleons off the coast of New Spain. Failing there, he crossed the Pacific and seized the silver-laden vessels from Acapulco as they approached the Philippines. It may be that his acquisition of Spanish charts of the Pacific facilitated British conquests in that ocean during the following decades. Fuenclara's reign was also a period of impressive construction in Mexico City, especially of government buildings and private residences. The embellishment of the capital was carried out in a style now much deplored, the *churrigueresque,* or extreme baroque, though later generations may admire it if the usual cycles of taste hold true. It was popular in colonial Latin America during the eighteenth century, with its profuse decoration, gilding, and numerous domes. Mexico City's lavish indulgence in this style made it the most magnificent city in the Americas. Yet the degradation of the foul slums contrasted sharply with these splendors. The same point could be made with equal force for contemporaneous Paris, London, or Rome, who lacked the good climate and natural scenic surroundings of Mexico City.

The Count of Revilla Gigedo reigned from 1746 to 1755, a period of general prosperity and growth, at least for the propertied classes. Revenues burgeoned, and giant steps seemed possible in elevating the productivity of the great viceroyalty. It should be admitted that Revilla Gigedo himself was widely accused of sharing personally in the rising prosperity. His description of the lower classes as vile, cowardly, lazy, insolent, incontinent, and drunken accords with the impressions recorded by many Spanish officials. So also did his complaints of the waywardness of the clergy. The royal instructions to his successor, the Marquis of Amarillas, took into account Revilla Gigedo's strictures about the clergy. Another cleanup was directed, and further efforts were made to force the friars farther into the wilderness. To be sure, the missionaries were displaying commendable energy, especially in the northern provinces and the present American Southwest. Improvement in government, rising revenues, and growing prosperity had characterized the first sixty years of Bourbon rule in New Spain. The viceroyalty was much less sluggish than it had been, and notable new advances seemed within reach.

New Spain at Its Peak

THE end of the Seven Years' War in 1763 marks a watershed in the history of colonial Mexico. Before, progress was steady and slow; afterward, for nearly a half century, progress was spectacular. The war itself had shaken the Spanish empire, which temporarily lost Manila and Havana. Had it lasted longer, the British might have carried out a project to invade New Spain simultaneously from Acapulco and Vera Cruz. Carlos III well understood the exposure of the viceroyalty and was prepared to take strong measures to make it safe in the future. The loss of

Florida and the acquisition of western Louisiana by Spain also posed formidable military problems. With such matters in mind, the sovereign sent to New Spain one of his ablest servants, José de Gálvez, who later became Marquis of Sonora. This Gálvez had served on the Council of Indies and knew much of the weaknesses of the overseas empire. He had ability, knowledge of the situation, and support of his royal master. After six memorable years in New Spain he returned to Madrid to become Minister of Indies for the last fifteen years of his life. No other minister of the Spanish empire carried out such thorough-going changes; no one else got so much done. Gálvez had his difficulties, for both men and circumstances sometimes resisted his will. He had his faults, for he favored his family unduly in official matters and was inclined to be tyrannical. Much of his thinking is unknown to us. His actions, however, offer eloquent testimony of his designs.

Gálvez arrived in New Spain in 1765 and at once clashed with the viceroy, the Marquis of Cruillas. The antagonism was natural, for no official liked to have a *visitador* move in on his preserve and take charge. Soon the viceroy was replaced by the Marquis of Croix, who remained for the duration of the *visita* and proved no obstacle to the determined Gálvez. Croix is chiefly known because he kept out of Gálvez' way and because he acquired the reputation of being the heaviest drinker ever to reign as viceroy. Perhaps the two points had a cause-and-effect relationship.

The chief problem was defense of Spanish North America. The British colonies had just been enlarged and were obviously full of aggressiveness. It was thought to be a question of only a few years until an Anglo-Spanish war would rock the continent. A much more remote, but real, danger appeared at this time in the Russians, who had lodged themselves in Alaska and were probing about the coasts of the present American Northwest and California seeking furs. There was nothing to prevent them from occupying empty islands and harbors and turning them into genuine bases. Then, it was apparent that Louisiana was going to be a problem. The 5,000 or so Frenchmen in New Orleans were unenthusiastic about becoming Spanish subjects and threw out the first Spanish governor who sought to assert His Catholic Majesty's power. Finally, the Indians of the north were acquiring horses and guns, often from "Anglo" and French speculators, and Spanish settlements were greatly imperiled. The existing defenses of New Spain were far from impressive. Perhaps 4,000 men, many of them convicts, comprised the regular army. These were concentrated in Vera Cruz or scattered in tiny *presidios* on the northern frontier. The viceroy had a small personal guard. A few of the major cities had tiny forces of militiamen, most of them mestizos who served for the small pay they received.

Somehow a transformation came about within a few years, a tribute to the administrative skill of Gálvez. To be sure, he was not the only Spanish official in the empire to be concerned with military matters. All over the Americas steps were being taken to create better defenses. In some cases Spanish regular army units bolstered the most vulnerable points. A considerable number of officers arrived from the peninsula to train and lead militiamen, who were drawn into the service both by better pay and conscription. Eventually, New Spain had 40,000 men in the various militia forces in the chief cities. Officered by both peninsulars and creoles, the former occupying the highest posts, they were manned by poor creoles and by mestizos. Uniforms, arms, and regular training served to give them a considerable spirit. Special privileges also endowed them with a sense of status. Ironically, the creation of militias did little to help the Spanish monarchy. They were eventually employed not to ward off the British but to eject the peninsulars. However, all this lay a half-century in the future, and men cannot be expected to see that far. As it was, Gálvez organized and others nourished a substantial armed force for New Spain, one that later proved a mixed blessing for the future Mexican republic.

While overseeing such matters, Gálvez and his party traveled widely over the viceroyalty, interviewing officials and checking accounts. The *visitador* found much that cried for reform: cheating officials, inefficiency, ignorance and flouting of the laws, and lack of purpose. He reprimanded and removed crown servants right and left, acquiring the reputation of being a most evil-tempered inspector. Gálvez decided that a wholesale renovation of the bureaucracy was long overdue, and when he returned to Spain he brought about the implantation of the intendant system in the mainland colonies, which replaced the decrepit administration fashioned by Felipe II two centuries earlier. He also discerned that great as New Spain's revenues were, they would be much larger if honest and efficient methods of collection were instituted. During his *visita* he accomplished something along these lines, and as minister of Indies afterward he did still more. He concluded that lower taxes would be collected more surely than unreasonably high duties. Accordingly, he ordered the reduction of the historic royal fifth (which in many cases had already become a tenth) to a much smaller rate, varying with conditions, with the result that mining production was stimulated and royal revenues spurted. Gálvez established a better customs house at Vera Cruz, an agency that was to provide the only steady source of income for the future Mexican republic for decades. While he toured New Spain, he grasped that more open ports and lower import duties would bring in greater revenues, and events proved him right after he had an opportunity to experiment. The imperial free trade edict of 1778 came about largely through his exertions.

Finally, he established a royal monopoly of tobacco products which proved highly remunerative, and a lottery, which to this day is a major source of income to Hispanic governments.

One of the most dramatic events associated with the Gálvez *visita* was the arrival of a secret order to be opened only on a certain day. It proved to be the command of Carlos III to arrest and remove all of the Jesuits. Only Gálvez, his nephew, and the compliant viceroy knew what was impending when special units were readied for the blow. One summer evening in 1767 these forces suddenly invaded the monasteries, colleges, and missions which contained the Jesuits and arrested nearly 700 of the black-robed brothers without explanation. Jailed and submitted to other indignities, these friars, who had done so much for Spain, were informed they were to be deported. It was necessary to move them at night in order to prevent popular demonstrations in their behalf. Finally, they reached the coast and boarded prison ships which carried them away to Europe for exile or prosecution. Whatever reason Carlos III had for his action, it was an outrageously ungrateful deed as far as his American domains were concerned. More than 100,000 Indians in Mexican missions were left without proper leaders, and the most qualified teachers in the colleges were removed. No other order could replace the elite Jesuits.

North and west of Mexico City, where the concentration of Jesuit missions was heaviest, resistance flared up in outspoken criticism of the king and in violent demonstrations. It was too late to save the black robes, who were well on their way to the coast, but the Spanish feared that worse disorders and even rebellion might ensue. Gálvez himself invaded the disaffected region with a substantial military force and personally oversaw the execution of ninety alleged leaders and the public whipping of many more. Perhaps the career bureaucrat enjoyed playing soldier. His strong-arm methods served their purpose, for the area calmed down, but it may be significant that this very region flamed up again fifty years later when Father Hidalgo gave the signal; the name of the royal government had remained hateful in many families. As for Gálvez, he underwent a mental crisis because of the strain or too much sun. Or, some suggested, cactus alcohol unbalanced him. For some weeks he imagined he was the king of Sweden, perhaps the mad Charles XII. Gálvez recovered, but for years afterward anyone who alluded to his temporary insanity was likely to feel his wrath.

During the Gálvez *visita* New Orleans was reduced to Spanish control, though Gálvez himself had little to do with this action. It was General Alejandro O'Reilly who, in 1769, led a fleet of twenty-one ships from Havana up the Mississippi to the recalcitrant city. Overawed, the Frenchmen did not resist. Instead, they watched with emotion while the lilies of the French Bourbon flag dropped and the lions and castles of the

Spanish Bourbon banner went up. O'Reilly punished some of the ring-leaders who had defied Spain in 1766 but scarcely deserved the name of "Bloody O'Reilly" which Louisianians gave him. The Spanish monarchy reciprocated the lack of enthusiasm for the annexation exhibited by the population. Yet, the crown had to make good its hold or see the Anglo-Americans move even closer to New Spain. At length Louisiana became part of the captaincy-general of Havana and thus was attached only remotely to Mexico City. Strangely, the chief imprint of Spain's domination, which lasted from 1769 to 1803, was on the architecture of the so-called French Quarter of New Orleans. By the latter date only a handful of Spaniards had penetrated upper Louisiana, while about 50,000 English-speaking Americans had moved across the Mississippi. New Orleans itself proved a nuisance to Spain, for its restless French inhabitants were seldom reluctant to flout Spanish laws regarding commerce, censorship, and revolutionary activity.

Gálvez was personally involved in the colonization of another valued component of the present United States, California. The Spanish had never attached much importance to this region because its natives were so backward and no treasures were in evidence. Yet, with the British probing about the Pacific and the Russians already operating a trading post in the San Francisco Bay area, it seemed clear that Spain should exert herself if she was going to hold the land at all. Already, the Jesuits under Kino and Salvatierra had established missions in Lower California, Sonora, and southern Arizona. On his western tour Gálvez determined to move the line of missions far into the north. By 1769, when he was ready, the Jesuits were no longer available for this task, and so it devolved upon the Franciscans. They performed creditably, carrying through one of the most humane imperialistic efforts ever known, as historian Rafael Altamira has described it. Two expeditions, one by land and one by sea, converged in 1769 on San Diego. Thanks largely to the vigor of Father Junípero Serra, and also to the discovery of a tolerable land route through the Sonora district, the Franciscans were able to set up a line of missions that reached San Francisco in 1776. The humble Indians readily built mission villages under Spanish tutelage and learned the mysteries of ranching, irrigation, and the cultivation of oranges, limes, lemons, olives, dates, and grapes. Yet they seemed no happier than they had been as innocent pagans picking berries and fishing. Many died or ran off. However, well-known cities have grown up about these missions. The indelible imprint of Spain was stamped on one of the choice lands of the future, and the Russians withdrew to Alaska.[2]

Gálvez and the bemused Viceroy Croix went home in 1771, to be

2. Had the Russians not retreated, the   to create bases on Kamchatka.
Spanish might have carried out a project

followed by one of the most admired colonial rulers of New Spain. This Antonio María de Bucareli, who served from 1771 until his death in 1779, was beloved during his lifetime, was buried in Mexico City, and is one of the two or three viceroys cordially remembered in Mexico today. Apart from his personal charm, he was liked because he presided ably during a period of beneficial changes. A striking increase in the number of cotton and woolen cloth factories occurred during his reign. Odious sweatshops, *obrajes*, though many of them were, they helped raise the standard of living for many Mexicans and gave the country some basis for future industrialization. And many new fortunes were made. Bucareli was in charge when the system of imperial free trade with lower duties was proclaimed in 1778. The results were those Gálvez had anticipated: much less smuggling and greatly increased revenues. New Spain enjoyed these benefits partially in 1778 and fully after 1786, when most of her ports were thrown open to commerce from any Spanish kingdom. Foreigners lost their markets to Spanish and creole business houses in the viceroyalty, bringing affluence to more and more persons in Mexican cities. A small middle class grew in numbers and power. Unfortunately for Spain, this element began to dream of genuine free trade with all nations and not just the mother country. Under Bucareli charitable institutions were organized under government rather than Church supervision, such as a poorhouse, a loan agency for the victims of usury, and an asylum for the insane. Much against Bucareli's will, the frontier provinces of the north and west were grouped into a new entity called the *Provincias internas*, or the commandancy-general. Madrid's ultimate intention was to create a new viceroyalty after this territory acquired sufficient cohesion. Bucareli, of course, saw the move as a clipping of his own power and a threat to sub-divide the viceroyalty the way Peru had been partitioned. An important measure which he favored was the creation of a guild of mine-owners in 1776. This organization assembled the principal miners, who were usually rich creoles, so that new methods could be utilized, capital made available for further prospecting, and a new mining code issued to replace the antiquated rules of the past. The mining code was finished in 1781, but it was not for another few years that beneficial results came from the modernized mining techniques and better financing. By 1790 the silver industry spurted in a most gratifying way. The mining guild functioned long after Mexico became independent.

Gálvez, now minister of Indies, had intended that his brother Matías succeed Bucareli. Perhaps for reasons of delicacy he had Matías designated president of the *audiencia* of Guatemala and then phrased an order so that Bucareli would be replaced by that official, unnamed. Unknown to Gálvez was the fact that Bucareli had died. Spanish legalism being what it was, and with various individuals pleased to spite Gálvez, the vacant viceregal post went to the president of Guatemala at the time of Bucareli's death and not to Matías, who had yet to take office. This absurd mixup brought Martín de Mayorga to Mexico City as viceroy, while Matías had to content himself for the time being with reigning over Guatemala. The reign of Mayorga from 1779 to 1783 is memorable partly for this confusion. It was also the period of Spanish participation in the American Revolution. An army from New Orleans led by Bernardo de Gálvez, Matías' son, carried out a brilliant campaign. Florida and the Bahama Islands were won for Spain, though the latter were lost in the peace treaty. Also, the fierce Comanches were making trouble for the more pacific Apaches, and both were depredating frontier settlements and missions in the north. The commandant-general of the *Provincias internas* had his hands full with this Indian violence. On the whole, the Spanish maintained themselves with difficulty. Finally, Mayorga's reign is associated with the creation of the Academy of Fine Arts, which today occupies one of the most garish buildings in the world. Instruction was open to Indians as well as to whites even in colonial times, and the academy has had much to do with the distinguished achievements of Mexican painters.

In 1783 Gálvez was able to unseat Mayorga, who died mysteriously on the voyage home, and Matías de Gálvez at last became viceroy. He died within a year and was succeeded by his son, Bernardo, now Count of Gálvez as a result of his war record and, one might suspect, his connections in Spain. This Bernardo de Gálvez was a very promising fellow, able, popular, and much admired. Rumors circulated that he planned to imitate George Washington. His costly reconstruction of the Aztec castle of Chapultepec, which became the favored residence of viceroys, emperors, and presidents until the 1940's, seemed to lend some support to these suspicions, but surely they were ill-founded. In any event, Bernardo died suddenly in 1786, and New Spain remained loyal to the king for another generation. He lived long enough to implement one of his uncle's favorite plans, the intendant system. With Mexico City as the super-intendancy, twelve provinces became intendancies, with an intendant in charge of each and sub-delegates reporting to him. The states of modern Mexico largely coincide with the boundaries of these units. Given a longer time and a better caliber of officials, the system might have worked well. But it served to tighten up the Bourbon autocracy under peninsular Spaniards at the very time creoles desired less arbitrary rule and more participation in government. And, while no one could foresee it, metropolitan Spain itself was soon to decline and fall.

The archbishop filled in for a year after Bernardo's death, and between 1787 and 1789 Manuel Flores was viceroy. At this time a Basque mining expert named Fausto de Elhuyer came to New Spain to head the mining guild. Demonstrating great energy and competence, Elhuyer brought about many improvements in mining techniques and sponsored the discoveries of many new silver lodes in districts supposedly worked out, in Zacatecas, Guanajuato, Taxco, Oaxaca, and Pachuca. Numerous new fortunes were the result, and a further rise in royal revenues. Even the workers, most of whom were well-paid free men, had some share in the heightened prosperity. Another commendable achievement of these years was the establishment of the Royal Botanical Gardens in 1788, which permitted a more scientific appreciation of the great wealth of plant life in New Spain.

The last of the able viceroys was the Count of Revilla Gigedo II, who reigned from 1789 to 1794. Born in Havana while his father was governor, this creole had once resided in New Spain as the son of the mid-century viceroy who had been such an admired revenue producer for Spain and, it was said, for himself. The vigor, wisdom, and, refreshingly, the integrity of the second Revilla Gigedo have given him a good reputation. Since few specific achievements can be attributed to him, the reason may lie in the fact that he understood and articulated the mood of New Spain far better than most other Spanish rulers. He had some sympathy for its growing restiveness under the imperial system and the interest of its educated groups in the Enlightenment. Yet, his reign coincided with the most intense phase of the French Revolution, and he found it necessary to persecute French residents in New Spain and to cast a rigid net of surveillance over New Orleans. Also at this time the Spanish clashed with the British at Nootka Sound and had to admit defeat, abandoning their pretensions to the Pacific Northwest. The Inquisition revived somewhat, for no other agency could discern and punish treason quite so effectively nor censor books and discourage revolutionary ideas. The nervousness of the Spanish authorities in New Spain over the French Revolution should not be ridiculed; Jacobin ideas were indeed mortally dangerous for all these officials stood for. On the constructive side, Revilla Gigedo II opened a college of mines in Mexico City which quickly acquired a high stature as a training ground for the country's most important industry.

The Last Phase

AFTER Revilla Gigedo II the quality of viceroys lamentably declined, reflecting the shoddy standards of the Spanish court during the dominance of Manuel Godoy. That worthy's brother-in-law, the Marquis of Branciforte, brought in great quantities of merchandise when he arrived in 1794 to become viceroy. Since these goods were his personal baggage and duty-free, he was able to undersell legitimate distributors. His wife pretended to disdain pearls and declared they were no longer fashionable in Europe. As the price dropped, the viceroy bought them up and shipped them profitably to confederates in Spain. War with France gave him an opportunity to seize the property of French residents and retain some of it himself. If such stories are not accurate in detail, the fact that they were widely credited suggests the lowered morale of the populace and their growing contempt for their rulers. José de Azanza served as viceroy from 1798 to 1800, a period of commercial hardship for legal traders because of the British blockade and increasing boldness of smugglers. Many Mexicans came to realize that Britain and the United States were better trading partners than Spain and drew the logical political conclusions. Of what value was the Spanish connection for Mexico? Contemptible and arrogant rulers, blockades, and heavy extortion of wealth were nothing to inspire loyalty to a mother country obviously too weak to defend herself against France and Britain.

The viceroy for the years 1800–1803, Félix Berenguer de Marquina, competes with several close rivals for the distinction of being the least esteemed. The cession of Louisiana to Napoleon was a relief to Spain, though his sudden sale of this territory to the United States produced much alarm. The Floridas, so recently recovered from Britain and never well Hispanicized, seemed destined for the expansionist republic to the north. New Spain was full of rumors concerning conspiracies to seize the government and declare independence, of Indians to rise and massacre all whites. Most of these tales were the fantasies of crackpots, yet a general uneasiness was diffused throughout the viceroyalty during the early years of the nineteenth century. The last viceroy of New Spain before the disruption of 1808 was José de Iturrigaray, another of Godoy's henchmen, who arrived in 1803. If he failed to restore respect for his high office, Iturrigaray performed one constructive service in permitting himself to be vaccinated in public with Jenner's smallpox serum. His example led others to accept vaccination, and the death rate from the affliction notably declined. Iturrigaray's undistinguished reign came to an abrupt close in 1808, when peninsular Spaniards deposed him for not supporting more passionately the cause of the Bourbons, who had just been unseated by Napoleon.

The wealth and importance of New Spain by the end of the colonial period made it by far the prize American possession of the king of Spain. Its proud capital was a worthy heir of the Aztec Tenochtitlán. Its cathedral, university, schools, newspapers, and theaters gave it much of the civilized appearance of famous European capitals. No other city in the Americas could equal it in fine government buildings, churches, and residences. Its slums could not have been much worse than those of other major cities. Anáhuac, the high central valley of Mexico, was still the heart of the country, full of long-settled Indians thoroughly dominated by Spaniards and creoles. Vera Cruz and Acapulco were good ports, the first a fine city in its own right. Puebla had factories and a strong clerical tradition. Guanajuato, San Luis Potosí, Pachuca, and Zacatecas were no mere frontier towns but long-established communities with a civilized veneer. Taxco, a mining town, was an unusually beautiful example of Italian architecture in the Mexican mountains. On the edges of central Mexico were plantations, ranches, and mines owned by white men but worked by mestizos and Indians. Still farther from the center were Indian tribes, some of them potentially rebellious, others under the control of missionaries and crown agents. Islands of Indian culture remained almost undisturbed in the most isolated mountainous areas and on the tropical coasts. Between Mexico City and Guatemala Spanish power was often frail. Northward, great expanses of desert and mountain were empty of humanity but for roaming Indians and occasional caravans carrying merchandise to frontier communities. In Monterrey, Saltillo, Tampico, El Paso, and the upper Rio Grande Valley Spanish culture had firm outposts, threatened as they were at times by marauding Apaches and Comanches. Both upper and lower California were held together almost entirely by the missions and a few white colonists. Texas was very weakly occupied, at least beyond San Antonio. It was mainly an Indian land. Except for Pensacola and a few missions and coastal settlements, Florida was a wasteland. Those esteemed paradises of the present United States—California, Arizona, and Florida— had so little to interest the Spanish, ironical as it seems.[3] Enormous and variegated was the Kingdom of New Spain, a splendid area stretching from the Columbia River to Central America. One is tempted to doubt that Spanish imperialism, even had it been given another century, could have welded such an expanse into a real nation.

An invaluable picture of the viceroyalty on the eve of independence is available to us from a remarkable work by Baron Alexander von Humboldt. A Prussian nobleman who became one of the world's most influential intellectuals during his ninety years of life, Humboldt had a unique opportunity as a young man. He and his companion, Aimé Bonpland, who later became a famous botanist, obtained permission from Napoleon to visit Egypt. Before they could sail, word came that the British had removed Napoleon's Army of the Nile, and the two young men went instead to Spain. There they met Carlos IV, who amazingly accorded them permission to make a scientific study of the Spanish In-

3. It might be added that the Riviera and other famous pleasure spots were not appreciated by the Europeans at this time either.

dies, a most unusual privilege in view of the general policy of secrecy. Humboldt and Bonpland sailed to Venezuela, where they suspected oil was to be found, as it was in 1918. Then they went up the Orinoco to its source, crossed jungles and mountains which even today are seldom traversed, and inspected Peru. Humboldt, who missed little, wondered why guano was no longer used as it had been in Inca times and would be again appreciated by 1840. Sailing northward in the cold, blue Antarctic current which now bears Humboldt's name, since he publicized it, they reached Acapulco. During most of the years 1803 and 1804 the travelers toured widely in New Spain and looked over official records that had always been kept secret. Humboldt's permission from Carlos IV opened every door. Afterward, he journeyed to Cuba and the United States, where he spent three weeks at Thomas Jefferson's home, Monticello, and then returned to Europe to write up his travels.

The account of his visit to Mexico was an enormous work entitled *Political Essay on the Kingdom of New Spain*, which he published in 1808 with a grateful preface to Carlos IV. The breadth and depth of this study made it a superlative work of political economy and, in some ways, of journalism. The statistics he obtained about Mexican population, mineral production, and the economy in general have seldom been challenged; rather, they are still cited respectfully. Analyzing each province and city, he offered a comprehensive picture of the vast territory which is invaluable to historians. Humboldt was inspired by New Spain. He thought it was the emerging great power of North America, one with a better future than the United States. This nascent nation he compared to the Russian Empire in political atmosphere and morality, surely not a heartening example though he may have intended it so. Its population, he estimated, was larger than the Spanish reckoned. Humboldt's figure was 6,500,000, two-fifths of them pure Indians, 1,200,000 Europeans, and the rest mestizos together with a few thousand Africans. The mixed bloods had already passed the whites in number. New Spain's wealth in agriculture was enormous and potentially unlimited. Much as had been done to stimulate mining and commerce in recent years, better methods within easy reach would produce still larger results, he insisted. Mexico City he thought by far the finest city in the New World, comparable to his own Berlin and to St. Petersburg in culture.

The reaction of the Prussian baron to the social situation reveal him as more than a solid German savant obsessed with statistics. The Indians struck him as phlegmatic and mysterious. The white man, he said, had made the natives cunning and vicious, and their Christianity was superficial. He was offended at the way the whites referred to Indians as perpetual minors, as brutes who were not endowed with human reason. He noted with disapproval the way Indian nobles sided with Spaniards to exploit their own people. Humboldt concluded that if the Indians were treated as equals, they would respond by acting like Europeans. With some compassion he described the place of the mestizo in society, uncertain, insecure, and not acceptable to either white or Indian. The debased masses of Mexico City horrified him as much as the notorious beggars of Naples. On the other hand, he noted the divisions among the whites, how hated the 70,000 or so peninsulars were by the Mexican-born Caucasians. That educated creoles now called themselves "Americans" rather than "Spaniards" he thought significant, suggestive of a new type of patriotism. Many of them felt that Spain was a decrepit power, unworthy to hold Mexico. Yet one still encountered provincial and ill-informed whites who imagined that Spain remained the leading power in the world. Humboldt described with admiration the culture of many Mexicans and the splendor of the lives of the wealthy.

Humboldt intended to be courteous to his royal patron and to present him with a reassuring portrait of New Spain. Yet his honesty led him to depict the gaping divisions of the races, the hatreds of the castes, and the passionate desire of all to be regarded as white and equal to the peninsulars. While he loved Mexico and responded with warmth to the beauties of this "delicious land," he sensed, as many still do, the undercurrent of violence, the harshness, inhumanity, latent explosiveness, and the pervading awareness of death. He perceived that the leading classes were about ripe for independence, and he told Jefferson that Mexico was in a mood to do what the United States had done. Humboldt did no favor to the Spanish monarchy when he also impressed a young South American he met in Paris, Simón Bolívar, with his views that New Spain was mature enough for freedom. For once the wise traveler's vision was cloudy.

15

The Grandeur and Misery of Colonial Peru

U<small>NTIL</small> late in the seventeenth century Peru was regarded as the most valuable Spanish kingdom in the Indies. Certainly she produced the most bullion. Yet the bureaucracy which governed in the king's name was often close to being autonomous, for Spain was so distant and, for most of the century, immobilized by her own troubles. Hence the administration centered at Lima was likely to be tyrannical. Under no circumstances could Peru be included among the fortunate of the world's societies during this period. The condition of the Indians was especially pitiable. Their own cultural evolution blocked, they were not assimilated by the European. In general, the white man despised the Indian and the Indian hated the white man, and each feared the other with reason.

The Seventeenth-Century Viceroyalty

T<small>HE</small> central Andean region had attained a measure of stabilization in the time of Viceroy Toledo, who departed in 1581; by then the Spanish political and economic system was functioning with some effectiveness. To many Spaniards it seemed that everything should contribute to the extraction of the largest possible amount of silver, especially at the great red mountain at Potosí, and both the government and the economy were shaped to this purpose. The native population was to be drawn upon to provide an unending supply of labor for the mines and also to support the European settlers in other ways. White men supervised the mining industry and the businesses which serviced Potosí and other productive areas. This in turn called for an effective governmental structure and for a flow of merchandise from Europe and means to ship bullion to Spain. The headquarters for this exploitative society was centered on the west coast at Lima, the City of the Kings. Here lived the viceroy, an archbishop, the provincials or generals of the several religious orders, the principal *audiencia* of South America, the inquisitors, and other major figures in the bureaucracy. Here also were the chief merchant princes who attempted to monopolize the distribution of imported goods throughout the continent, an increasingly difficult undertaking as the black market route from Buenos Aires persisted in growing. Back from the Pacific coast in the mountains and high valleys resided what was left of the Quechua- and Aymará-speaking subjects of the late Inca, now dominated by their own tribal rulers, who answered to the white man. These Indians were supposed to become Christians and to serve the economic needs of the Spanish establishment, above all to pour into the mines. Remote areas in South America—Chile, Quito, New Granada, Paraguay, and the Platine area—were also tied to the viceroy at Lima but possessed their own centers of control.

While the Spanish imperial system had many purposes, the viceroys well knew that their chief function was to see that the largest possible amount of silver reached the waiting galleons at Panama for shipment to Spain. Filling the viceregal post in Lima was a staggering challenge, the top position in the overseas hierarchy for most of the colonial period. Apart from the principal duty of shipping bullion, viceroys were to supervise the operation of the government, protect the Indians, regulate the Church, promote the welfare of their subjects in general, and to oversee the defense of the sprawling Spanish possessions in South America. Peru proper was the font and center of his power, the veritable heartland of Spanish imperialism. The land we know as Bolivia, but called during colonial times La Plata, Chuquisaca, Charcas, or Upper Peru, contained most of the silver mines to which such importance was attached. And then there were the more distance provinces or kingdoms over which the viceroy exercised as much authority as circumstances permitted. Apart from the normal difficulties inherent in ruling such a variegated expanse, he had to contend with the usual checks and balances within the Spanish system: the prestigious and well-endowed Church; *audiencias* in Lima, Quito, Santa Fe de Bogotá, Panama, Santiago, and Charcas; and the host of governors, *corregidores*, and other executives who often behaved as petty despots. One can sympathize with the Peruvian viceroy who complained that he carried a heavy burden on his shoulders but lacked hands to balance it.

The instructions left by most viceroys tell the modern student too little of what he would like to know. It is usually through allusion or inadvertence that they reflect the social history of this unique laboratory in the Andes for European-Indian amalgamation. The events are often monotonous to read about, however terrifying or memorable they must have been for the people who lived through them. Over and over one learns of steps taken to discipline wayward officials, to enforce humanitarian laws in behalf of the natives, to endow the Church with more virtue. The tragedies wrought by earthquakes were frequent and unpredictable, and the viceroy had to supervise the works of mercy and reconstruction following such catastrophes. Indian disorders were very much his concern. Sometimes it might be a matter of sullen non-cooperation or truancy. Outright rebellion flared up occasionally. Wild tribes on the edges of the Spanish pale—head-shrinking Jívaros and Aucas of Quito, Chiriguaros of Charcas, and Araucanians of Chile among others—often went on the rampage and pillaged white settlements. The rhythm of piratical and foreign assaults changed as developments on the international scene brought English, Dutch, or French fleets to vex the Spanish, or as buccaneers undertook to despoil coastal cities. Military defenses against Indian rebels or foreign enemies were always insufficient: only a few garrisons and cruisers and walled fortifications.

While the seventeenth century seems a little-known and somnolent period in the history of the Spanish empire, a few developments in Peru stand out. One of them is the steady growth and beautification of Lima. The City of the Kings became a proud capital with a cultural life not altogether bucolic when compared to European cities of the time. Lima has an unfortunate location in one respect, lying beneath a cloud bank that obscures the sky several months a year and oppresses the nerves of its inhabitants. Yet it never rains, it is always cool, and the buildings retain their whiteness year after year. Its chief enemy is the earthquake. One in 1687 destroyed much of the city, and others have wrought severe damage. Lima was and is a city of few Indians, most of its inhabitants during the colonial period being white or Negro, about evenly divided. The viceroys encouraged construction of charitable institutions and the organization of craft guilds on the European pattern. In 1619 a merchant guild, or *consulado*, was established to regulate—in fact to seek to monopolize—the distribution of imported goods over most of Spanish America. The cathedral, smaller churches, monasteries, and convents emphasized the presence of the ecclesiastical establishment. Clergymen tended to remain in the capital rather than face the perils and privations of the frontier. Expensive governmental palaces went up, for the highest officials wished not only to live in comfort but to impress the population with their majesty. Furthermore, Lima, like Mexico City, was the residence of many rich creoles who drew their incomes from mines or plantations in less civilized localities. Splendid homes and palaces housed this aristocracy, whose luxury the European upper classes might well have envied.

Despite the impression of torpor and incompetence that clings to the reputation of Spanish officials during the seventeenth century, it is apparent that some of the viceroys of Peru were outstanding men. Purchase their office most of them did. And they usually enriched themselves while collecting huge salaries and enjoying munificent allowances. Yet the viceroys of this century were often impressive. After such distinguished servants of the crown as Toledo, Martín Enríquez, and the Marquis of Cañete in the late sixteenth century came men of scarcely less luster: Luis de Velasco II, 1596–1604; the Count of Monterrey, 1604–1605; the Marquis of Montes Claros, 1607–1615; the Prince of Esquilache, 1615–1621; the Marquis of Guadalcázar, 1621–1629; the Count of Chinchón, 1629–1639; the Marquis of Mancera, 1639–1648; the Count of Salvatierra, 1648–1655; the Count of Alba, 1655–1661; the Count of Santisteban, 1661–1666; the Count of Lemos, 1667–1672; the Count of Castellar, 1674–1678; the Duke of La Palata, 1681–1689; and the Count of Monclova, 1689–1705. While these dignitaries are mere names, if that much, to the modern Peruvian, they were on the whole capable administrators in a most demanding position. Most of them had served creditably in New Spain before winning the promotion to Peru. Esquilache and Montes Claros were worthy figures in the cultural life of the viceroyalty. The Count of Lemos deserves much credit for the great burst of missionary activity that brought Christianity to the hitherto neglected Indians, and his energy in putting down a rebellion in Laicacota was in the tradition of the crown's most devoted servants. La Palata intelligently defended Peru from a multiplicity of foreign threats, launched a fleet of cruisers, and built a great wall around Lima. Monclova, the silver-armed former viceroy of New Spain, presided competently over the difficult period of wars with both France and England in the 1690's, the curious imperialistic effort of the Scots at Darien, and the early dangerous years of the War of the Spanish Succession.

Sad as the state of Spain itself had become under Carlos II, Peru was exhibiting a solid growth. New mines at Laicacota, Pasco, and other localities in Peru proper were supplementing those around Potosí. The colony was almost entirely self-supporting and yet shipped a huge bonus to Spain almost every year. The near collapse of the Spanish commercial system disturbed few colonials, who purchased all they could afford from accommodating smugglers. Cattle ranches, food farms, and sugar plantations served the basic needs of the population. If foreign attacks had produced many frights and often caused coastal populations to flee, there had been no permanent losses. In fact, these assaults were producing something resembling patriotism in this distant outpost of the Spanish monarchy. In 1701, soon after Felipe V mounted the throne of Spain, the authorities in Pacific ports were shocked at the appearance of French mariners as friendly allies with permission to trade. The goods and slaves they imported were eagerly bought, and licit commerce started to revive. Soon, Peru was forwarding large gifts to the mother country and rounding up suspected adherents of the Archduke Charles. The War of the Spanish Succession was to mark another turning point in its development.

Among the memorable personalities of seventeenth-century Peru was the wife of Viceroy Chinchón, who is usually credited with helping him publicize the value of quinine in treating fevers. The Spanish had ignored most of the medical knowledge of the ancient Andean cultures but learned to appreciate the bark of the tree eventually known as "cinchona." Another celebrated woman was a beautiful nun who caught the imagination of the populace by the extreme mortifications to which she subjected her flesh. Her death caused a great display of sorrow, and she was later canonized as Santa Rosa de Lima, the patroness of the capital and first saint of South America. Famous in a different way was the rowdy renegade nun, Catalina de Erauso, who had an aggressively masculine manner. Fleeing from a convent in Spain, she came to Peru dressed as a man. She went on to Chile to fight Indians and made such an impressive military record—among other deeds, she killed her brother in a soldier's quarrel—that when she was exposed and returned to Spain the crown pardoned her. Far from suffering punishment from her order, she was honored by the pope. In due course she went back to the Indies, this time to New Spain, for a long career as a muleteer (some say a highway robber) on the road between Vera Cruz and Mexico City.

The Solomon Islands, which acquired a somber fame during World War II, were explored by a party sent out from Peru in 1605 under Pedro Fernández de Quiros and placed under Spanish rule. And Peru, or at least its appanage, Quito, was itself the subject of an exploration when the Portuguese Texeira came up the Amazon from Brazil in 1638. The Spanish were annoyed at this display of Brazilian ambition to press past the Line of Tordesillas, though Spain and Portugal had a common monarch then, and the Inquisition in Lima pounced upon hundreds of suspected Jews of Portuguese nationality who had come to the capital as merchants. A dreadful auto-de-fé occurred in 1639, one of the worst in the history of the Indies. If the orthodoxy of Peru was thus defended, the Brazilians continued to penetrate the western reaches of the Amazon. Peru was also stirred by silver rushes from time to time, the greatest strikes being north of Lake Titicaca in mid-century. At Laicacota the Salcedo brothers, who had suddenly become immensely rich, also became defiant of the authorities. In 1668 Viceroy Lemos personally led a military force into the area and smashed what he regarded as an incipient feudal movement. This sort of thing seldom happened, however, for the whites in Peru usually appreciated the value of the government as an instrument to keep the Indians down.

The Indian in Peru

THE viceroys of Peru seldom approached the matter of dealing with the Indians as a single problem. Nor should they have done so. They were concerned in varying degrees with the cannibals on the coasts of Venezuela and the numerous tribes of primitive men west of the Andes from modern Colombia to Chile. Also, the wild natives in the pampas of the Argentine were their problem. So were the defiant nations in the Gran Chaco and the Araucanians in the rain forests of southern Chile. With such peoples alternate warfare and proselytizing efforts characterized the colonial period. The results were uneven, success with this or that group, failure with others. There was a relentless tension not unlike that between central New Spain and the tribes to the north.

For us to concentrate on the sedentary Indians of the former Inca society is to come closer to grips with a situation that demanded constant attention from the authorities. The survivors of the cataclysmic events of the sixteenth century, or their descendants, had largely withdrawn from northern and western Peru and concentrated in the general neighborhood of Cuzco. Perhaps the population was only half what it had been when Pizarro first came. If the Spanish presence had meant new plants, tools, animals, and religious symbols for these people, it had also undermined society as they had known it and brought them under alien rulers.

The *encomienda*, it will be recalled, was the original device for the invaders to dominate the conquered population. Some students still speculate that conditions would have been better if the crown had permitted the *encomenderos* to entrench themselves as hereditary feudal lords. After a few centuries of this system, the Indians might have emerged as Europeanized small farmers, runs the argument. It was not to be, however. The events of the mid-sixteenth century unnerved the monarch, suggesting as they did that *encomenderos* might well cut themselves off altogether from the crown. And moralists continued to insist that the natives be left alone as much as possible. Thus the *encomienda* was on the decline as a system and the government steadily found reasons to take up the holdings of deceased or disobedient *encomenderos*. During the seventeenth century most of them were on the frontier and were subjected to many restrictions, such as allowing royal officials to collect the tribute, having no right to employ the Indians, and being required to remain away from their subjects. In 1720 the *encomienda* was abolished entirely except for Chile. By that time the heirs of the original *encomenderos* were likely to own large estates worked by native peons, though the law had forbidden them to take up lands in this fashion. This was merely another instance of the disparity between law and practice.

As the *encomienda* system declined, the category of crown Indians had grown. As early as 1565 Governor García Castro had created a special office of *corregidor de indios* to represent the crown. His successor, Viceroy Toledo, regularized the office so that all Indians not living in missions would answer to a *corregidor*. If possible, they would continue to dwell in their ancient village communities or, in many cases, be forced to move to new settlements established by the crown. There they would obey their traditional tribal rulers, or *curacas*, who wielded immense authority in personal and economic matters. These Indian nobles had to be undeviatingly loyal to the Spanish, or else they were replaced. During the later colonial period there were probably 2,000 native rulers living amid their peoples but answering to the *corregidores*. By making their positions hereditary, the Spaniards attached these *curacas* to European imperialism. It was obvious that a *curaca*'s condition in life was a good one and that to keep it within his family he would have to satisfy his masters. Dealing through these tribal rulers with the native populations, the *corregidores* exercised three key functions: the tribute, the *repartimiento*, or forced sale of goods, and the *mita*, or labor draft.

The tribute was ordinarily the only tax the Indians paid. Exacted annually from each adult male, it was collected in money or in designated goods. Each Indian was checked carefully by his *curaca* and the *corregidor*. If he was delinquent, his relatives would have to pay up for him, or he might become something of a slave until he had worked out his debt. The great, multi-locked cash boxes were sent on to Lima and often to Spain, for the tribute was a substantial source of income. The *repartimiento* of goods took place every two-and-a-half years. The *curacas* lined up their tribes while the *corregidor* looked on. Goods would then be distributed—merchandise, tools, or domestic animals that might raise the Indian's standard of living and keep him from squandering his money on less useful articles—and the Indians forced to pay whatever the *corregidor* demanded for his "purchases." The *mita* was supposed to bring not more than one-seventh of the adult male population of any one community into a labor force for several months each year. The men would be sent to work in the mines, on public construction, or to individuals who hired them from the crown. The laws regulated the conditions: limitation on distances to be traveled, decent treatment, food and shelter, payment in the presence of royal officers, and release when the time was up. The theory, then, was that the natives should contribute a small tax annually, purchase goods that would make them more productive, and perform labor of value to the entire society. Had the Indians been left to themselves, it was reasoned, they would wallow in pagan idleness. Even the Inca system had employed compulsion to get the work of the world done.

Yet two things were wrong. One was that the Indian now worked under coercion without regard to the religious and fraternal stimuli that had once made his labor almost an act of reverence. Instead of toiling communally in measured tempo in the fields of his fellows, the Sun, and his Inca, he now marched off with a gang to dig into mountains, plant and harvest crops of aliens who despised him, and build walls, ports, and palaces for the invaders who had shattered his culture. Secondly, the *corregidores* occupied positions that could be satisfactorily filled, as it was said, only by angels. Even the finest official would fail to carry out his duties unless he resorted to forceful methods. In the happiest of countries people do not relish paying taxes, buying goods they do not want, and being forced to work for others. And few of the *corregidores* were gentle men. Most of them looked upon their positions as an opportunity for quick enrichment and were willing to pay heavily for the privilege of obtaining their posts. Until 1678 they usually received or bought their positions from the viceroy. Afterward they obtained them in Spain. This change brought piteous outcries from the viceroy, who prophesied all kinds of difficulties if he could not appoint his own *corregidores*. Notwithstanding his selfish interest in naming these officials, he was probably more correct than otherwise, for now he had little control over his nominal subordinates. It was the Indian who suffered the most, since now there was little to check the rapacity of the *corregidor*, only occasional bishops who might relieve injustices or visitors from the *audiencia* who now and again consented to listen to native woes.

Many other reasons might be adduced for the bad morale of the former Inca subjects. The Inca tradition itself, romanticized as it had become, was in fact harsh. And the conquistadors had gotten off to a bad start in Peru. Brutality was part of the atmosphere. Then, Peru was so far from Spain that impulses of the royal will might be weak when they reached the colony. Hence reform and humanitarianism could be postponed indefinitely, and no one would be the wiser. Whatever the explanations, conditions in colonial Peru were bad and remained so. And the authorities in Spain knew this, whether they grieved or yawned over the steady stream of reports depicting shocking conditions. Many sessions of the Council of Indies were devoted to devising remedial legislation. Kings often worried about these matters. Yet failure mocked even their most explicit commands. Madrid repeatedly ordered the colonial agents to treat the Indians better. *Encomiendas* were taken up, missionary activity was encouraged, and the abolition of the *mita* was considered, the Count of Lemos having suggested it. This last step was too dangerous, however, for the colonial economy might dissolve. Or worse, the colonials themselves might flatly refuse to obey. Peru was too valuable a treasure house to undermine.

Apart from the stream of exposures regarding the evil conditions in Peru, the census figures showed an appalling decline in Indian population. This meant that larger percentages of adult males must be drawn to work the mines and plantations, that the few hitherto enforced safeguards might be winked at. Visitors remarked on the emptiness of Peru, the bare valleys where evidence remained that numerous industrious inhabitants had lived and labored there in times past. The settlers were always complaining of labor shortages. Purchases of African slaves were stimulated by the government, but not even Peru was rich enough to import enough Negroes to replace the Indians. No one knew how many natives lived outside the Spanish pale. Clearly, the number was considerable, and a spirit of Inca nationalism was growing.

In the 1650's an adventurer from Spain named Francisco Bohórquez persuaded Indians of the back country that he was the true Inca and started a revolution. Natives in Spanish districts escaped to join the insurrection, but as usual, the Spaniards were able to crush it. Bohórquez was captured and, after eight years, executed. During this period a plot to massacre all whites was detected, the mestizos of La Paz rioted, and Juan de Padilla, a former employee of the *audiencia* of Lima, sent a shocking report on the situation of the natives to Madrid. Remedial measures were promptly taken under a strong viceroy, but no improvement was apparent. Other rebellions flared from time to time as Inca national feeling developed. In 1742 a mestizo named Juan Santos began a protracted insurrection in the *Montaña*, which is less mountainous than its name suggests but is rather a hilly, wooded transition area between the Andes and the Amazon jungle. Here lived the free Indians, those who enticed their enslaved countrymen to join them. This Santos was well-educated and had been sent by the Jesuits to Africa, Spain, and possibly England. He got into some kind of trouble, perhaps was accused of murder, and joined the Indians. For some years he led them in horse- and gun-stealing raids in Spanish territory and preached outright rebellion. The natives idolized him, many thinking him divine. Much as he troubled the authorities, Santos failed to raise up simultaneously the Indians in the mountains. One weakness was his use of the name "Atahualpa," which antagonized the Inca who still favored Huascar after two centuries. Santos died after about fifteen years and the rebellion quieted down.

THE REPORT OF JUAN AND ULLOA

The most readable and influential description of Indian conditions came about in an unusual manner. A party of scientists of the French Academy led by Charles-Marie de La Condamine sought to measure a segment of the earth at the Equator between the nearest meridians in order to determine the circumference of the globe. Since few areas on the Equator were suitable for such a project, they requested permission to go to the presidency of Quito. It was several years before Felipe V granted this privilege, for Spain was wary of letting foreigners, even allies, roam about her empire. The king also attached to the group two young Spanish naval officers, Antonio de Ulloa and Jorge Juan, to serve as aides and, perhaps, as spies. Ulloa, who was only nineteen when the expedition sailed, in 1735, spent six years in America and was captured by the British on his way home. Spending the rest of the War of the Austrian Succession in London, he impressed his hosts and learned a great deal about the world at large. Later he returned to America as governor of the mercury mine at Huancavelica, where he failed to correct deplorable conditions he had described. He was the Spanish commander who was ousted from New Orleans when he attempted to take over Louisiana in 1766, and he was in charge of the last treasure fleet to leave Vera Cruz under the old system. Juan, who was twenty-two when he joined La Condamine, was more of a scholar than man of action. He remained for eleven years in South America and wrote technical treatises on naval matters. Such then, was the caliber of the two young men who toured Quito and Peru between 1735 and 1741.

After a series of harrowing and hilarious experiences on the Equator with La Condamine's party, Juan and Ulloa traveled widely about the viceroyalty and wrote a detailed report for the Count of Ensenada, an enlightened minister of King Fernando VI. It is likely that this monarch and his successor, Carlos III, read it, and it may have played an important part in stimulating the famous *visita* of José de Gálvez to New Spain. So graphic were its details, and so damning was this study of the effects of the Spanish system on the natives, it was kept a close secret for many years. At last it was made public in English in 1826 in a mysterious manner, probably because a Spanish official with the London legation had an opportunity to sell it. In spite of Spanish protests the authenticity of the report has stood and is now acknowledged everywhere. Its effect on Spain's reputation has not been greatly less damaging than some of the effusions of Las Casas, which, unlike Juan and Ulloa's exposure, were often deliberately written as propaganda. In only one respect is the Juan and Ulloa study suspect. The two young men were knowledgeable beyond their years and quite likely relished the prospect of shocking the king's minister with an outspoken report.

"With sorrow and pity" they began their discussion of the oppression of the natives, caused, they said, by the thirst for wealth. *Corregidores* defrauded the government, tyrannized the Indians, and aggrandized themselves shamefully. Yet they were always absolved at the *residencia* because they bribed the investigating judges, paid off or threatened those who might bring forth complaints, and sometimes encouraged light charges that were easily refuted or obliquely flattering, such as working too hard. It was easy to secure abundant testimony that the *corregidor* had ruled well and treated the Indians kindly. And so the officials were either fooled or paid off. In practice, however, nearly every *corregidor* was a scoundrel who flagrantly violated the laws of the Indies. He suppressed the true number of Indians from whom tribute was collected, turned into the royal cash boxes the payments of a smaller number, and, further, levied this tax on many who were not supposed to pay it at all. Then, *corregidores* abused the laws of the *repartimiento*, which were supposed to place European tools in Indian hands. Instead of selling useful articles, they had the obliging *curacas* assemble their subjects in ranks like a military formation and pass out pell-mell unsaleable merchandise unloaded by the merchants of Lima: articles such as eye glasses that did not fit, hats, mirrors, razors for men who had no beards, and pens and paper for people who could not write. Whenever unsuitable goods were exhausted, mules might be forced on the unwilling buyers. The Indians wept and remonstrated, but they had no real recourse. They had to raise the money and buy whatever had been distributed to them.

The *mita*, reported Juan and Ulloa, was violated in almost every respect. This information was scarcely news, for everyone had been saying this for generations. The Indians were taken greater distances, treated worse, paid less, and forced to remain longer than the law provided. Quotas had stood firm while the population fell, so that a much greater percentage of the labor force was drafted. Yet the Indian seldom raised a fuss. It mattered little to him whether he worked for a *corregidor*, a priest, a miner, or the owner of a hacienda. Any white man was going to abuse and exploit him. There was no escape: not only did his own tribal ruler side with the Spanish to perpetrate these injustices, but mestizos and Negroes did so too. The Indian's life was one of toil and threats, whippings and curses. Even dogs were pro-white or pro-Indian, depending on their masters. Not only was the Indian situation depressing; it was degenerate. Natives lived in great poverty, often were diseased or crippled, and shared their huts with chickens and pigs. Incest and exchange of wives were common. Spanish civilization had not only failed to raise their standard of living except in a few items of food; it had also failed to raise the level of morality. Was it really necessary, Juan and Ulloa inquired, to oppress the Indians? The authors replied to their own question with emphatic negatives. Indians were not, they insisted, naturally idle and vicious. Free paid labor under honorable conditions was effective, even in the mines. Indians responded to decent opportunities for advancement and to sympathetic treatment.

Having supplied, perhaps too uncritically, the Indian side of the case against the imperialistic system, Juan and Ulloa offered His Catholic Majesty a very damning picture of the life and work of the clergy. "With diffidence," they pretended, they turned to this subject, though their spirited exposé of the seamy side of the Church suggests a great deal of eighteenth-century malice they possibly picked up from the French scientists. Parish priests, they declared, were unfeeling, openly immoral, and avaricious. They engaged in undignified intrigues and even employed force in order to obtain competitive posts likely to be lucrative. Once installed, a priest devoted his efforts to amassing wealth. He organized petty rackets among the Indians to stimulate the sale of ecclesiastical emblems during festivals and charged excessive fees for the sacraments. Sometimes priests passed on to bishops a percentage of their ill-gotten gains. Often they went into business, operating sweatshops where the Indians were treated like slaves. Incontinence among the clergy was general, a matter for boasting, worse than the frailty of human behavior would allow. Women lived in the monasteries with the friars, and illegitimate children ran all about the place. Whenever a new clergyman or any white man came to town, wise *curacas* offered him their daughters. (Juan and Ulloa virtuously disclaimed that they had taken advantage of such hospitality.) And the entertainments in the monasteries, the gross, lewd, obscene debauches . . . here our reporters, having built up curiosity and conveyed their impression, shrank from offending their readers.

As for the work of conversion, Juan and Ulloa reiterated points others had made since the earliest days of the Conquest. The behavior of the Christians so contradicted the teachings of the Saviour that few Indians could sincerely accept their cult. Not only was this true in the case of the ordinary Spaniard; the clergy, who numbered about 10,000 at this time, were often as bad. It was heart-breaking to see an earnest priest or friar arrive from Spain full of zeal, only to be confronted with the corrupt and cynical atmosphere that pervaded the Church in Peru. In most cases the immigrant would change his views and partake of the fruits of sensualism and materialism. A few might defy the trend and make themselves unpopular. Still fewer would march on to a determined martyrdom on the frontier. The lack of progress in missionary work on the barbarian edges of the Spanish domains provoked bitter comments from Juan and Ulloa, who were merely reinforcing a large body of critical reports of the same type. Only the Jesuits were an exception to the general picture of easy living and neglect of duty. Apart from the unedifying life of many clergymen, the system was indicted on the basis of ineffectiveness. Most of the Indians received only nominal instruction in Christianity. On Sundays they gathered outside churches, the whites being inside, and listened while an Indian, often a blind man, declaimed in Latin or Spanish. As he went through the service the timing was frequently off, and the congregation made the wrong responses unaware of the comic effect or blasphemies.

Other reporters on conditions in Peru, even after the supposedly massive conversions of the 1660's, described the superficial Christianization of the Andean natives. In 1818 a viceroy wrote a damning comment on this matter, this just on the eve of the final loss of the kingdom by the Spanish monarchy, and the end of Spain's opportunity to transmit the religion she cherished. It was customary all through the colonial period, and in some places it still is, for Indians to marry according to Inca rather than Christian rites, including trial marriages which permit the husband to shed an unsatisfactory wife after two years. At other important junctures of their daily lives they were likely to turn for consolation or inspiration to their pagan practices. On the other hand, Christianity perhaps brought more to the Indians in the way of holidays, which absorbed about a fourth of the days of the year. The natives loved festivals and the colorful aspects of Catholicism, the processions, decorated images, masses, music, and all the dramatic spectacles.

Juan and Ulloa's picture of Indian depravity and clerical ineffectiveness was only part of the truth. The young men intended to stress the defects of the Spanish system, not to offer a balanced study, and they surely were unable to resist the temptation to prick the sensibility of such august readers as the king's chief ministers and perhaps the king himself. Their description of colonial life in Quito and Lima, however, was typical of the educated European, admiring and yet patronizing. They noted the virulent hatreds among the whites, the ill will growing out of the tension between creoles and peninsulars. This animosity seemed to them almost like that of a people at war. Creoles were often proud and wealthy. Peninsulars were likely to be young upstarts who had left Spain for reasons one would not boast about. Yet they automatically outranked any creole and enjoyed official, social, and business preferment simply because they were born on the right side of the Atlantic. And while Juan and Ulloa did not stress the point, it is likely that peninsulars were more ambitious, imaginative, pushing, and able to discern opportunities than the Peruvian-born, very much as immigrant groups in the New World have often irritated and outplayed the older stock. In any event, a peninsular was a good catch for a creole girl. Marrying into the better families, he was likely to be reminded for the rest of his life by his wife and in-laws of his lowly condition when he arrived in Peru. He, on the other hand, could always flaunt the fact of his peninsular birth, which gave him an unanswerable advantage. So Juan and Ulloa explained many of the antipathies in Lima society. There may have been some shrewdness in their amateur sociology.

Society was obsessed with family pedigree, each clan rejoicing if it could trace its ancestry back to Spanish aristocrats of the Conquest and Inca royalty. Peruvians coveted titles and were ardent royalists, though the crown distributed titles very parsimoniously until the mid-eighteenth century, when at last it realized the advantages of attaching the stronger families by this means. The crown also encouraged the entailment of estates, thus tying up the larger holdings by primogeniture and enabling a family to maintain its wealth intact for generations. By the time of Juan and Ulloa's observations, Lima society was graceful and charming, very much absorbed in protocol and formality, eager to parade its ancestry and to puncture the pretensions of social rivals. The upper classes pursued pleasure and disdained work or seriousness. Often they were immoral and given to vice in ways accepted as genteel. In other words, they were not greatly different from the aristocracy of Europe, provincial as visitors from that favored continent might think them.

The Bourbon Viceroys

VICEROYS of the eighteenth century maintained and even increased the pomp that had surrounded their predecessors. They arrived in Callao in great style. Sometimes they visited the capital incognito while the official reception was being prepared. On the appointed day they met the outgoing viceroys halfway between Callao and Lima to receive the sash, truncheon, and other paraphernalia of office after their papers had been examined with the requisite solemnity. The entrance into Lima was a magnificent affair. The city would be cleaned, and arches were erected and tapestries and banners hung. A procession of the militia, the colleges, the university, the *audiencia,* the *cabildo,* and other officials passed in robed splendor. An elaborate reception at the cathedral, where the archbishop and thousands of spectators were standing, awaited the new viceroy. After his formal installation the city would erupt for twelve days of celebration. Even if most of the viceroys were remote and anonymous figures to the populace, their arrival was something to enjoy to the utmost.

The first Bourbon appointee was the Marquis of Castelldosorius, who came in 1707 and died three years later. Absorbed in raising loans, gifts, and revenues to sustain Felipe V, he was also plagued by attacks of the British and Dutch on the Pacific coast. Yet he offered Peru its first intimation of the new direction of the Spanish monarchy under French influence, particularly in the respectability he gave to the republic of letters. Cultivated men congregated at the palace for discussions, and Lima's cultural life received strong stimulation. This tendency had further impetus under the bishop of Quito, who served as viceroy from 1710 to 1716. He may have been, as it was charged, too partial to the Church, though bishops usually strove to prove they were good royalists and slighted the Church. The sanity of many subjects was threatened by the theft of the sacred hosts from the cathedral, if one takes literally the reports of the resulting popular furor. Following the bishop was the Prince of Santo Buono, whose reign from 1716 to 1720 is chiefly remembered for a terrible plague of fever, possibly typhus, which carried away countless Indians. For a time he stopped the *mita* at the Huancavelica mercury mine. Yet the work had to go on, and eventually this labor draft was restored. From 1720 to 1724 the Archbishop of Charcas served as viceroy. This was the nadir of the reign of Felipe V, the period when he was so melancholy he seldom got out of bed and never permitted his finger nails to be trimmed. Whenever the throne was immobilized by a sick king for a long period, the colonial administration suffered from lack of direction. That was the case with Peru at this time.

In 1724, after the seven-month reign of the child Luis I, Felipe V returned to the throne, so restored in health that he resumed his vigorous course. In the same year Peru received its first strong viceroy for many a year in the Marquis of Castel-Fuerte, a seasoned soldier like so many of the better Bourbon appointments. For twelve years Castel-Fuerte dealt energetically with three critical situations: smuggling, the dilapidation of the bureaucracy, and the torpor of the clergy. Finding, as he said, the ocean not pacific and the land not quiet, he made himself unpopular by attempting to enforce the laws. Dutch and English smugglers as well as Frenchmen who stretched the terms of the Bourbon amity were engaged in a huge, illicit commerce in South America. While their conniving American customers might be arrested and cruisers might occasionally interfere with the foreign ships, there was really no solution to the problem until or unless Spain herself supplied the goods Americans needed. This not being feasible for many years, Castel-Fuerte achieved little in this respect. Improving the administration yielded more satisfactory results, though again the situation seemed hopeless. As long as the Indians died out or ran away, *corregidores* were going to oppress the survivors to the limit. Not even a strong viceroy could prevent it. Castel-Fuerte was very much involved in the *comunero* affair in Paraguay, which will be considered in a later chapter. There he successfully asserted his authority and had his way, but only after several years of disorders and much opposition in that province and the capital too. In 1731 he courageously faced down a stone-throwing mob to see that the principal culprit was executed on schedule. With regard to the Church he anticipated the criticisms of Juan and Ulloa. So much was wrong: power-hungry prelates, truant friars, indifferent priests. Several noisy scandals involving the viceroy and the Church may have chastened the clergy somewhat, though improvements were not conspicuous. In one instance, Castel-Fuerte surrounded the Inquisition with troops and strode inside to inform the hooded judges that they were not a law unto themselves. It may be that this viceroy's severity awoke rebellious sentiments. People jokingly called him Pepe Bandos, or Joe Decrees, because of his frequent proclamations, most of them dealing with disagreeable matters. In retrospect, he seems an able man attempting to fill a difficult position.

The nine-year reign of the Marquis of Villagarcia, 1736–1745, brought little fame to the viceroy, momentous as the years were. Juan and Ulloa were forming their impressions and writing their devastating opinions of Peru. Lord Anson sailed around Cape Horn with a British fleet to attack Pacific ports and then to cross the vast ocean for other activities injurious to Spain. The British, it will be recalled, were seriously but vainly hoping to encourage independence sentiment in Spanish America. Possibly they circulated a little propaganda to this end, and they may, though it is unlikely, have furnished some incitement to the rebel Juan Santos, who was stirring up the Indians during these years. On the whole, Peru declined after the barracks rule of Castel-Fuerte. In 1739 the kingdom suffered the amputation of New Granada, which became a viceroyalty itself, and while this change brought no real injury to Peru, it diminished the prestige of its bureaucracy.

In 1745 another strong viceroy appeared in the Count of Superunda, who remained in office for a record sixteen-year reign. Promoted from the military governorship of Chile, Superunda set a precedent for several later viceroys of Peru; that Chile rather than New Spain served as the training ground for Peruvian viceroys indicates the lessening importance of the post at Lima. Superunda's first major task was to restore Lima and Callao after a particularly ruinous earthquake in 1746, one which was followed by a tidal wave that drowned almost all of Callao's population. The work was costly and tedious. Yet it was well done, and Lima became more beautiful than ever, not as large and magnificent as Mexico City but more lovely. One famous feature of its architecture was the enclosed wooden balcony which permitted ladies to observe the streets without being seen. Certainly a high society with dignity and tone continued to live luxuriously. Churches and government buildings were as ornate as iced cakes, the *churrigueresque* style attaining a fruition at Lima. The population, as before, consisted mostly of whites and Negroes, evenly divided. Callao also revived after the disaster. The official end of the fleet system to South America just before the War of the Austrian Succession permitted great numbers of privately registered Spanish vessels to enter and leave individually, and commerce flourished. The establishment of a tobacco monopoly in Superunda's reign brought in a substantial new source of revenue, almost as much as the native tributes.

Superunda's successor was still more illustrious a figure, Don Manuel Amat y Junient, an Aragonese aristocrat who had also served in Chile. His long reign, from 1761 to 1776, was full of events, but it is best known to us through romance, above all through Thornton Wilder's *The Bridge of San Luis Rey*. The aging bachelor viceroy made no secret of his infatuation with a mestiza comic actress of the Lima theater named Micaela Villegas, the famous *perricholi*.[1] Scandalous as his private life was, and extravagant with his mistress though he was, Amat was a respected viceroy. He acted his part well, insisting on unusual pomp and adulation. He had style, which the colonials admired. He enjoyed good talk in the palace and encouraged intellectuals to visit him. It was suspected that he was a free-thinker, which would not have been strange in a man of his class during the Enlightenment. The University of San Marcos and other educational institutions received much support, pulling out of a long dreary period when a few professors taught as many students the scholastic doctrines derided by the *philosophes* by this time. Now the modernists vanquished the ritualistic adherents of Aristotle and St. Thomas Aquinas, and the Enlightenment captured many of the best minds in Peru. Students flocked to the university, where they absorbed many of the new dogmas emanating from France. A cautious respect for experimentalism and rationalism weakened the hold of authority and prepared the way for revolution.

A cousin of the Count of Aranda, Amat may have shared that minister's enthusiasm for the expulsion of the Jesuits. Giving a party the evening before to avoid creating the impression that something serious was imminent, he pounced on the astounded brothers in 1767 and removed them from Peru as prisoners. As was true in other localities, the expulsion probably benefited the universities, for the Jesuits were mortal enemies of the new learning, but it badly crippled the colleges and the missions. About 400 were removed from Peru. It fell to Amat to organize a militia in Peru after the Seven Years' War, a task he apparently enjoyed hugely. Several thousand mestizos and mulattoes manned the various companies, which were segregated by race, and royalist creoles or penin-

1. Micaela's nickname may have been derived from the corruption of a Catalan term of endearment. Lima society liked to think, however, that her lover, when he was angry with her, called her *perra chola*, or half-breed female dog.

sulars officered these units. The militia had no foreign war to fight, but in 1765 Amat shipped a large force up to Guayaquil, which was now in the viceroyalty of New Granada, to help suppress a dangerous uprising in Quito. As it happened, the viceroy of New Granada was able to handle the situation. Perhaps Amat was seeking to demonstrate to the crown that the land of the Equator should be rejoined to Peru, a favorite idea in Lima for the next century or so. Amat also named a great number of creoles to the nobility, a tardy measure taken by the crown to tighten the loyalty of this group. He was a great builder, seeing that Lima was graced with a new bullring and cock-fighting pit, or Rooster Coliseum, as well as water ditches and hospitals. Indefatigable, he even sponsored expeditions to Tahiti, which Spain was not destined to hold despite several efforts at occupation. Full of years and honors, Amat retired to Spain in 1776, where he chivalrously married a girl of eighteen whom his nephew had jilted.

Manuel Guirior came down from New Granada in 1776 to become viceroy of Peru, only to discover that his jurisdiction had been drastically trimmed. After much deliberation Carlos III had decided to establish the viceroyalty of La Plata with its capital at Buenos Aires. Losing the Platine region was no blow to Peru, much as the Lima merchants had predicted it would be, but the annexation of Charcas or Upper Peru (modern Bolivia) to the new creation halved the output of treasure formerly credited to the Peruvian viceroys. Even if the free trade edict of 1778 greatly stimulated commerce and royal revenues at Callao, the bureaucracy at Lima refused to be consoled. It long bewailed the loss of Upper Peru and the prestige that went with it. As it turned out, Guirior's demotion had only begun. A *visitador* and superintendent of finances named José de Areche came out from Spain, hoping to perform in Peru the prodigies that his superior, José de Gálvez, had once brought off in New Spain. Elbowing aside the viceroy, Areche proceeded to look into the matter of tax collections over recent years. Apparently there had been much disorder, some of it deliberate so as to conceal delinquencies and official corruption. Striking fast and hard, the *visitador* extorted back levies with a vengeance, thereby frightening many wealthy Peruvians and royal agents. He also proposed to compel the Indians to pay the *alcabala*, or sales tax, an infliction they had hitherto escaped, and to devise means of forcing mestizos and mulattoes to contribute more to the government. This was not altogether an overzealousness to make himself popular in Madrid, though Areche was ambitious enough. Spain was by 1779 at war with Britain again (the American Revolution) and more funds were needed. His methods were high-handed in the extreme, however, and the whole viceroyalty was sullen. Complaints mounted, soon developing into defiance. Disorders took on a rebellious character. And then, in November 1780, the most formidable Indian insurrection since Manco Inca's attempt in 1535 shook the very foundations of Spanish rule in South America.

Tupac Amarú II

IN THE early years of the 1780's Andean natives in an area extending in an arc from modern Venezuela down into Argentina were stirred by a hope that the white man could be expelled. The origins of this alarming uprising went back to the earliest days of Spanish-Indian relations. Generations of ill treatment had built up a heritage of resentment, and dim, romanticized versions of pre-Spanish days had acquired a strong hold on the imagination of the oppressed. A veritable Inca nationalism had taken shape by the late eighteenth century. While the Spanish blamed British agents and embittered ex-Jesuits for stirring up this rebellion, indeed it is hard to see how they could have done so, glad as they might have been to do Spain a bad turn. The explanation was simply the final exasperations applied by Areche after generations of injustice and mounting hatred. Conditions had certainly grown no better in Peru after the indictment of Juan and Ulloa forty years before. If anything, they were worse, since the native population had continued to decline and greater pressures were being exerted for labor and revenues.

The leader of this rebellion was José Gabriel Condorcanqui Noguera, a devout, virtuous, educated mestizo who owned considerable land near Cuzco. He came into the position of *curaca* through inheritance and established to the satisfaction of the *audiencia* at Lima that he was entitled to call himself Marquis of Oropesa, a dignity reserved for a descendant of the Inca ruling family. For several years he inspected the miserable conditions of the highland natives and remonstrated with the authorities over the worst abuses. He went to Lima and, not satisfied there, talked of going to Madrid to obtain some redress of grievances. At some point late in the 1770's he began to consider himself Tupac Amarú II, the rightful monarch of the Inca population, and the enthusiasm of his followers went to his head. Months of plotting came to a climax in November 1780 when he seized an unusually detested *corregidor* at Tinta who had already been excommunicated for his outrages against the Indians. In trying this official before an irregular court of his own creation and having him executed, Tupac Amarú II gave the signal for a widespread uprising. The news flashed quickly up and down the Andes, becoming greatly distorted in the process but communicating nonetheless the essential fact that a reckoning with the white man was possible. Tupac Amarú issued appeals for mestizos, Negroes, mulattoes, and creoles to join him. Possibly he was sincere at the outset in protesting that he desired only reform, not revolution. In some localities the clergy supported him, for Tupac Amarú was a Christian and proposed to implement rather than abolish the religion of the Spaniard. Yet the vengeance exhibited by the Indians quickly terrified the other races. Crown officials were lynched, white people of all classes fled the affected areas or barricaded themselves in towns, and the mixed groups, as always, sided almost unanimously with the whites. Perhaps we should not take too seriously Tupac Amarú's declarations of loyalty to the king. Revolutions usually begin with a demand for reform. What had started at Tinta was no mere reform movement, but a wide-scale race war of Indian against white.

For some weeks the situation looked very dangerous. Horses, guns, and powder came into possession of the rebels through raids on towns and arsenals. Nearly half the population of Peru proper was in revolution and natives in Quito, New Granada, Upper Peru, and Venezuela were stirred into defiance or rebellion. The sullen Aymará of Upper Peru and spirited Araucanians of Chile were especially threatening. The possibility of British intervention and a trace—but only a trace—of disaffection among scattered intellectuals who desired a new system of government added further cause for alarm.

Yet the outcome proved to be the same as in all previous wars between Europeans and Indians. Even if the natives had vastly superior numbers and inspiring leadership in Tupac Amarú II, the whites had advantages the Indians could never match. More than 60,000 militiamen, most of whom were mestizos and mulattoes, adequately supplied with horses and guns and ably led, were enough to deal with the insurrection. Areche led his forces into the mountains and scattered the Indians in every skirmish. The viceroys of New Granada and La Plata took similarly vigorous, and successful, measures in their kingdoms. The few key battles over, elements among the rebels discerned advantages in betraying their leaders. It would be the same in Mexico in 1810–1814, and was perhaps implicit in such situations. Tupac Amarú II and his family were seized by defectors in their own following and turned over to Areche in the spring of 1781. After his wife and other members of his family were barbarously executed, the would-be Inca was pulled apart by horses. His half-brothers continued the struggle but to no avail. One of them was destined to spend the next forty years in prison and internment in Spanish Morocco. As the remaining bands were caught or betrayed, one after another, Areche punished them severely. In fairness, it should be added that the Indians had committed enough atrocities against the whites to justify savage retaliation, if it is ever justifiable. Areche employed this argument when he got back to Madrid, but it was coldly received. With Peru proper reconquered in 1781, the Spanish forces fought on for several years "pacifying" Upper Peru, where the Aymará had always shown more spirit than their Quechua cousins. La Paz underwent two fearful Indian sieges before the trail of atrocity receded deeper into the Andes.

The great fright to which the Spanish and mixed races had been put has a great deal to do with explaining the long unwillingness of the central Andean colonies to revolt against Spain thirty years later. Peru and Bolivia had to be pried out of the Spanish empire by liberators from the outside who were by no means entirely welcome. Once the massacres and economic disorganization had been written off, the crown took intelligent measures to heal the wounds of the Tupac Amarú rebellion. An *audiencia* was established in Cuzco so that Indian grievances could receive a faster airing. The *corregidores* were abolished and a new system of intendants and sub-delegates replaced them. The detested *repartimiento* ceased. The *mita* continued, would, in fact, remain well into the republican period (and the tribute even longer), but better safeguards were enforced to prevent abuses. The authorities at last accepted the fact that free paid labor would serve to remove silver from the mines, as it had long done in Mexico. The crown lavishly distributed pardons once order was restored. Sincere efforts were undertaken to encourage the Indians to become Christians and to use Spanish names. They were also supposed to wear European dress, and the circulation of works extolling the Inca system, such as Garcilasso Inca de la Vega's *Royal Commentaries*, was forbidden. The memory of the great insurrection was a strong force in Peru for many years. Projects during the Wars of Independence to create an Inca to rally the Indians to the new regimes stemmed from the recollection of how fierce the natives could be if their hatred of a government became unbearable.

Before the Deluge

SPAIN had again asserted her rule over Peru. The beaten Indians, now somewhat better off for their rebellion, were not to endanger the whites and mixed races further, much as the possibility remained in the minds of all. Viceroy Agustín de Jáuregui, who reigned from 1780 to 1784, had cooperated with Areche in suppressing the insurrections. Teodoro de la Croix, who had been commandant-general of the embryo viceroyalty in New Spain, the *Provincias internas*, assumed the vice-regal position in Lima in 1784 for a six-year period. These were the years of appeasing the Indians after the rebellion and of the instituting of reforms. At this time Peru, like New Spain, received a group of foreign technicians to modernize the mines. Baron Nordenflicht headed this mission and spent several years trying to improve production. While he did not fail, Peruvian mining underwent no striking transformation as that which occurred in Mexico under Fausto de Elhuyar's efforts in a similar mission. Peru was, in fact, no longer the brightest jewel in the crown of Spain, not even the second brightest. New Spain had surpassed her for a century, and by now New Granada and La Plata sometimes produced more revenues for the king. Little as this condition must have mattered to most of the population and to the king himself, it weighed on the spirits of the officials and older families of Lima.

Francisco Gil de Taboada served as viceroy from 1790 to 1796, a time of watchfulness against the ideas of the French Revolution, which nonetheless made some penetration among prosperous creoles and university circles. Revenues were increasing rapidly as a result of growing ocean commerce and the recovery from Tupac Amarú's rebellion. Patriotic and progressive creoles were looking about for further means of strengthening the colony within the monarchical framework. A "society of friends of the country," one of a number organized in the Spanish monarchy, reunited in Lima well-to-do men who learned of technological advances in other parts of the world. A tri-weekly sheet, *El mercurio peruano*, advanced comparatively modern, though entirely unrevolutionary, ideas. The fruits of the educational stimulation begun in Viceroy Amat's time were shown in greatly increased student enrollments and a higher caliber of academic life. A well-known scientist, Hipólito Unánue, was the center of much of this activity. A leading physician and surgeon and a professor of medicine at the university, he did much for both the medical training and the intellectual stimulation of the kingdom. In Arequipa the bishop attracted and inspired men interested in material progress. A few figures, some of them fashionable persons in Lima society, came close to revolutionary subversion in the privacy of their homes, and in talk-fests, known as *tertulias,* and coffee houses men ventilated their opinions of affairs, exchanged gossip, and, insofar as they could, discussed politics and ideas. Too much must not be made of these timid approaches to the confusing movements of the French Revolutionary period. Yet they must not be ignored, for a new generation was learning more than the authorities realized.

Ambrosio O'Higgins, Marquis of Osorno, arrived in Lima in 1796 as viceroy after a unique career. One of the numerous Irishmen who found their way to Spain, he had gone to the Argentine and Chile as a peddler and become immensely wealthy. In time he was appointed captain-general of Chile, where he served so well he was promoted to the viceregal post in Lima. His reign of four years was not particularly memorable, able and dedicated as he was. Conditions were comparatively good in spite of Spain's troubles in Europe and a new British war. Suddenly, in 1800, O'Higgins was removed from office. In spite of polite words he guessed the real reason: the revolutionary associations and activities of his illegitimate son Bernardo in Europe, of whom more later. The Marquis of Avilés reigned from 1801 to 1806, to be followed by Fernando de Abascal, whom we shall consider in connection with the independence period.

By 1808 Peru seemed secure enough, secure from Indian rebellion, from foreign seizure, and from revolutionary spirit. Shorn of its former prestige and adjacent dependencies, even Chile having become administratively free from Lima's control by this time, Peru was to prove in the difficult years ahead the abiding heartland of Spanish power in South America. Venezuela, New Granada, Argentina, Paraguay, and Chile would revolt or fall away. But Peru, which really meant the whites and mixed races on the coast, was fervently royalist until 1821, when Spain herself ceased to be so. It is sobering to learn how few these whites and mixed races were. The last census before the Wars of Independence reported only 135,000 Europeans and 244,000 mestizos. There were about 40,000 African slaves and 40,000 Negroes who were free, many of them mulattoes. The Indian population in the hinterland, which must have numbered in the millions in Inca times, was reported at 600,000. Regardless of its past as a valued Spanish colony and the continuing elegance of Lima, the viceroyalty was a depressing place in many ways by the end of the colonial period. Perhaps Simón Bolívar was right when he wrote, a few years later, that Peru was too corrupted by gold and slavery ever to have the makings of a nation.

The Steady Growth of Chile

IF PERU had declined in relation to other Spanish American kingdoms during the eighteenth century and New Granada and La Plata surged forward, another important land made sound, unspectacular progress. This was the kingdom of Chile, destined to become one of the most stable of American republics. Before 1776 Chile was not the long string of land squeezed between the Andes and the Pacific with which we are familiar, but rather a fat country looking on the map like a man's hat lying on its side, the brim composed of the pleasant, rich zone of central Chile and the crown reaching far across into the present Argentina. The kingdom was a province until 1778, when it became a captaincy-general ruled by a governor responsible to the man he hoped to succeed, the viceroy at Lima. This connection was mostly nominal, however, and in 1798 it almost lapsed. Yet governors or captains-general of Chile usually became viceroys of Peru during this century. Chile also had an *audiencia* in Santiago, its capital, after 1609.

Chile was not one of the favorite dominions of the Spanish crown, for it was too isolated, too lacking in loose treasure, and too full of hostile Indians. Its history since Almagro's unhappy expedition in 1535 until the eighteenth century was eventful enough but not of the type to encourage large-scale white immigration. The spirited Indians, above all the Araucanians, refused to settle into the Spanish system, defying soldier, missionary, and colonist alike. Earthquakes often mocked the efforts of farmers and town-builders. Smugglers crept around Cape Horn or bounced wildly through the Strait of Magellan to occupy islands off the coasts. This last is probably the main reason for the persistence of Spain in holding Chile at a high cost, though it must be admitted that the nature of Spanish imperialism was such that lands were seldom abandoned. In this instance, the Spanish feared that if they relinquished Chile, the Dutch or the British would move in. And, as time went on, it became apparent that enough gold could be wrung from the mountains to make the colony worth holding, though it was usually necessary for the royal treasury to subsidize the military establishment there.

The apparatus of government was typical of the Spanish system. It had a special atmosphere, however, because of the high point of tension between the settlers and the Indians. The colonists could not by themselves defend their holdings, and troops from Peru or Spain were constantly required. Chile was one of the very few parts of the Spanish empire where substantial garrisons were on duty almost constantly. As might be expected, the soldiers were often convicts or trouble-makers who did little to raise the moral tone of the colony. If they generally protected the central region from Indian conquest, they were unable to occupy the mountains and rain-forested islands which served as homelands for these natives, the Araucanians, Mapochos, Pehuenches, and others. For much of the colonial period the line of Spanish occupation rocked back and forth as the warfare went on. For once, Spanish gunfire and horses were not equal to the task of winning decisive victories, and the Indians acquired these advantages and used the *bola* with devastating effect. At times the Spaniards undertook campaigns of extermination, only to fall back in failure. Frightfulness as a tactic could be more than matched by the Indians. Truces and intervals of peaceful penetration by evangelists and traders nearly always ended in another outbreak of butchery. This constant warfare had at least two important effects: the continued importation of soldiers and the development of a vigorous, martial spirit on the part of the population. Chile was no somnolent colonial outpost but an alert garrison state. The aggressiveness of its inhabitants would long be a factor in South American affairs.

In spite of Indians and earthquakes, central Chile was a good place to live. This region, which is often compared to northern or central California, was fertile and temperate in climate, in fact invigorating. Wheat, fruit, and livestock flourished in the rich valleys and plateaus in the shadow of the imposing cordillera. Wheat had a steady market in Peru. Fruits and cattle were sometimes shipped into the mining regions of Upper Peru. Chilean wines attained a deserved fame which has by no means diminished today. And the Andes yielded enough gold to enrich a number of individuals. Copper, which was to become so important in modern times, had comparatively little value during the colonial period but for such homely articles as buckets, pots, wire, and sometimes bells and cannon. Chile, thus, was self-supporting in matters of food and had a few articles to export. Her trade was by no means impressive, but it served to maintain a modest flow over the Andes and the sea lane to Peru as well as occasional contacts with contrabandists. Cuyo, the trans-Andean province of Chile, did as well or better in trading with Upper Peru and Buenos Aires. When it was snipped away from Chile and added to the viceroyalty of La Plata, protests in Santiago were loud. The towns of Chile were squat and ugly, the capital, Santiago, having little to boast of but its climate and view of the cordillera. Concepción, to the south, was long the largest municipality, but it was almost destroyed by a tidal wave in 1734. Valparaiso had a splendid harbor but was much less pretentious than the Naples to which its inhabitants liked to compare it. Mendoza, in Cuyo, was more of a traditional colonial-type town. Others were mere settlements. More handsome than these municipalities were the missions of the religious orders, those of the Jesuits especially, which were often mammoth concentrations of fields, orchards, vineyards, homes, and small factories.

The social situation in Chile was not typical of the Spanish empire. For one thing, the whites were less disinclined to work with their hands than elsewhere. The climate was invigorating and many of the immigrants were Basques and Catalans, who have always been reputed more industrious than Castilians and Andalusians. More important was the comparative absence of Indian servile labor. While the *encomienda* had existed since 1540 and remained after 1720, when it was abolished elsewhere, few Indians fell into this form of tutelage, preferring to run away or fight back. This chronic war of the Spaniards and the natives prevented the stabilization of such Indians as lived in the Spanish pale, for they were often restless and able to escape. For much of the colonial period the whites were allowed to use prisoners of war as outright slaves, a method not overly satisfactory in such an uneasy situation. In 1610 a sort of truce was decreed by Madrid to keep both sides apart at the Bío-Bío River; it lasted only a few years. Also short-lived was a policy of drenching an Indian district with missionaries, for few of the friars returned. In short, nothing seemed to work, not terror, persuasion, nor compromise. An obvious alternative was to import Negro slaves. This was done on a steady scale through foreign shippers and the illegal caravans which came through unpatrolled passes of the Andes from Buenos Aires. Yet Chileans were seldom rich enough to purchase many Negro slaves, and the trans-Andean province of Cuyo was the only place where this form of servitude had much importance. What finally developed was that mestizos came to form the laboring class. Living as peons on the great estates owned by a few whites, these *inquilinos* are still an important factor in the Chilean scene. So also are the wandering, seasonal workers known as *rotos* (the broken ones), whose name conveys their tragic poverty and rootlessness. Alcoholism became one of the most conspicuous vices of the lower classes, a social evil that still exists on a shocking scale. Colonial Chile evolved, and republican Chile has maintained, a basic situation in which an aristocratic class of largely white landowners lives gracefully amid a huge, depraved, agricultural proletariat of mestizos.

The history of the colonial period is full of events of a violent character, but it lacks sufficient variation from the pattern to warrant detailed treatment. Campaigns undertaken against the Indians, depredations suffered at their hands, earthquakes and tempests, plagues, scandals, the doings of wicked rulers and estimable rulers, occasional terrors caused by the appearance of foreign enemies off the coasts—these would be too repetitious to chronicle. It should be noted that progress was uneven but steady. Chile slowly acquired a substantial white and mestizo population. Her gold mines, farms, ranches, orchards, vineyards, and minor factories grew more productive. An unhealthy social situation became intrenched, but the racial mixtures moved toward a homogeneity that would benefit the Chile of the future. The Spanish and Spanish-oriented population mounted, quintupling in the eighteenth century, again in the nineteenth, and apparently to do so in the twentieth.

The kingdom shared in the regeneration of the Spanish monarchy brought about by the Bourbons in the eighteenth century. Governors were more active and liberal-minded than their predecessors, more vigorous in promoting the economy and in collecting taxes, and more careful in providing better if more autocratic government. The Jesuits persuaded the crown to try a new policy with the Araucanians, to permit polygamy, drunkenness, and elements of traditional pagan worship in exchange for wearing European clothes and listening to Christian preachers. Results were not conspicuously heartening, and in 1767 the 300 Jesuits were ousted for reasons that had nothing to do with this experiment. Education remained backward, though the University of San Felipe was established in 1747 in Santiago after a century of petitions for such an adornment. A mint set up in 1750 testified to the growth of gold mining and provided a handsome building still used by Chilean presidents.[2] English and Dutch smuggling slowly declined as better administrative practices improved legal trade. One memorable incident of this practice was the marooning of Alexander Selkirk on the island of Juan Fernández, which inspired Daniel Defoe's story of Robinson Crusoe.

The decentralization of the Spanish empire directed by Carlos III led in 1778 to the elevation of Chile, shorn of Cuyo province, to the dignity of a captaincy-general. The imperial free trade edict of that year brought more commerce to Concepción and Valparaiso, along with greatly heightened royal revenues. Oblique but cogent evidence of Chile's advancement came in 1781, when so much of South America was experiencing rebellious sentiments, usually of Indian against white. In this case it was a plot for independence known as the conspiracy of the three Anthonys. Three men with this given name, one a landowner, another a French-born teacher, and the third an inventor or tinker, hatched a scheme to make Chile a republic. The amateurishness of the three Anthonys was at once hair-raising and heart-breaking. All three were apprehended and punished. The authorities kept the matter a secret so as not to give it more notoriety than it deserved. Not for another quarter-century were there enough advocates of independence or democracy to disturb the rulers of Chile.

Of the parade of Chilean governors who went to Peru as viceroys, Superunda, Amat, Jáuregui, and O'Higgins, this last left the deepest impress on Chile. The central mystery of the Irish boy Higgins who went to Spain and then to Buenos Aires as a peddler, moved on to wealth and influence in Chile, where he prefaced a snobbish "O" to his name and became captain-general, and then rose later to the viceregal post in Lima as the Marquis of Osorno, has never been satisfactorily explained. Certainly, his career was unique in colonial times. He seems to have been a highly successful governor of Chile, administering the kingdom with firmness while he chastized the Indians, planted towns, and improved the economy. Also he was popular, though a puritanical streak improbably appeared in this loose-living, self-made rich man. He attacked the chronic problem of alcoholism and tried to punish blasphemers and wife deserters. His term, from 1787 to 1796, was the apex of colonial Chile. The captaincy-general had more than a half million Hispanicized inhabitants. It was growing rapidly and, as an entity, was prosperous, though most Chileans were poor people indeed. With a stable economy and a population not overly divided on the basis of race, Chile was better prepared than most other Spanish American colonies for the upheavals so soon to begin.

2. The popular story that this mint was not meant for Santiago at all but was ordered through a bureaucratic fluke in Spain may be true.

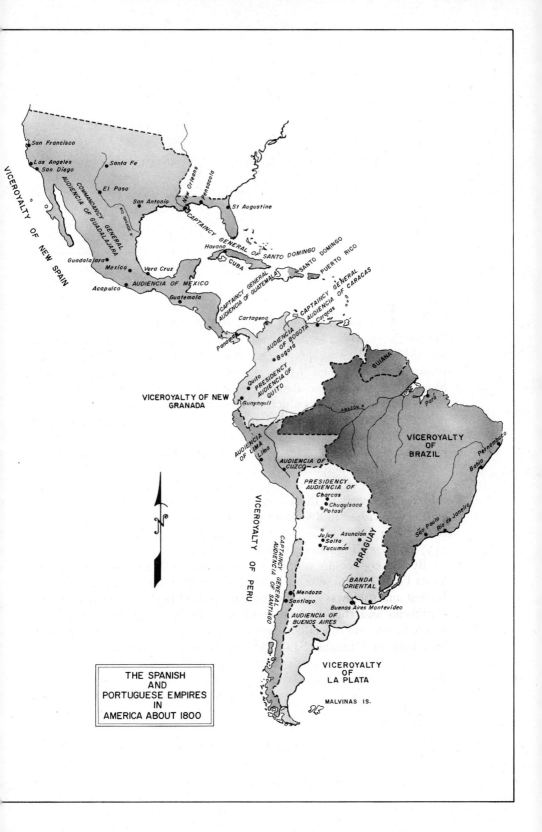

VICEROYALTY OF NEW SPAIN

San Francisco
Los Angeles
San Diego
Santa Fe
El Paso
San Antonio
New Orleans
Pensacola
St Augustine
AUDIENCIA OF GUADALAJARA
COMMANDANCY GENERAL
RIO GRANDE R.
CAPTAINCY GENERAL OF SANTO DOMINGO
Havana
CUBA
SANTO DOMINGO
PUERTO RICO
Guadalajara
Mexico
Vera Cruz
Acapulco
AUDIENCIA OF MEXICO
Guatemala
CAPTAINCY GENERAL
AUDIENCIA OF GUATEMALA
Cartagena
Panama
CAPTAINCY GENERAL
AUDIENCIA OF CARACAS
Caracas

AUDIENCIA OF BOGOTA
Bogotá
VICEROYALTY OF NEW GRANADA
Quito
PRESIDENCY AUDIENCIA OF QUITO
Guayaquil
AMAZON R.
GUIANA
Pará
VICEROYALTY OF BRAZIL
Pernambuco
Bahia
AUDIENCIA OF LIMA
Lima
AUDIENCIA OF CUZCO
VICEROYALTY OF PERU
PRESIDENCY AUDIENCIA OF CHARCAS
Chuquisaca
Potosí
São Paulo
Rio de Janeiro
Jujuy
Salta
Tucumán
Asunción
PARAGUAY
CAPTAINCY GENERAL OF SANTIAGO
BANDA ORIENTAL
Mendoza
Santiago
Buenos Aires
Montevideo
AUDIENCIA OF BUENOS AIRES
VICEROYALTY OF LA PLATA
MALVINAS IS.

N

THE SPANISH
AND
PORTUGUESE EMPIRES
IN
AMERICA ABOUT 1800

16

The New Kingdom of Granada;
The Platine Colonies

FOR much of the colonial period the northwestern corner of the South American continent was a land of mystery. Its geography was forbidding and its wealth suspected but not known. Hundreds of adventurers had lost their lives in the torrid jungles along both the Caribbean and Pacific coasts. Rising abruptly behind these shores were several chains of the Andes which divided the interior into isolated valleys. A few rich hauls of gold and emeralds and comparatively advanced Indians had induced the Spaniards to penetrate this region, but there was little to encourage large-scale settlement. The southwestern part of the kingdom was potentially good agricultural and grazing land. Yet colonists seldom got that far, settling instead in Peru or Quito. About half the area belonged to the Green Hell of the Amazon basin, where no white man wished to live. For two centuries following the three-pronged conquest by Jiménez de Quesada, Federmann, and Belalcázar in 1536–1539 the New Kingdom developed very slowly.

By the eighteenth century the land was still inchoate. Its capital, Santa Fe de Bogotá, was an isolated if beautiful town in the mountains. Its best approach was a tedious voyage up the Magdalena River from the Caribbean and then a steep climb on horseback. Contact with Lima was tenuous, and officials in Santa Fe exerted only weak authority over governors in Panama, Santa Marta, Riohacha, Cartagena, Popayán, and Antioquia and as many *corregidores* in less developed districts. The first four of these provinces were exposed to attacks by national enemies and corsairs. When conditions permitted, they were the scenes of sugar and indigo cultivation with the inevitable Negro slavery. Cartagena was a well-fortified and ornate port. Popayán and Antioquia were lightly inhabited ranching and farming provinces. Placer gold mining in the

mountains of this region was a stable industry which eventually produced thirty million fine ounces of gold, half of it in the eighteenth century. Yet gold mining had comparatively little effect on the rest of the
colony, for only a few thousand owners and workers were involved at any
one time, and the treasure itself was mostly shipped out. New Granada
was not even famous in the way other mining regions were.

The early history of the colony consists largely of those economic developments and the discouraging efforts of Spain to install an effective
government. In 1549 an *audiencia* had been established in Santa Fe de
Bogotá, and in 1564 the first of the two dozen royal governors assumed
office. Since the governor was also head of the *audiencia* he was known
as a president, and more often than not he bore the title of captain-
general. Not only was his connection with the viceroy at Lima fragile,
but he was also likely to clash with both his predecessor and his successor. It is almost absurd to recount the regularity with which a new set
of officials appeared in Santa Fe every few years, arrested the incumbents
for all kinds of misdeeds, and then were subjected to the same proceedings when their terms were up. Altogether, the government of the New
Kingdom was a sorry affair, as no one recognized better than the viceroy of Peru.

If only because the administration was so unedifying in political affairs, the work of the Church by contrast seems unusually admirable. An
archbishop in the capital and six bishops, together with the Dominicans,
Franciscans, Augustinians, Jesuits, and Capuchins, carried out their duties in such a way as to give the colonial Church in this area a good reputation. The Inquisition at Cartagena concerned itself almost altogether
with foreign heretics and African sorcerers. The Spaniards were too
few and too backward to be interested in forbidden religions. Apart
from the scandals and crimes that make up so much of New Granada's
early history, nature provided many memorable items in the way of hurricanes and earthquakes. Perhaps the only amusing occurrence of this
type was an incredible roar of March 9, 1687 which panicked the inhabitants of the capital. It turned out to be a matter of underground
gases loosened by recent tremors, not, as feared, the wrath of God or the
threats of Satan.

The Viceroyalty

AFTER the Bourbons were securely seated on the Spanish throne
a reappraisal of the American empire pointed up the weaknesses of New
Granada. For one thing, it was too vulnerable, pirates and national foes
long having found it easy to disembark on the Caribbean shore and make
mischief. The Scottish effort of the 1690's and a brutal French sacking

of Cartagena in 1697 had shaken the Spanish badly. Smugglers operated at will. With all the plans Felipe V and his ministers had to revive Spanish trade, it was imperative to build up a strong flank on the sea lane to Panama and Peru. Also, the lawlessness of the settlers in New Granada and the anarchical condition of the government had long been deplored. Much of the land ought to be occupied and cultivated. If the evidence was sound, much treasure lay in the mountains awaiting systematic excavation, and such mines as existed brought scanty revenues to the royal coffers. In 1717 it was decided to create a viceroyalty of the lands now contained in Colombia, Panama, Ecuador, and Venezuela. An official was sent to Santa Fe de Bogotá to organize this entity. Formidable as the challenge was, he performed capably under the circumstances and was succeeded in 1719 by the first man to bear the title of Viceroy of the New Kingdom of Granada, Don Jorge de Villalonga. After three years Villalonga concluded that his mission was premature, in fact hopeless, and he recommended that the effort be abandoned. The region was too large and varied, too lightly inhabited, its problems too forbidding. His advice was accepted, and in 1723 the several kingdoms reverted to their old status under the viceroy of Peru. One reason for this curious lapse of effort, this very un-Spanish surrender, was the mental depression of Felipe V at this time. His government suddenly lost direction, and projects such as this one were allowed to drop.

During the following sixteen years the viceroys of Peru again demonstrated their inability to govern northern South America, even under so able an administrator as the Marquis of Castel-Fuerte. One of the presidents of New Granada during these years wrote despondently of the area, which, full of gold and silver, emeralds and amethysts, fine woods, grasslands, and rich soils, offered little to the royal treasury. In the midst of these potential riches, he said, the inhabitants were mostly beggars. So few would toil: the whites not at all, the Indians only when driven, and the Negroes, whom he appraised as five-fold the worth of Indians as laborers, so scarce. Crown agents were as corrupt and ineffective as ever. They had few incentives to be virtuous, and it was tempting for them to facilitate contraband as a means of enriching themselves. The Church absorbed too much property, he reported, and itself suffered from low morale. Crime was common and seldom punished; disorder was endemic. In short, the same reasons that had led to the creation of the viceroyalty in 1717 clamored more loudly than ever.

When the War of Jenkins' Ear between Spain and Britain began in 1739, the British boasted they would detach portions of the American empire and dispatched imposing expeditions under Admirals Vernon and Anson to South America. In the face of these threats the Spanish again set up the viceroyalty of New Granada, composed as it had been in

1717. Sebastián de Eslava went to Cartagena as viceroy, spending most of his time organizing the defenses of that opulent city. His labor was fruitful. Vernon had seized Puerto Bello with scant difficulty and, over-confident, descended on Cartagena in 1741 with 28,000 redcoats. The Spanish have long exulted over the way London announced the capture of that city at a time when the British were dying outside its walls from Spanish fire and tropical diseases. After half his men were gone Vernon gave up the siege, his memory to be perpetuated not by medals struck in England for a victory that never was, but by a country home in Virginia named after him by one of his officers, George Washington's brother Lawrence. The whole affair was a demonstration that Spain had indeed revived considerably since the previous war with Britain. The viceroyalty had the makings of a sturdy colony. Viceroy Eslava went ahead with the labor of shaping it, organizing an improved system for collecting taxes, constructing fortifications and roads, laying out towns, and with a prodigal hand, as he said, multiplying officials of the crown to carry out the king's will. He came through his *residencia* nicely, parrying the charge that he had never gone to the capital with the evident facts that he had fought a good war and had set New Granada on a sound course.

The rather uphill work of making the new viceroyalty function went on steadily and generally successfully. Perhaps the crucial agents of this process were the missionaries and royal revenue collectors. The creation of a liquor monopoly early in the 1750's gave the government a further means of exerting authority and raising funds. In this case the crown was torn between the obvious social damage of providing the colored races with alcohol too easily, especially in the form of rum and sugar-cane brandy known as *aguardiente,* and the desirability of raising money. A decade later the establishment of a tobacco monopoly offered a less painful dilemma and produced more profits.

These royal monopolies could prove dangerous if they were mishandled. In Quito in 1765 an exasperated populace protested riotously against the practices of the government with regard to the liquor situation. The tumults blossomed into something bordering on revolution, though the crowds cheered the distant king of Spain. Quito, a beautiful colonial city nestling among snow-capped peaks, was undergoing a period of depression caused by the decline of its manufacturing owing to the improved shipments from Spain. Perhaps this accounts for the readiness with which the lower classes exploded against the liquor monopoly. In any event, the whites banded together. Troops from Peru and New Granada headed for the stricken city. It was the Jesuits, however, who pacified the population and restored authority. The viceroy at Santa Fe de Bogotá lavishly distributed pardons once his position was respected, and few punitive steps were taken. Two years later he had the ungrateful task of expelling the 200 Jesuits from his kingdom on orders from Spain. The population was stupefied by this action. Rich farms and orchards in mission areas quickly disintegrated as the black-robed friars were deported, and education was left in a shambles.

The viceroys themselves were not particularly interesting. One of them, José Solís Floch, 1753–1760, who had been a field marshal and a renowned lover of a good time, abruptly gave away his fortune and entered the Franciscan order, to live out his life in a monastery in New Granada. Pedro Messía de la Zerda, 1761–1773, left a depressing memorial regarding conditions in the viceroyalty when his reign was over. In treasury affairs he lamented the widely prevailing theft and fraud that continued despite improvements. He epitomized the difficulties of governing New Granada in two problems, disobedient vassals and barbarians. By the first he meant the lawless white settlers, the worse of the two conditions. Manuel Guirior, 1773–1776, found little to praise but the growing Church establishment, which then had 344 curacies functioning and a number of missions making inroads in what is now eastern Colombia and western Venezuela. While gold mining had made notable strides in recent years he felt that New Granada was far from attaining capacity output. Commerce was still largely in the hands of contrabandists. Agriculture and manufacturing he reported as greatly underdeveloped, and education was institutionalized only in the capital, and there weakly. In short, it would appear that New Granada's basic problems had yielded only slightly to the efforts· of the viceroys in almost forty years.

Revolt and Restoration

MANUEL ANTONIO FLÓREZ had an eventful reign between 1776 and 1782. His duties were simplified and his dignity affronted by the creation in 1777 of Venezuela as an autonomous captaincy-general. Free from this responsibility, Flórez had another British war to contend with. More revenues were needed at home, and he had to organize coastal defenses along the Caribbean to discourage another assault on the treasure shipments. In these undertakings the viceroy was afflicted with the presence of a royal *visitador* and superintendent of finances, Juan Gutiérrez de Piñeres, who, like his compeer Areche in Peru, was a difficult partner. Guitiérrez also resembled Areche in making himself at once unpopular by collecting back taxes, imposing the *alcabala* on the Indians, and raising the prices of liquor and tobacco. After the viceroy left the capital to attend to Cartagena's defense, the *visitador* remained as the symbol of autocracy and focus of resentment. In March 1781 a riot broke out in Socorro, a new town in one of the high valleys not distant

from Santa Fe de Bogotá. Soon the populace was tearing down proclamations announcing higher duties and restrictions on tobacco and liquor
sales. Enthusiasm for these activities grew so fast that neighboring communities joined the movement. Not only were the king's subjects unwilling to put up with the new exactions, but they also enjoyed looting the
warehouses and helping themselves to *aguardiente,* which heightened
their boldness. There was much talk of abolishing all taxes and monopolies. Meanwhile, a number of British vessels were off the coast, and a
marked apathy greeted the efforts of Viceroy Flórez to organize a militia.
In the capital, panic took hold. Only a small armed unit was available
to deal with the dissidents at Socorro, and it was quickly overpowered.
Now a crowd of several thousand men from the disaffected area stood
ready to march on the capital and enforce their demands for the end of
all taxes and monopolies. Led by Juan Francisco Berbeo, they were calling themselves *comuneros,* a term in Spanish history ominously signifying municipal rebellion.

Rather than face these outraged colonists, Visitador Gutiérrez
hastily departed for the coast. The respected archbishop, Antonio Ca-
bellero y Góngora, took charge with the agreement of the *audiencia.*
Late in May 1781, it sent a delegation to confer with Berbeo and his exultant followers. Berbeo's demands were not unreasonable in view of
the balance of power. The *comuneros* would be satisfied if the monopolies and new taxes were abolished and if creoles were given a large
share of government appointments. The authorities capitulated, signing
a pact to this effect in June, though one official wisely took the trouble
to swear that he had agreed only under duress. Berbeo came to Santa Fe
in triumph and seemed a hero to the creoles. But the absent viceroy and
visitador thundered from their respective headquarters that the whole
affair was illegal and promised punishment. Berbeo kept his followers
calm, but another leader, José Antonio Galán, roused the dissidents in
other localities and attempted to capture Gutiérrez. The second movement was smaller than the first, but more menacing, and its dangerous character was augmented when an Indian named Ambrosio Pisco
announced that he was the true heir of the Chibcha monarch. Inspired
by the Tupac Amarú rebellion in Peru, Pisco and his followers caused
considerable uneasiness among the whites but nothing on the order of
the convulsions farther south. These Indian threats served to demoralize
the followers of Galán and to rally the whites around the Spaniards.
Viceroy Flórez took an army from the coast into the interior and routed
the *comuneros* and Indians alike. Galán was executed, Berbeo stripped
of his newly-acquired office, Pisco imprisoned, and many others whipped
in public or shipped to the penitentiary in Spanish Africa. The pact
between Berbeo and the archbishop was, of course, cancelled. Once

Spanish authority was imposed, the usual generous supply of pardons calmed the kingdom.

After Flórez went back to Spain and his successor died, Archbishop Caballero served as viceroy from 1783 to 1788. He enjoyed considerable prestige, embittered as some of the *comuneros* were. A census he sponsored in 1788 showed 1,500,000 inhabitants in New Granada, considerably more than Peru reported. Royal revenues from the gold mines, monopolies, tributes, and, at last, from the customs were substantial and growing. The viceroyalty was beginning to flourish in most respects. That its long-suspected wealth was no illusion came out in a 25-year "expedition" organized by the archbishop-viceroy under the leadership of José Celestino Mutís, a priest from Cadiz who had come to New Granada in 1761. Sickly and too devoted to his work to be fond of people, the taciturn Mutís explored widely and collected an enormous variety of the kingdom's plant and mineral wealth. Greatly admired in South America, he also won the respect of European scientists for his labors in medicine, physics, and astronomy.

Under Viceroy José de Espeleta, 1789–1796, New Granada continued on its encouraging course, rapidly assuming shape as the nation it would soon become. Improvements were not limited to collection of revenue and missionary work among the Indians. A university in Santa Fe de Bogotá began to function, modestly but to good effect. The capital was already attracting foreign visitors who found this alpine community with its startling scenery, seemingly an isolated colonial town far from the routes to Europe, a would-be Athens of America. Its population was only 20,000, and it lacked the opulence of Lima or Mexico City, yet its inhabitants had an amazing respect for culture. The activities of Mutís were a great stimulation, and so was the press, which published news of the world and small volumes of poetry and fiction. This Shangri-la community was well started on its distinguished career as one of the most literary cities of the Americas—and one of the most literate, for schools were plentiful and reading was a pastime indulged in by many besides lawyers and priests.

Much as the printing press was to do for the capital, it brought tragedy to several young men in 1793. Their leader was Antonio Nariño, a collector of tithes, who came of a good creole family. Receiving a copy of the Declaration of the Rights of Man and Citizen framed in the early stages of the French Revolution, young Nariño was so moved he decided to circulate this thrilling message. Printed copies were widely distributed in Santa Fe, and some reached other American capitals. This fact disturbed the authorities less than the wild talk of Nariño's confederates regarding revolution, and the group was arrested after a few months. Shipped to Spain, Nariño escaped as his boat was being unloaded at Cadiz and went up to Madrid in disguise. After a time he went to England and then to France of the Directory, where he drank deeper at the fountains of liberty and met assorted radicals. He soon became an outright republican, one of the extremely few Spanish subjects to be so. With incredible rashness he returned to New Granada in 1797 and began a tour of the provinces to see if revolutionary sentiment was there to be fanned. Having no luck, he went to the viceroy probably in the hope of exchanging his store of subversive knowledge for a pardon. Instead he was betrayed, or at least rejected, and locked in a dismal cell for six years. Afterward he was sent into a rural community where he spent another six years in close internment. If the Nariño affair made little stir in New Granada and the man himself was almost unknown, he was to emerge later as a hero of the independence movement.

Pedro Mendinueta was viceroy from 1797 to 1803. His memorial to his successor is interesting testimony of the satisfactory state of New Granada at the turn of the century. Mendinueta declared that previous viceroys had painted too gloomy a picture of economic conditions. He reported no widespread misery but instead thirty or more cities and large towns and a multitude of haciendas, ranches, orchards, sugar plantations, and mines. Imports and exports were booming. Except for the frontier regions, the Indians were admirably settled in productive communities and, after a fashion, Christianized. The vast majority of the population were poor, as they were in every country, but they were far from brutalized. Smallpox vaccination promised to terminate one of the worst scourges of the people. Yellow fever and leprosy, this latter disease imported with African slaves, were still menaces. On the whole, however, he found the viceroyalty a heartening place. Not so long ago, he said, this area was a wilderness, full of mystery, savagery, an unfriendly nature, and enticing rumors. Now it was a real country with 2,000,000 civilized inhabitants and rapidly progressing. Improvements in all lines of endeavor were marked, particularly in the mining industry, which was producing more gold than ever. Glowing as Mendinueta's account was, the viceroy who received it was to see the viceroyalty shattered in revolution. Economic progress would be interrupted, and political life in New Granada would long be a mixture of chaos and sublimity.

Venezuela

THE history of colonial Venezuela followed a pattern of early attraction, disasters, violence, neglect, then a sudden spurt of growth toward the end, all leading up to an eventful career during the Wars of Independence. Spain's interest dated from the report of Columbus that he had located the site of the Garden of Eden in this bit of Caribbean coastland. It was Alonso de Ojeda, rather than the Discoverer, who first exploited the pearl fisheries there. Slave catchers from Hispaniola and Cuba frequently raided these shores, though the ferocity of the Caribs made their labors hazardous in the extreme. Father Las Casas made a calamitous effort to establish mission villages, and the German Welsers failed dismally to create a profitable colony. Before the middle of the sixteenth century Venezuela had an ominous reputation among the Spaniards. The few efforts at settlement resulted in a string of impoverished towns along the coast supported by primitive farms. Then the pirates and national enemies of Spain, particularly the Dutch, settled almost at will along this sector of the Spanish Main to grow food crops, tobacco, and sugar, and to dig for salt. The Dutch were to remain for long periods, operating veritable bases from which they could raid the Spanish empire and introduce contraband in defiance of the royal monopoly.

By the eighteenth century the Spanish had only a slippery foothold in this region. Nominally, the viceroy of Peru ruled the area, the *audiencia* at Santo Domingo supervised such justice as there was, and the bishop of Puerto Rico oversaw ecclesiastical affairs. Often the viceroy of New Spain was required to dip into his treasury to finance Venezuela's modest administrative and defense establishment. Contact with Spain was tenuous. A vessel or two might detach itself from the annual fleet to serve the little port communities, but once, for a period of thirty years after 1660, not a single authorized Spanish ship landed in Venezuela. After the War of the Spanish Succession it was obvious that more effort was needed if the colony was to become productive, indeed to be saved for the crown. Only a few thousand subjects lived in the string of coast settlements, most of them Canary Islanders, and were accustomed to being ignored by the home government. They produced sugar, indigo, tobacco, cacao, and hides in very modest quantities and traded chiefly with the Dutch, whose impudence grew steadily as nothing was done to dislodge them from the region.

One of the devices by which Felipe V hoped to renovate the Indies was the monopoly company, which would assume a privileged position in some of the underdeveloped colonies. Of the several such organizations formed with his support, only one succeeded very well over a long period, the Royal Guipuzcoan Company of Caracas which was chartered in 1728 to serve Venezuela. As its name implies, this organization centered in Guipúzcoa, a Basque city in northern Spain. The group of merchants who secured the charter planned to provide Venezuela with all its merchandise without competition and to monopolize the production and distribution of cacao, a commodity whose value was increasing as the European taste for chocolate grew. The crown was pleased to support the project because of the revenues it anticipated, the assistance the company promised in ejecting the Dutch, and the development of the colony in general. It was some months before the thrifty Basques could be induced to purchase all the company's stock, but by 1730 they were enthusiastic about the opportunity.

When the first representatives arrived in Venezuela and made known the intentions of the company, they found the inhabitants very cold to the prospect. They had long enjoyed official neglect, and they already had in the Dutch customers for their products and suppliers of their needs. With characteristic aggressiveness the Basques swarmed into the colony and prepared to channel all commerce to their advantage and to carve out plantations in the best areas. Spurred by the Dutch, the older colonists obstructed these proceedings as well as they could, sometimes employing Indian and Negro forces to intimidate the invaders. The Basques were able, however, to organize armed units of their own and to summon royal assistance when the going became too difficult for themselves to handle. By 1737 the company had made good its authority. Thriving cacao plantations, roads, warehouses, and port facilities were operating, and many Negro slaves were being imported. The colonists had to sell all their products to the company or see them rot. Royal and company ships all but broke the sea contacts of the Dutch, so that these accommodating smugglers could no longer bring merchandise into Venezuela. Hence the colonists had to purchase the company's goods or do without. During the war of 1739–1748 the company tightened its hold on Venezuela's economy and demonstrated its usefulness to the crown by employing its ships to chastise Dutch and British intruders. In all, the company was a huge success. Its profits were large, royal revenues were gratifying, and Venezuela was undergoing a profound development.

Unfortunately, the older colonists felt they paid the price for this progress. They complained of gouging on the part of the company, which palmed off cheap merchandise in Venezuela at high prices. In turn, the company set the price for cacao and raw materials, which naturally was to its advantage. The attitude of the officials was arrogant. It was clear that their interest was in making profits and that any benefit to Venezuela was incidental. And then the Canarians, like most Spaniards, detested the Basques. Tensions mounted during the war and came to the point of explosion as it ended.

Colonial grievances found a focus in 1749 when Francisco de León, a prominent planter and Canarian, was discharged from an official post by the company. The job itself probably meant little to León in a pecuniary way, for he was a substantial landowner, but his pride was injured. Again, the company had demonstrated its lack of consideration for the older stock. León's friends rallied to him with such fervor that a demonstration against the company developed. On two occasions mobs gathered in the central plaza of Caracas and demanded that the governor appear. This frightened dignitary did as he was told. With some orderliness representatives of the colonists listed their grievances and demanded that all Basques be removed from the company's management. Further, the governor was instructed to ask the king to have the company abolished altogether. The governor agreed, for he could do little else. For two years it seemed the colonists had won their point. The company remained, pending action in Madrid, but the most unpopular officials were ousted and the others were intimidated. León was something of a popular hero, no traitor to the king or subversive, but rather a responsible leader of outraged subjects.

The Spanish government was not accustomed to giving way to popular pressure. News of the riots in Caracas thoroughly alarmed the ministers, some of whom felt that a genuine secessionist movement was in progress. Under this misapprehension a potent expeditionary force was readied and shipped to Venezuela. There was, of course, no revolution to be quelled. Yet the military unit occupied the capital, arrested León, razed his home, and shipped him and other leaders to Spain. More trouble might have followed had the Spanish continued asserting their authority. Instead, they listened respectfully to the complaints of the Canarians and took a cold look at the manner in which the company had been operating. At this time, it will be remembered, Spain had a wise king in Fernando VI. After a lengthy airing of the issues, the authorities granted wide-scale amnesties, even releasing León himself, who lived out his life a free man in Spain. Then the Caracas Company was subjected to a thorough housecleaning. Its headquarters was removed from Guipúzcoa to Madrid, where the crown could keep a better eye on it. Extortionate practices were reduced and the worst abuses corrected. The company continued to function until 1785 with considerable success, and the Venezuelans shared its prosperity without notable grumbling. When it was abolished, it was not because of colonial complaints but because monopolistic companies had succumbed to the free enterprise doctrines of the physiocrats.

The growth of Venezuela in the last quarter of the eighteenth century moved the crown to set it apart as a captaincy-general in 1777, autonomous for all practical purposes from the viceroy of New Granada, its nominal suzerain after 1739. An *audiencia* was set up in Caracas in 1786, and the presence of bishops, intendants, and other officials indicated the colony had come of age. Caracas grew rapidly, attaining a population of 40,000 by the end of the century. Coro, one of the oldest ports, still functioned. Barcelona and Valencia grew to be small cities.

Along the torrid coasts were extensive plantations peopled by the usual creole aristocrats and Negro slaves. Behind the coasts were mountains, and then the grasslands began, extending to the Orinoco and beyond. Here were numerous Indian mission communities and great herds of wild cattle around whom a special society developed, the *llaneros*, or cowboys of mixed races who were to play such an important role in the Wars of Independence and after. Untamed Indians still lived farther to the south and in the Andes between Venezuela and New Granada. Perhaps three-quarters of a million people inhabited the captaincy-general. Then as now the Caribbean coastlands comprised the heart of Venezuela.

Because of its economic vitality—the sale of cacao, tobacco, sugar, indigo, and hides—Venezuela chafed more than many other components of the Spanish empire from the commercial restrictions. Britain and the United States, as well as the Dutch and French Caribbean colonies, were only too eager to trade with Venezuela. Yet the Spanish were generally able to prevent such intercourse until 1797, when another British war severely damaged Spain's naval power. Britain's acquisition of the island of Trinidad in that year forced an opening in Venezuela not only for contraband but for revolutionary ideas. And the rising of the Negro population against the French caused white refugees from Martinique and Haiti to throng into Caracas, bringing with them their modern and often radical notions. Illicit contacts with the United States had a similar effect. And a handful of Spanish radicals, who had attempted a republican uprising, no less, in Zaragoza in 1796, were sent to Venezuela for imprisonment. These advocates of revolution attracted kindred souls in Venezuela and were soon liberated. Their presence in the captaincy-general, along with that of other radicals, served to crystallize revolutionary sentiment. That precursor of the independence movement, Francisco de Miranda, was a Venezuelan. Dreaming that his compatriots were eager for freedom, he sent literature into the colony and indoctrinated Venezuelans he encountered abroad. A number of young men, among them Simón Bolívar, were responsive to such promptings. While Venezuela was not seething with subversive sentiment, its educated creoles were discontented with Spanish rule and interested in new ideas.

THE ORIGINS OF ARGENTINA

Argentina is the largest of the twenty Spanish-speaking nations in the world. Bigger in relation to other countries than it appears on conventional maps, the republic embraces a wide variety of climate and potentialities. In population Argentina follows Mexico and Spain, but her standard of living and her cultural level place her first in the Spanish family. Considering the slow start of this country during the long colonial period and its discouraging experiences in the first half-century of independence, its career is second only to that of the United States as an example of what European immigrants can accomplish in a productive land. This prosperous nation was close to being the least valued of Spain's American colonies until the last quarter of the eighteenth century. Then came a period of exhilarating growth under the viceroyalty and during the Wars of Independence, after which the nation fell on evil days. About 1860 it began another surge which brought it to the high position it holds today. It is our purpose here to examine not its whole history under Spanish rule but rather the living past, the aspects of that history which explain the phenomenon of its growth.

The Orphan Colony Buenos Aires

IT WOULD not be just to scold the Spanish for not appreciating the Río de la Plata basin during most of the colonial period. In the first place, they had misnamed it, for there was no silver anywhere near this muddy estuary and the monotonous flat land surrounding it. If the soil was such that almost any plant would thrive, this fact was no recommendation during the centuries when most parts of the world depended on themselves for foodstuffs. The improvements in food preservation and transportation that accompanied the population explosion of the nineteenth century brought the Argentine to the front as a producer. Before then, the region provided little of the sugar and chocolate craved by Europe. Nor did it possess minerals and woods that made colonies like New Granada valuable. And the nomadic Indians of the Plata area—the Puelches, Charruans, and still wilder tribes—were so hostile and scanty they scarcely aroused the cupidity of would-be exploiters or the proselytizing passion of the evangelizers. Almost the whole Spanish experience with this region, now so heavily populated and Europeanized, was discouraging for the first two centuries or more. The massive effort of Pedro de Mendoza in 1535 to establish a settlement had been a catastrophe. All that remained of it was a party that went up into Paraguay to organize a fairly solid community at Asunción. In 1580 the half-breed sons of these pioneers founded a permanent settlement at Buenos Aires, a windy point on the edge of the estuary. Their leader, Juan de Garay, had no reason to suspect that he was laying the foundation of the largest and most sophisticated city of the Spanish world.

Buenos Aires might have begun to flourish then had the crown encouraged it more. As it was, Spain herself was almost spent, and the imperialistic urge was to flag for more than a century. Peru was unquestionably a successful colony at that time, and respectful attention had to be paid to the merchants of Lima, who objected to the opening of a rival port at the other end of the continent. Accordingly, Madrid directed that no more than two ships a year could unload at Buenos Aires. Otherwise, the legal route for merchandise would have to be the channel from Sevilla to Puerto Bello, to Callao-Lima, and across nearly 2,000 miles of rugged terrain to the Plata colonists. A "dry customs" in the Andes would add 50 per cent to the cost of goods making this land passage. Naturally, this commerce was minute. The few and poor inhabitants around Buenos Aires could not think of paying such prices, especially when smugglers appeared off their coast to make more attractive offers.

For nearly forty years after its founding, Buenos Aires was ruled by the governor of Paraguay. For much of this period the governor was a capable man, Hernando Arias de Saavedra, who supervised the early development of the seaport. In 1617 Buenos Aires and the grassy flat-lands around it became a separate province with its own governor. A bishop, a few *corregidores* and *encomenderos*, a *cabildo*, and treasury officials completed the institutional structure. Once, between 1661 and 1671, an *audiencia* attempted to implant Spanish justice in this wild frontier. The task was too much, and judicial control reverted to the *audiencia* at Charcas, a thousand miles away. Lima was still farther, and the viceroy's authority was much diluted by the time it reached the Plata, though he continued to name most of the officials and to see that they were examined at the end of their terms. These officials might be tyrants if they instilled fear in the population. Otherwise they were likely to be ignored or to connive with contrabandists and other lawbreakers. Buenos Aires, in short, was usually a lawless community. This very fact may be at the root of the Argentine democratic tradition, for such a tradition indeed persisted despite all the colonial rulers and dictators of the country. More important than lawlessness in its development may have been the absence of sedentary Indians to form a lower caste or the fact that all the Spaniards were poor and hence egalitarian. Whatever the explanations, Buenos Aires from the first had a political atmosphere unique in Spanish America.

The commercial situation intensified the tendency of the *porteños*, as the inhabitants of Buenos Aires have always been called, to ignore crown authority. As southern South America slowly developed a few Europeanized communities, the need to import finished goods and to export raw materials grew proportionately. Buenos Aires, Paraguay, Chile, Charcas, and the foothill provinces on the Argentine side of the Andes had requirements that could not be filled by the cumbersome Spanish commercial system, especially after it became so dilapidated during the seventeenth century. No spot was quite so suitable for smuggling as the

Plata estuary, wide and smooth as it was and much closer to Europe than ports in Chile and Peru. The inhabitants were eager to do business, crown control was tenuous, and governors were more likely to participate in contrabandist activities than to be rigid about enforcing the laws. Furthermore, the casually-run Portuguese colony of Brazil was near by, and behind the Portuguese were the English. Even when the kings of Spain were also kings of Portugal, between 1580 and 1640, Brazil managed to ignore most of the commercial restrictions. After 1640 her monarchs sought ways to breach the Spanish pseudo-monopoly in the Plata. The results were what might be expected: the area was a large and growing leak in the Spanish commercial system. Foreign ships with goods and slaves put in almost at will and unloaded near Buenos Aires or across the estuary, a difficult feat, incidentally, for the waters were shallow and stevedores had to use horses to carry the cargoes to the shore. From Buenos Aires caravans of mule trains crossed the pampas into the cool interior and often across formidable passes of the Andes. Or smaller boats might sail up the complex of rivers that constitute the Platine system. Whatever the route, illegal merchandise and slaves in great numbers reached the western Argentine, Chile, Paraguay, Charcas, and sometimes Lima itself. These commercial arteries functioned in spite of the vast distances, marauding Indians, geographical obstacles, and occasional official interference. The heart of this system, Buenos Aires, pumped steadily for almost 200 years. Nothing the crown could do interrupted this process for long. Yet Buenos Aires did not become an attractive mart. It was no Constantinople or Venice. A squalid town with a few thousand whites and a smaller number of Negroes, it had mud huts with straw roofs, streets either dusty or choked with mud, and the morals of a frontier community. Indians sometimes raided this raw municipality and its own denizens, when drunk or riotous, could make quite an uproar themselves.

The Argentine of the future was to thrive on commerce, grain, and livestock. The beginnings of commerce in Buenos Aires are clear enough from the contraband trade of its earliest days. There was little, however, to suggest the potential of agriculture, though the rich, black topsoil of the pampas would nourish almost any crop of the temperate zone. Usually, the rude inhabitants cultivated only such grain as they consumed or could sell to the mining areas. No export trade was feasible, and the Argentines had little appetite for vegetables and fruits. One luxury article they relished was *yerba maté*, a tea-like plant long appreciated by the Indians. As for the livestock industry which has transformed modern Argentina, it showed little promise in early colonial times. A few animals had been left behind after Mendoza's ill-fated effort of 1535. Cabeza de Vaca imported more while he was governor of

Paraguay a few years later. These creatures multiplied quickly and were reinforced on a massive scale as their fellows wisely wandered down from Brazil into the cattle paradise that the pampas constituted. The grass was tall and rich. It even made the meat taste better to human palates.[1] The settlers were gratified as the wild herds increased on the grasslands, where the ostrich-like rhea, llamas, and armadillos also roamed. Livestock provided the early Argentines with food, hides, horns, and tallows to such an extent they scarcely needed to plant crops or concern themselves with procuring cloth or lumber. True, these animals were small, muscular, and long-horned. Yet they made human life comparatively easy on the frontier. There were so many of them that they were usually not regarded as private property, nor were the pampas where they throve. It was like the sea with all its fish. Men went out and took whatever they wanted—beef to eat, hides for clothes and tents, tallow for candles, bones for furniture—to return when they were ready for more.

The type of life which grew up around the herds of free cattle and sheep is now regarded with as much romanticism in Argentina as the Wild West is in the United States. The wind-burned men who preyed on the livestock, the *gauchos*, were a tough, adventurous lot. They might belong to any race or mixture of races. What they had in common was their life on the pampas centering around the cattle. Sometimes they were cowboys; but more often they were rustlers, highway robbers, Indian catchers, and contrabandists. They consumed beef and milk and, repulsive as it is to state it, blood. Their clothing was mainly of leather— jackets, gloves, caps, boots, and diaper-like *chiripás* which served as trousers. Their footwear was customarily fashioned by skinning a calf and placing the man's leg in the hide while it was still wet. Gauchos liked to leave the big toe free so it could be used to hold on to the stirrup or saddle-horn while they flung lassoes or *bolas*. These horseborne characters became very skilled in daredevil tricks and, as one would expect, in warfare. Their organization was essentially nomadic. They grouped themselves around leaders they feared or admired and raided towns or mule trains, fought one another, and chased Indians. They have a legendary reputation for being mystical and dreamy in the way of men who live outdoors, like fishermen. To civilized people they seemed superstitious, cruel, and mysterious. They developed a type of song that reflects these traits and strange, sad guitar music. By the end of the colonial period thousands of men lived the life of the gaucho. Soon after independence they overwhelmed the more advanced elements in Buenos Aires.

1. President Franklin D. Roosevelt once offended western ranchers with this assertion. Few who made the test would dispute him.

Tucumán, an Orthodox Colony of the Western Argentine

IF THE future lay with Buenos Aires and the surrounding pampas, it seemed during much of the colonial period that the most important part of the Argentine was the interior, the piedmont region of the Andes. The province of Tucumán ranked with Paraguay and Buenos Aires, having a governor appointed by the viceroy of Peru and falling under the jurisdiction of the *audiencia* at Charcas. Tucumán was originally settled by the off-pourings of Peru, disappointed Spaniards who had failed to make good or had been expelled for bad behavior. At first the province was called Nueva Inglaterra, since Felipe II was at the time king-consort of England. The towns of Córdova, Salta, Santiago del Estero, and Jujuy developed according to the conventional colonial pattern. Enough sedentary Indians were available to provide a laboring class. Crops of the type Spaniards liked, such as sugar, fruits, and grapes, could be raised here, and cattle and grain flourished in the more temperate sections. Upper Peru was close enough to serve as a market for food and hides. Also, millions of candles were needed for the mines each year, and this stimulated the cattle industry. Indians, of course, could be fed into labor forces that served the silver mines. Their fate was typical of the times. Some were converted and others rebelled and fled. Many became workers on the estates, and still more joined their fellow natives in the Andean mining region and never returned.

The province resembled other areas of Spanish occupation. As time went on, the towns grew to look like Spanish towns in architecture. Córdova became the home of a surprisingly good Jesuit university in 1624, and culturally it was much closer to Lima and to Spain than to crude Buenos Aires. Typical shops and markets functioned in the usual way, and small factories for cloth, furniture, bells, and carriages multiplied. Monotonous as the history of Tucumán seems for much of this period, the inhabitants underwent the usual shocks of Indian uprisings, scandals, and murmurs of defiance whenever the crown attempted to enforce the laws regarding Indian treatment and contraband. Both the white and the Negro population grew steadily, just as the Indian declined. Commerce, agriculture, ranching, and manufacturing made Tucumán seem far more advanced than its sister colonies in Chile, Paraguay, and Buenos Aires. But it had a sad destiny. The surge of Buenos Aires after 1776 was to bring economic stagnation to Tucumán, and the Wars of Independence were to leave it isolated and impoverished.

Paraguay, a Unique Colony

THE temperate climate and fertile soil of Paraguay offered the Spaniard an agreeable paradise, or so it seemed in 1540. Its Indians, mostly of the Guaraní group, were docile, probably because of their diet, and wandered about the land as classless and homeless folk. To the west and north were the fierce natives of the torrid Chaco whom the Spanish failed to subdue, though they did not try very hard. It was simpler to fasten the colonial system on the Guaraní.

Asunción, a Spanish settlement on the eastern bluffs on the Paraguay River, was the seat of Spanish authority in the Platine region until 1617, when Tucumán and Buenos Aires became provinces of equal stature. Yet Asunción failed to flourish, inviting as it was. It was simply too distant to tempt settlers from Peru or immigrants arriving at Buenos Aires. And it was off the principal trade routes from the ports to the mining regions of the Andes. Thus it was a stagnant province, its Spanish and mestizo inhabitants living comfortably enough off the labor of the Guaraní.

In a huge area to the southeast, on the banks of the Paraná River, was the great complex of Jesuit reductions comprising at its peak period 100,000 natives in nearly fifty villages. Two or three friars ruled each community with designated Indians as assistants. Livestock, yerba maté, sugar, grain, and other foodstuffs were cultivated with heartening success. The reductions were almost self-sufficient economically, and they had demonstrated their ability to fight off *paulista* marauders from Brazil and wayward Spaniards from Paraguay. From 1610 to 1768 the Society of Jesus operated this fantastic community. It seemed a splendid example of enlightened imperialism. Had the effects outlasted the presence of the Jesuits, one might draw enthusiastic conclusions from the experiment the way eighteenth-century writers did.

It was tantalizing to the thin crust of Spanish society in Asunción to have such large settlements of tamed natives living close by. They could put this labor to so much better use, or so they claimed, than the Jesuit friars. It was natural for them to believe and spread all kinds of tales about black-robed deviltry. They accused the Jesuits of exploiting their wards, of hiding vast treasures from the crown, of plotting to set up an independent state, and so on. After decades of tension between settler and friar, things reached the stage of crisis in 1720. The *cabildo* of Asunción disliked the governor of Paraguay and wanted to take the offensive against the Jesuits, no doubt to "liberate" some of the neophytes. The situation was so uncertain that the *audiencia* of Charcas sent a *visitador* named José Antequera to investigate. This Antequera locked up the governor and assumed his post, all with the approval of the *ca-bildo*, itself a suspicious circumstance. From 1721 to 1726 Antequera wielded the authority of governor, enriching himself and his support-ers while making threatening gestures at the Jesuits, who prudently militarized some of their wards to defend the reductions. Eventually the legal governor escaped and reported what was going on. When the vice-roy at Lima ordered Antequera to surrender the position he had usurped, the upstart suppressed the instructions and forged viceregal orders to legalize his position. Finally, armed forces from Buenos Aires closed in on Asunción and captured Antequera. He was taken to Lima, his home city and where he had many admirers among the creole ele-ment, who disliked the Jesuits. After five years of imprisonment there Viceroy Castel-Fuerte had him executed in the face of an ugly-tempered mob.

One would expect the matter to end here, amounting to nothing more than a rather startling example of a *visitador* running wild for a time. However, the citizens of Asunción had enjoyed their brief taste of freedom from crown control and still aspired to chastise the Jesuits. Soon they fell under the leadership of Fernando Mompox, who had been in jail with Antequera and was well-coached on conditions at Asunción. The *cabildo* declared that it was a commune and that Paraguay was a republic. Neither of these terms bore quite the revolutionary connota-tions they assumed in later periods, but it was clear that Asunción was asserting its intention of governing itself. If this so-called *comunero* movement was not frankly seditious, its implications were large indeed. For more than two years Paraguay held out against crown threats and military forays. In 1735 it collapsed, and Spanish authority returned. As a result of this affair Paraguay acquired a bad reputation in official circles as a province of rebellion and disloyalty. Asunción, never magnificent by any standard, declined. The ousting of the Jesuits in 1768 caused the ad-mired reductions to disintegrate rapidly. Soon Paraguay was a notoriously backward province.

The Viceroyalty of the Río de la Plata

MAINLY because of strategic reasons Buenos Aires came to the fore in the high policy of Spain during the second half of the eighteenth century. The sturdy little republic we know as Uruguay was the chief scene of a very long contest between the Spanish and Portuguese em-pires, and later between Argentina and Brazil. In 1679 a Portuguese ex-pedition appropriated a site on the northern side of the Plata estuary opposite Buenos Aires. The Spanish drove these intruders out with the help of Jesuit-led Guaraní soldiers, but Spain was compelled by European considerations in 1683 to concede Portugal a title to this spot, which the Portuguese named Colonia do Sacramento. The town throve as a smugglers' paradise, much to the discomfiture of both Spanish officialdom and rival contrabandists in Buenos Aires. During the War of the Spanish Succession, Colonia again fell to forces operating out of Buenos Aires, and once more a European peace treaty returned it to Portugal. In fact, commerce was growing so rapidly in the Platine area there was sufficient business for both competitors, legal and illegal. But the Spanish were irked at the impudence of the Portuguese and their British backers. Around 1725, Spaniards crossed the estuary to establish Montevideo on the Banda Oriental, or Eastern Shore. This town, composed originally of the scum of Buenos Aires, soon flourished as a commercial center and became what it has been ever since, a rival to its parent.

After a generation of violent competition between Colonia and Montevideo, the Treaty of Madrid in 1750 apparently settled matters by removing the Portuguese entirely from the Eastern Shore and giving them in exchange a district of Jesuit reductions with 30,000 wards. Much to the dismay of both Spain and Portugal, the Jesuits refused to change masters, beating off the Spanish, the Portuguese, and the combined forces until 1756, when they made a few concessions. This opposition, so understandable when one recalls the great harm the *paulistas* had inflicted on the reductions in times past, was probably a factor in convincing the rulers of Portugal and Spain that the Jesuits should be removed. In any event, the situation remained fluid. The Portuguese had remained in Colonia until the Seven Years' War, when they were expelled by a Spanish force. Still again, Spain returned it to Portugal in a European peace treaty. At this time Brazil was undergoing a drastic renovation and strengthening, and it seemed she would make good her control of the Eastern Shore.

Another strategic factor that concerned the Spanish was the ownership of the Malvinas Islands, which are now known as the Falklands by everyone but the Argentines. These rocky and starkly beautiful islands had long been useful to whalers in the South Atlantic. During the War of the Austrian Succession the British had discerned their greater significance as a base to dominate the waters of both the South Atlantic and the South Pacific. In 1764, Admiral Byron, grandfather of the poet, took possession of one harbor. In the same year a French explorer whose name was also to be remembered, Louis Antoine de Bougainville, led a party to another harbor. Spain protested and at length ousted the intruders, the French by persuasion, the British by force. In 1771, however, the British came back for three years, leaving again under Spanish pressure but threatening to return. The whole affair made Spain uneasy, linked as it was to Portuguese encroachments in the Eastern Shore and to the problem of oceanic control.

These dangers coincided with the projects of Carlos III to decentralize his American empire, the better to rule it. After years of consideration it was decided to create another viceroyalty with Buenos Aires as the capital. The inhabited parts of the republics we know as Argentina, Bolivia, Paraguay, and Uruguay were joined in this new entity. Only in Lima were strong protests made to the project, though Viceroy Amat himself recommended it. Much as the would-be monopolists in Lima objected to the severance of Upper Peru and its re-direction toward the Atlantic, their time was past. Monopoly itself was dead, and imperial considerations were far more important than historic pretensions. Thus, in 1776, the viceroyalty of the Rio de la Plata was announced. Its first viceroy, Pedro de Cevallos, set out from Cadiz with 115 ships and 19,000 men. It was an impressive force with which to begin an imposing new viceroyalty, to start, though he had no reason to suspect it, another well-starred nation in the New World that might truly date its birth with 1776. Cevallos landed at Montevideo and drove the Portuguese out of the Eastern Shore, this time for almost forty years. He also took the precaution of destroying Colonia altogether and scattering its population. Then, after a few months of organizing the new government in Buenos Aires, he was supplanted by another viceroy; the fall of Pombal in Portugal had brought about a friendlier atmosphere between Lisbon and Madrid, and Cevallos was too anti-Portuguese. Spain could now afford to conciliate Portugal, whose westward expansion beyond the Line of Tordesillas was again, and finally, recognized in exchange, among other things, for the loss of Colonia.

Juan José de Vértiz y Salcedo, who reigned from 1778 to 1784, performed the prodigious administrative labors needed to pull the huge viceroyalty together. It was indeed a gigantic task. Buenos Aires had about 24,000 white people and 7,000 colored, most of whom were Negro slaves or servants. The pampas surrounding it were lightly inhabited, and Indians and gauchos made life adventurous. Except for Montevideo the Eastern Shore was a grassy wilderness with a few gauchos and smugglers. Paraguay was in stagnation and official ill favor. Tucumán and Cuyo, the former Chilean province which had been annexed by the viceroyalty, seemed stable economically, if their creoles were not altogether happy over being wrenched from Lima and Santiago authorities. Upper Peru, whose treasure was now to come to Buenos Aires instead of Lima, had long since lost its pre-eminence in silver production and was, as we know, on the eve of the great Indian rebellion of the 1780's. Vértiz capably went about his duties, installing the eight intendancies ordered by Minister Gálvez, customs houses at the ports, and the rest of the paraphernalia that went with viceregal bureaucracy. When the Tupac Amarú insurrection spread into Upper Peru, he dispatched armed forces into the Andes and eventually pacified the region. A host of long-needed reforms in Buenos Aires was begun. An urgent one was public sanitation, which Vértiz undertook by directing the removal of dead animals from the streets and the digging of water ditches. A start was made in paving the streets, an exasperating task because of the soft mud, which refused to form a base. Streets were lit by lamps, the police were better directed, public schools begun, a park area set aside, and severe measures taken against alcoholism and card-playing. Vértiz opened a theater and won the applause of the population, or at least the fun-loving part of it, by expelling a clergyman who objected to the low tone of performances there. He was a good and a popular viceroy. And it was gratifying to see that revenues from hide exports spurted, the volume increasing eleven-fold in four years.

Firm administration continued under the Marquis of Loreto between 1784 and 1789. During this period an *audiencia* was established in Buenos Aires, which had for more than a century depended on justice from the distant court at Charcas. Commerce flourished in the Platine region, treasure pouring out of Upper Peru, and merchandise flowing into Buenos Aires, Montevideo, and the upriver town of Santa Fe. Every region seemed to benefit but Tucumán and Cuyo, who lost their markets on the coast for wines and finished articles to European competitors. Their decline had begun. They would be almost depopulated in forty years. On the other hand, the wizardry of Minister Gálvez had touched the subject of salted beef, a comparatively new process to preserve meat. Few people would eat such beef if they had any choice, but slaves in Cuba and Brazil had no choice, and a wonderful market expanded apace. To serve it, cattlemen somewhat regularized their practices. They began to claim some herds as their own, and not public, property and to mark out stretches of the pampas as ranches. In Buenos Aires slaughter houses were constructed near the shiploading points, stinking affairs with tell-tale carrion flopping above them. And hides continued to burgeon as exports.

Nicolás de Arredondo, viceroy from 1789 to 1795, organized the *consulado*, or chamber of commerce, an event which revealed how rapidly Buenos Aires trading firms were growing. He wrestled with the problem of paving the streets and enforcing hygienic measures. To be sure, the population continued its robust ways. Arredondo insisted that religious festivals did not justify the sacking of shops and homes, that fireworks must not be used as weapons, and that carnivals did not necessarily have to become city-wide debauches. It is apparent that civilized ways came slowly to the fast-growing, prosperous port city. The process was not helped by the greatly increased importation of Negro slaves from Fernando Póo, an island off Africa which Spain acquired in 1777 from Portugal. Many of the Negroes refused to serve as slaves and found ways to escape. Runaways from Brazil also swelled this element of the population.

Four viceroys served briefly between 1795 and 1804, Pedro Melo de Portugal y Villena, Antonio Olaguer Feliú, Gabriel de Avilés y del Fuero, and Joaquín del Pino. The administration of the viceroyalty continued stable; the regime was manifestly a success. The boom in Buenos Aires and adjacent areas more than balanced the decline of the interior. Commerce grew so fast that a delirious mood prevailed in some quarters. Whatever difficulties Spain had with France and Britain during these years, nothing seemed to interfere for long with the port's prosperity. Already it was displaying a mentality of its own, commercial and Europe-oriented, which would later cause much friction with the hinterland and make Buenos Aires almost a foreign city improbably planted on the coast with its back to South America. The city was also elevating its status culturally, though not to the extent of supporting a university in spite of repeated royal commands to begin one. There were newspapers, a reading public, primary education for all white males, and a College of San Carlos where political leaders of the future were learning much more than the authorities suspected.[2] And the city was finishing a cathedral, a huge, rectangular, colonnated affair modeled on the church of the Madeleine in Paris. Still unpretentious and muddy, Buenos Aires had a few domes and spires rising above the gray, one-storied barracks-type houses.

In 1804 the Marquis of Sobremonte arrived to assume the viceregal post. He observed, as his predecessors had, that the defenses of the port were far from imposing. Only a few cannon and an untried militia guarded this active city. Yet he was not mentally prepared for the news that reached him in June 1806. A British force of about 1,000 men had landed near the capital. This little army had sailed across the South Atlantic from an easy victory in Cape Town, which had been taken from Napoleon's unwilling Dutch allies. Its commanders, Admiral Home Popham and General William Carr Beresford, had no orders to invade the Plata, but for some time the British had been considering means to stir up independence feeling in the Spanish empire, another unwilling ally of Napoleon. Beresford simply marched his redcoats into Buenos Aires past stupefied citizens and silent cannon. Sobremonte took the treasury and fled to Córdova, not an altogether unintelligent action under the circumstances, but one which angered the *porteños*. Beresford was very

2. Many sons of Buenos Aires also im-   Chuquisaca in present-day Bolivia.
bibed modern ideas at the University of

correct, promising that Roman Catholicism would be respected and that open trade with England could now begin. He announced the separation of Buenos Aires from the Spanish crown. His troops had the most stringent orders to behave. Yet the inhabitants were aghast at this coup. Many escaped and joined a force of irregulars outside the capital being assembled by a French-born sea captain in the service of Spain, Santiago de Liniers. Meanwhile, Viceroy Sobremonte ordered the creation of military units in Córdova and Montevideo to liberate his capital. Liniers and his men struck first. Just six weeks after Beresford's entrance, Liniers marched his forces into the city to join the inhabitants, who were on a sort of general strike. Greatly outnumbered, the British asked for terms. Soon they sailed away.

The mood of Buenos Aires was one of exultation. Liniers was its savior, and the viceroy was threatened with death if he dared to come back. A few weeks later, in October 1806, news arrived that a huge British force had landed in Montevideo, 12,000 men under General John Whitelock. As luck would have it, Sobremonte was in Montevideo when the landing took place. Again he fled, reasonably but unheroically. At this point the *cabildo* of Buenos Aires, which for several years had been seething with ambition, proclaimed that Sobremonte was deposed and elected Liniers as military chief. This was not, of course, the way administrative changes were supposed to be made in the Spanish empire, but there was no one to prevent it. Whitelock went about his mission as Beresford had, keeping his men under order, promising respect for Catholic worship, and bringing in great quantities of merchandise which Britain had long been unable to sell in Europe because of the war with Napoleon. Also, the British were thirsting for a land victory, for they had suffered one disaster after another since the French Revolutionary wars had begun. Now they seemed to have an auspicious opportunity to take over a key portion of the Spanish empire. Yet the colonists would have none of it. Money and encouragement poured in on the beleaguered Plata from all parts of the American dominions of Spain. And if the inhabitants of the occupied towns traded with the British and read radical propaganda they had thoughtfully brought along, they were still fervently pro-Spanish. When, in the summer of 1807, Whitelock at last sailed his forces from Montevideo across the estuary to the Buenos Aires side, he found a well-organized army under Liniers facing him. And beyond these troops was an aroused city where people were ready with sticks, rocks, and scalding water to greet the heretics. After a few days of fierce fighting Whitelock gave up his attempt and re-embarked his forces. Britain would one day achieve land victories over Napoleon in the Spanish monarchy, but not in Buenos Aires.

Spanish America was jubilant over the triumph of Buenos Aires.

Congratulations from *cabildos* and authorities all over the empire rained on the *porteños,* who were bursting with self-confidence. Carlos IV expressed his gratification at the successes of his subjects and recognized Liniers' role by making him interim viceroy of La Plata. This was as close as Spain was ever to come to authorizing popular choice of officials in the days of her empire. It was obvious that Buenos Aires had beaten back the British offensives with little or no aid from the monarchy. The city had also tasted the fruits of free trade and found them pleasing. And the circulation of revolutionary propaganda by the British spread germs of ideas among the creoles. The mood of Buenos Aires on the eve of the fall of Carlos IV in 1808 was one of unlimited ambition. It is a pity that her leaders were not as well prepared to rule themselves as they thought.

17

The Later Colonial Period in Brazil

THE history of Brazil often seems formless, the events having little logical sequence or relationship to each other. Developments in some parts of this enormous land, which is almost a sub-continent, often had no bearing on the evolution of other sections. The white settlers from Portugal and their heirs tightened their hold on the coastlands and a few parts of the interior. Unwilling African immigrants became more numerous; many obtained their freedom from slavery and mated with persons of other races. The relations of the Portuguese and Negro elements with one another and with the native Indians gave Brazil a unique social history. Economic developments were sudden in some localities, steady in others; in all, Brazil grew much more productive in the later colonial years. Rather weak institutions kept the imperialist system from being overly autocratic and did little to unify the communities strung out over such an expanse. They were effective enough, however, to give Brazil an enduring Portuguese stamp. Inchoate as Brazil was during the colonial period, an outline of the future nation dimly appeared.

THE ADMINISTRATIVE MACHINERY

Brazil was the property of the Portuguese crown, very much as the Spanish kingdoms in America belonged not truly to Spain but to its monarchs. The early kings of the house of Braganza, particularly João IV (1640–1656) and Pedro, prince regent from 1667 to 1683 and king as Pedro II from 1683 to 1706, were respectful of Brazil's importance, particularly since it was their most profitable possession after the losses in the Far East earlier in the century. Usually they sought to govern in a responsible fashion and to conciliate a population who had displayed such initiative in ousting the Dutch in the years before 1654. An Overseas Council in Lisbon handled all official matters concerning the colonial empire but ecclesiastical affairs, which had a special agency. Officials were dispatched and recalled systematically as they were in the Spanish Indies, though they tended to remain in office longer. Taxes were similar to those in the sister Iberian colonies but were usually lighter and more haphazardly collected. Brazil continued to be divided into provinces ruled by officials known as captains-general or governors or, in one case, a *donátario*, vestige of the early sixteenth-century experiment. The governor of the most important province, Bahia, usually bore the title of viceroy, but not until 1763, when Rio de Janeiro became the chief province, did this dignity approach the significance of the viceregal position in the Spanish empire. Seldom were the other provinces under the viceroy's control. Their ties were with Lisbon, which helps explain the localism and eventual federalism that have been such strong forces in modern Brazilian history. Smaller units within each province were under the authority of a *capitão-mor*, whose functions resembled those of the Spanish *corregidor* or governor in Europeanized areas. A town of substantial size was likely to have a *senado da câmara* composed of creoles, usually the most important landlords in the district. Brazilian municipalities seem to have displayed more assertiveness than Spanish American towns. The courts, however, were much weaker than the *audiencias*. On the whole, the Portuguese administration was less effective and more easy-going than that of Spain, much as it resembled it in structure.

This was also true of the Church. As in Spain, the monarch enjoyed the power of patronage, which might have enabled him to dominate the ecclesiastical establishment. Often it was the other way around, for the royal court tended to be subservient to the clergy. The Brazilian Church was not as rich nor as extensive as the Spanish American Church, though Bahia and Rio de Janeiro were extravagantly endowed with Catholic buildings and there were numerous missions. An archbishop in Bahia and, by the end of the colonial period, nine bishops in other provinces composed the upper hierarchy of the Church. As was usual in a colonial land, parish priests were in short supply. The regular orders—Jesuits, Carmelites, Capuchins, Benedictines, and Franciscans—were perhaps less conspicuous in Brazilian towns than they were in those of Peru or New Spain. Their labors among the Indians, however, were often more notable than those of their Spanish brethren in South America. Large communities of missions in the far north and the southwest shielded thousands of natives from labor-hungry settlers and slave-catchers. The Inquisition had no permanent office in Brazil, though its agents sometimes toured the colony and bishops could apprehend suspects and send them to the Holy Office in Lisbon. It is obvious that heresy often went undetected or unpunished. Jews had been comparatively numerous since the earliest days of the colony and some of the Negroes adhered to Islam. Protestantism posed no threat at all to Brazil's orthodoxy, at least after the expulsion of the Dutch.

THE ECONOMY

Commerce

THE Portuguese commercial system varied considerably from the Spanish, even if its underlying assumption—that the mother country had every right to regulate the colonial economy to its own advantage—was the same. Fundamental differences from the Spanish monopoly arose from several circumstances. One of them was the absence, for much of the colonial period, of the precious metals that made the Spanish Indies such a desirable possession. Another factor was the official connivance of the Portuguese government in smuggling, not in its own territory, but in the Plata region at the expense of Spain. Pedro II in particular sought to win and hold a permanent base for this purpose. From 1683 to 1705 and at subsequent periods the contraband port of Colonia do Sacramento brought substantial profits to Portugal by virtue of illegal trading with Buenos Aires, the distribution mart for goods destined for Potosí, Chile, and other distant areas. The 200 or more vessels which sailed annually from Portugal often carried European merchandise not for Brazilians but for Spanish Americans. The chief distinction between Spanish and Portuguese commercial operations stemmed from the fact that England, the foremost naval power by the late seventeenth century, was an ally and not an enemy of Portugal. A treaty with Cromwell in 1654 authorized the English to send to Lisbon for trans-shipment all the goods they thought the Brazilians would buy. English representatives were permitted to live in both Portuguese and Brazilian ports to supervise this trade. This privilege was extended in a treaty of 1662, when Catherine of Braganza married King Charles II, and the Methuen treaty of 1703, which facilitated the exchange of Portuguese wines for English textiles. Seldom was less than half the freight carried in Portuguese ships from Portugal to Brazil of English origin. Thus England had every reason to protect and not harass Portuguese shipping and even to patrol South American waters to keep out smugglers.

Most of the trade was controlled by a monopolistic company protected by the crown, the General Company of Commerce, or the Company of Brazil, founded in 1649 and largely financed in the beginning by convicted Jews, who thereby purchased their freedom. Its original purposes were to supply flour, codfish, olive oil, and wine in four of the chief provinces in Brazil, to monopolize the wood trade, and to tax other important exports. As so frequently happened in these situations, the company paid its way but often clashed with the authorities and antagonized the colonists. In 1664 the crown withdrew the company's charter but continued to employ its machinery to dominate commerce in the principal areas for another thirty years. Under this arrangement a convoy system was organized so that two or three fleets a year might sail from Lisbon to Bahia, where branch fleets went to Rio and Pernambuco and Colônia. After the expiration of the company in 1694, annual fleets were usually dispatched until the reforms of the late eighteenth century.

Always eager to discover ways to make Brazil more productive, for the colony was economically stagnant during much of his reign because of competition from the sugar of the West Indies, Pedro II organized the Company of Maranhão and Pará in 1678. These two provinces, lying east of the mouth of the Amazon in the flat, forested tropics, had few and impoverished inhabitants, but they did not take kindly to the monopolistic practices of the company. In 1684, resentful of royal methods and, as will be seen, of Jesuit efforts to protect the Indians, a group revolted under Manoel Bekman and threatened to set up a plutocratic republic. The crown backed down and abolished the company. Another effort was made in that region in 1755 under a monopoly which achieved some success during its twenty-odd years of existence, especially in stimulating the slave trade and the cultivation of cotton and rice. The fourth such organization, the Company of Pernambuco and Paraiba, tried from 1759 to 1778 to dominate the trade of those richer provinces but caused so much dissatisfaction that it was abolished. Besides, mercantilistic agencies of this type were no longer in vogue.

The Production of Raw Materials

IT HAS been Brazil's fate to supply the outside world with luxury articles, which are eagerly purchased when times are good but are the first to suffer declining demand when conditions are bad. Sugar, fine woods, cacao, tobacco, cotton, gold, diamonds, coffee, and rubber, along with other items of the economy, have undergone boom-bust cycles which have given Brazil a turbulent economic history. The country has also been unfortunate in losing its best markets to foreign competitors. In the case of sugar, it was the West Indies; of fine woods, to some extent New Granada; of cacao, Venezuela; of tobacco and cotton, the United States among others; of diamonds, India; and of rubber, the Far East. Coffee, a late-comer in the colonial period, has lost ground to Spanish America and Africa but is still king in Brazil.

For the entire colonial period sugar production was Brazil's most stable and profitable industry. The long depression it suffered during the second half of the seventeenth century finally came to an end, for the European appetite for sweets and rum continued to grow. Dye-woods for the European textile industry and fine woods for furniture also had a steady if modest marketability during the whole colonial phase and after. In the general economic revival of the mid-eighteenth century, cotton, tobacco, cacao, and rice became significant exports that enriched certain landowners and traders. If the cattle industry had little value in international trade but for hides and tallow, the increase in herds, especially in the grassy provinces of the south, meant settlement of those areas by Portuguese and an ultimately sound ranching establishment. Beef and foodstuffs raised locally provided most of the nutrition required by the population. It was not abundant by any means, yet Brazil was not a land of starvation.

For nearly 200 years Brazil had been a great disappointment to her owners in the matter of minerals. While the Spanish colonies grew rich on bullion, the Brazilians supported themselves and exported nothing more valuable than woods and sugar. The difference was apparent in the comparative wealth and advancement of the two colonial empires, in which all the advantages were on the Spanish side. The Portuguese crown had long yearned for treasure and stimulated prospecting. Not until 1696, however, were significant sources discovered. In that year a roving band of *bandeirantes* found gold lying in shallow deposits in river beds in the bleak hilly area well behind Rio de Janeiro and São Paulo. The excitement provoked by this event can scarcely be described. Brazil was then a string of settlements, rather poor and somnolent and undergoing a long period of business depression. Suddenly there was gold! The good news circulated rapidly, the government itself committing the folly of advertising the discovery. A fantastic rush ensued. Officials deserted their posts, plantation owners took their slaves and started south, towns were depopulated of vigorous men, and when the news reached Europe, a new wave of immigrants arrived to plunge into the treasure hunt. As thousands of greedy and tough characters overran the area, general anarchy prevailed. Men fought over the placer gold deposits and slaves, who in turn escaped and often killed their masters, and epidemics raged. In the deserted areas stagnation and near famine for the stay-at-homes resulted. The crown had every intention of applying the ancient regulations concerning the royal fifth, but for a generation it collected little. Fiscal agents were intimidated, bribed, or fooled, and perhaps nine-tenths of the royal share evaded the king's officers. During this chaotic period the *paulistas* themselves were driven away in a bush war by the newcomers. So they continued to hunt for treasure, and found still vaster deposits of gold in Goyaz and Mato Grosso.

The gold regions were slow to settle down. As deposits were exhausted and more were discovered in the isolated interior, the prospectors migrated from place to place, keeping much of the colony in turmoil. Royal authority they flouted whenever they could. They fought over slaves and stole them from one another, a situation that enabled many Negroes to win their liberty. The crown regretted having publicized the new sources of wealth. When the Jesuit Antonil published a book locating accurately the mining areas, the crown sought to destroy every copy. That such precautions were not altogether fantastic was illustrated by the French occupation of Rio de Janeiro during the War of the Spanish Succession. Had the fortunes of war been different, some of the gold-producing regions might have experienced an invasion.

At length, royal authority was asserted over these areas. By taxing Negro slave workers and collecting at least some of the royal fifth, enormous revenues came to Lisbon. It was possible to establish some order in Minas Gerais, as the land came to be called, and the rowdy criminal atmosphere slowly sobered. As for the gold-seekers who were disappointed, many of them remained in Minas Gerais or São Paulo to become farmers, ranchers, or merchants. The center of gravity in Brazil began to shift from the north to the south.

In 1726 a group of *paulistas* learned that stones lying innocently on the surface in river beds of upper Minas Gerais were in truth diamonds. On this occasion the government was better able to deal with the situation and managed to encircle much of the area so that only licensed prospectors, in the main, could be admitted. The diamond rush in these so-called Forbidden Lands was far less sensational and less important than the gold discoveries. Fewer laborers were needed, and no stunning population shifts occurred on this account. For several decades great quantities of industrial and ornamental diamonds flowed to Europe. In time, the market became glutted and prices fell, but diamonds never fail to attract buyers, and Brazil had another steady source of income until late in the eighteenth century.

The revenues from gold and diamonds permitted the Portuguese monarchy to live in great style and to dispense with such trouble-making institutions as the *côrtes*, or parliament, which did not meet between 1697 and 1820. The kings grew not only much richer but also more autocratic. As in the case of Spain, the treasure was largely misused. Portugal did not imitate Holland or England in developing a sound commercial and industrial foundation. Rather, she employed her income to play a role on the international stage larger than her size warranted and to construct hundreds of churches, convents, monuments, palaces, and public buildings, most of them in the rococo style so admired in the eighteenth century and so deplored now. Except for lower taxes, the population as a whole received little benefit from the Brazilian revenues. The terrible earthquake which shattered much of Lisbon in 1755 seemed to many a divine punishment for the extravagance of the royal court. But while it lasted, until late in the century, the influx of gold and diamonds was pleasant for the king and other individuals who shared it. The scale of living and the ostentation made Portugal a glamorous kingdom for the upper classes.

BRAZILIAN SOCIETY

In considering social conditions of the later colonial period, it is natural to divide the population as the government did: Portuguese, Indians, and Negroes. Each race affected the others, but usually a type of segregation that went beyond the laws was maintained. The Portuguese immigrated at a small but steady rate and slowly imparted to the coastal areas their language, religion, and customs. They were a very small minority of the total population, and they were divided among themselves on class lines and on the basis of peninsular or creole birth. These whites were the owners of almost all the productive lands and the businesses. Peninsulars were likely to live in towns, where they were merchants or professional men. They tended, though not so much as in the Spanish colonies, to staff the organs of state and Church. While the creoles were scattered, their chief center of power was the sugar plantation area, where they lived as lords amid slaves and isolated from one another. Often they ignored the government. Whether the whites were peninsular or creole, rich or poor, rural or urban, they were the ruling element in the land and usually regarded themselves as Portuguese rather than Brazilians. They had little reason or inclination to resent the crown except, as people always do, to complain of being taxed and ruled from afar.

The Indians, who numbered possibly a half-million, were very much divided. The main linguistic types—Tupi-Guaraní, Ge or Tapuyan, Arawak, and Carib—had hundreds of·sub-divisions. By the eighteenth century perhaps a majority of natives lived as wild or free men, some of them cannibalistic savages in the Amazon vastness. Their contact with other races was usually hostile, a matter of *paulistas* invading their lands or escaped Negroes fleeing westward. As for those who lived in the civilized regions, some were slaves, this notwithstanding the brief effort of the crown in 1605 and 1609 and on subsequent occasions to outlaw this system. In the older areas groups of Indians lived under royal protection, or so it was called, somewhat like the crown Indians in the Spanish empire. Most of the Indians in white-controlled areas, however, were dominated by the church in mission settlements, where Franciscans, Capuchins, Benedictines, and Carmelites—above all, the Jesuits—isolated their wards.

The Society of Jesus had great momentum after the notable labors of Nóbrega and Anchieta in the sixteenth century. The success of this order in Paraguay early in the seventeenth century also served to strengthen its leadership. And after Portugal won its freedom from Spain, the Jesuits exerted, usually, an immense influence on the royal court at Lisbon. Important as these factors are, the Society enjoyed a great advantage in the services of Antonio Vieira, a remarkable friar whose career suggests comparison with Bartolomé de Las Casas in the early days of the Spanish empire. Even in temperament and longevity the two men were similar.

When Vieira arrived in the backward provinces of Maranhão and Pará in 1652, he was already famous as a preacher and very influential at court. What he found in Brazil shocked him. The laws regarding humane treatment of the Indians were totally disregarded, Christianity was not being taught, and the settlers were generally behaving outrageously, he reported. He attempted to shame the whites into acting with more decency, but, like Montesinos and Las Casas before him, succeeded only in stirring up their wrath against himself. Thus he returned to Portugal to obtain stronger royal backing; the crown usually meant well by the Indians, and Vieira secured the authority he wished. When he went back to Maranhão, the Jesuits had permission to take over all the natives. The brothers were to instruct them and to permit them to work for wages only half the time, in three two-month periods each year. To assure a respectful reception of this mandate Vieira brought with him a strong-willed governor and a military unit.

The work got under way with the energy characteristic of the more zealous missionaries. Indians were somehow persuaded to live in mission villages and to accept the guidance of the black-robed friars. As might be expected, the colonists complained piteously. Once, in 1661–1662, they chased the Jesuits out and saw to it that Vieira was hounded by the Inquisition when he reached Portugal. Turbulence around the Portuguese throne during the reign of Afonso VI (1656–1667)[1] permitted a lapse in Jesuit influence at court, but the order was in good graces again by 1679. In that year the Jesuits returned to Maranhão and Pará, and in 1680 the crown ordered that all Indians be freed. Again the colonists were unhappy, and when the Company of Maranhão further

1. This unhappy king was erratic and vicious. A plot by his wife and his brother Pedro led to his being confined to a large room in the Castle of Cintra. Pedro became regent and, in 1683, king; Afonso's queen obtained an annulment and married Pedro.

irritated them in economic matters, the Bekman revolt threatened to withdraw the area from the monarchy. The crown retreated, abolishing the company and ordering the Jesuits to share the natives with other friars. Vieira was in and out of this region, Portugal, and other parts of Brazil until his death in 1697 at the age of eighty-nine, a veritable scourge of those who abused the natives.

If the mission system had a limited effect in saving the Indian population from mistreatment and extinction, it is likely that thousands of natives lived out their lives in peace because of Vieira and less famous friars. Until the middle of the eighteenth century the missions sheltered thousands of Indians. Then, they were invited by the crown to become citizens on the same basis as whites if they lived and acted like Europeans.[2] Some accepted the opportunity but tended to become part of the lowest free classes in the towns. Others fled to the jungle or remained in mission reductions. In the long run, the aborigines in Brazil all but disappeared from civilized areas.

The Negroes retained their identity but had a sad enough history. By 1800 probably half the three million inhabitants of the country were pure-blooded Africans, most of them slaves. The slave trade itself went on with few interruptions, constantly bringing in more laborers. Everywhere the Negro was in evidence, above all on the sugar plantations. He was also in the mining regions, grazing lands, and plantations where cotton, rice, and other crops were raised. Negroes worked in the towns in nearly every capacity. Their influence pervaded nearly very aspect of life, affecting, among other things, the music, dialects, sports, pleasures, and Catholicism of the country. Much as they modified the language, customs, and religion of the Portuguese, they in turn adopted these practices, by and large. And, of course, the process of racial fusion went on continuously, producing the mulattoes, who were usually free plebeians, and the mixture of Negro and Indian, which was regarded as the lowest form of human life in colonial Brazil. The harshness of the institution of slavery and its degrading social effects do not need to be detailed. While there is no scientific way to verify the point, the tradition lingers that slavery in Brazil was less brutal than in other parts of the New World.

Strikes, mutinies, and organized escapes apparently occurred intermittently, though no general uprisings seem to have taken place. When Negroes broke away from their masters, they were likely to head for the forests or jungles, where *quilombos*, or settlements, might be founded. There the escaped slaves might kidnap whites and hold them for ransoms of guns, horses, or supplies. They might prey on the Indians. Some

2. This same option has been open to Negroes in Portuguese Africa in the mid- twentieth century. Apparently few have taken advantage of it.

of these larger communities in palm forests were known generically as *Palmares*. The most famous of these was begun in the hinterland of Pernambuco during the 1630's. Surviving a Dutch effort at destruction, this community of free Negroes, probably the largest in the New World until Haiti became free, maintained itself for most of the century. Surrounded by an extensive palisade of palm trunks, it was a fortified point. Inside were homes for thousands of Negroes, gardens, and a large lake stocked with fish. Fairly advanced social institutions existed: an elected king, a council, and laws. As the settlement grew, it became more and more a threat to the plantation lords in Pernambuco, not only as an attraction for their slaves but because of the pillaging for which it served as a headquarters. Spasmodic efforts to besiege or defeat Palmares came to nothing. The challenge it posed was growing. At last, in 1689, the governor procured the services of units of colored *bandeirantes* from São Paulo. For eight years these forces, militarized Indian and Negro organizations from the north, and white militiamen kept up the war. The number involved in these attacks must have been well in the thousands. In 1697 a protracted siege finally brought about the collapse of Palmares. Many of its defenders, including the king, jumped or were pushed over a cliff. The survivors were branded with the fugitive's "F" and widely distributed so they could not regroup. No other *quilombo* was ever again allowed to become so formidable.

REFORM, PROGRESS, AND A WHISPER OF REVOLUTION

The Portuguese monarchy underwent a drastic modernization comparable to the Bourbon reforms in Spain in the mid-eighteenth century. After the long reign of João V (1706–1750), a period of profligacy thanks to the gold and diamonds of Brazil, a new king came to the throne. This José I (1750–1777) had little taste for the cares of ruling and turned matters over to a dynamic minister, José Carvalho, better known as the Marquis of Pombal, a title he was given in 1770. Pombal was practically a dictator from the great earthquake of Lisbon in 1755 until the death of José I, when he was disgraced. Many reforms that had long cried for enactment now received it. The bureaucracy felt the results of his drive for efficiency and underwent improvement. Military and naval affairs, economic matters, and education received intelligent direction. With great relish the enlightened minister attacked the Church, reducing its wealth and numbers and, after a trumped-up charge of conspiracy to assassinate the king, expelling the Jesuits in 1759. This bold action was copied, as has been seen, by Spain and other countries within a few years. Portugal remained a comparatively backward and inefficient country, but the vigorous policies of Pombal gave her a new lease on life and enabled her to function with some effectiveness until Napoleon's troops arrived in 1807.

Brazil did not escape the critical eye of the despotic minister. Early in his rule, he dispatched his brother to the colony to make an inspection. The resulting report of Jesuit wealth, arrogance, and tutelage of the Indians may have had something to do with his action in 1759. Certainly Pombal had been chagrined by the role of the Society in preventing the cession of large areas of Paraguay to Portugal in accordance with the Treaty of Madrid in 1750. The injury which the expulsion of the Jesuits brought to Brazil's very frail educational establishment he attempted to repair by directing the *cámaras* in leading towns to create schools. As for the Indian wards left orphaned, he offered them the opportunity to become subjects on the same basis as the whites if they were sufficiently Europeanized. Pombal enunciated a policy that henceforth the Portuguese king would distinguish his subjects on the basis of merit and not color. If few practical effects flowed from this tolerant edict, it lent royal sanction to the direction Brazilian society was taking, one that would make it the least color-conscious country in the world. This direction was also shaped by laws to improve the treatment of Negroes, though slavery continued to flourish and the slave trade with it. Then, Pombal strengthened the administrative system and the law courts through better surveillance and greatly improved appointments. Two new trading companies and imaginative efforts to stimulate mining, agriculture, and commerce brought heartening results. Portuguese military units went to Brazil during the Seven Years' War and the crises with Spain that finally terminated with the Treaty of San Ildefonso in 1777. As in the Spanish empire, a colonial militia was created. In 1763 the capital was moved to Rio de Janeiro, an acknowledgment that southern Brazil was as valuable as the northern sugarlands.

Brazil was still a backward colony by the end of the eighteenth century, far behind New Spain, La Plata, and Peru in wealth, culture, and organization. The viceroy at Rio had little power over the sprawling provinces stretching from Maranhão to the Banda Oriental, and the administration remained lax. There were few *letrados*, or learned persons, on the colonial scene. Brazil had no university or college, only a few very unpretentious schools. No printing presses functioned in the entire viceroyalty, and book shops and private libraries were few. While brilliantly ornate churches and residences filled Bahia and Rio de Janeiro, Brazilian architectural achievements were far lower than those in Spanish America. A superior painter had appeared, however: Antonio Francisco Lisboa, a mulatto who decorated churches in Bahia and Ouro Preto despite the leprosy that ate away his hands. And another mulatto,

José Mauricio, composed worthy works of sacred music toward the end of the colonial period. Yet cultural life was very retarded in comparison to the United States and the Spanish viceroyalties. Rio de Janeiro itself was colorful and fun-loving despite its incredible dirtiness. Certainly it lacked the stateliness of Mexico City or Lima and the vitality of Boston or New York.

Brazil was not so backward that she failed to share in the revolutionary spirit of the age. During the 1780's a group of Brazilian youths who attended the University of Montpellier in southern France absorbed some of the Enlightenment. One of them wrote hopefully to Thomas Jefferson, the American minister in Paris, who did not reply. After they came home, their interest in revolution wore off, but a few of them discussed the new ideas that were about to bring France to such epochal convulsions. In both Rio de Janeiro and São Paulo a handful of "philosophers" enjoyed this kind of talk.

One man who became interested was a middle-aged army officer named Silva Xavier, who was known as Tiradentes because he had been, among other things, a tooth-puller. A failure in business and a long-unpromoted lieutenant in the army, perhaps he bore a grudge against the government and society in general. Or he may have been one of those inexplicable idealists who played such a role in the great revolutions of the times. Whatever his inspiration, Tiradentes spoke very indiscreetly of republics and rebellions without being molested. In the years 1789–1792, however, a period known as the *inconfidencia* produced many expressions of disaffection in São Paulo and Minas Gerais, not so much because of revolutionary events abroad as because the government sought vigorously to collect back taxes from mine owners and to impose new ones. Possibly a genuine plot to subvert the system was concocted. At any rate, crown officials thought so and arrested a number of known liberals, including Tiradentes. Most of the alleged conspirators were freed, but Tiradentes had been so outspoken it was decided to hang him. Perhaps his mistake was to be guileless enough to link grumbling against the tax collectors to the smattering of revolutionary thought he had learned from the former students. So far there was little material for martyrdom or hero-worship in his case, for he was altogether pathetic, but at the scene of his hanging Tiradentes made an eloquent speech, full of idealism and generosity. Somehow he left an enduring impression and was talked about for years, usually admiringly. While Brazil did not become independent until 1822 and remained a monarchy until 1889, Tiradentes eventually became a national hero and martyr to those who search history for such.

18

Eduation and Ideas

During the three centuries they controlled much of America, the Iberian nations imparted their civilization far more successfully than most other imperialistic powers. They gave what they had, and the daughter countries became firm participants in Hispanic culture. The Spanish and Portuguese languages have, of course, persisted, as have the religion, habits, customs, standards, and most of the attitudes of the former ruling powers. Of most importance in the diffusion of Iberian culture were the settlers, themselves often persons of little formal education but steeped in Western civilization. Clerical missionaries were also cultural agents of the utmost significance, and the constant coming and going of officials, the laws and decrees, and the circulation of peninsular literature likewise kept the European population oriented toward the homeland and slowly affected the colored and mixed races.

SCHOOLING

Until comparatively recent times the educational policy of the Spanish monarchy has been unfairly belittled. Only in the nineteenth century did universal schooling become a general ideal even in the most advanced nations of the world, and it is far from remarkable that in earlier times the rulers of Spain cherished no ambition to provide instruction for the masses. There as elsewhere it was assumed that literacy was desirable only for males of the upper classes and for certain categories of public servants. If, in the late eighteenth century, the most civilized country in the West, France, could claim that no more than one-fifth of its population could read and write, a lower fraction in Spain, Portugal, and Latin America could scarcely excite justifiable condemnation. In this context, it becomes evident that Spain provided a comparatively substantial apparatus for education in her overseas empire. According to law, every *cabildo* was supposed to maintain a public school; by the mid-eighteenth century, most of them did, though teachers were very scarce. Private schools existed here and there for the upper classes. Cities in which there were guilds offered further opportunities for education, since reading and arithmetic might be taught in addition to the craft skills. And most of the numerous monasteries throughout the empire had some facilities for teaching boys in the neighborhood.

It has been estimated that about one-fourth of white males in urban areas learned at least to read, write, and count. Mestizo boys, if their fathers were prosperous, were also likely to acquire the rudiments of education. Instruction for Indians was a rarity, though sons of tribal rulers who cooperated with the Spanish might be brought into schools to be indoctrinated. Negroes had no educational facilities whatever; their only opportunity for formal instruction was accidental, a matter of someone taking the trouble now and then to teach them either out of kindness or to make them more useful slaves. Female education was as haphazard and unusual in the Iberian empires as in such ancient centers of culture as Italy, China, or Persia. A girl might be taught on an individual basis and then proceed, as Sor Juana Inéz de la Cruz did, to educate herself, and a few convents offered instruction to upper-class women.

Spanish colonial universities existed from the earliest years of the empire, and they throve by the last quarter of the eighteenth century. On paper, the first was the University of St. Thomas Aquinas in Santo Domingo, which was started by decree in 1538. The first to function was the Royal and Pontifical University of Mexico, which began in 1553. Lima's University of San Marcos began regular courses in 1571, nearly two decades after its official establishment. In Santiago de Chile the authorities were rewarded after a century of petitioning with the University of San Felipe, and in Córdova and Chuquisaca, improbable as this seems in view of their location, universities of considerable excellence at various periods graced the interior of South America. Other universities stood in Caracas, Havana, Guatemala, Santa Fe de Bogotá, and Quito, while smaller institutions in provincial cities sometimes were called universities. John Tate Lanning, the leading student of this subject, places the number of schools that might be regarded as universities at twenty-three. Perhaps a hundred seminaries, colleges, and private institutions could be considered centers of higher learning. All of these were in Spanish America; Brazil had none during the colonial period.

A university was looked upon as a much-desired symbol of distinction by the officials and population of Spanish American cities. The king authorized it, usually after much pressure had been brought, and the royal treasury financed its construction and paid the faculty unless private endowments were available. As has always been true, the universities never had enough funds; yet most of them were handsomely housed. They were modeled on the University of Salamanca in Spain, an institution that was often the peer of Oxford, Paris, or Bologna. A considerable amount of autonomy was permitted, though the crown and the Inquisition exercised some supervision. Final authority resided in the cloister, composed of the faculties and the alumni who had received higher degrees, thus making of a university one of the few agencies in the Spanish empire where a limited amount of self-government was possible. Professors were initially clergymen, but as time went on many officials or professional men sought teaching positions for the prestige entailed and, one likes to think, for the love of pedagogy. In spite of very low salaries—a matter of small importance to clergymen and part-time professional men who taught—and considerable restrictions imposed by the authorities and the student body, the professorial life was apparently worth the struggle, for men competed vigorously to enjoy it. Important chairs were filled by competition, a public affair in which the candidates delivered long lectures to demonstrate their competence, and the winner was chosen supposedly by the authorities, but often as a result of enthusiasm on the part of the students. Perhaps the energy modern Latin American students devote to politics has a precedent in the colonial practice of voting, or fighting, for the competitors for chairs.

The universities had the usual collection of colleges: liberal arts, theology, law, and medicine. Courses were typical of European curricula: rhetoric, philosophy, civil and canon law, mathematics, Scriptures, and theology—and sometimes work in Indian languages was offered. Professors lectured in Latin or Spanish, or rather, read slowly so that students could copy, for books were scarce, so scarce that students had the right to insist that the faculty attend classes regularly and present a complete course.

Students were mostly creoles, though Indian nobles and mestizos in ever-larger numbers attended. They paid low fees to enter the university, but as they neared achievement of the coveted degree in the three or four years required, the rates became higher, and the graduation fee was formidable. Perhaps 150,000 men received degrees from Latin American universities during the colonial period, most of them sons of the well-to-do. The students were younger than those of today, and discipline was always a serious problem. Corporal punishments, whippings, and even campus jails were needed to punish adolescent boys for the brawls, battles with townspeople, crude practical jokes, and horseplay that characterized student life. Violent though much of their fun was, and dull as the long sessions of note-taking and memorizing must have been, a kindling of intellectual interests and exchange of ideas surely made university life rewarding for some.

The continuing prestige and growth of the universities suggest that people thought they were worthwhile; undoubtedly they were worthwhile for professional purposes. Lawyers and higher clergymen had to win degrees in order to carry on their careers, as did medical doctors, lamentable as the training of these last was. Government service was also an outlet for those who obtained degrees, even if the best positions went to peninsular Spaniards. A problem which Latin America has not yet outgrown appeared in the fact that too many people became educated for the jobs available to them, and something of an intellectual proletariat composed of letter-writers or scribes, copyists, clerks, and would-be men of letters developed in the larger cities. Their receptiveness to revolutionary ideas from about 1790 onward was no small factor in the disintegration of the empire.

LATIN AMERICA AND THE ENLIGHTENMENT

The Spanish American universities probably had more to do with circulating the ideas of the pre-revolutionary period in the eighteenth century than their counterparts in Europe did. These conceptions, combined under the imprecise term of "the Enlightenment," included faith in human reason, the implicit rejection of authority, a belief in the perfectibility of man, and the theory of progress based on the discovery of natural laws. Entering Spain with the Bourbons, and finding local traditions with which to work, these ideas slowly captured the minds of many learned, upper-class Spaniards. Their importation, usually by way of the universities, into the Americas was not long delayed. Descartes' theories were known and taught fairly early in some eighteenth-century colonial institutions of learning. Newton's writings, as well as those of Leibniz and Locke, found a good reception among several professors in influential positions, and a pioneer speculation on the theory of evolution by Lamarck was taught in Latin America within a year of its publication. While no sudden intellectual revolution occurred, by the end of the century an impressive number of faculty and students accepted experimental science and rationalism as truer guides than the hallowed authorities of the past. Thus the sacrosanct Aristotle and the reconciliation of his thought with medieval Christianity as St. Thomas Aquinas had arranged it—the neo-scholastic doctrine—were attacked here and there in the universities. While a considerable majority of academics probably clung to the old traditions and failed to grasp, or rejected, the new, those who accepted the Enlightenment did much to undermine respect for the ancient cosmology. By the early nineteenth century, more and more university intellectuals were turning the searching glare of "reason" on political institutions as well.

While the Spanish empire was sometimes held up to European "philosophers" of the eighteenth century as an embodiment of unreason, superstition, and cruelty (notably by William Robertson and the Abbé Raynal), its role as an arena for the new ideas had more lasting consequences. Peninsular officials, traders, and immigrants often brought into the Americas the irreverent and unorthodox attitudes of the French and of many educated Spaniards. Literate creoles were the most susceptible, particularly if they had already accepted, even without admitting it, the conception of a man-oriented rather than a God-oriented world and were coming to have more confidence in reason than in faith. In most Spanish American cities by the end of the colonial period, such men were likely to gather at coffee houses and discuss modern notions. The *tertulia*, that delightful Spanish custom in which friends meet at a home in a large circle to talk, was a means by which the exciting new doctrines were ventilated. There was little to impede such discussions. The Inquisition had only latent power and seldom functioned; the Index had long been a mockery, for libraries often contained forbidden books that had entered with the connivance of the port officials. While the twenty-five or so newspapers in the Spanish colonies contained little of a subversive nature, in fact not much news, they carried the bare facts of the American and French Revolutions, and intelligent readers could comprehend something of the ideas that were moving men in other parts of the world to drastic actions. Even the respectable Economic Societies of Friends of the Country, which appeared in most Spanish American cities to promote technical and economic knowledge, tended to serve as agencies for the spread of the Enlightenment and thus implicitly undermined the old regime. Possibly scattered secret societies propagated more revolutionary doctrines, though this cannot be proved for the last generation before independence. As events were to suggest, most educated and thoughtful urban creoles were acquainted with the ideas that facilitated revolutions in North America and France, and after 1808 would agitate Spanish America. Even Brazil contained a few "enlightened" souls who rejected much of the clerical and monarchical tradition.

The Wars of Independence

19

The Hispanic World
in War and Revolt

IT IS rare that either contemporaries or historians reach even a narrow area of agreement concerning revolutions. The men who are involved in these upheavals and posterity alike debate unendingly about their justification, what the parties really sought, how successful or calamitous their efforts proved, and whether life would have been better had the changes never taken place. No final answers can be provided in the case of the insurrection of Latin America that began in the era of the French Revolution. After a century and a half, students ponder the justice and wisdom of these rebellions and speculate about alternative directions they might have taken. Aware as it must be of the collapse of European colonialism in Asia and Africa, our own generation perhaps can ponder the Latin American movements known collectively as the Wars of Independence with more insight. All about us we see evidence that societies have a strong will to be independent, whether or not they are true nations, whether or not they are prepared for self-government. Any slackness on the part of the imperialist power is likely to loosen a will to be free.

BACKGROUND FOR REVOLUTION

From our review of the five Iberian viceroyalties we can appreciate the fact that all of them were experiencing improved administration and economic and cultural growth by the end of the eighteenth century. The occasional appearance of revolutionary sentiment should not mislead us into deducing that there was widespread, irresistible opposition to the imperial system of either Spain or Portugal. Since progress, however, frequently creates more dissatisfactions than gratifications, the betterment of conditions had put many of the creoles into a critical frame of mind. Moreover, examples and revolutionary ideas from North America and France inspired them to dream of changes in their own milieu. A New World sense of maturity, even nationalism, caused the enlightened classes to resent much of the colonial system. They aspired to control their own communities with less alien direction. Finally, an unparalleled opportunity presented itself with the clumsy aggression of Napoleon Bonaparte against the Iberian monarchies in 1807–1808. Under three general headings, then, the ideas of the Age of Revolution, the revulsion against colonialism, and the overthrow of the parent countries, we might approach the fateful period of Latin American history known as the Wars of Independence.

Latin America and the Age of Revolution

SPAIN and Portugal, together with their American possessions, experienced enough of the Enlightenment and its ideal of "reason" to be fundamentally unsettled thereby. At least after the end of the Seven Years' War in 1763, men of importance in government, intellectual, and economic affairs were likely to cherish concepts of reform and progress, so much so that they tended to prevail against the basic conservatism of Hispanic society. Even though modern ideas implicitly damaged the institutions of monarchy and the Church, royal officials and clergymen were usually the most effective dispensers of the Enlightenment. So long as kings such as Carlos III and powerful ministers like Pombal led governments along the lines of "reason," the ablest men of their countries were likely to follow them enthusiastically. When their successors stood in the way of modernity, discontent and sedition mounted. Even the nobilities of both Spain and Portugal, who had long since seen their political power wither away but still enjoyed wealth and prestige, were receptive to the leveling theories advanced by Rousseau, as long as they remained mere theories. While few persons in the Hispanic world ever confessed an erosion of their faith, many came to believe the Church should be stripped of its material possessions and demoted from its commanding position in society. An implicitly democratic and libertarian attitude seized the minds of men in the governing classes here and there. Wherever educated people were found, at the royal courts, universities, merchant houses, and social gatherings of the elite, a few individuals might enjoy some notoriety by advancing the beguiling tenets of radicalism. The majority of the ruling groups did not go so far, but they generally applied rationalism to the problems of government and society. If the effect of the Enlightenment was less pronounced in Latin America than in Europe, it nevertheless created a climate favorable to progress and reform. It dominated the thinking of nearly all of the men who led the independence movement and, often, that of their opponents.

Strangely, the effect of the American Revolution on the Hispanic world was only slowly realized. While Spain indirectly assisted that cause by warring on Great Britain, and while the events of the years 1775–1781 were generally known in Latin America, extremely few creoles were inspired to imitate the rebellious British colonists for some years. Perhaps the reason was the paucity of ties between English and Hispanic America. By 1815, however, the liberators in the south had come to appreciate the great success of the United States. Its initial rebellion and later its survival in the War of 1812 showed what might be done against a power far stronger than Spain. All this had been accomplished without producing a fundamental social upheaval, without provoking a slave or Indian revolt. And the propertied classes had demonstrated their ability to create a sound government that honored the principles of the Enlightenment. By the second half of the Wars of Independence, Latin American leaders drew their chief inspiration from the example of the United States.

The influence of the French Revolution was contradictory. During its first, the moderate, phase between 1789 and 1792, its lofty ideals appealed to many literate men of Hispanic American towns and cities. Then came the Reign of Terror and the great slave revolts in the Caribbean colonies, both of which caused genuine revulsion throughout Latin America. During the dozen years in which the Spanish monarchy was allied to the Directory and Napoleon, a modest circulation of the principles of the Revolution took place in America, despite some official discouragement. If these ideas were alien, they nonetheless appealed to all men, and by the time independence became a possibility, many Latin Americans were familiar with them.

If the Enlightenment, the American Revolution, and the French Revolution were living forces during the Wars of Independence, older ideals were not without potency. Among these we must count the long-won liberties of England. For various reasons London became the temporary home of a number of Latin Americans who later participated in the liberation of their homelands. They absorbed much of the love of freedom and civilized order that characterized their hosts. Almost to a man they remained Anglophiles even after the inapplicability of British experience to Latin American conditions had been demonstrated. Another source of British influence before and during the Wars of Independence was the flood of newspapers and journals from London and British America which poured into the seaports of the Americas along with merchandise. Educated Hispanic Americans were thus informed, often through translations in the press of their own cities, of the doings of a successful society centered in London which was free and moderately democratic. Another tradition as old as English liberty likewise had some force. This was the ancient constitutionalism cherished by Spaniards, much of it dating to a time before Felipe II. It was still taught in law and divinity schools of Latin American universities that kings must respect the rights of their subjects, that bad law was not law at all, and that rulers deserved obedience only if they were just. These antique doctrines, which long had little relevance in the Hispanic monarchies, suddenly assumed importance in the Age of Revolution, when the bases of government were under general re-examination.

Thus the Enlightenment began to affect Latin America about 1763 and grew increasingly more effective as a force to undermine attachment to the historic position of the crown, nobility, and Church while nurturing respect for liberty and even democracy. The American Revolution showed that a powerful mother country could be ejected from the New World without inciting a ruinous upheaval of colored men against white. That former colonials could rule themselves and prosper seemed another lesson from the United States. Tarnished as the French Revolution was in some ways, its fundamentals attracted liberal Latin Americans as they did men in many other parts of the world. And the revival of interest in ancient Spanish constitutionalism as well as the abiding example of English liberty strengthened the convictions of reformers in search of sanctions for what they wanted to do.

The Revolt Against Imperialism

FROM the earliest times it has been apparent that imperialistic control exerted by one society over another provokes resentment, usually of a helpless sort. In the Americas those who had the most reason to object to Hispanic colonialism were, by 1800, those who were most resigned to it. These of course were the Indians, possibly ten million or so, who had long been subjugated and exploited by the Europeans as they received many benefits from the same sources. After the disastrous Andean revolts of the 1780's the Indians of South America were not eager to rebel again. Most of them were almost altogether unacquainted with and unmoved by the ideas of the Age of Revolution; the great majority tended to obey their tribal rulers, who were profitably attached to the Spanish system, and to revere the distant lord in Madrid. Mission Indians were usually docile. Except for the explosive insurrection in Mexico in 1810, Indians were mainly passive factors in the Wars of Independence. They did not initiate the revolutions and were unlikely to participate unless they were conscripted into the forces of patriots or royalists. Both liberator and Spaniard promised the aborigines better conditions and an end to the worst abuses during this period. The Indians, rightly suspecting both sides, generally favored the royalist cause until the very last, when they partially shifted over to the patriots.

Negro slaves, who were as a rule slightly more rebellious than Indians, likewise had little inclination to rise against an imperial system that victimized them so badly. Those in Brazil were almost entirely unconnected with the independence movement. In Cuba and Puerto Rico the Negroes were given no chance, and seized none, to revolt in force. Africans on the Caribbean coastlands of South America were drawn into the independence side in the later stages of the wars by Simón Bolívar's promises to emancipate them. Similarly, José de San Martín attracted Negroes in the Argentine and the coasts of Peru. Yet no Negro leaders of importance appeared in the Spanish or Portuguese dominions, and slavery as an institution largely survived the formal end of colonialism. Mestizos and mulattoes took a more dynamic part in the liberation movements. Seldom initiating them, they were at first likely to fight with the side which offered them the better chance for pay or loot. Toward the last, however, many were sincerely moved by the opportunity to overthrow the old regime and rebuild society with an improved position for themselves. Their tendency to remain in armies or warring bands was to prove a lamentable factor in the early days of the republics.

It was the white man, the lord of the Americas, who most bitterly criticized the colonial institutions and, when opportunity beckoned, first rebelled. Most of these men were creoles, though a few peninsulars were prominent as revolutionists. Their fundamental complaint originated in the sixteenth century, when American-born Spaniards and Portuguese displayed resentment against the arrogance of Madrid or Lisbon. For generations these creoles had been developing the mines, plantations, ranches, and small businesses of the New World. They had built the cities, supervised the Indians and Negroes, and often had grown rich and proud. Yet the choice positions in the government and Church went to peninsulars, who looked down on the American-born whites. This situation had always rankled. It grew almost unbearable by 1795, when no one could seriously maintain that Spain and Portugal were great powers, or that their protection was necessary to keep heretics and colored races from taking over the New World. A generation before, the reforms of Carlos III and Pombal had seemed salutary. Now, with the tightened institutions mismanaged by lesser men, imperial controls were hateful. Whenever Britain or the United States breached the commercial monopoly Spanish Americans could dream of continuous profits if their ports were opened to world trade. Intellectual repression, even if sporadic, was intolerable because it was repression, and on behalf of weak powers.

And to what end were these monopolies perpetuated? So that hacks from the peninsula could swagger about colonial cities, extorting taxes, issuing decrees, and belittling the Americans as barbarians? It seemed so to increasing numbers of educated creoles. And whenever Americans went to Spain or Portugal they were made to suffer from having been born on the wrong side of the Atlantic. It is singular to note how many of the major figures of the independence movements underwent this humiliating experience, so galling to proud men who regarded themselves as aristocrats in their own milieu. On the rare occasions in which they replied to such complaints, Spanish rulers insisted there was no discrimination whatever against Americans. The king esteemed all of his subjects equally and appointed them to high positions if they were qualified, even in Spain itself. Portuguese authorities similarly denied favoritism on behalf of peninsulars. Brazilians were entirely welcome in the royal service, if any deserving applicants could be found. To the Americans such protestations were so much cant. They well knew the snubs and insults they endured. It was often repeated that of 170 Spanish viceroys only four had been born in the western hemisphere and that the proportion of *oidores*, bishops, abbots, and intendants was almost as low. More and more they talked of a colonial system that resembled a huge cow whose hungry mouth was in America but whose udder was in Europe, or of a vampire that sucked the riches of the New World for the benefit of the Old. It often seemed that the imperialist system performed no constructive good in America, not even in administration. Peninsular officials were only ravaging birds who flocked to America to steal its fruits.

Much of this bitterness was ill-founded. The American dominions were not heavily taxed, and most of their revenues by far remained in the New World. Colonial government, as events were to prove, was superior to any the creoles could devise. But it was a foreign government, and nationalism was becoming a compelling, even an unreasonable force among many creoles, as it so often is in its early stages, regardless of the tributes paid to reason. These American whites craved freedom from alien restraint and the opportunity to acquire status, titles, and power over their own communities. Some wanted to break once and for all the monopolies of peninsular merchants and to seize their properties. A radical minority even dreamed of demolishing the traditional system of privilege associated with monarchy and Church.

To acknowledge that ill feeling among the creoles was growing acute about 1800 is not to assert that revolution was inevitable. In the best of times people grumble; things are never perfect. And many of the conditions against which some Americans inveighed continued far into the republican period. Under happier circumstances the peninsulars might have realized the seriousness of creole complaints and made concessions.

The Americans might have contented themselves with gentle pressures for more recognition and, if they won it, with another generation or so of loyalty to a loose-jointed world empire. The *mystique* of royalty remained strong as a unifying force. As events were to prove, revolutionary forces in Hispanic America were not irresistible until years of blunders and bloodshed made them so.

Collapse of the Metropolis

BRAZIL, Haiti, and all of the Spanish mainland colonies became independent nations early in the nineteenth century chiefly because of an extraordinary series of events in Europe. A disastrous action by Napoleon Bonaparte in 1807–1808 brought tragedy to Spain and Portugal and cut their overseas empires adrift. It was then that the doctrines of the Age of Revolution and the discontent of colonials with imperialism came into play in Latin America. Independence movements, often disguised, were begun after some hesitation. Most of them were extinguished outright. In several localities they made considerable headway for a few years, but only one continued in Spanish America after the fall of Napoleon. The problems of reviving a devastated homeland were too great for the Spanish monarchy, and the restoration in the empire was not handled intelligently. Revolutions broke out anew and were proceeding successfully when a liberal revolt in Spain in 1820 cut the ground from the hitherto loyalist elements in the colonies. Much bloodshed was nonetheless necessary before Spain's power was broken late in 1824. The former French colony, Haiti, was ignored by the Europeans after 1804 and remained free. Brazil's secession from the Portuguese monarchy occurred easily in 1822, when the crown prince placed himself at the head of the independence movement. To these events, confusing in themselves and made all the more complex by the incredible changes of fortune in the era of the French Revolution and Napoleon, we must now look in some detail. They, rather than the grievances of Latin Americans against the old regime, were the immediate causes of the Wars of Independence.

THE DECLINE OF SPAIN UNDER CARLOS IV

The long and productive reign of Carlos III came to an end with his death in 1788. Not since that date has any Spanish sovereign been a stranger to exile.[1] Nor has any republic endured more than a few years. All of the dictatorships have proved short-lived until that of Fran-

1. Carlos IV and Fernando VII were forced into foreign residence in 1808. Isabel II was dethroned in 1868. Amadeo I gave up his crown in 1873. Alfonso XII was in exile as prince and titular king from 1868 to 1875, and Alfonso XIII left the throne in 1931.

cisco Franco in the mid-twentieth century. Brutal as it may be to say so, Spain has had no great or even successful statesmen since Carlos III. His immediate successor was his middle-aged son, Carlos IV, who so much resembled his French cousin Louis XVI in torpor, dullness, plain virtues, and fondness for outdoor activities. This simple king lived in terror of his wife, María Luisa, a woman of evil temper and domineering manner. Another quality of the queen was an excessive sensualism which she could freely indulge after she came to the throne, for she had by that time presented her husband with a number of children. This unpromising family has been immortalized for posterity by the frank portraits of the court painter, Francisco Goya, who depicted on numerous canvases the stupid-looking king, the lascivious queen, and the surly children along with various shoddy characters who frequented the royal court, a court that was the veritable nerve center of a great world monarchy.

This was Spain's leadership as the convulsions of the French Revolutionary period opened. In the summer of 1789 the ancient *cortes* of Castile was in session to ratify the accession of the new king. The news from France being disturbing, it was decided to dismiss the *cortes* before any thought of imitating the Estates-General in Versailles could be entertained. As the Revolution surged in France, the able ministers inherited from the previous reign took measures to brace Spain, such as closing the frontiers with France, arresting French residents, censoring the press, and alerting the long somnolent Inquisition in the peninsula and America alike. Yet, germs of revolution entered Spain and occasionally struck receptive persons. The official reaction was intensified, in America as in Spain. The mood changed, too, from a friendly curiosity in many quarters to genuine horror as the French abused the royal family and attacked the aristocracy and the clergy. By 1792, when it was apparent that the French Revolution was becoming a military as well as an ideological menace, the government of Spain fell into the hands of a despicable royal favorite, Manuel Godoy.

Godoy is one of the half dozen most detested men in the history of Spain. As a young man of the lower aristocracy from Badajoz, he had come to Madrid to enter the royal guard. Suddenly he was promoted rapidly and given access to the court, becoming in short order a grandee, field marshal, and Duke of Alcudia. Almost certainly he was the lover of the middle-aged queen, and everyone but the king knew it. Godoy's relationship with the queen was a scandal that became widely known far beyond court circles, eventually in Spanish America. Strangely, Carlos IV favored him, readily accepting his wife's opinion that he was a genius. Indifferently educated, Godoy thought himself a philosopher in the eighteenth-century fashion. He liked the company of liberals and wanted to make Spain more modern. While his beliefs were by no means absurd, he impressed nearly everybody as a charlatan, an opportunist of shallow convictions. Godoy was only twenty-five when, in 1792, the king made him first secretary or principal minister. In this position he was able to select officials for the imperial administration, to the notable and immediate detriment of its quality, and to collect payment for favors. The passive king permitted his growth of power and probably never heard that Godoy was his wife's paramour. Or did he hear and refuse to believe? Or believe and not dare to confront the hell-cat María Luisa? [2] As Godoy accumulated titles and wealth he became all the more arrogant. Able men quit the government or were cashiered. The court, the capital, the kingdom, and finally the whole world of affairs gossiped about the royal scandal. For the first time in nearly a century the Spanish reigning house grew contemptible, or worse, ridiculous, in the eyes of its subjects.

Carlos IV tried and failed to rescue Louis XVI. When this unfortunate monarch was guillotined in January 1793, the Spanish made ready to interfere in France to overcome the Revolution. Instead of awaiting this intervention, the Convention that ruled the French Republic added Spain to the list of its declared enemies. The war was immediately popular in all parts of the Spanish monarchy, even in America. France's long domination of Spanish diplomacy and cultural life had not kindled affection but rather dislike, and most Spaniards were fired by the idea of punishing the regicides and blasphemers of Paris. This enthusiasm flamed as Spanish armies invaded France and pushed some miles across the frontier. Then the crusade stalled. Soon it went into reverse, and troops of the French Republic crossed into Spain at both ends of the Pyrenees, compounding their sacrilege by creating republican committees to rule the towns they occupied and brazenly spreading revolutionary propaganda. *El Favorito*, Godoy, was roundly condemned for permitting these disasters to occur, but in all justice it must be recalled that the armies of Revolutionary France defeated and invaded all of the land powers that attacked her. By 1795, when more moderate elements were in control of France, Godoy terminated the war with the Treaty of Basel, by which Spain ceded to the French Republic her oldest colony in the New World, Santo Domingo, the one established by Columbus. Although the British moved to prevent French occupation of this area, Spanish Americans noted with dismay how casually their king and the favorite had disposed of an overseas colony.

2. Of course, there remains the slender possibility that it was not true.

THE FIRST SUCCESSFUL REVOLUTION IN LATIN AMERICA

France had insisted on the cession of Santo Domingo in order to restore her control of the former French colony, Saint-Domingue, the western third of the island of Hispaniola now included in the modern republic of Haiti. Since 1697 the French title to this tropical colony had been recognized by Spain. Its prosperity had made it the envy of other imperial nations. With scenic beauties, exceedingly rich soil, and a plenitude of plantations with elaborate irrigation and sugar-refining facilities, it was enormously profitable to France during most of the eighteenth century. Handsome towns, roads, and substantial country homes gave it a civilized appearance. About a half-million of its inhabitants were Negro slaves, most of them born in Africa. The remaining 70,000 or so were about equally divided between the owning and ruling whites and the mulatto freedmen. However secure an outpost of French civilization Saint-Domingue appeared, its huge black majority shared but feebly in the culture or religion of the white governing class.

Tensions of the most dangerous type arose from the French Revolution. "Great whites" of the planter class indignantly rejected the ambition of the "little whites" and free mulattoes to share in the democratic blessings proclaimed from Paris. A worse threat to the ruling group was the emancipationist propaganda issuing from France, where a society of *Amis des noirs* stimulated the Negroes to agitate for freedom. By August 1791 the whites were so divided by acrimony and the blacks so stirred that a revolution started. Before long it was a terrible civil war which awakened the fury of Africa in the hearts of the slaves. When Paris finally ordered the abolition of slavery, the colony was in the convulsions of a racial struggle. Torture, atrocity, death, and flight brought tragedy to thousands and the virtual elimination of the white race in Saint-Domingue. The French and creoles who survived fled to neighboring colonies, where they terrified other white populations with tales of the slave revolt. The abiding loyalty of Cuban and Puerto Rican creoles to Spain in the years ahead derived in large part from these frightful reports.

With the whites gone, the mulattoes began to feel the wrath of the Negroes. Most of this mixed group, too, were killed or forced to emigrate, though the few who remained enjoyed considerable deference from the blacks. The leader who emerged from this savagery was one of the great men of independent America, Toussaint L'Ouverture, who was born a slave in 1743. Somehow he had become free, rich, and well-read. Now in his fifties, he helped his former master to escape and assumed command of disorganized bands of black warriors. His masterful personality and manifest abilities established him before long as the foremost leader of the former slaves. Also he had, or learned, that cunning in deceiving men which characterizes most successful political figures. Whatever his secret, Toussaint was a natural leader. Such control of the wrecked colony as there was he exerted. He spoke knowledgeably of constitutions and laws. When, in 1801, he finally made good the cession of Spanish Santo Domingo by conquering it, he agreeably amazed the fearful white planters with his moderation. Toussaint undoubtedly had the instincts of a statesman and is rightfully revered. The material with which he worked, however, was pitifully unequal to his talents. His domain was a shambles, its economy ruined, the French and their works gone, the mulattoes decimated, and the former slaves free and idle in a tropical paradise. Napoleon, as it turned out, had ominous plans for Saint-Domingue.

THE ALLIANCE OF SPAIN AND FRANCE, 1796–1808

Spain's defection from the war against France greatly angered Great Britain, who promptly reverted to her traditional policy of attempting to wreck the Spanish empire. Because of this and Godoy's fatuous diplomacy, Spain drew close to the French Republic, now under the Directory, and signed an alliance in 1796. For several years Godoy sought to incorporate the milder reforms of the Revolution, attacking the Inquisition and the guilds, threatening land division and the trimming of aristocratic and clerical privileges, and encouraging the circulation of French liberal writings. This strong breath of radical air, more than any other circumstance, may have begun the militant liberal movement which has had such a calamitous effect on Spain at various intervals. Otherwise, it antagonized the conservatives and made Godoy more detested than ever. His flirtation with revolutionary doctrines had little effect on the Spanish overseas empire, where viceroys and intendants carefully watched the movements of Frenchmen and suppressed radical manifestations, often quietly so as not to stimulate interest. A curious affair with repercussions on both sides of the Atlantic was a republican conspiracy in Zaragoza in 1795 led by Juan Picornell. Easily scotched, the threat appeared in new form in Venezuela in 1797. Picornell and his companions had been sent to a prison in La Guaira, where they were liberated by local radicals. They schemed for a few weeks to throw the captaincy-general into an uproar and to free the servile classes. It was much too soon to foment such an uprising, but traces of this movement persisted for a few years, whereupon Venezuela proved herself ready for a republican adventure.

If Godoy's liberalism resulted in little but mischief for Spain, the military alliance with France brought one disaster after another, mainly at the hands of Great Britain. For much of the time after 1796, Spanish ships were unable to ferry officials and merchandise to the Americas on a regular basis, a deficiency the colonists partially made up by trading with the United States and Britain. For exasperating periods the flow of silver, which was now at its all-time peak, was delayed in reaching the peninsula. Furthermore, the British did not satisfy themselves with puncturing the Spanish commercial monopoly. Naval attacks on Puerto Rico and Central America were frightening intimations of possible conquests to come. The island of Trinidad, near Venezuela, was occupied by the British without notable opposition on the part of its Spanish inhabitants. And the British badly defeated a Spanish fleet off Cape St. Vincent in Europe in 1797, further diminishing the respectable navy Carlos III had assembled. The effect of all these events on the Spanish Americans was disastrous from the royal point of view. They knew about *El Favorito* and the venal officials to whom he sold imperial offices. They had seen the holy war against the French Republic followed by the cynical alliance of 1796. The cession of Santo Domingo, the loss of Trinidad, and the weakness of Spanish naval forces all had ominous implications. Not a few creoles allowed themselves to wonder out loud about the value of the tie with Spain.

By 1800 Godoy's unpopularity had brought about his supposed dismissal, though he continued in fact to be the closest adviser of Carlos IV. His Francophile policy was clearly misguided. Instead of growing weaker and more deferential to Spain, France, now under Napoleon Bonaparte, had become more powerful and aggressive; the court in Madrid cowered before his threats and imperious demands. Spain accepted the retrocession of Louisiana to France in exchange for the augmentation of the petty Duchy of Parma, which was ruled by the king's son-in-law. In 1801 Napoleon forced Spain to attack Portugal in order to compel that kingdom to close its ports to the British. This so-called "War of the Oranges" proved a simple affair, for Portugal put up no opposition. Spain grabbed her province of Olivenza, which made bad feeling between the two neighbors for many years and gave Portugal an excuse in 1816 to commit aggression against Spanish territory in La Plata. In 1802 Napoleon signed a short-lived peace with Britain, the Treaty of Amiens, to which Spain was pressed to adhere by recognizing the loss of Trinidad.

During the year that the Treaty of Amiens remained in force Napoleon undertook to restore France's former colonial empire in America, hoping to fortify Louisiana and to re-establish the lucrative sugar business in Saint-Domingue. An expedition of 20,000 Frenchmen, many of them Jacobins whom Napoleon wished out of the country, sailed to Saint-Domingue under the command of his brother-in-law, General Leclerc. Toussaint L'Ouverture had not proclaimed Haitian independence and was ostensibly agreeable to the resumption of French control. But it was soon obvious that Leclerc intended to restore slavery, an evil surprise to the Negroes. Toussaint himself was treacherously seized when he attended a parley and shipped off to France, where he soon died. His heir, Jean Jacques Dessalines, organized a revolt against Leclerc which brought about further butcheries between whites and blacks. Mainly because of yellow fever, the French lost. By 1803 Napoleon was at war with Britain again and thus unable to reinforce Leclerc, who perished with most of his men in the plague. The survivors moved into Santo Domingo, the former Spanish colony, and held out there until 1808. Saint-Domingue, now called Haiti, became entirely free in 1804, this time permanently, of European control. It was the first nation in Latin America to establish its independence.

When he realized the war with England was about to resume, Napoleon suddenly sold Louisiana to the United States, in violation of his earlier promise to Spain, thus bringing the ambitious Americans closer to the Viceroyalty of New Spain. Spanish interests had further sacrifices to offer at Napoleon's command. Carlos IV was browbeaten into declaring war on England again, for Napoleon needed Spanish shipping. An enormous force he assembled at Boulogne was supposed to invade the island kingdom, and in order to effect the Channel crossing, he required the combined forces of France and Spain, whose best units were placed under the command of a French admiral, Villeneuve. In 1805 the dictator, now an emperor, ordered the fleet to sail toward the West Indies in order to lure the British force under Lord Nelson into the far Atlantic. While Nelson was supposed to cruise about the Caribbean in search of his prey, the Latin allies were to turn about and hasten to Boulogne and escort the French barges to the shores of England. It should then be a simple matter for Napoleon to take London. The scheme might have worked but for the fact that the British found out about it, probably because of a leak in court circles in Madrid. All that happened was that the two fleets crossed the Atlantic twice, with Nelson dogging Villeneuve closely. Soon the French and Spanish were again anchored in the beautiful harbor of Cadiz while the British cruised outside. Napoleon's rage was fearful, and he made the fateful error of ordering Villeneuve, whom he reproached for cowardice, to break out of Cadiz as soon as he could. Meanwhile, the emperor was forced to divert his attention from the white cliffs of England to the massive armies which the Austrians and Russians were mobilizing against him.

Just as Napoleon executed the brilliant pirouette which took his *Grande Armée* into Germany in October 1805, Villeneuve carried out his unlucky orders to burst out of Cadiz. The result was the famous naval battle off Cape Trafalgar in which Nelson, with twenty-nine ships, destroyed or captured all thirty-six vessels of the Latin allies. Nelson's death in this, his greatest victory, did not spoil its effect. Never again was Napoleon able to plan an invasion of England. Another consequence of Trafalgar is less well-known but has immeasurable significance. Spain had by now lost almost her entire navy. What was left rotted in harbor, and she was never able to rebuild a fleet of any importance. When, by 1814, she was free, determined, and full of trained soldiers, she lacked sufficient shipping resources to dispatch enough men to deal with the Latin American independence movements. Almost to the degree that it spelled the salvation of England, the Battle of Trafalgar insured the ultimate freedom of Latin America.

As Napoleon struck down the great powers of Europe in 1805–1807, Spain watched helplessly. The British assaulted Buenos Aires and Montevideo, planned attacks on Venezuela and New Spain, and flouted the supposed Spanish monopoly of the empire's commerce; Spain's sense of frustration was extreme. At one point, in October 1806, Godoy thought he discerned an opportunity to switch sides and free Spain from the disastrous alliance with Napoleon. With his usual ineptitude the moment he chose was the eve of one of the Corsican's most striking victories, the Battle of Jena, which fairly smashed Prussia. A most untimely order to mobilize the Spanish army for a thrust at France was recalled when news of Jena arrived. Godoy was stupid enough to think Napoleon had not been offended by his planned treachery. He was, of course, marked for extinction. At the same time the maturing sons of Carlos IV began to chafe at the abuse they suffered at the hands of the favorite. The heir to the throne, Prince Fernando, was already the hope of a large party in Spain which looked to him as *El Deseado*, the desired one who would end the ignominy of Spain's situation. Rightfully afraid of his mother and Godoy, Fernando dared to do no more than appeal secretly to Napoleon. He wrote the emperor of his mother's adulteries, likening himself to Hamlet and asking Napoleon to become his godfather and to let him marry a Bonaparte princess. His pitiful importunings were carefully assessed by the sharp mind in the Tuileries.

THE FALL OF THE IBERIAN MONARCHIES

By the latter part of 1807 Napoleon seemed on top of the world but for British resistance, which he expected to bring to an end soon by economic measures, principally by keeping English merchandise out of the continent. He was now free to do something about Spain. To be sure, there was no need for him to do anything, for the Spanish government was eager to please him. Both factions in Madrid fawned on the great conqueror. While Prince Fernando was asking Napoleon to intervene against Godoy, that favorite and his royal master were seeking Napoleon's help for the conquest of Portugal, the creation of a stronger trans-

Atlantic empire, and other projects. The main idea was to maintain the pretense that imperial France and Spain were good partners. Napoleon really needed to do nothing but permit Spain to continue as his subordinate ally. But he had never forgotten how Godoy had attempted to betray him, and his contempt for the human race definitely included Prince Fernando. Therefore, he constructed a trap and fell into it himself. For no good reason, simply because he was acting the way power-mad despots have always done, Napoleon decided to degrade Spain further. He would intervene in the peninsula. It never entered his calculations that the common people of any country could cause him much difficulty.

Napoleon professed to believe that Portugal needed to be occupied in order to keep her from admitting British ships, something the little kingdom was unable to prevent even if it had been willing, which it was not. Carlos IV and Godoy readily fell in with the emperor's scheme, the king hoping to take the title of Emperor of the Americas (including Brazil) and Godoy to become king of Portugal. Late in 1807 a large French army led by Marshal Junot entered the peninsula and, with Spanish allies, overran Portugal. The mad queen, Maria I, her son, Prince Regent João, the rest of the royal court, and thousands of nobles gathered what they could and clambered on Portuguese ships just as Junot penetrated Lisbon. The fantastic expedition sailed out of the Tagus for Brazil, escorted by the British. Napoleon observed how easy it had all been. Now, perhaps the rotten Spanish Bourbons would disappear into the New World the way the Braganzas had. Portugal and Spain would then become satellite kingdoms ruled by Bonaparte monarchs, Britain could cruise the seas all she wished, and the Americas could absorb two unwanted dynasties forever removed from Europe.

Early in 1808 it became apparent even to the most trusting Spaniard that there was something menacing about Napoleon's attitude. Instead of giving Portugal to Godoy and withdrawing his armies, the emperor sent massive reinforcements. Then he stupefied the Spanish court with a demand for a belt of territory to form a corridor between France and Portugal. Carlos IV and Godoy at last realized that their policy of appeasement was exhausted, and the court moved south of Madrid to Aranjuez in order to place itself beyond the reach of Napoleon's armies. Terrified and confused, the Spanish rulers talked of withdrawing to Gibraltar, the Balearic Islands, or even to America.

At this point there occurred the first *pronunciamiento* in modern Spanish history, the intervention of the military which was to become the curse of Spain and her daughters in the New World. On March 13, 1808, a group of officers of the royal guard arrested Godoy and pressed Carlos IV to abdicate, whereupon *El Deseado* was proclaimed king as Fernando VII. This unconstitutional action, a fateful precedent, was greeted with hysterical rejoicing all over the country and soon in the American dominions. Yet no one had a clear idea of what the new monarch could accomplish with French armies in occupation of the northern third of the country. Fernando showed a commendable desire to set things aright. He saved his parents and Godoy from further indignities, allowing them to go to France, and he sought to please Napoleon in any way possible. But the emperor was not at all happy. From Bayonne, a French town on the Spanish border, he sourly regarded the unexpected turn of events. Instead of removing themselves, the Bourbons had now entrenched their hold on Spain with a highly popular new king. Napoleon kept his thoughts to himself for a few weeks, but his agents sounded out Spaniards reputed to be pro-French, or *afrancesado*, and his armies occupied Madrid and other strategic centers.

When he was ready to move, the emperor announced that he did not consider either Fernando VII or Carlos IV as the lawful king of Spain. In order to clarify the situation, he said, both claimants should confer with him in the "north of Spain," a location that proved to be. the imperial headquarters at Bayonne. Had Fernando VII been more intelligent he would have refused to enter the snare. Instead, he disregarded the importunings of his court and the instinct of the populace, who unhitched his horses on several occasions to prevent the journey, and made his way into Napoleon's hands, confident that he would win the emperor's award. A more heroic course of remaining with his people and fighting it out with the French and, when defeated, going to foreign soil or America apparently never entered his thoughts. Early in May 1808 the Spanish royal family was reunited at Bayonne. For several days Napoleon looked on, both amused and horrified, while Fernando VII and his brothers exchanged recriminations with their parents and Godoy. At length the emperor stepped in, compelling both Carlos IV and Fernando VII to abdicate and deliver the ancient crown of Spain into his hands. Carlos and María Luisa soon went to Rome with the inseparable Godoy. The royal couple died there in 1819. Godoy lived on many years but was never allowed to live in Spain. Fernando and two of his brothers became princes of the Empire of the French and were interned until 1814 on a pleasant if lonely estate in the valley of the Loire.

Rid of the Bourbons, Napoleon proceeded with his original plans. A number of *afrancesados* came to Bayonne at Napoleon's summons to receive a new liberal constitution for their country. They were also informed that they had a new king, Joseph Bonaparte, Napoleon's older brother. José I was a solid, good man and had, like Carlos III, served an apprenticeship as king of Naples. The resemblance ended there, however, for José I was not born royalty and he was manifestly being imposed by the autocrat of Europe. Nor was he a statesman. His accession was not a parallel to that of Felipe V in 1700, for the Bourbon had been named as successor to the legitimate monarch in a valid testament and was himself a royal personage by birth, a detail by no means unimportant. It is true that in Italy, Germany, Poland, and the Netherlands Napoleon I had created sovereigns in irregular ways and sponsored constitutions that swept away much that was archaic in the old regime. Now Spain had a chance to receive a king who could be no worse than Carlos IV and a constitution that embodied much of the Enlightenment and the French Revolution.

The nation would have none of it. No matter how ignorant and backward the Spanish people were, they rightly guessed what was happening and began to resist the Napoleonic dispensation from the first. Even before the settlement àt Bayonne, crowds in Madrid had tangled with French troops on May 2, 1808. In the resulting massacre of this celebrated *dos de mayo*, Spain's most hallowed national holiday, hundreds of Spaniards were killed or injured. The War of Independence, as the Spanish call it, had begun. When the proclamations arrived from Bayonne, the people reviled Joseph Bonaparte, and the *afrancesados* were denounced as the equivalent of quislings or collaborationists. All over the country the ancient localism asserted itself, the masses initially looking to the most respected aristocrats or clergymen for leadership against the French. Committees, or juntas, were organized to direct the fighting. Appeals went to England for arms. Opposition to Napoleon's brother was overwhelming, almost unanimous. A veritable peoples' war took shape, one more violent than the popular resistance Napoleon later encountered in Russia and the Germanies. The primitive Spaniards inspired occupied Europe with their challenge to the most modern of dictators.

King José I entered his capital in the summer of 1808 only to be snubbed by its population. Soon he had to withdraw as a British army moved in rapidly from the west. And Spanish forces astounded Europe by encircling an entire Napoleonic army in the south, at Bailén, and taking its surrender. Yet the French rallied from these setbacks and roundly defeated the British land forces, as they had done regularly since 1793, and poured more units into Spain. José I returned to the great royal palace in Madrid with its 2,800 rooms, appalled by the hatred of his subjects, who called him *El Intruso* (the intruder) and *Pepe Botellas* (Joe Bottles). His *afrancesado* advisers, many of whom were among the most distinguished men of the country, were bewildered by the reaction of their compatriots. Expecting to modernize Spain, they were cursed as traitors. It would be the same in the overseas empire. Emissaries of José I were insulted and thrown back, in complete contrast to the situation in 1701, when a new French king had been readily acknowledged throughout the Americas. Still, with the British pushed off into Portugal and the Spanish army disorganized, the intruder king and his enlightened supporters, backed by many French legions, hoped to bring regeneration to Spain. They drafted many admirable plans.

THE AGONY OF SPAIN, 1808–1814

The peoples' war grew more vicious. Those who could, fought with muskets and pistols; others employed knives, axes, stones, and scalding water. Many a French sentry was murdered in the night. Arson and ambushes accounted for numerous casualties. Acts of sabotage like those in the resistance movements of World War II became both a sport and a way of life. Furthermore, as irregular bands acquired practice in *guerrilla* methods, they sometimes took up banditry and political terrorism. In general, extreme elements moved into control. In Spain, as in Latin America a few years later, colorful military chieftains began to supplant the traditional authorities of a civilian society. The French failed utterly to establish an administration, even after Napoleon himself came to the peninsula and repeatedly battered the Spanish army. Occupation of the chief cities, sometimes achieved after brutal sieges, had no enduring effects. As soon as the French departed, the patriots would slaughter the remaining garrisons and *afrancesados*. Much as they tried, the French could not match the Spanish in atrocity. Yet the patriots were also unable to establish an administration, with their rightful king gone and the enemy in possession of the main strategic centers. Civilized society almost collapsed as Spain underwent years of battle and murder, seizures and theft, hatred and revenge.

Supposedly representing the absent Fernando VII (no one upheld the cause of the King Father, Carlos IV) were the various juntas. In September 1808 they concentrated their authority in a central supreme junta in Sevilla. From the old Moorish alcazar of that city, seat of the *suprema*, went appeals to the American dominions for loyalty and support. Offers of seats in this body were made to attach the colonials to the national cause. In lieu of any other legitimate source of authority most of the viceroys and captains-general in the overseas empire recognized the *suprema*, but many Americans were dubious about placing themselves at its orders. Early in 1810 the French occupied Sevilla and most of Andalusia. The *suprema* fled to Cadiz, which lies on a protected crescent-shaped peninsula, and disbanded itself. A committee of regency now claimed the authority of Fernando VII. Since that monarch had issued a call for the *Cortes* of Castile to formalize his reign just before he had left for Bayonne in 1808, the regency repeated his summons. It was to be a different type of parliament, however. Instead of the usual privileged groups sending representatives, an impossibility because of the French occupation, delegates were to be chosen by refugees from the peninsular provinces and elected by the *cabildos* in leading cities of the American empire from men of probity, talent, and education. Spain was to have seventy-five deputies, the Americas and the Philippines thirty.

The *cortes* gathered in September 1810, before the elections in America were completed and the deputies arrived. An orderly selection process in peninsular Spain was, of course, out of the question. What happened was that the original 105 members were mostly picked from refugees and stray Americans in Cadiz. The *cortes* was a most unrepresentative body, the most radical assembly the world had known in modern times, save only the Convention of the French Republic in 1792–1795. This was chiefly due to the energy and intrigue of ultra-liberal persons. Also, seaports are traditionally advanced politically, and the *cortes* needed to outbid the regime of José I with its imported modernism. Whatever the causes, the *cortes* abolished the Inquisition, destroyed many privileges long enjoyed by the Church, hacked away at the position of the aristocracy, ended many oppressive taxes, and with a zest that suggested genuine republican sentiment, curtailed the kingship itself. It would have liked to terminate the commercial restrictions that had long crippled free enterprise in the Americas, but the great merchant houses of Cadiz, for a century the chief beneficiary of the monopoly, were able to block such legislation. Measures to benefit Negro slaves and Indians in the overseas empire were also considered, for the deputies included colored races in their humanitarian plans.

The arrival of the elected American members served to cool such ardors, though they were otherwise inclined to be liberal and reformist. Their principal demand was for more representation. The colonial empire had about 15,000,000 people, they claimed, and peninsular Spain only 10,000,000. Therefore, they should have a majority of deputies in the *cortes*. To this contention the peninsulars replied that most Americans were in fact second-class subjects, Indians, Negroes, and mixed breeds. Impeccable as the peninsular logic was, it offended the Americans. They were also insulted by the tone of the peninsulars, for liberal as well as reactionary Spaniards made little secret of their contempt for the colonials. Thus the *cortes*, which lasted from 1810 to 1814, did little to endear the cause of Spain to the Americans.

The chief product of the *Cortes* of Cadiz was the constitution of 1812, a document destined for much usage.[3] Enunciating the doctrine of popular sovereignty, it asserted that the Spanish monarchy was not the patrimony of any one family but that Fernando VII would be recognized

3. This instrument was proclaimed in Spain and her American empire in 1812 and 1820, in Spain again in 1836, Portu- gal and Brazil in 1821, Naples in 1820, and Piedmont in 1821. It was a symbol to European liberals not greatly inferior to the *Marseillaise*.

if he swore to uphold the constitution. As king he would have little authority. Real power resided in the *cortes*, and a number of liberties and rights outlined the new era of freedom supposedly awaiting all Spanish subjects. A complete renovation of the government was projected, one that went beyond many of the claims of revolutionists in the New World. It was with restrained enthusiasm that viceroys in Mexico City and Lima proclaimed this constitution. Many creoles, however, believed that an age of liberty had dawned, and rejoicing was widespread.

Meanwhile, the war against Napoleon began to go well by 1812. A British army under the Duke of Wellington accumulated experience and became a superior fighting force. Spanish irregulars and what remained of the royal army continued to battle the French, though their effectiveness was often derided by Wellington's men, who saw them only as thieves and troublesome auxiliaries. Napoleon lost far more men in Spain than he ever admitted. The terrible bloodletting the French army endured in the peninsula was a major factor in the weakness it displayed in the Corsican's last campaigns. By the latter part of 1813 Wellington and the Spaniards drove Joseph Bonaparte's forces out of all but a corner of Spain. Then the British invaded southwestern France. Early in 1814, when the Allies were converging on Paris, Napoleon released Fernando VII. Within a few weeks the beaten emperor was on Elba.

It was a moving moment when Fernando VII, *El Deseado*, crossed into Spain, in March 1814. Napoleon had extracted a promise that the *afrancesados* should not be punished. This commitment could easily be forgotten, with the result that many of Spain's best educated men became convicts or exiles. The *cortes*, now removed from Cadiz to Madrid, had also obtained Fernando's promise to swear allegiance to the constitution of 1812; he was not to be recognized as king until he did so. After sampling military and popular opinion in northeastern Spain for a few weeks, the liberated sovereign comprehended that the *cortes* did not represent the opinion of the nation, that it was regarded as a usurper, and that most of the population had been outraged by its radicalism. A majority of the deputies also informed the king of their disapproval of recent legislation. Accordingly, on 11 May, 1814, Fernando ordered, from Valencia, the arrest of the liberal deputies. All the *cortes* had done since 1810 was denounced as illegal. A carnival of prosecution brought thousands of liberals and accused liberals into prisons with the *afrancesados*, except for those who escaped to foreign soil. The king's step was astoundingly popular nonetheless. All over Spain crowds surged through the streets and plazas crying *vivas* for absolutism, the Inquisition, and religion. In America, too, the reaction to the king's maneuver was generally favorable. The restoration was now a fact.

THE COLONIAL REVOLTS

The Loyalty of Spanish America, 1808–1810

THE news that Carlos IV had abdicated in March 1808 at Aranjuez was joyfully greeted in the Americas, where Fernando VII was proclaimed with sincere enthusiasm. Most of the peninsular Spaniards who staffed the bureaucracy knew about the royal scandal in Madrid and the sad state of the government. Many creoles, too, were aware of those conditions. Thus hopes flared when a new king came to the throne. Within a few weeks, however, ships appeared in American harbors with news that Joseph Bonaparte had become king of Spain. In every instance the Spanish officials, emphatically supported by the creoles, rejected the new dispensation. In thrusting back the representatives of the new pretender, Spanish officialdom and the Americans exhibited both gallantry and a respect for morality in public affairs. No one seriously believed the Bourbons had willingly sold out their rights to the tyrant Napoleon. Their unheroic behavior at Bayonne was entirely unknown. Fernando VII was widely thought to be chained up in a dungeon grieving for his peoples, and Napoleonic propaganda to the effect that he was quite contented as a French prince was indignantly disbelieved.

For two years the entire Spanish empire in America functioned along traditional lines in the name of the absent Fernando VII. The bureaucracy operated on the momentum of three centuries, necessary replacements being made at times on orders from the supreme central junta in Sevilla. Apparently sincere expressions of sympathy went to Spain; gifts and revenues were as generous as protestations of solidarity. The most conspicuous change in conditions was the accommodating attitude of Great Britain, who had been planning invasions of the Spanish empire until the very moment of the Napoleonic usurpation. Now, England was a friend of the stricken world monarchy, ready to ferry silver to Europe and officials and soldiers to the Americas. Most colonial authorities gave British vessels permission to land in Spanish American ports and sell the merchandise their subjects craved and which Napoleon had largely kept off the continent—and perhaps saved England's economy. Commerce on a small scale with the United States also became legal. While few people said it so bluntly, it was clear that the virtual obliteration of Spain was far from a disaster to many businessmen in Spanish America.

A threat to this state of affairs loomed in the announcement of Carlota Joaquina, the wife of Prince Regent João of Portugal and sister of Fernando VII, that she was willing to exercise the sovereign powers of her abducted brother. This princess was an unpleasant lady who had quickly alienated the Brazilians when the Portuguese court arrived early in 1808. Eager to play a large part in world affairs and to remove herself from her husband, who had caught her plotting against him a few years before and heartily distrusted her, she came forward with a proposal that she be recognized in Buenos Aires and Lima as regent until Fernando VII was released. Her offer was embarrassing. Obviously, Carlota Joaquina had a strong point, yet the colonial authorities preferred to rule in the name of an absent king and a beleaguered junta in Sevilla rather than place themselves at her orders. Nor were the creoles eager to have an imperious Bourbon-Braganza in their midst. Many thought she would only further the interests of Portugal and Brazil. Her husband, on the other hand, feared she would make war on him, or at least create trouble, if she installed herself in one of the Spanish viceroyalties. His most powerful British advisers insisted that she remain in Rio de Janeiro. She did, with much ill grace. In the viceregal capitals Spanish officials courteously considered Carlota Joaquina's offer to come rule over them, but no one of importance lifted a finger to implement it.

The constitutional situation was indeed perplexing, and at times chaotic. Men tended to fall back on legalism when they could. If they were going to be rigidly correct, the legitimate sovereign of the Americans in the Spanish monarchy was the King Father, Carlos IV, both of whose abdications had been forced and were therefore invalid. Yet no one championed his cause, and it was planned to ship him back to Europe if Napoleon, in order to create confusion, should send him to America. Joseph Bonaparte, of course, was universally rejected. But when his agents operating out of Baltimore offered the Americans freedom from Spain, a few thought he should be temporarily recognized as a gesture so as to achieve independence legally. Fernando VII, himself a usurper at Aranjuez, was supposed to be the true monarch, but he was incapacitated by being in French internment. The claim to exercise his sovereign prerogatives put forward by his sister, Carlota Joaquina, was really sounder in a constitutional sense than that of the supreme central junta in Sevilla and its successors. Yet the peninsular bureaucracy that ran the American empire chose to take its direction from the *suprema*. Meanwhile, many creoles were thinking for themselves and guardedly conferring. Informed men well knew that under ancient law enunciated since the time of Isabel the Catholic, the Americas did not belong to Spain but only to the monarch personally. If he was absent, they had as much right to exercise his powers as any self-appointed junta in Sevilla or elsewhere. While responsible creoles were debating these matters and seeking legal grounding for their aspirations, younger, more hot-headed men were saying that Fernando VII would probably never return. Now seemed a good time to rid the Americas of the Spanish tie altogether and to organize a new regime in accordance with the doctrines of the Age of Revolution. During the unsettled years of 1808 and 1809 a rapid shift to the left was taking place in Latin American centers.

Cut adrift from its sources of power, the imperial machine still was able to dominate the situation for two years. The only serious threat loomed in the Viceroyalty of New Spain in the beginning, and it was quickly repressed. Viceroy José de Iturrigaray had served in Mexico City for five years with some success, enough to live down the obloquy of being a close friend of Manuel Godoy. While the Mexicans generally liked him, he had offended the Church hierarchy by threatening to implement one of Godoy's policies of seizing clerical wealth held under disputed titles. Also, he had antagonized peninsular-owned merchant houses by planning to evacuate Vera Cruz in the event of a British attack. In short, his supporters were Mexicans, his critics Spaniards. The news from Spain in 1808 shook the powerful peninsular community in Mexico City particularly, for it was feared that Iturrigaray might betray Fernando VII, the enemy of his patron, Godoy. Rumors circulated that the viceroy was dealing with Joseph Bonaparte or planning to make himself king of Mexico. Apparently there was nothing to support such gossip, for Iturrigaray eventually cleared himself in Spain. But he courted popularity among the creoles and made it clear that the *cabildo* might have as much say as the peninsular-dominated *audiencia*. The Spanish element decided to allow him no chance to do mischief. On the night of September 16, 1808, a group of peninsulars led by a wealthy sugar planter named Gabriel Yermo bribed and forced their way into the viceregal palace. Before the creoles could rally, Iturrigaray and his family were on their way to Spain as prisoners. The junta at Sevilla named a more trusted viceroy, and the peninsulars remained in control of Mexico City without interruption until 1821. Many creoles muttered against *gachupín* arrogance and conspired through a secret society known as the Guadalupes. But they remained entirely subordinated to the peninsulars in the capital for thirteen years longer.

In 1809 four uprisings, all obscure and widely separated, gave an indication of turbulence to come. The large university in Chuquisaca in Upper Peru was a lively center where fundamental problems of government were debated. While modern revolutionary writings enjoyed some circulation, of more importance were the doctrines of St. Thomas Aquinas and Francisco Suárez concerning the relations of rulers and subjects. The crisis of the Spanish monarchy in 1808 had provoked a veritable frenzy of discussion. The two most important officials in the area, the president of the *audiencia* and the archbishop, were unpopular. It was known they had deliberated carefully about Carlota Joaquina's pro-

posals. When they finally chose to follow other Spanish officials by placing Upper Peru under the rule of the junta at Sevilla, a campaign of
slander ensued. On May 25, 1809, these dignitaries were suddenly deposed by a clamorous group, among which university students were most
conspicuous. A junta was established to represent the doctors and students of the various colleges, the creole *cabildo*, and dissident members of
the *audiencia*. This body asserted that Upper Peru had the same right to
govern for the absent king as similar bodies in Spain had claimed in
1808. More radical utterances were heard: of drastic social reforms, new
governmental institutions, even independence from a distant land
known as Spain with whom they once had shared a common monarch.
On July 16, 1809 the *cabildo* in La Paz, also in Upper Peru, rose up to expel peninsular officials and to proclaim its autonomy. In both cities the
creoles were in deadly earnest about resisting Sevilla's pretension. There
was nothing wrong with their logic or their law. The trouble was in their
timing. Other areas of the Spanish empire were not mentally prepared
for such self-assertion. From Lima the viceroy sent a force which conquered La Paz; the viceroy at Buenos Aires overpowered Chuquisaca.
The rebellions, however, made a deep impression on creoles in southern South America, as would be seen the following year. Upper Peru
was destined to be the last mainland colony to leave the Spanish empire.

The secluded city of Quito, long a clerical and intellectual center,
likewise claimed the right to govern itself instead of deferring to the
suprema at Sevilla. A group of liberal creoles led by the Marquis of Selva
Alegre transformed a not unwilling *cabildo* into a junta for this purpose
in August 1809. With impeccable logic, as in the cases of La Paz and
Chuquisaca, the junta professed its loyalty to Fernando VII while ousting Spanish officials. It was not long before a military force from Lima
conquered Quito, just in time to prevent its capture by a different army
dispatched by the viceroy of New Granada. Most of the rebels escaped,
and in Bogotá the viceroy came under severe criticism for refusing to
recognize the justice of Quito's position. A few months later Bogotá
would follow Quito's example. A less specific movement occurred in
December 1809 in Valladolid, in western New Spain. There the creoles,
long full of resentment against various aspects of imperial rule and antagonized by the arrogance of the peninsulars in Mexico City, conspired to set up an independent junta. Before they could act the authorities arrested some, but, significantly, not all, of the plotters.

For the time being it appeared that the viceroys had acted swiftly
and successfully against creole ambitions in four widely different cities.
By the beginning of 1810 the Spanish empire was functioning as it had
for so long, but with the *suprema* at Sevilla rather than the king as its
brain. Peninsulars in America were reassured. It seemed that they were

strong enough to maintain the traditional administration, with or without the monarch, and that the Americans had little desire and less chance of mounting a successful challenge.

The Imperial Crisis of 1810

FOUR rebellions in major South American cities during 1810 and a fierce race war in Mexico exploded whatever hopes the peninsulars had of presiding peacefully over a long interregnum. All of these uprisings were the result of carefully laid plans, the fruit of months of conspiracy and agitation. All of them were begun as ostensible efforts to establish self-government in the name of Fernando VII, but with little sincerity. They were touched off soon after news arrived that French troops had occupied Sevilla and had apparently brought Spanish resistance to an end everywhere but in Cadiz. The supreme junta, manifestly a failure, had dissolved itself. A call had gone out for the Americans to choose one-third of the deputies for a *cortes*. The summons seemed an impertinence to the creoles, an act of desperation to continue the pretense of a world-wide monarchy which had no king and no metropolis. Spain appeared to be finished as a nation in any case. Thus creole elements seized power in Caracas, Santa Fe de Bogotá, Buenos Aires, Santiago, and in western Mexico. None of these insurrections succeeded for long but the one in Buenos Aires. Ultimately, the reason for their failure was the abiding loyalty of the strongest sectors of the empire to the old regime and the royal symbol. Also, Spain was not as prostrate as she looked in the summer of 1810. Even if these revolutionary movements aborted, they were so important in shaping the eventual independence of Latin America that we must consider them in detail.

VENEZUELA, FUSE OF THE REVOLUTION

For some years the captaincy-general of Venezuela had seemed a danger spot of the Spanish empire. Foreigners and radical ideas circulated more easily there than in other colonies, possibly because of the considerable intercourse with the United States and Great Britain during periods of Spanish naval weakness. Frenchmen driven by slave revolts from the Caribbean islands reached Caracas in some number. Whatever their personal views, Frenchmen always seemed more modern than Spaniards, and while they related horrible stories of African savagery, they sometimes inadvertently inspired Venezuelan Negroes to dream of freedom. After they seized Trinidad in 1797, the British smuggled both goods and newspapers into Venezuela. Their plans to conquer this colony in the years 1804 to 1808 kept the Spanish on edge. The plot of Spanish and local republicans in 1797 had revealed some degree of latent revolutionary sentiment. It was known that radical idealists and assorted trouble-makers were at large.

The core of the country was the rugged strip of coastal land between the mountains and the Caribbean stretching from Coro in the west through Puerto Cabello, Valencia, Caracas, and on to Barcelona in the east. Here was a conventional colonial society, more brilliant than most and in recent years very prosperous. Beyond this area, in the mountains, the grassy swamps and plains of the Orinoco Valley, and the wilderness to the south were many Indian missions and also free communities of untamed natives. Of more importance in the years of revolution were the various half-breed types, most of them nomadic horsemen called *llaneros*. They hated civilization and were available for war and adventure when the time came. To be sure, the effective part of the colony was less secure than it might appear. Creole society was full of tensions. Descendants of the early Spanish settlers looked down on Canarians and Basques, who disliked one another. Radical intellectuals, the power-hungry, adventurers, and conservative, clerical-minded elements typical of Spanish colonial society were held together by slender ties, the most important of which was the imperial system. The large Negro population which supported economic life was a potentially explosive force.

The news from Spain in 1808 had brought about the usual reactions of indignation, dismay, and fervent expressions of loyalty to Fernando VII. To a greater degree than elsewhere, however, the creoles began to plan the overthrow of the peninsular officials. Many of these conspirators came from the wealthy planter and mercantile groups, and a number had drunk deeply from the fountains of revolutionary ideology. Some were sincere republicans and anti-clericals. Others simply coveted the positions held by the peninsulars. Very few gave serious thought to improving the condition of the colored races. Whatever their motives of greed and idealism, they recognized the opportunity provided by the fall of Sevilla and the apparent conquest of Spain, which British news reports announced in April 1810. Prepared for such a crisis, the conspirators engineered a mass meeting in front of the palace of Captain-General Vicente Emparán. They forced him to resign and ousted other peninsular officials. A junta, based on the *cabildo* of Caracas, asserted its right to exercise the powers of the absent king and invited other towns to follow its lead. The principal municipalities did as they were told. Soon a sovereign body in Caracas announced the freedom of Venezuela from all outside authority save that of Fernando VII. Largely as a gesture to attract the servile population, Negro slave traffic was forbidden and Indian tributes were ended. As the little congress contemplated a revolutionary future, highly unorthodox opinions were aired. These frightened the conservative elements, who had been caught off balance by the rebellion. A reaction set in quickly and gained control over some of the hinterland. And the beleaguered Spanish government at Cadiz was not as weak as the revolutionists had anticipated. By mid-summer 1810 it was able to enforce a blockade of the Venezuelan coast and to ship over royalist troops from Cuba. Hence, the Caracas government decided that British support must be won, and to this end it sent a delegation to London headed by Simón Bolívar.

Francisco de Miranda, el precursor

At this point it is necessary to digress in order to bring up to date the careers of two of the legendary heroes of the Independence movement. The first, Francisco de Miranda, is revered as the precursor of liberation. Born in Caracas in 1750, son of a Canarian who belonged to the lower gentry, Miranda acquired a fair education but was rebuffed by the inner circle of the local aristocracy. He went to Spain in 1771 and obtained a commission in the royal army. Again he was embittered by snubs, this time from peninsulars who disdained colonials. Miranda served for nine years in the army, mainly in the peninsula and North Africa. His reputation was dubious, for he was twice arrested for insubordination and was accused of stealing. Also, he read Rousseau and other forbidden writers. In 1780 he was transferred to the New World to participate in Spain's war against Great Britain. Long unpromoted, he advanced two ranks during these campaigns, to lieutenant colonel, and took the British surrender at Pensacola. A promising military career was cut short, however, when he was charged with illegal dealing in merchandise and possibly the sale of military secrets as he negotiated with British authorities on Jamaica. Years later, in 1797, he was absolved of these accusations by the Council of Indies, but this action may have been politically motivated.

Guilty or not, Miranda deserted and fled to the United States. An extensive visit in 1783–1785, during which he met Washington, Lafayette, Alexander Hamilton, and Tom Paine, failed to impress him particularly with the prospects of the new nation, but he made up his mind that Spanish America should also become free. After a short visit to England, which inspired him much more than the United States, Miranda made a spectacular tour of the continent. Between 1785 and 1789 he was a guest in nearly every capital, including Constantinople, St. Petersburg, and Stockholm. Posing as a liberal nobleman pursued by the Spanish Inquisition, he readily won admirers wherever he went. Wealthy ladies were eager to support him, among them the aging empress of Russia, Catherine the Great. Miranda cut quite a figure. He

widely advertised the supposed readiness of Spanish America for independence and fed the legends so dear to "enlightened" persons that
Spain was a benighted land of fanaticism and tyranny.

During a sojourn in England between 1789 and 1792 he won the
interest and some financial support from the prime minister, William
Pitt the Younger, by revealing his outdated secrets of Spanish defenses
in the Caribbean. Then, as a sincere radical, he went to Revolutionary
France and threw himself into the struggle against the kings of Europe.
Serving as a general for a few months, he participated in the invasion of
Belgium and possibly, though not certainly, exhibited military ability.
But he was involved on the wrong side when the Jacobins bested the
Girondins in 1793 and spent many months in a Paris prison. Somehow
he escaped the guillotine and became part of the gaudy Thermidorian
society. Expelled from France in 1797, probably because Spain and
France were then allied, he went back to England for several years of
good living financed by the British government and various female admirers. His most important activity during this phase was operating a cell
of a secret society which influenced dozens of young Spanish Americans
in London and sought to stimulate revolutionary sentiment in Venezuela by means of correspondence and propaganda. British officialdom
was interested in Miranda only sporadically, when it was thought he
might be useful in one or another of the projects to attack the Spanish
empire. The assault on Buenos Aires in 1806 was in part traceable to Miranda's inspiration, for he had been a friend of Admiral Popham.

Britain declined, however, to back a grandiose scheme of his to invade Venezuela, and so he went to the United States in 1805. With a
mysterious source of funds and the connivance of the American authorities, he obtained a sloop, the *Leander*, and a crew of adventurers drawn
from the New York waterfront. This unimposing expedition received
reinforcements in Haiti in the way of two small vessels and proceeded to
Venezuela. In April 1806, with splendid hopes and florid proclamations,
Miranda landed at Coro to announce the liberation of his homeland.
Apathy and suspicion greeted his invasion. He had not been in Venezuela for a generation and knew little of conditions there. Only a few
conspirators had ever heard of him. His attempt a complete fiasco, he
re-embarked and cruised some more. This time he obtained the protection of a British squadron, which facilitated another attempt, near Puerto
Cabello in August 1806. Again, the Venezuelans gave no sign of a
popular uprising, and the Spanish shore garrison captured many of the
invaders. Disgraced and not a little ridiculous, Miranda returned to England. His hopes soared again when he learned of an expeditionary force
being readied in Ireland for an assault on Spanish America. But when
Napoleon took over Spain in 1808 the British reversed their policy and

sent this army to the Iberian peninsula to save rather than strip the traditional Spanish enemy. Miranda ranted at British perfidy, totally unable to comprehend the overriding importance of defeating Napoleon. Now an aging voluptuary, he settled down comfortably in London, his life apparently wasted on hopeless causes. The Venezuelan delegation which reached England in the summer of 1810 had instructions not to treat with him.

Simón Bolívar, el libertador

The second Venezuelan who emerged into prominence at this time was a far more significant figure than Miranda. Simón Bolívar, chief of the little mission from Venezuela to London, was twenty-seven years old and belonged to one of the richest and most aristocratic families in South America. An orphan, he was turned over by his uncle and guardian to private tutors, the most influential of whom was Simón Rodríguez, as he called himself, a strange man and follower of Rousseau who indeed resembled that tortured genius and crackpot in so many ways. Bolívar's uncle would have been shocked had he known the type of education Rodríguez was giving his ward. Outdoing Émile in Rousseau's novel about pedagogy, the student was allowed to run wild, indulging his will, learning by doing, reading heretical books, and absorbing a natural religion. He learned to love nature, to express himself without inhibitions, and to play with ideas. During a gloriously free adolescence he acquired a strong taste for the forbidden radical literature of the Enlightenment. At last fate caught up with the tutor. Rodríguez was implicated in the republican plot of 1797 and had to flee Venezuela. The young Bolívar spent the next two years studying military affairs as a cadet and having a fine time riding and dancing.

In 1799 the youth went to Spain to join another uncle and complete his education. It was necessary for him to go via Vera Cruz, where he happened to meet the Viceroy of New Spain. On this occasion the sixteen-year-old boy aired some of his radical views in a defiant fashion, but the viceroy made no issue of this impertinence and Bolívar proceeded to Madrid. An unusually handsome youth with a small but iron-like frame, a captivating personality, and plenty of spending money, Bolívar was soon enjoying himself in the capital. He must have been an attractive fellow. Yet he had a serious side, and during this period he read more than ever and exhibited an intelligent curiosity about affairs of state. Like so many of the future liberators, he experienced the cruel and not always subtle slights directed by Spaniards at the American-born. Also, he had access to the royal court, where he verified to his satisfaction the truth of the salacious rumors concerning Queen María Luisa and Godoy and the disreputable behavior of other persons in high places. Surely, a

great deal of Bolívar's subsequent republicanism stemmed from his experiences in Madrid. He even had the opportunity to learn to dislike the
Prince of Asturias, the future Fernando VII, who repelled almost everyone who came to know him personally.

After nearly two years in Madrid, Bolívar had to leave under pressure.
His relatives had fallen from royal favor and he himself was involved in a
scuffle. He went to France, where he observed the wonders that Bonaparte was working in that revolution-wracked land. Then he married a
creole lady who, at twenty, was two years older than himself. The young
couple sailed to Venezuela in 1802. The owner of many houses, plantations, slaves, mines, and cattle, and a very happy husband, Bolívar was
ready to settle down to the agreeable routine of an aristocrat. But his wife
died suddenly, and his grief was so intense that nothing in Venezuela
could assuage it. Bolívar never re-married. As many women as he was to
possess in later years, he remained true in Romantic fashion to the belief
that he could never love another as he had his bride.

Returning to Madrid, the young widower continued to mourn. He
also underwent another disagreeable experience at the hands of the
government, which required all foreigners, including loyal Spanish subjects from America, to leave the capital because of a food shortage. Bolívar saw how off-handedly even important Americans were treated. In
Paris once more he fell in with a cousin, Fanny du Villars, who knew
many brilliant people. For two years Bolívar enjoyed being miserable,
always the Romantic, dissipating, drifting aimlessly in high society, and
despising the fortune he was wasting. Yet he read widely and observed
political affairs. He joined the masons, an indication that he was liberal.
Among the celebrities he met was Alexander von Humboldt, who committed one of the most ironical *gaffes* of all time by saying to Bolívar that
he did not see the man who was going to lead Spanish America to independence. Young Bolívar made no secret of his disillusionment when
Napoleon took the imperial crown in 1804. Possibly he did not boycott
the coronation ceremonies as he threatened, but he always condemned
the great general, whom he resembled in so many ways, for betraying the
republican ideal.

At this point Simón Rodríguez again entered Bolívar's circle and be-
sought him to stop wasting his life. Re-establishing his ascendancy, the
former tutor persuaded Bolívar to make a pilgrimage on foot to Rousseau's early homes in Geneva and Chambéry. In 1805 the two took this
trip and went on to Milan, where they saw Napoleon crowned king of
Italy, to Venice, Florence, Naples, and Rome. Bolívar saw Humboldt
several times more, once when they climbed Vesuvius together, and they
often talked of America. One evening in 1806 Bolívar and Rodríguez ascended the Monte Sacro in Rome at sundown. As they looked over the

ruins of the Eternal City in the twilight Bolívar sank to his knees and took an oath to free Venezuela from Spain, or so Rodríguez reported many years later. It may well have happened. In the Romantic Age poetic men like Bolívar were entirely capable of making such dramatic vows without feeling absurd or self-conscious. Certainly Bolívar no longer regarded himself as a Spaniard by this time. He avoided Spain as he made his way home, going by Hamburg and the United States. Early in 1807 he was back in Caracas.

During the next three years Bolívar looked after his extensive properties with an aristocratic insouciance, for he never showed much interest in business. More important were his clandestine activities in conjunction with other young men of his class who were enchanted with the possibility of promoting a revolution. They met frequently at affairs that were ostensibly social, at races, hunts, dances, dinners, and gambling parties. Also there were exciting gatherings of the secret society. When, in April 1810, the creoles overthrew the royal government at Caracas, this younger group was noisy and energetic. But it was not dominant; Bolívar and his associates were too radical for the others. This was perhaps one reason why Bolívar was chosen to lead the mission to London, to get him out of the country.

Bolívar really failed in his approach to the British government. He was supposed to obtain British recognition and military aid. He got neither. British officials refused to see him except on an informal basis. The reason, of course, was that England attached supreme importance only to the defeat of Napoleon. Spain was in the fight, a major battleground, and the resources of her empire in America were important to the cause. Bolívar played on the everlasting British desire for regular commercial relations with Venezuela and offered exaggerated prospects to British investors. But he got nowhere with the government, which loyally supported Spain. He violated his instructions by calling on Miranda, whom he found as fascinating as other impressionable South Americans had. Bolívar insisted that the Precursor come to Venezuela. Though he was now sixty and had a pleasant life in London, Miranda agreed to risk everything by plunging again into the cause of liberation. Perhaps he was not the cynical adventurer many people said he was.

The First Republic

The little "patriot" state of Venezuela, professing an unfelt loyalty to Fernando VII, was making very modest progress when Bolívar and Miranda arrived on separate ships late in 1810. Only the northern area adhered to the new government, and within its limits disaffection was strong. The worst problem was the inability of the creoles to organize a workable government, a grim portent of Latin America's future. They were quarrelsome, jealous, inexperienced, passionate, and despite the invocations to Reason, unreasonable. They could destroy but not build. There was no common agreement on what to do with the opportunity to establish a new regime. Into this distressing situation came Miranda, the friend of Europe's great, an experienced propagandist, and former lieutenant general of the French Republic. He grandly preened himself to take charge of the faltering state with the aid of Bolívar. Copying the method of the Jacobin Club in Paris some years before, they acquired control of a "secret" lodge that included the more radical and energetic elements. Gradually this society attained an ascendancy over the congress, chiefly because it had a determined program. On July 5, 1811, the congress under Miranda's prodding declared the independence of Venezuela, the first Spanish state in America to take such a step. The declaration was simple and dignified, free of embittered charges against the mother country. Venezuela, or a section of it, was now a republic.

The first republic lasted a year, from July 1811 to July 1812. While Miranda and Bolívar had many critics and disagreed between themselves, they were usually the most important figures of the regime. Many agreeable plans were announced. Civil liberties were to be scrupulously respected. Each community was to be self-governing, thus making the republic federal. All kinds of measures were to bring wealth and economic growth to the former colony. But realities were too intimidating. Among the most discouraging was the collapse of business that ensued from the expulsion of the peninsulars, the blockade, the recalcitrance of the hinterland, and the general uncertainty. In such an atmosphere political programs seemed hollow, even when ideologues could agree. Furthermore, many creoles regarded the whole proceeding as sacrilegious and iniquitous, for they were largely unprepared for so bold a step as repudiating the king. The military situation grew dangerous as Spanish reinforcements arrived.[4] Mission Indians, *llaneros*, and country folk in general were organized to oppose the rebel towns. A long deadlock might have resulted but for the intervention of nature on Holy Thursday in March 1812, when an earthquake literally shook the republic apart and killed thousands. The escape of royalist territory from this catastrophe did not go unmarked by those who contended the republic was wicked. Providence had intervened. While Bolívar angrily defied Providence and nature alike, it was clear that the earthquake was a devastating material and moral blow to his cause.

Spanish forces led by Domingo de Monteverde advanced from the west, recruiting Canarians in the area about Coro and Valencia. *Llaneros* who disliked the civilized coastlands and craved to pillage moved up

4. Regardless of their desperate situation at home, the Spaniards were able to transfer troops from Cuba to Costa Firme, often using British ships.

from the south. Under the circumstances the congress made Miranda a virtual dictator and proceeded to conscript men and supplies from the stricken republic in a brutal way. Much as he relished his position, the aging Miranda had little administrative experience or capacity. He drilled his troops in European style and inveighed against rum and gambling. He lived in grandeur, as befitted the head of a state. Yet he was indecisive, unable to take the initiative even when he had a numerical superiority in fighting men. Perhaps he hoped for foreign aid. More likely he was merely confused. After weeks of inactivity the republicans suffered a ruinous blow through a dereliction of duty on Bolívar's part. This young commander, who also lacked experience, neglected to take proper precautions with a number of royalist prisoners at Puerto Cabello. They escaped, completely unhinging the western defenses of the republic, and Monteverde made a deep advance. Bolívar was so chagrined he almost lost his reason.

Miranda was still in command of a larger force than Monteverde's, but it was demoralized and entirely on the defensive. Erstwhile patriots were now flocking over to the royalist side. Instead of fighting, Miranda sought terms. A perennial failure, the elderly adventurer had again lost heart. Monteverde agreed to a truce which provided amnesty for surrendering patriot soldiers and permission, within a certain time limit, for Miranda himself to leave the country with the republican treasury. If Miranda's negotiation was not heroic, at least it made sense. To flee with funds in order to fight some other day would become a standard practice in Latin American insurrections. But Bolívar, almost deranged from his own disgrace at Puerto Cabello, placed another interpretation on Miranda's action. He convinced himself the older commander was selling out. Possibly Bolívar was right, for men have always disagreed about the Precursor's character. Yet it is more likely that Bolívar, acutely conscious of his own contribution to the fall of the republic, acted through some perverse psychological compulsion to ruin Miranda in order to salvage his own sanity and reputation. Whatever his thinking, or passions, he and others arrested Miranda before he could board ship and had him turned over to the Spaniards after the time limit for the truce had expired, on July 31, 1812. Miranda spent the last three and a half years of his life in Spanish prisons, lastly in Cadiz. Bolívar was rewarded with a safe conduct, which enabled him to sail to New Granada. There is no reason to believe that his conscience ever disturbed him over this matter.

Revolution in New Granada

Bolívar and other refugees from the Venezuelan disaster made their way to the former colony in the west, New Granada. Like Venezuela, the viceroyalty had experienced considerable growth and prosperity during recent years. Except for a few impractical revolutionaries, such as Antonio Nariño, who had been in jail or internment since 1797, there was little evidence of subversion. In 1808 the viceroy was an aged and deaf general, Antonio Amar y Borbón, a competent official who expected to retire during the year. Instead of an honorable relief from duty, he was faced with the crisis of the Napoleonic intrusion into Spain. The reaction in his domain was typical. With apparent unanimity the peninsular and creole elements asserted their loyalty to Fernando VII and to the Sevilla junta which claimed the right to exercise his powers. Amar y Borbón took military measures to protect the viceroyalty in the event of a French invasion, and the clergy was ordered to inculcate loyal sentiments for the traditional Spanish system. A junta in Santa Fe de Bogotá called together by the viceroy, composed of leading peninsular officials and creoles, seemed to agree with his policies, though an eloquent lawyer named Camilo Torres made a strong plea for the right of the Americas to govern themselves. The uprising in Quito in August 1809, even if it failed, also indicated a creole ambition to take matters out of the hands of peninsular officials. During the early months of 1810, however, the viceroy and his entourage were reasonably confident of their position. They had little intimation that many prominent Americans were conspiring to unseat them and that a few radical revolutionaries were planning a real upheaval.

The reports of Spain's collapse in the late spring of 1810 and the successful rebellion in Caracas of April 1810 destroyed the illusion that New Granada was safe. The first city to revolt was Cartagena, on May 22, 1810. Long and lucratively as this seaport had been involved in the Spanish commercial monopoly, its most dynamic citizens wanted to trade with the rest of the world. A junta was founded and the port thrown open to all ships. Other towns up the Magdalena and Cauca valleys similarly organized self-governing bodies and ousted Spanish officials. The chain of rebellion reached Santa Fe de Bogotá on July 20, 1810, when the *cabildo* took charge and arrested the viceroy. Scattered municipalities in the highlands to the west and south of the capital also rose up. The whole process was relatively pacific. Few Spaniards were killed, few royalist heads broken. As usually happens after revolutions, a wave of good feeling swept over the affected areas. Most of the former officials were deported, and the creoles confidently took over their positions.

During the next five or six years the New Granadans were to

demonstrate a pitiful incapacity to govern themselves. The name Colombian historians have given this period, *patria boba* (foolish fatherland), conveys a sage verdict on the floundering of the creoles. New Granada, with its fantastic geographical variety and sparse population, was scarcely a fatherland of any sort but a collection of settlements with little affection or concern for one another. Moreover, the creoles who displaced the peninsulars were inclined to disagree wildly. Political opinions ranged from fanatical attachment to the old regime to extreme Jacobinism. Districts, towns, and families were split by fierce ideological struggles that had little bearing on the needs of a new state. The capital was the worst divided of all. *Bogotanos* had developed a taste for oratory and writing in their cool, green isolation. Now they poured words upon one another and preached to the other towns. It was far pleasanter to articulate their differences than settle down to the dull labors of state-building.

If the philosophical framework of the new freedom was confused, so was its geography. The junta at the capital issued a call for a national congress to legislate for the former viceroyalty. The response was very uneven. Two large areas which later became nations, Quito (Ecuador) and Panama, were full of Spanish soldiers and therefore spurned the invitation altogether. The ranching and mining region of the southwest, Pasto and Popayán, had a light population of isolated mountain folk who were fervently royalist. And the Caribbean port of Santa Marta, which was likely to do what its competitor Cartagena did not do, rejected the revolution altogether. Nor did Cartagena join the other insurrectionists. Declaring its independence of everybody in 1811, it remained aloof in its radical republicanism from all the other cities. All that was left for the congress to represent was Bogotá and the river towns between that capital and the Caribbean, plus a few mountain districts.

When the assembly convened late in 1810, it announced the severance of the bonds with Spain, though Fernando VII was still to be recognized as monarch if he came to New Granada in person. Then discord got altogether out of hand. Bogotá wished to dominate the new state while the other towns championed federalism. At length most of the congress withdrew to Tunja and organized a federalist state known as the United Provinces or the Confederation of New Granada, in which Camilo Torres was the most influential figure. Bogotá stood aloof in her mountainous isolation as the state of Cundinamarca. Antonio Nariño, whose long martyrdom at the hands of Spain appeared to have ended triumphantly, was its president. Thus only half of New Granada was in patriot hands, and that half had three quarreling governments: Tunja, Cartagena, and Cundinamarca.

Into this confusion Bolívar and other refugees from the Venezuelan debacle walked or sailed in the late summer of 1812. Bolívar was more or less the leader of these exiles, and he rose to the occasion superbly. He assured the New Granadans that only a battle had been lost, not a campaign, and that through Miranda's "betrayal." The 29-year-old officer was impressive even in defeat, obviously a man of compelling determination and persuasive eloquence. The Confederation placed him in charge of a small force with which he helped clear the royalists out of the lower Magdalena. Having proved he was a competent soldier, he sought and received permission to organize an army of Venezuelan refugees and New Granadan volunteers. Now a brigadier general of the Confederation, he assured his backers that he would obstruct an invasion that Monteverde was planning from Venezuela. He did not inform them of his plan to carry the revolution straight back to Caracas.

The Second Republic in Venezuela

In May 1813 Simón Bolívar began an undertaking that was to bring him international fame. With fewer than 600 soldiers, most of them indifferently armed and disciplined, he moved across the jungles and swamps of northeastern New Granada into the Andes and Venezuela. He had a Napoleonic ability to inspire his men to superhuman efforts, employing florid proclamations, appeals to cupidity and vengeance, poignant speeches, and just the right word here and there to individual soldiers. He was a natural military commander. The invasion of 1813, known justly as "the admirable campaign," revealed him a genius, or something close to it, in the art of war. In spite of his great numerical inferiority Bolívar was able to immobilize his enemy by striking unexpectedly at exposed positions. The configuration of the mountains served him well. Following not the valleys but the ridges, he avoided Monteverde's concentrations and descended at times to massacre isolated groups of Spaniards. Confused by these tactics, the royalists floundered. Also, republicans who had hidden in the eastern section of the Venezuelan swamps took heart and operated effectively in Monteverde's rear.

Bolívar's political warfare was often successful. Towns and communities were usually won over by his appeals or promises. Thus warriors, horses, supplies, and ammunition accrued to his forces as he penetrated the Venezuelan highlands. So well were things going he issued a "war to the death" order, which called on all to join his cause or face extermination as enemies. The pretext for this barbarous announcement was that Monteverde had violated his promise to Miranda regarding amnesty for the captured patriots. In reality, it was an act of terrorism, the old story of each side contending that it was retaliating for the crimes of the other. It led, as might be expected, to a carnival of atrocity on both sides. Bolívar continued his triumphant penetration, ignoring the protests of New Granada that the objective of his campaign was won and that he should return. In August 1813, with 2,500 soldiers, he staged a grand entrance into Caracas as *El Libertador*, his immortal title. A showman of the first order, he well knew how to make these pageants memorable experiences. There would be dozens more before his career ended. For many years people in South America would recall the great day when the Liberator came to town.

Again, the republic was proclaimed, though as before it consisted only of a sector of the north and not the entire country. Bolívar was less idealistic than he had been in 1810–1812. The mistake of those years, he believed, had been in allowing the various communities too much self-government and the population too much liberty. Thus he instituted a highly centralized regime he chose to describe as "the republic of wise and virtuous men," but which was really a dictatorship. Bolívar loved to play the ruler—much as he affected not to—but his abilities in administrative matters were not outstanding. Nor did he enjoy the details of statecraft half as much as the enunciation of political ideals or the pageantry of state occasions. Yet it must be admitted that he worked hard at this time to make the republic operate, and he had little assistance of value. The military situation was such that he needed to employ extreme measures, conscripting soldiers, seizing funds, issuing worthless paper money, and repressing opinions which might damage republican morale. For a year, from July 1813 to July 1814, Bolívar managed to keep the republic afloat. His ship of state was in reality a fragile raft tossed by waves of economic disorder and royalist vengeance.

The military pressures consisted mainly of regular Spanish forces under Monteverde, who had been out-manuevered rather than defeated in the *campaña admirable*. His forces were still organized and in a position to receive fresh supplies from Cuba and Puerto Rico. Of more importance each day were his allies, the barbarian *llaneros*, who were developing more taste than ever to loot the coastland. Leading the *llanero* bands, appropriately called the Legion of Hell, was an ex-convict named José Tomás Boves, an expert in mutilation and torture, a man who leered with sadistic delight while slaves raped womenfolk of republicans, when patriot prisoners of war walked over broken glass with their feet skinned. Bolívar's "war to the death" policy gave Boves a convenient justification for his atrocities. The Spanish advantage increased markedly in the spring of 1814, when it became known that Fernando VII was back on his throne. Royalists in republican territory took heart, and erstwhile patriots began to switch sides. For all his frenzy and eloquence Bolívar was unable to stop the tide. Once, recalling his experience at Puerto Cabello in 1812, he had 800 royalist prisoners massacred at La Guaira. Yet Boves and Monteverde could out-do the republicans in frightfulness. Sorrow, pain, fear, and death came to thousands as Venezuela was ravaged. Bolívar retreated from west to east, surrendering Valencia and then Caracas. By July 1814 his forces were decimated and the republic scarcely a pretense. He shipped his treasury to safety and prepared to sail away. At this point some of his officers, unconvinced he had done his best, considered arresting him. Bolívar was more fortunate than Miranda, however, and he talked his way out of the situation. In September 1814 he was on a boat headed for New Granada. The *campaña admirable* and the "republic of wise and virtuous men" had left Venezuela in ruins, at the mercy of vengeful royalists and savage *llaneros*. Boves was killed in October 1814, but others exacted punishment. Only a few hundred republican soldiers escaped the general debacle, some of them with the fallen Liberator, others in the swamps at the mouth of the Orinoco.

The Fall of New Granada

During Bolívar's absence conditions in New Granada, a veritable *patria boba*, had failed to improve. Royalists still held Panama, Quito, Santa Marta, and the southwest. Viceroy Francisco de Montalvo was in Panama awaiting the collapse of the "traitors" and "bandits," knowing that a large Spanish expedition was on its way. Cartagena was an ultra-liberal independent republic, the confederation was impotently calling for unity, and Bogotá-Cundinamarca was still at odds with the other patriots. Antonio Nariño, lately president of Cundinamarca, had led an army southward in 1813 to expel the royalists from Quito. Instead, his troops fled, and he was captured in May 1814. Nearly six more years as a prisoner of Spain, mostly in Cadiz, blighted his life. His old rival, Camilo Torres, welcomed Bolívar back from the second Venezuelan disaster in September 1814, chivalrously proclaiming the Liberator a great general if an unlucky political leader. The confederation invited Bolívar to conquer Cundinamarca and unite it to the other patriot city-states. This he did by December 1814. Another grand entrance and another title, this time Captain-General of New Granada, removed some of the sting of defeat from the Liberator. But when he went north to force Cartagena into the confederation, he was frustrated by stout defenses. All he achieved there was to weaken the little republic just before the Spanish expedition arrived to assault it.

In 1815 the confederation made Bogotá its capital and Torres its president. No amount of eloquent defiance could alter the fact that the cause of independence was sinking. A panicky mood gripped many of the erstwhile patriots. Utterly demoralized, Bolívar himself withdrew from the scene and sailed to Jamaica. A huge expeditionary force from Spain with 10,500 battle-hardened veterans landed in Venezuela. With about half of these men, the commander, Field Marshal Pablo Morillo, sailed to New Granada. A three-month siege of Cartagena brought the starving port into his power in December 1815. With a drive worthy of the conquistadors, Morillo's men moved up the Magdalena to join others who had crossed the Andes from Venezuela. In May 1816 the Spaniards entered Bogotá, and Viceroy Montalvo took his throne.

Fernando VII was sending many soothing appeals for reconciliation together with generous offers of amnesty to his rebellious colonists. Montalvo and Morillo implemented these proclamations with a remarkable lack of political wisdom. Their method was to visit extremely harsh punishment on the patriots but to follow it quickly with a shower of pardons. Thus they summarily executed the principal leaders, including Camilo Torres. They rewarded people for informing on their neighbors. In many towns they set up councils of purification which decided on executing or jailing former patriots, and councils of sequestration, which judged whose property was to be confiscated. Prisons and labor gangs were full of men who had come forward earlier to serve the one-time autonomous governments. Books with liberal or independence sentiments were burned in public. After a few weeks of such stern corrective action, as the royalists termed their activities, the king's mercy would flow liberally. Somehow the strategy did not win over the New Granadans. They remembered the cruelties and suspected the pardons. Furthermore, economic conditions remained bad after the restoration. After three years, as events were to prove, most of the population were eager to fling themselves into the arms of Bolívar.

UPRISING IN NEW SPAIN

It seemed that the Viceroyalty of New Spain would remain less affected than the other dominions by the demoralizing news from Europe in 1810, so firmly did the peninsulars control the imperial bureaucracy following their coup of September 1808. Preparations were soon under way for the election of representatives to the *cortes* of Cadiz who, as it turned out, were far more pro-Mexican than royalist. In the provinces, especially the mining districts north and west of Mexico City, peninsular authority was much weaker than in the capital. For months, creoles had been condemning the arrogance of the peninsulars. While their grievances were no more acute than in other parts of the Spanish empire, they were closer to the United States and thus more affected by its example. Furthermore, agents of the Bonapartes who operated out of Baltimore and New Orleans were in a position to foment subversion. A movement in 1809 at Valladolid (now Morelia) in western Mexico had been detected and frustrated by the authorities. In 1810 a rather able group of creoles, including former officials, army officers, clergymen, planters, and intellectuals, who had a secret center in Querétaro, considered ways to oust the peninsulars in Mexico City. Their plan was far advanced when, in September, it was discovered. One of the conspirators, Father Miguel Hidalgo y Costilla, decided to spring the plot, even though it was ahead of schedule. On the morning of September 16, 1810, he vigorously rang the bell at his parish church in Dolores, a town near Querétaro, and the inhabitants gathered to hear him. With much fervor the priest exhorted them to strike at once for independence, good government, and, paradoxically, for King Fernando VII. The Virgin of Guadalupe was invoked to bless the cause.

Father Hidalgo

It was a most improbable incendiary, a 57-year-old priest, who was summoning the village to revolt and inadvertently setting off a fearful Indian rebellion. Born in 1753, Hidalgo was the son of white parents and had grown up in the mining province of Guanajuato. He attended the College of San Nicolás at Valladolid and did well enough to earn a scholarship to the Royal and Pontifical University of Mexico, where he took his bachelor's degree in theology in 1773. Apart from being an able student, he was conspicuous for his sensitivity to the woes of the Indians and a rather mocking attitude toward the authorities. After his graduation he taught at Valladolid, where he indulged his taste for reading the proscribed literature of the Enlightenment. Although he was not particularly devout, he became a priest, probably in order to advance himself in the college. By 1791 he was its head or rector. Soon he was in trouble. Plans he submitted for a drastic change in the curriculum suggested ultra-liberal ideas. Also, there was a question of his misuse of college funds. Hidalgo was dismissed from his post and transferred to a parish in Michoacán, where he served as a mere parish priest. Embittered over the turn his career had taken, he neglected his religious duties, discussed revolutionary doctrines with imprudent abandon, and lived freely with various women.

In 1800 the Inquisition looked into his activities. Evidence was offered that he was not a real Christian, that he was a republican and a sinful man in general. After a year Hidalgo recanted and the Inquisition let him go. Next, still only a parish priest, he was assigned to the sleepy colonial town of Dolores. Again complaints arose: he was a most unorthodox clergyman, attended parties and hunts, played cards, gambled, had mistresses, and displayed forbidden books so freely that people called his home Little France. Yet a growing circle of creoles liked the sociable priest and his stimulating talk. He also won the affection of the Indians. On properties near his church he encouraged them to raise vines and mulberry trees, activities the Spanish authorities had long opposed because of the peninsular monopoly of wine and silk, and to manufacture small articles. Officials visited the parish in 1808 and destroyed the vineyards and trees. Again the Inquisition cast a baleful eye on the troublesome priest. Yet it took no action, and he went on living in Dolores until 1810.

Hidalgo's appeal on September 16, 1810, what is now celebrated every year in Mexico City by the president as the *grito* (cry) of Dolores, went in many directions: to the cautious for loyalty to Fernando VII, to the creoles for independence and good (or self) government, to the Indians for redress of ancient grievances. His use of the Virgin of Guadalupe as a symbol had fantastic consequences. A veritable tornado began at the church of Dolores, sweeping up in mass hysteria countless Indians who wished to settle scores with the whites. Also, the original conspirators of Querétaro and other provincial joined Hidalgo, whom they proclaimed chief of the movement. Among them were Ignacio Allende, commander of the militia at Querétaro, Ignacio Aldama, another officer, Miguel Domínguez, a manufacturer and former *corregidor*, and his impassioned wife, *la corregidora* so revered by later generations. Yet these rebels were soon bewildered by the ferocity of the Indians who were dropping everything to join the beloved Hidalgo. The holiday mood of the insurrection rapidly became a matter of terror as racial hatreds burst out. Indian masses made little distinction between creole and peninsular as they burned plantation houses, destroyed crops, and wrecked implements. Under the banners of the Virgin of Guadalupe, their very special protectress, they sacked Querétaro and then Guanajuato. At the latter city, homes were looted and whites maltreated. Five hundred militiamen who had taken refuge in the royal granary, a large stone warehouse, were slaughtered by maddened natives.

News of the rebellion spread quickly all over Mexico, informing the whites of the long-feared race war, the Indians of the day of vengeance and liberation. Workers left the mines and fields, came down from mountain communities, and defiantly walked out of homes where they had been servants. Father Hidalgo himself was abashed by the storm he had loosed. He scarcely had a master plan; all he could do was keep his forces in motion. They migrated over the scenic country from Guanajuato to Guadalajara, which the whites had evacuated, and then swung eastward to Toluca, near the mountainous gateway to the Valley of Mexico. The trail of revolution had exhilarated the Indians and scared most of the others to close ranks regardless of former tensions among creoles, peninsulars, and mestizos. It was race against race. Not for years could the material damage be repaired. Psychological or moral injuries could not be assessed other than to face the realization that the old regime would never be the same again.

By November 1810 Hidalgo had 50,000 or more undisciplined followers, almost all of them Indian, and a handful of white associates. They reached the mountain rim that encircles Mexico City and could see the capital so exposed to conquest or liberation. Hidalgo hesitated to fling his forces into this heartland of Spanish power. Perhaps he was prudent, for the garrisons and militia of Mexico City were formidably armed. Possibly the aging priest feared what the natives would do if they captured the city. In any event, he paused, and then ordered a withdrawal, just two months after the insurrection had begun. Allende and Aldama berated Hidalgo for destroying the morale of a surging movement by retreating. This is indeed what happened, for Indians suddenly lost interest and began to defect. They had for the time being satisfied their destructive instincts. The whites, huddling in the capital, took heart and seized the offensive. While Hidalgo withdrew to San Luis Potosí and talked of organizing a new regime, under Fernando VII but very different from colonialism, the whites prepared to strike back. Under an able general, Félix María Calleja, several thousand Spaniards and creoles marched toward Guadalajara. On January 17, 1811, they met a force under Hidalgo that must have outnumbered themselves many times over. As always, the Europeans held the key advantages in morale, arms, and organization. Fortune favored them too. A shell exploded a rebel magazine and started a grass fire which moved in the direction of Hidalgo's milling units. Panic and flight destroyed the Indian army altogether.

As Hidalgo and his closest advisers fled northward into Saltillo and then into the almost vacant province of Chihuahua, his followers melted away. The race war collapsed. Indians reverted to stolidity, but many never returned to labor on the white man's property. Hidalgo came under the most bitter criticism of his lieutenants, who deposed him from command as they rode into the empty arid spaces of northern Mexico. In March 1811 the haggard former leader was apprehended by pursuing royalist horsemen; perhaps treachery facilitated his capture. Imprisoned in the dusty provincial capital of Chihuahua for some weeks, he was subjected to anguishing pressures from officials of the Inquisition and the royal government. At length he signed a pathetic statement of recantation, after which, on July 31, 1811, he was stripped of his ecclesiastical emblems for having been a bad priest and shot as a traitor to his king.

José María Morelos

As much as Father Hidalgo had shaken the bases of Mexican society, his eventual significance as a historical figure lies in having set loose a spirit of rebellion. His political beliefs were too equivocal or unformulated to provide a program that attracted future generations. It is different with the man who took control of the movement, José María Morelos, for he organized better, fought longer, and left a solid tradition upon which Mexicans could build. Morelos, born in 1765, was probably a mestizo or mulatto, a short, heavy-set man with a scarred face and a grim expression. He was not as personable as Hidalgo, nor as intellectual. Once he had been a student of Hidalgo's at the College of San Nicolás, but the two men were not close until 1810. In the interim Morelos had worked as a farmer, a teamster, a teacher, and after 1797, a priest. His parish was a small one near Lake Pátzcuaro in western Mexico. He served with little distinction as a man of God, begetting several children and reading works on the Index. When he heard Hidalgo's call to revolt in 1810, he joined the movement and was soon recognized as an able military leader. Hidalgo commissioned Morelos to conquer Acapulco and other towns on the Pacific coast. When Hidalgo's insurrection collapsed, Morelos' forces in the south were about all that remained of the armed rebels.

In the aftermath of lost causes, politics tend to be unusually bitter. Morelos employed every artifice to establish his ascendancy over other refugees as willful as himself. At length the tough priest made himself leader of what survived of the revolutionary cause. He had considerable military ability, particularly in whipping small forces in and out of rugged terrain nominally held by the royalists. Of more importance was his clarification of the issues for which he asked men to fight: the complete independence of Mexico without any hypocrisy about Fernando VII, social and racial equality, termination of burdens that annoyed the whites and of ancient Indian injustices, and the maintenance of the Catholic religion without all the material apparatus of the Church. The warrior selected the title of "Servant of the Nation" for himself, setting a style for many Mexican caudillos of the future. He continued to regard himself a good Christian, indeed a true defender of the faith, and presided at mass as a priest.

After operating with only a few hundred irregulars Morelos finally, in 1813, took Acapulco. Then he "liberated" most of Oaxaca, a province full of Indians, where Spanish authority had always been thin. Next he interrupted traffic on the Mexico City-Vera Cruz road and briefly occupied strategic points commanding the Gulf port. Raids, sudden descents, and appearances out of nowhere were his tactics. They served well to keep the Spanish off balance. For all his skill and force, Calleja, now viceroy, was long unable to prevent these punishing darts into Spanish-controlled territory. Meanwhile, Morelos established contact with the secret society of Guadalupe which functioned in the capital, and he probably won to his cause a majority of the lower clergy in southern Mexico.

In 1813 he felt it was time to legalize his position. A congress was called, to meet at first in Apatzingán and then in Chilpancingo. With noble pretensions far out of keeping with realities, this body drew up a constitution. Independence, republicanism, Catholicism, and the aboli- tion of taxes, tributes, and slavery were duly proclaimed. Worthy a prece- dent as the congress later appeared, it was no national assembly but merely a fugitive body of revolutionaries. During 1814 and 1815 it migrated from one town to another, briefly instituting the new con- stitutional regime. From Chilpancingo the little government moved into the hills of the west and then, in an agonizing trek, south of Mexico City to the Gulf. Only the bravado of Morelos kept it going at all. Yet its very existence made the Indian masses in much of the viceroyalty rest- less and perpetuated the ideal of freedom, as the harassed Spaniards sadly admitted. At last, in November 1815, the government fell into an ambush. Morelos fought too long to rescue his subordinates and was himself captured. Enough of his partisans escaped to keep the movement alive.

Chained on a mule, the fallen leader passed through great, curious crowds on his way to Mexico City, where he was lodged in the prison of the Inquisition. Just what happened to him there has never been known in detail. He informed on the identity and probable whereabouts of his confederates. Yet he did not recant, as Hidalgo did, though the Spanish published a false statement to the effect that he had. Before the In- quisition had completed its labors the government took possession of the prisoner and executed him on December 22, 1815. Whatever the significance of these matters, Morelos had effectively continued the rev- olution for nearly five years after the fall of Hidalgo. He had obstructed the recovery of the viceroyalty so that Spanish rule remained shaky. And his enunciation of ideals for an independent, republican, egalitarian, Catholic Mexico were far from forgotten.

REVOLUTION AND DISINTEGRATION IN LA PLATA

Of all the Spanish American revolutions that started during the imperial crisis of 1810, the only one not smothered was in Buenos Aires. Conservative forces were entirely too weak to effect a restoration, and the cause of independence had too much vitality to succumb to mistakes and discouragements, however numerous these were. The revolt was the work of a very large faction, probably a majority, of the creoles. It is curi- ous that no truly great men came forward to dominate the cause, to lead it to triumphant fruition nor to disaster. It simply staggered along year after year.

Three major factors account for the potency of the revolutionary im- pulse in Buenos Aires. One was the absence of a powerful colonial-type society of planters and servile labor, for the economy of the area was such that individualistic cattlemen and merchants, most of whom were whites, comprised the dynamic class. Secondly, the victories of the inhabitants of Buenos Aires, the *porteños*, over the British in 1806 and 1807 had filled them with an overweening self-confidence. Their leader, Santiago Liniers, had even been elected by themselves to be military commander and named by the king as his interim viceroy. Finally, the importance of overseas commerce made the Spanish monopoly unusually odious, especially since the brief taste of free trade during the British occupations was so well remembered. The disastrous events that befell the Spanish monarchy in 1808 stimulated a fervently loyal reaction to Fernando VII. Yet the peninsular officials well knew how exposed their position was, despite all the brave talk of fealty to the absent king and the junta at Sevilla. And as creoles pondered the constitutional aspects of the situation, they discerned an opportunity to depose the peninsulars altogether.

Viceroy Liniers was in an especially awkward position because of his French birth. It was rumored that he had treated suspiciously with the Bonapartist envoy. And the governor of Montevideo, Liniers' subordinate, openly accused the viceroy of disloyalty. In cutting Montevideo off from the viceroyalty, the governor not only impugned the honor of Liniers but pleased the population of that port, which was traditionally opposed to Buenos Aires, its competitor. On New Year's Day in 1809 a pro-Spanish element in Buenos Aires sought to unseat Liniers, very much as their counterparts in Mexico City had deposed a suspected viceroy. Liniers, however, was still much too popular, and he continued in office. In July 1809 the situation seemed to be resolved when the Sevilla junta sent as permanent viceroy a survivor of Trafalgar, Baltasar Hidalgo de Cisneros. This naval officer assumed his duties with the full intention of placating all factions. It was apparent that the creoles were going to be difficult to please. Nearly all commerce had stopped, thus imposing great economic hardships on the leading groups and, incidentally, hampering the government's finances to a painful degree. A proposal to solve these matters emanated from a young liberal firebrand, Dr. Mariano Moreno, who wrote a pamphlet that devastatingly attacked the Spanish monopoly. Subversive as his denunciation was, it contained the highly sensible suggestion to throw open the port of Buenos Aires to world commerce. Considerable excitement arose from the pamphlet; both merchants and treasury officials agitated for something to start up the flow of trade again. With much trepidation Viceroy Cisneros acceded to their demand. Almost at once Buenos Aires was full of ships and money. Twice in recent years the creoles had had their way, the first time when they had Liniers appointed acting viceroy, and now with the lifting of trade barriers. Their appetite increased.

The crisis broke in May 1810 with imperfect reports that all Spanish resistance had terminated but for the isolated group in Cadiz. Creole elements had been awaiting such an opportunity and were not unprepared. With Moreno and others like him agitating for an open *cabildo*, Viceroy Cisneros bowed to the pressure in the hope of maintaining control of the situation. On May 22, the *cabildo* and many subjects gathered in what they called a general congress. It was not truly an open meeting, for alerted guards barred the doors to persons known to be pro-Spanish. The body was full of talkative men, most of them young and trained in the law. After two days of riotous discussion, extreme elements won the upper hand. A project to permit the viceroy to continue in some sort of honorific capacity was rejected. On May 25, now one of Argentina's great national holidays, a new ruling junta announced its sovereign right to govern the viceroyalty in the name of Fernando VII. Cisneros was arrested and, with members of the overturned *audiencia* and other officials, deported to the Canary Islands.

The junta feigned attachment to Fernando VII in order to disguise its real purpose: to detach the Plata territory from all Spanish authority. After deposing the numerous royal officials and appropriating their positions, the creoles re-examined laws, taxes, and other aspects of the old regime. It was clear they intended to start afresh with new institutions. Their immediate problem, however, was to carry with them the rest of the far-flung viceroyalty. Calls went out to other cities to secure their participation in building a new order. Montevideo, after a brief hesitation, denounced the proceedings in Buenos Aires as altogether disloyal and reprehensible. Warfare between the two rivals broke out, to continue until 1814, when Buenos Aires conquered Montevideo. Far up the Paraná River, in Asunción, Paraguay, the *cabildo* received the *porteño* summons coldly. Loyalty to Spain or the traditional dislike of the port city won out, and for another year Asunción professed its fealty to the old system. In 1811 Buenos Aires sent a force led by Manuel Belgrano to intimidate Asunción, only to see it turned back with losses. Then a small group deposed the Spanish governor of Paraguay and assumed control of the province as an independent state, one which Buenos Aires never succeeded in incorporating. There was little enough opposition in the course Buenos Aires proposed among the cities and towns of the western Argentine, in Mendoza, Salta, Santiago del Estero, and Jujuy, but also little enthusiasm except among young liberals. Armed resistance threatened in Córdova, mainly because of the leadership of Santiago Liniers, onetime hero and former viceroy, who had moved there. A year earlier his loyalty to the Spanish crown had been doubted. Now he proved it with his life. As an expedition from Buenos Aires approached Córdova he attempted to organize resistance, failed, and was shot, a martyr for Spain and, in a way, for decency.

Upper Peru was a most important prize, a veritable treasure house. In

1809 its creoles had tried rebellion prematurely and failed. Late in 1810 an Argentine army climbed up from the grassy pampas through rocky passes into the great, bare highland plateau, the *altiplano*, that constituted the effective part of the province. Most of the towns—Potosí, Cochabamba, Oruro, Chuquisaca, and La Paz—hastened to cast off Spanish authority and welcome the liberators. By the end of the year it seemed that Upper Peru was secure for the revolutionists, that its silver would flow to Buenos Aires and its mining economy draw upon the ranches and fields of northwestern Argentina. Equally attractive was the prospect that Peru proper could soon be invaded and torn from Spain. Yet these probabilities turned out to be illusions. Spanish power was very well-entrenched in Peru. Furthermore, the Argentines antagonized much of the population in Upper Peru by wholesale killings of peninsulars and offenses to the traditional conservatism of the whites. Much of this high-handedness was due to Juan José Castelli, the political representative of Buenos Aires, a fanatical radical who thought in terms of liquidating rather than conciliating his opponents. And, it can be assumed, the Argentine troops behaved badly, as soldiers usually do when they occupy a province even as liberators.

In June 1811 a royalist force fell on the Argentines at Huaqui and routed them. Enthusiasm for freedom in Upper Peru all but vanished as the liberators evacuated. After a terrible retreat through the cold *altiplano*, the surviving Argentines clambered down the Andes into Salta. There they rallied and checked the royalists who tried to follow them into the pampas. A deadlock was apparent. Highland Indians who composed most of the royalist ranks sweated and lost energy in the low country. Argentine gauchos and *porteño* recruits gasped and fainted in the mountains. Several campaigns and many skirmishes in the next few years demonstrated the force of this simple biological factor. Loyalist Peru could not overcome Buenos Aires, but neither could the Argentines traverse the Andean tableland to Lima.

Just a little over a year after the historic May 25, 1810, it was clear that the revolution had succeeded only in Buenos Aires and a few districts in northern and western Argentina. Territory of the former viceroyalty now included in the present republics of Uruguay, Paraguay, and Bolivia was hostile, while the wilderness extending southward through Patagonia acknowledged the rule of no government whatever. Liberation brought great economic benefits to Buenos Aires and its surrounding lands but hardships to the hinterland towns, who saw their brightest young men migrate to the port city and their former markets in Upper Peru denied by royalist officials. Already, the conflict of interest between Buenos Aires and the interior was dividing the land. The Argentine Republic still feels this tension.

In political affairs the new government was doing poorly. Within a few months most of the original leaders had seen their reputations and popularity disappear. Mariano Moreno, who had lost both, also lost his life at sea when he sailed to Europe on a mission to secure assistance. Briefly called "the soul of the revolution" for his fervent writings and oratory, he was almost the only leader to articulate the objectives of the movement. When provincial representatives arrived to join the junta little in the way of talent was added. These men were not founding fathers but quarreling brothers. Naïve, over-enthusiastic, inexperienced, and dogmatic, they disputed riotously and refused to compromise. In 1811 executive power was concentrated in the hands of triumvirs, an expedient that lasted for three years. The triumvirs changed rapidly, as others forced resignations and new appointments. Somehow the institution served to alienate both liberals and conservatives while antagonizing the provinces. A constituent assembly convened in 1813 as the sovereign body for the United Provinces of the Río de la Plata—really just the rebellious Argentine intendancies—and pushed the revolution a little farther, outlawing titles of nobility, the Inquisition (which the Spanish had also ended), royal symbols, and forced labor. As a sign of its equivocal position it made no reference either to Fernando VII or to independence. In 1814 the assembly ended the triumvirate and elected a Supreme Director, who proved unable to direct at all. Behind the aimlessness and confusion of the government were the passions of ambitious individuals, not the wisdom of patriotic statesmen. The free Argentine nation was off to a poor start, viable as it would eventually prove itself.

José Gervasio Artigas

While the flustered creoles in Buenos Aires discredited the cause of self-government, uglier forces were making themselves felt in the hinterland. These were the gaucho caudillos and their irregular bands. They really preferred no government at all but a life of hunting, fighting, marauding, and defiance to city men who denied these were the finest goals of existence. The first of these was José Gervasio Artigas, a colorful leader with a little education from the Eastern Shore (Uruguay). After protracted negotiations with the royalists he finally elected to champion independence. But he did not wish to see his territory incorporated by Buenos Aires. For a time he considered joining forces with the other liberators if extreme federalism were permitted. The *porteños* could not allow this solution, which would mean in fact the disintegration of the country into small territories ruled by gauchos like Artigas. The issue would long convulse the political life of the Plata region. In this case, Artigas struck out for independence. When an army from Buenos Aires conquered Montevideo in 1814, Artigas organized a vast force of gauchos to dislodge the *porteños*, which he did in 1815. Then he set about creating a sort of rural "democracy" under his own dictatorship, to include not only the Eastern Shore but also the adjacent provinces of Corrientes, Santa Fe, and Entre Rios. He nearly succeeded, and for a few months it appeared he might force Buenos Aires to accept his brand of federalism. But in 1816 the Brazilians, who had long chafed over Spain's refusal to surrender Olivenza (a district in Portugal seized in the War of the Oranges in 1801) and other wrongs, advanced into the Eastern Shore. Early in 1817 they entered Montevideo and annexed the whole area to the Portuguese-Brazilian monarchy. At length the rural hero tired of trying to establish a gaucho empire and retired to Paraguay, where he lived the remainder of his long life. An enigma to contemporaries and posterity alike, he is revered by Uruguayans. Yet his activities did much to frustrate the organization of civilized government in the Plata territory.[5]

Meanwhile, the Argentine assembly was alarmed by the restoration of Fernando VII and the failure of other South American independence movements. Hoping to mollify the provincials, the assembly gave way to another constituent body which convened in Tucumán instead of Buenos Aires in 1816. The new congress pondered many courses of action, such as reconciliation with Spain, a republic, offering the throne to a European prince, and submitting itself to an Inca in the hope of drawing Upper Peru. After much discussion the body finally agreed, on July 9, 1816, to declare full independence from Spain. Another Supreme Director was elected, the able conservative, Juan Martín Pueyrredón, who served from 1816 to 1819. Agents went to Europe to see if a suitable royal personage would grace the Platine throne.

CHILE'S ABORTIVE REVOLUTION

One of the most isolated outposts of Western civilization on earth, the captaincy-general of Chile found itself a scene of conflict between the forces that rocked the world during the Age of Revolution. Its social structure was inherently conservative, since only a few dozen white families owned most of the productive land—vineyards, plantations, ranches, and mines—while the mass of the population, mostly mestizo, labored in dreadful poverty. Only the capital, Santiago, was a city, and it was unprepossessing. Concepción, Valparaiso, and La Serena were modest towns. In the central valley lived more than half a million Hispanicized persons, about as many as there were in independent Argen-

5. Another interpretation is far more favorable. Perhaps the *porteños* were the ones who should be blamed. A loose federal structure, even if gaucho-ridden, might have survived better than the successive efforts of Buenos Aires. This Artigas, according to many historians, was not really a trouble-maker but a statesman.

tina in 1810. The magnificent cordillera of the Andes cut them off from the Argentine, the Atacama desert from Peru. The colony stopped abruptly at the Bío-Bío River in the south, for here began the Araucanian land which disappeared in the rain forests, fjords, and islands of the lower tip of the continent. Chile's main contact with the rest of the world was by sea.

Chilean creoles were proud and often rich. They bitterly resented the peninsular Spaniards who issued decrees, dispensed justice, and collected taxes. In 1808, when the Spanish monarchy fell, Chile had a new governor, an aging army officer with little taste for administrative chores. A certain amount of undercover agitation among the creoles during the next two years prepared some of the better-educated men to look for opportunity. The "day" was September 18, 1810. A junta, not unmindful of the experiences in Caracas, Bogotá, and Buenos Aires, assumed the sovereignty of the colony behind the mask of Fernando VII. After dislodging the Spanish officials and opening the ports to all traders, the rebels convened a congress to legislate for the new era of freedom. It was a delicious moment. Ejecting peninsulars and planning a new order were exhilarating activities for creoles who had been submerged so long.

The deliberations of the congress were soon cut short by an invasion of armed radicals led by José Miguel Carrera. Carrera was only twenty-six, a member of one of the most aristocratic families. He had been in Europe for several years and had participated in Spain's war against Napoleon. Like so many other liberators, he had suffered the disdain which Spaniards displayed to Americans. Now back in Chile with a head full of revolutionary ideology, he set out to remake the country. Such intellectuals as there were responded favorably for a time to his projects, and the masses were stirred by this upper class demagogue. The strongest class, however, the white landlords, were uneasy. Jacobin-type radicalism was not what they had envisioned when they broke with peninsular Spain. With some reservation they accepted the leadership of a young man hitherto regarded as an extremist himself but clearly less radical than Carrera. This was Bernardo O'Higgins, a wealthy and informed creole with a famous name.

Bernardo, as we have seen, was the illegitimate son of the late captain-general of Chile and viceroy of Peru, Ambrosio O'Higgins. He had spent many years in Europe, where he had fallen under the influence of Miranda and other sponsors of American independence. Much as he yearned for freedom and reform, O'Higgins regarded Carrera as a dangerous man who might well ruin the cause with his fanatical radicalism. O'Higgins' own doctrines were never so clearly enunciated that he could be typed. Depending on the point of view, he seemed liberal or conservative to his contemporaries. Men have seldom agreed as to whether he was an opportunist who first united, and then alienated, all sides, or whether he was detached and intellectually honest. At any rate, he came to represent those who favored independence but not a drastic social revolution.

O'Higgins and Carrera were poised for a conflict when a royalist reaction in southern Chile threatened to envelop the country early in 1814, a danger all the greater because of the restoration of Fernando VII in Spain. In this crisis the patriots rallied to O'Higgins and deposed Carrera. Then the Spanish forces captured Carrera and, in May 1814, negotiated a truce by which Chile would rejoin the Spanish monarchy without losing all the advantages won during the past four years. The cease-fire proved unacceptable to the viceroy at Lima, who sent large reinforcements by sea to Chile under an able commander, Mariano Osorio. The Spanish also released Carrera in order to divide the patriots. Carrera gathered an army and succeeded in winning over a faction from O'Higgins. For some weeks it was not clear whether he and O'Higgins would fight one another or combine to resist Osorio. In October 1814 the Spaniards advanced on O'Higgins and defeated him at Rancagua, south of Santiago. Carrera stood aside while his rival was crushed, making himself all the more odious to the moderate patriots. All the former rebels, whichever faction they favored, had to flee from the royalists by this time. There was nowhere to go but across the Andes into Argentina, where they reunited on the worst possible terms.

The revolutionary movements begun so hopefully in 1810 had all come to grief save in the Argentine, where conditions were far from auspicious, and in isolated Paraguay. In New Spain the capture of Morelos in 1815 had all but terminated serious resistance. Venezuela had twice failed to become a republic. By the middle of 1816 all of New Granada was back under Spanish authority. The defeat of Chile's national liberation was complete. Cuba, Puerto Rico, Guatemala, and Peru had not rebelled at all. Santo Domingo had cast off French rule in 1808 and was now more firmly attached than ever to the Spanish crown. On the surface, it seemed, the entire cause of independence was discredited, defeated more by entrenched royalist or loyalist elements in the colonies themselves than by forces sent from Spain. National feeling had not been powerful enough to overcome three centuries of attachment to the Spanish crown. Constitutionalism and reform did not match the ancient habits of obedience. No leader had emerged to rally society in any one colony long enough to repudiate the familiar regime. Yet the restoration would not endure, for it was not effected with wisdom or charity. And it opposed the currents which had deeply stirred Latin America, currents which led to the future and could not be resisted long.

20

The Achievement of Independence

A PROFOUND change of mood came over Spanish America when it became known that Fernando VII had returned to his throne and, in May 1814, restored the absolutist system. Royalists took heart, republicans were more than ever on the defensive, and moderates drew encouragement from the king's intimations of reforms to come. In Venezuela the republic collapsed and Bolívar departed a fugitive. Soon the various rebel states in New Granada began to succumb to a counter-revolution, which was completed in May 1816. Chile fell to the viceroy of Peru in the year of Fernando VII's restoration. In New Spain the insurrectionary movement lost force and was virtually ended with the capture of Morelos in November 1815. Only Argentina and Paraguay remained independent throughout the period of the reaction. The rest of the empire stayed as securely as ever, or so it seemed on the surface, within the Spanish monarchy.

Discredited as the cause of independence was after the king returned, it was soon to triumph. The very existence, not to mention the success, of the United States tempted Spanish Americans·to emulation. Nor were the heady doctrines of revolution easily forgotten, and with them the exhilaration of the open *cabildos* and congresses of 1810 to 1814. Important as these matters were, the primary reason for the resumption of the independence movement was the failure of the restoration. Once it was discerned that Fernando VII and his regime had nothing new and little good to offer the American dominions, the cause of liberation took fire again. Morally and psychologically the old regime did not succeed in recovering the hearts and minds of its most important subjects in the New World. A brilliant military blow in Chile in 1817, followed by another in New Granada two years later, fatally wounded the Spanish cause. And then a most untimely revolution in the peninsula made it possible for Brazil and the Spanish mainland empire to secure their complete independence shortly afterward.

RESTORATION AND RENEWED REBELLION

The Failure of Fernando VII

IN REPUDIATING the liberal movement sponsored by the successive governments during his absence, Fernando VII was acting as other European monarchs did after the fall of Napoleon and doing what his own people desired. His reactionary policies were not in themselves obnoxious to most Spaniards; rather, it was his inability to create an effective regime that caused many to turn against him. Here, it must be admitted, he deserves some sympathy, for the problems confronting him would have taxed an administrative genius of the first order. During the six years of the French intrusion almost every corner of the peninsula had been the scene of military action. Material destruction was enormous and economic disruption incalculable. The loss of life was estimated to be in the tens of thousands. Spanish society had been so torn that it would never be satisfactorily integrated again. Great numbers, perhaps a majority of the adult manhood, had learned to kill and loot, were still armed, and had developed a habit of following guerrilla chieftains rather than legitimate leaders. Spain's best talent had been tinged with liberalism or French sympathies during the long occupation. Now these men were barred from public life. The treasury was empty, the army assertive, and the navy and merchant fleet in shambles. Finally, Fernando VII was no administrator, for he was utterly without experience and scarcely gifted in any way. His parents had tried to ruin him, Napoleon had deceived him, and, while he was a captive, Spanish liberals and many of his American subjects had sought to steal his powers. Trusting no one but an earthy group who comprised his *camarilla*, the king had no idea of how to rule. With low companions he prowled about his capital by night and went through the usual motions of royalty in daytime. He offered no direction to the stricken country, and he was so suspicious that he rapidly changed ministers and rejected good advice.

With respect to America, Fernando sent out appeals for all of his subjects to lay aside their animosities and gather again as brothers under their father the king. Much of the New World was prepared, even grateful for the opportunity, to do just that. As the insurrections abated, the men about the throne pondered the grievances that had led to the colonial rebellions. Many folios in Spanish archives today offer evidence of

THE WARS OF INDEPENDENCE

VICEROYALTY OF NEW SPAIN

San Francisco
Monterey
Los Angeles
San Diego
Santa Fe
Albuquerque
St Louis
El Paso
Natchitoches
UNITED STATES
Chihuahua
San Antonio
Pensacola
St Augustine
New Orleans
Durango
Monterrey
Saltillo
La Paz
Havana CUBA
HAITI
Guadalajara
Dolores
Querétaro
Guanajuato
Apatzingán
Valladolid
Mexico City
Chilpancingo
Acapulco
Oaxaca
Veracruz
BELIZE (BR.)
Santiago
Port-au-Prince
SANTO DOMINGO
Santo Domingo
San Juan
PUERTO RICO
JAMAICA
Guatemala
San Salvador
León
Granado
San José
Panama
Cartago
Cartagena
Santa Marta
Trujillo
Caracas
Cúcuta
Angostura
Boyacá
Bogotá
Popayán
VICEROYALTY OF NEW GRANADA
Quito
Pichincha
Guayaquil
Pará
AMAZON R.
Ceará
Paraíba
Pernambuco
BRAZIL
Trujillo
Pasco
Junín
Huacho
Callao
Lima
Ayacucho
Cuzco
Bahía
VICEROYALTY OF PERU
Arequipa
Guaqui
Goyaz
Chuquisaca
Potosí
Diamantina
Suipacha
Ouro Preto
Salta
Asunción
Ypiranga
São Paulo
Rio de Janeiro
Tucumán
COCHRANE 1822-23
CAPTAINCY GENERAL OF CHILE
Córdoba
Santa Fe
Pôrto Alegre
Chacabuco
Valparaiso
Santiago
Mendoza
Maipú
Rancagua
Colonia
Concepción
Buenos Aires
Montevideo
PLATA ESTUARY 1806-7 (BR)
VICEROYALTY OF RIO DE LA PLATA
CHILOE IS.

N

HIDALGO 1810-11 _____
BELGRANO 1811 _____
BELGRANO-SAN MARTIN 1812-13 _____
BOLIVAR 1813 _____
SAN MARTIN-SOLER 1817 _____
O'HIGGINS 1818 _____
BOLIVAR 1819 _____
SAN MARTIN 1820-22 _____
COCHRANE 1822-23 _____
BOLIVAR 1821 _____
BOLIVAR-SUCRE 1822-25 _____

an extensive search for remedies that would reconcile the empire: committee reports, individual letters, cabinet minutes, crackpot schemes, and statesmanlike proposals. The British were particularly insistent that Spain reform abuses in America that had stimulated the liberation movement, but just because they had done so much to restore Fernando to his throne he resented them and brushed aside their advice. Nothing came of all the projects to renew American ties to Spain while the mood of loyalty lasted but for one military move, the dispatch of an expeditionary force of 10,500 battle-hardened veterans under Pablo Morillo in 1815. This single measure was almost, but not quite, enough to secure the empire militarily. Another such expedition might well have restored full Spanish control. It was not to sail, however, largely because of administrative ineptitude in dealing with the lack of shipping. In political affairs, too, Fernando and his regime were notably unsuccessful. The indefinite postponement of reforms in the imperial system exasperated the colonials, leading to the suspicion that none would ever take place. And the policy of harsh repression followed by generous amnesties produced more anger than gratitude in areas that had revolted.

José de San Martín and the Liberation of Chile

IN 1817 the delivery of an imaginative strategic blow placed the royalist cause in South America on the defensive. Its creator and agent was a stoic general named José de San Martín. An inarticulate man who cared little what posterity was to say about him and who was not overly concerned about the opinions of his contemporaries, San Martín was long unhonored and has never been well understood. Unlike Simón Bolívar, who said so much so well that one finds it difficult to know just which words represented his true thoughts, San Martín was exasperatingly laconic. At the height of his career he spoke and wrote as little as possible. In the long years of self-imposed retirement he kept his silence. Yet his actions were eloquent enough to establish him eventually as the leading rival to Bolívar for the gratitude of modern South Americans.

Born in 1778 in former Jesuit territory on the upper Uruguay River, where his father was a Spanish official, San Martín went to Spain at the age of eight. A student for a time at a school for nobles in Madrid, he became a cadet at twelve to train for officerhood in the royal army. A year later he witnessed some fighting in North Africa. The next twenty years reveal little about him. He was an officer who moved about the peninsula with his regiment. Apparently he was fairly studious, given to reading the works which influenced so many of his generation in the way of liberalism, but he was scarcely an intellectual. Probably he dabbled in secret societies and met radicals. The Napoleonic intrusion in 1808 involved him in battles and campaigns of Spain's war of independence. Apparently he acquitted himself well enough, since he held responsible posts and rose to the rank of lieutenant colonel. Suddenly, late in 1811, he deserted the Spanish army and made his way to London. This action has never been satisfactorily explained. An Argentine thesis that he felt the pull of his natal land when he learned of its rebellion in 1810 is too romantic to be taken seriously. Was San Martín in trouble, and fleeing to avoid prosecution of some sort? Was he tempted to adventure by secret agents of one type or another? Or did he decide, as well he might in 1811, that Spain was lost and there was no further purpose in risking his life for her?

In London he encountered other South Americans and was initiated into the masonic lodge that Miranda had founded. Early in 1812 he sailed to Buenos Aires. From the very beginning he was outstandingly successful in that rebellious port. Within a week he was given command of a unit which he built into an excellent regiment of mounted grenadiers. Soon he organized a Lautaro lodge,[1] whose real purpose was to manipulate the politics of the new patriot government. In October 1812 he participated in a coup that ousted the triumvirs and replaced them with another set. He married the daughter of a wealthy man. The effectiveness of his grenadiers he demonstrated by turning back a royalist thrust from Montevideo. In January 1814 this dark, taciturn officer with flashing black eyes was given command of the so-called Army of the North, which had already been defeated twice in attempted invasions of Upper Peru. Obviously, San Martín was well-regarded by the Buenos Aires government.

At this point he revealed the strategic vision that distinguished him from many other military leaders of the Wars of Independence. Lima, he realized, was the heart and brain of Spanish power in South America. No patriot victory could be permanent until this stronghold was captured. Yet it lay nearly 2,000 miles from the Army of the North over the roughest country in Christendom. Instead of leading this force into another hopeless invasion of Upper Peru, San Martín pleaded ill health, gave up his command, but wangled an appointment as governor of Cuyo. This province, which faced central Chile at the narrowest point of the Andes, was to be his springboard for the liberation of South America—to Santiago through a rocky pass, to Lima by sea! From April 1814 to February 1817 San Martín made his headquarters at the provincial capital, Mendoza, a city of considerable beauty and economically self-sufficient. Assembling the kind of task force he needed called for the utmost exertions; his health, as it happened, was sufficiently ro-

1. Named after the Araucanian youth   iards in Chile.
of the 1550's who had bested the Span-

bust for him to work with sustained fury.[2] Drawing on the manpower of Cuyo and volunteers from Buenos Aires, including his own grenadiers, he got together a respectable body of men he named the Army of the Andes. Also he attracted Negro slaves by promising them emancipation. And several hundred patriot refugees from the Chilean debacle of late 1814 made their way across the mountains to join the army. San Martín sent the troublesome Carrera brothers away and made O'Higgins his second-in-command. By 1817 the task force included about 4,000 trained fighting men and 1,400 auxiliaries.

More spectacular than the accumulation of soldiers was the organizational miracle wrought by San Martín in equipping this force for its mission. The resources of the province were mobilized with extraordinary thoroughness. Horses, mules, gunpowder, foodstuffs, muskets, lances, swords, artillery, and special clothing and footwear for men and horses were donated, fabricated, or seized. San Martín's experiences in Spain had taught him not only the ways of combat but also the complications of logistics. He also had worthy assistants. His wife exhibited talent in inspiring the women both of Mendoza and Buenos Aires to contribute money or articles for the cause. A patriot friar, Luis Beltrán, and a British adventurer, James Paroissien, were among the bizarre characters who helped the expedition in technical matters. Beset as he was with the problems of raising, training, and equipping the Army of the Andes, San Martín dealt confidently with political and diplomatic affairs. The government, such as it was, of Buenos Aires feared invasion by Spain or Brazil and coveted the new military force for its own purposes. San Martín fended off such demands with skill. By urging an outright declaration of independence at Tucumán in 1816 and by winning over the new Supreme Director, Pueyrredón, he stabilized his rear on the eve of the great offensive. As his army neared a state of readiness he solemnly negotiated with Indian leaders, knowing full well they hated all white men and would gladly betray him. Hence he gave them false information about his intentions, which they duly sold to the Spaniards in Chile. The Lautaro lodge had chapters in Chile, where patriots could carry on espionage and clandestine political warfare. And the appearance of Argentine ships off Chilean shores helped to keep the royalists in fear of a seaborne invasion and thus off balance.

Finally, in the dead of summer,[3] on January 9, 1817, the Army of the Andes began its march, an operation that inevitably suggests comparison with Hannibal's crossing of the Alps in 218 B.C. or Napoleon's passage

---

2. San Martín often complained of feeling bad. Perhaps he did, or possibly he was simply a hypochondriac, for he reached the age of seventy-two. Often he took opium and other drugs to soothe his pains.

3. The Andes are utterly impassable for surface travelers during the winter. In the southern hemisphere, of course, the seasons are reversed.

through the St. Bernard Pass in 1800, though San Martín's feat was really more difficult and its achievement more enduring. West of Mendoza the Andes loom as an awesome wall broken only by a few rocky, wind-swept passes, 12,000 feet above sea level, which drop precipitously into the central valley of Chile. Choosing the two main passes, Uspallata and Los Patos, for his principal forces and others for diversionary efforts, San Martín saw his units converge safely in Chile exactly on schedule, one month after their departure from Mendoza. Cold, fear, accidents, sick-ness, and sporadic enemy opposition took a substantial toll of his men and cost him more than half the 9,000 mules and two-thirds of the 1,600 horses. Yet his task force was in reasonably good condition after the An-dean passage. While the Spaniards knew about the invasion, they erred by anticipating that the liberators would emerge farther south; only an inferior royalist force opposed San Martín's army when it broke into Chile. At the battle of Chacabuco on February 12, 1817, San Martín won a signal victory that enabled him to move into Santiago.

An explosion of joy in the capital indicated the unpopularity of the Spanish regime. The open *cabildo* offered San Martín the headship of the liberated state, but he declined in favor of O'Higgins, who became Supreme Director. During the enthusiasm of these days it largely escaped attention that important royalist units had sailed from Valparaiso to join powerful Spanish forces in the south. In Santiago, O'Higgins went about the task of constructing a new regime, which officially declared its inde-pendence of Fernando VII on the anniversary of Chacabuco, in Febru-ary 1818. Just a month later, an ugly surprise alarmed the new state. Un-defeated royalist forces in the south, strengthened by seaborne incre-ments from Peru, marched northward under the command of General Osorio, who had overwhelmed the first Chilean independence move-ment in 1814. At Cancha Rayada he badly defeated O'Higgins. With the road to Santiago open, shaky patriots made plans to switch sides again or to flee into Argentina. It was San Martín who saved the situation. On April 5, 1818 he interposed his army between Osorio and the capital at Maipú. While the two forces were evenly matched in numbers, San Mar-tín's generalship was superior. After a dreadful carnage which took the lives of a fourth of the 10,000 combatants, the patriots won a complete victory. Chile was now safe.

The Peruvian Undertaking

IN PLANNING the next step of his grand design, the seaborne ex-pedition to Peru, San Martín had three major preoccupations: Chilean support, Argentine support, and acquisition of a fleet. The first entailed a great deal of bickering and tedious involvement in Chilean politics, but things went mainly the way San Martín hoped, thanks largely to the loyal support of O'Higgins. Many taxpayers in Chile had scant enthusiasm for financing a major share of the cost of the invading force; in fact, they cared little what became of the Peruvians, their competitors in commerce and so often in the past their oppressors. O'Higgins deepened his unpopularity in many quarters[4] by insisting on backing San Martín's project. With reference to aid from Buenos Aires, the difficulties defied solution. The politicians were too small-minded to grasp the importance of conquering Peru, and, besides, they still wanted San Martín's forces for their own purposes. Despite several trips to that capital, San Martín realized he would receive no real backing, particularly after the fall of his ally, Pueyrredón, in 1819. At length he resigned his commission as an Argentine general and sent half his forces back across the Andes. As an officer of Chile he resumed command of the expeditionary force and went ahead with his preparations with his usual thoroughness. It made little difference whether Argentina approved or not: governments were turning over so rapidly that his defiance, indeed the great general himself, was all but forgotten.

The naval problem, of course, was crucial. O'Higgins managed, by seizures and modest purchases, to accumulate a small fleet on which Chileans and adventurers from the United States and Great Britain developed into competent crews. His most important acquisition was Thomas, Lord Cochrane, an extraordinary personality who was hired by the Chilean representative in London in 1818. This Scotsman had sailed with his uncle in Caribbean waters in 1806, when the British assisted Miranda in his disastrous second landing in Venezuela, and he was the veteran of many naval engagements. He had been expelled from Parliament and imprisoned in the Tower of London for speculations based on false rumors, deliberately circulated, of Napoleon's death. Also, Cochrane had been cashiered from the Royal Navy amid noisy recriminations. This embittered aristocrat was to display a lifelong fondness for liberal causes, for the freedom of Spanish America, of Brazil, and of Greece. Yet it is difficult to escape the conclusion that his primary motivation was love of money; grasping, unstable, and evil-tempered, he was a trial to his associates.

His skill as a naval commander was something else. Cochrane had the touch of Drake and Nelson: superb self-confidence, brilliance, daring, and a delight in employing unorthodox weapons and dishonorable ruses. Soon after he arrived in Chile he showed what he could do with the little fleet. He got the Spaniards out of the port of Valdivia, captured

4. The nature of his problem will be discussed in a later chapter. A principal cause of antipathy was the killing of the three Carrera brothers in Argentina, which many people believed, perhaps rightly, O'Higgins had inspired.

a number of prizes, and sailed up and down the Pacific coast. Spanish naval defenses were utterly decomposed, and the Chilean fleet grew. Furthermore, Chile's ports were now open to vessels from all over the world, with the result that commercial prosperity spurted. Above all, he quickly won the naval supremacy necessary for the invasion of Peru.

By August 1820 San Martín was ready to sail. His force consisted of 4,000 or more Argentinians and Chileans, with the latter in a small majority, and a substantial fleet commanded by Lord Cochrane. The expedition disembarked at Pisco, about a hundred miles south of Lima, a sugar plantation and vineyard region full of Negro slaves and supplies of food and drink.[5] San Martín had a large supply of arms and uniforms with which he hoped to equip Peruvians who came over to his side. Only the slaves, to whom he promised freedom, showed much inclination to join him at this stage. It was also part of his plan to use a small force to cut Lima off from its sources of food in the south while shipping the main body of his army just north of the capital to interdict its provisions from other agricultural regions. Meanwhile, the effect of his presence in the viceroyalty and the operations of secret societies in Lima should serve to put the creoles in a receptive mood for independence. Lord Cochrane stormed at San Martín for this strategy, which he regarded as timid. His advice was to send the full force straight into the harbor at Callao, defying numerous Spanish guns, and from there directly into Lima. More aware of the realities of the situation, San Martín persisted in his plans. After a delay of several weeks, during which his agents negotiated with the viceroy of Peru to no purpose, he methodically carried out the transfer of his main army to the little port of Huacho, north of Lima, where he camped for many dreary months.

Lima and its surrounding district had been the bulwark of Spanish power for nearly three centuries. The bureaucracy was enormous and deeply involved in Spain's cause. No less committed to royalism were the ancient merchant houses and the many families who had grown rich on their ties with the peninsular monopolists. Even the Peruvians tended to be proud of their fealty to the king, much as they criticized the peninsular Spaniards. The lower classes were largely Negro, for few Indians lived in this area, and they were so suppressed they had no politics. Lima was a "little Madrid," the stronghold of royalism. Its inhabitants overwhelmingly preferred to keep the tie with Spain, they had not forgotten the fearful race war of the 1780's, and they frowned on liberals who might re-kindle the embers of Indian revolt in the hinterland. During the first phase of the Wars of Independence, from 1809 to 1814, Viceroy Abascal had displayed great energy in putting down revolutions in

5. The strong white brandy known as pisco is still one of the favorite intoxicants along the western coast of South America.

Upper Peru, Quito, and Chile, and an Indian rising in Cuzco. The present viceroy, Joaquín de la Pezuela, had shown himself inflexible and absolutist during the restoration. Yet he was caught in a cruel dilemma. On the very day he learned of San Martín's landing in Pisco he had been forced to re-promulgate the Spanish constitution of 1812. Both events were shattering blows to the royalist cause.

THE REVOLUTION OF 1820 AND ITS CONSEQUENCES

The Convulsions of Peninsular Spain, 1820–1823

DURING the three and a half years between San Martín's crossing of the Andes and his landing in Peru the cause of American independence had made considerable progress. Simón Bolívar had carried out a stunning offensive in New Granada, which will be treated presently, and unhinged Spanish might in the northern part of the continent. Yet his victory was far from complete, almost as far as San Martín's after the landing at Huacho, and in New Spain, Central America, and the Caribbean islands the cause had made no advance whatever. It still seemed likely that the huge expedition, at one time consisting of 22,000 men, that Fernando VII had gathered at Cadiz would overcome the liberating forces. At least a few responsible persons in Madrid believed with some reason that the American patriots would abandon the cause of independence if Spain loosened the commercial monopoly and elevated more creoles in the bureaucracy. In other European capitals there were powerful voices who asserted that Fernando VII's interests were those of all monarchs; every king in Europe had a duty to help him restore his full authority in the overseas empire. Even in London there was little desire to destroy the Spanish imperial system, at least if Spain would heed British advice about liberalizing some of its features. And while public opinion in the United States stridently favored aiding Spain's revolting colonies, officials in Washington were determined not to antagonize Fernando VII until the transfer of Florida was completed. In short, the liberators could expect no help from abroad and would be lucky if Spain received none. A protracted, uphill fight seemed to lie before them; independence did not seem likely for many years.

The picture changed radically in March 1820, when Fernando VII walked out on his palace balcony in Madrid and assured a threatening mob that he would restore the constitution of 1812. This extraordinary scene was the result of a mutiny in the expeditionary force which he had intended to send to South America. Thirteen times since his restoration in 1814, units of the Spanish army had pronounced against the absolutist regime, always in vain. Liberalism continued to fascinate the officer caste, however, sometimes for ideological reasons, more often because it offered army commanders a chance to thrust themselves into politics. Since Fernando VII was governing so ineffectively, it was easy to cloak selfish ambitions in patriotism. And, it seems likely, funds from American rebels encouraged Spanish officers to revolt against the king. However that may have been, the units gathering around Cadiz for eventual service in America were very susceptible to plots against the regime. For four years they had awaited shipment. Disease, demoralization, poor management, and propaganda by secret societies had long since removed any desire to fight rebels in the New World. News of the unseaworthiness of Russian ships purchased for their transfer was another blow to morale. Still more damaging were the tales of returnees from Morillo's expedition. And so the troops had drilled and cursed for endless months, listening to subversives and stories of hard conditions in America.

On New Year's Day in 1820 a regiment led by Colonel Rafael Riego revolted for the restoration of the constitution of 1812 and, without saying so publicly, for the abandonment of the expedition. Though loyal forces were unable to arrest the mutineers, no general movement followed for a few weeks. Then, as a result of conspiracies by the network of secret lodges that constituted a hidden government in the military, garrisons all over Spain pronounced in quick succession. When Madrid joined the movement Fernando VII sought to place himself at its head by his panicky appearance on the palace balcony. Soon the onetime *cortes* was re-assembled in the capital, many of its members emerging from prison or exile to take their seats. Viceroys in the overseas empire received orders to proclaim the constitution and to hold elections for the *cortes*.

It was not long before Naples, Piedmont, Portugal, and Greece followed the example of Spain. To the monarchs of Europe, who had been glorying in Metternichian reaction, it seemed that the Reign of Terror was about to be renewed. Bound together by the Holy Alliance, the continental rulers chose to crush liberalism wherever it appeared, and promptly did so in Italy. Britain, however, separated herself from these repressive policies. Reports from Spain indicated that royal institutions were seriously endangered. Fernando was insulted and abused the way Louis XVI had been in the months before his overthrow. Yet he saved himself by doing as he was told and, while smouldering inside, keeping amiably quiet.[6] Spanish ultra-liberals, or *exaltados*, not only degraded the king but violently assaulted the Church. If the abolition of the In-

6. When he could, Fernando VII unburdened himself bitterly to foreign diplomats. He earnestly pleaded for help from his brother monarchs.

quisition and the expulsion of the Jesuits (who had been restored by the pope in 1816) brought few regrets, terrorism against clergymen and church-burning dismayed the faithful all over the Spanish world. Conservatives in America were now in a most awkward position. Spain itself had gone red with revolution!

Less joy greeted the proclamation of the constitution in America on this occasion than in 1812, though many liberals were heartened. Newspapers were born, political prisoners released, and elections to the *cortes* held. Viceroys suffered some diminution of prestige by being renamed political chiefs, but these titles were seldom employed except in official documents. A certain federalism was also instituted, with each intendancy receiving permission to create elected assemblies known as provincial deputations. The *cortes* announced that no further expeditions would be sent to the Americas, which no doubt gratified the military leaders who had begun the revolution. Wherever there were independence movements, Spanish officials were to negotiate cease-fires with the leaders. Commissioners went from Madrid to see what the liberators really wanted and to seek an understanding with them. Perhaps these measures should have pleased the Americans, but usually they failed to do so. The spectacle of viceroys and Spanish generals holding parleys with patriot commanders undermined the confidence of royalists while inflating the rebels. The commissioners sent from Madrid found little to discuss with the former colonials, who wanted complete independence, not mere reform within a liberalized monarchy. The Americans soon realized that Spanish radicals had little interest and no understanding of their desire to achieve status and self-government. In the Spanish *cortes* the American deputies were usually regarded as tiresome and unreasonable inferiors. Constitutional Spain was not generally respected in America. Traditional conservatives thought it odious, the enemy of religion and justice. Liberals and patriots felt it was indifferent to their proper ambitions. It was obvious to all that it was weak; Spain was no longer an imperial power.

The Secession of New Spain

NOWHERE did the Spanish revolution of 1820 have larger results than in the Viceroyalty of New Spain. The recovery of this, the finest of Spain's overseas possessions, from the insurrections of Hidalgo and Morelos was well under way by 1820. Mines were slowly coming back into operation, and laborers who had run away to join the uprisings were returning. Viceroy Apodaca had informed the king that he needed no more royalist troops to maintain order and reigned with considerable serenity. It was true that remnants of Morelos' forces were still holding out in the southern mountains, but they posed no dangerous threat. The failure of the creoles to respond in 1817 to a liberating expedition led by Francisco Mina, a radical Spanish officer, indicated some degree of contentment with the regime. Then came the news of the Spanish upheaval and orders to restore the constitution of 1812. Doing as he was directed, Apodaca summoned provincial assemblies, often based on *cabildos* in the capitals, to choose deputies for the revived *cortes* in Madrid. These elections, together with a lively exercise of the right of free speech and the rebirth of newspapers, revealed that liberalism had by no means been eradicated during the restoration.

The resulting manifestations of liberal sentiments alarmed the creole aristocracy. Memories of Hidalgo's race war and Morelos' depredations were still very keen. As further news arrived from Spain of attacks on the Church and the dignity of the king, conservatives became more and more alarmed: radicalism in Spain might spell revolution in Mexico. Besides, Spain was no longer capable of running an empire, and peninsular officials were simply in the way. As for Mexican liberals, they were seldom won over by the mother country's sudden conversion to radicalism. Spain was eternally Spain, whether she was radical or reactionary, and the experience of 1814 had taught them how quickly conditions could be reversed. Within a few months the leading Mexicans, liberal and conservative, reached an obvious conclusion: the connection with Spain was no longer desirable.

The man who took the initiative in resolving the situation was Agustín de Iturbide, who lacked the appeal of Bolívar or the ability of San Martín. Yet he was destined to achieve as much as they did with far less effort. Born the year Bolívar was, in 1783, of a well-to-do landowning family in western Mexico, Iturbide had a comparatively poor education and was no student of political philosophy. He had served in the royalist army for several years, demonstrating both military ability and ruthlessness. On one occasion a unit he commanded inflicted very serious damage on Morelos' forces to the enhancement of Iturbide's prestige as a hard foe of the patriots. His allegiance to Spain was unquestioned. Soon after the restoration, however, he was accused of extortion and mishandling of funds, charges which so many of the liberators incurred at one time or another. Cashiered from the royal army, he spent several years fending off prosecution and attending to his business affairs in Michoacán. At some point he entered one of the secret lodges that attracted military men who were critical of Spanish rule. He seemed pious and solid to conservatives, no man likely to undertake a revolutionary enterprise.

Late in 1820 Iturbide journeyed to Mexico City and persuaded Viceroy Apodaca that the diehard patriot forces in the southern mountains, remnants of Morelos' armies, were becoming more dangerous. Since he had fought these "bandits" before with considerable success, it seemed both reasonable and commendable that he should offer to lead royalist troops in an effort to wipe them out. Perhaps the viceroy thought Iturbide was hoping to clear his name with the government. In any event, he agreed to the proposal and gave Iturbide command of a unit of 2,500 men whose officers, as it turned out, were covert partisans of independence. In December 1820 the army marched into the rugged south as though it intended to exterminate the rebels. Instead, Iturbide established contact with their principal chieftain, Vicente Guerrero, a tough guerrilla leader who was sincerely devoted to the late Morelos but was not particularly intelligent. After several weeks of maneuvering and negotiating, the two commanders proclaimed the Plan of Iguala, named for a modest town, in February 1821.

This was the first of innumerable Mexican "plans," those bombastic announcements of impending revolutions for noble ideals. This plan was indeed comprehensive, designed as it was to win over the strongest elements in the country. It had three fundamental points, or "guarantees." First, New Spain must be independent but should remain a monarchy, if possible under Fernando VII or one of his brothers, if not, under another prince of royal blood. Second, the Catholic Church should continue to enjoy the high, indeed privileged, position it always had. Third, racial equality was to prevail. To the colored peoples the last guarantee meant just that; to the whites it signified merely parity between peninsulars and creoles.

While Iturbide has never been admired as a profound political thinker, he had produced a beguiling program. It won over nearly everybody in Mexico: conservatives, liberals, Indians, mestizos, creoles, and even many peninsulars. Iturbide and Guerrero combined their forces into an Army of the Three Guarantees and called on the country to accept the Plan of Iguala. Since army officers all over the land were likely to be members of the secret network of lodges, it was simple enough to stimulate them to lead their garrisons into pronouncing for the plan, often to the whole-hearted enthusiasm of the population. Within a few months almost all of the viceroyalty was in the hands of the patriots. In the capital there was more resistance because of the large peninsular bureaucracy, but creole liberals were also at work. Furthermore, Apodaca had been relieved of his post and his replacement had not yet arrived.

When the new viceroy or political chief, General Juan O'Donojú, reached Vera Cruz in September 1821, he found his prospective realm united against him. He elected to deal with Iturbide and to accept the Plan of Iguala, a circumstance that gave rise to charges of bribery. Probably they were not sound. O'Donojú, who had been selected by the *cortes* because he was so liberal, may have had some sympathy with the Mexican patriots and realized there was nothing to be done but put a good face on matters. If so, he was almost the only Spaniard ever to display such wisdom and broad-mindedness. He received little credit for his action, which was angrily denounced by the *cortes* in Madrid. O'Donojú did not live either to be punished by Spain or rewarded by Mexico. He died within a month of his arrival, probably of natural causes despite rumors that suggested other explanations.

The Spanish government was indeed aroused by O'Donojú's "treason." The *cortes* indignantly disavowed his acceptance of the Plan of Iguala and threatened to coerce Mexico. Fernando VII was, if anything, yet more outraged. Even when he was free he never considered going to the New World. Now the *cortes* would not let him out of its sight. The same was true of his brothers, who had no desire to mount a Mexican throne and who would never have been trusted either by the king or the *cortes*.[7]

For some months Iturbide went through the motions of negotiating for a European prince, all the time maneuvering to place his partisans in key positions and cultivating popularity. Guerrero was all but removed from the scene. In May 1822 a noisy group of demonstrators surrounded Iturbide's residence and demanded that he become emperor. After an unconvincing show of reluctance, he capitulated to their wishes. The whole affair was manifestly staged, and few were deceived, least of all Guerrero and the liberals. It was necessary to use troops to persuade the congress, a majority of whose members had fled, to authorize the emergence of Agustín I to the imperial dignity. Regardless of his cynical role in these proceedings, Agustín Iturbide had torn Mexico out of the Spanish monarchy with little bloodshed and without disrupting its social system. Later generations have given him some credit.

Central America Follows Mexico

THE captaincy-general of Guatemala, which roughly corresponded to Central America as we know it today, was long the quietest component of the Spanish empire. For about three centuries there had been few rebellions, invasions, or scandals of enough consequence to disturb the crown. A chronic irritation had long been the theft, as the Span-

7. Since the history of both Spain and Mexico during the following decades was so tragic, one is tempted to speculate that it might have been well if Don Carlos de Borbón, the oldest brother after Fernando VII, had taken the Mexican throne. He might have served a good purpose in holding the country together. Instead, he caused the frightful Carlist wars and aggravated divisions that still plague Spain.

ish saw it, of logwood from Belize by British depredators operating out of Jamaica, but these activities had been so continuous that the authorities were almost resigned to them. Several towns had become fairly important as centers of business or culture; some of them would eventually be capitals of tiny republics. The colonial system functioned typically, with the usual peninsular bureaucracy and clerical establishment, creole planters, ranchers, and merchants, Negro slaves, and servile Indians. In some of the jungles and mountains the colored population lived as free men, at least as long as they avoided contact with the whites. An unusual district was the province of Costa Rica, which was full of settlers of Spanish origin who raised livestock and crops in that breezy section of the isthmus largely without assistance from servile labor. Otherwise, the captaincy-general resembled other parts of the Spanish empire. Its capital, Guatemala City, was almost a miniature Mexico City, with a scenic setting in which lakes and mountains were prominent, fine examples of colonial architecture, and the usual institutions of authority and culture.[8]

The catastrophes that shook the Spanish monarchy after 1808 had slight repercussions in Guatemala: only a row or two in the *audiencia*, a little agitation among creole liberals, and restless behavior in the various *cabildos*. There was no rebellion or any serious movement for independence. After the return of the king in 1814, the area settled back into its customary somnolence. In 1821 came the startling news of Iturbide's actions in Mexico, which threw the creoles into a rebellious frame of mind. Liberals clamored for freedom, while conservatives grudgingly admitted that radical Spain deserved no further support. Instead of combatting these manifestations the acting captain-general, a Spanish officer named Gabino Gainza, took the lead in bringing about the obvious solution. A provincial assembly was already in being as a result of the constitution of 1812. It was easy for the captain-general to persuade this body to become a junta and to declare independence. This was done on September 15, 1821, and Gabino Gainza was predictably elected to the post of chief executive. A confusing situation soon arose over whether the former captaincy-general should become a part of Mexico. Iturbide, naturally, favored this course, and so did the leaders in Guatemala City. Other provinces objected, however, indicating the nascent federalism which would soon disrupt the whole area. El Salvador went so far as to propose incorporation in the United States, an offer regarded with scant enthusiasm in Washington. Most of the year 1822 was taken up with the question of joining Mexico, an issue that was all the more contentious after Iturbide assumed the imperial title. The entrance of a Mexican

---

8. It was a new city, however, since an earthquake had destroyed the earlier capital, now known as Antigua, in 1773.

army did much to encourage the former captaincy-general to accept union with Mexico. It was a shaky solution, however. Local feeling, republicanism, and dislike of Mexico were strong enough to indicate that it would be of short duration.

Haiti's Freedom and Santo Domingo's Miscalculation

JUST what happened in Haiti after the departure of Napoleon's greatly reduced army in 1804 is known only partially, mostly through the reports of foreigners who regarded Africans as frightful or ludicrous. Jean-Jacques Dessalines seized the mantle of leadership once held by Toussaint L'Ouverture and stood triumphant as the French left to occupy the Spanish side of Hispaniola. Dessalines was born in West Africa and had been the slave of a free Negro in colonial times. He had risen to prominence as a lieutenant of Toussaint and possibly had betrayed him. According to tradition he was a fiend, a veritable monster who gloated over torture and killings. An often-told story is that he periodically examined the mirror of his snuff-box to see if it was moist. If so, he suspended the butcheries for a while; if not, they went on. Much as he boasted of having vanquished the great Napoleon, Dessalines imitated him by assuming the title of emperor. As Jacques I, he gloried in such imperial extravagance as the barbarized state could support. It is entirely possible that the traditional image of his reign of absurdities and bestialities is exaggerated. Jacques I seems to have displayed some constructive attitudes in attempting to relocate former slaves on the seized plantations and in reviving the country's agricultural production. Forced labor was almost a necessity if the latter purpose was to be attained, and it may have been his resort to this method that gave him a reputation for tyranny. In 1806 he was murdered.

After the inevitable squabble for power, Haiti came to be divided between the two leading contenders, though they kept up a continuous war of sorts against one another. The richest part of the country, the long, east-west peninsula in the south, fell under the control of Alexandre Pétion, a mulatto who had some education and who had lived in France. Pétion appears to have ruled in a fairly easy-going manner, perhaps because he assumed that people were naturally lazy and that government was necessarily corrupt. That he took the title of president suggested a certain leaning to contemporary notions of progress. His aid to Simón Bolívar in 1816 and 1817 was important in advancing the cause of independence in South America and in encouraging the emancipation of Negro slaves in that continent. On the whole, Pétion has a good reputation in history. Probably he did as well as anyone could have. He stayed in power until he died in 1818 and was succeeded by another mulatto named Pierre Boyer.

In the more primitive north of Haiti ruled Henri Christophe, a Negro who made himself king as Henri I. He may have been a madman. As in the case of his predecessor, Emperor Jacques I, legends of his vanities and cruelties give him a maniacal character. He abused his subjects with sadistic determination, forcing them to labor in gangs as they had under slavery, whipping and killing them as if they were animals. Henri I lorded it over the population as though he were a god-king. The paltry resources of his realm went into luxuries for himself, notably the great palace and fortress on Cap Haitien he called Sans Souci. Perhaps he was nothing more than a barbaric monster. Yet a more favorable interpretation can be drawn from the scanty information we have. His naming of Negro henchmen as Duke of Lemonade and Duke of Marmalade was not as ridiculous as it might seem, for there really were districts with those names. Compelling the people to labor could not have been done gently; it might have been better than allowing them to live in utter idleness. Considering the realities of the ruined tropical colony that constituted his kingdom, he may have been, at least for a time, nothing more than a pragmatist who dealt with conditions as he had to. However that may have been, a revolt threatened him in 1820, and he killed himself with a silver bullet. Not long after his suicide, the ruler of the south, Boyer, brought northern Haiti under his control. The republic was now united and independent but scarcely a part of the civilized world.

While Haiti was undergoing these shocks, conditions were less tumultuous in Santo Domingo. The planters, merchants, and officials of that sleepy colony had been badly jolted by the cession of the area to France in 1795. Fortunately, the transfer was not effected for ten years, until the survivors of Napoleon's expedition retreated from Haiti. Since France and Spain were then allied, the occupation was for a time conciliatory. The news of Napoleon's thrust into the peninsula in 1808 outraged the colonists, who overcame the tiny French garrison and placed themselves under British protection. This situation continued until 1814, when Fernando VII returned to the Spanish throne. For six or seven years thereafter Santo Domingo resumed her place as a quiet colony. Yet the Spanish-speaking mulatto and white population remained uneasy over the intentions of the Negroes of Haiti. To be sure, Toussaint had briefly taken over Santo Domingo on one occasion, but he had done little to injure the whites. Jacques I and Henri I had attempted invasions but had been turned back. Not until 1821 did the blow fall, and then because of the folly of the creoles. At that time the victories of Bolívar in Venezuela and the antics of the Spanish radicals in Madrid produced powerful sentiment for shifting allegiance from Spain to Colombia. Cáceres, the Spanish governor, joined with leading creoles to proclaim the freedom of the new nation on December 1, 1821 and to request Bolívar's protection. But the Liberator was far away and had few ships. Boyer, on the other hand, was just across the border ruling a recently united Haiti. In 1822 he led an army into Santo Domingo and received the surrender of the hapless Cáceres. For two decades Spain's original colony in the New World continued to be a colony, but now of Negroid Haiti.

Brazil's Fortunate Experience

THAT Brazil is now the largest and most important country in Latin America is not unrelated to the way in which she attained her independence. She became a nation with her basic institutions intact, without the shocks and disruptions suffered by the Spanish colonies. Nor was she splintered the way the other viceroyalties were when they became free; Portuguese America remained a unit. The results were so fortunate that many Spanish Americans in later years lamented their own bad luck in failing to attract a prince of a recognized royal family to open the careers of their homelands as independent nations. Brazil, who had been more backward than most of the Spanish colonies in 1808, surpassed the republics in nearly every respect within a half century. During this period her history was not so full as theirs of personal and national tragedies, of violence, of squalor in public life, or of bitterness toward the mother country.

The Brazilian independence movement began when Portugal lost her freedom to Napoleon in 1807. On that occasion, it will be recalled, the royal family and thousands of nobles and officials sailed away to Rio de Janeiro. In time the British liberated the homeland, but the little kingdom was so depressed she could never again exert her former authority over the gigantic American dominion which had flourished during her agony. The surge of Brazilian national feeling had begun when the refugee royal court arrived early in 1808 after an uncomfortable voyage of two months. At the head of the monarchy was the insane queen, Maria I, who had begun her reign in 1777 by dismissing Pombal and abandoning his program of modernization. Actually wielding the absolute royal authority was the prince regent, João de Braganza, a man of some ability who had long guided Portugal through the storms and stress of the early Napoleonic period until the French emperor abruptly cut short his game. His wife was Carlota Joaquina, a disagreeable princess who was the sister of Fernando VII of Spain.[9] All was confusion as the

9. Apart from making João's life unnecessarily hard and doing mischief in the Spanish American empire, Carlota Joaquina was destined to create many

royal exiles settled down in Rio. It was necessary to de-louse the noble
guests and to dislodge residents in order to accommodate the numerous
officials, aristocrats, and servants. While the colonials were surprised and
flattered at the appearance of the court in their midst, there were many
irritating adjustments to make. And the more perceptive Brazilians realized that the long period of easy-going colonial administration was about
to end.

On the whole, Prince João managed rather well, making the best of
the fact that Brazil was now to be the headquarters of the far-flung monarchy, which still included rich possessions in Africa and Asia. It was not
long before an effective executive bureaucracy replaced the slack rule,
indeed negligence, of colonial hacks. The judiciary was strengthened
and a supreme tribunal established. Both the royal army and the colonial
militia received needed invigoration. To an extent never known before,
the government collected taxes, inspected, and altered or enforced the
laws. Of greatest significance were the reforms João effected in commerce. Now that the Portuguese empire existed more than ever by the
grace of Britain, its ports were opened entirely to traders of that ally, who
responded by flooding Brazil with manufactured goods. This brought
about a considerable prosperity as well as an elevation in the standard
of living. João also established a national bank, a public library, two medical schools, an institute of fine arts, one of applied arts, a military
academy, a museum, and a botanical garden. Such learned men as
there were in Rio, most of them refugees from Portugal, were organized
in a National Institute. And a printing press, the first in Brazil, was soon
operating, mostly to publish government documents but also serving to
circulate news of the outer world. The glamor of the royal court began
to attract to Rio de Janeiro many bucolic Brazilian aristocrats who had
lived so long in isolation on their plantations. To encourage this migration and, further, to entrench the regime in the New World, João lavishly distributed titles and honors.

The sleepy colony suddenly came to life as a result of these activities.
If the jarring of Portuguese and Brazilian sometimes produced irritation,
it also heightened the colonials' awareness of the greater world outside.
A few creoles learned of the doctrines of the revolutionary age and the
technology of more advanced countries. While subversive movements in
favor of republicanism appeared here and there, most Brazilians were
quite contented under the regime. The court was also pleased to be in
Rio de Janeiro, a matter not difficult to understand in view of the attractions of that city. Long after Portugal was free, João found reasons to
postpone his return to Lisbon. In 1816, when his mother died and he

difficulties in Portugal during the 1820's   by inciting her absolutist son, Miguel,
against her more liberal elder son, Pedro.

became king as João VI, he honored Brazil by making her a kingdom equal to Portugal within the over-all monarchy, and he continued to reside there. All was not bliss, of course. Some Brazilians were sufficiently aware of their nationality to resent the hordes of Portuguese officials, who held the best positions and who manifestly enjoyed the sovereign's preference. A republican movement appeared in Pernambuco in 1817, reflecting this creole sentiment and the tradition of secession in that corner of Brazil. The revolt was suppressed, but a few embers remained. Also, the Spanish American insurrections inspired some Brazilians. Still, the situation at Rio de Janeiro in 1820 seemed to promise long years of stability.

Again, events in Europe dictated the course of Latin American affairs. Portugal was orphaned and neglected because of the protracted absence of the royal court. So restless had it become early in 1820 that General Beresford, the British officer who served practically as viceroy, went to Rio to warn the king. While he was gone a group of Portuguese military men in Oporto pronounced for liberalism and constitutionalism, obviously following the recent example of the Spanish army. Soon the movement spread throughout the kingdom, and, in the absence of a charter of their own, the Portuguese rebels proclaimed the Spanish constitution of 1812. They summoned a *côrtes* of 200 members, including seventy from Brazil. King João was affronted by the assertion of his subjects at home, and the Brazilians felt insulted over the small number of deputies offered their enormous land.[10]

Hoping to save the parent country for his crown, João decided to send his oldest son and heir, Prince Pedro, to Lisbon. At this point the large Portuguese contingent in Brazil thrust itself forward. Long homesick for Portugal and, in many cases, sincerely inspired by the liberal movement, they staged a threatening demonstration in Rio in April 1821. King João reacted by fainting, for he was always aware of the fate of Louis XVI. When he recovered his senses, he learned that no guillotine awaited him, but rather a demand that he accept the Spanish constitution of 1812 in Brazil as well as Portugal. He readily capitulated and, under further pressure, consented to go to Portugal to preside over the liberal government. The Portuguese nobles and officials were pleased at the prospect of returning home with the king. Many Brazilians likewise thought it was high time the court departed. João left as planned, taking with him most of the Portuguese element and the treasury, just as he had brought them from Lisbon when he fled in 1807. As he embarked he instructed Prince Pedro, who was to remain in Rio as regent, not to let

10. As in the case of the Spanish division of seats between peninsulars and Americans, it could be plausibly argued that the proportion was fair, given the low status of the huge colored population in the New World.

Brazil follow the Spanish countries in becoming an independent republic. If the separation movement became irresistible, the king told his heir, then Pedro should place himself at the head of it and not permit an adventurer to become ruler of Brazil.

For a year and a half Pedro ruled for his father in Rio, acquiring a taste for power and surrounding himself with men who encouraged him to be assertive. Some of these advisers were Portuguese absolutists, who resented the liberal movement on general principles. Others were Brazilians who felt the call of national independence. In this second group were three brothers of the Andrada family from São Paulo, the most prominent of whom was José Bonifacio, a learned man who had spent most of his life in Europe. He was enlightened, modern-minded, and had been for some years a professor of metallurgy at the University of Coimbra. Now a strong proponent of Brazilian independence, he inducted Prince Pedro into the masonic brotherhood and pressed him to take the lead in a patriotic movement. A few republican revolts indicated that there were alternatives should Pedro prove reluctant.

It is altogether likely that Pedro had sincere hesitations about lending himself to the cause of independence. On one occasion he wrote to his father in his own blood to deny any disloyal purpose. Yet the liberal *côrtes* at Lisbon antagonized the Brazilians, the Church, and the royal family in every way. Brazilian deputies were insulted and belittled like the American representatives in the Spanish *cortes*. Portuguese liberals had no consideration for these colonials who aspired to equality or more in the imperial system. They passed laws to break Brazil up into provinces that would be dependent on Lisbon and not on Rio. They invalidated the earlier decrees of João that had raised the stature of Brazil so markedly, restored the former commercial monopoly, and planned to reduce the Church to complete subservience to Lisbon. As a final insult, the *côrtes* ordered Pedro to return to Portugal and complete his education "in a civilized country." The prince-regent defied this command on January 9, 1822 by saying, "I remain," to the joy of his countrymen who still observe "I remain Day."

By mid-1822 the leading Brazilians were thoroughly alienated from the mother country. Pedro, a handsome, gallant fellow in his early twenties, was very popular. So was his wife, Leopoldina, a Habsburg archduchess, who had brought a number of savants from Europe to assess the riches of Brazil. Pressure on them both to cut Brazil away from Portugal was very strong. Perhaps it is remarkable they delayed as long as they did. On September 7, 1822 Pedro was in São Paulo when he learned of another command from the Lisbon *côrtes* to bow to its will. With this communication was a note from his wife which frantically urged him to seize the moment to carry out his father's original orders. Pedro therefore uttered a ringing statement in favor of independence or death, the *grito* of Ypiranga, named after a stream near São Paulo. His proclamation produced an outburst of joy among the patriots. To sweeten his appeal for the benefit of dubious liberals, he announced that he would be a constitutional monarch. Soon an assembly in Rio signified its enthusiasm for the step. Brazil would be free under a popular monarch. Since it was so large a country the new ruler would become no mere king but an emperor. On December 1, 1822 Pedro was crowned.

Only two potential sources of opposition existed within the new nation. One was the nucleus of republicans who refused to accept the promises of Pedro and the Andrada brothers to the effect that a constitution would insure their liberal ideals. This group was not large enough to pose a serious obstacle. Of more significance was the other, the lingering Portuguese officials and soldiers who had a vested interest in the continuation of the colonial system. Portugal herself, with a heady *côrtes* and a captive king, was in no position to do anything. Pedro got rid of the principal Portuguese garrison in the capital by using his personal prestige. He called the soldiers together, paid them off, and marched them down to ships in the harbor which carried them home. In Bahia, Pará, and Maranhão, which were almost unreachable by land, there were Portuguese garrisons who could not be handled so simply. It was Lord Cochrane, now free from his involvements in Chile and Peru, who came to Pedro's rescue. Employing the daring measures for which he was famous, the Scottish adventurer battered the loyalist forces at Bahia from land and sea until they surrendered. Those in Maranhão and Pará were bested by a ruse. Cochrane's fleet flew royalist flags as they entered these ports and tricked the commanders into coming aboard, whereupon they were compelled to capitulate. One final threat remained, some seventy Portuguese vessels which might blockade Brazil or, possibly, transport European troops. These Cochrane contemptuously scattered by the audacious employment of his crack fleet. Then, after the inevitable row with Pedro over payment for his services, the fiery naval hero went back to Europe at the end of 1823 for further adventures in the cause of Greek independence.

Portugal became absolutist again in 1824, soon after Spain did. King João proposed that all be forgotten and that Brazil rejoin his monarchy. Pedro was much embarrassed by this summons, because he was in a way loyal to his father and was heir to the Portuguese throne himself. Yet Brazil had tasted independence and had no wish to give it up. An awkward situation was brought to an end through the good offices of George Canning, Britain's foreign minister, who pressed both Portugal and Brazil into an agreement in 1826. Under the terms of this treaty

João would momentarily receive the title of emperor but would at once abdicate his Brazilian crown in favor of Pedro. A financial settlement that must have been fair, since both sides objected to it, provided that Brazil pay Portugal for confiscated property that once belonged to Portuguese loyalists. Finally, Britain compelled both nations to promise to terminate the African slave trade within a few years, a humanitarian measure dear to the British public but one which few Iberians or Americans could appreciate. On the whole, Brazil's secession was accomplished smoothly and with a minimum of ill feeling. Emperor Pedro I continued the Braganza dynasty in the New World, relations with the former mother country were decent if not cordial, and both the personnel and local institutions of the old regime continued into the national period.

THE FINAL VICTORY

Simón Bolívar in Oblivion and Glory

BOLÍVAR was thirty-two when he sailed from New Granada to Jamaica in May 1815, just before the collapse of the *patria boba*. His fortune long since spent in the cause of independence or confiscated by royalists and his reputation besmirched by defeat and failure, he was almost alone. It is symptomatic of the man's greatness that he recognized adversity as an impostor. Not all of the disasters that befell the liberation movement in 1814–1815 changed his conviction that the Americas would become free during his lifetime. A famous letter from Jamaica, written in September 1815 for publication, summarized the Liberator's thoughts in his darkest hour. American independence was morally victorious, he proclaimed, because the habit of obedience, a community of interest, understanding, and religion, mutual good will, and a tender regard for the birthplace and good name of their fatherland—all these were gone. The New World well knew its fundamental differences with the Old. A new race, a mixture of the original Americans and the heirs of the immigrants, had taken shape. It must and would work out its own destiny. Bolívar then analyzed the failures of the recent past and with acute insight forecast the probable development of the various territories of the Spanish empire, all of which he believed would win their independence. If the Jamaica letter was the most profound expression of the Liberator's thoughts during this period, he also composed many inspirational missives to refugees and beleaguered patriots. His soaring idealism and firm faith did much to maintain his leadership of the cause. Not all of his energies went into such noble activities, however. Often, like the temperamental actor that was part of his nature, or simply like the exhausted soldier, he delivered himself to seedy companions and loose women for long periods of debauchery.

During 1816 he alternated between dissipation and splendid exertion. Discovering a friend and supporter in Henri Pétion, the mulatto president of southern Haiti, Bolívar went to Aux Cayes to obtain material assistance in exchange for a promise to free the slaves in South America. Another ally appeared in Luis Brion, a Dutch adventurer from Curaçao who liked to make money by promoting independence, as did so many other helpful foreigners. In the spring of 1816 Bolívar and 200 or more men sailed from Haiti to the island of Margarita, off Venezuela, where patriots were maintaining a rather squalid hideout from the royalists. Doubling his force with these recruits, the Liberator sailed past the royalist fleet that patrolled the northern coast of Venezuela and landed at Ocumare, near Puerto Cabello. The expected popular uprising did not materialize, no more than it had for Miranda ten years before. Venezuelans perhaps recalled only too vividly the disasters Bolívar had brought them during the "liberation" of 1813–1814, and the Spanish restoration had not yet become unbearable. Another landing far to the east likewise failed to produce a favorable response, and the chastened Bolívar returned to Haiti.

It was characteristic of the Liberator that he asserted his will with confidence notwithstanding the stubbornness of realities. All great men probably do this. Conditions in 1817 were not in the least better for an effort to free Venezuela than they had been in 1816, but Bolívar determined to try again with different tactics. Patriot refugees were scattered about the wastelands of the mouth of the Orinoco River. A few were genuine lovers of liberty who were deeply committed to the overthrow of Spain. Many were just outlaws or primitive llaneros who enjoyed being led by men tougher than they, fighting, looting, and generally leading lives of violence. Freed slaves and formerly servile Indians were often allied with them. These forces were likely to be loyal to their leaders when things were going well, to quit when they were not. The leaders themselves, Piar, Mariño, Arizmendi, and many others unremembered, were difficult and quarrelsome men. Bolívar, however, discerned hope in these unpromising holdouts. For one thing, they could fight well. Their outlaw dominion was relatively safe from Spanish reconquest because of the swamps protected by mountains; yet the Orinoco gave the region contact with the sea and the outside world beyond, which might provide supplies and volunteers. Once he had mastered the chaotic personalities who clamored to lead these warriors and created an effective base, he could build up a real army that would oust the Spaniards. Bolívar's strategic sense was as sound as San Martín's. He saw truly, and he did exactly what he set out to do.

Landing early in 1817 at the delta of the Orinoco, the Liberator pushed up the muddy river to make his headquarters at a raw, frontier town then named Angostura, now Ciudad Bolívar. Much of his first year was occupied with establishing his leadership over the other chieftains. No doubt his prestige as an educated aristocrat and a general was initially an advantage. Of more enduring importance was his formidable personality, which could be seductively fascinating and terrifying as he wished. Also, he employed deceit, cruelty, something close to treachery, appeals to noble emotions, eloquence, subtle psychology—all the devices of great commanders and politicians. Somehow, he won the respect and often the fierce devotion of men as individualistic as these. Patriots in royalist territory heard of him and made their way to join up. And Bolívar achieved a notable victory in obtaining the allegiance of the most formidable force of *llaneros,* one led by the young folk hero José Antonio Páez. Under the command of Boves several years before, the *llaneros* had been a major cause of Bolívar's defeat. Now, with Páez as their principal chieftain, they were patriots. Probably their basic consistency lay in opposing Caracas and the developed area along the northern coast. Since it had become royalist, the *llaneros* turned into republicans. Bolívar attached Páez and his men to his command in a crucial interview held on the plains. Instead of ingratiating himself by acting like a rough cowboy, the Liberator presented a dazzling figure of a bemedalled, splendidly uniformed gentleman who had frequented the royal courts of Europe. His psychology was sound. The *llaneros* were impressed and followed Páez when he subordinated himself to the glittering Bolívar.

Another fruitful achievement of Bolívar in 1817 and 1818 was the attraction of foreign, mainly British, assistance. An agent in London was almost too effective in convincing British exporters that arms and supplies shipped to the patriots would be most liberally paid for. In time, many of the speculators were ruined and the agent got into trouble, for many merchants were as willing to believe that South America was a treasure house as their predecessors had been in the days of Drake and Raleigh. Dozens of ships from England ignored the Spanish blockade to bring in quantities of material to Bolívar's forces up the Orinoco. And several thousand volunteers migrated to Venezuela from Great Britain and Ireland. Failing to find diamonds and loose gold lying on the ground, as many had expected, these soldiers of fortune were often bitterly disappointed. Yet the gamble was preferable to enduring unemployment at home, the fate of so many veterans of the Napoleonic wars, and they remained. On the whole they made superb soldiers. In a moment when he failed, for once, to keep Latin American posterity in mind, Bolívar declared these fighting men from the British Isles the best he ever had.

For two years Bolívar labored in the hideous region of the lower Orinoco, much as San Martín had under pleasanter circumstances in Mendoza. Carefully studying the methods of the Spaniards and improving the training of his own men, he participated in numerous skirmishes. His original plan was to send his forces over the mountain range that separates northern Venezuela from the Orinoco Valley. At length he comprehended that it would be too risky. General Morillo was a very able officer, and the royalist infantry was large and well-equipped. For the patriots to invade the north would be to invite defeat. On the other hand, the skirmishes showed how ineffective the royalist infantry was in the grasslands against the patriot cavalry. Bolívar's final plan, then, was to permit the Spanish foot soldiers to reign in peace in the north while Páez' horsemen guarded the backlands. With a special task force the Liberator himself would strike in an improbable spot and deal Spain a body blow.

Before he opened his campaign, Bolívar again displayed his stature as more than a military commander. He well knew that war was not a mere matter of battles. Unlike San Martín, the Liberator appreciated the importance of proclaiming ideals to inspire his partisans among the civilian population and to weaken the convictions of his opponents. Calling a selected body of his followers to Angostura in what was euphemistically labeled a congress, he delivered a magnificent address on February 15, 1819. It was a virtuoso performance, full of allusions to the greater political philosophers and examples from history. He tactfully informed his hearers that Spanish America was not ready to experiment with complete liberty and absolute democracy. Years would be required to build up a sound national spirit, love of law, and respect for magistrates. The constitution of the future should provide for a period of tutelage. Thus the republic he envisaged should be unitary and not federal. There should be a strong president, an hereditary senate composed of the leading liberators, a lower house chosen by limited suffrage, an independent judiciary, and guarantees of civil liberties. Affecting to nourish no political ambitions, he closed the discourse with the words: "You may begin your labors; I have finished mine."

Bolívar's labors were, of course, only beginning. Within six years he would traverse a course in the shape of a reversed question mark from Angostura to Potosí, fighting most of the way in indescribably rugged terrain. Spanish power on the mainland would be broken for all time, and five modern nations would owe their independence directly to the famed Liberator. He started this campaign in May 1819 with about 4,000 men, including 500 British legionnaires. Páez circulated about the northern mountain range to confuse the Spaniards. In the corner of northeastern New Granada a less famous junior commander named

Francisco de Paula Santander was also engaged in distracting the royalists. Bolívar's force, most of which was mounted, made a spectacular dash up the torrid Orinoco and Arauca Valleys, a region that is even now largely unpopulated. As they penetrated the Andes, the heat gave way to cold. Incredible feats of exertion and ingenuity brought most of the army through, though almost all the horses were lost. Descending into the pleasant plateaus of New Granada the expedition fell upon a surprised royalist force at Boyacá on August 7, 1819 and disrupted it completely. Already, country folk were telling the Liberator how much they hated the Spanish, how glad they were to see him. That these intimations were not false indications of general sentiment was shown in the reaction of the viceregal capital when news of Boyacá arrived. Without a shred of dignity the viceroy and other officials fled. The *bogotanos* were in a state of delirium when the Liberator made his entrance. Only one battle, a minor one at that, had shattered the core of Spanish power in the Viceroyalty of New Granada.

Bolívar settled only briefly into the vacated executive post of the viceroy. Completing the war was then more important than administrative challenges, and so he called the 27-year-old Santander to serve as ruler in Bogotá, thus beginning a long career of this able patriot in that capacity. The Liberator made his way back to Angostura between September and December 1819, accepting the acclamations of many towns on the way. At his headquarters he mixed work with a full schedule of feasts and dances. His principal achievement was winning the consent of a reluctant congress to create a republic called Colombia, an inspired idea of Bolívar to do justice to the Discoverer. The new nation would initially consist of Venezuela and the liberated portion of New Granada known as Cundinamarca, and Bolívar was chosen as its first president. With this arrangement completed, the Liberator departed for the frontier region between the sister states in order to get on with military matters. These were not as neatly settled early in 1820 as they would appear in retrospect. Viceroy Juan Sámano, who had left Bogotá in such undignified haste, commanded more troops than the patriots numbered. General Morillo's large army in Venezuela was quite unbeaten. Quito was full of royalist troops, and behind Quito was Peru, which was not yet invaded by San Martín from the south. It was still possible that the tardy expedition in Cadiz might head for Costa Firme and undo all Bolívar had accomplished. With an air of urgency the Liberator planned new campaigns.

And then came the news from Spain about the revolution. It was clear there would be no further royalist reinforcements. And Morillo had orders to negotiate with the patriots, which he began to do in July. Bolívar responded to these overtures but for several months, until November, held out in vain for Morillo's recognition of Colombia's independence. This postponement was damaging for both sides, for desertions were very heavy during the period of inactivity. Morillo's forces suffered the more, however, for the cause of independence had momentum, and more British volunteers were joining Bolívar's army. When the two commanders finally met they got on surprisingly well, possibly as a consequence of the numerous toasts which mellowed their spirits. They arranged an armistice and exchanged felicitations. Almost immediately afterward Morillo gave up his command and returned to Spain. Universally respected as an able general, he had come close to restoring the overseas empire between 1815 and 1818. Now that Bolívar had destroyed his strategic position and the Spanish liberals had undermined the entire military structure, Morillo saw no reason to preside over a debacle. He left none too soon.

Within a few weeks the armistice was broken, each side accusing the other of violations. It was obvious that the patriot tide was surging. While the royalists were still numerous, they were demoralized and saw no real hope of victory. Bolívar now determined to clean them out of the northern coast of Venezuela, a task he especially relished because that area was his home and the scene of earlier failures. He combined his forces with those of Páez and approached this sector through the rugged terrain of the southwest, while Bermúdez made rapid advances from the east and occupied Caracas in May 1821. At Carabobo on June 24, 1821, in a hard-fought battle in which the British Legion carried off most of the honors, Bolívar won a signal triumph. The royalists rallied enough to hold some of the coastal towns, where they spent more than a year enduring privations not unlike those of the early conquistadors. Bolívar headed for Caracas to make a grand entrance, receiving the plaudits he knew so well how to stimulate. He was, at last, back home.

The Colombian congress removed from Angostura to Cúcuta in order to continue its labors of statecraft in a more central location. Bolívar was too occupied with military affairs to supervise every detail, with the result that many of the new members elected by Cundinamarca were men who wished to think for themselves and not serve as mere puppets. Ideologues of the *patria boba* type and self-seekers of the most sordid nature joined more responsible citizens to frame a constitution for Colombia. Bolívar was not at all pleased with the charter they prepared, the constitution of 1821. Like the *Cortes* of Cadiz, the congress claimed the title of "Majesty" and was held to be sovereign. The president was not as powerful as Bolívar had always advocated, and the upper house was not to be hereditary. Yet he accepted the new instrument and agreed to serve as president of Colombia. Scarcely had he done so when he went on leave of absence in order to lead his armies toward Peru. Santander remained in charge at Bogotá as vice-president. Already, many Venezuelans were grumbling because Bogotá was the capital instead of Caracas. No one but the Liberator himself had any strong enthusiasm for combining Venezuela and Cundinamarca in one centralized republic. Nearly every town, district, and faction craved the privilege of being left alone by higher authority. Although the future of Bolívar's creation was clouded from the very first days of its existence, he was too occupied to notice it. One man can do only so much.

Bolívar's Push Toward Peru

WINNING military campaigns, not educating willful individualists in the ways of guided democracy, was Bolívar's true metier. Now he turned to the huge royalist fortress in the central Andes, stretching from Pasto and Popayán through Quito and Peru to the edge of the Argentine. Bolívar was eager to finish off the Spaniards while the patriot cause was in full tide. Besides, San Martín was now on the coast of Peru and might win the glory the Liberator felt was his own. As he prepared his own force to march from Bogotá to Quito, he sent first a smaller one under the command of Antonio José Sucre, a Venezuelan not yet thirty whose military abilities would one day obscure Bolívar's own. Sucre went by sea from Colombia's Pacific coast down to Guayaquil, where the inhabitants had already declared their independence of everybody under the leadership of a poet. Sucre rather high-handedly proclaimed the torrid seaport a protectorate of Colombia and marched his forces nearly 10,000 feet upward to Quito. In the vicinity of that capital he defeated a royalist army on May 21, 1822 at the battle of Pichincha. The Spanish authorities then turned the kingdom over to Sucre, whereupon it became the Land of the Equator, or Ecuador, a part of the republic of Colombia.

Meanwhile, Bolívar had bogged down sadly in the mountains and valleys between this newly liberated territory and Bogotá. The geography of this country made any sort of military operation a test of physical endurance. Furthermore, the inhabitants had suffered at the hands of the patriots on earlier occasions and were fiercely royalist. Bolívar might not have made the passage at all but for Sucre's triumph at Pichincha, which opened the road for his penetration of Ecuador and eventual glorious entry into Quito. The usual parades, toasts, accolades, flowers, and Te Deum at the cathedral featured this event. Also, the Liberator fell immediately in love with one of his most fervent admirers, a wild young woman, Mrs. James Thorne, the wife of an elderly English doctor whom she had deserted. This Manuela Sáenz, as she is better known, was a doctrinaire radical who had longed to meet Bolívar. Now she captured him, to hold him in a tempestuous affair that inflamed and exasperated him for the remainder of his life.

By mid-1822 the former viceroyalty of New Granada was almost entirely in Bolívar's control. He had won Cundinamarca and Venezuela, Sucre had taken Ecuador, and Panama had almost bloodlessly shifted from peninsular to Colombian authority in 1821. New Spain and Guatemala had abruptly freed themselves in that same year, and Chile, Paraguay, and Argentina had been independent for some time. It remained to complete the liberation of Peru and Upper Peru, all that survived of Spain's mainland empire. At this point Bolívar and San Martín came together.

Liberator and Protector at the Summit

SAN MARTÍN's strategy in Peru had not produced the results he had expected. His occupation of the coast did not bring about a massive uprising, either among the people of Lima or the Indian population of the Sierra. Even the Negro slaves had joined his cause only in modest numbers. San Martín wanted the people to make up their own minds; he professed not to be impatient. Lord Cochrane was, however, and when the unavoidable quarrel over payment of his force arose, the terrible Scot seized the treasury of San Martín's government and sailed away, leaving the expedition stranded.

Awkward as San Martín's position was, it could not be exploited by the royalists, who were having troubles of their own. In January 1821 the leading Spanish officers deposed Viceroy Pezuela, supposedly because of his irresolution but also because he was too much identified with the absolutist system overthrown in Spain in 1820. The new viceroy (or supreme political chief, to employ the terminology of the constitution of 1812) was General José de la Serna, a constitutionalist more to the taste of the liberal and creole officers. La Serna made heroic efforts to whip up sentiment against San Martín, but nothing could obscure the fact that Lima was about to starve because the patriots occupied its principal food-producing sources. At length he conferred with San Martín about easing the situation. Like Bolívar and Morillo a short time afterward, the two generals sincerely embraced and found much to talk about. They were not far apart politically. Both favored self-government for Peru under a monarchy. But San Martín insisted on complete independence from Spain, a condition La Serna could not meet. While the conference failed, La Serna soon withdrew his forces from the hungry capital, in June 1821, taking with him thousands of civilians. San Martín thereupon entered Lima, not, however, as a conqueror, but as a liberator-by-default who was plainly flustered by the acclamations of the population. It was both appropriate and becoming that he assumed the modest title of Protector.

During the following year things had not gone particularly well for San Martín. His military position was very uncertain. He had only a few thousand homesick Chileans and Argentinians and a miscellaneous group of recruits from Peru. La Serna had a huge army, much larger than the patriot force, composed of Spaniards, creoles, Indians, and men of mixed race. The viceroy remained close enough to Lima to make its freedom highly precarious, and after Lord Cochrane's desertion, Spanish ships could bring hope, though little else, to the royalists. San Martín was also miscast as a ruler. His earlier republicanism having withered in the face of South American realities, he favored an autocratic government which would educate the people before giving them power. Yet he hesitated to provide this regime himself, possibly because he was, unlike Bolívar, temperamentally unsuited to govern. He dabbled in reforms, however, freeing the Indians from tribute and forced labor and newborn Negroes from slavery. He had a few constructive projects of a modest character; yet he gave the impression of half-heartedness in all he undertook. And his associates proved very unworthy of his ideals. The seamy side of liberation, with its corruption, seizures, immorality, and abuse of suspected royalists, made the regime seem oppressive. Finally, San Martín was not at his best personally. For weeks at a time he lived in retirement at the former viceregal country palace, in bad health and taking opiates. Hostile cliques grew up about him, and rumors about his health, irresolution, and disillusionment circulated widely.

That the Liberator and the Protector should confer and merge the two movements that had come so far, the one from Angostura, the other from Mendoza, seemed dramatically inevitable. The two generals had often corresponded and written glowingly of this prospect. South America anticipated this summit meeting as a grand climax to the long wars of liberation. As so often happens, the leaders harbored less lofty conceptions than the public or posterity and thought in terms of advantage. Guayaquil was a contentious issue: this valuable port and ship-building center had been part of both Peru and New Granada at different times and could thus be claimed by either. Its inhabitants preferred independence and had grudgingly accepted the protection of Colombia which Sucre had forced on them. San Martín planned to take it from the sea for Peru. Before he could do this, however, Bolívar overrode the local junta and incorporated the city outright into Colombia. An ideological issue loomed: San Martín believed that monarchy was essential for the period of tutelage he foresaw; Bolívar was a firm republican and wished to become an uncrowned autocrat himself. It was, of course, very much in order for the two liberating forces to cooperate in finishing off the Spaniards in Peru. San Martín had already provided assistance to Sucre's campaigns in Ecuador. Would Bolívar reciprocate? If so, what form was his aid to take? Who would be in charge? Who would make the basic decisions? Who would win the glory? No one familiar with the Liberator's character could doubt what his views would be.

On July 26, 1822 Bolívar welcomed San Martín at Guayaquil "to Colombian soil." They talked in private and then received the applause of the crowds. There was a banquet, with florid toasts and flourishes. On the following day the two generals conferred alone for four hours. Then, after a feast and ball, San Martín withdrew unnoticed to his anchored ship. Bolívar followed him for another short conversation, perhaps a mere farewell.

When San Martín reached Lima he discovered that the caretaker government he had established to rule during his absence had been overthrown. He did not seek to restore his authority. Nor did he deliver an exultant report of his long-awaited meeting with the Liberator; he said as little about it as possible. Soon he cryptically announced his resignation as Protector and his impending departure. In September 1822 he left for Chile. There he was saddened to find O'Higgins in deep trouble; he did, in fact, fall a few months later. San Martín tarried for some months in his beloved Mendoza, then went on to Buenos Aires. So confusing had the political scene been since his last visit nearly four years before, he discovered that he was almost forgotten. His wife was dead, and so he took his daughter and sailed away to England. Later he resided in Brussels and finally in France. For many years he lived close to poverty, until an old Spanish friend bought him a villa and his daughter made a good marriage. In 1850 San Martín died, having kept his peace all the years since the meeting at Guayaquil. His memory was not honored for another generation.

As to what happened at the famous encounter of Bolívar and San Martín, seldom has so much speculation arisen from so little authentic evidence. The two men who knew what had taken place said and wrote very little about the meeting. Hoaxes and forgeries, some of them in recent years, have badly confused the whole problem. Passions still rise quickly in South America whenever the issue comes up. In Argentina and Chile opinion is strongly in favor of San Martín; Venezuelans and Colombians are Bolívar partisans; Peruvians are comparatively neutral. It seems certain that Bolívar sternly rejected San Martín's proposal to create monarchical governments in the liberated states. On the other hand, San Martín was greatly offended at the way Bolívar had grabbed Guayaquil. Under the circumstances these matters were not sufficient to cause a rupture. The vanquishing of Spain was still to be accomplished, and it was obvious that Bolívar's assistance would be required.

This must have been the heart of the matter. Bolívar knew his participation was essential, but he was not a man to share leadership. If San Martín offered to subordinate himself to Bolívar's command, as he seems to have done, the Liberator may well have doubted the sincerity or endurance of such an arrangement, especially if he judged the Protector's nature by his own. Perceiving this, San Martín must have decided to remove himself from the scene as the sole obstacle to Bolívar's entrance. His bitter words, "The Liberator is not the man we thought him to be," might suggest such disenchantment in the face of suspicion or selfishness. But was Bolívar an unreasonable megalomaniac, as many southern South Americans affirm? He had history on his side if he believed that two famous generals were unlikely to cooperate satisfactorily. The realities of the power situation were altogether in favor of Bolívar, who had behind him a large, victorious army and the republic of Colombia. San Martín possessed a smaller force and only an uneasy authority in Lima and its environs. San Martín was the suppliant; Bolívar held the power to grant or withhold, or to lay down the terms of his aid. Also, San Martín's performance during the past year had clouded his reputation. His addiction to drugs, his inactivity, and his inability to dominate his subordinates suggested that he too was not the man many had taken him to be. The final truth of this poignant meeting of the demigods can never be known. San Martín's self-effacement has, long after his death, won him much respect. Bolívar may have been small-minded but fundamentally sound.

Bolívar did not rush into the vacuum, if such it was, left by San Martín's self-exile from Peru. His body was at last showing the effects of the rigorous campaigns, and, as on previous occasions, he indulged in long periods of indolence and amours. He offered the Peruvian congress his army, only to receive a cold reply. The creoles of Lima were not yet ready to place themselves at the mercy of so lordly an ally. Late in 1822 a royalist reaction in Pasto called for the Liberator's personal attention, which was effectively applied along with dreadful punishments afterward. In mid-1823, the same region rose again and had to be repressed. Bolívar was also occupied with the problems of Colombia, where objections were mounting to the cost of underwriting expeditions to liberate distant places. The advice and demands he showered on Santander made for ill feeling, though the tensions between the two men were not yet grave. Finally, in May 1823, the Peruvian situation was so bad the congress urgently requested the Liberator to come. He first sent several thousand troops to serve under Sucre's direction, but he himself tarried until he was certain the Peruvians would throw themselves at his feet. A Spanish reoccupation of Lima, which lasted only one month, provided this condition, and Bolívar sailed to Callao, where he arrived on September 1, 1823.

Fernando VII Again

THE constitutional period that began with Riego's revolt in 1820 had pulled the support from the landed aristocrats and clergymen in America who, by the nature of things, were most attached to the traditional Spanish absolutism. Already the defection of these groups, together with the confusion of the civil service and military, had cost the peninsula New Spain, Guatemala, and Santo Domingo in 1821 while undermining the loyalist elements in New Granada and Peru. A similar situation in the Portuguese monarchy had hastened the secession of Brazil in 1822. As the Liberator sailed to Peru in August 1823 for the final offensive, conditions were complicated by yet another reversal in Spain effected, as in 1808, by French armies. Fernando VII was restored to his full absolute powers.

Exciting as the liberal interlude in Spain had been, it deepened the chasm between the left and the right and made each side more intractable, to the tragedy of the nation's subsequent political life. By 1823 Spain was almost ungoverned. Madrid rang to the threats and oratory of the radicals; military leaders or bosses exerted such authority as there was in the provinces. The mother country itself was a political shambles while the empire was breaking up. After long hesitations the leading continental monarchies, the so-called Holy Alliance, decided to use force to crush the Spanish revolution. England separated herself from this enterprise but could do no more than warn the "Holies" to keep out of Portugal and not to take to the seas in order to interfere in Latin America. It was the France of Louis XVIII which received the mandate of the Holy Alliance to carry out this mission, supposedly to the interest of all civilization. A force of 100,000 "sons of St. Louis," as it was called, gathered on the Spanish border under the Duc d'Angoulême. Early in 1823 the invasion began. To the surprise of the world at large, the Spanish reacted with apathy or joy. With almost no opposition the French swept into Madrid. The *cortes* carried Fernando VII off to Sevilla and then to Cadiz. Angoulême followed, still encountering cordiality from the people who had risen up so furiously against his countrymen in 1808. After extracting from the king a promise not to take revenge, the liberals surrendered him in August 1823, only to find that he refused to honor a commitment made under duress. The worst of all Spanish reactions occurred. In 1824 Portuguese conservatives rose up against the liberal *côrtes* in Lisbon and restored King João VI to absolutism. The two Iberian monarchs understood American conditions as poorly as their liberal tormentors had. Forlornly and vainly, they appealed to their lost or slipping dominions overseas to return.

The Royal Navy and the Monroe Doctrine

ENGLAND was thoroughly angered by the intervention of the Holy Alliance. Fearing that the next step would be to suppress the revolutions in Latin America, George Canning, the British foreign minister, approached the United States to join in an Anglo-American declaration to deter such intervention. Flattered as the Americans were by this proposal from the world's premier naval power, they were deeply Anglophobic and regarded Canning with distrust. Furthermore, they disliked a point in his proposal that would have bound both powers not to acquire territory from the former Spanish empire, and they also feared Russian aggression in the North Pacific. After much deliberation, President Monroe and his cabinet, sure that Britain would interpose the Royal Navy between the Holy Alliance and Latin America in any event, decided to issue a declaration of their own. The Monroe Doctrine of December 2, 1823 warned the European powers not to seek colonies in the New World nor to spread their systems there. There was no disclaimer of American territorial ambitions, England was presumably included in the warning, and the United States promised not to interfere in Europe. For a moment, at least, both the American public and the Latin American liberators were delighted.

Canning, of course, felt that Monroe had played a shabby trick on him, and he hated the United States until he died. He had, however, secured a commitment from France not to send expeditions to Latin America prior to Monroe's message. Thus his proposal for a joint declaration with the United States had lost its relevance. In any case, Latin America was secure behind the British fleet, and the moral support of the United States was simply an additional comfort. It should be noted that neither Britain nor the United States threatened to prevent Fernando VII and João VI from seeking to reconquer their lost possessions. The likelihood that either could succeed in such an effort was exceedingly remote.

The End and the Beginning

THE restoration in Spain heartened the royalists in Peru, who unrealistically expected the arrival of great expeditionary forces from the mother country. Bolívar realized full well that his task, already formidable, was now even more difficult. In the stark mountains back of Lima were royalist forces said to number 15,000 or more. Most of them were Americans, loyalist creoles or colored men attracted by promises or simply drafted. Among his own forces, the Argentinians and Chileans who had come with San Martín served uncomfortably beside the Venezuelans and Cundinamarcans. Nationalism, which would soon mock his plans for a united America, was already showing itself. Bolívar was also aware that comparatively few Peruvians had joined the patriot army. And the Peruvian congress was frivolity itself, uncertain of conviction, resentful of foreigners, and inclined to intrigue. Conditions on the patriot side were so precarious that Lima was again retaken, but only briefly, by the Spanish forces. Bolívar at last browbeat the Peruvians into accepting a dictatorship. Obviously, the strongest measures would be needed if the final effort against Spain—the one that must not be mismanaged—was to be organized.

The Liberator was in Peru almost a year before he felt able to challenge the royalist forces. His health was bad, and he was continually vexed by the aimlessness or wrong-headedness of the men on whom he depended. At length he took the field with several crack units which fanned out in the Sierra in search of the royalists. On August 6, 1824, near the Lake of Junín in an altitude so high that he and many of his men suffered from mountain sickness, the Liberator established contact with the Spanish commander-in-chief, Canterac. Finding himself maneuvered into an awkward tactical position, Canterac ordered a cavalry charge, which Colombian horsemen met and broke with lances and sabers. Not a shot was fired, for the infantry had not become involved and the artillery was too far away for useful action. A picturesque battle, Junín was long and desperate and very demoralizing for the royalists. Canterac withdrew to Cuzco. Leaving Sucre with the army in the highlands, Bolívar went back to Lima.

Toward the end of November the Spaniards emerged from Cuzco with almost their full force, evidently seeking a decisive test. With Viceroy La Serna and Canterac were luminaries of the surviving Spanish officerhood in South America as well as 9,300 men, most of whom were Peruvians. Near Ayacucho, a town in one of the deep bowls of the Andes about half way between Lima and Cuzco, the royalists encountered Sucre with his 5,700 warriors. An unusually cordial exchange of courtesies took place, both on the part of the commanders and the ranks, for the independence cause had divided friends and brothers, often by conscription rather than conviction. On December 9, 1824, Sucre flung his forces against the royalists, who were well-entrenched with the cordillera to their backs. It was a short, violent battle, short because few men could fight on foot for long in such altitudes. Sucre's brilliant offensive and his patriot soldiers of high morale carried the day. If his report was accurate, the Spanish army suffered 1600 killed and the Americans only 300. A generous armistice gave the royalists the option of becoming citizens of an independent Peru or returning to Spain. While the suspicion has been ventilated that the Spanish defeat was pre-arranged, that the fighting was less serious than the commanders on both sides reported, and the losses lighter, it is inconceivable that thousands of participants could have hidden the truth. Sucre deserves credit for a glorious victory. Royalist resistance in Upper Peru and in a few points along the coast remained to be overcome, but Ayacucho marks the effective termination of the Spanish mainland empire in America. The era of independence had begun.

Adventures in Nationhood

21

The Twilight of the Liberators

T̲ʜ̲ᴇ̲ downfall of Iberian power was a joyous event in the Americas. Only the stranded former officials and merchants who retained their status as subjects of overseas kings seemed unhappy about independence, and they kept quiet. Hope and promise filled the air. The creole aristocracy still had its property, damaged though some of it was from recent violence. No longer would these landowners and mine owners suffer the insolence of low-born peninsulars or royal agents of better class. Merchants and small manufacturers looked for a lasting business boom now that colonial controls were cast off. Towns rang with the slogans of educated young liberals who intended to make the Americas over. Many Negro slaves had been freed, and Indians had been told that the tribute and other hateful aspects of imperialism were soon to end. Nearly all classes and groups experienced the delight of being free, of regarding themselves as masters of their own destinies. Congratulations showered from the United States and from such liberals as survived the reaction in Europe. In 1822 independence was a fact or clearly imminent throughout the Americas.[1] Argentina, Paraguay, Brazil, Chile, Venezuela, New Granada, Central America, and Mexico were free and, for the most part, in the hands of admired liberators, men of ability with armies, popularity, and programs. It was a delicious moment, one which soon became a bittersweet memory.

1. Cuba and Puerto Rico were to be disappointed, and the cause would take longer in Peru and Charcas than was hoped.

ARGENTINA

Now the most advanced Spanish-speaking country in the world, Argentina had a very disheartening start as a free nation. She became independent in fact on May 25, 1810, when an illustrious group of young men seized control of Buenos Aires, and officially so on July 9, 1816, when an unrepresentative congress at Tucumán formally cut the tie with Spain. During the ups and downs of the Wars of Independence the Spaniards were unable to restore their domination even briefly. Yet the patriots were unequal to the task of creating a true nation. Their conflicts of personal ambitions and ideals led to a squalid series of tumults in the first generation of independence. Buenos Aires could not establish a respected government for itself, and still less could it rule the vast expanse of the former viceroyalty of La Plata the way the royal government had. Rural elements in the province of Buenos Aires resisted the port city. Thirteen other provinces which sprang into existence were practically independent states. Wealth-producing Upper Peru was detached by the viceroy at Lima, who lost it in 1825 not to the Argentine but to Simón Bolívar, whereupon the new republic of Bolivia came into existence. Paraguay defied Buenos Aires from 1811 on and sank into a peculiar isolation enforced by the weird dictator, José Rodríguez de Francia. Uruguay was the scene of a four-cornered struggle for six years and was swallowed by the Brazilian monarchy in 1817.

Although the loss of the outlying provinces was disappointing, the failure to create in Buenos Aires an effective government for the remaining area was more portentous for the future. By 1819 there was no national government whatever, only provincial leaders who often warred with one another. The river provinces of the north and west had formidable caudillos who relied on semi-barbarian gaucho forces, who saw their nomadic way of life threatened by the spread of orderly ranching as the hide trade grew. In the more settled grazing areas livestock men feared, not without reason, that the detested *porteños* or port-dwellers of Buenos Aires would use and abuse their power to levy taxes on hides loaded in the Plata estuary. Thus commercial ranchers and gauchos combined to oppose the port. On their part, the *porteños* despised the rustics whom they nonetheless wished to rule. They also had little interest in purchasing the wines, cloths, and furniture produced in the Andean foothill provinces. European goods were better and cheaper, and they could be imported more easily, for it took seven weeks for bullock-drawn carts to cross the grassy pampas from Mendoza to Buenos Aires. The piedmont cities, which had been fairly prosperous under the viceroyalty, now found themselves declining rapidly. It was

UNITED STATES
OF
MEXICO

Texas

Mexico Vera Cruz

Acapulco

Guatemala

CENTRAL
AMERICA

CUBA (SP.)

PUERTO RICO (SP.)

JAMAICA (BR) HAITI (IND.)

Panama

Caracas

BRITISH

DUTCH

FRENCH

Bogotá

GUIANAS

COLOMBIA

Quito

Pará

PERU

Lima

EMPIRE
OF
BRAZIL

Bahia

La Paz

BOLIVIA

Charcas

PARAGUAY

Salta

Asunción

Rio de Janeiro

ARGENTINE
PROVINCES

Santiago

Buenos Aires

N

LATIN AMERICA
AT THE END OF THE
WARS OF INDEPENDENCE

apparent that the United Provinces of La Plata, a misnomer for the anarchical Argentine, had neither political nor economic unity. An issue
had already taken shape that would dominate the region for a half-
century: Buenos Aires disdained the provinces and could ruin them. She
wished to control them for her purposes, and they resisted. Yet neither
side was able to govern itself, still less to impose its will on the other.

The nadir came in 1820, known in Argentine history as "the terrible
year 20." At a time when Portuguese-Brazilian aggression and Spanish
reconquest threatened, the fourteen provinces were boiling with anarchy.
Buenos Aires itself underwent nine changes of government until September, when Martín Rodríguez became governor of the province. Somehow a corner was turned, possibly because the Iberian revolutions of
1820 removed the external danger. For the next few years Buenos Aires
the city cooperated with Buenos Aires the province, and several of the
leading provincial caudillos agreed to a pact of friendship that reduced
competition and allowed Buenos Aires to conduct foreign affairs for the
whole country. Hope began to shine through a murky political situation.
Economic conditions were promising except for the territory in the
Andean foothills, which had lost its markets in the mining areas of Upper Peru and was losing those in Buenos Aires. The cattle business was
good and expanding. Buenos Aires, though still a rather plain city, was
commercially vital and viable. Vessels from many nations arrived, unde-
terred by the need to anchor far out in the muddy Plata and be unloaded by stevedores on horseback. And with them came merchants,
speculators, technicians, and immigrants. As has always been true of this
amazing metropolis, business activity fed on itself, and newcomers,
whether from abroad or the hinterland, found outlets and rewards for
their skills.

Argentina's best-remembered figure of the 1820's is Bernardino Rivadavia, the first man to bear the title, however irregularly, of president of
the republic. Born in 1780, Rivadavia attended the Academy of San Carlos, the training ground for independence leaders, but did not finish.
Nonetheless, he acquired a good education on his own. He helped expel
the British in 1807 and married a viceroy's daughter. In 1810 he participated in the revolution, associating himself with the more idealistic
liberals. It developed that he was also quite practical, and he often dominated the triumvirate between 1811 and 1813, forcing the enactment of
laws that might, in happier circumstances, have proved foundation
stones for the new country. By 1814 he was out of power but on a diplomatic enterprise in Europe to find a king for La Plata. His mission failed,
but it was advantageous for him to be absent long enough to enjoy some
detachment from the feuds that rent Buenos Aires. He also learned much
of the great world outside, possibly more than was good for him, for

when he returned he was very much the European gentleman with expensive tastes and what seemed absurd affectations in the Argentine. Short, fat, dark, and pompous, he amused or annoyed many people. Here was no impressive executive, no solid San Martín, no glittering Bolívar, no man to cow gauchos. Rivadavia was not even a profound intellectual or a dreamer to kindle idealism. Rather, he was competent, practical, and modern. During his few years of power he devised a formula which later, much later, would bring fortune to Argentina. Only then would he be appreciated.

Rivadavia believed that Argentina should be like a European nation: civilized, tightly centralized, technically advanced, and independent. To this end the government should be unitary, but not in the way many *porteños* used the term, for Rivadavia wanted the capital city to lead without dictating and to share public revenues with the provinces. The country should be filled as quickly as possible with European immigrants. Foreign capital and technology should be imported, and the best of alien ideas copied. Naturally, the barbaric gaucho would have to be tamed and transformed. Business and professional men, artisans, and small farmers should eventually make up the population. The nation would be oriented toward Europe, the rest of South America serving mainly to produce the raw materials which would insure the flow of Europe's capital, culture, and emigrants to the Argentine. If Rivadavia never enunciated these ideas so bluntly, they were implicit in his activities; since things eventually worked out in this fashion, he may be counted among the great seers of his country.

From 1821 to 1824 Rivadavia served as minister of state for the province of Buenos Aires and as foreign minister for all the Platine provinces. As in all the new Latin American nations, financial problems were acutely frustrating. Rivadavia's plan was to collect revenues at the port on incoming and outgoing goods, to levy a direct tax on nearly every kind of economic activity, and to stimulate an influx of foreign capital. Only the first measure worked, for Buenos Aires was in a position to enforce it. Taxing other aspects of economic life was all but impossible in view of the lack of public administration. While foreign investors were often eager, they were almost as often disappointed. The loan of a million pounds from a British bank, the House of Baring, to improve the seaport and provide a city water supply was discounted so heavily that nearly half the amount did not reach Buenos Aires. Both to raise money and promote the distribution of land to small operators, Rivadavia began a program of emphyteusis, which enabled individuals to lease tracts for long periods at modest rents. He hoped to parcel out the public lands to small farmers and ranchers, acquire revenues from the process, and yet avoid the evils of latifundia by withholding permanent titles.

That the plan did not work out at all, that a few large buyers would make latifundia a curse to Argentina, was not altogether Rivadavia's fault.

Well-schooled in the anti-clericalism of the age, Rivadavia saw the Church as a drag on progress. Perhaps he was not wise in this, for so primitive a country as Argentina needed every civilizing influence it could have. Yet he was determined to assert the *real patronato* once enjoyed by Spanish kings and to curb the privileges of the clergy. Hence he abolished the tithe, substituting state payment of clerical expenses, which of course gave the government power to regulate the Church. He outlawed ecclesiastical courts, secularized cemeteries, and closed several monasteries. To fill the void thus left in charitable works Rivadavia organized a beneficent society of well-to-do ladies of Buenos Aires which has long served both as a fashionable and a humanitarian agency. Rivadavia's interest in encouraging women to take a modest part in public affairs and to become educated was startling for the time and place, and again it marks him as a man with a vision of the future. He sketched an ambitious plan for public education, modeled after Napoleon's, in which a secular University of Buenos Aires would embrace schools all over the province. He also sponsored public works to augment the city's facilities and to provide for future growth. Not the least of his services was fostering the practices of freedom and toleration in the hope that they would become habitual with the people.

As his power and prestige grew, Rivadavia persuaded most of the provincial leaders to send delegates to a constituent congress that would lay the juridical basis for a true nation. The assembly gathered while he was in Europe on a mission to gain support for Argentina against what seemed impending Brazilian encroachment. Before all the representatives had arrived, the Buenos Aires delegation named Rivadavia president of the Argentine Republic. His stature was so high the other members acquiesced in the step. Back home, President Rivadavia confidently pushed through the congress a unitary constitution that offered protection to the other provinces by removing the capital from Buenos Aires. It was a stunning blow to him when every one of the fourteen provinces rejected his proposal, even Buenos Aires, which had no intention of surrendering the seat of government. The rebuff was fatal to the president's career. Soon afterward he suffered another blow when his agent made a peace settlement with Brazil that left Uruguay a province of that empire. Now that he had stumbled twice, and badly, factionalism surged. Would-be leaders vilified Rivadavia for his arrogance and intransigence. Beset with critics, he resigned in July 1827 and went away, at first to Uruguay and Brazil, then to Europe. He died in 1845 in Cadiz, in the Spain against which he had revolted so hopefully, bitter about American prospects and regretting the part he had played in the liberation. His was a familiar ending already or soon to be experienced by nearly all of the founders of Latin American nations.

The Uruguayan situation that had helped to ruin Rivadavia was a crisis in the century-long conflict of Spaniard and Portuguese, or Argentinian and Brazilian, over domination of the Banda Oriental. The land was poor and sparsely-inhabited, but its potential for livestock-raising endowed it with value. Brazil's occupation of the area in 1817 had seemingly closed the issue, though neither Fernando VII nor the Argentine recognized this conquest. In 1825, however, a group of Uruguayan refugees, "the Immortal Thirty-three," sailed from Buenos Aires across the estuary and started a rebellion. Buenos Aires sprang to their assistance, for it was a traditional policy in that quarter to try to keep the Luso-Brazilians away from the estuary. An army of sorts was gotten up by the *porteños,* and Admiral William Brown proved willing and able to drive the Brazilian fleet from the Plata. While the military actions scarcely amounted to a war, disorders and violence went on for three years, with the Spanish-speaking elements gradually winning. In an effort to conclude the struggle Rivadavia had sent an emissary in 1827, but his acknowledgment of Brazil's title had brought grief, as has been noted, to the Argentine president. Finally, in 1828, Britain compelled the contenders to accept the creation of a buffer state, an independent Uruguay. Both Brazil and Argentina took the settlement with ill grace and intervened for many years in the tiny republic. Incidentally, José Artigas, the titular founder of Uruguay, was invited by his liberated homeland to return. But, comfortable in his Parguayan retreat and disillusioned with the chaos that Latin America had become, the liberator spurned the offer, in effect denying the paternity of a land that calls him its father.

It is scarcely surprising that Rivadavia's exile and the end of fighting in Uruguay brought no calm to the Argentine. Again, the hinterland caudillos and their gaucho forces refused to cooperate in building a nation. Buenos Aires province was in the hands of the federalist, Manuel Dorrego, who had helped make Rivadavia's life unendurable. In December 1828, the soldiers who had fought in Uruguay returned to Buenos Aires, full of resentment over the mismanagement of the war and the failure to win a victory. Their leader, Juan Lavalle, overturned the government and had Dorrego killed. Lavalle may have aspired to restore unitarism, or perhaps he simply wanted power. Whatever his motive, public morals had not sunk so low that what he did would be accepted, and he was driven out within a few months. The political situation could scarcely have been more confused. There was still no constitution, not even a nation, but only a congeries of local military leaders running their respective areas like despots and jostling one another. The Argentine seemed as far from nationhood as ever, and looming as the most promising strong man was no well-meaning Rivadavia but one of the most hateful tyrants in South American history, Juan Manuel de Rosas.

CHILE

On the surface Chile appeared to have a much better chance than most of her sister states in liberated America to find a basis for firm government. This she did in time, but only after an unseemly period of clamors and disorders. The new nation was virtually quarantined from the fevers that agitated her neighbors across the Andes and deserts. She was so isolated that Spanish reconquest was unlikely. The effective part of the country—the fertile, temperate central area bordered by the magnificent cordillera on the east, the ragged Pacific coast on the west, an impassable desert on the north, and great forests and fjords on the south —possessed a unity uncommon in South America. No large Indian masses existed to threaten the power of the whites, for the Araucanians had long learned to co-exist by staying, but for occasional raids, on their side of the River Bío-Bío. Within the central region about sixty families, many of them titled and most of them protected by the law of entail, firmly controlled the lives of the impoverished whites and mixed-bloods who lived as peons, almost as serfs, on their properties. These great landholders, many of them Basque in ancestry, generally lived on their estates like feudal lords. While a small business and professional class existed in Santiago, Valparaiso, and other towns, it too fell under the indirect domination of the rural lords. Still, the landed aristocracy could not agree easily on a program for running the new nation. A dozen years or so of anarchy and experimentation passed before it came into its own.

It is difficult to appraise the role of Bernardo O'Higgins as a founding father of one of South America's most admirable republics. In some ways he seems to have been unrealistic, to have misjudged the true bases of power, and to have set the nation on an impossible course. In other respects he appears wise and sound, a statesman who might, but for bad luck and the failings of his contemporaries, have laid foundations for even a healthier nation than Chile became. His vision in major matters was true. He realized that Spanish power in Peru must be broken before anyone was safe, and to this end he loyally supported San Martín's expedition in spite of much criticism from smaller-minded Chileans. O'Higgins also understood that Chile was not ready for democracy, that it needed a long period of paternalism. Like so many men of his period, he was eager to accelerate the enlightenment of the population through public schools and a lively press. He also grasped the importance of stimulating commerce with foreign countries and encouraging investments. Yet he miscalculated how far he could push the Church and the rural aristocracy. And he over-estimated the duration of the enthusiasm and gratitude the masses would bear for him once liberation was a fact.

O'Higgins dominated Chile for nearly five years after the victory at Maipú in 1818. He provided a temporary constitution which not only authorized him to be Supreme Director but also gave him power to appoint an advisory senate of five members. In a plebiscite the public overwhelmingly approved these arrangements, and the new regime was off to a good start. The Supreme Director was far from glamorous. Short, rather heavy, blue-eyed, and blond, he lacked the appeal of a classic Latin leader. He was certainly no orator, though he was well-educated, much-traveled, and rich. His temperament, like that of his father, the late viceroy, was autocratic and constructive, and he set about his work with great energy. He saw to it that an irrigation canal was built to serve fields in the Santiago region. Roads were improved, streets lighted, and an extensive network of urban and rural police put together to deal with the crime wave that inevitably followed independence throughout Latin America. O'Higgins re-opened the National Institute, a secondary school created early in the liberation phase, ordered town councils and monasteries to establish primary schools, and imported foreign instructors. Journalism was encouraged, and it was decreed that foreign books and pamphlets could enter Chile duty-free and circulate without postage. Not content with such wholesome measures, the Supreme Director abolished bullfights and cockfights and commanded the police to suppress gambling and alcoholism, the latter an enduring vice in Chile, where vineyards are so productive. Some of the population laughed at O'Higgins' puritanism and made jokes about his illegitimacy. Those who were punished were likely to be vengeful and to hate the kill-joy tyrant. Some of the landlords resented the interference of O'Higgins' police in the affairs of their peons.

Continuing to carry out his own ideas rather than meet popular demands, O'Higgins tackled the Church, beginning with the expulsion of such royalist critics of his regime as the Bishop of Santiago. He laid heavy restrictions on the nature and frequency of religious processions, which the populace loved, and also on the veneration of images he deemed spurious. Many were shocked when, for sanitary reasons, he forbade burials in church buildings and when, to appease English and American traders, he permitted the interment of non-Catholics in cemeteries.

A measure which greatly aroused the landed aristocracy was the abolition of entails on estates as a means of spreading property ownership. Nor were the rural lords pleased when titles of nobility were declared illegal. If the clergy and the oligarchy were becoming increasingly irritated with the Supreme Director, about whose bastardy they never ceased to harp, many liberals disapproved of the one-man rule O'Higgins thought necessary and of the arbitrary way he treated his critics.

Perhaps such dissatisfactions would not have mattered much if the economy of the country had improved and the government been able to finance itself. The rural areas were slow to recover from the ravages of the recent fighting, and business was generally bad except for the importers, most of whom were foreigners. Valparaiso was blooming as an international port, its lovely bay, so much like that of Naples, crowded with ships. Yet money for the government was hard to obtain, and O'Higgins insisted on devoting such as he had to the indecisive expedition of San Martín to liberate Peru. Ugly rumors circulated about the supposed ascendancy San Martín wielded over the Supreme Director, and there was much grumbling to the effect that the Peruvians could fight for themselves. Also, futile negotiations with Rome, statesmanlike as they were, to regularize the position of the Church made both the clergy and the anti-clericals uneasy. And a mission to Europe by the foreign minister to obtain credit, recognition, and possibly a monarch gave rise to dark speculations. By 1822 O'Higgins was sufficiently aware of mounting criticism to yield by calling a constituent congress to regularize his regime on a permanent basis. But, by picking a group of nobodies and dictating a constitution that might give him ten more years of autocratic power, he weakened his position. The hostility of conservatives and liberals alike now hardened. Matters came to a head when, for lack of money, government salaries were cut and soldiers' pay fell into arrears. And then an earthquake shattered Valparaiso late in 1822, darkening the one bright spot in the economic picture and seemingly justifying those who believed the anti-clerical decrees had brought down God's wrath.

General Ramón Freire, who commanded a considerable force in the southern state of Concepción that was guarding against a Spanish landing from Chilöe Island, proclaimed that O'Higgins must go. Other units in the northern end of the stringy republic joined him. In Santiago, O'Higgins beheld these movements in despair. He was also shaken by the visit of San Martín, passing from his incomplete liberation of Peru into exile, and by a disagreeable session with Lord Cochrane, who as always was demanding more money. Conservative factions and the masses alike in the capital were in a mood to topple the regime. An open *cabildo* and a defiant assembly of the new congress convinced O'Higgins that he could hold on, if at all, only by drastic military action. Early in 1823 he decided to resign. For once theatrical, he appeared before congress and announced his withdrawal. On his own suggestion he submitted to a *residencia,* where no serious charges were proved, and then left the country. With his mother and his illegitimate son he sailed to Peru, where an estate had been granted him, and lived quietly until 1840.

The Chileans might have done better to permit O'Higgins another ten years of strong rule. A period of sordid confusion followed, though it was educational and served to clarify the forces at work in the country. General Freire duly entered Santiago in triumph and sponsored a new conservative constitution and became Supreme Director. Some of O'Higgins' laws he undid, others he retained. The final abolition of slavery and the capture of Chilöe Island were achievements of importance, but the only ones for which he deserves any credit. Other problems refused to yield to his efforts. The economy dragged, and the government still could not support itself. Doctrinaire liberals railed at one another and reviled the Church and aristocracy, who grimly fought back. Criminality again became rampant, Araucanians raided white towns, and soldiers often joined the forces of disorder. Helpless to dominate such turbulence, Freire quit. Then, in 1826, the liberals won the upper hand and prepared another constitution, which proved to be Chile's sole experience with federalism. The new charter created eight states, weakened the central government, and called for popular elections to fill all offices, including that of parish priest. As first president of the republic the liberals named an almost-forgotten figure. In 1827, a rebellious colonel led a squad into Santiago and dispersed the government. After a few chaotic weeks the liberals rallied and offered another constitution, that of 1828, which was centralist. Elections held under this charter proved tumultuous and fraudulent. A new president was chosen, only to quarrel with congress and resign; he was promptly reelected, and he quit again.

In the midst of this uproar the landlords and clergy were joining forces with urban businessmen who craved stability. Called *pelucones* (big wigs) by their enemies, they labeled the liberals *pipiolos* (novices or raw hands). As often happens, this insulting nomenclature was accepted with pride and proved durable. At length, the conservatives solidified their ranks, chiefly by deciding precisely what they did not want, while the liberals debated among themselves. In the indescribably confused year of 1829 the conservatives conspired with General Joaquín Prieto, who commanded the largest military force, the garrison at Concepción. Important in these negotiations was a mysterious man of affairs, Diego Portales, who was soon to emerge as the stabilizer of the republic. The liberals rocked Santiago with their dissensions and finally removed the congress to Valparaiso, where they did no better. The former Supreme Director, Freire, who had played as complicated a game as any during the recent confusion, agreed to lead the liberal armies against Prieto, who was advancing in an ominous manner. In April 1830, on the banks of the Lircay, the conservative troops met the liberals and won a decisive victory. Prieto soon became president and Portales vice-president of the republic. Not for another year was it evident that something more significant than a tip of the see-saw had occurred. As it proved, the conservatives were in to stay. The baptism of chaos was over, over sooner in Chile than anywhere else in Latin America. At last the landed oligarchy and responsible urban leaders were ready to assume the power taken from the Spanish and lost by O'Higgins.

PERU

Would-be liberators of Peru were scarce until the very end of the Wars of Independence; the Spanish establishment was too lucrative and too prestigious to be shaken easily. While occasional liberals among the educated upper classes desired reform and autonomy, they seldom favored withdrawing from the Spanish monarchy, and in any case the predominant mood of the viceroyalty was royalist. Hence no group, or at least no important group, of Peruvians stood ready after Ayacucho to inherit the power of Spain. The experience of other countries suggests that such a party, had it existed, would have undergone sobering experiences. In any case, for Peru, liberation came from without. The process had begun inauspiciously when San Martín landed in 1820 with his force of Argentinians and Chileans and met an indifferent welcome. During the year that he reigned as Protector in Lima, he carried out some of the preliminary work of organizing a free nation: the creation of an army and fleet, laying a few bases for new institutions, and the dispatch of diplomatic missions. He also freed slaves born after 1821 and planned such matters as public education and improvement of Indian conditions. The departure of the Protector after his calamitous meeting with the Liberator at Guayaquil in August 1822 left most Peruvians unmoved. San Martín was quickly forgotten.

More than a year later, in September 1823, Bolívar arrived, to find the independent sectors attached to republicanism but willing to surrender all powers to him indefinitely. As a benign dictator, a demigod venerated despite his many human weaknesses, the Liberator presided over Peru for almost three years. Under his auspices the military logistics and strategy of the war against the royalists were handled with brilliant success. The victory of Sucre and his mainly Colombian army at Ayacucho late in 1824 destroyed the power of Spain in South America.

Idolized more than ever, Bolívar toured the war-ravaged country in a style reminiscent of ancient Inca potentates, confident of his popularity. Taxes were cut, convents turned into schools, food and money

distributed with regal abandon, wrongs righted, and the Indians told to
take possession of former royal lands. He commanded that new colleges
be opened, that primary education be provided in all towns, even that a
school for girls be started. The liberal Spanish code of laws promulgated
in 1812 was to stay in force until Peruvian legislation, no doubt still
more humane, could be devised. Since most of the mines were deserted
or ruined, Bolívar undertook to sell them to foreigners in an effort to
raise funds for the government and to fuel the recovery of Peruvian industry. The constitution he had written for Bolivia he now forced on
Peru, notwithstanding some uttered and much unspoken opposition.
The president would serve for life and choose a vice-president to succeed him. Tribunes were to legislate in routine matters, senators in those
of greater importance, and censors were to supervise the moral and educational life of the republic. While everyone was to enjoy liberty and
equality, only those who had property or incomes and could read
would be allowed to vote. This curious constitution, reminiscent of
Bonaparte's, was proclaimed in August 1826, and Bolívar was elected
president for life. In the following month he left Peru to deal with affairs in Gran Colombia that urgently required his attention.

By this time the Liberator's Panama Congress, a noble if premature
effort to bring about the diplomatic unity of all the Americas, was already
a fiasco. His Federation of the Andes, a project to unite Venezuela,
Cundinamarca, Quito, Peru, and Bolivia in a huge state to be ruled
by himself, was vanishing in the mists. In Colombia he was to find
heartbreak and an early death. And even Peru was to disappoint him!
Four months after his departure, the generals of the new republic ousted
Bolívar's representatives and renounced his leadership. For three years
the object of ovations and flattery in Peru, the Liberator was defamed as
a foreign tyrant with dangerous ambitions. By 1828 Peru had another
constitution and was in a state of war with Bolívar's regime in Colombia.

If the greatest of the independence leaders failed to establish an enduring government in a country he freed from colonialism, the futility of
lesser men in other lands can be appreciated the better. No particular
personal defects explain Bolívar's failure to build a regime in Peru. True,
he was often in bad health during the Peruvian phase, and his immoralities were widely known. He loved praise and courted applause, and he
threw money and gifts around freely. Yet these qualities often endear a
ruler to his people, and Bolívar seemed beloved when he left Peru. If the
constitution he dictated was not understood or liked, no one was able to
produce a better one. In fact, any explanation of the Liberator's failure
to hold Peru reflects on the population more than on him. The aristocracy of Lima, the natural heirs of Spanish power, respected Bolívar as a

blueblood as long as he was in their midst, but after he was gone, they were little inclined to perpetuate his regime and unable to devise one of their own. The Indians, of course, went about their way indifferent to public affairs. Poor whites, mestizos, and mulattoes were less apathetic, but they limited their participation in politics to fighting or rioting in behalf of the most reliable paymaster. Public opinion, by any acceptable definition, did not exist. Thus the power vacuum came to be filled by military leaders who seized control from Bolívar's lieutenants and then quarreled among themselves. With their stolen funds and armies of kidnapped or bribed youths, whom they often chained by day and jailed at night to prevent desertion, they made a mockery of institutionalized government. Bolívar may be fairly criticized for failing to extract from Peru's enormous wealth enough revenue to establish a loyal army and administrative apparatus. Even the Spanish had done that much, and more. But he had not addressed himself seriously to the problem, and his reliance on Colombian and Argentine-Chilean forces was no substitute, for the soldiers became disorderly and the Peruvians increasingly disliked them. Getting rid of these swaggering aliens was the first piece of business of the junta that overthrew Bolívar's regime.

Peru's defection was a hard blow for the Liberator, and a worse one for the country. It doomed the republic to years of anarchy and turbulence. The failure to create a workable political system meant that ungoverned whites would abuse the Indians and maintain Negro slavery. It also meant that there would be no public school system and that charity would have to depend on the uncertain support of a Church crippled by the Wars of Independence. Business conditions would remain poor for the many and beneficial, too often, for the dishonest. On the whole, Peru would be very slow to regain such prosperity as she had known under Spain. And justice, order, freedom, equality, and other goals of the liberators would remain far from realization.

BOLIVIA

Conditions were destined to be still worse in Upper Peru, which became the Republic of Bolivia in 1825. The Marshal of Ayacucho, Sucre, led his Colombian forces into the mountainous province early in the year and called an assembly of its notable citizens. Bolívar was somewhat annoyed by Sucre's presumption, for he liked to manage political affairs himself, but he acquiesced in it to save Sucre's face, or so he said. The assembly met in historic Chuquisaca and overwhelmingly declared for independence, rejecting alike proposals that the province join Argentina, with which it had been linked from 1776 to 1811, or Peru, of which it had been a part for more than two centuries. The question as to whether Bolivia should be a nation is still pondered, guardedly.[2] Only the few thousand European inhabitants were interested in its fate, for the large Indian majority lived to themselves as much as the whites permitted them to do so, and half the country was unpopulated. Yet nationhood the assembly chose, and Sucre was invited to remain with his army to enforce order. In the late summer of 1825 the famous Liberator entered the country named for him and received ovations as he visited La Paz, Chuquisaca, and Potosí. He climbed the famous silver mountain of Potosí and uttered words of eloquence appropriate for a man who seemed destined to be the master of South America. He showered blessings, scattering gifts and offering the brutalized masses an enticing view of the future. After he left, in December 1825, he presented the new republic with his celebrated constitution, the one which Peru later adopted under pressure from him.

It was for Sucre to fulfill these generous visions. The finest of men, with youth, ability, and prestige, Sucre was much less sanguine than his mentor. He was always skeptical of Bolívar's magnificent dreams, and the realities of Bolivia sobered him more than they had the Liberator. Further, Sucre wanted to go to Quito to be married, perhaps to quit politics. Yet he stuck with his task, proclaiming the constitution in 1826 and, later in the year, permitting himself to be chosen vice-president under Bolívar's life presidency. Sucre informed the assembly, however, that he would stay only two years. He sketched out new departments from the old intendancies and sought to man them with reliable officials. Schools were ordered to be opened, usually in vacated monasteries. He projected courts of law, a police force, ways to put the mines back into operation, a direct tax to replace colonial duties, and means to attract European immigrants. Personally honest, he was appalled by the greed of the officers who surrounded him. Upright and noble by instinct, he was dejected by the selfish individualism the new citizens were displaying. He was also distressed to see that the Colombian troops were regarded as unwelcome intruders. To race-conscious whites in Bolivia these men, only some of whom came from the Negroid tropics, were nearly always regarded as mulattoes.

Bolívar's departure from Lima and the subsequent overthrow of his government placed Sucre in an awkward position. Now the Peruvians sought to unseat him too and to annex Bolivia. Argentina, herself a thoroughly disorganized area, likewise craved to dominate the former province of the late viceroyalty. Sucre stood firm amid threats and temptations, a model chief of state in a land which was not really a state. Then the Colombian units, their pay in arrears and their morale ruined by in-

2. In 1959 a terrible anti-American riot arose from an alleged statement by a U. S. Embassy official that Bolivia ought to be divided among its neighbors.

action and insults, began to make trouble. The first major riot, in December 1827, Sucre succeeded in calming. Another, in April 1828, was uglier, and the Marshal of Ayacucho himself was wounded, something that had never happened, he bitterly observed, during the Wars of Independence. Across the border in Peru was an army under an ambitious general, Agustín Gamarra. Pretending that the Colombian riots constituted an invitation for him to liberate Bolivia, the Peruvian invaded. The Bolivian populace either fled or joined him, and the Colombian troops fought with notable lack of heart. Realizing that his government was crumbling and sick of the situation, Sucre resigned in August 1828, not long before his two years were up. Leaving a characteristically lofty address to the Bolivian people, which they scarcely heeded, he embarked his forces from the republic's small seaport on the Pacific and sailed to Ecuador, marriage, and murder. Peruvian units entered Chuquisaca in triumph, beginning an anarchical era of caudillos that may not yet be ended.

GRAN COLOMBIA[3]

The former viceroyalty of New Granada gave high promise of moving successfully from colonialism into nationhood, even of offering a splendid example to the rest of Latin America. It had an admirable constitution, the one drafted at Cúcuta in 1821, which seemed to assure liberty and the submergence of local interests in a large confederation. Having won British and American recognition, Colombia was taking the lead among the liberated Hispanic states in international affairs. The tone of its political discussions, in the elected assemblies, coffee houses, and press, was high, even sophisticated. Above all, the republic had Simón Bolívar as president, with his matchless prestige and faithful armies. Vice-president of Venezuela was the popular warrior, José Antonio Páez, and of New Granada, Francisco de Paula Santander, the competent soldier and upright republican whom the Liberator had called "the man of laws." Able leaders, military might, and attachment to constitutional procedures seemed to promise a happy destiny for this land of a million square miles and vast riches.

Yet things had not gone at all well since Bolívar had left to complete the destruction of Spanish power in the central Andes. Economic disorganization occasioned by the Wars of Independence, that pervading cause of frailty in the new Latin American nations, had unusual significance in this one. The plantations and cattle ranches of Venezuela had

3. The correct name for the large republic was "Colombia." Historians employ "Gran Colombia" from habit and to distinguish it from the later, truncated nation.

been raked over four or five times within a decade by Spaniards and patriots. The richest sections of New Granada had undergone similar devasta-
tion, and so had the province of Quito. It was very difficult for the new
government to finance itself, and so funds were seized and movable property carried off. Too often money disappeared in the gambling casinos or
foreign banks and never reached the common soldiers and civil servants.
The expense of Bolívar's army in Peru was a heavy drain, one which the
Colombians resented. Why, they asked, could not the Peruvians do their
own fighting and pay their own way? Furthermore, the Wars of Independence had divided families, towns, and provinces so that hatreds
seethed everywhere. It was easy to turn any political issue into fire. Lack
of cohesion among the upper classes prevented the development of a
solid conservative outlook. Liberals of that day were by nature disruptive,
unable to cooperate with one another. Finally, the Venezuelans chafed
at being tied to New Granada and having the capital at Bogotá. It was
the clash between the Venezuelans, artfully inspired by Páez, and the
federal congress that brought the Liberator back from Peru in September
1826.

Bolívar had changed. The vexations of waging the final war against
Spain had embittered him against the Santander regime, which had
often responded to his appeals with negatives or little help. And Santander was no longer an obedient junior partner but rather a major figure in his own right, a man of firm republican ideas and enough political
talent to organize something of a machine. In many ways he was following policies too Jacobin to suit Bolívar; in others, as in clerical issues,
he did not go far enough. As the Liberator returned by way of Guayaquil
and Quito, he behaved less like the president of Colombia than a man
bent on overturning the government. The old enthusiasm flared up all
the way, for Bolívar could always kindle the adulation of the population.
Everywhere he was regaled with tales of Santander's incompetence, tyranny, and corruption. A long list of towns, including some coastal
municipalities he did not visit, asked the Liberator to assume dictatorial
powers.

Back in Bogotá, Bolívar relished only for a few days the role of restored ruler. He patched things up with Santander, who of course was
a decent man and deferential to his superior, and both seemed confident
of the future. Then he went to Venezuela, where Santander and his
party of constitutionalists expected Bolívar to punish Páez. He embraced
him instead, and they entered Caracas together as old friends. In effect,
Bolívar sided with Páez but prevailed on him to remain within the Gran
Colombian state. With the authority and popularity Bolívar enjoyed,
Páez could scarcely have declined and remained in power or, possibly,
alive. For some months the Liberator lingered in his homeland, seeing

his relatives and attending to his long-neglected estates.[4] It was his last visit, and it was a happy one. Assuming extra-constitutional powers he issued decrees right and left, restoring the old Spanish *alcabala* and other colonial taxes and promoting officers as he wished. Most outward signs indicated that Venezuela would be satisfied to remain under his rule for an indefinite period.

Returning to Bogotá by September 1827, Bolívar addressed himself to his true purpose, the final establishment of a sound constitutional system. Nothing less than his brain-child, the constitution of Bolivia, would do, the basic law that provided for centralization, conservatism, and his own life tenure as near-monarch. Perhaps he was now in favor of a Napoleonic-style monarchy with himself as the imperial figure and Sucre as his heir. Charges flew thick and fast that this was his purpose, and some evidence points that way. In any event, Bolívar called for a constitutional convention to be chosen in order to revise the charter of Cúcuta. An outburst of liberal agitation ensued, which Bolívar attributed to the ambitions and prejudices of Santander. Before the convention met at Ocaña in the spring of 1828, the two men were known to be enemies. Santander said that Bolívar was erratic and unrealistic, that he was temperamentally unable to rule constitutionally. The Liberator told his old protégé not to correspond further. As matters turned out, a majority of the delegates at Ocaña refused to accept Bolívar's constitution, and the Liberator ordered his supporters to withdraw from the congress. For the last time he assumed dictatorial powers.

Only a few weeks later an assassination plot directed at Bolívar came very close to success. But for the quick action of Manuela Sáenz, who had rejoined her lover, the Liberator might have been knifed to death. He escaped and hid, but in an undignified manner that provided wits with material for cruel mirth. Uneasily in power as dictator, Bolívar watched his friends turn sad and his enemies intensify their bitterness. Santander was jailed and then exiled for supposed complicity in the assassination attempt, and the darkest of rumors circulated about Bolívar's alleged monarchical ambitions. And with it all, the Liberator was failing rapidly, his small frame no longer able to withstand the strains imposed upon it by strife and the demands of the burning brain and superhuman will that had set northern South America free.

Still another effort was required of the hero. The new government of Peru claimed Guayaquil and Quito and invaded Colombian territory. Although Sucre, now at last married and expecting to settle down, and Juan José Flores, another young general Bolívar had favored, beat the attack completely, the Liberator wearied himself further by making the hard journey to the south. Back in Bogotá by the end of 1829, he

4.   Also taking care to bank money abroad.

helplessly watched the disintegration of Gran Colombia. Liberals greeted him with virulent enmity because he had suppressed rights which, though sacred to lovers of freedom, often lead to chaos when exercised. Conservatives had cooled and offered only token support. Towns and garrisons broke away from his power. In December 1829, Páez again withdrew Venezuela from the mammoth republic, and soon Flores did the same for the land of the Equator. Sick and despondent, Bolívar resigned for the last time in March 1830. On this occasion no clamor arose that he resume power, and the Liberator made his way to the coast, apparently headed for Europe. On the way he learned that Sucre had been murdered and that his enemies in Bogotá were gloating over the ruin of the team whom they had suspected of seeking to establish a monarchy. When he reached the Caribbean, Bolívar was too ill with tuberculosis to undertake his voyage. With the unhappiest of thoughts, with an anguish over his wasted efforts that could scarcely find expression even in his matchless eloquence, he lay for weeks at an estate owned, ironically enough, by a Spaniard near that royalist center, Santa Marta. In December 1830 he died.

NEW GRANADA

After the great Bolívar left Bogotá, lesser men agitated and conspired in vain to create a viable state for two years, when Santander arrived. The capital city pretended to perpetuate the viceregal tradition to the extent of exercising power over the rest of the country. While by 1830 it had lost all control over Venezuela and Ecuador, an enormous land with a million and a half people remained. Now it was to be called "New Granada," partly as a gesture of repudiation aimed at the fallen Liberator.

It was as disunified a country as nature could make it. Along the Caribbean coast were torrid jungles and only two cities, Santa Marta and Cartagena. Panama was almost a wild province, reachable only by sea and economically active merely as it served trans-isthmian travelers. The Pacific coast resembled the Caribbean but was far more narrow. Immediately behind it rose the Andes, so that New Granada seemed to have its back to the seas, and to the world, and its face toward the Amazon and Orinoco basins. Between the three principal ranges of the Andes were the population centers that constituted the nation. The Cauca Valley was temperate and fertile, and cool in its southern or upper reaches. Here were strings of ranches, mines, farms, and small towns. It was fantastically difficult to cross from the upper Cauca Valley to that of the Magdalena, the cordillera being so high that white travelers usually had to be carried across by sturdy Indians. The Magdalena itself was as wide as the

Mississippi, but only a few settlements graced its shores. Beyond, up another range to the east, was the 8,500-foot-high basin in which Bogotá rested. And then other communities of long history filled valleys and depressions of the Andes. Past this region there was nothing of interest to the human race, only an awesome decline into the dank wilderness of the center of South America. The population was almost as varied as the geography. Negroes were thick in the coastlands and ·mining towns. In much of the country, Indians lived in a Stone Age culture. But a majority, probably, of the population had mixed blood, the result of three centuries of racial amalgamation. These and the whites, who lived mainly in the high valleys and plateaus, cherished fervent loyalties to their communities. What is remarkable is that a sense of nationhood existed, and waxed, in this complex land.

Much of the credit for the maintenance of this feeling is due Francisco de Paula Santander. He was in New York early in 1832 when he heard that he had been elected president of New Granada. Returning in July, this grave, upright soldier-statesman found a cordial atmosphere. Proud of his title, "the Man of Laws," and his stewardship of the region during Bolívar's presidency, he set out to enforce the constitution and to inculcate lawful habits among the people. He saw to it that officials were named and trained, that plans for honest elections were devised, and that order prevailed. A good Catholic, he wanted the Church to be strong and to extend its evangelism into the Indian country. Yet he was modern enough to resent the traditional privileges of the Church, and he invoked the powers of the *real patronato* to restrict ecclesiastical courts, secularize cemeteries, and to limit the clergy's role in public education. Santander hoped to revive the cultural life which had given the viceroyalty considerable tone. Thus he re-established the National Academy, re-opened the observatory, encouraged the institutions of higher learning, and increased elementary schools until there were 500 of them. He introduced the Lancastrian method of teacher-training from England, and English styles and manners in general were favored. So also were British trade and investments. But in order to revive the flow of goods it was necessary to restore credit. This Santander did by austerity measures, which caused much grumbling among his countrymen, and by settling the public debt, most of which was owed to Englishmen. Venezuela and Ecuador, as one-time parts of Gran Colombia, also shared this debt. When Santander arranged for them to assume half of it and New Granada half, great was the outcry in Bogotá, where it was popularly believed that Venezuela was immensely rich and could easily carry a larger share. On the whole, Santander's financial policies worked, but they did nothing to make him beloved.

Much as Santander had done to preserve order and to set his country on a sensible path, he found, as the other liberators had by now, that the people were in a chronically irritable frame of mind. Plots from surviving royalist elements and from Bolívar's faction became so serious that the Man of Laws resorted to drastic repressions, including public executions. Such actions intensified passions, and people began to say that Santander was a tyrant. The clergy had taken very ill his modest efforts to reduce their position, and local leaders in every district needed only the slightest encouragement to defy "dictatorship" from Bogotá. As happened elsewhere, factionalism appeared wherever men thought about politics. New Granada, in fact, was destined to become a nation of genuine clashes of principle. Santander, like so many others of the time, found himself vilified by nationalists and localists, by conservatives and liberals. His prestige declined so precipitously that he was unable to persuade, and unwilling to try to force, the country to accept his choice for a successor when his term ended in 1836. Santander hoped that General José María Obando would follow him. But Obando had been one of Bolívar's major enemies, was thought by many to have caused the murder of Sucre, and was handicapped by Santander's favor. The victor was an estimable jurist, Dr. José Ignacio Márquez, who had been vice-president under Santander but who had turned against him. For several years Santander was made to realize the estrangement of his countrymen from him. While it was grievous enough to be blamed for many ills, it was still sadder to see the republic endangered by civil war. By 1840 New Granada was torn with violence, and Santander was subjected to furious attacks. Shortly after making a passionate speech in defense of his record, he died, another liberator who had seen his country turn on him. At least he died of natural causes and at home. Years later he would be esteemed.

MEXICO

The Viceroyalty of New Spain had seceded from the Spanish empire with dignity and ease in 1821, though much bloodshed had preceded this event. Yet Mexico, as it was now called, was doomed to experience a full measure of violence and instability during its first half-century of independence, excelling other Latin American nations in romantic tragedy and idealism alike. The collapse of Spanish imperial control had left the sprawling land—which the wise Humboldt had predicted would become the great power of North America—in wretched confusion. The mining area had almost ceased to produce since the hordes of Father Hidalgo had wandered through it in 1810. The mountains and jungles that encircle the Valley of Mexico had relapsed into chaos during the protracted struggles of Morelos, Guerrero, and other heroes of independence. Everywhere in the rural areas strong men, "patriots" all but often bandits and terrorists too, were gathering forces of youths who craved a life of adventure. Nominally soldiers of a free Mexico, they were too often mere criminals who knew they would profit if their caudillos could seize political positions. Half the population, the Indians, played no conscious part in the public life of the new nation. They continued to labor as peons or to live in the missions. Many of them withdrew almost entirely from contact with the white man. The mestizos were on the resurgent, often comprising the local armies or making themselves felt as a political force as street-rioters in the cities. The whites, or those who were educated, had a tendency to fragmentize into countless factions. No principle of legitimacy united the effective elements of the country behind any cause, any government.

The true extent of the disruption experienced by Mexican society was not apparent in 1822, when Agustín de Iturbide made himself emperor. Agustín I imagined that his regime had a good chance to take root. It seemed that the important white element in the nation's heartland, the Valley of Mexico, favored monarchy, independence, and Roman Catholicism, all of which were identified with the new sovereign. He apparently enjoyed the support of the chief army units and the invisible apparatus of freemasonry. If they, along with the major landholders and business men, continued to favor him, he could beat down the liberal intellectuals and the guerrilla chieftains who wanted a republic. The conservative regime he planned would not differ greatly from the viceroyalty except for its freedom to import capital and goods and, of more importance emotionally, its independence from the detested officials sent from Spain.

Yet Iturbide failed miserably, even comically. Much of the fault was his own. He was ignorant and tactless, impatient and foolish. Much as he loved to strut, he was no Bonaparte with vast prestige and superhuman abilities. The conservative forces on whom he relied blamed him for taking the crown. They knew he had not tried seriously to find a prince of royal blood for Mexico's throne. When Agustín staged a gaudy and costly coronation, Mexicans laughed and grumbled. The imperial titles awarded to his parents and numerous children and the Order of Guadalupe he created for a new nobility pleased only those who got the honors. No one else was impressed, at least for long. Iturbide was an actor, not a monarch. His critics were aware that Bolívar would not recognize the empire and that the United States disapproved; his well-wishers were chastened by the refusal of the older monarchies in Europe to welcome the Mexican upstart.

While Agustín enjoyed playing emperor and did so with zest, he was soon forced to see that his pretensions collided with reality. The congress he summoned to legalize his regime proved recalcitrant, refusing to vote funds to pay the soldiers and officials. Soon the emperor was seizing whatever capital he could uncover and issuing worthless paper currency. These actions created animosity and yet failed to provide sufficient money to finance his government, a fatal flaw, for now his own servants saw no reason to remain loyal. Suspecting the congress of plotting against him, Iturbide arrested some of its members and sent the rest away in October 1822. Now, disaster stared him in the eyes. Conservatives froze into disapproving inactivity, and republicans became bolder. In reality, there was no imperial party. Military leaders in the provinces, the most notable of whom was Antonio López de Santa Anna in Veracruz,[5] openly defied the emperor and conspired to throw him out. For a few months Agustín strove to brave the hostile currents, but opposition became all the more formidable. Finally, in February 1823, the forlorn monarch summoned congress and went before it to admit his failure. Offering to abdicate, he was told that he had never legally been in power and was escorted to the coast, not without some show of respect.

Iturbide sailed to Italy, where agents of the Spanish Bourbons molested him. Then he fled to England, where he recovered his nerve and planned a comeback. In the summer of 1824 he sailed down the Gulf Coast with a very small party and a goodly supply of proclamations to his "subjects." Mexican authorities, aware of his schemes, were waiting, and when he landed in Tamaulipas he was captured and shot. Ignoble as his end was, Iturbide came to be honored in time by the Mexicans for his services in breaking the link with Spain. And for much of the nineteenth century nostalgic conservatives regarded him as something of a hero. Iturbide was not the worst ruler Mexico was to endure.

Independent Mexico's second political experiment, the federal republic, outlasted Iturbide's empire but was scarcely more successful. The fallen emperor was replaced early in 1823 by a committee of three generals. In November a new congress met to draw up a constitution. Still unaware of the appalling disintegration that was taking place, the delegates debated political theories as though they had some relevance in Mexico. For months flowery orations filled the air, and closely-reasoned pamphlets circulated. To be sure, some of the delegates were able men with experience in the recent Spanish *cortes*, and they showed much knowledge of English liberalism, the French and American Revolutions, and the constitutionalist movement in Spain. Already convinced republicans, a large majority also favored federalism, which the Spanish constitution of 1812 had implanted and provincial interests and sentiments promoted. Thus the constitution they proclaimed in 1824 copied many features of the American. Nineteen states and four territories would compose the United States of Mexico. The president would be

5. Usually spelled "Vera Cruz" in colonial times but one wor since then.

chosen by a majority of the states, and the second-runner would become vice-president. A bicameral congress and a judiciary would complement the executive. Roman Catholicism was declared the official state religion, and the familiar rights and liberties of constitutions of the Age of Revolution were proclaimed. It was a carefully-planned charter for a new republic, but, as it turned out, Mexico was grotesquely unprepared to live up to it.

The first president was a hero of the independence struggles, a warrior who called himself Guadalupe Victoria, surely an appealing if invented name, but one which was never to rank with George Washington. Along with the new president appeared the new flag, a banner of green, white, and red with the famous Aztec emblem—the eagle on a cactus on an island holding a serpent in its beak. It was popular then to glorify the ancient Indians, so long as the modern Indians kept their place.

Probably no one could have carried out the exacting task of laying a sound foundation for the republic in those years. Certainly Guadalupe Victoria was inadequate, though he achieved a melancholy distinction in being the only Mexican president for many years to serve out his term, and he was almost as unusual in that he was honest in financial matters. During his administration the Spaniards evacuated San Juan de Ulúa, a fortress that dominates the harbor of Veracruz, but it was known that Fernando VII was planning an invasion of Mexico in the near future. He also secured a loan from British banks at rates that were usurious, justifiably so in view of the risk, but much of the money failed to reach Mexico. In general, the first president helplessly beheld a country boiling in anarchy. Local caudillos made a mockery of the republican ideal as they ran state governments like private businesses. Ritualistic liberals mouthed phrases they usually did not grasp and drafted ambitious programs far beyond Mexico's reach. Most of the people could not understand public affairs or were quick to withdraw from them in disgust. And it was impossible for the president to command order among the various bands of soldiers and to pay the employees of the republic, though, or because, there was plenty of money for graft.

A complicating and sometimes amusing factor during these early years of the republic was the competition between Great Britain and the United States for Mexican good will, which was supposed to promote vast commercial benefits. This rivalry came to be personified by two men who disliked each other, the American minister Joel Roberts Poinsett and the British *chargé d'affaires* Henry George Ward. Poinsett was a rough-hewn republican who had exhibited his tactlessness and his scorn for monarchical Europe in South America during the early days of the independence movement. He wanted Mexico to be as much like the United States as possible, and thus he gravitated to the liberals. Ward was far more polished and skillful. Furthermore, he had a better case: Britain had many goods to sell and abundant capital to invest, and she harbored no aggressive designs against Mexico. Ward and Poinsett angled for social triumphs and economic favors, intrigued against one another, and sought to discredit each other's country. Ward easily got the better of the duel. He won the ear of President Victoria and, by working through the Masons who followed the Scottish Rite, helped solidify a pro-British conservative party in competition with the York Rite liberals whom Poinsett sponsored. Some of the Yankeephobia which Mexican official circles later exhibited stemmed from Ward's relentless preaching that the United States intended to expand at Mexico's expense, surely no slander, as events were to prove. Thanks in large part to his efforts, British traders, investors, and technicians entered Mexico in numbers the Americans could not hope to match. Though they rehabilitated some of the mines and lubricated economic life, most of them were disappointed in their pecuniary rewards.

As the first presidential term drew to a close in 1828, the conservatives and the liberals were identifiable not so much as political parties but as rival aggregations of factions. The election, to stretch the usual meaning of the word, resulted in victory for the conservative candidate, Manuel Gómez Pedraza, who won ten states to the liberal Vicente Guerrero's nine. Rightly fearing the outcome would be challenged, the conservatives struck first and attempted to seize the government. But the liberals, incited by Poinsett, brought about a hideous uprising in Mexico City by using the wretched *léperos*, not really lepers but Indian beggars and rowdies, and won the city.

The forlorn Guadalupe Victoria managed to sit on the presidential chair until the clock ticked out his legal term, when Vicente Guerrero took office. This rough and uneducated warrior had led irregular forces for years in the southern mountains and had participated with Iturbide in ousting the Spanish in 1821. He had little other claim to the high office his friends had seized for him. His incapacity was so apparent during the crisis of 1829 with Spain, described below, that he was replaced by the vice-president, Anastasio Bustamante, and driven back to the mountains. This shift in the presidency brought the conservatives into power and led to an order for Vicente Guerrero's arrest. The old fighter took refuge on an Italian ship, whereupon the captain sold him to his enemies. Guerrero, like his former partner Iturbide, was shot. It was both a pity and a disgrace, even though he had done something to bring this fate on himself. Eventually a state was named for him.

Guerrero's overthrow had been triggered by a Spanish invasion of Tampico, which revealed the president's impotence so brutally. Fernando VII had never recognized the independence of his former American kingdoms, and he sincerely believed that Mexico longed to return to his power. His repeated appeals, reflecting the emotions of a forgiving father and king, may well have stirred the thousands of Spanish subjects, most of them business and professional men and landowners, who had remained after 1821. Aware that an invasion was coming, Mexico offered these Spaniards the choice of leaving the country or becoming naturalized citizens. Rather than await their individual options, however, the government cruelly deported great numbers of them, further impoverishing Mexico by removing men of wealth and skill. The Spanish attack on Tampico, though it had long been planned, was supposedly Fernando VII's reply to the expulsion. The expedition was a fiasco of grotesque proportions. The royal fleet left the army stranded in the tropical port city, where inactivity and yellow fever ruined it. Finally, the demoralized invaders surrendered to a small force from Veracruz led by Santa Anna, who with characteristic vanity renamed Tampico after himself. This amazing man, one of Mexico's greatest misfortunes, had now established a reputation which he was not long in exploiting.

For more than two years the conservatives sought to govern an ungovernable land. They fared no better than the liberals, despite their apparent advantages of support by the Church, the landowners, and the British. One of their first actions was to send Joel Roberts Poinsett away with the flower that eventually bore his name. This may have pleased the British, but it solved no problems. Mexico was not recovering, but sinking deeper into poverty and disorder, pulled down by the indiscipline of the militarists and the anarchical tastes of the people. One figure at this time commands respect—the short, fat, pompous figure of Lucás Alamán, who until his death in 1853 articulated a frankly conservative political philosophy. As foreign minister in 1829–1832, and historian, pundit, and official at other periods, this aristocrat dreamed of a Mexican nation with a strong centralized government, perhaps a monarchy, based on a sound mining industry and manufacturing, enlightened through public education, and open to the culture, capital, immigrants, and technology of Europe. In a way he may be honored as a seer, very much like Rivadavia in the Argentine, who discerned the formula which would eventually shape his country.

As the second presidential term drew to a close in 1832, Santa Anna decided that he would like to be president and that liberalism was the stronger force. After making the necessary arrangements with other generals and issuing the appropriate manifestoes, he embraced the cause of liberal federalism and cooperated with one of its most important leaders, Valentín Gómez Farías, a physician from Guadalajara. The coalition served his purpose. Bustamante was easily unseated and, as a gesture toward legality, Gómez Pedraza brought in as president to serve for the last few months of the term to which he had been elected in 1828. Meanwhile, Santa Anna secured his own election for the new term and that of Gómez Farías as vice-president, it now being possible for the two to run on one ticket, the liberal federalist. But when the time arrived for the inauguration, Santa Anna mysteriously stood aside in favor of Gómez Farías, as honest and staunch a figure to Mexican liberals as Alamán was to conservatives. Not very convincingly pleading illness, the absentee president withdrew to his beautiful family plantation, Mango de Clava, near Jalapa in the state of Veracruz, where he lingered for many months while Gómez Farías proceeded to carry out the liberals' program.

CENTRAL AMERICA

The captaincy-general of Guatemala had long been a somnolent kingdom in the Spanish empire. Perhaps no more than 100,000 of its million and a half inhabitants were white, and they, lords of plantations, officials, and urban merchants and lawyers, formed no cohesive group. Entirely beyond political life were the million Indians, most of them broad-faced, almond-eyed Maya, and the few hundred thousand persons of Negro or mixed ancestry. The least backward part of the colony was in the cool mountainous regions of the western coast. In the jungles of the tropical oriental side the population was often uncivilized. The provinces, forebears of the modern republics of Guatemala, El Salvador, Honduras, Nicaragua, and Costa Rica, were isolated from the outside world and in little contact with one another. Nevertheless, the leading men of the towns had agreed in 1821 to break away from revolutionary Spain. The captain-general himself, Gabino Gainza, had connived with the advocates of independence and had led the rather half-hearted assembly to a decision to join Mexico. An army sent by Iturbide reinforced this policy,[6] but when the Mexican emperor fell, early in 1823, the imperial troops were withdrawn, detaching the province of Chiapas as they returned to Mexico.

Sovereignty thus reverted to a little assembly in session in Guatemala City. This body proclaimed independence and the creation of the Confederation of Central America. Like so many congresses of its type, this one was bewildered by the problems of organizing a new government and hardly knew how to begin. Political opinions had not yet crystallized, and the prevailing mood was one of timidity. Planters tended to favor autocratic government and possibly a return to Spain. They usually supported the Church. Professional and business men in the towns, together with various intellectuals, inclined toward liberalism with its

6. A group in the town of San Salvador objected to joining Mexico and asked to be incorporated by the United States.

broader participation in public affairs, federalism, and anti-clericalism. As the congress debated during 1823 and 1824 the two points of view became rather firm. In 1825, the liberals seemed victorious when Manuel Arce was somewhat irregularly chosen as the first president of the Confederation. Arce resembled most of the other beginner-presidents in Latin America by not being sure whether he was a liberal or a conservative and striving, with the best of motives, to be something of each. The results were typical: both sides were annoyed. Liberals believed he had misled them, conservatives that he was covertly their opponent. Within a year uprisings against his regime began to occur, a few of them ideologically motivated, but most of them the familiar outbreaks of personalism led by men who wanted to occupy the seats of power. But not until 1828 did Arce give up and leave Central America.

Succeeding him by election in the congress was Francisco Morazán, a strongly liberal Honduran who had shown military ability during the recent disorders. Morazán dominated the provinces for several years by giving his support to liberal groups in each one. His program of reform was partially successful in that monastic orders were abolished and their properties seized, a dubious standard by which reform could be measured, and he silenced or exiled obstructive clergymen and powerful conservatives. Morazán hoped to make the Confederation stable politically by permitting the several provinces some autonomy, and attractive to foreign traders and investors by sound fiscal practices. Economic conditions were not bad, for Central America had suffered no fighting during the Wars of Independence, and it held many resources to interest enterprisers. A few adventurous merchants entered the country, and a handful of immigrants from the slums of London founded a small colony. Things seemed to be going well for a time, and Morazán was popular and admired.

And then, in the pattern of tragedy that, like the operation of a meatpacking plant, was less Greek than merely mechanical in its inevitability, things began to go wrong. The immaturity and fickleness of the politically-educated element was a major factor, as always in Latin America of that day. The emergence of ambitious military leaders with their uncomprehending, greedy forces of mixed races was another. Most important of all was the rising wrath of the Church and its supporters in all ranks of the population. When Morazán proposed toleration and civil marriage, the provinces defied him, and they further regarded as suspicious plans for lay education and the promotion of immigration. The small English colony seemed especially sinister to the superstitious, xenophobic population; perhaps the colony was the cause of the cholera epidemic that swept the isthmus in 1836–1837. Or had Morazán provoked divine wrath with his anti-clericalism? Branded as un-Christian and pro-European, Morazán rapidly lost authority. When his second term ended, in 1839, all the provinces had left the Confederation but El Salvador. An ignorant young backwoodsman named Rafael Carrera, who seemed a messiah to the Indians and a deliverer to the conservatives, had taken Guatemala City and proclaimed the end of the Confederation. Morazán wisely left the country for Peru, but unlike some of the other founding fathers, did not content himself with lamentations over the woes of trying to establish a nation. By 1842 he was back in Costa Rica as a first step toward re-creating the Confederation. But few rallied to him, and he was defeated and shot. A united Central America remained a generally agreeable memory and a goal, but five squalid, tyranny-ridden republics constituted the reality.

BRAZIL

Independent Brazil began its career with optimism under a highly popular liberator the way its Spanish-speaking sisters often did. Disillusionment followed quickly, and a period of turmoil set in. Brazil, however, soon passed through the dreary phase and achieved an admirable stability that enabled her, within a half-century after independence, to surpass the Spanish states in most respects, an accomplishment all the more remarkable because at the beginning of this period Brazil lagged far behind them economically and culturally. This very backwardness is one reason why Portuguese America did not fly apart like the Spanish viceroyalties; most of the population was too unaware of public affairs to assert itself. Also, the sugar and cotton lords of the northeast had long been near-absolute masters of their own bailiwicks and usually dominated the town councils in their neighborhood. In effect, most of Brazil had been self-governing in colonial times, at least to this extent. Not only had the royal government been weak outside the mining areas and the capital, but its ally, the Church, was also comparatively frail. The shift from colonial status to equality with Portugal in 1816 and to independence in 1822 involved no real rupture with the past, and it occurred with little violence. Another key factor making for Brazil's unity after independence was the continuity of the monarchy in the person of Pedro I, who was proclaimed emperor in 1822 amid wide rejoicing.

This Pedro de Braganza headed an empire so huge and inchoate that the vital forces and power relationships at work in it could scarcely be identified. Almost four million persons lived within its sprawling frontiers. More than a million were Negro slaves; several hundred thousand were Indians living as pagan savages in the hinterland; and a million and a half were freed Negroes, civilized Indians, mulattoes, and mixtures of countless variety. Of the half-million or so whites, the ones who counted politically were the planters of the northeast, the ranchers of the south, the merchants and skilled artisans of the towns strung along the coast, the mine owners, and the bureaucracy. The antipathy between the Brazilian-born whites and those who had come from Portugal was acute, but the proclamation of the empire temporarily dulled it. Pedro I was a Portuguese who lived most of his life in Brazil. Only twenty-four in 1822, he was handsome, virile, and regal in manner, the ideal man, it seemed, to reconcile all parties and to be idolized by the masses. He was quite eager to play this part, and his wife, the popular Empress Leopoldina, a Habsburg, gave him strong moral and intellectual support. The emperor said and apparently believed that he wished to govern as a constitutional monarch. Strengthening this purpose was his chief minister, José Bonifácio de Andrada, the São Paulo scientist who had spent most of his life in Europe.

In 1823 Pedro fulfilled the promise he had made at Ypiranga to summon a constitutional convention. This body, like so many assemblies of this type in the Spanish countries, contained men of ability and culture who were at once well-meaning and power-hungry. No one, not the emperor, Andrada, nor the delegates, had much experience in the art of ruling or could gauge the sentiments of the country with sureness. An involved clash of personalities and purposes soon brought about Andrada's resignation. Pedro and the assembly collided directly over the issue of the source of power. Was the constitution the expression of the general will, the product of popular sovereignty? Or was it a gift from the monarch to his people? Pedro, naturally, preferred to regard it as the latter, and his position hardened as the Iberian constitutionalist movements were snuffed out during 1823. After putting up for some weeks with what he thought was impudence and even subversion on the part of the delegates, he forcibly closed the assembly in November. Andrada and other constitutionalists were sent into exile. Despite profound indignation in some quarters and stirrings of republicanism, the emperor had his way. In 1824 he appointed a committee of ten, five of whom had been members of the late assembly, which revised the constitutional draft prepared by that body. A free grant from the monarch to the nation, this basic law was promulgated in March and served Brazil well for the following sixty-five years.

The constitution of 1824 endowed the emperor with great but largely disguised powers. As moderator or mediator of the nation, he was to employ his executive authority to assure the operation of the government and to overcome obstruction by the legislative or judicial branches or by local organs. The monarch had a suspensive veto and could send parliament home. He could by-pass court judgments by granting pardons or modifying sentences. He also appointed presidents of the several provinces. Parliament had two houses: a senate with members named for life by the emperor from triple lists submitted by the provinces, and a chamber of deputies made up of men elected under a system of limited suffrage by those adult males who, whatever their color, met property qualifications. The provincial presidents were advised by elected councils, which clamored for more power and, in 1834, obtained it. As in colonial days, the Church remained under the monarch's control or patronage. Finally, a list of rights as liberal as any in Latin America adorned the charter, and it was destined to be much better respected than in other countries.

For nearly seven years Pedro I governed under this constitution as well as his temperament and training allowed. In a time of European reaction and growing Latin American anarchy, he seems to have performed adequately, though few of his critics gave him much credit. During the years in which Argentina fell into chaos, the Bolivarian creations collapsed, Chile suffered anarchy, and Mexico plunged into disorders, the Brazilian Empire grew to nationhood with comparative ease. Economic conditions were sometimes good, never desperate. Two law schools were established to train Brazilian civil servants and professional men who had formerly gone to Coimbra in Portugal or done without such instruction. Medical education also received an important impetus. Organs of government were established and put into operation, and the Church went on functioning as it always had. The army was kept either busy or quiet, except for some rowdiness on the part of mercenary troops.

Yet Pedro's difficulties got the better of him. Liberals had never forgiven him for scattering the constituent assembly of 1823; now they complained as this imperial Braganza snubbed the chamber of deputies and arbitrarily selected ministers in violation of their understanding of the procedures of responsible government. A republican-secessionist revolt sputtered in the heart of the northeast, where the sugar and cotton magnates were accustomed to ruling. Lord Cochrane, however, suppressed it with his customary verve. Unchastened, Pedro showed his impatience with opposition and denounced his critics as ignorant or wrong-headed. Sometimes, though not as a regular practice, he closed journals whose columns struck him as impertinent and allowed the police to violate the liberties of his subjects. Brazilians, who were flaunting the extravagant patriotism typical of newly-freed colonials, were also irritated by the presence of so many Portuguese in the emperor's immediate circle and the award of so many plums of office to these detested Europeans. And then Pedro's immoralities brought him unpopularity as it became evident that they had destroyed the happiness of the beloved empress and perhaps hastened her death in 1826.[7] Once the Brazilians had admired the youthful prince for his amatory prowess, for Brazil has never been a prudish land, but his mad love affair with an extravagant mistress disgusted many of them. His re-marriage in 1829 with a granddaughter of the Empress Josephine, Napoleon's first wife, failed to restore Pedro as a sympathetic figure. One by one, the emperor's personal and official acts brought condemnation. Since the other Latin American liberators underwent similar experiences, it may simply have been that independence left people fickle and in a mood to carp.

The rapid decline of Pedro's popularity was revealed in several important developments, in none of which does he seem to have blundered. Between 1825 and 1827 he negotiated agreements with Britain which brought recognition and a restoration of the age-old commercial relationship. Britain's foreign minister, George Canning, pressed Portugal into acknowledging the independence of Brazil, an important service, but one performed at the price of Brazil's promise to cease importing slaves by 1830, a requirement that injured the slaveocracy of the northeast and whose moral basis practically no Brazilian could understand. Still more luster rubbed off in the settlement with Portugal, which involved Brazil's acceptance of a large share of the debt of the Braganza monarchy, a stipulation that was not unfair but angered Brazilian patriots who remembered how João VI had taken the treasury with him back to Europe in 1821. And then the war with Buenos Aires over Uruguay between 1825 and 1828 discredited Pedro, since he took the field for a time and failed, and the loss of the Cisplatine province, as Brazilians called the area, disappointed nationalists. Pedro's employment of Irish and German mercenaries during that war and in suppressing internal disorders was another wound to Brazilian pride. Finally, the undying suspicion that Pedro was not at heart a Brazilian flared in 1826, when he inherited the crown of Portugal on the death of João VI. Pedro at once renounced the honor and named his infant daughter, Maria da Gloria, as queen. But this dynastic affair was not to be settled so neatly. Dom Miguel, Pedro's reactionary brother, seized the Portuguese throne, and Brazilian funds were used in an effort to unseat him. Thus irritation mounted against the emperor, most of it foolish and unfair, some of it well-founded.

Pedro might have ridden through these difficulties had he regarded the continuance of his reign in Brazil as worth a lifetime of patience and effort. His temper had grown short, however, as everything he did provoked opposition. No doubt he observed the way the Spanish states were expelling those founders who had not already quit in disgust. The French

7. It was widely believed, and possibly true, that Pedro had kicked her while she was pregnant and caused her death.

revolution of 1830 had a strong repercussion in Brazil, one of the nations that caught the proverbial cold whenever France sneezed, and people talked openly of deposing the monarch. Accompanied by his new empress, Pedro made an imperial tour of Minas Gerais, hoping to stir up enthusiasm but encountering apathy or hostility instead. Back in Rio de Janeiro, he tried for a few months to govern with the strictest constitutionality, the way the liberals wanted him to, and he found support again from Andrada, whom he had allowed to return. Yet defiance and frustration greeted him at every hand. Nothing seemed to work. Perhaps in an exasperated gesture of self-assertion, he installed an absolutist ministry. The liberals agitated wildly against this step, and superficially at least the population and garrisons of the capital sided with them. Confronted with a demand that he reinstate the former ministry, Pedro suddenly abdicated in April 1831 in favor of his five-year-old son and sailed away. His action produced far less rejoicing than might have been anticipated. Stupefaction and alarm dominated the minds of the more responsible leaders, who feared that the emperor's defection might mean the fragmentization of Brazil and the triumph of radicalism. Their dismay, however, could not bring him back. The emperor, for reasons that were debated then and afterward, had gone forever. He went to Portugal, where he fought for three years to install Maria da Gloria as constitutional queen. As soon as he won, he died. An unusual and gallant figure, he is still admired in Brazil.

The personal tragedies of the founders of Latin American independence were poignant indeed. Few of the key liberators remained prominent in public affairs by the 1830's. The disappointment of foreign well-wishers was as keen as the malicious delight of European autocrats, who had always prophesied the riotous anarchy into which the Hispanic American lands had fallen. Not that the erstwhile mother countries were in a position to gloat, or even to grieve. The dreadful Carlist wars in Spain and the Miguelist struggles in Portugal offered as depressing a spectacle as the failure of the liberators. Nor were the peninsular nations ever to recover the priceless quality of legitimacy: an unspoken, almost unanimous agreement that a certain political system is right and natural. The Latin American nations, of course, had still less in the way of legitimacy. A Braganza monarch, a self-made Mexican emperor, Bolívar, O'Higgins—all had failed. No set of ideals and basic laws had won general acceptance. Imperialist power was gone, but for lack of accord on what was to stand in its stead, chaos alone endured. Latin American realities in the 1830's contrasted miserably with the prosperity of the colonial world of 1790 and the high hopes of the Wars of Independence. As favorable as public opinion in the United States had been to the

Latin American cause, Americans nevertheless could not refrain from invidious—and at times, somewhat smug—comparisons between their own constitutional and economic progress and that of their brethren to the south. What had happened to the Washingtons, Franklins, Jeffersons, Madisons, and Adamses in Latin America? Why had wars solidified nationalism in the United States and torn society apart in South America?

The questions raised then are as hard to answer today. To invoke the familiar point of unfriendly geography is not to supply a true answer, unless we think in terms of the later nineteenth century and Latin America's absence of resources to support industrialization on a large scale. First of all, externally, thanks to the Atlantic Ocean and the British fleet, Latin America stood in no serious danger of European aggression. Secondly, internally as well, geography was not necessarily an enemy. Mountains, deserts, and jungles there were, but these had not prevented the Iberian powers from exercising authority over scattered and greatly varied centers of population. Nor had they been insuperable obstacles to the liberators, who had crossed them repeatedly and considered them no bar to hopes for either maintaining the old viceroyalties intact under new rulers or perhaps even combining them into greater states. To point to racial divisions as the immediate cause of the early political failures is equally unrewarding. Indians, Negroes, mulattoes, and mestizos made themselves felt on occasion, but European stock still dominated most of Latin America. And yet the whites were deeply divided among themselves.

What the liberators had not foreseen was the emergence, both appalling and glorious, of an individualism released by the destruction of the traditional restraints. As in the Reconquest in Spain and the Conquest of America, men learned to love a life of adventure. A strutting military leader with flair, color, and eloquence appealed to something deep in the American Spaniards and did not fail to attract mestizos and Indians. The upper-class caudillos who had ousted the peninsulars enjoyed a degree of popular adoration that enabled most of them to survive the next phase in which they dealt high-handedly with the constitution-mongers of the cities, the "lawyers," as they were contemptuously called. But then the people began to turn on these early heroes, blaming them for bad economic conditions, unresolved social questions, and failure to produce administration. A querulous, impatient mood became common. When the great liberators quit or fell, the successor liberators, the lesser officers of the Wars of Independence, emerged. Hard-bitten men, often little-educated, they were proud and difficult individualists, willful, imperious, unable to cooperate with others, and, by this time, cynical. Also, the rural masses and urban street mobs alike had learned to respect no one, and it was simple for these successor caudillos to appeal to their cupidity or love of violence.

These, then, were the true heirs of Spanish power in America; the caudillos with their irregular forces, tempted only by the material benefits and self-gratification that office brings. They brushed aside the lettered men of the cities, who craved power too but were responsive to ideals and were not altogether hypocritical as they quoted Jefferson and Rousseau. They also overthrew the liberators who dreamed of emulating Napoleon or Washington. But what of the most powerful class in America, the great landowners? The established creole families had prestige, wealth, and often cultured tastes and graceful ways. They had stepped forth at various stages during the independence movement, above all when Spain fell into the hands of radicals, and provided leadership. They would have liked to organize and run the new states as oligarchies, and indeed their plans were to this end. Yet they too were defeated and abashed by rude caudillos and their barbaric troops. The landed upper class, integrated as it was in social matters, revealed a critical lack of political cohesion. Its members might have tolerated Rivadavia, O'Higgins, Sucre, Bolívar, Pedro I, Morazán, and Iturbide longer, to their own immense advantage and that of their respective countries. Instead, they fretted over petty matters, quarreled over trifles, and undermined the men who might have founded solid regimes. After the general collapse of government in the 1830's, the great families were sick of politics and frightened. Concerned now with holding their properties and workers rather than with statecraft, they withdrew to their private estates and private affairs. Usually they financed caudillos as they had to in order to avoid destruction. When they had a choice, they tended to favor autocratic, centralized government and strong Church authority. Urban liberals were their natural enemies. Yet the landed aristocracy seldom offered leadership to the republics. It largely concerned itself with maintaining its privileges by adjusting to the unending crisis, and did so very well, thus perpetuating far into the national period many aspects of colonialism.

The failure to establish legitimate or even effective governments was not a mere matter of politics. Humanitarian reforms and social legislation could not be carried out. Business conditions remained generally bad for a generation or more after independence, due largely or altogether to the lack of government. Public administration was a disgrace, a matter of seizures and extortions, of brief luxury for the winners and abuse of the losers in power struggles. Most government consisted of attempting to thwart revolutions. Foreign traders, investors, and technical experts sometimes prospered in Latin America, but most of them found a more hospitable environment elsewhere, and of course none of the advanced nations at that time had foreign aid programs to assist newly-freed colonial areas. Public education could not make serious inroads in the wilderness of ignorance the southern Americas had become, because no regime could support it for long. The bad reputation of Latin America long prevented much immigration, even from Spain and Portugal. Years of shame and suffering had to pass before improvements were feasible. Little as the great majority of the population participated in public affairs, or cared about them, they were the victims of politics.

22

The Great Dictators
of the Early National Period

THAT so much of the history of Latin America must be told in the lives of individuals is itself depressing. It is still more depressing that so many of these men were personally contemptible, even when allowance is made for the extravagant language of their detractors. This was not true of the more famous leaders of the independence movement nor of most of the figures who tried to build states in the first decade or so of the national period. But in most of Latin America power had been lost by leaders who had vision, a sense of responsibility, and good will. Men of violence often seized control of the republics and held it by force until they were betrayed by caudillos as primitive as themselves. That they were sometimes colorful and attractive as personalities does not diminish the harm they did. The riotous character of public life discouraged the penetration of Latin America by educators, immigrants, investors, traders, and experts. If they came at all, it was usually for brief periods of exploitation, not for patient constructive labors. Europe, the United States, and other happier areas regarded Latin America with pity and scorn. And while many individuals of the region shared the artistic, literary, and scientific interests of the outside world, the general cultural level in most of these countries rose little, if at all, above that of colonial times. Social change was seldom in the direction of humanitarianism. Economic conditions remained bad almost everywhere, in contrast to the striking advances in other parts of the world. For a generation or two after independence, Latin America in general lost ground. The great dictators were both a cause and a consequence of this backwardness.

MEXICO

Antonio López de Santa Anna

FOR nearly a quarter of a century the public life of Mexico was dominated by as preposterous a figure as Latin America has produced, a unique dictator as little comprehensible now as he was to many contemporaries. Between 1832 and 1855 Santa Anna served as president eleven times. He adhered to no principles, had little respect for ideas, and apparently had no sense of pride or shame. An opportunist and self-seeker of the rankest sort, this man bore much responsibility for Mexico's loss of nearly half her territory to the United States. His showmanship debased Mexican public morals until the nation lost its self-respect and its reputation was scandalous. He stole, lied, and betrayed time and again. Almost nothing favorable can be said of his character or statesmanship, though he obviously had some talent. Certainly he could inspire troops, even if he failed to justify his self-granted title, "Napoleon of the West." One more or less constant advantage he enjoyed was the ability to raise a sizeable army at any time from among the Indians of his tropical hacienda, Mango de Clava, and its neighborhood in Jalapa. Also, his proximity to Veracruz enabled him to seize the customhouse, the only sure source of revenue in the Mexican republic. Santa Anna knew the soldiers and politicians of his country well, and, slippery though he was, he could usually line them up to serve his purposes. His crude and bombastic proclamations appealed, occasionally at least, to the ignorant or selfish. He was irresistible in personal contact, able to beguile such hard-bitten characters as Sam Houston and Andrew Jackson and, in fact, almost anyone else who met him face to face. After years of treacheries and follies he could spring back to the center of things and make himself welcome.

Born in 1794 of a well-to-do white family, Santa Anna (who added the second n to "Ana" as a gesture of defiance after some obscure quarrel with his parents) learned to ride, shoot, and fight Indians as a youth. He received only a rudimentary education, never becoming an industrious reader but learning enough to compose emotional proclamations and to count money. He was a dashing fellow, handsome and romantic, appealing and engaging, lecherous and fond of gambling. As a young officer in the royal Spanish army he exhibited a callousness to human suffering by mistreating soldiers and an ethical blindness by forging money orders. In 1821 the Spanish promoted him to lieutenant colonel when he promised to remain loyal. The very next day he accepted a full colonelcy in the Mexican army as a reward for switching to the cause of independence. During Iturbide's brief reign Santa Anna was one of the more unrestrained flatterers of the emperor. Then he joined the conspirators who plotted the overthrow of the empire, allowed Iturbide to win him back, and finally executed a triple-cross in which he wound up on the side of the rebels. During the first years of the republic Santa Anna did not shine particularly, probably because he was known to be so untrustworthy. But his decisive action against the Spanish expeditionary force in Tampico in 1829 elevated him to national glory, and later in the year he was instrumental in the ousting of President Guerrero. In 1832 he took the lead in organizing the liberal revolt which ousted Bustamante and resulted in his own election as president.

The peculiar behavior of the new president in retiring to the tropical estate he loved so well just after his inauguration may have been a matter of mood, for Santa Anna was very temperamental and never quite grew up. His habit of taking opium also accounts for much of his erratic behavior. Yet there may have been some calculation behind it. Valentín Gómez Farías, the acting president, was an earnest liberal who planned to make the constitution of 1824 work and to cripple the two major strongholds of conservatism, the regular army and the Church. In what proved to be a false dawn of the famous *Reforma*, Mexico's liberal movement, he and the congress attempted to decrease the army, create a civilian militia, reform the prisons and courts, abolish tithes, weaken the regular orders and missions, and establish a system of lay education. The army and the Church were quite capable of defending their privileges and straightway began to plot the overthrow of Gómez Farías. Much of the public was appalled at the "godless" administration and credited clerical assurances that the great cholera epidemic of 1833–1834 signified divine punishment. Well aware that the liberals had provoked much opposition, Santa Anna waited until April 1834, when he deemed the time right to intervene. Grandly emerging from his estate with his faithful soldiers and a good supply of manifestoes, he expelled Gómez Farías and the liberal congress, describing his actions as answering the call of the people to restore religion. After making a number of intricate financial arrangements beneficial to himself and his seedy followers, he then turned over the government to a conservative acting president and allowed a hand-picked congress to draft a centralist constitution to replace the charter of 1824.

THE LOSS OF TEXAS

Santa Anna's second retirement was disturbed a year later by the threatened secession of Texas. This large province had interested the Spanish only as a buffer to contain the French. Under free Mexico, the threat was not French but American, and Iturbide, who was never particularly shrewd as a statesman, confirmed a previous viceregal grant to

Moses and Stephen F. Austin to colonize the area with Catholics in the hope of blocking the Yankees. By 1835 the Austin enterprise had become a huge financial success, and Texas contained more than 30,000 Americans, very few of whom were Catholics. Friction of all sorts developed. The Yankees looked down on the Mexicans and aspired to join the United States. They preferred to trade with New Orleans merchants rather than purchase more costly goods from Mexico City. The settlers often disputed with Mexican officials, who tended to be corrupt and tyrannical, over customs duties, taxes, and all sorts of regulations. While they had been exempted from Mexico's law to abolish Negro slavery, they were nonetheless fearful of the future of the servile institution that seemed to go with the cotton culture that was so promising in the rich black soil of the eastern part of the province. To be sure, most of the Texans were outlaws or adventurous young men seeking their fortune. It was clear by 1835 that these tough colonists were no barrier to Yankee expansion but rather a fifth column. Their ardor to secede from Mexico became all the greater after Santa Anna sponsored a centralist regime that might jeopardize such autonomy as they had enjoyed.

After several clashes and much evidence of Texan defiance, Santa Anna emerged from Mango de Clava and collected an army of about 8,000 men, which was poorly outfitted by contractors who treated the president and his generals much better. Santa Anna's aim was to compel the wayward province to bow to Mexican rule, but his campaign was also a labor of love. He enjoyed being in the field, and as a youth he had fought Indians near Texas, an experience which convinced him that he could handle any situation there. As his forces enveloped San Antonio and besieged W. B. Travis, the immortal Davy Crockett,[1] and about 150 Texans in the old mission known as the Alamo, Texas declared its independence on March 2, 1836. The Alamo was overwhelmed and all its defenders killed. Then, Santa Anna moved eastward in pursuit of the fugitive Texas government, massacring 300 prisoners of war (or Mexican traitors, as with some reason he alleged) at Goliad. The Mexicans were utterly triumphant. The Texans were fleeing wildly, and with any luck or prudence Santa Anna should have smashed resistance in short order. But he lacked both. Now the Texans had an able leader in Sam Houston, a strong character who was fond of whiskey and wise to the ways of frontier fighting. As the pursued and the pursuers neared the site of the city that bears Houston's name, the over-confident Mexicans stopped to make camp on the banks of San Jacinto Creek on the morning of April 21, 1836. Stupidly, they neglected to take the most elementary precautions, had lunch, and began the inevitable siesta. Santa Anna was in a

1. A famous frontiersman in any case, presumably immortalized by the cult of his deeds among children of the mid-twentieth century.

tent with a slave girl. Inconsiderately, the Texans sprang at that time, and within eighteen minutes the Mexican camp was a shambles and Santa Anna had vanished. A day later, when he was picked up in the garb of an enlisted man, he tried to avoid recognition, but as soon as he entered the prisoner compound, shouts of *¡El presidente!* gave him away.

Santa Anna narrowly escaped lynching at the hands of the Texans. Houston, wounded and cursing, had the fallen ruler spirited to safety, finally to a ship anchored in the Gulf. The two men solemnly negotiated the independence of Texas, and Mexican forces were duly evacuated. Santa Anna then went to Washington, where he confirmed to American officials his treaty with Texas and promised to do all he could to persuade Mexico to accept it. As a prisoner in Texas, a passenger on steamboats pushing up the Mississippi and Ohio, and a guest in Washington, Santa Anna enchanted all who met him, from President Jackson on down. He did not stress the points that his promises were made under duress and that he had already been unseated as president of Mexico. A frigid reception awaited him in Veracruz, when he returned by ship late in 1836. But no matter, he was through with politics, as he assured the world, "forever."

Conservative politicians in Mexico City had undone the liberal legislation of 1833 and maintained themselves in power during Santa Anna's absence with the grateful support of the Church and the military. Though Mexico was now under a centralist constitution, that of 1836, it still had no true government. State leaders were militarist political bosses, and the national government functioned only to the extent that armed chieftains could enforce their will. Tyranny and corruption characterized such political life as there was. Everywhere, economic and cultural retrogression contrasted with the order and slow progress of Spanish times. There was little money to be had, with the Church hoarding its supply to buy off caudillos and foreign investors no longer proving gullible. Life went on—as it always does notwithstanding the antics of politicians— but the Mexican republic presented a sorry spectacle to the world and to the few of its own citizens who cared. The strong lived well when they were not quarreling with one another, while the masses were more depressed than in Aztec times.

Meanwhile, much ill will against Mexico was piling up abroad because of the outrages committed against foreigners who suffered equally from riots and the exactions of ravenous officials. A crisis of sorts occurred in 1838, when a French expeditionary force seized the fortress of San Juan de Ulúa, thus blockading Veracruz, and demanded payment for the losses endured by subjects of King Louis Philippe. That citizen-king followed a timid diplomatic policy in Europe, where he was ridiculed as the Napoleon of Peace, but he was willing to vent the aggressions of his subjects against a weak country like Mexico. As his army settled down for a long stay, Mexico declared war on France. This was the Pastry War, so-called because one of the French claims involved a baker whose shop had been looted by Mexican soldiers. Mexico had no way of ousting the invaders from the fortress, and in the capital people seemed more absorbed in an impending conflict between a Bengal tiger and a Mexican bull in the arena than in the liberation of the soil of the republic. The United States was not inclined to brandish the Monroe Doctrine. At length, Santa Anna came forth to "save" the fatherland, thus pitting the Napoleon of the West against the Napoleon of Peace. While the former president and his peon army dallied in Veracruz, the French made a surprise descent on the city and almost captured him. Finally, the Mexican government made promises and the French sailed away, bombarding the city for good measure as they withdrew. A cannon ball happened to strike Santa Anna's leg, which had to be amputated. With sickening publicity that worthy ("the immortal three-fourths," his enemies jeered) tirelessly informed his countrymen that he had expelled the French. The credulity with which the public received his claims illustrates the low level to which Mexico had sunk.

More chaos followed: Indian uprisings in isolated mountain areas and the jungles, a popular revolt in Yucatan which removed that state from the republic for five years, attempted liberal revolutions in Mexico City, and the collision of military leaders with one another. In 1841, Santa Anna participated in a bloody rebellion and became dictator. After a few months he was bored and his followers momentarily satiated, so he retired again to Mango de Clava while a puppet congress devised another centralist constitution, that of 1843. Under the terms of this instrument Santa Anna was elected president and returned in triumph to Mexico City. For more than a year he acted the part of a regal and adored autocrat. His stimulation of popular adulation anticipated some of the more vulgar measures employed by twentieth-century dictators: organized manifestations of gratitude, ritualistic cheering, and extravagant praise in public speeches and newspapers. His amputated leg was buried in the cathedral with great reverence, much as many citizens must have smirked and cursed the proceedings in privacy. Instead of honoring his vows to the United States to recognize the independence of Texas —which no Mexican president could have done—he made ardent oaths in public that the recalcitrant province must be restored, and he effectively blocked the Texans when they grabbed for New Mexico and Tamaulipas. Behind the scenes, while the populace focused its attention on lost limbs and provinces, Santa Anna's political machine did its wretched work, printing cheap money, extorting loans, and misapplying such legitimate revenues as were collected. Army officers and government officials wallowed in riches. The Church, now much depleted in the number and quality of clergymen, managed vast estates and business enterprises.

It was not long before the restless Mexicans were plotting Santa Anna's overthrow, some to secure a redistribution of spoils, others to get rid of a disgusting tyrant. The inability of the government to meet the public payroll precipitated a crisis, though Santa Anna made things easier for his enemies by marrying a sixteen-year-old girl disgracefully soon after his wife had been buried with spectacular public mourning. The signs of impending collapse only too clear, the president fled. He was caught by some barbaric Indians who thought it would be a huge joke to boil him, wrap his remains in banana leaves, and present them to the nation as a great tamale. Dissuaded from this course by bribes, they turned him over alive to the new government, which kept him in prison for many months. At last, he was allowed to emigrate to Cuba with his new wife, who turned out to be a hellcat, and the fighting roosters he loved so well.

THE WAR WITH THE UNITED STATES

A moderate general succeeded Santa Anna but within a year the conservative Mariano Paredes pushed him aside. Paredes, no paragon, was almost as treacherous as Santa Anna, whose alternate ally and foe he had been for years. By this time, 1845, the Texas issue had come to a true crisis. Mexico had steadily insisted, sometimes with sobriety and sometimes with bluster, that it would mean war if the United States annexed the rebellious province. For nine years the republic of Texas had pleaded with Washington for admission to the Union. The long delay came about less from fear of provoking Mexico than from the reluctance of the free states to incorporate another large slave area. Texas, however, spurred the United States by negotiating more or less insincerely to join the British Empire. The victory of the expansionists in the American election of 1844 and the peaceful settlement of the Oregon dispute made it possible, in 1845, for the United States to annex Texas by a joint resolution of Congress, which required only a majority, instead of by treaty, which would have necessitated a two-thirds vote. Thus the challenge was laid down to Mexico.

Official Mexico—that musical-chairs world of generals and office-holders—reacted with great indignation. Diplomatic relations were broken off, and after Paredes became president, Mexico flatly refused to negotiate with John Slidell, the emissary of President Polk, who also hoped to buy California. It is still debated whether the American president had concluded by early 1846 that war was both certain and desirable. "Manifest Destiny," which summoned the Americans to expand on a broad front to the Pacific, was an irresistible slogan in the United States. Yet, American appetites aside, Mexico bore some share of responsibility for the war that finally came. With her moral case already weakened by Santa Anna's commitments regarding Texan independence, she undermined it further by refusing to treat with Slidell. Wars usually begin through miscalculations, and the southern republic made her share of them. One of her delusions was that England and France would be obliged to come to her aid. While those two powers had encouraged this hope, they had had a falling out by now and were incapable of concerted action.[2] Furthermore, the ignorant men who ruled Mexico imagined that Polk's position was as precarious as that of a Mexican president, and they grossly misread the significance of the antiwar sentiment of certain Americans. Finally, they were not at all sure that Mexico would be beaten. The republic had a standing army several times larger than the American and a splendid cavalry, and of course every Mexican was said to be a hero. On both sides of the disputed border reigned over-confidence and something approaching an eagerness to fight.

It took a year for the war to begin, but neither party made intelligent preparations despite all the heady war sentiment. President Polk finally took the initiative when he ordered General Zachary Taylor into the disputed area between the Nueces and Rio Grande Rivers. Mexican forces gave battle and were defeated. Polk then informed Congress that the U.S. Army had been attacked on American soil, and war was declared in May 1846. For long months nothing much seemed to happen as both sides floundered in the unfamiliar complexities of waging foreign war. Taylor managed to move his army down into the Monterrey-Saltillo area, where it camped and slowly grew as reinforcements arrived. When it attained the size of 10,000 men, it was split in two, with one half remaining under Taylor and the other entrusted to General Winfield Scott for a seaborne expedition to Veracruz. There was much confusion on the American side: political conflicts between Whigs and Democrats, rivalries among generals, the reluctance of New England to wage war, overenthusiasm in the frontier states, inexperience, graft, desertions, and amateurishness in general. But the Americans were adept at chasing Indians and hunting and could be assembled into a respectable fighting force in short order. Furthermore, the national genius for logistics, which has always proved a decisive advantage in wars involving the United

2. Their entente had been ruptured by the scandalous affair of the Spanish marriages, in which France had engineered the double wedding of Queen Isabel II with an impotent man and of her sister with Louis Philippe's son. This arrangement did not result, as expected, in the accession of the Orleans dynasty to the Spanish throne. Queen Isabel contrived to have many children, and she so outraged her subjects by her immoralities that she was driven out in 1868.

States, shone through all the blunders. The Mississippi River steamboat was a particularly important means for enabling the Americans to supply their forces in Mexico.

Meanwhile, the Mexicans made even more mistakes. Liberals and conservatives struggled for possession of the capital and the privilege of controlling the war and all the profits it entailed. As usual, caudillos switched sides and betrayed the central government and one another. Mexico's army was quite large, perhaps 45,000 men, but it was absurdly over-officered and poorly armed and supplied. On the least excuse the enlisted men would desert. During the summer of 1846 the liberals, or *puros*, captured the capital and proceeded to raise funds by confiscating Church wealth and to try to raise morale by restoring the constitution of 1824.

During this phase, in August 1846, Santa Anna reappeared in the country, avowing modestly that he came as the "slave of public opinion." How this hero got to Mexico from his Cuban exile is a circumstance that clamors for explanation. The most informed deduction is that Valentín Gómez Farías, the admirable liberal leader, believed the peacock general had the ability to rally the country and hold off the Yankees. President Polk, on the other hand, apparently had reason to think that Santa Anna would make peace as soon as Mexico had put up enough resistance to save its honor, and Polk probably gave the Mexican secret permission to pass through the U.S. naval blockade and land at Veracruz. Whether Santa Anna kept his promise or not, Polk may well have reasoned that such a mischief-maker would further confuse and demoralize the Mexicans. Whatever the facts in the case, by the turn of 1847 Gómez Farías was president of Mexico, Santa Anna was in command of an army of 25,000 men and professedly loyal to the liberal administration, and Mexico seemed determined to wage an energetic war.

Santa Anna led his forces northward to dislodge Taylor's far smaller army from the Saltillo area. Late in February his tired and ill-equipped conscripts went into battle at Buena Vista, where they attempted to overwhelm the Americans with human sea tactics. They captured most of the strong points and some banners, and Taylor was prepared to withdraw. But Santa Anna retreated first, sending messengers ahead to Mexico City to announce a glorious victory. It may have been, as in most battles, that no one really grasped what had happened and that both Taylor and Santa Anna believed themselves defeated. In any event, the Mexican success in disentangling first gave the Americans a technical triumph. Santa Anna returned to the capital as though he had won, ousted Gómez Farías as unceremoniously as he had in 1834, and organized a new government with himself as president.

In March 1847, Winfield Scott landed 10,000 troops at Veracruz after administering a bombardment that aroused much criticism in Europe on grounds of inhumanity. Emulating Cortés and his conquistadors, the Americans moved easily through the tropics and mountains into Puebla, having to fight only one significant battle. Why was there so little opposition to the American invasion? Much injury might have been inflicted if bridges had been destroyed, roads blocked, and ambushes prepared. The answer may have been that Mexico was incapable of a sustained war effort. Or, Santa Anna may have wanted to lure the enemy deep into hostile territory. From London the aged Duke of Wellington expressed the belief that Scott was foolhardy to penetrate so far. Perhaps Santa Anna was living up to his supposed bargain with Polk. But just as his treason seemed certain, he began to fight, and with great skill as well, for he was a competent general if nothing else. When the Americans descended on Mexico City, they met ferocious resistance, immortalized by the teen-aged cadets at the Castle of Chapultepec, who were massacred in a heroic defense. These terrible battles around the capital saved Mexican honor, but Scott was finally victorious. At this point, in August 1847, Santa Anna accepted a large bribe to make peace. When the congress refused to agree, he dashed off again into exile. The governor of Oaxaca, Benito Juárez, denied him permission to enter his state, and a party of Texas irregulars, bent on a lynching, almost caught him. But, after a charming party at Mango de Clava, U.S. officials got the ex-president safely to a ship and sent him away to what was surely his final exile.

Not only did Mexico City fall, but Taylor swept down from the north, and Kearny pushed west through New Mexico to California, where American naval units and small forces under Frémont had already taken over. Peace negotiations dragged on for months, with the Mexican congress reluctantly acknowledging the magnitude of the disaster and the Americans quarreling among themselves. Finally, in February 1848, the Treaty of Guadalupe Hidalgo was signed. Under its terms the United States won Texas from the Rio Grande northward, paid $15,000,000 for the enormous territory known to Americans as the Mexican Cession, and assumed all outstanding claims of U.S. citizens against Mexico. American troops soon withdrew from Mexico, but several thousand deserters and ex-soldiers elected to stay behind and seek their fortunes in the conquered land, which has seldom failed to fascinate visitors.

Defeat stunned the Mexicans and aroused a resentment that still persists. The cession of nearly half their territory hurt their pride, though they had made little use of this vast expanse. Memories of this loss, plus the ravages of the invasion and the heroism of some, made it certain that Yankeephobia would be a powerful force in Mexican life for many decades. It was easy for Mexicans to forget their own tarnished innocence as a party to the war and to blame every calamity on the *gringo.* A deep sense of despondency settled on the country. The few citizens capable of responsible planning for the national future hardened in their determination, whether it was to solidify an autocratic regime or to sweep away the power of Church, army, and landowner and build anew. Many conservatives half hoped the Americans would remain in Mexico and establish order. Others thought the republic was a farce and that monarchy should be tried again. Liberals blamed conservatives for the recent national failure and studied with growing ardor the revolutionary literature of France and Spain. The upheavals of 1848–1849 in so much of Europe stirred them. Grimly, they looked for their day of power.

DICTATORSHIP AND DECLINE

The end of the war found a moderately conservative group in nominal control of the disorganized, truncated nation. Considering the problems it faced, the regime did not do badly. At least it established some fiscal order and curbed the American filibusterers. Also, the Indians had taken advantage of the chaos to rebel—in Yucatan, to try again to secede—and it was some time before the Europeanized elements were safely back in control. Before long the ultra-conservatives seized the government from the moderate conservatives. Lucás Alamán, who for so many years had preached the virtues of centralized autocracy, now openly advocated placing a royal prince at the head of such a government. During the early 1850's, when Mexico shared with Europe a mood of reaction from the recent revolutions, his plans found much support.

Alamán sponsored a dangerous scheme to bring about this monarchy. He imagined that Santa Anna would provide the proper authoritarian prelude to Mexican acceptance of a foreign prince. Santa Anna, of course, proved amenable when a delegation approached him at his pleasant villa in New Granada. In April 1853 he landed at Veracruz to what seemed the applause of the entire nation. The pageantry of the new regime the restored president enjoyed as usual, and with it, the pleasures of graft. The title of Serene Highness, ordinarily employed for princelings, he graciously accepted, and he recreated Iturbide's Order of Guadalupe and bestowed pompous titles of nobility on the seedy sycophants and sharpsters who crowded his court. Alamán's death only two months after Santa Anna's return removed a civilizing influence which the latter would surely have ignored anyhow.

The idea of importing a foreign prince faded, for Santa Anna enjoyed being a monarch of sorts and was encouraged by the example of Louis Napoleon, who had risen to imperial rank as Napoleon III in 1852. Monarchical trappings and corruption, whose mechanics none understood better than Santa Anna, required money, always in short supply in independent Mexico. Accordingly, the president sold a piece of desert in Arizona for $10,000,000 to the United States, which was convinced it needed the land for a railway to California.[3] This amount was enough to keep the army and bureaucracy contented for a year or more, but the Gadsden Purchase, as it is known in the United States, was a further injury to Mexican self-respect. Protests were rigidly suppressed as the dictator grew more arrogant. Liberals and personal enemies of Santa Anna were set to plotting, their hopes being articulated in the famous Plan of Ayutla of early 1854, the seed of the *Reforma* so soon to bloom. But Santa Anna was confident, and later in the year he conducted a Napoleonic-style plebiscite to prove the unanimity of the country's support for his regime. The results were what he ordered, and he apparently planned to continue indefinitely selling national territory for income, while sending funds out of the country as private insurance should the sales scheme ever cease to work.

That day came sooner than Santa Anna anticipated. During the spring of 1855 his authority clearly began to disintegrate. Intelligent political combinations by liberals were removing his supporters in key positions, armies were gathering, and the country was manifestly tired of his posturing. Knowing the signs only too well from several experiences in the past, Santa Anna decided in August 1855 to flee before the storm broke. He made it to Veracruz and on to the West Indies, where he lived comfortably until some swindlers gained most of his fortune. In 1864, attempting a comeback, he offered his services to the Emperor Maximilian but was deported. Three years later he returned, only to be sent away by President Benito Juárez. Finally, in 1872, he was rightly regarded as harmless and permitted to live out his last four years in Mexico City, poor, blind, and forgotten. He was a veritable curse to his country and a charlatan to rank with the worst of any age. Even allowing for the atmosphere of Mexico of that time, one wonders how he could have won so often the support he did.

Any progress Mexico achieved during the era of Santa Anna had nothing to do with him. Agriculture continued somnolently on the basis of hacienda and peon, providing few exports and insufficient food for Mexico itself. Possibly ranching increased in importance for the simple reason that animals multiplied. Mining of silver, copper, and lead recovered in some areas, thanks mainly to foreign enterprise. But Mexico failed to discover the great deposits in the lands lost to the United States when there was a chance to do so, and the republic had nothing of the pre-eminence in mining that New Spain had enjoyed in colonial times. Commerce and minor industrial developments were largely in the hands

3. The urgency of this need is open to question. Later, the Santa Fe Railroad used a more northward route successfully.

of aliens. Their growth was small compared to that in others parts of the world during these years. Despite a few luminaries in the field of literature, scholarship, and painting, Mexican culture was very retarded. If the Church was rich and powerful, it was understaffed, and the clergy showed unusually low intellectual distinction. Santa Anna left Mexico in 1855 much worse than he had found it when he first became president.

CENTRAL AMERICA

Rafael Carrera

THE dissolution of the Confederation of Central America in 1838–1839 left Guatemala, the heart of this area, in the hands of the primitives. Rafael Carrera, whose Indian followers saw in him a messiah who would free the land from well-poisoning foreigners, was scarcely twenty-five when he led his hordes into Guatemala City to oust Morazán and the liberal modernists. The messiah was mostly Indian in ancestry, had no education, and lacked experience in everything but the care of pigs and the command of ignorant masses in a skirmish. After "saving" his homeland he was inclined to retire to the backwoods. But the traditional wielders of power—the landowners, merchants, and clergymen— saw in him a protector who would insulate Guatemala from liberal anticlericalism and, perhaps more importantly, keep the Indians docile. Carrera obliged them for twenty-seven years, until 1865. The brutal warrior not only learned to read and to comport himself with dignity but also to manipulate the apparatus of government, crude as it was in Guatemala, and to rule the educated and the ignorant alike. By degrees he slid into respectability, becoming an instrument and a leader of the possessing classes. His wealthy supporters may have ridiculed his manners and deplored his primitive methods, but they well understood his services, not the least of which was keeping the large Indian majority obedient and full of awe.

Carrera's record was mixed. For more than a quarter-century he provided order. Military and police forces did his bidding. Oppressive methods kept his opponents, mainly liberals, quiet, but for a short period in 1848–1849 when they drove him from office. Much as he suspected foreign influences, Carrera did not dislike foreigners. They were the people he could trust most, he once declared, at least in running government monopolies and collecting taxes. If immigrants were not wanted as settlers, few indeed cared to come to the picturesque land. The Church enjoyed the privileged position it had known in colonial times, though its priests were not only sadly few but less zealous and less educated than before. Carrera himself came to scorn some of the Church's pretensions; nevertheless he used it to legitimize his authority and to discipline and entertain the masses. The internal peace maintained by Carrera's methods afforded some opportunity for business development, but it was on a small scale for the simple reason that Guatemala's economy was devoted mainly to feeding its own inhabitants. As yet, coffee and tropical fruits had few markets abroad.

Much as he inveighed against the liberal confederation of the Morazán period, Carrera in time recognized the benefits of maintaining some unity in Central America. Because he thought Guatemala's neighbors must have regimes congenial to his, the dictator supported conservatives in El Salvador, Nicaragua, and Honduras. Costa Rica, however, was distant enough to resist him and usually had liberals in power. The hated confederation was not revived.

Events in the backward republic of Nicaragua illustrate the mischief that foreigners and liberals could perpetrate during these years. Two rival towns adorned that colorful state, liberal Leon and conservative Granada. Thanks to Carrera, the conservatives usually held power. The annexation of California by the United States in 1848 and the discovery of gold there greatly affected Nicaragua, which served as a link between the Caribbean and the Pacific. The Nicaraguan route was much shorter than a voyage around South America, and it was safer than a covered-wagon trek across the American West. Presently, enterprising men were operating steamship lines to Nicaraguan ports on the Caribbean. At considerable cost travelers could go upriver into and across Lake Nicaragua and then by burros and carriages to the Pacific coast and ships bound for San Francisco. For a few years British businessmen seemed to be in the best position to exploit this lucrative transit traffic, for Britain had long occupied Belize[4] and had since the 1830's exercised a protectorate over the Indian and Negro Mosquito tribes on the eastern coasts of Honduras and Nicaragua. Involved was control not only of the route but of the eventual inter-ocean canal as well. In 1850 the Clayton-Bulwer Treaty between the United States and Great Britain stabilized matters by denying either a monopoly of the isthmus. Before long, the American Cornelius Vanderbilt got the better of British rivals and developed the most successful business.

Until 1855 Carrera was not urgently involved in Nicaragua's position as a highway. In that year William Walker, a Tennessee adventurer with a flaming imagination, descended on the little republic with fifty-seven cohorts and, with the connivance of the liberals, seized its government. Many foreigners attached themselves to him, attracted by the double

4. After Central America's separation from Spain, Belize became a British crown colony, later known as British Honduras.

possibility of dominating the isthmian trade and exploiting the nation. Walker himself dreamed of large profits and even of annexation by the United States, for Nicaragua would enlarge the bloc of slave states. Already a pawn in Anglo-American rivalry, the North-South struggle in the United States, and liberal-conservative factionalism in Central America, Walker committed his worst blunder by attempting to drive Vanderbilt out of business. Presently, the terrible commodore collected ships and adventurers of his own to throw out the interloper. Liberals from Costa Rica and conservatives dispatched by Carrera were thrust into the scene. After many skirmishes Vanderbilt (and Carrera) won. Walker was ousted in 1857 and shot when he tried to restore himself in 1860. Association with Walker had so discredited the liberals that the Granada conservatives dominated Nicaragua for years.

Carerra died in 1865 at the age of fifty-one, probably as a consequence of heavy drinking. The regime he had fashioned continued for some years under different management, still unprogressive and absorbed in maintaining the privileges of the owning classes. El Salvador and Honduras, for their part, experienced much disorder as the tiresome and often meaningless struggles of factions calling themselves liberal or conservative dragged on. So did Costa Rica, though her racial homogeneity and sounder economy made such contests less squalid. If order is a virtue, which it usually is, the passing of Carrera was somewhat unfortunate for Central America. He had kept most of the area stable most of the time. If progress is a virtue, which it usually is, Carrera's death removed an obstacle. In any event, Central America was not destined to enjoy the benefits of either virtue.

HISPANIOLA

Haiti: Jean Pierre Boyer and Faustin Soulouque

WHEN Jean Pierre Boyer became president in 1818, Haiti had long been independent from the French—independent and a shambles. Terrible massacres begun in 1791 had eliminated the whites altogether and decimated the mulattoes. The population of a half-million or so was overwhelmingly black, most of them African-born or first-generation Haitians. Their languages were African with a few garbled French phrases, their religions African with traces of Catholic practice. Gradually a French patois spread as a common tongue, and a curious mixture of paganism and Catholicism known as voodoo became the general religion. Little was left of the plantations of colonial times with their great houses, sugar mills, and irrigation systems. The population dwelt simply in huts that were comfortable enough in the warm climate and grew their own food. Officials of whatever government there was occasionally forced the people to toil, very much as the slavemasters once had done, but not for long periods. Freedom was undeniably a great benefit for these people, and they cherished it passionately. But there was little with which to build a new civilization, and Haiti languished in barbarism for a century.

The only human resources for managing this Africa-in-America were the few mulattoes who had escaped extermination during the convulsions of the independence era; Jean Pierre Boyer was one of these. An heir of Alexandre Pétion, who had ruled southern Haiti, he controlled the entire island of Hispaniola for most of the time between 1818 and 1843. While his regime was not gentle, he usually preserved order without resorting to the ultimate in harshness. His fellow mulattoes formed a dominant caste, the *élite*, as they have longed styled themselves, enjoying the few fruits of profit and power and disdaining the pure Negroes. Some of the *élite* attempted to maintain ties with civilization by importing French books and periodicals and, in a few cases, by going to Paris. Gallophile though they were, they also had a fierce national pride, which they expressed by boasting that Haiti had defeated Britain, Spain, and France—even the great Napoleon. Often they asserted they had nothing to learn from such nations, a notion that kept them from making the most of such foreign contacts as they had. Actually, the Haitians had an almost psychopathic fear of being conquered by imperialistic powers. If some craved contact with the great world outside, more believed in isolation. In the long run, Haiti's links with Western civilization weakened. Even Rome was given no opportunity to restore the Church.

During Boyer's long and rather uneventful rule Haiti overran and ruined Santo Domingo, the Spanish-speaking mulatto land that shares the island of Hispaniola with her. It was this territory which paid most heavily when France served Boyer with a bill for claims incurred during the independence struggles. King Charles X had sent a naval force to support his demand for 60,000,000 francs. Louis Philippe later halved the bill, but the payments bled Haiti and her conquered neighbor, creating at once more poverty and more xenophobia. In all respects—politically, economically, socially, and culturally—the only Negro republic in the world had the lowest position in Western civilization. Possibly this did not matter to the inhabitants, who enjoyed a good climate and much leisure. Work was light and pleasures were simple. However this may have been, Boyer finally accumulated enough enemies to be overthrown and exiled in 1843.

New depths lay in store for the island republic. After the mulatto Boyer came three pure Negro generals in succession. Their gangs seized the capital, looted whatever was available, exulted in brief periods of tyranny, and were ousted by force. Santo Domingo tore itself free in 1844. A clique of mulattoes regained control of Haiti in 1847 and named as president the ex-slave Faustin Soulouque, an illiterate captain of guards thought to be so stupid that he would obey orders. His ambitions proved to be nothing less than imperial, and in 1849, after he had ousted his mulatto backers and created a machine of his own, he declared himself emperor as Faustin I. For eight years the scanty funds of the country were squandered on monarchical pageantry. Faustin and his empress lorded it over the blacks, who adored them, the sneering foreign merchants, and the intimidated mulattoes. Nothing, of course, was done to improve the country. If Faustin was not quite as furious a despot as Henri Christophe had been, his misrule was deplorable enough to win him a place of infamy in Caribbean history. In 1857 the mulattoes rallied and deposed him.

The Dominican Republic: Pedro Santana

THE hopeful group of creole planters and merchants who in 1821 proclaimed the independence of Santo Domingo, Spain's oldest colony in the New World, had intended to associate their state with the great Bolívar's Colombia. Instead, the new nation met a brutal death at the hands of Negro armies from Haiti. From 1822 to 1844 the former Santo Domingo suffered an agony long and rightly dreaded, occupation by blacks. White people were killed or driven away, or most of them were, and their lands and business houses lapsed into disuse. Dominican mulattoes and former Negro slaves existed as well as they could in a disorganized society dominated by Haitians who bore little love for them. Although President Boyer, who freed the slaves, was far from the worst of tyrants, he brought few benefits to the country. Civilized life declined precipitously, and the Spanish-speaking Dominicans endured racial oppression as well as cultural and economic degeneration. The people tended cattle and raised enough food to support themselves, but that was about all. Commerce, including the once-lucrative export of sugar, almost ceased. Churches, schools, and charitable institutions were deserted. The University of Santo Tomas closed, and so did the newspapers. Swaggering Haitians almost broke the spirit of the Dominicans. To be sure, not many Dominicans were left to suffer these ills, perhaps fifty or sixty thousand compared to ten times that many Haitians. For those who survived, however, even a semi-barbaric life on the smiling island that once enchanted Columbus was not without its attractions.

The fall of Boyer and subsequent squabbling in Haiti gave the Dominicans their opportunity. In 1844 a group assembled and proclaimed independence once again, this time from an oppressor far worse than

Spain. Actually, appeals went to Spain itself as well as other powers to support the Dominicans against the Haitians, who certainly intended to reassert their control. During these events Pedro Santana emerged as the strong man of the new republic, though he had many competitors and never gained enough strength to become a despot. A mulatto, mostly white, he had a little education, some property, and a real talent for leadership. Commanding the most powerful military band, he was able to seize the capital and take the first steps toward organizing an administration under constitutional forms. When his presidential term was over, he allowed his better-educated rival, Buenaventura Báez, to succeed him. This coincided with the establishment of Faustin I's monarchy in Haiti. The violent Haitian tyrant vowed he would kill everything in the Dominican area, including the chickens. Fortunately, this threat broke against the valiant defense of the Dominican forces led by Santana.

Santana was president three more times, alternating uneasily with Báez. Both of these men did reasonably well, if allowance is made for their difficulties. Their country was poor; it was almost without schools or trained leaders; its shops were very modest, its farms and ranches unproductive, and its annual public revenue barely $650,000. If there was to be any chance for recovery, something must be done to discourage further Haitian aggression. Báez more than Santana understood this necessity, and he urgently sought the assistance of foreign powers. Santana's conception was simpler, and more disastrous. In power again after defeating Báez in 1858, he intrigued with the government of Isabel II of Spain for the re-entry of his country into the Spanish monarchy. In 1861, just as the United States was immobilized by the Civil War, the Dominican Republic became a captaincy-general in the Spanish empire. While the Spain of Isabel II was almost as ungovernable as her daughter nations in America, its self-confidence was still serenely untouched by realities. The reunion began auspiciously enough, with more enthusiasm in Madrid than in Santo Domingo.

Santana, who was named captain-general, expected to preside over a wholesome reconciliation. The Spanish, however, had learned and forgotten nothing. They dispatched more than 20,000 troops to the forgiven colony, and with them hordes of clergymen who found many traces of paganism and Protestantism to correct. Judges, tax gatherers, and *corregidores* from the peninsula were also over-active. Soon the Dominicans became restive. National independence seemed too precious to exchange for the collection of policies the Spaniards called "culture." Disappointed at the puny authority he was allowed to exercise, Santana resigned in 1862, when he was given a title of nobility. He stuck with his bargain and helped the Spanish thwart Dominicans who objected to the new regime. In 1864 he died, possibly by suicide, his reputation partially salvaged by his protests against Spanish methods. In Haiti, meanwhile, the government supported Dominican refugees and egged them on, for Napoleon III might take a notion to copy Isabel II and bring French civilization back to the former colony. Mutinies, killings, skirmishes, and small uprisings constituted what Dominicans call the War of Restoration. During 1864 the population grew increasingly rebellious. Spanish strong-arm practices made things worse, and yellow fever carried off enough Spaniards to cause the survivors to become all the more impatient with opposition. Of more importance were the end of the Civil War in the United States and a revulsion against imperialism in Madrid. In May 1865, Isabel II, prudent for once in her unfortunate reign, agreed to give up the attempt at reunion. Spain withdrew, more hateful than ever in Latin American eyes. Perhaps the most enduring result of Santana's scheme was a considerable whitening of Dominican complexions.

VENEZUELA

José Antonio Páez

VENEZUELA has been a land of dictators. Never experiencing for long either the calm life of a lawful democratic republic or the chaos of civil wars, she has known several very different and long-lived tyrants. The people, accordingly, have grown accustomed to hating while flatter-ing and expecting to be cheated after a brief period following the fall of each dictator. After the Bolivarian period, the first and possibly the best of the line of autocrats was José Antonio Páez, who was the dominant figure from 1819 to 1846. He returned to power in 1861–1863, to com-plete a span of almost thirty years as master of Venezuela.

A mestizo like most of his countrymen, Páez was a natural leader of men. He had begun as a daring cowboy in the *llanos*, the grasslands that stretch from the coastal highlands southward to an indefinite frontier beyond the Orinoco. His exploits during the Wars of Independence made him a national hero. During the years from 1819 to 1829, when Bolívar was usually titular president but absent most of the time, Páez held the true authority as the Liberator's lieutenant. He ruled with considerable flair, for he was no mere caudillo but a man who could grow. In the long intervals between the deliriously-welcomed visits of Bolívar, Páez devel-oped stature as a respected chieftain and a beloved figure above all par-ties and factions. They needed a firm hand. Enormous material damage had followed the several campaigns of liberation and restoration. Thou-sands had been killed, families divided, towns burned, Caracas sacked, and once-productive plantations returned to nature. Páez proved a unifier and won the respect of the populace. His withdrawal of Venezuela from Gran Colombia in 1829 was a highly popular step, much as it wounded the Liberator.

No leader in Latin America could rely for long on popularity. Páez' real source of power was the *llaneros*, whose emotional attachment to him was very much like the gauchos' veneration of Rosas in the Argentine. Whether organized as irregular bands or military units, they responded whenever their chieftain needed them. Negroes and Indians also revered Páez, for he had a psychical power, it seemed, that answered the longing of these groups for a master. His major preoccupation was keeping the whites from organizing against him. As in other countries, the plantation owners and business classes dominated the economic life of the republic. Often well-educated and elegant, they formed an aristocracy that was well-knit socially but chaotically divided in political philosophy. Because he was shrewd and had the *llaneros* to back him, Páez was long able to cow the upper classes. Yet he also sought to placate them, and, in so doing, he came more and more to ape them. His cronies had reason to suspect their old hero of selling out to his social betters.

Such a view was not altogether fair, though Páez' manners and dress improved and he disliked being reminded that he was a mestizo. While he was no philosopher, he understood better than most rulers of his type that primitive forces were never far below the surface in South America. If the traditional pattern of autocracy, latifundia, and clericalism were altered, as it had been during the Wars of Independence, much bloodshed could ensue. His policy, then, was to conserve and repair the fabric of society while conciliating all groups. He was far more successful than most of his contemporaries. A constitution he sponsored in 1830 established a republic apparently satisfactory to liberals but in fact oligarchical. A degree of liberty rare in Latin America was permitted, and in 1834 religious toleration was granted. The constitution, furthermore, by maintaining as reasonable a balance between local and national power as could be expected, postponed in Venezuela the inevitable clash of federalists and centralists. It was Páez' intention to instill constitutional habits in his people, and he outwardly respected congress, local authorities, the courts, and electoral processes. But when armed conspirators sought to spoil his handiwork, the caudillo-president was ready to spring at them with his faithful *llaneros*. For four years the country made considerable progress. Plantations, ranches, and Indian communities were restored to something like their colonial prosperity. Foreign trade flourished, Venezuela exporting hides, cotton, indigo, and cacao in exchange for finished goods. When his term was over in 1835,

Páez virtuously stepped down from the presidency in favor of his chosen successor, the rector of the University of Caracas.

Within a few months a group of soldier-politicians unceremoniously ousted the new president and proposed to initiate barracks rule. Like the father of his people he claimed to be, and to a large extent was, Páez summoned his *llaneros* to defend the constitution. The upstarts were chastised, and the rector resumed the presidency. In 1839 Páez again became president. During his second term the economic progress fostered by orderly government was all the more striking, so much so that immigration spurted briefly. In other directions modest constructive efforts were fruitful. The government built roads, ended the slave trade, opened a few schools, and revived the program to civilize frontier Indians, who had hitherto been outside the social structure. Finances were so well-managed that the national debt was paid. Páez withdrew special privileges from the Church and disbanded monasteries in an effort to appease the liberals and strengthen the state. He also had the remains of Bolívar brought to Caracas and interred with moving ceremonies that possibly assuaged the sense of guilt felt by many Venezuelans for their earlier defection from the Liberator. In 1843, Páez, now a patriarch bearing the title of "Most Illustrious Citizen," retired a second time to his rural properties, leaving the presidency again in the hands of a man who would obey him.

Páez probably intended to perpetuate his domination of the republic indefinitely. His popularity seemed secure and his supporters faithful. He believed he had won the aristocracy over while conciliating the liberals and retaining his hold on the masses. Yet his grip was looser than he knew. Liberals were not so easily quieted, and a strong undercurrent of left-wing feeling swept up many urban youths and assorted idealists and schemers. The masses had venerated the old *llanero* long enough; a new generation now wanted other heroes. Between 1846 and 1848 the realities of the situation became apparent as José Tadeo Monagas, a president expected to do the bidding of Páez, displayed a will of his own. Staffing the administration with his supporters and pressing for liberal legislation, Monagas was soon deadlocked with congress, which was loyal to Páez. Harsh words, defiant gestures, threats, shots, and killings led to a civil war in 1847. Páez bounded from retirement to protect the congress, summoning the *llaneros* as he had often done before. This time his appeal failed, and Monagas won the first crucial skirmishes. Exiled, Páez plotted to recover power by invading from New Granada but was imprisoned for his attempt and exiled again.

For a dozen years Monagas and his younger brother alternated in the presidency and fought off rivals. The final abolition of Negro slavery was

the most notable achievement of their regime, which was a tight dictatorship despite its liberal slogans. By 1860 the country was torn by a
confusing civil war over cloudy issues, one that supposedly pitted liberals
or "Yellows" against conservatives or "Blues," though in fact it was a
struggle for power by various caudillos and their uncomprehending irregular soldiers. Old Páez, now past seventy, returned and found himself welcomed again by the Blues. In 1861 he resumed the presidency
for an uneasy period of frankly conservative rule. Little as he realized it,
Venezuela had grown far away from him. His name no longer had
much appeal, and his followers would support him only temporarily. A
revolt toppled the old warrior in 1863. Páez lived on for another decade,
mostly in New York and Buenos Aires. He lectured for fees about the
great days of Bolívar and the Wars of Independence. To many he
seemed a garrulous bore, a professional liberator, a relic of times past.

NEW GRANADA-COLOMBIA

Tomás Cipriano de Mosquera

IT IS often observed that disorders in New Granada, or Colombia as it was called after 1863, had a dignity not ordinarily discernable in accounts of Latin American strife. Convictions counted for much,
men fought for ideals and took moral questions seriously, and rebellions
and civil wars had real issues. Another unusual quality of the republic's
evolution is that revolutions seldom unseated the government at Bogotá, and also that strong men were rarely able to hold their followers
faithful to them for long periods. On the other hand, it must be admitted that Colombian politicians have been notoriously tricky and
fractious, that intellectuals have been passionate but often foolish, and
that mere lawlessness, banditry, and teen-age criminality account for
many of the battles supposedly fought for principles. Whether or not
Colombia is regarded as a crucible of politics, it justified itself as a republic during the nineteenth century and emerged for a fine career in
the twentieth. All this occurred notwithstanding its awkward geography
that cut if off from neighbors and easy contact with the advanced nations of the world, a geography that permitted settlement in only one-
third of its territory and divided that section so badly with mountain
ranges and steamy valleys that nationhood seemed an impossible goal.

As has been seen, the great Santander was not to be typed easily as a
conservative or liberal. His successor, Dr. José Ignacio Márquez, was
elected in 1836 in spite of his disapproval but in the main continued
Santander's policies. For more than two years Márquez seemed suc-

cessful, until, in 1839, he made the mistake of suppressing four monasteries in the clerical province of Pasto in order to use the buildings as public schools and to send the friars into evangelical labors among the Indians. A nasty insurrection followed, one which curiously took the turn of opposing President Márquez for being too friendly to the Church. A civil war was still going on in 1840 when congress chose Pedro Alcántara Herrán as president to succeed Márquez. Herrán was admittedly a conservative, and he recalled the Jesuits, who had been ousted by Carlos III in 1767 and again by the republic in 1819. These black-robed marvels of efficiency, whom liberals considered demons of intellectual dishonesty and political conniving, straightway revived the teaching of Roman law in the colleges, thus implicitly supporting autocratic ideals, and began the exploration of the enormous jungle of the southeast. As President Herrán managed to calm New Granada's strife, another important development occurred, the beginning of coffee-raising on a massive scale in the western upper valley of the Cauca. This project was largely the work of Mariano Ospina, an enterpriser and publicist who articulated many of the ideas of the conservatives. Reactionary as he seemed to many, he perhaps inadvertently promoted social democracy by inspiring the government to sell public lands in small parcels to coffee farmers.

Herrán's successor was a strange man named Tomás Cipriano de Mosquera, who took office as president in 1845. A hero of the Wars of Independence, this conservative was so brilliant and unsettling that his own brother, the archbishop of Bogotá, is said to have opposed his election. Yet Mosquera ruled for four years as a conservative, though an enlightened one. He did not seek to obliterate liberalism and was even tolerant with his opponents, and, while he was attached to ideals of strong government and social stability, he shared the fervor of the liberals for material progress. By subsidizing the purchase of steamboats for the Magdalena River he facilitated the traffic of goods, persons, and ideas between Bogotá and the coast, and beyond. The province of Panama suddenly became prosperous as thousands of foreigners crossed it to reach California, and Mosquera negotiated the Bidlack Treaty of 1846 with the United States to ease the passage of American citizens, in exchange for which Washington promised to protect the isthmus from British encroachments. All in all, Mosquera's first term was one of comparative order, advances, and enlightenment. Somewhat wistfully, the president said he wished people would call him a progressive, and well they might.

By the time Mosquera's term ended in 1849, New Granada was in ferment as a result of the European revolutions of 1848–1849. Bogotá, whose citizens liked to call their city the "Athens of America," was more like an imitation Paris. As in France, many had made a cult of the great Revolution of 1789 and considered themselves Girondins; others, particularly students, had become interested in socialism. Not only intellectuals, but shopkeepers and artisans in several cities, concerned themselves with ultra-democratic ideas from Europe and participated in left-wing clubs. When it came time to choose a successor for Mosquera, the congress found itself under pressure, like the Legislative Assembly or the Convention in one of the great *journées* of the French Revolution. Clamorous students, intellectuals, and assorted liberal folk shouted from the galleries, and outside were menacing street crowds. In order to save their lives the deputies voted for the liberal candidate, José Hilario López.

During most of the years between 1849 and 1880 the liberals were to dominate the republic. In the delirious first months of the López administration, so like the mood of European capitals in 1848, the liberals joyfully attacked the ecclesiastical establishment. The Jesuits were pulled out of the jungle and the colleges and sent away. Tithes were ended, divorce legalized, Church courts abolished, the archbishop and two bishops expelled, and full religious liberty proclaimed. Church and state were separated,[5] though local governments were allowed to pay the expenses of public worship if they cared to. The López administration also ended slavery, which had persisted despite Bolívar's and Santander's decrees a generation earlier, and the death penalty. A constitution proclaimed in 1853 incorporated these measures and was so federalist that New Granada seemed to be aping Switzerland. Local governments were to be almost autonomous, all adult males were to be allowed to vote, practically all officials were to be elected, and, to assure the equality of these last with the rest of humanity, they were to be addressed as "Citizen," not by any other title.

President López complemented his political liberalism with the proclamation of economic freedom. He ended the century-old tobacco monopoly and most import and export duties. But the country did not respond by becoming more prosperous. Its economy uneven and often fragile since the revolt against Spain in 1810, New Granada became further depressed as ex-slaves walked away from plantations and mines and the weakening of government controls permitted disorders. Yet the liberals were able to elect another president in 1853, General José María Obando, who had been many things to many men in his time and was now an ultra-democrat. Within a year he was overthrown, and his liberal successor had to take to the field to put down a spate of conservative revolts in the provinces. Then he, too, was overthrown. New Granada seemed to be disintegrating. The federalist constitution had

5. For the first time in Latin America.

cut the communities loose from Bogotá and had turned the country into a riot of entities often ruled by local caudillos. Gradually, the conservatives gained the upper hand, enough to force the election, if it can be called that, of Mariano Ospina as president in 1857.

Staunch friend of conservatism and coffee culture that he was, the new president had been dismayed by the course of events since 1849. But he was unable to put the country back on what he regarded as its rightful course. He attempted to appease the liberals and federalists by proclaiming a new constitution, that of 1858, which re-christened the republic the Confederation of New Granada, a term that implied extreme federalism. This short-lived charter was about the only landmark of Ospina's administration—this and the return of the Jesuits. The country was, in truth, ungovernable, and the liberals were not to be deceived by the nation's new name. In 1860 a terrible civil war began when the national government presumed to inspect the electoral procedures of the states, thus assuring the perpetuation of the party in power in Bogotá. The secession of eleven American states in the next few months was also an inspiration to many parts of New Granada. By July 1861 Ospina was a prisoner, the Jesuits were on their way out again, and the liberals were back in Bogotá. General Tomás Cipriano de Mosquera was clearly in command of the situation.

Although he had been a conservative president from 1845 to 1849, Mosquera was by now a liberal. Some said he had undergone a conversion, others that he was erratic and opportunistic, and not a few that he was insane. There was basis for all three opinions. He undoubtedly planned to be a dictator, the first in the nation's history since Bolívar. Yet he obeyed the rules by calling a convention to draw up a new constitution, that of 1863, which re-stated most of the points of the liberal-federalist charter of 1853. Happily, Mosquera decided that it was time to abandon "New Granada," with its viceregal connotation, and to revert to the Liberator's choice, "Colombia," as the name for the republic.

The United States of Colombia, as it was now called, was no democracy. Mosquera killed, jailed, and exiled his opponents, censored the press, and cracked the whip over the population. It was typical of Colombia that the people refused to accept this sort of thing for long. The convention had the temerity to limit presidents to a two-year term without eligibility for immediate reelection. Thus Mosquera left the presidency in 1864, but he still managed behind the scenes. In 1866 he returned to the office, giving ever more signs of megalomania, though in his favor it may be recalled that South American countries were fearful of a Spanish reconquest at that time and some of his measures were designed to defend Colombia. It developed that he had violated the constitution by making a secret treaty with Peru against Spain. Mosquera's enemies in congress intrigued with military units in Bogotá to arrest the president in 1867. He was tried for abusing his powers, convicted, and sent into exile.

For the next dozen years or more the Colombians cherished the idea that dictators were not to be tolerated. A succession of weak presidents, serving two-year terms without immediate reelection, and an assertive congress, which was anything but a collection of sycophants, virtually gave the country a parliamentary form of government. Liberals and the more leftist democrats remained in power, and local bosses or governments had a large measure of autonomy. One of the conspicuous features of public life was the free expression of opinions. Numerous newspapers and journals were given to polemics; coffee houses were full of students, lawyers, writers, shopkeepers, and politicians who gloried in controversies; in congress, politicians were more likely to cultivate a splendid oratorical style and to affect learning than to boast of military prowess. Probably no other Latin American city was as sophisticated in the world of ideas as Bogotá. Politics was not the only concern. Currents in poetry, drama, and the novel stirred the *bogotanos*. They read, wrote, and criticized with real passion. Among the numerous writers of the time two are especially memorable. Jorge Isaacs (1837–1895), a Catholic of English Protestant and Jewish background, wrote a beautiful novel, *María*, which was both realistic and sentimental. José María Semper (1828–1888) was almost everything: money-maker, prolific writer, politician, lawyer, diplomat, and editor. Of his countless publications the most significant dealt with the fundamental concerns of the country: its heritage, problems, and prospects. He did something to prepare the way for an anti-liberal reaction. Colombian poets were numerous; then as now, nearly every self-respecting *bogotano* wanted to be a versifier.

While Bogotá was the political and cultural capital of Colombia, it had only forty or fifty thousand inhabitants and was not the largest city. Cartagena, long in decline since the great days of the Spanish monopoly, and Popayán, in the rapidly-developing Cauca Valley, surpassed the capital in size. In general, the republic was increasing its foreign trade, selling more coffee, sugar, rubber, cacao, and fine woods year by year. Road-building on a considerable scale improved business, and so did a few short railroads, though a country as rugged as Colombia could never expect to have an advanced system of surface transportation. Steamboats and barges on the great rivers, as well as donkey caravans, remained the chief means of travel. While Colombia was tasting enough fruits of the Industrial Age to crave more, the bulk of the population lived as though no material progress had been made for the past century. Such considerations preyed on the minds of intellectuals who knew what was going on in more advanced lands. A congressman and writer named Rafael Núñez caught the mood of many influential persons in 1878 and 1879 when he preached regeneration, the need of Colombia to pull itself together and join the march of progress.

Rafael Núñez

NÚÑEZ is indeed an odd historical figure, far more interesting and seminal than most of his contemporaries. Furthermore, his effect on succeeding generations has been very strong. Born in 1825 in Cartagena, this thin, nervous, articulate fellow was a fiery radical in his youth. He wrote easily and well, his essays being thoughtful and his poems appealing. At one time he was probably a socialist; at least he belonged to the extreme democratic wing of the liberals. After serving in various capacities in liberal administrations during the 1850's he went to Europe as a foreign service officer in 1863. There he remained for thirteen years, reading, writing, and above all, observing. This was the period of Napoleon III and Bismarck, the reaction from the revolutions of 1848. Núñez was impressed with the great material growth Europe was experiencing under their enlightened demi-autocracy and with the doctrines that were drawn from the Darwinian theory, the hard-headed ideas that the fittest survived and the weak succumbed. Political conservatism was thus indicated, though he continued to call himself a liberal.

Back in Colombia by 1876, he ran for president and lost. Then he became governor of the state of Bolívar, proof that he carried weight with the liberal bosses, and went to congress in 1878. By 1880 the moderate liberals, with more or less covert support from the long-suffering conservatives, elected him president. Apart from representing the dominant mood of his time, Núñez had another advantage in the $10,000,-000 which a French company paid Colombia for the right to dig a canal across Panama. The new president set out to tighten up the government in every respect, a purpose that attracted many supporters. Moderate liberals were weary of the democrats and tended to blame a fall in coffee prices on them rather than on the world depression. Conservatives had long been gathering strength, for Colombia remained basically Catholic and clerical and disapproved of the way the liberals had injured the Church. By 1882 Núñez was able to impose his heir in the presidency, and in 1884 he returned to that office for what proved to be the rest of his life, ten years. His technique was to man the administration with "reformed" liberals and conservatives at first, and then entirely with conservatives. Soon he created a new party, the National, which drew together the dominant elements of the country. This was not achieved without force. A civil war in 1884–1885 showed that the liberals were still potent. But Núñez won, and he was by now an outright dictator.

Núñez made his autocratic regime legitimate in the constitution of 1886, a frankly centralist and reactionary document. Henceforth the president was to be elected for six years, not two, by a restricted popular vote. States were to become departments ruled by officials appointed from Bogotá. The Church was restored as the official partner of the state, and national codes replaced local codes for civil and criminal procedures. The president could declare a state of siege whenever he feared resistance, and he could supplement laws by far-reaching decrees. In itself the constitution was not of momentous significance, for constitutions come and go in Latin America, though this one was to serve Colombia well until 1936. But Rafael Núñez proved equal to enforcing it, even if he resorted to censorship and violations of human rights. He was sensible enough to permit local governments to handle their own affairs so long as they were obedient to his over-all policies, and he consoled the anticlericals by permitting religious dissenters to be left alone. He· also brought back the Jesuits, who did not fail to strengthen his regime in the educational system and in Indian territory. On the last day of 1887 his representative signed a concordat with the Vatican which restored the Church to the high position it had enjoyed in colonial times. Núñez also lectured his congress, officials, and the population at large about regenerating the country within the historic framework of Catholic order and Christian charity.

So effective was Núñez' regime by 1888 he was able to retire for long periods to his plantation near Cartagena and to send orders and advice to his servants in Bogotá. He dreamed, wrote, and thought. Often he was troubled by doubts, for the youthful liberal sometimes haunted this aging adult. Yet he was convinced that he, like Díaz in Mexico, had found the solution for political instability and economic backwardness. One of his contributions to Colombia was its national anthem, whose words he wrote. Autocrat and mentor, his thoughts have long guided conservatives in Colombia. Núñez died in 1894, after giving his country the longest period of internal peace it had enjoyed since it left the Spanish monarchy. Not much else can be credited to him, though this is no small blessing. Alien investors were still unimpressed with Colombia's potential wealth. The population remained largely unschooled and impoverished, living on crops they grew but selling comparatively few of them abroad. Censorship and political oppression did much to destroy a long tradition of liberty. Núñez left the nation in peace but with its conservatives and liberals as self-righteous as ever and with the cleavage between them still very sharp.

ECUADOR

Juan José Flores

THE Republic of the Equator already had a ruler when it seceded in 1830 from Bolívar's Colombia. General Juan José Flores had been for several years in charge of the principal military force and had established himself as a spokesman for the ruling groups. A mestizo of Venezuelan birth, Flores was thirty at the time of the secession and had already spent half his life in the army. Despite undistinguished parentage and little education, he had advanced rapidly. Like most of Bolívar's lieutenants, he was a gifted man, a brave and able soldier, and, if aggressively ambitious, something of a statesman. His marriage into Quito's aristocracy, which was still full of noblemen and was not greatly changed since colonial days, made him acceptable as a political leader. But what was he to lead? Ecuador was not a nation but only the most artificial of states. Its eastern jungles were almost unexplored and entirely uncivilized. Guayaquil, the torrid, disease-infested seaport on the Pacific, was a reasonably busy city with a motley population and not a few liberals among its prosperous classes. Quito, a beautiful colonial city nestling among snow-capped mountains, was conservative and clerical. The rest of the country consisted of mountains and valleys. The population was overwhelmingly Indian. Not since Inca days had they lived well or felt themselves a part of society.

Yet Flores' creation has endured, and national sentiment has slowly formed, beginning with the few thousand whites and spreading gradually to the others. Flores ruled autocratically, as he had to, but he was no despot. He labored with intelligence to keep order, itself a full-time occupation, and to build the institutions essential for running an organized society. His seizure of the Galápagos Islands is accounted an achievement, though the giant tortoises remained undisturbed but for the terrible birds that prey on their young and the company of exiled Ecuadorian politicians. Guayaquil wanted to be the Buenos Aires of the area and resented the authority Flores exercised from Quito, which was almost inaccessible from the coast. Even in Quito a newspaper, *El Quiteño libre*, voiced criticisms of the president's tight rule. And the continued presence of "foreigners," the New Granadans and Venezuelans, including Flores himself, who had entered the country as liberators, was annoying to natives who classified themselves as patriots. Yet Flores remained in control of the situation and ostentatiously surrendered the presidency when his term ended in 1835.

Flores' successor was the opposition leader, Vicente Rocafuerte, a liberal orator and journalist from Guayaquil who had known Miranda in Europe and had been a member of the liberal Spanish *cortes*. His accession to the presidency was the result of a political bargain he had made with Flores while the latter's prisoner. The arrangement between the two men provided that they would alternate as chief executive, with Flores at all times keeping control of the military. It was by no means an evil agreement, and Flores loyally permitted Rocafuerte to carry out his own policies, vaguely liberal, between 1835 and 1839. Rocafuerte established eighty schools and otherwise sought to modernize the republic. When Flores returned to office, however, he swung away from liberalism and, instead, strengthened the forces of tradition identified with Quito. He even restored the Indian tribute. His taste for power growing, Flores decided to end the arrangement with Rocafuerte by having himself reelected president in 1843. Rocafuerte accepted a large bribe as consolation and emigrated, but the Guayaquil liberals were highly dissatisfied. In 1845 they rebelled and defeated the government forces. Now it was Flores' turn to receive financial consolation and remove himself.

For the next fifteen years Ecuador went through political convulsions as the two cities and the two philosophies competed, their instruments being, as usual, ambitious and often brutal caudillos who cared little for ideology. Economic conditions remained bad, foreign trade languished, and the security of property depended on the guns. The Church suffered punishment whenever the liberals had the upper hand and enjoyed favor when the conservatives won. Flores did not prove willing to remain out of the scene. Soon after his ouster he intrigued with María Cristina, the mother of Queen Isabel II of Spain, to restore Ecuador to the Spanish crown. An expedition gotten up for this purpose was kept from sailing only by British threats inspired by the pleadings of other South Americans. In the early 1850's Flores tried to invade Ecuador from Peruvian soil but was turned back. In 1860, however, his forces captured Guayaquil and probably expected to install him as president again.

Gabriel García Moreno

THE beneficiary of the military actions of 1860 was not Flores, who still had many enemies, but a younger man named Gabriel García Moreno. Born in 1821 at Guayaquil of white parents, Moreno gew up a studious lad inclined to resent the liberators both because they were foreigners and because his family had been impoverished during the independence period. Bold and willful, he once lay in wait all night hoping to kill President Flores, who happened not to pass that way.

Having acquired all the education he could in Ecuador through scholarships, young García Moreno attended the University of Paris during a period when he felt it unsafe to live in his native land. On his return he became a professor of science at the University of Quito and for two years was rector of that honorable institution. He was an able writer and orator, and as a senator he proved skillful in judging the political tides that swept his chaotic country; he advocated constructive conservatism and civilianism, two issues that had become popular during the recent period of radical demagoguery and militarism. Now allied to Flores, he loomed as the most satisfactory candidate for president, and the assembly so elected him in 1861.

It was not long before the civilian intellectual, so schoolmasterish in manner, demonstrated his political acumen. He deftly removed or obscured his potential rivals and benefited from the death of Flores. Liberals found themselves intimidated into silence or exile. The president became both popular and respected. Order, conservative policies, and clericalism satisfied the aristocrats and the nation in general. When his term was up in 1865, García Moreno went abroad on a diplomatic mission. The next two presidents in the line of succession failed to maintain order, liberals clamored and plotted, and a terrible earthquake in 1868 left such confusion that demands went up for a restoration of García Moreno's strong hand. This he supplied in 1869, when he resumed the presidency for a final tenure of six years, until murder ended his career in 1875.

García Moreno has a highly distinctive stamp as a Latin American dictator. A civilian, upright, modest in dress, and scholarly, he was the reverse of the typical caudillo. Conspicuous above all was his clericalism, based not on guile but on something bordering on fanaticism. He delivered Ecuador into the power of the pope as though it were a thirteenth-century kingdom. That symbol of reaction, the Society of Jesus, returned in triumph, and other orders were effusively welcomed. These friars came not only to clericalize the little republic but also to staff the educational establishment. Schools increased from fewer than 200 to more than 500, and some of them, surprisingly enough, were provided for women and Indians. The university was reorganized to combat what García Moreno regarded as the curse of the century, liberalism. Colleges were invigorated; a museum, conservatory, observatory, and fine arts school were established. Perhaps of most enduring significance was the creation of a polytechnic school to train engineers, architects, and scientists. Smothered as these institutions may have been by clericalism, they represented a giant step forward in modernizing Ecuador. As a culmination of his religious program García Moreno reverently dedicated the republic to the Sacred Heart of Jesus. If this action produced amusement abroad, another caused annoyance. Little Ecuador embarrassed diplomats by trying to organize a clerical army to rescue the pope from Italian power after the annexation of Rome in 1870.

In other ways the strange dictator promoted the progress of his country. Well-planned efforts to spur commerce and diversify the economy brought the first real stimulation to Ecuador since Spanish days, though of course poverty remained the norm for most people. A splendid road was built from Quito down to Guayaquil, one which won admiration from foreign experts. Others were completed in an effort to unify the small but mountainous land. A railroad was begun, and port facilities in Guayaquil were greatly improved. Furthermore, the regime was reasonably efficient and honest, García Moreno himself entirely so. Yet it was an autocracy that oppressed liberals and anti-clericals. In secrecy they met and plotted against the tyrant. Finally, in 1875, a group of youths ambushed the president as he entered the government palace and hacked him to death with machetes.

BOLIVIA

Andrés Santa Cruz

AFTER the departure of Sucre in 1828 the republic of Bolivia surprisingly remained upright. An assembly of notables composed of several hundred educated men—almost all the country had in this category—assumed the sovereignty of the nation. At first it was a howling mass of dissidents, then a frightened huddle of respectable men cowering before unruly soldiers outside its doors. Because of its confusion, this conventional assembly has gone down in history as "the convulsional assembly." Peruvian army leaders, who had "liberated" the republic by invading it and occupying Chuquisaca, suggested, and the assembly gratefully accepted, a solution. It was that Grand Marshal Andrés Santa Cruz, then in Arequipa, Peru, be invited to become president of Bolivia. Santa Cruz was willing and arrived for what proved to be a rule of ten years. He was far more successful than most of his contemporaries in South America and a worthy successor to Sucre but for one fatal flaw, inflamed ambition.

Santa Cruz was what the Peruvians and Bolivians call a *cholo*, a mestizo. His father was a Spanish sub-delegate in Upper Peru and his mother an Indian aristocrat who claimed descent from Inca royalty. Born in the area later known as Bolivia, Santa Cruz had served in the royalist army until he was captured by the patriots, at which point he wisely switched sides. He was an excellent officer, careful of his men and relying on sound

strategy instead of brilliant tactical strokes to win battles. He was promoted by San Martín for his services in 1821 and again by Bolívar. A
general and then a grand marshal, he was one of the half dozen ablest
leaders in Peru. Bolívar had twice left him in charge at Lima as provisional president, and he seemed as much a Peruvian as a Bolivian in
1829. He was solid rather than glamorous; broad-chested, dark, and
expressionless; except for the rare times when his eyes burned with
ferocity, he looked the Indian. Santa Cruz was cruel even for his times.
Whatever sensitivity he felt because he was part Indian he transformed
into an almost insane pride in his supposed Inca heritage.

The constructive work of Santa Cruz as president of Bolivia commands admiration. He drafted a constitution not greatly different from
the one Bolívar had given the country in 1826, which assured the president full powers while extending a semblance of authority to congress.
His prestige was sufficient to compel the army to obey, or at least to
discourage its officers from plotting against him. Santa Cruz continued
and extended the work of Sucre in organizing government administration and finances, and he was honest in handling funds. His plans for
improving the economy and raising the standards of the Indians were
commendable. He restored the two universities, opened a medical college, and expanded the courts of justice. In nearly every respect Santa
Cruz ruled with firmness and intelligence. For several years Bolivia's internal peace contrasted favorably with the chaos of her neighbors.

Unwilling to be content with the modest destiny of administering
Bolivia well, Santa Cruz surrendered to tempting dreams. In earlier
years he had said that Bolivia must be the Macedonia of South America,
a military state to conquer its more advanced neighbors. Now his reverie
turned to the glorious Inca past, romanticized in the central Andes just
as the Aztec past was in Mexico then. Santa Cruz knew that, as a great
soldier and administrator, he had many admirers among the propertied
classes in Peru. An heir of the Inca, he might unite the shattered Andean
world as no other man could. Perhaps a crown would be a suitable reward for such an achievement.

Santa Cruz did not rush matters. Not until 1835, when Peru had become a confused mess of military districts ruled by jealous generals, did
he force opportunity. After a highly complicated series of negotiations
with various generals, he marched into southern Peru and asserted his intention to rule. So far his move was on sound ground, for the population of the south was Indian and not displeased at being united with
Bolivia under a *cholo*. Northern Peru was a different matter, despite the
favorable signs among the Lima aristocracy that Santa Cruz had earlier
discerned. There the viceregal tradition was strong, and not a few patriots
felt that white Lima should dominate the mountains, not the other way

around. Personifying this conception was Felipe Salaverry, who took over as president of Peru. The partisans of Santa Cruz, plunging ahead, defeated and shot Salaverry. In 1836 Santa Cruz himself rode into the old capital. Public opinion changed again as it was argued that Santa Cruz was, after all, not only an estimable ruler of Bolivia but also a field marshal and former provisional president of Peru. Conservatives hoped he would bring order; liberals looked for reforms. Having triumphed with comparative ease, Santa Cruz announced a new state, the Peruvian-Bolivian Confederation. He would be protector of the whole entity and under him would serve presidents for Bolivia, southern Peru, and northern Peru. Perhaps other republics could be induced to join.

Probably the plan could not have worked for long, still less evolved into a Hispano-Inca monarchy, whatever Santa Cruz might have done. The *limeños* were too fickle and too quick to find fault. Peruvian generals were accustomed to defying the central government and competing with one another. The ruin of the confederation, however, came about from foreign interference rather than internal stresses. None of its neighbors was pleased with the new creation. Ecuador, whose army was controlled then by Flores during an interval between presidencies, well knew that Peru longed to annex the republic. The tyrant Rosas of Buenos Aires declared war and talked of invading Bolivia. But the most deadly peril came from Chile, which had never forgotten the colonial days when Lima lorded it over the west coast. If the confederation flourished, Chile might again be subordinated as during the viceroyalty. Besides, a number of boundary and financial disputes had poisoned relations between Santiago and Lima in recent years. Thanks to the foresight and energy of the great Chilean minister, Diego Portales, who was killed for his pains, an expeditionary force landed in southern Peru. Stalled for a time, it withdrew, sailed to a point near Lima, and marched into the capital. Santa Cruz found it as hard to contend with the Chileans as had the Spanish royalists to defeat the liberating armies in 1820–1824. After a few clumsy maneuvers he was badly beaten at Yungay, in 1839.

Santa Cruz rode back to Lima, which the Chileans had evacuated in order to do battle with him, and proclaimed his own defeat. His authority evaporated at once. Hoping to retain control of southern Peru, he led a diminished force into that sub-republic, only to see everyone desert his cause. It was the same in Bolivia. Exile was the only hope of saving his life, and so the fallen protector embarked on a British vessel and sailed away. Several years later he tried to return but was arrested as he crossed Chilean territory and, like the great Napoleon he had always admired, confined on a lonely island. Fate was kinder to Santa Cruz than to the Corsican. In 1849 Bolivia gave him a liberal pension and allowed him to serve in diplomatic posts in Europe. Though he had been officially branded a "traitor, unworthy of the name of Bolivian" at the time of his fall and otherwise reviled, Santa Cruz lived to see his reputation somewhat rehabilitated.

Ballivián, Belzú, Linares, Melgarejo

BOLIVIA's public life continued to center around colorful individuals. The great mass of Indians raised food on the mountainsides and stupefied themselves with coca leaves and chicha. Except when drafted for military adventures or street riots, they had no part in national affairs. Most of them paid the tribute as in colonial times and worked for the whites. Among the fifty or sixty thousand whites and a similar number of *cholos* there was no true cohesion, no group feeling to give society a real unity. Most of them looked after their own interests and tried to remain alive and hold their property while units of the army proclaimed this or that general as the savior of the fatherland. Despite the projects begun by Sucre and Santa Cruz, economic life was very sluggish, with most of the mines remaining unworked and commerce scanty. Bolivia's port on the Pacific was idle, almost depopulated. If a few of the educated citizens kept up with the outside world and talked of old ideals, they nearly despaired of their country.

General José Ballivián emerged as the strong man soon after the confederation went to pieces. A white aristocrat with a good education, he won prominence in 1841 by defeating an invading Peruvian army which was trying to return Santa Cruz' compliment by annexing Bolivia to Peru. Ballivián remained in power for more than five years, anticipating or frustrating rival generals who were likely at any time to "pronounce." His rule was harsh and arbitrary. Once he had a Franciscan friar shot as a warning to the disaffected, an incident which shocked the hardened Bolivians. Yet he was eager to promote public education, even for women, and to stimulate intellectual life. Refugees from the Argentine dictator Rosas were welcomed. Ballivián also had much of Bolivia explored and mapped as a prelude to economic development. Commendable as some of his policies were, the country continued to sink. A combination of generals threw Ballivián out in 1847, after which he went to Brazil and died. The upper classes cherished his memory and, forming a loose group known oddly as *rojos*, or reds, hoped to find another leader who would serve as well.

Manuel Isidoro Belzú, who eventually followed Ballivián, did not play this role. Another general, but of plebeian birth and tastes, he fought his way into power at Sucre, the new name of the ancient city previously called Charcas and Chuquisaca, and became president of the republic in 1850. Belzú represented a new force in Bolivian politics, the urban proletariat. Formidable in his ability to stir the street crowds into a frenzy, he enjoyed calling out the people to attack the army when he suspected it of disaffection and to intimidate the snobbish *rojos*. Particularly in La Paz, his home city, where he was adept at working this device. Much as the drunken mobs relished the sackings, and then the anniversaries of sackings, these demonstrations had no purpose other than to frighten Belzú's opponents. Demagogue that he was, Belzú had no vision of improving the lives of these ragged proletarians, most of them *cholos* or urbanized Indians. He had, in fact, no statesmanlike aims at all. By 1855, restlessness among various garrisons and other signs of danger shook his nerve. Suddenly he appeared before congress and, in a most unusual harangue, ridiculed the ungovernability of the republic. He became the first, and almost the only, Bolivian president to surrender his office voluntarily. Belzú's son-in-law assumed the presidency, held it for two uneasy years, and then was ousted in a barracks revolt.

José María Linares served as president from 1857 to 1860. The first civilian to occupy this post, he managed briefly to keep the generals divided. This administration represented a reversion to *rojo* control, and Linares proved a worthy servant of the white aristocracy. An aristocrat himself, well-educated, and long a resident of Europe, he was a conservative intellectual like so many political figures after the European revolutions of 1848 failed. Thin and sickly, Linares had little glamor. He was no man to enlist popular support for heroic policies or even to serve, as García Moreno of Ecuador would, as a schoolmaster for his country. Living frugally in the palace, the president conceived the worthy but disastrous idea of reducing the public payroll and decreasing the army from 10,000 to 6,000. This outrage could not be tolerated, and one day in 1860 Linares was curtly informed that he was no longer president.

It was four years before another strong man dominated the scene. The *rojos* still sought a benefactor, and Belzú's return complicated matters, as street crowds clamored for the restoration of this charlatan. Considerable sectional feeling was shaping up between northern and southern Bolivia, or La Paz and Sucre. Generals of all shades of opinion—if they had opinions—conspired, betrayed, and struck out for power. Out of this chaos emerged a frightening *cholo* of unknown parents who was enormously popular with the common soldiers and less cultured officers. This Mariano Melgarejo was a drunkard, probably mentally unbalanced. His small head and bulky body gave him a sinister appearance, which a terrible voice fortified. Melgarejo seemed a primitive force of nature with an urge to power that no logic or restraint impeded. Rash, intoxicated, or both, he was able to force his way through difficult situations. In 1865 it was by no means settled that he had won the latest game of power politics. Belzú, protected by his mobs and soldiers, seemed entrenched in La Paz and likely to become president again. Yet Melgarejo walked straight past a hostile crowd into the palace and up the stairs, seized a rifle on the way, and shot Belzú dead. Then he appeared on the balcony and boomed out: "Belzú is dead! Who lives?" After a brief hesitation, the response was "¡Viva Melgarejo!"

The five-year rule of Melgarejo debased Bolivia worse than ever. The president frequently invited his soldiers to join him in orgies at the presidential palace which usually ended with everyone lying on the floor in a drunken stupor, or with quarrels and shots. Sometimes he forced his officers to roll over like poodles. Again, he led them in horrifying surges through the streets, shooting wildly, looting, and raping.[6] Melgarejo enriched his seedy supporters as much as the impoverished state of finances would allow. While drunk at a banquet he suddenly proclaimed a new constitution, which he had never read. Debauches and terror, corruption and barbarism went on in a continuous carnival. When money ran short, he broke precedent by selling the communal lands of the Indians, bringing new poverty to the Aymarás and earning their dangerous hatred. Worthless coins he modestly called "melgarejos" were issued profusely. Another source of income was the sale of Bolivian territory and rights to other countries. A boundary settlement highly favorable to Brazil and a concession to exploit nitrates awarded to Chile temporarily enriched "the most illustrious man of the century," as Melgarejo liked to be called. At last his enemies found their courage. Early in 1871 Melgarejo was beaten in battle. His soldiers were massacred by Indians who avenged the sale of their lands. The ex-president himself escaped but was murdered a few months later by a relative of his mistress in Lima.

PERU

The Lesser Liberators: La Mar, Gamarra, Orbegoso, Salaverry, Santa Cruz

FOR several decades after independence the political history of Peru had a quality of dignity notwithstanding the absence of great issues and the dizzy sequence at which generals displaced one another. These

6. Once he had the British minister tied on a donkey and ridden through an abusive crowd. When she learned of this outrage, Queen Victoria is supposed to have literally crossed Bolivia off her maps and declared: "Bolivia no longer exists."

generals, usually veterans of the battle of Ayacucho, were neither bestial nor ridiculous. Like most strong men thrown up during periods of protracted crisis, they were vain, difficult, peculiar, and individualistic. Yet they meant well, and they truly desired pacification and progress for the new republic.

Less conspicuous, but not to be overlooked, were the educated men of Lima and Arequipa, for the viceroyalty of Peru had a number of luminaries who survived the change into republican times and kept their influence. These men, too, had ideas of some depth about the way to organize Peru, and they sometimes affected the generals. Political history is almost all there is to record in the case of Peru until mid-century. The social establishment changed little from viceregal days. The upper classes still had prestige and wealth. Negro slavery, Indian tributes, and the conscription of labor were restored in most localities. Commerce and manufacturing had grown little, if at all, since Spanish times, and mining had actually declined. Economically and socially, affairs proceeded at a sluggish pace. Likewise, cultural life was less brilliant than in the days of the viceroys. Yet few people dreamed of restoring Spanish power.

The overthrow of Bolívar's caretaker government in 1827 left sovereignty in the hands of a constitutional assembly, an able body dominated by the liberal priest, Luna Pizarro. It was also a free body, as it demonstrated by a divided vote for choice of provisional president. General José de la Mar, who won, was an Ecuadorian by birth but had served ably in Spain's war with Napoleon and had come to Peru as a brigadier of the royalist army. In 1821 he had changed sides and joined with the patriots. Modest, serious, and uncomplicated, he seemed something of a George Washington. His character and a liberal constitution adopted in 1828 gave promise of a sound basis for Peru's development. But in the following year La Mar was defeated in Ecuador during that depresssing struggle between Peru and Bolívar's crumbling Gran Colombia. This defeat ended his prestige, and General Agustín Gamarra overthrew him and assumed the presidency for four years. It all signified a bad start for the new republic, for Gamarra could do little in a constructive way but had to devote himself to striking down actual or potential opponents.

Hope flickered again in 1833, when the legislative body elected General Luis José de Orbegoso president. Orbegoso was acceptable to the white elite and, since for some reason he was adored by the masses of Lima, to the common people. With the timely aid of the capital's street crowds he defeated an effort of the garrison to dislodge him and managed to persuade commanders in other cities to support him. A constitutional assembly in 1834 broadened the nation's charter and legalized a prospective union of Peru and Bolivia. Judged by his actions, Orbegoso was a party to the project of Santa Cruz to unify the Andes lands in a mammoth confederation. As has been seen, Santa Cruz represented order and progress and was acceptable to both conservatives and liberals in Lima, at least to some degree. When the nature of Santa Cruz' plan became clear, and with it Orbegoso's complicity, a brilliant, cocky young general named Felipe Salaverry called upon northern Peru to defend itself. Forcing his way into Lima and the presidency, Salaverry went south only to be defeated and shot in 1835. Orbegoso was now in line to resume the presidency of northern Peru and to place it under Santa Cruz, the protector of the new confederation.

The matter of the confederation absorbed attention and energies from 1835 to 1839. To be sure, the system might have worked, for Santa Cruz was able and sentiment for stabilization was strong. Chile's opposition, however, spoiled whatever chance it had, and Santa Cruz' defeat at Yungay brought the several generals and their armies back to the political gaming table. Agustín Gamarra won the play. As before, he ruled autocratically but within the limits of decency. He was clearly conservative now, and he put through a constitutional change that legalized slavery and barred youth, so likely to be liberal or at least troublesome, from voting. Gamarra could not refrain from military adventures. In 1841 he confidently invaded Bolivia—as he had in 1828 to overthrow Sucre—but was badly beaten and killed. They mourned him in Lima, since he had at least brought order.

Ramón Castilla

FOR three years Peru was in the hands of Gamarra's conservative allies. All this time the situation steadily deteriorated as liberals clamored for reform and generals for power, power that would bring loot and promotions to their men and government jobs to their civilian followers. Out of the welter of riots and campaigns Ramón Castilla emerged in 1844 as the strong man of mid-century Peru. Now in his late forties, Castilla was born in Tarapacá on the southern coast, the son of a Spanish father and an Italo-Indian mother. He had an honorable record as a patriot during the Wars of Independence and was wounded at Ayacucho. Neither rich nor formally educated, he was plebeian in manner and had the common touch. For twenty years he attracted mass support in nearly every part of the republic, since he traveled over Peru as few others had and knew it well. Indians and *cholos* approved of his mixed blood and crude manners. Daring and caution were other assets, and he timed their display with either unusual sagacity or luck. His patriotism was childish, no more so than when he belittled Paris while comparing it with Lima, but it was sincere and it struck just the right note for the people of a formless nation just emerging from colonialism. They too were becoming nationalistic, little as they had to boast of. Aside from being a patriotic politician, Castilla was an honest one as well; he left office a poor man. Finally, he had a gift rarely found in Latin American leaders, an olympian detachment that enabled him to judge surely and to compromise. He was at once a conservative and a liberal.

Castilla ruled as president for two periods, from 1845 to 1851 and from 1855 to 1860. His first term was the more constructive, largely because of an economic boom. Peru, which had known prosperity in the great days of Inca agriculture and Spanish mining, had been depressed for more than thirty years, since the early days of the independence movement. Around 1840 another resource began to bring in foreign money and, with it, prosperity for many individuals. This was the vast accumulation of bird droppings on rocks and islands off the Pacific coast, the guano which the Inca had utilized centuries before. Now it developed that guano was highly marketable abroad as a fertilizer and as an ingredient in the manufacture of gunpowder. From all over the world ships began to arrive in Peru to fetch this commodity. That these vessels were veritable skunks of the ocean lanes to be avoided by other ships and denounced when they entered harbors mattered little to the entrepreneurs who profited from the traffic. The Peruvian government, which nationalized the guano deposits, also enjoyed huge profits.

During Castilla's first term the public income burgeoned. At last there was a source of revenue apart from the customs duties, Indian tributes, and that detested colonial sales tax, the *alcabala*. Castilla could pay and equip his army and purchase ships for a navy, which gave Peru status in the world. He could regularize the bureaucracy so that at least some public servants might be honest without starving to death. Roads, bridges, aqueducts, monuments, and public edifices, furthermore, could now be constructed on a large scale. Castilla was concerned as well with Peru's financial reputation. He improved its credit by balancing the budget for the first time and reducing the long-standing foreign and internal debt. A pension was awarded to the aged San Martín, who had long lived with inadequate funds. Public education, too, at last received attention, and intellectual life began to flourish in Lima as it had in the days of the viceroys. Another of Castilla's concerns was the nation's backward economy. To modernize it, he restricted the power of the guilds, which had long limited production, subsidized factories, built the first railroad in South America (a short line from Lima to its seaport, Callao), and advertised for European immigrants. Finally, he took the courageous step of abolishing the *mayorazgo*, by which the landed aristocracy had entailed its estates and thus kept them intact for centuries.

Castilla retired from office in 1851 in a blaze of popularity. A genuine political campaign with few issues but determined candidates ended in the election of General José Rufino Echenique as president. For three years Castilla beheld the demoralizing effects of guano prosperity on the new administration. Echenique presided benignly while financial scandals, speculation, and vulgar exhibitions of wealth by the newly rich tarnished the regime Castilla had founded. Then the winds of change began to blow as a new generation of Peruvian liberals belatedly drew inspiration from the European revolutions of 1848. Liberalism was so much in the air that Castilla adopted it when he pronounced [7] in 1854 at Arequipa, usually a liberal city. While no doubt bored with retirement, Castilla sincerely wished to oust the corrupt administration. Many towns and garrisons responded to his summons, but the revolt lagged until, in an inspired moment, he proclaimed the end of Indian tributes and Negro slavery. Then the masses acclaimed him with real fervor. Echenique, issuing the usual denunciations of "traitors," planned to stand fast in Lima, but his strategy failed when a wide-scale Indian strike threatened the capital's food supply. By January 1855 Castilla's triumph was complete.

A "government of morality" now proclaimed, Castilla called together an assembly to frame a new constitution. The dominant liberals proceeded to spend the next year or so edifying the country with learned orations that re-interpreted history and delineated a glowing future. For the first and only time the government of Peru was avowedly anti-clerical, though not rabidly so, and bent on attacking other foundations of the traditional society. Castilla observed these proceedings with diminishing enthusiasm. Himself a conciliator and pragmatist, he doubted that Peru was ready to follow Mexico's course of rampaging liberalism. Better than Júarez and other Mexican liberals, Castilla sensed the probable outcome of such adventures. What tipped the scales in his mind was the constitution of 1856, which proposed to clip the president's powers and to give control of the army to congress. For a time Castilla adopted a posture of frigid disapproval. Telltale movements among the military in various parts showed that he was well supported. Guessing he was plotting their doom, the congressional liberals fled from Lima and announced the re-assembly of the constituent body in the provinces. The liberals really had no chance of succeeding. With the army and the population standing by Castilla, all they could do was pro-

7. This rather awkward term in English must be used without italics, or quotation marks, since it occurs so frequently. It means to start a military move to overthrow the government.

tract the struggle by seizing the fleet and taking over the sale of guano from the islands. There followed a rash effort to take Callao, fiasco, and defeat; the brief liberal phase was over.

No man to attempt to exterminate his opponents, Castilla punished a few figures but was generally conciliatory. He ruled serenely for two years. In 1859 he was distracted by a war with Ecuador, a part of the tedious series of interventions in the affairs of that republic by Peru and disputes over possession of its Amazonian district that are still going on. Soon after Castilla returned from the campaign, a group of liberals assaulted and nearly killed him. In 1860 a new president and another constitutional assembly took over in a general mood of reaction. The result was a highly conservative constitution, one which remained in force for sixty years. Castilla exerted much influence over the regime until 1862, when some of his enemies were elected to the new congress. After that he steadily lost prestige. In 1867 he undertook a strenuous military effort to recover power, but now, at seventy-two, he was too old to withstand the rigors of campaigning in the alternations of heat and cold in the Peruvian countryside, and he died. A gallant man who did much for Peru, he is cordially remembered.

ARGENTINA

Juan Manuel de Rosas

THE splendid prospects of the Río de la Plata area at the dawn of the independence movement had turned to ashes by 1829. The utter inability of the "lawyers" in Buenos Aires to organize a government had resulted in the collapse both of the United Provinces and the administration of the city itself. Power then devolved upon the stronger, more primitive men of the pampas who cared little for civilization or constitutions, the gaucho caudillos whose own disunion was curbed by one of their number, Juan Manuel de Rosas. For nearly a quarter of a century this somber man dominated the Argentine. He created a tradition of autocracy, reaction, xenophobia, and, in spite of his slogans, centralization. Rosas' match in Argentina's history did not appear until the advent in the 1940's of Juan Domingo Perón, of equally disagreeable memory.

Rosas came of a family that was respectably Spanish in descent and wealthy by the crude standards of the Argentine. The eldest of twenty children, he exhibited his strong will even as a boy by defying and finally leaving his parents. As a gesture of repudiation he dropped the family name of his mother, whose imperiousness he inherited, and changed the spelling of his surname by using s in the middle instead of z. In the pampas this tough, blue-eyed rebel outdid gauchos and Indians in daring, athletic ability, and ruthlessness, and thus won their admiration. He had a psychic power over men as brutal as himself and became a natural leader. While still young he acquired vast properties and herds in the grasslands, which he complemented with extraordinary business acumen by establishing salt plants and slaughterhouses. His private army of gauchos was useful in this ranching empire, and it also made him a political force to be respected. In marrying María de Encarnación Ezcurra he found a wife whose ambition and shrewdness equalled his own. In 1829, when he was thirty-six, the legislature of Buenos Aires province, or what was left of it, asked him to become governor. With everything in chaos, Rosas loomed as the strongest figure on the scene. Though people respected or feared him, very few could yet discern in him the quality of mysticism that endowed him with superhuman determination and would make him one of the worst tyrants in Latin American history.

During his three-year term as governor Rosas achieved what had been expected of him. He calmed the province by strong-arm methods, governed with severity but not with intolerable autocracy. Through craft and terror he was able to unite the provincial caudillos who called themselves federalists and defeat those who championed unitarism. His program was defensible, possibly statesmanlike, given the realities of the situation. Buenos Aires would continue to control the invaluable customhouse and foreign relations for the whole Platine area, but the other provinces would still be free to go on under their own chieftains without interference, even to the point of issuing separate currencies and levying separate tariffs. There would be no serious effort to unify the area on any formal or constitutional basis. Instead, government would remain highly personal, not unlike a modern crime syndicate, with local bosses linked to one another by private pacts. Rosas built up an army to assure the cooperation of other leaders in this program. Liberals or men of laws would have to be silenced, and so would merchants who craved more contact with the outside world. The only foreign intercourse Rosas wanted for Argentina was the exchange of hides and salted meat for manufactured goods. This would enable ranchers to prosper and, thanks to the customhouse, bring in sufficient revenue to operate the regime. Alien capital and immigrants could stay away, and with them, modern ideas.

By 1832 Rosas had stabilized Buenos Aires province and persuaded most of the strong men in other areas to accept his brand of federalism. The powerful ranchers idolized him, and conservatives generally thought him a good thing for the country. His reputation as a gaucho made him a hero to the rural masses. Also, the lower classes, particularly the large Negro colony in Buenos Aires, were very much under the spell of the governor and Doña Encarnación. House servants and porters eagerly served as informers for the couple. And yet, when his term was up, Rosas dismayed his admirers by refusing reelection, thus seemingly setting a model for constitutional government. Possibly he was being temperamental, since a minority in the legislative body was critical of him and not all the "lawyer" partisans of Rivadavia and liberalism were suppressed. In any event, Rosas went south to attend to his business affairs and to drive the Indians farther into the grassy wilderness. This latter task was both congenial and useful. He loved to lead men in battle, and the Indians had become bold during the years of anarchy. Furthermore, the ranchers, including Rosas himself, desired more grass land because of a recent drought and the growing market for hides and beef. Rosas succeeding admirably, building up his popularity further and pushing the aborigines down the continent toward Patagonia. Not only were the ranchers pleased, but even the Indians were persuaded to be friendly. Rosas' skill in handling native leaders after he had beaten them was shown in the way they kept the treaties, which gave the whites security against attack and the Indians a dependable supply of horses, tobacco, salt, liquor, and *yerba maté* (Paraguayan tea). The Indians even agreed to furnish Rosas with military support whenever he required it. With more prestige than ever, he returned to Buenos Aires.

Meanwhile, that port city had again demonstrated its incapacity for self-government. Riots, political convulsions, and shrill charges from vocal, if ineffective, liberals characterized public life. Doña Encarnación had remained at the family hacienda in Palermo, now a handsome park in the Argentine capital, cultivating the leaders of the Negroes and other lower-class groups. She often saw politicians and reminded them that only her husband was powerful enough to rule. It seemed she was right. The times cried for a strong man, and when Rosas returned he was invited to resume the governorship. He declined. When the politicians insisted, he feigned reluctance. Finally, after they had beseeched him to restore order, he agreed only if a plebiscite showed that the population favored him. A vote announced as 9,300 to 5 compelled the "Restorer of the Laws" to bow to popular demand, and in 1835 Rosas resumed the post of governor. Soon Buenos Aires was quiet again, and the other provinces were tied to the port by private arrangements that Rosas persuaded or forced their caudillos to make. There was still no over-all government for Argentina—in fact, Argentina was not a nation at all but a geographical term—but Rosas, as governor of Buenos Aires and strongest of caudillos, was able to keep the other bosses quiet and subservient for nearly seventeen years. All this effective unification was done in the name of federalism. It depended on the personal force, craft, military prowess, and reputation of one man.

Back in power, Rosas revealed that his ideas of government had hardened during his absence in the pampas. Guided by his romantic, mystical conviction that his will was right and must prevail, he now suffered no interference or criticism whatever. Anyone who displayed unitarist or liberal sympathies was likely to feel the tyrant's power immediately. The considerable intellectual ferment that had characterized Buenos Aires since the end of Spanish power now ceased. Many of the ablest men left the country altogether. A few organized secret societies and communed with one another. The rest went over to Rosas or remained silent. Even the regular organs of government, the legislature and the *cabildo*, stopped functioning, for Rosas preferred to govern through cronies he trusted. Nothing stood in the way of his power; anyone who dared oppose him would be jailed or killed; critics not important enough to be disposed of so drastically might be beaten by unofficial gangs, the *mazorca* units, who foreshadowed the totalitarian "shirted" groups that obeyed Mussolini and Hitler. Informants and spies operated all over the city, so that no one spoke in the open except to praise Rosas. Pressure was such that every man who valued his freedom or safety would sport a red ribbon and exhibit a red banner in front of his business to honor the dictator's favorite color. "Unitarist" became a dirty word, not to be uttered unless coupled with contemptuous adjectives such as "savage," "impious," and "loathsome." It was unsafe to wear a rounded beard, lest the U-shape suggest unitarist sympathies. Slogans, chants, and worshipful displays of Rosas' portrait were the order of the day in Buenos Aires. After Encarnación died in 1838, the tyrant withdrew more and more from demagogic exhibitionism into a feline stillness, but he expected and received a steady stream of accolades from his subjects.

No intellectual and scarcely an educated man, Rosas did not bother to edify the world with his philosophy. An Italian journalist, Pietro de Angelis, did it for him, though Rosas' actions spoke eloquently enough. Federalism must be the compelling belief and slogan for the Argentine, a federalism that left each province autonomous except when the dictator chose to intervene. Ranchers should be favored and gauchos flattered. Conservatism of the type endured by central and eastern Europe was the ideal. The Catholic Church must be the ally and support of the ruler, even to the point of placing his portrait near the altar and participating in his adulation to a blasphemous degree. Since liberty in his mind meant license, there was no need to permit any at all, and therefore public education, newspapers, and books must be regarded as dangerous. The only foreign immigrants who could be tolerated were Spanish Carlists, themselves as atavistic as Rosas. Nor were alien investments desirable, not even for railways or modern port facilities, for foreign ideas might disturb Buenos Aires as they had earlier in the century. Rosas mistakenly believed the Jesuits would fortify his regime and al-

lowed them to return in 1836. Yet even this order, then so friendly to reaction in Europe and Latin America, balked at his demands for glorification in sacred buildings and was ousted after a few years. There was no
room for any opposition, however mild.

It was dismaying to many *porteños* to watch a peace of death close in
on Buenos Aires, once so stimulating if turbulent. Everything the original liberators and Rivadavia had stood for was mocked. Thousands fled
to Montevideo, Santiago de Chile, Bolivia, Rio de Janeiro, or to Europe.
If the usual figure for these emigrants, 30,000 in all, is even approximately correct, it signified that nearly a tenth of the population of
Buenos Aires province departed. Many of the exiles kept up a running
fire against Rosas by writing pamphlets and news sheets that were smuggled into the country. Those who visited North America and Europe
learned much of foreign conditions and were able eventually to introduce new ideas into Argentina. Some were influenced by socialist
and other radical doctrines, particularly after the revolutions of 1848, and
later created an important political trend in their own country. Yet great
numbers never came back. Naive and irresponsible as the Argentine
literate groups had shown themselves in the years before Rosas, their
loss must have retarded the emergence of the nation into the modern age.

Rosas created another mischievous tradition in the Argentine with
his truculent nationalism. His small-minded foreign policies both aided
and undermined his regime. He quarreled with every nation that had
any dealings with him and fanned the xenophobia of his people. England early incurred his hatred by reoccupying the Falkland Islands in
1834 as a base to control the route from the Atlantic to the Pacific and as
a whaling station. The resumption of the British claim to these bleak islands after a lapse of sixty years has never been accepted or forgiven in
Argentina, where maps still label them the "Malvinas." Nor has the
maladroit role of the United States in sparking the reopening of the issue
been forgotten. The relations of Rosas with Brazil were consistently hostile because of old memories and his refusal to open the Plata to commerce. Dictator Francia of Paraguay and Rosas largely left each other
alone in his sullen isolation, but when Francia died in 1840 his modern-
minded successor, who had reason to fear for Paraguay's independence,
chafed at the block to commerce that Rosas maintained in the Plata
estuary. Bolivia became involved in a brief war with Rosas in 1837, at a
time when Santa Cruz was trying to create his confederation. Rosas'
relations with Chile were scarcely less violent because of boundary fric-
tions and the hospitality Chile offered to Argentine refugees.

The most protracted dispute centered about Uruguay, whose independence Rosas resented. Hoping to reincorporate this state, the tyrant armed pro-Argentine gaucho elements and stirred up trouble. For

nine years Rosas' fleet tried to blockade Montevideo, but this rival of Buenos Aires managed to thrive nonetheless. Montevideo's sailors and such foreign adventurers as Giuseppe Garibaldi usually kept the sea lanes open, and Uruguayan hides and beef competed with those of Argentina. Before long, Britain and France became involved. Both powers wanted unhindered trade with the whole of the Platine area, and both were vexed by the way Rosas taxed, conscripted, and generally abused their nationals. In 1838 the French established a blockade of Buenos Aires, which gave Rosas a chance for two years to pose as a hero to his people. In 1845 the French again imposed a blockade, this time in league with the more powerful British fleet. Argentine business suffered badly, of course, and ranchers counted severe losses, though their herds multiplied because they had no markets. Not so Rosas himself, whose properties were south of Buenos Aires on the Atlantic coast. The enterprising dictator had his own fleet which carried his hides and salted beef abroad. Rosas' refusal to bow to the Anglo-French blockade delighted nationalists and enhanced his popularity, but his most important supporters, the ranchers, brooded over losses. In 1848 the European powers somewhat sheepishly gave up their attempt to chastise Rosas and lifted the blockade.[8] The tyrant exulted in his triumph. That forgotten exile, San Martín, who was generally so taciturn, had effusive praise for Rosas.

Late in 1851 Rosas confidently inquired of the heads of the other thirteen provinces whether they intended to renew the pacts by which he had led or ruled the entire Argentine. He seemed stronger than ever, with his most vocal enemies in exile and his victory over the British and French still a fresh memory. Much to his surprise he received a curt refusal from his long-time friend and ally, Justo José Urquiza, a man almost as wicked as himself. The reason was simple: Urquiza was the tyrant of Entre Ríos, a province that urgently needed free use of the river to assure the regular export of its products. He had at last come to realize that Rosas' policies were injurious to the commerce of the upriver provinces and that, for all the talk of federalism, the dictator was dominating the whole Argentine. Urquiza's bold nay at once struck the note that was required to crystallize the long-brewing dissatisfaction of many leaders. All but one of the provincial caudillos joined him. Brazil offered troops, ships, and funds to the rebels. Uruguay, eager to assist in the overthrow of her tormentor, sent armed forces. Paraguay and Chile were sympathetic to Urquiza and prepared to give help if he needed it. Refugees flocked to Entre Ríos from all over southern South America. Rosas faced the rebellion with calm assurance. At fifty-eight he was still vigorous, and he had been flattered for so long that he could not imagine

8. France, of course, was in revolution at that time. The English had already begun to consider the blockade a mistake.

the depths of his unpopularity. Hurriedly collecting an army of about 22,000 men, he went out to meet Urquiza's larger force, which Brazilian ships had ferried across the Plata. In February 1852 the two armies clashed at Monte Caseros. Victory went easily to the rebels. Rosas' conscripts had little zeal to battle for a prolongation of the tyranny.

A whipped bully, Rosas fled to Buenos Aires and took refuge in the British legation. His regime collapsed at once. The British, whom he had hated and baited so long, spirited the fallen dictator away from the vengeance of his victims and carried him and his daughter, Manuelita, to Southampton. Rosas had a huge fortune, but it was all in the Argentine and of no use to him. He lived for twelve years in a shabby hotel in Southampton, possibly on funds forwarded by Urquiza. Finally, after Manuelita had found a husband, he bought a few acres in southern England and lived as much like a gaucho as circumstances permitted. After brooding for a quarter-century on the ingratitude of the Argentines, he died in 1877 at the age of eighty-four. He was endlessly vilified in Argentina by men who rightly believed he had delayed their country's progress immeasurably. Yet there were still gauchos, Indians, and poor folk in Buenos Aires who nourished the memory of their hero. The literate regarded the Rosas system as an abomination, at least until the time of Perón. Rosas received credit for only one dubious achievement: the creation of an aggressively nationalistic spirit.

PARAGUAY

José Gaspar Rodríguez de Francia

THOUGH independent from Spain after 1811 and successful in preventing absorption by the Argentine, Paraguay was an ill-defined land that scarcely qualified for nationhood. Her single city, Asunción, stood on the bluffs of the Paraguay River, an impoverished, unpretentious capital whose commercial development was stunted by Buenos Aires' control of the Plata estuary. East of the river were fields and villages established by the Jesuits, who had departed in 1768. The state now owned most of these lands and compelled the docile Guaraní Indians to work them occasionally in labor gangs. A few persons of Spanish descent owned plantations or ranches where Negro slaves or Indian peons might toil. Most of the Guaraní did little work. Food was easily available from the manioc, citrus trees, and corn that grew so plentifully. The principal commercial crop, *yerba maté*, the Paraguayan "tea" so relished in southern South America, required little cultivation. Thus the large Indian population devoted itself to enjoying life, to smoking cigars and swinging in hammocks. The climate was hot but not disagreeably so. West of the River Paraguay were the trackless wastes of the Chaco Boreal where free Indians roamed wildly but not in dangerous numbers. The edges of the country were woods, jungles, swamps, or grassy plains.

By 1814 José Gaspar Rodríguez de Francia was master of Paraguay. Born in 1766 of a Portuguese father and a Spanish creole mother, he had attended the University of Córdoba and was entitled to call himself "doctor," or at least he did so. He had taught in the single college in Asunción, held a government position, and practiced law. A reader and something of an intellectual, he considered himself a disciple of Rousseau and as such had participated eagerly in the independence movement. Between 1811 and 1814 he achieved a degree of popularity among the creoles and served as a member of the triumvirate, and then the consulate, that governed the new nation. Thanks to his cunning and mass support in Asunción, he was able to oust his partners and divide his enemies. In 1814 the legislative body made him dictator on a temporary basis. Two years later it endowed him with lifetime dictatorial powers and dissolved itself.

By that time Francia, a striking man with frightening black eyes, a sharp nose, and a pinched mouth, had concluded that Paraguay had no prospect of becoming a community that might have pleased Rousseau. Not democracy but paternalism was needed. His own will must prevail in every matter, a will that steadily grew more unreasonable. For Francia himself had changed from the idealistic lawyer whom the patriots had liked. A bachelor disappointed in love, he was now neurotic and misanthropic, close to being a psychopath. Because he was a hermit, so must his nation be. Opposition to his rule could arise only from the whites, for the Indians had a slave mentality and gave no signs whatever of producing leaders. Therefore, the whites must be imprisoned, exiled, or killed. No more should enter the country, and intermarriage among whites was to be forbidden. During his first seven years of power *El Supremo*, as Francia styled himself, accomplished his objective. Almost the only Europeans left were the hundreds who had not yet died in the steamy prisons, the dozens who had kept out of the tyrant's way, and Francia himself. On the other hand, the Guaraní population revered and obeyed El Supremo, serving him loyally in the fields whenever work had to be done and drilling under his personal supervision in the large militia and army. The few foreigners who entered Paraguay were likely to suffer unpleasant experiences and to leave only too gladly when Francia had finished tormenting them.

Admittedly, Francia's regime provided the order that other Latin American countries longed for in vain. Yet the peace was one of death. No newspapers, no imported reading material, no political activities, and almost no schools were tolerated. The only foreign commerce permitted was the limited exchange of *yerba maté* and woods for military supplies, all handled by the state. Since Buenos Aires usually blockaded the streams which were Paraguay's sole outlet to the world, the fault was not wholly Francia's, though he approved of this seclusion. Not only did it suit his temperament, but it also kept the land-hungry Brazilians and the insatiable caudillos of the Argentine from penetrating his hermit nation. Francia had no interest in the opinion of the outside world or, apparently, of posterity, for he destroyed all his papers and never troubled to enunciate his policies or name a successor. He was, of course, at least partly mad.

From 1814 to 1840 Francia ruled absolutely, handling every detail himself. Paraguay had no constitutional apparatus of government, not even the puppet congresses that most despots allowed. Four or five underlings helped him with state business in Asunción. Local rulers he appointed and watched. Spies reported personally to him. The army, courts, and police were entirely his creatures, and even the Church, weak and demoralized since independence, answered to Francia, who despised it, and not to Rome. Melancholy and lonely, the tyrant wanted his subjects to believe, as Hitler later did, that he was utterly chaste and abstemious. The latter virtue was not a pretense, for he lived frugally in the gaunt former palace of Spanish governors. And if he personally received all the state revenues, he did not spend them on his own creature comforts. In his weird fashion he loved the people of Paraguay abstractly, contemptuous as he was of them as individuals. When he died in 1840 at the age of seventy-four, they were not joyous but stunned. They felt orphaned.

For all the gloom and oppression of Francia's dictatorship, the long years of isolation had saved Paraguay from the riotous anarchy of her neighbors. The country had been calm and peaceful, a veritable island of repose in that part of the continent. Despite appalling problems of health, the population had increased, possibly from about 200,000 to 300,000. Social classes had all but disappeared, and the policy of seclusion had fostered economic self-sufficiency. Hence cotton cultivation and cloth manufacturing had flourished. So had the raising of cattle and horses. Grain production, which had been so impressive under the Jesuits, had been partially restored. The economy of the hermit state was sound, and its inhabitants were provided with necessities. Apparently they wished for nothing more.

Carlos Antonio López

IT WAS some months before the Paraguayans could rally from the loss of Francia and organize a government. A group of army officers provided such administration as there was until March 1841, when some 500 of the leading citizens convened in an assembly at Asunción. This body reached back to the phase before Francia's dictatorship and revived the consulate. As had happened before, one of the consuls became dominant and, in 1844, had himself named president for ten years. In 1854 he was reelected; three years later he was made president for life, which as it turned out meant five more years. Francia's successor was Carlos Antonio López, an obese man with a pig-like face and a limp. Partly Indian, Carlos Antonio had acquired some legal education and a wealthy wife whose *estancia* lay far enough from Asunción to escape Francia's malevolent eye. Compared to his predecessor, López was good-natured and indulgent. He used the title of president instead of El Supremo, which indicated some relaxation of the dictatorship, and he often relied on genial persuasion rather than cruelty to gain his way, though he was perfectly capable of brutal methods when he thought them necessary. Soon the Paraguayans settled down contentedly under his rule. The habit of opposition had been obliterated by Francia, so that one could now govern Paraguay with more mellowness.

Carlos Antonio had elements of statesmanship. He was one of the best rulers Paraguay has ever had, weak as this tribute may be. He aspired to win diplomatic recognition and to open his country to foreign trade and technicians. But he could accomplish little until the fall of Rosas in 1852 removed the block to Paraguay's intercourse with the outside world. After that, the republic won international status and received foreigners. A few youths were sent to Europe to acquaint themselves with the advances of civilization almost unknown in Paraguay since 1811. The same period saw the building of a few roads and the completion of a short railroad. Laws and decrees gave public education a major stimulus, with perhaps as many as 500 schools opening. As a result, a comparatively high percentage of Paraguayans learned to read. A newspaper began publication in 1845. Carlos Antonio maintained and improved the army with foreign advice and erected a number of stockades or river ports. A small colony of Frenchmen known as *Nueva Burdeos* was established, the first of many, the president hoped. With a new theater in Asunción, as well as European clothes, furniture, and entertainment, life became more graceful. Out of step with the world for forty years, Paraguay made solid progress under Carlos Antonio.

Yet many things went wrong. Rosas, of course, stifled and threatened

Paraguay until his overthrow. Once the rivers were opened, Brazil demanded free use of the Paraguay for the benefit of her inland province of Mato Grosso. This was grudgingly permitted, but it led to much friction, a boundary dispute, and a near war. The French colonists at *Nueva Burdeos* claimed they had been swindled and mistreated, thus incurring the wrath of Napoleon III against López. Disagreements with British subjects brought warships of the Royal Navy up the river and dampened desires on both sides for commerce. Thereupon, Carlos Antonio ordered the closing of Paraguayan streams to foreign warships. This in turn led to a serio-comic dispute with the United States in 1855, when Carlos Antonio's soldiers fired on the American steamer *Waterwitch*, which was making a scientific survey. The president decided that Francia's isolationism had had some advantages after all. Apart from the abandonment of that policy, Carlos Antonio also differed greatly from his predecessor in other respects: he was no slave to honesty and frugality. In fact, before he had done, the extravagant López family came to control almost half the cultivated lands of the republic. Paraguay almost became, in the monarchical phrase, the patrimony of one family. Particularly greedy and spoiled was the president's oldest son, Francisco Solano, who became a general at the age of eighteen. This pampered braggart was made vice-president and heir apparent when Carlos Antonio guessed that death was near.

Francisco Solano López

WHEN his father died in 1862, Francisco Solano had no difficulty in persuading the congress to name him president. His troops surrounded that legislature, and the willful heir was not delicate in his methods. Long indulged by his father, the new president was accustomed to having his way, taking advantage of any woman who attracted him, bullying government employees, and abusing anyone with whom he had business dealings. Among other things, a visit to Europe in 1853–1855 had turned his head. He had been honored at the brilliant court of Napoleon III and had toured the Crimea during the war. His interest in imperial glory was whetted by a lovely woman of Irish birth, Madame Elisa Lynch, who followed him from France to Asunción and introduced to the drab city of 20,000 inhabitants some of the glitter of Paris. Francisco Solano was determined to be a great builder like the French emperor. Dozens of pretentious edifices were begun, though none but his own palace was ever finished. The dictator was more successful in other undertakings, such as the extermination of critics and potential opponents. In his terrorism he reverted to the days of the early Francia period. As usual, the Paraguayans flinched before such bestialities and followed their ruler wherever he chose to lead them. For some reason they idolized this man, who addressed them in Guaraní and liked to be thought a good fellow.

Francisco Solano's education and travels had not imbued him with virtue or even prudence. Inspired by Elisa Lynch, he craved imperial glory, nothing less than the creation of a huge Platine state with Paraguay as its core and himself as emperor. Unbalanced as the despot must be considered, his project was not altogether fantastic. Paraguay had the largest standing army in South America, and her inhabitants were disciplined fighters. The intended prey seemed weak. Uruguay was a pathetic, grassy entity, pawed over by her own factions and their Brazilian or Argentine backers. The Empire of Brazil was so disjointed that López had reason to believe it could never put an effective army in the field. Argentina had been united only recently, and some of her ripuarian provinces might join Paraguay against Buenos Aires. Furthermore, Argentina and Brazil had long been in conflict, almost at war. The Paraguayan tyrant, therefore, did not trouble to divide his enemies but attacked them all at once. Late in 1864, after Brazil had invaded Uruguay to suppress one of that unfortunate little republic's factions, he arrogantly intervened with a demand that the imperial troops withdraw. When Brazil rejected the ultimatum, he seized a Brazilian ship, occupied parts of Mato Grosso, and finally declared war, righteously summoning the Negro slaves of the empire to join him. Next, López proposed to send an army to Uruguay and the Brazilian province of Rio Grande do Sul, but such a move required permission from Argentina to cross her territory. When Argentina declined to be used as a highway, she too received a declaration of war.

Had Francisco Solano been the genius he imagined himself to be, he might well have conquered the entire Platine area in a sudden campaign. Instead, the war dragged on to 1870, characterized as were all mid-nineteenth century wars in Europe, the United States, and South America by amateurishness, epidemics, atrocities, and strong passions. The Paraguayan Indians fought with their traditional determination, enduring unbelievable suffering and inflicting unprintable barbarities. Their original offensive was spoiled by poor leadership. Then the war became a matter of a grinding, losing defensive against the allies. Brazil was slow to mobilize but eventually placed a large army in the field under competent commanders. With less effectiveness the Argentines assembled a fighting force led most of the time by President Bartolomé Mitre. Gradually, the allies forced their way into Paraguay. Facing disaster, Francisco Solano smelled conspiracies all about him and perpetrated a carnival of butcheries which killed thousands of his own countrymen. Disease and the overwhelming forces of his enemies eliminated most of the others. He fought to the end, as he had said he would. The Indians remained loyal to the very last. Finally, in 1870, the mad dictator was killed by lances as he retreated. Elisa Lynch hurriedly buried his remains and, after an interval of detainment, went to Europe, where she squandered the fortune stolen from the Paraguayans. Of the half-million population of Paraguay at the beginning of the war, only 220,000 were still alive, and of these no more than 28,000 were adult males. Paraguay was left in a state almost as primitive as when the Spaniards first came more than three centuries before. Yet López, though he had brought the nation near to annihilation, remained its favorite hero. He remains so today.

The Attainment of Stability: The ABC States and Porfirian Mexico

23

The Rise of the ABC States

ARGENTINA

W HEN the long tyranny of Juan Manuel de Rosas collapsed early in 1852, there was no true Argentine nation, only a huge expanse between the southern Andes and the Atlantic. Nationhood was the preoccupation of only a few men, for the ties that bound the rest of the people together were very frail, and the ambitions that had been aroused before the advent of Rosas were almost forgotten. Yet these few sons of the pampas proved to be founding fathers. They built well, creating a sound republic by 1860 and managing it with such ability and enlightenment that Argentina began to flourish. Soon she was the most admired country in Latin America, the freest, most prosperous, and generally successful. Her setting had much to do with explaining this progress. An agriculturally rich land in a temperate climate, she produced the meat and grain Europe needed. An effective partnership was soon operating, bringing immigrants, capital, and technology from the heartland of Western civilization and removing vast quantities of Argentine products. It was a partnership based on mutual interest and consent, and it did not involve military pressures or political subjugation. That it came about at all is largely due to Argentina's sound government, established by the generation of patriots who overthrew Rosas.

Argentina in 1852

ONLY one city graced the inchoate territory known as the Argentine: Buenos Aires, which had about 100,000 people who had long accepted the title of *porteños* by which men of the hinterland called them. While it contained a few handsome public buildings and churches, most of them built in viceregal days or in the booming years just after inde-

pendence, the city consisted largely of one-story stone and adobe structures. All but a few of its streets were either muddy or dusty, for the public works program planned by President Rivadavia in the mid-1820's had
made little progress. Everyone, even the poor, still rode horseback and
refused to walk if he could possibly avoid doing so. Much as Buenos Aires
had been isolated or blockaded during the Rosas period, its port was still
its reason for existence. It was a shallow harbor, however, and ships had
to anchor far from shore; goods and passengers would be unloaded by
mounted dock workers and carried on horses, large-wheeled carriages,
or small rowboats. And so it was with outgoing articles, chiefly the hides,
tallow, and salted meat that determined the city's commercial life. As
these crude products dominated business affairs, so the rawness and
brutality of the countryside hung over Buenos Aires. From the edge of
the city as far as one could see there was nothing but flatness, that of the
muddy Plata waters or the black-soiled pampas. The grasslands stretched
for hundreds of miles southward and westward, broken only occasionally
by strips of fields and the most primitive of rural dwellings: tents, adobe
huts, and shacks. Along the Atlantic coast the population was less sparse,
since the great landowners who had been favored by Rosas had their
ranches, or *estancias*, there. These had no fences, however, and the
homes even of well-to-do people were crude. In the interior stretched a
sea of grass with herds of scrawny wild cattle, horses, mules, and sheep.
Giving the land a special peculiarity were the armadillo, land turtle,
ostrich, and the large ombú tree. Furthermore, Argentines have some
justification for claiming that their skies have a unique blueness. Still, the
province of Buenos Aires was ugly and backward, and yet, despite this,
the foremost of the fourteen that composed the country.

Up the Plata, where the estuary becomes the point of convergence
for the Uruguay and Paraná Rivers, lay the province of Entre Ríos,
which was as grassy but more rolling than Buenos Aires province. To the
north, still between the rivers, was Corrientes, a state hotter and more
wooded than Entre Ríos but altogether as primitive, especially since it
contained a substantial Indian population. Westward, across the Paraná,
was Santa Fe, an upriver province that was beginning to shake off the
gauchocracy and absorb a little nineteenth-century technology. West of
it stretched the province of Córdoba, with its capital of the same name.
The area had once been a substantial foothold of Spanish colonialism.
Now it was semi-barbaric, and the capital was only a dusty town with
some dignified architecture to remind it of prouder days. As the pampas
rose into the upland piedmont region, there were other provinces which
had been more important in colonial times than now: Mendoza, San
Juan, San Luis, La Rioja, and Catamarca. Bounded on the west by the

Andes, this group had scant contact with Chile because of the mountainous barrier. They suspected and resented Buenos Aires, which had dominated them since the creation of the viceroyalty in 1776. Farther north were Tucumán, Santiago del Estero, Salta, and Jujuy, retrograde provinces whose economic functions had suffered when the Spanish empire disintegrated. Fertile and often semi-tropical, they possessed enormous agricultural potential, but they lacked the means to exploit this richness and had no markets of consequence.

These thirteen provinces and Buenos Aires were really all there was to Argentina in 1852. The southern half of the present republic, vaguely known as Patagonia since Magellan's time, was a grassland that grew more rocky and arid as one proceeded southward. A line of blockhouses and trading posts set up by Rosas generally kept the few thousand Indians away from the whites, who in turn refrained from penetrating the "desert," as they called this territory. Possibly a million people lived in the whole Argentine. Their racial composition was varied but predominately white, at least if mixed-blooded persons counted as white, as they wished to be. Pure Indians were mostly segregated in Patagonia, Corrientes, or the far north. Negroes, once so numerous in the city of Buenos Aires and in the colonial plantations of the northwest, seemed to be disappearing. Not particularly divided on the basis of color, the population tended also to egalitarianism because of ignorance, for at the very most only a fifth could be regarded as literate. Poverty was another leveler. The few who owned land had a brutish standard of living little above the gaucho type. Such *porteños* as had money or good businesses also lived crudely, because the Rosas regime had isolated them so long from the outside world. Nearly everyone, therefore, could be considered poor.

Urquiza's Effort at State-Building

JUSTO JOSÉ DE URQUIZA, the gaucho boss of Entre Ríos and long-time cohort of Rosas, had overthrown his former chief at the battle of Caseros in February 1852. To the cultivated men of the country, most of them *porteños*, he seemed as objectionable as the fallen tyrant. Urquiza began by unconsciously supporting this attitude. When he made his triumphal entry into Buenos Aires with detachments of gauchos, Uruguayans, and Brazilians, the victorious coalition, he sported the red ribbon that Rosas had made so hateful as a symbol of his dictatorship, which, it will be recalled, professed to be federalist. Urquiza had always considered himself a federalist and was still one. And it was he and not the Buenos Aires unitarists who had toppled Rosas. Thus he saw nothing provocative in wearing the detested scarlet nor in honoring the foreign troops who had helped him. Yet from this day a cleavage developed that complicated Argentine politics for years and threatened to keep the nation from organizing at all.

As in the 1820's, three major points of view prevailed. Urquiza and the federalists wanted a decentralized union in which all of the provinces would be juridically equal and would share the national revenue, most of which derived from the customhouse at Buenos Aires. The unitarists preferred a more tightly-organized republic, which would, in fact, be run by the province of Buenos Aires. A third faction wanted Buenos Aires to isolate herself from the other provinces, leaving them alone and denying them a share in the port duties. These divergences were not about issues which cause memorable wars and revolutions. There was no substantial disagreement on republicanism, representative government, democratic liberties, nor the privileged state of the Church. Yet the tension between Buenos Aires and the other thirteen provinces was serious enough to tear the country in two, just as it had been reborn through casting off the Rosas tyranny.

Urquiza, who had assumed the title of Director, went ahead with his plans to organize a federal republic, ignoring or insulting the *porteños*, who acted as if they had been the ones who overthrew Rosas. An *acuerdo* (accord) concocted at the town of San Nicolás in May 1852 constituted a promise by the major provincial leaders to call a constituent convention. Buenos Aires, however, refused to accept the *acuerdo* and in September rose successfully against Urquiza, who was now barred from the city. For a few months the Director planned a more or less bloodless way to conquer the recalcitrant port. An American adventurer named John Coe sold the services of himself and a fleet to ferry an expeditionary force into Buenos Aires. But then, as Mrs. Rennie has put it, this mercenary proved mercenary by selling out to the intended victim. Poor Urquiza now had no fleet, and he hesitated to pit his own army against an aroused Buenos Aires. Accordingly, he agreed to a truce by which Buenos Aires province could remain aloof while the other thirteen proceeded to organize a national government.

Just before the constituent convention met at Santa Fe late in 1852, its members received a large pamphlet composed by Juan Bautista Alberdi, an Argentine who had emigrated during the Rosas period to Chile, where he had become an able journalist. Much as Alberdi professed to love his native country, he seldom lived in it, even in the thirty years after Rosas fell. He had meditated long about Argentina's failure to become a real nation like the United States, about its poverty and backwardness. His conclusion was that a constitution like that of the United States might enable Argentina to develop in the same fashion. Above all, he insisted, the country must be populated, if possible by

European immigrants. "To govern is to populate," he affirmed, and his words became a slogan taken seriously by Argentine statesmen for decades. Alberdi's ideas had much effect on the constitution-makers at Santa Fe, who were easily convinced of the virtues of republican democracy and the need for industrious inhabitants. Argentines had not yet come to envy or dislike the "North Americans," and they were not hesitant about copying their methods. Thus, the constitution of 1853 written at Santa Fe greatly resembled that of the United States, except that the president served for six years without immediate reelection, the Catholic Church became the official partner of the government, and the right of the federal government to intervene in state affairs was more strongly expressed. Argentina's constitution was destined for a long career, even recovering from the distortions imposed by Juan Perón in 1949, and it is still in effect. Much as it reads like the American charter, however, liberties have been less protected and presidents have tended to dominate both congress and the courts to an extreme degree. Furthermore, national intrusion into state affairs, which has seldom been abused in the United States, occurred more than 150 times in half as many years in Argentina.

Urquiza took office as president of the Confederation—the republic minus its main province, Buenos Aires—in October 1854 for a six-year term. His old headquarters at Paraná became the temporary national capital. From this river town, a verdant but modest place in the state of Entre Ríos, he established diplomatic relations with the great powers, thus hoping to discourage Buenos Aires, 350 miles downstream, from interfering with the Confederation's foreign commerce. Alberdi accepted a mission to encourage Europeans to invest their capital and even to immigrate into the new nation; he was almost the only well-known man of the educated class who agreed to serve Urquiza. The president also sought to staff the government and courts, to create a system of taxation, to stimulate economic life, and to do all the other things so urgently needed. Yet his problems overwhelmed him. Nearly all literate men lived in Buenos Aires, and so the Confederation's administration had to continue on the old informal basis of gauchocracy, with Urquiza bullying the lesser caudillos. His government had no funds, credit, or currency. As a last resort he had to adopt the silver pesos of Bolivia as the legal tender. Urquiza hoped to establish a system of primary education and to revive the long-dormant University of Córdoba. It was no use; there was no one to teach, and academic traditions had been too long interrupted. As for European immigrants, only a few arrived, most of whom were appalled at the rawness of the Confederation and went home, or worse, to Buenos Aires. Railroad prospectors received every encouragement except the ones that counted, money and equipment. A national bank boldly begun on faith collapsed within six months. All Urquiza could do was enunciate plans which realities mocked.

The crucial need was money to finance the regime. After several projects came to nothing, Urquiza finally agreed to a plan he knew would provoke Buenos Aires, the taxation of imports. Most shippers preferred to unload at the port city, which had facilities of a sort and was at least on the ocean. In 1856 President Urquiza decreed that goods which paid duties at Buenos Aires would be taxed additionally if they entered the Confederation. Those which came directly to Rosario, a river port he was seeking to build up as a rival to Buenos Aires and Montevideo, would, however, be given every preference. For a time the system worked, Rosario enjoying some prosperity as a port of entry and the Confederation receiving a small but most welcome revenue. Then Buenos Aires became alarmed at Rosario's prospects and retaliated by punishing shippers who sailed there. She also threatened to obstruct commerce on the Paraná altogether. By 1859 it was apparent that a military test would have to settle the issue.

The Triumph of Buenos Aires

THINGS were going much better in the province of Buenos Aires during the 1850's. The victims of Rosas had mostly returned, bringing their knowledge of the outside world and their determination to prevent another period of domination by the hinterland rustics. Urquiza they wrongly considered another vicious gaucho boss of the type they had learned to despise. These former exiles were not the only *porteños* who distrusted Urquiza and the Confederation; nearly every articulate man of influence in public affairs felt that Buenos Aires should stay out of the nation unless she could control it. More than liberty or local pride was at stake now. Prosperity had arrived, the kind Rivadavia had foreseen and Rosas had hampered, a prosperity based on close ties with Europe. There seemed no limit to the markets for hides, tallow, wool, and salted beef produced in the Plata region. As these expanded, it was possible to purchase luxuries and equipment from Europe. Buenos Aires began its long career as the most fashionable city of South America, as Parisian dresses and hats and London suits were imported. Books, journals, and musical performers from the centers of culture stimulated the city, which has always liked to be considered a piece of Europe planted in the New World. Foreign capitalists saw opportunities and made investments in the province, and immigrants came in substantial numbers. Buenos Aires even built a railroad, a six-mile stretch of track made to fit an old locomotive the British had used in Russia during the Crimean War. Railways in Argentina all have the wide-gauge Russian bed, for in this, as in other matters, Buenos Aires was destined to set the pattern for the rest of the country. And the province, a little republic, had a good government, with elections, freedom of speech and press, and the usual advantages. With an adequate income from import duties it was able to provide training for administrators and to build schools. Before long it had the best educational system in Latin America.

The tension between Buenos Aires and the Confederation was harder on the latter, but it told on both sides; by 1859 the area of possible agreement had narrowed. It was the issue of the surcharges at Rosario that brought matters to a head. Urquiza had a large gaucho army made up mostly of cavalry. Buenos Aires had a smaller force, mainly of infantry but with modern equipment. Long facing one another in a protracted truce, they clashed over an incident connected with the unending interferences in Uruguayan affairs. Urquiza himself took command of the Confederation force, and General Bartolomé Mitre led the *porteños*. At Cepeda in October 1859 the two armies got into position for a real battle. Mitre, concluding that he was out-maneuvered, retreated and opened negotiations with Urquiza. After a few meetings representatives of both parties came to an agreement. Buenos Aires would join the Confederation of the Argentine after the constitution of 1853 had been altered in such a way as to assure her a special position.

Simple as the solution seemed, it did not correspond to the realities of power, for Buenos Aires was potentially the stronger and in a position to choose whether or not she compromised with the Confederation. On the other hand, the Confederation must make peace with Buenos Aires or face a future as bleak as her present. During 1860 an outbreak of gaucho anarchy in the western states revived precisely those fears in Buenos Aires which amounted to a phobia. Mitre became governor of the province just as Urquiza's term as president of the Confederation—which was re-christened the Republic—was ending and a personal opponent of his, Santiago Derquí, was chosen to succeed him.

The tension between province and republic tightened again for reasons that seem vague or unimportant a century later. Perhaps the real reason was that Buenos Aires was still bent on ruling the Argentine; or personal ambition, perhaps to become first president of the united nation, may have clouded Mitre's patriotism. Whatever the causes of this antagonism, Buenos Aires sent more delegates than the other states had expected to the convention that was to revise the constitution in her favor. Perhaps it was an honest move on the part of the *porteños*, who were acting according to their own understanding. Or perhaps they were deliberately trying to pressure the Republic. The Argentines refused to accept so many *porteños* delegates, and a rupture occurred. The armies now resumed control of the dispute, Mitre taking command of the

Buenos Aires infantry and ex-President Urquiza of the Argentine cavalry. At Pavón in October 1860 the two forces prepared for battle. After a few shots, Urquiza, who was physically sick and mentally downcast, suddenly went into retreat. Was he annoyed because President Derquí had not supported him sufficiently? Did he think Mitre was certain to win? Was there an uglier reason, one involving his own integrity? Argentines have long debated these questions and have reached no consensus.

The Nation Made. Bartolomé Mitre, 1860–1868

THE confrontation, scarcely a battle, of Pavón reversed the situation created by Cepeda. Now it was Mitre who was the commanding figure, and Buenos Aires could enter the republic not as an esteemed captive but as outright leader. And the fact that Urquiza had shrunk from battle also indicated that the balance of power had passed from horseman to foot soldier, and thus from the gaucho-dominated interior to the coast. Mitre had the sense to exploit his victory with grace and tact. He ruled the republic as provisional president for two years, feeling his way cautiously until the provinces accommodated themselves to the idea that Buenos Aires held the whip hand. The constitutional revisions went through as the *porteños* wanted them, but they were not arrogant enough to alienate the other states. In 1862 they went into effect, and Mitre was then elected president of Argentina for a full six-year term. It proved to be the beginning of seventy years of order and progress.

Mitre had both stature and ability, as well as the priceless trait of winning the confidence of men who knew him. Born in 1821, he had spent his youth in Uruguay, where his family had gone to escape Rosas, and he became a respected army officer and a skilled writer. Five years as a soldier in Bolivia and as a journalist in Chile had deepened his understanding of how not, in the case of the former country, and how, in the case of Chile, to run a Latin American republic. Even then a potential statesman, he learned to abhor riotous militarism of the type that degraded Bolivia and to value the stern but broad-minded regimen that Chile had. He returned to Buenos Aires after the fall of Rosas and thereafter filled important positions as a minister of the provincial government, a general, and an editor. Mitre was also a historian, being one of the first of modern South Americans to become interested in the Indian cultures of the past, and he wrote a biography of the independence leader, Belgrano. Long after his presidency he would compile an excellent history of the career of San Martín which established that forgotten hero's revered place in the South American pantheon. Soldier and scholar, polemicist and politician, Mitre personified above all the nascent nationalism of Argentina. The country must be one, he preached, oriented toward Buenos Aires but willingly so. His contemporaries caught his inspiration, and he remained, despite several serious false steps, a man of prestige and influence, almost a national monument, until his death in 1906.

As president, Mitre laid the fundamental bases for making the nation a success. Basic laws had to be compiled, courts established, officials trained and appointed, tariffs regularized, and currency created. To the gratification of the provinces he carried through the nationalization of the Buenos Aires customhouse, and he planned the eventual federalization of the capital city. These concessions, one real and the other promised, conciliated the hinterland without obscuring the fact that Buenos Aires set the tone for the republic. *Porteño* ideas were triumphant; the country must be Europeanized to the point of saturation. Commerce, immigration, and culture received every encouragement. William Wheelwright, an American who had done so much for Chilean shipping, came to Argentina to plan an ambitious railway system. It was British capital that carried it out, however, with the Argentine government cooperating by giving away lands along the roadbeds in the hope of populating the countryside so as to make the railroads profitable. The method worked, as it did in so many other underdeveloped countries. Mitre did not originate it, but he saw its possibilities and made the most of them. Lines were started which would link Buenos Aires with the north, to Córdoba and beyond, and with the west, toward Chile. The telegraph came to Argentina and helped to knit a national society. Immigrants, deterred during the 1860's by the Civil War and its aftermath from entering the United States, arrived in increasing numbers. Some of them discovered that wheat grew wonderfully in the pampas, a matter of large importance in Argentina's future.

At times Mitre had reason to feel abashed by the problems of organizing such a raw country, splendid a job as he was doing. There were never enough trained personnel to staff an administration equal to his ambitions, and money was always a problem. For example, primary schooling became available to three times as many children by the end of Mitre's term as at the beginning, but only a fifth of the eligible students could attend at all. This situation was true in so many other aspects; progress might be heartening, but it was far from enough. Mitre's vision, however, and his firmness in exercising the national authority over all the republic rallied Argentina in such a way that it continued to develop in a wholesome way. Life, liberty, and property became as safe as in any other part of the New World in that period. Constitutional government and economic progress gave much promise for the future. In 1865 the country was diverted from its foundation-building by the insane war brought on by the dictator of Paraguay, Francisco Solano López. Mitre rightly saw that Argentina was threatened by López' ambition to build a Platine empire, a plan mad enough to succeed. He led his nation into war and personally commanded the allied armies in the field. When his presidential term ended in 1868, the war was not over.

Domingo Faustino Sarmiento, 1868–1874

HAVING done so much to establish a republican tradition, Mitre did not wish to see it spoiled by an unfortunate successor. This possibility loomed large as 1868 approached, for two extremists wanted the presidency. One was Adolfo Alsina, a rabid *porteño* unitarist. The other was Urquiza, the federalist so distrusted by Buenos Aires, who was again serving as boss of Entre Ríos. Rather than see either win, Mitre prevailed upon his minister to Washington, Domingo Faustino Sarmiento, who was not overly identified with either unitarists or federalists, to be a candidate. Voting was controlled by the states, which meant that democratic balloting was out of the question and that local rulers decided major questions. Although Mitre affected to stand above the electoral contest of 1868, he really brought great pressure on the several bosses to elect Sarmiento as president and Alsina as vice-president. He had his way, and he had reason to congratulate himself for the way things turned out, though Sarmiento proved unwilling to return the favor in 1874 by arranging for Mitre to succeed him.

Many students rate Sarmiento as the greatest Argentine of all. Born in 1811 in the foothills of the Andes, in the province of San Juan, he acquired an education largely on his own initiative. It was no easy matter to find teachers or books in the remote back country, but somehow he did, and he read continuously even when he tended a store for his living. Sarmiento had scarcely thought about the semi-barbaric caudillo of his province, Juan Facundo Quiroga, until he was drafted into that gaucho's army. An act of insubordination brought him a short jail term, which had a traumatic effect. He rejected everything about this caudillo and gauchos in general. Making the difficult crossing into Chile, he found work there as a miner and teacher, still reading everything he could find. Between 1836 and 1841 he was back in San Juan, where he taught school and ran a country newspaper. He relished both careers to the fullest, but an open criticism of the Rosas regime cost him another arrest, a close call with official lynchers, and expulsion. During the next four years he worked in Santiago de Chile, much of the time supervising a teacher-training school under the direction of his friend, Manuel Montt, who was minister of education. Also he wrote prolifically for the newspapers, excoriating Rosas and stirring up many controversies. Of the most significance during this phase was a newspaper serial which finally became a volume, an essay named *Civilization and barbarism, the life of Juan Facundo Quiroga*. Nominally a study of the infamous Facundo, who by then was dead, the book was a mighty attack on the Rosas system and the gauchocracy. They represented barbarism, the author reiterated, as opposed to the European-oriented men of education, who stood for civilization. Romantic in style, with brilliant imagery and incisive sociological insights, the book made Sarmiento world-famous. Dictator Rosas well knew its threat, and he brought pressure on the Chilean government to expel the offending author. The Chileans found a pleasanter way to handle the situation. In 1845 they gave Sarmiento a mission of studying educational systems in Europe and the United States.

It was a magnificent opportunity for Sarmiento to see the world. He sailed to Montevideo and Rio de Janeiro and then on to France. From there he visited Spain, Algeria, Italy, the Germanies, and England, everywhere meeting people of influence. In some ways Europe was a disappointment to this bucolic intellectual, who had long regarded the continent as the font and center of all that was admirable. On the other hand, he was greatly stirred by the United States, a magnificent young democracy then tearing away half of Mexico and developing so swiftly its growth could not be measured. Sarmiento liked everything about the United States, which establishes him as a most unusual Argentine. Above all, he admired the public education system there. Horace Mann's normal institute near Boston gave him many ideas he later put to good effect in his own country, and he remained a Mann disciple all his days. Completing his mission in 1849, Sarmiento returned to Chile, where he married a wealthy widow and retired to a comfortable home at Yungay to study and write. With other Argentine exiles he kept up a running literary fire against Rosas that gradually undermined the gaucho despot. When he heard that Urquiza was organizing a rebellion, Sarmiento went to join him. Urquiza scoffed at this recruit but permitted him to use a hand press he had brought along to print propaganda. Before long Sarmiento was proudly issuing dispatches and letters from Palermo, the estate of the fallen Rosas.

After a conflict with Urquiza, another interval in Chile, and a permanent removal to Buenos Aires in 1854, Sarmiento definitely entered public life. For seven years he served in major elective and appointive offices in Buenos Aires province. In January 1862 President Mitre named him governor of San Juan, his home state. There Sarmiento interpreted his civilizing mission as the extirpation of the gaucho. He insisted that all males surrender their ponchos and chiripás for shirts and trousers. Everything about the gaucho he regarded as odious; he was evil incarnate, barbarism itself. When one of the last of the primitive caudillos, El Chacho, was killed, Sarmiento's glee was almost psychopathic. His campaign to abolish the gaucho was only one partially successful, and Sarmiento not only made himself ridiculous in some ways but also unpopular. He was, in fact, opinionated and disagreeable, and, as he aged and became deaf, he grew more so. Perhaps he would not have lasted much longer as governor of San Juan in any case. President Mitre rescued him from an uncomfortable position by giving him diplomatic missions abroad, lastly as minister to the United States, where he thrilled to Lincoln's personality and cause and developed attitudes that afterward affected his policies at home. He was returning from the Washington post in 1868 when a 21-gun salute in a Brazilian harbor informed him that he had been elected president of Argentina.

As chief executive of the republic Sarmiento relied little on personal charm, for his stock of this attribute was small. He alienated politicians by ridiculing their claims for spoils. The public resented his self-righteousness and called him *"Don Yo"* (Mister I). Nevertheless, he was a firm and capable ruler, his vision true and his actions bold. It took strength, probably this more than wisdom, for him to pursue the unpopular Paraguayan War until its apocalyptic end in 1870. Gaucho uprisings threatened all he stood for; these he combated with a manic relentlessness. He made a much-publicized visit to the seat of his old rival, Governor Urquiza of Entre Ríos, and became quite friendly with him. Then Urquiza paid for this reconciliation by being murdered, along with his family, by a barbaric caudillo named Ricardo López Jordán, who installed himself as governor. Gauchocracy again! Ironically, it rose over the dead body of Urquiza, whom Sarmiento and men like him had so long misjudged. The president mobilized the armies of the republic to expel López Jordán and did so. Sarmiento had proved again that Argentina could defeat the forces of barbarism and that the federal government was master, and the gauchos practically ceased to constitute a political force. Sarmiento also pursued the state-building endeavors started by Mitre: cables, telegraphs, railroads, immigration, national taxation, and the construction of long-needed docks at Buenos Aires. He took a census, which provided future rulers with statistical data for intelligent assaults on the nation's backwardness. It was characteristic of the times that when a costly plague of yellow fever struck Buenos Aires in 1871, the government reacted not in lamentations but by constructing a sewage disposal and public water supply system.

Energetically as he attacked a wide variety of problems, Sarmiento was happiest as the national schoolmaster. He lectured his people on the need to cultivate the orderly habits of more civilized nations, and he inspired the translation and publication of the writings of eminent foreign political thinkers, especially Americans. Largely through his efforts or inspiration there came into being an observatory at Córdoba, a school for agronomy and mining, naval and military academies, teacher-training institutes with American staffs, and schools, schools, schools . . . national, provincial, municipal, vocational, for the handicapped. In nearly every town he visited, the president was likely to designate a building and a literate man as a unit of primary instruction. He sent mobile parties to tour the most neglected areas and teach a few persons in each village to read and write. The results were remarkable. Argentina quickly became the most literate country in Latin America. The tradition established by Sarmiento was enduring, for the nation took pride in its system of public instruction and made sacrifices to maintain and improve it. If President Sarmiento was sometimes high-handed and wrong-headed, his work in the field of education suffices to make him one of Argentina's greatest builders.

Nicolás Avellaneda, 1874–1880; Conquest of the Desert and Buenos Aires

THE prospects for the presidential contest in 1874 reflected the improved condition of Argentina. Two of the nation's best men opposed one another, former president Mitre, now a senator, and Nicolás Avellaneda, a young minister who had worked closely with Sarmiento in the program of public instruction. In spite—or because, in the perverse human way—of his great indebtedness to Mitre, Sarmiento supported Avellaneda. Mitre carried the province of Buenos Aires, Sarmiento's home province of San Juan, and Santiago del Estero. Thanks to presidential pressures on the bosses of other states, Avellaneda carried the rest of the country and won the election. Mitre was sure he should have been the victor, and he rather surprisingly resorted to force. In a test of arms he was defeated and captured. After a few months of imprisonment he was pardoned and eventually restored to his seat in the senate and his rank of general in the army. Apparently he suffered little diminution of prestige, for he continued to be regarded as the nation's most eminent statesman for thirty years.

When he took office, Nicolás Avellaneda was thirty-seven and not particularly well-known. Soon he demonstrated that he was a worthy heir of Mitre and Sarmiento, since the presidential power continued to be the dominant force in political affairs. The country was reasonably orderly, its people far more absorbed in the exhilarating economic advances to be discussed presently than in politics. All of the usual indicators of progress, nineteenth-century style, were now known in Argentina: order, liberty, railroads, schools, investments, trade, machinery, and population growth. They were working about as well there as in the United States, Australia, Japan, indeed in Europe itself during those years, and some credit for these developments must be apportioned to Avellaneda. He was also involved in boundary questions, which he handled well enough. With defeated Paraguay there was a bitter dispute over a large area, now known as Formosa, in the humid north. At length Argentina compelled the little nation to acknowledge its loss. It was not so easy to adjust boundary conflicts with the Empire of Brazil, which, large as it was, had a voracious land hunger. Avellaneda sent his defeated rival, former president Mitre, to Rio de Janeiro to negotiate with Emperor Pedro II, but to no avail. The demarcation of the new frontier between the ancient rivals and short-lived allies of the Paraguayan War had to wait.

Another boundary trouble arose from the simultaneous extension in both Argentina and Chile of the white man's realm into Indian territory. In the case of Argentina, the campaign was deliberate and military, growing out of the rising price of land. Also, during the mobilization occasioned by Mitre's uprising in 1874 a number of garrisons had been withdrawn from the line established years before by Rosas, and Indians had penetrated the north. While the government was not reluctant to add more grasslands to the nation's already large holdings, it was sincere in fearing that a frontier war loomed, one of raids, torture, and thefts. Therefore, it was decided to end the Indian menace once and for all. General Julio A. Roca, the young army chief of staff, led the campaign during the last years of the 1870's. It was a difficult undertaking, made so by the desolation of the southern pampas and Patagonia as well as the hunger, cold, and loneliness. The foe proved capable of little opposition; somewhat sheepishly the government finally announced that the "countless hordes of barbarians" numbered only about 2,000. Those who survived were re-settled, and the vast southern expanse known somewhat inaccurately as the Desert was now opened to the white man. It was almost his last advance at the expense of the aborigine, who had been losing out since 1492. It also brought Argentina and Chile into collision. In 1881 the two republics agreed to divide Tierra del Fuego, the craggy Antarctic island, and to mark their frontier where the highest peaks of the Andes divided the watershed.

By 1880 the *porteños* were resurgent. For almost two decades the federal government had made Buenos Aires its temporary residence. Buenos Aires province had lost no ground relative to the other provinces but was actually growing at a faster rate than they. With the conquest of the Desert, its officials were determined to acquire a large share of the new lands. In order to assure this division the governor, Carlos Tejedor, announced his candidacy for the presidency. Also, a "rifle club" surreptitiously organized the militia and units of the army to lend force to Tejedor's pretensions. President Avellaneda and a group of provincial leaders known as the Córdoba League reacted vigorously to what they considered a renewed lunge for power by the *porteños*. Naming General Roca, the hero of the Desert campaign, as their candidate, they made the federalization of the city of Buenos Aires the issue. As usual, the president's heir won the election, whereupon Buenos Aires sprang to arms and put the national government to flight. Ousted from his capital though he was, President Avellenda still had great authority, and President-elect Roca enjoyed the army's support. A short campaign brought about the capitulation of Buenos Aires. The city was made a federal district as promised, and the province of Buenos Aires established its capital in the town of La Plata. It was one of those conflicts in which everybody won. The republic was the stronger for having the nation's only real city as its headquarters. Buenos Aires province got along fine without the city. And the great municipality itself continued to surge, practically dictating to the rest of the country in matters of culture and economics and more often than not in political affairs.

The Transformation of Argentina

JULIO ROCA was president from 1880 to 1886, and then was succeeded by his wife's brother-in-law, Miguel Juárez Celmán, who served to 1890. The political structure of the republic seemed sound. Though presidents were usually overbearing in their relations with congress, the judiciary, and the local governments, constitutionalism of a sort operated. Almost alone in Spanish America, the Argentine army was not oversized or excessively officered. It had a few special privileges and received modern weapons, but it obeyed the president, its commander-in-chief, and intruded into public affairs discreetly when it did so at all. Under the constitution of 1853 the Catholic Church enjoyed government support, which was forthcoming with little friction. In 1884 a law forbade religious teaching by the clergy in the public schools, a blow, but not a serious one, to the Church. Generally, Argentina had no major church-state problem, and the clergy was comparatively effective as a partner of the government. For much of the time Argentina seemed to have few fundamental issues at all to polarize political groups. Provincial laws granted suffrage, usually, only to the propertied and educated; the others did not object to disfranchisement with any great vehemence until 1890. State and municipal bosses counted the votes as they wished and intrigued among themselves for the spoils of office. The ruling group, loosely united in a National Autonomist Party, became known variously as the *Régimen,* the hierarchy, or the oligarchy. Politicians though they were, they made business the business of the government— the economic development of the country and their own reward for promoting it. They provided the climate which permitted Argentina to enjoy a delirious boom during the 1880's.

Forces for this boom had been accumulating even before the fall of Rosas, which spurred them by opening the country to foreign trade, capital, and immigration and brought life to long-dormant activities. Every president had proudly pointed to the multiplication of foreign commerce during his term. Hides and wool went overseas to an ever-expanding market, making possible an increasing volume of imported machinery and consumer goods. The steamship figured largely in this growth, as did the improved harbor facilities at Buenos Aires. Railways created an entirely new dimension for commerce. In twenty years after 1860, railroad trackage increased from thirty-nine to more than 7,000 kilometers. From Buenos Aires, lines extended to the north, the north-west, the west, and the south, tightening the dictatorship of the city over the countryside. Financed mostly by British investors, these road-ways were also fostered by extravagant gifts of land by the government, as was true in the United States during this period. Towns sprang up along the tracks, and land came into cultivation. If the government joined with the railroad companies in the wildest of corrupt practices, the nation as a whole nonetheless benefited. Argentina became a modern country and was known abroad to be such. More investors sent their money there for speculation with the result that business houses and public utilities flourished and land values spurted. Immigrants were entering as rapidly as capital,· nearly all of them from Europe. About 5,000 came in 1860; the number was 20,000 in 1870 and more than 100,000 in 1880, and by 1890 more than 200,000 Europeans were disembarking each year. Italians and Spaniards made up three-fourths of these immigrants, the Italians the more numerous. Among the Spaniards were large increments of Basques and Galicians, reputedly more industrious people than Castilians or Andalusians. During the 1870's the Argentine government usually paid their passage and exerted itself to house new citizens and to find them jobs. Later it was not necessary to be so solicitous, for the immigrant tide swelled without encouragement. A large proportion, it should be noted, were seasonal laborers or *golondrinas* (swallows) and not permanent settlers.

Until about 1880 these developments were testimony of Argentina's stable government and attractive climate but little else. The real spurt, came when the cattle industry underwent an amazing metamorphosis. Millions of "creole" cattle had long roamed the pampas, usually unclaimed, like birds or fish. Of small frame and with long horns and tough hides, they served to feed and clothe much of the population. Their value as an export item centered about their hides and tallow and salted beef, which tasted so bad that no one would eat it except the impoverished who could have nothing else, often slaves in Brazil and the West Indies. In 1876 a French ship, *Le Frigorifique*, carried a cargo of congealed Argentine beef to Europe. An experimental banquet had mixed results; some thought the meat admirable food, others said it had rotted. Several further efforts proved that frozen beef could be brought in large quantities to Europe and remain edible. Almost at once enterprising Englishmen perceived a great opportunity. Beef was much in demand in Europe, especially in England, where the population was rising so fast and industrialization was bringing the standards of living much higher. Now there was a new source of this food, Argentina. The number of refrigerated steamships multiplied almost every year, and so cheap meat from the Argentine could reach the tables of Englishmen of all classes. Their appetite was unlimited, and so was Argentina's capacity to satisfy it. Furthermore, continentals liked beef too, a need which British middlemen were only too eager to fill.

This simple formula had enormous consequences. Argentine landowners who had seldom bothered to survey their properties now put up barbed wire fences to confine their herds and steel windmills to assure them water. Before, it had not mattered if cows were scrawny or sickly; now it did, and the animals must be tailored for the market. Stockbreeding, a science long ignored by Argentine ranchers, suddenly assumed the proportions of a national craze. Fine bulls—Durhams, Herefords, and Angus—were imported from England to transform the creole herds. A *Sociedad rural*, organized in 1866 to promote the welfare of livestock, had been regarded with indifference before 1880. Then it became a most prestigious institution, holding great fairs every year to persuade the *estancieros*, some of whom were slow to adapt themselves to the new situation, of the advantages in changing the character of their herds. Cattle with huge, broad bodies, short horns, stumpy legs, and thin hides were by far the most desirable for beef production. Even the dullest rancher understood this when selling time came, for the hide business was almost insignificant compared to the beef. Profits and national pride soon made Argentina the most cow-conscious country on earth.

Paralleling the expansion of the cattle industry was the increase in the cultivation of corn and alfalfa to fatten the beasts. For this the pampas were ideal, and improved grasses likewise flourished. Slaughterhouses in and around Buenos Aires became more important than ever, with much foreign capital coming in to create new and modern establishments. Furthermore, what had been done for cattle could be done for sheep, which grazed by the multitudes in Patagonia on land too poor for cattle, or which ate short grass left by the cows. Little as the Argentines cared for mutton, Europeans were fond of it. Hence an outburst of activity led to more scientific breeding to produce the type of meat and wool desired by the customers. Fine Lincoln rams from England and other famous breeds effected a wholesale regeneration of Argentine sheep herds within a few years. And many herders from the less prosperous sections of the British Isles migrated to the Argentine. To this day many sheep men in Patagonia speak Gaelic English though they have never left South America.

This explosion in the livestock business brought into relief the fact that most of the land was held by a few thousand individuals, most of them descendants of Rosas' cohorts or other politicians who had been favored by territorial grants. In the case of Argentina, latifundia could not be blamed on Spanish colonialism, for the land had been divided after independence. Successive governments had distributed large tracts carelessly, often not knowing where they lay, as bribes, favors, or rewards. Of all the men of some statesmanlike qualities in Argentine public life, scarcely any had given a thought to homestead acts which might have populated the country with small owners. There had seemed to be an unlimited supply of land, and so few people. Now land was valuable, immensely so, and it was too late to do much about the *estancias* in the older settled regions. To be sure, there remained tracts of public lands, huge expanses of them, but the authorities had little idea of their nature or precise location. Besides, the temptation to sell them to speculators, most of them moneyed Europeans, was too strong. During the 1880's the disposal of public lands went ahead at a frenzied pace, to the enrichment of the investors and politicians and the discomfiture of Argentine society, which is still a major problem.

The climax of the boom came toward the end of the decade. By then the resident landowners had done much to improve their *estancias*. They were beginning to construct English-style manor houses in the pampas, for all good things seemed to originate in England. Many of them preferred to live in Buenos Aires, where they were more likely to build in the gaudy style of the French Second Empire or Victorian Britain. The Jockey Club in the capital was the center of this aristocracy, who took up polo and horse racing in preference to the less fashionable Spanish or gaucho sports. They owned the choicest sections of Argentina and indulged their new prosperity with gusto. Foreigners taught them the amenities of the great world outside and acquired control, in addition, of banks, meat-packing plants, and large commercial houses. Except for livestock or agriculture, Argentine-owned business tended to center about minor occupations: baking, groceries, tailoring, blacksmithing, and such. It was difficult for a native to rise into the upper ranks of society. In

rural areas the poor were warmed only gradually by the glow of prosperity. They usually lived on as cow hands, sheepherders, itinerant laborers, or tenant farmers. Where were the immigrants to go? Land-
holding was out of the question for most of them. Even farm labor had
its limits, though for some years thousands of *golondrinas* sailed to Argentina to harvest crops during the winter months back home and returned after a season or two with New World earnings. The immigrants
who remained had to settle in the towns, above all in Buenos Aires, a
majority of whose population was of foreign birth by 1890. Rather
quickly, much more so than the Argentines who migrated from the countryside, they became skilled laborers and started small businesses. Somehow, most of them were absorbed in the nation's economic life. Often
they were disgruntled, inclined to be contemptuous of their new homeland, and the government no longer made much effort to patriate
them. This rapidly-growing sector of the population would soon make itself felt in Argentine affairs. During the last decades of the century, however, it was the moneyed landed groups that gave tone and leadership to
society.

While Buenos Aires and the pampas profited most from the new
productivity, other areas shared the boom in different ways. Wood was
urgently needed in the treeless grasslands for fence-building and barns.
Thus the *quebracho* of the northern provinces assumed value. This hard
wood, named "axe-breaker" by the early Spaniards, was also a source
of tannin, an acid used in curing leather. Its enhanced importance
brought about a revival of economic life in the stagnant north. Sugar
had long been grown in that region for local usage, often for liquor.
The railroad presented this commodity with much larger markets in the
more populated sections of the country. For the first time since viceregal
days the semi-tropical states felt themselves linked to the Platine area,
and they began to face Buenos Aires rather than Chile or Bolivia. Yerba
maté, which for so long had been consumed by gauchos and other rustics,
became popular in Buenos Aires, and another profitable industry developed. Finally, the wines of Mendoza had been neglected by the
porteños, who could import European bottles cheaper. When foreign
immigrants rejuvenated this half-forgotten industry and the railroad
made Buenos Aires more accessible, viniculture and wine-making
flourished again. By the 1880's the Argentine Republic was, for the
first time in its history, a coherent economic unit. Politics first, then
the railroad, had made it so.

No longer was there a place for the gaucho, except in romance. The
might of the federal government had ruined his political power after
1860. A modern regular army had robbed him of his military significance.
Finally, scientific livestock husbandry destroyed his economic role. Thus

the gaucho became a mere cowboy who tended herds in fixed localities, colorful and picturesque in some ways but no longer a potent force in society. This transition was fast and smooth, and it was accompanied by the rise of a cult of the romantic past. Gauchocracy, like the American Wild West, seemed all the more glamorous to later, more civilized generations as it receded. Argentina's most beloved epic, *El gaucho Martín Fierro* by José Hernández, was published in the 1870's just as the gauchos lost status, to enshrine in popular lore the glory of a disappearing type. A supporter of the caudillo López Jordán against Sarmiento, this author took an enduring if rather painless revenge. As the years went by the cult of the gaucho waxed. The poet Leopoldo Lugones (1874-1938) did much to immortalize the appeal of life on the pampas to the modern, nostalgic Argentine. South America's greatest dramatist, the Uruguayan-born Florencio Sánchez (1875-1910), wrote several highly successful plays in which he stood Sarmiento's theme on its head by presenting the gaucho as a glorious figure compared to the civilized urbanite. Novels by Eduardo Guitiérrez (1853-1890) and Benito Lynch (1885-1952) both intensified and perpetuated the fond Argentine tradition of the gaucho as a man of admirable spirit.

Two of the best painters of Argentina, who are also among the foremost of Latin American artists, helped to immortalize the legendary gaucho. These were Prilidiano Pueyrredón, who had worked for Rosas himself and for Urquiza, and an Uruguayan immigrant named Juan Manuel Blanes. Posterity has admired their productions for their technical excellence but above all because they glorified the gaucho way of life. Similarly, Argentine music has drawn from the guitar-strummed melodies and lonely wails of the cowmen, not only in the ballads so beloved in Buenos Aires cabarets but also in more pretentious compositions. While musicologists are skeptical, Argentines loyally insist that their famous tango, which is danced everywhere in the world, is of gaucho origin.

Crisis and Rally

THE wonderful prosperity of the 1880's was made possible largely by the sound administration of President Julio A. Roca and the so-called Generation of Eighty. Unfortunately, they participated personally in this boom in ways that produced well-founded charges of official corruption. Under Roca the situation was kept within the bounds of decency, or at least it was not flaunted. But matters got out of control altogether under Roca's successor, Miguel Juárez Celmán. This president, who took office in 1886, sponsored intoxicating schemes for selling public lands to European speculators on a scale not known before, for watering railway stocks, and for allowing the national treasury to issue clandestinely great quantities of paper money. Meat exporters, the great ranchers and their allies in Buenos Aires, favored the cheapening of the Argentine peso because they were paid in sound European currencies. The more pesos they received for pounds, marks, lira, or francs the better— for them. Yet the devaluation of Argentina's money by repeated issues of paper money caused inflation. This too suited the *estancieros*, for their lands rose in value, but it damanged the nation's credit and it injured nearly everyone else in the country. Constantly expanding prosperity concealed the dangers of this course until 1889, when a world economic depression terminated the boom in Argentina and revealed the rickety structure of her system.

Late in that year bankruptcies and despondency abruptly replaced euphoria, except in the mind of President Juárez Celmán, who blithely persisted in being optimistic. Depression brought to light the many iniquities of his official family, and cries for reform mounted from·every side. Congress learned of the unauthorized issues of paper money and demanded explanations. There being none that could be admitted in public, the administration suffered a stunning loss of popularity. In April 1890 the entire cabinet resigned. Since there was really no political party but the National Autonomist, the vehicle of the regime, many divergent groups began to coalesce: military politicians, reformers, idealists, bourgeois, and labor representatives, and, above all, foreign-born elements who could not vote and who had suffered the most from the inflation. A natural leader of these factions emerged, if that is the word for it, since he was to remain in the background. This was Leandro Alem, a sad-faced lawyer and intellectual whose life had been embittered by the execution of his father, a Rosas henchman. The organization he assembled took the name of the Civic Union. During 1890, while the administration staggered toward catastrophe, the Civic Union plotted a popular upheaval in Buenos Aires that would overthrow it. The planning was excellent, a marvel of detail, and conditions were certainly ripe. Yet when the outbreak occurred, late in July, unlucky timing and a loss of nerve on the part of Alem caused it to fail. Enormous crowds of demonstrators gathered as planned, but they gave way before loyal troops, and the movement collapsed. Its purpose was attained, however, because Juárez Celmán's unpopularity had been dramatized in such a frightening manner. Congress, which so rarely displayed courage or even independence, was emboldened to demand the president's resignation. Early in August he capitulated.

Vice-President Carlos Pellegrini assumed the presidential chair only after the leading financiers assured him of their support for a policy of retrenchment. The regime was not to become democratic, and still less did it intend to satisfy the demands of the Civic Union. But a measure of honesty, economies, and fiscal responsibility in government were to be sought. Within a few months the new administration achieved its purpose. Inflation slowed down, the peso was stabilized, and Argentina's credit recovered. It was the same in many other countries, where governments set out to correct the supposed causes of the depression. That Argentina under President Pellegrini went with and not against the tide of world opinion indicated a certain maturity on the part of the ruling oligarchy.

The Civic Union was still hungry for power, if not through rebellion, then through the elections of 1892. Its opportunity seemed promising, though a majority of the population was disfranchised, because former president Mitre consented to be its candidate. Now seventy years old but still the idol of Buenos Aires, this statesman, who had put together Argentina's political system in the 1860's, would probably have attracted enough support to win. The campaign got under way with much force in 1891, perhaps with too much enthusiasm, because Mitre and many of his wealthy backers became uneasy about the ultra-democratic utterances of Leandro Alem. Finally, Mitre defected, fearing that he was being used as a mere front for the Civic Union. Sacrificing his own ambition to be president again, he negotiated with former president Julio Roca to unite the National Autonomist Party and the *mitristas*, a combination almost certain to win the election. One further threat loomed: a brilliant young soldier named Rocque Sáenz Peña was already well on the way to winning the nomination of the conservative group. The old soldiers thought him too modern-minded and cleverly headed off his candidacy by nominating his father, Luis Sáenz Peña, whereupon young Rocque withdrew. Leandro Alem and the Civic Union were, of course, outraged by Mitre's actions, which, among other injuries, had pulled out of their group many moderates. The remaining members reorganized, accepting the derisory term "Radical" as the name of their party, which has figured significantly ever since in Argentina affairs. The Radicals lost the election of 1892, as might be expected. Soon after Luis Sáenz Peña assumed office, they engineered a rebellion in several localities but failed miserably. Alem sank more and more into a depressed mental state, and in 1896 he committed suicide.

Years of Momentum

PRESIDENT Luis Sáenz Peña presided competently over the recovery of Argentina, but he was no man to deal with a turbulent political situation. The Radical revolts of 1893 unnerved him badly, for they seemed the beginning of a long phase of violence. Furthermore, he was distracted by the conflicting demands of his own party. Congress had unseated one president and was asserting itself with much confidence. Probably in imitation of Chile, where a parliamentary system had supplanted the autocratic presidency in 1890, the legislative branch in Argentina strove to acquire ascendancy. After three years of frustration, in 1895, Sáenz Peña resigned and was succeeded by the vice-president, José Uriburu. Somehow the oligarchy rallied to the executive, and nothing came of the congressional movement. In 1898 the *Régimen* decided to take no chances and nominated a strong candidate, former president Julio A. Roca, who was elected easily despite Radical threats. During the following six years President Roca served with the authority and firmness he had exhibited in his previous term of office. Order and prosperity had returned to Argentina.

The most publicized events of the Uriburu and Roca terms had to do with diplomatic affairs. One, an assertion against foreign intervention in Latin America, will be discussed below. The others were the resolution of long-standing boundary disputes with Brazil and Chile, matters in themselves of minor importance but of immense emotional significance to a people becoming as nationalistic as the Argentines were. Brazil and Argentina had never agreed on their common frontier after the Paraguayan War of 1865–1870. President Cleveland of the United States finally mediated the matter, deciding in 1895 largely in Brazil's favor, a decision accepted loyally but with resentment in Buenos Aires. In 1881 Chile and Argentina had seemingly settled the question of their long boundary by agreeing to mark it at the watershed of the continental divide. Much to their dismay, it soon developed that the flow did not always coincide with the highest ridge, and messy problems arose. Through the good offices of King Edward VII of England the boundary was drawn in 1902, and the famous statue, the Christ of the Andes, was erected to symbolize the perpetual peace the two republics intended to preserve.

Economic developments greatly overshadowed the world of politics after the early 1890's. European markets for Argentine beef, mutton, and wool resumed their expansion. *Estancieros* on the pampas became more scientific in managing their ranches and more elegant in their way of life. Investments poured into the country to extend the railways, improve docks and public utilities, and build meat-packing plants. The astonishing total of one-fourth of the national wealth was foreign-owned. There were still few factories, since the importation of finished goods from abroad was necessary in order to keep the volume of exports high. A new source of riches developed during the 'nineties: grain production, chiefly wheat. Of little importance in the Argentine economy until the last of the century, wheat suddenly achieved a commanding position in European markets, in some years bringing in twice the profits of beef. The pampas were ideal for grain production, their moisture, temperature, and fine black soil being just what this crop needed, and the growing population of Europe apparently offered a limitless outlet. So rewarding was this type of agriculture, many ranchers plowed up their pastures and invested in thrashers and reapers. The very size of the *estancias* made capitalistic agriculture on a large scale lucrative, and the supply of labor was never less than abundant. Realizing the possibilities of wheat production, the government wisely facilitated the construction of storage facilities and elevators, chiefly at Rosario, which Urquiza had once tried to build into a rival of Buenos Aires. Now it was the wheat capital of Argentina, the second city of the country, and after a spate of dredging and dock-building, the most important grain port in the world.

It is understandable that Argentina acquired a splendid reputation in the money marts of Europe. She was not one of those Latin American republics where they were always having revolutions. Her credit was sound, her currency respected; investors knew of fantastic profits speculation there might produce. In addition, the Argentines themselves advertised their nation's opulence. Sons of cattle barons often attended European universities, and it was fashionable for the Argentine aristocracy to go to Europe every year or two. They tended to be good spenders, often competing for space with Russian grand dukes at the best resorts. The Paris luxury trades drew much of their support from these South Americans. And then artists and performers of all types had long learned to respect the taste of theater-goers and musical audiences in Buenos Aires. French and Spanish publishers attached great importance to the Argentine reading public, who absorbed many of the best books and journals. Of course, most Europeans had only the dimmest idea where the country was, but they knew it was civilized and rich. About a quarter of a million Europeans elected to try their fortunes there every year.

As Argentina's economy and culture flourished, so did the ambitions of some of her nationalists. Only Porfirian Mexico could rival her in international prestige, for Brazil went through a squalid period after the fall of the empire in 1889. An increasing number of influential Argentines, politicians and writers, thought it inevitable that their country should assume leadership of Latin America. Some trace of this aspiration appeared at the first Pan-American Conference in 1889, where the Argentine delegation had been uncooperative. Another and a stronger indication came in 1902, when three European powers were blockading Venezuela because of unpaid debts, with the United States nervously acquiescing.

Luis M. Drago, the foreign minister under President Roca, issued a statement that thrilled many Latin Americans and became known as the Drago Doctrine, a condemnation of the use of force for purposes of collecting debts. Naturally, Argentina was acutely sensitive about this point, for she was the principal scene of foreign investments in South America. Yet she also desired to assert her leadership, and to a large extent succeeded in doing so.

In 1904, however, President Theodore Roosevelt issued his Corollary to the Monroe Doctrine, which contradicted the Argentine contention by intimating that the United States had a duty to keep Latin American countries from falling into such trouble as to provoke European intervention. From this time on—if not really from an earlier date —Argentine official and public opinion was hostile to the United States, and Argentina sought to exploit anti-American feelings all over Latin America so as to strengthen her own position. Much of this rivalry stemmed from an economic source, for the two nations were competitors. Both exported livestock products and grain, and both craved capital and immigrants. It is true that their commerce with each other grew sixfold between 1880 and 1906, but the total was insignificant when compared to the trade of either with Europe. If Americans seldom thought of Argentina at all, Argentines nourished a strong cult of anti-Yankeeism.

Illustrative of Argentina's determination to be European rather than American was the way Buenos Aires consciously imitated Paris and London in architecture, style of living, and pleasures. By 1900 the city had about three quarters of a million inhabitants, most of them of European birth. It had long been lighted and paved, and its sewage and water supply systems were modern. Banks and department stores copied the stateliness of London. The traffic pattern was English-style, on the left. Tree-lined boulevards with sidewalk cafes, mansions, theaters, and governmental palaces resembled those of Paris. Even the modest flats and shops that spread out into the pampas were drab like those of European cities, not squalid and colorful the way they were in Rio de Janeiro or Mexico City. Above all, Buenos Aires was bursting with energy and activity, charged with a nervousness of a city where money-making, not the traditional leisure of Spain, was the ideal. Rosario, which developed so rapidly as a flour-milling and grain port up the Paraná, was a miniature Buenos Aires. Córdoba and Mendoza had revived from their long sleep covering most of the nineteenth century and were now active, but they retained the appearance and low-keyed atmosphere of colonial times.

By any reasonable standard Argentina led the intellectual life of Latin America. Her school system, public-supported and under lay control, brought the illiteracy rate to the lowest in the Hispanic world. The appetite of her educated classes for the best of European literary production led to the establishment of publishing houses in Buenos Aires, many of which prospered. Literati in that capital seldom caught the attention of Europe for their originality, but they nurtured the Western cultural tradition in their own way, and worthily. In the world of ideas Argentina held a respectable position. Sarmiento's normal school at Paraná was the center of the positivist cult which so enraptured Latin Americans in the early twentieth century.[1] The University of Córdoba staunchly upheld the older Catholic orthodox philosophy, which insisted on being heard even in a materialistic age and did, as many later came to admit, hold much of importance for modern man. At La Plata there was a university unique by Hispanic standards. While it was customary for universities to offer professional training in law, medicine, theology, and other fields for the benefit of a few well-born students, La Plata specialized in basic research in the arts and science. Its influence was not easily measured, but it was clearly large.

Two Argentine thinkers, or *pensadores*, of this period had enormous followings in Latin America. The more prominent was José Ingenieros (1877–1925), who may have been the best-read author in the Spanish language. At first a physician, then a psychologist, finally a philosopher by profession, he traveled widely and wrote prolifically in a short life. Much of the time he popularized positivist, socialist, and Darwinian concepts. A fertile and original thinker with ideas bristling in every sentence, he sounded a call to idealism that Latin American youths found irresistible. At other times he might be cynical or inconsistent, but this would be overlooked. Carlos Octavio Bunge (1875–1918), likewise had great influence, though it is not easy to understand why. He appealed to the pessimistic strain that haunts Argentines even in days of glorious boom. Spanish Americans he pictured as arrogant and lethargic, condemned by racial heritage and the past to eternal frustration. Somehow his despondent criticisms articulated deeply rooted feelings which many people knew.

1. Positivism is a loose philosophical term that connotes dedication to "facts" of experience that can be verified in public. Implicitly, at least, it repudiates revealed religion or spiritual insight. While many Latin American, and other, positivists were able to reconcile Christianity and positivism to their satisfaction, there can be little doubt that the cult weakened the traditional faith and all that was implied in it. Positivists, particularly after the publications of the Frenchman, Auguste Comte, thought of themselves as modern men who emphasized the religion of humanity rather than the historic Judaeo-Christianity, and who favored unending material progress and believed that right dealing and ethical conduct could be regulated by mundane considerations with little or no reference to God. Of course, positivism was anything but new in the history of philosophy, but its terminology and popularity among Latin American intellectuals endowed it with a peculiar significance toward the last of the nineteenth century and the early twentieth.

The Emergence of the Radical Party

DURING the first years of the twentieth century the *Régimen* governed competently, even with traces of liberalism, like its contemporaries in Europe. But it also was haunted, as were its European counterparts, by the specter of revolution from below. Roca's second administration was probably the end of the confident period. There were too many signs of labor unrest and middle-class assertiveness for the ruling oligarchs to enjoy a sense of security. Roca was succeeded in 1904 by Manuel Quintana, an aristocrat in the grand manner. The Radicals had boycotted the polls in that year and attempted a rebellion in 1905. Quintana's death opened the Casa Rosada, Argentina's pink White House, to the vice-president, Figueroa Alcorta, for most of this term, which was a period of revolutionary agitation and uneasiness in spite of generally sunny economic conditions. For the elections of 1910 the entrenched oligarchy, whose National Autonomist Party was becoming more popularly known as the Conservatives, acknowledged the widespread dissatisfaction in the country by naming a reformer, Roque Sáenz Peña, as its candidate. Now nearly sixty, this able aristocrat was remembered for his service with Peru in 1879 during her war with Chile, for having been disagreeable to the United States at the Pan-American Conference of 1889, and for his championship of liberal causes while a member of congress. It will be recalled that he had been a formidable contender for the presidential nomination in 1892 until the bosses undercut him by selecting his father. Sáenz Peña had almost no opposition when he ran in 1910. The Radicals stayed away from the polls, and the Conservatives voted for him in the fervent hope that he could modernize the regime in time to save it.

The chief threat to the oligarchs was Hipólio Yrigoyen,[2] who had established a spider-like power over the Radical Power network since the suicide of Leandro Alem in 1896. A nephew of Alem, who was more like a brother than an uncle to him, Yrigoyen was born in 1852, the son of a Basque workingman and Alem's sister, a native Argentine. He had some education but was not by any means a cultured man. One of his few affectations was sporting the title of "doctor" on the basis of a single year's attendance at law school. While serving as a police commissar in Buenos Aires he absorbed a great deal of useful information about the way society worked and the motivations of people. As a member of the legislature of Buenos Aires province he acquired a contempt for parliamentarism. For many years he taught in a girl's school, a career that evidently encouraged him to read but not to respect the female intellect. His main

2. His own spelling of the last name,   which usually begins with an "I."

inspiration derived from the writings of Karl Kristian Krause, a German philosopher so obscure that he is seldom listed as a thinker of note. Krause's incomprehensible metaphysics happened to attract a group of Spanish students in Germany, who took it into the peninsula and started a *krausista* movement that had large effects there and percolated into Argentina during the 1870's and 1880's. Whatever the German intended to say, his adherents attributed to him a democratic idealism that would eventually lead to the brotherhood of man.

This was also true of Yrigoyen himself. While his true thoughts could rarely be inferred from his more or less unintelligible words, people felt a powerful appeal to democratic altrusim and credited to him the loftiest of sentiments. Perhaps the secret of the fascination he undoubtedly possessed lay entirely in this attractiveness. He was certainly not lucid in expression, nor eloquent. Physically he was not prepossessing; a tall, shabby, rather disagreeable bachelor, he had few of the charms of a successful demagogue. Yet individuals found themselves almost hypnotized, and the masses idolized him. As a protégé of Leandro Alem he had helped to organize the Civic Union and the Radical Party. He differed with his uncle and mentor as time went on, especially with regard to tactics, and just before he killed himself, Alem said that Yrigoyen had betrayed him. Others had reason to criticize his behavior. He was indeed a strange man. As Isabel Rennie wrote, "There has never been a character whose motivation was more obscure, or whose personality was more secretive. . . . Without being intelligent, he was almost unfathomable."

Yrigoyen's methods were as mysterious as his character. He seldom made speeches, and when he did, his oratory was uninspired and his meanings hidden. Yet his listeners sensed he had a great heart and would fulfill promises for reform and social uplift, promises that he in fact rarely made. His writings were equally unenlightening and often were published under someone else's name. He was uncomfortable before large conferences and made no secret of his distaste for public meetings. It was in the individual interview that he shone. Usually meeting people one by one in his unpretentious apartment in Buenos Aires, he talked for hours. His listener would leave the meeting entranced, convinced he had been in contact with undefinable but authentic greatness.

As the years went on Yrigoyen thus fascinated—or greatly repelled, for a few reacted strongly against him—nearly every Radical politician of importance in these private talks. In this way he constructed a large and devoted political machine. The center of his web was Buenos Aires province, where he began in 1890; twenty years later the organization was nation-wide, and Yrigoyen was its undisputed boss. Socialists and others who distrusted him had left the Radical Party to form splinter groups of their own. Basically, the attractiveness of Yrigoyen's organization was for the population of the cities, mainly the foreign-born or sons of immigrants, the lower and middle classes. First of all they demanded the right to vote which the oligarchy had contrived to deny them so long. Once they had the suffrage, they planned many steps to promote social welfare and to assure a more equitable distribution of wealth.

Yrigoyen was shrewd in guessing that the power of the Radicals would seem more ominous to the Conservatives if the party abstained from voting altogether. Since only a few Radicals were eligible to go to the polls, their showing would be demoralizing if not ridiculous. The crafty leader was not always able to enforce his views, for occasionally Radical groups submitted candidacies that were, as things turned out, roundly defeated. Nor was he able to prevent hot-heads from resorting to force before he thought conditions were ripe. A spatter of revolutions in 1905 showed the abiding power of the *Régimen* and the unreadiness of the population for violence. His policies vindicated, Yrigoyen continued to tighten his power and to undermine the confidence of the Conservatives.

The nomination of Roque Sáenz Peña in 1910 revealed that the oligarchs were worried. This president forthwith set out to meet the most urgent demand of the Radicals, universal suffrage. A series of bills known collectively as the Roque Sáenz Peña Law was forced through a hesitant congress in 1912. These required that every Argentine male register for army service and voting at the age of eighteen. Thereafter, the exercise of the suffrage was compulsory and secret; a booklet carried by each man showed his fulfillment of this duty at all elections, or else he was fined. Another stipulation was that a minority party must receive one-third of the seats in congress or state legislatures no matter how few votes it won. As so often happens in fortunate countries, the timely retreat of a ruling group spelled its survival. The Radicals soon came to power legally, and therefore were not so radical after all, and the Conservatives lived on even if they had to surrender office for a time.

In 1912 the congressional and local elections brought a formidable surge of Radical and Socialist representation. For almost the first time in Argentina, measures were passed to benefit the working classes and to restrict the employers. This taste of social legislation intensified the determination of labor groups, who were well aware of the Mexican Revolution and the teachings of European reformers. Yrigoyen offered little leadership in such matters; his approach was almost altogether political. Yet it was he and not the Socialists, whose appeal was limited to railroad and dock workers, who commanded the allegiance of the masses. As the elections of 1916 approached, it seemed clear that he would be swept into the presidency. Roque Sáenz Peña had died in office, and the Conservatives had no popular leader. Their candidate, as might be expected of a group so deeply involved with Great Britain, favored Argentine entrance into World War I, a stand most office-seekers in the western hemisphere, at least outside of Canada, considered impolitic. Oddly enough, the chief obstacle to Radical hopes was Yrigoyen's refusal to run. He may well have been sincere, for he was a recluse by nature. The most urgent importunings were necessary before he finally agreed to accept the nomination. His reluctance, whether it was assumed or genuine, increased his power over the Radical party and made him more beloved by the masses. He won a substantial popular plurality but fell short of a majority in the electoral college, where the provinces could make their distaste for Buenos Aires and the urban supporters of Yrigoyen felt. An ugly mood prevailed for some weeks. There was much talk, surely well-founded, that the Radicals would resort to force if denied victory. Finally, a small liberal party composed mainly of agrarian populists threw its support to Yrigoyen, and he was declared president of the Argentine Republic.[3]

Hipólito Yrigoyen as President, 1916–1922

YRIGOYEN'S inauguration in October 1916 typified much of his public career. He was uncomfortable amid all the ceremony and celebration, made no inaugural address, and tried to disappear in the crowds. On the other hand, the populace was delirious, unhitching his horses so they could pull his carriage and behaving as if the millenium had arrived. Great things were expected, and if Radical words meant anything, an avalanche of liberal legislation was about to smother the old regime. For some months, however, little happened. The president and his associates were absorbed in sweeping away thousands of office-holders to make way for power-starved Radicals. Because of their inexperience a certain amount of fumbling could be forgiven. But it finally developed that there was no real Radical program, no imperious demands by the president for congress to fulfill, nothing, in fact, but the joys of office sweetened by corruption worse than the Conservatives had indulged. Yrigoyen himself was honest and very frugal, preferring his shabby apartment to the Casa Rosada. He either was too blind to see how his followers were behaving or did not care. What he did care about was maintaining his hold on the Radical Party, which he did with a vengeance. During the campaign there had been much talk of shifting the

3. This was the doing of Lisandro de la Torre, one of the founders of the Radical Party who had become alienated by Yrigoyen's tyrannical methods. His Democratic Progressive Party, which was centered in Santa Fe, was long a force for liberalism, honest government, and agrar- ian reform. It cost De la Torre much anguish to throw the election to Yrigoyen, but he sincerely believed he was preventing a civil war by so doing. Long a respected figure in Argentine politics, he ran unsuccessfully for president in 1931.

center of government from the president to congress, presumably a democratic development and therefore desirable. Nothing of this sort happened. Yrigoyen ruled his machine as he always had, like a dictator, and through it, congress, the courts, and the provinces. It was soon apparent that he had scant respect for the niceties of constitutionalism. At times he told congressional leaders what he wanted done and proceeded to enforce his wishes as if they had already become laws. Even more than his predecessors he abused the presidential power to intervene in provincial affairs, setting aside elected officials and imposing his own choices on the grounds that the states were not truly republican. Now in his mid-sixties, Yrigoyen had held party control too long to share it, and he remained secretive and capricious. Sometimes he dreamed and dawdled, temperamentally refusing to read official correspondence or to see important visitors. His administration was aimless, corrupt, inefficient, and often tyrannical. No one but the Conservatives and the far left seemed to mind. Verbal liberalism apparently satisfied the common people, who virtually adored President Yrigoyen.

It was anti-climactic that the Radicals did not make the most of their long-awaited opportunity by enacting fundamental reforms. Apparently all they had craved was the universal suffrage law and office. Having won both, there was now nothing further to do. True, a few modest measures were passed. Congress outlawed child labor, specified that all workers should have Sunday rest, abolished licensed prostitution, forbade horse racing on working days, encouraged the arbitration of labor disputes, and specified a minimum wage for certain small groups. While these enactments were considerably less than revolutionary, hardly bringing Argentina abreast of other modern countries, the Radicals had, nevertheless, released currents of liberalism. Labor unionization made great strides. Numerous small industries were started, to manufacture articles the country could not import because of the war. A nationalized petroleum monopoly, YPF, represented a commendable desire to reduce Argentina's dependence on foreign oil, though it seemed for many years that she had none of her own to exploit.

Yrigoyen inadvertently sparked an important reform in university administration which other Latin American countries eventually copied. When he intervened in the conservative University of Córdoba in 1917, the students went on strike to protest his action. After much agitation there and in the other universities, student demands were crystallized in a series of statesmanlike proposals. Universities should become autonomous, governed by representatives of the state, alumni, faculty, and student body. More scholarships should be available, standards should be raised, and professorships should be filled by competition instead of appointment. These reforms, embodied in a law passed in 1918, notably improved the several Argentine universities and, in later years, many in other nations.

President Yrigoyen displayed great firmness of will in the face of much criticism with regard to Argentina's position in the last stages of World War I. He saw no need for his country to do anything but make profits from the sale of her war materials, which she was doing on an enormous scale, without bothering about the balance of power or international moral issues of questionable validity. Many believed him pro-German; others said he was simply ignorant. Again, he may have been much wiser than the highly vocal factions who advanced many arguments for Argentina to help Great Britain for business reasons, or France to save civilization, or Italy because she was the mother country of so many Argentines. The president spurned all such proposals and even heavier pressures. Probably the majority of the population supported him. To Yrigoyen, the entrance of the United States in 1917 was merely another good reason for Argentina to remain neutral. German atrocities, as the employment of submarines and poison gas were popularly characterized in those days, did not strike him as particularly odious. He was amazingly patient when the Allies presented him with a decoded message sent from Buenos Aires by the German minister, in which the diplomat urged that Argentine ships either be left alone altogether or else sunk without a trace, which involved gunning the survivors in lifeboats. It was poor psychology, he said, to allow news of such losses to be circulated, and he added a sneer at the Indianism of South America and an uncomplimentary comment about Yrigoyen. The unfortunate Teuton had to leave Argentina (to return, however, and die there many years later), but Yrigoyen ignored the clamor of the "best people" and continued diplomatic relations with Germany. Perhaps he enjoyed the impotent rage of the Anglophile cattle barons and the Gallophile literati whom he despised. In retrospect, he seems to have followed a correct course during World War I and to have represented the real sentiments of his people. After the war, when the League of Nations refused to include Germany and snubbed Argentina in a question about membership on the Council, President Yrigoyen withdrew his country from the world organization.

Shortly after the end of World War I, strikes and ultra-radical violence broke out in many cities of the world. The Red Scare, as people living in more serene times have derided this dangerous phase, swept through Buenos Aires in January 1919. While a weak revolutionary virus no doubt existed in the city, based mainly on Spanish anarchists and assorted immigrant radicals, there was little danger of a fundamental upheaval. Discontent was prevalent, rather, as a result of inflation and various economic dislocations caused by the end of the war boom. A series of strikes began and spread rapidly. When the police ambushed a group of dock workers who were on strike and caused casualties, the rest of the city's working population joined in a general strike. President Yrigoyen exhibited a stern sense of duty by siding with the forces of law and order against the lower classes, his strongest supporters, but his resort to brutal methods, including the shooting of demonstrators, went beyond the necessities of the moment. After the strike collapsed, popular aggressions were then directed irrationally upon the quarter of the city which housed thousands of Jews, apparently on the theory that most of them were of Russian birth and therefore must be Bolsheviks. Killings, injuries, and pillage reached an appalling level before the government finally restored order. Somehow President Yrigoyen emerged from this violent period with enhanced prestige. He won the grudging respect of the Conservatives while retaining the affection of the common people. He left the presidency in 1922 enormously popular.

Last Years of a Golden Era: The Presidency of Marcelo Alvear, 1922–1928

IT WAS easy for Yrigoyen to dictate his successor in the election of 1922, so strong was the Radical Party and his own hold on the population. He chose a liberal aristocrat name Marcelo T. de Alvear, who had joined the Civic Union in 1890 and had remained devoted to Yrigoyen through all the years of obscurity and triumph afterward. Much of Alvear's life had been spent abroad, either as one of the numerous moneyed Argentine tourists or as a diplomat. His chief claim to publicity stemmed from his marriage, years before he was elected president, to a Portuguese singer whom Buenos Aires high society persisted in cutting. Now in the Casa Rosada, the couple presided with dignity and charm during the prosperous 'twenties, disregarding the snubs of the aristocrats. Yrigoyen had assumed that Alvear would do his bidding. Alvear anticipated that the aging chieftain, now in his seventies, would be willing to relinquish his command of the Radicals. Both were mistaken, though it took two years for the tension to produce an outright rupture. Yrigoyen had dominated his party too long to tolerate independence of action, even in a president; Alvear had too much pride to be a puppet. Breaking in 1924, Alvear attempted to create a party of dissident Radicals known as the *anti-personalistas,* which allied itself with the Conservatives. Yrigoyen maintained his power over the larger numbers of Radicals who remained loyal to him.

Under the circumstances it was difficult for the administration to accomplish much. Alvear succeeded in having a few measures passed to protect the urban workers, notably a grandiose pension plan, but Argentina lagged far behind Mexico, Chile, and most Europen countries in welfare legislation. He also obtained a tax on land and inheritances which greatly disturbed the oligarchy, not because the rates were high, for they were not, but because a precedent had been broken. However, the wealthy classes once more, as in 1912, gave way to the trends of the times and were none the worse for it, at least in the long run. A dispute with the Catholic Church over the role of the president in appointing an archbishop caused an interruption of relations between Argentina and Rome for two years. The importance of the quarrel lay in the fact that it was so unusual; for decades exceedingly few disputes had disturbed the historic harmony between the republic and the Vatican. Alvear also sponsored an immigration law like that of the United States which required higher standards for admission and limited the number of new arrivals on the basis of quotas. Without admitting it, Argentina desired to remain a white man's country and also to prevent a flood of immigrants from eastern Europe. Another face of national feeling the republic displayed in dealing with other American nations. Argentina aspired more than ever to lead Latin America against the United States, who was depicted as a materialistic giant with malignant ambitions. Alvear was also angry when American tariff laws practically barred Argentine grain and wool, and his nation was insulted beyond apology when the United States banned Argentine beef because of hoof-and-mouth disease on the pampas. Outsiders were unable to comprehend how deeply involved was the pride of the Argentines in such matters, and few guessed the extent to which virulent nationalism was developing in the southern republic.

It was for the future to reveal the depths of Argentina's rabid patriotism and also to uncover the social forces that were at work below the surface in the 1920's. Outwardly, times were good, the best ever, and people seemed satisfied. England first, and then continental Europe, were paying good prices for all the beef, mutton, wool, and wheat that Argentina could export. Capital investments and finished goods poured over in payment for these raw materials. Immigrants in vast numbers still flocked to the Argentine with high hopes despite the new restrictions. Buenos Aires, which now rivalled Paris in size and splendor, continued to prosper as a sort of valve for the flow that poured out the republic's products and absorbed the people, money, and finished articles of Europe. Englishmen half-joked that Argentina was the most loyal dominion of the British Empire. And so it seemed. The *estancieros* were richer than ever, migrating in larger numbers to Europe for the social season, speaking British English or French, drinking Scotch whiskey, copying British tastes and sports, and fervently advocating the tightening of Anglo-Argentine ties while sneering at the United States. Even if the Radicals had driven them from political power they were far and above the dominant class. The middle classes were still unsure of themselves, ill-defined, and not yet pitted against the aristocrats in profound ways. It was well known that Argentine wealth and income were most unevenly distributed, but if the disinherited classes resented this situation particularly, there was little evidence of it during the Alvear presidency. The popularity of the novels by Manuel Gálvez (1882–   ), which exposed in detailed and authentic fashion the dissatisfactions of many Argentines, was taken only as a tribute to the author's skill. Argentina was a growing nation with the oldest and most successful system in Latin America, and she had a good reputation in the outside world.

Hipólito Yrigoyen had chafed for four years while President Alvear and the *anti-personalista* Radicals defied his leadership. If he had been reluctant to run for president in 1916, the old man, now seventy-six, was eager for office in 1928, probably out of spite. He was still a demigod to the masses, who credited him with deep humanitarian sympathies; only small numbers of the poor had defected to the Socialist Party. Yrigoyen stood even higher with the middle classes, who considered him one of themselves and believed him, strangely in view of his earlier term, to be the most sincere guarantor of democratic government. The polo-playing cattle barons and the rest of the elite knew by now that he was their foe only in relatively superficial matters. Thus his entrance into the presidential race brought widespread approval from most sectors of the electorate. Yrigoyen declined to campaign, and he revealed on one or two occasions that his mind was not vigorous. Yet he was triumphantly elected to the presidency, an apparent instrument of destiny and idol of his people. Very little happened, as in 1916, after his administration took over except a wholesale redistribution of the spoils of government. If anything, the loyal *personalistas* were more cynical, corrupt, and high-handed than they had been in the previous Yrigoyen term. The president himself gave more and more signs of his physical and mental decline. He refused to move into the Casa Rosada, neglected public affairs, was capricious and irritable, and held himself aloof, almost as a hermit, from national problems and presidential duties. During his first year all this made little difference, since Argentina was such a marvelous social organism that she flourished irrespective of politics. In October 1929, however, the Wall Street catastrophe plunged the world of international trade into disorder, and Argentina was one of the first countries to feel the effects. The depression threw into relief her social fissures and the flaws in her structure. Challenged by a vast economic crisis, Yrigoyen's government practically disintegrated.

BRAZIL: ORDER AND PROGRESS

The Empire

THE INTERREGNUM, 1831–1840

When Pedro I abdicated in April 1831, he did so in behalf of his five-year-old son, Pedro de Alcántara, for whom a three-man regency was to govern under the constitution of 1824 until the new emperor reached eighteen. Brazil was in a state of shock over the departure of its liberator-monarch. More than any others, the Portuguese, who were still numerous in the government and urban business circles, felt orphaned by Pedro I's defection. They knew themselves the losers in the recent upheaval. But who were the victors? The great native aristocracy, composed mainly of sugar lords, had apparently overcome the Portuguese element by securing the emperor's abdication, but it was an uneasy oligarchy indeed. Creole radicals in Rio de Janeiro and other cities, as well as the remaining peninsulars, were still in a position to make mischief and might yet prevent the planters from solidifying their power. In the southern provinces were *gaúchos* and ranchers who were drawn into the confused politics of the Spanish Platine area and who, essentially, preferred no government at all. Such educated Brazilians as there were divided sharply regarding ideology, the conservatives wanting to preserve a centralist monarchical regime and the liberals to repudiate the past by embracing federalism and radicalism. The bureaucracy, Church, and army seemed uprooted, scarcely capable of performing their historic functions for a monarch five years old. Most of the population had no interest in public affairs. Confusion and drift seemed to mark the future; it appeared very unlikely that Brazil would escape the anarchy and atomization that befell the former Spanish viceroyalties or that the monarchy would endure.

And yet Brazil survived this dangerous period, and so did the monarchy. Somehow the leading men found sufficient grounds for cooperation on essential matters, though this can be seen only in retrospect, for during the 1830's Brazil's public life was almost as riotous as that of her Spanish-speaking neighbors. Demagogues stirred the masses in nearly every town, garrisons rebelled, slaves rose up, and wildly partisan strife filled the press and the congress. The child emperor repeatedly had to be carried away from the capital for safety. Secessionist movements threatened to tear away Pará and Maranhão in the north, Minas Gerais in the center, and Rio Grande do Sul in the south. In the last-named province a civil war destined to last for ten years began in 1835. Republicanism, in some cases of the radical idealistic variety and in others of the plutocratic type, appeared at one time or another in every province. Still, the nation held together.

In times of extreme crisis, the principal leaders of competing factions could unite and compromise their ideological purity to save the state. At first their problem was to restrain the radical extremists in the capital and São Paulo and thus save the vital center of Brazil for constitutional monarchy. Severe methods by the minister of justice, a liberal priest named Diogo Antonio Feijó, supported by a flood of preachments by Evaristo da Veiga, the country's leading publisher, served to create a political synthesis. Then, the constitution was changed in 1834 by an "Additional Act" which appeased federalists by granting more powers to elected provincial legislatures and which strengthened the central administration by ending the three-man regency. In 1835 Father Feijó became sole regent, a position he filled for two years very capably, if autocratically. Determined to keep the ideal of a united monarchy alive, he created loyal national guard units and managed to maintain a core of military power that dealt effectively with revolutionary movements in the cities and the northern provinces. But he failed to pacify the south, and his harsh methods so alienated parliament that he was forced to resign in 1837.

Succeeding Feijó as regent was Pedro de Araújo Lima, a prominent congressional leader, who rallied for a time the parliamentarians and also attracted the Portuguese elements who had been left utterly without purpose after the death of Pedro I in 1834. With the moderate and reactionary factions combining to form a Conservative Party under Araújo's leadership and the remaining groups forming the Liberals, Brazilian political life reached an outwardly conventional stage. For three years Araújo attempted to hold the empire together, permitting considerable personal liberty and achieving some fiscal order. Yet the secessionist movement in Rio Grande do Sul, by now clearly a republican affair, was still out of hand, and revolts were likely to sputter anywhere. In 1840 the monarchical Liberals decided to supplant Araújo and the Conservatives by declaring young Pedro, then only fourteen, of age four years ahead of schedule. Committing perhaps the only questionable political action of his career—or did the adolescent sense that the regime might go to pieces unless he asserted the imperial prestige?—he lent himself to this unconstitutional scheme. The Liberals whipped up much agitation to have him declared of age, ostensibly to stabilize the country but in reality as a device to turn the Conservatives out, but they were unable to have congress authorize it. As for Araújo, he well realized that his administration was quaking, but he thought he might yet win Pedro by delaying matters a little longer. In an extraordinarily confused scene in July 1840 he lost control of the situation. The regent disbanded the lower house, only to see the Liberals flock to the imperial palace and beg the young emperor to assume full authority. Aware that public opinion and the emperor were on the Liberal side, Araújo and the Conservatives joined their rivals and likewise asked Pedro to take over. Elements of absurdity, patriotism, idealism, and practical politics were not absent as the sober-minded teen-ager bowed to the pressures. If the imperial authority had been invoked by the Liberals to win power and by the Conservatives to save the nation, both achieved their desires. The people went into transports of joy, and Pedro's coronation a year later was another event extravagantly celebrated by a nation which loves a good time. The magic of royalty was still a potent force.

THE PATTERN OF POWER IN THE SECOND REIGN

True to his bargain with the Liberals, Pedro II placed this group in power. Within eight months, however, he was displeased by the wholesale dismissal of Conservative office-holders and by Liberal proposals to weaken the central government, and he restored the Conservatives. During the next three years this party withdrew from provincial legislatures most of the authority granted them by the Additional Act of 1834 and created a national police system which largely dominated the judiciary. Liberals in São Paulo and Minas Gerais revolted but were defeated by a brilliant soldier who long served as a pillar of the empire, Luis Alves de Lima, the Baron Caxias, who later became a viscount and finally a duke. Caxias then terminated the republican-secessionist movement that had long torn Rio Grande do Sul. The last insurrection under der the empire occurred in 1847–1848 in the northeast, where a discordant collection of dissatisfied persons revolted for widely different purposes. After that the empire enjoyed forty years of internal peace, standing as a rebuke to the disorderly Spanish republics. By 1848 Pedro II was exercising his powers fully and in his own way. His success was demonstrated not only by the pacified state of the empire but by the fact that the Liberals had been in power for four years by that time and had adapted themselves to his aims as loyally as the Conservatives. Pedro had made it abundantly clear that he, rather than majorities in the lower house, would run the country, and he had even shaken off a palace clique that had aspired to envelop the throne.

Pedro II became the most admired individual of his time in Latin America. Indeed, he was one of the great rulers in the nineteenth-century world, possibly the most outstanding among those of the royal fraternity. He was unlike his father and the Braganza monarchs of Portugal, a generally undistinguished dynasty. Perhaps he resembled more the dutiful Habsburgs of his mother's line, though he was less rigid than most of their archdukes and emperors. Tall and dignified, he personified kingliness in all its majesty; yet people instinctively liked and trusted him, and he had no taste for the uniforms and parades that characterized monarchical pageantry in Europe and presidential ostentation in Latin America. Pedro's education explained much about him. During his minority the regents had seen to it that he received a good one, and he was by nature so bookish and serious-minded that he did not rebel against his solemn tutors. Intellectually he was humble, willing to be corrected, eager to learn—all this despite the fact that few men in South America were as learned as he was. He read, reflected, experimented in science, wrote verses, and studied fourteen languages. Furthermore, Pedro was virtuous. He was frugal and modest, careful about public expenditures and private conduct. Married at seventeen to a lame, homely girl four years his senior, Thereza of the Two Sicilies, he lived an impeccably moral life —as far as contemporaries knew—in a land no stranger to licentiousness. During a period of showy monarchism in most of the world the Brazilian imperial family were probably the least extravagant and the most democratic. Possibly it would have been better psychology to have flaunted the monarchy in all its gaudy splendor. But Pedro often said that royalty was out of place in the New World, and he devoted a lifetime to making his crown a symbol of republicanism in the best sense of the term.

For his personal respectability and long reign Pedro II inevitably suggests comparison with his contemporary, Queen Victoria. In more fundamental ways he resembled Queen Elizabeth I, in that he tamed disruptive forces and led his country superbly during a dangerous transition from near insignificance to near greatness. His rule had to be based on the approval of the great rural aristocracy, principally the sugar planters of the northeast, which gave the country such tone and direction as it had and which had really dominated Brazil for generations except during the reigns of João VI and Pedro I. A class with some culture and great patriotism, they respected the emperor and rejoiced that he, unlike his father, was Brazilian-born. Yet they were wary of his liberal tendencies, for this slave-owning oligarchy was inevitably falling farther behind the times as the century wore on. Pedro skillfully used this group but did not belong to it. He drew its abler men into public life and widely distributed titles—usually not hereditary—among them. With the emerging new planter class, the owners of cotton and coffee lands in the central regions, he was also conciliatory. For them the empire meant good government and a tranquillity helpful to economic progress, and also an opportunity to win status.

More than many of his contemporaries, the emperor appreciated the wonders that science, technology, and capitalism were bringing within sight of the masses. Accordingly, he encouraged inventors and tinkers, investors, bankers, and builders of mills, factories, and railroads. To this end it was important that Brazil have balanced budgets, honest administration, and sound credit, which it usually did under the empire. As amicably as possible Pedro needed to reconcile the protectionist desires of the manufacturing class with the free trade beliefs cherished by those who exported raw materials. The middle class, so frail, needed nourishment and received it. Ranching interests in the south had to be defended, even if this meant aggression on Brazil's part against Platine politicians who sought to enlarge the Spanish states. These, then, were the classes whose basic consensus was necessary if the empire was to survive. For many years Dom Pedro, as he was fondly called, secured this agreement, and the empire throve.

Pedro's methods of government revealed him an astute manipulator and a benevolent autocrat. The constitution of 1824 endowed him with great authority as chief of the executive apparatus, head of the army, and patron of the Church. He appointed his own ministers—a right he established when he was only eighteen—as well as department heads and presidents of the provinces, who in turn named the executives of the cities. A large, centralized bureaucracy reaching into the smallest units of government depended on the monarch. Police and judicial authority also channeled directly to him. He had the power of veto and could dissolve the lower house of congress and, extra-legally, to arrange that a new one favorable to his purposes was chosen by an electorate of taxpayers that seldom amounted to as much as one per cent of the total population. Instead of making himself an outright despot, however, Pedro chose to train the educated classes for self-government and to cloak his power. He liked to think of himself as the moderator of the country, the ultimate agent of sovereignty who could assert the public welfare (as he saw it) by using whatever branch of the government that served his purpose.

Brazil's imperial regime was therefore not constitutionalist in the British sense, though an effort was made to have it appear so. The emperor after 1847 appointed a prime minister who either enjoyed majority support in congress or would obtain it after a rigged election. Pedro made some effort to alternate Conservatives and Liberals, but the result was not the creation of a genuine two-party system; rather, the two parties grew more alike, being divided little by real issues and competing chiefly for the pleasures of office-holding and patronage in the large administrative apparatus. Each group was likely to complain of imperial arrogance whenever it was ousted and the electoral machinery was manipulated to favor its rival. Yet changes of this type were agreeable contrasts to the shots and bluster that accompanied overturns in the Spanish republics. Pedro changed ministries thirty-six times in forty-nine years, and on eleven occasions he disbanded the lower house rather than veto a bill. Brazil did not become a democracy, nor even a two-party oligarchy, but her government operated smoothly and well if allowances are made for the enormous area, the backward population, and the problems of the times. Moreover, personal liberty was respected in a way unknown in the rest of Latin America. One could say or write almost anything, even to urging the downfall of the monarchy, without fear of punishment. Life and property were safe from governmental tyranny and usually from outlaws. Pedro's appointments were exemplary; the members of his advisory Council of State, the provincial presidents, the ministers, and the life senators he named were mostly honorable and competent men. In making these appointments and in distributing titles of nobility, the emperor sought to reward talent, and not infrequently he honored men with Negro blood.

As the empire aged, criticisms of Pedro's methods became warmer. It was difficult to oppose him openly, such was his popularity and prestige. He was by far the most informed and experienced man in the country in government, and no ambitious person could long resist cooperating with him if he hoped to advance himself. Nor could the emperor's policies, which were simply good government and progress, be challenged very successfully. It was also difficult to make out a strong case against his veiled autocracy, for clearly the monarch was a modest individual of high integrity who respected the rights of others and manifestly loved his country. His magnaminity and broad-mindedness were characteristic of a large soul, and few thought otherwise even when they disputed some of his policies. Yet strong men chafed at the emperor's real power as opposed to the supposed constitutional system, disagreed with him at times, and resented the way he oversaw them like a German schoolmaster. An electoral reform in 1881 widened the suffrage and seemed to open the way for a true system of ministerial responsibility based on majority rule. It did not work that way for a variety of reasons, and by the end of his reign Pedro was still making the ultimate decisions of government. An artist in wielding power, he affected not to enjoy it, but politicians by that time saw him a convinced autocrat, an aging man who was out of touch with the democratic aspirations of the enlightened elements, no longer a leader but an obstacle.

THE EMPIRE AT ITS ZENITH

Brazil's sound political condition enabled her to participate in the general prosperity of the nineteenth century. With fiscal order and a good currency, it was now possible to re-establish the Bank of Brazil and to create other institutions of credit. Foreign capital arrived in significant amounts, partly because of the effective advertisement the emperor had given the country abroad. Factories, mills, business houses, railroads, steamship lines, telegraph systems, and public utilities were developed largely with foreign investment. Care was taken, however, to see that over-ambitious aliens did not dominate or monopolize the nation's re-sources, and Brazil was no one's economic colony. The most spectacular operator among the many who made fortunes during the empire was Ireneu Evangelista Mauá, later the Baron and then the Viscount Mauá. This promoter constructed the first railroad, from Rio de Janeiro to the highland resort Petropolis. He installed gas lights in Rio and São Paulo, financed telegraph lines and a cable to Europe, organized steamship lines for the Amazon and the high seas, constructed factories and shipyards, put together a network of ranches and plantations, and created a veri-table banking empire in Uruguay and Brazil. He made himself a mil-lionaire many times over and served, despite Dom Pedro's reserved atti-tude toward him, once as financier to the government. Unhappily, his speculations got out of hand, and he was improverished by the crash of 1875. If his credit failed, his material achievements had enriched the country, as did those of many enterprisers less famous. Moreover, the number of incorporated businesses multiplied, and foreign commerce in-creased ten-fold during Pedro's reign. Brazil gained her foreign earnings by exporting her historic products: wood, hides, sugar, and, by the end of the empire, coffee.

Word of Brazil's stability and economic progress circulated in Europe in contrast to the discouraging reports of other Latin American nations. While the United States was the first choice of knowledgeable emigrants, Brazil offered many advantages. Pedro II tried to attract young Euro-peans whose energies might contribute to Brazil's growth. Judicious ad-vertisement and the promotion of colonizing companies accomplished a great deal, though persons brought over by organizations tended to settle together and maintain their nationality, as the Germans did in the southern provinces. It was also helpful that the slave trade ceased in 1850 and that slavery itself diminished sharply thereafter, since the ensuing labor demand presented improverished Europeans with many opportunities. The stream of immigrants was steady in the 1850's and 1860's, and it widened greatly during the 1870's and 1880's. From Portu-gal, Italy, Austria-Hungary, Germany, and even from France, whose in-habitants have usually been loath to leave, these people came, most of them young, practically all of them poor and uneducated. Many returned after a season or two, but a majority remained in Brazil, concentrating in Rio de Janeiro, São Paulo, and the far south. While they usually went into business in the towns, not a few became small farmers or agricultural laborers as an apprenticeship to becoming larger farmers. On the whole the government treated them intelligently, seeking to place them where they were needed. Within a few years immigrants were likely to be run-ning successful businesses, starting factories, and taking over ranches and large coffee farms. Much as the new arrivals did to develop Brazil, the old stock often grumbled at their aggressiveness. To be sure, the atmosphere of the country noticeably changed: a modern, materialistic spirit appeared, one that was critical of the planter aristocracy who despised business and, eventually, of the monarchy itself.

Dom Pedro was by instinct a schoolmaster, one who loved to learn and loved to teach. His personal interests led him to visit schools endlessly, where he chatted with pupils and teachers. His own funds were sometimes devoted to purchasing books or sending bright students abroad for study. At his prodding congress passed a law in 1850 to make education compulsory all over the empire. And a few teachers were imported from Europe and the United States, especially after the emperor's tour of the former in 1871–1872 and the latter in 1876. Yet the results were very discouraging. If illiteracy declined during Pedro's long reign, as it must have, still no more than 15 per cent of adult males were able to read and write when it ended, in 1889, and next to nothing had been done to promote female education. Brazil had no university, only two law schools, a mineralogical institute, and a few medical colleges of little distinction. Boys who wanted university training still went to Coimbra or elsewhere abroad. On the other hand, a Historical and Geographical Institute attained a respected position in the learned world. The emperor nurtured this organization and spent many an hour of dubious enjoyment sitting through its sessions. His interests spread too thinly for specialized knowledge, he sometimes amused scholars or scientists with his smattering of information, but they were unjust if they thought Dom Pedro a mere dilettante. No other ruler could match his intellectual curiosity and devote so much time to public affairs. Any gadget or machine that seemed promising he would study and publicize. Artists and men of letters he subsidized and honored with his personal attentions. In his travels over the vast tropical empire he inspected, warned, advised, encouraged, and listened, enjoying his role of kindly schoolmaster to the nation.

Brazil's cultural life during the empire was earnest if not particularly rich in creativity, a pale copy of French civilization as it successively stressed romanticism, realism, modernism, and naturalism during the century. That Brazilian literature was not wholly imitative, however, was apparent in the verses of Domingos José Gonçalves de Magalhaies (1811–1882), who wrote lovingly of the countryside and Indians while baring a tortured soul in the best romantic fashion. The greatest Brazilian literary figure was a mulatto, Joaquim Maria Machado de Assis (1839–1908), a modernist or Parnassian poet of unequalled skill in imagery and a novelist whose reputation is still growing. Other novelists included Bernard da Silva Guimarães (1827–1834), who depicted the backwoodsmen and untamed *paulistas* sympathetically, and Alfredo d'Escragnolle, Viscount

Taunay (1843–1899), historian of the Paraguayan War and novelist of Mato Grosso, a master writer who typified the best of the expiring romantics and the emerging realists. Few of Brazil's cultural figures attained fame abroad, a commentary on Europe's provincialism more than their own lack of merit.

In foreign affairs Pedro II followed the historic Portuguese tendencies toward enlargement of an already inflated country, though he usually had law on his side in forcing or negotiating favorable boundary settlements. Certainly he made little effort to take advantage of the chaos in the Spanish republics. The army and fleet were modest in peacetime and so minimized by deliberate policy that a sense of grievance against the emperor developed among their officers. The emperor did not aspire to re-annex Uruguay, which his father had lost, but he intended that Rosas and other Platine caudillos respect its independence and that Uruguay's own gauchos refrain from tempting southern Brazil to secede. His support of a faction in Uruguay led to an attack by the crazed dictator López of Paraguay, who declared war on Brazil and occupied strong points in Mato Grosso while summoning Negro slaves to revolt. The terrible Paraguayan War of 1864–1870 cost Brazil a quarter of a billion dollars and 50,000 dead, many from cholera. The nation tired of the war and criticism flared against the emperor for pursuing it until López was annihilated, it was said, for dynastic, not national, reasons. A republican movement began as the war ended, inspired also by the establishment of the Third Republic in France in 1870.

Much as he admired Great Britain and sought her capital and influence, Dom Pedro had many difficulties with that power, most of them deriving from Britain's high-handed efforts to compel Brazil to cease importing African slaves, as she had promised to do by 1831. Other incidents led to ill feeling, though Brazil could scarcely afford to provoke her chief customer and money supplier, who also had the world's best navy. Pedro's friendship with the United States was sincere, and his alignment of Brazil with it in implied opposition to the Spanish republics laid an enduring basis for western hemisphere diplomacy. Despite Brazil's own problem of slavery, Pedro openly supported the Lincoln administration against the Confederacy. After that conflict a thousand or more former Confederates sought homes and slaves in Brazil, but this did not suggest Pedro's identification with the Lost Cause. A strenuous tour of four months' duration in 1876 took the monarch to every major section of the United States, where he delighted the republican Americans. With some wistfulness he wondered, as Brazilians often have, what the secret was that brought the Americans such material grandeur but refused to work for others.

The slave trade which caused so much antagonism with Great Britain had continued during the 1830's and 1840's regardless of Brazil's promise to stop it. Sugar and cotton planters and, to a lesser extent, coffee farmers were insatiable in their desire for an expanding labor force to meet the demands of growing markets. Very few Brazilians saw anything wrong with slavery as an institution, arguing as they had for centuries that Negroes were given an opportunity for eternal salvation by coming to a Christian country and that, after all, they were merely being removed from pagan slavemasters in Africa to more humane lords in America. When the British finally tired of Brazil's procrastination, they began, in 1845, to intercept slave ships and to enter Brazilian waters to make arrests of offending traders and effect liberations. The rage of Brazilian patriots was mighty, but Dom Pedro could do little but plan a larger navy to prevent such incursions in the future. Himself desirous of ending the traffic, he brought it to a close in 1850. Almost at once the volume of white immigrants increased, and capital formerly devoted to African slavery was diverted to purposes less inhumane.

The issue of slavery itself loomed as Brazil's enlightenment increased in mid-century. Educated persons realized that the institution was no longer morally or intellectually acceptable and that Brazil was scorned because she still supported it. Pedro himself held this view, for he associated himself with the best currents of the age. But what was to be done? Perhaps a third or more of Brazil's 8,000,000 people around 1850 were Negro slaves. If they were liberated, the economy of the land would go to pieces, or so it seemed, and the planters who comprised the real ruling class might be ruined. Pedro therefore elected to create an atmosphere in which gradual emancipation with compensation for the deprived owners might be achieved. He made known his disapproval of slavery by freeing his own slaves and ostentatiously complimenting those who followed his example. By advancing and even ennobling colored men, he implied that Negroes were not an inferior race. Abolitionists, like everyone else, had full freedom to agitate their cause, and the force of the law was invoked to remove slaves from persons whose titles were not impeccable. All this gave some impetus to the emancipation movement, and many individuals and organizations manumitted their bonded men. Yet the total was not impressive, and more drastic measures were indicated. During the 1860's Tsarist Russia freed the serfs and the Paraguayan War revealed to many Brazilians for the first time that their peculiar institution gave them a bad reputation among their allies and enemies alike. Moreover, in the United States slavery was ended under circumstances so tragic that Pedro vowed to proceed, but to proceed cautiously. At last, in 1871, the imperial government sponsored the so-called Rio Branco law for freedom of birth. Henceforth all persons would be born free, though children of slaves might serve their mother's master until they were twenty-one. In time, this would have brought freedom to all Negroes, but a million or more were doomed to live out their lives as slaves.

After the passage of the Rio Branco law the emancipation movement surged. A Negro named José Patrocinio and a white aristocrat, Joaquim Nabuco, toured the country whipping up abolitionist sentiment. In the northeast, where slavery was most entrenched, a failure to adjust to new methods of sugar production had brought about an economic decline and the consequent lessening of the slave's importance. Coffee and ranching activities in the center and south were less dependent on the institution, and more modern-minded owners were likely to manumit their slaves. Cities and provinces enacted abolitionist laws. Negroes in slave districts became restless and often escaped to free territory, where the authorities refused to send them back. The emperor approved of these developments but was rightly cautious about offending the sugar and cotton lords. But, not at his best physically and often abroad during the 1870's and 1880's, he fell behind his people in a cause that was growing daily. In 1885 he supported a law to free all slaves over sixty-five. Finally, when he was in Europe being treated for diabetes, his daughter, Princess Isabel, threw the full weight of the imperial power behind the abolitionists. In May 1888 the congress passed a law providing for the immediate freedom of all slaves without compensation to the owners. A veritable delirium of joy swept the country, and Isabel enjoyed a brief popularity as "the Redemptress." The nation exulted in a rightful act passed peacefully, one that liberated 600,000 or more slaves. Pedro, when he heard the news, is said to have wept with happiness. Yet the planter aristocracy, many of whom were impoverished and insulted by their former slaves, felt they had been shabbily treated by an empire they had supported so steadfastly. In a spirit of revenge they talked of ways to keep Isabel the Redemptress from becoming the next ruler of Brazil.

THE FALL OF THE EMPIRE

It seemed incredible that a regime that had provided Brazil with order, freedom, and progress unique in Latin America should be overturned, that so good a man as Dom Pedro II should be ousted ignominiously after years of service. This is what occurred, however, in November 1889. The emperor had received an ovation when he returned from Europe in 1888, and when an assassin tried to kill him a little later, a wave of indignation swept the country. A congressional election returned the majority he desired, with only one republican being sent to the chamber of deputies. The emperor seemed in better health, and such talk as there had been of his failing powers in recent years sounded foolish. Unquestionably he held the esteem of most of his subjects, though his personality was not one to excite fervent devotion, and behind criticisms of the monarchy there was usually an understanding that nothing should be done to destroy it as long as Dom Pedro lived. Yet a mere garrison *pronunciamiento* of the Spanish type, or so it appeared on the surface, brought him to grief and his regime to ruin.

Behind this extraordinary circumstance, which shocked most of the world and was long a cause of shame among many Brazilians, lay trends that had slowly come to a climax. One of them was the prospect that Princess Isabel would reign. The two sons of Pedro and Thereza having died in childhood, the older of the two daughters was in line for the succession. Isabel was known to be conservative and inclined to ultramontanism, or subservience to Rome. It was also feared that her husband would exercise undue influence, and he had always been unpopular. A French prince of the house of Orleans, the Comte d'Eu, this shy, deaf individual was thought to be very reactionary and oriented to Europe. He had never tried persistently to cultivate the Brazilians, who remained cold to him whatever he did or did not do.

Then, as no one realized better than Dom Pedro, monarchy was an alien plant in the New World, destined to stand on the defensive amid all the republics and, in the minds of many people, a bar to the fullest expression of national feeling. Pedro had often said half-seriously that he was a republican himself, but he knew that Brazil needed the tutelage that only a monarchy afforded. In fact, he was deeply committed to the institution he inherited and graced. He had reigned so long, in name since 1831. A people making so much progress as the Brazilians were bound to tire of him, to regard him as a relic of the past; new generations were unaware of his great services and regarded him as old-fashioned and out of step. The recent capitalist mood of Rio and São Paulo tended to reject the men and ideals of the rural aristocracy that had long found a focus in the monarchy. And many of the immigrants felt scant attachment to Dom Pedro or, for that matter, to their new nationality. All in all, these factors were not crucial, for no ruler is universally popular. The long-reigning contemporaries of Pedro II, Queen Victoria and Kaiser Franz Josef, underwent periods in which their subjects were apathetic or hostile but emerged later to higher levels of appreciation.

The collapse of support for the empire was far more basic than the tides of a fickle public opinion. One by one, the former slaveowners, the clergy, and the army hierarchy fell away from the regime. The defection of the rural lords began when the emperor ended the slave trade in 1850 and hacked away at the servile institution. The sugar planters in particular felt themselves on the defensive as capitalism and coffee culture rose in importance and their markets diminished in the face of foreign competition. Year after year they watched the spread of abolitionism that would rob them of their slaves. Their faith that the emperor would delay the movement and, if and when the awful moment came, reimburse them proved illusory, or mostly so. Eighteen months after Isabel signed the emancipation law, they refused to lift a finger in behalf of the empire in its death struggle.

Brazil had no fundamental Church problem such as that which plagued so many of her Latin American sisters. The continuation of the monarchy after independence meant that the Church would function as usual under the traditional royal (or imperial) patronage. The Church was not particularly strong in Brazil, since its servants were often out of touch with Vatican policy, few in number, and sometimes so undisciplined they ignored the laws of celibacy. Some devoted Catholics lamented Pedro's broad-mindedness and shook their heads when he visited Protestant, Jewish, and Mormon services while he was abroad. Nothing resembling a Church-state crisis, however, arose until 1872, when a bishop took it upon himself to punish a priest for celebrating mass for a freemason lodge. Legally there was nothing wrong in the priest's action, though the pope had denounced freemasonry in 1864. The Brazilian government had suppressed this papal syllabus, as it had a right to do under the patronage, and it was officially non-existent. Nonetheless, two other bishops decided to enforce the papal policies by ordering all faithful Catholics who belonged to lay brotherhoods—organizations for charitable and social purposes which were very important in Brazil—to forswear freemasonry. This brought much protest and anguish, for freemasonary had long been respectable in Brazil, having claimed Pedro I, the Andrada brothers, the present prime minister, Rio Branco, and possibly Pedro II.

While it was perfectly proper under Brazilian law for a man to be both a good Catholic and a freemason, the bishops undertook to challenge the regime. Clerical and anti-clerical arguments agitated the press, congress, and public forums. In the background, of course, was the campaign of Pope Pius IX to assert the power of the Church following the loss of Rome in 1870 to the Kingdom of Italy, which brought about a conflict of papal and national power in most countries with large Catholic populations. At length, Pedro II stood by his rights and had the offending bishops prosecuted and sent to prison, and he even obtained from the pope himself an equivocal condemnation of their conduct. A year and a half later the emperor pardoned the episcopal prisoners, but the damage had been done. Liberals and anti-clericals were wildly aroused by the ambitions of the Church and made to see that the empire had always been its partner. On the other hand, many important prelates and Catholic laymen came to think of the patronage as an insupportable oppression. Perhaps if it were ended, as it might be under a republic, the Church would flourish in freedom and carry out its policies without interference. Pedro II had lost another historic ally without winning over its enemies.

It was the defection of the army that proved fatal to the empire. Brazil's standing army had always been small, only one quarter the size of Paraguay's in 1864 and a mere garrison compared to many other forces in Latin America. It had no more than the appropriate number of officers and had been kept in its place. Unlike most monarchs, Pedro II did not enjoy playing soldier, and he really paid little attention to his army in peacetime. The Paraguayan War had caused the services to be greatly enlarged, and association with Argentina during that conflict acquainted many Brazilian officers with the profits and status that officers in other countries had long enjoyed. And the cost and mismanagement of that war pointed to the need for more sympathy from the imperial government in handling military affairs. Yet when the war ended, Pedro rapidly reduced the services to the size he deemed suitable despite protests from dismissed officers and enlisted men who believed they had been treated ungratefully. For some years thereafter the officer corps clamored for more funds and recognition. As long as the Duke of Caxias lived, to 1880, this agitation remained within bounds. Many officers, however, had already begun to flirt with republicanism, dreaming of large appropriations and opportunities to humble civilian ministers. Their demands were so forceful during the 1880's that the government made concessions. Each retreat produced more pressure. The emperor himself came to think, only too rightly, that the military was seeking improper privileges. His resistance had fateful consequences, and republicans made many converts in the army.

Who were these republicans? The older generation of republicans who had revolted now and again under João VI, Pedro I, and the youthful Pedro II had long disappeared. There was little connection between their efforts and the republican movement that developed about 1870. In that year, the end of the Paraguayan War and the establishment of the Third Republic in France started a ripple of anti-dynastic feeling in Brazil. The emperor had accommodated himself to it by liberalizing his government and suggesting that true ministerial responsibility would soon be observed. Yet his concessions were not far-reaching enough to please his critics, and his bad health and frequent absence abroad slackened his hold on the government. Republican clubs were organized, chiefly in São Paulo and other southern towns, attracting members of the young generation and immigrant groups. These republicans spoke and published widely, for Brazil was a free country. Sometimes the emperor himself was insulted in public, which he did not appear to mind. His own grandchildren were tutored by his friend Benjamin Constant, a known republican who lectured to more receptive students at the army's military college. The agitation seemed harmless, and it certainly made little headway. Very few republicans were elected to office, even when the polls were not rigged. Yet something was in the air. Positivism, the "religion of humanity" fathered by Auguste Comte, appealed to many youthful intellectuals who came to regard monarchy as incongruous in the progressive, secular paradise the positivists promised.

More calculating republicans were quietly at work in other circles. Slaveowners were told that the empire was destroying them and that the republicans would be more sympathetic in the matter of compensation if abolition occurred, an argument that held much force after the emancipation act of 1888. Clergymen were often convinced that a republic would liberate the Church from control by a government that restricted its rights. The officer corps well knew the emperor was an obstacle to their ambitions. Provincial politicians felt that the empire's centralist policies thwarted their own advancement and that a republic would respect federalism and allow each state to operate its own political machinery (and machines). Exaggerated stories about the emperor's failing health and mental sharpness were circulated. And a clinching argument could always be made by prophesying a reactionary, autocratic reign under Princess Isabel.

If declared republican sentiment was still small, many important sectors of the nation were cold to the empire and its prospects under Isabel. During the latter half of 1889 the army was plainly restless and disaffected. A Liberal prime minister, the Count of Afonso Celso, was determined to subordinate the military to civilian authority, if necessary by scattering key officers and units into distant parts of the country. The military hierarchy responded by plotting a lunge for power that would overthrow Afonso Celso and compel the emperor to appoint a ministry favorable to the army. The conspiracy involved Deodoro da Fonseca, the chief of staff and marshal of the empire, Marshal Floriano Peixoto, the minister of war, and the republican ideologue Benjamin Constant. Dom Pedro and his family were at Petropolis in the summer palace he loved so well. When the prime minister attempted to forestall the coup, the officers struck, on November 15, 1889. The emperor was informed of the crisis and hastened to the capital in the afternoon, finding it in the hands of the army. During a long and anguished night he deliberated his course. He could not honorably permit the army to dictate the dismissal and appointment of ministries. Possibly he could continue as monarch by allowing Deodoro, who was not sure he was a republican and who had sworn loyalty to the emperor on thousands of occasions, to assume all vital powers. This he would not do. While Pedro agonized, units of the garrison proclaimed the republic and manipulated a public demonstration in their favor. Pedro was then informed of his downfall and banishment. During November 16 the imperial family were held as prisoners in the palace. That night, while it was raining, they were taken to a ship and deported like dismissed servants. Plainly, the conspirators had not dared to remove Dom Pedro in daylight. The country at large, even Rio itself, did not realize what had occurred until the Braganzas were far at sea.

Not quite sixty-four at the time of his deposition, Dom Pedro lost his wife within a few weeks and himself died two years later in France. He was saddened less by the unceremonious treatment he had received than by the apathy with which Brazilians reacted to the news of the coup at Rio. Men whose careers had been made by the empire readily swore loyalty to the republic. The population gave little indication of disapproval. Alone with his thoughts and books, Pedro was careful to say or write nothing that suggested the bitterness he surely felt. As always, he was Pedro the Magnanimous.

The Republic

THE REPUBLIC'S EARLY TROUBLES

The advent of the republic was an exhilarating experience for some Brazilians. Those who had dreamed of the change abandoned themselves to euphoria, for in Brazil optimism bursts out easily, to subside as quickly. The sobriety and conservatism of manners under the empire now changed to exhibitionism and gaiety. Men who had always been free exultantly assured each other they were free. Certainly, old psychological restraints were gone. It was pleasant to believe that Brazil had crossed a threshold into a glittering period where riches and unlimited expansion were possible, where true social democracy might come about readily. Intellectuals quibbled over whether the republic should model itself after the United States or the First, Second, or Third French Republic. Soon, as always after a frenzy of exalted hopes, ugly realities obtruded.

Not the common man but the army held power, the gay, exulting soldiers who swaggered about the capital and paraded with a frequency never known under the colorless emperor. They did violence to monarchists, enjoyed an immediate raise in pay, and, in the case of the high-ranking officers, invaded profitable preserves of government which had been barred to them under the frugal empire. Officers shouldered aside the old imperial state servants and installed themselves as ministers, department heads, and bosses of provinces and towns. Close behind them were enterprising businessmen of Rio and São Paulo who recognized financial opportunities when they saw them, and a lucrative collaboration began. Meanwhile, intellectuals made themselves available to write the scenario for the dynamic new role the republic was expected to play and to explain to the world its high purposes. Also, an orgy of personal and official extravagance gripped the country. Inflation proceeded insanely, for the distribution of money seemed a simple way to capture the affections of the people for the republic. This mixture of idealism, carnival spirit, and rank self-seeking dismayed monarchical Europe, which discerned the militarism and economic follies behind the republican rejoicing, and recognition was slow to come from that source, even from the French Republic, which at the time was negotiating an alliance with tsarist Russia. The United States was less friendly to the republic of Brazil than might have been expected, and its recognition was delayed for many months. But the sister nations of Latin America promptly extended congratulations and diplomatic relations. At last Brazil had become one of themselves: a praetorian republic, autocratic and unstable.

Soon after his group seized power, Deodoro da Fonseca proclaimed the United States of Brazil a federal republic, announced the separation of Church and state, and extended suffrage to all literate males, about 15 per cent of the total population. He was not able, however, to compensate the former slaveowners. A committee he appointed went to work on a constitutional draft which a hand-picked constituent congress was allowed to examine and approve between November 1890 and February 1891. This constitution of 1891 was not really submitted for popular endorsement, and even the constituent congress was given to understand that few changes in the draft would be tolerated. Something of a blend of the American constitution and Pedro I's instrument of 1824, it provided for the usual three branches of the federal government with presidents serving for four years and not eligible for immediate reelection. Twenty states were recognized, all of them to be republics with more powers than the imperial provinces had enjoyed, elected governors and legislatures, and the right to levy export duties and to maintain militias. Despite the appearance of federalism, the central government controlled the national army and police force, both of which were enlarged, and reserved the right to intervene forcibly in state affairs and to suspend constitutional guarantees. Straightway, Deodoro (*cf.*, footnote, p. 642) began to assert his authority by removing state governors he did not trust. Ultimately, federalism came to be respected only in such large states as São Paulo, Minas Gerais, and Rio Grande do Sul, where political machines and local armies were strong enough to command such respect.

The constituent congress also legalized the position of Deodoro da Fonseca by electing him president of the republic and Floriano Peixoto as vice-president. The positivist slogan, "Order and Progress," was inscribed on the Brazilian flag. Thereafter the assembly did little but quarrel; it was unable to elect its own presiding officer and began to carp at

President Deodoro. The president's dictatorial temperament did not permit him to negotiate patiently with politicians, and when congress reacted to his proposed budget, which included enormous appropriations for the military, as though it planned to be obstructive, he simply sent troops into the chamber and turned the deputies out. The uproar that followed amazed Deodoro. For nearly two years he had bossed the nation and intimidated his critics. Now it seemed that some persons were impudent enough to take constitutional procedures seriously. As the storm grew and intimations of revolution emanated from various generals and the fleet, the president decided to resign. It was November 1891, just two years after he had ousted Dom Pedro.

Marshal Floriano Peixoto now inherited the presidency. This slippery officer, who was not above engineering some of the manifestations that convinced Deodoro it would be wise to resign, had maintained himself in high positions under the empire and republic without any discernable attachment to principle. Now he exhibited both strength and skill. The republican regime was in danger by 1892, its bloom vanished and its fiscal follies having bankrupted the government and depreciated the currency by half. Moreover, a world depression had set in, puncturing Brazil's speculative boom and reducing her foreign markets. So great was popular disenchantment that the monarchists were resurgent. With great dispatch Floriano removed state rulers who had been loyal to Deodoro and replaced them with his own followers. With more circumspection he shifted commands within the army, though not in time to prevent occasional revolts. As it happened, these manifestations of discontent, popular as well as military, were too uncoordinated to unseat Floriano, and his brutal suppressions of critical newspapers and individuals served their purpose, unprecedented as such harshness was in Brazil.

Nonetheless, Brazil was destined to experience the riotous disorders the Spanish countries had when they first became republics. In September 1893 a very threatening rebellion broke out, a monarchist affair in the southern provinces and a naval insurrection in Rio de Janeiro. The latter was led by Admiral de Mello, who insisted that the grasping followers of the generals had enriched themselves under the republic while starving the fleet, which was more aristocratic and therefore monarchist. De Mello's plan to bombard the capital into submission was frustrated by European and American warships, which refused to permit such a barbarity, and he sailed southward to join the monarchist forces. Fighting continued until the middle of 1894 and thousands were killed. The insurgents marched northward toward São Paulo but were defeated, whereupon the fleet surrendered and the republic rejoiced over its triumph. Tyrannical as he had been, Floriano now enjoyed considerable esteem for the courage and intelligence with which he had met the rebellion. It surprised many people when, late in 1894, he voluntarily retired from office and permitted a new president to be installed. Perhaps the reason was that he knew he was dying.

Dr. Prudente de Morais Barros[4] was an able lawyer from São Paulo, the first of three successive *paulista* presidents in Brazil. His election signified that, for the moment at least, the civilian politicians had wrested control from the generals. The political situation was somewhat more settled now that the rebellion was over, but things were tumultuous enough. Of the several attempted revolutions only one was serious, an incomprehensible folk movement in the arid land of Canudos back from the northeastern coast, which has always been one of the most impoverished regions of the country. Here a mystic leader called Antonio the Counsellor had ruled a theocracy of rural poor for many years. The inhabitants, known as *sertanejos*, were as backward as the legendary mountaineers of Kentucky and Tennessee, a folk given to superstition and feuding. Somehow the fanatical Antonio decided that the republic was sacrilegious and proclaimed a crusade to exterminate it, an undertaking which he said had the blessing of the "lost Sebastian," the Portuguese king who had disappeared in Africa in 1478. It should have been simple enough to suppress these backland warriors, but the governor of Bahia failed to do so, and federal forces required three years to break up the movement. While the weakness of the republic was thus advertised, the chief result of this civil war was Brazil's most famous literary work, *Os sertões*, or *Rebellion in the Backlands*, by Euclides da Cunha (1866–1909), an epic account compared not too absurdly with *Don Quixote* or *The Divine Comedy*. The end of the romantic insurrection and a narrow escape from assassination enabled Prudente to finish his term in a glow of popularity in 1898. Brazil was now calm.

THE ORDERLY REPUBLIC

Before he took office, the next president, another *paulista* civilian named Manoel de Campos Salles, made a pilgrimage to London to seek remedies for Brazil's desperate financial situation. The mismanagement of the early republic and the world depression had left Dom Pedro's fiscal system in ruins and the nation's credit a memory. The House of Rothschild agreed to make a huge loan to Brazil, guaranteed by prospective customs receipts. Within a few years the currency was stable, and foreign capital, especially British, had resumed its flow into the country. With the turn of the century prosperity was restored, and railroads, port facilities, public utilities, and small factories were being built. Commerce

4. In Brazil a man may choose the name by which he prefers to be known. Sometimes it is his given name; then it might be his father's or mother's family name or both. This president is often known as Prudente, but it is also correct to call him Morais, Barros, or Morais Barros.

was also expanding, for Brazil had all the rubber the world craved for bicycle and automobile tires, and most of the coffee. Sugar, cotton, timber, tobacco, cacao, and hides were also in steady demand, though the sugar industry sank in importance and with it the planter class who had so long dominated the country. As raw materials left Brazil, the various states taxed them. The federal government raised its revenues mainly by levying import duties on finished goods. There was enough money for all, enough to operate the government, construct public works, finance the voracious political machines, equip the army, and even purchase two dreadnoughts for the navy; these last gave the republic the appearance of being a great power. They terrified some of Brazil's neighbors, who had reason to regard the Portuguese-speaking residents of South America as inveterate expansionists; however, a mutiny of the crews indicated that Brazil was still Brazil, a land where the comic prevailed over the sinister.

The presidential terms of Campos Salles (1898–1902), Dr. Francisco de Paula Rodrigues Alves (1902–1906), and Afonso Augusto Moreira Penna and Nilo Peçanha (1906–1910) were comparatively sunny times. It was apparent that the republic was at least a qualified success, and monarchist sentiment all but disappeared. Brazil was again a free country where men spoke and wrote as they pleased. The army was far more important than it had been under the empire, and more costly, but it remained below the surface in political affairs. The separation of Church and state had gratified everyone, the Church because it was free from state interference, the anticlericals because they could ignore the Church. Brazil was not a conspicuously devout country in any case, and it had never been regarded as puritanical. Under the republic the bureaucracy had become larger, more corrupt, and less effective than it had been under Pedro II. The same was true of the judiciary. As for electoral processes, they were now managed by state machines usually allied with army garrisons in their districts. Voting was still a rare privilege, and there was no assurance that polls would be free or that ballots would be counted honestly. The greatest change from imperial days was the predominance of the central and southern states, particularly Minas Gerais and São Paulo (Rio de Janeiro had been federalized). Coffee barons, ranchers, capitalists, and traders now dominated the scene in place of the sugar and cotton planters of the tropics, at least so long as they did not provoke the army.

Brazil's good reputation won during the reign of Pedro II suffered during the troubled 1890's but was restored soon after 1900. The republic made sincere efforts to remove friction with her neighbors, who included colonies of three European powers and every South American country except Chile. Long-standing boundary problems were arbitrated, beginning with the Misiones dispute with Argentina in 1895 and continuing until Great Britain, the Netherlands, France, Venezuela, Colombia, and Bolivia had reached agreements with the Brazilian republic. More often than not Brazil came out well in these settlements, but it was clear that her land hunger was based on legal claims and was not likely to involve military threats. Most of these agreements were reached during the years when the Baron of Rio Branco[5] was foreign minister, from 1902 to 1912. Rio Branco also resumed the old imperial policy of cultivating the United States, a natural ally and by now the best customer of Brazil. Yet he also cooperated closely with Argentina and Chile, so that diplomats spoke of the ABC bloc. On one occasion, when Germany's trouble-prone gunboat *Panther*[6] violated Brazilian rights, he protested energetically and to good effect. This meant only that Brazil was determined to be respected; she was truly a pacific power and saw to it that the world at large understood that she was.

The stabilization of the republic and the resumption of economic growth after 1900 encouraged immigrants to seek opportunities in Brazil. Nearly every year a new record of immigration was set, as was true in the rest of the Americas in the decade or so before World War I. The cities of Rio de Janeiro and São Paulo and surrounding areas received the bulk of these settlers. The population of São Paulo the city, with its clear skies and energy-giving climate, increased more than ten-fold in the first thirty years of the republic and has doubled every decade since 1920. The red soil of the state provided the world's choice region for the production of coffee. As demand grew and seemed limitless, so did the ambition of the *paulistas*. Small farms, large farms, dairies, shops, banks, factories— every line of economic endeavor—prospered, and the immigrants poured in. Rio de Janeiro was not to be outclassed by her boastful rival. During the first years of the century her curse of yellow fever was finally lifted, thanks largely to Dr. Oswaldo Cruz, whose name is perpetuated by a renowned institute that studies tropical diseases. With yellow fever eliminated and other diseases reduced, the lovely capital city grew spectacularly. The harbor was improved, mountains were leveled and pushed into the sea to make room for buildings, and imaginative steps were taken to beautify this city, which already had magnificent natural scenery for its setting. Not only did the usual increment of Portuguese, Italians, Slavs, and Germans settle in this semi-tropical capital to become *cariocas*, but great numbers of rural Brazilians were lured. With some reason, other regions of the country complained that Rio was a vampire, draining the money and the best men from the provinces.

---

5. Titles were outlawed under the republic, but they are often used for the social and business advantages they bring.

6. The landing of the *Panther* at Agadir in 1911 precipitated the second Moroccan crisis.

A shift in mood came with the election of 1910, in the first truly national political campaign Brazil had experienced. Arrogant and corrupt as armies which fight no wars tend to be, the Brazilian military was no longer content to remain behind the scenes. Its ambition was to exercise the "moderating power" once wielded by the emperor, the right to make fundamental decisions when the politicians were deadlocked or when they acted contrary to national interests. For the first time since 1894 the political machines of São Paulo and Minas Gerais were denied the privilege of naming the next president. The army dictated the choice, Marshal Hermes da Fonseca, a nephew of Deodoro, who was an ambitious officer from Rio Grande do Sul. Strong opposition asserted itself, the liberals, civilianists, and many of the machine politicians throwing there support to the eminent lawyer and diplomat Ruy Barbosa, who had helped write the constitution of 1891. An exciting campaign ensued as Ruy Barbosa toured the country and seemed the obvious choice of the populace. Yet the vote tabulators gave Hermes a decisive victory. A general revolution seemed likely, but the military's hold was too formidable to permit it. A bombardment of Ruy Barbosa's home city, the old colonial capital Bahia, stopped the insurrection. His followers accepted defeat while planning to agitate for four years and then to try again in 1914. Certainly, Hermes' administration was an unhappy period. The army flaunted its power with little delicacy. Arbitrariness and graft were so prevalent that true republicans feared a permanent dictatorship had come.

Worse than the decline in the tone of government was the economic slump. First, the coffee market broke, for the *paulistas* had overexpanded and failed to reckon with competitors from Central America, Colombia, and Africa who were now invading their markets. Still more catastrophic was the collapse of the rubber boom in 1912–1913, when floods of rubber stocks poured into Europe and the United States from the Far East. This was an ugly surprise indeed, for the Brazilians had confidently expected their monopoly to endure indefinitely. Brazil had almost all the wild rubber trees in the world. For more than a decade great fortunes had been made by enterprising dealers who overworked Indians and Negroes in the limitless Amazon jungles. The tropical cities of Belém and Manaos had taken on a sudden gaudiness, and for the first and only time the Amazon had become an important commercial artery. So extravagant were the newly rich that an ornate opera house had been built in Manaos, a thousand miles up the great stream. This testimony of their optimism was destined to become a reminder to posterity of the transitory nature of prosperity, however, and no cultural center. In 1875 a Scotsman had stolen a few rubber plants and taken them to Kew Gardens, near London, where they were nourished in hothouses. Eventually trees were re-planted in Malaya, and then in the Dutch East Indies. It developed that cultivated plants were far more productive than wild trees in the jungle. Also, native labor was more plentiful in the Far East than in Brazil, and plant diseases could be controlled better. Experimental shipments in 1899 proving profitable, the British and Dutch planters enlarged their groves and overwhelmed the market within a few years. The Brazilian rubber industry was never to recover.

By 1914 the coffee and rubber situation had wrecked the optimism of Brazil. Tolerable government had disappeared with the Hermes da Fonseca administration, which had been characterized by militarism, corruption, and revolts. Now prosperity had departed. While perhaps there was no likelihood of a thoroughgoing social revolution, conditions were unsteady enough to induce the politicians to be cautious. It is noteworthy that the bosses, much as they feuded with one another, had enough common sense, or even statesmanship, to draw together when the ship of state was threatened by storm. The conservative factions wished to nominate Pinheiro Machado, the colorful *caudilho* of Rio Grande do Sul, who had been instrumental in electing Hermes da Fonseca in 1910. But he was too identified with that unpopular president and too repugnant a figure to many liberals. On their part, the liberal groups longed for Ruy Barbosa but feared that another stirring campaign like that of 1910 might disrupt the country. Accordingly, the leaders of both sides and the potentates of the army agreed to compromise on a safe politician, Wenceslau Braz, who was declared the winner in a dull election.

When Braz became president, the conflict of 1914–1918 that was once known as the Great War was under way. Further economic jolts were in store for Brazil, as the flow of funds and credit from Europe ceased and her raw materials could not be exported because of the shipping crisis. The government resorted to the issue of unsound paper money and pessimistically prepared for more depression and rebellion. Within a few months, however, the Allies restored the shipping lanes to Brazil and began to purchase great quantities of coffee, sugar, cacao, beans, nuts, and minerals, thus bringing prosperity to the possessing classes and good revenues to the government. Macabre a fact as it was, it became evident that great wars in distant places were good for business, and Brazil throve. Among the benefits of the war was the shortage of finished goods that could no longer be imported from Europe. Combined as it was with the large foreign earnings from the sale of raw materials, this condition led Brazilians to start at long last factories for textile and leather goods and thus enter seriously an industrial phase. Furthermore, the boom spurred the improvement of livestock and agricultural establishments and even brought a brief resurrection to the stricken rubber industry. The war also strengthened Brazil's ties with the United States, which had already surpassed Britain as a source for manufactured goods and would now eclipse her as a supplier of capital.

It was obvious that the republic's welfare depended on the Allies. British commercial and financial relations had long been crucial to Brazil's economy, the educated classes regarded France as the font of civilization, and the many Italians and fewer Japanese sympathized with their mother countries, which were on the Allied side in that war. When Portugal joined that cause (in order to keep the British from bargaining away her African colonies in the event of a negotiated peace), Brazil had overwhelming sentimental as well as economic reasons to oppose the Central Powers. The only dissent came from the half million or so Germans and smaller numbers of Austro-Hungarian residents in the republic. By October 1917 these pressures, as well as the example of the United States and sincere outrage over the sinking of Brazilian ships by German submarines, caused Brazil to enter the war, the only nation in South America and the only large country in Latin America to do so. Her declaration was little more than a gesture, but it was not an insignificant step in her rise to a respectable status in world affairs, and it also heightened the sense of nationalism in the huge, disjointed republic and fired democratic idealism, of which the Allies made much in the last year of the war. The contribution of Brazil was negligible: a few physicians, nurses, aviators, and naval patrols. And there was also a seamy side to her participation in the Allied crusade in the confiscation of German properties and the oppression—the harshness of which has long been a matter of debate—of German communities in the far south who rarely regarded themselves as Brazilian and who sometimes thrilled to the call of the Fatherland. The disaffection of this section of Brazil showed up later in the revolution of 1930 and was partially traceable to resentment of President Braz' wartime suppressions. At the Paris Peace Conference in 1919, Brazil played a dignified role under the leadership of Epitacio de Silva Pessoa. When the United States refused to join the League of Nations, Brazil eagerly presented herself as the leading western hemisphere power in that organization, and she won a seat on its Council.[7]

THE REPUBLIC IN DECLINE

In 1918 the presidency went, after the customary intrigues of the major state political machines, to Francisco de Paula Rodrigues Alves, who had served as president between 1902 and 1906. In frail

7. Brazilians greatly relished this honor. When, after the Locarno settlement of 1926, the German Republic was given a permanent place on the Council and Brazil was denied one, the latter withdrew in pique from the League.

health, this competent statesman died within a few months, and a special election brought to the presidential chair Silva Pessoa, who had publicized his country so well at the Paris Peace Conference. He assumed the position just as the war boom was transformed into a severe depression and the democratic idealism kindled by the war turned into general cynicism. Brazil shared lamentably in both of these developments. The rubber boom was entirely over. The price of rubber had fallen from 34 to six cents per pound in a mere ten years, and the monopoly of the Far East was such as to discourage the wild rubber industry of Brazil. Coffee, sugar, cotton, and other commodities suffered almost as badly. Scientific farming methods that had just gotten under way were frequently abandoned, and agricultural practices reverted to the slash-and-burn methods that had earlier wasted the fertile regions. Industries born of the war, however, usually managed to stay in business. The government was again embarrassed by a shortage of funds and resumed the issuance of currency of dubious value. And the disillusionment that followed the lofty hopes of 1918–1919 made thoughtful people critical of the republic, its inability to deal with economic problems, its corruption, and the bossism that made representative government a bitter phrase.

The postwar depression and cynicism produced also an atmosphere that encouraged military men to dream of drastic, unorthodox measures to make the government more effective. Curiously combining revolutionary sentiment with reaction, these aspirations clearly owed much to the Fascist movement in Italy, whose influence on Brazil is often weighty, and to kindred developments in Spain and Portugal. At the Military Club in Rio, where the officer caste met in luxurious surroundings, there was much talk of the dynamism needed to rescue a sickly country plagued by sordid politicians. As yet there was no true program. Outright fascism had not proved itself in Europe yet. Nor was monarchy their cause. The return of the Braganzas in 1921 with the remains of Pedro II and Empress Thereza had excited only affectionate curiosity and nostalgia, not political support. Yet the military was restless and assertive. Some kind of change was needed.

It was not yet time for the army to intrude, as the presidential campaign of 1922 demonstrated. Its candidate, former president Nilo Peçanha, ran against a machine politician from Minas Gerais, Artur da Silva Bernardes. As usual, about one per cent of the population voted, the vast majority disqualified by the literacy requirement and most eligible voters seeing no need to bother. The civilian politicians announced the triumph of Silva Bernardes, whereupon the son of former president Hermes da Fonseca undertook to seize Rio and install his father as dictator. But for unlucky timing he might have succeeded, disagreeable as the memory of Hermes da Fonseca's term in 1910–1914 was. As it happened, the regime survived, overpowering the rebels and inaugurating Silva Bernardes. His term, from 1922 to 1926, was one of the most tense in the republic's history. Again and again garrisons revolted, only to be punished as the population declined to join the army and state militias remained true to the civilian machines. Martial law, the ousting of local officials, changes in military command, and a thoroughly un-Brazilian suppression of civil liberties were features of the period that seemed to advertise the failure of the republic to function properly.

In addition to the demoralizing political situation, Brazil suffered from a very slow recovery after the brief, severe slump of 1920–1921. In most of the world the 1920's were called golden, but Brazil was depressed until near the close of the decade. President Silva Bernardes employed a British commission to diagnose his nation's troubles, which proved to be, according to their analysis, government wastefulness, graft, topheavy bureaucracy, need for a more favorable climate for foreign investments, and the removal from the states of their right to tax exports. Only by encouraging alien capital was Silva Bernardes able to carry out this advice, for New York financial houses were moving into Brazil on a formidable scale. An effort of the administration to govern the production and sale of coffee so as secure maximum profits was the creation of the Coffee Institute. Turned over to the state of São Paulo in 1924, it became a device for promoting the unlimited expansion of coffee production and a lever by which the *paulistas* could play politics with the nation's major industry.

During these uneasy years a man destined long to perturb Brazilian affairs appeared, Luis Carlos Prestes. An army captain of some education and a native of Rio Grande do Sul, he was a radical of uncertain commitment but leaning toward Communism. In 1924 he participated in a military uprising in the city of São Paulo which required three weeks to be suppressed. After the defeat Prestes chose to continue the fight. With about 2,000 followers—adventurers, idealists, misfits, and foreign revolutionaries—he undertook to preach class warfare in the rural areas. The little band moved, mostly on foot, through the desolate backlands from São Paulo almost to the northeastern corner of Brazil and then doubled back southward and finally traversed the wilds of Mato Grosso to emerge into Bolivia, where its members declared themselves political refugees. Government forces had vainly tried to capture the group and, of course, were made to look foolish as they repeatedly failed. This famous trek of 18,000 miles in two years endowed the Communist cause with a heroic character, at least as it was publicized, and numerous country folk heard radical propaganda for the first time. If Prestes was not already a dedicated Communist, he soon became one. After a time he went to Russia for five years of training in revolutionary techniques. Brazil had not heard the last of him.

The depression and disorders of the Silva Bernardes term formed the background for the revolution of 1930. Before that event, however, came the customary interlude of good times which, by classical formula, always seems to precede the collapse of a regime. This was the term of Washington Luis Pereira de Souza of São Paulo from 1926 to 1930. During his first three years conditions were comparatively good. The Coffee Institute stimulated production and sold its products for high prices without difficulty. The cotton industry made great strides, and other crops and businesses flourished. There was even some hope of a restoration of the rubber industry, for the American wizard, Henry Ford, established several mammoth plantations to cultivate rubber trees according to the methods that had proved so successful in Malaya and the Dutch East Indies.[8] Meanwhile, American bankers were pouring huge sums into a variety of Brazilian enterprises and the United States was buying more Brazilian products, mainly coffee, than all of Europe combined. And public utilities and light industries were growing, particularly in the golden corner of Brazil extending south from Rio de Janeiro. As a further sign of returning prosperity, European immigrants were again thronging to Brazil at the rate of 100,000 or more a year, the most ever.

Washington Luis encouraged these developments and stimulated the building of automobile roads, an urgent need in his enormous nation. He terminated martial law in the areas that had revolted under his predecessor and everywhere restored civil liberties. His administration was on the whole a time of optimism and growth. The president's home state of São Paulo was the dynamo of the boom, an area growing like California and exhibiting Yankee attitudes. Its seaport, Santos, became one of the busiest in the world, and its capital drew most of the European immigrants and young men of energy and talent from all over Brazil. Factories and commercial houses had only to be created to prosper. If many Brazilians grumbled that this strident giant was stripping the nation of its best men and seeking to run the entire republic, the *paulistas*, if they were not too busy to reply, were likely to boast that this was the way things should be. São Paulo was by far the most modern state in Brazil, had the best system of education, and paid more than half the republic's taxes. *Paulistas* had a saying of their own: Brazil's twenty states

8. Not even Ford was able to produce this miracle. After losing about $17,000,000 in the venture, the Ford interests turned the plantations over to the Brazilian government in 1946.

were empty freight cars, and São Paulo was the engine that pulled them.

The Wall Street crash of October 1929 destroyed Brazil's prosperity almost at once. New York bankers desperately sought to sell their foreign holdings in order to forestall bankruptcy at home, with the result that no more American capital flowed into Brazil. Worse was the collapse of the coffee market. Essentially a luxury, much as its addicts might protest, coffee suddenly had few American buyers. Its price fell by two-thirds within a few months, and the Coffee Institute found itself with enough coffee to supply the entire world for a year, if only it would buy. Panic spread into other industries, and then the federal, state, and municipal governments defaulted on their bonds. Eyes turned to the capital, where the rulers could do little; the administration was helpless to protect Brazil from disasters originating abroad. From all sides voices rose to blame the government for present poverty and generations of ineptitude. All of a sudden so much seemed wrong with the system.

Such was the mood of the country when the election of March 1930 approached. Washington Luis, who was really a fine man, had the unhappy inspiration to designate another *paulista*, Julio Prestes, to succeed him. In doing so he antagonized the political machines of Minas Gerais and Rio Grande do Sul, who had been led to expect an interruption of *paulista* control, and he also aroused the many Brazilians who thought São Paulo was too favored already. A formidable coalition gathered around the governor of Rio Grande do Sul, Dr. Getulio Dornelles Vargas, a so-called Liberal Alliance attractive to the military, Minas Gerais, and the discontented in general. After a lively campaign it was announced that Prestes had won, though Vargas' partisans protested. President-elect Prestes went to the United States to obtain loans for his ailing country. Getulio Vargas and his disappointed adherents prepared to overthrow the republic.

Brazil's history is characterized by boom and bust, by delirious optimism and despondency. In 1930 there was every reason for a depressing reappraisal of the nation's destiny. It was obvious that much of the achievement of the republican period had been hollow. The old clans among the rich, now widened to include a plutocracy that had developed since the fall of the empire, still ran the country, as they had since the mid-seventeenth century. The middle class was small, and an organized labor movement was frail. Most of the people lived precariously close to starvation and always in destitution. To regard the growth and high standards of living in the United States was a saddening experience for Brazilians. Since the advent of the republic, Argentina and Mexico had surpassed Brazil in industrialization, cultural life, and public education. Only in respect for personal liberty and in the relatively orderly rotation of presidents could Brazil take pride, and in 1930 these were about to change. The ancient saying, "God is a Brazilian," began to seem not only blasphemous but a mockery.

CHILE: LIBERTY WITHIN ORDER

The battle of Lircay in April 1830 proved more than a mere incident in the unending conflict of conservatives and liberals, or *pelucones* (big-wigs) and *pipiolos* (novices), as they called themselves in Chile. The conservative victory won by General Joaquín Prieto was decisive, settling the test of power until 1857 by one way of reckoning, to 1925 by another. The colonial-minded rural aristocracy of Chile formed a cohesive party that ruled absolutely until 1857. Then its basis shifted somewhat, divesting itself of the most reactionary elements and recruiting wealthy traders and professional men in the cities. Still an oligarchy, but enlightened, flexible, and able to adjust to the times, it managed the destinies of Chile until the great economic crisis of the twentieth century and is yet a powerful force. Not only did this oligarchy care for its own interests quite capably during this period, but it made the Chilean republic so stable and progressive that it was long the marvel of South America.

Just why Chile, and Chile alone, should attain stability so early in the national period cannot be explained simply. Certainly one factor was the concentration of its inhabitants in a fertile central valley between the Andes and the Pacific. Expansion to the frontiers of the north and south was slow enough so that the aristocratic agricultural society of the center was not disrupted. Nor was the growth of mining, commerce, and industry sudden enough to bring into political affairs new forces the landlords could not tame. The ruling oligarchy itself, largely of Basque and Catalan descent, tended to be practical, indifferent to the theories of doctrinaires and suspicious of the threats or temptations of soldiers. The country remained civilian-minded and materialistic. Even the ubiquitous racial factor failed to keep Chile from becoming an integrated nation. Most of her Indians were on the frontier, where to be sure they were often a menace, but not as much so as they would have been as a huge, sullen mass within the community. Great as the gap between rich and poor was, it did not have a racial basis, for Chile had grown so slowly during colonial times that the population of the central valley was generally mixed. Finally, the oligarchy that won control in 1830 was fortunate enough to have, and to follow, good leaders.

Diego Portales

FIRST and foremost of these leaders was Diego Portales, as strange a political genius as South America has produced and undoubtedly one of the most successful. Born in 1793, he was one of twenty-three children of the superintendent of the mint and a lady who claimed descent from the Borgias. His formal education was not impressive, coming as it did during the turbulence of the independence period. His talents seemed to lie in money-making. An import business he established in Valparaiso and in Peru brought him wealth at an early age. Soon he became interested in politics, writing editorials and poetry for newspapers he controlled and acquainting himself with men of affairs. His views were not particularly fixed, certainly not idealistic. As was natural in a man of property, he sided with the *pelucones* and craved order. Soon he was speaking of "the religion" of government, the only religion he admitted, for he had become a skeptic after the death of his wife and child in 1821. Portales declared that he believed in priests but not in God, by which he meant that the Church was to be esteemed only as an instrument to restrain the brutish masses. Snob though he was in politics, he avoided the society of the landed rich, preferring the company of actors, clowns, musicians, and assorted bohemians. His private life he kept private, though after his death it was revealed that a daughter of the late Baron Nordenflicht had borne him three children. When Portales entered the interim conservative government just before the battle of Lircay, he was known as a successful man of peculiar habits and compelling personal force, cruel in ridicule, brilliant in invective, complicated as a personality, and by no means lovable.

During 1830 and 1831 Portales held several portfolios as cabinet minister and easily dominated the interim government. Briefly vice-president as well, he scorned titles and was quick to give up his offices. In actions rather than utterances he revealed his ideas. Above all, Chile needed a government that would govern. The landlords and prominent traders must unite to impose their authority on soldiers, *pipiolos*, and the common people. The clergy must be their ally. Thus Portales, by force, guile, and ridicule, removed actual or potential opponents from public affairs and constructed a bureaucracy of conservatives. To prevent ambitious soldiers from thrusting themselves into politics, he reduced the regular army and created a national militia answerable not to professional officers but to the major landlords of each district. An efficient police force that ruled from Santiago gave the national government the sinews of power over outlying areas. Portales was ruthless in employing dictatorial methods to curb dissidents: censorship, summary courts, exile, and the other familiar means. The country was cowed but apparently recognized the need for strong-armed government. Portales achieved a certain popularity for all his mysterious ways and despotism. He was unwilling to risk his power by letting O'Higgins return from his Peruvian exile. Famous liberators were likely to be distracting elements, and dead ambitions might revive.

On September 18, 1831, General Joaquín Prieto was inaugurated as president of the republic. A few weeks afterward Portales returned to Valparaiso to husband his large business interests. For a time he retained a connection with the cabinet in Santiago and was governor of Valparaiso, but it seemed that he had tired of power. Prieto was by no means a nonentity, and his victory at Lircay had established his prestige over the army and the country, but he often sought Portales' advice and followed the ex-minister's views. Even when Prieto was reelected in 1836, it seemed that Portales was the real president.

Meanwhile, a convention produced the constitution of 1833, which established a centralized government with Catholicism as the state religion. Outwardly, the executive and legislative branches shared authority, but in fact the president held the key position with an absolute veto, almost unlimited appointive power, and machinery to dominate elections. He was eligible for one immediate reelection. Suffrage was restricted to property owners who were literate, and a complicated system of indirect elections assured many opportunities for the president to manipulate the selection of deputies and senators for the two houses and, of course, to reelect himself or pick his successor. A constitution designed to fit the needs of the times, it remained in force until 1925, though amendments altered its autocratic features in some respects.

Apart from the order produced by Portales and the legitimacy supplied by the constitution of 1833, the stolid Prieto enjoyed the services of another able minister, Manuel Rengifo, who served from 1830 to 1835 as the chief fiscal officer. The foreign and internal debts were consolidated and begun to be paid off—an almost incredible experience in Latin America of the 1830's—and a sound system of taxation brought in sufficient revenues to finance the government while falling gently on the landlords and such importers as Portales.

In 1835 Portales was induced to sacrifice his retirement from government by a threatening surge of *pipiolo* unrest. Within a few weeks he had set these liberals straight by the usual police methods. Then he perceived another menace. Bolivia and Peru had been brought into a confederation by General Santa Cruz. Was Santa Cruz a megalomaniac who would seek to annex other countries, including Chile? Portales thought he might harbor such designs, and a Peruvian-sponsored landing on Chile's coast by the liberal Chilean General Freire—which ended in fiasco with Freire being shipped to Australia—could be interpreted as the opening of a campaign against Chilean nationhood. Then, too, if the confederation proved a success, the growing commerce of Valparaiso, including Portales' own business, might be jeopardized by the old monopolists of Lima and Callao. And Chile held many grievances against Peru, such as the non-payment of the debts incurred during San Martín's liberating expedition. With this mixture of patriotic and personal purposes, Portales insisted that Chile break up the Santa Cruz creation. Despite urgent efforts by the Andean dictator to prevent war and much opposition within Chile itself, Portales, as usual, had his way. Chile declared war and organized an expeditionary force. Perhaps Portales hoped that a personal visit to this army on the eve of its departure from Valparaiso would diminish the grumbling and incomprehension of the men, and he enjoyed reviewing troops, civilian though he was. In June 1837, in one of the most unusual military parades ever held, the guest of honor was seized and made a prisoner. Then the army marched on Santiago with Portales handcuffed in a coach. In that predicament he had the pleasure of seeing the rebels soundly defeated by government troops, but little good it did Portales, for he was dragged from the coach and shot dead.

The brutal killing of Portales produced a wave of indignation in Chile. The minister had scorned public acclaim, but the people sensed that he had stabilized the country after years of disorder. His death made him a national hero whose stature has seldom been denied by later generations. Further, it made the war popular, for others finally realized that a Peruvian-Bolivian confederation would be a threat to Chile. The conflict was longer and more difficult than the Chileans expected. An expedition to Arequipa in 1837 failed to produce the expected mass desertion from Santa Cruz but brought defeat instead. Another expedition in 1838, led by President Prieto's nephew, General Manuel Bulnes, landed north of Lima and fought its way into the capital. After several months of floundering on both sides, victory at last came to Bulnes in January 1839 at the battle of Yungay. Santa Cruz fled and the confederation collapsed. It was generally agreed in Chile that Portales had been statesmanlike to arouse his country to the danger of the Peruvian-Bolivian combination. And the war had given Chileans a heady dose of confidence.

A Generation of Enlightened Conservatism

THE legacy of Portales formed the basis of Chile's order and progress during the mid-nineteenth century, a time of futile violence in most of Latin America. The Pacific coast republic flourished in nearly every way. Her government was efficient. Without mishap the presidency passed from Prieto to General Manuel Bulnes in 1841, and he was reelected in 1846. It was possible to maintain the regime with few of the dictatorial methods of Portales. It was safe to permit the *pipiolos* and the newer type of liberals to express themselves, though drastic measures were certain if opposition threatened to become revolt. O'Higgins was granted permission to return, another indication of a freer atmosphere, but he died before he could take advantage of the offer. The oligarchy was sure enough of its power to tolerate discordant elements.

Moreover, the economy throve in a way almost unknown in Latin America. Foreign commerce seemed to increase every year. Valparaiso was the prime distribution point of South America's western coast and was full of ships, warehouses, and merchants. Silver and copper ores were discovered north of the central valley. An unexpected and very profitable market for Chilean wheat developed when gold rushes brought settlers into California and Australia, distant areas to be sure, but closer to no grain sources than those of Chile. An American named William Wheelwright started a steamship line between Santiago and Callao, a veritable breakthrough in oceanic communications that would enhance Chile's position. A railroad from Santiago to Valparaiso was another indication of great developments of the future. Expansion into the forests and fjords of the Antarctic south gave promise of further economic activity. Coal was found, not choice coal, but the only deposits then known in South America. A colonizing company planted a group of Germans in southern Chile. They prospered, and many recruits joined them after the failure of the liberal revolutions in central Europe in 1848–1849. Presiding over the treasury under Bulnes was Manuel Rengifo, whose competent management made Chile attractive to foreign investors, traders, and immigrants.

Education also flowered under the orderly government of the Bulnes regime. Manuel Montt, the highly capable minister of justice and instruction, was largely responsible for an outburst of public school construction and teacher training. Chile had schools of fine arts, music, agriculture, engineering, science, music, and seamanship. The National Institute continued to supply teachers and trained public officials. The creation of the University of Chile in 1842 promised further advances, particularly when it secured as its first rector the Venezuelan Andrés Bello, the tutor and companion of Simón Bolívar. Bello long exerted a powerful influence on intellectual life as educator, writer, and elder statesman. His conservative views assured government support for his activities.

Chile also benefited from the presence of refugees from less happy countries, particularly from the Argentina of Rosas. A lively and relatively unhampered press stimulated interest in world affairs and the intellectual and artistic activities of Europe. A veritable school of writers and scholars developed in what had been one of the most bucolic of Spain's colonies a few decades earlier. Chile became and remained an enlightened republic where learning was admired. The illiteracy of the masses was no worse than that of older and richer countries of the 1840's.

The oligarchy was instinctively wise in regarding Montt's activities in promoting education with restrained enthusiasm. Contact with European currents made rebels or critics of many young Chileans, especially the sons of well-to-do traders in the cities. And foreign visitors, residents, or immigrants heightened the tendency to find fault with the reactionary landlords. José Victorino Lastarria, an academic man and often a deputy in congress, acquired a large following in his campaign to revive liberalism. A more radical spirit was Francisco Bilboa, descendant of one of the "three Anthonys" of 1780 who had tried to promote a revolution. Young Bilbao was so strident in his condemnation of the Catholic and autocratic tradition in Chile that he was invited to leave the country. He went to France, where he exulted in the revolution of 1848 and returned to introduce the new romantic democratic movement in his native republic. It fell to Montt to suppress much of the bubbling liberalism loosed by the European revolutions of 1848 and after. Much as he had done inadvertently to stimulate such feeling, he proved equally effective in stifling it by censorship, arrests, and other stringent measures. He earned the approval of the oligarchy, and President Bulnes determined that Montt should succeed him. This was easily arranged.

Manuel Montt was a civilian, a young middle-aged man of modest family background who had risen rapidly by his abilities. A brilliant student and teacher, he had served as rector of the National Institute. Bulnes had brought him into his administration, where Montt served the full ten years and emerged as the strongest figure in the government. By 1850 the liberals had decided he was a villain.

To Bilbao in particular Montt loomed as an obstacle to the inevitable revolution. Organizing a Society of Equality and publishing a newspaper called *Friend of the people*, Bilbao sought to bring Chile up to date on the French Revolution. By 1851 his activities were so conspicuous that he was again sent into exile, but the ferment continued. General José María de la Cruz, governor of the southern province of Concepción, came to Santiago during the summer of that year and learned of the restlessness of the youthful idealists and the lingering *pipiolo* sentiment of many older persons, including seventy elderly ladies who called on him in a group. Cruz returned to Concepción and when, in September 1851, Montt took over the presidency, he led a garrison in a typical Latin American "pronouncement." In La Serena, a port of the north, another revolutionary group seized an English ship and sought to raise the coast. The filibusterers were quickly chastised, and in December ex-President Bulnes defeated Cruz and thus saved his heir. What might be called Chile's revolution of 1848 terminated the way those in Europe had.

Begun in bloodshed, the Montt decade—for the president was re-elected in 1856—represents a period in Chilean history suggestive in some ways of the presidency of Theodore Roosevelt in the United States. Enlightened conservatism, then somewhat tarnished, became progressive, even liberal, and an astonishing display of energy brought both reforms and constructive work. Montt was far from colorful as an individual, severe and academic as he was. He could certainly be un-pleasant to his own countrymen when he thought they were endangering the precious stability that Chile had achieved. Yet he had the wisdom to engineer the transition of the republic from habitual conservatism to a cautious progressivism that satisfied most of the generation that had grown up under the oligarchy. It was time for adjustments; the landed aristocracy had become too smug with the long years of power, and prosperous businessmen of the growing cities demanded a larger share in government. Both the mining interests in the north and the settlers in the south claimed the right to participate in shaping the nation's poli-cies. Educated Chileans were less respectful of the Church and the ad-vantages of latifundia. They were entranced with the materialism and technology of the mid-nineteenth century, with factories, steamships, railroads, and other wonders that were remaking the Western world.

Montt was sympathetic to the modernists, though he moved slowly enough not to alienate the landlords during his first term. Every en-couragement was given railroad builders and steamship lines. The tele-graph came to Chile. Several banks attested to the republic's financial soundness and good prospects. Large numbers of Germans arrived to colonize southern Chile, founding the city of Puerto Montt and creating sturdy, attractive homes, manicured farms and orchards, and efficient small industries, including the inevitable breweries. Like the Basques and Catalans, the Germans played a conspicuous role in the nation's affairs. The prestigious Andrés Bello compiled a civil code for the republic. An observatory was established on the hill of Santa Lucía in Santiago, where Valdivia and Inéz Suárez had fought off the Indians more than three centuries before. Montt saw to it that 500 primary schools were built and staffed. Impressive as all this material progress was, the rural masses remained peons, destitute, given to vices, and powerless. The mine work-ers and urban laboring classes were at least as depressed as their equiva-lents in Europe. Alcoholism and gambling were national curses.

Little as he comprehended the basic social evils of the country, Montt courageously began to pry important privileges from the landlords and the Church. He outlawed the *mayorazgo*, which O'Higgins had tried to abolish, and thus encouraged the division of estates among the children of the owners. He even stimulated, though very modestly, the sale of farmlands to peons who were willing to try to improve their lot. A clash with the Archbishop of Santiago encouraged him to heed the liberals and take the first step toward anti-clericalism, elimination of the compulsory ecclesiastical tithe.

By 1857 Montt well understood that his progressive measures, mild as they were, had cost him the support of the die-hard *pelucones* without winning over the extreme liberals. A large center remained, and this he sought to integrate in a National Party with the motto, "Liberty within Order." The organization throve, and the defection of reactionaries and ultra-liberals from the Montt regime was welcomed. It was Montt's hope that his designated heir, Antonio Varas, would continue his policies in succeeding administrations. Varas was a close friend of Montt, like him a civilian of modest family and admirable intellectual attainments. He had served as vice-rector of the National Institute while Montt was rector, and he had been an influential cabinet minister throughout the Montt presidency.

Much as the two men were identified, Varas was disliked by many who supported Montt. Not only the democratic liberals, who were outside the National Party in any event, but many moderates blamed Varas for high-handed suppression of opposition and for various other unpopular actions. Agitation against his prospective candidacy grew until riots occurred in several cities early in 1859. And then a group of ultra-liberals in the mining area of the north started an armed revolution. By April 1859 Montt crushed all these manifestations. Soon Varas, possibly without being pressed into doing so, withdrew his candidacy, and the political situation quickly calmed.

Other troubles clouded the last years of Montt's administration. The Araucanians resumed their ancient habit of pillaging white settlements in the south and returning to the safety of the Andes and forested islands in the cold seas. A French madman reigned briefly in 1861 as king of Araucania until he was captured and shipped home. An economic crisis hit the country because of the fall in the price of copper and the decline in Australian and Californian demand for Chile's wheat. Nonetheless, Montt and his National Party successfully staged the election of 1861 so that their candidate, José Joaquín Pérez, a man admired by the liberals and trusted by the Church, was chosen president.

A Period of Moderate Liberalism and War

THE decade of Pérez, who continued the tradition of two-term presidents, was almost an era of good feelings in domestic politics. Amnesties allowed the victims of Montt's harsh policies to return, politicians made and unmade combinations with great gusto, and publicists applauded and derided various factions with cheerful inconsistency. There was no shooting. Chile was already a much freer country than her sister republics in Latin America. During the 1860's an increasing number of her citizens exercised this freedom by extolling or reviling clericalism, promoting or resisting further political liberalization, and advancing a variety of proposals to modernize the republic. In general, President Pérez sided with the liberals, though these liberals were usually members of the oligarchy that had long reigned and had little taste for bringing the masses into politics. It is fair to regard them as Whigs, as libertarians who prized the security of the propertied classes but did not believe in oppression. Probably more would have been accomplished had Chilean nationalism not been aroused to ferocity by a naval war with Spain in 1865. This futile conflict grew out of Spain's seizure of Peru's Chincha Islands in 1864 and attendant insults to her nationality, made all the more safe because of the Civil War in the United States. Chile rightly felt her own nationhood menaced and, when summoned to salute the Spanish fleet, responded by declaring war. For a time war was an exhilarating experience. A Chilean ship, the *Esmeralda*, captured a Spanish schooner, the *Covadonga*, after which the Spanish admiral committed suicide. Spain still possessed a superior navy and was able to enforce a blockade. When she gave up the Peruvian adventure, she subjected Valparaiso to a bombardment as brutal as it was stupid. Not until 1870 was peace made official. Apart from the fanning of patriotism which united Chile during that war, the Pérez administration was a period of continued growth of mining and commerce. Of all the reforms proposed during these years only two were important: the granting of toleration for non-Catholics and a constitutional amendment to prevent immediate reelection of the president.

The ban on presidential reelection had been passed with the acquiescence of Federico Errázuriz, the designated heir of Pérez, who served as president himself from 1871 to 1876. An aristocrat who had revolted with the liberals in 1851, Errázuriz secured the passage of several political reforms. The press was made almost entirely free. The clergy was placed under the law of the state instead of the Church. Elections were liberalized by a sort of proportional representation allowed to minority parties, and congress secured the right to name a majority to the council of state, a measure which apparently assured ministerial responsibility to the legislative branch. An almost unbelievable furor occurred when another law provided corners in cemeteries for the remains of those to whom the Church denied burial. Clearly, the mounting liberal feeling in Chile was moving toward a crisis with the surging ultramontanism of the clericals, a typical situation in most Catholic countries during the 1870's.

In 1876 the administration dictated the succession of Aníbal Pinto, though a genuine political convention and a heated campaign indicated that Chilean voters might have preferred less official management of elections. Politics could be great fun, as the strident enthusiasm, color, and acrimony of campaigns in the United States demonstrated. Chile was not to experience these pleasures for some years, however. Pinto was a satisfactory president, though he had a stormy administration. Son of a one-time president in the 1820's, an aristocrat, a liberal, a man experienced as deputy and cabinet minister, and a gentleman of culture, he was confronted with the fiscal calamity resulting from the world-wide depression of the 1870's. His response was regarded as sensible for the times: strict austerity in government expenses and a generous issuance of paper money. Things improved, though many businesses collapsed and numerous individuals went in want. An international crisis and war soon dominated Pinto's term.

The War of the Pacific waged by Chile against Bolivia and Peru between 1879 and 1883 can easily be regarded as the evil fruit of Chilean aggressiveness, and it often is. However, Chile had something of a moral case and impeccable legal justification for initiating this conflict. The war was terrible enough, with much suffering endured by soldiers in the desert and sailors on the high seas. Coastal populations were tragically involved. Lima endured years of occupation, and Peru almost disintegrated as a nation. Her rancor was kept alive for more than a half century, while Bolivia has never recovered from the blow to her pride and loss of territory.

The issue was utilization of the Atacama Desert, a strip more than 500 miles long stretching from Arica, Peru, to a point not far from the central valley of Chile. In 1536 Diego de Almagro had traversed this dreadful area with his thirsty and sunstruck party and appropriately called it "the land of desperation." Lying between tawny, utterly barren mountains and the frigid Pacific, it seemed to have nothing to offer the human race. Rain never falls, and no plants grow. The Spanish had never troubled to mark clearly the boundaries in this area for their various subdivisions. After independence, Peru asserted her sovereignty over Tacna, Arica, and Tarapacá. The central stretch known as Antofagasta was claimed by Bolivia, who desired a corridor to the ocean. Just where Bolivia stopped and Chile began, no one had bothered to determine. It made no difference for many years, for only a few adventurers entered the desert. It was known that guano islands were off the coast, and Chilean gatherers of this commodity had begun to scoop up a few shiploads now and then. Some of them discovered that unlimited quantities of mineral salts such as sodium nitrate and borax were available. Possibly mineral wealth awaited a lucky prospector in the Andes beyond the sandy expanses. It was not until the 1860's that the great commercial value of nitrate became apparent with the process discovered by Alfred Nobel of Sweden for manufacturing explosives. In an age when European armies were expanding apace and the use of dynamite was opening up new possibilities for mining and construction, the supplies of nitrate in the Atacama took on a sudden importance. Ever quick to exploit business opportunities, Chilean entrepreneurs and their workers invaded the desert.

Rather than quibble endlessly over boundaries and taxes, Chile made an agreement in 1866 with Bolivia to restrict her frontier at 24 degrees latitude and to share equally the revenues from 23 to 25 degrees. Chilean rather than Bolivian businessmen and laborers occupied the desert. Roads, docks, wells, machinery, and hideous little settlements for the workingmen developed rapidly. A town which Bolivia had failed to make a useful port, Antofagasta, became a veritable colony of Chileans. And then the enterprising men from the southern republic began to move into Peruvian territory, into Tarapacá, and proposed to expand farther into Arica and Tacna. While Chile faithfully kept her bargain of 1866 with Bolivia, Bolivians knew that that arrangement was favorable to Chile, and they remembered that it had been signed by one of their most venal presidents, Melgarejo, under suspicious circumstances. Peruvians, too, were disturbed that their own nitrates were being exploited by Chileans, whom they had always regarded as grasping and too materialistic. In 1873 Peru and Bolivia made a secret treaty to defend themselves should Chile attempt to follow up her economic control in their territory with political authority. Argentina, who was having many boundary difficulties with Chile, almost joined the allies. Meanwhile, many new Chilean fortunes were being established.

Another agreement between Chile and Bolivia in 1874 effected a few changes, the most important of which was that Bolivia would consent to Chilean operations in her territory at a certain rate of taxation which would not be increased. Soon afterward, Peru nationalized the nitrate sources in her provinces, much to the loss of many Chilean enterprisers. Bolivia decided to do likewise and, as a first step, decreed, in 1878, an increase in the rate of taxation for the removal of her mineral salts. Chile, of course, protested, but Bolivia went ahead with plans to compel payment. This was all quite contrary to previous treaties and international practices, but then Bolivia seldom concerned herself with her reputation. President Pinto dispatched an expeditionary force of 200 men who occupied the dreary little port of Antofagasta in February 1879. Bolivia declared war, and in Lima crowds howled for Chilean blood. After a few half-hearted negotiations, Peru decided to abide by her alliance with Bolivia. By April 1879 the three republics had exchanged declarations of war.

The most dramatic operations were those at sea. Chile had several warships, including two iron-clads of recent construction, and Peru possessed a fleet smaller by one ship and, as in everything else, less efficiently managed than the Chilean. Bolivia had no navy whatever. Chile took the offensive, propelling her sail-and-steam vessels up the Humboldt Current to Peru. The first major encounter resulted in the victory of Peru's iron cruiser *Huascar* over the wooden *Esmeralda*, but Chile's *Covadonga*, taken from Spain a few years before, ran the fine Peruvian frigate *Independencia* aground. The upshot was that the *Huascar*, under the intrepid Admiral Miguel Grau, sailed about freely for several months, disrupting Chile's shipping and bombarding her coastal towns. In October 1879, however, the Chilean *Cochrane* captured the *Huascar* in an operation which seemed to prove the fateful consequences of naming vessels of war after historical figures. After this, Chile had absolute naval supremacy, and Peru merely waited in helplessness for the landing of invading forces.

While Peru hastily purchased arms from the United States and shared some of them with Bolivia, Chile more wisely bought up munitions and artillery from the Krupps in Germany. Chile also had a better-managed army, one whose business was military and not, as in Peru and Bolivia, politics. And her soldiers seemed more obedient and sturdier than those of her enemies. In November 1879 a Chilean army confronted Dictator Daza's thirsty and ill-fed mob, who suffered from the low altitude among other things, near the desert port of Antofagasta. Daza unheroically but sanely declined combat and withdrew. There was nothing for his Peruvian allies to do but retreat. Thus the whole province of Antofagasta and the neighboring Peruvian area of Tarapacá quickly fell under Chilean occupation. Early in 1880 another Chilean force, 13,000 strong, landed north of Arica in Peru. Despite memorable sufferings from heat and stout resistance from the allies, they captured that town and Tacna, together with the surrounding territory. Chile had clearly won the war at this point, and negotiations were begun under the auspices of the United States and with the blessings of several European nations, all of whom had regarded the war with great revulsion. Yet Peru refused to accept Chile's demand for the province of Tarapacá, and the war resumed. Nor did Bolivia care to cede Antofagasta, but she scarcely mattered now.

Late in 1880 a huge Chilean force of perhaps 25,000 men was ferried to a point south of Lima-Callao. The Peruvians were thoroughly aroused and made plans both intelligent and extensive to fortify their capital. It was no use. In January 1881 the Chileans fought their way into the City of the Kings and, after a fearful sacking of shops and stores by Peruvian mobs, established a military government there. The war should have been over at this point, but Peruvian forces continued to harass the invaders from the mountains—very much as the Spanish had in 1821–1824—and two years passed before such authority as still existed in Peru agreed to peace terms. By this Treaty of Ancón, Chile agreed to evacuate the capital but to retain Tacna and Arica for ten years, after which a plebiscite would determine their future, and Tarapacá in perpetuity. Bolivia refused to make peace until 1904, but an armistice in 1884 allowed the Chileans legally to retain Antofagasta, which of course they already occupied.

Chile's series of victories, culminating in the acquisition of territory that increased her area by a fourth, heightened the already exalted nationalism of a confident people. Long the most successful country in Spanish America in governing herself, she now exulted in prosperity as her growth was resumed and re-doubled. The importance of the nitrate beds to the nation could scarcely be exaggerated. So great were the revenues from export duties on this commodity that internal taxes were gentle or dispensed with altogether, a matter that delighted none of her citizens more than the rich oligarchs. And, viewed as an entity, the Chilean nation utilized its income wisely. Corruption, militarism, and navalism absorbed as little as could be expected in an imperfect world. Most of the revenues went into public buildings, roads, canals, tunnels, docks, railroads, and beautification. It would be too much to expect a government of that time to employ its income in ambitious programs to eliminate the poverty of the masses, always the tragic undercurrent in the history of the Chilean republic, whose surface seas seem so smooth.

Such problems as the nation had during the 1880's were more or less minor adjustments to the times. Domingo Santa María was president from 1881 to 1886, his choice over the leading general of the war underlining the attachment of Chile to civilians. A liberal, Santa María took calmly the breach in relations with the Vatican over an archbishop's election. In retaliation, he sponsored legislation to permit secularized cemeteries, civil marriage, and a civil registry. Minute as these measures seem, they represented emotionally-charged victories of liberals who had agitated for years. Characteristically, this was as far as Chile would go in anticlericalism. The Church continued powerful and rich, a state Church, and the people were loyally Catholic. Santa María also declined to block, as he might have, a constitutional amendment to allow congress to override a presidential veto by a majority of two-thirds. He further permitted encroachment on his authority by agreeing to a law that endowed cities with a little home rule. The property qualification for voting seeming undemocratic, he sponsored a change which granted suffrage to all literate males over twenty-five, which scarcely changed the electorate at all, though the new principle was admirable. Finally, the Araucanians ceased, after 340 years, to be a danger to the white or half-breed man in Chile. During the War of the Pacific these Indians had taken advantage of Chile's preoccupation. Now at last, they were pushed into reservations in the southern Andes where they have ever since remained. Liquor, artillery, European immigrants, and the railroad account for this ultimate victory over the heroic nation the Inca and the Spaniard had failed to conquer.

The election of 1886, dominated as usual by the outgoing president despite noisy party conventions and electoral campaigns, brought José Manuel Balmaceda to the presidency. Cultured, of good family, prepossessing in manner, and long experienced in government, he also brought the best intentions into his office. He said he wished to unite the great liberal family, which had tended toward splinterization. Conditions were auspicious, for Chile's high reputation and booming prosperity were all that could be asked. He set about to promote public schools and to outdo all his predecessors in public works and other wholesome labors of construction. Many of these purposes he achieved. Yet Balmaceda ran afoul of political currents long gaining strength. The old *pelucón* groups, the die-hard reactionaries, still craved power that Manuel Montt had slipped out of their hands in 1857. A new Democratic Party, which had Marxist overtones, was organized when the urban poor were made unusually wretched by a cholera epidemic. The vital center which had run the regime since the days of Montt was no longer united. Personalism of the type suffered in France under the contemporaneous Third Republic seemed to make all politicians tricky, unreliable, and eager to knife anyone in power. Balmaceda himself had an unfortunate personal quality which is difficult to identify. Important men disliked him, and the masses were cool. His supporters tended to shift to the opposition once he had secured them positions. Fundamentally, perhaps, there were too many politicians in Chile. Also, parliamentarism was asserting itself ever more strongly against presidential autocracy. For the first time since the constitution of 1833 went into effect, the president lost control of congress as a result of the elections of 1888.

Irritation and suspicions mounted during Balmaceda's last years, but no urgent issues were at stake. In 1890 the president bowed to the demand of congress that the cabinet be responsible to itself. He made the usual preparations to assure the election of his chosen successor for 1891. While congress was adjourned, however, Balmaceda ousted the cabinet favored by the congressional majority and appointed one congenial to him. This breach in ministerial responsibility was less serious for a Chilean president than a European constitutional monarch, but it caused a great uproar all the same. Knowing that congress would be troublesome, he did not call it into session to approve the budget for 1891 but simply announced that the 1890 budget would remain in force for the following year. The challenge Balmaceda was raising was clear. Congressional leaders replied with spirit. In January 1891 a large group of deputies assembled and declared Balmaceda deposed. Issuing a ringing proclamation to the country in behalf of parliamentary government and free elections, these leaders joined the fleet at Valparaiso, where naval Captain Jorge Montt (no relation to the one-time president) carried them to the nitrate region.

For more than six months the congressional leaders remained in the north, collecting the vast revenues and purchasing arms abroad. A former Prussian army captain arrived to assume command of the army they were assembling. Balmaceda exercised an outright dictatorship in Santiago, punishing suspected enemies and seemingly assuring military support by raising the pay of all soldiers by half. Yet public opinion was against him, and he lacked the common touch to arouse the urban masses. Certainly the rural landlords with their peons could be counted among his opponents. In August 1891 the fleet brought more than 9,000 soldiers to a point near Valparaiso. Balmaceda believed he had 40,000 soldiers to support him, but he was deceived. Only a fourth of that number could be brought to oppose the congressional forces, and many of these declined to fight. An overwhelming victory of the *congresistas* opened Valparaiso and Santiago not only to their forces but to the crazed pillaging of a usually disciplined population. Balmaceda fled to the Argentine legation. He remained there several weeks, brooding over the ruin of his career and the wreckage of the presidential office he had been so determined to exalt. The punishment of his friends and supporters grieved him deeply. While he might easily have escaped to Argentina, he chose to sit out the remainder of his term in his asylum in Santiago. When it ended, on September 18, 1891, he dressed in his formal clothes and fired a pistol at his temple.

The defeat and suicide of Balmaceda terminated the long period of presidential autocracy but little affected the cultural and economic evolution of Chile. Most of the great luminaries of intellectual life who had glorified and molded so much of the republic's history had passed from the scene. Andrés Bello had died in 1865 at an advanced age. His influence had extended from the child Simón Bolívar to men powerful in public life as late as 1900. Long rector of the University of Chile, his lectures and personal counsels had immeasurable, but enormous, effects. So did his numerous works of criticism. Also, he was a poet, editor of the admirable civil code of the republic, and compiler of the best grammar of Castilian of his time. José Victorino Lastarria (d. 1888), as has been seen, was mentor to the moderate liberals whose triumph during the century was so steady if paced. Francisco Bilbao in a much shorter life founded and nurtured the romantic democratic movement of Chile which also emerged to victory by the twentieth century, though Bilbao himself died in 1866. Chile's historians had much to record with pride, for their nation was a success. Diego Barros Arana (1830–1907) and Miguel Luis Amunátegui (1828–1888) laid the basis for the country's historiography. Benjamín Vicuña MacKenna (1831–1886) wrote a hundred or more volumes, mostly of history, while risking his freedom and his life at times in political movements of an ultra-liberal character. José Toribio Medina (1852–1930) perhaps outdid all his contemporaries in historical productivity and bibiliography. Of essayists, poets, painters, and novelists there were many, though few but the poets won fame outside South America. Surely, the soundness of Chile as a state is one explanation of the richness of its intellectual life. Calm and prosperity provided the atmosphere; the republic's success offered an inspiration.

The Parliamentary Republic, 1891–1920

THE overthrow of Balmaceda ended a sixty-year period of what might be called monarchical presidents, executives who wielded ultimate power and who dictated the succession. It was also the only time in a 94-year period that the government was changed by means of force. For more than thirty years after 1891, Chile experienced that type of regime almost unheard-of in Latin America, a parliamentary republic. The experiment was not altogether edifying, refreshing as it was in contrast to dictators and all-powerful presidents in neighboring countries. The congressional party quickly solidified its victory after Balmaceda's fall in 1891, punishing its enemies and rewarding its supporters. The modest Jorge Montt was installed as president with the understanding that he would reign, not rule Congress at once made it clear that cabinet posts should go to men chosen by its own majority, not by the president, and that all government officials must be answerable to the legislative rather than the executive branch. The army, navy, and police accepted the new state of affairs with amazing amiability, another striking departure from Latin American practice. And a law of 1891 allowed towns all over the republic to dispense with presidentially-appointed rulers and to choose their own. The presidents filled the role designed for them with resignation. After Jorge Montt came Federico Errázuriz (1896–1901) son of the former president, Germán Riesco (1901–1906), Pedro Montt (1906–1910), Ramón Barros Luco (1911–1915), and Juan Luis Sanfuentes (1915–1920). Of these chief executives only Montt, son of the memorable President Manuel Montt, seemed to chafe under the restricted role. Successfully as he was resisted, his journey to Germany for medical treatment and his death there brought criticism from an oligarchy which was very hard to please.

In many respects this aristocratic *Fronda* (branch), so-called in reminiscence of the unsuccessful movement of the French nobility against Louis XIV in the seventeenth century, served well enough for the times. The republic's income was so great from nitrate duties that little taxation was required. Chile had a tradition of stability and civilianism. *Laissez-faire*, further building, beautification, and public enlightenment were all that the articulate groups demanded, and these they got. Chile continued to offer a model of steady progress. Economic expansion went on regularly in a businessman's and landlord's paradise. Foreign investments provided further development, and Spanish and German immigrants, while not "pouring in," arrived in a satisfactory flow. Commerce and education flourished, gathering momentum from the tranquil decades after Portales. In a period when Germany and England almost alone thought of providing elaborate welfare measures for the masses, the Chilean ruling groups should not be condemned too harshly for failing to anticipate the compelling trends of the mid-twentieth century.

On the other hand, the *Fronda* governed with little style. At least eleven political parties clamored for advantage in the congresses of this period, very much as they did in France of the Third Republic. Cynical combinations, ready treachery, and intrigue characterized the rapid rise and fall of cabinets, which occurred every three months or so. Few consistent policies could be carried out. Rich men paid enormous prices for election to congress, where members were unsalaried, and saw to it that local bosses provided the necessary majorities. Corruption at the local level was more than matched by graft on a grander scale in the national government. While this evil was common enough in all countries, even the most advanced, and certainly was smaller than in other Latin American republics, the reputation of the Chilean *Fronda* has always been clouded by its brazen encouragement of the condition.

Beneath the façade of the oligarchy with its proud landowning classes and high-spending businessmen, dangerous forces were at work. Only a small minority of the population immediately shared in the republic's prosperity. For all the handsome homes, fine public buildings, schools and libraries, railroads, mines, small industries, and shops, Chile was a poor country. The rural masses, the *inquilinos*, lived in isolation and poverty on the great estates. Homeless drifters or itinerant workers, known by the tragic word *rotos* (the broken), wandered in destitution from farm to town and back again. In the cities the majority who owned no property worked long hours for low pay, forming an urban proletariat of increasingly ugly temper. Alcoholism, gambling, poor health, and hunger characterized the lot of a shockingly large proportion of the population of the whole country. The old conservative and liberal parties, in whatever splinters they appeared, took little note of them while ruling the country. The Radical Party sought to organize labor unions and strikes. Marxist and other European ideologies found expression in the Democratic Party. Propaganda for the betterment of the working classes circulated widely, for Chile was a comparatively free country, and strikes became more frequent and more violent as the twentieth century aged. A few concessions from the oligarchy in the way of protective labor legislation and welfare measures served only to stimulate the demand for more, to show how much needed to be done.

The explosive character of Chile's social dilemma was not widely appreciated until the end of World War I. Meanwhile, the republic continued to enjoy a good reputation in international affairs. She bowed to the United States in the affair of the cruiser *Baltimore*, when the impatient northern republic demanded monetary compensation for the death of two sailors in Valparaiso after a street fight in 1891. It developed that the long dispute with Argentina over the boundary in the southern Andes and Strait of Magellan area had not been settled in 1881 by a treaty that prescribed the highest peaks and the watershed as the frontier. The mountain streams did not always flow in accordance with the continental divide! After much acrimony, the matter was turned over to King Edward VII for arbitration, which was accepted in 1902. The Christ of the Andes statue was then erected to symbolize the eternal peace the two republics promised to keep, and so far have. In 1904 Bolivia at last agreed to a treaty of cession of her lost province of Antofagasta, but the dispute with Peru over Tacna and Arica dragged on. Chile proudly took her place at Pan-American conferences and made useful contributions. It seemed fitting that she should also associate herself with Argentina and Brazil as one of the unofficial ABC powers, a bloc of internationally-minded and peacefully inclined states. Her fleet and German-trained army, and even her interest in aviation, assured the orderly republic of respect from other nations.

24

Mexico: Turmoil and Progress

REFORM AND RELAPSE: 1855–1911

DURING the first generation of independence, Mexico underwent disastrous experiences, having more than her share of tyranny, bloodshed, and economic and cultural retrogression. She endured a particularly painful blow in losing a war and half her territory to the United States. Yet, as in so much of Latin America, the mid-century years were a turning point, for a new generation came into power in 1855 and set out to uproot the lingering colonial evils they blamed for the nation's sorry situation and to infuse the republic with liberalism and technology as known in western Europe. Those efforts, *la Reforma* (the reformation), led to a fierce civil war in 1858–1861, which the modernizers won. Only a year after their victory, however, Mexico played the victim in one of the most outrageous episodes in the history of European imperialism, if it was also well-intended and romantic. It was utterly defeated in 1867 after much loss of life, whereupon the restored republic had nine fairly good years to fulfill the ideals of *la Reforma* and to patch up the country. This phase ended in 1876 as Mexico fell under the power of a firm dictator who for thirty-five years provided internal peace, enormous material progress, and a solid regime not too different from Spanish colonialism at its best. From this extraordinary period there emerged a radical and nationalist movement which became one of the more significant of all the twentieth-century revolutions in the world. The history of Mexico from 1855 to 1911 is stirring and meaningful, tragic, colorful, and fascinating. It is quite possible that the synthesis that has issued from this period is the truest guide to the destiny of Latin America.

La Reforma

THE BIRTH OF THE LIBERAL REFORMATION

Santa Anna's departure in August 1855 left Mexico full of pronouncing caudillos with their private armies, who were churning up the country in a fashion that had become only too familiar. This time, however, there really was a difference. Santa Anna was finished at last, and with him the toleration for peacock dictators of his stripe. The principal military leaders were adherents of the Plan of Ayutla, which had been proclaimed as early as March 1854 by the aging guerrilla boss, Juan Álvarez, who had controlled much of the mountainous south, notably the state of Guerrero, since the early days of the century. Uncouth as he was, Álvarez sincerely adhered to the cause of liberal constitutionalism, which Morelos had originally articulated. During the seventeen months from his pronouncement to the fall of Santa Anna, he and other caudillos had reiterated the central point of the Plan of Ayutla: that a constituent assembly be convened to devise a new basic charter for the republic. Lending this purpose real enthusiasm were members of the middle class, who were at last asserting themselves in politics. These lawyers, merchants, and intellectuals were determined to make the revolution of 1855 a true one so that Mexico would not revert quickly into its customary militarism. Above all, this objective meant breaking the power of the army and the Church. Once this reformation had been achieved, the country might build sound institutions as a liberal, federal republic where civil rights were respected and where economic freedom would facilitate the redistribution of national wealth.

Many of these reformers represented the new generation that had grown up during the squalid period of Santa Anna and the American war. Often serious and studious, they had cultivated the revolutionary ideals of Spain during her liberal periods and of France during the great Revolution and that of 1848. Yankeephobic as they were—as nearly all Mexicans were—they were aware of the success of republican democracy in the giant state to the north. Many of them had experienced during periods of exile in New Orleans and Texas that mixture of envy, admiration, and resentment that affects so many Mexicans when they regard the United States. Often ideologues with far too much faith in words, they nonetheless were a brilliant group; Benito Juárez, Santos Degollado, Ignacio Altamirano, Melchor Ocampo, and Miguel and Sebastián Lerdo de Tejada were soon to shine as the luminaries of this new generation. Of the older group there were still a few radical liberals, or *puros*, who had survived the long period of disillusionment since the days of Morelos and the constitution of 1824. The aged Valentín Gómez Farías, the most important of these veterans, was one of them, and so in a way was Álvarez. Also, many of the former moderates of the 1830's and 1840's joined the modern liberals, so that a formidable political party had taken shape. That so many of the liberal persuasion were mestizos was also a fact of greatest significance. A true Mexican nationality, neither white nor Indian, was asserting itself.

Álvarez and his ragged Indians took over Mexico City following the flight of Santa Anna, and in November 1855 this grizzled mestizo warrior of seventy-five became provisional president. He organized a cabinet and summoned the constituent convention so long desired. His minister of justice, Benito Juárez, precipitately revealed the direction of the new regime by a decree later known as the *Ley Juárez*, by which all special tribunals, usually kangaroo courts, were abolished. Also, the long-cherished right of ecclesiastical and military courts to judge cases not immediately under their jurisdiction was withdrawn. This measure was far from innocuous. It was a mortal threat to one of the fundamental sources of Church and army power over society, and as such it was recognized by the conservatives. The resulting uproar was so great that old President Álvarez, whose unfitness as chief of state had been obvious for some weeks, humbly retired.

The new president, Ignacio Comonfort, was a moderate creole lawyer who expected both to stave off a violent reaction and preside over further liberal reforms. Soon another decree, the *Ley Lerdo* of 1856, was brought forward, this time by his treasurer, Miguel Lerdo de Tejada, calling for the forced sale of corporate land holdings. The measure was really aimed at the Church, which possessed about a third of the cultivated land of the republic. Lerdo's intention was that landed property would be auctioned off to individuals so that a peasantry of small, free farmers would inherit the estates of the Church. From these sales the government would extract a transfer tax and thus finance itself in a way no Mexican regime had ever been able to do. The effects of a similar measure in France during the Revolution had been socially beneficial, so why not in Mexico? Nor would the Church be robbed, for it would receive payment for the land it lost. It should, if things went well, sink back into its proper role unencumbered by so many business interests. While the eager liberals of 1856 could not foresee it, seldom was a generous piece of legislation destined to be so distorted. Not land-hungry peons, but speculators and political favorites, were to strip the Church of its land, much of which had been used for humanitarian purposes or at least had been more productive under the clergy. And the phraseology of the *Ley Lerdo* was to permit the communal holdings of Indian tribes to be seized and parceled out so that once-free natives would become mere peons on large estates, or *haciendas*. This dismal process began almost immediately after the promulgation of the law, to continue until Mexico was further than ever from being a land of free peasants like France.[1]

Already horrified by the *Ley Juárez* and the *Ley Lerdo*, Mexican conservatives were further affronted by the constitution drawn up by the liberals and moderates. With that touching faith in the written word so characteristic of nineteenth-century politicians, the congress quickly put together a basic instrument for the republic. Its chief purpose was to prevent presidential dictatorship of the Santa Anna type. Thus a long list of inalienable rights, even more than in the ancestor constitution of 1824, supposedly posed bulwarks to tyranny. The deputies proclaimed the federal system, for the state capitals were full of ambitious men who wished to enjoy the satisfactions of ruling without interference from Mexico City. A single-house legislative branch was expected to constitute insurance against presidential autocracy, more so than a bi-cameral body which might be deadlocked. The longest and most bitter debates had to do with the issue of religious freedom: liberals favored complete liberty; conservatives thought it both wicked and dangerous to break the age-old partnership of state and Church; moderates were torn this way and that. At length, the congress decided not to mention either toleration or the Catholic Church.

It was a proud moment for the liberals when, in February 1857, the constitution was signed. The dying Gómez Farías was carried into the chamber, where he could be the first to take the oath to a document that seemingly represented the triumph of his lifelong devotion to democracy. Indeed, the constitution of 1857 was to enjoy a long life, to persist until 1917 with some changes. Yet, like the *Ley Lerdo*, it would become a mockery. Nothing could prevent presidents from dominating the political scene. Congressmen would be little more than creatures of the executive, as were magistrates and judges. State governors and legislatures would usually be installed or ousted as the potentate in the presidential palace decreed. Individual rights were observed only to the extent the president let them be. Admirable a symbol as the constitution of 1857 came to be in Mexico, it proved no guarantee of republican democracy, and still less of true federalism or separation of powers.

While this depressing future could not be visualized in 1857, other signs of opposition were only too evident. The clergy was up in arms, in some cases literally so, against *la Reforma* and all its works. Pius IX issued an extraordinary condemnation of the constitution, and the ecclesiastical hierarchy in Mexico warned that anyone who swore to uphold it was in danger of losing access to the sacraments of the Church. Nearly

1. The experience of Mexico in this respect resembled that of Spain at this period, when former Church and communal lands were carved into huge estates.

all the leading figures of the government and congress were excommunicated. Already, would-be purchasers of Church lands were being frightened off by threats of divine wrath, and the faithful were gathering funds and arms to discourage buyers. Yet the liberals stared these menaces in the face. Some, of course, were skeptics and cared little for Catholicism or any other religion. Others underwent acute mental torture as they chose between their faith and their long commitment to liberalism. As 1857 wore on, most of them stuck by the constitution and duly took their oaths. Conservatives, meanwhile, intensified their hostility.

For some time it had been apparent that a forceful reaction to *la Reforma* was shaping up; the circulation of anti-liberal tracts, the clandestine collection of weapons and ammunition, and the mysterious conferences of important generals and politicians indicated something was afoot. In December 1857 a unit pronounced at Tacubaya, near the capital, under the leadership of General Félix Zuloaga, professedly for changes in the constitution. Quickly engulfing Mexico City, the rebels seized the person of President Comonfort and jailed the new vice-president and chief justice, Benito Juárez. Many members of the congress and administration escaped to Querétaro, however, where they organized a rump government to represent the unchanged constitution. It looked for a time as though President Comonfort might effect a compromise. He had endured real anguish over the prospect of perpetual war between the republic and the Church, and he agreed to assume leadership of the new movement. In effect, he had revolted against himself! But then he changed his mind again. He saw to it that Juárez was released and, with his own pride and reputation gone, left the country. When lines were so sharply drawn, there was no place for a well-meaning moderate of his type. Comonfort's departure left the conservatives in the capital squared off against the liberals at Querétaro. In January 1858 Mexico's worst civil war began.

BENITO JUÁREZ AND THE WAR OF THE REFORM

The most admired individual in the history of Mexico was now emerging, as Benito Juárez went to Querétaro to be recognized as president of the true republic. A full-blooded Zapotec Indian from Oaxaca, a state where the white man had never implanted his system or his culture deeply, Juárez shared the fierce love of freedom his mountain people had so long asserted. As an orphaned sheep-herder, he made his way to the city of Oaxaca, where a kindly protector saw to it that he entered school to study for the priesthood. After some years in seminary he elected instead to become a lawyer, though he remained a pious, mystical, righteous man all his life. He was homely, short, copper-colored, and generally silent, not the kind of attorney to break racial barriers and rise

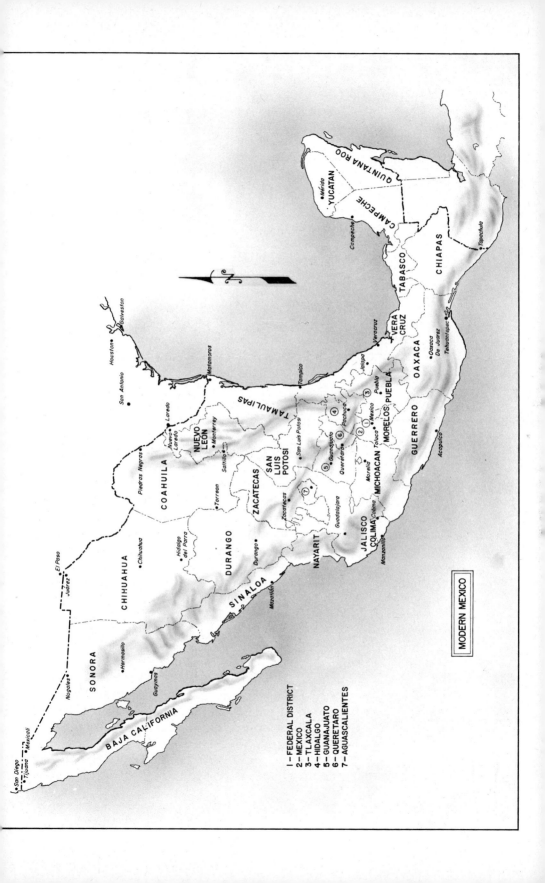

MODERN MEXICO

1 – FEDERAL DISTRICT
2 – MEXICO
3 – TLAXCALA
4 – HIDALGO
5 – GUANAJUATO
6 – QUERETARO
7 – AGUASCALIENTES

to fame. Possibly because he could obtain no other cases he was an advocate for the poor, and he built up a loyal following. He entered politics as a liberal, holding several secondary elective and appointive positions. As an official he displayed vast industry and a solid ability. Most conspicuous of all was his rectitude, a most unusual trait in a Mexican politician. In 1847 Juárez became governor of Oaxaca, a post he held for five years. While his constructive work as governor in itself might have made him famous, he won his stature as a national figure by denying asylum to Santa Anna on one of the occasions that the ex-president was fleeing. This action cost Juárez a two-year period of exile when Santa Anna returned in 1853, most of which he spent with other Mexican refugees in New Orleans, where they made cigars in the daytime and planned the future of their country in the evenings. Back in Mexico in time for the liberal triumphs of 1855, Juárez served as minister of justice, governor of Oaxaca, and chief justice and vice-president. Now, in January 1858, he claimed to be the lawful president of the republic. There was little to suggest that he was to become the most revered of Mexican rulers. He seemed to many an ugly, mute, modest little man with only plain virtues.

At the outset of the War of the Reform, the liberal or constitutionalist government was altogether on the defensive against Zuloaga and the conservatives. It had to flee from Querétaro before troops of Zuloaga, the congress disbanding and President Juárez and his cabinet setting out on a hegira in a black carriage that took them across the arid mountains of western Mexico. It was said that once the occupants of this famous vehicle, now an object of honor in the museum at Chapultepec, escaped arrest by asserting they belonged to a family ill with a contagion. This "sick family" incident gave liberals wry satisfaction, and they used it as propaganda. Reaching the Pacific coast after jolting over the country, Juárez sailed down to Panama. There he crossed the isthmus and embarked on an American ship which took him to Veracruz, a long-time stronghold of the liberals, and established the government of the republic, which only the United States among the larger powers saw fit to recognize.

The conservatives had a republic of their own in Mexico City. Controlling most of the army and the rich central region of Mexico, they had the chief advantages. By promising a restoration of the old regime and the undoing of la Reforma, they won the fervent adherence of the clergy and the devout in general. In fine, the War of the Reform pitted traditionalists against reformers, the army against civilianists, central Mexico against the provinces, the Church against the anti-clericals, and the sympathies of Europe against those of the United States. The conservatives had the most brilliant general, young Miguel Miramón, who supplanted Zuloaga in the presidency. Yet the liberals had the cause of the future, and in Benito Juárez a symbol of law and justice, civilian authority, Indianism, and Mexican patriotism. Also, Juárez, or perhaps someone in his entourage, was an artist in political warfare. Proclamations emanating from Veracruz struck deep into the hearts of the Mexican people, carrying an inspiration worthy of Bolívar, Lincoln, or Churchill.

It is a truism that civil wars are the cruelest of all. The War of the Reform, which went on for three years, illustrated the soundness of this axiom. Persecution and counter-persecution in the name of Catholicism was the principal cause of atrocity. Since the clergy had instigated and aided the conservatives, Juárez issued the Laws of the Reform, which completely separated Church and state, permitted toleration of all faiths, turned out the friars to civilian life, provided for the closing of all convents when the nuns died, ended tithing, required civil marriages and registrations of births and deaths, and virtually authorized the confiscation of all Church property other than that used directly for purposes of worship. These laws were carried out whenever the liberals occupied territory, but too often they were accompanied by injuries and indignities visited on members of the clergy and the pillaging of churches. Countermeasures of the most extreme type were the reply of the conservatives. Since they regarded the liberals as blasphemers, they were likely to kill all prisoners of war. The constitutionalists, of course, reciprocated, with the result that a hideous carnage went on. Atrocities, betrayals, and horrors of all kinds so poisoned the atmosphere that compromise became odious to both sides.

It was the Juárez regime that received the more censure in Europe; the revulsion against him in Catholic capitals was to have evil consequences. On the other hand, Washington sympathized with Juárez and performed the invaluable service of keeping the sea lanes to Veracruz open and endowing him with war material. President Buchanan wished to do even more for the Mexican constitutionalists. Since their financial position was desperate, he offered to purchase control of the isthmus of Tehuantepec, where Cortés had once dreamed of a canal. Juárez reluctantly agreed to his project, the McLane-Ocampo treaty, but the U.S. Senate refused ratification for fear the American slave states would somehow be strengthened. Much as they needed money, the Mexicans were not seriously chagrined.

For almost three years Miramón seemed to carry the offensive by striking out at his enemies from the Valley of Mexico. He won most of the battles; yet the liberals could retreat and rally, always drawing on the provinces for more recruits. Juan Álvarez was still an effective commander in the southern areas; Santos Degollado raised and trained hard-hitting armies in the west. Finally, Miramón undertook a forceful offensive to overwhelm Veracruz, the true heart of the liberal cause. He nearly succeeded—a fateful term in warfare—but in the end had to draw back. No longer could he hope for European supplies and aid. National enthusiasm for Juárez grew as the tide turned. Rather suddenly, it seemed, the liberals proved their superiority. As armies closed in on the capital from the west, other forces made the strenuous march from Veracruz up the route of Cortés and Winfield Scott. After a frenzy of atrocities Miramón fled, and the conservative republic collapsed. In January 1861 President Juárez, in civilian clothes, entered Mexico City in his plain black carriage, no conqueror, no liberator of the type of Bolívar, but an unsmiling, implacable symbol of law and the constitution of 1857.

The French Intervention

MEXICO'S VULNERABILITY TO IMPERIALISM

The fates allowed Benito Juárez only a year to establish the reformist regime before another war began. Problems of all types cried out for energetic attention. Yet the government had no funds and no trained bureaucracy to deal with them. And the conservatives had taken their defeat with the ill grace that typifies Hispanic politics. They still thought Juárez was contemptible and the constitution irreligious. Some made their way to Europe to peddle monarchical schemes. Others maintained small armies to disrupt the countryside. Conservative forces managed to kill Ocampo and Degollado, two of the ablest liberals, and a third, Miguel Lerdo de Tejado, happened to die about the same time. Juárez also lost men whom he urgently needed through defection. The end of the civil war permitted an explosion of individualism. While the reconvened congress elected Juárez president for another term, it fully intended, as the constitution of 1857 had encouraged it to do so, to exercise the sovereign power of the republic. Yet the deputies were fractious and irresponsible; so pleased were they to have a public forum, they debated and carped until the congress seemed an agitated chicken yard. President Juárez they badgered without mercy. On one occasion he was saved from a demand to resign by only one vote. Beset by conservative enemies, critical liberal friends, and circumstances alike, the stubborn president held fast to his ideals. To him the constitution of 1857 meant what it said; thus liberties must be respected and nothing should be done to suppress free speech or obstructionism. Lofty as his attitude was, the freedom which his critics so abused put a bad face on his administration. The extent to which he lost standing in Mexico would soon be revealed.

Of the riot of problems Juárez faced in 1861, the most hopeless was the fiscal. There was scarcely any money in circulation to be gathered as taxes. Nor could the sale of former Church properties yield significant amounts of hard currency. The loan sharks who so long had kept the Mexican government operating were now mostly out of business, and foreign credit was only a memory. And the pressure of aliens who demanded payment of ancient claims, some of them forty years old, was becoming much worse. Many foreigners had been killed or injured or had their properties seized by one side or the other during the recent civil war. Miramón had invaded the British legation to steal its funds, Santos Degollado had looted a silver train that belonged to foreigners, and bonds and promissory notes had been freely issued, mostly by the conservatives, to cover damages endured by subjects of several foreign powers. At that time it was acceptable international law and morality for a sovereign to enforce the claims of his subjects in a foreign land. Juárez had long had a bad reputation in Europe, where he seemed a vicious Indian bandit. Now there was no one to protect him from vengeful European creditors, for the United States had just become immobilized in a civil war of its own.

Juárez attempted to deal with the problem with his usual frankness and stubbornness. First, he scaled down the foreign claims to a figure that seemed insultingly low to the claimants. When they protested, he abruptly stopped all payments for two years. Defensible as his actions were under the circumstances, the outraged creditors brought great pressure in London, Paris, and Madrid to teach Mexico a lesson. Accordingly, the three governments agreed to occupy Veracruz, where they could either collect the customs until they were satisfied or shock Juárez into making reparations. In December 1861 a Spanish expedition sailed from Havana and encamped without opposition at the Gulf port. In the following month a British force joined the Spaniards, and then a surprisingly large French army. Because of the fevers around Veracruz Juárez gave the visitors permission to remove themselves to the uplands. A series of conferences ensued. The Spanish and the British satisfied themselves that Juárez would compensate them when he could, and they evacuated. But the French declined Juárez' assurances, and instead of leaving the soil of Mexico, they brought in reinforcements.

THE DREAM OF NAPOLEON III

Behind these odd maneuvers lay a plan hatched in the fertile brain of the emperor of the French, Napoleon III. His Second Empire was very prosperous, and many investors were eager to risk capital in business adventures abroad. If half of what Mexican conservative refugees said about their country was true, it should not be difficult to restore Mexico to the productivity it knew in the days of the viceroyalty, only now France rather than Spain would be the beneficiary. Mexico might become a client state something on the order of Algeria. Napoleon and his wife, the Empress Eugénie, were also intrigued by the possibility of restoring their standing with the French clerical party. France had recently assisted the runaway Italian unification movement that had endangered the Papal States. Now the imperial couple might demonstrate their loyalty to the pope by aiding his cause in Mexico. The dreamy emperor of the French had still another purpose. France aspired to the leadership of the Latin world, assisting Italy and Rumania and befriending Spain. The popularization of the term, "Latin America," was a French enterprise of some imperialistic implication. A bold undertaking in romantic Mexico might serve to bring Spanish and Portuguese America under French influence in ways that would strengthen the causes of Pan-Latinism, monarchy, Catholicism, and the glory of France. It was no mean illusion, if illusion it was. Mexican exiles in Paris did all they could to strengthen it.

Napoleon's objectives unfolded slowly, for that was his way. He did not confide in his allies in the Veracruz venture nor in the French or Mexican people. His first goal was to establish military supremacy. Once the British and Spanish had departed, the French commander had a free hand. In April 1862 he led his forces toward Mexico City. All went well for a time, until the imperial soldiers, over-confident and contemptuous of Mexican opposition, were badly defeated at Puebla on May 5. Mexico's continued observance of the *cinco de mayo* holiday is partially attributable to the fact that this was one of the rare occasions Mexicans defeated a foreign force at any time in their history. Proud a victory as it was, Puebla was ultimately calamitous for Juárez, for now the prestige of Napoleon III was involved. The emperor sent a new commander and massive reinforcements during the next year. President Juárez desperately attempted to rally his countrymen. But the response was very disappointing, largely because there had been so much disillusionment with his own government during the past year. In June 1863 a well-equipped French army of 30,000 entered Mexico City. With the core of the country pacified, the French established a puppet government under General Juan Almonte, who was said to be a natural son of the independence hero Morelos, and staffed by other conservatives who had been beaten in the recent War of the Reform. This regime invited Napoleon to nominate a monarch for Mexico. It seemed an obvious course, for the republic had failed for forty years to bring republicanism to the country. Now it was time to experiment with an imported sovereign, an emperor.

MAXIMILIAN OF HABSBURG

Napoleon III cast about carefully for a good prince. A parvenu himself, he was determined that the new American monarch command the respect that only born royalty enjoyed. At length he settled on the Archduke Maximilian of Austria, brother of Emperor Franz Josef. France had defeated Austria in war in 1859, and Napoleon saw a chance to patch things up a bit. He also remembered Maximilian as one of the first members of a major reigning family to visit him in Paris after he took the crown. Maximilian was a Catholic, a world traveler, a liberal, and an administrator who had distinguished himself as governor of Lombardy-Venetia during a period of rising Italian nationalism. Further-more, he was handsome, impressive, gallant, and, of course, a Habsburg. The tall, blond archduke postponed his acceptance until a plebiscite, which he did not know was rigged, showed that the Mexican popula-tion desired his services. His wife, Carlota, a high-strung Belgian prin-cess, ambitiously egged him on. At last he accepted the challenge, full of conviction that a man so well-meaning as himself could bring only good to Mexico. The pope gave him a personal blessing, all Europe wished him well, and Mexican delegates assured him of a heart-felt welcome from his new subjects. It was expected, of course, that he would protect the Church and procure justice for the European holders of claims against Mexico.

The imperial couple arrived in Veracruz in June 1864. Despite primi-tive traveling conditions and occasionally bad timings in arranging the receptions, the people seemed friendly, even enthusiastic. Maximilian and Carlota at once fell in love with their colorful empire. They visited many of its provinces and towns, usually without conspicuous protec-tion. They adopted Mexican-style clothes and averred they relished Mexican dishes. Things seemed to go rather well. The new French com-mander, Bazaine, had matters under control so that the former republi-can government was only a specter. He dispatched French units out from the Valley of Mexico the way Cortés had, and with similar results. President Juárez had taken to the road again with his nomadic govern-ment, moving to San Luis Potosí, then far into the north to Chihuahua, and finally to the city now known as Ciudad Juárez, across the Rio Grande from El Paso. Irregulars continued to defy the capital from the southern mountains, but that was an old story, almost a chronic situa-tion. Maximilian had little reason to doubt that his regime was a success. He felt confident enough to offer important positions to republicans, hoping to win them over. Juárez himself received such an invitation, which he refused with a dignity that chilled the emperor.

During 1864 and 1865 it seemed likely that the empire would take root. Most conservatives sincerely rallied to the new monarch, and so did many liberals, much as they later denied it. Even the Indians were impressed with Maximilian, whom some may have regarded as Quetzal-coatl. The pageantry and social life of the monarchy dazzled the masses and beguiled the upper classes, as it had in colonial times. Maximilian, who had once visited the Empire of Brazil, was determined that his regime be democratic, constructive, and a friend of all races. He believed he had the solution to Latin American turbulence, and he planned to take over Central America and to foster liberal monarchies in the southern continent. Mexico should be a showplace of progress and tolerance. Immigrants, Asiatic as well as European, must be attracted. He wanted to build railroads, start factories, raise agricultural production, rehabilitate the mines, and carry out vast public works. Maximilian had views of his own about the virtues of foreign investment. Capital should be encouraged, to be sure, but only on terms mutually beneficial to both Mexicans and foreigners. After some years of such policies, Mexico should be prepared for self-government. Thus an excellent constitution and generous statutes rounded out the imperial structure for the day when Mexicans could choose their own officials. To assure the continuation of the dynasty, the childless Maximilian and Carlota adopted a grandson of Iturbide, the one-time Agustín I.

For all the beneficent plans and the triumphant imperial progresses through the country, the empire lived under heavy clouds. The French had obligated themselves to remain in Mexico only a few years, supposedly enough to see Maximilian safely entrenched. To prepare for the day when they left, the emperor built up a Mexican army, based on the conservative units of the War of the Reform and again led by Miguel Miramón. Ostentatiously as the emperor favored the Mexican soldiers in preference to the French and the 6,000 or so Belgians and Austrians, it was apparent that his regime depended on the foreigners. Mexican soldiers were too accustomed to changing sides. Similarly, Maximilian took the conservatives for granted and courted the liberals. He hoped to train them, as Emperor Pedro II of Brazil was doing in his country, to alternate peacefully within a constitutional framework. It was a hopeless undertaking, one that flew in the face of Mexican traditions and habits. After making his will known to politicians, the emperor would turn to other matters, such as splendid travels and imperial pageants, or even fraternizing with the common people. Administration bored and bewildered him. Austrian archdukes were not trained in the dreary details of making governments run. Commendable as Maximilian's plans were, he had no real talent for putting them into effect.

In the two major problems he was expected to solve by those who had placed him on the throne, Maximilian displayed lofty idealism but poor political judgment. The Church had every reason to believe its properties would be returned, but the emperor refused to repeal the hateful liberal laws. Enormous pressure from the papal legate and even from Pius IX himself failed to budge him. While the clerical party had nowhere else to turn, a notable cooling of its support for the empire was an ominous sign. Then, the French intended to recover all their claims and to make Mexico an economic colony. Maximilian was committed to honor these demands, but he drew back when he grasped how large they were and how poor Mexico was. Particularly inexcusable were the Jecker claims for 15,000,000 pesos based on a loan of one-twentieth of that amount made to Miramón during the War of the Reform by a speculator who was not even a French subject until 1862! In order to collect anything at all, the French took matters into their own hands, grabbing what they could in the way of funds, lands, mines, and business houses. Careful as they were not to treat Maximilian like a puppet, they occasionally had to bring him face to face with the reality that he *was* a puppet. This was hard for the proud Habsburg to bear, and it embittered and enraged native Mexicans to an extreme degree. Avidly as they copied French tastes and styles, the Mexicans regarded these uninvited allies as pillagers. Maximilian sided with his subjects and helplessly protested as the French went about their seizures.

THE TRIUMPH OF BENITO JUÁREZ

All of these difficulties might have simmered on for years without producing a major crisis, for Mexico was accustomed to violence and hypocrisy. But the real flaw in Napoleon III's plan revealed itself in all its proportion by 1866. This was the fundamental miscalculation that the United States would be immobilized indefinitely by the secession of the southern states. All during the years of ordeal suffered by the sister republics, President Lincoln had given his moral support to President Juárez. As soon as the Union opened the Mississippi, arms found their way to Juárez' poorly equipped forces in the north of Mexico. After Appomattox in April 1865, great quantities of surplus war supplies and hordes of volunteers went to the Mexican republicans. This revival of liberal strength in Mexico drove the French to more drastic measures, to killings and suppressions. Vainly hoping to intimidate the *juaristas*, Maximilian issued, in October 1865, a decree that rebels should be shot. The United States also made representations in Paris, the source of Maximilian's power. Much as President Johnson might have exploited a popular foreign war to heal the wounds of the recent civil conflict, he confined himself to a polite insistence that the French withdraw. Napoleon III could but agree, which he did in February 1866. A few weeks later the stunning overturn in the balance of power in Europe resulting from Prussia's victory over Austria made it all the more urgent for Napoleon to return his troops. He now needed them to guard the Rhine, not to fight off the United States on the Rio Grande. He was not betraying Maximilian, much as this charge persists; he was trying to defend France.

Bazaine pulled the French forces out of Mexico ahead of schedule, so that by the end of 1866 most of them were gone. The Empress Carlota went to Europe to beg Napoleon to postpone these withdrawals. After a deplorable scene with the emperor her mind became unhinged, and she hurried to Rome. There, she tormented the Holy Father with her pleas for help and her wild charges that Napoleon was trying to murder her. She even embarrassed the pope by refusing to leave his quarters at night. Finally, her brother came and took her away. She lived on for sixty years in a secluded chateau in Belgium, hopelessly mad.

Meanwhile, her imperial husband looked on helplessly as his own supporters decided they were not monarchists after all and joined Juárez' growing forces. In majestic surges, the liberal armies swept down from the north with the Indian president who had suddenly become a national hero. Juan Álvarez and Porfirio Díaz collected formidable forces in the south. Maximilian was urged by the French to leave while he could. Hurt as he was by the fickleness of his subjects, he finally elected to die like a monarch rather than desert those who had placed their faith in his cause. In May 1867 the emperor and his remaining loyal units were surrounded at Querétaro. The proud Habsburg would not attempt escape, and so he surrendered. Despite a rain of humanitarian appeals from abroad, even from Washington, Juárez tried Maximilian as a rebel and filibusterer under the imperial decree of October 1865 and had him shot, in June 1867. The death of the archduke—as Mexicans to this day refer to Maximilian—was one of perhaps 50,000 fatalities resulting from the French intervention.

THE REPUBLIC RESTORED

Once again, on July 15, 1867, President Juárez entered Mexico City in his modest carriage, his stature immensely enhanced by his steadfastness during the five years of the intervention. More than anyone else he personified the nationhood of Mexico, its patience in suffering and its determination to bring about better times. Liberalism, patriotism, and Indianism, the forces that were molding the country, found their focus in the person of the diminutive president. He planned to bring them all to a glorious fruition. A strict legalist, he intended to make the constitution of 1857, now hallowed by the sacrifice of so many lives, an effective document. National feeling had been immeasurably inflamed by the European imperialists. Now Mexico could ignore its foreign debts and defy the monarchs of Europe, who in turn regarded the republic as a pariah among nations. If conservatives gibed that Juárez was subservient to the United States, whom most Mexicans disliked more than any European power, his Indianism served to rebuke any such reflections on his patriotism. And his kinship with the majority race in Mexico served to intensify a unique nationalism.

The problems facing Juárez were even worse than those of 1861, when he first entered the capital as president. First, he had to regularize his position. Congress re-assembled and elected him to another term as president. Then, it was necessary to keep the country from descending into another riotous era of militarism. Taking care not to antagonize the strongest generals, Juárez dismissed two-thirds of the army, a necessary step, but one which set thousands of soldiers loose without an income or, it seemed to many of them, a purpose in life. The situation would have been very dangerous had it not been handled wisely, for in pre-industrial societies there was no way to absorb a large increment to the labor force. Thanks to the minister of war, Ignacio Mejía, the crucial army units remained loyal to Juárez and prevented serious challenges to his authority and provincial anarchy. While no one could hope to make the republic financially sound for many years, another able minister, Matías Romero, established enough fiscal order to enable the government to function. The economy of the country, of course, suffered from the ravages of the civil war and the intervention. Mineral production remained low, and agricultural production had fallen off since the Church properties had passed into private hands. Foreign merchants and capitalists were understandably reluctant to take chances in Mexico by this time. Juárez dreamed of bringing public education to the entire population, and one of his aides, Gabino Barreda, did much to publicize this ideal and even established a few schools. This program collided with Juárez' determination to enforce the anti-clerical laws with energy and malice. The Catholic priesthood now consisted of only 3,000 men, and the regular orders had been disbanded. Hence the traditional custodians of education were in no position to provide this service. Protestant missionary activity, in which Juárez placed much hope, failed to overcome popular antipathy to "heretics," and so there was nothing to fill the void left by the depletion of the Catholic clergy. National literacy remained an impossible ideal.

On the balance, Juárez succeeded in stabilizing the republic in his term of 1867–1871 and in providing goals for the future. Mexico was a very different country now, with the Church greatly downgraded and the alien businessman a rare sight. Intellectual life was vigorous, for the coffee houses and legislative chambers were full of earnest men discussing philosophy, literature, and public affairs. As in his previous incumbency, Juárez permitted a wide latitude of expression. Unfortunately, politics absorbed much of the energy of the educated class, politics of a disruptive sort. As the end of Juárez' term approached in 1871, there were many who desired a change. Everyone in public life by this time classified himself as a liberal. Two "liberal" candidates announced their candidacies for the presidency. One was Sebastián Lerdo de Tejada, brother of the author of the *Ley Lerdo*, a lawyer and academic man who had long been a minister under Juárez. The other was an impressive general, Porfirio Díaz. But Juárez himself desired to run again, for the task of reconstruction was far from over. And demigod though he has become in modern Mexican mythology Juárez was human enough to love office and to regard himself as indispensable. The campaign was waged as the constitution specified, with the states choosing electors. Juárez received a plurality but not a majority, so that congress, which he largely dominated, made the decision and reelected him. Porfirio Díaz cried fraud and initiated an insurrection under a bombastic Plan of Noria, which really appealed to discontented soldiers and crypto-conservatives. The principal generals stood by Juárez, and the revolt was quickly beaten down. Lerdo, who had supported Juárez, became vice-president and chief justice of the supreme court.

A few months later, in July 1872, President Juárez suddenly died. Lerdo became provisional president and, later in the year, was formally elected for a full term. Again Díaz protested, and again he was bested in a power play. Lerdo's administration has an equivocal reputation. The president himself had many virtues and a good record, but people said he was lazy, arrogant, and dishonest, charges that should not be taken too literally. He presided over a generally peaceful term of nearly four years and permitted as much freedom as any Mexican president ever had. He built a few schools and showed himself one of the first Mexican leaders to appreciate the possibilities of the Industrial Age. It was now feasible to attract European traders and investors, an easier matter after Napoleon III fell, Spain became a republic, and Italy dispossessed the pope. Europe no longer seemed so hostile, and Mexico's renewed ties with that center of Western civilization quickened her intellectual, cultural, and economic life. More significant but less popular were Lerdo's dealings with capitalists of the United States, particularly with reference to the construction of railways, so extensive in the 1870's; perhaps his negotiations in this matter had something to do with the wave of criticism that engulfed the administration in 1876. Lerdo had confidently looked forward to reelection in that year, only to discover that powerful units of the army were against him and that civilian detractors in the capital were active. The election was held on schedule, Lerdo declaring himself the winner; yet half the country had risen up against him. One

battle caused him to flee in November 1876. As he left, he did not overlook the contents of the treasury, which enabled him to live out his days
comfortably in New York.

That Lerdo's generally serene administration had ended so disastrously was attributable less to his own failings than to the craft and
military skill of Porfirio Díaz. In this hard-bitten man Mexico had, by
the end of 1876, finally met her master, one she obeyed until 1911. His
advent terminated the period of the restored republic, even of *la Reforma* itself. In view of the bloodshed and tears, and the soaring idealism,
of the Reform, it is sad to conclude that the movement had not justified
the sacrifices it had cost. Only with the greatest generosity could the
federal republic have been regarded as functioning according to the
constitution of 1857. Economic life was still primitive. Mexico was a
beggar among nations, backward even by Latin American standards.
Social conditions had improved but little, though Indians and mestizos
held their heads higher. If the Church had been stripped, its former
properties had gone mainly to speculators or *hacendados* who were already land-rich. No free peasantry had emerged; the masses were no
better off. The republic had failed to fill the vacuum left by the Church
in education and welfare, heroically as Juárez and Lerdo had tried. All
the things that were supposed to be achieved by the Reform—republican
democracy, dismantlement of the Church, ejection of the foreigner,
curbing of the army, redistribution of wealth, and intensification of
nationalism—were to seem hollow in the decades after Lerdo's flight.
Still, the ideals were never entirely obscured. Their eventual resurrection
and fulfillment would remake Mexico in the twentieth century.

Porfirio Díaz

THE middle-aged general who took over Mexico late in 1876
had worked hard to reach the presidential palace. He had also come far.
Born in 1830 in the state of Oaxaca, Díaz was a mestizo with Spanish
and Mixtec blood. His family were in modest circumstances, his father
having been an innkeeper in a small town. Like Benito Juárez, he attended a seminary but decided against entering the clergy in favor of
the law. Juárez was one of the instructors in the law school Díaz attended and attracted the youngster to his liberal politics. Díaz was not
the student Juárez had been, and he did not complete his education.
Instead, he took such minor political jobs as the liberals dispensed during their intervals in power until he found his true vocation in the army.
A man's man, he rose naturally in military leadership. Díaz had courage:
in 1854 he boldly entered the voting plaza and insulted the officials by
shouting "No!" in the rigged plebiscite that was supposed to register

unanimous approval of Santa Anna. He got away safely, and word of his action circulated. When Santa Anna collapsed a few months afterward, Díaz was remembered for his defiance. During the War of the Reform he advanced himself both as a warrior and politician. He received credit as one of several leaders who defeated the French at Puebla on May 5, 1862. His fame increased when it became known that he refused to accept a pardon while he was a prisoner of Maximilian, and his daredevil escape from jail in 1865 gave Mexican liberals one of their rare opportunities to cheer a hero. As the empire went to pieces Díaz, now a general, commanded a formidable army in Oaxaca. It was he who first entered Mexico City after the imperial forces withdrew. Posing as the liberator of the capital, he staged an elaborate welcome for President Juárez in July 1867. Juárez is said to have snubbed him on this occasion. Already, he sensed that Díaz had too much ambition.

Possibly because Juárez made no place for him in the restored republic, Díaz privately deserted liberalism and began to cater to men who were, even if they did not admit it, conservative at heart. He retained command of the Oaxaca state army, which gave him an opportunity to deal with other generals, to dominate the political life of the state, and to pile up a fortune. His effort to win the presidency in 1871 failed because Juárez still controlled the liberal party, and his subsequent revolt revealed that he still lacked the military might to challenge both Juárez and Lerdo. Díaz learned from these failures and set out to correct their causes. During the administration of Lerdo he was in and out of the country, building his private estate, cultivating popularity as a military hero, secretly conferring with other generals, and making arrangements with liberal politicians. When he was ready to spring against Lerdo, in 1876, it was apparent that his machinations had been effective. A Plan of Tuxtepec denounced the idea of presidential reelection, called for effective suffrage, and criticized Lerdo for selling out to alien capitalists. Eventually this program would seem ironical in the extreme; Díaz was not the first, nor the last, politician to rise to high office with a platform he would proceed to turn upside down.

Díaz' capture of the government late in 1876 was primarily due to army support, for this mestizo hero had the respect of other officers and was popular among enlisted men. The rest of the population seemed to welcome his accession to power. He had long advertised his war experiences so as to build his reputation into a living legend. A liberal of long standing, he caused little uneasiness among the leading political figures or publicists. Now that Juárez was safely dead, Díaz fervently proclaimed himself the heir of the great man, whom he had in fact betrayed, and shamelessly exploited his memory, somewhat as Stalin would later invoke the name of Lenin to his own advantage. Conservatives, however, sensed or soon discovered that Díaz intended to smother the reform movement. Indians and the mixed races were inclined to idolize the mestizo Díaz as a man of the people. And then, nearly every sensible Mexican knew that the population both craved and needed a strong executive. Díaz seemed a safe man to trust with large powers. With masculine good looks, simple and unaffected manners, a tendency to blunt speech, and an honorable record, he had much appeal. In general, Mexicans liked and admired the masterful man who had forced his way into the presidency.

In the years that followed Porfirio Díaz revealed other qualities. An almost demonic will to power lay at the core of his motivation. He had waited long and struggled hard to win his position. Once he had attained it, he could not bear the thought of relinquishing it. Hence anyone who remotely threatened his power must be removed. Díaz was not a maniacal killer in the manner of a Hitler, but again like Stalin, he was entirely capable of employing murder as a means of ridding himself of rivals or obstructionists. Law and justice meant nothing to him if they interfered with his will. And while he no doubt believed with utter sincerity that he was a benefactor, he seldom said so himself, unlike fanatics who invoke noble ends with great eloquence in order to justify atrocious means. It was not that he disdained flattery, however. As time went on he craved it, and sycophants outdid themselves in glorifying the despot. Díaz also came to reveal an unsuspected racial snobbishness. Indians and mestizos failed to find preferment or even equality in his government, and anyone who referred to Díaz' own mixed blood was likely to regret his indiscretion. While he had never been as uncouth as wits among the cultured classes reported, he noticeably grew more dignified and fastidious after he married the aristocratic Carmen Rubio, his second wife.

THE POLITICAL STRUCTURE OF THE LONG DICTATORSHIP

Duly elected president after his military victory, Díaz skillfully constructed a political apparatus often called the *Díaz-potismo*, which rested comfortably within the constitution of 1857. In each of the states of the supposedly federal republic was a machine of the Liberal party. All of them answered to the party chieftain, the president himself. Through this power Díaz could make, unmake, and dictate to the several governors. The legislatures were filled with obedient politicians who depended upon Díaz not only for their positions, but also for their economic life, and often their freedom. In each district and city ruled a *jefe político* (political chief) who was immediately answerable to the president to a degree unknown in the days of the viceroys and their subordinate intendants and *corregidores*. The national congress, which was supposed to wield the strongest authority under the constitution, was composed entirely of loyal party men, even more so than in the days of Juárez and Lerdo. The judiciary, which was also expected to be independent of the president, was staffed with obedient judges who did the bidding of the dictator, as is usual in Latin America. Simply to fill the elective positions of the republic and the bureaucracy with Díaz partisans was enough to absorb most of the political talent and nearly all of the intelligentsia of Mexico. That Díaz could do this at all, keep these men in place, and finance the administration was a tribute to his abilities. But he went beyond these essentials to orderly government by spying on "public" servants, rewarding informers, and making available to the most loyal officials lucrative temptations for personal profits. His regime was by no means the most corrupt of the times. It was just corrupt enough to make government servants eager to please their master.

Important as it was to construct this nation-wide political machine, the task could never have been carried out unless the basic instruments of physical force had been at Díaz' disposal. The army he inherited was competent for its real mission, maintaining internal order. His problem was to keep it loyal. This Díaz was able to do partly because of his own prestige and personal force. But he was also crafty in appointing men he could dominate, in making it profitable for them to strive to retain his favor, and then in shifting them about frequently from command to command in order to prevent the development of deep-rooted private attachments within units that had made *pronunciamientos* so easy in the past. Officers enjoyed many special favors if they were conspicuously cooperative. Whether they were on active duty or not, they might receive regular pay or serve on useless commissions. It was not necessary to cultivate the favor of enlisted men, usually ignorant Indian boys who would take harsh discipline and mete out brutality to civilians. Mostly draftees, they were poorly paid and badly treated.

The police force, no less than the army, needed to be contented if the dictator's will was to be carried out. Here again, the federal apparatus was in reality centralized, and many favors were made available: control of gambling, profits from houses of vice, bribes, the privilege of oppressing private enemies, and freedom to indulge cruel or sadistic instincts. On the whole, the police force was highly effective from Díaz' point of view. He was even able to bring rural crime under control for the first time in the history of Mexico. Useful as the army was in this enterprise, more helpful still was a new organization of rural guards (*guardias rurales*). In establishing this force Díaz utilized one of the oldest devices in statecraft, the incorporation of bandits into handsomely-uniformed, armed, and mounted police units. Roaming the countryside and highways, the *rurales* soon made Mexico the most orderly country in the western hemisphere. They were also useful in terrorizing potential enemies of the regime or troublesome civilians.

When Díaz' term was over, in 1880, he had the decency not to seek immediate reelection, the principal crime for which he had denounced Lerdo in 1876. One of his client generals, Manuel González, occupied the presidential chair from 1880 to 1884, while Don Porfirio served as governor of Oaxaca and cabinet minister. He also took his bride on a long visit to New York during which he saw much in American life he determined to have Mexico imitate, mainly in the way of material development. While he was out of office Díaz retained control of the army and the political machine. To make sure that González retired when his term expired, he stimulated a press exposure of official corruption, which was in all likelihood as enormous as charged. In any event, the publicity disgraced González and made a return of Díaz all the more welcome. Meanwhile, González had served a useful purpose in carrying out a measure from which even Díaz had shrunk, the recognition of Mexican debts to Great Britain. Unpopular as this step was, it was essential to the growth of Mexico to have a good standing with the world's leading financial power, and the results were as beneficial as Díaz had hoped.

Don Porfirio allowed himself to be elected to the presidency in 1884. When he re-entered the presidential palace, he is supposed to have told his wife that he never intended to leave it permanently as long as he lived. He had the constitution altered to permit indefinite reelection, and he succeeded himself in 1888, 1892, 1896, 1900, 1904 (when the presidential term was lengthened to six years), and 1910. These elections were carried out in all seriousness, usually following an insistent campaign in which patriots beseeched Díaz to sacrifice himself again by running, but with no serious opposition. Further modifications were necessary to keep the regime operating well. Since the old liberal-federalist party of Juárez had become so dilapidated from years of fat, cynicism, and gilded dictatorship, Díaz reorganized it in 1892 as the Liberal Union, which was still only the *porfirista* party. It ran as before, but more tightly and with more arrogance. Not until the very last did Díaz lose his genius for keeping his party in a state of insecurity so that it would be loyal and responsive only to himself. The men who worked with the president were often better educated than he. Yet they struggled against one another for his favor and never combined against him for any length of time. It was a perpetual game of juggling personalities of cabinet ministers, generals, state governors, police officers, and congressmen; Díaz played it with unparalleled cunning.

It would be fatuous to pretend that the long regime, the *porfiriato*, was unpopular, at least until its last years. While important figures in the government may have grumbled at Díaz' secrecy and ruthlessness, they well knew he was the source of their authority and the profits that went with it. The general population was not encouraged to take an interest in public affairs. As far as any of the conventional signs can be interpreted, the people admired the dictator. It was good not to have civil wars and *pronunciamientos,* to go about one's business in peace, and to strive for the rewards of a materialistic age. Educated men who were not beholden to the regime were few. If they spoke or wrote out of turn, they might be jailed or beaten by the police. Mostly they kept quiet. Lawyers, publishers, and business men who had once been *juarista* liberals were usually won over by the administration's manifest success. If not, they knew that rapacious tax collectors or unfair judges could make their lives miserable. The whole system was built on the slogan of *pan o palo* (bread or club). Those who cooperated had bread, something of a status symbol in Mexico, where the poor ate corn tortillas. Those who obstructed might feel the policeman's club, or worse. Any inconvenient person could be eliminated through the *ley fuga,* by which a prisoner might be lawfully shot on the way to jail "while attempting to escape." Even the critics of Díaz bitterly acknowledged his skill in adopting the mantle of Juárez and using the constitution of 1857 so perfectly for his dictatorial purposes. The man was clearly a genius of sorts. Despite all the oppression and cynicism, he held the respect, even the affection, of most Mexicans until 1911.

A GENERATION OF MATERIALISM

Díaz was not consciously a political philosopher, nor an economist. His method was pragmatic, doing what seemed obvious or possible. Once his regime was firm and the country orderly, he simply let the winds from the outside world sweep over Mexico. These winds were strong, and full of dust from lands where great things were happening. They originated in Europe and the United States, both of which were undergoing the most striking material growth hitherto known in the history of the world. The Industrial Age had brought such developments in transportation, communications, mining, and manufacturing that unlimited material progress seemed possible. Enormous new sources of wealth appeared, and social structures were loosened or revised accordingly. With the Darwin theory often being interpreted, or perverted, to justify the ambitions of the strong and the survival of the fittest, materialism waxed and humanitarianism lagged. Furthermore, so rapid were many economic changes that social injustices developed among people who had not learned how to protect themselves. Since the gentler paternalism of the aristocracy and clergy was overshadowed by the surge of newly powerful groups, the lot of common men was likely to become worse. Mexico under Díaz fully shared in this materialism. It is to his credit that she did so, for the experiences of other backward countries during this era indicate how easily a poor government might have denied or delayed the benefits of the Industrial Age. Yet Mexico had more than her share of social imbalance that accompanied this materialism. And the indifference of the successful to the plight of the disinherited was more callous than in most countries, and the consequences more fateful.

Once Díaz had the republic in reasonably good order, its natural richness brought fiscal solvency to the government and wealth to the possessing classes. The dictator was well aware that the capital-exporting countries attached great importance to such matters and that a few years of stability was likely to obliterate the memory of past disasters in Mexican speculations. Above all, it was important that capitalists in Great Britain and the United States have confidence in the financial integrity of Mexico. By recognizing and paying off debts to these individuals, a politically dangerous step even for Díaz, the country's credit was restored. A sound banking set-up and an effective system for collecting taxes further strengthened this credit. Obstacles to commerce such as state tariff barriers, the ancient sales tax, or *alcabala,* and taxes on production Díaz modified or abolished. When, in 1894, his regime announced that the national budget was balanced for the first time in the history of the republic, the Mexican peso became one of the soundest currencies in the world. It did not take long for investors in the great financial centers to grasp that in Mexico they had a paradise. The government was friendly, potential wealth awaited exploitation, and labor was both plentiful and docile.

Money came into Mexico in very large amounts. At first it was mostly a matter of aliens purchasing haciendas. Then, as in most of the world, a frenzy of railroad-building brought enormous profits to foreign capitalists while opening up new sources of development in Mexico. The telegraph and the telephone involved foreign investments and management on a lucrative scale. As Mexico responded to these ministrations by growing ever more prosperous, the expansion of large distributing concerns attracted money from abroad. And then mining re-emerged into greatness. More than 3,000 silver, zinc, lead, and copper mines received the modernization, chiefly the cyanide process, that only foreign capital and techniques could provide. The historic industry of Mexico was again vastly productive. This in turn led to more railway construction . . . and the economic life the iron horse brought to stagnant areas between centers of production. As northern Mexico thus received stimulation, alien investors began to buy great ranches and enlarge the herds of livestock. Simultaneously, most Mexican cities began to insist on acquiring street railways, electrical systems, and other public utilities, which constituted sources of profits to the foreigners who alone could establish them.

Finally, in 1900, it became apparent that Mexico had some of the richest oil pools in the world, extending along the Gulf Coast from near Texas to Veracruz. British and American petroleum companies competed furiously for these fields, to the amusement of Díaz, who spurred their rivalry by selling very cheaply the subsoil rights that had always been guarded só jealously.

In many respects this development was just what Mexico needed. The out-pouring of oil and metals brought some profits to Mexicans and resulted in the creation of a fine mineral industry. Foreigners who bought up plantations and ranches introduced modern methods, machinery, and better breeds of livestock. Large commercial houses and merchandising firms benefited not only the entrepreneurs but also raised the standard of living for Mexicans by making more goods available. An abundance of small factories, also financed more often than not by foreign investors, had the same effect, though labor conditions were indescribably evil. In short, the beginnings of the Industrial Age in Mexico spelled the creation of an impressive productive system, modern technology, and an elevation in the standard of living for some classes.

On the other side of the picture were the curses that went with such developments, notably in the way of exploiting miners and oilfield and factory workers. The Díaz regime had little sympathy for labor, and union organizers were likely to be treated as enemies of society. As the industrial working class continued to expand, its grievances became all the more unbearable. The eventual explosion would reveal that a time bomb had long been lying beneath the *Díaz-potismo*. Another destructive force inadvertently nourished by the regime was xenophobia. Long before Asia and Africa, or even other parts of Latin America, Mexico was building up a terrible, often irrational, hatred of Yankee and European "imperialism." The country was rapidly becoming under Díaz a mere colony operated for the benefit of aliens, or so it seemed to nationalists. Often the foreigners were arrogant, elbowing aside native capitalists or managers by outmatching them both in money and in skill. They tended to look down on Mexicans as a people who might be picturesque but who were too stupid and unmechanical to operate complicated machines or supervise significant enterprises. As the natives beheld the *norteamericanos* buying up ranches, mines, and oilfields and employing their own nationals for managing them, their Yankeephobia smouldered. The condescending British, with their fingers in nearly every type of economic activity, kindled little affection. Even the *gachupín*, the peninsular Spaniard, had returned to monopolize the tobacco business and to buy up vast agricultural properties. Factories, public utilities, or large commercial houses were often the preserves of Germans, Belgians, Frenchmen, or other Europeans who looked upon Mexicans as a subject population. Certainly, the Díaz administration did all it could to encourage the foreigner. He was protected from the police and law courts, and government censorship and tax laws functioned to his advantage. It was increasingly difficult for Mexicans to take the long view that all the economic development brought about by aliens was ultimately good for the country.

If something can be said in favor of Díaz' patronage of foreign investors, scarcely any case can be made out in defense of his policies with regard to land holdings. At the time he came to power, it was apparent that the *Ley Lerdo* had miscarried, the lands of the Church having gone mostly into the hands of speculators or of men who were already rich. Instead of seeking to remedy this situation, Díaz greatly worsened it and added vicious new features of his own devising. Don Porfirio had a low opinion of the peon and saw no virtue in making him a free farmer. It was much easier to entrench the *hacendados* by offering them low taxes and a solution to labor troubles in exchange for supporting his regime. Thus the peons continued to live in squalor, perpetually in debt to the owner, and to do as they were told. Should they riot or strike, the forces of the state were available to suppress them. Then, as both foreigners and moneyed Mexicans became more numerous, they sought to purchase ranches and estates. Díaz accommodated them by applying the *Ley Lerdo* to Indian tribes who still held communal lands. This was legal, for the law authorized the forced sale of corporate holdings, and an Indian tribe was juridically as much a corporation as the Catholic Church. Thus the government proceeded to deprive the natives of their ancient holdings and to sell them cheaply to political favorites or anyone with capital. If the Indians resisted, as they often did, the army and the *rurales* were in readiness to make war on them and reduce them to peonage. This was done with less hesitation than in the early days of the Spanish conquest with its "just wars," and with similar results. One particularly defiant nation, the Yaquis of northwestern Mexico, long resisted these encroachments with barbaric fury. At length Díaz had many thousands rounded up and shipped down the Pacific coast to Acapulco, from where they were driven across the south to Yucatan. That unhappy province, which suddenly emerged as the world's chief source of henequen, and therefore of twine and cords, had earlier been depopulated when rebellious Maya had been sold as slaves in Cuba. While the transplantation of the Yaqui was the most notorious outrage of this nature, it was far from unique. Many unassimilated Indians revolted and died when the government took their lands. Others simply settled into peonage.

Another means of acquiring haciendas to sell was for the authorities to confiscate the property of individuals who had made themselves obnoxious to Díaz. This could be done through the courts with a semblance of legality. In addition, the government sold or gave away much acreage in the reserves of public lands. There was no Homestead Act to populate these empty regions with land-hungry settlers or war veterans. What finally resulted was a latifundia worse than that of Spanish colonial times. By 1911 Mexico had 900 large land-holders, some with ranches of several million acres, and a rural proletariat of 9,000,000 who owned no land at all. Conditions were what might be expected under these circumstances. The owners had impressive homes on their estates and could live as feudal lords. Often they chose to spend their days in Mexico City and in Europe, leaving their properties to be managed by professionals who were seldom as humane as the clergymen who had often looked after these lands before la Reforma. The lot of the Mexican peon was probably as bad as it had been in Aztec or colonial times. He was underfed, badly housed, brutally treated, and often drunk. His real income was probably lower than it had been in the days of Santa Anna or the viceroys. Mexico's food production rose more slowly than the population, though luxury articles for export flourished. Hunger was chronic in many parts of the country, and food often had to be imported.

The despair of the peon was not apparent to the many visitors to Mexico during the heyday of Díaz. A foreign traveler, who in any case was most unlikely to be a social reformer, might admire the excellent railways, which had increased thirty-fold in mileage under Don Porfirio and were splendidly operated by foreign crews.[2] While the provincial cities would have their adobe slums and the dignified relics of colonial days, they also boasted light industries and modern shops and homes. In the mining regions and the oilfields all was active; efficient alien managers and a disciplined labor force apparently went about their work with the benevolent protection of the regime. From a passing train the ranches would seem well-fenced and well-stocked, the corn and cane fields rich and productive. For all one knew, the population ought to be contented. Mexico City itself would inevitably inspire admiration. Its surrounding mountains, cool and sunny climate, and colonial architecture were as wonderful as men had long reported. Hundreds of lovely homes, ornate government palaces, wide, tree-lined avenues, and magnificent shops and theaters made it almost as striking as Paris. Statues and monuments in the flowery style so admired in the late nineteenth century adorned this large city, obviously a great capital and cultural center. It was also an active headquarters for business affairs. The streets were clean, and one seldom saw a beggar, or for that matter, a poor person of any type in the principal parts of the city. The face of Mexico was indeed agreeable.

2. A half-truth often circulated after the fall of Díaz was that the railway network did not integrate the republic's various territories but served only to facilitate the removal of Mexico's raw materials to the seaports.

Numerous foreign visitors came away with praises for Porfirio Díaz, who had made it so.

In handling the Church or clerical issue, Díaz illustrated his genius for doing what he pretended not to be doing and somehow pleasing all factions. He well knew that Mexico was not fundamentally anti-Catholic or even anti-clerical. He could safely allow the Laws of the Reform to drop into disuse. Yet he had no intention of permitting the Church to recover its former position and thereby encroach on his own power. Nor did he care to set the old-fashioned liberals, who were still quite articulate in the clichés and slogans of the Reform period, to complaining again. His policy was to pose as an unrepentant anti-clerical of the days of Juárez but not to enforce the laws. Soon the Church was quietly gathering back some of its lost property and accumulating cash reserves. Monastic establishments were occasionally allowed to exist, supposedly as clandestine convents but really open secrets known to entire cities. If the liberals inveighed against reviving clericalism too stridently, the dictator might throw them a bone now and again by raiding the monks or nuns, but only after his wife had sent out warnings. Doña Carmen was known for her piety, and she openly befriended important prelates. During the Díaz regime the Church hierarchy knew it had the despot's favor and, furthermore, that he respected its power. The number of priests rose from 3,000 to 6,000 during his terms of office. Still, as he did in the case of his other supporters, Don Porfirio kept the clergy in a thoroughly insecure state. The Laws of the Reform would be unenforced only so long as he chose. Thus the clergy had no course but to strengthen his regime and cultivate his good will. Their admittedly powerful hold on the common people was no protection against a resurgence of anti-clerical politicians.

So successful did the regime seem after 1890 a new rationale became popular among the ruling groups. It was based on the rejection of the old *juarista* type of liberal, who had been left behind the times, and the elevation of Díaz into a demigod, a remote father and teacher of his peoples who no longer fraternized so familiarly with his subjects. It was not the Hispanic-Catholic tradition that should be restored, but rather the recognition of a new materialistic creed, Positivism. José Limantour, who became minister of finance in 1892 and helped reorganize the liberal-federalist party as the Liberal Union, was the leader of this group, whose members called themselves "scientists" (*científicos*). They were not a party, but rather a clique within the Liberal Union and the administration. These men believed they possessed the formula for making Mexico run. It was simply to let the richest people, who by definition were the most intelligent, exploit their opportunities to the fullest. Mexico would become ever more productive. Inevitably, efficiency would be rewarded while the unfit sank into semi-servitude, where they belonged.

Naturally, many of the favored few would be foreigners, but that did not matter. The *científicos* made no secret of their fascination with Europe, whose civilization must be copied and imported until Mexico was saturated, until the disreputable Indian past and the somewhat depressing Spanish heritage were submerged. Racism was an avowed part of their thinking. It was the white man who must rule Mexico, even if he did so under the mestizo Díaz for a time, until Limantour replaced him. Indians were unlikely ever to rise out of the proletariat and should not be encouraged to try. The eventual disappearance of the native race was a possibility that could be faced with equanimity. Meanwhile, the whites should be progressive and modern, closely tied to Europe as the font and center of culture but not disdainful of techniques that could be learned from the clever Yankee.

The cynicism of the *científicos* was nowhere better illustrated than in the educational policies of the *Porfiriato*. It was the Indian, Benito Juárez, who had enunciated the ideal of schools for everybody. Díaz never in so many words repudiated this aspiration, but the number of primary schools during his long and prosperous administration increased only in proportion to the rise in population. So much more could have been done had he wished it, as many other countries were demonstrating during these years. Yet cultural life among the upper classes was unusually rich. In 1910 the National University, which had functioned intermittently since the days of Santa Anna, was reorganized and strengthened as an institution to train the elite. Other establishments for higher education received official support. The cultural and artistic life of the capital was the equal of that of most great cities its size, with concerts, theaters, operas, and the circulation of books and periodicals of high quality. Mexican painters, sculptors, and architects were quite respectable members of Western civilization, though they seem in retrospect to have lacked originality, to have imitated European models altogether. Poets were also numerous; yet they too copied the style and approach of the Europeans, notably the Parisian modernists. Of these the physically repulsive but exquisitely sensitive Manuel Gutiérrez Nájera (1859–1895) and Enrique González Martínez (1871–1952) were the most famous. Writers such as Justo Sierra, a historian, jurist, educator, and novelist who commanded respect abroad, and Francisco Bulnes, an essayist who articulated the *científico* point of view, did credit to the country's intellectual life.

Since literary and artistic souls, in fact, the Mexican intelligentsia in general, lauded Porfirio Díaz, it is not strange that the outside world also admired the dictator. Honors and praise showered on him from everywhere, from monarchs, politicians, diplomats, financiers, intellectuals, even from humanitarians. From a distance he seemed a wizard who had raised Mexico from squalor to its present admirable state as a worthy member of the European family. If only other Latin American nations could enjoy such leadership!

THE COLLAPSE OF THE DÍAZ REGIME

Don Porfirio was seventy in 1900. During the following decade men could not keep from wondering how much longer he would last. There was no sign that the dictatorship was likely to disintegrate; it was a matter of how it could be continued without the founder. José Limantour preened himself to inherit the leader's mantle. He was justly respected for much of the financial management that had made Mexico so prosperous. Another aspirant was General Bernardo Reyes, who had long been a helpful satellite of Díaz and was now governor of the state of Nuevo Leon. Other members of the official family allowed it to be known that they were willing to be considered as heirs of Díaz. Yet the old president seemed vigorous. He enjoyed the maneuverings of his would-be successors. Sometimes he would encourage one hopeful for a time, only to remind him later what had happened to another presumptuous heir who had been shot under the *ley fuga*. Men who thought they stood well with the despot would suddenly be demoted or sent on frivolous missions abroad. In 1904 Díaz allowed the nation to reelect him for a six-year term, though he made a concession to those who thought he was too old by permitting the installation of a vice-president. Yet this dignitary, Ramón Corral, was such an egregious person, so unfit and so detested, that no one would dream of killing Díaz. The game went on, with the feline old president serenely in control of things as usual. No prospect was groomed for the succession, and there was no clear sign of revolution.

A break in the tension came about inadvertently in 1908 when an American journalist published an article about "the greatest man on the continent" after an interview with Díaz. He reported that Don Porfirio had expressed the hope that Mexico might develop another strong party, one that could put up respectable opposition in the election of 1910. While the article was published in the United States and Díaz had attached no significance to it, politicians in Mexico City started buzzing when they heard of it. Did the old man intend to indicate that he would not run in the next election? Díaz soon became annoyed with the speculation and sent both Limantour and Reyes, the probable beneficiaries of his retirement, abroad in disguised exile. Yet the talk would not die, and the more likely it seemed that Díaz would at last step down, the more attractive the possibility became. A series of troubles indicated serious symptoms that things were not well: strikes in Sonora, Veracruz, and Yucatan, all of which were suppressed with ferocity; a short business depression following the New York panic of 1907; rural disorders resulting from droughts and food shortages; and evidence of disaffection even in the army. A handful of Spanish anarchists somehow escaped the police network to promote radicalism among the industrial proletariat. Two native revolutionists, the Flores Magón brothers, sent propaganda and agents from their headquarters in St. Louis, Missouri. Obviously, the working class was receptive to such agitation. And here and there rural radicals moved about the country stirring up the peons to demand a division of the land.

The decisive figure in the undoing of Porfirio Díaz proved to be Francisco Indalecio Madero, a funny little man whom few took seriously at first. He came of an aristocratic family in Coahuila which had grown wealthy as Díaz supporters. Born in 1873, he had attended schools in France and the United States. As manager of his properties in Mexico he had been quite successful but, uniquely, also concerned with the welfare of his peons. If he was urbane, original, and full of ideas, his physique and personality seemed to disqualify him for leadership. Madero was short and shrill, apparently lacking in dignity. He had a nervous twitch in his shoulder. A prohibitionist and vegetarian, he also practiced a variety of spiritualism, to the amusement of many people. Still, he had qualities that drew able men to him, among which were a soulfulness and a transparent goodness that made him seem a saint, or at least a welcome contrast to the hard-bitten politicians to whom Mexicans were accustomed.

His ambitions at this stage seemed modest enough. In 1908 he published a book on the presidential succession for 1910. Quite respectful of Díaz, whom he praised for many achievements, Madero suggested that the vice-presidency be filled in 1910 by a man popularly chosen and not dictated by Díaz, who presumably would run for the presidency again. Perhaps he was proposing himself for this second position. Whatever his intention, the reception of the tract was so enthusiastic that Madero issued two more editions, changing them so as to criticize Díaz in moderate terms. In 1909 he was encouraged enough by his fame to announce his own candidacy for president. He would use Díaz' old slogan of 1876, "effective suffrage—no reelection," and call his party the Anti-reelectionist. At this point Díaz summoned Madero for an interview, the upshot of which was that each man formed a low opinion of the other. Díaz thought Madero a near lunatic, so ridiculous that his candidacy would prove that only crazy people opposed the regime. Madero discerned that Díaz was failing badly as he neared eighty.

Madero stayed in the race, happily elaborating his program as potential supporters brought him ideas. Most of his plans had to do with political reforms, for he had not thought deeply about social or economic questions. He traveled widely over Mexico, making ever bolder attacks on Don Porfirio, and he manifestly stimulated much excitement, for he was saying things many people had wanted to hear for years. Meanwhile, he sent funds to Mexican radicals in exile who printed propaganda for clandestine circulation in Mexico. In many cities and towns "Democratic" clubs sprang up. Both industrial and agrarian laborers gave signs of serious unrest. So did many among the better-educated classes, who had long chafed over the arrogance of foreigners and the suppression of liberty. Madero was clearly raising a storm.

Just before the election, Díaz decided he had tolerated Madero long enough and had him jailed in San Luis Potosí. The election went off on schedule, and when the votes were announced some months later, Madero was accorded 196 ballots in contrast to the million received by Díaz. In September 1910 a protracted and costly celebration was held to commemorate the centenary of Father Hidalgo's uprising. Díaz, who turned eighty during the ceremonies, dutifully rang the sacred bell of Dolores and uttered the immortal *grito* before vast throngs of cheering patriots in the main plaza of Mexico City. He entertained numerous distinguished guests from abroad and received honors from foreign governments. His own people seemed to venerate him as much as ever.

Yet all was not well. Madero, who had been released in October, fled to the United States to organize a true revolution under his Plan of San Luis Potosí, dated as if he had composed it in prison.[3] His program had mostly to do with liberty and political reform, though there were vague references to land division and other social changes. In nearly every town in Mexico there were men who circulated this plan and vowed to rise when the time came. A strange outlaw, who called himself Pancho Villa, organized a horde of cowboys and bandits in Chihuahua which surprisingly overthrew the Díaz machine in that state. South of Mexico City in the little mountain-ringed state of Morelos, a rural hero of more idealism, Emiliano Zapata, was leading hundreds of peons in a jacquerie. In daytime they worked innocently in the cane fields; by night they terrorized officials and *hacendados*. These rural disorders spread into Guerrero and thrilled peons in other states, where the slogan of "Land and Liberty" excited thousands of the disinherited. All over Mexico it was apparent that revolution was about to burst. Many were ready to risk their lives to end the long dictatorship, if only a leader would take the initiative. Madero had been the first to challenge the tyrant, and he had funds and a national reputation. Thus he loomed as the natural focus of revolutionary hopes.

To combat these undermining forces Díaz depended on governors

3. The Revolution, with a capital *r*, is thus regarded as commencing in 1910, though it was not successful until 1911.

and generals often as old as himself. A whole generation of rulers had become senile. Most of them were bewildered and helpless before the signs of revolution. The army, whose officers had been pampered so long, suddenly proved demoralized and incompetent; the enlisted men were caught up in the national movement. The rotten state of the regime was apparent early in 1911, and now its nerve was gone. Díaz was realistic enough to comprehend that his forces were unequal to the challenge. He begged Limantour to return from Europe and work his familiar magic. Instead of going straight to Mexico, the financier went to New York, where he conferred with Gustavo Madero, the older and more capable brother of Francisco. There they concocted in a hotel room a compromise by which Díaz should remain in office but make many concessions to the *maderistas*. News of this confession of weakness proved ruinous to Díaz. Everywhere, his supporters sensed the game was up at last and prepared to change sides. Pancho Villa's private army and irregular forces with Madero himself received many arms and supplies from the United States, not, as charged, because of any official policy, but because merchants on the border liked to make money by selling military hardware. The climax of six months of uneasiness came in May 1911. Zapata's forces captured the important railway center of Cuautla. Villa stormed Ciudad Juárez. This news led to mutinies of many garrisons and to riots in Mexico City.

Díaz realized that his hour had come. Suffering mental anguish and dental pain, he finally gave way to the pressures of his family and friends, probably just in time to prevent a dreadful bloodbath in the capital. On May 25, 1911, the old man resigned the presidency he had held so long. Except for a few shots fired at his train, he was treated with courtesy as he journeyed to Veracruz, where he boarded a German vessel, the *Ypiranga*, and sailed to Europe. Four years later he died in Paris.

Modern and Contemporary Latin America

25

Mexico

La Revolución

THE TRAGEDY OF MADERO

THE departure of Porfirio Díaz in May 1911 delivered Mexico over to the ecstasy and euphoria that characterize the first stage of a revolution. Francisco I. Madero made his way from the north to the capital by slow train, greeted along the way as a messiah. There was something at once pathetic and ominous about the delirium of the crowds. So much faith centered on the tiny aristocrat who had surprisingly broken the power of the Díaz dictatorship, this kindly man who truly believed he received guidance from the spirits of the dead. The masses hailed him in unconscious blasphemy as savior and redeemer, often shouting the slogan, "Land and Liberty." Madero really had small experience in the world of affairs, and none whatever in government. His plans consisted of little more than holding free elections and establishing a democratic government. In October 1911 the first of these goals was fulfilled. The caretaker regime that had followed Díaz staged the elections with an honesty never known before in the Mexican republic. Madero himself was chosen president, and *maderistas*, whose opinions were still largely unformulated, were elected to most of the positions in the national congress and the state governments. To have ousted the Díaz regime with so little bloodshed and installed a representative government were no minor achievements. But what was to be done with the opportunity?

It was obvious that the opportunity was vast and, as usual in such cases, full of danger. Neither Madero nor scarcely anyone else comprehended the titanic forces released in 1910–1911, exactly a century after Father Hidalgo had loosed terrible and sublime urges he did not understand. To Madero and his immediate circle the main objective appeared to be political rather than social. If Mexico functioned according to her excellent constitution, that of 1857, her problems could be approached thoughtfully and, above all, legally.

This attitude paid the Mexican nation a compliment it did not deserve, for it was far from prepared to settle down into order. The northern states of Sonora and Chihuahua were almost in anarchy, as Pancho Villa and men of his stripe assembled armed masses of cowboys and bandits. In Morelos and Guerrero, the folk hero Emiliano Zapata was leading his peon forces against the landowners, the *hacendados,* killing some of these hated monopolists, burning records, and often distributing the farmlands pell mell. The federal army, now supposedly *maderista,* was full of hard-minded generals who chafed at legalism and itched to assert themselves. Even the liberal politicians and professional classes behaved with an unseemly lack of restraint. So long suppressed during the *porfiriato,* they carped at Madero for not solving all problems at once, the way their counterparts had found fault with Juárez a half century before. Radical idealists and revolutionary adventurers had drastic plans to remake the social order and entrench themselves as a new upper class. In the background, the clergy, the great landowners, and the ubiquitous foreigners regarded the new regime nervously. They had reason to be fearful of the future and to take steps to protect themselves. In all, the dimensions of Mexico's ferment in 1911 exceeded the estimates of everyone.

Perhaps no mortal could have dominated the situation; Madero made a valiant effort. He attracted some of the best men in the country into his administration, but he tolerated many unrepentant *porfiristas* and, to his discredit, far too many of his relatives. The old Díaz bureaucracy underwent a purge but was not swept away, a seemingly wise compromise to assure continuity of administration. Madero also sought a balance in dealing with alien interests, pleasing Mexican nationalists with strident denunciations of the privileged foreigner but reassuring other governments that their subjects would not be abused. He addressed himself energetically to preliminary challenges from the army, the inevitable pronouncements of generals now freed from the stifling controls of the Díaz dictatorship. Generals Pascual Orozco, Bernardo Reyes, and Félix Díaz, this last a nephew of the fallen tyrant, led premature insurrections in Veracruz and the north. Their prompt defeat seemed an indication that Madero's regime was solidly based. Zapata was less easy to handle. After several stormy sessions with the president, who characteristically went to great lengths to reach an agreement with him, Zapata finally refused to disarm his followers. He rightly feared a reaction that might cheat them of the lands they had seized; to hasten the forcible division of the sugar plantations he issued a grandiose *Plan de Ayala* and continued his operations.

This defiance was serious enough, but worse was the manifest diminution of Madero's prestige during 1912. His undignified behavior in public and the comic aspects of his personality and physique furnished material for ridicule. The cynical doings of his brothers and other supporters dimmed his halo. Now that the Mexicans had freedom of press and speech, they exploited to the fullest their opportunities to criticize. Madero was not particularly distressed by the decline of his popularity, for he knew the population was fickle. Nor, trusting and well-meaning as he was, could he credit rumors of conspiracies among important men who seemed friendly in personal contact.

The fatal stroke, indeed the felon blow, that ruined him came not from querulous liberals, *zapatistas,* or revolutionaries but from those who favored a restoration. Generals Félix Díaz and Bernardo Reyes, who had been imprisoned in Mexico City following their abortive revolt, managed to weave a conspiracy involving much of the military hierarchy and large financial interests. In February 1913 a garrison on the edge of the capital pronounced and released these generals. Reyes was killed in a skirmish with loyal troops, but Díaz placed himself at the head of a strong rebellious unit with headquarters in the citadel of Mexico City. At first it seemed that only a barracks revolt, or *cuartelazo,* had sputtered, for there was little response elsewhere in the country.

However, Madero made a grievous if typical error. Innocent as always, he summoned to his defense one of the most sinister figures in Mexico, General Victoriano Huerta. True, Huerta was a competent general and had earlier demonstrated his loyalty to the president by fighting rebels. But Madero had afterward offended him by demanding an accounting of his use of public funds, a bad breach of the code in Mexico. Besides, Huerta was in on the conspiracy. For ten days, the "tragic ten," from February 9 to February 18, Huerta's forces at the national palace and Félix Díaz' at the citadel lobbed shells and mortars on the center of the capital but avoided hitting one another. Many civilians were injured or killed, and the population was terrorized. Outside Mexico City the country was calm, loyal to President Madero. During this senseless bombardment the American ambassador, Henry Lane Wilson, who had often berated Madero for his deafness to the importunities of foreign investors, was suspiciously active. Wilson had made no secret of his belief that Madero was a fool and that he was bound to fall. Administering a push, he dealt with both Huerta and Díaz during these tragic ten days. On February 18

Huerta suddenly arrested the gentle president he was supposed to defend and announced that peace was restored. Meeting Félix Díaz at the American embassy, he arranged to assume the presidency himself until an election could be held. Ambassador Wilson proudly presented President Huerta to the diplomatic corps and sent jubilant reports to Washington, where the expiring Taft administration comprehended little of what he had been doing. Despite profuse promises that Madero could leave the country, in exchange for which the betrayed leader resigned his office, both he and his former vice-president were shot down on the night of February 22 as they were being removed from the national palace. Whether this crime arose from confusion or, as was more likely, from planned cruelty, it made Madero a national martyr. And it spoiled whatever chance Huerta ever had of becoming an effective ruler.

AN INTERLUDE OF BARBARISM

Huerta was able to establish himself as provisional president before the facts of Madero's murder became generally known. He remained in this office what he had been before, an alcoholic soldier of base instincts. First, he betrayed the conspirators who had raised him to the presidency in the expectation that he would soon step down and let Félix Díaz restore the system of his uncle. Instead, Huerta shipped Díaz to Japan and proceeded to install his own brutish henchmen in key positions, including the main commands of the *federales,* or the federal army. For seventeen months he governed central Mexico (much of the country resisting him) in the fashion of an underworld king, making his headquarters in tawdry bars. Gang rule, corruption of the most brazen type, and a liberal employment of the *ley fuga* enabled him to hold together a fantastic administration. Huerta had no plans, even when he was sober, other than perpetuating his rule. Thus foreign investors, the clergy, the large landowners, and the generals tended to support him, for at least he let them alone. Congress, the one elected with Madero in 1911, showed signs of disapproval. This body he intimidated by arresting more than a hundred deputies. As for the election he had promised when he became provisional president, Huerta disarmingly announced in October 1913 that so little interest was evident in this poll that he would simply remain in office without one. He was not unduly disturbed when Zapata and other provincial leaders broke away from the government, or when Pancho Villa escaped prison to re-enter Mexico from the United States and start a rebellion. After all, it was enough to rule the vital center of Mexico, where most of the population and wealth were, and to control the valuable customhouse at Veracruz, source of most of the revenue.

An unexpected complication in Huerta's plans arose in connection with Mexico's relations with the United States. President Woodrow Wilson, who took office in March 1913, was dismayed when he learned how Madero was overthrown. He recalled Ambassador Wilson in something bordering on disgrace. Instead of replacing him and thus establishing diplomatic relations with the Huerta regime, as the European powers had done, President Wilson violated custom by embarking on a course whose merits were long debated. It was traditional to recognize any *de facto* government, however it originated. So repelled by Huerta was the moralistic American president, however, that he decided to extend no recognition whatever to his regime and to try to unseat the monster. Huerta professed to believe this disapproval would do him no injury, for Mexicans were passionately resentful of the United States. Besides, European competitors might gladly replace the numerous *gringos* who had entrenched themselves so profitably in Mexico. Yet President Wilson's attitude strengthened those Mexicans who opposed Huerta, and it also made it easier for them to obtain arms in the United States.

Huerta's enemies increased rapidly. The surviving *porfiristas*, cheated of their ambitions for Félix Díaz, were not won over by a president so debauched and capricious as Huerta. Pancho Villa, who had gotten away from Huerta's clutches, proceeded to expand his outlaw empire in the state of Chihuahua. The bandit king found it easy to finance himself by stealing cattle and selling them across the Rio Grande and by robbing anyone he pleased. Emiliano Zapata's power was also mounting. His domain now stretched, as that of Morelos had a century before, almost from Veracruz to Acapulco. His peons had become so confident they now enforced a leveling doctrine that compelled all men to dress the way southern Indians did, with loose-legged uniforms like white pajamas and enormous straw hats. These surging folk movements were bursting out of their native habitats into other parts of Mexico, and they were attracting lettered men who articulated sophisticated political programs. In vain the *federales* fought them; opposition simply hardened their determination.

As anarchy grew, something of a directing force appeared to channel these trends in the person of Venustiano Carranza, the patriarchal governor of Coahuila. Long a staunch partisan of Díaz and a former senator, Carranza had changed sides in time to save his reputation and had built up a large private army in his state. Educated and less primitive than Zapata or Villa, he had a dim statesmanlike purpose. First, the egregious Huerta must be removed. Then, a constitutional regime should be restored, hence the favorite name he applied to his partisans, the *constitucionalistas*. Finally, a small group of intellectuals in his entourage, who made the desert town of Nogales their headquarters, insisted that social justice be done, that militarism, latifundia, clerical privilege, and foreign ownership be eliminated from Mexican life. While Carranza took this program rather casually, he tolerated and used these idealists, who were effective propagandists for his cause, and he invented the title of First Chief and bestowed it on himself. He made an uncertain alliance with Villa and his Chihuahua group. The two men were too different to trust one another long. With Álvaro Obregón, a young general who called himself a socialist and who ruled the northwestern state of Sonora, Carranza established a more solid relationship after making a spectacular march across the deserts and *sierras* to meet the young caudillo, who agreed to subordinate himself to the First Chief.

That Huerta would soon fall seemed inevitable as Carranza, Villa, Obregón, and Zapata withstood the *federales* and took the offensive. It was "the eternal enemy of the north," however, which dealt the fatal blow. The arrest of a few American sailors in Tampico gave President Wilson an opportunity to humiliate Huerta. Already irritated because the Mexican had jeered at his lofty preachments, Wilson demanded an apology and a 21-gun salute to the Stars and Stripes. No Mexican president could grant the latter, unless it were reciprocated, and stay in office, and Huerta refused. Thus Wilson, in April 1914, ordered the seizure of Veracruz, whose customs were Huerta's principal source of income. An awkward incident arising from the successful attempt of the German merchantman *Ypiranga*, which had carried Díaz off to exile in 1911, to land arms for Huerta led to an American bombardment of the city and the killing of perhaps 300 Mexicans. Much as Huerta sought to arouse nationalistic fury against the Yankees, he was immobilized by the loss of revenue from the Veracruz customhouse and, besides, about to be overwhelmed by his domestic enemies. He resigned in July 1914 and fled, finally, to the United States, where drunkenness and schemes to invade Mexico led to his death in a Texas jail.

It was far from clear who was to inherit the position Huerta had vacated. Pancho Villa was leading a veritable folk migration of perhaps 100,000 down the railway from Chihuahua to Zacatecas, a frightening horde called the "Army of the North" that could loot with scientific skill and slay with barbaric abandon. Furthermore, Álvaro Obregón was making a rapid descent down the Pacific coast with his better-disciplined force of cowboys and Yaqui Indians. With more deliberation Venustiano Carranza, who had by now broken with Villa, was moving toward the capital from Coahuila. And Zapata's hordes were climbing over the rim of mountains that separated their homeland from the Valley of Mexico to probe cautiously around the capital's environs. Obregón got to Mexico City first, in August 1914, where he proclaimed Carranza as First Chief of the nation. In October representatives of the leading factions assembled at Aguascalientes, supposedly neutral territory, to organize a government satisfactory to all. The constituent congress thus gathered heard splendid philosophical debates and witnessed outrageous scenes. About all it accomplished, however, was the election of Eulalio Gutiérrez as provisional president of the republic and the alienation of the Carranza and Zapata deputies. Villa soon took possession of the town. Rather than face the government and Villa and, possibly, Zapata all at once, Carranza and Obregón withdrew from Mexico City to Veracruz. There, in the manner of Juárez during the War of the Reform, they maintained a *constitucionalista* regime, purchased arms and supplies from abroad, and built up an effective army.

During the winter of 1914–1915 the First Chief labored wisely and well. While Obregón trained his army, Carranza's publicists drew up an ambitious program to renovate Mexican society, notably in the way of improving conditions for the industrial working class and promoting the distribution of land to the peons. Wide-scale publicity was given to his decrees, which attracted, as he had hoped, the support of responsible elements throughout the country as well as the confidence of the proposed beneficiaries of these reforms. Meanwhile, *villistas* swaggered about Mexico City, singing *La Cucaracha*, their rollicking song, terrorizing the rich, and taking women and property as they liked. Zapata joined Villa for a bucolic summit meeting of apparently amiable atmosphere in Xochimilco, the suburb with the celebrated floating gardens. The two rustics enjoyed parading through Mexico City and being photographed as they sat in the presidential chair. Poor provisional President Gutiérrez soon escaped and announced for Carranza. For some weeks Mexico City underwent experiences not unlike those Havana would know after the advent of Fidel Castro. Oddly enough, the *zapatistas* behaved with much more humility than Villa's men. They soon went home.

In January 1915 Obregón temporarily occupied the capital, which proceeded to change hands several times in the next few months. Villa, however, was definitely on the defensive and began a retreat to the north. When he elected to give battle, in April, at Celaya in the state of Guanajuato, he found Obregón not only in possession of an excellent army but also informed of the advantages of trenches, barbed wire entanglements, and machine guns, which were being used in World War I to such murderous effect. A three-day battle, the worst ever fought in blood-soaked Mexico, was a decisive victory for Obregón and the *constitucionalistas*. Villa could only flee homeward, to Chihuahua. In retreating he tore up the railway tracks for hundreds of miles to discourage Obregón's pursuit. His forces melted away by the thousands, and when he reached his native province he was a whipped bully, a hero only to the homefolks but a nuisance to everyone else. Zapata likewise withdrew, into Morelos, where he defied Carranza and Obregón for four years. In 1919 he agreed to attend a parley with Carranza's representatives, only to be shot dead as he approached by *federales* from whom he expected a salute. For many years peasants in the south refused to believe he was gone and often reported seeing him at night on his famous white horse riding through the sugar cane.

IDEALISM AND CRIME, 1915–1920

Venustiano Carranza resumed the presidency in Mexico City in August 1915, with Obregón as his minister of war and principal prop. The state of the republic could scarcely have been worse, having declined in nearly every respect since the fall of Díaz in 1911. Economic disorganization had reduced business life to the primitive level of barter and theft. At a time when World War I was bringing prosperity to much of the planet, Mexico had lost her credit and markets. Except for oil exported for the British fleet she was largely unable to take advantage of Europe's agony. No national currency was recognized; of the dozen or so issues sponsored by various leaders only Zapata's had any value, because he used gold and silver pieces. Militarism, which Díaz had curbed, was now the most pressing curse. The huge federal army was top-heavy with officers and laden with corruption. It was not really a good army; events would soon prove it could not put up any defense against a small American expeditionary force. And its units were too autonomous to preserve internal order. Private forces, such as those of Pancho Villa and Emiliano Zapata as well as countless lesser caudillos, were a continuous threat to the national government. Crime made life and the possession of property in all sections precarious. Furthermore, little progress had been made since 1911 in tackling the great social inequities. The Church was still a state within a state, and a comparatively well-endowed one at that. If southern *hacendados* and northern ranchers had been killed or driven away, latifundia still prevailed, and most peons were worse off than they had been under Díaz but for ever-receding hopes. While the working classes had been promised many benefits, most of them had no work. With good reason Porfirio Díaz, as he lay dying in Paris in July 1915, had a feeling of vindication.

Carranza undertook with considerable vigor and foresight the administrative reconstruction of the country, following which he hoped economic problems would diminish and social injustices might be healed. He had scarcely begun when Pancho Villa deliberately embarrassed him by attracting the wrath of the United States. This he did by murdering sixteen American engineers on their way to re-open a mine in Sonora in January 1916 and then, in March, by senselessly raiding the town of Columbus, New Mexico. The indignant President Wilson at once sent an expeditionary force led by General John J. Pershing to chastise the bandit leader. Villa had a fine time being pursued across the arid brush country of the north he knew so well. He delighted in the publicity which American journalists were only too eager to give his bizarre forces. Pershing's mission proved a fiasco, though it gave the American army important experience soon to be needed in France. President Carranza blustered mightily at American arrogance in hunting Villa on Mexican soil, but he was unable to handle Villa at all, much less Pershing. The failure of the expedition made the Americans look foolish, and they withdrew in February 1917.[4] About the same time Germany, anticipating the United States declaration of war, offered Carranza a far-reaching alliance and return of the territory of the Mexican Cession of 1848. Tempting as this proposal was from an emotional point of view, Carranza well knew that Germany could not aid Mexico. When the British secret service published this offer, the Zimmerman note, American hatred of Germany and suspicion of Mexico flared to new heights. On the whole, the antipathy of the Colossus of the North was an asset to Carranza.

Some measure of stability came to the republic during the Carranza administration, an achievement of no small importance. The most lasting accomplishment of that period, however, was one which the president regarded with restrained enthusiasm. This was that famous affirmation of policies and ideals known as the constitution of 1917. Hoping to restore legality to political affairs and to redeem some of the promises made in his name, Carranza assembled a convention to revise the constitution of 1857 in December 1916 at Querétaro. Its product was an altogether new basic charter, hurriedly put together to attract peasant and worker support during the period of the American invasion, a time when it appeared Carranza might collapse. Unrepresentative and hasty as the delegates were, they were an able group, even brilliant. Their work became a hallowed document in la Revolución, the continuing movement which is dated back to 1910 but which really began about 1916 with the Querétaro convention. The constitution of 1917 replaced that of 1857 as the bible of political liberalism in Mexico. It did more, for it became a beacon to reformers all over Latin America, and many of its ideals were actually transformed into realities. Much as this document extolled freedom, it incorporated the collectivist principle to a degree unrealized anywhere prior to the Russian Revolution. The state was to take precedence over the individual. Reaching back into Roman and Spanish law and borrowing from socialist doctrines, the delegates asserted that property in the last analysis belonged to the state and could be reclaimed from individuals, with compensation, if the national welfare demanded it. The subsoil—the mineral deposits and oil pools—could never be alienated;

4. Villa was never caught, either by the Americans or the federales. He lived a life of crime until 1923, when a relative of one of his victims ambushed him.

it too was the state's. If these principles were as old as Rome, their new context was revolutionary.

The constitution specified that communal *ejidos* should be restored and enlarged, and that oversized individual land holdings should be divided. Farm and industrial workers were guaranteed the right to unionize and to strike; limits on working hours and bases for minimum wages were also proclaimed. Debt peonage must be abolished, along with child labor. The president of the republic could require any foreigner to leave the country. Finally, the old anti-clerical laws were strengthened and restated. The Church must own no property whatever, not even houses of worship. Monastic orders were again outlawed, and priests were to be rigidly restricted. The Church must have nothing at all to do with public education; in fact, it seemed destined to wither into insignificance as a factor in Mexican affairs. It was obvious that the most fundamental questions were raised by the constitution. Were landowners to be dispossessed forthwith? Were all foreign holdings to be confiscated? Were the working classes to attain conditions not known elsewhere in the world? Was the Church to lose all of its property and influence in the immediate future? Hopes and fears ran high as the product of Querétaro became known.

Carranza was annoyed with much of the new constitution, though he liked the section which increased the president's power and downgraded that of congress. He felt the radicals had run wild, taking advantage of a chance to reform the old constitution by issuing one of revolutionary character. Yet he needed all the support he could get, and if the new instrument flattered the ideologues and the lower classes, he was willing to acknowledge it. Without offering either threats or assurances, he proclaimed the constitution in February 1917. Nothing much happened. The intended beneficiaries of the new charter were pleased for a time to have their hopes codified. Prospective victims comprehended that nothing was to be done to them for awhile, perhaps never. As Carranza's term wore on, the country settled into an acceptable equilibrium.

Carranza's administration came to an end in 1920. Presidents were not eligible for reelection under the constitution of 1917. Unaware that many adherents of the Revolution were becoming restless, he thought himself popular enough to dictate a successor. He made a poor choice in picking Ignacio Bonillas, a relative nonentity and one-time diplomat. Bonillas was regarded as a Yankee toady by the few who had heard of him at all. The most significant objection to his candidacy came from Álvaro Obregón, whose victories had put Carranza in office in 1915 and who had served as minister of war. Now he was governor of Sonora and commander of the best of the state armies. Obregón, like many others who took the constitution of 1917 seriously, regarded the First Chief as having lost his revolutionary virtue, and his summons to resist the imposition of Bonillas aroused most of the republic. Carranza was grieved at the disaffection he saw all about him. Like Porfirio Díaz, Francisco Madero, even Pancho Villa, he pondered the inconstancy of men he had led. After some hesitation, he elected to remove himself from the scene. To that end he filled twenty railway cars with treasure and property that legalists said belonged to the nation and set out for Veracruz, assured by the ranking commander on the route that he was still regarded as "president and leader." Nonetheless, this same admirer derailed the train and had Carranza hunted down in the hills. Murder was the fate of still another Mexican ruler. Yet, hearteningly enough, this more or less peaceful revolution of 1920 has been Mexico's last to succeed.

THE REVOLUTION RESUMES UNDER OBREGÓN, 1920–1924

In 1820, on the eve of Mexican independence, it looked as though the revolution begun by Hidalgo ten years before had failed utterly and brought only tragedy. A similar parallel suggested itself in 1920 to those who remembered Madero's challenge of 1910. Despite all the promises and idealism, the decade that followed, like 1810–1820, had been one of lawlessness, impoverishment, and death. Mexico's population was believed to have fallen by a million. The habit of obedience and tradition of order established under Porfirio Díaz were lost in violence and confusion. Except for the oil fields, Mexico's production was shockingly lower, and her inhabitants were hungrier than ever. The constitution of 1917 seemed as unrealistic as Morelos' charter of 1813 had a century before, its revolutionary vision a mirage. Many individuals had, of course, improved their situation in life, but more must have been killed or despoiled, and the nation was much worse off than in the days of the *Díaz-potismo*.

It was Álvaro Obregón who salvaged the Revolution in 1920 and proceeded to consolidate it, really to institutionalize its main objectives so that the country remained in the mold he cast. When he rose against Carranza, Obregón was forty years old, with an empty sleeve and a brilliant military record to remind the population of his attachment to the Revolution. Like Madero and Carranza, he was a northerner, continuing what came to be called the Northern Dynasty. Indeed there was a clannish spirit among the numerous mestizo warriors from Sonora, Chihuahua, and Coahuila who somehow managed to monopolize the key positions in the republic until the mid-1930's. They were generally serious about the aims of the Revolution without being ideologues, and they were impatient with the *gringos*, clergymen, *porfiristas*, or landowners who might get in their way. Yet they had little respect for the imported radicalism of Europe and the extremists of the Zapata type.

Above all, Obregón and his associates were pragmatists. They would borrow, copy, modify, and distort revolutionary doctrines as they needed them. If they re-kindled the Revolution, their intentions were only partially idealistic. Like Napoleon's marshals after years of warfare, they had become middle-aged men who craved enrichment rather than more adventure. Obregón, their natural leader, typified these mixed ambitions. He was sincere about the Revolution; yet he saw ways to make it a good thing. Elected president in 1920 after Carranza's flight and death, he set out to insure his power, to make the constitution of 1917 effective, and to exploit his position for private gain. In aspiring to accomplish these purposes he was far from original. It was his success that distinguished him from the numerous caudillos the Revolution had thrown up from obscurity and then destroyed.

Obregón discerned the three basic elements in the confusion that was Mexico in 1920. These were not the historic bases of power: the landowners, clergy, and foreign investors. Now they were the Revolutionary generals, labor leaders, and agrarian spokesmen, men who held authority in the crucial sectors of the new society. The generals yielded rather easily to Obregón's magnetism. Like Porfirio Díaz, the new president was a respected commander who knew how to handle these officers, how to mix threats and bribes so as to attach them to his regime. Lavishly endowing the somber Revolutionary leaders with rank and financial opportunities, he then proceeded to reduce their forces so that many generals became decorative parasites. Yet the potential power was available if he needed it, for soldiers could always be drafted to fill up the commands. Generals enjoyed not only wealth and status; they were also an excessively pampered class, usually above the law, whether murder or traffic offenses were involved. Most of them responded to this treatment by remaining loyal to Obregón and his system for the rest of their lives.

Industrial workers had been steadily increasing since the middle of the *porfiriato* as railways, mining, and small factories developed. Long oppressed, they had blossomed out with the Revolution of 1910 as an aggressive force in politics. Union organizers and foreign radicals had been active in creating a proletarian psychology. Yet the disorders and economic decline following Madero's triumph had worked against the emergence of this class as an effective power in the new society, and Carranza had done almost nothing to stimulate a real labor movement. However, a 300-pound unionist of notorious ruthlessness named Luis Morones had started an organization called CROM (*Confederación regional obrera mexicana*) in 1918 which, set up on craft union lines, won the brotherly support of the American Federation of Labor. Under the Obregón administration Morones enjoyed enthusiastic government sponsorship. Union membership, he informed a skeptical world, spurted from 50,000 to more than a million; at least it increased very markedly. His methods were far from gentle. Reluctant or hesitant workers were forced into unions by strong-arm organizers who often carried pistols and who insisted on abject obedience. Employers learned they could be driven into bankruptcy by strikers who had the full backing of the police, army, tax collectors, and courts. Under the circumstances, it is not surprising that collusion among union leaders, employers, and government officials settled most labor problems and became an accepted feature of Mexican business life. Everyone gained something in these arrangements except the consuming public. Morones was able to indulge his taste for diamonds and armored Cadillacs. His juniors in CROM likewise learned to spend freely, live high, and purchase desirable real estate. The workers received better wages and the owners made profits. Since the Obregón administration had blessed CROM from the beginning, it enjoyed powerful support from this quarter.

It was far more difficult to organize the agrarians, as might be expected in a land where nine-tenths of the population devoted itself to farming or ranching. The Northern Dynasty was not overly inclined to sympathize with the southern, or *zapatista*, reformers who wanted to break up all estates and divide them among Indian tribes or individuals, probably because land division would be ruinous for the ranches with which they were familiar. Obregón made the ritualistic gestures and utterances about land reform expected of a son of the Revolution, and he employed Zapata's old publicist, Antonio Díaz Soto y Gama, to advertise his interest in the cause, but he did comparatively little. About one per cent, or 3,000,000 acres, of the land available for redistribution was awarded, mostly in the form of *ejidos* to Indian communities. This paltry achievement was nonetheless of significance; the very fact that the program had at last started after a decade of sloganeering was indescribably heartening to the land-hungry population. And as part of his agricultural program Obregón stimulated the education of farmers in modern methods and technology, something that was urgently needed in order to raise productivity. The deprived owners, incidentally, were not altogether swindled, for they received government bonds, sometimes of doubtful worth, in payment for their lost properties.

That generals were arrogant, labor unions corrupt and tyrannical, and land reform mostly token was not the whole story of the Obregón regime. The Revolution was surging through all sectors of Mexican society, bringing new attitudes, changes, and sometimes improvements. A great awakening of the nation's talent and energy was beginning. Mexicans were doing things for themselves, learning how to use modern machinery and apply their ingenuity to problems ranging from improving the poorest farms to the development of the highest artistic expression. The foreigners who now came were no longer capitalists and their managers, but Latin American refugees and European radicals. Often they stirred up new currents and enriched the Revolution.

For the first time since Juárez and Lerdo, public education received strong official support. The minister of education, José Vasconcelos, a writer and philosopher of high standing, and his successor, Moisés Sáenz, began a movement that caught the approval of the outside world. Vasconcelos wanted the Mexicans to learn from both their Spanish and Indian heritage, for, like Bolívar, he felt the American race was the product of a fusion and should respect all its ancestors. In creating a thousand new schools and sending out many hastily-trained primary teachers, he stimulated a great outburst of missionary zeal to make Mexico literate. Itinerant instructors moved from village to ranch to hacienda to slum, teaching adults the letters and numbers and, often, basic Spanish. Thousands of children were set to singing, dancing, painting, and making pottery in the hope, which was fulfilled to an amazing degree, of awakening creative instincts that would bring both money and esthetic satisfaction to the poor. Cultural missions taught backward communities the rudiments of hygiene and nursing. The motion picture was another invaluable means of modernizing Mexico, at least in showing the population something of the outside world. Earnestly as Vasconcelos and his associates strove, their task was indeed overwhelming. Four out of five Mexicans were illiterate in the early 1920's. And when rural folk learned a little, they were far more likely to emigrate to the United States or flock to Mexican cities than to remain in their home communities.

The cultural awakening pervaded more sophisticated circles. Always appreciative of foreign music and performers, Mexico City came to realize it had talent of its own. Carlos Chávez began his long career of orchestral conducting and the composition of music based on Indian themes. Mexican literature had usually copied European models until the Revolution, which absorbed most of the writers in pamphleteering or politics. Now with the stability of the 1920's, they began to write poems in praise of the machines that promised to help the masses and to compile turgid autobiographical novels that built up a mythology glorifying the Revolution. It was Mexican painting that attracted the most admiration from abroad. A school of artists undertook to immortalize the Revolution on acres of murals in public buildings, blatantly idealizing the colored races and other victims of the old regime in paintings larger than billboards. Radical propaganda though much of it was, and likely to inspire defacement from outraged conservatives or Christians, some of the work had great artistic merit. Mexico, like Haiti, produced the

first truly creative American art, indigenous and not imitative. Diego
Rivera, David Alfaro Siqueiros, and José Clemente Orozco became the
most admired of these political artists. Along with their efforts were less
famous experiments in reviving pre-Columbian painting and sculpture.
This blossoming of Mexican talent was not poor advertisement for the
Revolution.

Obregón presided over these developments while he was building a
cohesive political machine that permeated the entire republic, from the
federal district of Mexico City to every isolated *patria chica*. His fanning
of the Revolution did not include attacks on the Church and, with a
few exceptions, the great landowners. With foreigners, too, he was hesitant. The oil industry, which British and American companies all but
monopolized, was functioning at its peak and was too important a source
of revenue to the Mexican government to be disturbed. The United
States demanded assurances that the holdings of its citizens not be
confiscated under the constitution of 1917. Obregón demurred, for to
bow to *gringo* pressure was to invite deposition. At length, in August
1923, Mexico informally promised not to seize American oil properties
acquired prior to 1917. In exchange, the United States restored full diplomatic relations with her neighbor after a suspension of ten years.

This rapprochement came none too soon for Mexico. As the election
of 1924 approached, it was apparent that Obregón might need American
support in order to continue the Revolution under his hand-picked successor. This choice was his friend and fellow Sonoran, Plutarco Elías
Calles, who had taught school and tended a bar before he rose as a
political general in the Northern Dynasty. Opposition to Calles came
from a wide variety of sources, mostly discontented liberals backed by
conservatives who were pleased to aggravate any difficulty of the ruling party. A revolt began and threatened to spread. American arms were
made available to the loyalist army, however, and Obregón even received
permission to ship his soldiers through a part of Texas in order to flank
the rebels. Victorious in this test of arms, Obregón also succeeded in imposing his heir. On December 1, 1924, he retired, and Calles took office.

GILDED SOCIALISM AND CHURCH-BAITING UNDER CALLES,
1924–1934

Under Calles the regime continued in the direction Obregón had
set. Its atmosphere was somewhat more harsh, for Calles was less willing to tolerate free speech than Obregón had been. Also, he was a harder
man than Obregón, who killed only when he felt it necessary, and then
discreetly. Under Calles a larger number of troublesome persons were
executed or "suicided." Policies begun in the previous administration
continued much the same. Luis Morones waxed richer and more confi-

dent than ever, and the CROM rewarded its leaders so lucratively that men began to speak of gilded socialists. Generals and ranking politicians continued to luxuriate in the friendly climate provided by the regime. However, land reform moved much faster, with about 8,000,000 acres being apportioned in Calles' term, and the government also pushed work in public health and sanitation with commendable vigor. Articulate Mexicans gloried in their Revolution, in books, newspapers, and painting. Much as there was to be proud of, some of this boasting was in antipathy to the exultant capitalism of the United States. Not a little was mere demagoguery inspired by the government to convince the Mexican people that they were achieving more than they were.

In one respect Calles demonstrated his revolutionary virtue with a vengeance. At last the Church came under the concentrated attack that had been threatened so long, implicitly since the fall of Díaz, directly after the constitution of 1917. The clergy were, of course, and had reason to be, enemies of the Revolution. Many in the ruling government clique were irreligious as well as anti-clerical. They also wanted the wealth of the Church, to break its power over the masses, and to neutralize potential rallying points of the opposition. President Calles went out of his way to humiliate several members of the higher clergy. Then, he required the registration of all priests and the closing of seminaries. Faced with the long-dreaded assault, the clergy elected to resist. On July 31, 1926, a cessation of clerical activities was ordered, a strike as the government labeled it. Church bells stopped ringing, causing an eerie silence in a land where chimes had always paced the day. Priests no longer administered the sacraments or held mass in public. The government replied by hunting down clandestine friars and nuns, of whom there were still a few, and by taking over Church lands, artistic objects, and funds. In many localities the authorities hounded priests and bishops. Also, the teaching of atheism was encouraged, and parochial schools were shut. Devout citizens were often troubled and hurt. As in the French Reign of Terror, some hid priests and helped them move about the land in disguise. Often they found ways to strike back by assassinating officials and beating up important men of the Revolution. A *cristero* movement took shape, chiefly in the western mountain states, to mobilize the faithful in war against the godless republic. Chalking "V. C. R." (*viva Cristo Rey*) on walls became an act of devotion to Christ the King and a threat to the persecuting regime.

By 1929 both sides had enough of the tension. The government relaxed its campaign, and the strike ended. But within two or three years several state governments were acting on their own to ruin the Church and, in some cases, to extirpate Christianity. All priests were expelled from Sonora. Most were deported from Yucatan, Tabasco, and Veracruz;

in this last state the authorities proudly announced there was only one priest left. In the entire republic perhaps only 300, five per cent of the number in 1911, were openly carrying out their duties, and they could wear clerical garb only in their churches.⁵ Calles accomplished much of what he intended. Anti-clericalism gratified the ideologues and made property available for distribution among his henchmen. Yet he widened the antagonisms that had beset Mexico since the Reform, and he unnecessarily agitated and distressed much of the population.

The persecutions of the Church caused a revulsion in many quarters of the United States. A powerful campaign to intervene got under way, fostered by some Catholic circles but backed also by many other elements. Intervening in Mexico was by no means unprecedented, and many Americans felt that the excesses of the Calles regime called for punishment. Holders of defaulted Mexican bonds or worthless currency, absentee owners of lands long seized or ruined by the Revolution, and oil companies and mine owners who smelled doom were likely to come forward with many altruistic reasons for American rescue of the Mexican people. Opponents of such proposals made themselves heard too: the American Federation of Labor, many liberals, and some Protestant groups. In the end, the non-interventionists carried more weight than those who demanded another expeditionary force, at least in the mind of President Calvin Coolidge.

In the autumn of 1927, when American criticism of Mexico was at its peak, Coolidge began what would later be known as the Good Neighbor policy by sending as his ambassador to Mexico City a Wall Street financier who seemed the worst possible choice for this post. Instead, Dwight Morrow became the first of the current generation of ambassadors who regard their chief function as the cultivation of good will among all classes of the nation to which they are accredited. Morrow at first startled, and then pleased, the Mexicans by approaching them in an informal, friendly manner. Here was no arrogant capitalist threatening invasion or insulting Mexican nationalism, but a kindly fellow who was most *simpático*. Morrow and his wife and daughters went about casually, sincerely admiring things Mexican and addressing themselves to all who would respond. The Mexicans were delighted and took them to their hearts. Soon the ambassador was on excellent personal terms with President Calles, with whom he dealt as a confidential friend. And when Charles Lindbergh, who had thrilled the world with his solo flight across the Atlantic, flew down to Mexico City and married one of Morrow's daughters, the Mexicans were so joyful it seemed that generations of ill will had evaporated. This was not really the case, but both Mexico

5. When outside, they often wore their   collars around their thighs, inside the trouser legs.

and the United States, officially and popularly, were happy to be friends again after a century. Morrow persuaded Calles not to molest the oil companies for awhile and to be reasonable about American claims. Probably he influenced him to let up on the anti-clerical campaign. It is less likely that the financier slaked the fires of the Revolution, as some Mexicans have charged, for Calles had abandoned much of the radical program quietly and on his own.

In 1930, when Morrow retired in a glow of warm feelings, Plutarco Elías Calles was no longer president of Mexico. But he was still its ruler. He had manipulated the election of 1928 so as to restore his old partner, Alvaro Obregón, with whom he planned to play leap-frog in the presidency. Before the date set for his inaugural Obregón was assassinated by a fanatical youth who had permission to sketch the president-elect during a public luncheon at San Ángel, near the capital. Ambassador Morrow deftly supported President Calles in an effort to ward off an unseemly struggle for control of the government, or worse, a bloody convulsion. Calles called in various national leaders and made a dramatic announcement. Mexico was through with caudillos, he said. The time had come for true constitutionalism without an overly strong president. He himself would never be president again, not even to cover this emergency. Therefore, he sought and obtained the approval of those who mattered to install a rather neutral figure, Emilio Portes Gil, as provisional president until the next year, when an election could be held to choose a regular executive to fill out the term Obregón had intended to serve, a term recently lengthened to six years. It seemed a statesmanlike measure, and Calles' international prestige was very high.

Calles may have saved the republic from bloodshed by his exhibition of authority and apparent selflessness. It soon became clear, however, that he had no intention of giving up his power. Pulling together the principal parts of the machine which Obregón and he had constructed so capably, he officially made Mexico a one-party state. Organizing the PNR (*Partido nacional revolucionario*) with himself as *jefe máximo* (supreme chief), he was able to perpetuate his domination of the government at all levels, national, state, and local, while controlling the army and the agrarians. The CROM was left out. Luis Morones had finally antagonized Calles, possibly because he pressed too hard or was too greedy. Or, it may have been that Calles had become conservative and wished to subordinate the unions to business. Whatever his reasoning, the CROM began to wither away.

Calles' own power did not wither at all. Although he moved to Cuernavaca, where his neighborhood was known as "the street of the forty thieves," he continued to rule. A rigged election in 1929 brought

Pascual Ortiz Rubio to the presidency.[6] Rubio was the most abject of puppets, but he failed on one occasion, in 1933, to consult Calles about an appointment. His consequent resignation and journey abroad caused cynical smiles. Abelardo Rodríguez obediently filled out the remainder of the term. During the cloaked *callista* rule of 1928–1934 it seemed to many that another *porfirista* system was taking shape. There was only one party, which Calles managed in the style of Díaz. Politicians mouthed the demagogic slogans of the Revolution while disregarding its ideals but for one—baiting the Church. Calles even announced that land reform was a failure and intimated there would be no further divisions. A new class of business men enriched by the Revolution now had the favor of the government; it was safe to discipline or discharge employees regardless of the unions. The corruption and cynicism of the PNR with its moneyed politicians, venal army officers, and gunmen were blamed, more or less correctly, on Plutarco Calles.

The times, however, were not congenial for this type of system. The world-wide depression was bringing about violent changes all over Latin America, and the New Deal in the United States. To Mexico the latter was more influential. In spite of herself, she had often followed the rhythms of American politics and was about to do so again. A new generation had grown up which deplored the corruption of the Revolution's founders. Marxists were becoming increasingly prominent; they had practically taken over the ministry of education and much of the public school system. From the ruins of the CROM a radical labor movement was being reconstructed, led by an off-again, on-again Communist named Vicente Lombardo Toledano. The landless were still largely unsatisfied, their appetites whetted and then frustrated. More than twenty years had passed since the slogan, "Land and Liberty," had stirred the rural masses. Most Mexicans had neither, though they had heard propaganda until they distrusted all politicians. As the election of 1934 approached, Calles sensed that it would be wise to make concessions to the resurgent left. The PNR announced a bombastic Six Year Plan to please radicals who admired the contemporaneous Soviet Five Year Plan. Publicists were cut loose to stimulate the tired, and atrophied, Revolution. Perhaps Calles believed it would release resentments harmlessly to talk about these matters a bit.

6. Not without armed opposition, however, and considerable popular ferment. José Vasconcelos, the former minister of education and a famous intellectual, ran against Portes Gil. When his defeat was announced, he fled to the United States, and a few army units made menacing moves, which Calles thwarted. It seemed to many that Mexico had become unsafe, or at least uncomfortable, for men of ideals like Vasconcelos.

Lázaro Cárdenas and the Revolution in Flower, 1934–1940

CALLES dictated the choice of General Lázaro Cárdenas, the 39-year-old governor of Michoacán, as the PNR candidate for the presidency in 1934. A Tarascan Indian from a family not quite as poor as most Mexicans, Cárdenas had fought on the side of Zapata, Villa, and finally the victorious Carranza-Obregón forces against the *zapatistas* and *villistas*. A general at twenty-five, he had served the Northern Dynasty in several capacities, most conspicuously as governor of his native state. In 1934 he was generally respected as an adroit politician who had said "Yes" to the right people and as a refreshingly incorruptible official. There was little to suggest that he would rival Juárez as the most popular president in Mexican history, which he presently did.

Cárdenas began his rise to greatness soon after his nomination by the PNR late in 1933. He needed to do nothing but await the announcement of his victory at the polls in July 1934, but instead he undertook a most strenuous campaign, penetrating nearly every section of the republic, publicizing the Six Year Plan as though the election were not predetermined. He continued his speeches and travels after his triumph, indicating that he wanted the population to understand and approve this program. It was obvious that he stirred up much enthusiasm, both for himself and his platform. When he took office in December 1934, some of the older heads in the PNR felt slightly nervous. Did the new president really think the Six Year Plan was in earnest, and was he too dense to grasp that he was expected to be a *callista* puppet? Calles himself professed great confidence, saying that Cárdenas was more a son to him than his own offspring. Cárdenas repeatedly hailed the *jefe máximo* as "father and teacher."

It was not long before Mexico became too small for both Cárdenas and Calles. The president, who had a puritanical streak, precipitated the breach by closing gambling casinos and brothels owned by important *callistas*. Then he announced a number of far-reaching educational and social programs without securing the approval of the *jefe máximo* and his neighbors on the "street of the forty thieves" in Cuernavaca. When a wave of strikes broke out in the spring of 1935, President Cárdenas openly supported labor and alarmed the older oligarchs by saying that the factories ought to be taken over by the workers. Calles was no man to shrink from a challenge. Still in control of the PNR, he stirred up anti-clericalism in certain states in order to embarrass Cárdenas, who was known to be "soft" on the clergy. In June 1935 the *jefe máximo* publicly condemned the runaway radicalism of the new administration in economic affairs and alluded to the fate of Ortiz Rubio, the puppet president he had ousted in 1933. The political crisis reached a state of unbearable tension. Around Calles in Cuernavaca grouped the familiar generals, politicians, and union bosses of the PNR hierarchy. In Mexico City Cárdenas lined up faithful military units and surrounded himself with the new crop of agrarians, intellectuals, and labor leaders. A hint that he would nullify the anti-clerical laws brought him much popular backing in all sections. Meanwhile, the poor politicians and office-holders did not know whose side to take; as well as they could, they kept lines open to both leaders. At last it became clear that Cárdenas had out-manuevered Calles both militarily and in popular appeal. Thereupon he dismissed *callista* officials and won a stirring vote of approval from congress, which had long been a supine collection of claques for the *jefe máximo*. The straddlers then rushed to the president's side. Calles was closely guarded for some months until, in April 1936, he was suddenly forced on an airplane and flown away to Los Angeles.

The dramatic victory of the young president signified a massive renewal of the Revolution. In a triumphant administration Cárdenas came as near as was humanly possible to fulfilling its promise—or threat—and in doing so he established himself as a living myth among leftists and the poor. His personality greatly impressed the common people. The fact that he was an Indian, as Juárez had been, gave a vicarious satisfaction to the majority of the population. Cárdenas' stamina in traveling all over the republic by rail, automobile, horse, burro, and foot was justly admired. In exhausting himself thusly he learned much about the country that escaped official reports, and he convinced many neglected communities in isolated sections that he truly cared about their needs. He seemed eager to do good and to hear about the humblest troubles. Every Mexican had a standing invitation to wire him free and to take up his time in interviews, whether the presidential headquarters was in the capital or migrating about the rough country. Even if the theatricality, indeed the demagoguery, of these methods is admitted, Cárdenas drew the lowly into the common fraternity of Mexican nationalism as no other leader had, and they almost deified him.

Peripatetic angel of mercy though the president seemed, he was hard-minded enough to master the grim forces that determined Mexican politics. Several highly important generals and governors he deposed by force or threat of force; the assassination of others he must have condoned. Democratic liberties he usually respected, but always with the admonition that no speaker or writer threaten the regime too pointedly. Many potential dissidents were appeased with the fruits of corruption in office. As safely as he could without disrupting the party, Cárdenas removed the tarnished profiteers of previous administrations and replaced them with younger, more idealistic men and, sometimes, with radical fanatics committed to Communism. Whomever he used, he displayed a superb skill in extracting from men what he required and keeping them circumscribed. In this he resembled Profirio Díaz. He imitated Obregón in gathering into his own hands the ties that bound the three main pillars of the new society: the military, organized labor, and the agrarians. The generals remained above the law but subject to the president's will. Cárdenas undermined them by having the enlisted men indoctrinated with the slogans of the Revolution and by giving them more status and numerous material benefits. Since they had previously been treated like brutes, they responded warmly to the president's solicitude, and it was generally believed they would support him instead of their immediate commanders should a breach occur. It was much the same with organized labor. Cárdenas strongly backed Vicente Lombardo Toledano in uniting the workers in the CTM (*Confederación de trabajadores mexicanos*), a highly militant organization. In disputes with management there was no question where the government's sympathies lay. Lest the leaders of the CTM, who perpetuated the gilded socialism and tyrannical methods of the CROM, become too assertive, Cárdenas carefully cultivated the workers themselves. Should the top officials and the president ever clash, it was likely that Cárdenas would be the stronger. Finally, the agrarians were brought into a mammoth union, the CNC (*Confederación nacional de campesinos*), which Cárdenas set up so that its organization was quite separate from the CTM, even likely to compete with it, and so that he could undercut its leaders by reaching the simple farmers who almost idolized him. The modernization of the power structure was formally recognized in 1937, when the PNR was dissolved and the PRM (*Partido de la Revolución mexicana*) took its place. This change signified not only the alterations Cárdenas had effected in the old Obregón-Calles machine but a higher position for intellectuals, and it gratified those who agitated for a leftist popular front of the type so common during the 1930's. Cárdenas had done more than re-shuffle the alphabet. He had created an efficient party which reflected the political realities of his time.

LAND, INDUSTRY, AND OIL

At long last the program of land reform, about which so much rhetoric had been expended since 1910, received vigorous impetus. Cárdenas distributed about 44,000,000 acres, more than twice as many as all of his predecessors combined. Often he ordered the immediate division of haciendas on the spot, the way Zapata used to do in Morelos, and left instructions for piped water and a schoolhouse before he invaded another community. In other cases a more deliberate process was carried out by government commissions, who loaned the peons money to purchase holdings. A collectivist, Cárdenas really preferred the *ejido* to the sub-division of haciendas to individuals. Thus villages would take possession of large estates and supervise their operation on a communal basis. The largest experiment in collective farming was in the Laguna district of Durango, where 30,000 families took over a tract of more than a half-million acres. This undertaking posed many dangers, not the least of which was the substitution of bureaucratic tyranny for that of the vanished *hacendado*, and also the inequitable division of labor and profits. The Laguna experiment appeared successful enough, however, to justify the creation of other vast collective farms in the coffee regions of the Pacific coast, the henequen country of Yucatan, and the cotton and sugar cane areas of the torrid south. While the ranches of the north did not lend themselves to either collectivization or sub-division, Cárdenas initiated ambitious irrigation projects to transform certain arid areas into farmlands which would ultimately be partitioned.

These reforms lifted the hearts of the rural proletariat, whether they won a few acres of their own or shared them with their fellows in *ejidos* or the great collective farms. Yet there was simply not enough land to go around, and the majority still lacked opportunity. Furthermore, the splitting up of the haciendas tended to lower production, despite urgent efforts on the part of the government to pour tractors, plows, mules, harvesters, and technical experts into these areas. Both critics and proponents of agrarian reform could make out convincing cases. For better or worse, however, the land reform was fully launched. No politician would dream of trying to undo it.

Cárdenas' championship of industrial labor enabled the CTM to become mighty and improved conditions in nearly every respect for urban workers. These were increasing considerably, for the Industrial Revolution was again making itself felt in Mexico after many interruptions. Many small factories for food processing, textiles, and cement were started. Towns and cities grew, absorbing some of the surplus farm workers. And the depression of the 'thirties dampened conditions in Mexico only occasionally and in spots. Cárdenas and the men about him had large ambitions with respect to industrialization, aspiring to nothing less than the transformation of the national economy. Mexico had always exported raw materials and imported most finished goods. Now the regime wanted to create an industrial plant which would process these raw materials, thus providing employment for a large proletariat, raising the purchasing power of the general population, and improving the standard of living.

While he would have been offended by the term, "national social-ism," which Hitler was using for his system, the words epitomize the gen-eral objective Cárdenas had in mind. His frequent anti-capitalist utter-ances and denunciations of foreign investors discouraged those entrepre-neurs who might have facilitated the program, but it went ahead rapidly nonetheless. Domestic rather than alien capitalists established new in-dustries, most of which succeeded and caused the labor force to expand. Conditions blessed the owners, who somehow looked after themselves, often in collusion with supposedly socialistic labor leaders and officials. The Cárdenas administration and the CTM blessed the workers. Both the middle class and the urban proletariat accordingly prospered, and Mexican industrialization flourished. One peculiarly difficult problem re-fused to yield to Cárdenas magic, the railway system. Constructed long ago by foreigners and bought up for the republic by Díaz, it was now in a very decrepit state. The president despaired of straightening it out, much as he needed good transportation for the industrialization pro-gram, and turned the railroads over to the workers. Joyful as socialists and the labor force were, the change was scarcely beneficial. Feather-bedding, inefficiency, and costs mounted to appalling heights. So did the accident rate—on what had once been one of the model networks of the world. This experiment in socialized industry gave little comfort to collectivists and poor service to the republic.

Cárdenas' most sensational experiment had to do with the petroleum industry, which was one of the most productive in the world and had long brought large revenues to the government. The British and Ameri-can companies who operated it had come under increasing harassment from the Cárdenas administration, which accused them of failing to ob-serve Mexican laws with respect to labor. The president himself had scant patience with these foreigners; as a bucolic socialist he had an ab-surd mental image of the wicked capitalists of Wall Street and London. A protracted dispute between the oil firms and the CTM, whose merits were obscured by righteous propaganda on both sides, led to a complete deadlock. As might be expected, Cárdenas backed the workers and saw to it that the courts decided in their favor. The companies refused to submit. Suddenly, on March 18, 1938, President Cárdenas announced the expropriation of the foreign oil properties. It was a stunning action, for the world had not yet become accustomed to such confiscations. But the Mexicans were exultant; all factions rallied joyously behind the presi-dent. It was the British who lost the most property and who most ur-gently needed Mexican petroleum. When they protested in frigid wrath and intimidated drastic action against the republic, Cárdenas broke off diplomatic relations. He could not resist reminding Britain that she had refused to pay her World War I debts to the United States.

As for the Americans, vigorous protests emanated from New York and Washington. Relations of the two republics had been very cordial since Dwight Morrow's mission in 1927. Between the Roosevelt and Cárdenas administrations there were especially strong ties of sympathy. Ambassador Josephus Daniels had become popular in Mexico in spite of his connection, as one-time Secretary of the Navy, with the bombardment of Veracruz in 1914. Now, with Cárdenas defying the United States and Britain, it remained to be seen how strong the new friendship was. After some weeks of indecision President Roosevelt, prompted by Daniels, decided not to chastise the Mexicans. International threats from the Axis made western hemisphere unity a paramount consideration; besides, large oil companies were anything but pampered favorites of the Roosevelt administration. Since Daniels had sided with Mexico, he enjoyed another surge of popularity south of the border, and Latin Americans in general were relieved to see that the Good Neighbor policy was no mere cloak for Yankee imperialism.[7] Not until 1941 was a settlement arranged. Mexico agreed to pay the American concerns $24,000,000 for their lost properties, about one-tenth the amount they claimed.

The immediate effects of these confiscations were not heartening to Mexico. Cárdenas nationalized the oil fields and refineries, creating a government monopoly known as PEMEX (*Petróleos mexicanos*), only to find he had few technicians, tankers, or customers. Production and revenues declined drastically, exports to nothing. The rest of the world managed well enough without Mexican oil, even during the worst of all wars. Among the several morals of this famous incident was one which many small nations were slow to recognize: a minor power which considers its special export essential to the international economy and attempts a sort of blackmail on this supposition may well be deceiving itself.

FLOWERS AND WEEDS

During the stirring 'thirties much of the outside world became enthusiastic about Mexico's cultural renaissance. No longer did it need to be affirmed on faith alone that a New World society could draw from its native past and from Europe to produce an admirable fusion. To the satisfaction of many students Mexico had proved it, and her example encouraged other Latin Americans who had long debated the merits of acculturation, the combination of European and Indian ways, and assimilation, in which the native was rejected as Western civilization engulfed their countries. Mexican painting and music demonstrated the

---

7. More than one Latin American also entertained tempting thoughts about American property in their countries. If Mexico could take over oil installations without being punished, then other republics might do the same.

success of acculturation. Rivera, Orozco, and Siqueiros, together with their disciples, made themselves and their nation world-famous by producing works that fused Indian and European techniques. Carlos Chávez did the same in his musical compositions, and as director of the national symphony orchestra he was a much-sought guest abroad. Mexico, as influenced by Hollywood as perhaps any country in the world, developed an excellent motion picture industry of her own which earned both money and prestige in other nations, particularly in Latin America. The publishing industry of Mexico City waxed until it surpassed in some years those of Barcelona and Buenos Aires both in output and merit. Of the many novelists inspired by the Revolution, the one most acclaimed abroad was Mariano Azuela, (1873–1952) whose numerous novels narrated the dramatic events especially after 1910 with compassion, insight, and realism. José Vasconcelos, who had done so much to build the public school system in the 'twenties, had many admirers both within and beyond his country, eccentric as some of his essays became. Of more stature was the eminent philosopher, Antonio Caso, whose mysticism, Catholicism, political conservatism, and puritanical preachings appeared to be completely at variance with the mood of his country but which somehow gained him great prestige.

Mexico's active cultural life was not only a matter of creative individuals, who might appear unpredictably and inexplicably in any milieu. It was, rather, something of a patriotic enterprise, resting on government subsidies in many cases, deliberate stimulation of interest by the authorities, and a cult among the educated classes. The circle of enlightened persons grew not only in numbers, which it did very rapidly in the Cárdenas years, but also in sophistication. This circle rested ultimately on the system of public education, especially after the Church lost most of its functions as custodian of the nation's culture. Universities and colleges expanded very fast. They were lively centers for the social sciences, fine arts, humanities, and, as always in Latin America, political ferment. They lagged badly in libraries, laboratories, and other facilities and were notoriously weak in the physical sciences and technology, a deficiency which would retard the nation's development in future years. Cárdenas revived the cultural missions to bring the letters and public hygiene to backward sections. He personally ordered the opening of countless schools as he traveled over the country, and he imparted to teachers everywhere a missionary zeal. That the ministry of education fell into the hands of Communists caused much rancor. Leftist teachers were often ejected from villages with sticks and stones. Not a few suffered worse fates. Whatever their politics, however, the huge instructional staff reduced illiteracy from about 60 to 50 per cent during the 1930's. People who learned to count and read did not necessarily appreciate the complexities of Marxism.

Another factor in the cultural revival of the times was the arrival of thousands of refugees from Spain, many of them men of letters, scientists, professional people, and technicians. Cárdenas was almost alone among Latin American rulers in taking the side of the Spanish republic in the memorable civil war of 1936–1939. Generous as his decision to admit the exiles was, they stirred up ancient hatreds of the peninsulars and created numerous complaints of Mexicans being dislodged from positions by better-qualified foreigners. That many of these Spanish refugees were Communists or anarchists disturbed Cárdenas not at all. He might have said with sincerity what the Chinese Communists later said in bad faith, "Let a hundred flowers bloom!" The president gloried in the diversity of political opinions. At the same time that he consorted amiably with Stalinists he befriended Leon Trotsky, who lived in Mexico a few years until he was murdered by an orthodox Communist. While he permitted a considerable revival of Catholicism by neglecting to enforce the anti-clerical laws, he also encouraged the schools to teach atheism. An increase of Communist power in the CTM was matched by a growth of conventional bourgeoise sentiment among the business classes, both of which Cárdenas blessed. Fascists, Nazis, Trotskyites, Communists, and other groups frequently demonstrated insolently in public without government curbs. However contradictory or disruptive these manifestations might be, Cárdenas regarded them as signs of a healthy ferment in Mexican life. Approaching the problems of his time realistically and tolerantly, he succeeded better than most of his contemporaries, the gay utopians and the glowering dictators.

Farewell to Revolution

THE REVOLUTION COOLED: MANUEL ÁVILA CAMACHO, 1940–1946

Cárdenas' great popularity did not tempt him to change the constitution and run for reelection. For a successor in 1940 he picked the colorless General Manuel Ávila Camacho of his cabinet. Opposing Ávila Camacho and the PRM was another general, Juan Andreu Almazán, a wealthy man who was as conservative as anyone in public life dared to admit. The campaign was waged as though the results were not already settled, lasting eighteen months and provoking much popular passion. Almazán rallied nearly everyone who resented the PRM or the Cárdenas administration, including the militant right which admired Mussolini, Hitler, and Franco. Ávila Camacho had everything in his favor: the vast party machine, the army, labor, and the agrarians. All the resources of the republic were readied to impose him by force if the voters failed to cooperate. On election day in July 1940 "only" 350 Mexicans were killed or injured. President Cárdenas sadly observed that Mexico was not yet a democracy. Though Ávila Camacho probably had a good majority, the twenty-to-one margin announced by the authorities insulted the nation's intelligence. Crying fraud, Almazán fled to Texas to organize a rebellion, as Madero had after his defeat in 1910. In this case Uncle Sam subtly interfered, refusing to allow Almazán, at this time of Hitler's greatest victories, to set fire to Mexico. Thus Ávila Camacho took office in a peaceful atmosphere with American approval. Cárdenas withdrew gracefully into private life, to spend the next twenty-odd years serving in important temporary posts and championing leftist, often Communist, causes.[8]

From the beginning it was evident that President Ávila Camacho was going to moderate the Revolution. During the campaign his affirmation, "*Soy creyente*" (I am a believer), suggested an end of anti-clericalism. The laws oppressing the Church he omitted to enforce altogether, or nearly so. Priests again dared to appear in public wearing their clerical habits, at least occasionally, and once in awhile religious processions made their way through the streets. While the laws remained on the books and could be enforced if a local leader happened to be anti-clerical, the national government no longer sought to extirpate or even hamper Catholicism. It was no threat to the state, and at best the country was now only tepidly devout, women more so than men. Other evidence of a change in mood came in labor disputes. To their dismay, labor potentates found the government far less friendly than in the days of Cárdenas. Workers learned to their hurt surprise that the authorities would not invariably take their side if they clashed with management. The new administration was far more interested in promoting economic growth than further social benefits; business interests accordingly enjoyed a much more favorable climate. The railroads, which had been turned over to the workers so airily by Cárdenas, went back under government ownership. However, Ávila Camacho was not a reactionary. What he sought was a balance or a consolidation, to discipline those who had been too long spoiled and to mollify those who had been mistreated in the Revolution. As a demonstration of the new conciliatory mood, he appeared with all six of the living ex-presidents of the republic on the balcony of the national palace during the celebration of Hidalgo's summons, on September 16, 1942. A gathering of this type would

8. He was one of the recipients of the Stalin peace prize in 1959 after a much- publicized tour of Communist East Europe and China.

have been unthinkable at any other period since the inflamed priest rang the bell at Dolores in 1810.

One important factor in bringing about the studied calm of Mexican politics was World War II, with its promise of riches for those who were not deeply involved in the fighting. Mexico had failed to share in the prosperity that World War I had stimulated. As the second struggle deepened, Ávila Camacho aligned his country beside the United States in an anti-Axis posture. Strident criticism of this policy from the left, which was very articulate, abruptly ceased in June 1941, when Hitler invaded the Soviet Union. Rightist agitation mounted, however, some of it directed by Axis agents but most of it deriving from native-born conservatives and clericals of the *cristero* type. A *sinarquista* (without anarchy) movement which extolled Franco Spain, Vichy France, and Mussolini's Italy attracted many followers in those segments of society most opposed to the Revolution, often rural clericals and well-to-do youths in the cities. *Sinarquismo* caused some concern but was not strong enough to affect national policy. Ávila Camacho stayed on course, vigorously supporting the United States after Pearl Harbor and getting congress to declare war on Germany in May 1942 when a Nazi submarine sank a Mexican tanker. Soon Mexico was at war with Japan as well, partly because she feared a descent on her long, exposed Pacific coastline.

Many Mexicans were dismayed to find themselves outright allies of the United States, but the benefits of this partnership were too obvious to deny. Uncle Sam eagerly loaned money to his neighbor and dispatched droves of technical experts to improve the railroads and highways, to start factories, and to advise Mexican agrarians on means of improving food and cotton production. All the minerals Mexico could extract the United States purchased at high prices. Surplus American war equipment went to the Mexican armed forces. So serious was the manpower shortage in the United States, the two republics agreed on a plan to bring thousands of Mexican workers as contracted laborers, or *braceros,* north of the Rio Grande. Probably a much greater number migrated unofficially by swimming that river, hence the term *mojados* or "wetbacks." Whether they were legal or informal immigrants, countless Mexicans harvested crops in the United States, worked in factories, or joined the U.S. armed forces during the war. While this situation was marred occasionally by anti-Mexican outbreaks in border areas, it generally benefited both countries. And many moneyed Americans, cut off from Europe by the war or from resort areas by military establishments, flocked to Mexico, where rationing was unknown and night life flamboyant. Mexican ships participated in the patrols against Axis submarines, and one fighter squadron of aviation flew with the Far East Air

Forces for a few weeks prior to V-J Day. To Mexico the war meant identification with the democracies, improvement of her productive system, a
release from agrarian pressures, and glorious profits. It also gave her favorable international publicity. President Roosevelt conferred with Ávila
Camacho in Monterrey in 1943, and the important inter-American conference of 1945 was held in the castle of Chapultepec.

Many changes occurred in the nation's economy, largely as a result
of the war-time prosperity. Above all, industries grew to a startling degree, pushing Mexico toward self-sufficiency, widening her middle class,
expanding her labor force, and generally elevating the standard of living. Most of this development was the work of Mexicans themselves,
much as they owed to the Americans who helped finance it or who advised them on technical matters. Given half a chance, the Mexican population responded to new opportunities with alacrity. So much was going
on in the industrial scene: food processing, steel manufacture, beer-
making, meat packing, fabrication of textiles, glass, and cement, and
assembly of imported machine parts. Much as individual enterprises differed, some failing and more succeeding, the national economy as a
whole was taking giant strides. Progress outran the skills of the people,
and great effort went into training workers. One group of businessmen in Monterrey created a technical institute, which quickly became
an imposing college for preparing young Mexicans for further industrial expansion. Along with the production of so many new products
went the creation of distribution facilities. With modern wholesale
houses and shops springing up everywhere, the familiar village markets
survived as mere vestiges of an older Mexico.

The Ávila Camacho administration did more than provide a climate
for such spirited economic development. Dam-building, irrigation projects, electrification, and other public works went ahead vigorously, with
even more progress than Cárdenas had obtained. The foreigner reappeared in Mexico as an owner and enterpriser, often surreptitiously, for
the laws were strict and the population more nationalistic than ever. Yet
it was easy for the government to connive with moneyed alien investors,
devising sham corporations to conceal their subsidization of Mexican
business or simply ignoring them. This cynicism was not really new in
Mexico, and no one appeared to object very much. Ávila Camacho did
many other worthwhile things, such as establishing a far-reaching social
security system and fostering education on a scale never before known.
With the brilliant Jaime Torres Bodet as his minister of education, he
built and staffed schools and distributed textbooks. One law which
caught the imagination of the public and which produced splendid results was the requirement that each literate Mexican teach an illiterate
to read and write, "Each one to teach one," as the slogan went, sounding

better in English than in Spanish. It may have been, as the government reported, that the rate of illiteracy dropped from 50 to 30 per cent during these years. In summary, Ávila Camacho consolidated and cooled the Revolution. It was so victorious by now that it could afford to accommodate itself to its former enemies, even to permit almost full democratic freedom. In 1945 the PMR changed its name to the PRI (*Partido revolucionario institucional*). The Revolution was victorious, at peace, and institutionalized.

THE NEW PLUTOCRACY: THE ADMINISTRATION OF MIGUEL ALEMÁN, 1946–1952

For its entry in the presidential race of 1946 the PRI selected a civilian, Miguel Alemán, who at forty-four had already received important awards from his party, notably the governorship of Veracruz and the ministry of interior. Handsome, manly, and likeable, he faced Ezequiel Padilla as his opponent. Just why Padilla, once ambassador to Washington, foreign minister, and delegate to the United Nations, exerted himself so strenuously to win an election bound to be predetermined is a mystery. Perhaps he enjoyed the publicity, or hoped to make the Mexicans more international-minded. The fact that he left the PRI to start a new movement suggests the more relaxed atmosphere of the country. In what was said to be, and possibly was, an honest election, Alemán won more than three-fourths of the votes.

During the campaign Alemán had intimated anti-Yankee sentiments, probably because Padilla was so identified with the United States. It was soon seen that such utterances had no significance. Alemán well knew the importance of the United States to Mexico's economic welfare, and the wartime intimacy continued. He became the first Mexican president to visit Washington while in office. And he extended a lavish welcome to President Truman, who delighted the Mexicans with an unannounced early morning visit to lay a wreath on the monument of the *niños héroes*, the cadets killed in 1847 as the Americans took the hill of Chapultepec. Liberal loans from the United States continued to pour into Mexico through the Export-Import Bank. American investors found themselves cordially treated in Mexico, no matter what the laws said. Tourists from the northern republic taxed Mexico's facilities as they discovered a poor man's substitute for Europe, a land at once picturesque, romantic, friendly, and inexpensive. If the Mexicans imported American goods to the limit of their purchasing power, they also sent nine-tenths of their exports to the United States, as well as uncounted thousands of workers, many of whom remained. So great was the intimacy of the two countries some prophets anticipated an eventual amalgamation.

Such predictions were quite far-fetched, for aggressive patriotism in

Mexico sometimes became chauvinistic and xenophobic. And Mexicans were making heartening progress in solving their own problems. The ultimate problem, political stability, was settled by the one-party system which ruled firmly but in an atmosphere of relative freedom. Usually, the worst that happened to enemies of the PRI was a denial of jobs or business opportunities. As much credit as the regime deserved for creating an acceptable political system, its cynical methods did little to raise the tone of public morality. Alemán's administration was the most corrupt of any since the Revolution, his associates brazenly sharing in the profits so many were making. Most officials of any rank or importance spent freely, lived luxuriously, and found opportunities to invest, usually in urban real estate, money that evidently came from somewhere.

One reason for the unashamed venality was the exhilarating prosperity of postwar Mexico. An incredible construction boom was remaking the country. Mexico City was transformed into a modernistic showplace, dazzling to Americans as well as to Europeans. Despite its unfortunate soggy base, which causes it to flood and sink in a frightening way, the capital attracted provincials like a magnet, draining the nation of talent, as some complained. Becoming the principal industrial center of Mexico, it grew into one of the dozen largest cities of the world and showed no signs of slowing down. Other cities also were swollen with migrants and engaged in rebuilding themselves in the new industrial era: Monterrey, Guadalajara, Puebla, and Veracruz. Acapulco developed into a fantastic tourist center on the tropical Pacific coast. The extravagant building boom in the cities was no more spectacular than the creation of thousands of small factories and assembly plants which largely accounted for the prosperity. The *Nacional Financiera* greatly facilitated these enterprises. Established in 1934 as a purchasing agency, it expanded into a huge credit institution to finance all types of economic activity the government wished to foment. Many of its funds were really of foreign, mainly American, origin, but the nature of the *Nacional Financiera* was such that this awkward fact could be disguised, as could the illicit personal profits gained by officials in its operations. Apart from the growth of industries, Mexico also experienced many improvements under Alemán. Farm-to-market roads, airports, docks, highways, telephone lines, radio stations, and new railways were built. Alemán started a master program to construct hydroelectric installations that would provide irrigation, potable water supplies, and electrification on a scale undreamed of a scant ten years before.

As happened in most of the world during these years, the farming population of Mexico found itself declining relatively as an urban, industrial society grew. To be sure, the Alemán administration combated this trend in various ways. The land distribution program continued, though small holdings to individuals were favored over the *ejidos* so dear to the collectivists of the Cárdenas period. Furthermore, the government strengthened several inherited projects to educate the farmers to appreciate the possibilities of mechanization, fertilization, soil conservation, and improved seeds, particularly hybrid corn. Yet centuries of wasteful agricultural practices and innate rural conservatism were difficult to overcome. All of Mexico produced only a fraction of the corn Iowa did, and food still had to be imported. Indeed, it seemed by mid-century that the Mexican agriculturist had nothing but the pride of ownership to compensate him for all the promise and furor of the land reforms. He lived almost as poorly as he had under Díaz. The agrarian population had diminished to about half the national total, and its income was only one-fifth. Among the depressing factors in the situation was that farms or shares in *ejidos* could become available to only 40 per cent of the rural populace. There was simply not enough land to go around, and many students of the problem wondered if the whole program had not been misguided. It was better in the cattle industry, though the per capita consumption of meat grew much slower than the increasing numbers of livestock would suggest. Apparently the more prosperous classes and the export market absorbed most of the ranch products. Hard times afflicted the latter, however, when it developed that large numbers of Mexican cattle suffered from the dread hoof-and-mouth disease. A remarkable program of American-Mexican cooperation in attacking this malady led to the vaccination of 60,000,000 cattle and slaughter of more than half a million animals in the southern republic during Alemán's administration.

Mexico's new mood of unashamed materialism enabled President Alemán to carry out two policies unthinkable a few years before: the settlement of the British oil claims of 1938 and the termination of socialist teaching in public education. The first was arranged easily enough in 1949 with the British Labor Government with Mexico's promise to pay more than $20,000,000, a sum much smaller than the petroleum companies had demanded earlier. By this time PEMEX had established some order in the wrecked oil industry. While its efficiency was a subject of joviality both to honest Mexicans and to foreign experts, the fields produced, the refineries operated, the tankers sailed, and the government again drew substantial revenues. As for the changes in public education, Alemán yielded to the clericals and to common sense. There was no point in seeking to transform the school system, which was strained as it was to provide basic instruction to the growing population, into a socialist missionary enterprise. While a considerable number of Communists and other radicals remained as teachers, they were cowed into some degree of conformity with the rest of a society which demonstrated every day its attachment to the profit motive.

Alemán's most spectacular boon to education was the construction of a university city for the ancient University of Mexico in the volcanic wastes south of the capital. This wonder of modernistic architecture and flamboyant colors offered a splendid plant for 25,000 students, everything, in fact, but a good full-time faculty. Students and instructors alike found it awkward to ride buses more than twenty miles each way every day, and they were distracted by frequent indignation meetings and political riots. Conditions were much the same in the six regional universities and the various professional and technical schools. If fine buildings could be provided and enthusiastic youths gathered, then eventually, perhaps, sound learning might be nourished. There was reason for hope.

ADOLFO RUIZ CORTINES, 1952–1958: A PURITAN IN PLUTOCRACY

Rumors concerning the indecent prosperity of Alemán's associates, perhaps of the president himself, seemed well-supported as the election campaign of 1952 approached. A popular general and wealthy contractor named Henriquez Guzmán set out to reform the PRI and to run for president as its candidate. Although he had for a time the support of Lázaro Cárdenas, whose prestige was immense, the PRI hierarchy declined to name him, instead choosing a most unromantic statistician, Adolfo Ruiz Cortines, from Veracruz. Guzmán organized a "peoples' federation" and undertook to mobilize that section of the public whose animosity toward the PRI had long been increasing. He campaigned most vigorously and stirred up wide support. Ruiz Cortines, on the other hand, seemed a dull and mediocre time-server in the party. President Alemán contributed to the campaign by, among other things, promoting a "depistolization" movement to prevent murder on election day. With its usual brazenness, the official machine announced Ruiz Cortines' victory by the ratio of more than three to one, a probable exaggeration. When he took office in December 1952, the plain-looking president astonished the country by making a public announcement of his estate, which was quite modest, and insisting that other ranking officials do the same. A shower of resignations removed some of the most egregious grafters.

Ruiz Cortines suggested Calvin Coolidge. Himself frugal, he sought to encourage integrity in others. Yet his campaign for honesty gradually lost vigor as the public tired of it, though officials became more circumspect than they had been under Ávila Camacho or Alemán. The new president's successful promotion of woman suffrage achieved far less than he had hoped in bringing about public morality, but it was a further sign of Mexico's desire to be as modern as other countries. By reacting against former President Alemán, who had many uncomfortable months wondering whether he would be prosecuted, and cultivating former President Cárdenas, Ruiz Cortines brought further respectability to his administration.

Mexico was growing so fast that few could comprehend what was going on. Her population, which had been about 16,000,000 when Cárdenas took office in 1934, was twice that number in 1955, and it appeared to be growing at the rate of a million a year. Monetary statistics regarding increases in wealth, trade, and production were almost meaningless in view of the devaluation of the peso, dictated by continuous inflation, but it was obvious that expansion in nearly every field was enormous. As barrels of oil, head of livestock, bales of cotton, bags of coffee, bars of steel, and production of almost all other types were reckoned, new records steadily appeared, only to be broken in a short time. The completion of dams and electrical projects in Michoacán, Veracruz, and along the Rio Grande furnished further stimulation to the economy. Huge irrigation schemes turned some of the arid northwest into productive areas like those in California and Arizona. A dramatized "march to the sea" led to the clearing of much of the torrid south. With all of these developments the Ruiz Cortines administration had some connection, either in fomenting them or in permitting them to occur. It was the energy of the general population, however, awakened as it was by modern technology and stable government, that explained most of this progress.

Mexico's relations with the United States continued to be as intimate as successive presidents had proclaimed they ought to be. About as many Americans entered Mexico each year—several hundred thousand —as tourists or enterprisers as Mexicans went north as seasonal laborers. Mexico sent 57 per cent of her exports, mostly perishable food, coffee, and mineral products, into the United States; 77 per cent of her imports came from there. Impressive as this commerce was, it was declining steadily, an indication that Mexico was finding other customers and suppliers. In matters concerning the Cold War or the United Nations, the Mexican government cooperated with the United States, though it was obvious that latent anti-Yankee feeling of the historic type was far from extinct and that Communists were active in stirring up hostility to the northern republic. Generally, Mexico had a very high reputation during the 1950's, particularly among Latin Americans. There was much to admire: a dynamic economy, a considerable culture, and above all, an

effective government. Inhabitants of Caribbean or Andean dictatorships had reason to look with envy on the liberties Mexican citizens usually enjoyed.

THE REVOLUTION SUSPENDED: ADOLFO LÓPEZ MATEOS, 1958–

As the Ruiz Cortines administration drew to a close in 1958, it
seemed apparent that the president had failed to extirpate venality and
to purify public life. Also, the potentates of the PRI were no longer in a
mood to experiment with reformers. Accordingly, they declined to hold
an open convention but, rather, chose the 1958 candidate in a conclave
of party bosses. This selection proved to be Adolfo López Mateos, minister of labor under Ruiz Cortines, an athletic fellow from the state of
Mexico. For the first time in many years the principal opposition was
frankly conservative, a nationalist party which nominated Luis Álvarez.
The campaign was, as all Mexican campaigns have been since the Revolution, long and noisy, and as earnestly conducted as though the outcome
might really be in doubt. There was little pressure other than occasional
rough street mobs which molested Álvarez' gatherings and government
loudspeakers which drowned out some of his speeches. López Mateos, of
course, won the election by a vote announced as ten to one in his favor.

When López Mateos took office in December 1958, the PRI was as securely in control of the republic as ever. Since 1920 the official machine
had been in power without interruption or serious threat. By achieving many of the Revolution's aims it had rendered age-old political controversies irrelevant. It had absorbed many elements of the former opposition and indoctrinated successive generations. By the early 1960's the
chief complaints emanated from state party officials, who charged the
national leaders with being too dictatorial and with monopolizing government revenues. Federalism, a good cause in the 1820's when the republic was born, was still potent. Yet the presidency had been so institutionalized and policy-making so centralized, prospects were poor of reversing the trends. The PRI gave no sign of fearing overthrow or drastic
reformation. On the contrary, it permitted other parties to organize
and the population at large to express themselves freely. Only in vote-
counting could democratic practices not be endured.

Was the Revolution dead? One would not gather as much from the
fervent invocation of its heroes and ideals, the slogans, and names applied to streets and projects. It was, however, clearly suspended. Mexico
was no longer seeking to become a socialist paradise but, instead, to develop as a state capitalist enterprise where the profit motive was far from
scorned. The government made basic economic decisions and set policy,
as under Porfirio Díaz, as under the Spanish colonial system. Private

property in anything but farmland was accumulated avidly. The high-living moneyed classes, who out-numbered wealthy American tourists in most centers of luxury, might be regarded as the new aristocracy. If so, it was a fluid one, drawing on the old landed class of former days, government princelings, and economic royalists, all of whom were likely to be adept at tax evasion and other forms of law breaking. The middle classes had been growing since the last years of Díaz; now they were a formidable force in society. Rural proletarians were moving to the cities and becoming urban proletarians, at least superficially Westernized. Industrial workers were powerfully organized and, in many ways, privileged. They were less class conscious than before, however, and many of them were productive or fortunate enough to rise into the bourgeoisie or higher. The clergy was much more in evidence than it had been during the 1920's and 1930's. Indianism, which the Revolution had set out to promote, seemed a forgotten cause in the 1960's in a Westernized capitalistic society. That was really what Mexico had become, and few of her citizens objected to it.

López Mateos dealt with the problems typical of a country growing fast and unevenly. Inflation was a chronic concern, for profits outpaced wages and living standards rose in jerky motions that brought suffering to many families. Soon after he assumed office, he had a crisis on his hands in the way of a huge strike caused by this inflation. Mexican workers saw their undoubted progress being overtaken by constant rises in the cost of living. Much to their dismay, López Mateos, the former minister of labor and long-time champion of the unions, mobilized the entire force of the government to defeat the strike. His action signified that big labor had, at least temporarily, reached its peak and could expect no more special favors. Another labor problem was embarrassing for the Mexican government to acknowledge, since it reflected the fact that a large labor surplus existed in the country. This was the continuous seepage of Mexican farm workers into the United States, sometimes as seasonal laborers, sometimes as illegal immigrants. When the *bracero* program for contracted workers at last ended, only official statistics registered a decline in this movement. The "wetbacks" continued to flow into the United States in unknown numbers, doing so even when tales of American exploitation circulated widely and their own government sought to discourage the current. Manifestly, they could do better in the northern republic than at home, whether they settled there or merely worked a few weeks harvesting crops. It was physically impossible for the two governments to patrol the 1600-mile frontier at all times. The only indicated solutions were for Mexico to industrialize at a still faster rate and to create a domestic market to absorb her products.

Mexico's progress was remarkable even when similar or greater strides in other countries are considered. But was it sufficient? In the early 1960's the answer loomed as negative. The magnificent efforts made in the field of education could not accommodate the growing population, and half the children of school age were receiving little or no instruction. Heroic increases in agricultural production did not parallel the rise in population, and half the inhabitants continued to be under-nourished, as they had always been, partly because of unwise eating habits and ignorance, but fundamentally because food was inadequately produced and distributed. Few countries had done as much as Mexico to educate their peoples in hygiene and to provide sanitation and good water supplies. Yet a majority of Mexicans were in fragile health, and all the efforts of the government to improve conditions lowered the death rate and thus aggravated the problem by prolonging the lives of many sickly people. In short, the population explosion, which threatens so much of the planet, loomed as a specter that might eventually defeat the Revolution. Frightening as this possibility was, hope rather than dread dominated the atmosphere of Mexico in the early years of the 1960's.

26

The Caribbean Island Nations

Where Spain Lingered

D URING the long centuries of Spanish power Cuba played a major role in naval strategy but was otherwise almost insignificant. The *flotas* and galleons converged in Havana's well-defended harbor to be refitted before undertaking the voyage to Spain with American silver. This port and, to a lesser degree, Santiago de Cuba and San Juan in Puerto Rico, were also useful bases for royal naval units and convenient points to concentrate garrisons in time of war. Otherwise, the islands were not rich jewels in the Spanish crown, being only modestly valuable as exporters of horses, hides, sugar, coffee, and tobacco, this last the most important item. The population engaged mostly in subsistence agriculture and was not large. Indians had long since been killed off or absorbed, peninsular immigration was light, Negro slaves composed a probable majority, and many persons of mixed blood had appeared. Sleepy backwaters of the Spanish empire Cuba and Puerto Rico may have been, but they were not hateful places. Gentle hills and valleys, beaches, grasslands, fertile areas, and a few mountains offered a pleassant site for living. The climate, but for hurricanes and a rainy season, was also kind. It was never cold, and winds usually blew away the accumulations of torrid atmosphere. Somehow the population adapted itself comfortably to conditions, its attitude likely to be careless and relaxed, often gay.

Much as the Wars of Independence rocked Latin America, Cuba and Puerto Rico remained steady, the former earning the title of "ever-faithful isle" from a grateful monarchy. Three principal reasons accounted for this situation. First, the presence of royalist garrisons and fleets served to dampen temptations to rebel. Second, creole refugees from other islands terrified the white elements with tales of Negro atrocities and caused them to be wary of provoking a race war. And third, the usual criticisms of the Spanish system had less relevance on the islands than the mainland, since the former already traded considerably with foreigners and Spanish rule, at least in Cuba, was fairly efficient and conciliatory after the British occupation of Havana in 1762–1764. Thus the two islands passed through the fervid period of revolution with little more than a few small scares caused by isolated patriots or secret societies. Liberation from the outside was also deterred by lack of Mexican or Colombian naval power and the tacit agreement of the Anglo-American powers, both of whom coveted Cuba, that it was just as well to let a weakened Spain continue her domination.

Fernando VII had no inclination to deal seriously with the issues that had caused his other possessions to rebel, and so the islands remained under the peninsular bureaucracy headed by a governor or captain-general in Havana and San Juan. Things went on much as before, the Spanish imperial regime being no worse than that of mainland dictators and rather lenient about permitting trade with foreigners. Conditions in the islands improved very slowly, and mass poverty continued to be the norm. Tobacco was the most promising crop for export and also the most socially desirable, for its cultivation encouraged small landowning. Sugar cane raising was also lucrative, enough so that African slaves were imported after Spain had officially abolished the traffic and Maya laborers were sometimes bought from Mexican rulers. Havana and San Juan, as well as other towns, had the trappings familiar to a colonial system: a peninsular elite, a few cultured creoles, small middle classes, and squalid slums. If there was much resentment of Spanish rule it seldom showed. A Negro poet who called himself Plácido agitated for Cuban independence, but he was shot in 1844, and his memory was revered only much later.

The worst problems arose from the fact that Spain kept degenerating as the century wore on. Beset with civil wars, radical outbursts, and military dictatorships under Isabel II (1833–1868), the monarchy governed worse than before, trying the nerves of the colonials by alternating between phases of slackness and ferocious oppression. A slowly growing impatience with Spanish rule was not sufficient during the 1840's to stimulate a desire to be annexed to the United States, who tried to purchase Cuba in 1848 and met a cold rebuff from both Madrid and Havana. Narciso López, a filibusterer of uncertain or no convictions, landed in Cuba in 1850 with a small force of liberators but met no response. When he tried again in 1851, he was easily captured and killed. In 1854

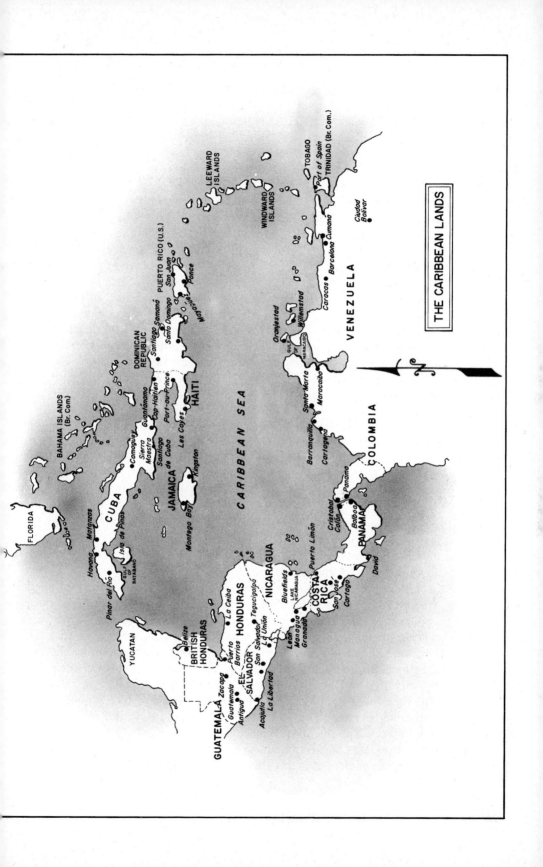

THE CARIBBEAN LANDS

three bucolic American ministers to European courts met in Ostend, Belgium, to issue a manifesto calling upon Spain to sell Cuba or see it taken by the United States, but their own government repudiated them, Europeans smirked, and the intended beneficiaries of this transfer ex-, hibited little interest. Other projects for American annexation, which usually had to do with increasing the number of slave states, likewise came to nothing.

Not until 1868 were considerable numbers of Cubans mentally prepared for freedom from Spain. In September of that year the exasperated subjects of Isabel II expelled her in what they called "the glorious revolution." A month later a group of Cuban patriots echoed them with the *grito de Yara*, which called for Cuba's independence, and thereby started the terrible Ten Years' War in the island. As always, Spain proved stubborn, though she was undergoing a fantastic sequence of revolutions and civil wars during that decade. At first, the liberal interregnum government invited Cuban and Puerto Rican deputies to participate in the *cortes* in Madrid, which, like the *Cortes* of Cadiz earlier in the century, was sincere in planning reforms but utterly unwilling to relinquish Spanish sovereignty. The issue of Negro slavery was awkward; the Spanish reformers favored emancipation, but a planter lobby and creole fears of racial strife induced restraint, and all that emerged was a law of 1870 providing for the freedom of all new-born Negroes. Meanwhile, the insurrection in Cuba worsened, with each side seeking to outdo the other in atrocities. Spanish forces held Havana and most of the key points, but the rural areas became anarchical. Under Amadeo I (1871–1873) and the republic (1873–1875) the war refused to abate, though the latter abolished slavery. Not until the restoration of the Bourbons in the person of Alfonso XII in 1875 was Spain able to end the rebellion by making many concessions, and in 1878 the fighting finally halted, leaving Cuba in dreadful condition. The principal leaders made no peace and went abroad to rally for another day.

During the following seventeen years comparative order prevailed. Spanish immigrants entered both Cuba and Puerto Rico in large numbers, and economic life revived. While the royal administration was supposedly liberal, and a measure of self-government was conceded, its weakness and ineptitude continued to be irritating to the colonials. Several developments in these years affected the future significantly. One was the effective and final abolition of Negro slavery. Another was the decline of tobacco production in both Cuba and Puerto Rico relative to sugar, which meant the growth of large plantations at the expense of small farms. Yet the sugar cane industry suffered because of the competition of beet sugar and superior methods in other Antillian islands. Since Spain could not supply the modern means for extracting juice from the cane and the United States could, planters looked to the northern neighbor for machines and capital. Thus American investors, with the approval of the royal government, began to purchase sugar plantations, or *centrales*, in both Cuba and Puerto Rico and build modern refineries. In 1890 the United States granted preferential tariffs to Cuban sugar, and for three years the island's economy boomed.

This wave of prosperity broke with the world depression of 1893 and the American tariff act of 1894 that ended the preferential treatment. By that time intellectuals in the islands had become deeply anti-Spanish for ideological reasons, and the masses were inclined to blame the mother country for their poverty. From outside came torrents of propaganda by exiles in other Caribbean lands, New York, and Florida. Rebellion, which had continued like a low-grade infection in the mountains of Oriente province even after 1878, flared up in other regions. By 1895 groups of Cuban refugees were ready to sail home and join the rebels, among them Tomás Estrada Palma, who still claimed he was head of the government set up during the Ten Years' War, Antonio Maceo, a brilliant Negro commander, and old Máximo Gómez, the most famous hero of the 1870's. The most colorful, however, was José Martí, a Cuban now forty-two, who had known the chain gang and guerrilla warfare in his youth and years of wandering in Central America, Mexico, and the United States since 1878. Martí was an emotional orator who could make his audiences weep or exult as he wished, a great poet and journalist whose words are highly quotable. Among his conquests were many Americans, who shared his passion for *Cuba libre*. This talented man and Maceo were both killed soon after their return to the island, but the revolution proceeded.

For the last time Spain dispatched large expeditionary forces to America. General Valeriano Weyler planted himself firmly in Havana and undertook an offensive in the eastern provinces. For two years he fought the rebels, who now claimed most of the population, but failed to subdue them. While both sides committed barbarities, Weyler received by far the worse publicity in the United States, where the "yellow press" found colored reports of his misdeeds a good way to sell newspapers. As "Butcher" Weyler entered revolutionary areas, he had women and children re-settled in garrisoned towns while Spanish forces hunted down their menfolk in the fields. Contagious diseases broke out in these concentrations, and cruel food shortages occurred when the rebels cut off supplies. In 1897 the Spanish government recalled Weyler and made determined efforts to pacify Cuba with gentle means, vainly, for Cubans by this time were thoroughly aroused by hatred of Spain, desire to enjoy power, and will to be free. Besides, they knew that Spain was seldom consistent enough to abide by any policy for long.

The Spanish-American War and Liberation

BY THE beginning of 1898 the Spaniards had the upper hand in Cuba and almost complete control in Puerto Rico. Enough danger to American residents remained, however, to induce the United States to send the battleship *Maine* to Havana, both as a warning to Spain and as a haven for U.S. citizens. In February the ship blew up, killing 260 sailors. Whether the cause was mechanical or the result of mischief by Spaniards, Cubans, or private parties has never been determined, but the American public had had enough of Spanish activities in Cuba, and their government was eager to obtain Caribbean bases. President Mc-Kinley thereupon demanded that Spain offer Cuba self-government, which was reluctantly conceded, and then allowed himself to be pushed by public opinion into insisting that the island be granted independence. On April 20, Congress voted that Spain must either leave Cuba or be forced out, and it also promised that the United States would not annex it. The Spanish-American War thus began, to end three months later with Spain's catastrophic defeat and, as it turned out, cultural regeneration. The United States, which had disregarded the opposition of all the continental European powers, emerged as a great power itself. Cuba was to become independent, but Puerto Rico (or "Porto Rico," as the Americans long called it) was destined for a very different career, as were the Philippines and Guam.

Even had the American public not been awakened to the delights of ruling other peoples, it was truly unthinkable to leave the Cubans unguided. Thousands of Spanish civilians were in danger of expulsion or worse, and the United States felt obliged to see that they were not despoiled. Traitors and heroes had not been identified beyond all doubt in the island, so that the fate of all property titles was uncertain. Poverty, hunger, and sickness were everywhere; much of the population was armed and migrating about the island to no good purpose. Accordingly, the Americans elected to install a workable government before leaving the Cubans to their own devices. Brushing aside the pretensions of the provisional Cuban government, which in fact had little control of the situation, the liberators established a military regime, which in 1899 was placed in the capable hands of General Leonard Wood. In two years Wood disarmed the population by paying off the warriors of independence, created a civil administration, put together a makeshift system of courts, designated 3,000 buildings as schools, and had roads and telephone lines built. A census he supervised reported the population at 1,500,000, one-third of whom were Negro by American reckoning. For once grasping the intense nationalism of the Cubans, the American authorities did not staff the new schools with imported teachers but sent a thousand or more Cubans to the United States for training. After Dr. Walter Reed verified the theory of the Cuban, Dr. Carlos Finlay, that yellow fever was carried by the mosquito, the Americans nearly wiped out this insect, and not only Cuba but most of the world afterward conquered the disease.

Much as the Cuban experiment had fired the emotions of the American people, it was not intended to last long, for the government was committed to the cause of independence. Under the eyes of the U.S. Army the adult males elected an assembly to frame a constitution, which created a centralized republic and, no doubt to the gratification of the occupying power, separated Church and state. And then the Americans, who believed they had given Cuba her independence with little help from her own patriots, presented the bill for this service in the form of the so-called Platt Amendment. The most important of its conditions was Article III, which gave the United States the right to intervene in Cuba to preserve its independence and to maintain a government adequate for the protection of life, property, and individual liberty. Furthermore, dispossessed Spanish subjects were to be compensated by Cuba, and no Cuban government was to contract a debt whose servicing surpassed current revenues after defraying the ordinary expenses of administration. Nor could it make treaties with foreign powers that might impair its sovereignty. Cuba was not to claim the Isle of Pines, and she must sell or lease to the United States shore property for naval bases. The Cuban assembly was greatly affronted by these demands, but when it realized that the United States would not evacuate until they were accepted, it incorporated them in the constitution in 1901 and in 1903 further formalized them in a treaty. In May 1902 Tomás Estrada Palma, who had borne the title of president of the republic for a quarter-century, became so in fact. The republic, however, was really an American protectorate, and Estrada Palma wondered aloud whether it contained any citizens.

The First Generation

NO LATIN AMERICAN country joined the ranks of free countries as auspiciously as did Cuba in 1902. An island, she had no immediate neighbors to quarrel with; with so many of her people mixed-blooded, gaping racial distinctions were not to be a determining factor in her society; the traditional caste system had departed with the Spaniards, and there were few planters or rich men; the Church could not perpetuate colonialism, since it was separated from the state and most of the clerics who opposed the republic had been ejected; and the United States had set the new nation up and was ready to defend it, to buy its products, and modernize it. Furthermore, the climate was pleasant and the population healthy for the tropics and inclined to enjoy life. Most Cubans were fervent patriots, eager to make the republic a success. There was every reason to hope that Cuba, avoiding the unhappy experiences that befell the other Latin American republics in their first decades, would become a showcase of peace, brotherhood, and plenty. Scarcely anyone foresaw that the reverse would be its fate, that Puerto Rico instead would be favored by fortune.

Tomás Estrada Palma, the first president of *Cuba libre*, was a venerated leader of sixty-seven when he took office in May 1902. Long as he had served as provisional president in the hard times, he had developed little capacity for administration. Or were the Cubans ungovernable? Whatever the trouble, the nation was tasting the delightful fruit of freedom for the first time and ignored the president when he called for restraint. Riotous factionalism appeared, caused less by ideological issues than the desire to work for the government, the only sure way to win a living, often without doing any labor. Congress was also irresponsible, not attending to the basic laws necessary to make any new nation viable but occupying itself with patronage and bonuses for war veterans. From the very first a degenerate character overwhelmed Cuban political life. Only in settling various issues with the United States was the first administration effective: the treaty of 1903 that incorporated the Platt Amendment; the leasing of Guantánamo Bay and Bahía Hondo (which was not used and reverted to Cuba in 1912); the acquisition of the Isle of Pines, not formalized until 1925; and a reciprocity treaty which gave Cuban products a 20 per cent discount—and therefore an immense advantage in the American tariff structure.

Having failed to float above partisan strife, Estrada Palma associated himself with the conservative coalition, the Moderate Party, and was reelected in 1905. The Liberals, however, charged that the election was being rigged and mostly boycotted the polls; by 1906 they were in full revolt, already displaying the intractability that so often mars Hispanic political life. Estrada Palma found himself unable to cope with the situation and appealed to President Theodore Roosevelt to support him. Roosevelt was most reluctant to send troops, since Europeans had, no doubt with envy, been charging him with imperialism, and instead of an army he dispatched a mission headed by Secretary of War William H. Taft to seek a reconciliation of the Cuban factions under Estrada Palma. But the old president, now a broken man with little prestige, resigned his office and retired to a farm to live out his last years in poverty, as disenchanted a liberator as his Latin American predecessors eighty years earlier. His precedent in dying poor was one no other Cuban president has been willing to follow.

Things were now so chaotic that Roosevelt sent American military units. Taft managed to disarm many Cubans and set up another administration, which he turned over in October 1906 to Charles E. Magoon, a Nebraskan who had been governor of the Panama Canal Zone. Magoon ruled for two years, enforcing order, training native administrators, and decreeing basic laws the Cuban congress might have enacted sooner. Hoping to placate the factions, he distributed government jobs among Liberals and Moderates alike and probably fattened the bureaucracy to satisfy the claimants. His liberal award of pardons and contracts may also have sprung from a desire to make everyone happy, but they won him little credit among the Cubans, who charged him with extravagance, favoritism, dishonesty, and tyranny. Subsequent assessments show that Magoon did not deserve the hateful reputation that still clings to his name in Cuba. His real offense was personifying Yankee tutelage, and for this he could not be forgiven.

It was apparent by now that American interest in Cuba transcended humanitarian and strategic considerations. The island had so perfect a setting for a vast sugar cane industry that American investors were eager to purchase ever more plantations and modernize them with machinery. Between 1901 and 1923 such outlays were destined to grow from $80,000,000 to $1,500,000,000. Since the price of land mounted rapidly, Cuban owners were willing to sell their properties, though they often had little to do with their capital but gamble it away. As a result, onetime farmers often wound up as workers on scientifically-operated plantations owned by non-residents. If it was comforting that they had to work only three months out of the year, at harvesting time, there remained the matter of securing an income for the other nine months, and the rural masses found themselves little better off than in colonial days. Beneficial as the inundation of Yankee gold was to Cuba as an entity, its social effects were sad in many cases, a situation that lay beyond the concern of the United States and, it must be admitted, of Cuban politicians.

Late in 1908 the American authorities judged the island ripe for another try at self-government and conducted an election. The winner was General José Miguel Gómez, a Liberal who was shrewd and magnetic and, like all Cuban politicians for a generation, had been a "hero" of the War of Independence. Cubans liked the way he restored cock-fighting and the official lottery, two features of the colonial regime they remembered with enchantment. And since revenues from sugar exports now gave Cuba the highest per capita tax income of any Latin American country, Gómez had ample funds to build up an inflated bureaucracy that readily became noted only for its efficiency in making office-holders wealthy men. Gómez himself acquired a large fortune, and his administration established a precedent for venality that all subsequent Cuban governments have respected. In a negative way he set another evil example by failing to recognize or deal with the absorption of the nation's economy by foreign capital. Although a few other Latin American leaders regulated the activities of aliens so they would not overwhelm or distort their countries, nothing of this sort occurred to Cuba's rulers. In later years Cubans would blame the Americans for buying so much of their sugar and for investing money in the island. None of their politicians was statesmanlike enough to control the situation until the republic had long been an economic colony of the United States.

President Taft, whose administration coincided with that of Gómez, and who had reason to remember the strong nationalism of the Cuban people, hoped to avoid intervening again in their affairs. Two incidents in 1912, however, served to break his resolve. The first intervention was merely verbal, a word to Gómez that it would be unwise to sponsor a bill before the Cuban congress calling for the dismissal of all public servants who had ever been tainted with royalism in the War of Independence. Gómez complied, probably grateful for the excuse to block its enactment, for a storm was already brewing. The second occasion was a rising in the heavily Negroid section in eastern Cuba, where black leaders maintained that, though their race had performed most of the fighting in the struggle for independence and had faithfully supported the Liberal Party, it had been denied a proper share of the spoils of government. While the insurrection was suppressed quickly, the United States landed a small marine force at the town of Daiquiri, ostensibly to protect American citizens but probably to sober the rebel leaders and enable Gómez to re-establish his control.

Gómez was entirely willing to be reelected in 1912, but stronger men than he wished to run the carnival of graft. Alfredo Zayas managed to steal the Liberal nomination from the president, whereupon Gómez, largely out of spite, threw his support to the Conservative (formerly Moderate) candidate, General Mario García Menocal. Since the army obeyed the president, voters were manhandled and boxes seized, thus assuring the victory of Menocal. The new president had been educated at Cornell, worked with American interests in Nicaragua, had a good war record, and was rich enough to inspire hopes that he might be honest in office. Yet his administrations, for he was reelected in 1916, were quite as tawdry as that of Gómez and the Liberals. By now it was cheerfully accepted that all politicians were venal and that public officials devoted themselves to amassing wealth rather than to carrying out their duties. Few seemed to care if appropriations for schools or public works were rarely translated into visible improvements. In this way Cuba was weirdly democratic. Her upper classes were not landed aristocrats or other holdovers from Spanish times but former warriors, now in politics, who had started out poor, might have any mixture of racial strains, and were subject to some rotation in office, the real source of prosperity. And gambling, the obsession of the population, also served to redistribute wealth on bases other than birth. At least Cuba had a fluid class structure, and anyone could hope to become rich.

Menocal's tenure from 1913 to 1921 featured the first so-called "dance of the millions" in Cuban history. Immense loose wealth came into the island from the United States because of rising sales of sugar and continued investment. During World War I the boom reached its peak, with the government enjoying revenues enough to support tens of thousands of office-holders, who nonetheless found ways to supplement their salaries, and with owners of sugar *centrales* taking enormous profits. Not all of these owners were American by any means, for flamboyant new homes, clubs, and casinos in Havana and occasional gaudy villas in the countryside testified to the opulence of a native plutocracy. Almost none of Cuba's political leaders and few indeed of her intellectuals seemed to think of spreading the bounty to the masses or otherwise displayed a strong social conscience. A conspicuous exception was Enrique José Varona (1849–1933), a professor of philosophy at the University of Havana, whose preachments spread beyond the student body, though with little effect. Varona condemned the United States for arrogating the right of tutelage over Cuba, and yet he freely criticized the republic's own leaders and electorate for their blindness to real needs. After a short excursion into public life he retired in disgust. Fascinated with lucrative opportunities which only a few could really exploit, Cuba, like the Congress of Vienna, danced but did not advance.

World War I not only stoked Cuba's boom but caused another armed intervention by the United States. President Menocal's reelection in 1916 was the occasion for disorders, since the Liberals claimed their candidate, Alfredo Zayas, should have won. After much pressure, Menocal agreed to hold fresh elections in certain districts, but, fearing that these too would be rigged, Zayas and his followers revolted in February 1917. To President Woodrow Wilson, who was then preparing to take the United States into the war, a Cuban upheaval would have been most inconvenient. Accordingly, American marines landed in Oriente, the Liberal stronghold, and Zayas was unable either to win the new elections or to overthrow Menocal. With the marines remaining until the end of the war, President Menocal was secure, and it is not surprising that he was a fervent supporter of the Allied cause.

By the time for another election, in 1920, Cuba had fallen on evil days, her dance of the millions broken up by the fall of sugar prices from 22.5 cents a pound in May to 3.75 cents in December. Many Cuban farmers who had hitherto held out against buyers were now bankrupt and, frequently in panic, sold their lands far too cheaply. Rural workers now were without even seasonal labor, though most of them could raise foodstuffs, for Cuba was not over-populated and it was fertile. Every bank in the island owned by Cubans failed, and the Menocal administration had so disintegrated, it could not even conduct a proper election. Thus the main political leaders invited General Enoch H. Crowder, an American who had served with the Magoon regime earlier, to supervise the test at the polls. The campaign was bitter. Liberals blamed President Wilson for depriving them of victory in 1916 and had rallied under former President Gómez on an anti-American platform. Conservatives were so disgraced by Menocal's administration that they assumed a new name, the National League or Popular Party, and nominated their opponent of 1912 and 1916, Alfredo Zayas. The elections were not quite the model General Crowder had hoped for; American poll watchers stood by helplessly as troops dispersed voters and carried off the ballot urns, thus enabling Zayas to win by a close margin.

The Americans hoped that Zayas, who took office in May 1921, would set Cuba aright. A man of charm and intellectual gifts, he was supposed to be a reformer. Prosperity was returning by then, and Zayas deferred to General Crowder, now the American ambassador, who all but took charge of the government, trimming the budget, canceling contracts for public works that never materialized, seeking out responsible men to staff the administration, and reforming the national lottery. After making good progress, Crowder won a $50,000,000 loan for Cuba from the United States. As soon as the loan was secure, however, President Zayas suddenly became a patriot and rebelled against his mentor, stridently denouncing American interference. He stressed his new independence by dismissing most of the officials Crowder had picked and by squandering both the loan and public revenues on mythical enterprises that fattened the purses of his henchmen. The Americans who had looked for a reformer-president in Zayas now labeled him cowardly, vicious, and crooked. If the Zayas regime dropped to new depths in public rascality, literary circles were expressing an awareness of the evils in Cuban life to which the politicians seemed indifferent. Perhaps the most influential writer was Carlos Loveira (1882–1928), whose novels depicted the destitution of the poor and the vulgarity of the moneyed rulers. Two admired poets, Nicolás Guillén (1904–   ) and Emilio Ballagas (1908–1954), composed experimental verses to dramatize Negro themes and the hard life of the masses.

Cubans were not so devoid of responsibility as to smile on Zayas, and in 1924, former President Menocal, who was scarcely one to be righteous, persuaded the conservative coalition to nominate himself instead of the president. In revenge Zayas returned to the Liberal Party, which he had deserted in 1920, to support its candidate, General Gerardo Machado. This successful businessman, who promised "moralization" of the government, won the election. Conditions were propitious for a good administration. The all-important sugar industry was succeeding so well that its problem was now to curb production. Furthermore, vast numbers of Americans had discovered in Cuba a winter paradise and, of more significance, a glorious oasis during Prohibition. Not only did thirsty tourists flock to the island, but so did bootleggers and gangsters, and Cuba's income from rum sales added new delights to the dance of the millions. Race tracks, gambling casinos, luxury hotels, night clubs, and bordellos in Havana flourished as they never had before. In addition, American capital investment mounted rapidly, now spreading from sugar and tourism into public utilities and factories. President Machado smiled on this prosperity as though he had brought it about. He did, in fact, accomplish more than his predecessors by diversifying the economy, building railroads and highways, and regularizing sugar exports so as to steady them. His special prides were a modern automobile road running the entire 750-mile length of the island and a boast that Cuba had more teachers than soldiers, a preposterously misleading claim, for servicemen had prestige and were paid regularly.

In 1928, President Machado was popular and successful enough to persuade (or bribe) the leading politicians to unite behind him to reelect him for another term, which was now to run for six years. While he was ostentatiously friendly to the United States and enjoyed its official approval, Americans were made more and more aware of disagreeable incidents in his country. News reports occasionally mentioned riots, bloody strikes, and charges of terrorism. After the stock market crash of October 1929 sent sugar prices into a downward spiral, the defects of Cuba's social system showed in all their magnitude. The republic was a sham, a plutocracy run by scoundrels. A large majority of the people was uneducated, indolent, and very poor. Economically, the island was an American satrapy, regarded as a naval base, a glorified tavern, gaming house, or brothel, and a place where easy profits could be made. To the rising chorus of accusing voices President Machado was a perfect target, the incarnation of all the evils of a system that violated the gospel according to Marx.

No doubt there were Communists in Cuba, but there were also plain citizens who had become aware that other lands had decent governments and that a great variety of material benefits could be made available to the masses. Agitation against Machado grew in volume and desperation. Cuban exiles in New York and Florida—a familiar sight in Spanish days—advertised the poorhouse and place of terror that Cuba had become. President Machado was in no mood to pacify his detractors through reforms; in fact he continuously underestimated their numbers and fancied himself popular. His army and police tightened things until a harsh dictatorship was a fact, with censorship, the closing of institutions of learning, arbitrary arrests, beatings, and invocation of the *ley fuga*, the shooting of prisoners while allegedly escaping. The practice of dropping his victims through chutes in the Morro Castle prison to sharks in the harbor caught the imagination of the world as a typical atrocity of the regime. Students and teachers threw bombs and organized militant gangs called the ABC, only to find themselves beaten down by club-wielding *porristas* loyal to Machado. Between 1930 and 1933 unrest spread into the slums and the rural areas, making conditions as bad as they had been in the days of "Butcher" Weyler. Things got so grim that many Americans who deplored intervention in Latin America in principle insisted that their government do something about Machado.

In 1933, soon after President Franklin Roosevelt took office, the diplomat Sumner Welles was sent to Havana to see if Machado could be eased out. Since Cuba's foreign trade had by then dropped more than nine-tenths since 1929, its people were suffering and sullen, many of them in rebellion. Machado was confident of the army and, strangely, of his hold on the population's affection, but the political and military leaders Welles approached were only too eager to end the regime. It took a general strike and a surge of revolutionary violence in August to convince the president that he should remove himself. Welles' activities could not be classified as anything but Yankee intervention in Cuba's domestic affairs, but by obtaining the deposition of the most tyrannical ruler the land had known he was generally applauded. Yet he well realized the perils of such interference, and in 1934 he was instrumental in persuading the Roosevelt administration to abrogate the Platt Amendment. For some years thereafter the United States pretended to no right to intervene in Cuba and was cordial to any dictator, however odious, who would accept its friendship there or elsewhere in Latin America.

The Rise and Eclipse of Fulgencio Batista

GERARDO MACHADO had scarcely left Havana when the provisional government set up with Welles' approval was also overthrown. On September 4, 1933, a sergeant with a pistol in his hand walked into the office of the army chief of staff and calmly supplanted that officer. The new chief of staff, who advanced himself to the rank of colonel, was Fulgencio Batista, a stocky fellow with a pumpkin-shaped head and a pagan grin, thirty-two years old. Batista had Chinese, European, and African ancestry, came of a poor rural family in the eastern tip of the island, had been a barber and cane-cutter, and finally had made a career of the army. Learning to read and write in the service, he had become a stenographer and confidential secretary to high-ranking officers, a position that gave him a chance to learn the inner workings of the military. Now, as leader of an ingenious conspiracy, he was ruler of Cuba. Batista was sensible enough to see the inherent absurdity of this turn of affairs, and he wisely stayed in the background. For president he selected the idol of the students, in those days very much in evidence in Havana, Dr. Ramón Grau San Martín, a former dean of the medical school who was a high-grade rabble rouser and a self-proclaimed socialist and foe of the Yankee. The new regime was soon threatened when 500 cashiered army officers gathered in one of the capital's best hotels to defy Batista and Grau San Martín. But the street crowds and the army besieged them for twenty-five days, and after a number of shells and shots—and after the ubiquitous Sumner Welles interceded—the rebels surrendered.

Fulgencio Batista ruled Cuba for seven years, from 1933 to 1940, through seven different puppet presidents. He was not a classic dictator, but just a strong man, an army commander, an astute political operator, and a popular fellow to the common people, who could identify themselves with his success. Critics could make themselves heard in congress or in election campaigns, the courts were not entirely supine, and newspapers and students were free to accuse or advocate. So free was the ferment that pro-Axis or Communist elements agitated in ways that went beyond the conventional bounds. Batista gave women the right to vote and encouraged the working classes to unionize on a large scale. He sponsored an ambitious law to establish a genuine public education system, for Cuba's progress in this direction had been pathetically small since the days of General Wood. Cubans had reason to believe Batista had their interest at heart, as he instituted measures to provide better working conditions and safeguards against unemployment, accident, and indigence in old age. They were a passive people, despite a fondness for demonstrations; these benefits were not won through popular pressure but handed down by a brotherly leader. Finally, Batista had a good reputation abroad. He was a staunch Good Neighbor who affirmed the need for a common American democratic front, made no issue of the U.S. Navy base at Guantánamo, and accepted loans from a United States government that had now replaced the investors of yore as financier of Cuba's development. Batista visited Mexico, where he had a cordial reception, and otherwise identified himself with popular movements abroad. If he had increased the Cuban army, toppled a president every year, and occasionally borne down on opponents, he seemed for the most part a force for social democracy.

By 1940 this tough little ex-sergeant could point to seven years of comparative stability in the midst of a wholesome ferment. He had changed, becoming very fond of luxury and more decorous in his habits, but he retained the appeal of a common peasant who had made good. Batista decided to occupy the presidential palace himself and was duly elected under a constitution approved in 1939. In office he continued to manage skillfully, shifting with the currents of left and right, favoring this faction or that as expediency dictated. Without alienating the sugar potentates he allowed international Communism to make Havana a prime center for Caribbean subversion.

As another dance of the millions began in World War II, business classes and rural workers alike enjoyed better incomes, since the United States purchased every pound of sugar Cuba exported and helped improve the airports, docks, and roads of the island. The Americans also stimulated the extraction of nickel and manganese, which became substantial industries, and helped the ailing tobacco business. Wartime Havana may have dimmed slightly, but the American servicemen who replaced the tourists seldom thought its pleasure spots and vice dens failed to deserve the formidable reputations they enjoyed. In all, Batista's Cuba was as cooperative an ally as the United States could have wished.

During a visit to Washington before the war, Batista had been advised by Franklin Roosevelt, of all people, that presidents ought not to succeed themselves. While he was not eligible to run for reelection in any event, the beaming little Cuban, now fatter and more confident than ever, was so impressed with this counsel that in 1944 he did not even attempt to dictate the outcome of the election. Much to his amazement, the candidate he preferred lost to Dr. Grau San Martín, the first puppet of the Batista period, who was now estranged from his former chief. Since Grau San Martín called himself a socialist, and really was a liberal reformer, his victory suggested deeper dissatisfactions in Cuba than most observers had detected. Batista good-naturedly allowed his critic to become president and went on a tour of South America, where he made speeches praising democracy. Before long, enough evidence of malfeasance during his rule was turned up to make it unwise for him to stay in Cuba, and so he made his residence in Florida, where he lived on a most extravagant scale on millions acquired from unspecified sources.

Again a new administration proved a sad disappointment to respectable Cubans and friends of democracy. It was not because Cuba under Grau San Martín was undemocratic, for it was as free as it had ever been, with the press and students assertive and the politicians riotous. The president was really not a strong enough ruler to keep his leftist coalition from falling apart, largely because the Communists, not permitted to take it over, set out to ruin it. They also extended their power into the labor unions and rural areas, with the result that gangster tactics in the cities and lawlessness in the countryside almost reduced the island to anarchy. It was prosperous, however, for the end of World War II made Cuba's sugar, cigars, and minerals still more marketable, and American tourists swarmed to the delights of Havana in the greatest numbers ever. Just why the learned and social-conscious Grau San Martín did not try to channel the dollar income into improvements for the common people is a mystery concealed in his breast. What happened was that government officials became outrageously rich, and the president ruined his reputation by constructing an air-conditioned palace in the country with a private zoo and racing stable. One of his ministers drove a truck into the national treasury, loaded millions into suitcases, went to the airport and flew to Miami, where he sought asylum as a refugee. Not even in Cuba had graft and thievery ever been so brazen.

Carlos Prío Socarrás was elected president in 1948 with the approval of Grau San Martín, his victory being a nominal one for the liberal-reformist coalition, though it was apparent that political labels meant nothing. Prío addressed himself to the nation's worst immediate problem, dishonesty in government, by exposing his predecessor's misdeeds. More than $175,000,000 had supposedly been stolen from the public, or even more, as many suspected. By submitting former President Grau San Martín to a trial the new president indicated that he was not being grateful for past favors at the nation's expense; his acquittal was open to the contrary interpretation. Many of the accused grafters were not available for trials rigged or otherwise, having found attractive spots in other parts of the world to enjoy their money.

Certainly no marked improvement in the situation occurred under Prío Socarrás, whose administration was as grasping as its predecessor. The dance of the millions went on for the benefit of those in a position to enjoy it. American payments for sugar made the industry enormously rewarding, though it was subject to fluctuations. If the United States purchased most of Cuba's sugar exports, its citizens no longer owned most of the plantations. Cubans were now wealthy enough to buy back into their nation's prime industry, their share rising very steeply from 22 per cent in 1939 to 60 per cent in 1950. American investment capital went mainly into public utilities, mines, light industry, and distributing businesses. Havana, a glamorous residence for Cuba's own plutocracy and for moneyed aliens, was nearly rebuilt, with emphasis on luxury dwellings. It also drew tourists in such a volume that miles of new hotels had to be erected, along with restaurants, night clubs, race tracks, country clubs, casinos, and houses of vice. The surfeit of honey gave Cuba a false façade, for it remained a poor country in spite of appearances. A great majority of the people were uneducated, poorly clad and housed, and unable to buy the material symbols of modern civilization flaunted by their own rich and by foreign visitors. Their government offered them no hope, for it had practically ceased to function, sated as it was with corruption.

Batista Restored

A FALSE dawn stirred the island in March 1952. Fulgencio Batista was back in the country, had become a senator, and was expected to be elected president later in the year. To the masses he remained a charismatic hero, a farm-worker and enlisted man who had risen to be president and had done more for them than any other ruler. Batista and his friends in the military believed the Prío Socarrás administration might influence the election to their disadvantage and therefore struck first. A mere barracks revolt one night brought Batista into power in a few hours, practically without any shooting, and sent Prío Socarrás into flight. The population seemed pleased, and the international reaction was favorable. Batista acted as though a significant revolution was occurring and aroused hopes for reform. It was natural that he should devote his first efforts to making the military and the police happy, which he did with great success, but then he settled down to enjoy his position and do nothing more. Various groups, including intellectuals, students, and Communists, became restless as the grinning dictator shelved his projects for social welfare. Batista was a seasoned ruler and well knew how to handle dissidents, and soon he quieted them, employing methods far harsher than he had used in his earlier administration. On July 26, 1953, a hare-brained attack on an army post in eastern Cuba led by the brothers Fidel and Raúl Castro ended as might be expected. Batista was so confident of his power that he soon changed their prison sentences to exile, whereupon they departed for Central America. A "Twenty-sixth of July" movement they proclaimed appeared to have little significance.

Batista held an election in 1954 which duly made him president for four years. In contrast to his rather fruitful activities in 1933–1944, he seemed content to bask in a prosperous sun and leave Cuba's basic problems alone, seeing to it, of course, that his army, police, and bureaucracy had good incomes. Outwardly, times were good all during his administration. Cuba was the number one producer of sugar in the world, and the American market seemed insatiable and everlasting. The growth of mining, light industry, and tourism also kept the population at work, at least in the insouciant fashion of the island, with public works taking up any slack in employment. Cubans enjoyed a relatively high standard of health, were not reproducing too fast for their facilities, and seemed to have enough food, cigars, rum, and amusement to keep them contented. But they were not. Their problems were cruel and were growing worse; and enough educated people were aware that improvements were possible to convince the masses they were being cheated. Too much of the land, perhaps three-fourths, was held by owners, Cuban or foreign, who never came near their properties, which were worked by underpaid peasants. Labor conditions in the cities were less favorable than Cubans knew them to be in other countries. Their government was as inefficient and dishonest as it had always been, and citizens still had little say in its operation. Public schools were too few and too poor; much-advertised appropriations had never been translated into a sound system of education but, like so much else in the island, had disappeared into the pockets of politicians. Worst of all, most Cubans saw no hope of improving their conditions of life under the fake republican system, which Batista was turning into a callous dictatorship.

The growing disgust with the Batista regime manifested itself in acts of sabotage and bombing, which the authorities attributed to Communists. They also blamed student riots, the circulation of incendiary pamphlets, strikes, and rural violence on such subversives. Yet restlessness grew worse as the government sought to suppress it. Things were almost as bad as they had been in the last days of Spanish colonialism or the Machado regime. It was not enough for the educated classes to charge Batista with neglect and tyranny. Uncle Sam loomed as the creator of Batista and of all unworthy rulers in the past. While Communists circularized this idea, Cuban intellectuals were entirely capable of conjuring for themselves an image of a vulgar plutocracy to the north which had bought up their land, reduced the population to the status of employees, turned on and off the flow of income, made and unmade rulers. The Yankee was the source of Cuba's distress, they said, and Batista its transient symbol.

The Emergence of Fidel Castro

THE instrument of this accumulating wrath proved to be Fidel Castro, a doctor of laws born in 1927. Scion of a wealthy Santiago family, he had become a radical in his youth. He played some role in the Bogotá street riots of 1948 and had consorted with Communists and other revolutionaries in various parts of the Americas, including the United States. His brother Raúl was admittedly a Communist and so was his close associate, the Argentine physician Ernesto ("Che") Guevara, but Fidel's opinions were either vaguely leftist and unformed, or else he was fantastically successful in concealing a true Communist fanaticism, much as he loved to talk. In December 1956 he led a seaborne invasion in the best filibuster tradition onto the shores of eastern Cuba, to the accompaniment of bomb explosions and premature cheering in scattered parts of the island. Batista firmly suppressed the rebellion and tightened his dictatorship, this time closing down the University of Havana. Defeated, Castro went with a dozen cohorts into the Sierra Maestra mountains, whose cliffs and woods had long offered a haven to Cuban outlaws and patriots.

During the next two years as unusual a political campaign as the New World ever saw, and one as fateful, took place. Camping in the mountains, attracting recruits from the rest of the island, and receiving supplies from abroad, Castro drew the bones from the Batista regime while cultivating Cuban and world opinion. The legend grew that this bearded, cigar-smoking lawyer was an authentic folk hero who represented the common Latin American laborer in his defiance of an unfair social system. That this image flourished most wherever Communist influence was strong perplexed not a few students of affairs. Yet anyone could see that much in Cuba cried for reform, and since Castro laughingly denied Communist sympathies, most people believed him. With a portable radio station and printing press, Castro was able to pour out torrents of propaganda to a population that grew more receptive as the tyranny of Batista worsened. Individuals and parties made pilgrimages into the Sierra Maestra to listen for hours to the big, magnetic fellow. While his harangues were incoherent and offered no precise program of action, the message was clear in essence: Batista must be ousted and Cuban society remade. During 1957 much of the rural populace went over to Castro, and in 1958 the urban proletarians were won in a campaign that offered a brilliant lesson in political science.

President Batista professed to belittle the Castro movement and repeatedly announced Fidel's death. The censored press treated the threat contemptuously. Cuban naval craft patrolled the island to interdict seaborne supplies that poured into Castro's area from unknown sources, the army tried to strangulate rebel territory, and airplanes periodically gunned and dropped incendiaries on the Sierra Maestra. Batista grinned as disarmingly as ever, a picture of serenity, but he stopped appearing before crowds for fear of provoking a revolution, and he was almost assassinated in March 1957. A much-publicized effort by his enemies to call a general strike in April 1958 was a fiasco and thus seemed to confirm his confidence. With good reason Batista pointed to Cuba's excellent business conditions; it was in fact one of the four countries in the Americas that had suffered no serious inflation. He also revived his old promises to promote the social welfare of the masses and improve the government. And in November 1958 the elections were held as scheduled, resulting in an overwhelming victory for Batista's chosen heir. Yet everyone knew the election was a farce, that Cuba was an armed camp, and that Batista was a hated tyrant.

During 1958 Castro's prestige abroad grew as it did in Cuba. Respected organs of opinion sent reporters to the Sierra Maestra, often by parachute, who sent back dispatches with effusive praise for the true, if somewhat cloudy, idealist that Fidel represented himself to be. Any suspicion that he was a Communist was likely to be denied vigorously by these observers, who had quotations from the bearded patriot to disprove it. And while the Batista regime was not the worst Cuba had ever known, its evils were bad enough to create sympathy abroad for anyone who sought to destroy it. The cult of Castro in the outside world heartened educated Cubans, who had always kept in touch with things, and perhaps influenced the Catholic clergy to take a stand against Batista. The United States, where the Castro campaign was very effective, stopped permitting Batista to purchase arms, though Great Britain to the last sold him military aircraft. Nonetheless, most Cubans passionately and erroneously believed that Washington was propping up the dictator.

While the outside world was warming to him, Castro was winning in succession the peasants, the urban workers, and lastly, the middle and professional classes in Cuba. All that remained to support President Batista was his own bemused political machine, the army, and the police. In December 1958, just after the false election, these crumbled entirely. Castro emerged with his armed "peasants" to engage Batista openly. A few skirmishes showed the army was unwilling to fight, and early on January 1, 1959, Fulgencio Batista flew away to that nest of deposed dictators, Ciudad Trujillo.

Fidel Castro, master of Cuba at the age of thirty-two, walked most of the way from the eastern end of the island to the capital, receiving accolades due a messiah, pausing here and there to order the shooting of former officials. Havana was in a carnival mood as thousands of Batista supporters fled its docks and airports and the liberator approached. When at last Castro entered the city he found it ecstatic, the island rejoicing, and the rest of the world applauding. His warriors, hirsute, filthy, and rum-swilling, invaded the hotels to prod bewildered tourists with rifles, though they seemed good-natured as they did it. Havana, they made clear, was no longer a play spot for rich foreigners. And thousands of countryfolk took over luxury apartments and fine homes from wealthy natives who had either left them or nervously let the visitors in. The "peoples' revolution" seemed completely victorious.

Castro was content to let Manuel Urrutia take over the dignities of the presidency and Miró Cardona those of the premiership as well. He would be only the peoples' instrument. After a protracted period of debaucheries and celebrations, as well as a friendly visit to Venezuela, he settled down to attend to business. First, a purge of Batista followers must rid the island of "enemies of the Cuban people." Public trials and prompt shootings brought death to many hundreds within a few weeks, while squeamish persons shuddered at the arbitrariness of revolutionary justice. In April 1959, Castro paid a theatrical visit to the United States, where the crowds were curious and amiable, perhaps a little amused. Affirming that his heart was with the West in its struggle against Communism, he made himself welcome to the Eisenhower administration, which received him cordially and made tentative offers of massive aid for Cuba. And then he returned to Havana to harangue vast audiences for hours about the far-reaching agricultural reforms he was going to institute.

In July, President Urrutia resigned, letting it be known that he was disturbed about Communist influences in the regime, and was replaced by Oswaldo Dorticós Torrado, who thought Communists grand fellows. Castro soon assumed the premiership after his first appointee in that post defected. He vowed that elections would be held within four years, presumably long enough a period to work out the basic reforms he had in mind. He furthermore declared that his program would not involve aid from the United States, a jolt to Washington made the more pointed by Castro's refusal to see the American ambassador for three months. To the many Americans who had rejoiced at the advent of the bearded leader the situation was becoming very mysterious. Bombings, leaflets dropped from airplanes, and acts of individual terrorism in Cuba suggested that opinion there was not unanimous. Another surge of persecutions by the revolutionary tribunals made Castro seem as vicious a figure as more conventional dictators. And then that sight, familiar in the days of Spain, Machado, and Batista, Cuban refugees in Florida, disenchanted many former Castro enthusiasts abroad.

Late in 1959, as if by cue, the controlled Cuban press began to rail at the United States for crimes that might have shamed Hitler. Its naval base at Guantánamo Bay was made out to be an intolerable affront to Cuba, and Castro finally stated what he had for some time implied: American property would be nationalized. Cubans fell into the habit of punctuating Castro's pronouncements with cries of *Cuba sí, yanqui no.* In March 1960, Cuba denounced the Rio de Janeiro pact of 1947 by which all the American republics bound themselves to help one another in the event of attack from the outside. Meanwhile, there was much cordial intercourse between the Castro administration and the Communist bloc nations.

By the summer of 1960 the true situation was lamentably clear. Whatever Fidel Castro had been, whatever reservations he still had, his regime was being manipulated by international Communism. The expropriation of American holdings worth more than a billion dollars was one telltale sign. The presence of Russian submarines in the Caribbean was another. Wildly anti-American denunciations and spectacular receptions to Communist representatives spoke for themselves. American journalists, some of them ardent apologists for Castro, were jailed and deported. The Eisenhower administration bore these provocations patiently, not wishing to injure the Cuban people for the excesses of their leaders and hoping that the revolutionary venom would play itself out. But in July 1960 the president asked Congress to cancel the arrangements by which Cuba had, in one form or another since independence, enjoyed a favored treatment for her sugar exports to the United States. This was done, and soon the Americans were purchasing no Cuban sugar whatever, nor were any but clandestine tourists of leftish sympathies visiting what was once a popular land.

This stoppage of American dollars into Cuba seemed to trouble Castro little; on the contrary, he became more defiant. He went to New York in September to attend the opening session of the United Nations General Assembly, where he ostentatiously courted Premier Khrushchev and other anti-American leaders, who delightedly returned his friendship, and agitated the colored population. His rustic companions made a shambles of their quarters in two hotels. The press reported that they picked chickens in their rooms and never took baths. But Castro was no longer a comic figure. So worried had the American public become, both candidates in the campaign of 1960 vied in denouncing him. In January 1961, after Castro made violent threats against the United States and ordered the immediate reduction of its embassy staff, Washington broke off relations with Havana.

Deplorable as was the estrangement of the United States and Cuba, it was only one aspect of Castro's foreign policy. He sent small forces against Haiti and the Dominican Republic, vainly hoping to unseat their dictators. After promoting disorders in other Latin American nations, Castro found Guatemala, El Salvador, Nicaragua, Honduras, Paraguay, and Peru hostile enough to sever diplomatic ties. The Betancourt regime of Venezuela, initially his friend, became very cool. Throughout Latin America, governments regarded Castro as an unsettling influence if not worse. This was only too true, for the *Cuba sí, yanqui no* slogan had enormous appeal to students, middle-class intellectuals, and the large impoverished groups. Many contended that the Castro movement was as significant an upheaval as the French Revolution had been. Cuba was easily the prime problem in Latin America faced by the new administration that took office in Washington in 1961. How the island could function, even if helped by Russia and China, without American markets, investments, and tourists was a mystery, but it was one that Castro clearly intended to probe.

That Cuba had become a Communist foothold was not merely an American fear or a leftist hope. Thousands of Cubans verified it. Havana's press, radio, and television were faithful organs of Marxist orthodoxy, and the substitution of a peasants' militia for the regular army was another indication. Castro's long-heralded land reform program did not console believers in free enterprise, for plantations were transformed into collective farms, soviet-style, rather than divided among independent owners. The mines and refineries were also collectivized under national monopolies, and the labor unions were consolidated as a state agency run by Communists. Clergymen, who had usually stood aside during the last days of Batista or openly favored Castro, now warned that godless Communism was rampant, suffering persecution for their assertion. Most revealing of all were the floods of defectors and refugees. Cuban delegates to the United Nations or diplomats abroad deserted Castro so regularly that their actions were a predictable item of news. Worse yet were the exiles who left Cuba altogether, giving up their homes, professions, and business. By the end of 1960 there were 60,000 refugees—an appalling number for a land of only 6,000,000 people—in Florida alone, and more were arriving constantly. These were not capitalists or dispossessed planters, for such persons had long since departed. The major increment was composed of doctors, dentists, attorneys, teachers, and other professional men as well as skilled workers and shop owners, the very people whose talents Cuba could least afford to lose.

Whether they would remain in exile long was problematical. Like refugees from the "Pearl of the Antilles" in other years from other tyrants, they made plans to free their homeland. The United States government armed and trained many of them for a military descent from bases in Central America, but the landing of April 1961 at the Bay of Pigs was tragically mismanaged, resulting in imprisonment for 1,200 filibusterers, a ferocious wave of oppression in Cuba, and the humiliation of the Kennedy administration. Apparently the fiasco showed that Castro had a far stronger hold on the island than the exiles had reported, and it greatly sobered any ardor some Latin American governments might have had for trying to intervene in Cuban affairs. Washington was shocked into re-examining, among other things, the wisdom of its thirty years of effort to make the Monroe Doctrine multi-lateral and its countless promises never to intervene in Latin American domestic affairs. While Castro's excesses had disenchanted many of his erstwhile admirers, he stood strong and defiant after the Bay of Pigs affair, and more beholden to his Communist allies than ever. The perversity of man had long kept Cuba from becoming the paradise it ought to be. The world might be fortunate if only the latest of its tyrants could be removed without setting off a nuclear war.

HAITI

Haiti, the only Negro republic and French-speaking nation in the New World, is still unformed in character, its ideals and sense of direction almost as dim as they were a century and a half ago. No government is really legitimate or supported by legal and popular sanctions. Militarism, rebellion, and corruption persist as though things had changed little since the days of Dessalines or Christophe. There are far too many inhabitants for the resources of this land, the smallest in the Americas but for El Salvador. A rapid population growth in recent decades has sent the number of Haitians past the 3,500,000 mark, swamping public services that had been inadequate even for a smaller number. Since only a third of the country is arable, and inadequately cultivated at that, undernourishment is a familiar condition. The people raise manioc, corn, yams, and fruit, but not enough of them. They have little to export, about $50,000,000-worth a year of sugar, coffee, sisal, cacao, bananas, and vegetable oils, an amount insufficient to finance the finished products they need to import. Poverty claims all but a few of these people, and illiteracy about four-fifths. Poor health is general, a cause of indolence and fatalism, and repeated failures have robbed the Haitians of national ambition. Two or three per cent of them consider themselves of the *élite* class, mostly mulattoes who have a fair livelihood and who speak French. The rest are Negroes whose tongue is Creole, a patois of French, Spanish, and various African languages with sprinklings of Carib, English, and Dutch words.

Yet all is not gloom. If they are the poorest, they are the least despairing people in the Americas. They like color, music, and fun, and a generally prevailing system of free love stimulates a cheerfully pagan attitude toward life. An official but shallow Catholicism shares the allegiance of the masses with the cult of Vodun or "voodoo" in an apparently satisfying amalgam. Haiti's primitive-style painting has won the approval of many sophisticated outsiders, and her music and dance forms are greatly admired. Furthermore, the country's natural beauty—its mountains, woods, valleys, and beaches—please ever-growing numbers of tourists, most of whom also find the people fascinating. Like so many of the Caribbean lands, this one is a slum that might be a paradise, with a climate comfortable for the tropics, though dry spells and hurricanes occasionally bring disaster. Haiti is not divided among aliens or aristocrats but is owned mostly by the common people. A recent decline in their historic xenophobia suggests that heavy doses of aid from more fortunate countries might alleviate their worst ills.

Self-Government, 1859–1915

AFTER the overthrow of the egregious Faustin I in 1859, a signal improvement in Haiti's fortunes came about. The new president, Fabre Geffrard, was a dark enough mulatto to win support from both the *élite* and the masses. In a rule of eight years he restored the republic on nominally constitutional lines, won for the first time Haiti's recognition by the United States, re-established the *corvée* to put idle males to work, and restored relations with the Holy See. This last measure had great importance. Trained Catholic clergymen came back into the country for the first time since the French Revolution, and while they were too few to do much about the superstitions or cults that held most of the population, they won back the *élite*. They also began schools which eventually restored Haiti's ties with the centers of civilization. President Geffrard established a few schools too, among them a center for the study of medicine. But his hope of linking Haiti further with Europe by inviting foreigners to do business collided with the passionate nationalism of the people, and his popularity declined. Since he had halved the overblown army that Faustin I had created, he found himself unable to fight off guerrillas who followed rebel leaders, and in 1867 he was thrown out of office.

Subsequent Haitian presidents established themselves in Port-au-Prince, the capital, almost invariably by force. Most of them were Negroes with bands of supporters known as *cacos*, rural soldiers from the northern mountains. Unable to rule the republic, the *élite* had to be satisfied by holding most of the secondary positions in the government and by handling most of Haiti's business affairs. Some of the African presidents were minor statesmen, though they fought their way to power, filled their purses, and oppressed their opponents. Lysius Salomon, who ruled from 1879 to 1888, created a national bank and tried to improve education and agricultural practices. The latter problem was crucial, for since the massacre or expulsion of the French aristocracy in the 1790's, irrigation works had fallen into disuse, crops were not rotated, and much of the soil was allowed to wash away. It must be admitted that Salomon's efforts bore paltry results; sugar production was only a third of what it had been a century before. Most of the men refused to work, for the *corvée* was usually unenforceable and women were willing to toil in the fields. Moreover, females carried in most of the commerce, which was on the humblest level, largely because men were afraid of coming into towns lest they be drafted into one guerrilla band or another.

Under another competent Negro ruler, Florville Hyppolite, who was president from 1889 to 1896, traces of the outside world at last brushed Haiti. French and German traders established firms in Port-au-Prince, exporting sugar and coffee and importing a few finished articles. A telegraph and telephone system was begun and a railroad started. Docks were constructed and a few bridges rebuilt. While such activities did not effect the modernization of Haiti by any means, they helped acquaint the population with the machine age and fostered the growth of the *élite*. And clever members of this group discovered ways to turn the activities of the caudillos to advantage. Bonds might be issued, sold to speculators in Europe, and then repudiated. The pattern was for the leaders to hire a gang of *cacos* to rebel and declare themselves a government, issue bonds or currency, seize the capital city long enough to legalize these scraps of paper, whereupon the holders could sell them to gullible foreigners at large profits. Then another revolution would begin and the same formula be repeated. As debts piled up abroad trouble loomed, although for several decades nothing of importance happened other than the appearance of French or German warships in Haitian waters, ultimatums and threats that could be ignored, and fluctuations in money capitals abroad as investors tired of being swindled. Native Haitians made a good deal of money in this way, and the *cacos* were satisfied if they were paid after putting up or pulling down a president.

The American Phase, 1915–1931

THE character of Haitian politics became particularly tawdry by the second decade of the twentieth century. In rapid succession six presidents took over and suffered removal, one blown up in the palace with 300 followers, another probably poisoned, and the most unfortunate torn limb from limb by his erstwhile subjects. This last incident, which occurred in July 1915, resulted in the temporary loss of Haiti's independence through a sequence not altogether logical. It seems that a New York bank had acquired an important share in the National Bank of Haiti, which served as treasurer for the republic. A breach between the National Bank and the Haitian government gave rise to fears that the former would be confiscated, and so its funds were secretly shipped to New York. At the same time a scandal broke concerning the financing mainly by French and German investors of a railroad from Port-au-Prince to Cap Haitien, which after years of expenditures consisted only of eighty miles of track in three useless segments. Thus the Haitian government had justification for taking over both the bank and the railway. If it did, very serious complications might follow, because by that time, late in 1914, France and Germany were at war with one another and either would be pleased to retaliate against Haiti by occupying one of its harbors as a naval base. President Wilson sent an American fleet to Haitian waters in order to discourage such an adventure.

In July 1915 came the tragedy of the president, Vilbrun Guillaume Sam, who was dragged from the French legation in Port-au-Prince and dismembered by a mob that blamed him for the massacre of political prisoners. Rather than give France a pretext to intervene, Wilson ordered the U.S. Navy to take over the capital. To Yankeephobes then and later, this action stood as a flagrant example of dollar diplomacy; according to their interpretation, the United States simply exploited an excuse to destroy the independence of a little country, hypocritically invoking the cause of neutrality but really trying to save the investments of a few capitalists. Yet to anyone who respects President Wilson's integrity, this explanation is nothing short of slander. The United States had been attempting for ten years to make the Caribbean republics behave, and in a time of world war no great power should be given a pretext for taking over an important strategic base like Haiti. So runs the case for the defense.

Whatever the reasoning of the American leaders, the fact was that 2,000 marines now ruled Haiti. They turned back the inevitable *caco* invasion from the north and induced the frightened congress to elect as president Sudré Dartiguenave, who was to serve from 1915 to 1922 as an American puppet. A treaty forced on Haiti turned the customs over to American authorities, who used the proceeds to satisfy foreign creditors, and created a *gendarmerie* under United States direction to replace the riot of *caco* bands. As the protectorate settled down into some condition of order, Washington decided to favor it with a constitution. One, which Franklin D. Roosevelt said he wrote (though it is disputed), was handed the Haitian congress in 1918 only to be rejected, at which point the marines disbanded the congress and staged a plebiscite which obtained the expected "popular" approval. It was obvious that the United States was acting in a most arrogant manner; yet it went further by requiring that all bills should be approved by the American authorities before being taken up by the Haitian congress and by presuming to veto any expenditure that might pass that body. On a lower level the Americans also behaved harshly. Many marines showed their scorn for Negroes, including in this category the *élite*, who prided themselves on white blood and high status. A well-meaning attempt to put the rural populace to work by reviving the *corvée* led to a desultory civil war, which dragged on for two years under a native hero named Charlemagne and killed 2,000 Haitians. After President Harding came into power things improved slightly, with American controls being concentrated in the hands of a tactful high commissioner and a new Haitian president, Louis Borno, who served from 1922 to 1930.

Painful as the moral issues and practical problems of the American occupation were, some benefits accrued to Haiti. It may have been worth something to the republic to have its foreign and internal debts funded and fiscal order established. The Americans built public works on a large scale, finishing the railroad, introducing automobiles and trucks and constructing 800 miles of roads for them, and repairing ancient French irrigation facilities. They also paved streets, set up electrical systems, extended telephone lines, and established pure water supplies. Of the greatest significance were the hundreds of rural clinics and hospitals they created, which employed modern methods to curb malaria, yaws, yellow fever, smallpox, and leprosy. The Americans also built a number of schools, including much-needed rural institutes to teach farmers scientific methods, and of course they kept order through the *gendarmerie* commanded by marines. While these improvements were imaginative for the 1920's, they pale before uplift programs of later decades and were pitifully inadequate to meet the needs of Haiti. The traditional illiteracy, poverty, sickness, and resistance to modern methods yielded but little to humanitarian efforts; an unwholesome population growth was their principal result. Furthermore, the *élite*, who had been restored to prominence by the Americans because they were the only educated group, chafed over paying taxes and being barred from sources of graft and, more than the black masses, resented the segregationist practices of the American military.

Free Again

LATE in 1929 conditions deteriorated as the world depression destroyed Haiti's modest foreign markets. The American presence seemed all the more obnoxious, and there was much fear that President Borno, who was looked upon as a Yankee toady, would prolong his term. Perhaps believing that the original reason for the intervention was no longer valid, President Hoover decided to have a new regime installed and to proceed with its immediate Haitianization. An election honestly supervised by the well-known Latin Americanist, Professor Dana C. Munro, brought a new congress together in 1930. This body chose as president of the republic an active critic of the United States, the mulatto Sténio Vincent. In 1931 the occupation was formally terminated and the bureaucracy turned over to the Haitians, and by 1934 all the marines were gone.

Vincent remained president all through the 1930's, irregularly having himself reelected in 1935 for a term he extended to six years. If its progress during these depression years was not notable, Haiti at least remained peaceful, and the educational and public health facilities continued to function. In 1941 another mulatto, Elie Lescot, became president for a period in which World War II afforded another infusion of American assistance: public works, attacks on disease, more schools, and high prices for Haiti's products. During the war the republic acquired a new export item in sisal, which replaced the hemp of the Philippines, but a costly effort to re-settle thousands of Haitians in a rubber-cultivating project was a fiasco.

Lescot had congress extend his term to 1951, but he was not destined to last that long. The small Haitian army, the *Garde d'Haiti* based on the *gendarmerie* of the occupation, contained ambitious leaders, chiefly among its palace guard. When the end of the war produced economic dislocations and popular restlessness, the *Garde* took over. It was apparent that racism played a role in Lescot's deposition. Negro leaders had gotten the upper hand in the *Garde,* and they resented the complacent *élite* with their airs of superiority and French pretensions. The new president, Dumarsais Estimé, was a Negro, an idealist who had long taught school and encouraged his race to assert itself. He had the pleasures of ending the foreign financial controls, for Haiti's debts were now all paid, and of ousting the *élite* from key positions and making them pay an income tax. Addressing himself to Haiti's most painful problem, the undernourishment of the people owing largely to improvident agricultural methods, he collectivized a number of farms which he hoped would become scientific showcases for production. He was also helped extensively by American public and private agencies as well as by one of the first of the United Nations' programs in promoting better health, which meant inoculating every Haitian who could be caught and improving sanitation. During his administration Haiti was really ruled by the *Garde,* but it enjoyed a high degree of freedom for the Caribbean, and its educated groups, who still looked to France for inspiration, read, wrote, and discussed avidly.

In May 1950, President Estimé proposed that his term be extended and thus brought about the opposition of Colonel Paul Magloire, the commander of the *Garde.* With little difficulty Magloire overthrew his former friend and took his place as president. Magloire was an appealing figure, beloved by the masses and much admired abroad. Regal and handsome, he lived as majestically as a monarch, though he was thought to be honest and undoubtedly was full of benovolence. Discerning the needs of Haiti as industrialization, greater productivity, diversification of the economy, and improved health and education, he attracted much foreign support. Private investments, tourism, technical assistance, and official grants or loans stimulated the nation's economy. Magloire was also statesmanlike enough to seek to end the tension between the *élite* and the Negroes, and for a time he was looked upon as one of the most promising rulers in Latin America.

Whether Magloire was really a first-rate president or merely had a good press is difficult to determine. After several years of apparent popularity and success, he was suddenly deposed in 1956 by a junta of army officers who claimed that he had been hypocritical and dishonest. Their regime was scarcely a reformation, and for nearly a year they rent the land with unedifying squabbles over obscure issues. An election was finally held in September 1957, bringing one of their associates, a physician named François Duvalier, into the presidency. Since then the government of Haiti has deteriorated sadly, and so have conditions in general. Strikes, riots, fiscal crises, and states of siege have given the republic a gloomy atmosphere. Labor leaders and newspapers have accused the Duvalier regime of ruining unions and going beyond the customary limits of censorship. The clergy has been critical, and university students have been so rebellious the schools were often closed down. Furthermore, Haiti's trade has fallen almost by half, the result of the collapse of coffee and sugar prices in world markets, and tourism has declined sharply because of the unsettled conditions. In foreign affairs Duvalier has had the habitually bad relations with the Dominican Republic and exchanged ferocious threats with Castro's Cuba. After Duvalier declared his own reelection to a six-year term in 1961, the United States, whose aid constituted half of Haiti's budget, began to withdraw its support.

THE DOMINICAN REPUBLIC

Two-thirds of the island of Hispaniola falls within the boundaries of the Dominican Republic, the land founded by Columbus as a colony for Isabel the Catholic in 1493. Europeanized the longest of any country in America, with the oldest city and perhaps the oldest university, it is a humble adornment of Western civilization. The Dominicans have achieved little since they left the Spanish monarchy in 1821, and in fact have aspired to little. Perhaps they have been defeated too often. Under Spain they were backward and neglected; as soon as they declared independence, they endured invasion and oppression by the Haitians. Since the end of the Negroid occupation, they have known chaos alternating with tyranny and unpleasant pressures from the great powers. The product of this dismal history today is a land of about 2,500,000 people, most of them of mixed European and African ancestry, living in constant tensions with the 3,500,000 Haitians who share the island. The Dominicans have as lovely a homeland as Columbus reported in his first letters, a country of smiling valleys, woodlands, pastures, farms, and mountain ranges. It is usually comfortably cool, and, unlike Haiti, it enjoys a dependable rainfall. The people live far better than the Haitians, are more educated and healthy, and have more economic opportunities. Their commerce is twice that of their rival, and their agriculture, mines, ranches, and factories far more productive. Yet this is not a happy land. Freedom and self-respect have long been strangers here, as has been shown by their timid reappearance following the assassination of Generalissimo Rafael Leonidas Trujillo in 1961.

The Failure of Self-Government, 1865–1905

OF ALL the caudillos who have strutted across the Dominican landscape, not the least interesting is Buenaventura Báez. Long a rival of the rustic leader Pedro Santana and usually on the losing end, he escaped the obloquy suffered by Santana for restoring the country to the Spanish monarchy in 1861. This is not to say that Báez was a staunch patriot, for he too accepted honors and money from the Spanish crown, but when he saw the restoration was failing, he took the field again with an army. In 1865, after the Spaniards had left, Báez entered the city of Santo Domingo as president, was soon pushed out again, and returned triumphantly in 1868. While he frankly declared that the republic was incapable of self-government and likely to succumb to another Haitian occupation, his proposed remedy was ill-starred. Báez thought the Dominican nation should be annexed to the United States, a suggestion well-regarded by Presidents Johnson and Grant but not by successive American senates. He also sought to lease the Bay of Samaná, an excellent harbor in the north, but again a balky Senate frustrated him. These proposals had the effect of propping up his rule until 1874, since American naval craft and credits were at his disposal, but in that year he fell. He fought his way into power in 1876, only to be ousted for the fifth and last time in 1878. Out of these maneuverings little good came to the Dominican nation, which continued as poor, backward, and isolated as before and had already accumulated foreign debts that would one day plague it.

In 1882 another caudillo appeared, to last until his murder in 1899. This was a Negro named Ulises Heureaux. Although the mulatto population was fearful of Negroes, Heureaux was able to win general support and to provide an interval of peace. Most of these seventeen years he was president; when out of office, he ruled through puppets. While his enemies were not wholly unfair when they called him cruel—what successful Caribbean ruler is not?—he had some education and was sincerely anxious to improve the country. During his rule the sugar industry began to blossom, partly as a result of enterprise on the part of Cubans who had left their rebellious island. And the traditional Dominican export, hides, continued to furnish foreign earnings. Most lucrative of all were the loans which Heureaux obtained from European investors, a flow of money that enabled him to build a few schools, roads, and public edifices and support himself and his regime in considerable style. Multiplying the foreign debt ten times, he occasionally had difficulties with importunate creditors, but he met their demands by paying them off with debased currency, which pleased them little. Before they could persuade their governments to act against him he was killed, the last Negro to rule this land.

The mulatto caudillos who followed Heureaux were, if anything, less capable than he. Ramón Cáceres, who had killed him, was in and out of power several times, taking the capital with rustic warriors and being driven away again. A tiresome see-saw developed among various groups based partly on personal rivalry, Haitian support of one faction or another, and the covetousness of plunderers—never on real issues. Something of a cynical game developed for several years: men would organize behind one caudillo to win the administration and treasury for a few months of looting, and then ditch him for another front man, inevitably a "liberator" or "restorer," and divide up the national income on a slightly different basis. While most of the population was apathetic, participating only when they were conscripted, their interests necessarily suffered.

The American Protectorate, 1905–1924

BY 1904 several European governments were willing to assist their subjects in collecting bad Dominican debts, which amounted to $32,000,000, the service of which would absorb the republic's revenues. One incitement to action at this time was a decision by the new international court at The Hague concerning the Venezuelan claims, which stipulated that nations using force against defaulting governments had prior rights. President Theodore Roosevelt foresaw a race to the Dominican Republic by several powers, any one of which might be a potential enemy of the United States and quite capable of acquiring naval bases on the route to the Panama Canal then being dug. Accordingly, he took possession of a customhouse in the Dominican Republic in October 1904, and proceeded to separate proper from improper debts and to pay off the former with import duties. He also proposed that the United States assume direction of all Dominican customhouses and settle the foreign claims. While the Senate refused, he went ahead anyhow. By mid-1905 American forces had occupied Santo Domingo and taken over all the republic's customs stations, giving 55 per cent of the revenues to the creditors and 45 per cent to the Dominican government. It is testimony of the previous Dominican methods of collection that their share of this income amounted to more under this arrangement than all of it had been before. In addition, American loans, thus guaranteed, to the extent of $20,000,000 reassured both foreign creditors and Dominicans. In 1907 the Senate finally authorized Roosevelt's actions by ratifying a treaty.

As far as European debts were concerned, the method worked satisfactorily, but the Dominicans had other problems too. Their political factions were almost as unruly as before. Ramón Cáceres, between 1908 and 1911, presided to the satisfaction of the Americans, but then he was murdered and succeeded by other leaders with their disorderly factions. Annoyed by the turmoil, the United States landed 750 marines and indicated that further revolutions would not be tolerated. Its effort to create a durable elective regime failed utterly, however, since the factions would not accept any one of themselves as dominant and even refused to combine under the Archbishop of Santo Domingo. Washington, under both Taft and Wilson, regarded the Dominican scene with mounting exasperation and worried that customs revenues might fail to meet foreign claims and yet provoke a European intervention. Finally, the republic put itself in the wrong technically by raising its debt limit, thus violating the treaty of 1907 with the United States. Concerned less with this than the possibility of German mischief, President Wilson ordered the marines to take over the entire republic in 1916, which was done with little opposition from its inhabitants.

Wilson did not even attempt to create a Dominican figurehead ruler like the then president of Haiti. Rather, he set up an American military governor with full executive and legislative authority, permitting Dominican nationals to hold most governmental posts but none of decisive importance. Even if the stringencies of World War I justified a certain arbitrariness in American methods, the occupation was carried out with an arrogance that aroused Latin America. For much of the time martial law prevailed, an unnecessary censorship made a mockery of democratic ideals, and American marines swaggered about as offensively as occupying troops usually do. It was particularly offensive to the racial-minded Dominicans to be regarded as Negroes, as they often were, and pushed around by all-white invaders. When a critic of the occupation, the poet Fabio Fiallo, was jailed, an outburst of indignation occurred in parts of

Latin America, where any Yankee misdeed quickly became an atrocity. While it was true that American troops brought peace to a country that had abundantly demonstrated its incapacity for self-government, and while the republic could now sell more sugar and cacao than ever before, and at wartime prices, these benefits were obtained at the cost of Dominican dignity. Long after the war, in December 1920, President Wilson announced the impending end of the occupation, whose purpose from start to finish had been of questionable morality. Under President Harding the withdrawal started, but it proved difficult to work out the details, and so Sumner Welles, who later became an architect of the Good Neighbor policy, skillfully arranged to get the marines out by 1924 without leaving a complete vacuum. Financial advisers remained until all foreign debts were settled, in 1940. The Americans had done little but rule the Dominican Republic, without undertaking the humanitarian measures that softened their protectorate over Haiti.

The first election in eight years was held in 1924. General Horacio Vásquez, who had struggled to win power since the death of Heureaux in 1899, became president of a pacified republic buttressed with the support of a model army based on the constabulary organized by the Americans. For five years he governed easily enough, and the republic shared modestly in the general world prosperity. In 1929, Vásquez indicated that he would seek reelection in the next year. Then he fell seriously ill, leaving the government in the hands of his vice-president. It happened that the vice-president had a bitter enemy in the head of the army, General Rafael Leonidas Trujillo. A man who never cared for genuine elections, Trujillo decided not to let the voters determine whether they wished Vásquez or his heir to continue. By a well-managed military coup he overthrew the regime and, in May 1930, had himself formally elected president.

The Era of Trujillo, 1930–1961

TRUJILLO's advent proved no mere power shift but the beginning of the most enduring dictatorship of twentieth-century Latin America. Born into a poor mulatto family in 1893, he had been trained by the U.S. Marines in the military art and less honorable pursuits. Soon after he became president, a hurricane that ravaged two-thirds of Santo Domingo in September 1930 gave him an opportunity to demonstrate his high administrative talents and to establish himself as a humanitarian. It is probable that at any time in the next thirty years he could have won an honest election, because he ruled competently and was a genius in public relations.

His approach to the problem of governing the Dominican Republic was to treat it as a business enterprise to be run efficiently: productive, its employees kept in a good humor, and spruced up so as to reflect credit on the proprietor. Also, it should bring its master good profits; thus Trujillo and his family accumulated properties said to be worth hundreds of millions of dollars. Other Dominicans fared well materially, however, and achieved the highest per capita income of any of the small Caribbean republics. The budget was balanced, all debts paid off, and the currency so stabilized that the Dominican Republic enjoyed the unique distinction of knowing no inflation in the mid-twentieth century. A businesslike approach resulted in the application of scientific, modern methods to all aspects of the economy. Sugar cultivation mounted, coming to comprise half the exports, and the cacao, coffee, and livestock industries flourished. Factories diversified the economy and elevated the standards of living. Many fine public works were completed: the best roads in the Caribbean lands, ports, airdromes, electrical plants, and pure water systems. The capital, impudently renamed Ciudad Trujillo in 1936, became one of the cleanest and most modern in Latin America, and crime and mendicancy were reduced to the lowest level throughout the republic. Many farmers obtained their own land through government aid. Low-cost housing and welfare benefits kept the urban workers contented, though they lacked labor unions. Most of the children attended schools, vocational training on a very extensive scale raised the skills of the population at large, and the university, endowed with a handsome campus outside the capital, was full of obedient teachers and students.

It is no wonder that Trujillo allowed himself to be hailed as "Benefactor of the Fatherland," "Genius of Peace," "Father," "Protector," and "Rebuilder." His statue graced every plaza, his photograph every shop and home, and the sign, "God and Trujillo," many a street. The years progressed serenely for the Benefactor, with elections being held regularly, though only one party, the Dominican, ever seemed to have any members. From 1938 to 1942 and from 1952 to 1961 he allowed others, usually his relatives and always his creatures, to serve as president. Political life consisted of little but accolades for the Benefactor. Economic affairs were featured by full employment, expanding production and foreign markets, acceptable labor conditions, and a steady elevation in standards of living. As the years went on, the Dominican Republic experienced more industrialization in the way of plants for food preservation, clothing, furniture, meat-packing, cement-making, sisal bag manufacture, and engine assembly. It built the largest sugar refinery in the world and a huge shipyard. National wealth and income were comparatively well distributed among the population, though a few became exceedingly rich, among whom the Trujillo family must be included.

In international affairs Trujillo also pleased his people. He was friendly with all American administrations until the end of President Eisenhower's, thus assuring good markets, military equipment, and technical assistance. When Hitler was persecuting the Jews, he grandly announced room for 100,000 refugees in the republic, which has always desired white immigrants, but only a few hundred went to his much-advertised colony of Sosua, and even they used it as a staging area for moving to other countries. Trujillo's chronic vituperation of Haiti and Cuba was consistent with Caribbean traditions, but an atrocity against Haitian squatters in 1937 went beyond acceptable practices. Disliking Negroes in general and Haitians in particular, the Dominicans had long fretted about the farm workers who spilled over from Haiti to camp in their republic. Trujillo had his soldiers pounce on these migrants and kill unknown thousands of them. Surprised by the uproar that followed abroad, he then paid Haiti an indemnity and, in 1941, made a state visit to Port-au-Prince, apparently feeling he had made amends. World War II came and went, leaving Trujillo as firmly entrenched as ever, and as one dictator after another came down in the 1950's the Benefactor offered them refuge but seemed little disturbed about the possibility of sharing their fate.

Opposition was, however, manifesting itself as time went on. The calm of the Dominican Republic, the outside world slowly realized, was due less to unanimous support of Trujillo than an amazingly effective system of terror. His spy agency was superb, and most critics were caught before they could do any damage. Improbable "accidents" and "suicides" removed inconvenient persons, but still the number of exiles grew and became more voluble in spreading stories of the Benefactor's inclusive tyranny. While no informed person could truly be surprised at censorship or political persecution in a Caribbean republic, reports of Trujillo's oppression were too shocking to be discounted. His long arm may have reached into the New York subways to kidnap a Basque writer, Jesús de Galíndez, who was preparing a book damning the regime. A world-wide scandal developed, but it has yet to be proved that the Benefactor was culpable. Exposures and protests reached the flood stage by the late 1950's, though not a few American congressmen and publicists defended Trujillo, maintaining that he ruled his country with an enlightenment that other Latin American leaders might imitate.

Rich in years and honors—and in properties—Trujillo steadily lost ground in world opinion. His relations with Haiti and Cuba could scarcely have been worse, amounting to unofficial warfare and vivid public insults, and several other Caribbean republics accused him of malignant interference. Bad publicity concerning his playboy son, Lt. Gen. Rafael Trujillo, Jr., "Ramfis," for spending a ten-month course at the U.S. Army's Command and General Staff College in gambling and extravagant entertainment of motion picture stars, advertised the low character of the Trujillo family. When that institution declined to issue Ramfis more than a certificate of attendance, Trujillo defiantly promoted him to full general and threatened to accept no further American aid. And then Washington joined with the other members of the OAS in accusing the Benefactor of trying to assassinate President Betancourt of Venezuela and of other violations of human rights. In 1960 most of the American republics broke relations with the Benefactor, thus causing a sharp fall in Dominican exports and tourist income. Trujillo parried these efforts at isolation by flirting with Castro and the Communist bloc. He also increased the oppressiveness of his regime and even provoked the clergy, which had long been aloof from politics, into bold steps of defiance.

One night in June 1961 the indestructible caudillo was destroyed by gunfire on a lonely road as he motored to see one of his mistresses. A bloodbath was visited upon the suspected members of the plot, who apparently sought personal revenge rather than revolution, and, to be sure, there was no explosion, but rather public mourning so emotional as to reach hysteria. Ramfis Trujillo and the puppet president, Joaquín Balaguer, were confident enough to invite members of the OAS to see for themselves whether the Dominican Republic was a despotism. Yet growing popular unrest made it impossible for the regime to operate without its founder. All the Trujillos had to leave and new leaders groped for means to give the freed republic a better system.

27

Central America

THE five republics that derive from the Spanish kingdom of Guatemala together with Panama, which is often included as part of Central America, have an area and a population about equal to those of Texas. While ancient civilizations throve here and contacts with Western culture are four and a half centuries old, Central America ranks near the bottom of the world's societies. Its inhabitants, a mixture of Indian, European, African, and Asian, generally have poor health and little education. They are technologically retarded and culturally backward, buffeted by forces from the outside they seldom comprehend. As a rule they do not work hard, since a bounteous nature makes subsistence easy. Their economy is still largely colonial or pre-capitalist, a matter of producing raw materials for more advanced peoples to take away and utilize. No republic has a national budget as large as that of one of the major American universities. In government, the frailty of institutions, absence of legitimacy, and depravity of political practices have given several of these states the contemptuous name of "banana republic." Ridiculous things happen there: the strutting of dictators who are often unconsciously comic if sinister, corruption so open that it causes amusement rather than indignation, shooting scrapes, wild popular outbursts, revolutions, and repeated invasions of one land by another. Tempting as it is to adopt a patronizing attitude toward the region, respect and compassion are in order, and recent developments offer a basis for optimism.

Central America is an interesting and attractive part of the world. It possesses great natural riches in forests, minerals, and fine farming and ranching areas. While about half the land consists of torrid, low territory, the other half, where most of the people live, has a good climate and considerable scenic beauty. As a human laboratory it is also fascinating, es-

pecially since recent trends point to great improvements in living standards and more political consciousness. Education is doing much to
acquaint the enlightened classes with the forces that are dominating the
world. The middle sectors are growing in power and ambition; urban
proletarians are on the march; even the long-dormant rural masses are
being Westernized. While the traditional landed aristocracy and
moneyed soldier-politician are still conspicuous and ultimately direct the
republics, they are on the defensive. Tawdry examples of democracy as
most of the Central American lands have been, and still are, they pro-
fess devotion to its ideals. Recent tyrants have been unable to prevent
popular discussion of issues and clear demonstrations of sentiment.
This political ferment is no doubt related to the steady growth of commerce and production, which expanded twelve-fold in the first half of
this century and have now reached a level where highly rewarding
strides are possible. Even the humblest of Central Americans is likely to
know of the comforts other peoples enjoy and to insist upon a rapid at-
tainment of the abundant life.

One of the most interesting features of Central American history has
been the groping for unification by the republics. This tendency often
seems unrealistic, since the population centers are divided by jungle and
mountain. Yet the ideal beckons, whether to power-hungry dictators
who crave to expand or to responsible elements who see unity as a means
of promoting progress. In 1907, thanks to pressure from the United
States and Mexico, the little republics vowed not to interfere in each
other's affairs, to scorn rulers to who came into power by violence, and to
establish an international court of justice, which actually functioned un-
certainly until 1918. This commendable program soon became a trash
pile of broken promises and unratified conventions, but in 1923 the republics again pledged their attachment to it. Little improvement could
be recorded thereafter; yet in 1951 representatives of the various states
gathered in El Salvador to reiterate their desire to strengthen ties, avoid
conflict, and solve their common problems. Talk of a customs union,
standardized law codes, highways, and a University of Central America
aroused hopes, and in 1954 several governments combined after a fashion
to overthrow Communism in Guatemala. In 1955 they established an
Organization of Central American States (ODECA) within the framework of the Organization of American States and the United Nations.
By 1959, the advent of Fidel Castro with his policies against foreign
ownership and the emergence of free African nations who aspired to dislodge Central America from certain world markets led the republics to
take up serious discussions for a common market that might eventually
lead to a political union. Perhaps these efforts will end, like previous
ones, in a mess of recrimination. But the ideal of unification, with its

undertones of democratic stability and economic development for the masses, is likely to persist. Central America is certainly no longer a dormant area.

GUATEMALA

The home of nearly one-third of Central America's population of 11,000,000, Guatemala has long asserted over the other republics a preeminence based on her role in the Spanish empire. This pretension has been successfully resisted by the others since 1839, however, and there is little to justify it. Guatemala is not and has not been the natural leader of Central America. While she has had fewer revolutions than her sister republics, she has endured longer periods of despotism and her people have shown little capacity for self-government. One retarding factor has been the gaping division of the people on a racial basis, which sets a few Westernized mestizos, or *ladinos*, apart from the large Indian majority. The former own and manage the country's sources of production; the latter, descendants of the great Maya, usually live as an orphaned segment of the population, speaking their traditional dialects, raising their corn, and obeying tribal rulers for generation after generation. Only superficially have they absorbed the religion, habits, and technology of the Spaniards and their heirs. Until very recently they have resided in northern jungles, where anthropologists have studied them with great interest, or gone about their ways in mountainous communities, subject only to occasional labor conscription or military service by the ruling *ladinos*. Now they may be changing, for events of the past three decades have awakened them to the idea of progress as Westerners understand it.

This apartness of the Guatemaltecan Indians explains much of the history of the nation since the days of Rafael Carrera. Since the Indians have not been integrated into national life, Spanish-speaking elements monopolized economic and political power. These were not a cohesive aristocracy, however, and they too tended to be passive in politics as long as strong men were able to intimidate them. Rafael Carrera, the idol of the Indians who had done so little for them, was the first of these autocrats, and after his death in 1865 the Conservative machine he built continued to rule for another six years. By that time factions who called themselves Liberals were gaining the upper hand all over Central America; in 1871 they overthrew Carrera's heirs in Guatemala.

Three Dictators, 1873–1944

JUSTO RUFINO BARRIOS, a white aristocrat of some education, was the dominant figure in the new Liberal government and became president in 1873. A man who knew something of the outside world, he was eager to bring railroads, steamships, teachers, modern administrative methods, and foreign capital and immigrants into Guatemala. Having a low opinion of the Indian's capacity for adaptation to civilization, Barrios, like so many others of this time, really wished to transform his country by and with aliens, to which end he made a tour of Europe and the United States. Few foreigners could be enticed, however, and the rest of Barrios' program progressed but little. Seeking to destroy what he and most other liberals considered the most stubborn impediment to advancement, he struck the Church, which he separated from the state. Furthermore, he required civil marriage and registry, confiscated the properties of the regular orders, banned processions, forbade clergymen to wear their prescribed garb outside churches, and exiled the Jesuits. More influenced than he cared to admit by the *Reforma* in Mexico, Barrios did in truth cripple the Church so badly that it was never to recover its traditional position in Guatemala. As always, such policies pleased most liberals, who prided themselves on being enlightened, but they had a baneful effect on the country by injuring the principal agents of education and mercy: the friars, nuns, and priests.

More consciously did Barrios copy Mexican practices of the time by instituting the *jefe político* system of Porfirio Díaz, by which powerful executives assumed control in the Spanish-speaking districts in the name of the dictator. He also shared Díaz' interest in economic development, but he emulated his success only in starting the large coffee industry that was destined to become Guatemala's main earner of foreign exchange. His methods were simple enough: government agents distributed coffee plant seeds to landowners and whipped them in public if they failed to cultivate the crop satisfactorily. Barrios' admiration, well mixed with fear, of the scowling Porfirio played a part in his agreement to abandon Guatemala's title to Chiapas, which Mexico had detached a half-century before.

In another respect, however, he risked the displeasure of the Mexican despot by trying to revive the Confederation of Central America, a project for which he thought, probably wrongly, that he had the approval of the United States following a visit to Washington in 1882. The little republic of El Salvador was first on the list. Mexico revealed her attitude by mobilizing troops on Guatemala's frontier, but Barrios defiantly invaded his intended victim in 1885. In one of the first skirmishes the would-be unifier was killed, a circumstance that saved El Salvador from further molestation and probably prevented a Mexican invasion of Guatemala. All told, the dozen years of Barrios' presidency represented a modest stimulation of the country, at least in that he acquainted many with the need to import modern ideas and began the coffee industry. He is generally treated kindly by historians.

Barrios' successors were usually Liberals, though none had his vaulting ambitions and none effected as many changes. Guatemala remained independent and gradually increased its coffee sales to the extent that foreign machines, luxuries, publications, and finished goods could be imported. In 1898 a civilian Liberal became president, to initiate a rule that proved to be the longest and worst the republic has yet endured. This was Manuel Estrada Cabrera, who remained president for twenty-two years, regularly renewing his regime by holding elections in which he was the sole candidate and the voters were marched to the polls by soldiers. His dictatorial methods were the familiar ones: an obedient army, a servile police, a puppet congress and judiciary, censorship, and crowded jails. Unlike some tyrants, Estrada Cabrera was not loved and made little effort to be, though the upper classes may have been grateful for the strong rule he provided. Even the elite feared him, for Guatemala became a land of whispers, and its proverbially jolly population acted like cowed slaves. The Indians were his chief victims, since he made peonage more systematic, and therefore worse, and drew heavily on the free communities for forced labor. Only in one respect can Estrada Cabrera be regarded as having benefited Guatemala: he attracted German and American capital so that public utilities and better transportation and communications systems were built, and also hundreds of thousands of acres were placed in the hands of energetic foreigners. The pre-emption of vast tracts of hitherto economically useless coastlands by American banana companies, especially United Fruit, signified the beginning of a second large industry for the republic.

Estrada Cabrera's regime was profitable from the standpoint of these aliens, himself, his family, and his most useful supporters. He ruled so long that his head was turned, and possibly he became insane. Behaving more and more like a royal personage, he had the birthdays of his family and his own public appearances staged with majesty, and the populace did not dare fail to applaud appreciatively. By 1920 the people were so resentful that the military leaders began to conspire. They were delighted to learn that the United States was willing to encourage them, in this case the Wilson Corollary—that governments must not be overturned by force—being denied by its author. When the plot was ripe, the Guatemalan congress suddenly voted to declare Estrada Cabrera mentally incapable, and a rebellion broke out. The tyrant still had enough army units to bombard the capital, which had recently suffered from two severe earthquakes, but this was his last atrocity. He was taken captive and died a few years afterward. Nothing favorable could be said about his administration. The order he had enforced was won at the price of the population's self-respect, and the material improvements Guatemala had undergone were probably fewer than twenty-two years of a different regime would have brought. A considerable betterment in public health was the work of the Rockefeller Foundation in reducing yellow fever and malaria. Guatemala's most famous novelist, Rafael Arévalo Martínez (1884–   ), wrote odd books on the resemblance of human beings to animals and other weird theories both pathological and tender, but his productions could scarcely be regarded as conscious achievements of the regime.

There followed an interval between dictators that lasted for eleven years, from 1920 to 1931. Politics was still the game of the landed *ladino* lords and their military associates. While they intrigued, gave battle, and manipulated the government to their own profit, the period was not wholly barren. The currency, debased by Estrada Cabrera, was stabilized, and American capital poured into Guatemala during the 1920's as it did into other parts of the world. Banks, railroads, and electrical systems expanded as this money entered. Most important of all was the consolidation by the United Fruit Company of still greater banana-raising lands on both the Atlantic and Pacific coasts, the need for large tracts arising from the fact that banana cultivation required shifts from one locality to another at frequent intervals. Indian laborers performed most of the hard work at wages and under conditions that were extremely favorable by the country's standards. And the world's craze for chewing gum led to the penetration of the Petén jungles by hunters of chicle, who inadvertently discovered the sites of marvelous Maya ruins. Coffee continued to be a rewarding industry in the Pacific highlands, where decomposed lava provided an excellent soil for coffee of the finest taste. Since the government was less badly managed than in Estrada Cabrera's time, and since it enjoyed regular revenues as a result of export duties, civil administration improved, and more than 100,000 students were said to be in public schools by 1927.

In 1931, Guatemala's fourth long-term dictator began a rule destined to last for thirteen years. General Jorge Ubico was a short *ladino* with an authoritative manner, who fancied that he resembled Napoleon and who did not always hide his admiration for Hitler. Refreshingly enough, Ubico had a puritanical streak which restrained the acquisitive tendencies of his family and henchmen, and thus some national income was devoted to public purposes. Giving the country relatively effective and energetic administration, the president inspected his domain frequently, terrifying officials with sharp questions and demands to examine their accounts. In addition, Ubico had a sincere concern for the Indian population, who for the first time in decades were treated as though they were not part of the animal kingdom, and he ended the ancient labor draft that dated back to early colonial days and issued laws to protect natives from the worst excesses of peonage. It would still not do to permit the people to toil or not as they pleased. As the Spaniards had justified their labor conscription system by a right of eminent domain, so Ubico decreed that the Guatemalans must perform some work; those who did not have regular jobs had to submit themselves for a specified number of days a year to the state, which might hire them out to contractors. This vagrancy program, as he called it, was nonetheless a considerable improvement over the older arrangement, and the Indians began to stand straighter. With less reluctance some of their abler young men abandoned the traditional Maya aloofness for real participation in modern society.

Despite the world depression, Ubico's regime had fairly good credit, and it built roads and schools and improved public health and sanitation. The University of San Carlos became a source of pride, though many of its graduates had no place in such an underdeveloped land and tended to take up radical causes. World War II brought Guatemala little but benefits. By declaring war on his esteemed Hitler, Ubico could legally appropriate German-owned land, then worth about $150,000,000, sell all of Guatemala's exports at gratifying prices, and enjoy American technical and military aid. As happened in so many other Latin American countries during these years, a little progress awoke the ambitions of the people at large by revealing to them how much more they might make under beneficent rulers. Undirected restlessness became outright discontent, which caused the dictator to take drastic steps of oppression by 1944 and thus intensify rebellious feeling. Soon after a popular revolt in the neighboring republic of El Salvador toppled an autocrat, university students began to riot in Guatemala City. These demonstrations inspired enthusiasm in many quarters, and suddenly Ubico fell.

In Search of a Synthesis

SOMETHING was clearly in the air, for the revolution of 1944 was no mere shift in dictators. The people had shown that they could overthrow a tyrant, a lesson that caused joy to penetrate all of the country and brought to the surface many unsuspected forces. After some months of agitation, which in itself indicated an eagerness of the masses to take an interest in public affairs, a free election of December 1944 made Juan José Arévalo president. A civilian who had spent the past ten years teaching in Argentina, Arévalo was a benevolent person who exuded goodness and assured the Guatemalans they could transform their society. He said he was a socialist, and as soon as he took office he snubbed representatives of foreign interest, hitherto treated with such respect, and ignored the traditional landed oligarchy. Reformers with plans for a social overhauling gathered around the national palace, and new, often young, faces were seen behind government desks. For the first time Guatemala began to seem like something more than an artificial nation. A literacy campaign emulating that of Mexico sent itinerant teachers into the rural areas, where the Spanish language as well as patriotic purposes were now spread. Labor organizers from Mexico flocked into Guatemala to unionize the workers, including those on United Fruit plantations whose welfare had long been conspicuously superior to that of other laborers. And the Arévalo administration passed laws to offer clerks, factory workers, and peasants the protection that working classes in other lands knew.

It was not long until an ugly current manifested itself. President Arévalo was almost a caricature of the well-meaning intellectual in politics, inexperienced and confused, really competent only in enunciating lofty goals. He let someone persuade him to raise his own salary and expense account to a figure beyond that of most monarchs or executives, thus tarnishing his image before the people. As it happened, there were men available who were only too eager to undermine him and to fill the power vacuum. From all over Latin America came Communists, some professed, others covert. While the total was only a few thousand, these men had no intention of winning this tropical land by majority rule. Into key government positions, the army, labor unions, newspapers, and radio broadcasting stations they burrowed, quickly attaining an influence far beyond their numbers. A strident leftist claque began to belabor the propertied classes and to preach Marxism. Combining nationalism with Communism, it aroused real passion for the cause of forcing Britain to surrender Belize, or British Honduras, whose 80,000 inhabitants indicated little interest in being liberated. More menacing were the demands that United Fruit and other "capitalistic imperialists" relinquish their holdings, an agitation that regularly filled the plazas with shouting students and workers. President Arévalo was probably honest in protesting that he was a mere socialist and democrat, but his influence was nearly gone, and more willful men were working toward more drastic goals.

In 1950 the elections, which were subject to pressure and miscounting but were not notably farcical by Guatemalan standards, brought Colonel Jacobo Arbenz Guzmán into the presidency. Arbenz was a blond, blue-eyed radical of long standing, half Spanish, half German-Swiss. Very slowly promoted in years past in the army, he had become bitter during the 1930's and had turned Marxist. His wife had been rejected by her family for marrying him and was also full of hate for society. Both had lived abroad and had associated with Communists. Arbenz, further, was so fond of liquor that he was likely to be erratic in the evenings, testy in the mornings, and groggy in the afternoons. As president he stepped up the attacks on Britain and the United States as perpetrators of an appalling list of crimes. After ignoring the efforts of United

Fruit to come to terms, he issued an agrarian law in 1952 that practically confiscated its properties on the Pacific coast, and other foreign businesses were forced to sell out at low prices. Native owners who resisted his social program were also likely to lose their properties. Accordingly, the government came into possession of vast and valuable lands, but instead of dividing them Arbenz turned them over to government corporations. Few collective farms absorbed the proletariat, however; instead, Arbenz and his cohorts were spending immense sums on automobiles and living on a splendid scale. Much as outsiders, including many Americans, wished to see Guatemala achieve a long-needed social reformation, they were forced to witness a looting of the little country in the worst fashion of strutting dictators of old.

That the revolution was being cheated was sad enough. It seemed almost as grievous that liberty, which had flourished since the fall of Ubico in 1944, was also being extinguished. Radio and press outlets devoted themselves almost entirely to propaganda of Communist orientation, and critics were silenced. Guatemala became the only country in the Americas where an anti-Communist demonstration would be dispersed by the government. When Josef Stalin died in 1953, the puppet congress in Guatemala City stood for a moment of silent reverence. Yet Arbenz was unable to keep everyone quiet. The Church, which had been intimidated since the days of Barrios, found ways to rebuke the regime, and whenever it did so, popular approval showed itself. And the educated groups, who had emerged so hopefully in 1944, muttered their concern over the activities of self-confident professional revolutionaries who had almost ruined Guatemala's economy to no end but the glorification of a foreign-directed tyranny.

In March 1954, at the Inter-American Conference in Caracas, Secretary of State Dulles heard the United States abused by Guatemalan delegates as it had never been at such a forum. He finally obtained the reluctant consent of the other republics to condemn international Communism wherever it appeared in the Americas and to take steps to defeat it. No one could ignore the fact that some of the Latin Americans enjoyed Uncle Sam's discomfiture. But what was to be done? If Washington regarded Guatemala's regime as a Communist virus, it was deeply committed to non-intervention and acutely sensitive to charges of American intimidation. The matter was handled in a way still untold in full. In May 1954, it was known that a shipment of arms from the Communist bloc was headed for Guatemala. Professing fears of aggression, that nation's neighbors bristled in protest, and Guatemalan exiles were allowed to arm on their soil. From Honduras a force of 2,000 Guatemalans led by a onetime minister of war, Carlos Castillo Armas, invaded their homeland, ragged but well-equipped and with airplanes to drop leaflets on the capital. They quickly penetrated Guatemala, encountering little re-sistance from Arbenz' army, which for some reason declined to fight. Lashing out drunkenly to bestir the people to defend the regime, Presi-dent Arbenz aroused only sullenness and soon gave up. Probably he gathered a considerable fortune before taking diplomatic asylum, as did hundreds of his followers. After some months of wrangling, all of them were permitted to leave Guatemala, with the Communist world as their destination.

Castillo Armas' victory was due partly to his effective methods and the failure of Arbenz to win the army and populace. Was there some-thing more? All over the world, leftists and many liberal purists de-nounced the United States for staging a clandestine invasion, assuming that American intelligence agents had bribed Guatemalan army leaders to desert Arbenz and had supplied Castillo Armas. While Washington's denials were often discounted, many were relieved that the first Com-munist foothold in America had been removed so easily, and there was little disputing the favorable reaction in Guatemala itself. Castillo Armas abolished most of the government monopolies Arbenz had set up and, with liberal American subsidies, swiftly revived economic life. He also restored liberty to all but Communists, a category that may have been too inclusive by his reckoning, and otherwise indicated that Guatemala would achieve social democracy without guidance from Moscow. Some of the confiscated properties were returned and others, including the former German lands, were distributed as homesteads. United Fruit agreed to share 30 per cent of its profits with the government and to strengthen its program of welfare capitalism, but for the following six years there were few profits to divide, so ruinous had been Arbenz' dis-ruption.

In July 1957, Castillo Armas was shot dead by an adherent of the fallen regime who had infiltrated the presidential bodyguard. While he had rarely been wildly popular after his initial victory, his regime had seen the country develop faster economically than any other Central American nation, and the level of life for the rural masses had unques-tionably risen sharply. Political advancement by the Guatemalans was suggested in the way they conducted themselves in choosing another president. After a free campaign the election was held in October. It was so close that no candidate had an uncontested plurality, and so another election took place in January 1958. It too was close, with the re-sult that the unicameral congress decided that General Miguel Ydígoras Fuentes, who had a very narrow margin, should be declared president.

Ydígoras was sixty-two, a cultured man with much experience in Europe and a former official of the Ubico regime. On assuming the presi-dency he proclaimed a "democratic creed" which he promised to follow.

During his first two years foreign observers complimented the republic on its respect for human rights, many leftist exiles returned, and students and teachers expressed vociferous opinions about a variety of issues. Only when bomb-throwing became too common did Ydígoras, on two occasions, impose states of siege. He kept up the ritualistic clamor for British Honduras, where indifference toward union with Guatemala continued; he caused Mexican fishermen in Guatemala's claimed territorial waters to be shot, thus bringing about a break in diplomatic relations, and he cut diplomatic ties with Castro's Cuba, which was full of former participants in the late Arbenz regime. Ydígoras pursued the various projects to advance Central American unity and, except for politic outbursts in public that have become standard in Latin America, was friendly with the United States, who bought three-fourths of Guatemala's coffee exports and subsidized her budget to the extent of one-third.

Much as political events and foreign affairs dominated the news from Guatemala, the more significant developments had to do with its economic growth. Progress was steady, despite ups and downs in the price of coffee; this crop and bananas and forest products had a consistent demand abroad, and there was hope of finding oil and minerals in abundance. Scientific methods could produce all the food the people needed, and the growth of light industry and shops all pointed to a diversification of the economy. If the past is any guide, leftist turbulence or rightist reaction is likely at any time to interrupt Guatemala's advance, for her institutions are still fragile. Yet if fortune favored the country for another decade or so, she might well attain administrative stability and a decent standard of living.

EL SALVADOR

The Republic of the Savior is not as devout a land as its name implies. It is, however, a comparatively wholesome and stable country. The smallest in the Central American group, it is second to Guatemala in population, a rather rugged land, cool, and endowed with rich lava soil ideal for coffee-raising. The 2,000,000 or so Salvadoreans are little divided on a racial basis, nearly all of them being mestizos, though Indian communities persist in a few isolated areas and some of the older families claim to be entirely white. Nor are they very class-conscious. If a few Salvadoreans are coffee magnates or unusually successful in business or politics, the others are likely to own at least some property and to enjoy an income that holds them above the mass poverty so common in Latin America. Salvadoreans impress foreigners with their energy; they seem nervous, quick, and industrious, not at all fitting the cartoonists' stereotype of a languid Latin propped against a palm tree. El Salvador's overwhelmingly important business is raising coffee, which constitutes nine-tenths of her exports and finances the machines and finished goods the republic must buy abroad.

A major aspect of El Salvador's history has been its determination to be independent of Guatemala, whose political rhythms it nonetheless has followed. Thus it has been a strong proponent of Central American unification as a means of keeping Guatemala from becoming a Prussia, and in recent years it has worked fervently for the Central American common market and the Organization of Central American States (ODECA). El Salvador's sense of difference from her neighbors has roots in colonial history, and in 1821 some of her leaders offered to join the United States. Perhaps it perversely follows that its stout defense of its own freedom has inclined this republic to meddle in the affairs of its neighbors, especially Honduras.

During the nineteenth century this isolated land was divided by liberal and conservative factions in a series of power seizures and civil wars that no longer seem instructive to chronicle. Few of the victors stayed in office long enough to shape the character of the country or win the attention of posterity. By the end of the century whatever differences there were in ideology had been blurred; what is more worthy of recording is that from 1898 to 1931 no revolutions were successful. Between 1913 and 1927, furthermore, a Meléndez family almost established a presidential dynasty but was peacefully prevented from doing so. During this long period Salvadorean society jelled in the pattern we know today. Small farmers raised and sold coffee year after year. Gradually they acquired a few of the ideas, luxuries, and techniques of the industrialized world. The capital, San Salvador, became a nice-looking city, and education was more general than in most of Middle America. So aware were the republic's leaders of the need for foreign capital, they voluntarily subjected their customhouse to American bankers in 1923 in order to attract investments. While aliens built short railroads, telephone lines, and public utilities—and also eradicated yellow fever and malaria—they did not buy up the country, which has therefore avoided much of the rancor of lands regarded as exploited.

In 1931, when the coffee market was bad and El Salvador was depressed, a revolution finally succeeded. The new ruler was Maximiliano Hernández Martínez, a vice-president who used force to dislodge the president and catered to the rural elements in a demagogic fashion. Handicapped by the refusal of the United States to recognize his regime, Martínez faced in 1932 a serious rebellion, which he labeled Communist, a palpable exaggeration, and suppressed it with a fury unknown in El Salvador. By 1934 there was no question that he was in power, really as a dictator, and the United States recognized him. Martínez was enough of a tyrant to be attracted by European fascism, but when World War II involved the United States he prudently shifted his stance and cooperated with the anti-Axis coalition. For this action he was rewarded by good prices for coffee, military equipment, and American assistance in developing mining and transportation. Meanwhile, the Martínez regime served the interests of coffee planters large and small reasonably well.

Yet Salvadoreans had a tradition of liberty which Martínez flouted, and they have often shown themselves volatile. In March 1944 the death of a child triggered an outpouring of schoolchildren which somehow expanded into a demonstration against the government. Elements of the military then revolted and gave the capital a severe bombing, and a general strike followed. Martínez duly departed, possibly edified by the realization that the Salvadoreans wanted the freedom he had denied as well as the prosperity he had provided. A revolution of a different sort occurred in 1948, when a group of young military men forced their way into power with a social program, a reflection of the fact that El Salvador had been successful enough as a society to demand a better distribution of material things. Thereafter the articulate groups of the republic talked confidently of industrialization, electrification, modern housing, and other advances that would support a general rise in living standards. Oscar Osorio, who was elected president in 1950, carried out much of this program, and his successor, José María Lemus, who became president in 1956, likewise supported these goals and provided a businesslike if oppressive administration. Yet the pace was not fast enough to suit students and middle-class intellectuals, who looked to Communism or Fidel Castro in many cases as offering more material blessings. Apparently fearful of a leftist revolution, a military group struck in October 1960, unseating President Lemus and replacing him with a junta. One of the group, Col. Julio Adalberto Rivera, was elected president in 1962.

It would be premature to judge that El Salvador has achieved democracy, since the army is something of a state-within-state that wields ultimate power, as the revolts of 1948 and 1960 showed, and the population has no real sense of legitimacy where constitutions or regimes are concerned. Yet the Salvadoreans have repeatedly made it clear that they are aware of and devoted to human rights and will resist a government that denies them too long. Perhaps the basic problem now is whether any administration can promote economic growth at a rate fast enough to satisfy the people. El Salvador really has little but the coffee industry to finance its development, and by its nature this source depends on prices abroad. Cotton cultivation, a little mining, and light industry offer some hope of widening the economic base, but most important of all at present is the willingness of the United States to promote Salvadorean growth. Theoretically, a few years of hard work and technical advancement could accomplish wonders and might make this pleasant land almost as comfortable as some of the smaller European nations. The Communist virus, however, poses a threat, and a Central American habit of failure imposes caution on optimistic forecasts.

HONDURAS

Honduras has long been typed as the most backward nation in Central America, perhaps in all America. Second in area in Central America and third in population, it has not proved a viable nation, in fact scarcely a nation at all. Until recent years it has simply been a territory with rubber-like boundaries and governments that either failed to govern at all or did so only briefly. It has had an average of one president a year. While much of Honduras is rugged, it lacks the lava soil that has made the western portions of Central America such fine regions for raising coffee, and tropical rain forests and unfertile savannahs retard even subsistence agriculture. Its people, more than a million and a half of mixed European, Indian, and African ancestry, are victims of what the present president calls the "four 70's": 70 per cent illiteracy, illegitimacy, avoidable deaths, and rural status. Thanks largely to the welfare capitalism of the United Fruit and Standard Fruit companies, as well as to revolutionary agents, the Hondurans have awakened to the possibilities of conquering their awful poverty, and like all Latin Americans, they appear to yearn for democratic republicanism, little of it as they have experienced. It does not seem fantastic to hope that a massive program of economic development, which the United States is eager to support, might transform Honduras into a rather pleasant country, but an awareness of the republic's history tempers optimism of this type. Honduras has always had bad luck.

When this state fell out of the Central American Confederation in the 1830's it had only one town of consequence, the hilly capital of Tegucigalpa. Scattered about the jungles, low mountains, and grassy plains were primitive communities, some of them mere temporary centers for a largely nomadic population. Enough planters and ranchers existed, however, to compose a bucolic aristocracy, and they were sufficiently dedicated to the republic to try to organize and run it, a process usually involving raising ragged armies to fight other would-be leaders. Caudillism at its worst therefore flourished for almost a century after independence. Warriors seized the seat of government for a few months, found themselves betrayed or defeated, and gave way in dizzy succession to others. There was scarcely any administration in the usual sense, only usurping officials who tried to make their brief terms profitable. And yet a dim respect for constitutions, ideals, laws, and elections persisted all through these dreary decades, and a few people were educated enough to talk seriously of ideologies. However divisive the political factions were, the Hondurans maintained a national consciousness and usually resisted whenever Nicaraguans, Salvadoreans, or Guatemalans invaded their country. They had no occasion to rise up against major powers, who threatened Honduras only rarely, when their more adventurous subjects got into trouble there.

By 1900 Honduras' national industry was taking shape. This of course was the banana business, most of which was controlled by the United Fruit Company. It and other foreign firms came into possession of hundreds of thousands of acres along the humid coastlands, employed scientific methods to reduce the toll of the Panama disease that so often ruined the fruit, and drew workers from the interior into company towns, where conditions were pitiful but far better than in the rest of Honduras. As the years went on, the alien concerns protected their workers by eliminating tropical diseases and promoting health and social services. The world's appetite for bananas kept expanding, and so did this establishment.

That was one Honduras. The other had little to do with it except as laborers migrated there and the government drew revenues from banana exports. Tegucigalpa remained as backward a capital as Latin America knew, a trophy for warring factions who invariably failed to hold it long. When they were not engaged in civil war they were likely to be resisting invaders or seeking to borrow money abroad. So dismal was the republic's plight, it was mainly responsible for the conferences of 1907 and 1922–1923 in which the United States attempted to foster international legality among the Central American states. Washington was not inclined to intrude in Honduran affairs except to the extent necessary to ward off European intervention or molestation by imperialistic little neighbors. Thus it supported the unification movement and in 1924 interfered for the purpose of keeping a warrior-politician regarded as a trouble-maker from seizing the government.

This caudillo, General Tiburcio Andino Carías, was not as evil a person as the State Department had thought, as he proved when he finally became president in 1933 for a fifteen-year administration, the longest by far that Honduras has ever known. A tough soldier who knew how to discourage opposition, he also had instincts of statesmanship. Relatively disinterested financially, Carías saw to it that fiscal affairs were set aright for almost the first time in history and proceeded to construct an acceptably effective bureaucracy superimposed on the ruins of a municipal system that had never worked well. He also had some social consciousness and took steps to promote the welfare of the working classes and to build schools. During his administration many roads were scraped out, thus bringing the modern world to isolated parts of the republic. A few silver and gold mines came into operation, and it was possible to exploit the fine forests of hardwood and to build a livestock industry. While Honduras remained appallingly retrograde, there was no denying that the paternalistic Carías had prodded it gently toward the paths of Western progress. Meanwhile, United and Standard Fruit continued to expand and more white ships carried great quantities of bananas from Honduras to New Orleans. While the alien firms stepped up their program of welfare capitalism, building model communities and providing schools and clinics, their reward often seemed to be demands by educated Hondurans for the expulsion of the companies. Labor unions organized and struck for higher wages, the government demanded more taxes, and Communists and left-wing incendiaries penetrated the banana regions.

In 1948, President Carías permitted an heir to take his place as ruler: Juan Manuel Gálvez, who served for six years. During his term Honduras became the base for Guatemalan exiles to organize against the Arbenz regime, and the United States, partly for that reason, liberally poured funds and technical assistance into Honduras. The United Fruit Company negotiated the same agreement with Honduras that it made with Guatemala to the effect that 30 per cent of its profits would go to the government. A taste of progress during these years whetted the appetites of the educated classes, who aspired to increase the tempo of modernization. Efforts of less idealistic motivation caused repeated strikes in the banana regions, where it was apparent that some labor leaders desired nothing less than the ruin of the foreign companies. Obviously, some of these agitators were Communists; others were nationalists who convinced themselves that any alien concern was necessarily an exploiter.

That public opinion had finally developed was evident in those matters and in the increasing ferment of political life. The election of 1954 was marked by much excitement and an inconclusive result, which led the vice-president to take over forcibly. In two years he fell, and then in 1957, the faction which had ousted him lost control, and so another election was held, one which outsiders reported as honest. In this test the victor was a physician, Dr. Ramón Villeda Morales, a liberal civilian who had been ambassador to the United States. Dr. Villeda identified Honduras' major concern as the need to elevate the living standards of the people quickly but within the framework of democratic procedures. That a popularly-elected president could set such goals was an indication that the days of the banana republic, in the invidious sense, might be ended for Honduras. His administration supported the optimists, though it was possible to discern abuses of liberty. Many schools and roads were built, a large hydroelectric project was started, the economy improved, and a labor code gave status to the working classes. As often happens in an underdeveloped country, people received university education faster than satisfactory positions were available for them, and trained young men sometimes became bitter at the lack of opportunity and looked with sympathy toward Communism or Castroism. On the whole, Honduras appeared to be emerging from primitivism, though no one could confidently predict a future free of strife.

NICARAGUA

The history of Nicaragua has been the most eventful in Central America. From a distance it seems a procession of low comedy and pathetic folly, but to the participants it has frequently been a tragic affair, and in truth, much of the trouble has been caused by foreigners. Most Nicaraguans have gone about their humble affairs for generations, unaware that their republic was the prime illustration of Theodore Roosevelt's term, "chronic wrongdoing." The million or more Nicaraguans are mainly of mixed blood, though there are pockets of Indians and Negroes and a few whites claim undiluted European ancestry. Their land is almost evenly divided between monotonous flatlands with swamps and jungles and one of the most beautiful areas of mountains, lakes, and volcanoes in all America. Bananas and woods are taken from the former, the eastern, section; coffee and cotton come from the arable patches of the latter. San Juan del Norte (formerly Greytown) is the Caribbean port, while Managua, Leon, and Granada are the leading cities of the interior. A varied country with likable inhabitants, Nicaragua deserves, according to the wistful, a happier fate than she has known.

After centuries of torpor under the Spaniards, this country found the outside world crashing in during the days of the California gold rush. Travelers landed at Greytown, were rowed up the San Juan River into Lake Nicaragua, sailed across it, and went by wagons or mules to the Pacific coast to embark for San Francisco. These activities stimulated the little republic, but they also involved it in the riotous events centering about Cornelius Vanderbilt and William Walker, and they made it for a time a pawn between Great Britain and the United States. By 1863 a calm settled on the country. Panama, with its railroad, was attracting most of the trans-isthmian traffic, Walker was gone, and the great powers were occupied elsewhere. Since Walker had made use of the Liberals, this party was in disgrace and its stronghold, Leon, was no longer the capital. Instead, the Conservatives ruled Nicaragua from Granada or Managua from 1863 to 1893, a period known, with some latitude, as the "Thirty Years' Peace." The peace was only relative, for Liberals waged war from time to time and the Conservatives scrapped among themselves. On the whole, government was crude, and so was the nation. A few minerals, woods, and coffee exports brought in enough foreign exchange to enable the rich to purchase finished goods.

Strangely enough, it was here during these years that one of the greatest of modern poets grew up and began his career. Rubén Darío (1867–1916) was a Nicaraguan prodigy of uncertain parentage. Uneducated as most of them were, his fellow countrymen recognized him as a poet of immense power. When he was grown, he went on to Chile, Argentina, Spain, France, and the United States for a life of romantic suffering and dissipation, but also to compose poems and poetic prose that made him the first and the greatest of the "modernists," French-inspired perfectionists who used abstract problems as themes rather than the realities they knew personally, and who treated with exquisite grace the mysteries of life as a modern civilized man might respond to them. Darío returned to Nicaragua to die.

A man almost as famous, but in a different way, advertised Nicaragua for sixteen years after 1893: José Santos Zelaya. In that year the Conservative regime finally collapsed, and Zelaya, a Liberal from Managua, became president. He made up for the long Liberal exile by oppressing Conservatives with a ferocity rare even in Central America. An absolute tyrant, depraved, brutal, and thoroughly contemptible, he ruled the little republic like a jailor. A man of preposterous vanity, he imagined himself a great benefactor and offered to spread his Liberal "reforms" into lands as far away as Guatemala and Ecuador. So cruel were his persecutions of aliens who had come to do business, Britain twice sent warships to threaten him—the United States not being the only power to throw its weight around the Caribbean at that time. It was a grievous blow to Zelaya that the Americans built the canal through Panama instead of Nicaragua, which in truth might have been a superior route, and he blustered vainly about selling Nicaragua's transit rights to a potential Yankee enemy, such as Japan. Debasing as his rule was, it afforded sixteen years of internal peace. A few students went abroad, the coffee industry grew considerably, the ubiquitous United Fruit Company developed a banana establishment, and railroads and lake steamers modernized the country in modest ways.

Washington's ill will proved Zelaya's undoing. Already worried about a possible British intervention to collect debts, the United States made an issue of Zelaya's killing of two of its citizens in 1909. Soon the president's official family eased him from power, only to be ousted itself in the following year. At this point President Taft allowed the State Department to negotiate with the new administration a deal whereby American bankers would loan Nicaragua $15,000,000 to stabilize its currency and make payments on the debt, for which service the bankers would receive many favors. The U.S. Senate regarded the project as suspicious and smelled collusion between the State Department and Wall Street. The upright Taft was sure his course was correct, however, and went ahead with a modified plan, after the Senate rejected his proposed pact, on his authority as chief executive. For a year or two it seemed to work well enough; Nicaragua obtained loans and pacified her creditors, whose claims were shown to be outrageously high. In 1912, when a revolution threatened, Taft dispatched marines to protect the pro-American administration and thereby grabbed a bear by the tail. Not until 1933 were the marines to be finally withdrawn from Nicaragua, and the notoriety of the American intervention has not yet been lived down.

Woodrow Wilson righteously condemned Taft's actions in the campaign of 1912 and promised to remove the marines, but after taking office he underwent a conversion. If the American forces left Nicaragua to her own devices, she would surely get into trouble again and probably provoke European intervention. And so the marines stayed, usually only a hundred strong unless disorders threatened. Since the simplest way to prevent violence was to control the government, Wilson found himself advising, then almost dictating, and, in 1916, arranging that a pro-American Conservative win the election. Meanwhile, he appeased Nicaragua's outraged feelings over losing the canal by means of the Bryan-Chamorro Treaty of 1914, which was ratified in 1916. This pact called for the United States to pay the republic $3,000,000 for an option on the Nicaraguan route and the right to establish bases on the Corn Islands, at San Juan del Norte, and on the Gulf of Fonseca. The treaty only made matters worse. Most of the money went to Nicaragua's creditors, not her politicians; Costa Rica loudly asserted her claims to San Juan del Norte; and, as a glance at the map should have made clear in the beginning, the Gulf of Fonseca involved two other countries, El Salvador and Honduras, both of whom set up a clamor. Eventually, the United States settled for the Corn bases, but her maladroit diplomacy had angered everyone.

It is entirely possible that the presence of the marines at first gave Nicaragua a few years of comparative peace. Some progress in sanitation and education occurred, and American investments livened the national economy. After the election of 1924, which the United States supervised in the interest of a fusion candidate, it seemed in order to end the protectorate. The marines departed in August 1925. A revolution broke out in October, led by Emiliano Chamorro, who had negotiated the treaty of 1914. Exasperated officials in Washington decided to send the marines back, only to incur the opposition of Mexico, at that time engaged in much acrimony with the United States, and to see a savage civil war begin. The Americans were greatly embarrassed by world-wide reflections on their motives, which to be sure were not particularly clear and were open to harsh interpretations. Finally, in 1927, President Coolidge sent Henry L. Stimson, a onetime and future cabinet officer, to pacify Nicaragua. This he did after a fashion by holding an election, courtesy of the U. S. Marines, in which voters had their hands dyed as soon as they had passed the ballot box in order to prevent repeating. Victory by a close margin went to the anti-Yankee Liberals, and Washington decided to prolong the stay of the "legation guard," as the marine occupying force was called.

By this time Latin American opinion was furiously aroused against the United States, and many Americans also believed that the marines were oppressing an innocent nation. Washington feared a complete breakdown of Nicaraguan society if the marines left; little as others believed it, officialdom could not have cared less about the few millions of private American loans in Nicaragua. Another factor was the defiance of a Nicaraguan junior officer, Augusto César Sandino, who organized guerrilla parties to ambush the marines and commit isolated acts of terrorism. On several occasions his forces nearly defeated detachments of marines. The thrill of hero-worship for this grizzled leader, a "bandit" to many Americans, throughout Latin America further distressed Washington. Sandino vowed he would never leave Nicaragua until the last marine was out, and he presented a program of social reform. While in fact he did leave Nicaragua several times for debauches in Mexico, and while the sincerity of his social projects was open to doubt, Sandino became a popular idol. Finally, in 1932, an election carried a Liberal leader the Americans had long opposed, Juan Bautista Sacasa, into the presidency, whereupon President Hoover decided to pull the marines out. Certainly the long intervention had done great injury to the reputation of the United States, though it probably benefited Nicaragua. As for Sandino, once the Americans were gone the Liberals and Conservatives united against him as a nuisance, and, after dining with President Sacasa in 1934, he was treacherously murdered. His ghost is still invoked by Yankeephobes.

The killer of Sandino belonged to the *guardia nacional*, a constabulary created by the United States to keep order after the marines had left. The leader of this force was a tough little warrior named Anastasio Somoza but familiarly called "Tacho." Somoza was also the nephew of President Sacasa, during whose administration he acquired a strong grip on the mechanisms of power. Soon he was announcing his advent to the presidency, implying that no one had better try to stop him. No one did. Somoza was the sole candidate in 1936, and he remained in power until he was assassinated twenty years later. During its second protracted dictatorship Nicaragua made much progress, materially and culturally. Perhaps she would have done so regardless of her government, but Tacho claimed full credit. Greater output of farms, mines, forests, and ranches, as well as wholesome measures in education and public health, compensated in part for the highly-organized tyranny he imposed, and he was abreast of his times in providing social welfare measures. The vast Somoza family also made much progress, acquiring properties said to be worth tens of millions of dollars.

In the spring of 1939 President Somoza was invited to make a state visit to Washington. He had lived in the United States as a youth and had been cordial to the Americans as president, but his reception was truly extraordinary. President Roosevelt, his family, the cabinet, the Supreme Court, and the entire Congress met his train. A most elaborate parade and a majestic series of festivities honored the Nicaraguan dictator, about whose true character few informed persons could be ignorant. Gossips gaily reported that these ceremonies for Tacho were in reality a dress rehearsal for the forthcoming visit of King George VI. If Somoza heard this, he was not offended. During World War II he was highly cooperative, and he was rewarded as handsomely as other Latin Americans, perhaps more so, for he received a special bonus in the way of a $12,000,-000 highway the United States built to connect the Caribbean coast with the lake cities. After the war he continued to pose as an intimate friend of the United States, his country's best customer, banker, and rich uncle. When he stepped down from office in 1947 in favor of a puppet, the Truman administration thought it time to let Nicaragua know that dictators were no longer in style. But an error in thanking the new president for sending flowers to the funeral of Truman's mother constituted an act of recognition, and relations continued. Tacho resumed the presidency in 1950. When he was assassinated in September 1956 his son, Luis A. Somoza Debayle, was prevailed upon to become provisional president and was elected to a full term in the following year. The dynasty continued.

The Somozas, however, were beginning to relax the dictatorship after so many years of power and profit. The new president was very sensitive to charges that he censored the press, oppressed political opponents, and caused trouble among his neighbors. Much evidence as there was that he did just those things, it was something of a gain that he was ashamed of them and that he did them covertly and on a smaller scale than his father had. To disprove charges of dynasticism he promised a completely free election for 1962, one in which neither he nor any of his relatives would be a candidate. Skeptical enemies were not willing to wait that long.

Planes and ships full of invaders, often of the Caribbean Legion, an irregular group that professed to hate all dictators, frequently descended upon Nicaragua only to be, at this writing, repeatedly turned back. Fidel Castro of Cuba was a favorite enemy of the Somoza regime, and there was much coming and going of armed men between Cuba and Nicaragua, all bent on revolutionizing one another's country. Somoza the younger insisted that his rule was both beneficent and popular. He could point to one considerable achievement: Nicaragua had the best credit rating in all Latin America during 1959, a change indeed from the days of "chronic wrongdoing." Cotton exports had grown so fast they surpassed coffee, which had also expanded, and economic activity in other areas was fairly vigorous. The republic was still no paradise—far from it—but its progress had been substantial enough to encourage cautious hopes for the future.

COSTA RICA

Costa Rica does not seem to belong in Central America, and it often has spurned intimacy with the other republics. This admired little country also ignores the dreary catalogue of handicaps from which most Latin American lands suffer. No geographical, racial, or social divisions have held it back. Nor has it ever been mortgaged to foreigners or badly abused by the great powers. A major producer of bananas, this is no banana republic. Costa Rica is a high, cool, breezy segment of the isthmus, happily isolated from such wayward neighbors as Panama and Nicaragua by jungle growth. While the coasts are torrid, most of the population lives in pleasant uplands, particularly in the verdant *meseta* around the capital, San José, where the climate is so good Canal Zone residents have long taken their vacations there. Most Costa Ricans, or *ticos*, are of Spanish descent. In colonial days word spread through Spanish Galicia that this was a land of opportunity, and many hardy, industrious *gallegos* migrated there. The Indians were driven away and few Africans were ever imported; thus the racial composition of the colony, and afterward of the republic, has been remarkably uniform. Furthermore, the inhabitants worked on their own farms and ranches, avoiding the latifundia pattern, and if some were richer and more successful than others, an egalitarian spirit nonetheless prevailed. Isolation and obscurity were other advantages in colonial times, for Spain seldom bothered with Costa Rica, and pirates and foreign enemies had little temptation to loot an agricultural region.

Independence from Spain in 1821, and then from the Central American Confederation by 1838, left this little society on its own resources. One of its first rulers, Braulio Carillo (1835–1842), was wise enough to divide up the municipal lands among the inhabitants, thus increasing the number of small farmers. He also encouraged the planting of coffee on these holdings, thus starting an industry that has long been the backbone of Costa Rica's economy. Juan Rafael Mora, who ruled from 1849 until he was shot in 1859, further strengthened the republic's institutions and helped defeat the intruder William Walker in Nicaragua. Tomás Guardia was dominant from 1870 to 1882, winning the respect of posterity by breaking the power of a potential ruling class of the larger property owners and sponsoring the constitution of 1871, which remained in force until 1917. In addition to being generally observed, this charter gave Costa Rica a distinction in providing for legislative ascendancy over the executive. The numerous splinter parties that accordingly developed often stood for something, and they fostered democratic habits. In 1889 an outgoing president did nothing to prevent an opposition candidate from winning the election, perhaps the most free held in Latin America until then, and taking office. In fine, the republic was a reality, though politicians often fell short of perfection.

Of more importance than politics during the last of the nineteenth century were the activities of an American entrepreneur, Minor C. Keith. President Guardia wanted a railroad built from Puerto Limón on the Caribbean up to San José and called on the fabulous Henry Meiggs, whose prodigies of railroad construction in South America were well known. He obtained instead the services of Meiggs' nephew, Keith, who proved himself altogether as astonishing a managerial genius as his uncle. Keith built the railroad, a difficult feat in itself, finished in 1891 and necessitating the importation of West Indian Negroes who were immune to tropical diseases. After enriching himself and cooperative politicians in the usual ways, he further set out to find more freight for the railway to carry. The banana industry loomed as a great opportunity, for Americans craved the fruit but could seldom obtain it. Hence Keith bought a fleet of steamers to deliver them in a refrigerated state to New Orleans. His business prospered so well that he developed great banana plantations in the humid coastal lowlands, and in 1899 he helped organize a number of firms as the United Fruit Company, which acquired a near monopoly not only in Costa Rica but in other states of Central and South America. With substantial exports of coffee, bananas, and a few minerals, Costa Rica enjoyed a steady income for decades.

The little republic seldom figured in international news. Its inhabitants minded their own affairs, and foreigners rarely intruded except to expedite commerce. Gradually, public education was extended to everyone, and it became a boast that Costa Rica had more teachers than soldiers. Sometimes, however, the soldiers made trouble. They helped Federico Tinoco into power in 1917, but in only two years the republic resumed its democratic ways, thanks to popular insistence and American opposition to Tinoco. During the early 1920's Costa Rica nearly became involved in war with Panama over an ancient boundary dispute. An American award had given the town of Coto to Costa Rica in 1914, but

Panama refused to surrender it, whereupon Costa Rica occupied Coto by force in 1921. The Panamanians were prevented from waging war by a veto by the United States, but quarrels, agitation, and occasional skirmishes continued until 1941, when Panama finally gave up. By that time both Costa Rica and Panama had no standing armies, only militias and police forces. Costa Rica seldom concerned herself with the meddling that so often brought the other Central American republics into conflict.

With her orderly habits and self-respecting population, and her quaintness and scenery, Costa Rica inevitably suggested comparison with Switzerland. Together with Uruguay, which was far less colorful but much like her in behavior, she gave students of affairs reason to doubt the clichés that so confidently explain the political turbulence and mass poverty of Latin America. By the mid-twentieth century this rural paradise began to change its character somewhat without losing the attributes that had made it so admired. Light industry was creating a small urban proletariat and expanding the middle class, and also awakening the population at large to the comforts of modern technology. By the end of World War II, labor organizations were receptive to radical preachments, and intellectuals often became sympathetic to Communism. A crisis occurred in the election of 1948, which was won by a liberal publisher named Otilio Ulate. Leftist elements sought to annul the verdict for no very sound reason, a circumstance that inspired a small civil war. Conspicuous among Ulate's followers was a planter, José Figueres, who collected a force of irregulars called the Caribbean Legion, a declared enemy of all dictators. Figueres, the beloved "Pepe" to his men, was a graduate of the Massachusetts Institute of Technology and was married to an American; a major spokesman for the cause of social uplift within the framework of democracy, he was strongly anti-Communist. The movement he led won. The leftists of totalitarian sympathies were routed, Otilio Ulate took office in 1949, and Pepe Figueres succeeded him in 1953.

Costa Rica's prosperity continued with few interruptions during the 1950's. Fluctuations in coffee or banana prices or hurricanes and plant diseases occasionally injured the economy, but the growth of meat-packing, mining, and light industry more than compensated for them. Figueres secured from United Fruit the familiar 30 per cent arrangement for a share in its profits. He also built low-cost housing for workers, strengthened the social welfare system, and nationalized several large businesses. Accused of socialism, he pointed to his record as an enemy of Communism with its bogus socialism and chided critics who demanded that Latin America become more efficient but condemned as socialism state efforts to make it so. His position on this issue was, in truth, equivocal, as his domestic opponents and American observers pointed out. And the

Caribbean Legion proved a mixed blessing, since it lost its original anti-Communist character which gave rise to suspicions that it served Moscow. On several occasions the legion attempted to overthrow the Somoza dictatorship in Nicaragua, which likewise sought the fall of Figueres. In January 1955 a war between the two republics was averted by the strong intervention of the OAS.

Popular as Pepe Figueres was at home and abroad, he was unable to persuade a majority of his countrymen to elect his candidate in 1958. In an election reported by United Nations observers as honest, the conservative Mario J. Echandi won by a narrow margin after charging the Figueres regime with disguised socialism. While Echandi promised to reverse the trend, no major changes occurred, and Figueres' choice, Francisco J. Orlich, was elected in 1962. More than a million *ticos* appeared to be confident they could perpetuate and strengthen their democratic republic.

PANAMA

The republic of Panama is an artificial state that came into being because President Theodore Roosevelt grew impatient with the rulers of Colombia in negotiations for an isthmian canal route. At that time, in 1903, about 300,000 persons lived in the region. While they had often revolted, they were not really nationalists striving for freedom but regionalists who rebelled for a variety of causes, the way other Colombians did. National feeling was not initially crystallized by the immigrants, many of them Negro workers from the West Indies and Americans, who came in to build the canal. The two leading towns, Colón on the Caribbean and Panama on the Pacific, became real cities, and other communities developed along the canal route. Nowhere else was there much activity; even now only a few towns and settlements are found away from the Canal Zone, most of them devoted to banana cultivation. Indians in the Darien region live almost as primitively as they did four centuries ago, and much of Panama is uninhabited.

The million Panamanians, a very high percentage of whom live near the famous "ditch," derive their livelihood mainly from serving the garrisons and employees of the Canal Zone and living off the requirements and vices of those who pass through it in the 10,000 or more transits made by vessels each year. The tone of Panama is therefore low, as it was when the area served a similar function in the days of the Spanish colonial monopoly. Sailors and travelers are seldom interested in book shops, concert halls, and art galleries, and the Panamanians cater to other desires. Another degrading factor is the availability of duty-free merchandise, which encourages visitors to look for bargains and swindling merchants to palm off shoddy goods on the unwary. Thus Panama means to many a passenger or serviceman a land of servants, unskilled workers, prostitutes, gamblers, entertainers, and sharpsters. It happens, however, that its population now has a fierce national pride and an educated element. Panamanians are demanding the material benefits of modern life in a threatening way, and often the focus of their frustrations is the very canal that accounts for their livelihood.

The United States meant to do well by Panama once it was separated from Colombia. The Hay-Bunau-Varilla Treaty of 1903 gave the new state $10,000,000 and promised an annual rental of $250,000 for the Canal Zone. It also provided for American intervention in the interest of public order or sanitation. A constitution in 1904 seemed a veritable model of republicanism, with all the civil rights, a centralized government, and separation of state and church being specified. In the same year the army was disbanded at the behest of the Americans, whose protection was all that Panama needed. But acrimony arose almost at once. The Panamanians knew so little of democratic practices that they were unable to conduct elections, and the Americans repeatedly intruded themselves to place candidates in office and keep them from being forcibly ejected. Soon the natives were objecting to the large number of Negroes whom the United States imported to dig the canal, and they also resented the Chinese and East Indians who swarmed into the country to handle the business entailed by the hundreds of millions being spent on the channel. Panamanians also protested when the Americans established their own postal system and customhouses and set up commissaries, which deprived Panama's shops of well-heeled customers. And they were acutely offended by a pay scale in the Canal Zone which rewarded non-Panamanians on a far more liberal basis than citizens of the host nation.

These irritations troubled the Americans little enough at first. The construction of the canal, by far the greatest engineering feat in the world until that time, was a wonderful enterprise that enlisted the enthusiasm of the United States. The Chagres River was dammed, to become Gatun Lake, and channels were dug in the harbors of Colón and Panama City. Intricate locks were constructed to elevate ships into Gatun Lake and lower them again. A very difficult operation finally produced Gaillard Cut, which completed the channel. While the canal was being built under the direction of Colonel George W. Goethals, another army officer, Dr. William C. Gorgas, was supervising the extermination of mosquitoes and other health measures. Malaria and yellow fever, which had defeated the earlier French canal enterprise, were at last conquered. When the first ship sailed through in 1914, the American nation congratulated itself on a magnificent achievement. From the first, the canal justified itself, commercially, financially, and militarily, and was a boon to Latin America as well as the United States. To Americans, it seemed that the Panamanians ought to rejoice that Yankee enterprise had touched their land and given them health, freedom, business, protection, and order.

The Panamanians were not always inclined to look at matters that way. The transit route had filled their country with outsiders, some who stirred envy, others racial prejudice. Many natives objected when the Negroes were not shipped back to the West Indies after the canal was finished and yet found themselves looked upon as colored men by white Americans who discriminated against them in the familiar ways. The Panamanians' pride was injured by the evident disdain the Americans bore for them, by the way they lived aloof in the Canal Zone like a foreign ruling class amid despised natives, emerging only to find servants, drink liquor during Prohibition, buy drugs, and be entertained. While the American element had done much to give Panama schools and better health, its very opulence reminded Panamanians how poor they were. Even the manifest benefits of the American presence seemed patronage or charity carelessly tossed off to inferiors.

By 1918 the United States paid enough heed to Panamanian sensitivities to remove most of the political controls and let the people, as it proved, misgovern themselves. A few Panamanian families were aristocratic, or at least rich: Arias, de la Guardia, Porras, Arosemena, and others. This native oligarchy was badly divided by clan pride and ambition rather than political ideologies. Since Panama had no army, an inflated police force served to furnish a basis for militaristic politics, and so Panama did not escape the Latin American curse of caudillism. When one family was in power, it mistreated its rivals and made vast profits, for Panamanian administration was corruption itself. Force or the threat of force was likely to make any tenure fairly brief, and Panama failed completely to become a showcase of republican virtue.

In 1936, as part of the Good Neighbor policy, the United States agreed to raise the annual rental to $430,000, a step Panama demanded because of the devaluation of the dollar in 1933. Furthermore, the republic was no longer to be considered a protectorate of the United States but an ally, no less, and the Americans vowed not to intervene in its internal affairs. Not until 1939 did the U.S. Senate satisfy itself that the agreement would not prevent American measures on Panama's soil to defend the canal and ratify the treaty. While relations improved considerably thereafter, many Panamanians by this time had become educated and therefore vulnerable to anti-American propaganda emanating from European totalitarians. An opportunity for the republic to assert itself appeared in the use of Panamanian registry for merchant ships, often a device for shipowners to circumvent safety regulations or the imperatives of labor unions in their own countries. Thus Panama became one of the greatest shipping nations on earth, at least on paper. Ironically, this practice was very handy for the United States government early in World War II, since it could send armed ships under the Panamanian flag to British and French ports despite the Neutrality Act. A difficulty appeared in 1940, when Arnulfo Arias became president. An ardent nationalist and admirer of Hitler, Arias attempted to stop the arming of Panamanian ships for this purpose. His abrupt removal from office a few months later suggested that American influence was still potent in Panama's affairs.

During World War II, Panama caused no trouble for the United States. A friendly administration leased more than a hundred sites to the Americans for military bases and loyally joined its ally in declaring war. To the relief and surprise of everyone, the Axis made no attack whatever on the canal. But when the war ended, a surge of anti-Yankee feeling came to the surface. Stiffened by rioting students, the Panamanian congress declined to accept an American request to continue the lease on a few of the wartime bases. And in 1948, Arnulfo Arias, backed by extreme nationalists and Communists, was again elected to the presidency. For the second time he was ousted under confused circumstances, and a pro-American president took his place.

The elections of 1952 gave the presidency to Colonel José Remón, who as chief of police was the most powerful man in the republic and, some charged, the richest. Since he was very friendly to the United States, a lull in Yankee-baiting ensued. The canal was jammed with traffic, so much so that ships had to queue up for days. Many Panamanians resentfully eyed the tolls, which came to $40,000,000 a year, though of course expenses were heavy too, and the United States agreed to raise the rental from $430,000 to $2,000,000 a year. Also, much of the lock machinery was modernized, and Gaillard Cut was widened to enable ships to go in both directions at once. These activities, of course, stimulated Panama's economic life to some degree, but not fast enough to satisfy its inhabitants. Moreover, the obliging Remón obtained much technical assistance from the United States to improve food production, schools, and roads. But one of his pet projects, the resettlement of the idle proletariat on farmlands, was a failure. Life in the cities on any terms seemed preferable to Panamanians, as it did to most other peoples, to economic independence and hard work in the country. Other possibilities appeared within reach to improve Panama's economy: a fruit and rice industry; tourism, with fine hotels, beaches, and casinos; oil refining for imported petroleum; and that status symbol of small nations, a steel mill, which in this case would have to process imported iron. While the population was better off than it had ever been before, it shared the world-wide realization that a few fortunate lands were immensely richer and blamed the United States for not helping Panama more.

In January 1955, President Remón was shot dead at a race track by unknown persons just after he had returned from a triumphal tour of the United States. After a confused interval, an election was held in 1956 which was won by Ernesto de la Guardia, the candidate backed by Communists and ultra-nationalists. Panama was greatly stirred by the Suez crisis of that year, though her situation was quite different from Egypt's. Unlike the British, the Americans had formidable garrisons around the canal and were in firm possession of it, and their rights under international law were incontrovertible. Nonetheless, President de la Guardia encouraged his countrymen to demand the canal. For several years the little country seemed to become a sea of angry men demonstrating at will, screaming insults at Uncle Sam and abusing American nationals who strayed out of the Canal Zone. Students, journalists, and politicians accused the United States of crimes that might have made Hitler envious. On one occasion, in November 1959, human sea tactics by great masses threatened to overwhelm the zone, and it looked for a few hours as though a bloodbath were inevitable.

President Eisenhower decided to conciliate the Panamanians. First, the wage differential that had offended them for decades was abolished, though the 14,000 Panamanian employees continued to draw lower pay than the 5,000 Americans because they performed less skilled labor. Then, Eisenhower consented to permit the flag of Panama to fly in the Canal Zone, where the United States had rights under the treaty of 1903 as "if it were the sovereign." Not a few Americans argued that the canal should be internationalized, for it had become such a symbol of hate throughout Latin America, it was no longer a military necessity, and it could not be defended in a nuclear war. Others maintained that submission to pressure would simply ignite more. Anti-Yankee agitation continued throughout 1959 and 1960, the streets of Panama City and Colón often being filled with striking students, some of them children, and others who had readymade slogans of probable Communist origin. Comic relief was afforded in April 1959 when a rebellious member of the Arias family tried to raise a revolution but succeeded only in having his wife, the illustrious ballerina, Dame Margot Fonteyn, put in jail for a night.

That the Panamanians were not altogether a collection of furies became evident in the elections of May 1960, which put things back in balance. A fairly conservative figure, Roberto F. Chiari, was chosen president, succeeding the strident de la Guardia, the first Panamanian for a quarter-century to complete a four-year presidential term. Chiari indicated that anti-American violence would no longer have official sanction, and his tone with Washington was reasonable. Besides, he urged,

Panama should not be so obsessed with the canal. With American aid that was amply available, she could diversify her economy and raise her standards of living. In preparation for this program she must undergo a "national redemption," cleaning up her administration, reducing graft, and restraining Communist agitation. His words were well received. Many Panamanians realized that their demands had been extreme, that even if they won the canal and all its tolls there would still not be enough money to help many of them. As for the students, they knew better than many alarmist observers that their earlier rioting had largely been fun-making, or at most a protest against a world that had not favored their country as well as others. In the last analysis, Panama could not possibly take the canal away from the United States against its will, a hard fact that might not sit well with Americans who wanted to be loved but which was obvious even to Panamanian extremists. Whatever their feelings about the Panama Canal, Americans could only regard with uneasiness the potential rage of an impoverished million people living beside the famous artery.

28

Venezuela

A CENTURY ago Venezuela was full of vitality and had many men who took political issues seriously enough to kill and die for them. Today, the country is almost as vibrant, and no Latin Americans are more assertive or demanding than the Venezuelans. But during the intervening hundred years this condition did not prevail; unusually severe despotisms, four in particular, nearly smothered the country. They coincided with its entrance into the age of machines and capitalism, which failed in this instance to be also an age of democracy.

It is not easy to isolate the reasons for Venezuela's political decline after the 1860's. The early republic may not have been a glorious affair, but it had fostered a respect for popular government. The country was comparatively large, rich in natural resources, and unusually varied. Primarily tropical, it was favored by mountains rising steeply out of the Caribbean, which gave it cool, fertile valleys near the coast. In the western end of the country were the Andes, in the southern part the Guiana Highlands. The enormous valley of the Orinoco River was full of *llanos*, or grasslands, and beyond them was the *selva*, or jungle forest. Most of the people lived in the rugged belt along the Caribbean coast. Racial divisions had not been for a long time a determining factor in their history. While the whites usually asserted—and the others in subtle ways acknowledged—a superiority, they were not numerous. Most of the population by far was a mixture of Spaniard, Basque, or Canarian with Indian or African. And yet a bountiful nature and a relatively homogeneous population did not make for a happy career as Venezuela entered the modern age. She had the worst and most protracted dictatorships of any of the larger Latin American nations.

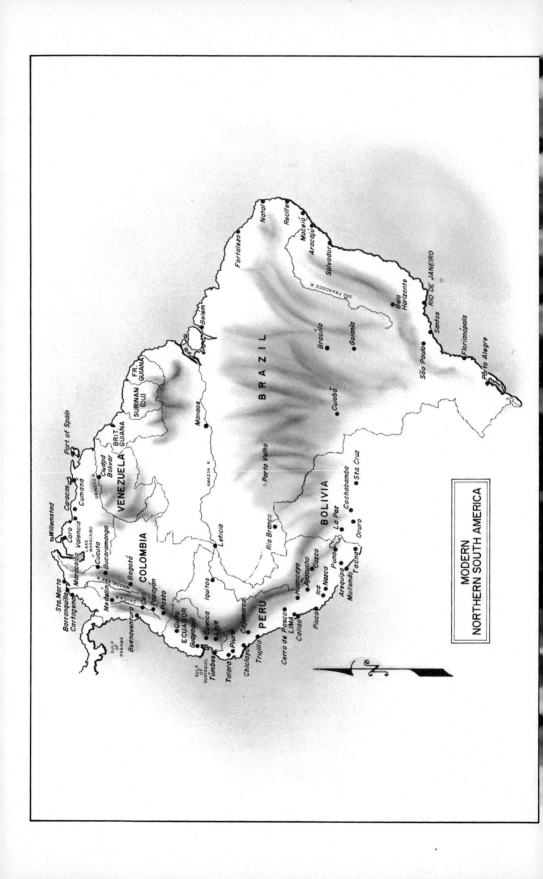

MODERN
NORTHERN SOUTH AMERICA

ANTONIO GUZMÁN BLANCO,
AN ARISTOCRATIC DEMAGOGUE

For a quarter-century after the first fall of José Antonio Páez in 1846, Venezuela was disrupted by caudillo-politicians who professed to fight over the issues of liberalism and federalism versus conservatism and centralization. The "Yellows," as advocates of the former cause were called, came into their own in 1863 after the second fall of Páez and almost produced the disintegration of the republic. Their opponents, the "Blues," made war to restore Caracas as the font of authority. After a confusing sequence of battles and revolutions, Antonio Guzmán Blanco entered the capital in April 1870. It required about two years for him to make his will respected throughout the whole nation, or at least in its major population centers. He was leader of the "Yellows" and presumably a liberal federalist.

Guzmán Blanco was a handsome fellow of Spanish ancestry. His father had been an influential liberal journalist and politician and had seen to it that Antonio was well educated. Something of a patrician, the new ruler had a gift for conveying his sympathy for the poor. Thus he enjoyed the confidence of the planters and merchants—for he was one of them—and the adulation of the masses. He was also a competent soldier and a shrewd manipulator of men and public relations. Once his power was firm, he made it clear that he had no intention of permitting the nation to be confused with a welter of opinions. He censored the press, jailed or exiled his critics, and otherwise instituted the familiar instruments of dictatorship. Nor was he really the federalist that liberals claimed to be, for he wanted state rulers to represent his will, not that of their respective localities. The Church, which was usually "Blue" in sympathy, offended him for that reason and because he was a high-ranking Mason, possibly a skeptic. Therefore, he exiled the papal nuncio and the archbishop, disbanded the religious orders and confiscated their properties, laicized cemeteries, required civil marriage and a civil register of vital statistics, and proclaimed complete religious freedom. While the real effect of these actions was to weaken education and deprive Indian missions of their leaders, they did not seriously injure his popularity. He also did much to stimulate public esteem for his administration. Aware of the endurance of the names of Justinian and Napoleon, he compiled a code to perpetuate his. Newspapers and books were required to praise him as the "Regenerator," the "Pacifier," and the "Illustrious American," and his name was inscribed conspicuously on every public building. These methods of advertisement, in addition to placards and monuments, were partly the result of a puerile vanity, but they were also a time-tested way of strengthening a leader's hold, as monarchs of the past and democratic rulers of the present have amply demonstrated.

Guzmán Blanco's policies were well-adapted to the immediate needs of the republic. Once order was enforced, foreign capital and enterprise could be attracted. The railroad made its entrance, with several small lines being begun, and ports were improved, bridges erected, and wagon roads built on a considerable scale. The telegraph represented a significant advancement, as did banks, a sound currency, and a tidy financial system, all of which he provided. Soon the graceful colonial aspect of Caracas changed as the dictator constructed boulevards and ornate public edifices. These years of internal peace and material development served to stimulate coffee exports, Venezuela's principal means of earning foreign exchange, and sugar and cacao also won more markets abroad.

Such prosperity as there was benefited the planters and business classes. Rural masses labored in ignorance of the greater world outside, and the *llaneros* lost ground as the livestock industry, in contrast to the situation in other countries, went into decline. Guzmán Blanco was resigned to the poverty of the lower classes and also to their illiteracy, for he did very little for public education. He was content to flatter the literary groups of Caracas, who often returned the compliment, especially when he subsidized them. While he no doubt deserved some credit for trying to stimulate a cultural flowering, it seems that few of the productions of this period went beyond imitations of realistic fiction or precious poetry of the type stylish in Paris and Madrid. An exception would be the romantic poet, Antonio Pérez Bonalde, who died in 1892. And Manuel Romero García (1865–1917) later wrote a famous novel, *Peonía*, that immortalized the dictator in a way that he would not have appreciated.

Guzmán Blanco stayed in the presidential chair for seven years, until 1877, when he permitted a puppet to take over. In 1879, however, he returned for a five-year term, during which he hit upon a charming scheme that would permit him to live luxuriously in Paris on a Venezuelan income without burdening himself with the chores of the presidency. His method was simply to pick a henchman to serve for two years, not long enough to entrench himself, he supposed, and to be followed either by another puppet or by the great man. Frequent visits and the trans-Atlantic cable, together with Guzmán Blanco's prestige, should be enough to assure an indefinite continuation of the regime. This arrangement worked until 1888. In that year a president began to show signs of independence, notably by refusing a concession that Guzmán Blanco had corruptly granted to a French firm. Then he greatly offended the absentee dictator by permitting the remains of General Páez, long an enemy of his family, to be installed in the national pantheon. Soon it became apparent that Guzmán Blanco's saints' days and anniversaries were no longer being observed with the customary reverence. And in October 1889, crowds shattered statues and monuments honoring the dictator. While the government still feared him and hoped to avoid an open break, these popular actions forced its hand. Realizing that he had been "betrayed," Guzmán Blanco wisely remained in Paris, living extravagantly for his last ten years on money he had pilfered from his homeland. In so many ways a contemptible figure, he had undoubtedly sponsored the greatest outburst of material growth that Venezuela had yet known.

CIVIL WAR AND NOTORIETY

It is not surprising that the end of Guzmán Blanco's rule unleashed the dogs of strife. Local guerrilla leaders sprang back into action, clamoring for federalism or some other tenet that might spell power for them. The army divided, as commanders went this way and that. Politicians schemed and orated, behaving in the fashion that so often robs Latin American government of dignity, though of course some of them were sincere patriots. After much confusion, a onetime marionette of Guzmán Blanco, General Joaquín Crespo, fought his way into the capital. Representing the lingering attachment of many to the fallen tyrant, he nonetheless dissuaded his erstwhile patron from abandoning the delights of Paris.

Possibly Crespo might have restored the stability Venezuela had known under the earlier regime had he not been absorbed in a foreign quarrel, one not wholly of his making. The British had long disputed with the republic the boundary of Guiana, but the issue dragged on desultorily year after year because the area in contention was the hot and soggy lower valley and delta of the Orinoco, where almost no one cared to live. In the 1890's, however, an unsound rumor that gold could be found there caused prospectors to clash and governments to take an interest. Britain claimed nothing less than the Orinoco itself for the boundary. Venezuela stridently protested and appealed for help. It was this dispute that inspired President Cleveland to assert the Monroe Doctrine, which the European powers had never openly recognized, and his secretary of state, Richard Olney, truculently informed Great Britain that the United States would defend the rights of Venezuela, employing the unfortunate words: "To-day the United States is practically sovereign on this continent, and its fiat is law upon the subjects to which it confines its interposition." Venezuela was gratified, but Olney's phraseology has long been invoked by critics of the United States. Eventually, Britain gave in and agreed to an arbitration, which gave her a good share of the disputed territory but not what she most wished, the banks of the Orinoco.

Crespo's term ended in 1898, and in 1899 his "Yellow" successor lost his position in a civil war that lasted four years. From its outset, however, Caracas was in the hands of a new type of caudillo, a rancher from the extreme western state of Táchira, which would provide Venezuela with rulers without interruption until 1945. The first of this series, which compares unfavorably with Mexico's Northern Dynasty, was the "Blue" leader, Cipriano Castro. A rustic of some education, Castro had been a lawyer of sorts and governor of Táchira, a bleak honor for the state or the man. An enemy of Crespo, he had been forced into exile in Colombia, where he devoted himself to stealing cattle and gathering an effective army of cowboys. Having won a sanguinary battle and penetrated Caracas in 1899, he slowly reduced the rest of the country. Ignorant, cruel, and shamelessly venal, he ruled as a tyrant and banked large sums in Dutch Curaçao and New York, sometimes forwarding the money directly from the Venezuelan treasury. While he liked adulation, he was somewhat less brazen than Guzmán Blanco and was content to be known only as the "Moses" of his people.

Most of his countrymen came to regard Castro as a hero because he found a popular issue: defying the outside world. During the difficulties of the 1890's many foreigners had been despoiled or maltreated and, when they resorted to Venezuelan courts, gotten no justice, whereupon they turned to their home governments. The European powers had known this sort of thing to happen before, and they had ways to deal with it. Threats were usually sufficient. On this occasion, however, Castro not only refused to bow to their demands but jeered at them, to the delight of many Latin Americans. Germany, Great Britain, and Italy, whose subjects were the chief claimants, then got up a fleet to blockade the coast of Venezuela, first clearing their intended action with the United States, who did not object. The blockade of 1902–1903 proved fateful. Latin America was aroused, and Argentina's foreign minister, Luis Drago, won fame for demanding that all forcible interventions be outlawed. The Venezuelans rallied stoutly behind Castro and became more xenophobic than ever when their navy was seized and their fortresses at Puerto Cabello and San Carlos were subjected to a stupid bombardment.

At this point the American public became aroused too, and President Theodore Roosevelt began to fear that the Europeans might take over Venezuela as the British had Egypt, protestingly but quite thoroughly. Using pressure the exact nature of which is still controversial, he secured the withdrawal of the monarchical fleets and had the claims question turned over to the new international court at The Hague. Castro made much of "his" victory, and when the world tribunal scaled down the claims very considerably, it appeared that he had been right all along. At any rate, this mountaineer tyrant boasted of having defeated the great powers, Latin America flared up against intervention, and the United States undertook to see that such situations did not arise again, thus beginning the phase of diplomacy of sad memory associated with the Roosevelt Corollary to the Monroe Doctrine.

JUAN VICENTE GÓMEZ

For five years after the European withdrawal Cipriano Castro ruled Venezuela unchallenged. Perhaps he heightened his popularity by expelling the Dutch minister for publishing a criticism of his ways, though the Dutch retaliated by molesting Venezuelan shipping for some months. Somehow this super-patriot, the "little Andean cattle thief," as foreign journalists called him, managed to keep everyone intimidated. In November 1908 he went to Europe for medical treatment, leaving the presidency in the hands of his companion in exile and war, Vice President Juan Vicente Gómez. Posing as a faithful, rather dull sycophant, Gómez had concealed his treacherous nature from Castro for years. It was an unpleasant surprise to the latter while in Berlin to learn that he had been deposed by this plodding junior. The cheated tyrant could not accept this turn of events philosophically, and for eight years he sailed about the Caribbean, seeking to organize forces for the "liberation" of Venezuela. Foreign powers were far from eager to see this trouble-maker restored, and if any Venezuelans favored him, they were kept in check by Gómez. In 1916 Castro settled in Puerto Rico, where he died eight years later, still railing at his betrayer.

Juan Vicente Gómez was widely believed to have supernatural powers; people called him a wizard, and indeed he seemed capable of smelling conspiracy or disaffection. Men were tortured and killed because he read their thoughts. Like Castro a rustic from Táchira, he had learned to rustle cattle and fight with that master. All but illiterate, he was coarse and uncouth, brutal and insensitive to suffering in others. While he never married, he sired eighty or more children, or so people admiringly reported, and he stole from the treasury as openly as Castro had. His fortune did not reach the proportion of $100,000,000, as so many journalists reported, but merely a third of that amount. Nor was it all banked abroad. Venezuela eventually recovered most of it. Not only immoral and venal, Gómez was cruel in a feline way. Fiendish tortures for critics, macabre punishments for onetime associates, and jails and labor gangs of the worst sort for thousands featured his regime from start to finish. He thought it a great joke to close the University of Caracas and send its students into chain gangs to build roads after they rioted for a government that would enable them to serve their country. Many of the tales of Gómez' cruelties must have acquired color through frequent narration, but the proved facts were horrifying enough, and his name has lived in infamy.

Gómez had no exalted purpose in dislodging his chief; he simply wanted power. Yet his regime represented some improvement over Castro's. For one thing, Gómez was determined to have good relations with other countries, and he welcomed foreigners as residents or investors and saw to it that all debts were settled and that no new ones were contracted. The result was what might be expected: alien investors and enterprisers flocked to Venezuela and did much to liven its economy. Furthermore, Gómez had the wisdom to employ talented men as administrators, so that his bureaucracy functioned smoothly and well, at least from a mechanical point of view. Gómez also was modern enough to recognize the value of good public relations, to which end he suborned a corps of literary men and journalists. Some intellectuals even devised a perverted philosophical justification of the autocracy, starting with the assumption that Venezuela was a land of impoverished, ignorant people who lacked self-respect and who craved a masterful leader like Gómez who would tell them what to do. While Gómez allowed himself to be hailed as "El Benemérito," he was modest in some ways, disliking to strut about the capital in uniform or formal dress. He preferred to wear sandals and plain clothes at his rural residences. Between 1914 and 1922, and again from 1929 to 1931, he was not even officially the president, turning the honor over temporarily to puppets, though he was, of course, always the boss. At the town of Maracay near Caracas he constructed many homes for his family and associates and a monstrous wooden palace for himself. This resort area was virtually the headquarters of the government. Congressmen, officials, and foreign diplomats came hat in hand to hear the dictator's will.

During his first decade as ruler Gómez financed his regime adequately and enriched himself and his coterie on the traditional products of Venezuela. Coffee exports from the western highlands brought in by far the most foreign exchange, while cacao, sugar, and indigo increased it and supported the landed aristocracy in its accustomed opulence. While the livestock industry did not keep pace with others, rangy creole cattle were still driven by the thousands from the *llanos* to slaughtering facilities on the coast, and hides and beef were exported. Venezuelans seldom had milk or meat for their own consumption, however, and the population generally ate corn and other home-grown products. The vast majority were undernourished, and Venezuela ranked as a very poor land.

And then, in 1918, came the oil strike. The republic was soon to enter a class all by itself in Latin America, to become technically the richest land per capita south of the Rio Grande.

The "discovery," which Indians, friars, and Alexander von Humboldt had long before anticipated, was that enormous pools of petroleum awaited extraction around and in the great shallow bay known as Lake Maracaibo on the western coast of Venezuela. This was a torrid area, almost the hottest in South America, and scarcely anyone lived there. Now foreign oil companies competed wildly for the privilege of exploiting it. Gómez, who resembled Mexico's Porfirio Díaz in so many respects, fostered this rivalry to his advantage, as Díaz had done, but he was wiser, or perhaps aware of the Mexican constitution of 1917, in that he insisted from the outset upon Venezuela's receiving a large share of the profits. The rate changed from time to time, but the government always thereafter obtained a generous division. Standard Oil, eventually through its subsidiary, Creole Petroleum, acquired the largest holdings, and then Royal Dutch Shell, a predominantly British company despite its name. The Dutch, however, were very much involved in Venezuela's oil business, since they owned Curaçao and Aruba, well-governed islands with good technicians who could refine the crude oil that was piped or shipped there from the mainland. As the years went on the magnitude of Venezuela's petroleum resources defied comprehension. This republic apparently had almost as much oil as the United States or the entire Middle East, and it was not limited to the miserable Maracaibo region. Large pools were located in many pleasanter spots all across the country from west to east.

As the gushers and the wonderful profits multiplied during the 1920's, the Gómez dictatorship was able to indulge in many luxuries. The income was delightfully simple to manage, for foreign managers, experts, and, often, oil-field workers performed the labor, and the corporations merely turned over huge revenues to the Venezuelan treasury. All Gómez had to do was think up ways to spend this windfall. He greatly embellished his resort at Maracay and acquired further properties for his numerous progeny. Large fortunes became available to politicians, contractors, and generals who outdid themselves in pleasing the tyrant. The army, which was already far too sizeable for a country not in danger of immediate attack, was liberally endowed with airplanes, heavy guns, and modern vehicles, which served to keep it loyal to Gómez and formidable to anyone who dreamed of overthrowing him. Brilliant uniforms, good barracks, recreational facilities, and motorcycles delighted the enlisted men, who had little reason to complain of the regime and much to fight for it. Officers formed a class privileged even by Latin American standards. Gómez further improved the army's effectiveness and indulged his own desires by constructing many roads and bridges suitable for the automobile age. Fine government buildings went up on a scale that Guzmán Blanco could scarcely have imagined, and the possessing classes acquired much taste for living in the style of twentieth-century plutocrats. Venezuela had such a large income that it could avoid levying most forms of taxes, and the world depression after 1929 hardly affected it at all. Also hardly affected were the masses, either by the oil money or world conditions. They had as poor food, housing, schooling, and health as ever.

Gómez showed little decline until he reached his mid-seventies. He was erect, smooth-faced, and charming whenever he chose to impress a visiting celebrity. Around 1933, however, he began to suffer from uremia, and he seldom left the sprawling wooden palace at Maracay. It made no difference. The regime ran on its own momentum, lubricated by the petroleum income. Terroristic methods had silenced anyone who might have conspired against him, and the people had a superstitious venera-tion for the "catfish," the whispered nickname of the dictator. During the last months of his illness a peace of death continued, the army and police remaining obedient, congress mute, and the appointed state presi-dents attentive only to their immediate duties. Venezuelans had almost forgotten what it was like to assert their opinions. The only ones who made themselves heard were the exiles, and frequently they exaggerated so badly that they alienated those who might have been sympathetic. Finally, in December 1935, word went out that Gómez had expired. It hardly seemed possible, and for two or three days an incredulous pause hung over the republic.

AN INTERVAL BETWEEN DICTATORS, 1935–1948

When the populace at last accepted the fact of the despot's death, they celebrated deliriously and violently for many days. The explosive holiday must have been fun, coming as it did after so many years of oppression, but it was marred by many acts of brutality against Gómez henchmen and the numerous illegitimate children of the dead dictator. After it ran its course, some of the less detested figures of the regime who had escaped lynching or beating assessed the situation and realized that the sinews of the regime were still intact. The minister of war, Gen-eral Eleázar López Contreras, went on the radio to summon the nation to calm down, assuring it that the tyranny was over and that reforms were now in order. With a surprising sense of sobriety the Venezuelans re-turned to work. The surviving Gómez congress elected López Contreras president, and the administration was re-manned with persons not notoriously identified with the old regime. The return of many refugees and the revival of a free press signified the restoration of a relative degree of liberty.

López Contreras, another mountaineer from Táchira, presided competently over the transition of Venezuela from an old-fashioned despotism to something much better, though none of the usual terms quite fit. The republic was given a new constitution in 1936 which supposedly established a model government, but there was no tradition of law to make it successful. In 1937, for instance, the results of the congressional elections were far more leftist than López Contreras liked, whereupon he proclaimed a massive red scare and declined to seat many of the victors. There were, of course, influential and ambitious Communists at work in the country, but few observers agreed that the president's drastic action was justified. Having suppressed the far left, however, López Contreras now cultivated moderates and liberals. His pro-Allied policies in the early stages of World War II could not have been more gratifying to the democracies, and Venezuela continued to be, officially at least, fervently anti-Axis all during the war, though she did not declare a state of hostilities until February 1945. Much of the government's attitude could be explained by the importance of exporting oil to the United Nations and anger over German anti-shipping activities. López Contreras stepped down from the presidency in 1941, to be followed by his associate, Isaís Medina Angarita, another son of Táchira.

Under Medina the country continued along a moderate course, neither a democracy nor a dictatorship, but a stable land with gratifying revenues from oil. This money spread much farther down the social scale than it had under Gómez, and the regime permitted labor unions to organize and provided a few welfare benefits for the masses. President Medina generally relaxed the government's powers, especially when López Contreras fell sick and was no longer able to control his heir through the military. Medina went so far as to allow the creation of *Acción Democrática*, a non-Communist socialist and leftist group that appealed to youth, organized labor, and the lower middle classes. It also reached into the army, where ambitious young officers shared some of the democratic sentiments that swept over the world as the war drew to a close. A presidential election was due in 1945. President Medina hesitated about choosing a successor or allowing congress to do so. While he was deliberating, *Acción Democrática* formed an alliance with the Communists and, in October, struck. Medina, who deserved a better fate, was jailed, and a new era of democracy was proclaimed.

Acción Democrática was at this time greatly influenced by the Labor Government of England, which had recently come into power, and it planned to make Venezuela a socialist state. Its most important leader was Rómulo Betancourt, a veteran of student riots against Gómez and the harsh imprisonment and exile that followed such activities. At one time a Communist, Betancourt had seen enough of the Americas to decide that guided democracy and socialistic gradualism were preferable to totalitarianism. As head of a junta that included military reformers and liberal politicians, he embodied exciting hopes for the reconstruction of the country. Nothing less than the diversion of the oil income to the improvement of the masses was his main purpose. Henceforth, he decreed, all business firms must distribute 10 per cent of their profits each year to their employees, but the oil companies must treat the workers even better and, besides, turn over to the government half their income, an amount larger than before but not enough to drive them out of Venezuela. This expanded income enabled the junta to undertake a far-reaching program to establish schools, hospitals, public water and sanitation facilities, and low-cost housing developments. Furthermore, the proletariat was to be unionized further and to share in the distribution of landed estates. Reasonable as this program might appear, and long overdue, it signified a veritable revolution, and formidable opposition was bound to arise. Betancourt insisted it could be achieved, and as proof of his good intentions sponsored the constitution of 1947, which created the basis for much of it. He also announced elections in which he would not be a candidate. *Acción Democrática's* nominee was an elderly novelist, Rómulo Gallegos, whose *Doña Bárbara* had advertised the harsh life of the Venezuelan backlands and the need for reform. He was elected in 1947 in the nation's first free test at the polls, one in which everyone over eighteen was required to vote. Colored ballots made it easier for the illiterates, who composed a large majority of the electorate, to choose their favorite.

The respected writer and educator took office in February 1948 in an atmosphere of wild hopes on the part of middle-class liberals and the masses. Well-wishers in the outside world also expected Venezuela to be transformed, to prove that a Latin American country could both enjoy freedom and use oil income to further social democracy. It was not to be. The benevolent Gallegos guilelessly encouraged the urban working classes to expect socialism, and they repeatedly gathered in the main plaza of Caracas, mis-named El Silencio, to create a din. More portentous was his proposal that landed estates be divided. Most disastrous of all was his suggestion that the army be drastically reduced and that a peasants' and workers' militia assume most of its functions. At this point, only nine months after his inauguration, a military coup engineered by three lieutenant colonels abruptly removed Gallegos. For three years these officers had cooperated with *Acción Democrática*. Now they outlawed this organization, promising, however, that most of its program would be carried out. Their sincerity was rightly suspected, but, as so often before, the Venezuelans settled back abjectly under a dictatorship.

THE MILITARY IN GLORY: MARCOS PÉRÉZ JIMÉNEZ, 1950–1958

The new provisional president was Delgado Chalbaud, a moderate reformer whose utterances seemed in harmony with the ideas of the men he had helped oust. Yet he had mortally offended the followers of *Acción Democrática* by his actions against Gallegos, and as leader of the new junta he necessarily had to rely for support on the conservative army officers, big businessmen, oil companies, and planters. In 1950, after he had snuffed out the reform movement, he was kidnaped and murdered by, it was announced, a personal enemy who conveniently died soon thereafter. Whether Chalbaud's successor was the author of the crime or not was never proved, plausible as this deduction was. This man was his brother officer and defense minister, Marcos Pérez Jiménez, a short, stocky Táchiran who wore glasses and stammered. No figure to kindle popular adulation, he had remained in the background under Betancourt, Gallegos, and Chalbaud and had now, by unknown methods, emerged as dictator. At thirty-six he was the youngest American president of his time.

Since Venezuelan dictators have usually been unlovable personalities, it mattered little that Pérez Jiménez was unappealing. The population cheered him only routinely or not at all, apparently warming to him only when he gave them vicarious pleasure by racing fine automobiles over the countryside. When he made the mistake of holding an election in 1952, a free one but for a ban on *Acción Democrática*, early returns showed that his opponents were heavy winners. Rather than permit the count to be completed, he confiscated the ballots and announced an overwhelming triumph for his supporters. The congress thus elected issued a new constitution at his bidding in the following year and named him president for a five-year term. The people scarcely stirred. Pérez Jiménez had clamped his power on Venezuela skillfully, relying above all on the army. In a revival of Gómez' tactics he allowed the soldiers to stand as a privileged aristocracy, enjoying graft on an enormous scale and indulging their aggressive instincts as they would on the civilians. The officers' club he built near Caracas was perhaps the finest in the world, and the armed services had not only every comfort but a handsome collection of weapons and equipment to intimidate the populace. Policemen were also pampered and respected. A matchless spy system permeated the country, serving not only to frustrate plots against the regime but also to provide the police with manifold opportunities for graft, blackmail, and immorality. Pérez Jiménez maintained concentration camps for people who refused to admit the blessings of his regime and restrained students by shutting the university whenever restlessness got out of hand. Inside Venezuela there was little his enemies could do other than throw occasional bombs or scatter subversive literature. Exiles, however, especially former presidents Betancourt and Gallegos, filled the columns of the free press abroad with denunciations of the young dictator.

Prosperity continued to sweeten life for Venezuelans in a position to enjoy it. The Korean War and the Suez crisis, as well as the conservation policies of the United States and the general increase in world demand for oil, kept Venezuela's leading industry busy. Nearly 3,000,000 barrels a day poured forth, making Venezuela the largest producer after the United States. The fifty-fifty arrangement proved quite satisfactory for the government and the foreign companies. Venezuelan nationalism was gratified by the employment of natives to replace aliens wherever possible, by welfare capitalism on the part of the foreign firms, and by the construction of a token refining industry in the republic. Most of the oil by far went in tankers or pipes to other countries; oil, in fact, was about all Venezuela exported, seldom amounting to less than 95 per cent of her total sales. The income permitted the government to function without levying more than a few taxes, and it endowed the administration's favorites. Moreover, some of it spilled over into the business life of the country. High wages for oil workers meant construction and luxuries in the productive districts, which in turn benefited Caracas, the arbiter of the nation's economic life. That capital grew in size, passing the million mark in population, and was so graced with handsome mansions, business buildings, governmental palaces, and apartment houses that it rivaled Mexico City or São Paulo as a monument to modernistic architecture. As in those cities, the construction of low-cost houses was insufficient to prevent the expansion of horrid slums. Pérez Jiménez devoted one-third of the national budget to public works. Magnificent freeways and avenues in Caracas, a very costly *autopista* with a three-mile tunnel from that capital to La Guaira, superhighways along the northern coast, and countless lesser roads, many of which the dictator opened by racing a sports car over them, made Venezuela one of the most modern nations in the world with respect to communications. All this construction also kept the grafters rich, the contractors prosperous, and labor occupied. Pérez Jiménez said that Rome was remembered for its roads; certainly he sought to immortalize his name in this way.

Not all of the income went to the army, the officials, and public works projects. Some progress against illiteracy was recorded, and clinics and hospitals sprang up. Venezuela's population passed 6,000,000 during these years, partly because such diseases as malaria were almost eliminated, and partly because immigrants, for the first time, arrived in significant numbers. A new infusion of European stock, largely Italian, brought factory workers, shopkeepers, and professional men into the republic. Though, or because, rural conditions improved, agricultural workers also flocked into Venezuelan cities, for Pérez Jiménez did not wholly neglect the hinterland. A minute part of the budget was devoted to setting up schools in farming regions to instruct agriculturists in scientific methods. Nelson Rockefeller, who owned a ranch in Venezuela, cooperated with the government in such undertakings through the International Basic Economy Corporation, of which he was a sponsor. This organization also stimulated food production and taught the Venezuelans to purify milk, though they rarely elected to drink it. The iron industry held great promise. During World War II it was discovered that the largest supply of high-grade iron ore in the world lay near Ciudad Bolívar, where the Liberator had planned and preached, in the lower Orinoco. Mainly through the exertions of subsidiaries of U.S. Steel and Bethlehem Steel, a new industry grew apace, and its requirements caused the initiation of dam-building and electrification projects. On the surface, Venezuela was a thriving nation during the Pérez Jiménez regime, though the dictatorship bore down heavily on the people and most of them were still desperately poor. At least the nation had been awakened and was sharing in the mania to catch up that characterized so many of the backward parts of the world.

Pérez Jiménez had the grace not to pretend to be a great democrat. He frankly stated that his people needed an autocratic government and would abuse liberty if they had it. In fulfillment of this theory he canceled the elections scheduled for 1958 and held instead a plebiscite in 1957, which was announced as approving a renewal of his tenure by an almost unanimous vote. This time the country stirred. In January 1958 units of the air force rebelled unsuccessfully. Soon a general strike filled the streets of the capital with idle crowds, who were plainly in a bad humor. Since cabinet members and the army hierarchy, supported by important prelates, well knew the cause of these threatening motions, they conspired to get rid of their target. Early on the morning of January 23, Pérez Jiménez and his family were placed in an airplane and flown away to that haven of dictators, the Dominican Republic. As in 1935, after Gómez died, the nation gave way to a joyous but destructive carnival of celebration. As also in that year, a surviving member of the fallen regime established himself as provisional president. Venezuelan revolutions seldom go very far.

ANOTHER EFFORT AT DEMOCRACY

A handsome admiral, Wolfgang Larrazábal, became chief of the new regime. He said he did not plan to continue the dictatorship at all, even on a reformed basis, and he demonstrated his sincerity by prosecuting such of the malefactors of the fallen administration as could be apprehended. As the exiles flocked back, it was obvious that former presidents Betancourt and Gallegos still enjoyed immense popularity, for these liberals received tumultuous ovations. Larrazábal wanted to be considered a liberal too, and for much of 1958 he cultivated the left, particularly the urban masses. Yet his hold on the country was frail, as was demonstrated during the terrible riots attending the "good will" visit of Vice President Nixon in May 1958. That Nixon and his wife came close to being torn to bits by street rioters, many of them Communists, and had to slip out of Caracas ahead of schedule came as an evil surprise to American opinion. It seemed that the United States was being blamed for the late tyranny of Pérez Jiménez! If Larrazábal apologized, the rest of the nation gave little evidence of shame for its lack of hospitality. The people were obviously in an ugly mood. Having been cheated so long of their proper share of the national wealth and with their appetites greatly sharpened, they were ready to do violence to anyone who was identified, rightly or wrongly, with the past.

Larrazábal liked the taste of power he had sampled, and he succeeded in having himself nominated by a left-wing coalition known as the Democratic Republican Union. Rómulo Betancourt, whose determination to rule and to carry out his original program had been hardened during his long exile, was the candidate of *Acción Democrática*. The election of December 1958, which was fair if bitter, gave Betancourt the victory. Before he took office, however, Larrazábal anticipated one of his main promises by changing the fifty-fifty arrangement with the foreign oil firms to a sixty-forty proportion favoring Venezuela. Annoyed as they were, the petroleum corporations were relieved that he had gone no further. Close students of the Mexican expropriation of 1938, responsible elements in Venezuela feared that a harsher settlement might ruin their oil sales altogether, and with them three-fourths of the government's income. Venezuela was by no means the only oil-producing country in the world, and much as demagogues clamored for it, confiscation might have been disastrous.

Rómulo Betancourt was inaugurated in February 1959. Two years later his anniversary marked the longest period any democratically elected regime had survived in Venezuela. It was observed less with joy than with a sense of miracle that he had lasted that long. The country remained confused and angry, both hopeful and fearful. Communists were very much in evidence, their ranks greatly strengthened by the advent of Fidel Castro in Cuba. Yet rightist plots were of more immediate concern, for Pérez Jiménez and his friend, Dictator Trujillo of the Dominican Republic, kept Venezuela's armed forces in a state of titillation. An assassination plot aimed at President Betancourt in June 1960 led the Organization of American States to censure and isolate the Dominican Republic, almost certainly the source of the plot. Furthermore, a restless proletariat in Caracas and the oil districts, where there was considerable unemployment, was in a mood to do anything, whether it benefited the fallen regime, a new dictator, or international Communism. Late in 1960 the Democratic Republic Union, which had been sharing office and responsibility with *Acción Democrática*, withdrew from the coalition and greatly weakened Betancourt's administration thereby. The future of representative government in Venezuela was far from assured.

Shaky as his regime was, Betancourt gave substantial evidence of statesmanship. At least he permitted civil rights and human liberties except for a few months after the assassination attempt. He described the national purpose in ways that appealed to many educated Venezuelans, stressing the importance of not driving away foreigners, who had the technical knowledge Venezuela needed and who bought almost all its petroleum and iron. The country must take heroic steps to improve housing, the worst grievance of the urban population, one made all the more unbearable by the contrasts of shacks and luxurious apartment houses. The cost of living must be restrained, and social welfare spread more evenly. One day Venezuela's oil might play out, or the world might use other sources of energy. For such catastrophes Venezuela must prepare by diversifying her economy, a task that was theoretically not beyond human capacity. Ranching and dairying could be developed into great industries, and almost any crop would grow in some part of the republic under the ministrations of scientific methods. Other countries had shown how easy it was to industrialize rapidly, often without Venezuela's advantages in oil, iron, and manpower. Rivers and waterfalls, including Angel Falls, the world's highest, could be harnessed for electrification. In all, tremendous opportunities awaited Venezuela if her people could discipline themselves and receive good leadership. If moral authority and high principles counted, Rómulo Betancourt might prove the man to meet this challenge. On the other hand, the history and traditions of the nation pointed to strife and its usual product, dictatorship. Venezuela, a beautiful country favored by nature, still seemed ill at ease in the modern world.

29

Colombia

At the beginning of the twentieth century Colombia was still a stranger to the new world of machinery and middle-class culture. Only her intelligentsia and coffee exporters had any contact with the outside world. Her inhabited areas, so divided from one another by geography, had scarcely emerged from the slumber of colonial times, and a patriarchal society continued. On the humid Caribbean coasts this society was a matter of white upper classes—sugar planters of the countryside and merchants of Cartagena and Santa Marta—living amid Negroid masses. The strip of hot coast along the Pacific was largely uninhabited; where there were communities at all, they were likely to be those of impoverished, primitive Negroes. Far more lively was the upper valley of the Cauca, where whites and mestizos were little aware of racial distinctions. Planters, ranchers, miners, and, in numbers unusual in Latin America, small farmers, they were on the eve of a rise from a subsistence economy into a much better situation. To the east, across a magnificent cordillera of the Andes, lay the Magdalena Valley, a region so hot that few lived there and important mainly because of its stream. Beyond another range, east of it, was the 8,500-foot-high basin in which rested Bogotá, the capital, a city of nearly 200,000 people, fine government buildings and mansions, and extensive slums. Remote as it was, this community boasted a vibrant intellectual life and familiarity with the culture of Europe. Of its scholars, critics, novelists, and poets, the most famous was José Asunción Silva, who killed himself at thirty-one in 1896 after producing many death-obsessed verses. Northeast of Bogotá were other basins and other communities, most of them bucolic and poor. The enormous lands stretching downhill toward the Amazon were practically unknown to Colombians. This varied land had somehow justified itself as a nation. Its citizens were absorbed in politics, aware of genuine issues, patriotic, and hopeful of a great destiny for the republic.

THE PANAMA AFFAIR

The reluctance of this destiny to manifest itself had not caused the Colombians to be passive or disillusioned. After the death of Rafael Núñez, the great Conservative president, in 1894, public life revived with a vengeance. Liberals, who had dominated the republic between 1849 and 1880, were still potent as a political force. In 1895 they rebelled in several departments but were put down, mainly through the efforts of General Rafael Reyes, of whom more later. They remained quiescent while Miguel Caro finished out the term to which Núñez had been elected in 1892 and watched the Conservatives install Manuel Sanclemente in 1898. Wrangling among the victors offered them another opportunity to revolt in 1899, and they did so on such a large scale that a three-year civil war, the so-called War of the Thousand Days, brought death and damage to nearly every part of the republic. The figure is always given that 100,000 men perished in this fighting, a gross exaggeration, one hopes. But it was undoubtedly a ruinous affair, and the economic life of the country was badly disorganized. When the civil war ended in June 1903, Colombia was in a pitiable condition. Again the Liberals had lost; in this republic the government nearly always wins. President Sanclemente had been deposed in 1900 by his vice-president, José Manuel Marroquín, and the Conservatives still ruled.

Marroquín had almost despaired of the country's prospects even before the War of the Thousand Days. As he surveyed its condition in 1903, he was still more despondent. Yet Colombia was about to suffer more ignominy, the worst blow of its history, at least in the eyes of patriots. This was the amputation of Panama. Its appearance on maps notwithstanding, this department had no passable land connection with the rest of Colombia. Much of it was still wild, and only about 200,000 persons, who lived around the railroad connecting Colón with Panama City, could be considered citizens. While Panamanians had been turbulent, like other Colombians, and a few had even agitated for independence, they scarcely had a public life. For two intervals after the expulsion of Spain in 1821 Panama had been prosperous. Around 1850 the trans-isthmian route was very active because of Americans and Europeans going to California, and the Panamanians had fleeced or served these travelers profitably. Later, the Nicaraguan route had almost destroyed its prosperity, and Panama became stagnant. Then it revived for a few years after 1878 when Ferdinand de Lesseps imported French supervisors and Negro laborers to dig a canal, an enterprise dreamed of since the days of Balboa. But the French undertaking ended in utter failure. Financial mismanagement and dishonesty had brought disgrace to many in Paris, including the president of the French Republic, and engineers could not deal with the difficulties of construction. Thousands had died of yellow fever, and again Panama had sunk into misery and depression.

Even though construction had long since ceased, the French company still had rights to the route and a considerable amount of machinery along the abandoned ditches. Its agent, Philippe Bunau-Varilla, peddled these interests to several European powers but found no takers, for he asked a huge price. During the Spanish-American War the United States came to realize how valuable a canal could be in shifting its fleet from one ocean to the other in a hurry. And when the American navy began to be enlarged under President Theodore Roosevelt, the convenience of a canal became a necessity. Accordingly, Washington considered the possibility of cutting a canal across Nicaragua and listened to Bunau-Varilla's proposition. Meanwhile, in 1901, the British obligingly agreed to cancel the Clayton-Bulwer Treaty of 1850, thus leaving the United States a free hand. At length Bunau-Varilla offered specific terms: the French rights and properties would be sold for $40,000,000, a sum acceptable to the United States. Now it was necessary to obtain the approval of Colombia, which was being ravaged by civil war and was in urgent need of money. In January 1903 President Marroquín promised to sell his country's rights to a strip ten kilometers wide for $10,000,000 plus a rental of $250,000 a year. All seemed in order for the Americans to start digging.

It was an ugly surprise to President Roosevelt when the Colombian congress refused to ratify the treaty later in 1903. Was patriotism the cause of its recalcitrance? It might have been, for Colombian parliamentary bodies were not as supine as most other Latin American congresses. Had Marroquín instigated this opposition in order to obtain a higher price? Or had another power tempted him? The truth is not known for sure. Nor can we verify the doings of Bunau-Varilla, who was busily lobbying in Washington and New York. He had reason to fear that the Nicaraguan route might yet win out over the Panamanian, and the concession he was selling was to expire within a few years and would then be valueless. To him, at least, it was very important that the Panama project go through promptly. On November 3, 1903, a group of railroad workers and street rowdies in Colón rebelled and proclaimed the independence of Panama. A Colombian expedition led by General Rafael Reyes sailed to deal with them but found itself interdicted by the U.S. cruiser *Nashville*, which "happened" to be in those waters. On November 6, President Roosevelt recognized the new republic and its representative in Washington, Bunau-Varilla. This ubiquitous personage at once negotiated a treaty which gave the United States a strip ten miles wide in perpetuity in exchange for $10,000,000 and an annual rental of $250,000. The United States guaranteed Panama's independence and paid $40,000,000 to the French company for its rights. At least three important mysteries have never been solved: the reason for the action of the Colombian congress, President Roosevelt's foreknowledge of the Panamanian revolution, and the identity of the recipients of the $40,000,000.

While other Latin Americans were little ruffled by these events at the time, they later found them convenient for berating Uncle Sam. Roosevelt did not help matters when, in 1911, after he had left the presidency, he publicly declared: "I took Panama." Nor did his earlier denunciations of the Colombian government as "a gang of bandits" and the people as "a bunch of Dagoes" fail to receive wide circulation. His reputation in Colombia today remains on a par with that of Francis Drake, or even lower. The sense of grievance felt by the Colombian nation was long important in its politics and diplomacy. For some years, however, the American public and the world at large cared little what the Colombians thought. The canal was started and soon proved as beneficial as Roosevelt had hoped, and Panama has exhibited no interest whatever in reverting to statehood under Colombia.

THE SYSTEM OF RAFAEL REYES, 1904–1930

This painful jolt to Colombia's dignity, as well as the financial and territorial loss, did something to sober the uncompromising ideologues of that republic. In 1904, General Rafael Reyes was chosen president by the Conservatives, the Liberals, who had just been beaten in the civil war, not participating in the election. Like his opposite number in Washington, Reyes led a strenuous life. Born in 1850, he built up a good business selling forest products. While he was young he had made a sensational expedition into the Amazonian jungles with his two brothers, both of whom perished, one a victim of yellow fever, the other of cannibals. Returning to civilization in 1884, Reyes found his business firm in poor condition but himself famous. He joined the army and proved so useful in putting down a Liberal revolt that he was soon made a general. For some years he held major posts in the administration, was a congressman and diplomat, and continued to serve as general, as noted in connection with the civil war of 1895 and the Panama uprising of 1903. A man of little formal education but far from ignorant, he seemed somewhat crude to the well-born. His imperious personality and his achievements, however, won him respect. When he headed the Colombian delegation to the Pan-American conference in Mexico City in 1901–1902, he made a good impression. He also received a favorable impression of Porfirian Mexico, a land of discipline and amazing material growth. Now that he was president, he set out to copy some of the methods of Porfirio Díaz.

Rafael Reyes soon realized that congress was going to be difficult about his plans for regeneration. Hence he arrested some of its members and sent the others home. To replace them he convoked a national assembly with three representatives, most of them his choices, from each of the nine departments. He also thought it necessary to chastise political opponents who might be obstructive. In short, Reyes was practically a dictator. Yet his policies laid the base for years of tranquillity. The Liberals, he said, must vote and not revolt. Thus all literate males who owned property must be encouraged to exercise the franchise in the assurance that their ballots would count for something. While there was no danger of letting them vote the Conservatives out of power as long as the administration conducted the elections, the Liberals should be given a minority of plums in a sort of system of proportional representation. The device worked well enough to entice the Liberals back into political life on a peaceful basis. Reyes also stabilized the currency, repaired Colombia's credit standing, and encouraged foreign investment. The sale of coffee and rubber spurted as a result of these activities, and the government had enough revenue to build schools and make public improvements on a modest scale.

However promising these beginnings were, Reyes was brought to realize the force of Colombia's traditional intolerance for dictators. In 1909, when he negotiated a pact with the United States by which Columbia would recognize Panama in exchange for $2,500,000 and the right to use the future canal, students and other demonstrators filled the streets of Bogotá, shouting protests. Then Reyes sought to strengthen his position by changing the constitution to establish a four-year term for presidents and to fill the first one himself. By now the rioters got completely out of hand, the army glowered, and Reyes decided to leave the presidency and the country. Autocrat though he was, he had at least brought order to a weary and torn nation and capitalized on its national shame to bring its best men back into public life.

The Reyes system operated without its founder for another twenty years. While the treaty with the United States was abandoned, presidents were now elected for four years instead of six, and the Liberals, who voted without hope of winning full control, consoled themselves with a considerable share of elective and appointive positions. The first president after Reyes, a former rector of the University of Antioquia named Carlos Restrepo, even allowed Liberals to serve in his cabinet. José Vicente Concha, who succeeded him in 1914, did not go that far, but he shared various offices with the Liberals and maintained an atmosphere of freedom. Marco Fidel Suárez, who followed him in 1918, did not disturb the system, but he was induced to resign in 1921 because of financial difficulties and furious opposition over his efforts to negotiate another treaty with the United States regarding Panama.

These first years of the Reyes settlement brought not only internal stability but also the economic development the founder had desired. Coffee exports rose, especially from the numerous small farms in the Cauca Valley. Gold, lead, platinum, and emerald production increased, more sugar and rubber were sold, and official efforts to stimulate the sale of fine woods had good results. World War I, in which Colombia was sternly neutral because the United States sided with the Allies, had the familiar effects: economic disruption followed by a boom, then a crash, and quick recovery. Other international affairs had a less dramatic impact, as Colombia sensibly settled her boundary disputes with Ecuador, Brazil and Venezuela.

The first election of the golden 1920's, that of 1922, probably favored the Liberals, but the Conservatives announced the voting results and therefore won. The new president, General Pedro Nel Ospina, was sure enough of his strength to accept an American offer of $25,000,000 for the loss of Panama. While Colombia received no apology—a rebuke to Roosevelt for which the Republicans had delayed the treaty during the Wilson years—the money was a major factor in giving the republic an excellent financial basis, and it opened the way for an inundation of American investments. During the decade about two billion dollars' worth of Colombian bonds were sold to Americans. The market for Colombia's splendid coffee, which many regard as superior to Brazil's, doubled and trebled. Minerals, precious stones, timber, sugar, and immense quantities of bananas flowed abroad, more to the United States than anywhere else. All this meant prosperity for many individuals along with jobs for countless thousands who had previously done little but grow their own food. Ports and highways were constructed, and rapid urban growth began. Colombians discerned the possibilities of aviation in tying their disparate land together as early as 1920, when the German-operated Scadta system went into business. Fortune smiled as vast oil pools were located in the torrid northern coast, and British and American firms set up derricks, pipelines, and refineries. Barranquilla became a major outlet for oil and other exports, far outclassing the lovely fortress-city of Cartagena, which remained a relic of colonial times to attract tourists.

During the 1920's Colombia indeed enjoyed something of a "dance of the millions," a familiar term for Latin American prosperity. Its height came during the administration of Dr. Miguel Abadía Méndez between 1926 and 1930. Expanding prosperity had enriched the propertied classes, widened the bourgeois, and drew many of the lower classes into the Industrial Age. Since the government was as efficient and honest as any in South America, this wealth spelled greater revenues, even an income tax, to finance dams, electrical power plants, automobile and truck roads, modernized cities, public sanitation, and above all, schools. Enlightenment long having been a privilege of the rich, now Colombia undertook to bring free education to the masses. Perhaps one-third of the boys of school age received some instruction. As for the ardent and sophisticated intellectuals of Bogotá and other cities who had long penned verses and devoured literary journals from Europe, they were comparatively unproductive in works that endure. José Eustacio Rivera published the most renowned work, a novel of the jungle entitled *Vortex*, in 1924, four years before he died. But Colombia's cultured classes, if not particularly creative, continued to win the admiration of critical visitors, and their Castilian has long been reputed to be the purest in the Americas.

THE LIBERAL PHASE, 1930–1946

Trouble was forecasted in 1928 when a terrible strike in the banana plantations led to much violence and long-lasting class hatreds. And then the crash of 1929 abruptly inhibited the American investor and sent coffee prices into a downward spiral. Restlessness and latent rebellion were in the air as the electoral campaign of 1930 approached. The Conservatives were jaded from their long years of power and weakened by personal rivalries and a sense of losing touch with the population. When the Archbishop of Bogotá, who had long lent his support, so important in this clerical nation, to the party, declined to choose between rival factions, the Liberals organized to win. Enrique Olaya Herrera, the minister to Washington, ran as a Liberal, conducting a three-week campaign in which he used the airplane and radio to promise drastic social and political reforms. The masses were delighted with both his theatrics and his program, and since the Conservatives for once permitted an honest count of the votes, Olaya Herrera won. During this year of South American revolutions Colombia transferred power from one party to another peacefully. No wonder she received the applause of editorial writers the world over. The world's second largest exporter of bananas, Colombia was no banana republic, but a mature nation.

Olaya Herrera proceeded very slowly, for the Conservatives still controlled congress. During his four years of office he gradually fulfilled many of his promises and did so without antagonizing the moderates among the Conservatives. Important to his success was the rapid recovery which Colombia experienced from the depression. She resumed her growth without large outlays from American speculators and enterprisers, though an American facility, the Panama Canal, ironically did much to promote Colombia's good times. In particular, such west coast ports as Buenaventura prospered mightily as outlets for the products of the upper Cauca, a region that resembles some of the more fortunate parts of the United States, full as it is of independent farmers and ranchers and energetic businessmen. Bogotá also boomed, expanding in the fashion of capital cities all over the world, and the lower Cauca and Magdalena responded under the impact of modern methods. The Caribbean coastlands, disagreeable though they were in climate, had seemingly inexhaustible sources of wealth in oil and lands suitable for bananas and sugar.

Colombia also hoped to develop that half of her area drained by the tributaries of the Amazon. In 1924 the republic had won a great diplomatic triumph in securing from Peru a boundary settlement that gave her Leticia, a protrusion in the extreme southeast that included a port on the Marañon River. In 1932, however, a group of Peruvian irregulars seized it, and the Lima government allowed itself to be pressed by public opinion into supporting them. While the area was all but uninhabited and the town had only a few warehouses, it promised Colombia an outlet to the Atlantic via the Amazon and ultimate development of the huge jungle territory. Peru, threatened with war by Colombia and scolded by the League of Nations, backed down in 1934.

Instrumental in settling the Leticia dispute was Dr. Alfonso López, a Liberal who had gone to Lima to deal with the Peruvian government. He was nominated for the presidency in 1934 and elected by a huge majority, one especially large because the Conservatives, smelling defeat, had generally abstained from voting. Since the Liberals also carried congress, they were now able to carry out far-reaching reforms. López, a scholarly journalist of the type Colombians admire, indeed a publisher, was quite wealthy. Like so many rich liberals he hoped to emulate Franklin D. Roosevelt. His slogan was "Revolution on the march," and what he effected was something of a revolution. A constituent convention so amended the constitution of 1886 that a veritable new charter, that of 1936, became the basic law. Now all men, not merely literate property owners, could vote. Labor was provided with many guarantees and government protection, with the consequence that unionization on a large scale began. Socialistic suggestions to the effect that property must be used for national interests, that squatters could claim lands they occupied, and that foreign holdings might be confiscated satisfied the demands of the times. It is interesting to note that the Liberals did not restore the federalist system, a fetish to their predecessors in the nineteenth century. Nor were they passionately anti-clerical. After some years of negotiations, they signed a concordat with Rome in 1942 which did not disestablish the Church but deprived it of control of education, marriage, and cemeteries.

By the end of Dr. López' administration in 1938, Colombia was the most respected country in Latin America. She was free, progressive, and stable. Uruguay might be as admirable, but she was such a small nation. Brazil and Argentina were less free, and Mexico and Chile less stable. The election of another Liberal publisher with scholarly tastes, Eduardo Santos, appeared to be further indication of Colombia's remarkable maturity. Having long prospered from the sale of raw materials, the nation was now diversifying her economy and beginning a phase of industrialization that might bring her into the first ranks of advanced countries. Her sunny prospects were scarcely clouded by the war of 1939. By now very friendly with the United States, her best customer and home of the New Deal she was copying, Colombia followed the northern giant into an anti-Axis posture. Her airlines were de-Germanized, Scadta being replaced by Avianca, and German-owned properties near the Panama Canal that might be used as airfields were guarded. During the war years Colombia permitted American transit over her air lanes and use of her airports and seaports, sold her goods to the United States, and undertook with American guidance the usual developmental projects to uncover raw materials. After four years of good times under President Santos, the electorate returned Alfonso López to the presidency in 1942.

It is perhaps a measure of Colombia's advancement that her educated classes grasped the ideological issues of World War II and debated their merits as though this corner of South America were a Europe in microcosm. Every cause that led Europeans to kill one another at this time had adherents in Colombia. There were, of course, Communists and many others who followed them, first in favoring Germany and after June 1941 in reviling her. Lovers of western European or North American democracy were predominant, holding the key positions in the government and press. Then there were mild authoritarians who praised Vichy France or Fascist Italy, more than a few Nazis or Naziphiles, and finally, a very potent faction of Hispanicists who admired Franco Spain. Wherever Colombians talked politics—in their homes, public forums, coffeehouses, or clubs—their opinions of the great world struggle were likely to provoke clashes. Bogotá, in particular, always famous for its love of talk, was a babel. Old-fashioned aristocrats spoke of their admiration for the Catholic and ultra-conservative aspect of Franco Spain (only one of its faces); the surging middle classes were sometimes democratic, sometimes touched with fascism; and the laboring classes, who were emerging under skilled leaders, were confusion itself, demanding something that would raise their level of life and importance but unsure whether it was Communism, fascism, or democracy. In a sense not intended by President López, revolution indeed *was* on the march.

It was this president's fate to preside, in spite of himself, over the disintegration of the political system that had won so much approval abroad. Wartime prosperity, too many electoral victories, and a general bemusement caused the Liberal administration to become slack. Corrupt and cynical men replaced the idealistic utopians of the 1930's. A left-wing faction led by Jorge Eliécer Gaitán, one of the protagonists in the terrible strike of banana workers in 1928, who now had a devoted following in the labor unions, seceded and made startling progress among the urban masses with a program of national socialism. This man had an almost malign craving for power. Strident, theatrical, and immensely appealing, he seemed to some a messiah, to others a fascist demagogue like Perón. Gaitán's defection split the Liberal Party so that the Conservatives could tip the balance of power in congress. They too were resurgent, particularly under the proddings of the engineer-publisher Laureano Gómez, who pitilessly exposed the flaws of the López administration and preached national regeneration along antique Hispanic and Catholic lines. As extremists on the left and right divided the land, inflation began to injure the middle and lower classes. Dissatisfaction or confusion manifested itself in many ways. Once, in 1944, President López and some of his ministers were kidnaped and held prisoner for a few days in Pasto, a shameful blot on the history of this civilized republic and one that embarrassed its better elements. It also made the president look ridiculous. In 1945, when the end of the war caused economic dislocations and a bubbling of discontent in many quarters, López gave up and resigned. His prestige had vanished, and he was dispirited.

For a time the more responsible politicians rallied behind a provisional president in the hope of staving off chaos. Alberto Lleras Camargo was entrusted with the presidency. Only thirty-nine, this well-known man of letters had behind him an amazing career. He had been a cabinet minister and ambassador under the Liberals, while writing prolifically and profoundly on the problems of his country. At the Chapultepec and San Francisco conferences in 1945 he had attracted international attention as one of the most enlightened of Latin Americans. Now as provisional president he announced elections for 1946, in which he would not be a candidate, and steadied the country under a coalition government. He well understood the dangers that threatened the republic: Liberal extremism under Gaitán and Conservative extremism under Gómez, nothing less than a renewal of the violence that had marred Colombia's history from Santander to Reyes. Lleras Camargo inspired many of his countrymen to be restrained, but he was not able to prevent a shockingly bitter campaign. In the election of May 1946 the Conservative candidate, Mariano Ospina Pérez, won a plurality over a moderate Liberal, Gabriel Turbay, and the radical Gaitán, the ratio of votes being five-four-three, respectively. The Conservatives had at last elected a president, but they were still a minority party, and they did not win control of congress.

SINCE 1946: TYRANNY, TROUBLES, AND RENEWED HOPE

As in 1930, the transfer of the presidency from one party to another was carried out peacefully. Yet there was something ominous in the determination of the Conservatives and the bitterness of the left-wing Liberals. Ospina Pérez, a wealthy man of honorable intentions, offered the Liberals several cabinet posts and a share of the patronage, which they, except for the Gaitán wing, accepted. Yet the old formulas would not work. Colombia resembled the rest of Latin America at this time by experiencing a fantastic economic development that few understood or could gauge, and one that involved a cruel inflation. The old symbols had lost relevance, and the nation's familiar moorings were gone. An orgy of materialism and lawlessness on one side, and a fierce ideological competition on the other, left the population both confused and bad-tempered. Government in the usual sense was almost impossible; there were too many voices and too many leaders and, paradoxically, too much indifference. Ospina Pérez was unable to give the country strong guidance, and his prestige drained away. Somewhat wistfully, patriots and friendly outsiders expressed the conviction that Colombia had been a democratic republic too long to fall into real danger.

An incident in April 1948 proved this hope unfounded. While Bogotá was playing host to the crucial Ninth Inter-American Conference, Gaitán was murdered. All of a sudden the capital exploded with a violence unknown in Colombia for at least half a century and frightening even by the standards of less orderly lands. Angry proletarian followers of the martyred Gaitán, assisted by such foreign revolutionaries as Fidel Castro of Cuba, surged through the streets, killing Conservatives, sacking shops and offices, and burning governmental palaces. The delegates to the all-American congress fled to the suburbs in order to resume their sessions. Officials of the government had to hide or leave town. Order did not return until days of furious demonstrations, much of it mere looting and hooliganism, had passed, and echoes of these brutal events stirred other cities throughout the republic. The national capital was prostrate, its principal buildings burned or ravaged, and the number of killed, though never precisely known, was considerable. The identity of Gaitán's killer was never known for sure; people said he was a personal enemy, a Russian agent, a Yankee agent, a Conservative, a Liberal, or whatnot.

Worse than the sense of shame felt by Colombia's responsible citizens were the oppression and chronic civil war that followed the Bogotá upheaval. President Ospina Pérez appealed to the Liberals to cooperate with him, which they did for a year, but he set out to destroy their Gaitán faction. In doing so he was so harsh that the moderate Liberals were alienated, and then they too began to feel the exterminating zeal of the Conservative administration. By May 1949, Conservatives and Liberals all over the country were either at war or manifestly preparing for a test of force. Under these circumstances were held the elections in November. The Liberals chose to abstain, and that most reactionary of Conservatives, Laureano Gómez, was elected and inaugurated.

Gómez had fled to his admired Franco Spain after the Gaitán murder, but his name inspired the traditional Conservatives, propertied classes, army officers, Church hierarchy, and Hispanicist ideologues. Well aware that a majority of the nation detested him, he did nothing to win over his enemies. He maintained a state of siege, which permitted arrests and seizures on a scale that most Colombians had never personally experienced, indeed thought their country had outgrown. Censors moved into newspaper offices and ruined a genuine tradition of a free press. Irritated by Protestant missionaries, who had long worked in the Colombian backlands, Gómez encouraged attacks on their persons by patriots or fanatics. The missionaries reacted by becoming notably tactless and defiant, and further prosecutions, some of a shocking nature, resulted. From the national palace the president preached, as he long had done in his newspaper, that "Anglo-Saxonism" was almost as odious as Communism, that it was a deadly threat to Latin and Catholic culture. While he shipped a thousand Colombians to Korea to cooperate with the United Nations forces—Colombia being the only Latin American country to do so—he was not credited with internationalist sentiments, but only with a cynical desire to obtain American aircraft and weapons and to remove Liberal army personnel from the republic.

By 1952 Colombia's reputation as a land of freedom was gone. Perhaps, as some students said, her democratic stability had always been over-rated; she had stood above her sister republics only because their systems were so much worse, not because her own was good. However that may have been, Colombia had not been dominated by the military for a half-century. Now this was to change too. Civilianism joined liberty, domestic peace, and religious toleration in exile, partly because Gómez suffered a heart attack in 1952 and the army assumed some of his powers. Another reason was the continuance of civil war in almost every department, sometimes organized fighting between Liberal bands

and government units, frequently mere lawlessness, a matter of aveng-
ing personal enemies and sacking warehouses and plantations, or even
violent adventure for its own sake. Whatever the causes, the civil war
was very destructive of life and property, and it grievously impeded the
economic growth of the country. The army, which had been pampered
by the Gómez regime and which now had abundant modern weapons
donated by the Americans, at length concluded that the ailing, hated Gómez was no asset, and several generals conspired to remove him. In
June 1953 the president was flown away to Spain, with few lamenting
his removal, and an obscure general named Gustavo Rojas Pinilla assumed the presidency. Promising the people everything, he traveled all
over the republic by airplane, receiving hysterical expressions of gratitude. Colombia's holiday went on for weeks, and nearly everyone believed the nightmare was over.

Rojas Pinilla enjoyed playing the role of deliverer. He was so impressed with the applause he got and so fatuous that he believed the
popular gratitude would permit him to do anything. After the celebrations died down, the committee of generals he headed indicated that
Gómez' useful apparatus of autocracy would continue under their auspices. A little more freedom might be permitted, but not much. Perhaps
the Protestants should not be mishandled quite so openly, for American
and British newspapers were making much of their suffering. The principal change between Rojas Pinilla's and Gómez' rule, however, was the
unashamed alliance of the military-politicians and businessmen. Colombia was inherently so rich, and modern technology could work such marvels, that the country would boom if given half a chance. This it did, and
the mid-1950's featured another "dance of the millions." A riot of speculation, construction, urbanization, and industrialization ensued, and the
output of mines, forests, oil pools, farms, and ranches expanded. The regime smiled on this prosperity and also catered to the foreign expert and
investor who greatly promoted it. All of this might have been entirely to
the good had not inflation and corruption accompanied it and if the administration had not squandered foreign exchange on luxuries. Furthermore, the Rojas Pinilla regime made no real effort, apart from inspiring
words, to provide the country with schools and public services that were
now lagging sadly as the population shot past the 12,000,000 mark. The
president was apparently satisfied that he had done enough to provide
a strong government and to liberate the nation's energies. So sure was
he of his power that he spoke confidently of abolishing the traditional
political organizations and consolidating the entire citizenry into a single
new party. Admitting that he was willing to be elected president for a
legal term by such a party, he unconsciously parodied Louis XIV by declaring, "I am public opinion."

It happened that Rojas Pinilla absurdly overestimated his popularity. Complaints about his oppressive measures became more strident, with the result that the oppression grew worse, and so in turn did the complaints. Fighting in the backlands resumed; whether it was mere lawlessness or earnest resistance to tyranny, it was unsettling to the country and harmful to the regime. While respectable Liberals and Conservatives bemoaned the crudeness of the military dictatorship, Communists were strengthening themselves with the laboring classes and the intelligentsia. Even the clerical hierarchy, including the archbishop who had at first applauded Rojas Pinilla, became critical. It was widely believed that the president and his cohorts were indecently enriching themselves, and in any event they were tyrants. Jeers for the dictator and his family in public places indicated growing opposition, and Rojas Pinilla's action in having hundreds of people shot down in the Bogotá bull ring for hissing his daughters infuriated the population. Yet, in April 1957, he convoked a carefully selected constituent assembly and had himself named president for a four-year term. This action set in motion a variety of revolutionary forces, not the least important of which was a civic union directed by former president Lleras Camargo. In May a general strike paralyzed the capital, and riots and demonstrations clearly showed the temper of the people. A junta of generals who had borne the dictatorship with equanimity up to this point now became nervous. After a flurry of rumors and secret conferences, they placed Rojas Pinilla on an airplane and sent him off. Again, as in 1953, the nation went into transports of joy, this time with better reason.

The junta survived the fall of Rojas Pinilla, but it had more wisdom than to try to perpetuate the dictatorial regime. Not only were the people aroused, but the government was no longer a prize for plunderers. Foreign credits had been used up, the currency was falling, and the economy was faltering. Furthermore, as after the loss of Panama in 1903, the more responsible leaders of the country were determined to set things aright. Lleras Camargo went to Barcelona, Spain, and concocted an ingenious pact with the exiled Conservative former president, Laureano Gómez, who realized as well as his visitor that Colombia was in bad condition and needed a long truce. Hence they agreed to share power between the Conservatives and Liberals for sixteen years, giving each party half the seats in congress, the departmental legislatures, and the municipal councils. Patronage would also be divided evenly, and the presidency was to alternate every four years for four terms. If this seemed an artificial, even a childish, way to restore constitutional government, it had precedent in the nation's history, and it served the purpose of pacifying the country.

The pact being acceptable to leaders of both parties, it was submitted to a popular plebiscite in December 1957 and overwhelmingly approved by 4,000,000 voters. Other provisions called for women suffrage, the maintenance of Catholicism as the official religion, and the devotion of one-tenth the national budget to education. In March 1958 the voters chose the congress. While Liberal candidates received far more than a majority, the two parties loyally executed their pact by dividing the two houses equally. Next came the presidential election in May, which the Liberals, owing to a split in Conservative ranks, were allowed to monopolize without difficulty. Alberto Lleras Camargo won and was inaugurated for the second time in August. Pursuant to the agreement, he created a National Front administration with cabinet ministers divided evenly between Liberals and Conservatives.

For almost two years the coalition functioned well. The state of siege that had been in force since the Bogotá riots of 1948 was finally ended, and the civil war in rural areas that was said to have cost 100,000 lives in nine years tapered off until it was wholly a matter of a chronic crime wave. Urban crime also yielded to stringent efforts of the administration, and of course the administration was relieved of the more blatant grafters. Former dictator Rojas Pinilla embarrassed the regime by coming back to Colombia voluntarily to face those who had accused him of monumental venality and abuse of power. While he insisted that he was legally president and denied the jurisdiction of the senate, he submitted to a trial by that body in January 1959 with composure. After several months the senate stripped him of his rights and pensions for misuse of authority, and later the supreme court convicted him of financial malfeasance. After more than a year of house arrest, he was freed, apparently no longer a danger to the nation and yet cleared of the most extravagant charges that had been made against him. Meanwhile, President Lleras Camargo fastened an austerity program on the country, and soon Colombia, which is so productive that only a few months of sensible management is sufficient for financial matters to right themselves, had restored a favorable trade balance. So peaceful and prosperous was the country after two years under Lleras Camargo that the politicians began to indulge in the pleasures of quarreling among themselves. Whether this revival of partisanship was a healthy sign or not, the coalition held and in May 1962 elected the Conservative Leon Guillermo Valencia president.

Colombia's problems in the early 1960's varied little from the general pattern of Latin American difficulties. The interruption of her tradition of freedom had lowered her political morality to the level of that of her sister states, which meant that she was a land of comparative liberty, but uneasily so. Communism, an outlawed movement for many years, was a force of unknown but considerable potency, but conventional fascism was dormant. Officially, the country was friendly to the United States, the source of most of her foreign capital and the leading customer for her coffee, which accounted for four-fifths of her foreign exchange. While the population was outgrowing the schools, public services, and housing facilities, the government was determined to deal with such challenges, and the United States eager to aid it. Airlines, waterways, railroads, and highways were expanding apace but were far from adequate, perhaps always would be because of the unfortunate, if scenic, geography of the country. Colombia's educated classes had not been notably creative for some decades, but they were alert and well-informed participants in Western civilization, and the University of the Andes near Bogotá was one of the best in Latin America. One familiar Latin American problem that Colombia knew only in small degree was latifundia; already 2,000,-000 of her farmers owned their own land.

On the whole, there was reason to be optimistic about the future, and Colombians were. Much wealth remained in their oil fields and mines, there was no visible limit to the expansion of agriculture that mechanization and scientific methods could bring, and half the country, the wooded region of the southeast, remained to be tapped. Industrialization was proceeding very rapidly. Colombia had coal, oil, and water power; she had a steel mill and was about to manufacture automobiles. Above all, its human resources were impressive. If most Colombians were still poor by present standards of Western civilization and likely to be uneducated, they had become acquainted with the possibility of striking self-improvement and seemed well on the way to achieving it.

30

Ecuador

THE murder of García Moreno in 1875 is a convenient point at which to resume the account of the Republic of the Equator. This state had seemed entirely artificial at the time of its secession from Colombia in 1830, but it had proved viable enough to survive. Except for its two major cities, the seaport Guayaquil and the highland capital, Quito, which were very much at odds with one another, Ecuador's composition was somewhat vague. Filling in 400 miles of space between disputed frontiers with Colombia and Peru, the republic extended from the Pacific coast to an unmarked boundary on the edges of the Amazon basin. Its maritime region was fairly narrow, very hot, and over-saturated with rain. Except for Guayaquil, a shallow port fifty-five miles from the ocean on the Guayas River, this section was lightly inhabited but rich in soil and woodlands. Ecuador's heartland lay in the high basins between two ranges of the Andes. Here was Quito, with an elevation of 9,000 feet and awesome vistas of snow-topped peaks, including the famous Avenue of Volcanoes; southward were Cuenca, Loja, smaller towns, and a number of hacienda villages. Most of the population, about ten per cent of whom were of European descent, lived in this region, raising livestock and food on the mountainsides as they had in Inca times or engaging in more advanced methods in the basins, where lava had enriched the earth. Toward the east, as the Andes sloped down into the Amazonian vastness, there were woods and grazing lands, but scarcely anyone lived there except the barbaric Auca and Jívaro Indians. Ecuador's social system was either patriarchal, as it had been in Spanish times, or primitive. While that mystical dictator, García Moreno, had exalted the Church, gotten a few schools started, and done something to introduce modern technology, the republic was still very backward.

MILITARISM AND HESITANT
CONSTITUTIONALISM, 1875–1924

One of the most potent opponents of García Moreno had been the liberal poet and man of letters Juan Montalvo, who boasted that his pen had killed the dictator, though a group of youths had actually administered the blows. Liberalism had never died out in Ecuador, partly because it had a strong geographical base in the city of Guayaquil. Furthermore, this retarded land had a small elite of cultured souls, some of whom were ideologues. As it happened, the liberals were not yet prepared to assume direction of Ecuador in place of the dead dictator. Only a year after they killed him, in 1876, General José de Veintemilla re-asserted the power of the conservative army and maintained himself as president-dictator for seven years, a period which lacked the style and dynamism of García Moreno's rule but which perpetuated the oligarchical system identified with Quito's ascendancy. In 1883 he was overthrown by a semi-popular revolt, though political life still turned on the military pivot in the last analysis, and Ecuador fell back into the hands of conservatives as radical as García Moreno, a condition as paradoxical as the little republic itself.

During these years of rightist domination the activities and writings of Montalvo and liberals like him gradually drained the force from the conservative oligarchy. By 1888 enough of this group had become alienated from the extreme conservatives to join with liberals in a "progressive" coalition, which elected Antonio Flores as president. The son of Ecuador's founder, Juan José Flores, he presided over four years of domestic peace, a relatively upright administration, and an unusual period of liberty. This relaxation in factionalism was probably made possible by the growth of the cacao industry in the maritime region, which caused the exporters and bankers of Guayaquil to be prosperous and gave the planters more opportunity to travel abroad. Antonio Flores was followed by another progressive, Luis Cordero, whose exemplary administration ended abruptly in disgrace. It was revealed in 1895 that he had permitted the use of Ecuador's flag to cover the surreptitious sale of a warship by Chile to Japan, who was then waging a predatory war on China. Because of the dishonor he had brought on the republic, Cordero was thrown out of office.

Now it was time for the traditional liberals, long in eclipse but firm in morale, to seize the government. Their leader was General Eloy Alfaro, a pugnacious man who had profited from years of exile by making a fortune, mainly in Panama. A friend and follower of Juan Montalvo, who had died in 1889, Alfaro had definite ideas about transforming Ecuador.

Among his chief aims were the promotion of constitutional procedures, respect for civil rights, and a financial soundness that would attract foreign capital. He also planned schools, public sanitation measures, modern law codes, and improvements for the Indians, so many of whom still lived in a servile state. The most controversial of his projects, however, was the reduction of the power of the Church, so all-pervading since the time of García Moreno. Thanks to the conciliatory attitude of the archbishop, it proved fairly simple to remove most of the regular orders from the republic and to trim the power of the secular clergy. But when he suggested disestablishing the Church, cries of "atheism" filled the air.

Perhaps Alfaro would not have pressed for this extreme measure, but his successor did. This was the capable General Leonidas Plaza, president from 1901 to 1905, who fathered a new constitution which omitted to name Roman Catholicism the state religion. When this charter was proclaimed, in 1906, Alfaro was president again, and it was he who bore the brunt of outraged conservative and clerical feeling. His second administration, from 1905 to 1911, was full of acrimony over this issue, the rural priests arousing the masses, urban prelates prophesying doom, and liberal intellectuals angrily denouncing "fanaticism" and "superstition." Alfaro reacted by suppressing his critics, using familiar methods that made a mockery of his supposed views in favor of liberalism and toleration. He further quarreled with his supporters in a way that suggested extreme irascibility. Bitter as his second administration was, it saw the fulfillment of most of the liberal program. Among the greatest achievements was the completion of a 288-mile railway from Quito to Duran, a town across the Guayas from Guayaquil, a marvel of engineering that went from sea level to 11,000 feet and brought pride and joy to Ecuadoreans, who made veritable holidays of railway trips. More important, it linked Quito to its rival city and the sea and did much to knit the republic.

Alfaro, "the Great Fighter," as his partisans acclaimed him, left office in 1911. Soon he became displeased with his successor and gathered an army to remove him, but he was defeated and lodged in the penitentiary at Quito. In January 1912, a pro-clerical crowd pulled him out of the prison, tore him to bits, and burned his remains, an atrocity that reflected the kind of passions he had aroused. Alfaro's followers were fanatical in their way too. For many years they troubled Ecuadorian politicians who had been his enemies, and they still make a cult of his memory. The immediate victor in the savage fracas of 1912 was Alfaro's former friend and protégé, ex-President Leonidas Plaza, who served again as president until 1916 and was followed by two other liberals, each of whom filled four-year terms.

While the political equilibrium of Ecuador now depended on the loyalty and effectiveness of liberal army units, the republic was outwardly constitutionalist. Of more importance than politics during these years was the expansion of cacao pod exports, the fabrication of Panama hats, the growth of banking and light industry, and the success of British oil scouts and American gold hunters. Also, the Rockefeller Foundation ridded Guayaquil of yellow fever, malaria, and the bubonic plague. For decades shippers had avoided this diseased port if possible; now they concentrated on it, or as near to it as their vessels could come. The harbor was so shallow that large ships anchored at the island of Puná and used rafts or lighters for loading.

MODERN ATTITUDES, MODERN PROBLEMS

By the mid-1920's Ecuador had only sampled the advantages of the Industrial Age and was still, in a loose sense, feudalistic. A few hundred creole families owned the major plantations and business houses and ran the political parties and the army. Few immigrants had entered the republic, so this white element was small. Mestizos were likely to be workers in the towns, small shopowners, and managers of haciendas, while a few thousand Negroes lived in dire poverty along the coast. Most Ecuadorians were Indians, mainly highlanders who lived in peonage on the haciendas or in mountainous communities still largely untouched by Western civilization. The period of transformation was beginning, however, with the automobile, truck, motorcycle, and airplane as well as the motion picture and radio. Ecuador's upper classes, who had long regarded themselves as members of the modern world community, were now feeling themselves crowded by the growing middle class and even some elements of the urban proletariat. The country's proud cultural tradition made it easier for attitudes of Europe or the United States to find acceptance, particularly through the agency of the University of Quito, an admirable institution with the usual Latin American student body of politically-conscious sons of the well-to-do. In addition, a school of novelists, of whom Jorge Icaza (1902–) was the most influential, was making the literate somewhat aware of social problems, especially the plight of the Indian workers. If students and writers were often Marxist-oriented and anti-Yankee, and if they prided themselves in violating the restraints of polite literature, they awakened their fellow countrymen. Ecuador, in short, was feeling the impact of forces that were stirring the rest of the world.

The first important evidence that times were changing came in 1924, when a radical member of the liberal faction, Dr. Gonzalo Córdoba, was elected president. Córdoba called for an end to militarism, imperialism, and plutocracy, protection for labor, social services, and land reform. Only a few months of his regime was sufficient to convince the possessing classes that their ascendancy was endangered. Accordingly, a "Ninth of July" movement in 1925 removed the offending radicals and restored the familiar politicians. And yet, as in Peru and Chile during these years, the traditional oligarchs were conscious of the need to make concessions to the poor. Something in the way of benefits for urban labor, public works, school-building, and sanitation was supplied. Perhaps the achievement of which the ruling groups was most proud was the establishment of a sound system for government financing and currency, a labor carried out with the advice of an American party of experts.

Before long, the world depression undermined the new rationale, and Ecuador went through a very turbulent period. The cacao industry had been declining for several years because of plant diseases, and the disappearance of world markets for other products left the country commercially stranded. Labor unrest, strikes, radical agitation, and confusion among the ruling groups reflected the hard times. Political changes came thick and fast as urban crowds, insubordinate army units, and, curiously enough, rebellious congresses pulled down presidents and set up others. After several years of acute instability the military literally closed ranks in 1935 and re-established itself as the guardian of Ecuador's destinies. Many officers were attracted to Nazism during this period, which led to truculent denunciations of "pluto-democracy," and one president tried in 1938 to deport all Jews who were not farmers.

By 1940 the embittered radicals and liberals united long enough to secure the election of Dr. Carlos Arroyo del Río, who remained in power for four years. Of no small importance in making his tenure possible was the aid which the United States provided Ecuador in exchange for bases at Salinas and the Galápagos Islands, those stark protrusions that had offered many specimens to Charles Darwin in the 1830's and had served Ecuador principally as a penal colony. From American sources came loans and grants to re-equip Ecuador's railways, to construct highways, and to provide rural medical service. Also, Americans helped Ecuadorians conduct a survey that revealed the richness of so much unused lands and forests and the possibilities of mining. Ecuador's sale of cacao, rubber, quinine, balsa wood, and kapok brought in much money during the war, money that produced an inflation but also expanded the middle class. Absorbed in the novelty of prosperity, Arroyo did not attempt drastic social reforms, but the few modest ones he sponsored further modernized the country. One of his actions, however, was unforgivable. In 1942, under immense pressure from the other American republics, he agreed to a settlement of the ancient boundary conflict with Peru, which that country had anticipated by barbarously driving out Ecuadorians from the province of El Oro. Ecuador lost a huge amount of land, mostly in the Amazon basin. While this territory had never been exploited, scarcely explored, its cession to Peru left Ecuador little more than a strip along the Pacific coast, to the everlasting chagrin of her nationalists.

Wartime prosperity and oppressive measures enabled Arroyo to stay in power as long as he did following this cession. In May 1944 a coalition of patriots, Communists, conservatives, liberals, and other ill-matched groups combined to overthrow him. He was replaced by a former law professor who had lived much of his life in exile, Dr. José María Velasco Ibarra. Velasco had served as president once before, in 1934–1935, and had shown himself tyrannical. Now he capitalized on the leftist and nationalist turbulence that was such a consistent feature of many countries during the mid-1940's. His administration, which lasted from 1944 to 1947, was full of bombast but singularly undistinguished. An effort to cooperate with the Communists soon ended in acrimony and persecution. Inflation, a growing awareness of social evils, and the persisting determination of the old oligarchs to rule made him unpopular and led to his overthrow. The junta which replaced him found three presidents in rapid succession to occupy the national palace until, in June 1948, it turned the fate of the republic over to the electorate. The result was a narrow victory for the liberal grouping and its candidate, Galo Plaza Lasso, son of onetime President Leonidas Plaza.

No Ecuadorian has been so well-known in the United States as Galo Plaza, who was born in New York, educated at Cornell University, and had served as ambassador in Washington. A winning and eloquent man, he advertised not only his country's woes but its determination to overcome them. During his periods of residence in Ecuador he had made a point of studying its problems at first hand. His family estate became a veritable experimental farm to demonstrate the usefulness of scientific techniques. Now that he was president, Galo Plaza concentrated on two major lines of policy. First, the republic must be a showcase of liberty. This meant an end to political terrorism, restraint of the military, and encouragement of free expression, even criticism of himself. The Ecuadorians responded commendably to this opportunity, notwithstanding the slanders of Communists and other extremists. It seemed that Ecuador, if given half a chance, might be capable of responsible government. Plaza's second purpose was to tackle the fundamental social and economic problems of the country in realistic ways. Rather than prepare grandiose projects for the millenium, he thought it better to teach farmers how to exploit the land better, to breed better livestock, and to bring new areas under cultivation as free homesteads, for small as Ecuador was, she had abundant lands in rich areas that had never been turned to human use. Under the president's personal leadership and with the aid of the International Basic Economy Corporation and loans from a variety of sources, the rural population responded enthusiastically. Furthermore, Plaza encouraged Indian women to improve their domestic skills, particularly in weaving, and to turn them to commercial purposes. Other programs that blossomed were reforestation, schooling, rural road construction, and the provision of potable water. Although one of the most tragic earthquakes in history magnified the republic's problems in 1949, the Plaza administration was one of unprecedented progress.

A correct constitutionalist, Galo Plaza Lasso did not seek to prolong his term of office nor influence the choice of a successor. While all men were supposed to vote and women were allowed to, only a tenth of the population participated in the election of 1952. The result was somewhat disenchanting, since the winner was General Velasco Ibarra, president in 1934–1935 and 1944–1947. Having just returned from a long residence in Perón's Argentina, Velasco employed the vocabulary of nationalistic demagoguery and berated the United States for unclear but sinister intentions. Yet his four-year term was less retrograde than many had feared, though he ended the holiday of freedom the country had enjoyed under his predecessor. For the most part he continued the economic programs of Plaza and, despite his strictures about imperialism, allowed foreign, private, and United Nations agencies to effect many improvements. Ecuadorians reacted in the familiar way: by clamoring for further material benefits and by reproducing. As the population passed 4,000,000, the specter of over-crowding peered over the Andes at Ecuador. Fierce patriot that he said he was, Velasco revived the boundary dispute with Peru. The settlement of 1942 was found to be full of geographical and technical errors which gave him an excuse to make threats, for students to riot against Peru and the powers, including the United States, who had allegedly favored her, and for the nationalistic press to rage. The chronic border war, which had gone on for more than a century before 1942, resumed its unedifying course.

The election of 1956 was acceptably honest. With the covert backing of President Velasco, the conservative-bloc candidate, Camilo Ponce Enríquez, won. Directing his attention to fiscal affairs, he stabilized the currency and limited inflation. Ecuador's foreign trade had been growing steadily since World War II, with banana exports making her the world's prime source of this food and with sales of coffee and rice mounting and cacao at last reviving as an export item. Such old staples as Panama hats, of which Ecuador has long had a near monopoly despite the name, and tagua nuts, the ivory-like fruit used for buttons, also brought in foreign exchange. While little oil could be located in the republic, there was much evidence of mineral ores that had never been tapped. Ecuador was potentially productive; a brief period of intelligently directed human energy ought to be enough to raise her to the level of her neighbors. This was supplied in part by various teams of foreign experts and financed by the World Bank and United States official and private sources. Ecuador acquired an airline, a steel mill, an oil refinery, and had prospects for an indefinite expansion of light industries, communications, and electrical power systems. A huge project to make Guayaquil a deep-water port and one to complete the Pan-American highway offered bright hopes for advancement. The transformation of the Galápagos Islands into a national park and game refuge and efforts to entice foreign tourists also promised new items of income.

If material improvements seemed altogether within the range of the possible, what of the human element? Here the answer remained discouraging. Only about a tenth of the population could be classified as effective citizens. While a few thousand of them were as enlightened and energetic as directing classes in other countries, they were still divided about the course their nation should follow. The patricians were abidingly powerful and not inclined to surrender their privileges. Communists and other totalitarians were vocal and well-organized. Middle-class liberalism was a frail cult indeed, however able some of its adherents were. And despite all of the changes in recent decades, the Indian rural population mainly lived in destitution and ignorance and obeyed rich men. A brutal massacre of American missionaries in the Auca region and the continued practice of head-shrinking advertised to the world the primitive character of eastern Ecuador. Notwithstanding the culture of the elite and several campaigns to promote public education, illiteracy claimed a large majority of the population. To pessimists it seemed that the principal result of all the uplifting programs had been to lower the death rate, thus permitting a population growth that overtaxed existing facilities and threatened further impoverishment.

Another discouragement to those who wished this picturesque land well was the election of 1960. Galo Plaza Lasso, who was so much admired abroad, ran for president against Velasco Ibarra and a leftist candidate. Velasco won by a huge majority, an indication partly of a peculiar method of counting votes but, it had to be admitted, also that his crimes against liberty in previous tours of duty were not particularly resented. His espousal of virulent nationalism, now patterned after Cuba's Castro rather than Argentina's Perón, had much appeal to Ecuadoreans. Violent attacks on the U.S. Embassy and angry anti-Yankee demonstrations disturbed the Americans, who were generally eager to assist the little republic and harbored not the slightest intention of enslaving it. Velasco's fanning of the Peruvian border war and his claims to a 200-mile limit for Ecuadorian rights in the Pacific—a common assertion in the late 1950's as the fishing industry grew more lucrative—showed that he was a trouble-maker. His talk of social justice and orderly agrarian reform did not satisfy the people. In November 1961 a wave of popular and military opposition resulted in his overthrow and the installation of the vice-president, Carlos Julio Arosemena Monroy.

31

Peru

I<small>N HER</small> first forty years of independence the republic of Peru
had known more than a dozen constitutions and had abided by none of
them. Constant invocation of the words "liberty" and "democracy" by
her leaders had done little to create a republican spirit or representative
institutions. Peru's failure to become a real republic prolonged the tragedy of the area dating back as far as the civil war between Atahualpa and
Huascar. If it had sometimes been stable as a component of the Spanish
empire afterward, its social basis was too corrupted, to paraphrase Simón
Bolívar, by treasure and human servitude to make for a wholesome
growth into nationhood.

Peruvian society had changed little since the formal end of colonialism in 1824. The creole aristocracy continued to preside over the best
lands and business houses and was conservatism itself in politics, religion,
dress, and manners. Middle-class development had been halting, uneven,
and on the whole minute, though militaristic politics and guano sales had
somewhat re-distributed wealth to the benefit of some bourgeois citizens.
As for the lower classes, who composed 95 per cent of the population,
some were persons of mixed blood who were likely to be ragged peons
or slum-dwellers, often hungry, drunken, and given to crime, although a
few had risen in the army or trades. Far more Peruvians were pure
Indians who spoke Quechua, deferred to tribal rulers, and mixed Christianity with ancient paganism. Many of these lived in servitude on haciendas; others were in native communities in the highlands, where their
contact with Westernized elements was sporadic, only a matter of being
drafted for labor on the white man's lands or for service in his armies for
incomprehensible purposes.

Peru was disjointed not only with respect to race and class. Her geography shredded the country. Near the Pacific coast, where the creoles, mulattoes, and Westernized Negroes and mestizos, or *cholos*, were concentrated, the land was either desert or rugged. Some of the coastland was a tawny strip of sand seldom more than thirty miles wide, crossed with rivulets that shot out of the mountains and only haphazardly irrigated since the days of the Inca. Sugar cultivation was almost the sole economic activity here. West of it was the ocean, where the cold blue Humboldt current flowed northward from the Antarctic, never producing rainfall for the parched string of sand except in years when *El Niño*, a phenomenon much dreaded, caused storms. To the east the mountains rose abruptly as they do all along the Pacific coast of the Americas. Rich valleys in the western cordillera of the Andes accommodated fine estates for cotton and food production with the familiar landlord-peon social pattern. The arid plateaus between the western and eastern *sierra* were often uninhabited or devoted to grazing. Farther eastward the mountain chains were higher and more likely to be snow-topped. In these highlands were the masses of the Indians, living in drab communities as they had since time immemorial, raising corn and potatoes, drinking *chicha*, and tending herds of European origin and alpacas, llamas, vicuñas, and guanacos. The prospect of this region as it might have appeared to a condor was one of emptiness. Beyond the Andes, covering about a third of the republic, were jungles and wooded mountains, a climate generally torrid, and a descending terrain stretching toward the Amazon. This area was practically a wilderness, its Indians primitive and nomadic.

Peru's cities were few, small, and contentious. Lima, the City of the Kings, the handsome relic of colonial grandeur covered by a cloud bank several months of the year, asserted a right to rule all Peru and to regulate its intercourse with the outside world. Smaller towns like Ayacucho, Cajamarca, Huancayo, and Trujillo changed exceedingly little over the decades. Arequipa, a charming city in the south, where the plateaus are not quite so stark and arid, competed with Lima rather ineffectively but, as a nest of revolutions, caused it frequent trouble. And there was Cuzco, the unofficial Indian capital, full of Inca ruins and Quechuas, which played almost no part in national life. Divided as nature and man had made republican Peru, its government was as unitary as in viceregal times, only now there were departments instead of intendancies or *corregimientos*. Lima nearly always dominated the rest of the country.

WAR, MISMANAGEMENT, DEFEAT

The history of modern Peru is unhappily free of great events or developments that carry a country into spectacular good fortune. She has never uncovered a source of wealth that did much to favor the nation as a whole, achieved a political equilibrium of long duration, elevated great numbers of her population to a higher level of comfort and welfare, or come into a rich cultural period. Yet all of these benefits she has sampled in a tantalizing way. During the 1860's the outside world began to intrude on Peru. First, the European market for guano, which for twenty years had brought money into the country, continued to flourish. Sales of these bird droppings from islands off the coast were sufficient to finance the government and to permit it such luxuries as public works and modern weapons, status symbols then of great significance to small nations, as airlines and steel mills would be a century later. Also, a considerable number of individuals had become rich by advancing to the government, always improvident, funds at high interest rates in exchange for the privilege of excavating this repulsive commodity. These persons and wayward public servants prospered considerably, though the guano income brought few advantages to the rest of the population.

In 1864 this game was threatened by aggressive moves by Spain, whose subjects or their heirs had never received satisfaction from Peru for losses sustained during the Wars of Independence. Spain also had a convenient excuse to bring pressure on Peru in that a group of Basque immigrants had complained of being maltreated by the Peruvian government. Of more importance was the fact that the United States was absorbed in the Civil War. The appearance of a large Spanish expeditionary force off the coasts aroused fears in Peru, though it was said to be engaging in scientific findings and did, in fact, include a few oceanographers and meteorologists. Particularly disturbing was the attitude of Don Eusebio Salazar y Mazarredo, a diplomat who later was to play a calamitous role in bringing on the Franco-Prussian War. This personage demanded settlement of the old claims and compensation for the Basque immigrants, but he insisted on being recognized as the "royal commissioner," a term that implied to the Peruvians an ambition to restore their country to the Spanish monarchy. Before long the Spanish squadron occupied the Chincha Islands, which provided half the guano, and Spain formally demanded settlement of her claims as the price for relinquishing these stinking rocks.

The president of Peru, Juan Antonio Pezet, favored coming to terms with the Spaniards, but most of his countrymen, as well as other Pacific coast republics, foresaw further demands if these were conceded and ultimate re-colonization. Soon a *golpe de estado,* or coup d'état, ousted Pezet and installed as president a liberal colonel named Mariano Ignacio Prado. Peru then adopted a high tone, ordered the Spanish to evacuate the Chinchas, and, when they declined, declared war on the former motherland. Chile, Bolivia, and Ecuador joined Peru. The war proved awkward to fight, since the Americans could not contend with the naval power of Spain, who did not attempt to land an army on the mainland. Mostly it was a matter of Spanish sailors and coastal populations threatening one another with small arms and of popular attacks on Spanish residents. The only major actions took place in 1866, after the United States was through with its civil war and Spain had sold enough guano to compensate her for her exertions. As a brutal parting shot, the Spanish fleet bombarded Valparaiso, Chile, where they did little damage, and Callao, Lima's port, where they did much, and sailed back to Europe. In 1871 a truce was arranged, and in 1879 Spain and Peru signed a peace treaty. Perhaps the worst effect of this curious war was the renewal of hatred by the South Americans for the erstwhile mother country, which inhibited the flow of peninsular immigrants that Peru was so eager to attract.

Mariano Ignacio Prado was little different from the usual military presidents of Peru except that he was, by local standards, more liberal. Surrounding himself with an able group of young men, he talked of moralizing the government, and he tried to express the liberal conscience by taking the side of Cuba's revolutionaries, partly of course to vex Spain, and of Paraguay in her struggle against Argentina and Brazil. An effort to reduce the continuous clanging of church bells antagonized the priestly and feminine portions of the population and aroused latent anti-clericalism in other quarters. A constitution which he sponsored in 1867 promised a revival of the liberal promises thwarted by Ramón Castilla in 1856, but by this time Prado had been in power for two years and had alienated a number of people. Castilla himself took the field to overthrow him but died in the campaign. In January 1868, other enemies, mainly military, succeeded.

Colonel José Balta, an engineer officer of conservative sympathies, was the victor in the latest *golpe*. He set aside Prado's constitution of 1867 and restored the conservative charter of 1860, which was destined to remain in force until 1919. Balta stayed in power for a full term, from 1868 to 1872, a period of comparative freedom but better remembered because of a significant financial arrangement associated with his minister, Nicolás de Piérola, a man who would figure prominently in Peruvian politics for almost half a century. Piérola regarded the public debt as unmanageable, since the government had too long borrowed from local and foreign financiers in anticipation of future guano income and, of course, had tended to squander the money. With an Alsatian jeweler and importer long resident in Lima named August Dreyfus, Piérola negotiated in 1869 a different arrangement, one by which a company of French capitalists organized by Dreyfus would monopolize 2,000,000 tons of guano annually and take over most of the marketing. In exchange, it would service the consolidated foreign debts of the republic. Stridently as Peruvian money-lenders objected to the Dreyfus contract, Piérola secured approval for it, and for several years the arrangement worked well. The government had ample funds, though it continued to direct them to channels other than national needs, and the Parisian financiers were so pleased they advanced further sums for railroad building.

Railway construction, so prevalent in the West during this period, had touched Peru to the extent of several short lines. It did not appear to have a great future, given the mountainous nature of the republic, but such realities did not deter adventurers who dreamed that this profitable activity could make Peru a modern state and themselves rich. By far the most famous enterpriser in South America was Henry Meiggs, a New Yorker who had made and lost a fortune in California and had then migrated to Chile, where he had constructed many miles of railway. While he had again been bankrupted, he was still revered as a wonder-worker, and the Peruvians lured him to Lima. He presented an attractive scheme: the construction of costly railroads in improbable places under government rather than private auspices, financed by French capitalists. For several years he achieved fantastic results, building a trans-Andean line with numerous bridges, tunnels, and frightening grades and curves to connect Callao with Oroyo. He also started a road from Arequipa to Puno, which is so high that modern travelers inhale oxygen during the journey, and another difficult connection between Cuzco and Juliaca. Meiggs gloriously conquered engineering obstacles, though some of his solutions proved expensive and unsafe. He also handled labor problems with great success. Since Peru's lower classes would not or could not work to his satisfaction, he made extensive use of Chinese coolies, most of whom had been kidnaped or deceived and shipped on slave ships to Peru as indentured workers. For a few years all went well. Money filled the pockets of politicians and Peruvians in general were excited by the prospect of a wonderful future thanks to railways. Meiggs was so admired that, simple and unpretentious as he was, he dominated Lima socially and was entrusted with other public works. He built a great palace for a national exposition in 1872, a status symbol for the time, tore down ancient walls that constricted Lima's expansion, and planned grand boulevards and monuments. He also subsidized artists and writers to a generous degree and was charitable to the poor. A man who loved life, he took and shared.

The activities of Dreyfus and Meiggs during the Balta administration gave Peruvians an intimation of what might be done to transform their nation. Their new mood was reflected in the abandonment of viceregal dress and the adoption of Second Empire styles. Yet the dawn was false, for bad luck and ineptitude were to postpone Peru's entrance into the modern industrial era. Political instability continued to be a drag on progress, as the election of 1872 showed. In that year a large party set out to lift the curse of militarism that had plagued the republic so long, and to the surprise of everyone these *civilistas* won the election, which meant they secured a majority of the few thousand votes cast by property-owners. It was the first time in Peru's history that the "outs" had defeated the administration party in a test at the polls. Manuel Pardo, the victor, came of a good Lima family, had studied and traveled extensively abroad, and had prospered as an importer. His inauguration seemed certain as outgoing President Balta bowed to the election results. However, a group of four brothers, the Colonels Gutiérrez, decided to save Peru from the civilians and locked Balta up. Usually this action would have settled the matter, but this time the civilianists were not to be cheated. Winning over many soldiers in Lima—by bribes and alcohol, their opponents charged—and arousing the street crowds, they produced an explosion of wrath against the Gutiérrez brothers. After a few days of savage fighting, during which President Balta was murdered in prison and President-elect Pardo took refuge on a ship, the *civilistas* won. The Gutiérrez were barbarously killed and burned, and Pardo entered the capital in exaltation.

Begun with such a stirring triumph, the Pardo administration, which lasted from 1872 to 1876, was a mixture of misfortune and promise. As the depression of the 1870's settled on the world, Peru's unorthodox finances suddenly appeared insane. Not only did the price of guano fall, but its markets disappeared when Europeans discovered other types of fertilizers. Dreyfus was no longer able to raise money in Paris and became the focus of antagonism in Peru, where native financiers had always deplored his activities. Even Henry Meiggs ran into trouble. Unable to meet his payroll, he had to abandon construction on the rail projects, went broke again, and died. By 1875 Peru's credit standing collapsed when she suspended payment on her large foreign debts. One hopeful development, however, was the growth of a lucrative demand for *salitre*, or nitrates, of which Peru had an abundance in her southern coastal provinces. Since Chilean enterprisers had already established themselves in these regions, President Pardo decided to remove them tactfully by creating a monopoly for nitrates under the Peruvian government. It was a fateful step, contributing before long to the war with Chile.

In other respects Pardo and his civilianists fared better. They set up a faculty of political science at the University of San Marcos to train government servants, and schools of engineering, mines, agriculture, naval science, and artillery. Pardo created a few public schools, established a normal institute, and imported some foreign instructors. Such efforts, together with the freedom of press and association Peru enjoyed then, livened the intellectual interests of the capital. Peruvians were awakening to the wonders of their past. An Italian-born geographer, Antonio Raimondi, virtually "discovered" Peru, uncovering many resources and historical relics long undetected. A society of fine arts fostered the disciplined study of Inca times. During these years Ricardo Palma began the publication of a multi-volumed popular history of Peru, and Sebastián Lorente became one of the first scholarly historians the republic had produced.

Humanitarianism was another characteristic of the Pardo period. The president attacked the scandal of Chinese immigration, which had led to the forcible importation of perhaps 85,000 coolies between 1861 and 1875. A treaty with the Celestial Empire reduced this flow and humanized its nature. Pardo's efforts to entice European immigrants were, however, almost wholly fruitless. While the census of 1876 showed that Peru now had nearly 3,000,000 people, twice the number of 1836, little of the increase was due to an influx of white men. To some extent this condition, together with abiding fear of racial strife, explained the conservatism of the ancient Spanish element in Peru, for they were seldom jarred by the energies or new ideas of European immigrants. Perhaps the republic would be more attractive if it were freed of militarism. Pardo undertook to reduce the role of the army by reducing the army itself to a mere 3,000 men. Henceforth, recruitment was to be voluntary, officers were to be schooled in service academies, and soldiers were to be treated as human beings. A federalized national guard of short-term draftees was supposed to provide for order and defense. Commendable as these aims were, Pardo could scarcely have chosen a worse time to undermine the military, for war was already in sight as his term ended in 1876.

Pardo was succeeded by Prado, the General Mariano Ignacio Prado who had served as a liberal autocrat in 1865–1868 and was acceptable both to the *civilistas* and moderate militarists. As his term wore on, the civilianists fell away from him, the country refused to prosper, and, in 1879, the War of the Pacific began. Much as Admiral Grau and the heroic vessel *Huascar* did to lift Peruvian spirits, their deeds did not prevent the Chilean conquest of the nitrate-laden southern provinces, Tacna, Arica, and Tarapacá. After a visit to the crumbling front, President Prado, late in 1879, avoided an overthrow by setting out for Europe to buy warships and munitions. He was succeeded by Nicolás de Piérola, the onetime finance minister, who was given dictatorial powers when an invasion of the Lima area became imminent. Piérola strove to brace the capital, drafting manpower and wealth, enlisting the fulsome support of the clergy, and proclaiming himself protector of the Indians. Neither morale-building nor military preparations served to deter the Chileans, and all was lost save honor. By degrees the men of

Chile closed in on Pisco, Callao, and Miraflores, and finally fought their way into the City of the Kings in January 1881 and later into Arequipa. Piérola moved to Ayacucho with a congress that soon deserted him. Peruvian resistance was then personified by General Andrés Avelino Cáceres, who became a national hero by leading red-capped guerrilla forces in punishing attacks on the invaders. In Lima, where the Chileans remained for three years, the inhabitants complained of oppression and looting. Finally, in October 1883, a rump congress agreed to the Treaty of Ancón, and the Chileans began to evacuate the capital.

By the Treaty of Ancón Peru lost Tarapacá and, for at least ten years, Tacna and Arica, and with these departments the nitrate revenues she needed so badly. The war had not only injured her national pride but had thrown her economy into such disorganization that conditions were almost primitive. Fortunately for the landholding classes, the Indians re- mained aloof in their highlands, caring little about the sufferings of the coastal regions and taking no advantage of them to revolt. The country as a whole seemed to be in a trauma after the shock of war and occupation. General Miguel Iglesias, now the provisional president, assumed the onus for signing the Treaty of Ancón, but he found himself denounced as a traitor rather than a patriot by General Cáceres, who still commanded spirited forces in the hinterland. In November 1885 Cáceres entered Lima and assumed the task of putting the stricken republic on its feet.

TOWARD STABILITY AND
ECONOMIC GROWTH, 1885–1919

Cáceres stayed in power from 1885 to 1890, somewhat more than the four-year term allowed by the constitution of 1860. It served a useful pur- pose to have a national hero as president during a period of recovery from the war, especially when he strove without too much hypocrisy to be correctly constitutionalist and even organized a Constitutionalist Party. Cáceres was also eager to restore Peru's long-lost reputation with foreign creditors. Since the debt was enormous, more than $200,000,000, and it was unthinkable to levy heavy taxes on the leading families, who did not care to pay, or the rest of the people, who could not pay, an ingenious arrangement was devised to obtain British money. Two American broth- ers, Michael and W. R. Grace, who had created a very successful guano- exporting business and other enterprises in South America, were instru- mental in preparing the scheme, which was nothing less than to turn over to a Peruvian Corporation the servicing of the debt in exchange for a large share of the guano and the profits from Peru's railways, seven of her ports, and shipments across Lake Titicaca, all for a period of sixty-six years. The method worked well, and Peru rapidly recovered a good credit rating while obtaining better railway and port service. Another development at this time brought benefits. Vast oil deposits were discovered in the desert coastland of northern Peru, around Talara, whose proximity to the sea somewhat compensated for the loneliness of this hideous area.

By 1890 Peru had partially recovered from the War of the Pacific, though she was doomed to many decades of disappointment in the Tacna and Arica issue. Her historic creole aristocracy was still supreme, but now it felt the challenge of a democratic movement inspired, as so often happens, by defeat in war. Nicolás de Piérola, whose reputation had survived the Dreyfus loan and the capture of Lima, had returned and organized the Democratic Party. His efforts to campaign in 1890 led to his imprisonment for a few months, but during the presidency of Cáceres' heir, Colonel Remigio Morales Bermúdez, he managed to instill determination in his followers. When Morales died in 1894, General Cáceres seized the presidency in defiance of the constitutionalism he claimed to espouse, a circumstance that caused the Democrats and the old *civilista* party to combine against him. Piérola engineered a revolt in 1895 that, after several battles and much hard street fighting in the capital, succeeded.

The presidency of Piérola, which commenced in 1895 and lasted for four years, was something of a turning point in the history of Peru, though the basic social pattern changed but little. This leader was fifty-six in 1895, a man so short as to arouse ridicule and yet, with his curly white beard and great shock of hair, impressive. He had had much experience in business, travel, journalism, and even in Church affairs. Aristocrat though he was, and married to the granddaughter of an emperor (Mexico's Iturbide), he nonetheless captured the affection of the poor, who sensed that he sympathized with their aspirations. His plans were not so much to elevate the masses, whose plight seemed hopeless in any case, but to strengthen the small urban middle classes who hoped to wrench control of the republic from the traditional oligarchy. Piérola seemed to snap with energy; yet he was thoughtful. He was a curious combination of dreamer and doer, of rebel and builder.

Piérola had the advantage of an improving economic situation, though Chile still refused to return Tacna and Arica, whose nitrates would have made Peru much more opulent. With a sound currency and the servicing of the debt by the Peruvian Corporation, the country was able to participate in international commerce. Guano still had some marketability, so did a few minerals, and there was the growing income from the oil at Talara. Further, rubber entered the business picture as the largely unexplored trans-Andean territory of Loreto was tapped. There, where Gonzalo Pizarro had once searched for the Land of the Cinnamon Tree, numerous rubber forests awaited exploitation. By shipping the crude product down the Amazon, the Peruvians could obtain profits, and their government revenues. Along with some economic prosperity, Peru enjoyed a taste of democracy under Piérola's auspices. He widened the suffrage so that all literate adult males could vote, and his congress was active, often the scene of riotous debates that suggested an awakening political consciousness. Mindful of his support from the *civilistas*, or the Civilianist Party, Piérola ended forced recruitment and substituted a national conscription, supposedly a more democratic procedure, and imported French advisers to train the army. He encouraged towns to start laic schools and allowed the press a good deal of freedom. His was a period, in fine, of some prosperity and considerable ferment, enough to establish a tradition that civilian and mildly democratic rule was preferable to the familiar militarism.

A more or less free election in 1899 gave Eduardo de Romaña the presidency, thus prolonging the influence of Piérola and his coalition. In 1903 the Civilianist Party named the president, and, when he died the following year, this organization again won. By now Piérola's power was in decline and the Democrats had broken with the Civilianists. But the two parties were viable, and so also was the Constitutionalist group of former President Cáceres. While none of these parties displayed much solicitude for the Indians or the poor, their very existence indicated that Peru had gone far from the days of neo-colonialism. The president who served from 1904 to 1908, José Pardo, son of the civilian president of 1872–1876, had a particularly fruitful administration. An enormous deposit of copper at Cerro de Pasco that is still being worked by an American corporation offered prospects of great wealth. And cotton cultivation on the irrigated coastland as well as sugar plantations in the north, around Trujillo, added greatly to the national income. In order to increase the number of landholders, Pardo allowed the Church to sell some of its properties long held in mortmain, and he was the greatest patron of public education Peru had yet seen. The number of schools doubled during his administration and the scholastic population rose to 168,000, a figure that signified a striking improvement but still a desperate inadequacy.

Another Civilianist won the election of 1908, this being Augusto Bernardino Leguía, a provincial of modest background who had an amazing talent for making money, often but not always at the race-track. By this time the Democrats were convinced that the repeated Civilianist victories at the polls derived from informal understandings with the military and bribery of the handful of voters. In 1909, the family and partisans of Nicolás de Piérola—who almost certainly was implicated in the plot, for he was restless when he was not in the thick of things—organized a revolt. The conspirators seized President Leguía in the palace and dragged him out to the Plaza de la Inquisición, where he was threatened with death unless he signed an order for the garrison to subordinate itself to the rebels. Resolutely refusing, Leguía probably escaped extinction on the spot by the timely clatter of hoofs that signified the arrival of loyal soldiers. This close call may have gratified Leguía's supporters, but it did little to make him a respected president. His term was one of plots and rumors, of strident partisanship and scanty accomplishments. If Peru won 96,000 square miles in a boundary dispute with Bolivia in 1909, the credit was due to the arbitration, not the government. Leguía's prestige was so low in 1912 that he failed to install another Civilianist as his heir. Instead, the Democrats revolted again, this time successfully, and sent him away before his term was over.

Guillermo Billinghurst was the new Democratic president. He was full of plans for drastic reforms that would give his party a permanent advantage and that, further, would cripple the power of the *patrones*, or bosses, over the rural masses. Congress was reluctant to revamp the political system, especially since Billinghurst's proposals would have reduced its functions. The *patrones* were so accustomed to a plentiful labor supply and abject obedience that any suggestion of arousing the poor outraged them. And Billinghurst went so far as to take the side of rubber workers in the backland *montaña*, whose exploitation had been advertised by several novelists but most effectively of all by the British diplomat, Sir Roger Casement, who was to be executed in 1916 for seeking to raise Ireland. No one was surprised when, in 1914, a garrison inspired by the Civilianist Party threw Billinghurst out of office. This force was led by Colonel Oscar Benavides, who would be president of Peru in less than twenty years, but the immediate beneficiary of his action was former President José Pardo, who returned to the palace for another term.

Pardo's second term, extending from 1915 to 1919, was stormy, despite his efforts to appease all factions. First, World War I had initially thrown Peru's export business into a depression. Then, as demands for copper, cotton, rubber, oil, and guano spurted, some elements of the country enjoyed a dizzy prosperity for two or three years, only to fall back into a crisis of surpluses and low prices after the war ended. A general strike in Lima in January 1919 revealed for the first time the determination of militant labor. Pardo met it by limiting the hours of work in government concerns and recommending the same course to private employers. He also ordered planters to pay their peons in cash, and he created an agricultural bank to alleviate the distress of the rural poor. And he took a step that was pleasing to liberals but shocking to traditionalists in authorizing religious toleration. Of more enduring consequence than any of these actions, however, was probably the government's campaign against the mosquito, and hence yellow fever and malaria, which greatly lowered the human death rate.

When the election of 1919 loomed, the bosses, mostly Civilianist, decided to return to Augusto Leguía, who had been absent from the country since 1912, a period long enough to enable people to forget that he had been little more than a nonentity during his previous term of office. Leguía had spent his exile profitably, mostly in England, where he had played the races with his proverbial good luck and had otherwise increased his fortune. He had also meditated about his past mistakes and ways to make a better showing if he ever had the chance. His sponsors almost certainly were unaware of his new ideas and felt he would be easy to manage. For some reason, apparently no sound one, they feared that President Pardo would intervene at the last minute to keep Leguía from being inaugurated, though he had easily been elected. A bloodless coup in July 1919 removed Pardo and installed Leguía ahead of schedule. He was to remain in the presidency for eleven years that would change the face of Peru.

PERU IN QUEST OF ITS DESTINY

Augusto Leguía defied classification, other than the admission that he was a dictator. He must have been influenced by Yrigoyen's career in Argentina, by Alessandri of Chile, and the Mexican Revolution. Probably he was a student of Bolshevism in Russia, Fascism in Italy, and Primo de Rivera's methods in Spain. While Peru was not confused and rootless the way Europe was during the 1920's, she was enough so to inspire a strong ruler to try to integrate her formless constituents into a coherent social entity. Whether this entity was fascism or merely a modernized version of *caudillaje* or even a groping for that balance toward which Latin America has been striving in this century, whatever it is, Leguía gave his country a sense of direction. He reassured the army, Church, and gentry without letting them dominate him. To a greater degree he cultivated the newly-rich and the growing middle class, who included a thriving colony of foreign residents, and was eager to please investors abroad. Yet he did not sell Peru to foreign thralldom; rather the reverse, for he inadvertently swindled most of the aliens who invested in it. He allowed the top layers of society to hold their privileges while stimulating the layers below, even to the extent of helping the urban working classes and encouraging the Indians. While he professed to be fervently nationalistic, a fashionable pose for the times, he negotiated amicable settlements with Peru's strongest rivals. Apparently Leguía was popular, even beloved, despite a tyranny that was more harsh than Peru was accustomed to. For ten years the country responded to his ministrations with a memorable economic growth. His hold ended when the good times did, and then the Peruvians savagely turned on him.

Leguía was a modern dictator. No strutting militarist, he was a very small man, dignified, subdued, and cold-eyed. Yet he loved to mingle with the people and exhibit himself at the interminable fiestas, carnivals, banquets, balls, sports events, and pageants that have made Lima since its earliest days a city where life seemed full, even if it was full of trivialities. Leguía attended the races on Sunday afternoons so faithfully that an occasional absence would serve to start a spate of rumors. Not long after his accession to the presidency for the second time, the public decided that it liked him, a condition that made it all the easier for him to slide the country into a dictatorship. He gave his government the respectability of a new name and a new constitution. The *Patria nueva* (new fatherland), as he called it, was based on the constitution of 1919, a document full of social guarantees that pleased the masses. It also reduced the power of congress and made a concession to federalism by abolishing the meaningless departmental juntas of the past in favor of three regional congresses, which proved equally meaningless. The Church was now freed from government patronage, which pleased the higher clergy who could now fill vacancies without reference to the state. The power of the Church, as well as its holdings, continued undiminished, though very many Peruvians were practically untouched by Catholic doctrine and practice. While the customary list of rights appeared in the new constitution, the regime had no hesitancy about invading the courts or congress itself to remove troublesome persons. Since the University of San Marcos was often a scene of political demonstrations, Leguía closed it down for long periods. The press likewise learned the hard way not to be severe in judging the regime. It was safer to hail Leguía as the "giant of the Pacific" or "Jupiter president" than to risk prison and ruin by criticizing him. When the centenaries of Peru's proclamation of independence and the Battle of Ayacucho fell due, Leguía and his countrymen hailed a century of "liberty" and "democracy."

The success of the dictatorship depended more on money than on Leguía's popularity. His solution for obtaining this commodity was amazingly simple. During these years New York was full of bankers who, sometimes compromising their reputations, would sell bonds to Americans. All Peru had to do was print these certificates and present only mildly plausible evidence of economic growth. The flow of money started and grew fantastically. In eleven years Leguía multiplied the national debt ten times, and not until 1929 did he have any difficulty in finding Americans who would buy Peruvian bonds. The dollars enabled him to reward his associates, buy off his enemies, build up the army and police, and construct public works that delighted the populace and kept them busy. Some of them, of course, proved magic wands that kindled economic life in a variety of ways. Of the most immediate importance to this dictator, as to any, was the loyalty of the military forces. Leguía's system was to keep the armed services happy with money, privileges, and equipment. The army was liberally endowed with airplanes, tanks, machine guns and artillery, items that made it all the easier to handle the populace, for the day had come when street fighters had little chance against a determined garrison. And the Peruvian navy was also enriched by a variety of craft, including submarines, of dubious utility for the defense of a country in Peru's location.

Leguía's affluence enabled him to carry out many useful projects. As the automobile age included Peru, road-building became an obsession, notwithstanding the fact that few countries are as exasperating as this one for permanent modern highways. Even if there were deserts, mountains, and jungles, and even if the rainy season and thaws washed the roads away every year, built and re-built they had to be. Leguía not only invested heavily in this form of transportation but also instituted a general labor draft which brought citizens out to the roads as regularly as the Inca and *corregidores* had in the days of the *mita*. Furthermore, railroads were extended, better dock facilities built, airports scraped out, and Lima modernized so that it became again one of the finest cities in the Americas. Foreign residents—Americans, Italians, Germans, and Japanese especially—found it easy to establish themselves. Usually prospering, they also facilitated the rise of business activity and living standards among the general population. A sense of enterprise took hold of Peru, benefiting natives as well as foreigners, local capitalists as well as New York bankers. So secure did Leguía feel as conditions improved that he instituted an income tax, a daring step in view of the oligarchy's reluctance to support their government, and he catered to the working classes by establishing systems for accident insurance and arbitration of labor disputes. A new bureau undertook to improve conditions among the large Indian population and to give them a sense of participation in national life. Leguía directed the re-creation of the *ayllu* in some localities, which had the effect of restoring common lands for Indian clans. While the aristocracy was not hurt and the working classes and Indians not conspicuously uplifted during these years, the *Patria nueva* took the first bold steps toward a reformation of Peruvian society.

As an ultimate sign of his self-assurance, Leguía settled two seemingly eternal boundary disputes in ways not overly favorable to his country. After several years of negotiation he conceded Colombia's urgent request for a port on an Amazon tributary, Leticia, which jutted deep into Peru's claimed territory. From Chile, whom Peruvians had cordially hated since the War of the Pacific, he tried, as all presidents of Peru had, to obtain fulfillment of the treaty of 1883, which called for a plebiscite in Tacna and Arica. After the fiasco of the American-sponsored effort to accomplish this in 1926, Leguía negotiated a treaty that permitted the return of Tacna to Peru but admitted the permanent loss of Arica. This pact of 1929 flew in the face of nationalistic aspirations, but it made sense, and gradually the long-existing tensions subsided. It was ironical that once Peru acquired Tacna she neglected it so badly that the inhabitants became discontented.

Leguía went through the motions of having himself reelected in 1925 and 1929. The second occasion was once too often, for the world depression soon staggered Peru by cutting off the flow of American money and curtailing her sales of raw materials. The regime received the blame, not wholly unjustly, since its financial practices worsened what would have been in any case a bad situation. And, of course, it had unsettled the aristocrats and awakened ambitions among the Indians and proletariat. A few dedicated revolutionists had also been sowing dragon's teeth by acquainting young idealists with the alleged achievements of the Russian and Mexican Revolutions. José Carlos Mariateguí was a Marxist who had worked effectively along these lines, and also influential was a voice from the grave, that of the poet Manuel González Prada, whose largely posthumous publications included bitter protests against Indian conditions and the lack of liberty and true Christianity in Peru's social system. Defending Leguía, however, was the ineffable poet, José Santos Chocano (1875–1934), whose bizarre life included many tawdry romantic escapades and panegyrics for various dictators in Latin America. All the same, he was an influence for cosmopolitanism and unquestionably a great poet.

Not writers and agitators but army officers and political bosses made decisions in Peru. When it was obvious that Leguía had stumbled on catastrophe, the predictable uprising occurred on August 22, 1930, the garrison at Arequipa led by a young *cholo*, Colonel Luis Sánchez Cerro, taking the initiative. Two days later, on a Sunday, President Leguía left the horse races only to find the Lima garrison in rebellion and the streets filled with students. A civilized arrangement was made for him to leave at once on the cruiser *Grau* for exile. Before this vessel had sailed far, however, Sánchez Cerro entered Lima and ordered it to turn back. Leguía, now close to seventy, remained in prison for more than a year until his death. The revolution was both gay and violent, typical of the overturns of 1930. Extravagant hopes for the dawn of democracy seemed well-founded as Sánchez Cerro gave way to a junta which promised free elections within a year and announced his candidature.

The most striking development at this time was the outburst of enthusiasm which greeted the return from exile of Víctor Raúl Haya de la Torre. Haya was still in his thirties, an intellectual and former professor who had studied radicalism at first hand in Moscow, Berlin, London, and Mexico City during his residence abroad. A man of great personal magnetism and a compelling speaker, he also was admired for a unique program called APRA (*Alianza popular revolucionaria americana*). While much of this program was unintelligible, a pretentious metaphysics supposedly based on Einstein's theory of relativity and full of such phrases as "historical time-space," the rest was quite lucid. Haya proclaimed the emergence of an Indo-America which would erase political boundaries and establish a society in which wealth would be socialized, land worked cooperatively, and women and Indians emancipated. APRA was anti-capitalist and anti-American but non-Communist; its methods were peaceful and persuasive, and Christianity was exalted. For twenty years it, together with the Mexican Revolution, was to excite many students of affairs as the most promising native movement to emerge in Latin America.

The campaign for the election of October 1931 became a contest between Sánchez Cerro and Haya de la Torre. It was exciting in the extreme, but if the race had been open the vote-counting was not, and the ruling junta announced the victory of Sánchez Cerro by 150,000 ballots to Haya's 110,000. Ignoring the charges of fraud, Sánchez Cerro took office and jailed his recent opponent. He also, however, undertook to placate the elements who had supported APRA by improving social conditions. An agricultural bank facilitated the purchase of land by peons, and new laws gave more protection to employees. As a concession to liberal anti-clericals, the new administration made civil marriage obligatory and authorized divorce. Flaunting his *cholo* background, Sánchez Cerro tried to make himself popular with the Indians, and some of his racist remarks made the white elite uneasy for one of the rare times since Tupac Amarú II's rebellion in the 1780's. A law that required four-fifths of the personnel in any business to be Peruvian may also be interpreted as an effort to steal an APRA issue. To capitalize on nascent nationalism Sánchez Cerro took the side of a group of civilians from Iquitos who had seized the Colombian river port of Leticia in 1932 and threatened war. Peru not only defied the League of Nations in this issue but sent the *Grau* and two submarines up the Amazon to defend her "rights." And then, on April 30, 1933, Sánchez Cerro was assassinated by an *aprista*.

Congress, with the approval of the generals, thereupon elected as acting president General Oscar Benavides, who had overthrown the Democratic regime in 1915. Benavides was an authentic representative of the creole oligarchy variously known as the "twenty-five" or "forty" or "sixty families." Since he was as sure of their backing as they were of his, and since the depression had ended in Peru, he concentrated on mollifying APRA and its potential followers. Haya was let out of prison and officially ignored while he agitated and constructed an APRA machine.

Meanwhile, Benavides created a ministry of public health, labor, and social welfare to meet lower class needs and instituted a modest social security program. The building of a workers' hospital and numerous low-rent flats in Lima alleviated the condition of the urban poor while, exasperatingly, drawing into the capital many impoverished migrants. An industrial bank backed by the government was helpful in fostering business enterprise. With such policies and the resumption of economic growth, the Benavides administration could claim that it had saved Peru from social upheaval.

The elections of 1936, however, revealed that APRA had grown strikingly, that it was surely the majority party even though it was not allowed to name candidates. This organization more or less covertly backed one of the presidential nominees. When the first returns indicated that he was certain to win, Benavides cancelled the count, thus depriving Peru of a new president and congress. Prolonging his rule with the relieved thanks of the army and the aristocracy, he took steps to throttle *aprista* agitation. When he was satisfied with conditions he drew up a constitutional reform providing for a weakened congress and a potent presidency with a six-year term, which the public approved in a plebiscite. In the election of 1939 APRA was disqualified from participating on the grounds that it was not a Peruvian political party but an international movement, which in fact it professed to be, and Benavides' choice, Dr. Manuel Prado Ugarteche, won.

While many foreign observers looked for APRA to triumph eventually, it was truly beaten. The mild autocracy and partial reforms of Sánchez Cerro and Benavides had gotten the oligarchy over the dangerous period, and Haya's opportunity was gone. He still addressed hysterical mass meetings and circulated over the country in spite of police bans, wrote, schemed, and encouraged his followers to paint signs and agitate. Yet the traditional rulers of Peru were firmly in the saddle. President Prado continued the policies of his immediate predecessors without serious fear of social revolution. His methods resembled those of the Axis dictators so much that democrats suspected him of favoring that alliance during World War II, particularly since German, Italian, and Japanese residents enjoyed such pre-eminence in Peru's business community. Yet Prado faithfully cooperated with the other American states, permitted the United States to establish coastal guns and air bases on Peruvian soil, and sold almost all of the republic's guano, petroleum, rubber, copper, wool, lead, and cotton to the United Nations. As was customary, the United States fostered developmental corporations to promote production of raw materials, transportation, and hydroelectric projects. While the material advantages of cooperating with the Americans no doubt accounted for much of Prado's accommodating spirit, he was not unmindful of the highly favorable boundary settlement with Ecuador which the United States helped to win for his country in 1942. In time, Peru declared war, confiscated Axis property, received numerous surplus weapons from the United States, and sent President Prado on a state visit to Washington.

The end of the war and of Prado's six-year term coincided. Bowing to the leftish effervescence that was stirring most of the world in 1945, Prado decided to let the electorate express itself as it would, in full freedom. It was puzzling to many that Haya de la Torre did not run for president. Was he intimidated by the regime? Did he doubt that he would win, despite years of claiming that the majority yearned for *aprismo?* Or was he fundamentally nothing more than an actor and demagogue who drew back from responsibility? Whatever the reason, APRA changed its name to the Peoples' Party and joined other democratic forces in a front behind an estimable but unimpressive candidate, José Luis Bustamente, who won the election handsomely. Despite confusion in the names it employed, APRA gained a majority of seats in the lower house and half of those in the senate and, after a hesitation, accepted three cabinet posts. Most students of Peru thought Haya was in control of the government and looked for the nation to begin a wholesale renovation of its antiquated structure.

It was not to be. Perhaps Haya de la Torre was not the genius his followers had long imagined. Certainly he had changed, for he no longer hated the Yankee, a shift in attitude explained largely by his admiration for Franklin D. Roosevelt, and he was now not merely non-Communist, but anti-Communist. He astonished the world and many of his followers by advocating successfully that Peru compensate American investors for the worthless bonds they had bought in the 1920's, and he disenchanted many admirers by insisting on a strict law for press censorship. Meanwhile, *aprista* members of congress came forward with abundant projects to divide the land among peons, build schools and irrigation systems, and promote extravagant social welfare benefits. President Bustamente felt he was being pushed too far too fast. When he agreed with everyone else in attributing the murder of a conservative publisher in Lima in January 1947 to the *apristas,* the three cabinet members of that party stalked out, and then the non-*aprista* members of the senate refused to attend sessions, thus preventing a quorum and blocking all legislation. Communists loudly derided APRA as a fake revolutionary movement, while the powerful conservatives denounced the *apristas* as true rebels. Beset by the left and the right, APRA turned, or was driven, to violence. A bloody revolt of fleet units in Callao in 1948 inspired by *apristas* proved a fiasco, and Bustamente rallied the other factions to outlaw APRA altogether.

Still fearful of the latent power of Haya's organization, the military insisted on more drastic oppression than President Bustamente was willing to sponsor, and he, of course, was tarnished by his earlier friendship with APRA. Later in 1948 he was removed from office and shipped to Argentina. General Manuel Odría, a hard-faced officer of immense determination, assumed the presidency and held a rigged plebiscite in 1950 to authorize his tenure for a six-year term. He hunted down the *apristas* with fury and skill. While several hundred escaped through diplomatic channels, Haya de la Torre was not permitted to leave the Colombian legation in which he had taken refuge. For five years the world's imagination was held by the plight of this lonely leader, who could not even walk in the gardens or appear at the window for fear of being shot. Hundreds of policemen and soldiers guarded his residence constantly and flooded it with searchlights at night. Disregarding private and diplomatic appeals, Odría refused to let him go until 1954, when he thought it was safe to do so.

As president from 1948 to 1956, Manuel Odría left little doubt that he was in truth a dictator, though he was certainly in no class with such contemporaries as Perón, Batista, Somoza, Trujillo, Rojas Pinilla, or Pérez Jiménez. His approach to the problems of Peru, which resembled that of Augusto Leguía in the 1920's, may have been sound for the times. He regarded the country as needing a huge dose of foreign capital and technology rather than a social transformation. Accordingly, he made it hospitable to aliens, especially Americans, and gave free enterprise every opportunity to flourish. Whether Peru was admired or deplored as a paradise for capitalists, it enjoyed an unprecedented economic growth. Odría did his part by stabilizing the currency, which saved the republic from the kind of inflation that plagued her neighbors, by accepting financial guidance from an American mission, and by easing conditions for foreign enterprisers. He even provided a trained and relatively honest bureaucracy, so that Peru enjoyed effective, and sometimes good, public administration. His autocratic rule distressed friends of democracy, and he did little to alter the traditional society of rural areas, which much of the world knew through Ciro Alegría's novel published in 1941, *Broad and Alien Is the World*. But his enlightened conservatism channeled the energies of the nation and created a basis for eventual reformation.

Among the important developments of the booming 1950's was a nation-wide attack on illiteracy. Even in Indian communities, schools were built and instructors provided. Uniformed boys and girls nearly everywhere attended schools at least for two or three years. Libraries and university buildings went up, though the acquisition of books and competent faculty members lagged and Peru's relative position in Spanish

American culture was far below that of viceregal days. Transportation was another vital need for the republic which received much impetus. Peruvians were as avid as anyone else for automobiles, buses, trucks, and motorcycles, and the roads they required. Aviation promised to skip over several stages of progress by knitting the country together; it was not uncommon for airplanes to fly the most primitive of Indians to work in ancient ways on distant lands. Resistant as they had been for four centuries to the culture and vices of the Western world, highland or jungle folk inexorably felt their impact as the radio, television, motion picture, and popular press intruded. Lima, and to a lesser degree the other cities, even Cuzco, became more and more an agency which drew backward peoples from rural areas and changed them, for better or for worse, into Europeanized citizens. Lima grew the way most Latin American capitals did, surpassing 1,000,000 in population and becoming a city where modernistic structures crowded colonial relics and where the poor dwelt in tents and shanties until they could find room in older slums, then progressing to government housing and, if they became rich, into opulent apartments. Elegant shops, flowery plazas, and handsome villas made it one of the most charming of South American cities, but it was a dynamo too.

Manuel Odría was wise enough not to let the people become too tired of him. In 1956 he held an open election, with women voting for the first time. Manuel Prado Ugarteche, who had been president for the years 1939–1945, was returned to the office with the approval of Odría, the generals, and the aristocrats, and over no strong opposition on the part of the rest of the electorate. While he perpetuated the enlightened conservatism that had become Peru's formula of progress, Prado permitted far more freedom than his predecessors had. University students used and abused this liberty as they had in years past, as the unfortunate visits of Vice President Nixon in 1958 and Ambassador Stevenson in 1961 dramatized. Prado also allowed APRA to come to the surface and Haya de la Torre to come home for a messianic welcome.

The apparent serenity of Peru evaporated during the presidential campaign of 1962, when Haya de la Torre, Manuel Odría, and Fernando Belaúnde Terry stirred passions of a fierce sort as they sought the office. The elections in June gave Haya a small plurality but not the percentage required by law. The military intervened, deposing President Prado and announcing fresh elections. From Washington, where the administration had been hopeful that Haya might lead Peru through a peaceful social and economic revolution, came sharp criticism of the military's action. So long a sham republic with its society frozen into castes, Peru seemed again to be on the eve of profound changes or dictatorial efforts to prevent such changes.

32

Bolivia

THE Andean republic named for the Liberator was fated to illustrate all the handicaps that he foretold would retard the Spanish American nations. Chief among these were an impossible geography, severe racial cleavages, militarism, and absence of public spirit on the part of the directing classes. A nation as mountainous as Switzerland or Tibet, Bolivia has been so subject to partition that she also resembles Poland or the Ottoman Empire. The Andes here are at their widest, about 400 miles, and almost at their highest. The *altiplano* of the western section contains most of the Indians as well as the principal city and capital, La Paz. High valleys and plateaus to the south and east have numerous Indians and also most of the whites and mixed-blooded *cholos*. Sucre, a sometime capital previously known as La Plata, Charcas, and Chuquisaca, adorns this region, as does Cochabamba. While these alpine sections of Bolivia represent one-third of the nation's extent, they contain more than four-fifths of its population. The remainder of the republic consists mainly of almost uninhabited valleys, forests, and flatlands, or *selvas*. Western Bolivia, then, is the effective part, a veritable land in the clouds, monotonously rugged and perpetually chilled, bleak yet beautiful because of the snow-capped peaks. Most of its people live in rural communities, for the cities are few and small. They are also a notably unhealthy population. Chicha-drinking and coca-chewing partially account for this condition while at the same time making it and other misfortunes bearable.

As has been seen, the political history of Bolivia from the departure of Sucre in 1828 to the fall of Melgarejo in 1869 was largely a sequence of white and *cholo* caudillos overthrowing one another. Once in power the successive presidents were likely to pillage the meager treasury and bend the courts and congresses to their purposes. Nine constitutions had been proclaimed and violated; yet lip service to democracy, popular institutions, and human rights had at least kept ideals alive, and a strain of decency is apparent in all phases of Bolivia's history, despite the appalling behavior of most of her leaders. With a large majority of the population, the pure-blooded Indians—living in remote mountain communities, speaking Aymará or Quechua, barefooted, practicing unorthodox Christianity, and deferring to tribal rulers—practically estranged from the creoles and Westernized *cholos*, no real nationhood was possible. Even the upper layers of society were divided on the basis of white and mestizo and within each category by caste and clan. After nearly a half-century of independence they had arrived at no consensus strong enough to make them an effective ruling group. Bolivia's economic progress too had been small or altogether lacking. Its once-famous mines were often deserted, there were practically no factories, modern commerce was all but unknown, and agricultural production was of the subsistence type, insufficient to feed the population adequately. For income the government depended on the sale of nitrates from the Pacific coast province, which Chileans usually extracted, and pickings from the once-great mining industry.

THE LOSS OF THE COAST

Agustín Morales, who had been instrumental in overthrowing the egregious tyrant Melgarejo, proved a man almost as base during his presidency of 1869 to 1872, which ended with his being murdered by his nephew. There followed four years of rule by short-term presidents whose character and efforts suggested that Bolivia was not devoid of responsible men, chief among whom was Adolfo Ballivián, son of an earlier president, José Ballivián. His death from natural causes in 1874 spoiled the chance, if there had really been one, for the republic to become a constitutionalist state. After an uneasy interim, General Hilarión Daza secured the presidency in 1876 by military pressure on the congress and the few thousand voters. Daza was one of the worst of Bolivian rulers: he tore up the constitution and prepared a new one of equal uselessness; he had politicians, officers, and publishers beaten whenever they crossed him; in public life a swaggering tyrant, in private he was a drunkard and ignoramus. While such men had come and gone in Andean public life for some years without inflicting enduring injury, Daza made a unique and disastrous contribution to the degradation of Bolivia. In 1878 he violated existing arrangements with Chilean companies which were profitably scraping nitrate from the Atacama desert on the Bolivian coast and proceeded to levy higher taxes. When Chile protested, he confiscated these firms. Just as Bolivian authorities began to carry out Daza's orders, Chile replied by sending forces into the Atacama, thus beginning the War of the Pacific in February 1879.

Daza may have thought that his army of Indians could repel the Chileans, who had to be ferried and supplied by sea, especially after Peru joined Bolivia in the war. If he did, he was quickly disenchanted. In December 1879, when he was in the field and about to participate in a Bolivian-Peruvian offensive against the invaders, he suddenly concluded that the Chileans were too formidable and withdrew his army, leaving the Peruvians to face defeat alone. When news of this deed reached La Paz, a revolution proclaimed that Daza was no longer president. Accused of cowardice, drunkenness, and treachery, he became the focus of Bolivia's shame, and when he returned to the country under an amnesty several years later, he was promptly murdered.

General Narciso Campero became president after the overthrow of Daza. He went to the coast to take charge of the Bolivian army, whose Indian soldiers were brave but so poorly equipped that they sometimes had to use clubs and stones against the well-armed Chileans. The only advantage the Bolivians enjoyed was an ability to withstand thirst better than their enemies, and this was not sufficient to save them from being badly defeated at Tacna early in 1880. For all practical purposes Bolivia was knocked out of the war. Chile annexed her coastlands and went on to defeat Peru. In 1884 Chile and Bolivia agreed to an indefinite truce which twenty years later was formalized in a permanent treaty. With the loss of military honor, the outlet to the sea, and the revenues from nitrate extraction, Bolivia was a forlorn country indeed. It seemed that Queen Victoria's curse had all but come true.[1]

THE CONSERVATIVE ASCENDANCY, 1884–1899

Yet the republic held together, thanks to the fact that its wealthier families united enough to assume direction after the catastrophes blamed on the militarists. This became apparent in 1884, when the candidate blessed by President Campero lost the election to a civilian, Gregorio Pacheco, one of the few Bolivians who had ever risen from poverty to wealth apart from politics or the army. His victory, which the outgoing Campero and the militarists did not dare to challenge, began a fifteen-year rule by the conservative faction known as the Constitutionalist Party. This group was based in Sucre and the southern highlands, which had been the core of the Spanish colony, and was still unconvinced about the merits of democracy. Accepting with deep reluctance, but accepting,

1. Cf. p. 569, n. 6.

the loss of the coastland to Chile, the new administration addressed itself to maintaining order and to finding ways to improve the economy. It was an uphill struggle, but the government at Sucre generally managed to dominate the other towns and to restrain the army, which was discredited and small because there was no way to pay the soldiers. President Pacheco, who was low-born and earthy in tastes, achieved a good deal by visiting the enlisted men and granting them favors behind the backs of their officers, who were likely to be his opponents. The building of railways, cart roads, and telegraph lines and the creation of banks brought Bolivia a taste of modern life, and the reopening of silver mines led to the discovery of copper and lead ores. While the country experienced no spurt in prosperity as a consequence of these activities, its economy began to flicker somewhat.

President Aniceto Arce, who ruled from 1888 to 1892, achieved further success in taming the military by building better barracks and holding regular messes for the soldiers, thus providing fixed facilities for units who, followed by their womenfolk, had been accustomed to wander over the country and participate in rebellions whenever they took it into their heads. While Arce was once compelled to flee from Sucre disguised as a priest during a revolution, he returned in triumph and usually succeeded in keeping the army loyal.

Under the third conservative president, Mariano Baptista, who served from 1892 to 1896, a railroad was built from Oruro to Antofagasta, now a Chilean port, and Bolivia was permitted to use it as an outlet to the world. Baptista also made a boundary settlement with Argentina which stripped Bolivia of more land but offered the prospect that she might use rivers to the Atlantic that Argentina controlled. Severo Fernández Alonso, the last of the conservative executives, came to power in 1896. By this time Bolivia had enjoyed some years of an orderly, centralized regime and civilian domination. Railroads and mines were proving helpful to its economy, and a modest public school system had been started. Overestimating the strength of his party, however, Alonso pushed his luck too far by proposing that Sucre, long the seat of government, be made the permanent capital. This was too much for La Paz, where a furious rebellion took place, and for other cities which had chafed at the administration's centralist policies. After several battles and much rioting, the insurgents defeated Alonso and assumed power in the name of federalism and liberalism.

LIBERAL RULE, 1899–1920

The victorious combination took the name of the Liberal Party. Its leader, and the new president, was Colonel José Manuel Pando, who had won fame by exploring Bolivia's territory in the Amazon basin. While Pando soon abandoned federalism—for the republic would surely have flown apart without tight rule from the capital—his administration made good on its promise to designate La Paz as the national capital, leaving Sucre with the supreme court as consolation. About this time tin, to which Bolivia's fortunes have since been tied, began to be mined, thus furnishing the government with steady revenues, the mineowners with large incomes, and thousands of workers with new jobs. Tin production also led to close bonds between Bolivia and Great Britain, who bought most of the commodity, and an increase of British trade and enterprise in the republic.

While President Pando's administration was now solvent enough to pay the army adequately and to invest further in public schools, it could not escape one of Bolivia's chronic afflictions, the covetousness of her neighbors. It happened that Brazilian rubber-tappers had entered Bolivian territory and proclaimed an independent state there. A sordid mess in the jungles was avoided in 1903 when Brazil and Bolivia reached an agreement that Brazil could buy 191,000 square kilometers of the land and construct a railway from northern Bolivia to a deep port on the Madeira River. This would give Bolivia ultimately an outlet to the Atlantic and immediately a tidy sum. Another settlement, the treaty of 1904 with Chile, involved railway construction in Bolivia by Chileans and a line from La Paz to Arica, which Bolivians could use as a free port. When these connections were completed, Bolivia was land-locked only in a geographical sense. Her commerce could move through Brazilian and Chilean territory with little or no inhibition, a matter of small comfort to patriots who looked at maps and bewailed the isolation of their country.

In 1904 one of Bolivia's most admired presidents took office. This was Ismael Montes, a Liberal, once a law professor at La Paz and later a prominent general. It was time, he judged, for the republic to reduce the power of the Church, which was conservative in sympathy. Accordingly, he sponsored laws to permit religious toleration, abolish Church courts, and authorize civil marriage. While the pope denounced these measures, no serious conflict developed. The Church continued to be influential in many quarters and to own much property; yet its clergy was so sparse and untrained that it fell far short of its aims in providing charity and instruction for the Indians. Having asserted a fashionable anti-clericalism rather tardily, the Bolivian Liberals thereafter co-existed comfortably with the ecclesiastical authorities.

Co-existence with her neighbors Bolivia had achieved by surrendering territory, at least in the case of Chile, Argentina, and Brazil. There remained Peru and Paraguay, with whom boundaries in uninhabited areas were vague. The dispute with Peru was submitted to the president of Argentina for arbitration. His award favoring Peru stood regardless of riots in Bolivian cities and a break in relations between La Paz and Buenos Aires. Having regularly lost territory, Bolivia waited another twenty years to make the final settlement with her last neighbor, Paraguay, which involved the worst loss of all. In 1909, when the Peruvian cession occurred, Montes' term ended but he continued as president, not, however, for the reason so familiar in Latin America, but because his Liberal successor had died before he could take office. Another election brought Heliodoro Villazón, a Liberal, into the presidency for the years 1909–1913, and then Montes was returned for the term extending from 1913 to 1917.

Montes, who by now was so powerful and respected as to dominate the country, retired in 1917 in favor of his Liberal heir, José Gutiérrez Guerra. By far the most important aspect of the Bolivian scene at that time was the tin industry, which grew larger than ever as the British carried the metal away for their wartime needs. Convenient as it was as a source of income for the government, the tin trade had unhappy social consequences: fortunes for a few, toil and low pay for the many. Educated Bolivians were becoming aware of this condition, many of them quoting a book published in 1909, *The Sick People*, by Alcides Argüedas, a Bolivian pessimist who made a thorough-going critique of his country and urged education, immigration, and morality as remedies. If tin was a mixed blessing, so also was the fine railway network completed early in the twentieth century, for if it gave the republic some unity, it also served to carry its products away to those who knew how to exploit them, permitting, in the words of social critics, foreigners to loot Bolivia. The nation was still very disjointed and backward. Its upper classes had the mentality of colonial times, the middle class was very small, and the masses, mostly Indians, worked in mines, plantations, and ranchlands for pitifully low pay. After a season of labor they tended to creep back to their mountain homes to raise corn and potatoes, tend llamas, chew coca, and drink chicha as though nothing had changed—as perhaps nothing for them had—since the heyday of silver and the Spaniard.

REPUBLICAN PREDOMINANCE, 1920–1930

The boom and bust caused by World War I in the Bolivian tin industry served to whet the appetites of many for the fruits of the Industrial Age and then to disappoint them. By 1920 there was much restlessness, some of it due to unemployment and strikes, but some attributable to the emergence of a new political party, the Republican. This group drew upon the ranks of the Liberals, who had grown fat and slack in many years of power, and even lured onetime Conservatives of the now moribund Constitutionalist Party. The Republican leaders represented, moreover, a younger generation of politicians who thought of accelerating the economic development of Bolivia and, less seriously, of long overdue social reforms. The Republicans also capitalized on a highly popular issue by prophesying that the League of Nations would soon usher in an era of international justice, which to Bolivians meant the return of the coastland from Chile and the redress of other boundary grievances. A bloodless coup served to overthrow President Gutiérrez in 1920, and a few months later the Republican chieftain, Bautista Saavedra, was installed as president.

Saavedra's administration had much in common with contemporaneous regimes in Latin America of the 1920's. Like them, it was a strong government, practically a dictatorship, that censored the press, curbed freedom of speech, and arrested inconvenient critics, even members of congress. It was also very eager to obtain American money, which was forthcoming on a big scale through capital investments and the sale of Bolivian bonds to unwary buyers in the United States. While Bolivia's national debt multiplied ten times in as many years under the Republicans, more mines were worked, automobile roads built, and distributing businesses established. The wonders of the modern world trickled into the country, even affecting the Indians, so that the so-called revolution of rising expectations began. The more Bolivians knew of these benefits, the more they craved them. Successful as Saavedra was in maintaining strong government and in luring American capital, he failed to redeem his pledges to win back the coast. The League of Nations made short work of Bolivia's importunities, and Chile, who in any case could defend her interests, showed no tendency whatever to mollify Bolivia.

Saavedra permitted the election of another president in 1925, a year in which the republic was celebrating its centennial of independence and "freedom." His successor, however, was soon thrown out of office because he sought to reconcile the Republicans with their opponents. Another Republican, Hernando Siles, a law professor and rector of the ancient University of Chuquisaca, came in to fill a stormy term. Bolivia's prosperity was producing enough ferment to cause labor organizations to seek a larger share of the national income. Also, for the first time since the 1780's the Indians were becoming restive, partly, as loudly charged, because of Communist incitement, but mainly as a result of the intrusion of the outside world. And then Bolivian hopes for the coastland were again cheated, after an intoxicating period of optimism, when Chile returned Tacna to Peru. It turned out that neither Chile nor Peru would lift a finger to satisfy Bolivia. Absurd as it seemed to foreigners, the lack of a seacoast caused true mental anguish to Bolivians, and it was this feeling that inspired President Siles in his ultimate folly, the war with Paraguay to be discussed presently. Siles used the conflict as an excuse to prolong his term, but this and the world depression of 1929 caused many to conclude that he had outstayed his welcome. A garrison revolt at Oruro, student riots in La Paz, and a popular movement in other parts of the country spelled out the inevitable. In June 1930 President Siles fell, the first of a series of South American presidents to be overthrown in that eventful year.

THE WAR FOR THE CHACO

Within a few months, by January 1931, Bolivia had elected a new congress and seen her leaders, usually so intransigeant, organize a national regime. Daniel Salamanca, who seemed to personify the best hopes of the republic, became president. The reason for this display of sobriety was an undeclared war with Paraguay, the last neighbor with whom Bolivia had not yet made a boundary settlement. Between the population centers of the two republics lay much of the Gran Chaco, about 500 miles of steaming flat or lightly-rolling country, some of it grassy and filled with lagoons, other parts of it densely wooded with the axe-breaking *quebracho*, practically none of it inhabited by civilized human beings. This vacuum had long assured a peace of isolation between Paraguay and Bolivia. The frontiers were unascertained and, in view of conflicting Spanish documents going back to 1536, perhaps unascertainable. In a desultory way both republics had asserted their authority over the Chaco Boreal, the Chaco north of the Pilcomayo River, but no one had cared very much until the 1920's. By that time Paraguay had begun to develop it to some extent, but more, the belief grew that great oil deposits were to be found there. Patriots in both countries became agitated over its future, the Bolivians developing a particularly ugly mood because they had finally lost hope for recovery of the Pacific province. Since Paraguay had only a third of Bolivia's population and was more backward, it offered a tempting release for Bolivian frustrations. Besides, the Paraguayans were in an aggressive mood too.

Both countries sent scouting parties into the Chaco and built fortified camps at various localities. Skirmishes began as early as August 1927
and an undeclared war in December 1928 with a Paraguayan attack on
the Bolivian fortlet at Vanguardia. An uproar in La Paz in which women
and young people were very prominent suggested the temper of Bolivia,
and the populace of Asunción was likewise bellicose. Since the governments of both republics were weak, no concession could be made, and
so Bolivian army units descended from the *altiplano* to meet Paraguayans
who had penetrated more easily from the plains. As the fighting intensified, the frail Pan-American organization came into action, setting up a
committee composed of the United States, Mexico, Cuba, Colombia,
and Uruguay, all of them distant enough to be objective, which urged
both parties to cease fighting. They agreed reluctantly, but both used
the armistice as an opportunity to build up their armies and purchase
modern weapons. In the case of Bolivia, this involved the expertise of a
German general long resident in the country, Hans Kundt, and the importation of tanks, aircraft, machine-guns, mortars, carbines, flame-throw-
ers, and other equipment. More than 250,000 Bolivians were destined to
be mobilized, and much of the population was set to work to support
such a force. While most of the soldiers were illiterate Indian conscripts,
their discipline was good and they had the advantage of numbers and
fire-power over the Paraguayans. Skirmishing resumed in 1931, Paraguay
launched an offensive in 1932, and she declared war formally in May
1933. Foreign diplomats wrung their hands, but both parties had an aggressive spirit and they ignored warnings by the other American states
that no boundary changes would be recognized if effected by force.

The Chaco War may have been a tawdry quarrel between two of the
most backward nations in Christendom, but it was also grim and tragic.
Modern equipment flowed to both parties, who, despite their unfamiliarity with engines and advanced weapons, inflicted terrible casualties on
one another. Their manpower was thrown into the desolate Chaco, where
reptiles, insects, and disease added to the horrors. Sometimes the soldiers
bogged down in mud; in other seasons they fought like animals for the
privilege of drinking polluted water in occasional holes of the parched
Chaco. Buzzards flapped about, by no means in vain, for human prey.
The Bolivians, who usually had the extended lungs of highlanders, suffered the more, with 52,000 dying in action, though the Paraguayans,
with 36,000 deaths, lost a larger percentage of their men. The course of
the war was principally a steady Paraguayan advance toward the Bolivian
altiplano between 1932 and 1935. During those years the League of Nations deplored the war and the munitions-makers who fed it but could
do nothing to stop it. After the Bolivians saved their military honor with
a limited counter-offensive, Argentina took the lead in persuading them

to make peace in 1935. The fighting ceased, but it was not until 1938 that Bolivia agreed to a settlement that gave Paraguay most of the Chaco Boreal. Consoled only with a river port for this cession, Bolivian patriots lamented the loss of territory to the fifth and last of their neighbors, and the weakest one at that.

Many currents were loosed by the Chaco War, among them the advertisement of the League's ineffectiveness and the determination of the American republics to prevent further outrages against humanity in the western hemisphere. Xenophobia grew, for it was very widely if erroneously believed that American interests had fostered the war on Bolivia's part and that Anglo-Argentine "imperialism" had egged Paraguay on. If Paraguay had won the war and most of the land in dispute, Bolivia probably underwent a more beneficial shaking up. Her loss of pride and life did not obscure the fact that she had made signal advances toward modernity. Workshops and factories had been improvised on a large scale, and countless Bolivians had become familiar with automobiles and trucks, as well as rifles. Nearly all of the population had been affected by the war and had become more nationalistic and more skilled as a result of it. Never again would remote mountain communities stand in cool isolation, utterly unaware of the rest of Bolivia or the outside world. The Indian had been awakened and would soon be heard from.

CHANGING FORCES, 1935–1952

President Salamanca had had little opportunity to vindicate the idealism of the revolutionaries of 1930, since the Chaco War necessarily absorbed his attention. When, in 1934, he visited the front after a series of disasters in order to remove the commanders, he himself was arrested, and army leaders in La Paz placed the vice-president in power. The change failed to save Bolivia's cause, and after the armistice of 1935, embittered veterans returned to the *altiplano* bearing little respect for those who had been in charge of the government. In May 1936 a conspiracy brought about the downfall of the administration and the installation of a "mixed" junta of four civilians and four officers. Colonel Germán Busch, a war hero of Indian and German ancestry, was the dominant figure, though he permitted a young colonel named David Toro to become president. Toro proclaimed a sort of national socialist program, one that would satisfy the veterans by restoring Bolivia's self-respect and dividing up the national wealth. About all he achieved, however, was the confiscation of Standard Oil's properties in Bolivia, a spiteful action reflecting a popular view that this corporation had promoted the Chaco War. Toro, who articulated the desire of many young war veterans to renovate the social system, lacked the strength to undertake such a program, and in July 1937 Germán Busch pushed him aside and assumed the presidency himself. He had a new constitution issued in 1938, one full of jargon about liberty, equality, and social welfare.

Germán Busch was an enigmatic figure. A well-read military leader, he may have defined Bolivia's eventual course by making a better life appear within reach of the masses while fostering nationalism in the way so stylish during that decade of fascism. Again, he may have been out of his depth in politics. His rule was autocratic; within a year he set aside the new constitution. He talked of trimming the power of foreigners in Bolivian affairs, which in fact meant weakening the British interests who extracted most of the tin. Bolivian officers blustered about the Chaco settlement and threatened to renew the war, all with the president's apparent approval. And the bestirred masses regarded him as one who might deliver them from the poverty that had until recently been thought a natural condition. On the other hand, his high-handed methods did not give Bolivia internal order, and his threats against foreigners melted before their counter-threats to stop buying tin from Bolivia altogether. Whatever the final judgment of this figure may be, he made enemies, and in August 1939 it was announced that he had become so neurotic over the nation's problems that he had taken his own life. Many thought he had been "suicided."

In April 1940 another war veteran, the commander-in-chief who had followed the German Kundt, took office as president. This was General Enrique Peñaranda, whose administration saw Bolivia's recovery as a result of World War II. Her copper, lead, silver, and tungsten were in great demand, but above all tin, of which she had a near monopoly after the Japanese conquest of Far Eastern sources in 1942, was required by the United Nations. Peñaranda posed no obstacles; he readily compensated Standard Oil and de-Germanized Bolivia's armed forces, with the result that American largess became available. By constructing a tin smelter in Texas the United States shifted the traditional channel of Bolivia's tin exports away from Britain and laid the basis for what was intended to be a permanent arrangement. Peñaranda created a developmental corporation with both native and American funds to increase the output of the mines, establish small factories, raise agricultural production, and build roads. Considerable success attended these efforts, and the military was also pleased to acquire American equipment, which made the enforcement of order easier and enabled Peñaranda to keep labor unrest from interfering with the boom, as when he had strikers shot down at the mines of Cataví. While Peñaranda was always a brutal autocrat, he gave the lower classes a few social benefits and preened himself as an adherent of the United Nations cause. In April 1943 he declared war on the Axis, an action he had no right to take on his own, but later in the year congress legalized it. In December 1943 Peñaranda was thrown out of office.

This turn of events puzzled and disturbed the Allied capitals. Obviously, the Bolivian military had engineered the deed with considerable popular support. Washington studied the evidence, which pointed to Axis and Argentine inspiration, for six months but finally concluded that even if anti-democratic forces had been involved they could do little. Bolivia had to export tin in order to live, and only the United Nations powers could fetch it. Recognition was then forthcoming, and Bolivia ceased to be a source of international concern. The new regime manifestly represented a combination of powerful if mysterious forces. Organizing a strong party known as the MNR (*Movimiento nacional revolucionario*) under the new president, Gualberto Villarroel, they enunciated more decisively than ever ideals of national socialism. A strong anti-Yankee strain in the "movement," as the party was called, reflected the growing belief that Americans were responsible for the exploitation of the miners. Undisguised anti-Semitic actions, some of them involving violence to individuals, echoed Axis policies but also indicated hatred for the Hochschild family, who owned one of the three largest tin complexes, and resentment against the several thousand Jewish refugees who had purchased visas from venal Bolivian officials. These exiles were supposed to become farmers, but most of them awaited an opportunity to migrate to more advanced countries and spent their time in Bolivia by engaging in business or professional life, easily besting the lesser-trained natives in their pursuits. In spite of the seamy aspects of the MNR regime, it produced a spate of decrees to benefit the workers, labored hard to raise the nation's primitive economy, and stimulated hope among the masses for unlimited material blessings.

Villarroel's administration became shaky after the end of the war because of the fall in mineral prices, inflation, unemployment, and other familiar effects of peace. Furthermore, the propertied classes, mining potentates, and older army officers were not yet ready to abdicate. In August 1946 a shocking rebellion occurred in La Paz as soldiers and street crowds went on a rampage. President Villarroel was beaten, shot, and hanged from a lamp-post, a barbarity that had no parallel in Bolivian history since the mid-nineteenth century. Its meaning was hard to assess beyond the admission that powerful forces had overcome the MNR and that the Bolivian populace was becoming very volatile. The new government stayed in power for six years, but it was weak. A constitution proclaimed in 1947 and two almost anonymous presidents, Enrique Hertzog and Mamerto Urriolagoita, signified little but that a nervous alliance of the oligarchs and the military had postponed a social crisis.

More important were developments below the surface of political affairs. The MNR was secretly rebuilt into a formidable machine under the direction of Víctor Paz Estenssoro, a former economics professor and key figure in Villarroel's administration, who operated from Perón's Argentina. Communists became much more powerful, making use of a far-left party under Juan Lechín's leadership. Favored by unemployment, wretched labor conditions, and anti-foreign sentiment, Lechín organized well-disciplined labor unions among the miners. Teachers, students, and other members of the educated middle class convinced themselves and preached to others that the core of the nation's trouble was the Yankee, who had, they alleged, connived with British capitalists to build a one-sided economy in Bolivia and then proceeded to debase the workers. In fact, the tin industries belonged mostly to two Bolivian families, Patiño and Aramayo, and if the Anglo-Americans had bought Bolivian tin it was because they needed it. Furthermore, their purchases fell drastically by the late 1940's because cheaper metal could again be imported from the Far East, not as part of a plot to make the Bolivians suffer. Such defenses received little credit among the miners, who listened avidly to Juan Lechín and his corps of agitators. And Indians in general were no longer the dreamwalking primitives of the mountains they once had been but resurgent masses who craved to break into modern civilization and were willing to believe that wicked capitalists or imperialists had long held them back.

THE NATIONAL REVOLUTIONARY MOVEMENT IN POWER

National elections were held in 1951, with all literate adult males being allowed to vote. A majority of these 200,000 citizens voted for the MNR candidates, an ugly surprise for the ruling *junta*, which set aside the results and proceeded to install a member of the Ballivián clan as president. While he was the third member of this family to hold the office, the people were in no mood to give him a chance. A wide-scale rebellion broke out in April 1952, obviously the product of a well-organized conspiracy involving many segments of the population.

Paz Estenssoro returned in triumph from Argentina and assumed the presidency. Many outsiders feared that the hand of Juan Perón had finally grasped Bolivia, the one-time presidency of Charcas which Buenos Aires had ruled, but Paz proved to be a strong man in his own right and no puppet. Soon he established cordial relations with the United States, which proceeded to give Bolivia more aid than any other country in Latin America: funds to stabilize the currency, technical assistance to improve all aspects of the economy, and various grants that, together with native and United Nations programs, filled the republic with foreign experts. Paz Estenssoro proposed nothing less than the nationalization of the tin industry, to which the United States did not object and which was rapidly carried out, leaving the former owners to console themselves as best they could with fortunes banked abroad. Now the miners were to operate the tin mines, which meant the unions, which meant Juan Lechín. The MNR also ridded itself of the army by disbanding it and creating units of workers' militia all over the country, a measure that failed to bring about general pacification. In further imitation of the Mexican Revolution Paz proclaimed the division of landed estates, which absorbed about two-thirds of the arable territory of Bolivia. Peasants were now invited to purchase holdings of their own and to repay the dispossessed owners in long-term bonds. The number of small landowners jumped from a few thousand to three-quarters of a million within several years. Finally, the MNR undertook to diversify the economy by creating light industries, promoting oil exploration, and cultivating new crops.

Things went amazingly well for several years, or so it appeared to observers. At last Bolivia had popular and skilled leadership and was, with generous aid from foreign taxpayers, making great strides into modernity. No longer was this land a false republic run by contentious creole aristocrats at the expense of Indian peasants but, it seemed, a true nation with a sense of direction and purpose. Economic activity was making the cities flourish and the countryside take life. Massive road-building programs had much to do with this, as did the improvement of railways and the creation of bus lines. Aviation grew so fast that it seemed the highland Indians might compress generations of progress by advancing from the donkey to the airplane. And then nature suddenly smiled on Bolivia by revealing considerable deposits of oil, which fortunately lay in a north-south direction beside the *altiplano*, safely beyond Paraguay's reach. Brazil, which was hopeful of tying Bolivia's economy to its own, built a railroad from the isolated tropical town of Santa Cruz in Bolivia to São Paulo. A bright future for Bolivia's eastern lowlands thus dawned. Argentina needed oil almost as much as Brazil did, and she exerted herself to improve commerce and communications with Bolivia. Paz was enlightened about the petroleum windfall, making foreign enterprisers welcome as long as they shared their profits with his country. And he broke the "code" of recipients of American aid by publicly and repeatedly expressing his gratitude for it.

Enthusiasm for Bolivia's "movement" waxed high. It seemed justified by the elections of 1956, which were almost a model of good political behavior. Every adult citizen, male or female, lettered or not, was permitted to vote. Vice President Hernán Siles Zuazo, a close collaborator of Paz and son of a onetime president, won by a large majority. Auspi-

cious as his induction seemed, it soon became obvious that the movement had passed its glorious phase. First, Siles fell out with the powerful
Lechín, the former favoring an end to inflation and the latter not, and
the president demanding greater productivity from the workers and the
labor leader more favors for his unions. At length Lechín resigned as a
cabinet minister and began a campaign of harassment. The nationalized
mines he controlled became monuments of inefficiency, with feather-
bedding, scanty production, and gestures instead of work. Some of the
government factories his unions operated made nothing whatever but
paid their "workers" regularly. And then the Soviet Union suddenly
dumped great quantities of tin on the world market and took half of
Bolivia's accustomed sales. Furthermore, agrarian reform proved troublesome to achieve. Although the haciendas were really being divided very
expeditiously, the rural masses were in a hurry and had no patience with
the need to clear titles before making grants. Now that they had militias
they often resorted to force, ousting the original owners, government
agents, and then one another. Rural lawlessness became a feature of
Bolivian life. Nor did the division of land result in greater production.
Quite the contrary, for the new farmers chose to turn their plots into
gardens for their own use, and the population as a whole was more
short of food than ever.

Finally, xenophobia at last turned against the thousands of well-
meaning foreign experts who had been seeking to introduce modern
methods. Many of them were chased away, their tractors and implements
being discarded as the farmers and miners reverted to their ancient ways.
Indians who had been removed from bleak mountainsides into the fertile
eastern zones frequently deserted model farms after a few months and
returned home. A far-reaching program of public education had organized seven universities and countless primary schools and had dispatched
peripatetic units to instruct the rural population. Yet professors, teachers,
and students were usually the ones who most resented the foreigners.
Riots and furious anti-American propaganda, much of it Communist-
inspired, occurred when the United States briefly debated reducing its
quotas for Latin American minerals in order to benefit its own industry
in the West. Gradually, credible evidence reached Washington that the
various aid programs in Bolivia had been badly managed. The "do-
gooders," it was charged, had wasted American money in order to create
a pampered labor class that did no work and hated the United States besides and to encourage Bolivia in economic follies. Early in 1959 a violent
anti-American outbreak occurred in La Paz and other cities when the
Latin American edition of *Time* supposedly quoted a U.S. Embassy official as repeating an ancient joke to the effect that Bolivia was so hopeless a proposition it ought to be divided among its neighbors so they

could share its problems, a proposal that did not amuse Bolivians, who felt their neighbors had always tried to partition their country. President Siles Zuazo himself quieted the crowds in a courageous tour of La Paz, but it was apparent that the population remained full of spleen, and popular anti-Americanism was never far below the surface.

By the time of the 1960 elections, nothing could hide the disenchantment that had settled over the Bolivian national revolutionary movement. Strikes, jacqueries, riots, and wild inflation kept the nation tense. The traditional conservatives had organized a party they disingenuously called the Socialist Falange and were full of confidence. So were the Communists. President Siles Zuazo admitted his disappointment when he informed the country at the end of his term that his administration had accomplished little. And yet a long view of what Bolivia used to be, and what she was striving to become, offered grounds for some optimism. Much progress was being made in the field of public education and health. At last Bolivia's population was beginning to grow, making a mockery of predictions that high altitudes would forever discourage human reproduction. Not even the most demoralizing temptations of the welfare state nor the tendency of Indians to cling to their traditional ways had prevented real progress. Productivity had increased, transportation was much improved, and isolated parts of the republic were being Westernized.

The elections of 1960 were almost frustrated by an attempted coup of the Trotskyite Workers' Party in May and then by continued turbulence that affected all regions and all groups. Clearly, the republic was boiling. Even the MNR was breaking apart, a moderate wing that called itself the "Authentic" MNR seceding from the main organization. Yet nearly a million voters reported at the polls in June and overwhelmingly returned the original MNR, whose candidates were Paz Estenssoro for president and none other than Juan Lechín for vice-president. Lechín's return to the administration insured at least some months of political harmony, and by now the army had been restored to the extent that it might keep order without becoming ambitious to take over the government. Paz faced a financial crisis that $150,000,000 in seven years from the United States had not alleviated and an irritable, demanding population of almost 4,000,000, whose appetites had been aroused but who were confused about means for satisfying them. Friendly outsiders could scarcely hope for much in Bolivia in the immediate future, but then they could not dare not to hope.

33

Chile

CHILE is a land so long that it might stretch from the British Isles to Siberia, and yet it is seldom more than a hundred miles wide. One of the most scenic countries in the world, it also enjoys immense natural riches and a fine climate, at least in the central portion where two-thirds of its people live. In this basin or valley around Santiago practically any crop or livestock common to temperate zones flourishes. South of it, where most of the remaining third of the population lives, grazing and forest lands, together with coal mines and oil fields, contribute to the wealth of the republic. Not even the desert expanse to the north is a waste, since nitrates have long been scraped up there and shipped abroad to make iodine, fertilizer, and explosives. The gigantic cordillera that dominates the whole nation has untold sources of wealth, of which copper has played the major role in Chile's history.

Chilean society is as protected from others as though it were on an island, and it has much choice as to contacts it will have or influences it will accept. Until the period of World War I this nation was by far the stablest in Latin America, one where liberty seemed secure, progress unlimited, and, thanks to the shipment of nitrates, of which Chile had a near monopoly, prosperity certain. While Chileans were little affected by racial divisions, since most of the people were mixed white and Indian, they were badly stratified by caste. A few hundred families owned the choice lands in the central region and formed an aristocracy not greatly different from those of Spain or central Europe. They were also likely to own business houses in the cities: Santiago, Valparaiso, and Concepción. Having dominated Chile since the days of Diego Portales under the constitution of 1833, they constituted the *Fronda* in political life, a true oligarchy with morale and pride. Since 1890 their rule stressed parlia-

LAKE TITICACA

LaPaz

BOLIVIA

Arica

Oruro

Sucre

Potosi

Iquique

PARAGUAY

PARAGUAY R.

PILCOMAYO R.

C H I L E

Antofagasta

Jujuy

Salta

Asunción

Villarrica

Iguasú

Tucumán

Santiago del Estero

Corrientes

PARANA R.

URUGUAY R.

Coquimbo

La Rioja

Santa Fe

Salto

Córdoba

Rosario

URUGUAY

Valparaiso

Mendoza

Mercedes

SANTIAGO

A R G E N T I N A

Buenos Aires

Montevideo

Chillan

Concepción

Valdivia

Bahía Blanca

Mar del Plata

Osorno

San Carlos de Bariloche

GULF OF SAN MATIAS

Puerto Montt

I. Chiloé

Comodoro Rivadavia

GULF OF SAN JORGE

N

STRAIT OF MAGELLAN

Punta Arenas

MODERN
SOUTHERN
SOUTH AMERICA

mentary ascendancy over the executive, civilian predominance, centralization, clericalism, suffrage limited to literate males—and a wide degree of freedom. Contrasting with this aristocracy was the great mass of the poor, who were largely rural, living on the *fundos,* or landed estates, as peons, or *inquilinos.* If they had no fixed dwellings but migrated from *fundo* to *fundo* or into and away from the towns as hunger and mood dictated, they comprised a class known as the *rotos,* or the broken. Mostly resigned to a poverty that seemed eternal, or at least sanctioned by the ages, the lower classes were given to alcoholism and frequently to crime. They seldom voted unless their employers bribed or herded them into the polling places to cast ballots for *Fronda* candidates.

Chile was a proud member of the Western or Europeanized community in 1914. The imbalance of her social system was scarcely more pronounced than it was in most of Europe itself. The nation rated with Argentina and Brazil as one of the ABC powers, and it was respected as a country where constitutional government was well-entrenched. Chile also had one of the best public education establishments in Latin America, sound institutions of higher learning, a flourishing publishing industry, and a wide reading public. The early years of the twentieth century and the spectacular boom of nitrate and mineral exports during World War I brought her to a climax of what passed for national success.

THE END OF THE CALM

As in Europe, the revolt of the masses against the classes that exploded after the end of the war had earlier given many evidences of its approach and had done so in a period that seemed serene to the upper classes. Since half the Chileans could read, they were able to learn from newspapers about the great material improvements in the life of common people in more fortunate countries. Naturally, they became more resentful of the oligarchy, who seemed to deny them opportunities while enjoying their own privileges to the fullest. Nitrate excavators and copper miners, who lived often in barracks in the bleak northern zones, as well as railway workers came to covet the benefits that organized labor was winning in the United States and Europe. Not lacking were men eager to shape the opinions of the disinherited. The historian Francisco Encina, no radical, preached that education should be furthered so that all Chileans could win a better place in society, an optimistic attitude common to many intellectuals of the time. Luis Recabarren, who was a radical, went to Europe and became a convinced socialist, then returned to Chile to organize a labor party. Chile's novelists had long followed European men of letters in romantic and realistic trends; now they pursued them in naturalism, which gave them opportunities to publicize social injustices. Alberto Blest-Gana (1830–1920), one of Latin America's most admired novelists, and later Joaquín Edwards Bello (1888–   ) dwelt on the irresponsibility that characterized the rich and the miseries that were the lot of the far more numerous poor.

A suggestion of turbulence beneath the placid surface of Chilean life came with World War I, when labor unions organized and struck in the midst of what the *Fronda* regarded as unparalleled prosperity. The election of 1915, in which the oligarchy's candidate, Juan Luis Sanfuentes, a financier whose speculations had a bad odor, had difficulty in defeating a coalition of leftist parties, also indicated a new atmosphere. Soon afterward the *Fronda* made a few concessions to the plebeians by legislation requiring Sunday rest for all workers, a compensation law for certain laborers, and a weak employers' liability act. Railway workers, the most vociferous group after the miners, were given the first of many *cajas*, funds to which owners and workers contributed to provide security for old age. Generous as these measures seemed to the *Fronda*, they served chiefly to whet the appetites of urban or industrial workers, and agitation continued. Recabarren, who was thrilled by the Russian Revolution, organized a Communist Party, which aroused much interest among the unemployed after the end of the war threw thousands out of work in the nitrate fields. During 1919 a class struggle seemed imminent in Chile, though the agricultural workers were scarcely involved at all.

A NEW ORIENTATION, 1920–1931

Chile was a stricken nation when the presidential campaign of 1920 began. Business was very bad, unemployment was heavy, and the government could no longer finance itself from nitrate revenues. Not since 1890, when the presidency had been clipped so badly by the parliamentary politicians, had elections amounted to more than adjustments among the twenty-five or so parties. Now, however, fifteen more or less liberal factions formed a coalition behind Arturo Alessandri in the Liberal Alliance, while the conservative groups united in a National Union. The age-old division of *pipiolos* (novices) and *pelucones* (big wigs) had been revived. While the Communist Recabarren refused to back Alessandri and soon took his own life, it was apparent that the angry, partially organized proletariat wanted the Liberal Alliance to win. Handsome, or at least striking in appearance, and with a marvelous voice and magnetic personality, Alessandri was the first of a long series of wealthy demagogues in Chile. "The Lion of Tarapacá," as this shaggy, roaring, and fierce-looking son of the northern province liked to be called, was descended from an Italian diplomat and belonged to a rich clan. Little in his previous career suggested a passionate concern for the common man. Now, however, he toured the stringy republic making rousing speeches everywhere. Knowing that the Chileans had been inspired by Yrigoyen's regime in Argentina, Alessandri promised even more radical changes by advocating a new constitution which would strengthen the president, separate Church and state, and permit all citizens, even women, to vote. An income tax and increased land taxes would compel the oligarchy to share the nation's wealth, and a program of social welfare could be financed. While Alessandri stirred the masses and was undoubtedly the popular choice, the *Fronda* almost defeated him by voting their rural workers in mass. A court of honor selected by congress finally decided that Alessandri had won. As in Argentina in 1916, the traditional conservatives agreed by a narrow margin not to risk social revolution by denying the peoples' hero his victory.

The gamble was worth taking. Alessandri was not personally radical, and his election temporarily pacified the masses. Congress still held the critical position in the republic, and while the Liberal Alliance had a majority in the chamber of deputies, the oligarchy controlled the senate. For more than three years a deadlock prevailed, with Alessandri able to redeem only one of his promises, the levying of a gentle income tax. While the copper industry was beginning to boom, the country as a whole languished in depression. The outside world no longer needed nitrates now that it was at peace; besides, German scientists had found during the war a way to obtain nitrogen literally out of the air. Thus the Chilean government had few revenues. President Alessandri demanded that congress do something about raising money to pay the army and bureaucracy, but to no avail. He sent message after message urgently requesting action on his constitutional and social program and even threatened to resign; yet the infuriating deadlock continued. Finally, in the spring of 1924, the fifteen parties of the Liberal Alliance won enough seats to take control of both houses of congress, and the country looked for wholesale reforms.

Congress, however, seemed determined to prove the inadequacy of parliamentary government. It devoted weeks to passing a bill, probably unconstitutional, to provide salaries and expense accounts for its members, for no longer could all deputies be presumed to be rich *frondistas*. The reformers regarded the situation with acute irritation, but not as bitterly as the army, whose pay was far in arrears. For the first time in generations the military stepped into politics. Following a series of conferences at the *Club militar* in Santiago, army officers filled the galleries of congress on September 5, 1924 and managed to have a few quiet words with the party leaders. All of a sudden, thirteen bills that Alessandri had long demanded were passed in one sitting. Then the officers called on the president and ordered him to sign them but to veto the bill for reimbursing the deputies. Alessandri did what he was told, but because of an honorable indignation at the methods employed, he resigned on September 9. First going to the American embassy as though he sought asylum, he soon departed for Argentina with a huge, bewildered crowd watching his train pull out. A military junta took charge of the government and sent congress home.

Was Chile a dictatorship now? The junta earnestly professed that the republic was intact, but appearances were not deceiving. A self-exiled president and a dismissed congress, as well as a circumspect reticence on the part of the press, were testimony of a changed order. The army, however, was not monolithic, for younger officers had political ambitions and many favored drastic reforms. In January 1925 a group led by Colonels Carlos Ibáñez del Campo and Marmaduque Grove bloodlessly slid the original junta out of the seats of power. Their first step was to recall Alessandri, who by now was in Mussolini's Italy. The Lion of Tarapacá returned in March to the acclamation of the populace and resumed the presidency. A constitutional convention wrote the new basic charter he had promised when he first ran for president, the constitution of 1925. Henceforth presidents would be popularly elected and would enjoy the decisive power in government. Congress could no longer oust his ministers by censure, nor could its members serve in the cabinet. Church and state were separated, with the government promising to support the ecclesiastical establishment for five more years, and a paper concession was made to the surviving instincts of federalism, once the principal cause of the liberals, by allowing the provinces to elect assemblies which, however, had little power. And while Alessandri had no intention to evict foreign business interests or to force a redistribution of property, his constitution explicitly proclaimed the priority of the state over private ownership and enterprise.

Gratified by seeing most of his program of 1920 at last enacted, Alessandri, who was not eligible to succeed himself, hoped to see a liberal civilian follow him in 1926. However, Carlos Ibáñez, now the war minister, had developed a taste for power and chose to be a candidate. An obscure clash between him and the president brought about Alessandri's second resignation in October 1925 and his return to Fascist Italy. A stop-gap president chosen irregularly served for the following eighteen months, really as a puppet of Ibáñez, who waited until a rigged election in April 1927 to assume the presidency himself.

Carlos Ibáñez del Campo played many roles in Chilean politics between 1924 and 1955 and can scarcely be typed. He was, of course, an army man, and he saw to it that the services were rewarded with better pay and more privileges and as much equipment as the nation could buy. A splendid organization of carabineers loyal to the national government largely supplanted the decentralized police system. Yet he firmly proclaimed his devotion to the constitution and the rule of law, and while he discouraged strident criticism of his policies and even jailed or exiled a few opponents, he was apologetic about using such measures. His regime was no military dictatorship; yet it was not a democracy either.

In effect, Ibáñez carried out most of the program that Alessandri had popularized in 1920, but with a different spirit and without antagonizing the landed aristocracy seriously. Nor was he as beholden to organized labor, whom he firmly restrained from presuming to direct policy, though he strengthened the rights and favors they had already won. He began a program to transfer former nitrate workers to public lands in the south of Chile, where they might join large groups of German colonists and become farmers. Ibáñez' policies were above all designed to please modern-minded and moneyed urban groups by expanding commerce, diversifying the economy, industrializing, and attracting foreign capital. The copper industry was growing rapidly and, with American financing, showed promise of meaning as much to Chile as nitrates once had. The sale of Chilean bonds in New York and elsewhere also brought money into the country, thus sparking a business recovery in many lines. Now the government had a considerable income again, with the result that public works—automobile roads, docks, canals, and irrigation and electrification projects—could absorb the unemployed and improve the country's productivity. As prosperity fed on itself, textile factories were begun and shipping boomed.

Little could be done to benefit the *inquilinos* on the landed estates and the migratory *rotos*, for the rural aristocracy was still potentially strong. The Ibáñez administration tried, however, to promote public education in the rural areas, and several hundred new schools were built and staffed. In foreign affairs the principal issue was Chile's tedious dispute with Peru over Tacna and Arica. Now that nitrates were no longer lucrative, Ibáñez was willing to be reasonable. Many Chileans, however, were not, and more or less popular resistance frustrated the efforts of an American commission to hold a plebiscite in 1926, and when Ibáñez agreed to return Tacna to Peru in 1929, Chileans tore down the cathedral of that district out of spite. In all, Ibáñez violated civil liberties to some extent, but he was otherwise an adequate ruler, one who was in tune with the times in promoting foreign investment and the expansion of the economy, and he kept the landed aristocrats and radical labor groups from tearing the country apart.

A comparatively progressive period ended with the Wall Street catastrophe of 1929, which deprived Chile of most of her customers for bonds and copper. The only constructive step that Ibáñez could take was to

nationalize the sick nitrate industry in the first of government corporations that would soon be so common in Latin America, COSACH
(*Compañía del Salitrera de Chile*), which was organized in 1930. Before
long COSACH was a target of liberals and nationalists, who charged
that it was run for the benefit of grafters in the government and foreign
interests and that, besides, it did not restore prosperity in the stricken
north. Conditions kept getting worse. No nation endured as steep a decline in foreign trade as Chile; business almost ceased, and the government faced bankruptcy. Aware that his popularity had fallen as much
as the economic index, Ibáñez publicly congratulated himself on getting
through the year 1930 without being overthrown. But it was only a
reprieve he enjoyed, for his turn came in 1931.

In an attempt to forestall a revolution, President Ibáñez appointed
José Estéban Montero as minister of interior and Pedro Blanquier as
finance minister. The former removed all controls over the press, with
the result that a roar of criticism abashed the administration. The latter
let it be known that the government was out of money. Ibáñez tried to
repair the damage by appointing a military junta, to which the population of Santiago responded by going on strike. At first students and
teachers, and then professional men and white collar workers, and finally
almost everybody took to the streets. On July 26, 1931, Ibáñez resigned
and left for Argentina. Peaceful and exhilarating as the revolution had
been, it jolted the many admirers of Chile who had long complimented
the republic on its orderly ways. Those days receded into memory as the
nation now began at least three decades of turbulence. The spell of Diego Portales that had kept the republic amazingly firm since 1833 was
now definitely broken.

SHIFT TO THE LEFT, 1931–1941

Prostrated worse than other countries by the world depression and in
rebellion against familiar symbols, the Chilean republic went through
nearly a year and a half of anarchy. Left and right hardened their positions and faced one another in deadly hostility, though gaiety was in
the air too, perhaps the delirium of desperation. For a time moderate
factions sought to keep a balance. They put down an insane mutiny
by the navy and restored enough order to conduct elections, in October
1931. Arturo Alessandri, the former president who had just returned,
ran against Montero, the minister of Ibáñez who had ended the repression. Montero won, or was reported to have won, and set out to
steady the quaking republic. He intended to maintain civil liberties, enforce an austerity program, and leave COSACH alone for the time being. He tried valiantly for six months to hold things together, but Com-

munist, socialist, and other forms of agitation, mostly extremist, kept the
scene turbulent. Since he had no money, Montero cheapened the currency to create the impression that there was some, bringing about inflation and further dislocations. In June 1932 a group of socialists
literally drove him from the presidential palace and set up a junta dominated by Carlos Dávila and the air commodore Marmaduque Grove.

Now a socialist republic was proclaimed, to the horror of the *Fronda*
and the delight of the radicals. Dávila, who became provisional president,
was a half-hearted socialist, having been an Ibáñez supporter in years
past and an advocate of nationalization more on the order of state capitalism than Marxism. Grove, however, said he was an orthodox socialist.
The two were soon at odds, but they cooperated long enough to suspend
the constitution, dissolve congress, and inaugurate a memorable "hundred days" of the socialist dictatorship. As a prelude to a thoroughgoing
revolution, it was planned to confiscate money from the rich to distribute
to the poor. Relations between Dávila and Grove became so bad that
Dávila arrested his fire-eating associate and appealed to the army to rally
behind the dictatorship. Instead, the army ousted Dávila in September
1932 and then was itself elbowed out of power by a moderate group,
which maintained itself long enough to hold elections on October 30,
1932. The two chief candidates were Marmaduque Grove and Arturo
Alessandri. The victory of the latter, who had once seemed a blood-red
radical to the *Fronda*, really signified the successful coalescing of conservative and liberal factions against extremists of the left, and revolutionary fevers subsided.

Alessandri had not lost his ability to thrill the crowds with impassioned speeches, but he was now in his sixties and had come to view
Mussolini's methods in handling a once-riotous Italy with favor. Thus
he surprised many Chileans agreeably and disgusted others by placing
his emphasis on order rather than reform. His handiwork, the constitution of 1925, was restored, but it did not keep him from dealing high-
handedly with congress, restraining the press, exiling inconvenient critics,
and keeping trouble-makers like Marmaduque Grove in prison. Propertied classes feared worse if Alessandri fell and therefore supported him,
while moderates and liberals had long admired him and continued to do
so. He also enlisted the Church to inculcate a sense of Christian responsibility among the working classes, which it strove to do, though Alessandri had caused its disestablishment, which, incidentally, had been
handled very gracefully. Without offending the armed services he created the Republican Militia, a sort of *jeunesse dorée* that intimidated
enemies of private property throughout the country. Alessandri catered
to the rising nationalist passions of his country by ending COSACH,
which had the reputation of being an instrument of aliens. He also re-

quired British and American interests to sell most of their public utility, airline, and railroad holdings. Finally, as conditions improved, he was able to finance public works on a wide scale, mainly in the way of low-cost urban housing and school construction.

Although Chile returned to a semblance of her traditional orderliness as a result of Alessandri's firm rule and economic recovery, chaos threatened to break out almost constantly. A nation-wide strike on the republic's excellent railway system early in 1936 almost reduced the country to paralysis. At length Alessandri dissolved congress, arrested labor leaders, and turned the railroads over to the army for a few months. The Left broke completely with Alessandri, whom it regarded as a traitor, and organized a Popular Front, of the type France and Spain knew, with Communist support. And many persons of German birth or ancestry in Chile, who often held important positions in the business or professional life of the cities and formed virtually a rich colony in the south, were fascinated with Hitlerism, or at least fearful of the Popular Front. In former president Ibáñez, who might have been flattered by the way his old enemy Alessandri imitated his regime, they found a leader. A well-disciplined party of *nacistas* seized several public buildings in Santiago in September 1938 and was narrowly defeated in an effort to set up a pro-German government. Despite the suppression which followed, Chile was nervous for the next five years about the German element, and her rulers were careful not to antagonize it.

The elections of 1938 were quite exciting. Conservatives and moderates rallied behind Gustavo Ross, a wizard of a finance minister under Alessandri but also an outspoken reactionary who had infuriated the Left. The Popular Front nominated a wealthy ultra-liberal named Pedro Aguirre Cerda who, among other distinctions, had been a professor and a dean in the National University. A conscious imitator of Franklin D. Roosevelt, "Don Tinto," as Aguirre Cerda was called, did not prove as successful a vote-getter, but he won the election by a hair. The closeness of the vote did not indicate an evenly divided electorate, for nearly all of the articulate groups, even the *nacistas*, had supported him, but rather the abiding power of the *Fronda* to herd their farm workers to the polls.

The Popular Front administration opened with one of the worst earthquakes that Chile had ever known, familiar as she was with these disasters, and a costly relief and reconstruction program was necessary. General Ibáñez disturbed matters in August 1939 with an abortive rebellion, though a worse furor arose when the Nazis and the Communists in Europe signed a non-aggression pact and threw the Popular Front into confusion. And then the outbreak of war in September brought about a sharp rise in foreign demands for Chile's copper and nitrate, to which Aguirre Cerda reacted by raising prices and cheapening the currency.

The inflation that ensued has been with Chile ever since. The Popular Front government also established a developmental corporation, CORFO, which reunited government and private funds on a massive scale to promote the industrialization of the country. Like other such organizations in Latin America, it came to be financed mostly by the United States. Chileans could take pride, however, in the prodigies of CORFO in modernizing the mines and transportation system, establishing small factories for textiles and cement, and building power plants. Economic stimulation reached into the long-neglected fishing industry and ranches, where livestock breeding was improved, as well as the great forest reserves among the scenic fjords and Araucanian reservations of the south. The Popular Front had less success, however, in introducing scientific methods on the benighted *fundos*, where the landed aristocracy resisted most forms of progress.

While economic growth inspired by World War II was the dominant aspect of the Popular Front regime, social reforms were by no means forgotten. *Cajas* came to prevail in almost every occupation, with employees and employers contributing to funds that would protect the workers against the hazards of toil and old age. A powerful beginning was made to provide better public sanitation and health for a country whose ratio of deaths to births was horrifying. Medical insurance, free clinics, and low-priced government housing did much to raise the standards of living among the poor. By 1941 Chile had the most comprehensive program of social welfare in Latin America. Yet not even the Popular Front dared to force a distribution of the great landed estates; all it did was to revive the old Ibáñez program of re-colonizing surplus miners of the north on small farms established on former public lands in the south.

SUNNY INTERVALS AND CLOUDINESS, 1941–1952

Early in 1941 the Popular Front disintegrated owing to strife between the Communists, who were then friendly to the Axis, and leftists and liberals who were not. This situation left the Radical Party, which had long been gaining strength among groups who would be considered moderate in most countries, the most cohesive force, as was demonstrated when President Aguirre Cerda died in 1941 and new elections were held in November to choose his successor. The Radical candidate, Juan Antonio Ríos, defeated that perennial office-seeker, General Carlos Ibáñez, who was now the darling of the conservatives. Ríos was another wealthy president, a successful businessman from Concepción, but he was several shades less liberal than Aguirre Cerda. Doing nothing to alarm the propertied classes and little to estrange the powerful labor and

leftist groups, he was destined to govern for nearly five years in comparative peace. These were years of immense economic growth, thanks to
the war and CORFO. Iron ore in the north began to be excavated on
a large scale and a steel mill was built in Concepción, far to the south,
to process it. Chile also constructed a wire plant, so that not all her copper had to be shipped abroad. Coal mining in the southern regions grew
into an impressive industry, and various programs for industrialization
and power went ahead rapidly. While strikes and proletarian agitation
reflected continuing social unrest, it was less conspicuous than the economic development of the republic and the attendant growth of a middle class.

All was not agreeable for Chile, however, during World War II. The
destruction of the American fleet at Pearl Harbor left her long coastline
exposed to Japanese attacks, and there was great fear, perhaps exaggerated, that the German element might rise. These dangers deterred Ríos
from breaking relations with the Axis for a year after all the other
American nations but Argentina had, not until early 1943. After that
he cooperated intimately with the United States in removing spies and
saboteurs and in surveilling the countless harbors that might have provided nests for Axis submarines. Chile was never, however, fervently pro-
United Nations; her declaration of war was very tardy, just in time to
permit her inclusion in the world organization.

The end of the war predictably threw the economy into disorder.
Loss of markets, inflation, strikes, and a powerful surge of Communism
threatened chaos. President Ríos died in 1946 before his term had ended,
and a special election reflected the confusion by giving no candidate a
mandate, with the result that congress made the choice by electing
Gabriel González Videla. The third member of the Radical Party in
succession to win the presidency, González Videla was leftist enough to
revive the Popular Front. A rich man from Tarapacá who had wrested
political control of that province from Alessandri, the new president did
not disconcert the conservatives unduly. He spoke well, was handsome
and theatrical, and loved to mingle with his fellow citizens as a good
fellow. He suffered, however, from one serious delusion: he believed the
Communists might be useful allies, and he included three of them in his
cabinet. Disenchantment was not slow in coming. The Communists
tried to take over the military and the bureaucracy and abused González Videla without mercy when he blocked them. After more than a
year of utter frustration, he dismissed them from his cabinet, broke diplomatic relations with the Soviet bloc, had congress outlaw the party, and
sent many of its members into the far south as Siberian-style colonists.
After this the president was no longer the idol of the left. Since conserva-

tives had never really trusted him, it was a tribute to his skill that he managed to stay in office for the rest of his term.

Reform was no longer the preoccupation of the Chileans after the days of the Popular Front, which legislated so much of it. Subsequent administrations carried out welfare programs but devoted most of their attention to the uneven prosperity, inflation, and constant adjustment to the frenzied economic situation that characterized Chilean life. Among the more significant developments under González Videla were the discovery of oil in Punta Arenas and the building of a refinery in Valparaiso. The completion of a railroad from Antofagasta over (and through, for there were extensive tunnels) the Andes into Argentina opened a prospect for heightened economic growth. González Videla made himself ridiculous to the outside world but immensely gratified Chilean patriots by sailing in a warship to Graham Land in the Antarctic and proclaiming it O'Higgins Land, a possession that might prove rich.

SINCE 1952: CONTINUING INSTABILITY

By the presidential compaign of 1952 it was difficult to discern the true forces that moved Chilean opinion. No politician had much prestige, and the parties were so splintered and misnamed as to have little significance. General Carlos Ibáñez, now seventy-five, presented himself as usual as a presidential candidate. Perhaps it was the vote of women, who participated in national elections for the first time, or the accumulated irritations of the population in general, that gave him an impressive showing when the votes were counted. Again congress had to choose the victor from among several candidates who had large votes but no majority, and Ibáñez received the award. Earlier he had been a semi-dictator, from 1925 to 1931; he had rather openly befriended the Nazis on several occasions afterward and indicated fascist sympathies; and he was known to be very cordial toward Argentina's Perón. During the campaign of 1952 he had denounced the United States, promised to recognize the Communists, urged the division of landed estates and the nationalization of industry, and vowed to provide an honest administration. His was a catch-all political platform, and it is not strange that many Chileans and friendly outsiders believed the old man would be a Peronist puppet.

If President Ibáñez did not justify these misgivings, it was largely because he did so little of anything. True, he was not personally inactive, for he was vigorous and crisp in manner, he traveled widely in Chile and abroad, and he carried out ceremonial duties with gusto. But, like Vargas in Brazil, he could no longer understand or direct his country. Still the army's man, he could count on the military to keep order, which on several occasions meant enforcing martial law in strike-bound areas. He did not provoke the public by violating civil liberties, though he was far from pedantic about observing all of the constitutional amenities. And in spite of his harsh statements during the presidential campaign, Ibáñez was friendly to the United States. Communism was not recognized as an authentic movement on a par with other groups. Also, investment capital and loans from the United States were so essential to Chile that Washington could not be antagonized. Ibáñez was circumspect with his ambitious neighbor, Juan Perón. The Argentine made a flamboyant state visit to Santiago early in 1953 but failed to enchant the Chileans with his proposal for a commercial union. Ibáñez had a most impressive reception in Buenos Aires when he returned the call, but effusive words could not conceal the odium with which Chileans regarded Peronism and, it was obvious, the Argentine nation. Perón's fall in 1955 was probably a relief to President Ibáñez.

Such matters were largely negative in character. The Ibáñez administration was a period of executive inaction and congressional squabbling while the republic floundered. Its dilemma lay in the fact that a vigorous and vocal segment of the population, the urban, wanted a highly modernized nation. This could be attained only if other lands purchased Chile's products regularly and at high prices. Otherwise the country would collapse in revolution or revert to the control of the *Fronda* and their docile farm workers, the former fate meaning chaos, the latter mere subsistence at a very low level. No government in Santiago had the power to compel the world to buy Chile's products at a rate that would provide the basis for the material improvement many Chileans wanted, and when copper prices sagged during the 1950's, irritations mounted. Nor could the government court foreign investment too openly, for nationalism or anti-Americanism flared so quickly. An attempt to carve up the large estates was too risky to try; surely it would have meant civil war, and, as most thoughtful students were concluding, other Latin American experiences with this process were not at all encouraging. Thus Chile, a lovely, temperate land with awesome vistas of cordillera and sea, was tragically split between a reactionary countryside and a radical urban society that wanted more than the country could afford.

Of all Chile's problems, the most exasperating was inflation, which had begun modestly during the 1930's, surged during the 1940's, and gotten hopelessly out of hand in the 1950's. The rise in the cost of living was so steep that it spoiled the effects of all the pension plans and wage increases. Every month or so the peso hit new depths, and the government helplessly conceded raises in everything, everything but the price of copper that foreigners would pay. In a cosmic way the situation was mirthful, and the Chileans seemed more resigned than angry about it. Of course, runaway inflation did not injure the owners of tangible property, and there are always clever persons who manage to prosper amid conditions that are disastrous for the majority. The *Fronda* remained, if anything, richer than ever, and many enterprisers successfully rode the inflationary tides, making one fortune after another. Chile's wealthy had ironically survived the Popular Front and other political disasters meant to ruin them, while the laboring classes had to struggle to stay alive. As in other Latin American countries, the prosperous thought little of sharing their good fortune.

Since the Ibáñez regime was so weak, the campaign for the presidency began a year ahead of the election scheduled for September 1958. The air was long filled with the vows and accusations of politicians. Since by now all of the parties were mere factions, a general grouping of conservatives, moderates, liberals, and radicals reduced them to four coalitions. It was now a custom that no candidate could win a majority and that congress would have to select the president. This happened again in 1958, when the moderate candidate, Jorge Alessandri, son of the Lion of Tarapacá and an engineer who was no stranger to the world of business and politics, was named to the office. As had been true with few exceptions since 1925, Chile's destinies were confided to a man who was a puppet neither of the *Fronda* atavists nor the ultra-radicals of the cities. Optimists hoped that Chile was developing a new tradition suitable to modern conditions, a rationale between Communism and aristocracy.

The nation continued to be a puzzle to its own thoughtful elements and to students abroad. So much about it was wrong. Alcoholism and criminality had become worse, and morals in general were degraded. The lower classes in rural areas were still destitute, poorly housed, and undernourished. The countryside produced far less than it might—some said that wheat and grape cultivation should exchange locales, that the former would do better on the central *fundos* and the latter on small southern farms—and resistance to scientific farming methods was holding it back. In the cities, of which only Santiago with its 1,500,000 people was really large, public housing and other benefits had done little to slake the radicalism of the working classes. They were frankly receptive to Communist preachments and irrationally hostile to the United States. No one had a right to be surprised if they one day captured the machinery of government. As for the upper classes, they had expanded far beyond the historic four or six hundred families of the *Fronda*, since so many industrial and commercial magnates, and speculators, had joined their ranks. With skiing in the Andes, swimming at Viña del Mar, gambling, horse racing, and other fashionable activities easily available, they indulged themselves with little inhibition and sometimes berated Uncle Sam for not being more generous to Chile's poor. It was doubtful that the old restraints, whether of religion, decency, or law, could still command enough allegiance to prevent an ugly class war.

And yet so much was admirable about Chile. Scenery, climate, soil, resources, and racial mixture were all in her favor. This ribbon of a land still attracted European immigrants in a stream strong enough to enrich it without drowning its character, and the Araucanians were at last entering national life. The curse of earthquakes, such as the disaster of May 1960, might bring tragedy to hundreds of thousands in a few seconds, but the nation always rallied with assurance. Chileans had faith in themselves and a patriotism that sometimes transcended good sense; like Argentina, Chile had become truculently nationalistic. The republic had one of the best educational systems in Latin America, and her four universities were fervid centers of intellectual activity. It had produced a Nobel prize winner in literature, the poetess who called herself Gabriela Mistral (1889–1957), who was almost as admired for her compassionate and social works as for her verses. Pablo Neruda (1904–   ), who like Mistral employed a pen name and served Chile abroad, has extraordinary popularity, though as a surrealist he is often difficult to fathom and as a political radical he makes enemies. Chile's educated class continued to read avidly, to participate in the republic of letters and ideas. The abundance of forests made paper cheap, and so Santiago's publishing houses were able to do justice to native writers. Eduardo Barrios (1884–   ), with his novels about abnormal personalities, and Pedro Prado (1886–1952), a master stylist who wrote of ideas and human dilemmas, were perhaps the most conspicuous of a stellar group of prose writers.

In other respects Chile offered room for optimism. The health of her population was beginning to improve, as the burst of human growth that lifted it beyond 7,000,000 suggested. And despite immediate vexations, the economy was really making great strides. Industrialization had proceeded so far that it had a momentum of its own. Welfare capitalism introduced by the American firms Anaconda Copper and Bethlehem Steel made the life of miners less grim and inspired some emulation among native firms. While Chile was dependent for half of her foreign earnings on copper exports, steel and oil might become significant sources of income. Nitrates were already being sold in as great a volume as during the heyday of World War I, though they brought much lower prices. Chile's wines were relished all over South America, as were her non-tropical fruits and vegetables. If the economy did not seem hopeless for the long run, neither did the political situation. The republic functioned fairly well under the constitution of 1925, with liberty, some separation of powers, a multiplicity of parties, a seasoned if over-staffed public administration, a military establishment that had learned to be subtle in using its influence, and a Church that was not strong enough to be monopolistic nor weak enough to fail in ministering to the people. With so much in its favor, Chile was far from the hopeless mess that foreign pessimists sometimes said she was.

Nonetheless, President Jorge Alessandri properly addressed himself to the nation's problems with great seriousness. First, he said, there must be austerity, an end to governmental extravagance and the importation of luxuries. He received full powers for a year to direct the economy and reorganize public services. Since the treasury was empty, he had to accept direct assistance from the United States, something no other Chilean president had dared to do. He won the gamble, and the nation responded. Confidence crept back, business improved, strikes declined, and the rise in living costs slowed down. In local elections of April 1960 the voters, long said to be so grasping and irresponsible, endorsed the austerity Alessandri had imposed. Scarcely had a treasury surplus been noted, however, when an earthquake and tidal wave destroyed 65,000 homes around Concepción, and very expensive measures were needed to bring relief. The tragedy set the administration's program back, of course, but the mood remained determined. A generous welcome accorded to President Eisenhower in 1960 indicated that the population still had a warm spot in its heart for the great capitalistic democracy of the north. With luck and good management, Chile might also, it seemed, elevate her population to higher living standards without succumbing to dictatorship.

34

Paraguay

R OMANTICS who long for a Garden of Eden on earth have frequently looked to the Indian society that lives between the Paraguay and Paraná Rivers. In so many ways Paraguay should qualify for this title. Its climate is good, warm without being tropical, much of the soil is exceedingly favorable to vegetation, and animal life flourishes. Water is plentiful during most of the year, with the rivers affording all that could be desired in the way of navigation. The country has hills, but no spot is more than 2,000 feet high. If nature is kind, man is not particularly vile. The Guaraní Indians who compose the majority of the population have always struck visitors as friendly and amenable, even though they have made superb warriors on occasion. They were docile under the first Spaniards, Irala and Cabeza de Vaca, and during the long generations of Jesuit tutelage. Afterward, viceroys in Buenos Aires and dictators in Asunción have ruled these multitudes with little difficulty. Political clashes nearly always pitted Spaniard against Spaniard, creole against creole, or mestizo against mestizo, but rarely white against colored. Not even the modern immigrants or alien enterprisers who control so much of the little country have experienced much resistance from the Indians. Therefore, in one sense, Paraguayan life is easy. Most of the people cultivate gardens of a few acres, live in thatched huts in intimacy with chickens and pigs, imbide their "tea," or *yerba maté*, smoke cigars, and wear few clothes. On the other hand, they are sickly, they die young, and they are so detached from modern civilization as to covet few of its gadgets and better offerings. Observers often feel both envy and pity when they look upon the Paraguayans.

Arcadia though Paraguay had seemed at various times, it was in the most wretched state imaginable after the five-year war that closed with the death of Dictator Francisco Solano López in 1870. Perhaps half the population had perished, leaving about 220,000, only an eighth of whom were men. Argentine and Brazilian armies occupied most of the republic, the latter being dominant in the capital, Asunción. These two powers might have partitioned Paraguay had they been less contentious. As it was, the Brazilians remained until 1876, when they withdrew their soldiers—many of whom must have been reluctant to leave such a heavily female population—and detached a huge slice of territory. Argentina had to content herself with a smaller cession, thanks to the arbitration of President Hayes of the United States in 1878, for whose decision the grateful Paraguayans named a river port Villa Hayes, after him. Both Brazil and Argentina eventually gave up hopes of collecting a war indemnity from Paraguay, for the country had no portable wealth at all.

A few educated and propertied men who had survived the wrath of López and the hazards of war assembled under Brazilian auspices in Asunción to draw up the constitution of 1870, which remained officially in force until 1940. Its provisions matter little, since the population never reached the level of abiding by representative government and their self-appointed magistrates paid it little note. Not even the leaders themselves often rose above anonymity as far as history is concerned. Between the Paraguayan and Chaco Wars, that is, from 1870 to 1932, the republic had twenty-nine presidents. Paraguayans were skittish about allowing anyone to remain long in office after their experiences with the long-term dictatorships of Francia and the two López, and every occupant of the presidential chair well understood that it had, usually figuratively, a bomb beneath it. In any case, military commanders and civilians who shared their outlook ruled the nation for decade after decade, gradually achieving a political rationale.

The first postwar president, Cirilo Antonio Rivarola, was memorable only because he was the first. General Bernardino Caballero was more important because he founded in 1874 a group known as the *Colorado*, or Republican Party, which dominated public affairs until 1904. For most of the 1880's Caballero and his associate, General Patricio Escobar, or their clients held the presidency. The overturn of 1904, which had something of a popular character, brought in the Liberals, who had become a party in 1887. Their tenure lasted until 1936, which just about equalized things with the *Colorados*. The Liberals gave Paraguay three able presidents: Eduardo Schaerer (1912–1916), the first to serve an uninterrupted four-year term; Eligio Ayala (1924–1928), who undertook many fine projects during the smiling 1920's; and Dr. Eusebio Ayala (1932–1936), an architect of the successful war against Bolivia.

During these years between the wars the Guaraní went about living and dying with little reference to the shifts of regime in Asunción.

The sexual balance was restored after a generation, thanks partly to the cooperation of the occupying armies, but Paraguayan males continued to be bemused and pampered creatures. The bounty of nature and the accommodating character of the women made it unnecessary for men to work. Marriage was much less usual than informal unions, and most of the population was illegitimate. Supposedly Catholic, it knew little of the details of this faith and its practices. Schooling marred their childhood days hardly at all; not until the 1920's were there more than a few dozen primary schools, and then only a few hundred were established. The rural masses might have enjoyed their languid lives better had they been healthier. Yet they displayed little eagerness to purify their water or to put up screens or to adopt modern methods for combating sickness. When the Rockefeller Foundation sent a mission early in the twentieth century to establish clinics and health centers, it was found that nearly every Paraguayan suffered from hookworm, typhoid, tuberculosis, or leprosy. Yet the population responded indifferently to efforts to raise their level. Mostly, they were content to raise a little food, mostly the mandioca, corn, and sweet potatoes they had always consumed, tend fowls and low-grade livestock, suck *yerba maté* through tubes placed in gourds, and smoke black cigars. They made their own clothing and shelters and, for luxury articles, beautiful laces.

The outside world would not leave Paraguay entirely alone. A few adventurers penetrated the hermit republic and discovered opportunities for enterprise. Not Paraguayans but foreigners bought up land for commercial farms and sugar mills, supervised the cutting of timber for the woodless Argentine, and erected plants for the extraction of tannic acid from the *quebracho* forests. If they prospered, and many did, they might further develop cotton plantations, tobacco farms, and rice fields, and tap rubber. Oranges from Paraguay came to have a good market in Buenos Aires and other downriver cities, and the acid from citrus trees known as petitgrain was useful in the preparation of French perfumes. As such businesses grew, modest commercial empires came to distribute imported finished articles among Paraguayans. Yet it was almost always the alien who carried out these activities, who saw to it that steamboats and barges filled the rivers to ship Paraguay's products away. A few Paraguayans continued to own estates, as they had for generations, but most of the population either lived in abstraction from economic life or served as low-paid workers. An unwholesome social system accordingly took shape.

The role of Paraguay's rapidly-changing governments in these beginnings of capitalism was mostly passive. Members of the ruling groups discerned the value of steamboat lines, banks, telegraph wires, and the single rail line that connected Asunción with a ferryboat crossing to Argentina, which was completed in 1885, as well as other touches of modernity.

Yet they had little talent for encouraging native enterprise or securing significant amounts of foreign capital. They vaguely hoped that European immigrants would come into Paraguay on a large scale as residents. All they could attract, however, were Italians who had no better place to go and a few Spaniards. That so many of these new citizens quickly made good testified less to their abilities than to the backwardness of the people into whose midst they moved. The government resorted to the encouragement of colonies of misfits as a way of inducing white settlement. Australian socialists unwelcome at home, stray religious sects, and persecuted minorities of one sort or another were likely to find hospitality in Paraguay. Of these the most interesting were the pacifist Mennonites, who felt abused in Canada, the United States, Russia, and Manchuria. Beginning in 1926, five or six thousand established settlements in Paraguay, chiefly in the Chaco region. Despite these migrations and the slow growth of a mestizo element, the population was mainly Guaraní.

By the 1920's Paraguay showed some response to the penetrations of modern civilization. More than 2,000 steamships and barges put in annually at Asunción. A railway, as noted, tied the country to Argentina, and short lines served to transport raw materials to river docks. Perhaps 100,000 children out of a total population of 1,000,000 were in school. A National University in Asunción, which had been established in 1882, trained a few hundred students for the professions, government, or white-collar proletariat. Sadly, many graduates despaired of finding a place for themselves in Paraguay and went to more advanced countries. The republic had a few newspapers and boasted several historians, poets, and critics —presidents among them—whose renown, however, was strictly local. Foreigners might smile at claims of a Golden Age of literature that supposedly began early in the twentieth century, but in fact Asunción had a small cultured elite who were not entirely alien to the world of ideas. And while a visitor might see a scattering of well-run plantations, orange groves, tannin extraction facilities, and sugar and lumber mills, he could not fail to notice that most of the land was undeveloped. As for Asunción, which had a few government buildings and some solid homes and shops on the bluffs of the Paraguay River, it was the smallest and poorest capital in South America.

THE CHACO WAR AND
A NEW DIRECTION

Her primitive condition allowed Paraguay to escape the worst effects of the world depression. Troubles of another nature, however, soon intruded: conflicts with Bolivia that led to the terrible Chaco War. While the League of Nations ultimately branded Paraguay the aggressor in this struggle, it has been seen that Bolivia's rulers had thought they could safely enforce their interpretation of the boundary dispute and were in a bellicose mood. It happened that Paraguay had a competent president in 1932, when the war really began, in Dr. Eusebio Ayala, a Liberal as were all presidents between 1904 and 1936. Abandoning his plans for domestic improvements, Ayala threw himself into the labor of winning the war, which cost far more than either the Paraguayans or Bolivians had expected. The smaller republic had to draft nearly every adult male and draw heavily on Argentine credits—which facilitated the economic ascendancy in its affairs that Buenos Aires was already winning—in order to contend with Bolivia. Paraguay's war effort was surprisingly effective with regard to equipment and logistics, but it should not have been surprising that her soldiers were sturdy and disciplined. Moreover, they fought in a terrain and climate that caused them less suffering than the Bolivians, who had to descend from their lofty Andes. By 1935 the Paraguayans had pushed their enemy almost out of the disputed Chaco Boreal and withstood a strong Bolivian counter-offensive. At this point President Ayala acceded to urgent pressures from other American republics, chiefly Argentina, and agreed to an armistice. His action was unpopular, for even if Paraguay had lost 36,000 men and was exhausted, the cause had enlisted the passionate enthusiasm of her population, and the army, at least, was disappointed at not being allowed to conquer La Paz.

A war hero who commanded the respect of the veterans, Colonel Rafael Franco, brought about the downfall of President Ayala in February 1936, hence the name *"Febreristas"* which his faction assumed. The *Febreristas* initially promised to resume the war, but once in power they were prudent enough to content themselves with ultra-patriotic bluster. Franco was more than a mere chauvinist. Reflecting the neo-fascism which so many South Americans exhibited during the 1930's, he aspired to "integrate" the traditional conservative forces with the awakening masses who were thought to desire social and economic betterment. Franco and his court ideologue, Dr. Juan Stefanich, articulated this doctrine and popularized notions of reform. Thus land division was preached and even begun, on 5,000,000 acres hitherto uncultivated. An eight-hour day and labor unions were offered the small industrial proletariat, and hopes for more extensive social benefits were aroused. Students, veterans, and many who had been torn from their native communities by the war reacted enthusiastically to the prospect Franco laid before Paraguay. They also liked his balcony appearances and other imitations of the dramatics of European dictators. It was significant that Franco invoked Francisco Solano López as the nation's greatest hero, tyrant and author of ruin though he had been, for at least he had been popular and nationalistic. Seminal as Franco's regime was for the future, it lasted only eighteen months. In August 1937 rival army officers unseated the *Febreristas* and restored the Liberals.

As had happened before, the Liberal Party gave the nation a good president, at least after two years of shifting rulers and intrigue. This was General José Félix Estigarribia, a glamorous and handsome officer who deserved as much credit as any for Paraguay's victory in the Chaco War. In 1938 he had courageously signed the treaty that ended this war, something no one but a successful veteran could have done, and he had also served as ambassador to Washington. Estigarribia took office in August 1939, when the country had almost recovered from the dislocations of that war and was about to enjoy a boom as a result of a far greater war in Europe. Soon, Paraguay was exporting her products, especially cotton, beef, and forest products, in the largest volume ever. President Estigarribia continued Franco's program of dividing unused lands among the rural poor and encouraging them to use scientific methods. Public works and further benefits for the urban working elements also indicated his desire to modernize the country. And he prepared a new constitution in 1940, which the population ratified in a plebiscite, to replace the basic law of 1870. While the constitution did not keep him from governing autocratically, Estigarribia struck most observers as a highly promising ruler, for he was able, energetic, and popular. In September 1940 he was killed in an airplane accident.

General Higinio Morínigo, the minister of war and navy (the latter consisting of a few armed river boats), succeeded the late president. The Liberals, who sponsored his accession, soon had reason to regret it. Morínigo dismissed them in favor of *Colorados*, who had been out of power since 1904, and *Febreristas* after a complicated series of private negotiations with various army officers. He remained in power for nearly eight years, setting a new record for Paraguayan presidents since 1870, surviving barracks revolts, student riots, strikes, and a variety of intrigues. During 1946, when Paraguay suffered from the collapse of the war boom, a general strike was called to liquidate the Morínigo regime. Yet he suppressed it and also a civil war of five months' duration in 1947 inspired by ex-President Rafael Franco and the *Febreristas*, who by now had fallen out with Morínigo. As was customary in Paraguay's history, these disorders were not racial in character nor even class strife, but only struggles for power by individuals or factions. One secret of Morínigo's success was the loyalty of key army officers, who were heady and assertive following the Chaco War but willing to be influenced by favored treatment. Morínigo devoted 45 per cent of the national income to the military, and he received practically as gifts American surplus war equipment designed to keep Argentina's Perón from taking over Paraguay. Not that his relations with Perón were disagreeable; he flattered that dictator by imitating his methods and cultivated his friendship as effectively as he did that of every other nation. Argentine interests expanded until they controlled three-fourths of Paraguay's foreign holdings.

By the late 1940's Paraguay counted some achievements despite the political retrogression she had undergone. American and Brazilian capital joined Argentine in opening up new activities, and the expanded commerce of the war years largely continued. An increment of white immigrants, most of them displaced persons from behind the Iron Curtain, brought in techniques and skills badly needed by the hermit republic, though it remained a tight autocracy, ruled by a small oligarchy, and the most backward state in South America. Morínigo, who had had himself elected to a five-year term in 1943, decided to step down while things were going well. In February 1948 his chosen heir was elected president. It turned out that no one could play off the factions as well as Morínigo had, and five presidents moved into and out of the national palace during the following eighteen months.

In September 1949 an elderly conservative, Federico Chávez, was installed as president with the blessing of Perón and the *Colorado* Party. The hundreds of Liberals and *Febreristas* had little incentive to return home from exile, and few did. For the next five years Chávez ruled, or served as a front for a tiny *Colorado* oligarchy, in a dull fashion while rebellions sputtered, Perón's wishes were followed, and dictatorship continued. Perhaps the most significant activities in Paraguay were carried on by outsiders working under the American Point IV Plan and United Nations experts, who improved market roads in rural areas and taught the inhabitants more about public health, sanitation, and scientific techniques. Paraguay seemed tailor-made for a splendid project of uplift—if only her government did not obstruct and her people responded. A few years of education and economic stimulation might accomplish wonders. While the regime was not hostile to these efforts, the population remained nonchalant before the exhortations of experts. Some students admired the Indians for relying on their atavistic wisdom and rejecting the well-meaning modernizers and thought them the happier for it.

At length, President Chávez ceased to please the army and *Colorado* oligarchy and, in September 1954, was abruptly removed in favor of General Alfredo Stroessner, a hard-faced man in his early forties. The new president resembled Morínigo, for he was skillful in handling the difficult personalities who composed the ruling group and made little effort to cultivate the masses. Paraguay now endures another long dictatorship, one that is worse than previous regimes or at least more publicized abroad. In a period when dictators were being deposed all over Latin America, Stroessner reigns year after year, surviving barracks revolts, street demonstrations, and small-scale invasions. No one knows how many Liberals and *Febreristas* are in exile; certainly the number is in the tens of thousands. In nearly every capital in South America, refugees attack Paraguayan diplomatic posts and proclaim to the world that torture, oppression, and concentration camps defile their homeland. Some of their charges are undoubtedly true. Yet Stroessner maintains his rule, and he flaunts his confidence by making frequent trips abroad, usually a dangerous course for a tyrant.

One of his most formidable critics is the Church, which has seldom asserted itself so openly in Paraguayan public affairs. A Jesuit priest, Ramón Talavera, circulated throughout the western hemisphere denouncing Stroessner and attempted to bring him down by hunger strikes and one-man invasions. Armed parties of Liberals and *Febreristas* at times have crossed the frontier to proclaim liberation, so far in vain. A general strike of 1958 that suggested wide-scale unrest among the workers crumpled before police-state methods. Then a sector of the *Colorado* Party seceded from the regime, only to find itself isolated and impotent. That Paraguayans might prefer liberty was suggested by the emotional reception given Vice President Nixon in 1958, when it was rumored that he might persuade Stroessner to relax his autocracy. Three years later Ambassador Adlai Stevenson carefully avoided smiling while he was with the dictator in the presence of photographers, lest the people think the United States approved of Stroessner. No improvement is evident, however, as the dictatorship begins its ninth year. The Paraguayans are still the poorest and most oppressed nation on the continent.

All is not gloom, however. Paraguay's currency is sound, thanks mainly to aid from the International Monetary Fund and the United States, and inflation is not a serious problem. Her export markets are holding up well. The population, more healthy now, is growing but not too rapidly for the nation's resources, and it has abundant mandioca, corn, rice, and meat. Housing and clothing are primitive but not unsuitable for the warm climate. Large commercial farms and ranches prosper, and a few small factories are being established. Asunción is still the most backward capital in South America, but it has finally acquired a pure water supply and a sewer system. An airline, a few highways, and railways to Argentina and, recently, to Brazil supplement the heavy river traffic. While Paraguay was disappointed to find only dry holes in the Chaco Boreal, which was rumored to have great deposits of oil at the time of the Chaco War, she still has many articles that the outside world will buy: cotton, *quebracho*, timber, sugar, *yerba maté*, and coffee. So much fertile land is available that there is little incentive to fragmentize the estates. And schooling is improving, with 300,000 pupils reported by the government. A very humble member of the Western community, almost an outcast, Paraguay still pleases those who admire a quiet society with ancient ways and inspires those who see an opportunity for a wonderful transformation. It could either live with its problems or attack them. Apparently the people care little which course is followed.

35

Argentina Since 1930

AFTER seventy years of comparative political stability and economic progress, the Argentine Republic went through a turbulent period, beginning in 1930. Her reaction to three decades of depression, totalitarianism, World War II, and the Cold War dismayed her admirers abroad, who had long regarded this nation as the model for Latin America, and it badly damaged her international reputation. Argentina seemed to turn on the ideals and practices by which she had grown astonishingly modern and civilized. During this period her own people were confused and unstable, surprisingly timid before their own oppressors, surprisingly aggressive toward foreigners. And yet patriotism, at least of the type that implies political virtue and maturity, was scarcely their outstanding characteristic. None of the catastrophes that revolutionized the world at large intruded immediately on the Argentine scene. The depression affected her severely but only briefly; she recovered far ahead of most countries, including the United States. Totalitarianism entered not through invasion or conquest but through willing captives, her most influential citizens. The only shots Argentines heard during World War II were those of German and British naval guns off her shores, and the great conflict generally benefited the nation's economy. As for the protracted Cold War, it too has stimulated Argentine economic life and so far has threatened this land as little as any on the globe. Yet Argentina has rocked and reeled with the convulsions of the outside world. In doing so she perhaps unwittingly proved her membership in the European community. Exhausted, dispirited, and wounded after a long experience with a totalitarian dictatorship of her own, the republic has struggled to recover the peace and self-respect it once knew. Argentina's importance to the world at large and her inherent greatness cannot be denied. With wonderful resources and a gifted population, she is unlikely to flounder indefinitely.

THE RISE OF THE ARMY

The Revolution of September 1930

THE great world depression that began in October 1929 jolted Argentina with stunning force. Within a few months her grain and meat exports dropped to less than half the customary volume. This alone was enough to produce a severe shock to the nation's economic structure. All at once banks closed, thousands became unemployed, prices and values collapsed, and businesses went bankrupt. In other countries the same calamities occurred, but usually their effects were cushioned by a diversified economy, which Argentina did not possess. Nor was the Argentine government, no more than those of many other nations, capable of understanding or coping with the disaster. President Hipólito Yrigoyen, the builder of the Radical Party that had been in power since 1916 and now serving his second term, was almost eighty years old. For a year or more people had been saying he was senile, and he had no associates or prospective heirs who could assume his responsibilities. Only sycophants, time-servers, and the most brazen of grafters stood out among his official family. The administration had distinguished itself in nothing but corruption and high-handedness in dealing with local governments or opponents. In the face of the depression the government seemed to have disintegrated altogether. Therefore, responsible citizens patriotically took matters in their own hands and replaced a discredited regime. So runs the legend of the significant revolution of 1930.

As usual, the truth is far more complicated and less likely to identify heroes and villains. Most of the world was initiating far-reaching revolutions of one type or another about 1930. Some regimes fell because of momentary weaknesses in the face of irritations. In Argentine, as in other large countries, the cause was more fundamental: a loss of confidence in democratic institutions. For thirty-five years the Radical Party had stirred the Argentine middle and lower classes. About all it had achieved was to make them aware of the improved conditions they ought to enjoy—but without bringing these conditions about. By 1930 these prospects seemed farther out of reach than ever, and Yrigoyen's clique had dissipated the idealistic purposes so long associated with the party. In the face of such demoralization in a time of economic crisis, it was not difficult for energetic groups to act. General José Félix Uriburu, a former Radical turned Conservative, nephew of a onetime president, and admirer of

Italian Fascism, was the instrument of change in this instance. A few months of discreet negotiations, inspired student demonstrations and street riots, a rumor campaign exaggerating Yrigoyen's mental failings, and a well-briefed (and bribed) garrison were all that he needed. By the end of August 1930 President Yrigoyen realized the extent to which his administration had lost confidence, and he turned his office over to the vice-president. Had the conspirators been what they professed, this should have satisfied them. What they desired, however, was not merely a new president but full power for themselves. On September 6, Uriburu led his troops into the heart of official Buenos Aires and proclaimed himself provisional president of the republic. Only a few people were killed or injured. There was little visible evidence that the population objected to his action.

In many countries such an event might not have been particularly important. In Argentina it was: for the first time since 1860 a legitimate government had been overthrown by military action. The Argentine army, for seventy years the guarantor of lawful succession in the presidency, was itself the agency of revolution. It is always difficult to restore a tradition once it has been broken, and military leaders who have tasted political power are usually reluctant to return to a subordinate status. The democratic republic, imperfect as it was but still a creditable system, especially in Latin America, has been ever since only a dim ideal in the Argentine. It is the military which is sovereign. It has deposed presidents in 1930, 1943, 1944, 1955, and 1962; now it decides for itself whether or not to permit an administration to continue, and if so, on what terms. Thus, 1930 is a fateful turning point in the history of Argentina.

From the first a new atmosphere was apparent, an ugly one. It was symptomatic that former president Yrigoyen was treated with shameful lack of decency. Rioters stripped and desecrated his poor flat in Buenos Aires, where for years he had lived and intrigued. The old man was imprisoned first on a gunboat, then in the penitentiary on Martín García Island in the Plata. Finally freed to live in obscurity, he died a few months later, in 1933. The enormous popular outpouring for his funeral suggested that he was not as discredited as the revolutionists had proclaimed. Uriburu's soldiers roughed up and physically ejected thousands of Radical office-holders. No doubt many of them were rascals who deserved no better treatment. Yet the spirit behind these tactics was something new in Argentina as far as living memory went. Furthermore, army men were not yet prepared, psychologically or otherwise, to fill the major administrative posts. Their choices almost invariably fell upon members of the Conservative Party, which had been beaten regularly in free elections since 1912. The revolution, then, signified among other things the installation of the minority party by force.

President Uriburu had more in mind than a mere overhaul of the bureaucracy. As time went on he spoke with increasing confidence about organizing an altogether new regime to replace the republic of the constitution of 1853. What he delineated seemed more on the order of Fascism as exemplified by Benito Mussolini, a state in which a select minority would lead those intelligent enough to follow, and coerce the uncomprehending masses. That Uriburu was no friend of democracy was also made clear by the beatings of Radicals and Socialists by his troops, by censorship of all but the most prominent newspapers, such as *La Prensa* and *La Nación*, and by searches and arrests in violation of civil rights. Familiar as such activities were in many Latin American countries, they represented a reversion to times which most Argentines knew only from history books. Nor was Uriburu respectful of the electorate. He neglected to rig an election in Buenos Aires province in April 1931, with the result that the Radicals won handsomely. Without hesitation the provisional president intervened to reverse the decision, and precautions were taken to assure that future elections did not offend the regime.

Uriburu quickly became unpopular, even though the new officialdom was generally more effective than the ousted administration. Economic conditions improved in 1931 so that extreme measures had little justification. Furthermore, his acts of oppression and fascist utterances had antagonized large groups without winning over many others. Probably all this would have made little difference had Uriburu been clever enough to construct a machine among his own partisans in and out of the army and if he had been appealing enough to capture the masses. A general-president needed both popularity and an effective organization if he was to make a dictatorship palatable to a people so long accustomed to representative government. The lesson was there for those who could learn; one who did was Captain Juan Domingo Perón, who had participated in the uprising of 1930. At this point, however, the beneficiary of Uriburu's ineptitude was not Perón but General Agustín P. Justo, a powerful figure among the generals. Justo and some of his associates had already decided that Uriburu was likely to get into trouble sooner or later. One of Justo's supporters was minister of interior, a position that enabled him to establish control of the electoral machinery. Secretly and skillfully the conspirators undermined Uriburu, who awoke one day to realize that his removal was imminent and that it would doubtless be applauded by the people. Like the sports-loving army officer he was, he decided to put a good face on matters by leaving gracefully. He announced that elections would be held, a promise made at the beginning of the revolution but conveniently forgotten, and that he would not be a candidate. Uriburu was, in fact, not the man to revolutionize Argentina; he had only taken the lid off.

General Justo, as might be expected, won the nomination of the official party, a union of Conservatives and *anti-personalista* Radicals who now called themselves the National Democrats. The original *anti-personalista*, former president Marcelo Alvear, who had been president from 1922 to 1928, set out to rally the Radical Party, from which he had cut himself loose in 1924. He might have been a formidable candidate, for the Radicals were surely the most popular party, but the administration chose to observe at least one clause in the constitution of 1853, the one which stipulated that a president could not succeed himself until a full term of six years had elapsed. The only opposition to Agustín Justo, therefore, was that of Lisandro de la Torre, the Santa Fe populist who ran on the Democratic Progressive ticket with Socialist support. No one knows how the Argentine voters felt about the election, which went off on schedule in November 1931. Landlords collected the voting books of their workers and listed them for the National Democratic candidates. Known Radicals were not allowed to approach the polls, and the government counted the votes in any event. To the surprise of no one, General Justo was announced as the winner of an impressive mandate.

New Wine in Old Bottles: The Administration of Agustín P. Justo, 1932–1938

AGUSTÍN JUSTO's stewardship of the Argentine presidency can scarcely be characterized without many qualifications. It was prescient and blind, enlightened and retrograde; the man himself emerged with a fairly good reputation. For one thing, his administration was much less oppressive than that of Uriburu, and Argentines were soon enjoying again their familiar civil liberties. Only if they presumed to elect Radical candidates to local offices was the federal government likely to intervene, topple their chosen officials, and install National Democrats. While this practice was by no means unprecedented, it was all the more odious in view of the open secret that the Radicals were really the majority party. Besides, the provincials had long nurtured a mental image of Buenos Aires as an exploiter, a selfish giant that drew their products and their ablest young men and gave nothing in return but disdain and governmental tyranny. This situation, however, was an old story, nothing to make or break Justo's administration. It was obvious that the firm government he provided was effective but fell far short of the dictatorships that were flaunting themselves in so much of the world during the 1930's. Furthermore, Justo showed an unusually strong international spirit, in contrast to the blustering militarism so much in fashion then. And he broke the dictator's code in still another respect: when his term was up, he made no effort to prolong his rule.

In the last analysis the regime of President Justo may be judged as an attempt at restoration: the recovery of political authority by the old oligarchy of cattle barons, capitalistic wheat farmers, and their allies. As in the days before Yrigoyen's victory of 1916, this element tolerated democratic institutions so long as their power was not jeopardized. They were international-minded because their income largely derived from the sale of meat and grain to Europe and also because their own culture and habits were cosmopolitan. In fact, many of the upper classes were not patriotic Argentines at all. Aping the aristocracies of Europe as they did, they were frequently apologetic for the homeland which financed their way of life. For an interval between the depression and the war, a period coinciding with Justo's administration, this class obtained what it had always wanted, a moderately autocratic order and a continuation of the economic intimacy with Europe that had made it rich in the first place.

The chief dilemmas arose from the fact that their outlook no longer fitted the facts of life, and therefore the comparative serenity of the Justo years was based on false assumptions. Argentina was rapidly growing out of the phase in which she was a mere ranch and wheat farm operated for the benefit of Europe. During World War I she had begun to industrialize on a modest scale. The depression, which had lowered the prices of her own products faster than those of imported finished goods, had caused enterprising Argentines to manufacture many more articles for home consumption. These were usually humble consumer goods: shoes, hats, dresses, radios, furniture, household appliances, and toys. The important items of the Industrial Age—steel, coal, oil, automobiles, construction and farm machinery, and heavy equipment in general—all still came from abroad. A shift was taking place in this traffic, however, one scarcely detected for some years. This arose from the increasing preference for American goods that was becoming almost a mania.

Although the new currents were not generally understood until about 1940, the historic relationships of Argentina were changing all during the 'thirties. Industry was surpassing agriculture and livestock in value of production and crowding them in the utilization of human energies. Peons and cowboys were migrating to the cities to join the labor force. European immigrants were no longer flooding Buenos Aires, and thus the new working class was changing character. Industrialists began to elbow the landed aristocrats in places of luxury and in business. It was they who created the more capital, started new enterprises, and bought up urban real estate. Most difficult of all to classify was the ill-defined middle class which battened on the new industrialism and was developing more far-reaching objectives than Hipólito Yrigoyen had bequeathed them. Yet the Justo administration behaved as though conditions were unchanged since 1900, as though all Argentina needed to do was to please Europe, especially Great Britain, by shipping out raw materials and importing capital and finished goods.

Being no better endowed with the gift of prophecy than other mortals, Argentine statesmen failed to foresee that Britain would soon lose her world position but that Germany would not replace her, and that virulent nationalism would presently play itself out in Europe but flourish malignantly in Argentina. Therefore, they hastened to placate the British at all cost and disregarded Argentine chauvinism. The Ottawa conference of 1932, where the British Empire proclaimed a new policy of fomenting imperial trade at the expense of outsiders, greatly alarmed the rulers of Argentina, who saw their country losing its best market, England, to Australia, New Zealand, and Canada, who produced the same products Argentina did. Accordingly, they agreed to the Roca-Runciman Pact of 1933, by which England and Argentina promised to continue their prevailing volume of commerce. England would not reduce her purchases of chilled beef. Argentina would let British goods enter with very low duties, coal with none at all, and protect British interests with the utmost solicitude. While nationalists in both countries felt their own governments had conceded too much, the Argentines had a special grievance in alleging that England was trying to stifle their industrialization. In 1936, when the Roca-Runciman terms were renewed, another outcry revealed a threatening temper in Argentina.

Further ill will with the British arose from an inconclusive agitation about the Argentine railways, long the pride of the country and by far the best in South America. British capitalists and engineers had built about three-fourths of the network late in the nineteenth century, and British stockholders still owned a majority interest. Now they claimed they were not drawing adequate profits from their investments and demanded a revision of rates. The Argentine people well knew that the railroads had become decrepit through poor maintenance and that much of the equipment was old and unsafe. In the course of the discussions, which had no immediate result other than the exasperation of feelings, it became known that the value of railway stocks had been absurdly inflated from the earliest days, to the enrichment of politicians long since dead. President Justo in this one instance braved the disfavor of the British by refusing to ban automobile highways that might compete with the railways. Instead, he encouraged both road-building and commercial aviation. However, he capitulated to British investors who wanted to reorganize a company which owned the street railway system of Buenos Aires so as to obtain better profits. The tracks were bad and the cars ancient. It was the *porteño* lower classes who paid the price for the government's appeasement of the foreign stockholders. Their fares were higher and service remained as unsatisfactory as before. It was the same with the electrical plant of Buenos Aires, which British investors controlled through a Belgian dummy corporation. More scandalous yet was the government's needless and expensive renewal of a concession to a French company which had built the grain elevators and loading devices at the port of Rosario in 1902 and operated them with fantastic profits ever since. One common theme in this series of surrenders to alien investors, all of which caused noisy rows in congress and the press, was the strong possibility that government officials received pecuniary rewards for their actions. One public figure who said as much, Lisandro de la Torre, the Democratic Progressive leader from Santa Fe, finally despaired of exposing such corruption and took his own life in 1938. A few years later, when Argentine public opinion was raging against foreign exploitation, it was apparent that such incidents as these had been carefully noted and well remembered.

In other respects the Justo administration was more edifying. By trimming the expenses of the government the president restored fiscal stability to the country, and soon it was sharing the economic recovery that Europe experienced, though prices for Argentine exports remained rather depressed for some years. An income tax could be delayed no longer, as even the oligarchy realized, and Justo introduced this mixed blessing. He also increased inheritance taxes slightly, another affliction the wealthier classes bore with resignation unless they managed to escape it by incorporating entire families. Protective tariffs not in conflict with the Roca-Runciman Pact benefited certain Argentine manufacturers. President Justo showed more judgment than most of his contemporaries by being concerned about the deteriorating international situation. He led Argentina back into the League of Nations in 1932 after more than a decade of aloofness occasioned by Yrigoyen's petulance. Justo's foreign minister, Carlos Saavedra Lamas, was elected president of the League Assembly and was both effective and publicity-conscious in bringing to an end the terrible Chaco War between Paraguay and Bolivia. The award of the Nobel Peace Prize to this diplomat was an honor much appreciated in Argentina. Justo cordially joined with the United States at the Montevideo Conference of 1933 in advocating the lowering of trade barriers in exchange for American renunciation of intervention in Latin America. When the Inter-American Conference opened at Buenos Aires in 1936, Justo and the rest of the country gave a surprisingly warm reception to President Roosevelt, who sailed down for the occasion. During this gathering, an odd and fleeting moment when the American republics could seriously proclaim the western hemisphere an island of peace in a war-prone world, all was agreeability for most of the time. But then Argentina opposed a strong pact of neutrality to bind the New World which the Americans presented. If she was wise to reject this concept in 1936, which the United States itself repudiated three years later, she nonetheless aroused the undying animosity of Secretary of State Cordell Hull, who would have further dealings with her in the near future. Aside from being an uncommonly "Good Neighbor," especially for an Argentine, President Justo abolished visas for entrance into the republic and encouraged the re-writing of public school textbooks to remove chauvinistic excesses.

The Descent to Totalitarianism: Roberto M. Ortiz and Ramón S. Castillo, 1938–1943

IT WAS a grateful surprise to most observers that President Justo made no effort to alter the constitution and have himself reelected when, in November 1937, the time came for filling the next presidential term. He had no intention, however, of allowing the Radicals to recover the presidency. His choice fell upon the minister of interior, an overweight corporation lawyer named Roberto M. Ortiz. The vice-presidential candidate on the same ticket, the National Democratic, was the dean of the law school of the University of Buenos Aires, a well-known reactionary, Ramón S. Castillo. Opposing this team was former president Alvear, who ran as a Radical. The campaign was suspiciously calm and dull. Sure as they were that they were the majority and avid as they were for office, the Radicals generated little enthusiasm. With full confidence the National Democrats faced the polls and counted the votes, great numbers of which appeared to come from persons long dead. Despite much evidence of fraud, there seemed amazingly little indignation when the large victory of the administration candidates was announced. Perhaps, as the word circulated among journalists, a deal had been struck some time before. According to this theory, which events evidently vindicated, Ortiz had promised Alvear a return to representative democracy in exchange for an easy victory at the polls. However that may have been, Ortiz was inaugurated in February 1938 before the frigid glares of his countrymen; almost immediately he began to thaw their hearts by living up to his reputed bargain. Congress was permitted to convene and to carry out its constitutional duties, even though the lower house was Radical. Whenever there was evidence of fraud in provincial elections, the president exercised the intervention power firmly, as much so against his own partisans as the Radicals. Conservatives thought Ortiz a traitor. Radicals looked forward to future elections they were sure they would win. Everyone was free to indulge his views: Nazis with their strident newspaper, *El Pampero*; Communists, who suddenly began to act like Nazis after the Russo-German pact of August 1939; Anglo-French propagandists; Hispanists, those nostalgic conservatives who admired Franco Spain; strange pseudo-intellectuals who cultivated the memory of the gaucho tyrant Rosas; socialists, liberals, Trotskyites, and whatnot. From 1938 to 1940 Argentina, under President Ortiz, was a gloriously free country, and this at a time when Hitler was winning his greatest diplomatic and military victories.

World War II naturally dominated the atmosphere. No other country of equivalent importance, however, could afford to take so detached a view of that struggle as Argentina. There was no serious likelihood that any of the belligerents would molest the republic with armed force. No national minority was large enough to pose a danger save the Italian, which was so well assimilated and so unresponsive to Mussolini's promptings that subversion was not a real threat. All Argentina needed to do was sell her meat, hides, wool, and wheat to anyone who would come and fetch them. If Britain could do so, well and good. But German ships would be equally welcome, or Italian, or Japanese, or Vichy French. The outcome of the war could be regarded with equanimity. A Germanized Europe would desire Argentine products as much as a continent dominated by England and France. This essentially simple situation was complicated, however, by emotions and passions; it would be too much to add, by moral issues. The oligarchy remained pro-British to the core, as they had been in the other war. Yet many Argentines remembered the long years of British economic ascendancy with less warmth and were inclined to gloat over Britain's setbacks in 1939 and 1940. While the fall of France in June 1940 grieved the cultured classes, the Vichy regime appealed to many reactionaries. Argentina's army had a strong pro-German tradition which dated back to 1911, when German officers had arrived to advise the military establishment. Above all, the armed forces admired success, of which Nazi Germany appeared to have a monopoly until 1942. And then Argentines who resented England were likely to indulge their spite by parading pro-German sympathies. In all, the country was churning with undirected and contradictory currents. Since it was really aloof from the issue of the balance of power, expressions of ideologies or opinions tended to be superficial and confused.

Under such circumstances it made much difference who the president was. Ortiz was firmly opposed to the Axis, probably because he was associated with the oligarchy and, possibly, was sensitive to the threat of Hitlerism to human decency. In 1938, before the war began, he had taken the initiative at the Lima Inter-American Conference in obtaining a commitment that all the American republics would consult if emergencies arose—a not altogether meaningless covenant. At Panama in

1939 Argentina accepted with a cooperative spirit the arrangements to establish a safety-belt patrol around the Western hemisphere. In 1940 at Havana she agreed to the no-transfer principle regarding European possessions in the New World (with a reservation concerning her own right to occupy the Falkland Islands if Britain could no longer hold them). There was no reason to suppose that Argentina would depart from her course and become a concern instead of a comfort to Hitler's enemies. Fate, however, intervened just at the most desperate moment of the entire war, in July 1940. President Ortiz, obese and long a victim of diabetes, began to go blind. Unable to carry out his duties, he honorably turned over his office to Vice President Ramón S. Castillo. Two years later Ortiz resigned altogether, and soon thereafter he died.

Castillo was a frail, chilly, and withdrawn person, said to be the most unpopular academic official who had ever presided at the University of Buenos Aires. He immediately dismissed the Ortiz cabinet and installed a highly conservative group. Where Ortiz had intervened in provincial affairs only to correct fraud, Castillo at once reverted to the historic use of that prerogative, upsetting Radical governors and seating National Democrats. Censorship and repressive police measures of the type experienced under Uriburu in 1930–1931 again characterized the scene. The authorities protected pro-Axis groups, especially when they hounded Jews, liberals, and socialists. A pro-British group, *Acción Argentina*, whose program to renovate the country later was pillaged by Juan Perón, found itself hamstrung and abused by the government. German propaganda filled the air waves, newsstands, and motion picture houses, while British propaganda was muted. No one knew for sure whether Castillo was an isolationist as Yrigoyen had been in World War I, whether he expected, not too unreasonably, that Germany was going to win the war, or whether he was at heart a fascist. His murky public utterances and, more, his actions suggested this last possibility. Official and semi-official pronouncements from Buenos Aires jolted the anti-Axis world with their prophecies of a Hitlerian triumph and the unconcealed implication that such was desirable. Castillo proceeded to suspend part of the constitution to justify his punishment of anyone who criticized his foreign policy. Since the Radicals controlled the lower house of congress, he dismissed both houses and governed by decree. No one was immune from his repressive measures but *La Prensa* and *La Nación*, the famous Buenos Aires journals which were apparently too respected for him to intimidate.

Soon after the Japanese attacked the United States, Castillo revealed the extent of his commitment to the Axis cause. The Argentines, surprised like other people, generally felt a spontaneous sympathy for the Americans and a thrill of fear that the New World had been violated in even so remote an outpost as Pearl Harbor. Castillo made no statement that might comfort the United States. On the contrary, he ordered the troops in Buenos Aires to disrupt a mass demonstration in behalf of the Americans. And when the Inter-American Conference was gathering at Rio de Janeiro in January 1942, the Argentine acting president made a point of seeing some of the delegates who passed through his capital in the hope of persuading them not to go along with Yankee blandishments. The United States hoped to align all the American republics to speak with one voice before the world by having them agree unanimously to break relations with the Axis or to declare war. Argentina spoiled the dramatic psychological effect by refusing to join in such a declaration and by cooling the ardor of other states. Finally, the Americans had to settle for an innocuous statement to the effect that all of the republics would consider severing diplomatic ties with Axis nations. They also agreed, including Argentina, to curb the activities of Nazi spies and saboteurs on their soil.

If Castillo even considered the Rio proposals at all, he rejected them. He found many ways to irritate the United Nations and to hearten the Germans. Swarms of Axis agents operated in Argentina with a brazenness the Americans found hard to endure. A long "black list" of Axis firms was supposed to be respected by all of the American nations through boycotts. Castillo jeered at the compilers of the list and actually favored the businesses which had Axis connections. He would not permit ships that flew the Argentine flag, many of them confiscated Italian or French vessels seized legally under wartime arrangements, to sail with Allied convoys. If the beleaguered British wanted Argentine products, they would have to come and get them. When Brazil declared war late in 1942, a sputter of democratic sentiment in Argentina was manifest, only to be followed promptly by a fiercely nationalistic reaction in which Brazil was ridiculed for her Negroid character and her alleged subservience to the United States. Former president Agustín P. Justo, who was certainly no radiant liberal, showed his disapproval of Castillo's course by joining the Brazilian army. Castillo retaliated by intervening in Justo's stronghold, the state of Corrientes, and dislodging his supporters. In the Argentine army there was much heady talk about an eventual showdown with Brazil, who was belittled as a soft and mongrel country incapable of intelligent effort. The fury of nationalists in the Argentine army could not be contained when the United States proceeded to lavish great quantities of military hardware—airplanes, guns, tanks, jeeps, trucks, and ships—on Brazil, which was done with ostentation so as to compel the Argentines to see what they were missing and also to deter any adventures. Argentina's Axis friends could reach her only by means

of uncertain submarine voyages, and in any event they had less equipment to distribute to their admirers.

Even in the freest of countries it is often difficult to ascertain what
the population thinks. Argentine public opinion during World War II
was especially confused, misled, uninformed, and limited in expression.
Geographically remote from the fighting and indifferently affected by
the ideological issues, most Argentines may well have been neutral even
in thought. Furthermore, foreign critics have often commented on a
cruel strain in the Argentine mentality and a lack of humor or understanding. Perhaps these factors would account for the tendency of the
population to gloat over the defeats suffered by either side during the
war and to deny or minimize stories—or even proof—of atrocities. Germany's misdeeds could be matched by a passionate if somewhat unfair
analysis of Great Britain's imperialistic career and, of course, by the
barbarisms of Russian Communism. Supposed historic wrongs perpetrated by the United States were presented as crimes as bad as Hitler's. In
short, Argentine public opinion was unlikely to crystallize firmly in
favor of one side or the other, and the people tended to support their
government in whatever policy it followed. There is no reason to believe
that Castillo's pro-Axis course either pleased or offended the majority of
the population. In any case, he did not consult them.

Whatever World War II did to Argentina morally and politically, it
greatly helped her economically, at least after the initial dislocations.
Enough convoys got through to collect the great surpluses of livestock
and agricultural products, whose sale piled up great surpluses of another
type in London and New York, credit and gold. Since the war cut Argentina off from many consumer articles and more important items, industrialization surged even more to supply the domestic market. Factories,
and with them newly enriched capitalists and inflated labor forces,
sprang up in many cities, above all in Buenos Aires. This growing industrial plant required fuel, better transportation, and more power. Argentine governments, least of all Castillo's administration, were not in the
habit of thinking in such terms. Nor was it solicitous of the clamors of
enterprisers or the working classes, though both were stirred, for different reasons, by the promises implicit in national socialism. Castillo paid
them little mind. The president, as he became when Ortiz resigned in
June 1942, disregarded advice in domestic affairs as he did in foreign relations, indulging his prejudices without reference to public opinion. Of
all his mistakes, the most consequential was his neglect to consider the
fundamental change in Argentina's economic structure that World War
II hastened.

Castillo apparently thought the real sources of strength in the republic abided in the old cattle and wheat oligarchy. Actually, manufacturing and distribution had become more important than livestock and agriculture, but he was oblivious to the stirrings of the new forces as were his conservative official family. And yet he himself had demoralized the oligarchy by his anti-British policies. Bull-headedly pursuing his own predilections, he chose Robustiano Patrón Costas as his heir when the elections of November 1943 loomed. This selection flew in the face of many important groups. Patrón Costas was a highly reactionary member of the *Régimen* who had enriched himself as a sugar magnate in the far northern province of Salta. It was common knowledge that he had long and illegally imported Bolivian Indians to work as little more than slaves on his properties. Liberals and labor spokesmen found him abhorrent. Industrialists and the middle classes of the cities detected little in him to inspire enthusiasm. Also, Patrón Costas was outspokenly pro-Allied in his attitude toward the war. One may conjecture that President Castillo had, by 1943, guessed that the United Nations were going to win but that he was too obstinate to admit it himself. His successor, however, might carry the country along with the tide without losing face. As it happened, the Argentine army was not prepared for such a shift, for to the last it expected the Axis to triumph and perhaps has never understood why it failed. Thus Patrón Costas was offensive to those who resented the oligarchy for whatever reason and also to the military. In the face of the nation's sullen and contradictory attitudes, opportunity awaited those who would seize the initiative.

For the second time since the founding of the republic, the army struck. A widespread conspiracy within the inner circles of the army came to a head on June 4, 1943 and was carried out swiftly. President Castillo and his intimates fled to a minesweeper that sailed them to Uruguay, unmourned by the Argentines. Forces stationed near Buenos Aires moved into the governmental district and took over. General Arturo Rawson, the first to reach the Casa Rosada, there declared himself provisional president, a violation of the conspirators' scheme but justified in his own mind by his determination to bring Argentina into the camp of the United Nations. Within forty-eight hours the other generals concentrated in Buenos Aires and sent Rawson away, replacing him with General Pedro Ramírez. Jubilation had reigned in Buenos Aires as soon as it was known that the unpopular Castillo had departed; the provinces were somewhat more cautious in celebrating the revolution but gave no sign of regretting it. No one really knew what had happened, and the leaders themselves gave a queer impression of confusion. In the outside world the great powers hailed the ouster of Castillo, each expecting advantages. The Axis governments immediately recognized the new regime, probably having reason to believe it would favor them. A day

later so did Great Britain and the United States, and then the other republics of Latin America. Democratic leaders congratulated the Argentines and expressed the fervent hope that they had found their collective
soul. Perhaps they had, but it was a spirit the United Nations would soon
find very uncongenial.

Pedro Ramírez, Edelmiro Farrell, and the Colonels, 1943–1945

THE revolution of June 1943 was in the tradition of that of September 1930, but it was far more ominous. In the latter case, the middle-
class Radicals had been removed and the oligarchical regime had been
restored. After thirteen years this dying effort of the historic ruling
group collapsed, leaving the country, in Ysabel Fisk Rennie's excellent
summary, ". . . disunited, deeply cynical, without purpose or direction.
Its spiritual bankruptcy was as patent as its physical prosperity in the
war boom. . . . A nation, a society with all its values, was adrift on a
wide ocean, with no one to set the course and no one even to point a destination." And now, in June 1943, another revolution had installed the
military. Perversely acting as though the world would soon come under
Axis control, these leaders floundered and blundered as though they had
no real plan other than preparing Argentina to adjust to such an unlikely
situation.

Argentina was indeed a changing country, so much in flux that its
crucial power groups were difficult to identify. It looked as though the oligarchy might have ceased, at last, to be the group which provided national leadership, though the cattle and wheat barons were to continue to
enjoy their riches and social eminence. The large and expanding middle
class was vaguely loyal to the bankrupt ideals of the Radical Party, which
no longer functioned as a potent political organization. On the whole,
the Argentine bourgeoisie was inchoate, unstable, and lacking in leadership. It was well understood by now that the urban proletariat had become a massive force in society. Its nature had also changed in the past
decade, for the Italian and Spanish immigrants of the past, or their sons,
were repudiating Europe and becoming fanatically nationalistic Argentines. Many had risen in the social scale and were no longer to be classified as workingmen, their places in that category filled through auto-
immigration from Argentina itself. Former peons, tenant farmers, and
cow hands, many of whom had Indian blood, had been flocking into
Buenos Aires. While they did not comprehend alien radicalism the way
so many of the European immigrants had, they knew they were poor in
the midst of a sophisticated city where the rich inspired class hatred by

spending so extravagantly. Accustomed to obeying ranchers and planters, these rustic migrants formed a potential source of power for demagogues who knew how to exploit their grievances and to command.

The countryside was changing much more slowly than Buenos Aires, which was still regarded as a vampire. Herdsmen in Chubut and Patagonia lived almost as primitively as Indians. Livestock tenders on the great ranches of the pampas were poorly paid and arrogantly treated. In the grain regions northwest of Buenos Aires countless thousands of farm workers moved in misery from field to field, living little better than European peasants of a century before. Those who owned or rented small patches of the rich Argentine earth were likely to be hungry, ill-housed, and barefooted. Conditions were even worse in the *yerba* groves of the damp, semi-tropical northeast and in the spacious sugar cane fields of Tucumán, and worst of all in the arid northwest of the Andean piedmont. While the prevading latifundia had produced a glittering upper class to grace Buenos Aires and the resorts of Europe, it had left the rural population unhealthy, undernourished, and destitute. The only escape from such poverty was to move to the city, which increasing numbers did, only to encounter slums, low wages, and harsh working conditions. Contact with Buenos Aires, as well as the radio and the motion picture, served to inform the Argentine masses that a better share of modern civilization might be theirs. But who was to translate this dream into reality? There were few who pointed the way.

If Argentina's fundamental problems stemmed from an unhealthy social imbalance, the generals who seized power in June 1943 showed little indication of recognizing it. Instead, as noted, they acted as though the principal task of the nation was to prepare itself for a Hitlerian world, an eventuality which every war bulletin made more remote. Liberals, socialists, Communists, and Jews were subjected to persecution, perhaps a thousand or more being sent to concentration camps in Patagonia and Tierra del Fuego. Many of them had guilelessly come out in the open to celebrate the fall of Castillo and the presumed end of the fascist threat, only to learn that democratic ways were not yet in fashion. The intervention power, which Argentine presidents had always used with reference to provincial governments, was now brandished at universities, labor unions, and corporate bodies of other types. When students and professors protested, they were likely to be subjected to physical violence and ejected from institutions of learning. While labor organizers were not accustomed to government benignity in recent years, they now found little warmth except from Juan Perón. It seemed that the only beneficiaries of the Ramírez regime were the officers of the armed services, who moved into important government posts and even into executive positions in businesses which dealt with the state. And the appropriations for the military rose dizzily, from a quarter of the national budget to half the total within a year. The much-acclaimed revolution of 1943 appeared to signify only the exaltation of the officerhood with nothing, not even promises, for the civilian population. Lieutenant Colonel Juan Perón, an influential figure in the regime, astutely assessed the weaknesses of the Ramírez government, dreaming how much could be accomplished if the army's strength could be combined with mass popularity.

In foreign affairs the Ramírez administration mocked the United Nations about as boldly as Castillo had. This did not interfere with business, however, for Britain was half-starved for meat and flour and could buy them at high prices. German agents moved about freely, and Nazi propaganda was still very strident. The surrender of Italy during the summer of 1943 and other Axis setbacks inluced a slight change of mood. In September the foreign minister proposed that the United States send equipment to Argentina in order to redress the balance of power upset by American arming of Brazil. In return, Argentina promised to honor the commitments she had made at Rio in 1942 regarding Nazi saboteurs. It would be unchivalrous, however, for Argentina to employ these armaments against Germany now that she was on the defensive. Secretary Hull's refusal was so wrathful and sarcastic that the hapless foreign minister was dismissed, not because the regime was going to change its policies, but because he had exposed his country to such a re-buke. Soon afterward, reckless threats in Buenos Aires about a thrust toward democratic Uruguay caused the United States to send a fleet to Montevideo. And then Britain began to drop hints that she might do without Argentine products. In January 1944 the United States inti-mated that Argentina's large reserves in New York might be frozen un-less her government behaved better. Probably it was this possibility that caused Ramírez to announce the severance of diplomatic relations with Germany and Japan. This mild measure, which did not retard the activi-ties of Axis spies and propagandists, was too much for a dynamic group in the military known as "the colonels." A bloodless coup late in Febru-ary removed Ramírez from the government. General Edelmiro Farrell took his place as president.

Although he served as president of the republic for more than two years, Farrell made little impression on Argentina or the outside world. He was scarcely more than the front man for a secret military lodge of a type not unfamiliar in Latin American history. Known as the GOU, *Grupo de oficiales unidos* (United Officers' Group), with a motto with the same initials, *Gobierno, orden, unidad* (Government, order, unity), the society acquired an ascendancy within the army and pulled wires that manipulated much of the government. Though most of its leaders were generals by February 1944, they had been colonels at the time of the

June 1943 coup, and journalists persisted in calling them "the colonels." It was not long until the most influential among them was identified: Juan Domingo Perón, who became vice-president of the republic and minister of war under Farrell. Perón was soon the most publicized spokesman of the regime in domestic affairs. He was also heard in foreign affairs, in which area he enunciated the weird idealism of the GOU. For example, just after the Normandy invasion in June 1944 he stated that Argentina was indifferent to the outcome of the war. She would attain her great destinies through her own might and special brand of totalitarianism. Secretary Hull, whose distaste for Argentine individualism had mounted steadily since 1936, could contain himself no longer, and he replied to Perón's bluster with a number of threats designed to compel Argentina to live up to her commitments under the Rio declaration of 1942. It was to no avail. Argentine public opinion rallied behind the Farrell-Perón position while other Latin Americans secretly, more or less, applauded this defiance of *Tío Sam*. International courtesy reached a new low, at least for recent times in the Americas, as Washington and Buenos Aires exchanged criticisms, the former always being careful to cloak its condemnations as Inter-American and United Nations sentiments. Argentina did not receive an invitation to participate in the Chapultepec Conference of February 1945, where the American republics planned their role in the United Nations Organization soon to be established. In March, however, a *détente* occurred. It was clear that the Axis was on its last legs, and Secretary Hull had resigned for reasons of health. Argentina declared a "state of tension" with the Reich, and the United States recognized the Farrell regime by sending an ambassador to Buenos Aires. This personage, Spruille Braden, was studiously cool to the Argentine government but made a great point of encouraging its opponents, particularly the cowed Radicals. Finally, on March 27, Argentina declared war on Germany and Japan, tardily, reluctantly, and for the cynical purpose of qualifying for admission to the United Nations.

THE RISE OF
JUAN DOMINGO PERÓN

Perón's conspicuous activities from the first days of the Farrell administration caused him to be regarded, correctly for the most part, as the real power of that regime. Born in 1895 in the southern part of Buenos Aires province, he was of mixed Spanish and Italian ancestry and middle class. After spending his childhood in the ranch country, he moved to Buenos Aires with his parents. His academic and athletic abilities won him entrance into the national military college, where he prepared for a career in the army. An intelligent and industrious officer, respected as a fencing champion, a man's man, and something of a scholar, he none-theless crept up slowly in a service where considerations of pedigree fa-vored the landed aristocracy. In 1930, when he participated in Uriburu's rebellion against President Yrigoyen, Perón was a captain. During the following six years he moved up two grades. He taught at the war college for some time, becoming a respectable historian and author. Then he served two years in Chile as a military attaché, his tour of duty being cut short, or so it has been said, by accusations on the part of his hosts that he was engaging in espionage. In 1939 he went on a mission to Italy to train with the magnificent army that Mussolini claimed would soon astonish the world. During the next two years Perón traveled over several countries in Europe, read, observed, and pondered. He became conscious of a historic destiny reserved for himself, a Napoleonic star. He was vain enough to believe that he could copy the successful methods of the great dictators—Mussolini's perfidy, Hitler's technique with threats, and Franco's feline relentlessness—without making their mistakes. A tour of Spain soon after the end of the civil war filled him with a determination that such a struggle must be avoided at all cost in his own country. His ends must be gained, but gained less ruinously. When he went home in 1941, Perón was aglow with dreams to capture Argentina's government and to transform the nation into a worthy partner of Nazi Germany, Fas-cist Italy, and Nationalist Spain.

In only three years he rose to the top. His personality had much to do with his success. Perón was an extrovert with extraordinary magne-tism; he was very persuasive—or frightening. A big man, athletic, mascu-line, and handsome, he conformed to the Argentine ideal of a hero. A hypnotic speaker like Hitler, he could inspire, console, and enrage vast crowds as he pleased. In one speech he could personify tenderness and seem a sincere humanitarian; in another a few minutes after, he would be a bloodthirsty terror. In short, he was a marvelous actor, as so many suc-cessful politicians have to be. Perón was no ignoramus. He was thought-ful and very well-read; when he cared to, he could impress a discriminat-ing audience. Yet he fraternized casually with enlisted men, rustics, and unlettered workers as a good fellow who shared their attitudes and under-stood their problems. Apparently he had no moral sense whatever.

This close student of Mussolini had understood far better than his associates how important it was to complement naked military power with popular support. This meant, in fact, organizing the poor and igno-rant through blatant appeals to envy and class hatred, through dema-goguery and vulgarity. Such methods might be repugnant to the colo-nels as a group, for they were socially close enough to the upper classes to have snobbish attitudes and, indeed, to be inhibited by civilized re-straints. Perón had no hesitancy whatever in exploiting these means, and while he was certainly not the first demagogue to appear in Argentina, he gauged the aspirations of the masses better than any other. His real opportunity came during the eight-month administration of President Ramírez. Perón won two positions, neither of first importance; he was undersecretary of war and head of the department of labor. The former enabled him to learn what he needed to know about the officerhood and to manipulate appointments and promotions so as to strengthen his position as the nerve center of the GOU. The second post, which might have been an honorific affair, a mere sinecure, he elevated to cabinet rank within a few months. Despite his scanty experience with labor unions or industrial affairs, Perón learned quickly. Labor unions, which had been intimidated so long by the government and were still belittled by Ramírez, learned that the new minister was eager to cultivate them. If the leaders did his bidding, they were likely to obtain excellent terms in disputes with employers. A rash of unionization, long overdue in Argentina, garnered hundreds of thousands of workingmen into organizations controlled by Perón's creatures. The minister himself seldom failed to exploit an opportunity to associate his name with a settlement favorable to labor or with promises of new benefits.

The installation of General Farrell as president early in 1944 placed Perón near the front of the government. As vice-president, minister of war, and minister of labor and social security, he enjoyed even more advantages than before. While his power over the top army commanders was by no means total—in fact, this was never to be, even at his height—it was sufficient to assure him immense importance. A story much in circulation that might have been true, and was certainly in character, was that Perón would not assign or promote an officer until he wrote out in his own hand a letter of resignation—which Perón could date and publish at his pleasure. Another technique, which he may have copied from Cárdenas of Mexico, was to stimulate the loyalty of junior officers and enlisted men to himself by paying them personal attention and providing them with better pay and conditions. In a showdown between the war minister and their immediate commanders they might well side with Perón or at least inhibit ambitious generals. There were several occasions during the next eleven years in which this method served Perón well, since generals were not always sure of their troops. Of course, the considerable benefits won by the lower ranks of the army might not have been entirely attributable to Perón's craftiness. He may have had some humanity.

Even more revolutionary than Perón's attachment of the army were his efforts to win working class support. Within a few years he raised the proportion of unionized labor from one-tenth to two-thirds of the working force. The leaders of these unions were seldom the original organizers of years past, for Perón made a clean sweep of the old hierarchy. Usually they were men he chose and felt he could manage through office and bribery, even blackmail. They professed fervent loyalty to him if they wished to remain in their posts, which tended to be very lucrative. Social security benefits were extended to almost every type of workingman, white-collared or overalled. Even the forgotten rural proletariat fell into Perón's power by means of agricultural unions which he sponsored. It was both a slow and a difficult process to unionize certain regions, where the company store and private police discouraged organizers, but it made considerable headway. Copying the Brown Shirts of Hitler and the Black Shirts of Mussolini, those extra-legal policemen and militiamen who served the official parties, Perón developed an organization of the *descamisados* (shirtless), who really had upper garments but not the white shirts worn by men of affairs. Thousands of young men, many of them rowdies from the poorer districts, notably La Boca in Buenos Aires, were trained into experts at beating up opponents, looting shops or factories, and otherwise terrifying gentlefolk. Reminiscent of Rosas' *mazorca* gangs of a century before, the *descamisados* well knew the signals by which Perón could fill the Plaza de Mayo in front of the Casa Rosada within a few minutes with shouting enthusiasts or set armed mobs surging through the fashionable sections of Buenos Aires. Even regular army troops feared them. Finally, Perón used his position to grant holidays, wage increases, and bonuses to labor simply by announcing these benefits whenever he thought he needed the publicity. Employers had to pay or see their businesses smashed, in many cases literally. The Argentine workingman was no longer an orphan. He had a friend and leader who had delivered material benefits and endowed them with status and power. Who cared if his methods were arbitrary?

Perón's political genius and his good fortune enabled him by mid-1945 to contemplate taking over full authority in the republic. While he scoffed at the idea of running for president, saying it was "impossible" that he would ever seek the office, every indication pointed to this ambition. Conditions seemed ripe, though the army gave him some cause for uneasiness at this time. Labor fairly idolized him and apparently had forgotten the older politicians. The rural masses seemed to be deserting the Radical and Democratic Progressive parties which had held their allegiance so long. And as a defiant champion of Argentine nationalism, Perón appealed to miscellaneous groups everywhere who yearned for new values. Still, much of Perón's program ran counter to world opinion. The outcome of World War II suggested that Argentina's foreign policy for the past five years had been madness. Intellectuals gathered enough courage to denounce Perón as a would-be Hitler. Ambassador Braden's encouragement to the opposition had done something to revive the old parties. In most of the world the mood of 1945 was restlessly democratic, as was natural at the close of a long war, and Argentina shared some of this attitude. And too, the country had an accumulation of irritations arising from the war: inflation, shortages of consumer goods, and decrepitude of machines too long used. During September and early October a number of demonstrations in Buenos Aires showed the popular temper to be nervous and critical. Misled into believing that Perón was going out of fashion like the other fascists, a group of army and navy officers concocted a plot to remove him. On October 9 a garrison near the capital pronounced and compelled him to resign. Just before he signed away his power, however, the wily vice-president decreed another general wage increase and a paid holiday for October 12, a day celebrated more for the glorification of the Spanish "race" than for the Italian who discovered America. Then he was taken to the penitentiary on Martín García island. It seemed a ridiculous end for so promising a career.

The conspirators allowed General Edelmiro Farrell to remain as president, for he was a pliable nonentity. They undid much of Perón's work, including the cancellation of the paid holiday for October 12, a disastrous mistake. A false spring of revival swept through the country, heartening to liberals and democrats who rejoiced over Argentina's narrow escape from totalitarianism. As in previous coups of this type in 1930 and 1943, the new ruling clique was not exactly sure what was to be done next. None of its members was an outstanding figure. While they hesitated, others acted. Perón's most loyal lieutenants accurately assessed the situation as not lost beyond recovery. Summoning the *descamisados,* they found these street fighters still obedient and capable of arousing the rest of the working class. For several days huge mobs stalked through the splendid avenues of Buenos Aires, all the more ominous because they were subdued in manner. Gradually they began to assert themselves more forcefully, chanting slogans and roughing up opulent or intellectual persons. An important contribution to their morale came from Perón's mistress, a minor actress and radio singer named Eva Duarte. This strident beauty proved herself as effective a demagogue as her lover. As isolated acts of violence took on a pattern suggesting proletarian revolution, the generals nervously calculated the chances of pitting the troops against the grim popular mass. Soon they decided it was too risky. On October 17 the movement reached a crescendo of wrath when untold thousands gathered in the Plaza de Mayo shouting "Give us our leader back." A reign of terror seemed imminent. For once, the only time, President Farrell asserted himself and dismissed the new government. Perón returned to the balcony of the Casa Rosada to thank his followers, a hero restored to his people by popular demand. From that fateful evening on October 17, 1945 to the summer of 1955 no one could doubt that Juan Perón was the ruler of Argentina.

It was now in order for him to become president of the republic. Elections were called for February 1946 with the army, which was still independent of Perón, pledging its honor to see that they would be conducted properly. Perón collected his various blocs of supporters in an organization he named the Labor Party. The Radicals attempted to rally their scattered members and to put together a massive coalition including the Progressive Democrats, Socialists, and Communists. They named as their candidate José Tamborini, an estimable man who was greatly handicapped by the unfamiliarity of his name and a colorless personality, from neither of which Perón suffered. Perón enjoyed every advantage in fame, political appeal, and dynamism. He particularly exploited the fervant patriotism which second-generation Argentines were now displaying. Britain, the historic embodiment of imperialism, he defied with a passion that appealed to many Argentines. The United States, which had so long been an object of envy and dislike, was an even more convenient bugbear. Although Braden had gone home some months before, Perón shouted up and down the country that the voters must choose between "*Braden o Perón*," a slogan chalked on many walls. Hoping to discredit Perón, the United States issued a Blue Book which was designed to prove beyond doubt that recent Argentine governments had shamelessly cooperated with the Axis. Instead, it offended more Argentines than it converted, turning more voters to Perón as a patriot. The most influential clergymen favored Perón; a pastoral letter read in every church instructed the faithful to vote against his opponent. While the campaign was open, Tamborini had a difficult task to establish himself as a man of stature and patriotism. The election was also free, as every qualified observer, foreign and domestic, agreed. Perón won a huge electoral majority and carried his followers into control of both houses of congress and into most of the provincial posts. His popular plurality was less impressive, 1,500,000 to 1,200,000, but quite substantial.

Juan Domingo Perón as President-Dictator

NOTHING in Perón's previous career suggested that his electoral victory might induce him to govern constitutionality, as well he might have. The defeat of fascism in Europe meant to him only that he must avoid the tactical errors of Hitler and Mussolini, not renounce their perverted philosophies. His regime, officially inaugurated on June 4, 1946, therefore contained few surprises. From the outset it was clear that the president was everything, the other branches of the national government and the local organisms having no independent power whatever. Congress remained obedient because most of its members were Peronists and could be disciplined through his political machine. This organization, after considering several jaw-breaking names, sensibly decided to call itself the *Peronista* Party. Membership was restricted, as in the case of the Communists in Soviet republics or the late Nazi and Fascist parties, and made a privilege which opened the way to political and financial favors for the faithful. Congressmen who were not *Peronistas* were intimidated, expelled, and frequently imprisoned under a law punishing *desacato* (disrespect), which could be interpreted to include sharp questioning or any type of criticism even on the floor of the legislative body. Perón also crushed the judiciary, which had enjoyed considerable prestige for its probity and an independence unique in Latin America. He had four of the five supreme court justices impeached and ousted on spurious grounds. Other federal judges were simply turned out wholesale by the device of having congress refuse to confirm their positions. The replacements for these jurists were, of course, reliable party men. Finally, all officialdom was "purfied"; state or local rulers were dislodged by means of the familiar right of intervention unless they were ardent *Peronistas*.

Re-staffing the administration from top to bottom was a conventional practice, even in democratic countries. To control the officers of government through a party dictatorship was less customary, though Yrigoyen and the Radicals had gone almost as far as Perón in earlier days. However, Perón utilized many refinements which almost extinguished the republican spirit and the democratic tradition. His informal militia, the *descamisados*, were most useful in breaking the heads and shattering the offices and shops of men suspected of being opponents. A critic of Perón might at any time lose his health, dignity, livelihood, or freedom at the hands of these hoodlums, whom the police never chastised. The secret police conducted searches, pilfered the mails, and made arrests without regard for the niceties of civil liberties. As time went on, members of the upper classes and the intelligentsia wryly took pride in the number of times they had been jailed. Torture was a common practice in police stations. Argentines learned to look over their shoulders before they spoke, to expect invasions of their homes and offices, and to inform foreign visitors in a special language of the doings of some character known as John Sunday (Juan Domingo—Perón). Argentina's excellent press and her great publishing establishment, in both cases the finest in Latin America, had learned something of censorship since 1930. Now they acquired much more familiarity with this practice. An impertinent editorial for an inconvenient news story might be followed by a strike, a sharp rise in the tax rate, the arrest or beating of the offending writer, a curious unobtainability of paper or ink, or one of the dreaded "spontaneous" incursions of *descamisado* gangs who would wreck the premises. Managers of publishing houses learned what not to print, and book dealers what not to display, if they wished to remain in business. Only *La Prensa* and *La Nación* seemed safe from the worst pressures, and they were cautious.

Among the most stubborn of Perón's critics were university faculty members and students. Already they had suffered considerably under President Castillo and the colonels prior to 1946. Now they were thoroughly beaten down. Nine-tenths of the faculty in the six universities lost their positions. Students were expelled by the hundreds, their limited rights to self-government under the reform of 1918 being flouted with contempt. Perón showed no mercy in denying outspoken students their degrees, which often meant they could never enter the professions for which they had trained. Students also learned that hoodlum mobs were available to break their bodies any time a public meeting or demonstration took on an anti-Perón character. Meanwhile, Perón spoke glowingly about destroying the aristocratic university system and replacing it with one more "democratic," where vocational training would supplant the historic disciplines and there would be no fees. Fortunately, he never gave this matter persistent attention. It was easier to revamp the public school system so that textbooks and courses would glorify the regime. While Perón crippled and debauched Argentina's fine educational establishment, it was sturdy enough to survive him.

Perón was probably sincere in maintaining that his system was original, eclectic, and truly adapted to Latin American conditions in a way no other had ever been. The name he attempted to affix to this system was Justicialism, which, perhaps mercifully, was never made very specific or even coherent as a doctrine. It would not do for so great an innovator as himself to stand in history merely as another Argentine president under the constitution of 1853. A new basic charter must embody Justicialism. After much fanfare he assembled a constituent congress in 1948. Its product, the constitution of 1949, outwardly had much in common with the instrument of 1853, though Argentina was now a very different country from the truncated Confederation of the days of Urquiza and Alberdi. Nominally, it maintained the federal system, along with the separation of powers and civil liberties. Women were allowed to vote for the first time in Argentina's history. Presidents were to be chosen by direct election and could succeed themselves (Perón laughingly let this provision slip through; he affected to have no interest in the matter). A list of "rights" for the aged indicated the warm humanitarianism that supposedly suffused his philosophy. Another bill of rights for labor included every demand the working classes could think of except the right to strike. There were kind words for children. Also, wide and vaguely defined powers were entrusted to the national government in matters of economic affairs, foreign trade, and ownership of minerals and public services. As a document the constitution of 1949 did not depart radically from the windy and misleading charters of other Latin American countries. But it was a sad bit of cynicism for Argentina, a republic which had for so long made progress in living up to her political ideals.

Perón's economic program deserves a variety of contradictory judgments: insane, patriotic, unrealistic, pragmatic, magnificently conceived, sinister, disastrous, amazingly successful, and so on. No epigrammatic assessment really fits, for Justicialism was all of those things in the economic area, and more. Experts abroad became convinced that Perón was bent on destroying his country's prosperity as though he were a captive of a suicidal mania. Yet he repeatedly surmounted crises and confounded his critics. His policies were so daring as to be irresponsible, and they were carried out amid extreme corruption and degrading misrepresentation. They came close to ruining agriculture and the stock-raising industry. Yet when Peronism was a thing of the past, it could be fairly said that Argentina had strengthened and diversified much of her economy, that standards of living had improved, and that her people were devoted to the new ways. It should not be overlooked, however, that nearly every country made giant strides in the decade after World War II, and that Argentina might have progressed much faster under a less erratic government.

Some glimmer of consistency emerges from Peronism when Argentina is seen as undergoing a rampage of nationalism like that of Mexico during the 1930's, or belatedly participating in a world-wide revulsion against imperialism. Since nationalism is largely non-rational, the warnings of economists and bankers had little relevance in the fevered atmosphere stimulated by Perón. Basically, the Argentines wanted to terminate their material dependence on Britain without substituting for it a new semi-colonialism under the United States, West Germany, or the Soviet Union. Perón understood this longing and turned it to his own advantage. British markets and good will he cast away with a frivolity that appalled sober students but delighted the masses. Americans were defied and insulted, always a popular activity for an Argentine public figure, but Britain was the initial enemy. Just before World War II it was known that alien investors held more than two billion dollars worth of Argentine property, in railroads, public utilities, street railways, packing plants, and land. British owners accounted for about three-fourths of this total. For the time being, during the years of austerity following the war, the British still urgently needed Argentine meat, wheat, and wool. Therefore, Perón deemed it safe to strike at this long-time partner who now

seemed an exploiter. In doing so he was also hurting the landed aristocracy, the "hierarchy" he abused with such vulgarity in his speeches, the
fashionable and cultured classes who despised him as an upstart or madman.

On July 9, 1947, the anniversary of Argentina's declaration of independence from Spain in 1816, Juan Perón stood in the very room in the
city of Tucumán where this announcement had been made and proclaimed the economic independence of the republic. An officially-
inspired campaign of Anglophobia and bald threats by the dictator
readily brought the British Labor Government to terms. An agreement
in 1948 resulted in the exchange of most of Argentina's railways for about
$600,000,000 in credits and food products. It was a proud moment for
the Argentines when their government took possession of the transportation system, and they looked forward to enjoying better service and
equipment. As for the British, they had not survived and prospered over
the centuries for nothing. They were really pleased to be rid of this huge
investment, which was exposed to confiscation and was not any longer
very profitable. It later developed that they had obtained a much more
equitable bargain than contemporaries thought, perhaps had even gotten the better of Perón's negotiators! Heady with what he boasted was a
great success, Perón proceeded to purchase nearly all the foreign-held
utilities. By 1948 the national government owned practically all the
banks, insurance companies, means of communication and transportation, ports and elevators, and public service installations. Whether it operated them well or ill, most Argentines felt a gratification difficult for
foreigners to appreciate. Their country was no longer in any sense a
colony.

Perón exhibited a certain degree of statesmanship in making a mammoth effort to industrialize Argentina, something that had been going
on for some years without much official encouragement or even understanding. His underlying design was for the republic to convert her
economy so as to favor capitalists and labor and to strengthen the middle
classes by building up the domestic market. If his program succeeded,
Argentina would have a much higher standard of living and would be
dependent on no outsider. The decline of the cattle barons and wheat
lords he could accept with satisfaction. The creation of a large industrial
establishment necessarily involved importing capital goods abroad,
mainly heavy equipment from the United States. For several years an
enormous volume of these imports could be financed with the credit
and gold reserves accumulated during the war and just after. The
reserves were huge, for Argentina had charged unmercifully for her
products during the war and the period of hardship following. It is to

Perón's credit that he expended these funds wisely, not squandering them on luxuries as Brazil and a few other countries did, and on the whole the purchases had the effects he intended.

It was also important to acquire means of fueling the industrial plant he was constructing. Coal from Wales, Chile, and the Ruhr, and petroleum from Venezuela or the Middle East cost heavily in foreign exchange and would become more expensive as Argentina's requirements grew. For the first time scientific surveys were made of the Andes, whose resources had long been neglected, and enough coal and minerals were found to reduce Argentine dependence on outsiders. Oil had long refused to appear in the republic, but the national monopoly, YPF, increased its efforts and discovered substantial pools in Chubut, the windswept southern province, Salta in the extreme northwest, and the tropical Argentine Chaco (renamed Presidente Perón). At least the country could look forward with some reason to supplying a considerable share of its own fuel. With reference to electric power, all that was needed to supply all the nation could use was effort, and this was forthcoming on a heroic scale. A very expensive but well-planned program accomplished wonders in harnessing power from the streams that sprang out of the Andes. The mighty Iguasú Falls in the northeast awaited utilization, which the government began to project. To be sure, Buenos Aires grew so fast she periodically outran her electrical power resources. Streets were often dark, factories were hampered, and apartment dwellers had to walk up the stairs when elevators balked for lack of current. A sense of patriotic sacrifice, much stimulated by officialdom and the press, helped to compensate for these inconveniences.

Since all of these projects were expensive, the administration developed an agency to handle the export of raw materials and the importation of capital goods and other finished products. A mammoth monopoly known as IAPI, *Instituto Argentino para la promoción del intercambio* (Argentine Institute for the Promotion of Exchange) bought up beef, wheat, and other raw materials, stored them, and exchanged them for such foreign goods or credits as the authorities could arrange. This nationalization of exports failed to function as efficiently as Perón promised. IAPI often paid lower prices to ranchers and farmers, who were orphans under the regime in any event, than foreign concerns once had; yet it sold their products abroad at exceedingly high rates. The explanation of the discrepancy was the venality of the officials who managed IAPI, who had added a new dimension to the corruption that Argentines had long learned to expect from their public servants. In the long run IAPI defeated the purpose for which it was supposedly created. Argentine agriculture and stockraising suffered and declined, while foreign customers stopped buying from IAPI as soon as other suppliers made themselves available.

By 1949 Perón's program was in deep trouble. Europe was no longer compelled to buy Argentina's products at blackmail prices, and the Marshall Plan benefited American food exporters at the expense of Argentine. And Nature frowned on the southern republic at this time by inflicting a terrible drought on the pampas, causing the failure of crops and the diminution of herds. With her exports falling off disastrously and her wartime credits almost exhausted, Argentina was hard-pressed to finance her industrialization program. Perón professed to be unworried. Credit, he said, was only a state of mind and economists were short-sighted. He boasted that Argentina would never again accept a loan from abroad. In 1950, however, he was greatly relieved when the United States saw to it that the Export-Import bank granted a loan (though it was not called this, in view of Perón's sensitivities) of $125,000,000. This advance and the sharp rise in prices occasioned by the Korean War staved off a financial collapse, and Argentina creaked along miraculously for several more years. Bankruptcy was ever close, however, and inflation, which plagued almost the entire globe, refused to obey the president's orders to cease and desist. The cost of living overtook the enormous wage increases Perón had decreed, leaving the working classes little better off. He made desperate efforts to halt the rise in prices and to enlist the public's cooperation in several imaginative campaigns for this end. Yet the financial precariousness of his regime defeated even the most sincere anti-inflation measures. It was doubtful whether the factories being constructed everywhere, the dams, power plants, and public works would be finished before the nation's economy went to pieces.

Nothing whatever had been done about dividing the great ranches and farmlands except in a few cases when Perón nationalized the estates of his personal enemies. This was not because he wished to favor the "hierarchy," but because the experience of Mexico and other countries had indicated a certain economic unwisdom in breaking up large rural units. Nor was Argentina yet able to do without the income, shrinking though it was, that meat and flour exports brought her, and which would surely have declined further had the land been distributed. Perón could point to many achievements, however, in other directions. Nearly every section of the republic had taken life. Everywhere buildings were going up, testimony not only of urban industrialization but also of a provincial revival. Foresty and mining in the Andean areas had become important industries with promise of much future growth. Ocean fishing was no longer neglected, little as Argentines were inclined to substitute fish for beef. The republic was now the possessor of a large merchant marine, purchased abroad, which Perón said would make her forever independent of foreign shippers. However shaky the economy appeared to bankers and creditors, electrification, new sources of fuel, and the largest industrial establishment in South America were realities. Argentina's human resources had also grown faster than most demographers imagined and had done so recently without much immigration. Her population stood at 18,000,000 by the end of Perón's rule, twelve times its size a century before. No one could doubt that the nation was tapping its riches with some effectiveness. Men had long admired Argentina as an economic wonder. After a decade of Perón they regarded her as a miracle, for she developed so rapidly under such an erratic government.

Early in his career Napoleon Bonaparte said that the French people cared little for liberty: equality was what they craved. Juan Domingo Perón applied this cynical thought to the Argentines. Freedom he degraded in nearly every way, but egalitarianism flourished until the masses idolized Perón as *El Líder* (the leader), their unique benefactor. He brought them unionization, higher wages, paid vacations, shorter working hours, dignity, status, free medical care, improved housing, and safeguards against accident, illness, and old age. Even the rural workers shared these benefits, to which they responded in the usual twentieth-century way by departing from the countryside and moving in droves to the cities. Of course, many criticisms of Perón's achievements were valid: that he had done little but insult and threaten the oligarchy, who were still rich; that his agglomeration of labor unions, the *Confederación general de trabajo*, was honeycombed with tyrannical and grafting officials; that inflation consumed most of the wage increases; that the *descamisado* gangs gave the whole lower class a totalitarian tradition that would long linger. These disagreeable points, however, could not and did not obscure the enormous gains Perón had delivered to the workingmen of Argentina, especially since the official propaganda apparatus dinned the benefits in their ears.

Eva Duarte Perón

PERÓN's social policies cannot be separated from the astounding career of Eva Duarte Perón. Of illegitimate birth in a provincial town in 1919, she had gone to Buenos Aires as a young woman to become an actress. Her success in this capacity was very modest. She had a few minor parts on the stage but found a better livelihood by singing in cabarets and on the radio. Soon she was circulating in the fast society of high-ranking army officers, who seldom troubled to present her to their wives. Thus she acquired fine clothes, jewels, and a bad reputation. Eva was an extraordinarily beautiful woman, blond and brown-eyed. While her education was very limited, she was intelligent and, in a sentimental way, idealistic. Perón met her during the summer of 1943–1944. He was a widower just then rising to power with an obsession to remake the country. Eva became his mistress, but more; she was a truly fanatical *Peronista* and an assistant with much acumen. Perón recognized her important role in liberating him on October 17, 1945 by having her appear with him in the celebrated balcony scene at the Casa Rosada. A few weeks later they were married.

For six years Eva Perón was the most famous woman in the world. She was the real secretary of labor and welfare in her husband's government. She wrote a newspaper column and acquired a controlling interest in several journals. After agitating successfully for the right of women to vote, she organized and headed the woman's branch of the *Peronista* Party. Her voice, which lost much of its musical quality in countless public harangues, was heard all over the country, on the radio, the balcony of the Casa Rosada, in street meetings, before labor unions, children, and, in fact, nearly every imaginable group. Her message was not consoling or compassionate but full of hatred. She inveighed against Perón's enemies and scolded those who failed to contribute their best to his "crusade." Her special foes were upper-class womenfolk, the society ladies who sneered at the titular first lady of the republic. Since Rivadavia's time, in the 1820's, the aristocratic women of Buenos Aires had supervised a host of charities in their *Sociedad de beneficencia*. Eva Perón set out to ruin it, first by acts of spite, such as having garbage dumped in inconvenient places or by creating servant troubles. Then she outbid it, creating an Eva Perón Foundation to which workingmen "voluntarily" contributed a day's pay now and then and which businessmen who wished to avoid a visit by the *descamisados* liberally endowed. There was no accounting of the fantastic sums involved since, as Señora Perón disarmingly stated, "Everyone knows I am honest." Misdirected though much of its money was, the foundation did a great deal of good. Charity was now possible on a tremendous scale, available to anyone who dropped by the Casa Rosada and had a few words with the president's lovely wife. She even threw coins into crowds like medieval monarchs, which possibly helps account for the fact that she never lacked a large audience. Many Argentines received clothing, medicine, and grants to help them through difficult days. Eva Perón had a wicked sense of humor, which on one occasion she combined with national vanity to delight her countrymen. When the Argentine embassy in Washington received a routine appeal for contributions to local charities, the great-hearted lady in Buenos Aires shipped a large quantity of food and clothing. Argentina, she explained, was generous enough to share her riches with Yankee beggars.

Valued partner of her crusading husband, scourge of the "best people," angel of mercy, Lady Bountiful—these were the roles the onetime
frustrated actress played with immense success. Another and more subtle
characterization was filling the position dominated by film stars in some
countries and by royalty in others. Eva Perón had the most expensive
clothes and the most spectacular jewels of any Argentine. By flaunting
them as she did, she gave vicarious satisfaction to countless women of
the lower classes who relished seeing one of their own so lavishly be-
decked. Instead of resenting her extravagance they admired her brazenness. And they enjoyed being told that such clothing might come within
their reach in the better Argentina Perón was building.

No delicacy or modesty inhibited Eva Perón as she forced the Argentines to become familiar with her. *Descamisados* were encouraged to
chant "Evita" as though invoking a holy spirit. Her portrait appeared on
posters all over the nation and in the display windows of merchants who
valued their safety. Syrupy tributes came forth in speeches of almost
any type, in newspapers, magazines, radio broadcasts, and newsreels. Of
course, surreptitious means were found to circulate jokes and rumors
about her morals or the indecent enrichment of her family. Her pretensions grew with her power. In 1951 a campaign was initiated to have
her nominated for vice-president when Perón ran for reelection in the
following year. The pressures mounted, doubtless with much inspiration
from the Casa Rosada, and an ostensibly popular campaign gained great
force. However, the army hierarchy was socially conservative and could
scarcely contemplate such an affront to Argentine manhood. In one of
the rare occasions when they crossed Perón, the generals made their feelings clear, and the campaign suddenly ceased.

Soon afterward it became known that the first lady was sick. An operation for cancer of the throat failed to deliver her from this ailment. As
long as her failing strength permitted, she appeared before her beloved
descamisados, pale and wrinkled, croaking horrendous threats to her
husband's enemies and urging undying loyalty to his mission. When she
died on July 26, 1952 at the age of thirty-three, thousands of mourners in
front of the Casa Rosada wept. All over the country clocks were stopped
at the hour of her passing, many to remain so for two or three years. Black
banners were draped about the innumerable portraits in public places.
The painted word "Evita" still appeared wherever a wall or facing was
blank, and anyone who scoffed risked violence or worse. For years people
would travel great distances to stand in reverence before her remains,
which were expected to be placed in a tomb of incredible magnificence.
The province of La Pampa took her name, as did the city of La Plata,
and every province received an order from the national congress to re-
name a town after her. The absurd and rather pathetic autobiography,

which had been ghost-written, *La razón de mi vida* (The reason for my life), became a required textbook in every Argentine school. There was undoubtedly much true feeling in the blasphemous orgy of national grief that followed the death of Eva Perón, which included demands that she be declared a saint by the Catholic Church. But much of it was also artificially stimulated by President Perón, who wished to exploit her popularity and use it to strengthen his own. As for the widower's own feelings, it was later learned that he had little difficulty in finding consolation.

Peronism and the World

UNDER the Perón dictatorship Argentina gave the fullest play to the spirit of belligerent nationalism. The country was full of aggressions, which had long been turned within itself, since it had not been involved in a foreign war since 1870. Now these unpleasant sentiments were directed against malevolent outside forces as Perón successively pointed them out. Chronologically, Great Britain was the first enemy. It was not enough for Argentina to over-charge this good customer for meat and flour during the war and the period of austerity afterward, when these commodities were in pitifully short supply in Britain. Perón also ranted at supposed British perfidies in the past and present, and the inspired press poured out vile abuse. For a time Perón seemed determined to seize the Falkland Islands, which Argentines call the "Malvinas," but ultimately he shrank from challenging the Royal Navy, demobilized as it was. No particular purpose can be found in this official bluster unless it was to humiliate the Anglophile oligarchy within Argentina. Or perhaps dictators simply like to concentrate popular hostilities on distant objects. After the sale of the foreign-owned railways in 1948, some of the venom went out of the anti-British campaign. Perhaps Perón was also chastened a little when the British reduced their purchases in Argentina as world conditions improved. Yet he had needlessly repudiated a century of good will and a most fruitful period of collaboration that had benefited both countries.

With the defeated Axis nations Perón cultivated close ties, perversely defying world opinion but, perhaps, displaying a considerable vision. Refugees and war criminals from Hitler's fallen empire found a welcome in Buenos Aires, with great numbers living in peace despite the clamors of their victims. Italy, West Germany, and Japan were soon doing as much business with Perón's Argentina as conditions permitted. While Franco Spain was being ostracized by the United Nations for several years after the war, Perón ostentatiously offered that country his friendship, keeping his ambassador in Madrid though few other countries did.

Eva Perón made a much-publicized visit to Spain in 1947, where she was greeted like a beloved royal tourist.[1] Perón and Franco hoped to carry on an immense volume of commerce that would enrich both of their countries and signed an agreement to this end. It soon became apparent, however, that Spain was far too impoverished to pay for goods in any significant amount, and relations between the two Hispanic dictators noticeably cooled. Perón also irritated Britain, the United States, and other democracies—whom he seemed to equate with the "nice people" he derided at home—by deliberately playing up to Communist Russia. He recognized the Soviet Union, something previous Argentine governments had never done, and permitted the Communist Party to function openly in Argentina. Several barter arrangements between Argentina and the Iron Curtain countries were mutually profitable, though not to the degree Perón had prophesied. As for the domestic Communists, they got along comfortably in Perón's Argentina. *Peronistas* and Communists were convinced they were taking advantage of one another, and perhaps both were correct.

Perón's friendliness with the Communist world was a useful lever to win favors from the United States, a device other national leaders were not above using. After the few months' experience with Ambassador Spruille Braden in 1945, the Americans reverted to the role of a long-suffering Good Neighbor who refused to be provoked. As the Cold War intensified, Perón exploited Washington's dilemma by insulting and threatening the *yanqui* to the delight of many Argentines and other Latin Americans. This abuse did not arouse a hostile reaction in the United States, at least officially. On the contrary, it made the government all the more eager to please Perón, as witnessed by the loan in 1950 that probably saved his regime from a financial debacle. The forbearance of *Tío Sam* was based on the fundamental realities that lay beneath the shower of vocal offenses from Buenos Aires. Argentina had no military might whatever in the stark new world of power politics after 1945. Her large and showy army and her minute air force and navy were insignificant factors in an age of inter-continental bombers and nuclear weapons.[2] The only way Perón could harm the United States was by granting bases to the Russians. This he was unlikely to do for many reasons, chief among which was Argentina's urgent need for American machinery and other capital goods. This need was not reciprocal; Argentina produced nothing the United States could not obtain elsewhere. Al-

1. Eva went on to visit Rome and Paris, where officially she was well-received. On this celebrated tour only the British royal family dared to snub her, which accounts for her abandonment of a cherished intention to visit London.
2. Perón jarred the world with an announcement that his scientists had discovered a simple means of producing nuclear fission. It all turned out to be a hoax, merely false publicity to cover the failure of Argentina's costly experiments in this field.

though the Americans purchased canned meat and other Argentine products, even though they were in some years Argentina's prime customers, they could easily turn to other suppliers. In ignoring or placating the strident dictator the State Department was not being pusillanimous. Rather, the American policy grew out of the conviction that inter-American solidarity and long-range relations with the people of Argentina were worth the price of enduring the provocations of a tyrant.

Toward other Latin American nations Perón exhibited signs of aggressiveness that alternated with expressions of pacific intentions. He had many admirers in the Hispanic world, and he cultivated the militaristic dictators who aped him and attempted to influence labor organizations through his own CGT. Paraguay, which was economically at the mercy of Argentina, was ruled by an army group inclined to be sycophantic before Perón. Bolivia fell into the power of a party inspired by Argentina and hostile to American "exploitation." The army junta which ruled Peru was generally friendly to Perón, if nervous about his ambitions. The same was true of Colombia and Venezuela and sometimes of the small republics of the Caribbean. In 1952 Chile, who has always been cool to her great neighbor, surprised the world by electing Carlos Ibáñez as president. This former fascist professed to be a great friend of Perón's, and the two exchanged dramatic visits in the manner of Hitler and Mussolini. However, Perón overplayed his hand by assuming too confidently that Chile planned to remake itself on the Justicialist pattern and become a satellite of Argentina. No basic change in the relationship of the two countries occurred despite the fraternizing of their presidents. Brazil had reason to be nervous about Perón. Much reckless talk in the Argentine army about the supposedly imminent disintegration of the mammoth, spongy republic allegedly weakened by its Negroid character both offended and frightened the Brazilians. Perón harassed the liberal regime of President Dutra in minor ways between 1946 and 1951 and was possibly disappointed when the return of Getulio Vargas to power in Rio indicated a strengthening of the country. Uruguay was Perón's worst annoyance. This small democracy was by its very existence a rebuke to the Argentine dictatorship, and its prosperity made a mockery of some of Perón's policies. It was also a nest of Argentine refugees, as it had been in the days of Rosas a century before. Perón retaliated as much as he dared by forbidding Argentines to travel to the little republic, thus depriving it of a large source of income from *porteños* who had long made a habit of visiting its casinos and beaches. The Mexican Revolutionists, who competed with Perón for Latin American leadership, were perhaps aware that the Argentine dictator had copied many of their measures, but they consistently made known their disapproval of his regime.

Perón pretended to profound aspirations. On several occasions he said that World War III had already begun and that it would lead to the inevitable destruction of both the United States and Russia. Therefore, Argentina should groom itself as a third force—a popular ambition among many nations—to inherit the world. This she should do by following a course midway between capitalism and Communism, which Perón claimed Justicialism signified, and by being militarily strong and socially united. While his metaphysics were rarely taken seriously, perhaps not always by himself, it was possible to make a persuasive case for the success of his diplomatic policies. A pariah among the United Nations in 1945, Argentina had come to enjoy some influence in the world organization and to be courted by all of Hitler's erstwhile enemies while enjoying the friendship of the former Axis partners themselves. Her Latin American neighbors either feared or imitated Argentina; in any case they respected her. And yet Perón's regime had little but nuisance value in international affairs. Few could truly esteem a government so vulgar, so defiant of world opinion, so changeable. When Perón's achievements were weighed against what Argentina might have accomplished between 1945 and 1955 under a democratic system with a sound economic policy, there was little to admire, much to inspire pity and disgust.

Decline and Fall

EVIL days for liberty or democracy might be tolerated by most Argentines with comparative equanimity as long as there was reason to believe they were being led into a paradise of material well-being. By 1951 or 1952, however, it became increasingly apparent that El Líder was faltering rather badly on this path. Meat exports were only a third as great as they had been fifteen years before. Perón thought it necessary to exhort his people to consume less beef, by far their favorite dish, and to command them to observe one meatless day a week.[3] Every citizen could now experience for himself at least one effect of Perón's alienation of the nation's customers, no matter how much the drought or oligarchical obstruction was blamed. More and more there appeared to be a sound basis for the rumors concerning the fantastic profits the potentates of IAPI were making at the expense of farmer and rancher, and also the consuming public. And for all the public boasts of iron and oil discoveries, Argentina was still expending the major share of her diminished credits on imports of these products. Heavy machinery could no longer be bought in sufficient quantities to keep pace with the scale of industriali-

3. This really meant only a beefless day, since fish, fowl, hog meat, and mutton were not included. Even so, most Argentines felt themselves deprived, the Peronistas proud to suffer, the others with different emotions.

zation. There never seemed to be enough electrical power, despite *Peronista* claims and genuine accomplishments. Luxuries from abroad were almost unprocurable. Dislocations and inconveniences plagued almost every aspect of the nation's economy, though the rest of the world was booming as never before in all history. Buenos Aires, for so long the pride of the Hispanic world, became a conspicuously shabby city, unrepaired, unpainted, dirty, with antiquated services and very old and not many automobiles—all this at a time when other Latin American cities were experiencing a frenzy of construction and chaotic traffic problems because of so many shiny new cars. Inflation, which most countries had tamed by this time, broke loose in Argentina worse than ever, impoverishing a population which had long been told that Perón knew the secrets of economics. All over the country people would see the sign, *Perón cumple* (Perón fulfills). It seemed more and more a mockery as business worsened and promises remained unmet.

While economic conditions were becoming more precarious, several events shook the faith of the population in the regime. One was the revelation, clandestine but rightly believed, that Eva Perón had looted her celebrated charity foundation, enriching her family and favorites and banking huge sums abroad—all this at a time when the government fostered a prolonged period of public mourning for this departed benefactress. Another incident was the strangulation of *La Prensa*, the very symbol of the old days of Argentine liberty and enlightenment. Having already subdued *La Nación* after a long campaign of harassment, Perón closed in on this final bastion of a free press. In 1951 the noble journal was stilled, its publisher, Dr. Alberto Gainza Paz, fleeing abroad to receive honor and sympathy wherever there was freedom of the press. The CGT took over the plant and name of *La Prensa*. An impudent banner, *Ya es argentina* (Now it is Argentine), was wrapped all the way around its building facing the Casa Rosada. With control of the nation's press at last absolute, the government next barred all foreign journals which had been, or might be, critical of Perón. To a literate people such as the Argentine these matters were acutely oppressive and humiliating. Finally, the presidential election of November 1952 revealed the helplessness of the voters to change the system. The first Argentine president to run for immediate reelection, Perón was unwilling to allow an open campaign and honest tabulation of the votes, in contrast to 1946. He had an opponent in Ricardo Balbín, the candidate of the Radical Party and its allies, but this challenger rarely received permission to speak on the radio, and the controlled press all but ignored him. His public speeches were usually disorderly affairs, with *Peronista* violence lurking in the foreground. According to the announced results, Perón obtained 65 per cent of all votes cast. Possibly this percentage represented the loyalties of the general electorate, for no one could seriously doubt that Perón still held the support of the masses.

Since his secret police was exceedingly effective in reporting on the state of opinion and, of course, Perón himself was very astute, the president could not have failed to know that his popularity was slipping. Like Franco of Spain, he had known many close calls and always seemed to emerge the stronger after a period of danger. An incident in April 1953 demonstrated his technique. While he was delivering one of his frequent harangues from the balcony of the Casa Rosada several bombs exploded, far from him, to be sure, and quite possibly planted by his supporters. The atrocity at once became an excuse for the *descamisados* to push in mass through the avenues of Buenos Aires in search of Perón's enemies. By some design they concentrated in the downtown area at the Jockey Club, which for seventy years had been the sanctuary of the landed aristocrats, the lair of the "hierarchy," as *Peronistas* believed. The fine old building was sacked and burned. Valuable paintings, books, furniture, and wine stocks were destroyed while the fire department occupied itself in other sections of the city. For months nothing was done to clear away the debris, which filled the fashionable shopping area with a memorable stench. It was a warning to the oligarchy—and to all of Perón's enemies —that no one could fail to grasp. Having made his point, Perón typically sought to captivate his victims. An obvious shift in official favor from organized labor to big business featured the mood of the administration in the next few months.

This reversal of policy received explicit verification in July 1953, when Dr. Milton Eisenhower, brother of the American president, paid a brief visit to Buenos Aires in the course of an extensive tour of South America. The stopover in the Argentine capital had been designed to be so short as to constitute a snub; it was included at all only after much hesitation. However, President Perón exploited the occasion to dramatize his new spirit of reasonableness to business interests. Dr. Eisenhower was lionized in every way in full view of thousands of citizens, and Argentina made known her willingness to change her mind about the iniquity of foreign capital. While the Americans did not rush to take advantage of the new hospitality, a definite change of mood was apparent. Before long an American promoter began the construction of a large automobile and truck plant. Perón shocked devout nationalists with the suggestion that YPF share its oil monopoly with foreign companies, who could presumably win better results than Argentines. And, most significant of all, he began to speak of the need for labor to earn its wage increases instead of relying on the beneficence of the government. Perón was serious about revamping his regime in a conservative sense, for Argentina's economic plight was nearly desperate; he even permitted some mellowness to creep into the system, apparently to make the country attractive to the moneyed classes and to foreign investors. It was fascinating by late 1954 to speculate whether or not he could succeed without losing the common people who had so long obeyed him.

At this critical point, however, Perón committed a folly which defies comprehension, recalling the magnificently insane basic errors that previous dictators have made. This was his assault on the Catholic Church. Most students of Peronism had long, and perhaps not always justly, counted the hierarchy of the clergy as a silent partner of the regime. Certainly the Church enjoyed a privileged position under Perón which the republic had denied it before. While the Argentine people were not conspicuously devout or clerical, they were overwhelmingly Catholic, and there seemed no reason for Perón to make any changes whatever in the situation, especially now that he was courting the conservatives. Possibly his megalomania got the better of him and, like most absolute rulers, he was hyper-sensitive to any suggestion of dissidence. At any rate, Perón apparently became alarmed at a Christian socialist movement among the lower clergy that was kindling a considerable response among the masses. In November 1954 he spoke menacingly about Church "meddling" in student and labor groups and warned of "intrigues" on the part of various unnamed prelates. Suddenly, he announced an intention to legalize divorce and to restore licensed prostitution, thus re-opening issues which had long been settled to the satisfaction of the Church. A modest outburst of protest following this announcement led to the dismissal of a number of priests, particularly those tainted with Christian socialism, who had been teaching in the public schools. In reply to this astonishing attack, the clergy rather stiffly made known its opposition to the proposal to insist on the canonization of "St." Eva Perón. The situation deteriorated very rapidly early in 1955, and it became apparent that an inexplicable breach had divided Perón and the clergy. Demonstrations by the faithful in front of cathedrals resulted in severe police measures. Perón was clearly aggravating matters, for reasons never determined. Congress did his bidding in permitting divorce and prostitution, and the remaining priests were ordered out of the schools. Religious holidays were no longer to be respected. In May 1955 Perón commanded congress to disestablish the Catholic Church, destroying a position it had held since 1853. On June 11 a massive demonstration in Buenos Aires by 100,000 of the devout pushed Perón to the most extreme measures. He at once deported two major Church officials and set the police and the *descamisados* to sacking the residences of priests and to submitting them and well-known clericals to indignities. On June 16 Pope Pius XII excommunicated all government authorities in Argentina who used violence against the Church, presumably, though the point is debated, including President Perón himself.

This sudden war of Church and state was a bewildering development and one that was altogether senseless for Perón. He doubtless aroused much of the country, including a large proportion of the female population and the conservatives he had recently been wooing. Now his other enemies had a popular issue, and conspiracies developed for the first time since 1945 in an atmosphere of hope. And yet, no twentieth-century totalitarian dictator had ever been overthrown without the benefit of a foreign liberating army. The first efforts to destroy Perón fizzled out ignominiously. Several naval aircraft dropped bombs on the Casa Rosada, barely missing Perón, but missing him, and the aviators flew abroad. A sputter of garrison revolts in various parts of the country came to nothing. During July it seemed that Perón was surviving another crisis, to emerge with enhanced strength as he had before. If labor had cooled because of his recent policies and women because of the anti-clericalism, the population as a whole seemed as cowed as ever. The key to the situation was the army, as it had been since 1930. Never quite as bound to Perón as most outsiders believed, the generals knew a declining dictator when they saw one, though most of them had attained their rank by toadying to him. In August 1955 Perón sensed that the military was full of intrigue. He reverted to his old formula, pitting the *descamisados* against the army and gambling that the enlisted men would defy their own officers. He spoke in this sense at a mass meeting of the CGT on August 31, dramatically offering his resignation if that was what the country desired. As he expected, the reaction of the workingmen was a furious protest and a threat to call a general strike until he promised to remain in office. Perón bowed to their will in a barbarous speech in which he threw down the challenge to his enemies. A desperate man, wild and bloodthirsty, he shouted: "Kill five for one," and his audience roared its enthusiasm for this course.

It was not long until Perón's defiance received its reply. The generals conferred at army maneuvers near Córdoba. Officers of the navy and air force, who had always been tepid in their Peronism, came into contact with the army conspirators. On September 16 a military revolt broke out simultaneously in several provinces, all army-led. From Córdoba, where the radio station was seized, broadcasts went out to raise the entire country. Naval units steamed toward Buenos Aires, threatening by radio to bombard the city unless Perón resigned. Airplanes flew over the capital in ominous waves. Against such forces the street-fighters were helpless. In truth, the *descamisados* exhibited little spirit to die for Juan Perón. On September 21 the garrison near Buenos Aires announced its adherence to the rebellion and occupied the city, the only bloodshed occurring when they overcame a group of die-hard *Peronistas* who had barricaded themselves in an office building. Deserted on all sides, Perón slipped away on a rainy night from the Casa Rosada to the legation of Paraguay, and then to a gunboat of that nation anchored in the harbor.

INHERITORS OF WRECKAGE

As it was said, this may not have been a popular revolution, but the revolution was popular. As soon as Perón's flight was known, hordes poured into the streets and plazas of most Argentine towns to rejoice. The arrival of the temporary chieftain of the military group, General Eduardo Lonardi, was the occasion for a tumultuous welcome in Buenos Aires. While celebrants on such occasions tend to obscure mourners, no one could seriously question the relief felt by a majority of the population at the fall of Perón. The decline of his popularity had been obvious for two or three years. But what was to fill the awful vacuum left by his departure? As in 1930 and 1943, the generals who controlled the rebellion were almost anonymous dignitaries as far as the public was concerned, and they were also unorganized regarding the program for the future. Once in power they seemed bewildered. Most of the new officials were conservatives, even civilians, who had been out of affairs of government for years and had little notion of what to do. About all they accomplished in the first confused months was to dismiss the most important *Peronistas* and to publicize the malfeasance of the fallen regime. Some of the revelations were indeed shocking: business was far worse than official statistics had reported, graft much larger than suspected, the transportation system in chaos, fuel reserves desperately low, credit almost exhausted, and the export volume far too small to support the scale of imports needed to keep the country functioning. Pleased as most Argentines were to be rid of Perón, they had reason to be dismayed by the problems he had left and to question the ability of the new government to deal with them.

In November 1955 Lonardi was discreetly ousted in a palace coup. The other generals apparently felt that he had fulfilled his function in overthrowing Perón and that now a stronger president was needed, or perhaps one not so identified with the conservatives. It is possible that the official reason, Lonardi's bad health, had some basis, much as he denied it, for he died a few weeks later in Washington. It appeared unlikely that the generals would break their code by explaining this action. In any event, the army chief of staff, General Pedro Eugenio Aramburu, succeeded Lonardi as provisional president and held the position until May 1958. His administration did much to restore the reputation of the Argentine army and, further, the nation's own self-respect. Yet it was not, and could scarcely have been, a brilliant or even a popular regime. No one had political appeal to match Juan and Eva Perón. And the preoccupation of the government was necessarily with affairs that seemed drab after the extravaganzas of the dictatorship. Aramburu created a National Consultative Committee to represent all of the major parties and to advise him in matters of high policy. No other formal organ of representative government existed for many months. While the constitution of 1853 was declared the law of the land, a state of siege remained in force until 1957, and the provisional president ruled by decree, often without reference to the committee. Freedom, however, was permitted to all groups but the *Peronistas*. The slow revival of political life reflected not so much the autocratic methods of Aramburu but the long somnolence of the country under Perón and his immediate predecessors. Argentines had almost forgotten how to behave like free men.

News accounts of Argentine affairs during 1956 and 1957 were monotonous and dreary, dealing as they did with the difficulties of restoring orderly government, restraining inflation, recovering a measure of solvency, and preventing a counter-revolution. A number of wrongs were righted. *La Prensa*, of course, was returned to its lawful owner. Most confiscated properties, including a financial empire of $100,000,000 taken from the Bemberg family, were duly restored. Some of the most oppressive *Peronistas* were sent to prison; many, however, had earlier provided for themselves by banking large sums abroad and managed to escape to spend it. A series of revelations about Perón himself disgusted many people. He had accumulated a fortune of $7,000,000 in Argentina and perhaps many times that amount in Switzerland. For some months prior to his overthrow he had been having lewd relations with a 14-year-old girl named Nelly Rivas. Strong as the demand to punish the ex-dictator was, the new regime was fearful of arousing the street gangs who were still loyal to him. Since Paraguay was too close to Argentina, pressure was brought to have him sent to a more distant exile. He went to Panama for some months, then to Venezuela, the Dominican Republic, and finally to Spain, a beaten bully who excited little sympathy abroad. From exile the former dictator was still capable of making mischief. On his orders *Peronistas* conducted a steady campaign of harassment, stopping trains, cutting off electric power, rioting, sabotaging, and scribbling slogans on walls. Perón himself blustered as self-righteously as ever. On one occasion he challenged President Aramburu to meet him on the frontier for a duel. Aramburu ignored Perón, a former fencing champion and expert shot.

Aramburu plunged ahead with the task of purging *Peronistas* throughout the administration. It was a major step when he returned most of the teachers Perón had expelled, restored the autonomous character of the Argentine universities, and had textbooks purified of chauvinism and pious references to the Peróns. Aramburu easily suppressed an isolated but potentially significant garrison revolt on behalf of the former dictator in June 1956, thus preventing any further expressions of latent Peronism in the army. Later in that year he felt the regime strong enough to forbid all strikes and to announce that no further blanket wage increases would be forthcoming until an elected government took over. With some nervousness the authorities publicly encouraged foreign capital and business firms to enter Argentina, as Perón himself had done during his last two years. Nationalists grumbled but did nothing. It was only too plain a fact that outside help was needed to exploit the oil and iron, build the dams and roads, and expand the industrial plant. Aramburu also chose to abandon most of the economic controls so that the people could work out their economic salvation under the free enterprise system. The first results were equivocal; some sectors of the economy responded hearteningly while others lagged. Some of the problems would require years to settle, particularly the restoration of agriculture and the livestock industry. Under Perón, farm machinery had rarely been imported so that industrial equipment might be favored. Livestock herds needed to be built up and better types of cattle, such as the Santa Gertrudis or the Brahma, were required in order to develop larger animals that could resist heat and disease. All of these plans to revive Argentine prosperity were sensible enough, but inflation continued to rage, the working class was sullen, and the uneven division of wealth persisted as a dangerous factor in the nation's life.

In July 1957 the government held elections for a constituent assembly, with voting compulsory for all citizens of age. The results offered as true a picture of Argentine attitudes as could be obtained by any process. More than 2,100,000 voters turned in blank ballots, which meant that they favored Perón. Almost as many voted for the Peoples' Radical Party and a slightly smaller number for the Intransigeant Radicals, reflecting a split and re-alignment of the historic political group associated with the name of Hipólito Yrigoyen. Minor parties still had some following, but it was something of a surprise that the Communists, who had been so articulate, polled only 225,000 votes. Since about one-fourth of the electorate had indicated a lingering allegiance to the exiled dictator, the constituent assembly was timid. Instead of reorganizing the republic on a heroic or even an imaginative scale, about all it did was to confirm the restoration of the constitution of 1853 that Aramburu had earlier decreed. The assembly was cool to Aramburu's recommendation that the presidency be weakened in order to reduce the danger of dictatorship in the future.

Although disorders and uncertainties gave his administration an appearance of frailty, President Aramburu continued to prove himself a

worthy custodian of his nation's affairs. He would not be deflected from
the economic policies that, he hoped, would eventually right material
conditions. As Argentines became accustomed again to civil liberties,
their old intellectual life showed signs of recovering its vigor. In February 1958 it was time to hold the national elections which Aramburu had
promised. He admonished the people to vote with a sense of responsibility and civic conscience. Not a candidate himself, the general-turned-
statesman took pride in showing the world that at least one military man
could lead a Latin American nation from dictatorship to democratic republicanism. As things turned out, his own civic conscience must have
been tempted. Aramburu's preferred candidate, Ricardo Balbín, lost the
election. Although Balbín had courageously run against Perón in 1952
and was known to have the favor of the regime, he received only half as
many votes on the Peoples' Radical ticket as his chief opponent. The victor was Arturo Frondizi, who had been Balbín's running mate in 1952
and was now the candidate of the Intransigeant Radicals. Frondizi's
branch of the former Radical Party also won control of both houses of
congress and a majority of the states. In some respects his victory was as
disturbing as it was surprising. Frondizi had courted both the *Peronistas*
and the Communists and was widely believed to have made a bargain
with Perón himself. Also, he had played the demagogue during the campaign, catering to the left in the style of Perón, flattering the nationalists,
and promising the clericals that he would restore the Church to the high
status it had enjoyed during most of the Perón years. While Frondizi had
shown great political skill in re-creating the coalition that had long supported the former dictator, it could not be denied that a majority of the
Argentine people had shown something about their own opinions. They
were still loyal to much of Perón's program.

Arturo Frondizi was inaugurated in May 1958, and within a few
weeks he was in trouble. *Peronistas*, who were now very aggressive, accused the president of moving too slowly in restoring their civic rights
and in admitting the exiles. On the other hand, former president Aramburu and the other generals guarded him carefully and growled whenever he made a gesture to appease the *Peronistas*. At length Frondizi was
able to carry out what must have been a pre-election promise to return the
Peronistas to political life, but he did not dare permit the ex-dictator to
return to Argentina. For this attitude he received a bitter criticism in October 1958 from Juan Perón, then in Ciudad Trujillo, who believed the
country would rise *en masse* to acclaim him if he set foot in Argentina.
He might have been correct in this conviction, and the generals did nothing to loosen their hold, lest he attempt to prove it. Frondizi also encountered difficulties in meeting his promises to the clericals. Only after
many student riots and liberal protests was he able to obtain passage of

his proposals to ban divorce and legalized prostitution and to permit the Catholic Church to establish private universities.

The more fundamental problems of the country yielded with agonizing stubbornness to the pressures of the administration. Frondizi was courageous enough to inform the population in December 1958 that hard times were ahead. Argentina had been living an economic fiction, he said, and for fifteen years had been spending far more than she earned. She had dissipated her credit and injured her most productive industries while outgrowing her facilities to such an extent that she had lost ground. Many Argentine intellectuals also voiced the belief that the republic had compromised its destiny and lost its magic formula. Yet a majority of the people would not be denied the social welfare programs Perón had taught them to expect. Nor were they prepared to slake the fires of malevolent nationalism. While Frondizi visited the United States in 1959 and 1961, the only Argentine president ever to do so while in office, and sincerely sought to entice American technical and financial assistance, his countrymen were deeply suspicious of Yankees and other foreigners. Just how these prejudices and ambitions could be reconciled with the facts of life was by no means clear in the early 1960's. In the local and congressional elections of March 1962 the *Peronistas* won more than a third of the votes, the most of any party. The army deposed Frondizi for having let this happen and confined him on Martín García Island, where he protested that he was still legally president. José María Guido became the army's puppet president and annulled the elections. Argentina still offered an attractive prospect of a country with great natural richness, a good climate, and a literate, industrious population of about 22,000,000. In view of the fragility of her government and the disturbed mood of her people, however, it was not easy to be optimistic about her immediate future.

36

Brazil in Ferment

As EMPIRE and republic prior to 1930, Brazil had a placid political history by Latin American standards. Imperfect as her government had been, the population had become accustomed to freedom. And the nation had held together in spite of powerful local loyalties and the distances between population centers. During the nineteenth century Brazil had adjusted to world currents slowly but with few shocks. By World War I these currents were stronger as scientific and technological advances further affected economic life and social equilibrium. Popular journalism, motion pictures, the automobile, and the radio began to enlighten the masses about the outside world and to make them discontented with the poverty they had long endured with resignation because they knew of nothing different. Thus the rural poor migrated to the cities, where they formed a restless proletariat ripe for reformers, idealists, and demagogues. The Brazilian middle class continued to be modest in numbers, but it expanded somewhat in size and greatly in influence. The traditional upper class remained powerful, while abandoning some of its historic clannishness and recruiting new members from the business community. The military, whose hierarchy was aristocratic, became more querulous about the inadequacies of the republic and looked with interest at European totalitarian movements. Finally, among the awakening forces that made Brazilian society restless by 1930 were women, who were beginning to insist on political and economic equality.

It has been seen that the republic of the constitution of 1891 was a fair-weather regime. As tensions mounted under the impact of new developments, it fell behind the dynamic elements of the country in offering leadership, and it seemed unresponsive and cynical. With the collapse of the coffee market in 1929 an economic crisis of huge proportions

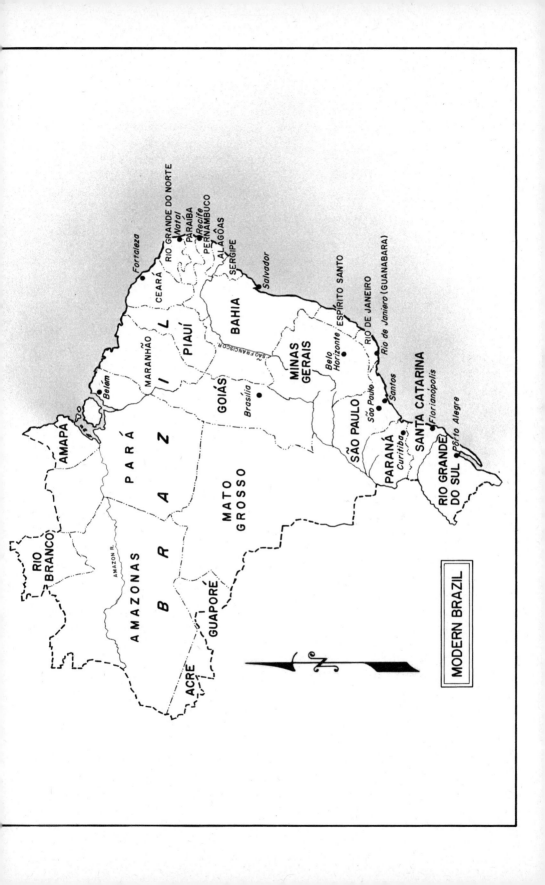

MODERN BRAZIL

came to a head. For such a catastrophe the administration had no remedy. Brazil, in common with many other countries at that time, had psychological readiness and genuine causes for repudiating the symbols and ideals of the recent past. All over Latin America there was uneasiness, with militant labor, totalitarians, nervous propertied groups, nationalistic army officers, and impoverished masses clamoring for drastic measures. In 1930 Brazil underwent a revolution, the first to succeed since the republic was established.

THE ERA OF GETULIO VARGAS

After the proclamation of Julio Prestes' victory over Dr. Getulio Vargas and his Liberal Alliance in the elections of March 1930, the nation remained tense. Many complained that the elections had been rigged in order to perpetuate the domination of the state of São Paulo and the conservative machines. The losers assessed the situation and concluded that they could rally the country. Accordingly, negotiations between politicians in Rio Grande do Sul, where Vargas was governor, and Minas Gerais, which resented *paulista* betrayal of an agreement to alternate the presidency, led to a plan to enlist the military and upset the announced verdict. Dr. Oswaldo Aranha, a lieutenant of Vargas, undertook a discreet tour of army commands and found support among the generals as well as real enthusiasm among the *tenentes,* or junior officers, for adventure. In October 1930, when the net was ready, Vargas grandly summoned the nation to rise, charging that the votes had been miscounted to cheat him of the presidency. To sweeten his appeal he made many promises: a reformed electoral system, the promotion of public health and education, land distribution, social welfare, and favors to industries other than coffee and to states other than São Paulo. Nearly everywhere the reaction was favorable, for the depression had created an urge to change things. Vargas assembled a large force of state and national troops with many popular auxiliaries for a march on the capital. Actually, the journey from his headquarters, Porto Alegre, to Rio de Janeiro was made by slow train. Only in São Paulo did opposition threaten, and it vanished soon after the rebels approached. When he entered that city late in October, Vargas even received a few cheers, and from there to Rio the triumphal "march" was a holiday affair, a gay revolution. Brazil would not have been true to itself had violence and bloodshed characterized even so important an event as the fall of the republic, as the Vargas revolt ultimately signified. Outwardly, at least, the seizure of power was well-received, and Julio Prestes, the president-apparent who had been elected in March, took refuge in the British legation, while the retiring president, Washington Luis, was arrested and deported.

There was little to suggest that Getulio, as Brazilians familiarly called their new leader, had the makings of a dictator. At forty-seven he had behind him a respectable but not spectacular career. Born in the ranching state of Rio Grande do Sul, he had completed the study of law, hence his title of "doctor." Successful in business and ranching, he liked to be known as a gaucho but was, in truth, much more the suave banker. He had served briefly as minister of finance for the republic in 1926 but had resigned to become governor of his home state. While he had been something of a puppet in this capacity, for Rio Grande had a rustic *caudilho* as boss, he had shown administrative talent and an unexpected popular appeal. His campaign for the presidency had revealed him astute in handling politicians. Circumstances and his own flair had made him the embodiment of a wide variety of aspirations. Short, rather distinguished-looking, and thought to be moral and upright, he was also very charming. Vargas smiled often, so much and so winningly that few detected the coldness and craft, or the somewhat sinister mystical quality, that lay behind his agreeable face.

Brazil in 1930

IT WAS time for Brazil to reach again for the destiny of greatness that had been repeatedly prophesied since 1500 but which the fates or human ineptitude had kept it from capturing. The country was fabulously rich in natural resources. Vargas' own state of Rio Grande do Sul and its neighbors to the north, Santa Catarina and Paraná, were fertile and temperate. Their potential as livestock areas was almost as great as that of Uruguay and Argentina, and they had minerals and seaports as well. All they needed was the intelligent application of modern technology, which so far had been spasmodic, to become immensely productive. This was being demonstrated in the envied state to the north, São Paulo, which had better agricultural lands—above all the red soil and warmer climate needed to produce most of the world's coffee—and a head start in industrialization. Its inhabitants had energy and the habit of success. With the incredible city of São Paulo, the dynamo of the continent after Buenos Aires, and the excellent port of Santos, the state had advantages that placed it in the first rank of the favored regions on earth. North of it was the smaller state of Rio de Janeiro, which was almost as rich.

In the federal district was one of the great capitals of the world, Rio de Janeiro, with its outstandingly beautiful setting: Guanabara Bay and its islands and inlets, the noted mountains, Sugar Loaf, Corcovado, Tijuca, and the Organs, and spacious beaches. In this loveliest of all tropical cities were flamboyant palaces and residences that housed an aristocracy that still had the elegant habits of monarchical days. Migrating to the mountainous Petropolis in hot weather, often adorning the fashionable spots of Europe, and attending horse races, balls, and beach parties, they had great style. Merging into their ranks were successful business-men, generals, and politicians. Rio also was the headquarters of a swol-len bureaucracy that conducted the affairs of the republic in a reputedly lackadaisical fashion. The pageantry of the Church, the army, and the navy was much in evidence. The city loved fun. Its saints' days, national holidays, and pre-Lenten carnival were world-famous for their giddiness and extravagance. Also, the *cariocas* (inhabitants of Rio) supported the best that the Western world offered in the way of cultural activities: musical performances, art exhibits, and books. More than that, it was a mecca for Brazilian painters and writers, many of whom were more orig-inal than outsiders appreciated, and through Rio had gone Brazil's pe-culiar dances and rhythms to centers of entertainment the world over. The capital devoted itself to more than pleasure. Banks, commercial houses, and light industries were much in evidence. These evidences of a workaday world, together with the slums and shanty-towns, were sof-tened by the tree-lined streets, flowery parks, colored balloons in the air, and inspiring views of mountain and sea. Like Paris, Rio made a cult of beauty. Capital, seaport, center of business and culture, it was one of Brazil's major resources.

Behind the capital was the large, rugged state of Minas Gerais, which still produced gold and diamonds and was about to reveal the world's largest deposit of iron ore. Laggard in everything but politics, the state was in need of a strong dose of modern technology; its latent energies and natural riches awaited strong leaders. The Brazilian west—the states and territories of Goias, Mato Grosso, Pará, Amazonas, and smaller units—were undeveloped. The government had long neglected this area, which, to be sure, contained nearly every discouragement that climate, disease, and wildlife could present to human enterprise. The northeast-ern corner of Brazil, whose principal states were Bahia, Pernambuco, Rio Grande do Norte, and Paraiba, had been in decline since the 1880's, when the sugar industry had fallen behind foreign competitors and the slaves were freed. Rubber from the western section of this region was no longer a real industry, despite the efforts of Henry Ford to establish plantations there. On the hot, wet coasts there were still sugar plantations and large commercial cotton farms, but they were not of critical impor-tance to Brazil. The interior of the northeast was arid, subject to droughts and famines, and full of wretchedly poor inhabitants. Efforts beyond human capability as then known would be needed to make this part of Brazil productive.

While students occasionally projected the human geography of Brazil as leading to the fusion of a cosmic race, with Europeans, Indians, Africans, and Asians coming together as one common family, this process was not working itself out except in terms of blood mixture. If it was true enough that the various races were interbreeding, the population was steadily becoming whiter. Most immigrants were European, and colored persons often aspired to pass as white. Nor was there a high degree of acculturation, for Brazil was ever growing more Western in its civilization. Traces of non-European habits and ways lingered in enclaves here and there, and in other areas as peripheral or nostalgic aspects of life. Dim as it was in some places, the goal was to be Western.

Of full-blooded Indians there were perhaps half a million. Mostly they were primitives who lived apart in the wilderness, the Amazon "Green Hell," divided into tribes. General Cándido Rondon, himself an Indian, was doing much to impart the civilization of the coastlands among the aborigines. His loving labors in medical care and spiritual regeneration earned him the comparison with Dr. Albert Schweitzer, whose career in central Africa was on the same order. Vargas said he intended to draw the Indians into Brazilian society as useful citizens. The 300,000 or so Asians in Brazil were already useful citizens, but they were scarcely Brazilians. Most of them Japanese who had been imported since 1908 to work on rubber plantations and coffee farms, they maintained a separate identity.

The Negro population was still concentrated in the northeast, with liberal sprinklings in the mining regions and in every city slum. Having been strengthened by practically no immigrants since 1850, and suffering more than anyone else from early mortality, they were relatively declining. Moreover, they had long been mixing with other races and discarding their Africanism. Generally they were uneducated and poor, employed as menials or forming a rural proletariat of seasonal laborers. Those who had the fortune or ability to rise in the social scale were seldom obstructed by color bars, and a few Negroes were affluent and prominent. Brazil had less color prejudice than any other country with large blocs of various races, and since early colonial days both the structure and sanctions of its society had encouraged Negroes to mix with other races. Those Africans who could not pretend to pass as white or mulatto had every incentive to become Westernized in their ways. Without considering the Negro population a problem as such, Vargas had promised massive efforts to introduce free education, sanitation, and social betterment to the poor, a category which included most Africans.

Europeans were probably less numerous than Negroes and mulattoes combined, though no one knew for sure. From Rio de Janeiro south the population was overwhelmingly white, many of them of European birth, for the immigrants had always headed for the less tropical areas. Strong family and sentimental ties linked many of them, as well as first- or second-generation Brazilians to their country of origin. Sometimes, as in the case of the German communities in the far south, they lived in isolation and made little effort to conceal a patronizing attitude toward other Brazilians. Slavonic settlers were also fairly slow to assimilate. But the Portuguese, Italians, and Spaniards, who were by far the most numerous among the whites, tended to become loyal Brazilians readily. While the doctrine of white supremacy was seldom asserted bluntly in public, it was implicit in the attitudes and writings of the dominant groups even when they were tolerant about accepting non-whites who made good. Certainly, Caucasians composed the possessing and directing groups of Brazilian society. Those who were unsuccessful lived as miserably as the poor in any country did, and of these there were considerable numbers. The plight of the *caboclos*, the rural poor often but not necessarily white, was coming more and more to the attention of the country through the writings of Monteiro Lobato (1883–1948), a coffee planter of São Paulo who became one of Brazil's finest novelists.

Census figures and government estimates offered only a hazy picture of the population. Probably Brazil had 35,000,000 inhabitants in 1930. On the whole, they were a sickly population, particularly in the tropics. Yellow fever, malaria, and smallpox had largely been eliminated in the cities, thanks to the heroic efforts of such individuals as Dr. Oswaldo Cruz. And Brazil had several renowned centers for studying diseases, snake venom, and biology. Yet nearly every illness known to mankind claimed many victims in this republic. Leprosy persisted and tuberculosis was rampant. Infant mortality was appallingly high, and the average span of life was among the briefest in the Western world. Moreover, physicians and hospitals were concentrated in the cities, leaving the sick elsewhere to the ministrations of faith healers and charlatans. In few localities outside the largest centers had official efforts to provide a pure water supply, public hygiene, or sanitation been effective, if indeed the authorities had tried at all. And while Brazil produced more than enough food for her population, poor transportation and distribution facilities kept it from reaching communities sticken by disaster. Nor were wise eating habits the general rule; malnutrition was often a matter of ignorance rather than food shortage. The inadequacies of public health policies and the tropical character of so much of the country combined to make Brazil a land of lassitude. Too many of its people simply felt bad.

Varied as the population was, it was bound by solid ties to the concept of a single nation. During the colonial and imperial period the unity of Portuguese America had become a powerful tradition, and the federal republic had by no means weakened it. The Portuguese language itself was a strong factor for unity, the tongue of most whites and Negroes and one which the new rulers of 1930 intended to spread to Indians and unassimilated immigrant groups. Roman Catholicism was another important bond that held Brazil together, though the Church was pitifully understaffed. Also, the cult had become distorted, really heretical, in many localities because the clergy was so small. Moreover, Protestantism, Judaism, and Islam claimed some followers. Even so, the historic Church maintained some hold on all sections of the country and was a force for unity. Vargas planned to restore Catholicism to the role of partner to the state, as it had been under the monarchy, though he was cautious about saying so. Another unifying factor was the concentration of the population, for the Brazilians were a far less dispersed nation than the map would suggest. Nine-tenths or even more of the people lived near the coast and knew something of the traditional ties that had held the area together politically for four centuries. A fervent patriotism was appearing by 1930, one that would diminish regional attachments and exalt national feeling.

Among the factors that proved unifiers to a smaller degree than might be supposed were the transportation and educational systems. Only coastal steamers and river boats were significant agents of a national communications network. The railroad system was stunted, mostly connecting inland centers and seaports, and wretchedly equipped. No lines linked Rio de Janeiro with the populated areas in the northeast. It took a week to travel by train from São Paulo to Uruguay, and most of the country had no railway service whatever. Brazilian highways were almost altogether mere dirt roads, and all automobiles and trucks had to be imported. Aviation—which Brazilians claim they originated in the person of Alberto Santos-Dumas, one of the first men to fly—was mainly a matter of stunts and thrills. As for the educational establishment, it did little to integrate the republic. Much as public enlightenment had been proclaimed as a national goal, the system was weak. The secondary schools for which the federal government was responsible were few and generally poor. The states, which were supposed to maintain primary schools, had not created enough to keep up with the growth of population except in the case of São Paulo, which had developed a splendid system. Brazil's literacy rate, about 20 per cent, was almost as low as when the republic was founded. There was no university whatever in Brazil, a gaping dereliction for a country more than four centuries old. Several colleges and institutes, however, had fair reputations as centers to provide training for the law, fine arts, mineralogy, and medicine. The

Oswaldo Cruz Institute was famous abroad for its research work in public health, and the Biological Institute of São Paulo was distinguished. The Mackenzie Institute in São Paulo, which was founded in 1870 by a group of American Presbyterians, trained students from the primary grades through professional schools and exerted much influence on the educational system as a whole. Extra-institutional agencies of instruction were comparatively weak. Brazilian newspapers were often good, but a large majority could not read them. The radio, which would soon amuse and enlighten the masses, was in 1930 a gadget for the urban rich.

People seemed to sense that the "gay revolution" of 1930 represented a significant turn in the nation's career. It was time for heroic measures to make Brazil over, really to bring her into the twentieth century. A new set of rulers was full of optimism and energy; Vargas and his followers had described the nation's needs and caught its imagination. The challenge was indeed enormous, nothing less than the awakening of the latent powers of 35,000,000 people who lived in a land that ought to be, but was not, fabulously productive. Diversification of the economy, industrialization, improved transportation and communications, the harnessing of the sources of power, education, social justice, public health, and the instillation of a sense of national purpose—these and other goals were being proclaimed. Yet depression, ignorance, sickness, languor, and a ramshackle administration were the points of departure. Getulio Vargas scarcely seemed the daring and resourceful man to undertake the task of renovating the country. Fifteen years later it was clear that this strange little man had delivered better on his promises than most politicians. While Brazil would no doubt have undergone many changes without him—as any country would in that length of time—Vargas deserves at least a junior position among the titans of the 1930's and early 1940's.

The Vargas Years: First Phase (1930–1937)

THE first task of Dr. Getulio Vargas was the obvious one of consolidating his power. In doing so, he effected a major overhaul of the bureaucracy, removing his enemies and many long-entrenched beneficiaries of the old political machines. While his replacements were not always improvements, it resulted that a new class of administrators rejuvenated the government. The familiar clans who had dominated the previous regimes gave way to men generally younger and more social-conscious and national-minded. Local bosses were retired, demoted, or absorbed into the new Vargas machine. Federal interventors dislodged all of the state governors (or presidents, as some were called), and the states lost their right to tax exports and saw other powers wither away. Federalism, as in the United States during this period, became a losing cause, a matter of nostalgia for conservatives. Rio de Janeiro, so long a trophy tossed from one set of state politicians to another, became the true nerve center of Brazil. And Rio was Vargas. As provisional president he ruled without a congress and bent the judiciary to his will. And he took the precaution of shifting army commanders about so that none could challenge him for long. Furthermore, the military felt the infusion of the *tenentes*, the younger officers devoted to Vargas.

A flood of decrees set in motion the projects Vargas had promised: public works, school-building, minimum wages and a 48-hour week for labor, the establishment of the University of Rio de Janeiro, sanitation, and the initial steps to revive and diversify the economy. The immediate problem, however, was to raise the price of coffee, for without the foreign earnings this product of São Paulo brought there was no hope of financing the new programs. Vargas tackled the problem boldly if perhaps wrong-headedly by curtailing production through forbidding further plantings of coffee trees and, to the awe of many, the burning of the surplus. During the next few years Brazil destroyed 76,000,000 bags, each containing 132.5 pounds of coffee, an amount that represented a three-year supply for the world. Callous as this measure seemed, it served its purpose, and coffee again became a great income producer for the nation. It is pertinent to note that the United States during these years could devise no way to distribute its food surpluses to a hungry planet but resorted to the destruction of crops and young livestock. Sometimes acts of desperate madness seem rational in an imperfect world.

The *paulistas* had no great objection to the continuous burning of coffee, for prices rose and prosperity returned. But they did not like Vargas, who they felt had deprived their state of its rightful position as director of the nation. To be sure, the *paulistas* paid half the federal taxes and received only a fraction of the revenues in return. And as inhabitants of the most advanced state they took more seriously than others the importance of constitutional behavior. Devoted to lawful procedures and convinced they had fathered the republic and been its true custodians, they abhorred Vargas for concentrating all power dictatorially and in Rio. Two years passed without his calling a constituent convention, or a congress of any sort, and the *paulistas* decided to force his hand. On July 9, 1932, a well-planned rebellion involving nearly every faction in the state broke out. As might be expected of so successful a people, the affair was cleverly designed, orderly, and efficiently managed. The entire state was mobilized for battle, an army of 50,000 being assembled and the population set to work fabricating weapons and ammunition. So strong was the spirit of these *paulistas* it seemed they might secede from Brazil unless they had their way. However, they were chagrined to find that no other state would join them, and Vargas proved very energetic in collecting forces from the rest of the country. Soon, the largest armies ever seen in South America were facing one another. Though little fighting took place, the *paulistas* realized that they were overpowered and in October 1932 wisely surrendered. President Vargas was magnanimous, prudently conciliating his challengers. Only light punishments befell most of the *paulista* leaders, and he summoned a constituent convention as though he had intended to do so all along, thus conceding the professed aim of the *paulista* rebellion. In no important way was the state made to suffer; it continued to thrive under Vargas, and São Paulo became the fastest-growing urban center on earth. When, a few years later, the municipality opened the great freeway that slashes through the ancient streets, defiantly named the Ninth of July, President Vargas himself officiated at the ceremonies, smiling as usual.

The constituent congress was elected in the spring of 1933, with women voting for the first time in the history of Brazil. Its product, the constitution of 1934, was not altogether to Vargas' liking, but it incorporated his principal ideas and gave him legal authority to proceed. with his program. While the Church was not restored to its position of monarchical times, the wording of the constitution implied that it was no longer separate from the state. The lower house of congress would include as one-fifth of its membership representatives of occupational groups rather than of geographical divisions, a favorite idea of Italian and Portuguese fascism. And presidents were to be elected by popular vote rather than by states, though the first president under the new dispensation, Dr. Getulio Vargas, was chosen by the constituent congress.

This term of President Vargas, stretching from 1934 to 1938, was the only lawful tenure of his fifteen-year regime. On the whole it was a fruitful period. By 1934 Brazil had largely recovered from the depression, and the government was able to carry out extensive enterprises. Of course, the country made much progress apart from, or some would say in spite of, the ministrations of Vargas, but in general the administration gave strong leadership. Rural areas received improved roads and a knowledge of modern agricultural techniques. Vargas aroused interest in this type of progress by traveling widely over his tropical empire, as Dom Pedro used to do, inspiring local authorities to exert themselves. As he had promised, he spurred the opening of the great Amazon west, and many Indians were enticed from the jungle into Westernized communities. The radio and the motion picture did much to accustom the isolated rural areas to the ways of the modern world. Slowly and steadily the hinterland took life. Sugar cultivation was another government concern. It spread into nearly all of the states and acquired larger domestic and foreign markets. Coffee was a sound industry again. Cotton and cacao, beans and *yerba maté*, rice and livestock, and nuts and rubber received enlightened official attention. Vargas' home state of Rio Grande and its neighbors likewise prospered, as ranchers were taught more about scientific stockbreeding. But the greatest advance was the growth of light industry, chiefly in Rio and São Paulo. Many factories were started, creating new wealth, absorbing hordes of skilled laborers, and elevating the standard of living. And the Vargas regime attempted to keep its social programs abreast of this industrial development. Education, which included instruction in basic Machine Age skills as well as letters, likewise improved the status of many individuals. The regime claimed to have lowered the rate of illiteracy from 80 to 60 per cent during the 1930's, a probable exaggeration but nonetheless a wholesome trend.

The popularity of Getulio Vargas waxed steadily as the masses received social benefits. The possessing classes usually remained critical or skeptical, but it was evident by now that Vargas was no revolutionist, and they were reassured. Politicians learned that he was either phenomenally lucky or far more cunning than he looked. His victory in 1930, the revamping of the bureaucracy and the army, and his defeat of the *paulistas* suggested the latter. By the mid-thirties he faced another challenge in the Communists. Luis Carlos Prestes, the hero of the hegira of 1924–1926, returned from Russia and set about organizing a Communist network. Hailed by his followers as "the knight of hope," Prestes concentrated on the junior ranks of the military caste, many of whom were bitter over not being promoted with Vargas' *tenentes*. In 1935 a series of mutinies revealed the effectiveness of Prestes' labors. While agitation in the military was a serious problem of itself, Vargas used it to encompass the ruin of many other opponents, all of whom he labeled "Communists." A noisy uprising by aviation forces in Rio late in 1935 gave the president an opportunity to arrest hundreds of real or accused Communists inside and without the military. While the world has since had many demonstrations of the truth that a handful of radicals can capture an army and a state, the Communist purge of 1935 seemed to many a mere excuse for Vargas to rid himself of enemies. After a time Prestes was sent to the penitentiary, and while Vargas ruled on in safety from Communism for another decade, the outlawed movement continued to attract intellectuals and spokesmen of urban workers.

Getulio Vargas was strangely tolerant of a danger that appeared far more threatening than Communism. This was a fascist movement led by an eloquent pseudo-intellectual named Plinio Salgado. Obviously copying Mussolini and Hitler, Salgado organized units of green-shirted warriors who marched, saluted, and chanted in the fascist manner. Making a symbol of the rising sun, these *Integralistas* talked of "integrating" Brazil—whatever that meant—and jeered at liberals, Jews, capitalists, and Communists. Their appeal was most effective among middle class conservatives of German or Italian descent. For several years the regime left them alone, though it was rightly suspected that Nazi Germany was providing funds and direction for their activities. This may have been because their objectives coincided with those that Vargas more or less covertly cherished, and also because he sought the support of Brazilians of German, Italian, and Japanese origin. Also, Nazi Germany had many finished goods to barter for Brazil's raw materials, and in some years of the decade she replaced Britain as the republic's second-best trading partner.

Salgado had reason to expect a rise in his fortunes in the elections scheduled for January 1938. President Vargas was ineligible for immediate reelection, and so one of his cabinet ministers ran as his heir presumptive. But then Vargas fell out with his candidate for unexplained reasons, and other office-seekers had little appeal. Thus Salgado became a serious contender as the *Integralista* nominee. By late 1937 it seemed that he could scarcely fail to be elected president, quite likely with the blessing of the administration, and the Nazis were openly gloating over the prospect. Yet the foxy Vargas did not commit his prestige, allowing himself only to mutter occasionally that he was depressed over the situation. In October 1937 he suddenly declared a state of siege, which permitted him to alert the police and the military, and he named his brother chief of police for Rio. On November 10, Getulio went on the radio to announce that the elections were called off. He himself would continue as president, and a new constitution would be prepared. Except for the disappointed *Integralistas* there was little open protest over this step. In delivering the country from Plinio Salgado the president appeared to be acting more like a patriot than a tyrant.

The Vargas Years: Second Phase (1937–1945)

PRESENTLY a new constitution was ready for public inspection. Drafted by a hand-picked committee, perhaps by only one man, this document dismayed liberal Brazilians and friends of democracy abroad. For the republic Vargas substituted an entity he called *O estado novo* (the New State), clearly inspired by the corporate states of Italy and Portugal. The president was to have autocratic powers, to be practically a dictator. A National Economic Council was to represent business, professional, and labor groups in advising the president. A congress was called for, but its powers were vague. Local government practically disappeared, a situation Vargas dramatized by having Girl Scouts burn all the state flags in a spectacular ceremony. Civil liberties were apparently to be respected only at the president's pleasure, and a rather ominous statement of duties suggested the subordination of the individual to the national government. And the Catholic Church was to form an integral part of the political structure. Full of undemocratic implications as this constitution of 1937 was, adherents of representative government could draw some comfort from the fact that it was never ratified nor promulgated. Vargas simply ruled on as dictator, using parts of the constitution when they served his purpose and ignoring the rest. The National Economic Council was called into being, but congress was not. With all political parties being dissolved, the nation's public life all but ceased, and Vargas ran the vast republic without open challenge or criticism.

Ideologically satisfied as the *Integralistas* must have been with O *estado novo*, they felt that Vargas had robbed them of certain victory by his coup. After months of planning, a great number of Green Shirts enveloped the Guanabara Palace, then the presidential residence, in May 1938. According to one version, they forced their way into Vargas' presence, only to find the little president in pajamas and holding a pistol, surrounded by a few armed members of his family. For several hours he bravely stood off the intruders, time enough for General Eurico Gaspar Dutra, his minister of war, to learn of the affair and to gather loyal troops. At length the *Integralistas* surrendered, joining the *paulistas* of 1932 and the Communists of 1935 among those Vargas had vanquished. Plinio Salgado fled to Europe for first-hand studies of successful fascism, and his organization was shattered. Fascinated as Vargas had been by Adolf Hitler, his narrow escape was decisive in convincing him of the mortal danger of befriending the Nazis. Satisfactory proof came to light that the German embassy in Rio knew more about the attempt than was proper, and the ambassador left Brazil. If Vargas continued to ape fascist methods in ruling his own country, he was well aware that Nazi Germany could mean no good for himself or for Brazil.

The dictatorship tightened its hold over the population, though Vargas' own sense of moderation and the good-natured casualness of things Brazilian kept oppression within bounds. Secret police agents opened mail and spied on suspected dissenters. Perhaps a hundred political prisoners were confined on the tropical island of Fernão de Noronha. Ever more stringent censorship kept the newspapers from publishing information unpalatable to the regime, and gradually the journals were compelled to print false news or official propaganda as directed by Vargas' department of public information. Sometimes they fought back by omitting to record news of the president's speeches or anniversary celebrations, but any serious recalcitrance could be avenged by increased taxation or the withholding of paper by the government. A famous journal, O *Estado de São Paulo*, was punished for refusing to fall into line by being shut down altogether on the patently spurious charge that its building was used to store weapons. Few others were so unyielding, and so Brazil came to have a controlled press. Naturally, democratic friends of Brazil were distressed by this development. As Hitler went from triumph to triumph between 1938 and 1942, it became a matter of deep concern that this historically easy-going country should imitate his methods in domestic affairs. Yet Vargas insisted that all he was doing was promoting "disciplined democracy," one not less free than Mexico with its one-party system and other Latin American republics. The personality of the genial dictator with his perpetual smile and the optimistic attitude of the *cariocas* were arguments that things were not really as bad as they seemed from a distance.

With his authority strengthened under the New State, Vargas applied renewed energy to the several programs which had been remaking Brazil since 1930. Industrialization was his central goal at this stage. Light industries sprang up apace: textiles, newsprint, household appliances, sporting goods, chemical products, cement, and the assembly of automobiles and trucks. Officially, Vargas was a staunch advocate of economic nationalism, as testified by tariff barriers, requirements that alien concerns hire Brazilians, and speeches against "capitalist imperialists." In fact, foreign money and enterprisers poured into the country and found their way smoothed by the government. Officially, the New State frowned on the free enterprise system and reverted with a vengeance to the paternalism of colonial days and of modern totalitarianism. In fact, businessmen were usually free to create and experiment as they wished. It was through no oversight that Vargas neglected to reform the historic tax structure that favored free economic growth. Industrialization also sped the tempo of urbanism, with Rio de Janeiro and São Paulo drawing talent and surplus labor from the hinterland to man the new factories. It required, furthermore, drastic improvements in the transportation system, which the regime attempted by enlarging the railways and by constructing highways, airports, and docks. Brazilians delightedly took to the air age, which promised to compress their mammoth country. Electric power and irrigation of garden areas near the cities were urgently needed to support industrial growth. Accordingly, the administration plunged ahead with plans for dams on an enormous scale, the most spectacular project being that of the São Francisco Valley, which runs northward some distance behind the coast. São Paulo, which had already reversed the course of streams so they would form lakes for hydroelectrical purposes and empty into the Atlantic instead of the Amazon, went ahead with further developments. Such projects caught the imagination of the Brazilian people, who admired daring plans, contempt for costs, and disregard of nagging realities.

A survey of national resources undertaken by the regime revealed that Brazil was even richer than suspected. The variety of plant life was staggering, by far the greatest of any country. Almost any food, medicine, or wood could be produced, and the government had some success in fostering the cultivation and sale of such items. In Minas Gerais, Goias, and Mato Grosso new minerals were discovered: bauxite, from which a flourishing aluminum industry grew; industrial diamonds; manganese, which the United States lacked and therefore purchased avidly during the war; and most important of all, iron, the world's largest deposit at Itabira, a region convenient to Rio and São Paulo. Coal was also found, both in the northeast and the far south, but not enough to fuel a large industrial plant. Petroleum eluded the surveyors, thus, pessimists feared, condemning Brazil to a perpetual status as a secondary industrial power. Complementing these activities was the continued growth, partly attributable to government sponsorship, of agriculture. Farmers were taught new techniques in plant culture and soil usage, while modern methods of fighting insects helped them to increase production. Coffee, cotton, sugar, cacao, rice, beans, citrus fruits, *yerba maté*, and other crops felt the benefits of improved methods.

In promoting social welfare Vargas was emulating his contemporaries in both totalitarian and democratic countries. While he outlawed strikes under the New State, syndicates of labor, government, and management usually offered justice and sometimes favors to industrial workers. He further mollified the proletariat with a labor code of 1943, which offered the Brazilian workingman social security, pensions, limitations on hours, and insurance. The government also built enormous low-cost dwelling developments and financed free-care clinics and cheap restaurants. Such benefits seldom reached the rural poor, who continued to live at a subsistence level as sharecroppers or ill-paid harvesters. It is not strange that so many betook themselves to the cities. Vargas' hold on the masses deepened during these years. They venerated him as Getulio, *O pai do povo* (the father of the people), a benefactor who had brought them dignity and hope. To more fortunate classes, particularly among *paulistas*, such idolatry was a source of bitter jokes, but Vargas was genuinely popular.

A far-reaching educational program likewise encouraged the common people, though it was pathetically inadequate in view of the need. Vocational institutes transformed many a primitive peasant into a skilled worker or scientific farmer. Under Vargas the number of primary schools doubled and the secondary schools, whose graduates might be addressed as "doctor," quintupled. As in Mexico, rural schools were social centers where physical training and health education improved standards of life and where adults as well as children might learn their letters and numbers. In 1937 the University of Rio de Janeiro became the University of Brazil and advanced rapidly into prominence as one of the finest institutions in Latin America. São Paulo, never willing to be outclassed by the capital, started a university in 1934 which also developed in giant strides, before many years acquiring an elaborate University City in what was fleetingly the countryside until the city grew about it. Other universities were organized in Rio Grande do Sul and Minas Gerais. While medicine and science were the most respected academic specialities in Brazil, the country produced a world-renowned anthropologist in Gilberto Freyre, whose own training had been at Baylor and Columbia. His insights into the racial evolution of Brazil stimulated a vast amount of research in this field, where the nation provided a unique laboratory for problems the rest of the world was concerning itself with more urgently each year. Finally, Brazilian education experienced some betterment as the Church, now favored by the government, became more active in blighted areas.

In foreign affairs Vargas succeeded in confusing his countrymen and outsiders alike. He ostentatiously befriended President Roosevelt during his visit in 1936 and South American leaders, all in the best Good Neighbor style. Yet he exchanged cordial communications with Hitler and Mussolini and lionized the latter's son and daughter when they came to Brazil. Since no one knew just where he stood, dictators and democrats alike courted Vargas. It was a basic fact of life that Brazil urgently needed the United States, her chief customer and supplier. British interests, especially in the way of investments, were also deep, and England was traditionally the ally of the Portuguese-speaking world. To educated Brazilians France was almost a mother country. But Italy was literally a mother country to many citizens of Brazil, as were Germany, Spain, and Japan to a lesser degree, and German trade was larger than British. In such a pluralistic society it was natural that different blocs responded in different ways to World War II. Vargas seemed sympathetic ideologically to the Axis but was usually careful not to alienate the Allies. However, when Hitler conquered France in June 1940, an event most cultured Latin Americans took as a personal tragedy, Vargas derided liberalism as decadent and spoke of an imperative new ordering of the world's power structure. It was well-known that the armed forces of Brazil admired the success of the Nazi war machine and were fearful of getting in its way. And the press, largely controlled by the regime, was more friendly to the Axis than to the Allies. In Washington there was an alarm bordering on panic that Hitler might establish an air base at Dakar in French West Africa, which was only 1,600 miles from a Brazil that could become his ally.

Vargas was not as foolish as that, however. He had experienced Nazi "friendship" in several hard-driven barter deals and during the *Integralista* rising. No amount of conciliatory words from Berlin could conceal the ultimate doom of Brazil should Hitler ever succeed in organizing Europe and Africa. Accordingly, late in 1940 Vargas agreed to permit the United States to construct air and naval bases on Brazilian soil in exchange for arms and funds. While he minimized the likelihood of a Nazi invasion, he also consented to transfer garrisons to the undefended northeastern bulge, where most of the bases were. By 1941 American naval units were using them to help the British in the Battle of the Atlantic, and hundreds of aircraft were stopping to refuel as they flew to British units in the Middle East. During 1942 the bases were vastly important for the war at sea and, for a time, the sole route for American airplanes headed for the Far East, Russia, and England. Had Vargas declined to make them available, the United States might have occupied them, but matters never came to that point. It may have been Brazil's foreign minister, Oswaldo Aranha, rather than Vargas who aligned the Land of the Southern Cross so firmly with the United States at the Rio de Janeiro conference of American states in January 1942, following Pearl Harbor, but the dictator permitted it, and in August Brazil declared war.[1] She contributed liberally to the naval forces that patrolled the Atlantic and became the only Latin American country to send men in any significant number to the fighting front. Air units trained in the United States—where their deliriously individualistic approach to the art of pilotage was the despair of their instructors—and afterward performed very creditably in the Mediterranean theater. An army of 25,000 Brazilians also served in that theater. Hoping to illustrate their racial theories, the Nazis deliberately struck hard at sectors held by the Negroid Brazilians, only to encounter stout soldiers who fought as well as any others.

Brazil's natural resources were also of great importance to the United Nations. American agencies purchased practically all of her surplus coffee, sugar, rice, wood, cacao, cotton, beef, and minerals—more than could be shipped for months at a time. A heroic effort to restore the rubber industry, whose products the Americans desperately needed because of the Japanese conquest of Far Eastern sources, did not come to fruition in time to be of much assistance. A large steel complex at Volta Redonda was completed with Anglo-American funds and technical advice. Lend-Lease aid to the extent of $560,000,000, which Brazil later repaid, improved railway, highway, harbor, and airport facilities. Lavish gifts of military hardware, by far the most any Latin American country got, greatly strengthened Brazil's armed forces, to the acute annoyance of Argentina. With abundant foreign earnings, loans, and advice from outside experts, Brazil was stimulated and enriched during the war years. Her industries grew faster than ever, and she won markets for textiles

---

1. German submarines had sunk thirteen Brazilian vessels, including a troopship that involved a heavy loss of life.

in Spanish South America which European factories had previously supplied. Perhaps Vargas had been calculating when he sided with the
United Nations, who had seapower, air power, and purchasing power.
Yet selfish interest and national interest coincided, and Vargas did what
a responsible Brazilian leader should have done, however much he may
have grumbled in private, as many said. If he was ideologically an embar-
rassment to democratic elements in the United Nations, he proved by
deeds that he supported their cause.

THE REPUBLIC RESTORED

During the war years the Vargas dictatorship showed few signs of becoming mellow, but its henchmen grew slothful as they ate the fruits of
power year after year. And, as in 1918–1919, the idealism professed by
the winning side in the war filtered into the country, re-kindling sentiments never extinguished by the New State. During the spring of 1945
much restlessness was evident, with riots, demonstrations, and illegal
strikes. The people seemed to be tiring of Vargas after fifteen years and
also irritated by the inflation and shortages caused by the war. Some of
the incidents were merely rowdy, others grim. Still others had a comic
aspect, as when lepers escaped from a leprosarium and terrified a town
by parading for better conditions, or when exasperated commuters near
Rio aggravated their plight by burning dozens of rickety railway cars in
protest over a shortage of equipment. Sensing that the populace was
about to boil over, Vargas announced that elections would be held to
ratify the constitution of 1937 and to choose a congress and a new president. These concessions brought politics out of a long slumber with a
bound, possibly to Vargas' amazement. Passions long suppressed charged
through the atmosphere, and the impending dissolution of the dictatorship was taken for granted. As usual, Vargas kept his thoughts to himself. He stood aside while political parties resurrected themselves and
nominated candidates. For reasons never made clear, he released Luis
Carlos Prestes from an imprisonment of nine years and established relations with the Soviet Union. Prestes seemed anything but vengeful over
his long incarceration. Apparently he ordered the Communists—of
whom there suddenly were a great number—to praise the retiring Getulio.

But was Vargas really going to retire? All over the country appeared
the sign, *Queremos* (We want), which was known to be officially inspired as a slogan for Vargas to remain. The Communists behaved in a
very puzzling way, as though they wanted Vargas to continue in office.
Otherwise, the campaign was off to an exciting start, three parties besides
the Communist having organized. The Social Democrats nominated

General Eurico Gaspar Dutra, a longtime minister of war under Vargas. An air force officer who had distinguished himself in the war, Brigadier Eduardo Gomes, was the candidate of the Democratic Union. Plinio Salgado returned to Brazil to revive the *Integralistas*. Although Vargas was expected to support Dutra, he remained aloof, smiling less warmly now and more like Mona Lisa. As 1945 wore on, he intimated now and then that none of the candidates was big enough to fill his shoes. Rumors circulated about military and police precautions. And then, in October, Getulio appointed his brother to be chief of the Rio police. The parallel with 1937 was too ominous to be ignored, and the country became tense as another coup appeared imminent. At this point the highest-ranking officers held serious discussions at the Military Club in the capital. On October 29 a committee of generals called on President Vargas. When they left, they had his resignation. Getulio was soon on an airplane headed for his ranch in Rio Grande do Sul.

Eurico Gaspar Dutra, 1946–1951: Boom Out of Control

THE dictatorship had been terminated bloodlessly, almost in a gentlemanly way, pleasing most of the people as it seemed. With Vargas deposed, the presidential election scheduled for December 1945 could proceed, and political life was fervid. The test, which was probably the most honest ever held in Brazil, showed General Dutra the victor by a considerable margin. He was a solid man, one who enjoyed much prestige long before and long after his term. Pro-fascist utterances he had made in the 1930's were not held against him, for moderates and liberals apparently cast their votes in his favor. After his inauguration early in 1946, the first order of business was to regularize the constitutional situation. A convention chosen for this purpose devised the constitution of 1946, which established a centralized republic that called itself federal. While the delegates were perhaps disingenuous in creating a powerful national government while pretending not to, they were quite serious about establishing a true separation of powers. The office of president was downgraded so that its occupant could no longer dominate the states, congress, judiciary, and armed services as though he were a law unto himself.[2] It was the congress that was to exercise the sovereign power, but the other branches were intended to be sturdy enough to protect themselves from encroachments. In this way Brazil might develop

2. A further restriction on the president was the provision that the vice-president might be elected independently of him and from an opposing party, as happened in 1960.

into a sound political organism providing both equilibrium for democratic practices and responsiveness to social needs. All adults who could
inscribe their names, addresses, and occupations in registration books,
a number generously estimated at 40 per cent of this age group, were to
be enfranchised. The constitution, which came into effect in 1946, contained the familiar lists of freedoms and social objectives found in
Latin American charters of this type.

President Dutra strove commendably to fill his constitutional role.
He traveled extensively and officiated at many public ceremonies. A visit
to the United States, the first of a Brazilian head of state since Pedro II
went in 1876, bolstered his prestige, for the northern country was still
popular. Dutra also exhibited a workmanlike earnestness in dealing with
the nation's problems without inflating his constitutional position. Yet
he was personally colorless, and the times clamored for more dynamic
leadership. Before long he seemed a rather somber figure overwhelmed
by his difficulties. Perhaps he was, for Brazil was churning with undirected
passions and restless forces that few politicians could gauge. The Communists, who had astonished students of politics by winning 600,000
votes, a tenth of those cast in 1945, were particularly threatening. Prestes
was noisy and troublesome, bent on disrupting the deliberations of congress by undignified tactics and throwing business life into chaos through
strikes and demonstrations. His alliance with Getulio Vargas, who had
modestly reappeared in Rio as a senator, indicated an ambition to inherit the former dictator's popularity with the masses. Vargas himself
was thought to be senile enough, or spiteful enough, to cause trouble by
lending his name to the Communist cause. Agitation mounted until it
seemed possible for Prestes to immobilize the chief cities and seize power.
In 1947, President Dutra broke off relations with Russia, ostensibly because of insults directed at him by the Moscow press. Early in 1948 he
persuaded congress to outlaw the Communist party, whereupon the
army and police fell upon many of its cells and made numerous arrests.
Prestes went into hiding and spent some years flitting into and out of
Brazil in disguise. It was obvious that he wielded much power over a
Communist organization that was by no means broken.

Noisy as politics were, economic affairs dominated the atmosphere of
postwar Brazil. The boom that had begun in the late 1930's and surged
through the war years now carried the nation into transports of optimism. The large reserve of foreign credits built up during the world conflict was now squandered. Dutra's administration made little effort to direct the nation's spending into such sober purposes as constructing a
larger industrial plant or improving agriculture through farm machinery.
Much of the reserve vanished in order to import automobiles and luxury
articles. It seemed that Brazil was determined to reverse the rules by

enjoying a high standard of living before establishing a sound economic foundation to support one. Not only was there questionable spending, but corruption on as large a scale as the republic had known demoralized the government and clogged the wheels of commerce. A thriving black market, wastage in building highways, airports, dams, and dwellings, and percentages taken by underpaid bureaucrats were accepted features of society. Nobody seemed to care particularly; Brazil has been singularly free of spoilsports who preach the dull virtues. Private individuals were quite as free-spending as their government. The construction of palatial mansions and luxury apartments turned the urban centers into monuments of modernistic and futuristic architecture—with buildings on stilts, lavish use of glass, daring (occasionally fatal) experiments in stress, riotous colors, imaginative exploitation of sunlight, breeze, and shade— that were so functional and so revolutionary they seemed an American advertiser's depiction of the world of tomorrow. All of this would have been to the good had the slums not grown even faster.

While automobiles cost thrice what they did in the United States and gasoline was a dollar per gallon, countless Brazilians found the means to buy them and to drive with an abandon that made Rio the most unsafe capital in the world. In defense of the Brazilians, it should be realized that real estate and vehicles were sound investments when prices rose steeply, as they were doing. As usual, the continuous spurt in prices outran real income. Strikes and constant agitation for wage increases kept the business world tense, almost in a state of chronic hysteria. Wage increments were frequently granted, but then prices always shot up again. In contrast to the United States, possessing classes in Brazil favored inflation, for they found ways to re-invest their capital so as to stay well ahead of the cost of living, and many individuals were clever enough to make one fortune after another. Wage earners, of course, were usually victims of this process.

The experiences of better-governed countries during the postwar period indicate that these conditions might have been curbed. Brazilians are not the most disciplined of peoples, but they are far from devoid of public spirit. Yet the Dutra administration shared the euphoria and refused to apply restraints. It may be instructive to note that some good came of its policy, though moral philosophers and orthodox economists shook their heads. Another campaign of school-building and an imaginative attack on illiteracy by mobile units reduced the percentage of unlettered from sixty to fifty, or so the authorities maintained. The São Francisco Valley project went ahead, its hydroelectric dams providing irrigation and power for vast areas. This and other projects made Brazil the fourth nation on the planet with respect to electrification, though there never seemed to be enough current to keep up with the needs of Rio and São Paulo, whose streets were often dark because of power rationing. The government began a railroad to link Bolivia with Santos, the seaport of São Paulo, in the hope of tapping the wealth of that land-locked nation. Volta Redonda succeeded so well in producing steel that it was greatly expanded, and new mills were projected. Toward the end of his term Dutra proclaimed a typically ambitious plan, SALTE, to promote public health, nutrition, transportation, and electrification. In all, the material development of Brazil proceeded despite the inflation and fiscal policies that outraged foreign economists. And just when the boom showed signs of collapse, early in 1950, the Korean War suddenly restored high prices and good markets for Brazilian exports.

Getulio Vargas Again, 1951–1954

THE presidential election of 1950 attracted that perennial candidate, Plinio Salgado, who now pointed to Portugal rather than the late Nazi Germany as an ideal. President Dutra's party, the Social Democrats, nominated Christiano Machado, a politician of little appeal. As in 1945, the Democratic Union selected Brigadier Eduardo Gomes. It seemed curious and a little pathetic that Getulio Vargas, now sixty-seven, should enter the race as the candidate of a hastily-organized Labor Party which had covert Communist support. As the campaign proceeded, it became apparent that he was still revered by the common people as O pai do povo and that he was not, as the journalists said, a politician whose future was past. Even so, most foreign students were unprepared for his astonishing victory in December, when he won sixteen of the nineteen states. His popular plurality was less impressive, however, and his party failed to carry congress. It was a gratifying time for the former dictator, nervous as it made friends of democracy. The masses evidently remembered him for the favors he had brought them before and still looked upon him as a magician who would make their dreams come true. Since the military hierarchy had reason to be fearful after its role in deposing him in 1945, the generals took steps to protect the armed services from the president's grasp and to make sure the dictatorship would not be revived. Getulio may have been innocent of any such design. He was humble in victory and chastened by his previous experiences. When he took office in January 1951, he spoke admiringly of Britain's Labor government and of socialistic measures in Scandinavia, but he offered no program of his own. It turned out that he really had no plans in particular.

The absence of leadership was not wholly a matter of Vargas' personal decline. Other elements than the presidency had weight under the constitution of 1946. Congress, which was dominated by the president's opponents, frequently ignored his recommendations and harassed his administration. The national judiciary was no longer a mere implement of the presidential will. On several occasions the supreme court condemned Vargas and interdicted actions proposed by his subordinates. Most important of all was the military, which tended to usurp from congress the ultimate sovereignty of the republic, and the generals were so independent of Vargas as to be defiant. Praiseworthy as this balance of power was as an exercise in republican democracy, it did not make for effective government. Brazil had near-chaos at the top resembling that of the Third and Fourth French Republics, with the result that public spirit was low and consistent official policies were made impossible. Perhaps things were not as bad as they appeared to foreign commentators and political scientists, who repeatedly prophesied a Communist or military dictatorship in Brazil. There may have been a self-regulatory character among all of the elements clamoring to govern the gigantic republic. At least Brazil was a free country, in contrast to many of her Spanish-speaking sisters and to Portugal, her motherland.

With Brazil's central problem, spending more abroad than was earned, no one had the strength to deal. While exports—two-thirds of which were coffee—were high and expanding, imports consistently stayed ahead of them. All of the crude oil and petroleum products, automobiles, airplanes, railway cars, and heavy machinery, and most of the coal, wheat, capital goods, and luxuries came from abroad. A stern government in Rio might have regulated foreign commerce at least to the extent of keeping exports and imports in balance. Instead, successive administrations permitted popular demands and corrupt pressures to play havoc with the trading system. On one occasion, just after the Korean War ended, Vargas called in the eminent diplomat Oswaldo Aranha to impose rigid controls on foreign commerce, but his austerity program lasted only a few months. Neither officials nor the public would stand for it. And so Brazil continued to incur larger obligations to overseas creditors than could be met. The International Monetary Fund and various official and private agencies of the United States repeatedly bailed the Vargas administration out of its deficits, but increasingly harsh scoldings from those sources suggested that rescue missions might someday cease.

Foreign investments did something to redress the economic imbalance, though every politician or publicist who valued his popularity denounced "exploitation" and talked of restricting or even confiscating alien investments. Notwithstanding such threats, which often were not serious, capital poured into Brazil from the United States and, after it revived, western Europe. Yet the volume would surely have been larger had there been more hospitality. The case of Petrobrás, the national petroleum monopoly, was revealing. Badly as Brazil needed oil and its derivatives, Vargas catered to nationalist passions by insisting that foreigners not be employed. It was regarded as a great concession when Petrobrás hired American geologists to search for oil pools. When a few were discovered, mainly in Pará, the monopoly jealously kept foreign technicians at a distance and operated so inefficiently that Brazil continued to devote a third of her foreign credits to the importation of petroleum. Moreover, the government neglected a great potential for foreign earnings in tourism. As spectacular and picturesque a land as Brazil might have drawn hordes of visitors. Yet neither the authorities nor private agencies stirred themselves particularly, with the result that tourists often found inadequate facilities, little guidance, and sometimes an indifferent reception.

Vargas continued to gamble, and not in vain, on Uncle Sam's unwillingness to let Brazil go bankrupt. The material development of the country belied the grim statistics in trade balances, and it could be argued that fiscal difficulties were superficial matters. Agriculture, still the basic industry, progressed as mechanization raised production and improved transportation permitted the better distribution of crops. An American, Nelson Rockefeller, worked through the International Basic Economy Corporation to spread knowledge among farmers of soil erosion prevention, insect eradication, fertilization, and scientific crop breeding. The livestock industry also improved markedly as imported bulls, often Brahmas from India and Santa Gertrudis from Texas, changed the character of the herds. Southern Brazil began to rival the Argentine pampas in numbers of cattle. The domestic market for beef also grew rapidly, so much so that hordes of cattle were smuggled from Uruguay to meet it. While the manufacture of small articles continued to expand hectically, Brazil was also determined to build a heavy industrial plant. Steel-making at Volta Redonda had been so successful that a half-dozen other plants and rolling mills were erected, largely with European and Japanese capital. Having long imported automobiles and trucks, Brazil began to assemble them from imported parts and then to undertake their entire manufacture, a process that involved the distasteful participation of foreign experts. At the same time highways were being improved and new dirt roads cut into isolated areas. The government also began the long-delayed project to consolidate the railway system into an effective north-south network. Brazilians liked to assert, however, that they had skipped the railway age by leaping from horses into airplanes. Probably no other people are as addicted to flying as the Brazilians, and a mushrooming aviation industry has brought modern civilization to areas that never knew a train and regarded an automobile as a curiosity.

The growth of Brazilian cities, especially São Paulo, both inspired and alarmed students of urbanism. The *paulista* capital was now the dynamo of South America, quite likely its largest city, and, its citizens maintained, a threat to New York's pre-eminence in the western hemisphere. Both São Paulo and Rio de Janeiro drew people far faster than they could provide homes for them, with the result that *favelas*, communities of tents and shacks, surrounded them. Apparently rural Brazilians preferred the *favelas* to their places of origin, for they flocked into them by the thousand every year, living in squalor until they could be absorbed into the labor forces and older slums of the cities. Skyscrapers gave São Paulo the appearance of Los Angeles or Chicago. Rio specialized more in modernistic grace and elegance and was so beautiful that no city could be compared to it. Brazilian builders and architects were likely to imitate the style of the native pioneers Oscar Niemeyer, who was one of the designers of the United Nations headquarters, and Lúcio Costa. Those who could afford it constructed luxury apartment houses, villas, and magnificent residences and hotels in their style, and the government was by no means parsimonious in building palatial offices. São Paulo and Rio were only the most spectacular scenes of pell-mell construction. Porto Alegre, an old state capital and seaport, was transformed into a modernistic marvel, and a new capital, Goiana, was planned to the last tree and curb before being started. Ancient São Salvador, the colorful capital of colonial times, suddenly began to grow after two centuries of stagnation, and Manaos, the relic of the rubber boom far up the Amazon, came back to life. Brazil seemed to be leading the worldwide trend by allowing her urban agglomerations to expand beyond comprehension, rebuilding her lesser cities, and seeing small towns and the countryside become depopulated. If her slums spawned even faster than the new housing, she was by no means unique.

Getulio Vargas could no more grasp the miracle that made Brazil what she was than could others. The country was defying economic laws and thriving nonetheless. It was dizzy from growth and yet in a bad temper. Politicians from all sides cried out for him to do something, but they abused him whenever he tried. Responsible men lamented that the country was in a desperate condition despite appearances, and everyone seemed critical. The president's prestige sank as reports of impending ruin came in daily; he was also shaken by rumors of forthcoming disclosures of corruption enormous even by Brazilian standards. Congress openly defied him, the supreme court slapped him, businessmen shouted warnings, and the military growled. The aging Getulio seemed helpless amid the clamor. In August 1954 things came to a head with the attempted assassination of Carlos Lacerda, a journalist who had often proved a gadfly to the ruling groups and had stridently denounced Vargas. While Lacerda was only wounded, an air force officer died, and a national scandal grew out of the suspicion that the killing was attributable to someone very close to Vargas. Pressures of an extreme nature were brought to bear on Getulio, more than his broken morale could sustain, and military rebellion impended. After a few days of crisis, he agreed to turn over his office to Vice President João Café Filho (John Coffee, Jr., as American newspapers liked to explain). Then, on August 24, Vargas shot and killed himself, an act utterly out of character for a man so genial. One of his suicide notes, which may have been spurious, blamed foreign (American?) interests for driving him to self-destruction, but no one seemed to know the truth of the tragedy. The politicians and generals had reason to be alarmed by the explosion of popular anger and sorrow, for Getulio was beloved by many. After a few days of demonstrations and lamentations, the situation quieted to the extent that the late president's remains could be flown to Rio Grande do Sul for burial.

João Café Filho, 1954–1955, and Juscelino Kubitschek, 1955–1961

THE new president was a Presbyterian from Rio Grande do Norte whose caliber was untested. Straightway he affronted the leading figures of the government and business world by pleading for morality in public affairs. Soon he came to be regarded as a killjoy who might puncture the boom with his dour preachments, and in any case only a caretaker president. While he was personally upright and was earnestly desirous of reforming the maddening economic structure, Café lacked the prestige to compel respect for his ideas. And so things went on as before, with the cost of living spurting and the cruzeiro falling. Many well-to-do persons who had learned to turn these conditions to their benefit repeatedly made fortunes, and the less fortunate majority threatened and complained. American financial aid was still available to avert a fiscal collapse. More dangerous than the financial situation was the growth of Communism, a supposedly outlawed movement whose ubiquity was advertised wherever there was space on walls for placards or painted signs. Prestes, who had undergone a temporary decline after the death of Josef Stalin in 1953, restored his position by 1955 and was known to be operating confidently from Bolivia, Uruguay, and secret hideouts inside Brazil. Congress and local organs of government behaved riotously, and a total administrative breakdown appeared imminent to many students, who probably under-estimated the continuities beneath the boiling surface. Only the armed services, particularly the army, seemed firm during the mid-fifties.

Maneuvers for the presidential election of October 1955 began early. President Café's warning that the nation was too tense to risk a contest at the polls went unheeded, as all of his warnings did. Governor Juscelino Kubitschek of Minas Gerais, a physician of German-Polish descent, won the nomination of the Social Democrats. He also captured the Labor Party by choosing its leader as his running mate. This João Goulart, known as "Jango," had been a neighbor and long-time protegé of Vargas and a minister of labor whose demagoguery suggested a close study of Perón's labor-union fascism in Argentina. Left-wing support of the Kubitschek-Goulart coalition appeared complete as the Communists swung into line behind the ticket. The Democratic Union chose the army chief of staff, General Juarez Tavora, who attracted conservatives and moderates with his appeals for morality and patriotism. Two extremist candidates drained some support from the major parties. One was the unrepentant Naziphile, Plinio Salgado; the other was Adhemar de Barros, an opportunist who had become immensely rich as governor of São Paulo but had excited thereby more jovial admiration than indignation. In a close vote that showed the right and left almost evenly divided, Juscelino Kubitschek and João Goulart won a small plurality and the election.

For some weeks Brazil quivered on the brink of political collapse. President Café had a heart attack and was succeeded, not as president but as occupant of the office, by the next in line, Senator Carlos Luz. Rumors flew about that Luz was intriguing to prevent Kubitschek's inauguration, whereupon the army removed him and installed the following in line, Senator Nereu Ramos. Luz protested that he was still acting president, and then Café confused matters by announcing his recovery. Brazil had three claimants for the presidential office! For more than two months the generals saw to it that Luz and Café did not leave their homes and permitted Nereu Ramos to sit in the president's chair, where he did little but sign routine papers. Serious as the crisis was, it struck many citizens as funny, and the *cariocas* comported themselves with their usual gay nonchalance. Meanwhile, President-elect Kubitschek made an air tour of the United States and Europe, where he assured important leaders that his Communist supporters would not deflect him from fidelity to the cause of the free world. Perhaps the most significant aspect about the situation by the end of 1955 was the army's full assurance that it would see to Kubitschek's installation, though the chief of staff himself had been narrowly defeated in the election. It was a good precedent for the military to set, one that would soon be followed in Argentina. As self-appointed custodian of the moderating power once exercised by Emperor Pedro II, the officer caste showed a true dedication to fair play and to constitutionalism.

At his inauguration on January 31, 1956, Juscelino Kubitschek, who was fond of grandiose projects, promised to make "fifty years of progress in five." It was a slogan to lift the hearts of Brazilians. His attitude toward the future perfectly suited the mood of his countrymen. Brazil must "think big," dream of greatness, and expand in all directions regardless of tiresome facts. Somehow it would all come out right. Thus, after taking one look at the financial situation, which he pronounced "desperate," Kubitschek proceeded to ignore it and to lay plans for further construction. The cruzeiro dove from 96 to the dollar to 221 between late 1957 and early 1960. Inflation, strikes, riots, and the collapse of credit had been so familiar to the nation that their abiding presence, and worsening, could do little to dampen spirits. While the International Monetary Fund and various foreign creditors washed their hands of Brazil, Uncle Sam remained a reliable source of funds. To make sure the rich uncle did not tire of helping Brazil, Kubitschek resorted to the polite threats other nations had found successful: he talked of shifting the axis of Brazilian commerce to the Communist world, though realists pointed out that Russians and Chinese were not fond of coffee.

President Kubitschek also volunteered a solution to the fundamental problems of Latin America. Operation Pan America, as it came to be called, would pool the resources of all the nations in the western hemisphere to increase agricultural production, stabilize markets, and elevate the standard of living of the masses. The United States was mildly receptive to this costly venture, most of which it would have to underwrite, and then fervently so after the rise of a new Communist threat in Cuba. At the Bogotá conference of 1960 a modified version of Operation Pan America was authorized. Kubitschek also excited his countrymen with the prospect of developing all of the Brazilian hinterland, so much of which was still untouched by Western civilization. Some enthusiasts asserted that the Amazon basin, which contained about four million people, could accommodate a half-billion. Kubitschek saw no reason why jungle-clearing and air-conditioning on a massive scale might not transform this area into a suitable home for Brazilians of the future. And he built Brasília.

Many citizens scolded Kubitschek for reviving the long-dormant project to remove the capital from Rio de Janeiro to a more central point. It was typical of the president, and of the appeal he had for Brazilians, that he brushed aside all objections as small-minded and plunged ahead. Brasília was a symbol of the nation's determination to become great, regardless of nagging realities. The site was a sunny, arid spot in the high plateau of the state of Goias (wicked tongues said Juscelino liked the climate because it was good for his asthma), connected neither by rail, river, nor highway to anything else. Foreign embassy staffs disliked the idea of leaving glamorous Rio, where they had already invested in expensive headquarters. Long-entrenched merchants and caterers of the federal district were entirely unenthusiastic about losing so many customers. Important officials were dismayed by the prospect of giving up their residences in one of the world's great cities to move into the middle of nowhere. Hosts of minor bureaucrats saw real hardship if they had to transfer their families to new homes. And, of course, Brazil could not afford it.

Yet Kubitschek played on the nation's faith in the future and won his game. At fantastic expense, with the usual discounts for graft, ultra-modernistic buildings sprouted like mushrooms from the bleak plateau, many of them designed by the renowned Oscar Niemeyer and Lúcio Costa. The president decided that the move must be made on Tiradentes Day, April 21, 1960, come what may. Work went on night and day under clouds of dust, not even halting for President Eisenhower's visit early that year. On the day set, thousands of airplanes, trucks, and buses delivered the skeleton administration of the national government with its civil servants and office equipment. Somehow the grumblings were drowned out by the carnival-like merriment and the delirious chaos. Juscelino correctly anticipated that the nation would approve of Brasília.

The publicity about the new capital could not obscure the basic problems of the country. Perhaps the worst of these in the long run was the population expansion, which carried the number of Brazilians well past the 60,000,000 mark in 1960. Inadequate as public health measures had been, they had, together with the fabled fecundity of the Brazilian people and medical advances, caused the population to burst the republic's facilities, which themselves had increased mightily in recent decades. Immigration was not the cause of this growth. Although Europeans and Orientals were still arriving in modest numbers, they came on their own volition; the government had ceased to encourage them after 1930. Now it appeared that the reproduction of the existing population alone might make it difficult for Brazil to feed itself in the future. Housing and public services were over-taxed and could scarcely be enlarged in time to meet requirements. In the public schools conditions were worst of all. Heroic as its efforts had been, the government saw education falling behind. Only half the children of school age could be accommodated, and they for only two or three years in most cases. Nor had the Church been able to keep up with the multiplication of human beings. Brazil had only one-tenth the number of priests for her sixty millions that the United States had for its 39,000,000 Roman Catholics. Measures of the most ambitious sort were going to be necessary to house, feed, clothe, employ, and educate the exploding masses. Furthermore, the people had learned to insist that the government provide for their needs. Ugly street incidents and revolutionary movements indicated that prolonged inattention to their demands might be avenged. Communism and its close relative, the *fidelismo* inspired by Cuba, fed on such conditions. When Prestes was allowed to operate openly in 1958, he found much material with which to work, and Brazilian politicians went out of their way by 1959 to ingratiate themselves with the bearded dictator in Havana.

Jânio Quadros and João Goulart, 1961–

THE election campaign of 1960 was very hard-fought, with the candidates rivaling Kennedy and Nixon in the United States at the same time in exhausting themselves. The National Democratic Union nominated Jânio Quadros da Silva, a 43-year-old former mayor of São Paulo and current governor of the state, an owlish fellow famed for reducing expenses and for honesty. His campaign emblem was a broom, which he brandished as a sign of his determination to clean up the federal government. His leading opponent was Marshal Henrique Texeira Lott, who had Social Democratic, Labor, and Communist support. Adhemar de Barros, whose regime in São Paulo had contrasted so sharply with the model administration of Quadros afterward, ran as a Social Progressive but seemed more of a symbol of Brazil's worst weaknesses. Vice President "Jango" Goulart ran for reelection, nominally on the same ticket with Lott but covertly fostering a "Jan-Jan" movement to attract Jânio Quadros' supporters, though Jango and Jânio could not abide one another personally. It was no great surprise that Quadros' promises to halt inflation and corruption proved highly appealing. He was elected in a landslide on October 3, and Goulart won the vice-presidency again. Both promptly went abroad for many weeks, Quadros to Europe and North Africa incognito, Goulart to the Communist republics in the pose of a popular hero. Both returned in time for the inauguration of January 31, 1961, the first to be held in Brasília.

As president, Quadros indicated that he would not betray his vows to stop inflation and venality. Openly blaming his predecessor for Brazil's "terrible" financial situation, he imposed a long-needed program of austerity and spoke as though he would resort to orthodox economic measures to right matters, including the encouragement of foreign investments. On August 25, 1961, Quadros stunned the nation by resigning and taking a slow voyage around the world. Perhaps he expected to be recalled with full powers, like de Gaulle of France in 1958. Or, as many Brazilians charged, he may have been mentally and emotionally unstable. Afterward, Quadros spoke darkly of political threats and American pressures as the cause of his action, and he re-entered politics.

The resignation found Vice President Goulart on a trip to Red China, a circumstance that gave the military and congressional leaders an opportunity to deny this untrusted leftist the complete executive authority. When he reached Brazil, Goulart was allowed to become president only by accepting a constitutional change that placed crucial power in a cabinet responsible to congress, ultimately the army. The new system worked poorly and Goulart was restless under it. Meanwhile, Brazil's problems were growing worse, especially in the impoverished northeast, where Castroism was gaining rapidly. Yet Brazilians remained confident about the long-range future. Theirs was a rich and talented country, all told, the foremost tropical civilization in the world, and greatness still beckoned.

37

Uruguay

To CLOSE our survey of Latin American nations with Uruguay is to end with a note of optimism. The Eastern Republic of the Uruguay (River), as it is officially known, has been for a half-century almost a model of political stability and social democracy. It is also an enlightened country, with perhaps the highest rate of literacy in Latin America, a large cultured class, an important publishing industry, and humanitarian practices. In civic virtue and governmental structure Uruguay has consciously copied Switzerland. It is, however, more like a miniature Australia, a land that finances itself with wool exports and has an elaborate welfare system and where one-third of its people live in cities, mainly the beautiful capital, Montevideo.

Conditions, of course, are not ideal. Uruguay's financial problems have been unusually vexatious in the past few years, and its citizens have not always been paragons. It is also true that Uruguay has not known many of the handicaps that have retarded its Latin American sister states. In violation of the guide-book cliché, this is no land of contrasts; it is very uniform, with a temperate climate and gently rolling countryside. Ranching is its major economic activity. There are few forests or mines and not more than one-seventh of the land is in fields. The sea and its arms embrace this compact country, shielding it from Argentine pressure and offering it contact with distant continents as well as matchless beaches and a flourishing fishing industry. The population of about 3,000,000 is also strikingly uniform, with only 10 per cent being non-Caucasian, and their standard of living is not only relatively high, but little marred by disparities between the more and the less prosperous.

A PAWN BETWEEN ARGENTINA
AND BRAZIL, 1825–1872

The *banda oriental*, or Eastern Shore, as has been seen, was long a center of strife between Spaniard and Portuguese in the colonial period. During the Wars of Independence it fell under the domination of Brazil, and the Uruguayan folk hero, Artigas, emigrated along with thousands of his rural followers. In 1825 a group of former residents, the "Immortal Thirty-three," led by Juan Antonio Lavalleja, crossed the Plata to drive the Brazilians out. After nearly three years of warfare, which amounted to a contest between Buenos Aires and Brazil, Great Britain forced a settlement by creating a buffer state, the republic of Uruguay. It was a pitiful entity, with fewer than 100,000 people, most of them gauchos, or tenders of herds scattered over the grasslands, or living in the port city of Montevideo. In 1830 the leaders agreed on a constitution that was to remain nominally in effect until 1919 and elected as first president a hard-bitten rustic named Fructuoso Rivera. His administration was mostly a matter of seizures and shootings, typical of political life in that part of South America that is now its showcase—Uruguay, Buenos Aires, and southern Brazil—but was then torn by gauchos and men of civilization. In 1835 Manuel Oribe became president, by which time the chaos subsided enough to permit identification of the two major parties. These were the familiar liberals and conservatives into which the human race seems inevitably to divide. In this case, were *Blancos* (whites) and *Colorados* (reds), names which have persisted into present-day Uruguay and still have significance. The *Blancos* were the more conservative, favoring ranchers and the clergy, and their strength lay back from the coastal towns. For some years they tended to ally with Dictator Rosas in Buenos Aires and the imperial government of Brazil. *Colorados* were strong in Montevideo and other sections of the coastlands, they were more modern and interested in foreign commerce, and they looked for support to Rosas' enemies and the *farrapos* of Brazil who resisted the imperial regime.

The political history of Uruguay for its first forty years can scarcely be related coherently, and it was certainly not clear to many contemporaries. President Oribe, a *Blanco*, soon found himself in chronic war with his old associate, the *Colorado* former president Rivera. The clash of personal ambitions, treacheries, expulsions and restorations, and barbarities kept the country in turmoil and restricted its growth. When the French blockaded Buenos Aires in 1838 and again, with British help, from 1845 to 1848, Oribe's cause was in the ascendant. Yet Rivera and the *Colorados* usually occupied Montevideo and thus prevented consolidation of the republic. For a period of more than eight years, stretching from 1843 to 1851, Montevideo was largely isolated from the hinterland and under partial blockade by Rosas. This "Great War," as Uruguayans call it, had the unexpected effect of strengthening Montevideo, since its port was open to European commerce and considerable numbers of immigrants landed there instead of heading for Argentina. And Montevideo was culturally stimulated by exiles from the wrath of Rosas, among them the best-educated and ablest Argentines. A national university was established in 1849, and a lively press existed. Just when Montevideo and the *Colorado* cause seemed doomed, in 1851, after the Anglo-French blockade, a turn of fortune brought them salvation. The Urquiza rising in Argentina caused the *Colorados* and *Blancos* to join in a successful coalition against Rosas and thus blunt their fratricidal tendencies.

Bipartisanship lasted only two years, to 1853. Then Brazil, who had troops in Uruguay, forced a greedy boundary settlement on the little republic, a circumstance that provoked a *Colorado*, Colonel Venancio Flores, to seize the government. Two years later, in 1855, the Brazilian forces saw to it that he was overthrown in favor of a *Blanco* and withdrew in the expectation that the *Blancos* would be pro-Brazilian. A *Blanco* president who took office in 1860, however, violated this premise by refusing to settle certain claims with the great northern neighbor. Again, in 1864, the Brazilians intervened and supported a *Colorado* uprising that also had Argentine backing and was led, confusingly enough, by the same Venancio Flores whom Brazil had opposed in 1855. Improbable as it seems, this involved situation was the origin of the terrible Paraguayan War of 1864–1870. When it was over, Uruguay was firmly controlled by the *Colorados*. A civil war was begun by the unhappy *Blancos*, who reluctantly came to terms in 1872 when Argentina upheld the *Colorados* and offered the former a gift of money and domination of four of the fifteen departments as a price for laying down their arms. Not until 1959 were the *Blancos* to assume direction of the republic.

MEASURED PROGRESS, 1872–1903

Cynical as it might appear, the arrangement of 1872 was a sensible way to allay conflict between *Colorados* and *Blancos*. Revolutions almost ceased, and presidents were less likely to be rustic caudillos than officers of the regular army. One of them, Lorenzo Latorre, tried to rule as a dictator from 1876 to 1880, when he suddenly gave up the effort because, he said, the Uruguayans were "ungovernable." This was really a compliment to these citizens, for their way of life had made them addicts of liberty and equality, though not of fraternity. During the last third of the nineteenth century politics did not seem important except to the soldiers, for Uruguay was absorbed in material development. Enormous sales of wool, hides, and skins were now possible, and canned or chilled beef and mutton had a seemingly unlimited market abroad. Uruguay's growth at this time resembled Argentina's, though it lagged considerably. Ranchers began to fence their lands, erect windmills, and import fine bulls and rams to improve their herds. Gauchos gradually turned from lives of adventure to more orderly pursuits on the range. Montevideo filled up with European immigrants who opened business houses and banks to serve the growing export trade, and a British company built an excellent rail network to bring rural products to the port. Flour mills, docks, public utilities, wineries, and breweries took their place in the bustling capital. While the republic's economy still rested on the ranching industry, its middle class and urban proletariat were becoming important.

No one knows precisely how many European immigrants made Uruguay their permanent home during these years, but the volume was very large. The population grew strikingly, and by 1900 Uruguay had more than 1,000,000 people. Their educational level was unusually high largely because of the efforts of José Pedro Varela, a writer who had visited the United States and been impressed by Horace Mann and who was also a devoted follower of the Argentine president-pedagogue, Sarmiento. During the Latorre dictatorship Varela had started two normal schools and had gotten a public education system authorized. His death at an early age soon thereafter did not end his influence; from his time onward Uruguayans, like Argentines, have been dedicated supporters of general enlightenment. Montevideo, which had been an intellectual center since the days of the Rosas exiles, continued to be hospitable to those who read, talked of ideas, criticized, and wrote. Its vigorous newspapers and its contacts with the outside world through traders made it a stimulating city.

Montevideo did not lack a writer of stature at this time. José Enrique Rodó (1872–1917), an aristocratic ascetic, began a literary journal while quite young and made his home a mecca for men of letters. An essay he published in 1900, *Ariel*, became famous as the most successful of all efforts to define the true character of Latin America as Latin Americans liked to think of it. This image, as he described it, was idealism, the life of the spirit. Contrasting with it were the materialism and pragmatism which he pictured as being the obsessions of the United States, causes of bad taste, mediocrity, and brutality. Thus the Yankee was Caliban and the southern American Ariel. Caliban was successful but not sensitive, democratic but common, while Ariel represented higher, more precious values. While Rodó's publication contained many qualifying subtleties that escaped most of his readers, it has long inspired those Latin Americans who grope for justification of the feelings of superiority to which they often pretend.

By the turn of the century Uruguay was not in a position to boast of any kind of superiority. Much as her political life had calmed, *Colorados* and *Blancos* were still armed parties often in hostilities. A civil war in 1897 had permitted the expansion of *Blanco* territory from four departments to six. Elections were regular, but they were always won by the incumbent party in each department, with the *Colorados*, of course, monopolizing the national government. If presidents left their office on schedule, they ruled arbitrarily while in power and were succeeded by political associates. And while Uruguay had made conspicuous economic progress, she could not compete seriously with Argentina in beef, since her soil was not as rich and would not grow the fine grasses and alfalfa that the pampas did. Uruguay did not yet have a meat-packing plant. And while Argentina was prospering because of a wheat boom, Uruguay had only limited regions suitable for this grain. Industry, of course, was on the smallest scale in Uruguay, and the republic was in no respect a leader or a model. Things were soon to change, however, as a highly successful statesman appeared on the scene.

THE ERA OF BATLLE, 1903–1929

José Batlle y Ordóñez became president in 1903 and began forthwith to unify Uruguay and to introduce the type of democracy, social welfare, and economic nationalism other Latin American countries have come to champion, often at the cost of violence and injustice. Batlle was born in 1865 into a *Colorado* family. His father was president of the republic from 1868 to 1872, and young Batlle naturally enjoyed many advantages, including a good education and travel in Europe. In 1886 he founded a newspaper in Montevideo which preached the virtues of democratic republicanism and humanitarian ideals. Perhaps Batlle's columns were all the more effective because of his plain style, which set them apart from the colorful effusions of his contemporaries. In and out of government, he became the boss of the *Colorados* and president. He served from 1903 to 1907 and then again from 1911 to 1915. During the interval his follower, Claudio Williman, upheld his policies, and until his death in 1929 Batlle remained the mentor of Uruguay's ruling party. He was a man of immense personal force and commanding appearance, a thinker and a doer, a realist and an idealist.

Batlle first attacked the cleavage in the republic's political life, an action forced on him by a *Blanco* uprising in 1904. After winning the test, he cancelled the territorial arrangement and unified Uruguay's departments for the first time, consoling the *Blancos* with proportional representation, by which they were promised a specific share of positions in the government. Next, Batlle paid off foreign creditors simply by managing the republic's finances better and ended thereby any possibility of unpleasant pressures. His next move was original and destined to establish him as a pioneer in economic nationalism. It was unthinkable, of course, for little Uruguay to drive off her customers and discourage capital investments and business activity by aliens; yet they should not be allowed, Batlle said, to make it an economic colony like other undeveloped nations. Accordingly, he set out to regulate the effects of foreigners on Uruguayan life without driving them off, something any other Latin American country of the time might have tried, perhaps saving itself from "imperialism." Batlle's policies included creating state insurance and mortgage banks and strengthening the national bank, so that Uruguayans might borrow money at reasonable interest rates and not depend upon foreign money-lenders who were often usurious. He also set up a few tariffs to protect Uruguayan industries. The state took over electric light and power from foreign interests who were alleged to be exploiting Uruguay, and Batlle even planned to purchase the British-owned railways, though this project had to be postponed until 1948. Alien traders and enterprisers were not by any means expelled; in fact, they came in greater numbers, establishing at this time meat-packing plants that greatly increased Uruguay's income, but they well understood that doing business did not mean creating monopolies.

Batlle was even farther ahead of his times in adopting social welfare measures that only Germany and England accepted early in the century. He encouraged labor union organization and proclaimed an eight-hour day for industrial workers. During his presidency and afterward through his influence, old age pensions, minimum wages for urban and rural workers, and accident insurance became fixtures of the welfare system. It was a costly system, of course, but the well-to-do paid their taxes, in contrast to the upper-class practices of most Latin American nations. An educational establishment already sturdy was so improved that Uruguay claimed the highest literacy rate in Latin America, and the National University and Montevideo's literary circle continued to flourish. Destined for praise and imitation as many of Batlle's innovations were, their functioning occasioned at least the normal amount of maladministration. The state banks were in themselves disappointing, though they served to curb the cupidity of private competitors. So strong was resistance to the social legislation by employers, especially those in rural areas, that the welfare provisions were frequently nullified in practice.

Having unified the republic, tamed foreign interests, and instituted a welfare system, President Batlle might well have been content, but he dreamed of settling once and for all the curse of dictatorship. The heart of the matter as he saw it was the excessive power of the executive. Yet parliamentarism, as the experience of Chile was then indicating, might be almost as undesirable in a different way. To Batlle, the government of Switzerland, a land he had visited and studied, offered a fruitful example of a plural executive, and he devoted years to writing and speaking in behalf of this form. After he had left the presidency in 1917, a constituent convention convened to take up the question of reform. Batlle's ideas were not wholly victorious, but the constitution drafted in that year and put in force in 1919 provided for a split executive. The president, who was to be chosen by the direct vote of all adult males, would handle foreign affairs, defense, and internal order. Other executive powers were entrusted to a National Council of Administration of nine members, with three chosen every two years by direct vote and with six seats always reserved for the majority party, then the *Colorados*, and three for the minority, the *Blancos*. A bicameral congress, which must also include one-third representation for the minority party, had the usual legislative functions and settled disputes between the president and the council. Liberties were to be scrupulously respected, and a limited measure of local self-government was to be permitted.

For more than a dozen years the constitution of 1919 worked smoothly. Militarism all but disappeared, elections were honest, and freedom reigned as in no other Latin American country. Uruguay's prosperity during the 1920's seemed a reward for her commendable political behavior. Exports doubled every few years, thus financing a higher standard of living for the population and further adventures in state capitalism. A national meat-packing plant was set up in 1928 to serve as a yardstick for the profits made by the American firms of Swift and Armour, and a state monopoly assumed the distribution of liquor, cement, and gasoline. In addition to enjoying republican democracy and economic advance, Uruguay continued to shine in the world of Spanish letters. Perhaps the greatest of modern romantic poets, Juan Zorrilla de San Martín (1855–1931) adorned the republic. A poetess named Juana de Ibarbourou (1895–   ) wrote joyous verses about the landscape and the good life as she gradually shifted from paganism into mysticism. Carlos Reyles (1868–1938) became the foremost of Latin American novelists who dealt with peninsular Spain, and Justino Zavala Muñiz (1897–   ) traced in several novels the evolution of the gaucho from grassland hero to subdued proletarian. In general, Uruguay's experience seemed proof that Spanish American countries were not necessarily doomed to perpetual revolutions, dictatorship, poverty, and ignorance. It was symbolic that the life of José Batlle, a pioneer and giant among Latin American statesmen, ended in 1929, just when good times did.

SINCE 1929: PARADISE ENDANGERED

The world depression threatened to undo the marvelous mechanism that Uruguay had become. Exports dropped more than 80 per cent to a point slightly above half the figure for 1900. The piles of unsold wool, hides, beef, and mutton spelled disaster for the ranchers and the workers who depended on them. Business in the towns almost halted, so that the middle class faced universal bankruptcy and the workers unemployment. The expensive welfare system began to sag badly and seemed on the point of collapse as government revenues dried up. Many voices in the early 1930's demanded socialism or Communism to restore economic life, though Uruguay's basic difficulty—her inability to sell her products abroad—would scarcely have yielded to any remedies undertaken in Montevideo.

During the worst of the depression Gabriel Terra was president. A *batllista Colorado,* he found himself at odds with a majority in the National Council and the congress over the socialist and Communist threat. He felt that force was needed to prevent revolution; most of the council and congress disagreed. In 1933 he sent soldiers into the chambers to eject members of both bodies, whereupon the *Blancos* and many moderate *Colorados* rallied to him, as did the military, and made his coup a success. A new constitution he fathered in 1934 restored the president to his old-time powers and rewarded the *Blancos* by giving them half the seats in the senate and a third in the cabinet. Terra then proceeded to have himself elected under the new constitution for a four-year term. His administration was the most repressive Uruguay had known for a generation. Baltasar Brum, a former president and one of the first statesmen to urge that the Monroe Doctrine be made multi-lateral, became so despondent over the end of democracy in Uruguay, it was said, that he committed suicide. Other liberals did not take such drastic steps, but enough of them felt the sting of Terra's oppression to brand him without qualification as a dictator. Revolts in 1935 and a Communist conspiracy served to tighten the regime. Yet business conditions improved, low-cost housing and other benefits pacified the laboring classes, and Terra made no effort to prolong his rule when his term ended.

Subsequent presidents under the constitution of 1934 reverted to the traditional democracy the republic had boasted. All of them were *Colorados,* though the *Blancos* were strong enough to make a good showing at the polls. World War II brought about an exhilarating rise of exports that made the depression a mere memory. The scuttling of the *Graf Spee* in Montevideo's harbor in 1939 and an alleged plot of local Nazis to seize the government in 1940 assured Uruguay's attachment to the Allied cause. Argentina's strange diplomacy and bluster aroused genuine fears that "the colonels" might be rash enough to attack the little country, though American bases, arms, and warships in Uruguay served to deter aggression from Buenos Aires. The United States also bought all of Uruguay's wool clip for several years, equipped its armed forces, and loaned funds to develop a steel plant and one of the largest hydroelectric projects in South America. Not all Uruguayans were pleased with these attentions. The *Blanco* leader, an intellectual politician named Luis Alberto de Herrera, praised Vichy France and Franco Spain while reviving in somewhat distorted form Rodó's familiar strictures against the United States as Caliban personified. Many Americans were bewildered at the strength of anti-Yankee feeling in this model republic.

After the war Uruguay seemed set for a long period of advancement. Her popular institutions were secure and her economy boomed. A slight decline in the late 1940's was quickly reversed by a flood of exports to the United States during the Korean War of 1950–1953. Further projects for electrification compensated for the land's refusal to yield coal and oil, and roads, airports, docks, and housing were built steadily. Some diversification of the economy resulted from official efforts to stimulate light industry, olive tree culture, tourism, and dairying. The greatest worry was Perón. While it was no longer likely that he would attack Uruguay, he avenged himself on that country for harboring Argentine exiles by cutting off the flow of tourists, who long had found the "Oriental" beaches and resorts a vacation paradise. The braying voice from the Casa Rosada, however, had the effect of increasing the attachment of Uruguayans to democratic ways. With their state-directed theater and radio establishment they had a means· to shame educated Argentines for enduring the vulgar Perón. His collapse in 1955 was in no small part attributable to the example and propaganda of the sturdy little republic across the Plata.

A liberalizing reform was proposed in 1951 by President Andrés Martínez Trueba and authorized by the population in a plebiscite— nothing less than the diminution of Trueba's own office. Henceforth the executive power was to be wielded very much as it had been under the constitution of 1919. A nine-man Federal Executive Council came into being, with the minority party having a third of its seats and equivalent representation in other elective bodies. The presidency should rotate every year among the council members. The change was popular, and Uruguay continued to be gloriously free among the dictatorial regimes so common in Latin America in the early 1950's. By now the chief threats to democratic institutions came almost wholly from the Communists, who dominated many key offices in labor organizations and captivated the most vocal students and intellectuals. While Herrera was still active as the major *Blanco* leader and maker of opinion, he seemed reconciled to the failure of Franco Spain to attract a significant following in Latin America, and he supported the republic.

After a sunny period of about twenty years, Uruguay fell on bad times again in 1957 when the wool market collapsed. An American tariff hurt Uruguay's leading business, but European sales also declined, and a conspicuous effort of the Soviet Union to befriend Uruguay by purchasing more wool did not right matters. Business depression spread rapidly into other lines of activity, and the government began to have difficulty financing its costly social program. It also became evident that inefficiency and graft were making a mockery of the state credit institutions and monopolies. It was a stunning blow to Uruguay when Swift and Armour closed down on account of bureaucratic intimidation. And then inflation and strikes, the familiar Latin American troubles of those years, aggravated a bad situation. The Communists grew bolder, the Russian embassy in Montevideo serving as an acknowledged center for South American leftists. The jeering of Vice President Nixon in 1958 indicated their hold on student and labor groups. But Communist agitation was a consequence and not a cause of Uruguay's difficulties. Her fundamental problem was the fact that the outside world was no longer purchasing her products in sufficient volume to keep her running. An important secondary cause, however, was the decline of the *Colorado* Party, which had grown cynical and slack after more than ninety years in power.

All during 1958 the news from Uruguay was bad. It developed that the peso was unsound, almost as weak as the Brazilian cruzeiro. A price spiral that followed this disclosure caused more inflation, strikes, wage increases, price rises, and more inflation. A meat shortage became acute largely as a result of poor management of the nationalized marketing and packing agencies, and also because cattlemen illegally drove their livestock across the Brazilian border, where prices were better. For a long time rural workers had complained of being orphans while urban groups got repeated favors from *Colorado* governments. Property-owners had reason to believe that the welfare system had degenerated into a racket to support the improvident or the pampered. And yet the supposedly spoiled urban laborers were not well off; they suffered severely from unemployment and inflation. All groups agreed in condemning the administrative morass that the government had become. Yet it was a surprise that the elections of November 30 gave a majority of votes to the *Blancos*, who had not been in power for ninety-three years.

After assuming direction of Uruguay early in 1959, the *Blancos* promptly bogged down, which was not remarkable in view of their disunity and lack of experience. They were also weakened by the death of Herrera on the morrow of their accession. No other leader could approach him in stature unless it was Benito Nardone, a former *Colorado* and one-time stevedore who had built up a devoted following through years of broadcasting a folksy radio program. Nardone served as president for the 1960–1961 term and perhaps achieved something in alerting the country to the danger of Communist infiltration in its schools. An austerity program designed to halt inflation, however, was such a fiasco that the International Monetary Fund refused to bail Uruguay out again. It was taken as a measure of desperation when an income tax, which most countries had known for years, was imposed on Uruguayans. Fiscal collapse was averted by American aid, but anti-Americanism grew in spite (or because?) of it. During President Eisenhower's South American tour of 1960, the only unpleasant incident occurred in Montevideo, when tear gas had to be spewed on a group of hostile demonstrators. In the same year expressions of outrage in Uruguay over the execution of a criminal in California reflected not only the republic's opposition to the death penalty but also its desire to denounce the eternal Caliban. Much as demoralization and drift characterized the scene in Uruguay of the early 1960's, the nation's history during the twentieth century pointed not to dissolution but to a resumption of progress.

38

The United States
and the Other Americas

IN COLONIAL times the English and Iberian dependencies of the western hemisphere had extremely little contact with one another. Such public attitudes as existed in British America and Spanish America tended to be mutually hostile. After the United States became independent, feelers went from the northern to the southern continent for the purpose of fomenting commercial intercourse. Yet the primitive economies of both offered little to exchange. The Americans could obtain tropical goods from the British or French West Indies, and the Hispanic Americans regarded England as a better trading partner than the United States. Except for a few souls in the viceroyalties who dreamed of independence, the United States held little allure.

THE MONROE DOCTRINE AND MANIFEST DESTINY

During the Wars of Independence, interest in the American experience grew until, toward the last, the United States became the major inspiration for the conflict with the mother country. But while both the American government and public sympathized with the liberators, there were few useful ways to assist them. The United States itself was a weak power, greatly endangered until 1814 by both Napoleonic Europe and Britain, and its experiences during the War of 1812 were not conducive to a policy of taking risks. Thus all the Americans could do was to send encouraging words and friendly agents and to promote the occasional sales of military supplies to the insurgents. After the general restorations of 1814–1815 the United States continued to be timid, as befitted a frail republic in a world of resurgent autocracy. Furthermore, the project to purchase Florida made it important that Fernando VII not be alienated until the final transfer of that territory, which took place in 1821. Despite the clamors of Henry Clay and a few others for open support of the liberators, President Monroe refused to be pressured into a perilous course. Not until 1822, when Florida was secure, Spain in revolution, the Americas mostly free through their own efforts, and Britain committed to Latin American independence, did Monroe begin to extend diplomatic recognition to the new nations. His famous proclamation of December 1823, later known as the Monroe Doctrine, caused a momentary excitement, but it was soon made plain that the United States would not interfere if Spain or Portugal attempted a reconquest. Thus most of the liberators felt that the northern republic had let them down throughout their long trials. At the Panama Congress of 1826, Bolívar planned to invoke British rather than American protection for the new nations.

It was truly England, with her peerless fleet and economic power, who was the guardian of Latin American independence. As her foreign minister, George Canning, exulted, the area was British, at least in sympathies and commercial matters. Nearly everywhere British investors and traders had the advantage over their American competitors, a dubious benefit in many cases, for so many were bankrupted in ventures that refused to succeed. Yet enough were rewarded to make the British businessman a prestigious figure in nearly every Latin American city, and not far behind him were bankers or diplomats and the Royal Navy or merchant fleet that advertised Britain's omnipotence. In time, other Europeans penetrated Latin America, a few as distributors or planters but the most conspicuous as adventurers. Some caused trouble, some were maltreated, and a few grew rich in introducing the wonders of nineteenth-century technology to underdeveloped lands. Nearly always they outclassed Yankee enterprisers, at least until mid-century, and did far more to stimulate the economy than the landed aristocracy of Latin America. To these intimate economic ties with Europe was added an increasingly tight cultural connection. The educated classes of Latin America knew and cared little about the raw United States. It was the foreign colony in their own cities, the books and journals from European capitals, and the pilgrimages to Europe that made them sophisticated and cosmopolitan, or to seek to be so.

It is clear that the United States had only slight connections with Latin American business or intellectual life for much of the nineteenth century. Comparatively uncultured itself, the Union was absorbed in Manifest Destiny, the occupation of the northern continent. Bound to Europe almost to the degree Latin America was, the United States often regarded the southern nations as rivals who were gratifyingly falling behind. While a few Americans lamented the failure of the New World to become a community of defiant republics in a monarchical world, the nation as a whole had little interest in South America. The Monroe Doctrine, which the European powers did not recognize, was seldom mentioned. In 1833 the British re-occupied the Falkland Islands over shrieks of protest from the Argentine gauchocracy. In 1838 the French began a two-year blockade of the Plata and interfered in political affairs there. Again, in 1845, France and Britain went beyond admissible limits of defending their interests by meddling in Platine politics. Only obliquely did Washington make known its displeasure, and the Monroe Doctrine was not brandished.

In Mexico, Central America, and the Caribbean the Americans were more assertive. Mexico, of course, fell a victim to Manifest Destiny and its own follies, a circumstance that England and France bewailed but did nothing to prevent. In Central America the Americans and the British collided ominously during the 1840's and 1850's. England rather off-handedly, in one of those fits of absentmindedness that are said to have built the British Empire, stretched her previous treaties with Spain regarding logwood-cutting in Belize into the right to incorporate that torrid area as a crown colony, a clear violation of the Monroe Doctrine. She also extended her sovereignty to include the Bay Islands off Honduras and assumed a protectorate over the Mosquito Indian nation in Nicaragua and Honduras. An obscure move to add Yucatan to the British Empire was also indicative of large ambitions. American opposition took the form of an agreement with New Granada in the Bidlack Treaty of 1846 by which the United States indicated that she would obstruct further British expansion and received preferential rights to use the Panamanian isthmus. In 1850 a *détente* seemed to begin. By the Clayton-Bulwer Treaty of that year England and the United States bound themselves not to acquire further territory in Central America and to control jointly the isthmus crossing, which had assumed great importance following the discovery of gold in American California. But, as it turned out, the Americans had deceived themselves in interpreting this pact as signifying a British retreat from the Mosquito lands. Thus acrimony resumed, with the Americans backing the filibusterer William Walker and the British opposing him, and with the Americans (while Britain was occupied in the Crimean War) bombarding Greytown, a British settlement in Nicaragua, and finally breaking off relations with Her Britannic Majesty. The United States also negotiated the abortive McLane-Ocampo Treaty with the beleaguered Juárez government for a transit right across the Tehuantepec isthmus in Mexico. There was much wild talk about "liberating" Cuba on the part of Americans and other evidences of turning Manifest Destiny southward. But the Tehuantepec plan fell through, Walker was killed, and the free states had no inclination to add Cuba to the Union. And, in one of those timely shifts of opinion with which British history is filled, responsible men in London reached the conclusion that it was both futile and uneconomic to oppose American expansionism. Actually, as the California experience had proved, American rule was better for British business than Latin American rule. Let the Yankees expand as they pleased! English traders would not be far behind.

If England had, by the eve of the American Civil War, withdrawn her opposition to American imperialism in Middle America, what did the inhabitants of the southern republics think? Brazilians apparently thought little one way or the other, for they had only the slenderest of contacts with the Yankees and were strong enough to believe they could take care of themselves. In the Spanish-speaking states, however, much odium for the burgeoning northern republic was building up. They had a long colonial tradition of regarding the "Anglo" as an eternal aggressor, a tradition that included Drake, Hawkins, Raleigh, Morgan, Anson, Vernon, Popham, and the other great captains. They knew that the English settlement in North America had been an affront to the papal award of 1493, and that the astonishing expansion of this nucleus from the Virginia coast to the Rio Grande and Pacific had been mostly at Spanish or Mexican expense. If England would no longer restrain the Colossus, there was nothing to keep it from engulfing more and more of the Spanish-speaking republics. Apart from a sincere distrust of the Americans, educated Latin Americans often bore them much scorn. The Yankee seemed to embody the crudeness, the aggressiveness, the cult of power and materialism, and the Protestantism that mocked the traditions of Latin and Catholic civilization. Besides, he was so successful. Then as now, Spanish American intellectuals who could boast of little in their own countries convinced themselves that they were superior to the boorish, overgrown adolescent they imagined the United States to be.

The Civil War of 1861–1865 did something to modify Spanish American apprehensions concerning the United States. While the great northern republic was immobilized, the French, with the initial connivance of England and Spain, established a client state in Mexico under Maximilian I which was intended to restore the institution of monarchy and to expand into Central America and beyond. Spain re-annexed Santo Domingo and waged war on the Pacific coast republics of South America. That these intrusions were liquidated soon after the end of the Civil War offered a moral plain to those who would hear: a weak United States was more dangerous for Latin America than a strong one. European imperialism would be a certainty in the former case, while Yankee imperialism was only a possibility.

THE BEGINNINGS OF PAN-AMERICANISM

For thirty years after the Civil War there was little to arouse Latin American fears of the United States. Negotiations for a naval base in Haiti or the Dominican Republic, or even projects to annex the latter, came to nothing. The United States did not lift a finger when Sweden sold France the tiny island of St. Bartholomew in 1878. Nor was the Monroe Doctrine invoked when a French company began to cut a canal across Panama. Meanwhile, such American enterprisers as Henry Meiggs and Minor C. Keith were doing much to develop Latin America without Washington's backing or interference. American investments in Cuba and Mexico were growing, but they were far from absorbing those lands. It occurred to the American secretary of state, James G. Blaine, that the New World might, at last, draw together to promote commercial intercourse. In November 1881 invitations went out from Washington for a congress of the American states, but the gathering was called off because, mainly, of American domestic political developments. But the idea did not die, and during the 1880's, the European powers indulged in a frenzy of imperialism that brought much of Africa into colonial status. Would Latin America be subjugated also? While there was little alarm, the partition of Africa kindled warmer feelings throughout the Americas for developing a community of sorts. In 1888, President Cleveland decided to revive the idea of a congress, and in the following year Blaine, again secretary of state (under Harrison), saw it realized. Between October 1889 and April 1890 delegates from all of the American nations but Canada and the disorganized Dominican Republic convened in Washington.

It was here that the Pan-American movement, with a salute to Bolívar's earlier project, was born. Eventually it developed into the inter-American community of the 1930's and the Organization of American States. The start was modest enough. At the first gathering the delegates were treated to a railroad tour of the United States and countless speeches. Blaine's project to begin a customs union elicited no enthusiasm; Latin America was still oriented toward Europe, and American commercial penetration was looked upon as something to be feared rather than welcomed. The major concrete result was the creation of an information clearinghouse that eventually became the Pan-American Union. It was also worth something that the representatives of the American republics (Brazil becoming a republic during the Washington meeting) assembled, came to know one another, and aired their opinions. To Washington it was a disturbing revelation to learn how suspiciously the Spanish-speaking states regarded the United States. Since

Brazil shared little of this feeling, an unspoken Brazilian-American axis took shape, to intensify in future years as the United States became such a voracious consumer of coffee. Fragile as the Pan-American movement was, it was strong enough to sustain further meetings, at Mexico City in 1901–1902, Rio de Janeiro in 1906, Buenos Aires in 1910, Santiago de Chile in 1922, and Havana in 1928. These conferences were wary about compelling political or diplomatic affairs. Most of their labors centered about copyrights and patents, regulations for routine commerce, standardization of laws, and sanitary matters. While it was worthwhile to bring the American states together now and then, and while the ventilation of opinions may have done some good, the period before the 1930's was, as an eminent Mexican has said, one of "blah-blah Pan-Americanism."

Shortly after the first Pan-American Conference, the United States angered Chile by demanding compensation and apologies for the killing of sailors from the cruiser *Baltimore* in a Valparaiso street fight, a case in which both sides had good arguments. In 1895 Argentina felt affronted when President Cleveland favored Brazil in an award concerning the disputed onetime Jesuit mission territory. Aspiring to lead the Spanish-speaking states against the United States and Brazil, largely in vain, Buenos Aires regarded Cleveland's decision as biased. Brazil, on the other hand, honored Monroe as something of a hero, the only Latin American country to do so. Also in 1895 Cleveland sided with Venezuela in a boundary dispute with British Guiana, deliberately taking advantage of Britain's preoccupations elsewhere. While this pleased Venezuela, Secretary of State Richard Olney wrote a dispatch which both offended Great Britain and gave Yankee baiters in Latin America everlasting proof of their accusations. Olney bluntly declared that the United States was "practically sovereign" and that its "fiat is law" in the western hemisphere. After rebutting this contention with frigid dignity, Britain nonetheless acceded to the basic American demand, which was to arbitrate the dispute with Venezuela. And with an exquisite timing that a kindly fate rather than human prescience dictated, she recognized the Monroe Doctrine and cultivated the friendship of the United States, just as Europe entered the period of repeated crises that led to World War I.

The short, astonishing war between the United States and Spain in 1898 produced many conflicting emotions in Latin America. Hispanophobia was still very strong, despite efforts at reconciliation on the part of the mother country and a general celebration in 1892 of the anniversary of Columbus' voyage. The Latin Americans also sympathized with Cuba in its bitter and protracted fight for freedom. Yet the amazing series of American victories in "the splendid little war" touched a chord of sympathy in many Latin American breasts for the motherland. Again, the "Anglo" materialists were demonstrating their brute superiority over Latin civilization! A Pan-Hispanic movement began bringing the former members of the Spanish empire together in a cultural solidarity that probably had more potency than the Pan-American program. And the Yankee protectorate over Cuba and the annexation of Puerto Rico and the Philippines seemed ominous advances that might easily lead to further seizures of Spanish lands. When the American voter in 1900 seemingly authorized an essay in imperialism, all in the name of humanitarianism, many Latin Americans looked for dangerous pressure from the north. Their alarm was not ill-founded, if the reasons they advanced were.

The Roosevelt Corollary

IT WAS certainly true that the government and population of the United States believed that they had a duty to compel backward nations in their neighborhood to improve. Of more importance were strategic considerations. Theodore Roosevelt, who succeeded to the presidency in 1901, was perhaps less of an officious meddler than Latin Americans thought. Continental defense was uppermost in his mind as he planned for a big navy, a canal across the isthmus, and Caribbean bases. Both he and the people were in an exultant frame of mind and craved to place the United States among the greatest of world powers. The desire to attain this stature was partly, but not wholly, the vanity of a young giant aware of its strength. The benevolence of the mighty British Empire could not be taken for granted. Japan was forcing her way into the society of major nations. Pan-Slavism and Pan-Germanism were not illusions, and the German navy was a reality too conspicuous to be ignored by any responsible statesman. In a world drunk with militarism the United States must be powerful and take steps to protect her weaker neighbors. So Roosevelt seems to have thought, and, like many of his countrymen, he was not oblivious to the moral implications of the policies he proceeded to enunciate.

The Venezuelan affair of 1902–1903 threw light on the problems the warlike twentieth century was forcing on the United States. Tired of having their bills for past loans denied, Great Britain, Italy, and Germany decided to blockade Venezuela until its dictator, Cipriano Castro, came to terms. Since it was customary for great powers to take such steps, the Americans at first interposed no objection. As the blockade continued, however, the president and the public became more critical. For one thing the Germans and British were unnecessarily brutal. And then there was reason to believe that their claims were too high. Most of all, it made the Americans nervous for European fleets to sail about the Caribbean. At length Roosevelt brought enough pressure—its exact nature still being mysterious—to secure the withdrawal of the warships and arbitration of the demands, which to be sure were greatly modified in Venezuela's favor. What if other Latin American countries got themselves into serious trouble with great naval powers? The outcome might not be as deftly arranged as it had been in Venezuela. Germany, in particular, might refuse to bow to Washington's will, and she might obtain permanent bases in the Caribbean such as those France and England already had. Roosevelt concluded that the United States must have a huge fleet and the trans-isthmian canal. As for preventing European intervention in unruly Caribbean lands, there were two important proposals. Argentina's foreign minister, Luis M. Drago, advocated that debts should never be collected forcibly, a doctrine the great powers would not take seriously. Roosevelt had a more practical solution: the United States should see to it that small Latin American nations did not act so as to provoke European intervention. This Roosevelt Corollary to the Monroe Doctrine, announced in December 1904, met general approval in the United States and Europe, but to many Latin Americans it seemed a mere cloak to authorize further Yankee annexations.

As usual, American policy in the Caribbean was influenced by strategic rather than humanitarian or economic reasons. Roosevelt had determined on the isthmian canal, and by November 1903 he was ready to promote the secession and independence of Panama, who promptly sold the Americans the strip they needed and placed itself under the protection of the United States. With work on the canal soon under way, Roosevelt was more than ever convinced that European intervention in any Caribbean land might result in the establishment of a potentially hostile naval base on the flanks of the route to Panama. In 1904 conditions in the Dominican Republic appeared to invite foreign interference. Anticipating military action by the aggrieved powers unless debts were paid, Roosevelt pressured the Dominican government into accepting an American receivership for customs receipts so as to make payments on these claims, an arrangement that lasted until 1934 and for long periods involved outright American rule of the little nation and large-scale occupation by the marines. In Central America, too, scandalous financial affairs might give European nations an excuse for intervention. Cooperating with President Díaz of Mexico, Roosevelt tried in 1907 to promote the confederation of the little republics so as to establish political and fiscal order. While this effort came to little, Roosevelt had, with the tardy consent of the U.S. Senate, made his corollary accepted American policy. Henceforth any small American nation guilty of "chronic wrongdoing" might be disciplined by the United States, even occupied and administered, in order to deter European intervention. To most Latin Americans the Roosevelt Corollary was arrogance in its most hateful form. Under the pretense of keeping European powers out the United States might come to dominate all of Latin America. The "Big Stick" might be used to club even the larger nations of Latin America.

During the administration of William Howard Taft the new American policy was further exercised in ways to give rise to the worst possible interpretations. Taft reluctantly and briefly intervened in Cuba and intensified American controls in the Dominican Republic. Disregarding the opposition of the Senate, he sent marines and fiscal agents into Nicaragua. The Nicaraguan affair seemed a blatant instance of "Dollar Diplomacy," the use of force to benefit Wall Street bankers in collusion with Washington. While this charge was outrageously unfair to the upright Taft, it has become part of the lore of anti-Americanism which most of the world—and many Americans—accept as fact. Under Woodrow Wilson occurred still more acts of high-handedness. Wilson's lamentable relations with Mexico led to bloodshed, ignominy, and an exacerbation of Latin American feelings toward the United States. An ugly quarrel over the Panama Canal tolls clouded the good name of Uncle Sam. In 1915 the Americans took over Haiti and established a puppet government. They gave the Dominican Republic no such consolation in 1916, when marines occupied the country and an American military administration was set up. On two occasions Wilson sent armed forces to Cuba for reasons that were not worthy of the finest principles. The United States purchased the Virgin Islands from Denmark, further strengthening its position in the Caribbean, and interfered somewhat clumsily in Nicaraguan affairs. On the other hand, the Americans decided in 1918 to allow the Panamanians to govern themselves without tutelage.

And yet Wilson appealed to the Latin Americans. In a famous address at Mobile in 1913 he promised that the United States would never "seek one additional foot of territory by conquest" and proposed a Pan-American pact for liberty. Wilson repeatedly and emphatically denied that he was an interventionist despite his actions in Latin America and, of course, in Europe and Siberia, and the tendency of Latin Americans was to credit him with sincerity. Argentina, Brazil, and Chile were flattered when he invited them to arbitrate some of the issues between the United States and Mexico. American participation in World War I had the approval of the most influential elements among the politically conscious in Latin America, and Wilson's idealistic utterances gratified lovers of democracy and international decency. His performance at the Paris Peace Conference won the respect, on the whole, of Latin Americans, who proved more eager to cooperate in the League of Nations than Wilson's own nation. Wilson also sought to conciliate Colombia for the loss of Panama, though the Senate refused to approve his project, which implicitly cast a reflection on former president Roosevelt.

The "Friendly Neighbor"

DURING the 1920's it was apparent that the United States had further increased its lead over her neighbors in the western hemisphere. No longer could European powers consider aggressive actions in Latin America, nor inhibit the United States from doing so. Perhaps this situation accounted for the passionate attachment of so many Latin American countries to the League of Nations. They seemed to think it might protect them from the Yankee! Furthermore, the United States had replaced Europe as the source for loans and investments and, often, for choice finished goods. Hitherto American financial penetration had been conspicuous in Mexico, Cuba, and a few spots in Central America and western South America, but was far from significant in other localities. This too was changing, for now Americans had money to buy bonds galore from any government that issued them. The Yankee banker and trader seemed everywhere, and numerous American salesmen appeared in Latin American cities on e monopolized by European merchants. Much of this contact resulted in friction rather than fraternity, for Latin Americans frequently complained of being sold inferior goods, a notion by no means discouraged by European distributors. Even more than before, the cosmopolitan intellectual elite decried Yankee boorishness and, with incitement from a demoted France, lamented the emergence to world power of a people so given to gangsterism, divorce, immorality, and materialism, as the Americans were popularly represented in the press. Yet the impact of the motion picture, radio, and automobile ineluctably drew Latin America closer to the northern colossus. For their part, the Americans awakened to Latin America not only as a business partner but as a fascinating area for study and travel. For the first time many of them became aware of this area and liked it.

The currents of opinion on both sides of the Rio Grande were too numerous and conflicting for official policies to reflect, still less to direct, all of them. As a rule, the formal relations of the governments were correct and outwardly friendly, but often uneasy and embarrassed. Brazil, Peru, Chile, Cuba, Colombia, Venezuela, and Bolivia openly welcomed American enterprisers and money, but friction arose in many situations and animosity was often close to the surface. Over the Caribbean islands and Central America the United States maintained actual or potential protectorates while its citizens invested funds hand over fist. Such political stability as the Americans enforced often spelled tyranny to the inhabitants of these countries, and to many it seemed that the American presence was purely exploitative. A legend with enough truth in it to convince great numbers of Latin Americans was built up, picturing the Americans as creators, or at least perpetuators, of dictatorships and unwholesome economic systems that benefited only aliens and their toadies. This image appealed particularly to middle class intellectuals who enjoyed so few opportunities for advancement. As the impoverished masses saw moneyed Americans in their midst or in motion pictures, their envy could easily take the form of blaming the Yankee for their own destitution. Frank hostility to the United States, however, was a luxury that only Mexico and Argentina could indulge, at least officially. Mexico's defiance was an old story by now. Argentina was still bound economically to Europe, and she had an acute grievance in the American ban on her beef on grounds (sounder than most Argentines realized) of disease.

During the Harding administration Secretary of State Hughes addressed himself to an improvement of inter-American relations with great energy, proclaiming a "Friendly Neighbor" policy. By lightening the burdens, if such they were, of some of the protectorates and liquidating others, he diminished fears that the United States was engaging in a creeping imperialism that would not stop short of the Antarctic. The Bucareli conference patched up Mexican-American relations somewhat, and a gathering in Washington renewed plans for a Central American confederation. American forces left Cuba and the Dominican Republic. Commendable as Hughes' efforts were, the frosty statesman lacked the political talent to dramatize the "Friendly Neighbor" policy and mobilize public opinion, which was in reality a true ally of those Latin Americans who abhorred intervention. Under Coolidge the Americans made no further inroads at the expense of Latin America and tried, with very unfortunate results, to terminate the Nicaraguan protectorate. Mexico, the most bitter critic of the United States, began the process of becoming a hesitant comrade when Coolidge sent Dwight Morrow there as ambassador. The taciturn president also attended the Inter-American Conference at Havana in 1928, where all was decorum and platitude until one session turned into a riotous scene in which the United States was accused of imperialism and oppression.

Most Americans were bewildered that their country should be so misrepresented south of the border. It was obvious that the incident at Havana revealed far more faithfully the state of Latin American opinion than the courteous utterances of the diplomats. Why should a good-will flight of U.S. military aircraft around South America produce a flurry of alarm? Why were garrisons in Puerto Rico and the Canal Zone depicted as nests of aggressors, or naval manuevers as preparations for invasion? What was going on in the heads of the politicians and journalists who made careers out of berating *Tío Sam* and of the people who manifestly agreed with them? During the late 1920's responsible citizens earnestly pondered such questions. Gradually, the prevailing air of injured innocence gave way to an appreciation of the Latin American point of view. More and more, men in public life and framers of opinion admitted that the traditional American attitude toward Latin America was deeply insulting. More restraint in describing Latin Americans as frivolous, irresponsible, ungovernable, and inept crept into writings and speeches. Sincere efforts to understand the southern neighbors led to an appreciation that many of them had admirable cities and cultured groups, that phenomenal advances were being made, and that a genuine attachment to democratic and Christian ideals persisted in spite of all the dictators and revolutions. Small and weak as they were, the Latin American nations were nations, and the American protectorates outraged their pride in a way that no amount of material betterment could redress. Like India and China of that period, Latin America was becoming passionately nationalistic, and the United States made matters worse by presuming to chastise or tutor it. And, many Americans said, there must be something to all the talk of Dollar Diplomacy, the Big Stick, imperialism, and exploitation.

When Herbert Hoover was elected president in 1928, he set out to remove the irritants that made Latin Americans so critical of the United States. The times seemed ripe for a real reconciliation on the popular level, the governments already being cordial enough. Direct American investments in the area now amounted to $3,500,000,000 out of a world total of $7,500,000,000. The volume of trade seemed to set new records every year, as did the flow of tourists, students, and businessmen. Hoover made an extensive tour of South America between his election and inauguration and found a warm response to his friendly overtures everywhere, except perhaps in Buenos Aires. After he took office, he published a State Department paper, the so-called J. Reuben Clark Memorandum, that in effect assured Latin America that the Roosevelt Corollary was no longer in force. He began the withdrawal of the marines from Haiti and Nicaragua, and he set a terminal date for the financial controls in the Dominican Republic. With Mexico he strengthened both official and popular ties. Hoover was a devout admirer of Woodrow Wilson and followed his policy of discouraging revolutions. In 1930 he sent military supplies to the Brazilian president in a vain effort to prevent his overthrow by Getulio Vargas. He refused to take advantage of the Platt Amendment to upset a Cuban tyrant, Gerardo Machado, whose unpopularity was turning the island into a revolutionary stew. Hoover also stimulated to a degree hitherto unknown the movement of American students, humanitarians, and technical experts to Latin America. Much as he did to change the image of an oppressive Colossus of the North, however, Hoover was too beset with the problems of the depression and too lacking in political flair to dramatize effectively the fact that American policy had fundamentally changed, that the United States truly respected the sovereignty of Latin American nations and was eager to strengthen them.

THE GOOD NEIGHBOR, 1933–1953

It was for Franklin D. Roosevelt to capture the mood of Americans both north and south and to immortalize in a happy phrase the new relationship. This he did in his inaugural address of March 1933, when he promised that the United States would be "a good neighbor." To the Americans, whose economic problems were such they wanted no further difficulties anywhere, it was heartening to believe that bickering with Latin America would cease. While more skepticism prevailed in the south, events soon showed that Roosevelt was sincere in desiring good relations, as indeed his predecessors had been too. It was even helpful that the flow of American capital had stopped with the depression, at least in the sense that economic penetration could no longer be denounced. At the Inter-American Conference held in Montevideo in 1933, the United States delegation emphatically declared that the days of intervention were over. The highly informal methods of Secretary of State Cordell Hull at this gathering at first shocked, then amused, and finally captivated the Latin American representatives. The idea grew that Uncle Sam was like Hull, a benign fellow without guile or style, a friend who would respond if needed but who would never force himself on anyone. The Good Neighbor policy was off to a splendid start. Beginning when it did, on the eve of a series of crises leading to World War II, it was nothing less than providential.

Roosevelt plunged ahead with the Good Neighbor policy with characteristic verve. American financial agents left the Dominican Republic. Panama was relieved of the indignity of being a protectorate, and the last marines departed from Haiti and Nicaragua. Latin American leaders were given to understand that they would be warmly received in Washington regardless of their character. Any government that came to power was to be recognized by the United States, who would not inquire into the means of its advent nor attempt to undermine or overthrow it. This right to govern or misgovern themselves without foreign participation had long been dear to Latin Americans; now Washington promised to keep hands off. In only one instance did Roosevelt violate this policy, in Cuba in 1933. There, his ambassador, and later undersecretary of state,

Sumner Welles, frankly supervised the negotiations that ridded the island of the tyrant Machado. Yet Welles realized that this action, in itself beneficent, was of questionable wisdom, and he took the lead in ending the Platt Amendment and in assuring Latin America that Uncle Sam would intervene no more. Thereafter the United States has not attempted to unseat dictators at all, or has done so very indirectly. It was also during the Roosevelt period that the words "Pan-American" and "Monroe Doctrine" became taboo. Substituting for them were "Inter-American solidarity." The republics were free, equal, and twenty-one. With some seriousness, American leaders proclaimed that the voice of Honduras was as weighty as that of Uncle Sam.

Not only the incomparable personality of Franklin D. Roosevelt, but the New Deal itself, appealed mightily to most Latin Americans, who were undertaking drastic social reforms of their own during the 1930's. At last they responded to those northerners who had long preached that all of the Americas had common ideals for democracy and material progress. For the first time, a true sense of western hemisphere unity was evident, though it was accepted with varying degrees of enthusiasm from country to country and man to man. This feeling was best demonstrated at an inter-American gathering in Buenos Aires late in 1936. President Roosevelt, fresh from a great electoral victory, sailed to Rio, Montevideo, and the Argentine capital, in all of which he was heartily welcomed. This was during the brief period when the United States aspired to pure neutrality as war clouds gathered over Europe, Asia, and Africa. Together with her southern partners, the United States would hold herself aloof from a war-prone world. Therefore, the conference proclaimed the Americas "an island of peace," an isolated stronghold of democracy. Much as this episode appears as a figment of a never-never land today, it represented the real desires of the New World to be peaceful, democratic, and associated together. These ideas had deep appeal, much as subsequent events were to dispel the notion of isolation. The conference also agreed firmly that the Monroe Doctrine was multi-lateral, the responsibility of all the republics, and that intervention by one state in the affairs of another for any purpose whatever must be barred.

It was not long until Mexico posed a test for the Good Neighbor policy and the Buenos Aires pact by confiscating the vast oil properties owned by foreign interests, including American. The United States soon acknowledged Mexico's right to seize such holdings, thus proving her sincerity as a good neighbor and inspiring other Latin Americans to emulate the Mexicans. It is quite possible that Washington's forbearance had something to do with the alarming diplomatic situation in Europe. Shortly after the Munich affair, another inter-American conference met, at Lima in October 1938. The theme was democracy versus dictatorship, the American republics in solid union denouncing the advances of the Nazis. While cynics pointed out that no more than nine of the twenty-one American nations qualified as democracies, the Lima conference was not unimportant. The United States and Mexico were still friends, the ideal of freedom received fresh vows from the western hemisphere, and the republics promised to have their foreign ministers gather promptly if international emergencies arose.

World War II

SUCH emergencies came thick and fast during the next four years, destroying the earlier pretense that the Americas might stand aloof during a world convulsion. A few weeks after the war began in Europe in September 1939, the foreign ministers of the republics met in Panama. The United States dropped hints of economic aid to dull the shock of war on Latin American commerce, and talk of the western hemisphere as a citadel of democracy filled the air. With declining conviction the American nations proclaimed their determination to be neutral, but most of them feared the Axis and hoped that Britain and France would hold firm. On the initiative of Washington a "safety belt" of 300 miles was projected around the American continents. Naval craft of the various republics were to keep vessels of the warring powers out of these waters. But only the United States possessed the ships to attempt such a blockade, and they were insufficient, as the famous battle between the *Graf Spee* and the Royal Navy in the Plata revealed. The fiasco of the safety belt was soon forgotten as the United States moved rapidly away from neutrality into an anti-Axis posture during 1940. Yet naval cooperation by the American republics had begun, a matter of some consequence in the years ahead. The fall of France and the Netherlands, as well as the apparently impending defeat of Britain during the summer of 1940, brought the foreign ministers together again at Havana in July. There they enunciated the "no-transfer" principle, which specified that New World possessions of European powers could not be ceded to another nation but would, instead, become wards of the American republics. A reservation regarding the Falkland Islands satisfied Argentina, who had never recognized the British title to these bleak rocks, and complications arose concerning some of the French colonies whose officials adhered to the Vichy government. On the whole, however, the Havana arrangement was in the best tradition of inter-American cooperation. An announcement by Washington of a half-billion dollars in aid to be made available to Latin America, mainly for armaments, made the conference in some ways a happy occasion.

Among the least of the worries of the United States during 1940 was the title to the Caribbean possessions of England, France, and the Netherlands. The very independence of the Americas seemed in jeopardy. If Hitler acquired the French and British fleets, it would be possible for him to send expeditionary forces, most likely against the "bulge" of northeastern Brazil, which had no defenses whatever. American army planners had reason to draft desperate projects for the poorly-armed and minute U.S. forces and to urge the Latin Americans, whose armies were relatively larger but utterly inadequate for anything but shooting civilians, to prepare themselves to face invasion. During this emergency two major difficulties confronted the United States in this matter. First, the Latin Americans maintained an exasperating—if eventually justified—equanimity about the danger of a German invasion. Not even Brazil was alarmed enough to do more than permit the United States, through the "front" of Pan-American Airways, to build and improve airfields in her territory and offer seaports for use by U.S. naval craft. She flatly refused permission for American land forces to occupy exposed points and was very desultory about transferring some of her own garrisons, who, as it turned out, possessed almost no weapons, from the Rio-São Paulo area to the danger zone. The other republics were quite as reluctant to see American armed forces on their soil. Second, the United States had promised extensive arms to Latin America, but she had none to spare except for outdated weapons which the Latin Americans spurned. Only a few antique searchlights and coastal artillery guns were available, and they were duly installed on the coasts of Venezuela, Chile, and Peru. Naval patrols continued and made use of ports throughout the Americas, and Pan-American Airways was allowed to create airfields in the Spanish-speaking areas of northern South America as well as Brazil. Much visiting by military and diplomatic officials between Washington and the southern capitals occurred.

Thanks to British hardihood no desperate crisis in the Americas materialized during 1940. In the spring of 1941 came another period of alarm, at least in the minds of Washington authorities. Then it appeared that Hitler might move through Spain and French North Africa and, possibly with air-borne troops, occupy the Brazilian bulge. At great sacrifice the United States sent a few items of modern equipment to stimulate Brazilian efforts. President Roosevelt seriously considered sending President Vargas a personal letter imploring him to admit U.S. troops. Had this happened, and Vargas refused, the question of intervention would have been raised in a most acute form and with the country that had been most friendly to the United States. But, Hitler invaded Russia instead of North Africa, and the alarm was off. Postwar examination of captured files has shown that the Nazis never at any time projected an invasion of the Americas. Much as this justifies the Latin

American attitude of calmness during these years, it might be remembered that German plans were capable of quick formation and stunning execution. Washington was being realistic, not hysterical.

By the time of the Pearl Harbor attack the Americas were outwardly unified in common determination to defend themselves. An Office of the Coordinator of Inter-American Affairs under Nelson Rockefeller was supplying considerable direction to a variety of programs to foment a group spirit. Most of the airlines in South America had been de-Germanized or de-Italianized; the continental naval patrol was operating after a fashion; air and sea bases for U.S. usage were being developed in Mexico, Brazil, Central America, and some of the Pacific coast republics of South America; and a trickle of American supplies was reaching Latin American forces. Strong as pro-democratic and pro-Communist opinion was in all of the countries, an undertone of Axis sympathy was manifestly powerful. Probably most Latin Americans were not deeply involved in the ideological or political issues of the world struggle. Yet the Roosevelt administration had been remarkably successful in putting a good face on matters and in persuading the most influential authorities that Latin America should follow the United States in opposing the Axis, though in fact Washington had gone ahead in this departure from neutrality alone. The Japanese attack of December 7, 1941 put the Good Neighbor policy to its hardest test. It was by no means obvious that the United States would ultimately win the war, nor that it could protect South America from invasion. Yet nine Latin American republics promptly declared war on the Axis, and at the inter-American conference held in Rio de Janeiro in January 1942, all agreed to recommend consideration of breaking relations with the enemies of the United States. This decision, to be sure, represented a quasi-defeat for the United States, which had hoped for a unanimous declaration of war, or at least a total rupture of diplomatic relations, but it was still gratifying. Also at this time inter-American boards for defense, economic affairs, and political problems were established, though they were seldom allowed to deal with genuine issues. The Peruvian-Ecuadorian border dispute was settled so as to minimize friction among the New World nations.

Brazil proved the keystone of the Latin American defense structure. For a few weeks early in 1942 her air forces afforded the only route for ferrying American aircraft to Britain, the Middle East, and even the Far East and Russia. In order to protect them, the defenses of New York Harbor were weakened by the withdrawal of anti-aircraft guns. President Vargas and his officers continued to clamor for modern equipment, which the United States could supply in quantity by 1943. Ultimately, Brazil received three-fourths of all the Lend-Lease weapons and munitions the Americans sent to the southern republics, itself only one per cent of the total for the world. These supplies were sufficient to make Brazil secure against Argentine aggression, a possibility never entirely discounted during these years. Moreover, Brazil demanded to participate in the war. An expeditionary force of 25,000 men went to the Mediterranean theater and fought competently. While thus asserting herself as a great power, Brazil also came closer to being one economically, thanks to vast programs of improving her communications, production, electricity, and commerce, often with valuable help from the United States. While the North African landings of November 1942 removed the danger of a German invasion of the bulge, Brazil contributed enough to the war effort to be a valued ally of the United States.

Other Latin American nations were helpful in important ways. Mexico was cooperative to a degree unimaginable a decade earlier, permitting American airplanes and ships to use her bases and technical experts to advise her land forces and industrial authorities. The settlement of American oil claims in a way highly favorable to Mexico made this cordiality all the more warm, as did the American policy of buying up all of Mexico's exports at good prices. Furthermore, uncounted thousands of Mexicans made their way to the United States to toil or to serve in the armed forces. Having declared war on the Axis in 1942, Mexico dispatched a squadron of fighter pilots to the Far East in 1945. While only Brazil and Mexico sent forces overseas, all the other nations but Argentina permitted a high degree of American supervision in punishing pro-Axis business firms and in hunting spies and saboteurs. Colombia, Ecuador, and Peru granted use of air and naval bases which were helpful in the Pacific campaigns, and the small Caribbean republics offered nothing but hospitality to U.S. armed forces whom they had denounced a few years before as imperialists. In the last two years of the war the United States distributed much modern war equipment in Latin America, often as virtual gifts. Washington stipulated, however, that most of these be defensive weapons, lest the republics be tempted to employ them against one another.

Argentina, of course, was a most unhappy exception to this picture of harmony. Already selling all the meat and grain that she could to the United Nations, the only powers with shipping resources to fetch these products, she indulged in bitter anti-Americanism and encouraged the activities of Axis agents and propagandists. Her influence over Chile in such matters all but disappeared early in 1943. Toward the end of fhat year it appeared that she had seduced Bolivia, but this land-locked republic, so urgently in need of American markets for its tin, was in no position to defy Uncle Sam. As things went worse for the Axis, Argentina's rulers perversely and irrationally became more partisan for that alliance. Yet, in 1944, an economic threat from London and Washington led the Argentine president to break relations with the Axis, whereupon he was overthrown by "the colonels." The rise of Perón intensified the discordant character of Argentine behavior, but the course of the war made his international ambitions ineffectual.

During the war, then, the Americas offered a picture of near unity. All of the republics, even Argentina by March 1945, declared themselves belligerents. The international naval patrols, the Mexican air force, and the Brazilian army bespoke a concerted if modest military effort. Sales of raw materials to the United States and Great Britain were truly of the greatest importance. By providing bases for United Nations airplanes and ships, the republics of the western hemisphere compensated Uncle Sam for whatever concern he had about defending them. Intercourse among Americans north and south on a personal basis was the strongest ever. Not only servicemen in transit, but students who did not qualify for military service went from the United States to Latin America, and in the other direction went young people as students in universities or armed forces training centers. Tourists, barred from Europe, went instead to other American republics. Journalists, artists, entertainers, athletes, and literary figures went in great numbers from the United States to Latin America, and their equivalents were treated to tours of the northern republic. Furthermore, nearly every country had its mission of United States experts who advised governments and armed services, industrialists and planters, and explorers hoping to uncover new natural riches. Latin American ports, airdromes, railways, and roads underwent major improvement under American prodding and aid. Outwardly, it appeared that Yankee and Latino had never been so close, and on so many different levels.

A different interpretation sometimes, though rarely, received publicity. Latin Americans in the United States as guests of the government were not always reticent in expressing their disapproval of what they saw, and often they showed little patience for the irritations of life produced by the war. Not all Americans who went to Latin America were tactful. Among young people, friction inevitably arose between servicemen and citizens of the republics in which they were stationed, and teen-aged Mexican "zoot-suiters" tangled in several shocking riots with U.S. military personnel in California. Among Latin Americans in general there were important reservations about the war aims of the United States. On their part, Americans were often aware that commitment to the United Nations cause in Latin America was only half-hearted. A U.S. senator, Hugh Butler, said what many others hesitated to express when, in 1943, he condemned the prodigality of the United States in attempting to buy the friendship, as he saw it, of Latin America with unnecessary purchases of materials and with loans for questionable enterprises. He felt

that the Latin Americans discerned this purpose and despised the United
States for it. The effusive "good-willing" of politicians, motion picture
stars, and literary figures affronted the more intelligent Latin Americans.
Many others wondered if the southern Americas really cared about the
war or were seeking bribes from the United States and opportunities to
despoil Axis property-owners. And did the endowments of military hardware strengthen Latin America against dangers that no longer existed?
Even worse, did they serve to entrench tyrants—those smiling presidents
greeted in Washington as brother democrats—against their suffering populations?

As the war wore on, more disturbing factors came to the surface. The
forced resignation of Sumner Welles in 1943 significantly coincided with
the demotion of Latin America in the minds of United States officials.
The facts of life were, as always, essentially brutal. Latin America really
amounted to little in the world of giants emerging from the war. Courteous explanations by Washington about the dealings of the mammoth
powers did not obscure the fact that Latin America was being left out.
After devoting years to the construction of an inter-American system,
the United States was now taking it for granted. It seemed that this system would have no status in the new power balance that was being created except as a very junior client of the United States. While such misgivings both wounded and disturbed Latin American leaders, another
force was making itself felt: international Communism. All of a sudden,
beginning in 1943, the Soviet Union greatly stepped up its efforts in
Mexico City, Havana, and other centers to cultivate popularity. Before
long the campaign showed results. Believing themselves saved from Hitlerism, the Communists were now readying themselves for a long contest with the "capitalist" powers, notably the United States. Anti-Americanism had acquired its most potent supporter ever.

The Organization of American States

AS THE end of the war came in sight, the United States undertook
to tighten the unity of the Americas and to lodge them all as a body in
the United Nations. At the Chapultepec conference in Mexico City
early in 1945, this matter was solved in a way pleasing to Washington.
Every American nation who declared war on the Axis was, according to
the agreement, to become a charter member of the world organization.
With contempt and cynicism Argentina met this qualification in March
1945. At the San Francisco conference a few weeks later her admission,
along with that of all the other Latin American republics, was granted
after strenuous and somewhat embarrassing efforts by the United States.
Twenty of the original forty-six members of the United Nations Organ-

ization were thus Latin American. There was reason to hope that they would enjoy great power, and most of them entered upon United Nations activities with even greater enthusiasm than they had displayed for the League of Nations. Spanish was recognized as one of the four major languages within the organization. Yet Latin America was in no position to cut a great figure in the power politics of the world. Only the United States had the atomic bomb and a strategic air force. Russia and her satellites were immensely strong in other respects, and aggressive too. It was not long until the very minor role of the Latin Americans was apparent, regardless of their numbers in the United Nations. Only by siding with the United States—or by threatening to vex it—could they exert any influence at all.

During the early postwar years the Truman administration became sensitive to the criticism that the United States had mobilized and used Latin America but was now neglecting it. In 1947 the president and his family sailed to Rio de Janeiro for an intended revival of the Good Neighbor policy. The occasion was a conference of all the American republics to rejuvenate the atrophied ties of western hemisphere fraternity in order to obstruct the spread of Communism. The gathering itself was splendid, by far the most extravagant of the inter-American series, and all effusive friendliness. Only the presence of Eva Perón, who managed to attract maximum attention with her well-staged entrances and exits, was a reminder of latent discord. By the end of the conference the United States had secured its aim, the adoption of a permanent mutual defense treaty by which all of the republics agreed to resist an attack upon any one of themselves from within or without the New World, "all for one and one for all." The Rio treaty was a splendid monument to the Good Neighbor policy and the memory of war-time cooperation as well as a signpost for the future.

Other forces, however, were already working to undermine that pillar. After a brief flurry of democratic restlessness following the end of the war, most Latin American nations—with the important exceptions of Brazil and Mexico—settled down deeper into political autocracy. Lovers of liberty tended to blame this development on the United States, who sold weapons at low prices from her wartime surpluses to Latin American governments. While Washington was hoping to strengthen each country against Communist mischief, it laid itself open to the charge of seeking to buttress dictatorships. Yankee economic imperialism was another complaint. The American investor was back in Latin America, buying land, mines, oil fields, and bonds, starting industries, and often circumventing local rules that restricted alien business enterprise. And for some years after the war, only the United States could sell Latin America the capital equipment and finished goods it desired. Thus leftists could point to the renewed invasion of capitalists and monopolists of the northern colossus and draw ominous inferences from it. Further supporting this impression was the fact that the United States regularly loaned money to Latin American governments who were often getting themselves into fiscal trouble because of inflation and expensive social welfare measures. Even the egregious Perón regime was bailed out. If Americans protested their interest in nothing but promoting solvency, southern critics charged that intervention of a most insidious sort was taking place, that Washington was practically underwriting dictatorships in order to interdict the spread of Communism.

Yet lack of American activity was also condemned. Popular interest in the United States for Latin America lagged during the first postwar years. Travel or study in other parts of the world attracted Americans most, despite a surge in popularity for winter cruises in the Caribbean and short vacations to Mexico. And Washington was preoccupied with the plight of Western Europe, the Communist victories in China, and the emergence of India and the Middle East. At the inter-American conference held in Bogotá in 1948 Secretary of State George C. Marshall had the somber duty of informing the other American republics that the recovery plan (which eventually bore his name) was for the benefit of Europe, not Latin America. The United States did not enjoy unlimited resources, and Europe was in great peril of economic collapse and Communist aggression and thus had the first claim on American assistance. The laments of many Latin Americans suggested that intervention, the bugbear of earlier years, was desirable if it spelled Yankee financial support. Nonetheless, the Bogotá conference authorized the transformation of the old Pan-American machinery into the Organization of American States, a regional grouping within the United Nations. The new agency would have its headquarters in Washington and far more elaborate machinery for dealing with disputes and other common problems. Soon afterward the beginning of the Korean War caused significant purchases by the United States of Latin American materials and the distribution of further military equipment under the Mutual Security Program of 1951.

THE "GOOD PARTNER" AND THE ALLIANCE FOR PROGRESS, 1953–

It has become customary in American politics for the party out of power to condemn the administration for neglecting or abusing Latin America. So it was in 1952, when General Dwight D. Eisenhower accused the Truman regime of permitting the dissipation of Good Neighborliness. When he became president, he sent his brother, Dr. Milton

Eisenhower, on an extensive tour of South American capitals during the summer of 1953, after which numerous plans were made to re-knit the old ties. As a "good partner," the United States would listen sympathetically to Latin American requests and seek to provide aid. By now it was evident that the most urgent need was to raise production in all lines, for the inhabitants of the southern republics were reproducing at a fantastic rate, the highest in the world, and were surpassing the United States in numbers for the first time in several generations. During the 1950's countless projects were undertaken to increase industrialization and agricultural output in Latin Americas. Some were the work of the United Nations, but most were inspired and financed in one way or another by the United States. Financial aid through the Export-Import Bank, the World Bank, and the International Monetary Fund was designed to curb inflation. The American Point IV program brought many benefits, as also did the investments fostered by the International Finance Corporation. Technical assistance through various O.A.S. agencies were helpful, and the International Basic Economy Corporation, essentially a Rockefeller-supported institution for stimulating self-aid in Latin America, had rewarding results. Numerous and imaginative as these efforts were, they were insufficient; population growth outran facilities, runaway urbanism complicated both rural and municipal problems, and governments were generally too weak to risk antagonizing their populations by enforcing the austerity measures necessary to restrain inflation. Latin America's basic problems multiplied.

A long-dreaded dilemma arose in the republic of Guatemala, where a popular movement to reform a sorry political system and to redistribute wealth came under the domination of Communists. Much of the movement excited sympathy in the other nations, including the United States, but Washington was determined to keep Communism out of the New World. Secretary of State Dulles obtained a declaration from the inter-American conference held at Caracas in 1954 to the effect that the O.A.S. would act should any of its members be threatened by international Communism. It was apparent that the Caracas agreement was unpopular in many quarters, that it had been wrung from several unwilling delegations. Soon thereafter, rebels who had been mysteriously equipped invaded Guatemala and easily overthrew the regime, which apparently had little popularity. Details of this event have never been fully explained and are subject to many interpretations. Most leftists were eager to announce, however, that the United States had armed the revolutionists and undermined the government, and many who were not leftists reluctantly agreed with them. If it was a gain to rid the Americas of a Communist center, the revival of anti-Yankee slogans and credible charges of intervention disturbed American public opinion. And the

Communists, whether they were outlawed or not, grew more formidable as the decade wore on.

Meanwhile, the United States was deeply involved with matters of more immediate urgency than the attitudes of its southern neighbors. Once Russia had obtained nuclear weapons and guided missiles and the Communist dust had settled over China, American foreign policy was necessarily preoccupied with issues that might spell the end of civilization. Again, Latin Americans began to complain of neglect, this time on the part of the Eisenhower administration. Washington was accused of assuming the support of Latin America while making major decisions without consulting it. By the late 1950's most Latin American republics felt a little less dependent on the United States, for a recovered Europe was re-asserting its old position as a major investor, customer, and supplier, and even Japan was active again. The new situation produced many conflicting currents. Latin America desired more aid from the United States and begrudged the small share it was receiving compared to Europe, Africa, and Asia. Yet it also wanted to control its own destinies, even if this meant dealing with the Communist bloc. In general, Latin Americans were inclined to feel that the United States cared little about them as long as they refrained from becoming Communist.

Absorbed in so many other matters, the Americans were largely unaware of the mood of Latin America during the decade, which was really nothing new but a deepening of an atmosphere that started to appear in 1943, if not earlier. Things seemed satisfactory on the surface. Dictatorships were falling. Argentina, Colombia, Venezuela, Peru, and other lands showed a heartening return to popular institutions. Brazil and Mexico remained democratic republics, at least by Latin American standards, and the future of other countries appeared far from bleak. Business was booming. If Latin America had problems, they were the problems of growth and not of stagnation. Direct American investments were climbing to $9,000,000,000, and commerce was good. A serenity based on ignorance and indifference prevailed among most Americans. It came as a grievous shock when, in 1958, Vice President Nixon's goodwill tour of South America turned into a nightmare. Hissed in Montevideo and Buenos Aires by sizeable groups, threatened in Lima and Bogotá by still larger crowds, Nixon and his wife were trapped and in great danger of being murdered by howling mobs in Caracas. They had to be extricated from that capital under frightening circumstances. While much was done afterward to put a good face on the affair, which was publicly attributed to Communists, the United States was forced to realize how much popularity it had lost in Latin America. Not the least disturbing aspect of the Nixon reception was the absence of apology or a sense of shame on the part of many articulate elements in that area who had once been Good Neighbors.

Again, to a chorus of editorial lamentations that Latin America had too long been neglected, Washington revived its efforts to restore cordiality. Official visits, protestations of fraternity, stronger programs to promote cultural exchange, and more agents of technical and humanitarian progress gave an appearance of renewed concern by the United States, and correctly so. However, nothing could long obscure the fact that Latin America could not claim the major share of Washington's attention. The area was militarily impotent in an age of nuclear weapons, guided missiles, and earth satellites. The primary concern of the United States was and must remain the containment of Communism and the prevention of total war. As for competing with the Communists for the allegiance of the underdeveloped areas, Africa and Asia ranked as more urgent problems than Latin America. Thus American diplomacy, and the foreign aid programs that supported it, continued to concentrate on other parts of the world. As long as Latin America remained non-Communist she could expect little more than sympathy, friendship, and modest assistance from the United States, who was not as rich as most foreigners fancied. This situation greatly irritated all groups in Latin America. Leftists charged that while assistance meant enslavement, the United States mistreated Latin America by not offering her more of it. Other elements, whatever their political ties, saw their problems getting far out of hand while Uncle Sam did too little.

In 1958 President Kubitschek of Brazil proposed "Operation Pan-Americana," involving an inter-American bank to promote economic development on a heroic scale, particularly in raising the living standards of the lower classes. Obviously, most of the financing would have to come from the United States. Washington responded by agreeing to organize such an agency, the Inter-American Developmental Bank, which would loan money but on a smaller scale than Kubitschek had recommended. Scarcely had it been approved when a surprising turn of affairs alarmed the United States. The new dictator of Cuba, Fidel Castro, made it quite clear by 1960 that he was a servant of Communism. Soon, by the Act of Bogotá in that year, Washington offered to expand the new bank. Thus the decade opened with considerable hopes that American financial aid might relieve some of the social and economic pressures in Latin America before the masses turned to Communism or Castroism. Efforts by several South American and Central American nations to create a common market also raised the possibility that commerce would be increased on a large scale.

President Eisenhower made a triumphant visit to South America early in 1960, where his reception at times bordered on hysterical acclamation. Warm as this welcome to a hero and personable head of state was, the absence of ugly incidents was due to the temporary lull in the Cold War, which caused the Communists to refrain from mischief. By the summer of 1960, after the U-2 incident, the Communists were again baiting the United States with skill and energy. As in 1952, 1932, 1920, 1912, and other presidential election years, the anti-administration forces, in this instance led by John F. Kennedy, denounced the regime for not doing enough for Latin America. Kennedy's election brought the United States to a point of re-appraisal of its policies. The new president announced an "Alliance for Progress" and increased programs for aid. Again, a flood of editorials on both sides of the Rio Grande praised the "new" policy and expressed optimism about the future. About three months after his inauguration, however, Kennedy aroused a great furor by lending his support to anti-Castro invasion forces who failed pitiably to overthrow the bearded tyrant of Cuba. It was problematical whether he could ever restore the warm glow that his accession had originally inspired. At Punta del Este, Uruguay, in January 1962, the major Latin American nations declined to vote with the United States for the expulsion of Cuba from the OAS. Yet Kennedy's visits to Caracas, Bogotá, and Mexico City evoked good responses. And the Alliance for Progress, with its emphasis on Latin American self-help and economic reforms as a condition for American assistance, slowly gathered momentum.

What could, in truth, be done that had not already been tried? The possibility of mobilizing hemisphere opinion against dictators of all types, whether Castro or Trujillo, had only fair prospects at best. Too often in the past Americans north and south had chosen to ignore tyrannical regimes for various reasons. It would be extremely difficult to obtain a unified course of action against dictators, and if the United States proceeded alone, a tradition of non-intervention that had been growing for forty years might be destroyed, with unpredictable results. Programs of cultural exchange could always be increased, as they had been repeatedly. Yet few Americans cared to attend Latin American universities, and southerners who came to the United States were frequently ill-prepared for higher education. Furthermore, student bodies in Latin America were usually centers of virulent anti-Americanism, and most intellectuals professed antagonism toward the United States. Nearly everyone in the United States acknowledged that massive economic aid for its neighbors was imperative. Yet results of earlier programs were far from encouraging, and it was well known that the wealthy classes in Latin America paid low taxes and exhibited a disheartening indifference toward the poor of their own countries. While the spectacle of crowds in Latin America demanding the hide of Uncle Sam might frighten the

United States into offering more aid, it might, contrarily, disgust and alienate the American public. Latin America had no way to force the United States to lower its standard of living in order to eliminate poverty elsewhere. The decision was for the United States to make, subject to a thousand vagaries of public pressures and statesmanlike impulses.

For a century and a half, the United States had been interested in fluctuating degrees in a free Latin America. It is sobering to reflect how little the basic problems had changed. In principle, all the Americas professed an attachment to democratic republicanism and human rights. Yet no country in Latin America had achieved as much as the United States in institutionalizing these ideals. Legitimacy, that unspoken agreement on the bases of society, still eluded most regimes in the southern nations. Violent crowds and ambitious soldiers still had far too much to do with political solutions, and civil liberties, though ardently desired by most Latin Americans, prevailed only spottily and briefly. Amazing as much of the technical and economic progress had been, Latin America had lost ground in comparison to most of its companions in the community of Western civilization. The temptation of its masses to turn to other systems could not be minimized with safety. As the decade of the 1960's opened, however, the United States was determined to assist her southern neighbors in satisfying the material needs of a greatly expanding population within a framework of democracy. The response in Latin America, though dim in certain localities, was one of hope. Already the home of a fine culture, Latin America might yet, in partnership with a sympathetic United States, build a free and prosperous society.

Further Readings

GUIDES

R. A. Humphrey, *Latin American History: A Guide to the Literature in English* (New York, London, Toronto, 1958); C. K. Jones, *A Bibliography of Latin-American Bibliographies* (2nd ed., Washington, 1942); Benito Sánchez Alonso, *Fuentes de la historia española e hispanoamericana* (rev. ed., 3 vols., Madrid, 1952). *The Handbook of Latin American Studies* (Cambridge, Mass., 1936-1951; Gainesville, Fla., 1951-   ) is an outstandingly valuable guide, containing summaries of books and articles, published annually since 1936. Somewhat similar is the quarterly *Índice histórico español* (Barcelona, 1953-   ).

The principal professional journal in the field is the *Hispanic American Historical Review* (Baltimore, 1918-1922; Durham, N. C., 1926-   ). Summaries of articles in this quarterly publication are found in Ruth Lapham Butler, *Guide to the Hispanic American Historical Review*, 1918-1945 (Durham, N. C., 1950), and Charles Gibson, with E. V. Niemeyer, *Guide to the Hispanic American Historical Review, 1946-1955* (Durham, N. C., 1958). Other important journals are *Revista de historia de América*, published twice a year in Mexico; *Americas*, published by the Organization of American States in Washington since 1949 (formerly the *Bulletin* of the Pan American Union, 1893-1948); *The Americas: A Quarterly Review of Inter-American Cultural History* (Washington, 1944-   ); and *Inter-American Economic Affairs* (Washington, 1947-   ). Various statistical reports and other studies published by the United Nations are also highly useful.

BACKGROUND

F. A. Carlson, *Geography of Latin America* (3rd ed., New York, 1952); Preston E. James, *Latin America* (2nd ed., New York, 1950); Robert S. Platt, *Latin America: Countrysides and United Regions* (New York, 1942); J. L. Rich, *The Face of South America: An Aerial Traverse* (New York, 1942); A. C. Wilgus, *Latin America in Maps* (New York, 1943); John Collier, *The Indians of the Americas* (New York, 1947); Kenneth MacGowan, *Early Man in the New World* (New York, 1950); Clark Wissler, *The American Indian: An Introduction to the Anthropology of the New World* (3rd ed., New York); Friar Diego de Landa, *Yucatan before and after the Conquest* (William Gates edition, Baltimore, 1937); Sylvanus G. Morley, *The Ancient Maya* (3rd ed., Stanford, Calif., 1956); Tatiana Proskouriakoff, *An Album of Maya Architecture* (Washington, 1956); Herbert J. Spinden, *Maya Art and Civilization* (Indian Hills, Colo., 1957), and *Ancient Civilizations of Mexico and Central America* (3rd ed., New York, 1958); John Lloyd Stephens, *Incidents of Travel in Central America, Chiapas and Yucatan*, ed. by R. L. Predmore (2 vols., New Brunswick, N.J., 1949); J. Eric S. Thompson, *The Rise and Fall of Maya Civilization* (Norman, Okla., 1954); Victor Wolfgang von Hagen, *The Maya Explorer* (Norman, Okla., 1947).

Alfonso Caso, *The Aztecs, People of the Sun*, tr. by Lowell Dunham (Norman, Okla., 1958); Francisco Saverio Clavigero, *The History of Mexico* . . . (2 vols., London, 1787); Miguel Covarrubias, *The Eagle, the Jaguar, and the Serpent* (New York, 1954); E. L. Hewett, *Ancient Life in the American Southwest* (Indianapolis, 1930); Francis Borgia Steck, *Motolinia's History of the Indians of New Spain* (Washington, 1951); Bernardino de Sahagún, *Historia general de las cosas de Nueva Espana*, tr. by Mrs. Fannie Bandelier (Nashville, Tenn., 1932); Jacques Soustelle, *La vida cotidiana de los aztecas en vísperas de la conquista*, tr. by Carlos Villegas (Mexico, 1956); J. Eric S. Thompson, *Mexico before Cortes* (New York, 1933); G. C. Vaillant, *Aztecs of Mexico* (New York, 1941).

Louis Baudin, *A Socialist Empire: The Incas of Peru*, tr. by Katherine Woods, ed. by Arthur Goddard (New York, 1961); Wendell C. Bennett and Junius B. Bird, *Andean Culture History* (New York, 1949); Wendell C. Bennett, *Ancient Arts of the Andes* (New York, 1954); Hiram Bingham, *Lost City of the Incas, the Story of Machu Picchu and its Builders* (New York, 1948); Gregory Mason, *South of Yesterday* (New York, 1940); J. A. Mason, *The Ancient Civilizations of Peru* (Harmondsworth, England, 1957); P. A. Means, *Ancient Civilizations of the Andes* (New York, 1931); Sally Falk Moore, *Power and Property in Inca Peru* (New York, 1958); Harold Osborne, *Indians of the Andes* (London, 1952); Paul Radin, *Indians of South America* (New York, 1942); Julian H. Steward (ed.), *The Handbook of South American Indians* (6 vols., Washington, 1946-1950); Julio C. Tello, *Origen y desarrollo de las civilizaciones prehistóricas andianas* (Lima, 1942).

Rafael Altamira y Crevea, *Historia de España y de la civilización española* (4 vols., Barcelona, 1900-1911; also available in several one-volume English abridgments); Américo Castro, *The Structure of Spanish History*, tr. by E. L. King (Princeton, 1954); Bohdan Chudoba, *Spain and the Empire, 1519-1643* (Chicago, 1952); Havelock Ellis, *The Soul of Spain* (Boston, 1926); Richard Herr, *The Eighteenth-Century Revolution in Spain* (Princeton, 1958); Ramón Menéndez Pidal, *The Spaniards in Their History*, tr. by Walter Starkie (London, 1951); Roger B. Merriman, *The Rise of the Spanish Empire in the Old World and the New* (4 vols., New York, 1918-1934); Sir Charles Petrie, *The Spanish Royal House* (London 1958); Claudio Sánchez Albornoz, *España: Un enigma histórico* (2 vols., Buenos Aires, 1956); Jean Sarrailh, *L'Espagne eclairée de la second moitié du XVIII siècle* (Paris, 1954); R. Trevor Davies, *Spain in Decline, 1621-1700* (London, 1957); Pío Zabala y Lera, *España bajo los Borbones* (4th ed., Barcelona, 1945).

W. J. Barnes, *Portugal, Gateway to Greatness* (London, 1950); Jaime Cortesão and Antonio Ballesteros y Beretta, *Los portugueses* (Barcelona, 1947); B. W. Diffie, *Prelude to Empire: Portugal Overseas before Henry the Navigator* (Lincoln, Neb., 1961); James Duffy, *Portuguese Africa* (Cambridge, Mass., 1959); H. W. Livermore, *A History of Portugal* (Cambridge, England, 1947); Charles E. Nowell, *A History of Portugal* (New York, 1952); J. P. de Oliveira Martins, *A History of Iberian Civilization*, tr. by A. F. G. Bell (London, 1930); Elaine Sanceau, *The Perfect Prince: A Biography of the King Dom João II* (Oporto, Portugal, 1959); H. Morse Stephens, *The Story of Portugal* (New York, 1891).

Note: The extensive publications of the Hakluyt Society of London since 1846 include many volumes of translated, annotated chronicles dealing with the African and Indian background of Latin American history, as well as the principle narratives relating to the discovery and conquest of the New World.

DISCOVERY AND CONQUEST

Antonio Ballesteros y Beretta, *Génesis del descubrimiento* (Barcelona and Buenos Aires, 1947); E. G. Bourne, *Spain in America, 1450-1580* (New York and London, 1904); J. B. Brebner, *The Explorers of*

North America, 1492-1806 (London and New York, 1933); R. B. Cunninghame Graham, *The Horses of the Conquest* (Norman, Okla., 1949); Lewis Hanke, *The First Social Experiments in America* (Cambridge, Mass., 1935), *The Spanish Struggle for Justice in the Conquest of America* (Philadelphia, 1949), *Bartolomé de Las Casas* (The Hague, 1951), and *Bartolomé de Las Casas: Bookman, Scholar and Propagandist* (Philadelphia, 1949); Antonio de Herrera y Tordesillas, *Historia general de los hechos de los castellanos en las Islas y Tierrafirme del Mar Océano* (New edition, Madrid, 1953); F. A. Kirkpatrick, *The Spanish Conquistadores* (London, 1934); Bartolomé de Las Casas, *Historia de las Indias* (New edition, 3 vols., Mexico, 1951); Roberto Levillier, *América la bien llamada* (2 vols., Buenos Aires, 1948); Peter Martyr d'Anghera, *De Orbe Novo, the Eight Decades of Peter Martyr d'Anghera*, tr. by F. A. MacNutt (2 vols., London and New York, 1912); Amando Melon and Ruiz de Gordejuela, *Los primeros tiempos de la colonización* (Barcelona, 1952); Diego Luis Molinari, *El nacimiento del Nuevo Mundo, 1492-1534* (Buenos Aires, 1941); Samuel Eliot Morison, *Portuguese Voyages to America in the Fifteenth Century* (Cambridge, Mass., 1940); Bernard Moses, *The Establishment of Spanish Rule in America* (New York and London, 1898); Edmundo O'Gorman, *The Invention of America.* (Bloomington, Ind., 1961); Edgar Prestage, *The Portuguese Pioneers* (London, 1933); Justin Winsor, *Narrative and Critical History of America* (8 vols., Boston, 1884-1889); Silvio Zavala, *The Political Philosophy of the Conquest of America* (Mexico, 1953).

Antonio Ballesteros y Beretta, *Cristóbal Colón y el descubrimiento de América* (Barcelona and Buenos Aires, 1945); *The Journal of Christopher Columbus*, tr. by Cecil Jane (New York, 1960); *Life of the Admiral Christopher Columbus by his Son Ferdinand*, ed. by Benjamin Keen (New Brunswick, N.J., 1958); Salvador de Madariaga, *Colón.* (London, 1949); Samuel Eliot Morison, *Admiral of the Ocean Sea: A Life of Christopher Columbus* (2 vols., Boston, 1942); J. B. Thacher, *Christopher Columbus: His Life and Work* (3 vols., New York and London, 1903-1904).

Germán Arciniegas, *America and the New World: The Life and Times of Amerigo Vespucci*, tr. by Harriet de Onís (New York, 1955); Frederick J. Pohl, *Amerigo Vespucci:Pilot Major* (New York, 1944); E. F. Benson, *Ferdinand Magellan* (London, 1929); Charles McKew Parr, *So Noble a Captain: The Life and Times of Ferdinand Magellan* (New York, 1953).

Ángel de Altolaguirre y Duvale, *Descubrimiento y conquista de México* (Barcelona, 1954); Anonymous Conqueror, *Narrative of Some Things of New Spain . . .* , ed. by M. H. Saville (New York, 1917);

C. S. Braden, *Religious Aspects of the Conquest of Mexico* (Durham, N. C., 1930); *The Letters of Cortes*, ed. by F. A. MacNutt (2 vols., New York and London, 1908); Bernal Diaz del Castillo, *A True History of the Conquest of New Spain* (New York, 1958); C. Harvey Gardiner, *The Constant Captain: Gonzalo de Sandoval* (Carbondale, Ill., 1961), and *Naval Power and the Conquest of Mexico* (Austin, Texas, 1956); *The Discovery of New Spain in 1518 by Juan de Grijalva*, ed. by H. R. Wagner (Berkeley, 1942); J. E. Kelly, *Pedro de Alvarado, Conquistador* (Princeton, 1932); *The Broken Spears: The Aztec Account of the Conquest of Mexico*; ed. by Miguel Leon-Portilla (Boston, 1961); Salvador de Madariaga, *Hernán Cortés, Conqueror of Mexico* (2nd ed., London, 1955); W. H. Prescott, *History of the Conquest of Mexico* (3 vols., New York, 1843, and many other editions); Robert Ricard, *La "Conquête Spirituelle" du Mexique* (Paris, 1933); Henry R. Wagner, *The Rise of Fernando Cortés* (Los Angeles, 1944).

Hoffman Birney, *Brothers of Doom* (New York, 1942); Pedro Pizarro, *Relation of the Discovery and Conquest of the Kingdoms of Peru*, ed. by P. A. Means (2 vols., New York, 1921); W. H. Prescott, *History of the Conquest of Peru* (2 vols., New York, 1847, and many other editions); Charles L. G. Anderson, *Life and Letters of Vasco Núñez de Balboa* (New York, 1941); Kathleen Romoli, *Balboa of Darien* (New York, 1953); Germán Arciniegas, *The Knight of El Dorado* (New York, 1942); Stephen Clissold, *Conquistador: The Life of Don Pedro Sarmiento de Gamboa* (London, 1954); Herbert E. Bolton, *Coronado* (Albuquerque, N. M., 1949); G. P. Winship, *The Coronado Expedition, 1540-1542* (Washington, 1896); H. C. Heaton (ed), *The Discovery of the Amazon According to the Account of Friar Gaspar de Carvajal* (New York, 1934); Paul Horgan, *Great River: The Rio Grande in North American History* (2 vols., New York, 1954); José de Oviedo y Baños, *Historia de la conquista y población de la provincia de Venezuela* (1723 ed. reproduced, New York, 1941); Ida S. W. Vernon, *Pedro de Valdivia, Conquistador of Chile* (Austin, Texas, 1946); Robert S. Chamberlain, *The Conquest and Colonization of Yucatan, 1517-1550* (Washington, 1948); and *The Conquest and Colonization of Honduras, 1502-1550* (Washington, 1953); J. G. and J. J. Varner (eds.), *The Florida of the Inca* (Austin, Texas, 1951); Ione S. Wright, *The Early History of Cuba, 1492-1586* (New York, 1916).

COLONIAL PERIOD

Cayetano Alcázar Molina, *Los virreinatos en el siglo XVIII* (Barcelona, 1945); Rodolfo Barón Castro, *Españolismo y antiespañolismo en la América Hispana* (Madrid, 1945); Harry Bernstein, *Origins of*

Inter-American Interest, 1700-1812 (Philadelphia, 1945); *Greater America: Essays in Honor of Herbert Eugene Bolton* (Berkeley, 1945); Charles E. Chapman, *Colonial Hispanic America: A History* (New York, 1933); Hugnette and Pierre Chaunu, *Seville et l'Atlantique,* 1504-1650. (6 vols., Paris, 1955); Bailey W. Diffie, *Latin American Civilization: Colonial Period* (Harrisburg, Pa., 1945); Lillian E. Fisher, *The Intendant System in Spanish America* (Berkeley, 1929); Henry Folmer, *Franco-Spanish Rivalry in North America, 1524-1763* (Glendale, Calif., 1953); Earl J. Hamilton, *American Treasure and the Price Revolution in Spain, 1501-1650* (Cambridge, Mass., 1934), and *War and Prices in Spain, 1651-1800* (Cambridge, Mass., 1947); Lewis Hanke, *Aristotle and the American Indians* (London, 1959), and *The Imperial City of Potosí* (The Hague, 1956); C. H. Haring, *Trade and Navigation between Spain and the Indies in the Time of the Hapsburgs* (Cambridge, Mass., 1918); and *The Spanish Empire in America* (rev. ed., New York, 1952); Cecil Jane, *Liberty and Despotism in Spanish America* (Oxford, 1929); Pál Kelemen, *Baroque and Rococo in Latin America* (New York, 1951), and *Medieval American Art* (New York, 1956); Richard Konetzke, *Colección de documentos para la historia de la formación social de hispanoamérica, 1493-1810* (2 vols., Madrid, 1953-1958); George Kubler and Martin Soria, *Art and Architecture in Spain and Portugal and their American Dominions, 1500-1800* (Baltimore, 1959); John Tate Lanning, *Academic Culture in the Spanish Colonies* (New York, 1940); Henry Charles Lea, *The Inquisition in the Spanish Dependencies* (New York, 1908); Irving A. Leonard, *Books of the Brave* (Cambridge, Mass., 1949), and *Romances of Chivalry in the Spanish Indies* (Berkeley, 1933); Salvador de Madariaga, *The Rise of the Spanish American Empire* (London, 1947), and *The Fall of the Spanish American Empire* (London, 1947); Bernard Moses, *Spanish Colonial Literature in South America* (New York, 1922), and *The Spanish Dependencies in South America* (2 vols., New York and London, 1914); José M. Ots Capdequí, *El siglo XVIII español en América* (Mexico, 1945); J. H. Parry, *The Spanish Theory of Empire in the Sixteenth Century* (Cambridge, England, 1940), and *The Sale of Public Office in the Spanish Indies under the Hapsburgs* (Berkeley and Los Angeles, 1953); Carlos Pereyra, *Las huellas de los conquistadores* (Madrid, 1929), and *Historia de la América española* (8 vols., Madrid, 1920-1926); *Recopilación de leyes de los reynos de las Indias* (new edition, 3 vols., Madrid, 1943); J. Fred Rippy and J. T. Nelson, *Crusaders of the Jungle* (Chapel Hill, N. C., 1936); Wilhelm Roscher, *The Spanish Colonial System,* tr. by E. G. Bourne (New York, 1914); Ángel Rosenblat, *La población indígena de América desde 1492 hasta la actualidad* (Buenos Aires, 1945); Luis Alberto Sánchez, *Historia de América* (2nd ed., 2 vols., Santiago de Chile, 1942); Ernesto Schäfer, *El consejo real y supremo de las Indias* (Sevilla, 1935); Robert J. Shafer, *The Economic Societies in the Spanish World, 1763-1821* (Syracuse, 1958); W. Eugene Shiels, *King and Church: The Rise and Fall of the Patronato Real* (Chicago, 1961); Robert S. Smith, *The Spanish Guild Merchant, a History of the Consulado, 1250-1700* (Durham, N. C., 1940); Juan de Solórzano Pereyra, *Politica Indiana* (3rd ed., Madrid, 1736); Frank Tannenbaum, *Slave and Citizen, the Negro in the Americas* (New York, 1947); Juan de Torquemada, *Monarquia Indiana* (3rd ed., 2 vols. Mexico, 1943); José Tudela, *El legado de España a América* (2 vols., Madrid, 1954); John T. Vance, *The Background of Hispanic-American Law* (New York, 1943); Antonio Vázquez de Espinosa, *Compendium and Description of the West Indies*, tr. C. U. Clark (Washington, 1942); Juan Vicens Vives (ed.), *Historia social y económica de España y América* (3 vols., Barcelona, 1957); Arthur P. Whitaker (ed.), *Latin America and the Enlightenment* (New York, 1942); A. C. Wilgus (ed.), *Colonial Hispanic America* (Washington, 1936), and *Hispanic American Essays: A Memorial to James Alexander Robertson* (Durham, N. C., 1942); Silvio Zavala, *New Viewpoints on the Spanish Colonization of America* (Philadelphia, 1943).

Mexico and Spanish North America

A. S. Aiton, *Antonio de Mendoza* (Durham, N.C., 1927); H. H. Bancroft, *History of Mexico* (6 vols., San Francisco, 1883-1888); J. F. Bannon, *The Mission Frontier in Sonora, 1620-1687* (New York, 1955); P. J. Barth, *Franciscan Education and the Social Order in Spanish North America, 1502-1821* (Chicago, 1945); H. E. Bolton, *The Spanish Borderlands* (New Haven, 1921), *Rim of Christendom* (New York, 1936), and *Texas in the Middle Eighteenth Century* (Berkeley, 1915); Sherburne F. Cook and Woodrow Borah, *The Indian Population of Central Mexico, 1531-1610* (Berkeley, 1960), and *The Population of Central Mexico in 1548* (Berkeley, 1960). Woodrow Borah, *Early Colonial Trade and Navigation between Mexico and Peru* (Berkeley, 1954), *New Spain's Century of Depression* (Berkeley, 1951), and *Silk Raising in Colonial Mexico* (Berkeley, 1943); Carlos E. Castañeda, *Our Catholic Heritage in Texas* (6 vols., Austin, Texas, 1938-1950); Charles E. Chapman, *A History of California: The Spanish Period* (New York, 1916); Verne E. Chatelain, *The Defenses of Spanish Florida, 1565 to 1763* (Washington, 1941); François Chevalier, *La formation des grands domaines au Mexique* (Paris, 1952); P. M. Dunne, *Pioneer Black Robes on the West Coast* (Berkeley, 1940); Charles Gibson, *Tlaxcala in the Sixteenth Century* (New Haven, 1952); Charles

W. Hackett, *Revolt of the Pueblo Indians* . . . (2 vols., Albuquerque, N. M., 1942); G. P. Hammond and Agapito Rey, *Don Juan de Oñate* (2 vols., Albuquerque, N. M., 1953); Walter Howe, *The Mining Guild of New Spain* . . . (Cambridge, Mass., 1949); Alexander von Humboldt, *Political Essay on the Kingdom of New Spain*, tr. by John Black (4 vols., London, 1811); *Instrucciones que los vireyes de Nueva España dejaron a sus sucesores* (2 vols., Mexico, 1873); J. V. Jacobsen, *Educational Foundations of the Jesuits in Sixteenth Century New Spain* (Berkeley, 1938); Lawrence Kinnaird (ed.), *Spain in the Mississippi Valley, 1765-1794* (2 vols., Washington, 1949). Irving A. Leonard, *Baroque Times in Old Mexico* (Ann Arbor, Mich., 1959), and *Don Carlos de Sigüenza y Góngora* (Berkeley, 1929); Lyle N. McAlister, *The "Fuero Militar" in New Spain, 1765-1800* (Gainesville, Fla., 1957); Josephine Y. McClaskey, *Inquisition Papers of Mexico* (Pullman, Wash., 1947); Brantz Mayer, *Mexico* (2 vols., Hartford, Conn., 1854); Clement G. Motten, *Mexican Silver and the Enlightenment* (Philadelphia, 1950); J. H. Parry, *The Audiencia of New Galicia in the Sixteenth Century* (Cambridge, England, 1948); Philip Wayne Powell, *Soldiers, Indians and Silver* (Berkeley, 1952); Herbert I. Priestley, *The Mexican Nation, a History* (New York, 1923), and *José de Gálvez, Visitor-General of New Spain, 1765-1771* (Berkeley, 1916); Franchon Royer, *The Tenth Muse, Sor Juana Inés de la Cruz* (Paterson, N.J., 1952); Carl Sauer, *Colima of New Spain in the Sixteenth Century* (Berkeley, 1948); France V. Scholes, *Troublous Times in New Mexico, 1659-1670* (Albuquerque, N. M., 1942); W. L. Schurz, *The Manila Galleon* (New York, 1939); L. B. Simpson, *Studies in the Administration of the Indians of New Spain* (Berkeley, 1934-1940), and *The Encomienda in New Spain* (Berkeley, 1950); A. B. Thomas (ed.), *The Plains Indians and Mexico, 1751-1778* (Albuquerque, N.M., 1940); Robert C. West, *The Mining Community in Northern New Spain: the Parral Mining District* (Berkeley, 1949).

Peru

Charles Gibson, *The Inca Concept of Sovereignty and the Spanish Administration in Peru* (Austin, Texas, 1948); *Gobernantes del Perú* (14 vols., Madrid, 1921-1926); Jorge Juan and Antonio de Ulloa, *A Voyage to South America* (5th ed., 2 vols., London, 1807), and *Noticias secretas de América* (2 vols., London, 1826); Guillermo Lohmann Villena, *El corregidor de indios en el Perú bajo los Austrias* (Madrid, 1957); P. A. Means, *Fall of the Inca Empire and the Spanish Rule in Peru, 1530-1780* (New York, 1932); José Toribio Medina, *Historia del tribunal de la Inquisición de Lima* (2 vols., Santiago de Chile, 1956);

John Preston Moore, *The Cabildo in Peru under the Hapsburgs* (Durham, N. C., 1954); Javier Prado, *Estado social del Perú durante la dominación español* (Lima, 1941); Moisés Saenz, *Sobre el indio peruano* (Mexico, 1933); Antanine Tibesar, *Franciscan beginnings in Colonial Peru* (Washington, 1953); Daniel Valcarcel, *Rebeliones indígenas* (Lima, 1946), and *La rebelión de Tupac Amarú* (Mexico, 1947); Rubén Vargas Ugarte, *Historia del Perú, virreinato* (3 vols., Lima and Buenos Aires, 1949-1956); A. P. Whitaker, *The Huancavelica mercury mine* (Cambridge, Mass., 1941); A. F. Zimmerman, *Francisco de Toledo* (Caldwell, Idaho, 1938).

Brazil

C. R. Boxer, *The Dutch in Brazil, 1624-1654* (Oxford, 1957), and *Salvador de Sá and the Struggle for Brazil and Angola, 1602-1686* (London, 1952); João Pandia Calógeras, *A History of Brazil*, tr. and ed. by P. A. Martin (Chapel Hill, N. C., 1939); Jaime Cortesão and Pedro Calmon, *Brasil* (Barcelona, 1956); Luis Edmundo da Costa, *Rio in the Time of the Viceroys*, tr. by Dorothea Momsen (Rio de Janeiro, 1936); Gilberto Freyre, *The Masters and the Slaves*, tr. by Samuel Putnam (2nd ed., New York, 1956); Mathias C. Kiemen, *The Indian Policy of Portugal in the Amazon Region, 1614-1693* (Washington, 1954); Pedro de Magalhaes de Gandova, *The Histories of Brazil*, tr. by John B. Stetson, Jr. (New York, 1922); Alexander Marchant, *From Barter to Slavery* (Baltimore, 1942); Roy Nash, *Conquest of Brazil* (New York, 1926); José Francisco da Rocha Pombo, *Historia do Brasil* (10 vols., Rio de Janeiro, 1905); Roberto C. Simonsen, *Historia economica do Brasil, 1500-1820* (2 vols., São Paulo, 1937); Robert Southey, *History of Brazil* (3 vols., London, 1810-1819); Affonso de Escragnolle Taunay, *Historia geral das bandeiras paulistas* (Sao Paulo, 1930); F. A. de Varnhagen, *Historia geral do Brasil* (3rd ed., 5 vols., Sao Paulo, 1927-1930); Arnold Wiznitzer, *Jews in Colonial Brazil* (New York, 1960).

Central America and the Caribbean

H. H. Bancroft, *History of Central America* (3 vols., San Francisco, 1883-1887); John Tate Lanning, *The University in the Kingdom of Guatemala* (Ithaca, N. Y., 1955); José Alejandro Bermúdez, *Compendio de la historia de Colombia* (Bogota, 1945); Jerónimo Becker and J. M. Rivas Groot, *El nuevo reino de Granada en el siglo XVIII* (Madrid, 1921); F. R. Hart, *The Disaster of Darien* (Boston, 1929); Jesús Maria Henao and Gerardo Arrubla, *History of Colombia*, tr. and ed. by J. Fred Rippy (Chapel Hill, N. C., 1938); *Relaciones de Mando. Memorias presentadas por los gobernantes del Nuevo Reino de Granada* (Bogotá, 1910); Roland D. Hussey, *The Caracas Company, 1728-1784* (Cambridge, Mass., 1934); Nellie M. Crouse, *French Pioneers in the West Indies, 1624-1664* (New York, 1943); John Esquemeling, *The Buccaneers of America*, ed. by W. S. Stallybrass (New York, 1923); Thomas Gage, *The English American . . . or a New Survey of the West Indias.* (1648 and various editions); Alexander von Humboldt, *The Island of Cuba*, tr. by J. S. Thrasher (New York, 1856); P. A. Means, *The Spanish Main, Focus of Envy, 1492-1700* (New York, 1935); A. P. Newton, *The European Nations in the West Indies, 1493-1688* (London, 1933; Richard Pares, *War and Trade in the West Indies, 1739-1763* (Oxford, 1936); J. H. Parry and P. M. Sherlock, *A Short History of the West Indies* (London, 1956); W. Adolphe Roberts, *Sir Henry Morgan* (New York, 1933); Rayner Unwin, *The Defeat of John Hawkins* (New York, 1960).

Argentina and Chile

Guillermo Céspedes del Castillo, *Lima y Buenos Aires* (Sevilla, 1947); Enrique de Gandia, *Buenos Aires colonial* (Buenos Aires, 1957); R. B. Cunninghame Graham, *A Vanished Arcadia; some account of the Jesuits in Paraguay, 1607-1767* (rev. ed., London, 1924); Ricardo Levene, *A History of Argentina*, tr. and ed. by W. S. Robertson (Chapel Hill, N. C., 1937); John Lynch, *Spanish Colonial Administration, 1782-1810: The Intendant System in the Viceroyalty of the Rio de la Plata* (Fair Lawn, N. J., 1958); Magnus Mörner, *The Political and Economic Activities of the Jesuits in the La Plata Region*, tr. by Albert Read (Stockholm, 1953); Elman R. Service, *Spanish-Guaraní Relations in early Colonial Paraguay* (Ann Arbor, Mich., 1954); Ricardo Donoso, *El Marqués de Osorno. Don Ambrosio Higgins* (Santiago de Chile, 1941); Agustín Edwards, *Peoples of Old* (London, 1929); Luis Galdames, *A History of Chile*, tr. and ed. by I. J. Cox (Chapel Hill, N. C., 1941).

INDEPENDENCE

Rafael Altamira y Crevea, *Resumen histórico de la independencia de la América española* (Buenos Aires, 1910); Melchor Fernández Almagro, *La emancipación de América y su reflejo en la conciencia española* (Madrid, 1944); C. C. Griffin, *The United States and the Disruption of the Spanish Empire, 1810-1822* (New York, 1937); Julio F. Guillén, *Independencia de América* (3 vols., Madrid, 1953); Alfred Hasbrouck, *Foreign Legionaries in the Liberation of Spanish South*

America (New York, 1928); John Burch Kyle, *Spain and its Colonies, 1814-1820* (Ph. D. thesis, Duke University, 1951); Bernard Moses, *The Intellectual Background of the Revolution in South America, 1810-1824* (New York, 1926), *Spain's Declining Power in South America, 1730-1806* (Berkeley, 1919), and *South America on the Eve of Emancipation* (New York, 1908); W. S. Robertson, *France and Latin-American Independence* (Baltimore, 1939), and *Rise of the Spanish-American Republics* (New York, 1918); J. M. Spell, *Rousseau in the Spanish World before 1833* (Austin, Texas, 1938); C. K. Webster, *Britain and the Independence of Latin America, 1812-1830* (2 vols., Oxford, 1938); A. P. Whitaker, *The United States and the Independence of Latin America, 1800-1830* (Baltimore, 1941).

V. A. Belaúnde, *Bolívar and the Political Thought of the Spanish American Revolution* (Baltimore, 1938); Francisco A. Encina, *Bolívar y la independencia de la América española* (Santiago de Chile, 1957); Waldo Frank, *Birth of a World: Bolívar in Terms of his Peoples* (Boston, 1951); Vicente Lecuna, *Crónica razonada de las guerras de Bolívar* (3 vols., New York, 1950); Vicente Lecuna and H. A. Bierck (eds.), *Selected Writings of Bolívar* (2 vols., New York, 1951); Salvador de Madariaga, *Bolívar* (London, 1952); Gerhard Masur, *Simón Bolívar* (Albuquerque, N. M., 1948); *Memorias del general O'Leary* (Caracas, 1879-1888).

Nettie Lee Benson, *La diputación provincial y el federalismo mexicano* (Mexico, 1955); J. A. Caruso, *The Liberators of Mexico* (New York, 1954); Jaime Delgado, *España y México en el siglo XIX* (3 vols., Madrid, 1950); Jack Allen Haddick, *The Administration of Viceroy José de Iturrigaray* (Ph.D. thesis, University of Texas, 1954); W. S. Robertson, *Iturbide of Mexico* (Durham, N. C., 1952); John Rydjord, *Foreign Interest in the Independence of New Spain* (Durham, N. C., 1935); Wilbert H. Timmons, *The Life of José Maria Morelos* (Ph.D. thesis, University of Texas, 1949); William Forest Sprague, *Vicente Guerrero* (Chicago, 1939).

J. C. J. Metford, *San Martín the Liberator* (London, 1950); John Miller, *Memoirs of General Miller in the Service of the Republic of Peru* (2nd ed., 2 vols., London, 1829); Bartolomé Mitre, *Historia de San Martín y de la emancipación sudamericana* (Buenos Aires, 1888-1889); José Pacífico Otero, *Historia del libertador, Don José de San Martín* (2nd ed., 4 vols., Buenos Aires, 1949); Herbert Raffeld, *The Viceroyalty of Peru: Bulwark of Royalism, 1808-1821* (Ph.D. thesis, University of California, Berkeley, 1951); Ricardo Rojas, *San Martín, Knight of the Andes*, tr. by H. Brickell (New York, 1945); Rubén Vargas Ugarte, *Historia del Perú: Emancipación* (Buenos Aires, 1958); Thomas, Earl of Dundonald (Lord Cochrane), *Narrative of Services* . . . (London, 1859).

Stephen Alexis, *Black Liberator: The Life of Toussaint Louverture*, tr. by W. Stirling (New York, 1949); John Armitage, *The History of Brazil* (2 vols., London, 1836). Charles W. Arnade, *The Emergence of the Republic of Bolivia* (Gainesville, Fla., 1957); Agustín Edwards, *The Dawn* (London, 1931); Basil Hall, *Extracts from a Journal . . .* (2 vols., Edinburgh, 1824); R. A. Humphreys, *Liberation in South America, 1806-1827* (London, 1952); Benjamin Keen, *David Curtis DeForest and · the Revolution of Buenos Aires* (New Haven, 1947); Ralph Korngold, *Citizen Toussaint* (Boston, 1944); Edna D. P. Nelson, *O'Higgins and Don Bernardo* (New York, 1954); W. S. Robertson, *The Life of Miranda* (2 vols., Chapel Hill, N. C., 1929); T. Lothrop Stoddard, *The French Revolution in San Domingo* (New York, 1914); John Street, *Artigas and the Emancipation of Uruguay* (London, 1959); Joseph F. Thorning, *Miranda: World Citizen* (Gainesville, Fla., 1952); Octavia Tarquinio de Souas, *José Bonifacio, Emancipador del Brasil* (Mexico, 1945); J. W. Vandercook, *Black Majesty: The Life of Christophe, King of Haiti* (New York, 1928); José Ricardo Vejarno, *Nariño* (Bogota, 1945); J. B. von Spix and C. F. P. von Martins, *Travels in Brazil* (2 vols., London, 1824).

MODERN AND RECENT

Richard N. Adams et al, *Social Change in Latin America Today* (New York, 1960); R. J. Alexander, *Prophets of the Revolution* (New York, 1962); Germán Arciniegas, *The State of Latin America* (New York, 1952); William Benton, *The Voice of Latin America* (New York, 1961); Harry Bernstein, *Modern and Contemporary Latin America* (Philadelphia, 1952); James Bryce, *South America: Observations and Impressions* (rev. ed., New York, 1914); Carlos Dávila, *We of the Americas* (Englewood Cliffs, N. J., 1949); Harold E. Davis, *Makers of Democracy in Latin America* (New York, 1945), and *Latin American Leaders* (New York, 1949); F. García Calderón, *Latin America: Its Rise and Progress* (London and New York, 1913); Victor W. von Hagen, *South America Called Them* (New York, 1945); C. H. Haring, *South American Progress* (Cambridge, Mass., 1934); R. A. Humphreys, *The Evolution of Modern Latin America* (Oxford, 1946); John J. Johnson, *Political Change in Latin America: The Emergence of the Middle Sectors* (Stanford, Calif., 1958); Tom B. Jones, *South America Rediscovered* (Minneapolis, 1949); Benjamin Keen (ed.), *Readings in Latin-American Civilization* (New York, 1955); Edwin Lieuwen, *Arms and Politics in Latin America* (New York, 1960); Austin F. MacDonald, *Latin American Politics and Government* (2nd ed., New York, 1954); J. Lloyd Mecham, *Church and State in Latin America.* (Chapel Hill,

N. C., 1934); William W. Pierson and Federico G. Gil, *Governments of Latin America* (New York, 1957); Frederick B. Pike (ed.), *Freedom and Reform in Latin America* (Notre Dame, Ind., 1959); Galo Plaza Lasso, *Problems of Democracy in Latin America* (Chapel Hill, N. C., 1955); Luis Quintanilla, *A Latin American Speaks* (New York, 1943); A. C. Wilgus (ed.), *South American Dictators during the First Century of Independence* (Washington, 1937).

Economics

R. J. Alexander, *Labor Movements in Latin America* (London, 1947), and *Communism in Latin America* (New Brunswick, N. J., 1957); *Economic Survey of Latin America* (United Nations, 1949-   ); W. C. Gordon, *The Economy of Latin America* (New York, 1950); J. Fred Rippy, *Latin America and the Industrial Age* (2nd ed., New York, 1947); George Wythe, *Industry in Latin America* (2nd ed., New York, 1949).

Culture

Alfred Coester, *The Literary History of Spanish America* (2nd ed., New York, 1928); W. Rex Crawford, *A Century of Latin American Thought* (rev. ed., Cambridge, Mass., 1961); C. C. Griffin (ed.), *Concerning Latin American Culture* (New York, 1940); Pedro Henriquez-Ureña, *Literary Currents in Hispanic America* (Cambridge, Mass., 1945); Christopher Isherwood, *The Condor and the Cows* (New York, 1948); Salvador de Madariaga, *Latin America between the Eagle and the Bear* (New York, 1962); José de Onís, *The United States as Seen by Spanish American Writers, 1776-1890* (New York, 1952); A. Torres-Rioseco, *The Epic of Latin American Literature* (rev. ed., New York, 1946).

Note: *The Hispanic American Report* (formerly *The Hispanic World Report*), edited by Ronald Hilton and published monthly at Stanford, Calif., since 1948, contains invaluable summaries of events in Latin America.

Inter-American Relations

Samuel Flagg Bemis, *The Latin American Policy of the United States* (New York, 1943); Harry Bernstein, *Making an Inter-American Mind* (Gainesville, Fla., 1961); Stetson Conn and Byron Fairchild, *The Framework of Hemisphere Defense* (Washington, 1960); Alexander DeConde, *Herbert Hoover's Latin American Policy* (Stanford, Calif., 1951); Donald M. Dozer, *Are We Good Neighbors: Three Decades of*

Inter-American Relations, 1930-1960 (Gainesville, Fla., 1959); J. W. Gantenbein (ed.), *The Evolution of our Latin American Policy: A Documentary Record* (New York, 1950); C. H. Haring, *South America Looks at the United States* (New York, 1928); R. D. Hussey and R. N. Burr (ed.), *Documents on Inter-American Cooperation* (2 vols., Philadelphia, 1955); W. R. Manning (ed.), *The Diplomatic Correspondence of the United States. Inter-American Affairs, 1831-1860* (12 vols., Washington, 1932-39); J. Lloyd Mecham, *The United States and Inter-American Security, 1889-1960* (Austin, Texas, 1961); Dexter Perkins, *The Monroe Doctrine, 1823-1826* (Cambridge, Mass., 1927), *ibid.,* 1826-1867 (Baltimore, 1933), and *ibid.,* 1867-1907 (Baltimore, 1937); J. Fred Rippy, *Latin America in World Politics* (3rd ed., New York), and *Globe and Hemisphere* (Chicago, 1958); J. B. Scott (ed.), *The International Conferences of the American States, 1889-1928* (New York, 1931), and *ibid., First Supplement, 1933-1940* (Washington, 1940); Graham H. Stewart, *Latin America and the United States* (5th ed., New York, 1955); A. P. Whitaker, *The Western Hemisphere Idea: Its Rise and Decline* (Ithaca, N. Y., 1954); Bryce Wood, *The Making of the Good Neighbor Policy* (New York, 1961).

Mexico

Lucás Alamán, *Historia de Mejico* . . . (5 vols., Mexico, 1848-1852); Eugene C. Barker, *Mexico and Texas, 1821-1835* (Dallas, 1928); Carleton Beals, *Porfirio Díaz* (Philadelphia, 1932); Alfred Hoyt Bill, *Rehearsal for Conflict: The War with Mexico, 1846-1848* (New York, 1947); W. H. Callcott, *Santa Anna: The Story of an Enigma who was once Mexico* (Norman, Okla., 1936), *Church and State in Mexico, 1822-1857* (Durham, N. C., 1926), and *Liberalism in Mexico, 1857-1929* (Stanford, Calif., 1931); Mme. Calderón de la Barca, *Life in Mexico during a Residence of two years in that Country* (2 vols., Boston, 1843); Howard F. Cline, *The United States and Mexico* (Cambridge, Mass., 1953); Count Egon Caesar Corti, *Maximilian and Charlotte of Mexico*, tr. by Mrs. C. A. Phillips (2 vols., New York, 1928); Daniel Cosío Villegas, *La republica restaurada: La vida política 1867 a 1876* (Mexico, 1955); T. E. Cotner and C. E. Castañeda (eds.), *Essays in Mexican History* (Austin, Texas, 1958); Charles C. Cumberland, *Mexican Revolution. Genesis under Madero* (Austin, Texas, 1952); Josephus Daniels, *Shirt-sleeve Diplomat* (Chapel Hill, N. C., 1947); Daniel Dawson, *The Mexican Adventure* (London, 1935); Moisés González Navarro, *El porfiriato. La vida social* (Mexico, 1957); Graham Greene, *Another Mexico* (New York, 1939); Ernest Gruening, *Mexico and its Heritage* (New York and London, 1928); Robert S. Henry, *The Story of*

the Mexican War (Indianapolis, 1950); Aldous Huxley, *Beyond the Mexique Bay* (London, 1934); H. Montgomery Hyde, *Mexican Empire: The History of Maximilian and Carlota of Mexico* (London, 1946); F. A. Knapp, *The Life of Sebastián Lerdo de Tejada* (Austin, Texas, 1951); Sanford A. Mosk, *Industrial Revolution in Mexico* (Berkeley, 1950); Henry Bamford Parkes, *A History of Mexico* (rev. ed., Boston, 1960); David M. Pletcher, *Rails, Mines and Progress: Seven American Promoters in Mexico* (Ithaca, N. Y., 1958); J. Richard Powell, *The Mexican Petroleum Industry, 1938-1950* (Berkeley, 1956); J. Fred Rippy, *Joel R. Poinsett, Versatile American* (Durham, N. C., 1935), and *The United States and Mexico* (rev. ed., New York, 1931); Ralph Roeder, *Júarez and his Mexico* (2 vols., New York, 1947); Stanley R. Ross, *Francisco I. Madero: Apostle of Mexican Democracy* (New York, 1955); Antonio López de Santa-Anna et al., *The Mexican Side of the Texas Revolution*, tr. and ed. by C. E. Castañeda (Dallas, 1928); Alfred Tischendorf, *Great Britain and Mexico in the Era of Porfirio Díaz* (Durham, N. C., 1961); W. P. Tucker, *The Mexican Government Today* (Minneapolis, 1957); Erico Verissimo, *Mexico* (New York, 1960); Walter V. Scholes, *Mexican Politics during the Júarez Regime, 1855-1872* (Columbia, Mo., 1957); Robert E. Scott, *Mexican Government in Transition* (Urbana, Ill., 1959); Justo Sierra (ed.), *Mexico, su evolución social* (2 vols., Mexico, 1900-1902); Eyler N. Simpson, *The Ejido, Mexico's Way Out* (Chapel Hill, N. C., 1937); Lesley Byrd Simpson, *Many Mexicos* (rev. ed., Berkeley, 1952); Justin H. Smith, *The War with Mexico* (2 vols., New York, 1919); Frank Tannenbaum, *Mexico: The Struggle for Peace and Bread* (New York, 1950); H. G. Ward, *Mexico in 1827* (2 vols., London, 1828); Nathan L. Whetten, *Rural Mexico* (Chicago, 1948).

Central America

Mavis Biesanz, *Costa Rican Life* (New York, 1944); Robert S. Chamberlain, *Francisco Morazán, Champion of Central American Federation* (Coral Gables, Fla., 1950); Chester Lloyd Jones. *Guatemala Past and Present* (Minneapolis, 1940), and *Costa Rica and Civilization in the Caribbean* (Madison, Wis., 1935); Thomas L. Karnes, *The Failure of Union: Central America, 1824-1960* (Chapel Hill, N. C., 1961); J. H. Kemble, *The Panama Route, 1848-1869* (Berkeley, 1943); Vera Kelsey and Lilly de J. Osborne, *Four Keys to Guatemala* (rev. ed., New York, 1961); Gerstle Mack, *The Land Divided* (New York, 1944); Dana G. Munro, *The Five Republics of Central America* (New York, 1918); W. O. Scroggs, *Filibusters and Financiers: The Story of William Walker and his Associates* (New York, 1916); Ronald M. Schneider,

Communism in Guatemala, 1944-1954 (New York, 1959); W. S. Stokes, *Honduras* (Madison, Wis., 1950); Nathan L. Whetten, *Guatemala: the Land and the People* (New Haven, 1961); C. M. Wilson, *Challenge and Opportunity: Central America* (New York, 1941).

The Caribbean

German Arciniegas, *Caribbean: Sea of the New World* (New York, 1946); C. E. Chapman, *A History of the Cuban Republic* (New York, 1927); H. P. Davis, *Black Democracy: The Story of Haiti* (rev., New York, 1936); R. H. Fitzgibbon, *Cuba and the United States, 1900-1935* (Menasha, Wis., 1935); Jesús Galindez, *La era de Trujillo* (Santiago de Chile, 1956); Willis F. Johnson, *The History of Cuba* (5 vols., New York, 1920); Chester Lloyd Jones, *The Caribbean since 1900* (New York, 1936), and *Caribbean Backgrounds and Prospects* (New York, 1931); J. G. Leyburn, *The Haitian People* (New Haven, 1941); R. W. Logan, *The Diplomatic Relations of the United States with Haiti, 1776-1891* (Chapel Hill, N. C., 1941); Jorge Mañach, *Martí: Apostle of Freedom*, tr. by Coley Taylor (New York, 1960); *The America of José Martí; Selected Writings*, tr. by Juan de Onís (New York, 1953); Arthur C. Millspaugh, *Haiti under American Control, 1915-1930* (Boston, 1931); Lowry Nelson, *Rural Cuba* (Minneapolis, 1950); Fernando Ortiz, *Cuban Counterpoint: Tobacco and Sugar*, tr. by Harriet de Onís (New York, 1947); Dexter Perkins, *The United States and the Caribbean* (Cambridge, Mass., 1947); Herminio Portell Vilá, *Historia de Cuba en sus relaciones con los Estados Unidos y España* (4 vols., Havana, 1939-1941); Basil Rauch, *American Interest in Cuba, 1848-1855* (New York, 1948); J. Fred Rippy, *The Caribbean Danger Zone* (New York, 1940); Selden Rodman, *Haiti: The Black Republic* (New York, 1954); Robert F. Smith, *The United States and Cuba: Business and Diplomacy, 1917-1960* (New York, 1960); Charles C. Tansill, *The United States and Santo Domingo, 1798-1873* (Baltimore, 1938); Sumner Welles, *Naboth's Vineyard: The Dominican Republic, 1844-1902* (2 vols., New York, 1928); A. C. Wilgus (ed.) *The Caribbean Area* (Washington, 1934), and *The Caribbean . . .* (Gainesville, Fla., 1951-   ).

Colombia

David Bushnell, *The Santander Regime in Gran Colombia* (Newark, Del., 1954); P. J. Eder, *Colombia* (London, 1913); Vernon L. Fluharty, *Dance of the Millions: Military Rule and the Social Revolution in Colombia, 1930-1956* (Pittsburgh, 1957); J. M. Henao and G. Arrubla, *History of Colombia.* tr. and ed. by J. Fred Rippy (Chapel Hill, N. C.,

1938); John D. Martz, *Colombia* (Chapel Hill, N. C., 1962); E. Taylor Parks, *Colombia and the United States, 1765-1934* (Durham, N. C., 1935).

Venezuela

John Lavin, *A Halo for Gomez* (New York, 1954); Edwin Lieuwen, *Venezuela* (New York, 1961), and *Petroleum in Venezuela: A History* (Berkeley, 1954); W. D. and A. L. Marsland, *Venezuela through its History* (New York, 1954); Thomas Rourke (pseud.) *Gomez, Tyrant of the Andes* (New York, 1936); Mary Watters, *A History of the Church in Venezuela, 1810-1930* (Chapel Hill, N. C., 1933); A. P. Whitaker, *The United States and South America: The Northern Republics* (Cambridge, Mass., 1948); George S. Wise, *Caudillo: A Portrait of Antonio Guzmán Blanco* (New York, 1951).

Peru

Jorge Basadre, *Historia de la república del Perú, 1822-1908* (rev. ed., 2 vols., Lima, 1949), and *Chile, Perú y Bolivia Independientes* (Barcelona, 1948); G. H. S. Bushnell, *Peru* (London, 1956); W. C. Davis, *The Last Conquistadores; The Spanish Intervention in Peru and Chile, 1863-1866* (Athens, Ga., 1950); W. J. Dennis, *Tacna and Arica* (New Haven, 1931); Charles R. Enock, *Peru* (London, 1925); Thomas R. Ford, *Man and Land in Peru* (Gainesville, Fla., 1955); Francisco García Calderón, *En torno al Perú y América* (Lima, 1954); Harry Kantor, *The Ideology and Program of the Peruvian Aprista Movement* (Berkeley, 1953); Sir Clements R. Markham, *Historia del Perú*, tr. by Luis C. Infante (2nd ed., Lima, 1952); Watt Stewart, *Chinese Bondage in Peru* (Durham, N. C., 1951), and *Henry Meiggs, Yankee Pizarro* (Durham, N. C., 1946).

Ecuador

George I. Blanksten, *Ecuador: Constitutions and Caudillos* (Berkeley, 1951); Albert Franklin, *Ecuador* (New York, 1943); Lilo Linke, *Ecuador: Country of Contrasts* (2nd ed., London, 1955); Richard Pattee, *Gabriel García Moreno y el Ecuador de su Tiempo* (Quito, 1941).

Bolivia

Robert J. Alexander, *The Bolivian National Revolution* (New Brunswick, N. J., 1958); Alcides Argüedes, *Historia general de Bolivia, 1809-1921* (La Paz, 1922); N. A. N. Cleven, *The Political Organization of*

Bolivia (Washington, 1940); Harold Osborne, *Bolivia: A Land Divided* (2nd ed., London, 1955).

Paraguay

George Pendle, *Paraguay: A Riverside Nation* (2nd ed., London, 1956); Philip Raine, *Paraguay* (New Brunswick, N. J., 1956); Harris G. Warren, *Paraguay: An Informal History* (Norman, Okla., 1949); Pablo Max Ynsfran, *The Epic of the Chaco* (Austin, Texas, 1950); David Zook, *The Conduct of the Chaco War* (New York, 1960).

Chile

Diego Barros Arana, *Historia general de Chile* (2nd ed., 16 vols., Santiago, 1930); Domingo Amunátegui y Solar, *Pipiolos y pelucones* (Santiago, 1939); G. J. Butland, *Chile: An Outline of its Geography, Economics and Politics* (3rd ed., London, 1956); Ricardo Donoso, *Alessandri, agitador y demoledor* (Mexico, 1952), and *Desarrollo político y social de Chile desde la constitucíon de 1833* (2nd ed., Santiago, 1942); Alberto Edwards, *La fronda aristocrática* (Santiago, 1945); P. T. Ellsworth, *Chile, An Economy in Transition* (New York, 1945); Francisco A. Encina, *Resumen de la historia de Chile* (2 vols., Santiago, 1954); Francisco V. Frias, *Historia de Chile* (4 vols., Santiago, 1947-1949); George M. McBride, *Chile: Land and Society* (New York, 1936); J. R. Stevenson, *The Chilean Popular Front* (Philadelphia, 1942); Jordan M. Young, *Chilean Parliamentary Government, 1891-1924* (Ph.D. thesis, Princeton University, 1954).

Brazil

Fernando de Azevedo, *Brazilian Culture*, tr. by W. R. Crawford (New York, 1950); George C. A. Boehrer, *Da monarquia a república* (Rio de Janeiro, 1954); Sergio Correa da Costa, *Every Inch a King*, tr. by Samuel Putnam (New York, 1950); Gilberto Freyre, *New World in the Tropics: The Culture of Modern Brazil* (New York, 1959), and *Brazil, an Interpretation* (New York, 1945); C. H. Haring, *Empire in Brazil* (Cambridge, Mass., 1958); Marvin Harris, *Town and Country in Brazil* (New York, 1956); Lawrence F. Hill, *Diplomatic Relations between the United States and Brazil* (Durham, N.C., 1932), and *Brazil* (Berkeley, 1947); H. G. James, *Brazil after a Century of Independence* (New York, 1925), and *The Constitutional System of Brazil* (Washington, 1923); Karl Loewenstein, *Brazil under Vargas* (New York, 1942); Alan K. Manchester, *British Pre-eminence in Brazil: Its Rise and Decline* (Chapel Hill, N. C.,

1933); Richard M. Morse, *From Community to Metropolis: A Biography of São Paulo* (Gainesville, Fla., 1958); Carolina Nabuco, *The Life of Joaquim Nabuco* (Stanford, Calif., 1950); J. F. Normano, *Brazil: A Study of Economic Types* (Chapel Hill, N. C., 1935); Donald Pierson, *Negroes in Brazil: A Study of Race Contact at Bahia* (Chicago, 1942); Samuel Putnam, *Marvelous Journey: A Survey of Four Centuries of Brazilian Writing* (New York, 1948); Arthur Ramos, *The Negro in Brazil* (Washington, 1939); Charles W. Turner, *Ruy Barbosa* (New York, 1945); Erico Verissimo, *Brazilian Literature: An Outline* (New York, 1945); William L. Schurz, *Brazil, the Infinite Country* (New York, 1961); Roberto C. Simonsen, *Brazil's Industrial Revolution* (São Paulo, 1939); T. Lynn Smith, *Brazil: People and Institutions* (2nd ed., Baton Rouge, La., 1954); T. Lynn Smith and Alexander Marchant, *Brazil, Portrait of Half a Continent* (New York, 1951); Stanley J. Stein, *The Brazilian Cotton Manufacture* (Cambridge, Mass., 1957), and *Vassouras: A Brazilian Coffee County, 1850-1900* (Cambridge, Mass., 1957); Charles Wagley (ed.), *Race and Class in Rural Brazil,* (Paris, 1952), and *Amazon Town: A Study of Man in the Tropics* (New York, 1953); Mary W. Williams, *Dom Pedro the Magnanimous, Second Emperor of Brazil* (Chapel Hill, N.C., 1937); George Wythe, R. A. Wight, and H. M. Midkiff, *Brazil: An Expanding Economy* (New York, 1949).

Argentina

R. J. Alexander, *The Peron Era* (New York, 1951); George I. Blanksten, *Peron's Argentina* (Chicago, 1953); A. W. Bunkley (ed.), *A Sarmiento Anthology* (Princeton, 1948), and *The Life of Sarmiento* (Princeton, 1952); Miron Burgin, *The Economic Aspects of Argentine Federalism, 1820-1852* (Cambridge, Mass., 1946); J. F. Cady, *Foreign Intervention in the Rio de la Plata* (Philadelphia, 1929); Thomas B. Davis, Jr., *Carlos de Alvear* (Durham, N.C., 1955); H. S. Ferns, *Britain and Argentina in the Nineteenth Century* (Oxford, 1960); V. Fidel López, *Historia de la república argentina* (8 vols., Buenos Aires, 1949-1950); Manuel Galvez, *Vida de Hipólito Irigoyen* (2nd ed., Buenos Aires, 1939); Samuel Haigh, *Sketches of Buenos Ayres, Chile, and Peru* (London, 1831); S. G. Hanson, *Argentine Meat and the British Market* (Stanford, Calif., 1938); José Ingenieros, *La evolución de las ideas argentinas* (3 vols., Buenos Aires, 1946); Mark Jefferson, *Peopling the Argentine Pampa* (New York, 1926); W. H. Jeffrey, *Mitre and Argentina* (New York, 1952); Ray Josephs, *Argentine Diary* (New York, 1944); John J. Kennedy, *Catholicism, Nationalism, and Democracy in Argentina* (Notre Dame, Ind., 1958); F. A. Kirkpatrick, *A History of the Argentine Republic* (Cambridge, England, 1931); Clifton B. Kroeber,

The Growth of the Shipping Industry in the Rio de la Plata Region,
1794-1860 (Madison, Wis., 1957); Ricardo Levene, A *History of Argen-*
tina, tr. and ed. by W. S. Robertson (Chapel Hill, N.C., 1937); Thomas
F. McGann, *Argentina, the United States, and the Inter-American Sys-*
tem, 1880-1914 (Cambridge, Mass., 1957); Madaline Nichols, *The Gau-*
cho (Durham, N.C., 1942); Woodbine Parish, *Buenos Ayres and the*
provinces of the Rio de la Plata (2nd ed., London, 1852); George Pendle,
Argentina (London, 1955); J. M. Ramos Mejía, *Rosas y su tiempo* (2nd
ed., 3 vols., Buenos Aires, 1907); Ysabel F. Rennie, *The Argentine Re-*
public (New York, 1945); José Luis Romero, *Las ideas políticas en Ar-*
gentina (Mexico, 1946); L. S. Rowe, *The Federal System of the Argen-*
tine Republic (Washington, 1921); Domingo F. Sarmiento, *Life in the*
Argentine Republic in the Days of the Tyrants: or Civilization and Bar-
barism, tr. by Mrs. Horace Mann (New York, 1868); A. P. Whitaker,
The United States and Argentina (Cambridge, Mass., 1954), and *Ar-*
gentine Upheaval: Peron's Fall and the New Regime (New York, 1956);
John W. White, *Argentina, the Life Story of a Nation* (New York,
1942); A. C. Wilgus (ed.), *Argentina, Brazil, and Chile since Independ-*
ence (Washington, 1935).

Uruguay

Russell H. Fitzgibbon, *Uruguay: Portrait of a Democracy* (New
Brunswick, N. J., 1954); S. G. Hanson, *Utopia in Uruguay* (New York,
1938); W. H. Hudson, *The Purple Land* (London, 1885); W. H.
Koebel, *Uruguay* (London, 1911); George Pendle, *Uruguay* (2nd ed.,
London, 1957).

Index